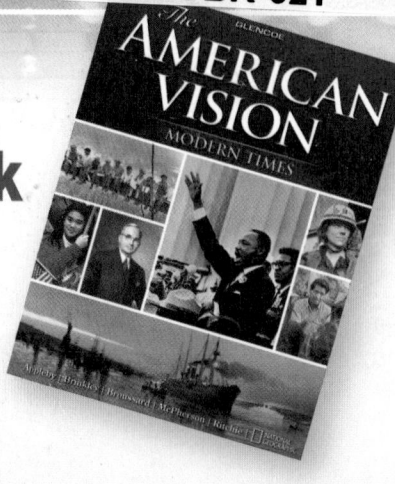

QuickPass™

More Than a Textbook

Find it faster.

Visit **History ONLINE** at <u>glencoe.com</u> and enter a (QuickPass)™ chapter code to go directly to the chapter resources you need.

TAVMT5147c1

Enter this code with the appropriate chapter number.

Find what you need.

- StudentWorks™ Plus Online
- Section Spotlight Video
- Chapter Overview
- Study Central™
- Chapter Audio
- Workbooks
- Self-Check Quiz

Find extras to help you succeed.

- Study-to-Go
- In Motion Animations
- Multilingual Glossary
- Student Web Activity
- ePuzzles and Games
- ...and more

You can easily launch a wide range of digital products from your computer's desktop with the McGraw-Hill Social Studies widget.

The AMERICAN VISION

MODERN TIMES

Joyce Appleby, Ph.D.   Alan Brinkley, Ph.D.   Albert S. Broussard, Ph.D.

James M. McPherson, Ph.D.   Donald A. Ritchie, Ph.D.

NATIONAL GEOGRAPHIC

Mc Graw Hill Glencoe

About the Cover The images on the cover are (from left to right): Construction workers eating lunch on a construction site at Rockefeller Center in New York City; Martin Luther King, Jr., gives his "I Have a Dream" speech in Washington, D.C., in 1963; female U.S. soldier during the Gulf War; Asian American girl holds flags at a Chinese New Year celebration; Harry S. Truman; César Chávez talks to workers in a vineyard; and *Shipping Near the Statue of Liberty* by Christian Cornelius Dommerson.

The McGraw-Hill Companies

 Glencoe

Send all inquiries to:
Glencoe/McGraw-Hill
8787 Orion Place
Columbus, OH 43240-4027

ISBN: 978-0-07-877514-7
MHID: 0-07-877514-0

Printed in the United States of America.

7 8 9 10 RJE/LEH 12

Joyce Appleby, Ph.D., is Professor Emerita of History at UCLA. Dr. Appleby's published works include *Inheriting the Revolution: The First Generation of Americans; Capitalism and a New Social Order: The Jeffersonian Vision of the 1790s;* and *Idcology and Economic Thought in Seventeenth-Century England,* which won the Berkshire Prize. She served as president of both the Organization of American Historians and the American Historical Association, and chaired the Council of the Institute of Early American History and Culture at Williamsburg. Dr. Appleby has been elected to the American Philosophical Society and the American Academy of Arts and Sciences, and is a Corresponding Fellow of the British Academy.

Alan Brinkley, Ph.D., is Allan Nevins Professor of American History at Columbia University. His published works include *Voices of Protest: Huey Long, Father Coughlin, and the Great Depression,* which won the 1983 National Book Award; *The End of Reform: New Deal Liberalism in Recession and War; The Unfinished Nation: A Concise History of the American People;* and *Liberalism and Its Discontents.* He received the Levenson Memorial Teaching Prize at Harvard University and the Great Teacher Award at Columbia.

Albert S. Broussard, Ph.D., is Professor of History at Texas A&M University from which he received a Distinguished Teaching Award and has served as a distinguished lecturer. Before joining the Texas A&M faculty, Dr. Broussard was Assistant Professor of History and Director of the African American Studies Program at Southern Methodist University. Among his publications are the books *Black San Francisco: The Struggle for Racial Equality in the West, 1900–1954* and *African American Odyssey: The Stewarts, 1853–1963.* Dr. Broussard has also served as president of the Oral History Association and was chair of the Nominating Committee for the Organization of American Historians.

James M. McPherson, Ph.D., is George Henry Davis Professor of American History, Emeritus at Princeton University. Dr. McPherson is the author of 14 books about the Civil War era. These include *Battle Cry of Freedom: The Civil War Era,* for which he won the Pulitzer Prize in 1989, and *For Cause and Comrades: Why Men Fought in the Civil War,* for which he won the 1998 Lincoln Prize. He is a member of many professional historical associations, including the Civil War Preservation Trust.

Donald A. Ritchie, Ph.D., is Associate Historian of the United States Senate Historical Office. Dr. Ritchie received his doctorate in American history from the University of Maryland after service in the U.S. Marine Corps. He has taught American history at various levels, from high school to university. He edits the Historical Series of the Senate Foreign Relations Committee and is the author of several books, including *Doing Oral History; Electing FDR: The New Deal Campaign of 1932; Reporting from Washington: The History of the Washington Press Corps;* and *Press Gallery: Congress and the Washington Correspondents,* which received the Organization of American Historians Richard W. Leopold Prize. Dr. Ritchie has served as president of the Oral History Association and as a council member of the American Historical Association.

The National Geographic Society, founded in 1888 for the increase and diffusion of geographic knowledge, is the world's largest nonprofit scientific and educational organization. Since its earliest days, the Society has used sophisticated communication technologies, from color photography to holography, to convey knowledge to its worldwide membership. The School Publishing Division supports the Society's mission by developing innovative educational programs—ranging from traditional print materials to multimedia programs including CD-ROMs, DVDs, and software.

Contributing Author

Dinah Zike, M.Ed., is an award-winning author, educator, and inventor known for designing three-dimensional hands-on manipulatives and graphic organizers known as Foldables®. Foldables are used nationally and internationally by teachers, parents, and educational publishing companies. Dinah has developed over 150 supplemental educational books and materials. She is the author of *The Big Book of United States History, The Big Book of World History,* and *The Big Book of Books and Activities,* which was awarded Learning Magazine's Teachers' Choice Award. In 2004 Dinah was honored with the CESI Science Advocacy Award. Dinah received her M.Ed. from Texas A&M, College Station, Texas.

Consultants & Reviewers

Academic Consultants

David Berger
Broeklundian Professor of History
Brooklyn College and the Graduate Center
City University of New York
Brooklyn, New York

Paul Cimbala
Professor of History
Fordham University, Rose Hill Campus
Bronx, New York

Linda Clemmons
Assistant Professor of History
Illinois State University
Normal, Illinois

Charles Eagles
Professor of History
University of Mississippi
University, Mississippi

Neil Foley
Associate Professor of History
University of Texas at Austin
Austin, Texas

Allison Gough
Assistant Professor of History
Hawaii Pacific University
Honolulu, Hawaii

K. Austin Kerr
Emeritus Professor of History
The Ohio State University
Columbus, Ohio

Jeffrey Ogbar
Associate Professor of History and Director of
   the Institute for African American Studies
University of Connecticut, Storrs
Storrs, Connecticut

Elizabeth Pleck
Professor of History
University of Illinois at Urbana-Champaign
Urbana, Illinois

William Bruce Wheeler
Emeritus Professor of History
University of Tennessee
Knoxville, Tennessee

Shawn Johansen
Professor of History
Brigham Young University Idaho
Rexburg, Idaho

Teacher Reviewers

Joanna Ackley
John F. Kennedy High School
Taylor, Michigan

Pat Ambrose
Adlai E. Stevenson High School
Lincolnshire, Illinois

Sharon K. Anderson
Cookeville High School
Cookeville, Tennessee

Fred Barnett
Cibola High School
Albuquerque, New Mexico

Shawn Barnum
Tonawanda High School
Tonawanda, New York

Vincent Beasley
Eastern Wayne High School
Goldsboro, North Carolina

Jeremiah Bergan
Baker High School
Baldwinsville, New York

Randy Bishop
Middleton High School
Middleton, Tennessee

Patrick Boyd
Ravenwood High School
Brentwood, Tennessee

Suzanne Brock
Vestavia Hills High School
Vestavia Hills, Alabama

Joyce Brown
LaFayette High School
LaFayette, Georgia

David Chapman
Bentonville High School
Bentonville, Arkansas

Teresa Cooper
Battle Creek Central High School
Battle Creek, Michigan

Timothy Davish
Lakota East High School
Liberty Township, Ohio

Peter DeWolf
First Colonial High School
Virginia Beach, Virginia

Glenn DiTomaso
Norwell High School
Norwell, Massachusetts

Kimberly Dunn
Chase High School
Forest City, North Carolina

Bre England
Warren Central High School
Indianapolis, Indiana

Robert Fenster
Hillsborough High School
Hillsborough, New Jersey

James A. Field
Morgantown High School
Morgantown, West Virginia

Shane Gardner
Freedom High School
Morganton, North Carolina

Diane Gebel
Attica High School
Attica, New York

James Gill
Binghamton High School
Binghamton, New York

Mary Ellen Goergen
Amherst High School
Amherst, New York

Teacher Reviewers

Robert Haley
Cleveland Hill High School
Cheektowaga, New York

Ken Hall
Larkin High School
Elgin, Illinois

Anne Harper
Del Sol High School
Las Vegas, Nevada

Roberta Heath
Capital High School
Charleston, West Virginia

Cliff Hong
Liverpool High School
Liverpool, New York

George Irby
Miami Killian Senior High School
Miami, Florida

JeTaun Jamerson
Lake View High School
Chicago, Illinois

Carol Johnson
Cary High School
Cary, North Carolina

Harry F. Jones
Panther Creek High School
Cary, North Carolina

Shirley Jones
Hillcrest High School
Memphis, Tennessee

Joe Leonard
Southport High School
Indianapolis, Indiana

Tom Long
Buffalo Gap High School
Swoope, Virginia

Rebecca Mabrey
Central Cabarrus High School
Concord, North Carolina

Amy MacIntosh
Fairfield Warde High School
Fairfield, Connecticut

Shannon W. McDonald
Harding University High School
Charlotte, North Carolina

Chad McGee
Warren County High School
McMinnville, Tennessee

Marty McNeil
Akron East High School
Akron, Ohio

Kathryn Merritt
Hillcrest High School
Tuscaloosa, Alabama

Rita Morgan
Beaverton High School
Beaverton, Oregon

Jimmy Neal
Beech High School
Hendersonville, Tennessee

Teresa Pardee
East Mecklenburg High School
Charlotte, North Carolina

Patricia Radigan
Thomas Dale High School
Chester, Virginia

Steven Reeder
Cordova High School
Cordova, Tennessee

Debi Reeves
Liberty High School
Bedford, Virginia

Connie Schlieker
Atherton High School
Louisville, Kentucky

Mark Schuler
North Springs High School
Atlanta, Georgia

Russ Smith
Ashley High School
Wilmington, North Carolina

Mitzi Terry
Franklin High School
Franklin, Tennessee

Dal Tomlinson
Dixon High School
Holly Ridge, North Carolina

Penny Toneatti
Half Hollow Hills High School East
Dix Hills, New York

Lisa Valentine
Harding University High School
Charlotte, North Carolina

Stan Vickers
Westview High School
Martin, Tennessee

Danielle Walsh
Emmaus High School
Emmaus, Pennsylvania

Joshua White
Charlotte High School
Rochester, New York

Gerald Wild II
Alden High School
Alden, New York

Amy Working
Central High School
Memphis, Tennessee

Table of Contents

Table of Contents

Unit 2

The Birth of Modern America 154
1865–1901

Table of Contents

NO MOLLY-CODDLING HERE

Unit 4

Table of Contents

Table of Contents

Table of Contents

Appendix

Features

ANALYZING PRIMARY SOURCES

POLITICAL CARTOONS PRIMARY SOURCE

Turning Point

ANALYZING SUPREME COURT CASES

Time Lines

Primary Source Quotes

A variety of quotations and excerpts throughout the text express the thoughts, feelings, and life experiences of people, past and present.

Primary Source Quotes

Primary Source Quotes

Primary Source Quotes

Maps

Maps In MOtion See *StudentWorks*™ *Plus*
or glencoe.com.

Map entries in **blue** have been specially enhanced on the StudentWorks™ Plus DVD and on glencoe .com. These In Motion maps allow you to interact with layers of displayed data and to listen to audio components.

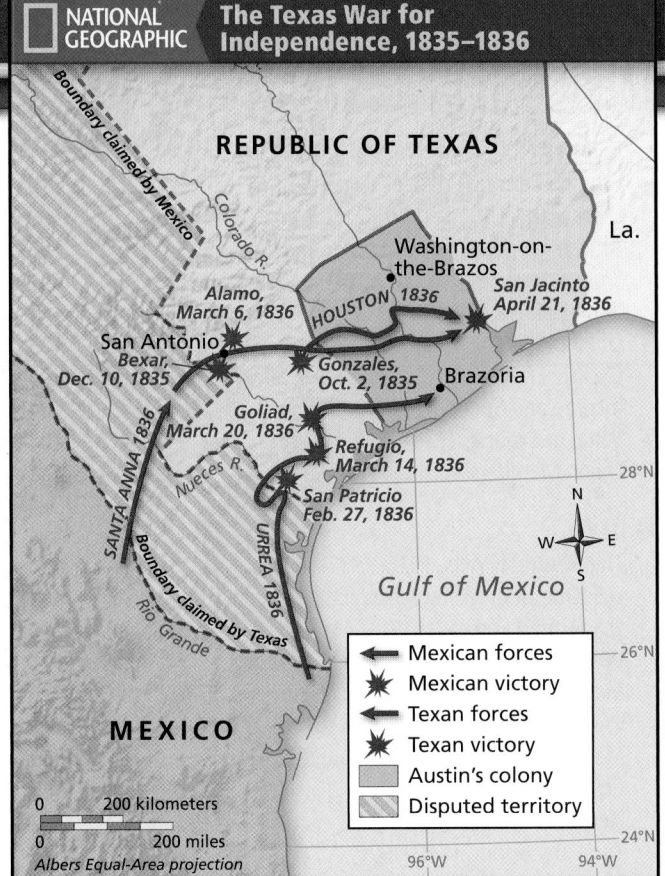

NATIONAL GEOGRAPHIC

The Texas War for Independence, 1835–1836

REPUBLIC OF TEXAS

Boundary claimed by Mexico

Colorado R.

La.

Washington-on-the-Brazos

Alamo, March 6, 1836

HOUSTON 1836

San Jacinto April 21, 1836

San Antonio Bexar, Dec. 10, 1835

Gonzales, Oct. 2, 1835

Brazoria

SANTA ANNA 1836

Goliad, March 20, 1836

Refugio, March 14, 1836

Nueces R.

URREA 1836

San Patricio Feb. 27, 1836

28°N

Boundary claimed by Texas

Rio Grande

Gulf of Mexico

26°N

MEXICO

0   200 kilometers

0   200 miles

Albers Equal-Area projection

N W E S

→ Mexican forces
✶ Mexican victory
← Texan forces
✶ Texan victory
▨ Austin's colony
▨ Disputed territory

24°N

96°W   94°W

Charts & Graphs

The American Vision: Modern Times contains a wealth of information. The trick is to know where to look to access all the information in the book.

If you go through this scavenger hunt, either alone or with your teacher or parents, you will quickly learn how the textbook is organized and how to get the most out of your reading and study time. Let's get started!

1. How many units and chapters are in the book?
2. What is the difference between the glossary and the index?
3. Every chapter contains primary sources—quotes or documents from the era. Where else can you find primary sources in the textbook?
4. In what special feature can you find the definition of a physical map, a political map, and a special-purpose map?
5. If you want to quickly find all the maps, charts, and graphs about World War II, where in the front do you look?
6. How can you find information about civil rights activist Martin Luther King, Jr.?
7. Where can you find an overview of the major events of the Vietnam War discussed in Chapter 19?
8. Where are the key terms and names for Chapter 8, Section 3 listed, and how are they highlighted in the text?
9. The Web site for the book is listed six times in Chapter 16. After finding all six, list how the Web site can help you.
10. Which of the book's main features will provide you with strategies for improving your studying and writing skills?

Themes in the
American Vision: Modern Times

As you read THE AMERICAN VISION: MODERN TIMES, *you will be given help in sorting out all the information you encounter. This textbook organizes the events of your nation's past and present around 10 themes. A theme is a concept, or main idea, that happens again and again throughout history. By recognizing these themes, you will better understand events of the past and how they affect you today.*

Culture and Beliefs

Being aware of cultural differences helps us understand ourselves and others. People from around the world for generations have sung of the "land of the Pilgrims' pride, land where our fathers died," even though their ancestors arrived on these shores long after these events occurred.

Past and Present

Recognizing our historic roots helps us understand why things are the way they are today. This theme includes political, social, religious, and economic changes that have influenced the way Americans think and act.

Geography and History

Understanding geography helps us understand how humans interact with their environment. The United States succeeded in part because of its rich natural resources and its vast open spaces. In many regions, the people changed the natural landscape to fulfill their wants and needs.

Individual Action

Responsible individuals have often stepped forward to help lead the nation. Americans' strong values helped create such individuals. These values spring in part from earlier times when the home was the center of many activities, including work, education, and spending time with one's family.

Group Action

Identifying how political and social groups and institutions operate helps us work together. From the beginning, Americans formed groups and institutions to act in support of their economic, political, social, and religious beliefs.

Government and Society

Understanding the workings of government helps us become better citizens. Abraham Lincoln explained the meaning of democracy as "government of the people, by the people, for the people." Democracy, at its best, is "among" the people.

Science and Technology

Americans have always been quick to adopt innovations. The nation was settled and built by people who gave up old ways in favor of new. Americans' lives are deeply influenced by technology, the use of science, and machines. Perhaps no machine has so shaped modern life as the automobile. Understanding the role of science and technology helps us see their impact on our society and the roles they will play in the future.

Economics and Society

The free enterprise economy of the United States is consistent with the nation's history of rights and freedoms. Freedom of choice in economic decisions supports other freedoms. Understanding the concept of free enterprise is basic to studying American history.

Trade, War, and Migration

Events much bigger than any individual also shape the course of history. Being aware of global interdependence helps us make decisions and deal with the difficult issues we will encounter. Trade, war, and the movement of people between nations have altered the nation's history.

Struggles for Rights

For a democratic system to survive, its citizens must take an active role in government. The foundation of democracy is the right of every person to take part in government and to voice one's views on issues. An appreciation for the struggle to preserve these freedoms is vital to the understanding of democracy.

USING THE BIG IDEAS

You will find Big Ideas at the beginning of every section of every chapter. You are asked questions that help you put it all together to better understand how ideas and themes are connected across time—and to see why history is important to you today.

REFERENCE ATLAS

NATIONAL GEOGRAPHIC

ATLAS KEY

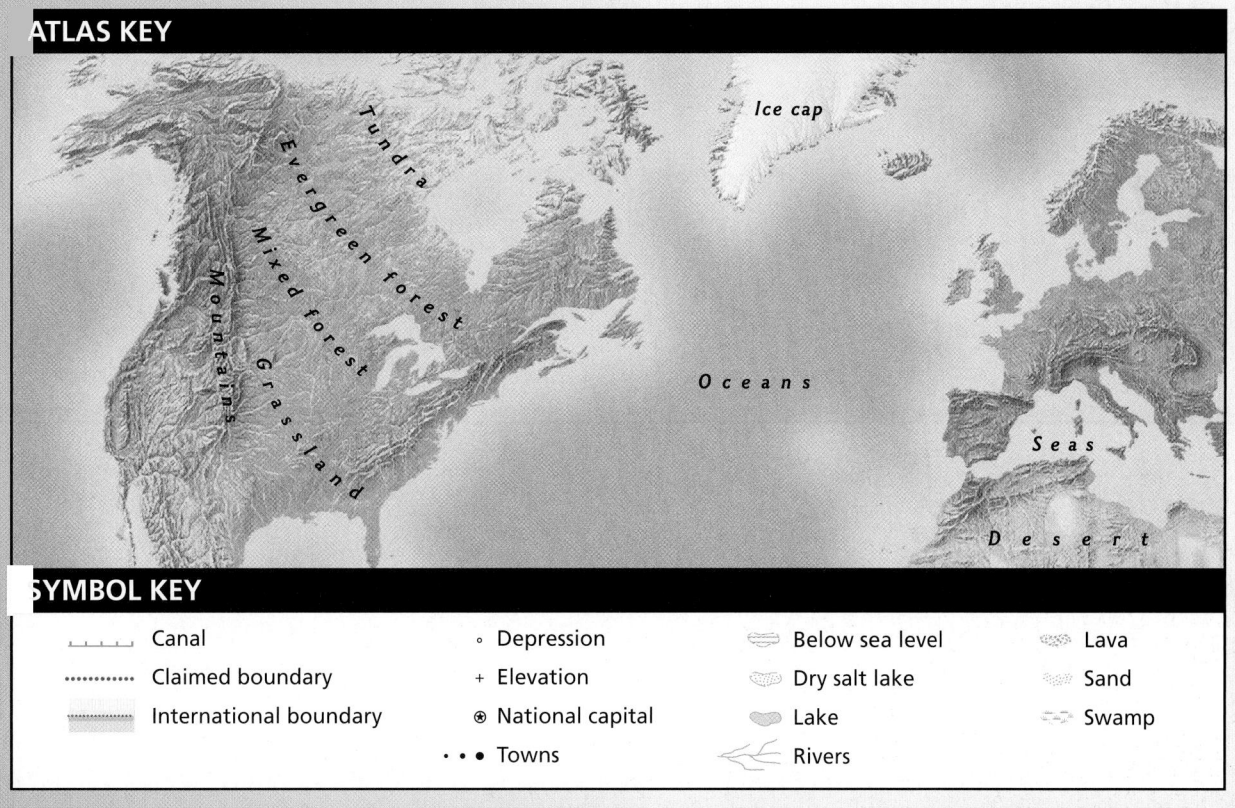

SYMBOL KEY

Canal	∘ Depression	Below sea level	Lava
Claimed boundary	+ Elevation	Dry salt lake	Sand
International boundary	⊛ National capital	Lake	Swamp
	• • Towns	Rivers	

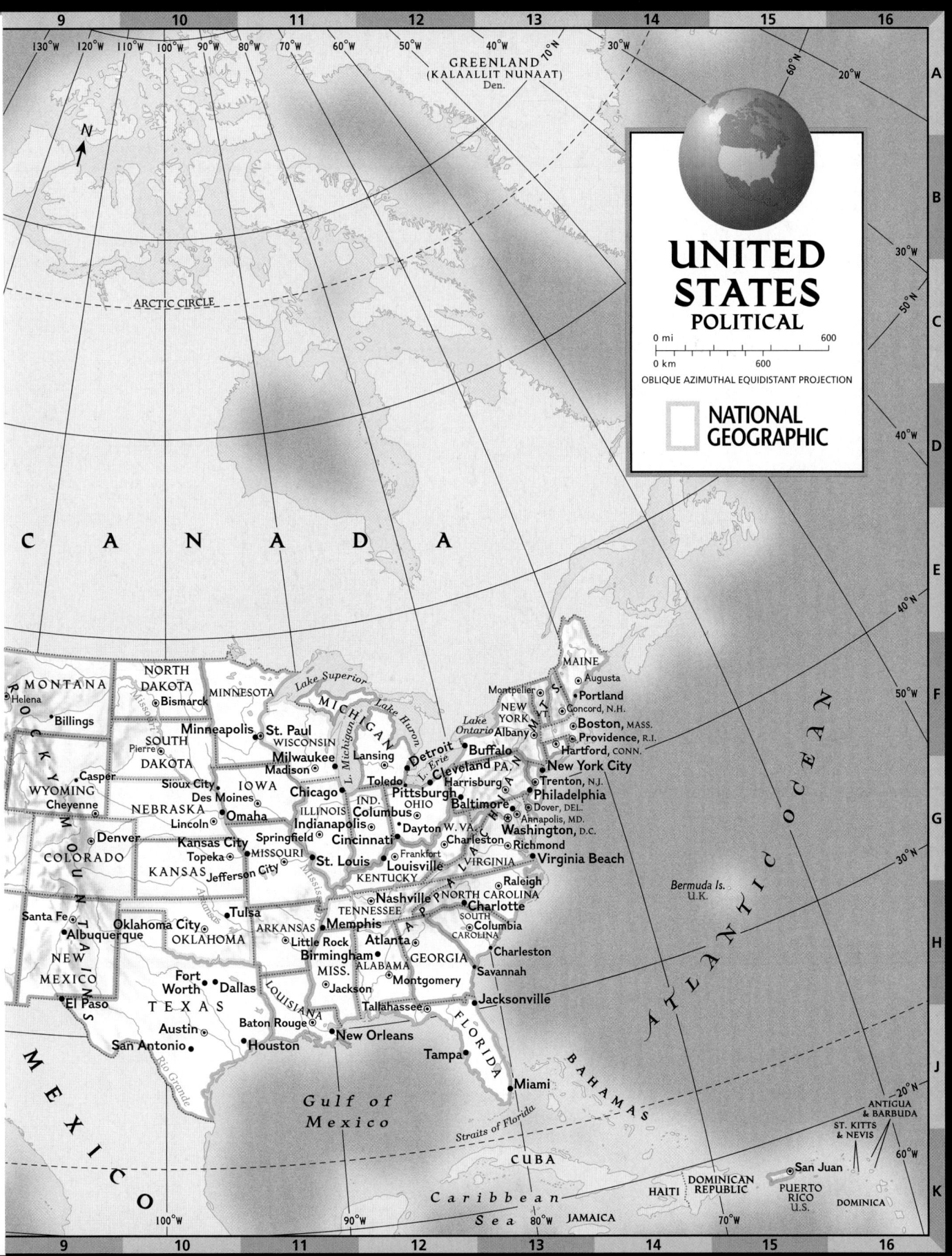

UNITED STATES POLITICAL

0 mi 600
0 km 600

OBLIQUE AZIMUTHAL EQUIDISTANT PROJECTION

NATIONAL GEOGRAPHIC

A 1 2 3 4 5 6 7 8

130°W   125°W   120°W   50°N   115°W   110°W   105°W   100°W

Cape Flattery
Mt. Olympus
7,965 ft
2,428 m
Seattle

45°N

C A N A D A

Columbia
CASCADE RANGE
COLUMBIA PLATEAU
Blue Mts.
Clearwater Mts.
Bitterroot Range
ROCKY
Missouri

Great Sandy Desert
Salmon River Mts.
Absaroka Range
Bighorn Mts.
Laramie Mts.
Black Hills

130°W

40°N
Cape Mendocino

Snake
Snake River Plain
Shoshone Falls
Wind River Range

N. Platte
GREAT
Sand Hills
Missouri

SIERRA NEVADA
Central Valley
Lake Tahoe
Great Salt Lake
Wasatch Range
Uinta Mts.

Platte
Platte

PACIFIC
OCEAN

GREAT BASIN

MOUNTAINS

Denver
14,433 ft
4,399 m   Mt. Elbert

High Plains

35°N

Mt. Whitney
14,494 ft
4,418 m
Death Valley
-282 ft -86 m

Lake Powell
Colorado

Arkansas

Point Conception

Mojave Desert
Lake Mead
Grand Canyon
Colorado Plateau
San Juan Mts.
Sangre de Cristo Mts.

Los Angeles

Channel Islands

Salton Sea

Colorado

Phoenix

Sacramento Mts.

Llano Estacado

Red

San Diego

30°N

Sonoran Desert

Rio Grande

Dallas
Brazos

125°W   120°W   115°W

G

ARCTIC OCEAN
Point Barrow
Beaufort Sea

68°N
180°
Chukchi Sea
North Slope
Brooks Range
68°N

CANADA

Edwards Plateau

RUSSIA
Bering Strait
ARCTIC CIRCLE
Seward Pen.
ALASKA

C O

St. Lawrence Island
Yukon
Kuskokwim
Tanana

172°W
60°N
Nunivak Island

Alaska Range
Mt. McKinley (Denali)
20,320 ft, 6,194 m
Anchorage

110°W

60°N

25°N

H

J

Bering Sea
Bristol Bay
Gulf of Alaska
Alexander Archipelago

Alaska Peninsula
Kodiak I.

M E X I C O

52°N
ALASKA
0 mi   300
0 km   300

PACIFIC OCEAN

52°N

TROPIC OF CANCER

K

164°W   156°W   148°W   140°W   132°W   105°W   100°W

1 2 3 4 5 6 7 8

A4 Reference Atlas

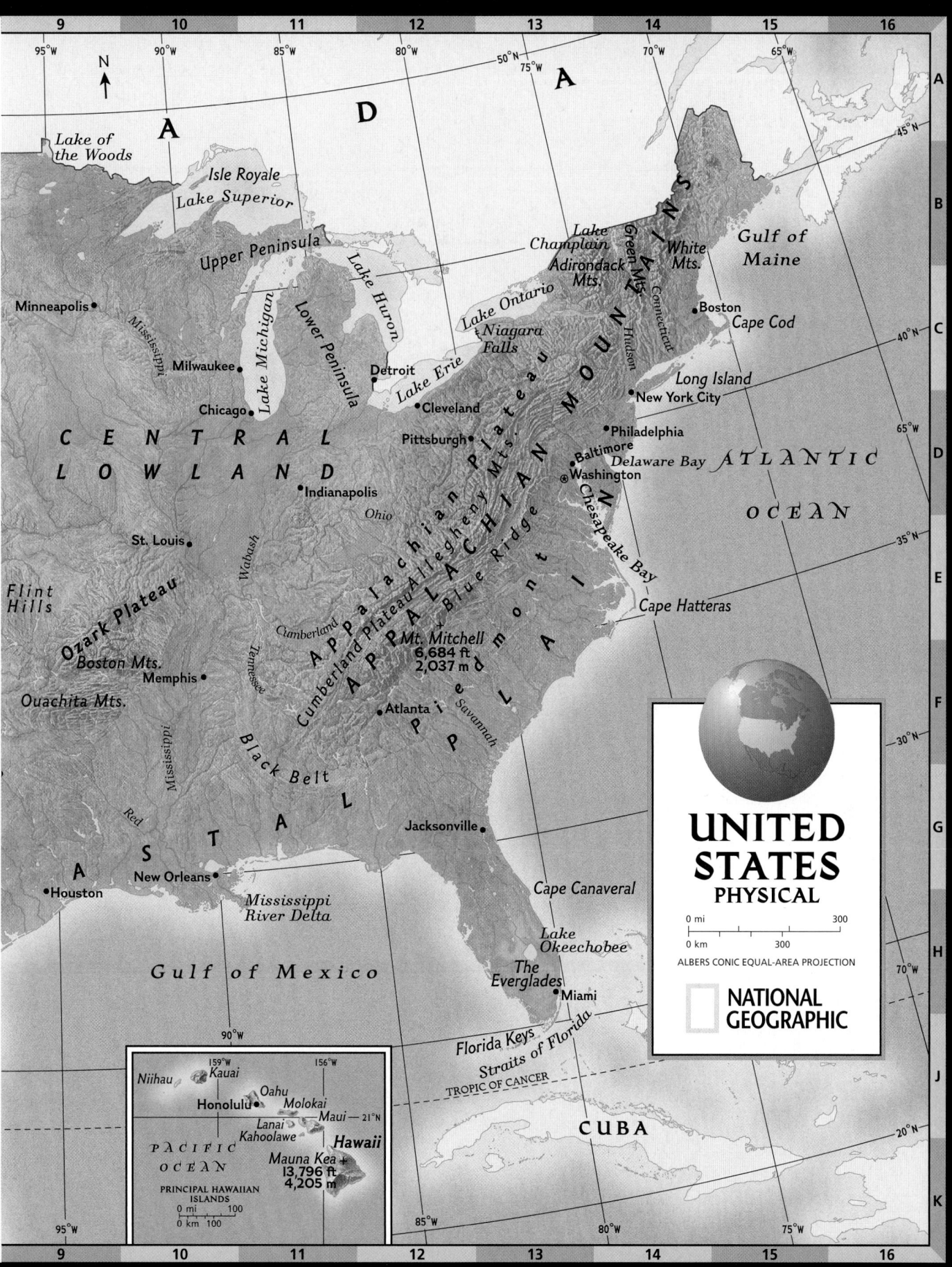

9 10 11 12 13 14 15 16

95°W 90°W 85°W 80°W 50°N 75°W 70°N 65°W A

N

A   A   D   A

Lake of
the Woods

45°N

Isle Royale
Lake Superior

Upper Peninsula

Lake Champlain
Adirondack Mts.
Green Mts.
White Mts.
Gulf of Maine

Minneapolis

Lake Huron

Lower Peninsula

Lake Michigan

Boston
Cape Cod

40°N

Milwaukee

Lake Ontario

Niagara Falls

Connecticut

Chicago

Detroit

Lake Erie

Cleveland

Long Island
New York City

65°W

C E N T R A L

Pittsburgh

Appalachian Plateau
Allegheny Mts.

Philadelphia

Baltimore
Delaware Bay

ATLANTIC

L O W L A N D

Indianapolis

Ohio

Washington

Chesapeake Bay

OCEAN

St. Louis

Wabash

Appalachian Plateau

Blue Ridge

APPALACHIAN MOUNTAINS

Hudson

35°N

Flint
Hills

Ozark Plateau

Cumberland

Cumberland Plateau

Piedmont

Cape Hatteras

Boston Mts.
Memphis

Tennessee

Mt. Mitchell
6,684 ft
2,037 m

30°N

Ouachita Mts.

APPALACHIAN

Atlanta

Savannah

Black Belt

Mississippi

Red

A   S   T   A   L

Jacksonville

New Orleans

P L A I N

Houston

Mississippi
River Delta

Cape Canaveral

Lake
Okeechobee

G u l f   o f   M e x i c o

The
Everglades

Miami

Florida Keys
Straits of Florida
TROPIC OF CANCER

CUBA

20°N

UNITED STATES
PHYSICAL

0 mi   300

0 km   300

ALBERS CONIC EQUAL-AREA PROJECTION

NATIONAL
GEOGRAPHIC

70°W

75°W

Principal Hawaiian Islands inset:

159°W 156°W

Niihau Kauai

Oahu

Honolulu Molokai

Lanai Maui — 21°N

Kahoolawe

PACIFIC
OCEAN

Hawaii

Mauna Kea
13,796 ft
4,205 m

PRINCIPAL HAWAIIAN
ISLANDS

0 mi   100

0 km 100

90°W 95°W 85°W 80°W 75°W

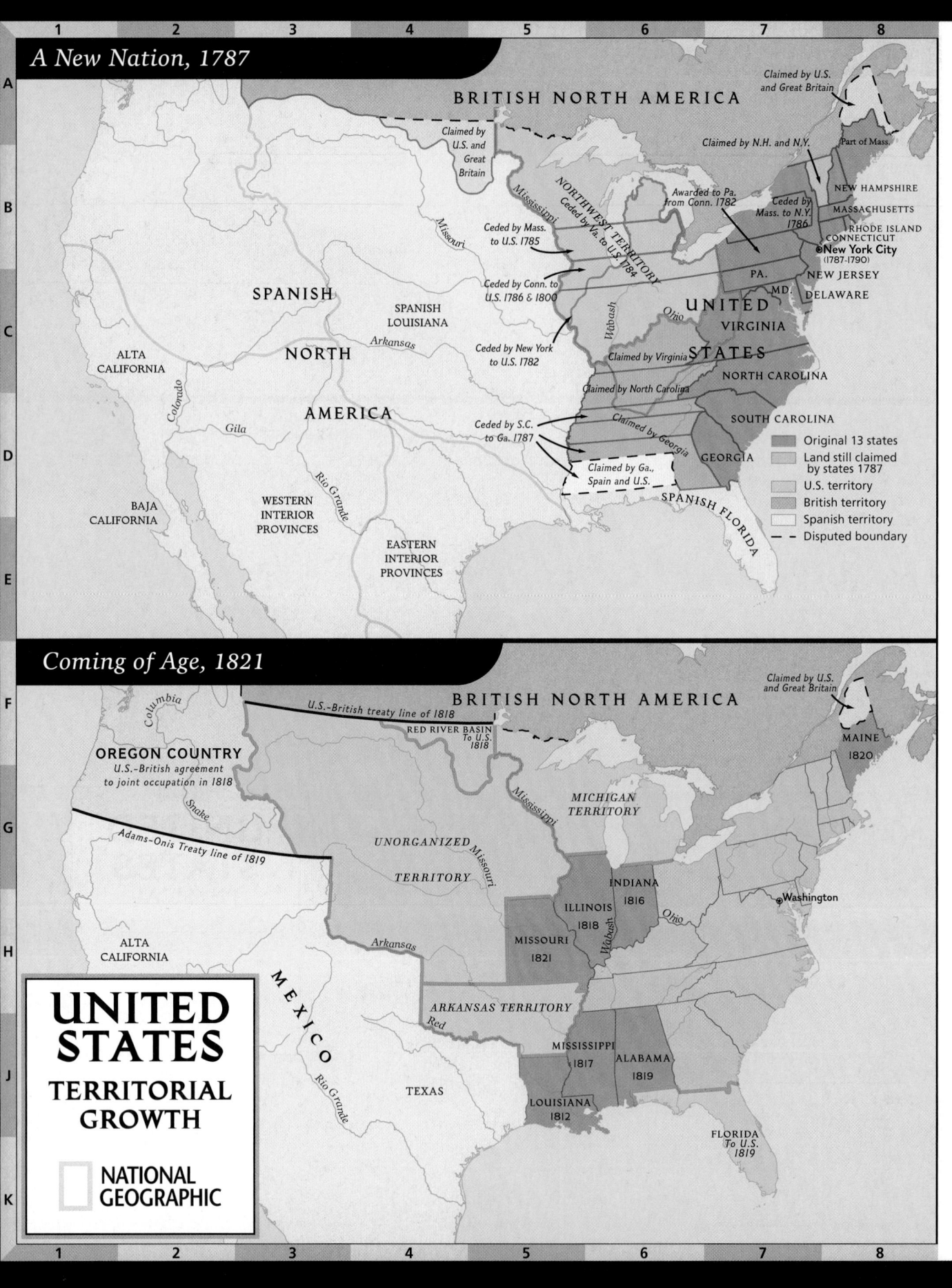

A New Nation, 1787

BRITISH NORTH AMERICA

Claimed by U.S. and Great Britain

Claimed by U.S. and Great Britain

Claimed by U.S. and Great Britain

Part of Mass.

Claimed by N.H. and N.Y.

Awarded to Pa. from Conn. 1782

Ceded by Mass. to N.Y. 1786

NEW HAMPSHIRE

MASSACHUSETTS

RHODE ISLAND

CONNECTICUT

New York City
(1787-1790)

PA.

MD.

NEW JERSEY

DELAWARE

Ceded by Mass. to U.S. 1785

Ceded by Va. to U.S. 1784

NORTHWEST TERRITORY

Ceded by Conn. to U.S. 1786 & 1800

Mississippi

Missouri

SPANISH

NORTH

AMERICA

SPANISH LOUISIANA

Arkansas

Colorado

Gila

Wabash

Ohio

UNITED

STATES

VIRGINIA

Ceded by New York to U.S. 1782

Claimed by Virginia

Claimed by North Carolina

NORTH CAROLINA

SOUTH CAROLINA

Ceded by S.C. to Ga. 1787

Claimed by Georgia

GEORGIA

Claimed by Ga., Spain and U.S.

SPANISH FLORIDA

ALTA CALIFORNIA

BAJA CALIFORNIA

WESTERN INTERIOR PROVINCES

Rio Grande

EASTERN INTERIOR PROVINCES

Original 13 states
Land still claimed by states 1787
U.S. territory
British territory
Spanish territory
– – – Disputed boundary

Coming of Age, 1821

BRITISH NORTH AMERICA

Claimed by U.S. and Great Britain

U.S.–British treaty line of 1818

Columbia

RED RIVER BASIN To U.S. 1818

MAINE 1820

OREGON COUNTRY
U.S.–British agreement to joint occupation in 1818

Snake

Adams–Onis Treaty line of 1819

Mississippi

MICHIGAN TERRITORY

UNORGANIZED

TERRITORY

Missouri

INDIANA 1816

ILLINOIS 1818

Ohio

Washington

ALTA CALIFORNIA

Arkansas

MISSOURI 1821

Wabash

M E X I C O

ARKANSAS TERRITORY

Red

MISSISSIPPI 1817

ALABAMA 1819

Rio Grande

TEXAS

LOUISIANA 1812

FLORIDA To U.S. 1819

UNITED
STATES
TERRITORIAL
GROWTH

NATIONAL
GEOGRAPHIC

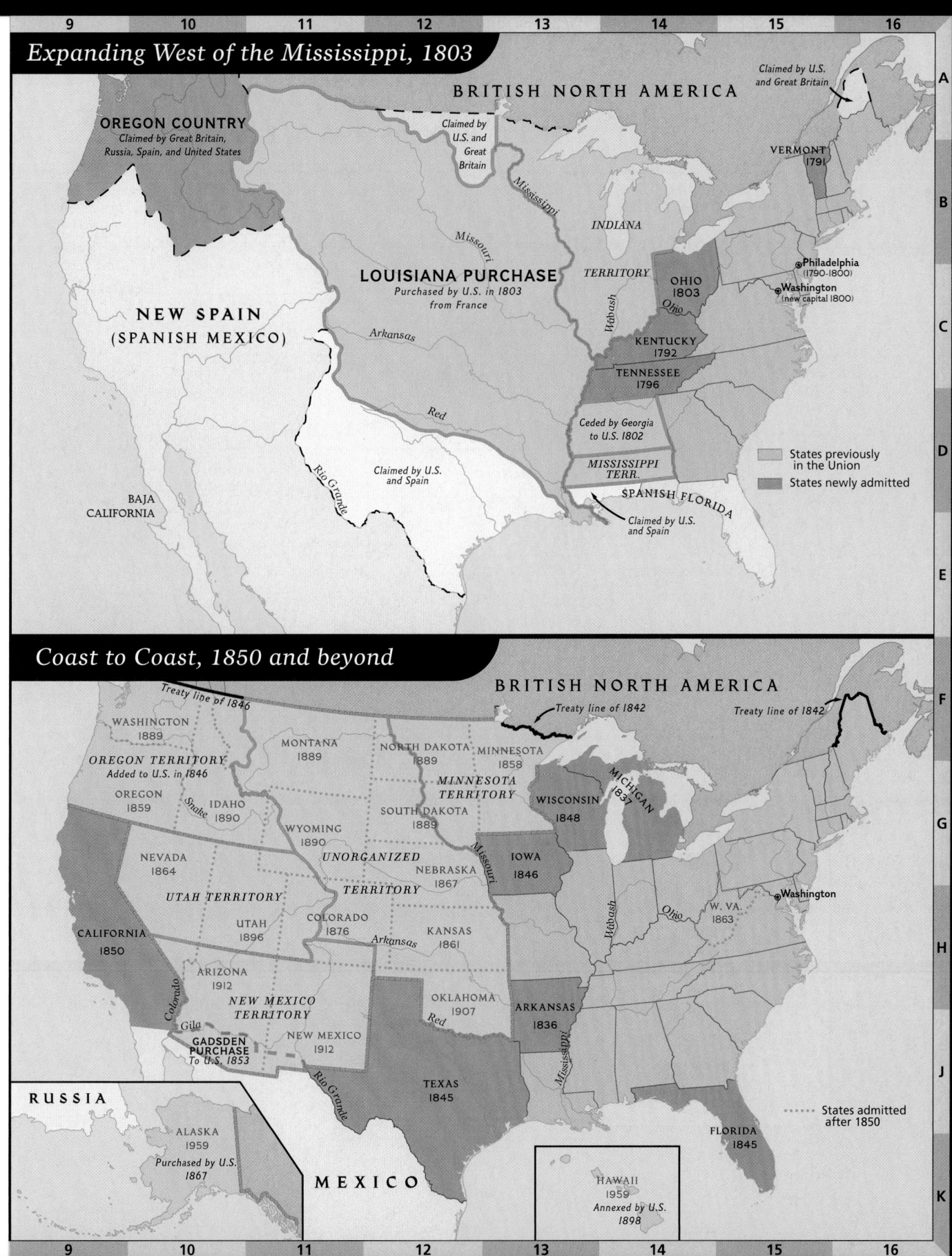

Expanding West of the Mississippi, 1803

BRITISH NORTH AMERICA

Claimed by U.S. and Great Britain

OREGON COUNTRY
Claimed by Great Britain, Russia, Spain, and United States

Claimed by U.S. and Great Britain

VERMONT 1791

Claimed by U.S. and Great Britain

Mississippi

Missouri

INDIANA

TERRITORY

LOUISIANA PURCHASE
Purchased by U.S. in 1803 from France

OHIO 1803

Wabash

Ohio

●Philadelphia
(1790-1800)

●Washington
(new capital 1800)

NEW SPAIN
(SPANISH MEXICO)

Arkansas

KENTUCKY 1792

TENNESSEE 1796

Red

Rio Grande

BAJA CALIFORNIA

Claimed by U.S. and Spain

Ceded by Georgia to U.S. 1802

MISSISSIPPI TERR.

SPANISH FLORIDA

Claimed by U.S. and Spain

States previously in the Union

States newly admitted

Coast to Coast, 1850 and beyond

BRITISH NORTH AMERICA

Treaty line of 1846

Treaty line of 1842

Treaty line of 1842

WASHINGTON 1889

MONTANA 1889

NORTH DAKOTA 1889

MINNESOTA 1858

OREGON TERRITORY
Added to U.S. in 1846

MINNESOTA TERRITORY

MICHIGAN 1837

OREGON 1859

Snake

IDAHO 1890

SOUTH DAKOTA 1889

WISCONSIN 1848

NEVADA 1864

WYOMING 1890

UNORGANIZED

Missouri

IOWA 1846

UTAH TERRITORY

TERRITORY

NEBRASKA 1867

W. VA. 1863

●Washington

CALIFORNIA 1850

UTAH 1896

COLORADO 1876

KANSAS 1861

Arkansas

Wabash

Ohio

Colorado

ARIZONA 1912

NEW MEXICO TERRITORY

OKLAHOMA 1907

ARKANSAS 1836

Gila

GADSDEN PURCHASE
To U.S. 1853

NEW MEXICO 1912

Red

Mississippi

Rio Grande

TEXAS 1845

RUSSIA

ALASKA 1959

Purchased by U.S. 1867

MEXICO

FLORIDA 1845

HAWAII 1959

Annexed by U.S. 1898

States admitted after 1850

Reference Atlas A7

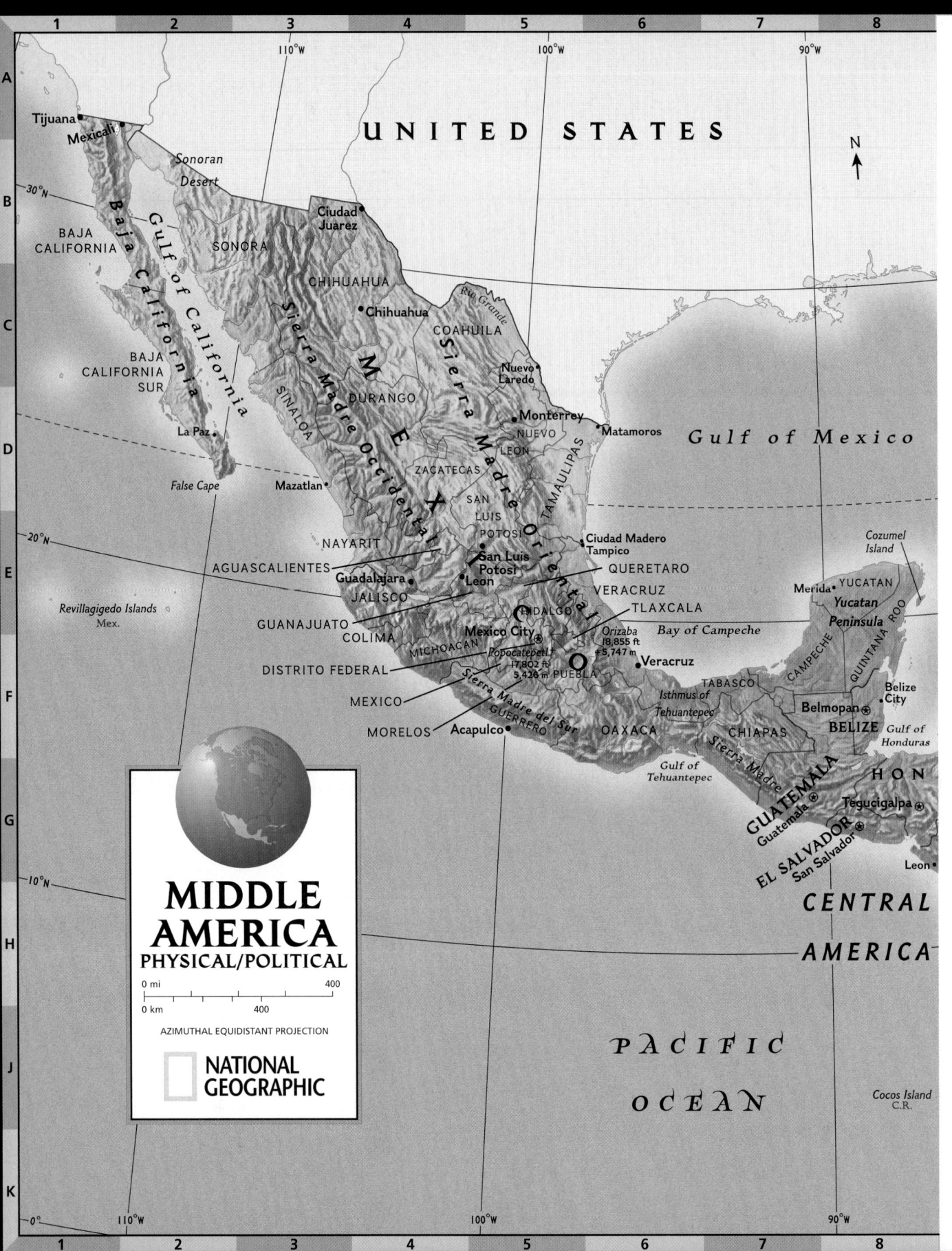

MIDDLE AMERICA
PHYSICAL/POLITICAL

0 mi   400
0 km   400

AZIMUTHAL EQUIDISTANT PROJECTION

NATIONAL GEOGRAPHIC

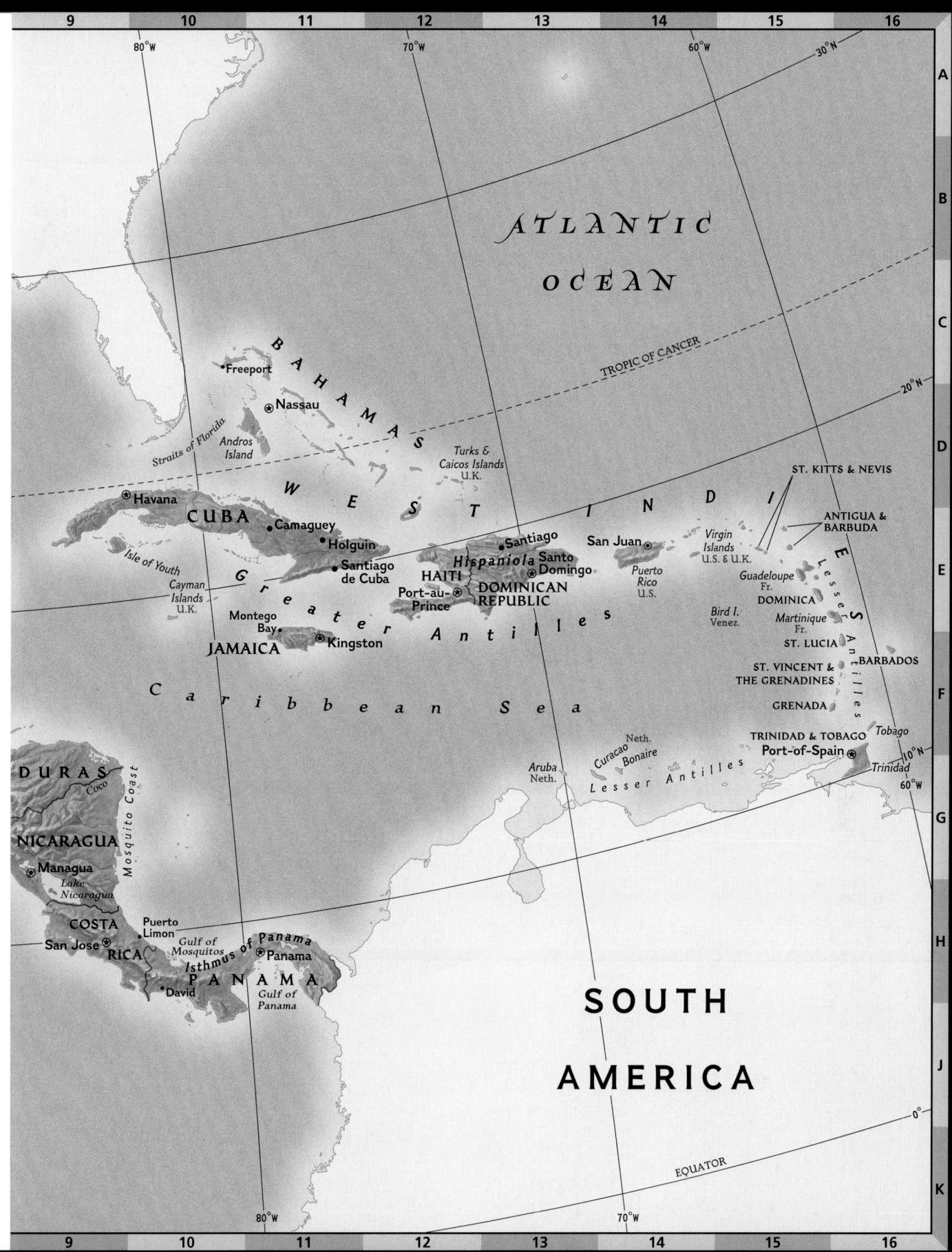

ATLANTIC

OCEAN

TROPIC OF CANCER

30°N

20°N

BAHAMAS

•Freeport

⊛ Nassau

Andros
Island

Straits of Florida

Turks &
Caicos Islands
U.K.

WEST INDI

ST. KITTS & NEVIS

ANTIGUA &
BARBUDA

⊛ Havana

CUBA

Lesser Antilles

•Camaguey

•Holguin

•Santiago
de Cuba

Santiago•

Hispaniola Santo
HAITI   Domingo
Port-au- ⊛
Prince   DOMINICAN
          REPUBLIC

San Juan ⊛

Virgin
Islands
U.S. & U.K.

Puerto
Rico
U.S.

Guadeloupe
Fr.

DOMINICA

Isle of Youth

Cayman
Islands
U.K.

Greater Antilles

Bird I.
Venez.

Martinique
Fr.

ST. LUCIA

Montego
Bay

JAMAICA

⊛ Kingston

BARBADOS

ST. VINCENT &
THE GRENADINES

GRENADA

Caribbean Sea

Neth.

Curacao
Bonaire

TRINIDAD & TOBAGO
Port-of-Spain ⊛

Tobago

Aruba
Neth.

Lesser Antilles

Trinidad

10°N

60°W

DURAS

Coco

Mosquito Coast

NICARAGUA

⊛ Managua

Lake
Nicaragua

COSTA

San Jose ⊛

RICA

Puerto
•Limon

Gulf of
Mosquitos

Isthmus of Panama

⊛ Panama

PANAMA

•David

Gulf of
Panama

SOUTH

AMERICA

0°

EQUATOR

80°W

70°W

A10   Reference Atlas

CANADA
PHYSICAL/POLITICAL

0 mi   400
0 km   400

AZIMUTHAL EQUIDISTANT PROJECTION

NATIONAL
GEOGRAPHIC

ICELAND

GREENLAND
(KALAALLIT NUNAAT)
Den.

Ellesmere
Island

Devon Island

Baffin
Bay

Melville
Peninsula

Foxe
Basin

Baffin Island

N   U   N   A   V   U   T

Southampton
Island

Iqaluit

Davis Strait

Hudson Strait

Labrador
Sea

Ungava
Bay

Cartwright

NEWFOUNDLAND AND LABRADOR

Hudson
Bay

Belcher
Islands

Schefferville
Happy Valley-
Goose Bay
Smallwood
Reservoir
"Churchill Falls

Island of
Newfoundland

James Bay

QUEBEC

Manicouagan
Reservoir
Sept-Iles

Anticosti I.

St. John's
Avalon
Peninsula

St.-Pierre & Miquelon
Fr.

Gulf of
St. Lawrence

S   H   I   E   L   D

Chicoutimi

Gaspe
Pen.

PRINCE
EDWARD
ISLAND

Cape Breton I.

ATLANTIC

ONTARIO

Lake
Nipigon

Rouyn-Noranda

Quebec

Fredericton

Charlottetown
NOVA
SCOTIA

Thunder
Bay
Lake
Superior

NEW
BRUNSWICK

Saint John

Halifax

OCEAN

Sudbury

Montreal

Bay of Fundy

St. Lawrence

Ottawa

Lake
Huron

Lake Michigan

Toronto

L. Ontario

Niagara Falls
London

L. Erie

Map labels (main map):

1 2 3 4 5 6 7 8

A

40°N
B

Sea of
Marmara
Istanbul

Black Sea

ANATOLIA

Ankara

TURKEY

C
Tunis

TUNISIA

Mediterranean Sea

Taurus Mountains

CYPRUS   SYRIA   Aleppo

LEBANON
Beirut   Damascus

ISRAEL   Syrian
Desert
Jerusalem

Alexandria
Cairo   Amman
El Giza   JORDAN
Sinai
Pen.

See inset below

Tripoli

30°N
E

LIBYA

F

EGYPT   Nile R.

Hejaz

Aswan
High Dam

Red Sea

SAHARA   Boundary claimed
by Sudan

SUDAN

AFRICA

Khartoum

30°E

Eastern Mediterranean Area

TURKEY

N

CYPRUS   Aleppo

SYRIA

LEBANON
Mediterranean
Sea   Beirut   Damascus

Sea of Galilee   Golan Heights
Jordan River
Tel Aviv–Jaffa   West Bank
Jerusalem   Amman
Suez Canal
Gaza Strip   Dead Sea
ISRAEL   JORDAN

El Giza   Cairo

EGYPT   Nile River

Gulf of Suez

Gulf of
Aqaba

30°N

SAUDI
ARABIA

0 mi   100

0 km   100

Red Sea

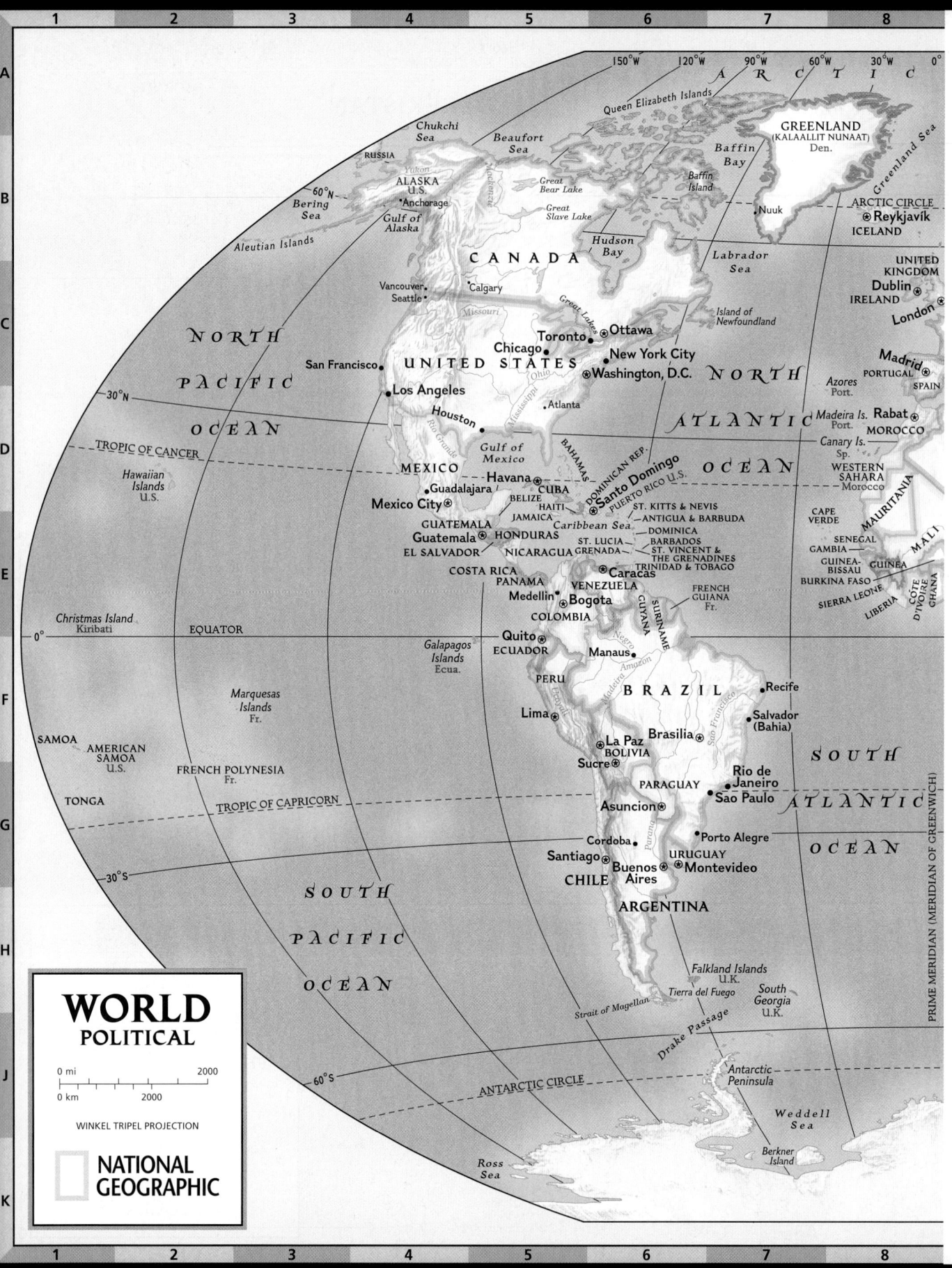

WORLD
POLITICAL

0 mi   2000

0 km   2000

WINKEL TRIPEL PROJECTION

NATIONAL
GEOGRAPHIC

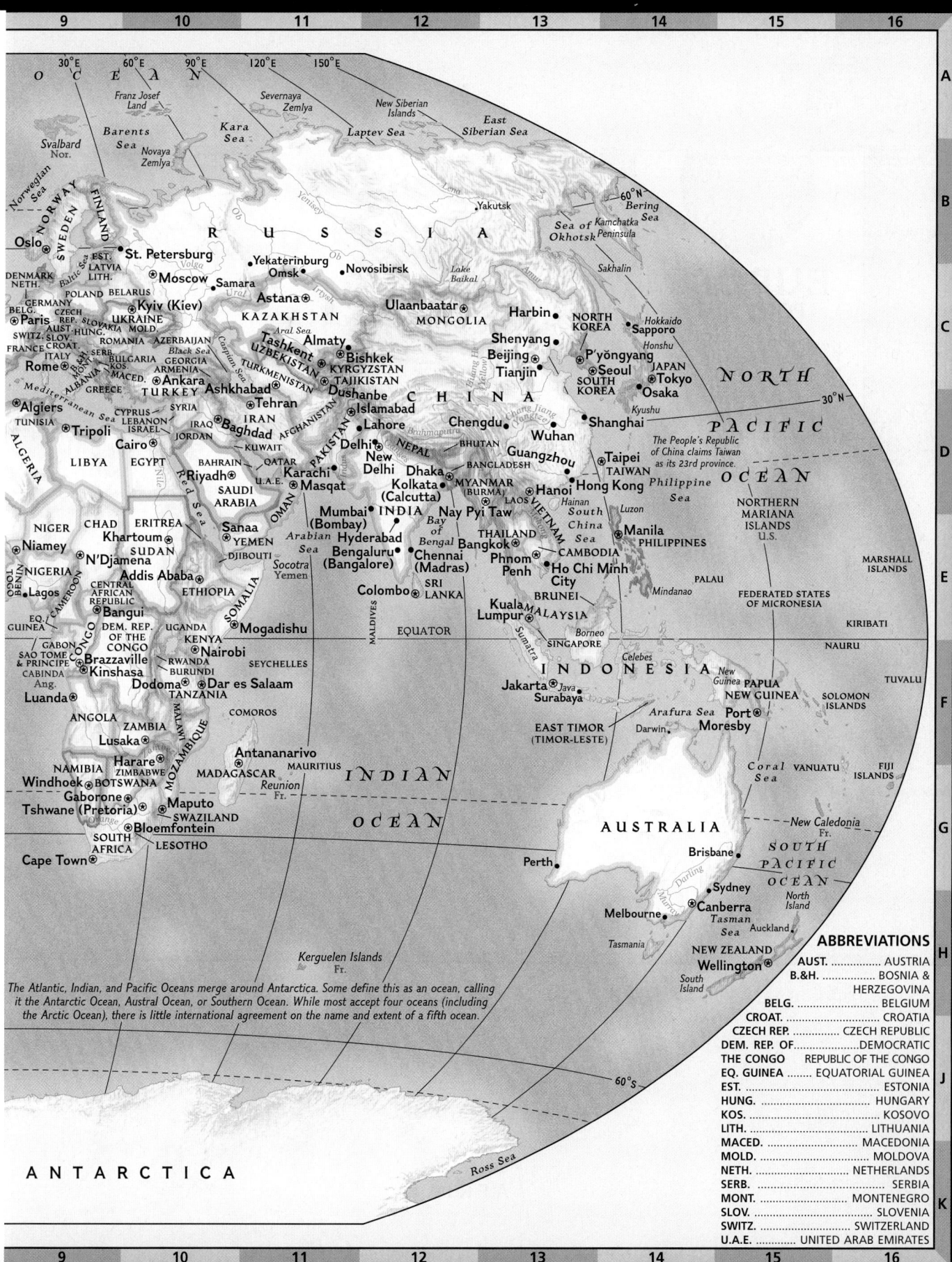

The Atlantic, Indian, and Pacific Oceans merge around Antarctica. Some define this as an ocean, calling it the Antarctic Ocean, Austral Ocean, or Southern Ocean. While most accept four oceans (including the Arctic Ocean), there is little international agreement on the name and extent of a fifth ocean.

The People's Republic of China claims Taiwan as its 23rd province.

ABBREVIATIONS

AUST.	AUSTRIA
B.&H.	BOSNIA & HERZEGOVINA
BELG.	BELGIUM
CROAT.	CROATIA
CZECH REP.	CZECH REPUBLIC
DEM. REP. OF THE CONGO	DEMOCRATIC REPUBLIC OF THE CONGO
EQ. GUINEA	EQUATORIAL GUINEA
EST.	ESTONIA
HUNG.	HUNGARY
KOS.	KOSOVO
LITH.	LITHUANIA
MACED.	MACEDONIA
MOLD.	MOLDOVA
NETH.	NETHERLANDS
SERB.	SERBIA
MONT.	MONTENEGRO
SLOV.	SLOVENIA
SWITZ.	SWITZERLAND
U.A.E.	UNITED ARAB EMIRATES

EUROPE
POLITICAL

0 mi   400
0 km   400

AZIMUTHAL EQUIDISTANT PROJECTION

NATIONAL GEOGRAPHIC

A commonly accepted division between Asia and Europe—here marked by a gray line—is formed by the Ural Mountains, Ural River, Caspian Sea, Caucasus Mountains, and the Black Sea with its outlets, the Bosporus and the Dardanelles.

Europe-Asia boundary

ASIA

RUSSIA

KAZAKHSTAN

UKRAINE

BELARUS

ESTONIA

LATVIA

LITHUANIA

RUSSIA

FINLAND

LAPLAND

ROMANIA

MOLDOVA

SERBIA

BULGARIA

KOSOVO

MACED.

GREECE

TURKEY

GEORGIA

AZERBAIJAN

ASIA

CYPRUS

Barents Sea

White Sea

Kola Peninsula

Murmansk
Kirovsk
Umba
Kiruna
Kiruna
Ivalo
Kemi
Lulea
Oulu
Umea
Vaasa
Kuopio
Pori
Tampere
Turku
Helsinki
Tallinn
Riga
Daugavpils
Vitsyebsk
Vilnius
Kaunas
Warsaw
Krakow
Lviv

Tobseda
Pechora
Arkhangel'sk
Severodvinsk
Syktyvkar
Perm
Kirov
Ufa
Kazan
Yaroslavl
Nizhniy Novgorod
Tver
Moscow
Ryazan
Samara
Orenburg
Oral
Penza
Saratov
Smolensk
Bryansk
Minsk
Homyel
Kursk
Chernihiv
Sumy
Kyiv (Kiev)
Kharkiv
Poltava
Vinnytsya
Donetsk
Dnipropetrovsk
Rostov
Volgograd
Astrakhan
Stavropol
Grozny
Baku

Lake Onega
Lake Ladoga
St. Petersburg
Velikiy Novgorod

Chişinău
Odesa
Sea of Azov
Crimea
Kerch
Simferopol
Yalta
Sevastopol

Belgrade
Bucharest
Constanta
Pristina
Sofia
Varna
Skopje
Thessaloniki
Dardanelles
Aegean Sea
Peloponnesus
Athens
Crete
Iraklio

Istanbul
Bosporus
Sea of Marmara

Black Sea

Caucasus Mountains

Caspian Sea

Ural Mountains

Dniester
Carpathian Mts.
Balkan Mts.
Danube
Volga
Ural

Nicosia
Rhodes

Sea

30°E
40°E
70°N
50°E
70°E
60°N
80°E
70°E
50°N
60°E
40°N
30°N
50°E
30°E
40°E

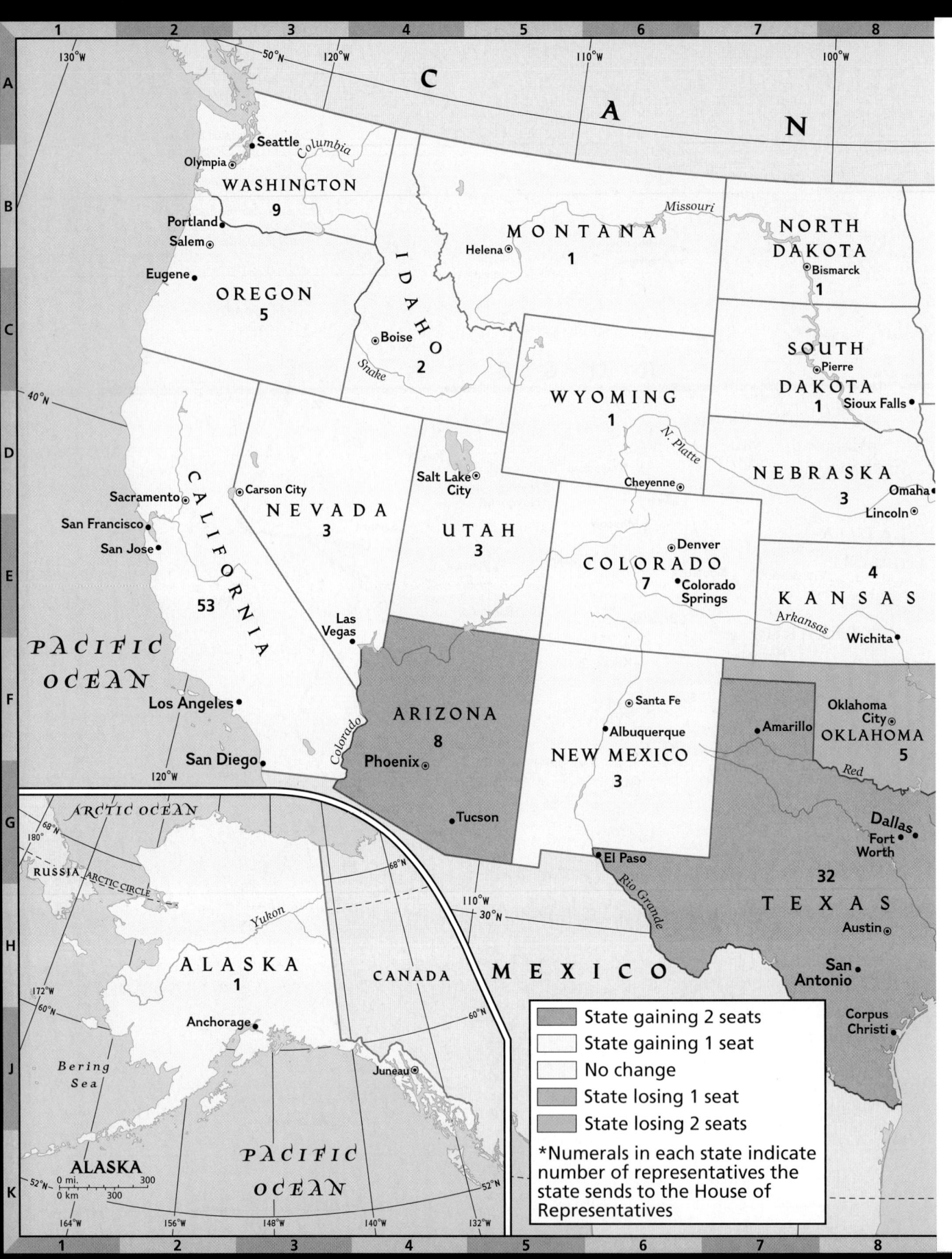

1	2	3	4	5	6	7	8

130°W 50°N 120°W 110°W 100°W

A

C A N A

Seattle Columbia
Olympia ⊙

WASHINGTON
9

Portland
Salem ⊙

Eugene

OREGON
5

I D A H O

Helena

M O N T A N A
1

Missouri

**NORTH
DAKOTA**
Bismarck ⊙
1

B

⊙ Boise

2

Snake

WYOMING
1

Cheyenne ⊙

N. Platte

**SOUTH
DAKOTA**
Pierre ⊙
1 Sioux Falls

C

40°N

Sacramento ⊙ Carson City ⊙

San Francisco

San Jose

N E V A D A
3

Salt Lake ⊙
City

U T A H
3

⊙ Denver

COLORADO
7 Colorado
Springs

NEBRASKA
3 Omaha
Lincoln ⊙

D

C A L I F O R N I A

53

Las
Vegas

4

K A N S A S

Arkansas
Wichita

E

**PACIFIC
OCEAN**

Los Angeles

Colorado

ARIZONA
8
Phoenix ⊙

Santa Fe ⊙

Albuquerque

NEW MEXICO
3

Amarillo

Oklahoma
City ⊙
OKLAHOMA
5

Red

F

San Diego

120°W

Tucson

El Paso

Rio Grande

Dallas
Fort
Worth

G

ARCTIC OCEAN
68°N
180°

RUSSIA ARCTIC CIRCLE

Yukon

68°W

110°W
30°N

T E X A S
32

Austin ⊙

H

172°W
60°N

A L A S K A
1

Anchorage

CANADA

M E X I C O

60°N

San
Antonio

Corpus
Christi

J

Bering
Sea

Juneau ⊙

	Legend
▨	State gaining 2 seats
□	State gaining 1 seat
▢	No change
▨	State losing 1 seat
▨	State losing 2 seats

K

ALASKA
52°N
0 mi. 300
0 km 300
164°W 156°W 148°W 140°W 132°W

**PACIFIC
OCEAN**

52°N

*Numerals in each state indicate
number of representatives the
state sends to the House of
Representatives

1	2	3	4	5	6	7	8

MINNESOTA
8

Lake Superior

M I C H I G A N

WISCONSIN
8

Minneapolis
⊙St. Paul

Mississippi

Milwaukee
Madison

Lake Michigan

Lake Huron

15
⊙Lansing
Detroit

Lake Ontario

Lake Erie

Buffalo

MAINE
2

⊙Augusta

Montpelier⊙ N.H.
VT.　　2
1　　⊙Concord

Boston

29
Albany⊙
10 MASS.
Hartford⊙ 5
CONN. RHODE ISLAND
2

Providence

40°N

50°N 70°W

I O W A
5
⊙Des Moines

Chicago

ILLINOIS
19
Springfield⊙

Fort Wayne

INDIANA

Indianapolis⊙

NEW YORK

O H I O
18
⊙Columbus

Cleveland

PENNSYLVANIA
19
Harrisburg⊙
Pittsburgh

N.J.
13
⊙Trenton
Philadelphia

New York City

M A R Y L A N D

Dover
DELAWARE

1

ATLANTIC
OCEAN

Kansas
City
⊙Topeka
Jefferson⊙
City

St.
Louis

Cincinnati
Ohio
Louisville
⊙Frankfort

9

WEST
VIRGINIA
3

Washington,
D.C.
8
Annapolis

11
Richmond⊙

⊙Charleston

•Virginia Beach

MISSOURI
9

KENTUCKY
6

V I R G I N I A

Tulsa

9 ⊙Nashville
TENNESSEE

13 ⊙Raleigh
NORTH CAROLINA
•Charlotte

N

ARKANSAS
Little
Rock ⊙
4

Memphis

Tennessee

Mississippi

Birmingham

⊙Atlanta

SOUTH
⊙Columbia
CAROLINA
6

4
MISSISSIPPI
Jackson⊙

ALABAMA
7
Montgomery⊙

GEORGIA
13

Savannah

Savannah

30°N

7
LOUISIANA
⊙Baton Rouge
New Orleans

Mobile Tallahassee⊙

•Jacksonville

70°W

•Houston

Gulf of Mexico

Tampa•

F L O R I D A

25

UNITED
STATES
2000 CONGRESSIONAL
REAPPORTIONMENT

90°W

0 mi.　　　　　　300
0 km　　　　　　300
ALBERS CONIC EQUAL-AREA PROJECTION

•Miami

NATIONAL
GEOGRAPHIC

159°W　156°W
Niihau　Kauai
Honolulu⊙ Oahu Molokai
Lanai Maui — 21°N
Kahoolawe *Hawaii*

*PACIFIC
OCEAN*

PRINCIPAL HAWAIIAN
ISLANDS

0 mi.　　100
0 km　　100
156°W

2

TROPIC OF CANCER

C U B A

80°W

20°N

Geography Skills Handbook

How Do I Study Geography?

Geographers have tried to understand the best way to teach and learn about geography. In order to do this, geographers created the *Five Themes of Geography*. The themes acted as a guide for teaching the basic ideas about geography to students like yourself.

People who teach and study geography, though, thought that the Five Themes were too broad. In 1994, geographers created 18 national geography standards. These standards were more detailed about what should be taught and learned. The Six Essential Elements act as a bridge connecting the Five Themes with the standards.

These pages show you how the Five Themes are related to the Six Essential Elements and the 18 standards.

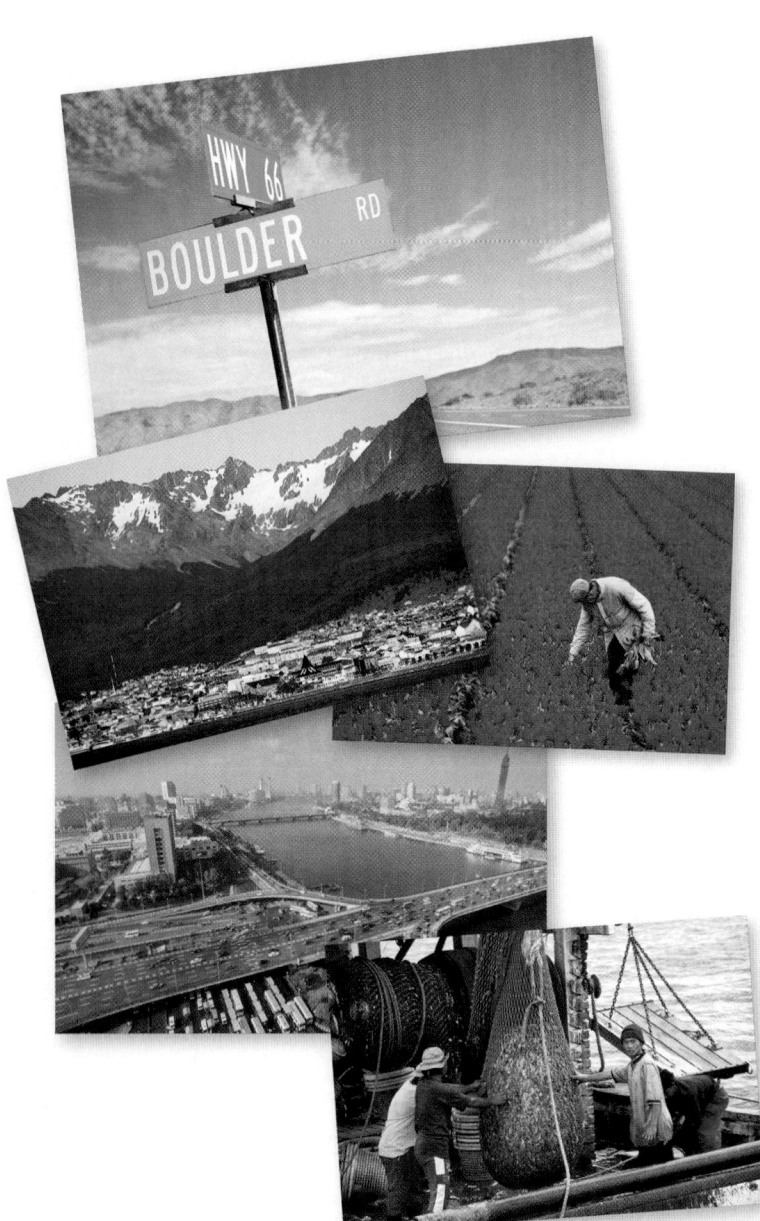

5
Themes of Geography

1 Location
Location describes where something is. Absolute location describes a place's exact position on the Earth's surface. Relative location expresses where a place is in relation to another place.

2 Place
Place describes the physical and human characteristics that make a location unique.

3 Regions
Regions are areas that share common characteristics.

4 Movement
Movement explains how and why people and things move and are connected.

5 Human-Environment Interaction
Human-Environment Interaction describes the relationship between people and their environment.

6 Essential Elements

18 Geography Standards

I. The World in Spatial Terms
Geographers look to see where a place is located. Location acts as a starting point to answer "Where Is It?" The location of a place helps you orient yourself as to where you are.

1 How to use maps and other tools

2 How to use mental maps to organize information

3 How to analyze the spatial organization of people, places, and environments

II. Places and Regions
Place describes physical characteristics such as landforms, climate, and plant or animal life. It might also describe human characteristics, including language and way of life. Places can also be organized into regions. **Regions** are places united by one or more characteristics.

4 The physical and human characteristics of places

5 How people create regions to interpret Earth's complexity

6 How culture and experience influence people's perceptions of places and regions

III. Physical Systems
Geographers study how physical systems, such as hurricanes, volcanoes, and glaciers, shape the surface of the Earth. They also look at how plants and animals depend upon one another and their surroundings for their survival.

7 The physical processes that shape Earth's surface

8 The distribution of ecosystems on Earth's surface

9 The characteristics, distribution, and migration of human populations

10 The complexity of Earth's cultural mosaics

11 The patterns and networks of economic interdependence

IV. Human Systems
People shape the world in which they live. They settle in certain places but not in others. An ongoing theme in geography is the movement of people, ideas, and goods.

12 The patterns of human settlement

13 The forces of cooperation and conflict

14 How human actions modify the physical environment

15 How physical systems affect human systems

16 The meaning, use, and distribution of resources

V. Environment and Society
How does the relationship between people and their natural surroundings influence the way people live? Geographers study how people use the environment and how their actions affect the environment.

VI. The Uses of Geography
Knowledge of geography helps us understand the relationships among people, places, and environments over time. Applying geographic skills helps you understand the past and prepare for the future.

17 How to apply geography to interpret the past

18 How to apply geography to interpret the present and plan for the future

NATIONAL
GEOGRAPHIC

Contents

Geography Skills Handbook

Throughout this text, you will discover how geography has shaped the course of events in United States history. Landforms, waterways, climate, and natural resources all have helped or hindered human activities. Usually people have learned either to adapt to their environments or to transform it to meet their needs. The resources in this handbook will help you get the most out of your textbook—and provide you with skills you will use for the rest of your life.

The study of geography is more than knowing a lot of facts about places. Rather, it has more to do with asking questions about the Earth, pursuing their answers, and solving problems. Thus, one of the most important geographic tools is inside your head: the ability to think geographically.

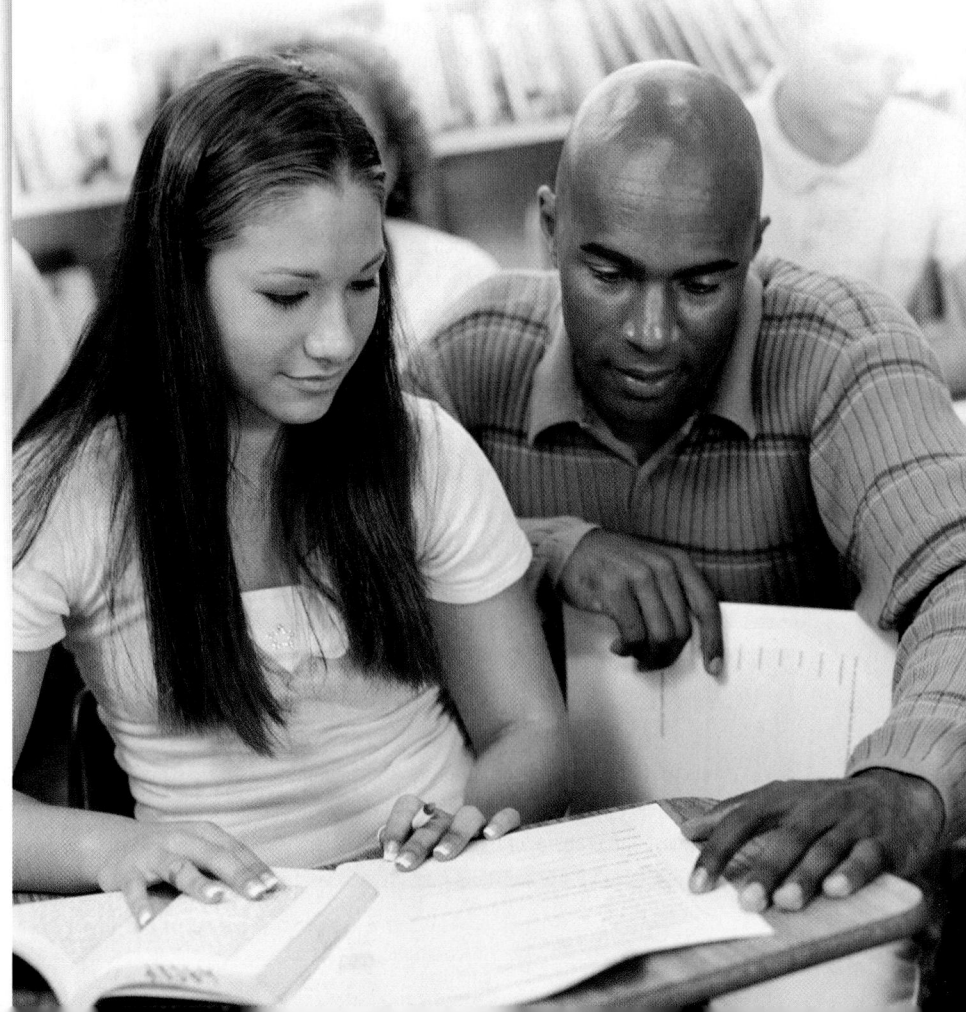

Globes and Maps

A **globe** is a scale model of the Earth. Because Earth is round, a globe presents the most accurate depiction of geographic information such as area, distance, and direction. However, globes show little close-up detail. A printed **map** is a symbolic representation of all or part of the planet. Unlike globes, maps can show small areas in great detail.

From 3-D to 2-D

Think about the surface of the Earth as the peel of an orange. To flatten the peel, you have to cut it like the globe shown here. To create maps that are not interrupted, mapmakers, or **cartographers**, use mathematical formulas to transfer information from the three-dimensional globe to the two-dimensional map. However, when the curves of a globe become straight lines on a map, distortion of size, shape, distance, or area occurs.

globe accurately shows a great circle route, as indicated on the map below. However, as shown on the flat map, the great circle distance (dotted line) between Tokyo and Los Angeles appears to be far longer than the true direction distance (solid line). In fact, the great circle distance is 345 miles (555 km) shorter.

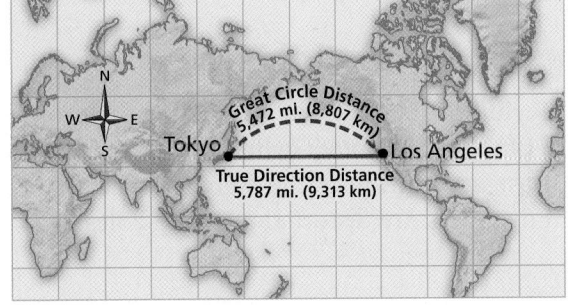

Great Circle Routes

A straight line of true direction—one that runs directly from west to east, for example—is not always the shortest distance between two points. This is due to the curvature of the Earth. To find the shortest distance, stretch a piece of string around a globe from one point to the other. The string will form part of a *great circle*, an imaginary line the follows the curve of the Earth. Ship captains and airline pilots use these **great circle routes** to reduce travel time and conserve fuel.

The idea of a great circle route is an important difference between globes and maps. A round

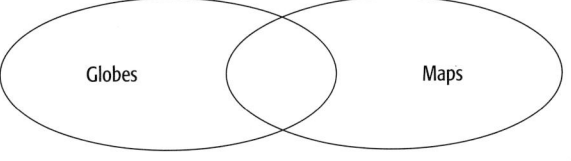

Practicing SKILLS

1. **Explain** the significance of: globe, map, cartographer, great circle route.
2. **Describe** the problems that arise when the curves of a globe become straight lines on a map.
3. **Use** a Venn diagram like the one below to identify the similarities and differences between globes and maps.

Globes   Maps

Projections

To create maps, cartographers project the round Earth onto a flat surface—making a **map projection.** Distance, shape, direction, or size may be distorted by a projection. As a result, the purpose of the map usually dictates which projection is used. There are many kinds of map projections, some with general names and some named for the cartographers who developed them. Three basic categories of map projections are shown here: **planar, cylindrical,** and **conic.**

Planar Projection

A planar projection shows the Earth centered in such a way that a straight line coming from the center to any other point represents the shortest distance. Also known as an azimuthal projection, it is most accurate at its center. As a result, it is often used for maps of the Poles.

Cylindrical Projection

A cylindrical projection is based on the projection of the globe onto a cylinder. This projection is most accurate near the Equator, but shapes and distances are distorted near the Poles.

Conic Projection

A conic projection comes from placing a cone over part of a globe. Conic projections are best suited for showing limited east-west areas that are not too far from the Equator. For these uses, a conic projection can indicate distances and directions fairly accurately.

Common Map Projections

Each type of map projection has advantages and some degree of inaccuracy. Four of the most common projections are shown here.

Winkel Tripel Projection

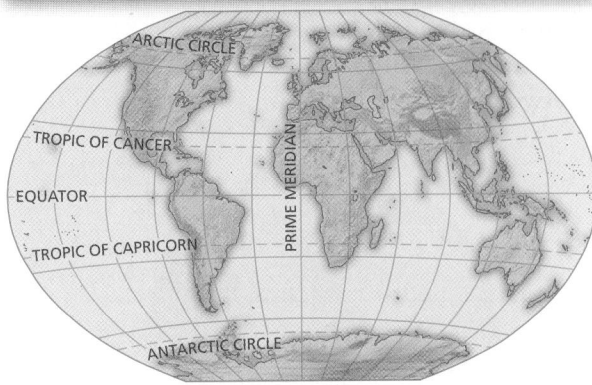

Most general reference world maps are the Winkel Tripel projection. It provides a good balance between the size and shape of land areas as they are shown on the map. Even the polar areas are depicted with little distortion of size and shape.

Goode's Interrupted Equal-Area Projection

An **interrupted projection** resembles a globe that has been cut apart and laid flat. Goode's Interrupted Equal-Area projection shows the true size and shape of Earth's landmasses, but distances are generally distorted.

Robinson Projection

The Robinson projection has minor distortions. The sizes and shapes near the eastern and western edges of the map are accurate, and outlines of the continents appear much as they do on the globe. However, the polar areas are flattened.

Mercator Projection

The Mercator projection increasingly distorts size and distance as it moves away from the Equator. However, Mercator projections do accurately show true directions and the shapes of landmasses, making these maps useful for sea travel.

Practicing SKILLS

1. **Explain** the significance of: map projection, planar, cylindrical, conic, interrupted projection.

2. **How** does a cartographer determine which map projection to use?

3. **How** is Goode's Interrupted Equal-Area projection different from the Mercator projection?

4. **Which** of the four common projections described above is the best one to use when showing the entire world? Why?

5. **Use** a Venn diagram like the one below to identify the similarities and differences between the Winkel Tripel and Mercator projections.

Winkel Tripel projection   Mercator projection

Determining Location

Geography is often said to begin with the question: *Where?* The basic tool for answering the question is **location.** Lines on globes and maps provide information that can help you locate places. These lines cross one another forming a pattern called a **grid system,** which helps you find exact places on the Earth's surface.

A **hemisphere** is one of the halves into which the Earth is divided. Geographers divide the Earth into hemispheres to help them classify and describe places on Earth. Most places are located in two of the four hemispheres.

Latitude

Lines of **latitude,** or parallels, circle the Earth parallel to the Equator and measure the distance north or south of the Equator in degrees. The Equator is measured at 0° latitude, while the Poles lie at latitudes 90°N (north) and 90°S (south). Parallels north of the Equator are called north latitude. Parallels south of the Equator are called south latitude.

Longitude

Lines of **longitude,** or meridians, circle the Earth from Pole to Pole. These lines measure distance east or west of the **Prime Meridian** at 0° longitude. Meridians east of the Prime Meridian are known as east latitude. Meridians west of the Prime Meridian are known as west longitude. The 180° meridian on the opposite side of the Earth is called the International Date Line.

The Global Grid

Every place has a global address, or **absolute location.** You can identify the absolute location of a place by naming the latitude and longitude lines that cross exactly at that place. For example, Tokyo, Japan, is located at 36°N latitude and 140°E longitude. For more precise readings, each degree is further divided into 60 units called minutes.

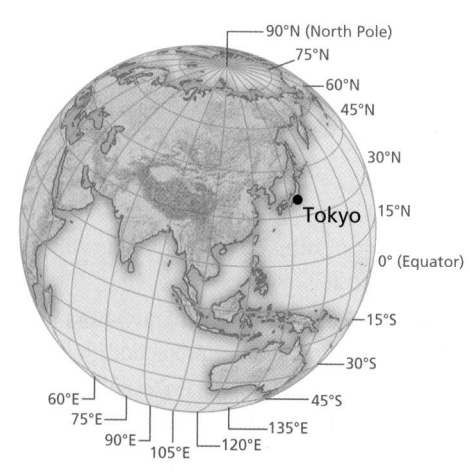

Northern and Southern Hemispheres

The diagram below shows that the Equator divides the Earth into the Northern and Southern Hemispheres. Everything north of the Equator is in the **Northern Hemisphere.** Everything south of the Equator is in the **Southern Hemisphere.**

Northern Hemisphere

Southern Hemisphere

Eastern and Western Hemispheres

The Prime Meridian and the International Date Line divide the Earth into the Eastern and Western Hemispheres. Everything east of the Prime Meridian for 180° is in the **Eastern Hemisphere.** Everything west of the Prime Meridian for 180° is in the **Western Hemisphere.**

Eastern Hemisphere

Western Hemisphere

Practicing SKILLS

1. **Explain** the significance of: location, grid system, hemisphere, Northern Hemisphere, Southern Hemisphere, Eastern Hemisphere, Western Hemisphere, latitude, longitude, Prime Meridian, absolute location.

2. **Why** do all maps label the Equator 0° latitude and the Prime Meridian 0° longitude?

3. **Which** lines of latitude and longitude divide the Earth into hemispheres?

4. **Using** the Reference Atlas maps, fill in a chart like the one below by writing the latitude and longitude of three world cities. Have a partner try to identify the cities.

5. **Use** a chart like the one below to identify the continents in each hemisphere. Some may be in more than one hemisphere.

Hemisphere	Continents
Northern	
Southern	
Eastern	
Western	

Reading a Map

In addition to latitude and longitude, maps feature other important tools to help you interpret the information they contain. Learning to use these map tools will help you read the symbolic language of maps more easily.

Title

The title tells you what kind of information the map is showing.

Key

The **key** lists and explains the symbols, colors, and lines used on the map. The key is sometimes called a legend.

Scale Bar

The **scale bar** shows the relationship between map measurements and actual distances on the Earth. By laying a ruler along the scale bar, you can calculate how many miles or kilometers are represented per inch or centimeter. The map projection used to create the map is often listed near the scale bar.

Compass Rose

The **compass rose** indicates directions. The four **cardinal directions**—north, south, east, and west—are usually indicated with arrows or the points of a star. The **intermediate directions**—northeast, northwest, southeast, and southwest—may also be shown.

Cities

Cities are represented by a dot. Sometimes the relative sizes of cities are shown using dots of different sizes.

Capitals

National capitals are often represented by a star within a circle.

Boundary Lines

On political maps of large areas, boundary lines highlight the borders between different countries or states.

Using Scale

All maps are drawn to a certain scale. **Scale** is a consistent, proportional relationship between the measurements shown on the map and the measurement of the Earth's surface.

Small-Scale Maps A small-scale map, like this political map of France, can show a large area but little detail. Note that the scale bar on this map indicates that about 1 inch is equal to 200 miles.

Large-Scale Maps A large-scale map, like this map of Paris, can show a small area with a great amount of detail. Study the scale bar. Note that the map measurements correspond to much smaller distances than on the map of France.

Absolute and Relative Location

As you learned on page GH6, absolute location is the exact point where a line of latitude crosses a line of longitude. Another way to indicate location is by **relative location,** or the location of one place in relation to another. To find relative location, find a reference point—a location you already know—on a map. Then look in the appropriate direction for the new location. For example, locate Paris (your reference point) on the map of France above. The relative location of Lyon can be described as southeast of Paris.

Practicing SKILLS

1. **Explain** the significance of: key, compass rose, cardinal directions, intermediate directions, scale bar, scale, relative location.

2. **Describe** the elements of a map that help you interpret the information displayed on the map.

3. **How** does the scale bar help you determine distances on the Earth's surface?

4. **Describe** the relative location of your school in two different ways.

5. **Use** a Venn diagram to identify the similarities and differences of small-scale maps and large-scale maps.

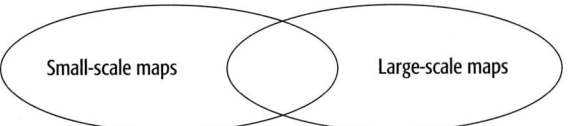

Physical Maps

A **physical map** shows the location and the **topography,** or shape of the Earth's physical features. A study of a country's physical features often helps to explain the historical development of the country. For example, mountains may be barriers to transportation, and rivers and streams can provide access into the interior of a country.

Water Features

Physical maps show rivers, streams, lakes, and other water features.

Landforms

Physical maps may show landforms such as mountains, plains, plateaus, and valleys.

Relief

Physical maps use shading and texture to show general **relief**–the differences in **elevation,** or height, of landforms.

---

1. **Explain** the significance of: physical map, topography, relief, elevation.

2. **Complete** a table like the one to the right to explain what you can learn from the map about each of the physical features listed.

Physical Feature	What You Can Learn from the Map
Davis Mountains	
Red River	
Gulf Coastal Plains	

Political Maps

A **political map** shows the boundaries and locations of political units such as countries, states, counties, cities, and towns. Many features depicted on a political map are **human-made,** or determined by humans rather than by nature. Political maps can show the networks and links that exist within and between political units.

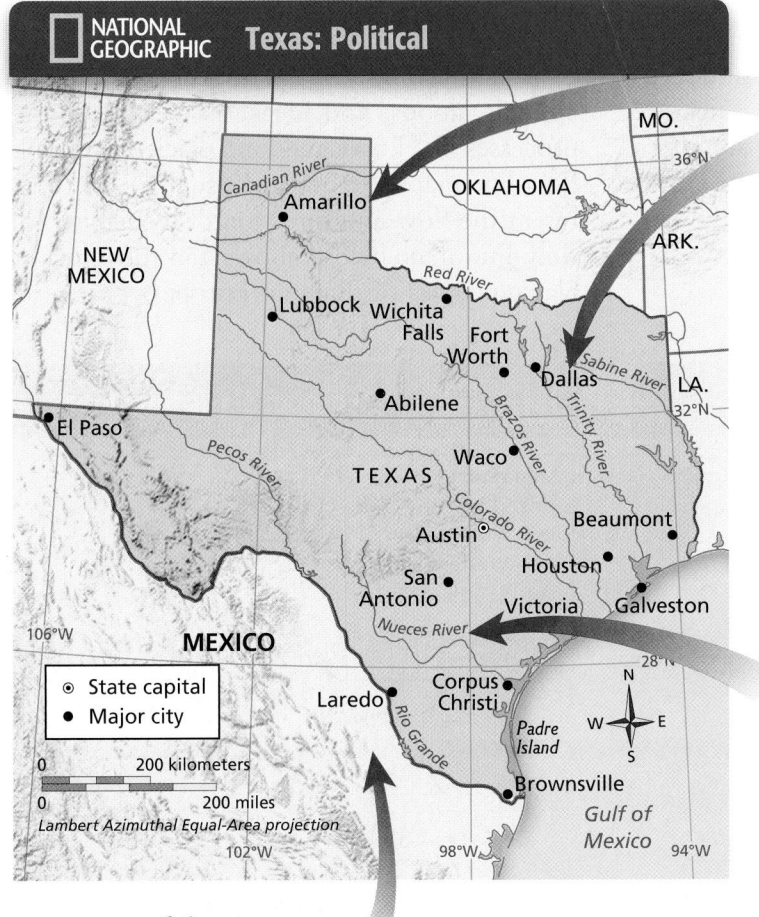

Human-Made Features

Political maps show human-made features such as boundaries, capitals, cities, roads, highways, and railroads.

Physical Features

Political maps may show some physical features such as relief, rivers, and mountains.

Nonsubject Area

Areas surrounding the subject area of the map are usually a different color to set them apart. They are labeled to give you a context for the area you are studying.

Practicing SKILLS

1. **Explain** the significance of: political map, human-made.
2. **What** types of information would you find on a political map that would not appear on a physical map?
3. **Complete** a table like the one to the right to explain what you can learn from the map about each of the human-made features listed.

Human-Made Feature	What You Can Learn from the Map
Austin	
El Paso	
Texas state boundary	

Thematic Maps

Maps that emphasize a single idea or a particular kind of information about an area are called **thematic maps**. There are many kinds of thematic maps, each designed to serve a different need. This textbook includes thematic maps that show exploration and trade, migration of peoples, economic activities, and war and political conflicts.

Qualitative Maps

Maps that use colors, symbols, lines, or dots to show information related to a specific idea are called **qualitative maps**. Such maps are often used to depict historical information. For example, the qualitative map below shows the primary exports of Latin America.

Flow-Line Maps

Maps that illustrate the movement of people, animals, goods, and ideas, as well as physical processes like hurricanes and glaciers, are called **flow-line maps**. Arrows are usually used to represent the flow and direction of movement. The flow-line map below shows the movement of Slavic peoples throughout Europe.

Geographic Information Systems

Modern technology has changed the way maps are made. Most cartographers use computers with software programs called **geographic information systems (GIS)**. A GIS is designed to accept data from different sources—maps, satellite images, printed text, and statistics. The GIS converts the data into a digital code, which arranges it in a database. Cartographers then program the GIS to process the data and produce maps. With GIS, each kind of information on a map is saved as a separate electronic layer.

1 *The first layer of information in a GIS pinpoints the area of interest. This allows the user to see, in detail, the area he or she needs to study. In this case, the area of study is a 5 mile (8 km) radius around Christ Hospital in Jersey City, New Jersey.*

2 *Additional layers of information are added based on the problem or issue being studied. In this case, hospital administrators want to find out about the population living in neighborhoods near the hospital so they can offer the community what it needs. A second layer showing African Americans who live within the 5 mile (8 km) radius has been added to the GIS.*

3 *Complex information can be presented using more than one layer. For example, the hospital's surrounding neighborhoods include other groups in addition to African Americans. A third layer showing whites who live within the 5 mile (8 km) radius has been added to the GIS. Administrators can now use this information to help them make decisions about staffing and services associated with the hospital.*

Practicing SKILLS

1. **Explain** the significance of: thematic map, qualitative maps, flow-line maps.

2. **Which** type of thematic map would best show the spread of Islam during Muhammad's time?

3. **Which** type of thematic map would best show average income per capita in the United States?

4. **How** does GIS allow cartographers to create maps and make changes to maps quickly and easily?

5. **Complete** a chart like the one below by identifying three examples of each type of thematic map found in this textbook. Note the page numbers of each.

Qualitative Maps	Flow-Line Maps

Geographic Dictionary

Volcano
Mountain peak
Strait
Sound
Valley
Cape
Island
Ocean
Cliff
Isthmus
Bay
Harbor
Peninsula
Gulf
Delta
Seacoast

As you read about the history of the United States, you will encounter the terms listed below. Many of the terms are pictured in the diagram.

absolute location exact location of a place on the earth described by global coordinates

basin area of land drained by a given river and its branches; area of land surrounded by lands of higher elevations

bay part of a large body of water that extends into a shoreline, generally smaller than a gulf

canyon deep and narrow valley with steep walls

cape point of land that extends into a river, lake, or ocean

channel wide strait or waterway between two landmasses that lie close to each other; deep part of a river or other waterway

cliff steep, high wall of rock, earth, or ice

continent one of the seven large landmasses on the earth

cultural feature characteristic that humans have created in a place, such as language, religion, housing, and settlement pattern

delta flat, low-lying land built up from soil carried downstream by a river and deposited at its mouth

divide stretch of high land that separates river systems

downstream direction in which a river or stream flows from its source to its mouth

elevation height of land above sea level

Equator imaginary line that runs around the earth halfway between the North and South Poles; used as the starting point to measure degrees of north and south latitude

glacier large, thick body of slowly moving ice

gulf part of a large body of water that extends into a shoreline, generally larger and more deeply indented than a bay

harbor a sheltered place along a shoreline where ships can anchor safely

highland elevated land area such as a hill, mountain, or plateau

hill elevated land with sloping sides and rounded summit; generally smaller than a mountain

island land area, smaller than a continent, completely surrounded by water

isthmus narrow stretch of land connecting two larger land areas

lake a large inland body of water

latitude distance north or south of the Equator, measured in degrees

longitude distance east or west of the Prime Meridian, measured in degrees

lowland land, usually level, at a low elevation

map drawing of the earth shown on a flat surface

meridian one of many lines on the global grid running from the North Pole to the South Pole; used to measure degrees of longitude

Mountain range · Source of river · Channel · Glacier · Highland · Plateau · Lake · Hills · Canyon · Desert · Mouth of river · River · Upstream · Downstream · Plain · Lowland · Basin · Tributary

mesa broad, flat-topped landform with steep sides; smaller than a plateau

mountain land with steep sides that rises sharply (1,000 feet or more) from surrounding land; generally larger and more rugged than a hill

mountain peak pointed top of a mountain

mountain range a series of connected mountains

mouth (of a river) place where a stream or river flows into a larger body of water

ocean one of the four major bodies of salt water that surround the continents

ocean current stream of either cold or warm water that moves in a definite direction through an ocean

parallel one of many lines on the global grid that circle the earth north or south of the Equator; used to measure degrees of latitude

peninsula body of land jutting into a lake or ocean, surrounded on three sides by water

physical feature characteristic of a place occurring naturally, such as a landform, body of water, climate pattern, or resource

plain area of level land, usually at a low elevation and often covered with grasses

plateau large area of flat or rolling land at a high elevation, about 300–3,000 feet high

Prime Meridian line of the global grid running from the North Pole to the South Pole at Greenwich, England; starting point for measuring degrees of east and west longitude

relief changes in elevation over a given area of land

river large natural stream of water that runs through the land

sea large body of water completely or partly surrounded by land

seacoast land lying next to a sea or ocean

sea level position on land level with surface of nearby ocean or sea

sound body of water between a coastline and one or more islands off the coast

source (of a river) place where a river or stream begins, often in highlands

strait narrow stretch of water joining two larger bodies of water

tributary small river or stream that flows into a larger river or stream; a branch of the river

upstream direction opposite the flow of a river; toward the source of a river or stream

valley area of low land between hills or mountains

volcano mountain created as ash or liquid rock erupts from inside the earth

Creating A Nation

Beginnings to 1877

Why It Matters

The history of the United States of America began with the decision of the thirteen colonies to rebel against Britain. After emerging victorious from the Revolutionary War, the United States created a new form of government. The new republic struggled to balance federal versus states' rights as the nation grew in size and the North and South divided over the issue of slavery. Unable to reconcile these differences, the country fought the Civil War.

Signing the Declaration of Independence

A Nation Is Born

Beginnings to 1789

George Washington at Valley Forge

1492
• Christopher Columbus lands in the Caribbean

1521
• Cortés conquers the Aztec

1619
• First meeting of the Virginia House of Burgesses

1607
• The English found Jamestown in Virginia

1630
• Massachusetts Bay Colony established

U.S. PRESIDENTS

U.S. EVENTS

WORLD EVENTS

1500

1600

1498
• Vasco da Gama sails around Africa to India, locating a water route to Asia from Europe

1520
• Magellan sails into Pacific Ocean

1517
• Protestant Reformation begins

1642
• English Civil War begins

MAKING CONNECTIONS
Why Do People Rebel?

Even today, Americans grow frustrated when the government raises taxes. In the early colonial era, Americans grew accustomed to running their own affairs. So when Britain tried to reestablish control, tensions mounted over taxes and basic rights.

- *Why do you think colonists became angry at Britain?*

- *When do you think it is acceptable to rebel against a government?*

FOLDABLES™

Generalizing on the American Revolution Create a Concept-Map Book Foldable that details the causes and the course of the American Revolutionary War. Select the most important causes of the war and list them inside one-half of the Concept-Map. Use the other half to list the outcomes of battles during the war.

American Revolution

| Causes of the War | Course of the War |

1788
• Constitution of the United States ratified

Washington 1789–1797

1776
• Declaration of Independence signed

1754
• French and Indian War begins

1700

1800

1688
• Glorious Revolution establishes limited monarchy in England

1748
• Montesquieu's *The Spirit of Laws* published

1776
• Adam Smith's treatise on mercantilism, *Wealth of Nations*, published

1789
• French Revolution begins

History 🖱 **ONLINE** Visit glencoe.com and enter *QuickPass*™ code TAVMT5147c1 for Chapter 1 resources.

Converging Cultures

Guide to Reading

Big Ideas
Government and Society European settlers established colonies in land inhabited by Native Americans and developed new forms of government.

Content Vocabulary
- joint-stock company (p. 8)
- Pilgrim (p. 8)
- subsistence farming (p. 10)
- proprietary colony (p. 11)
- indentured servant (p. 12)

Academic Vocabulary
- cultures (p. 4)
- immigrate (p. 8)

People and Events to Identify
- Jamestown (p. 8)
- William Penn (p. 11)

Reading Strategy
Taking Notes As you read about the early settlements of America, use the section headings to create an outline similar to the one below.

Discovery and Settlement
I. The Earliest Americans
   A. Early Civilizations in America
   B.
   C.
II. European Exploration
   A.
   B.
   C.
III.
IV.
V.

While a number of civilizations flourished in the Americas, Europeans looking for trade routes began settling in the region. Their colonies developed different forms of government, and many depended on slave labor.

The Earliest Americans

MAIN Idea Native Americans adapted to their environments and developed diverse cultures.

HISTORY AND YOU Do you remember getting used to a new school? Read to learn how the first American settlers adapted to their new environments.

No one knows exactly when the first people arrived in America. Scientists have pieced together many clues by studying the Earth's geology and the items left by early humans. Such studies proved that people were here at least 10,000 years ago. More recent research, however, suggests that our ancestors may have arrived much earlier—between 15,000 and 30,000 years ago.

These newcomers to America were probably nomads, people who continually move from place to place. With time, Native Americans learned how to plant and raise crops. The shift to agriculture led to the first permanent villages and to new building methods. As early societies became more complex, civilizations emerged. A civilization is a highly organized society marked by advanced knowledge of trade, government, the arts, science, and, often, written language.

Early Civilizations in America

Anthropologists think the earliest civilization in the Americas arose between 1500 B.C. and 1200 B.C. among the Olmec people in southern Mexico. The Maya and the Aztec later developed their own civilizations in Central America, building impressive temples and pyramids and establishing trade networks. Many anthropologists believe that the agricultural technology of Mesoamerica eventually spread north into the American Southwest and beyond. Around A.D. 300, the Hohokam began farming in what is today Arizona. They and another nearby people, the Anasazi, were able to grow crops in the dry Southwest by building elaborate irrigation systems.

About the time of the early Olmec civilization, the people in North America's eastern woodlands were developing their own **cultures.** The Hopewell built huge geometric earthworks that served as ceremonial centers, observatories, and burial places. Between A.D. 700 and 900, the Mississippian people in the Mississippi River valley created Cahokia, one of the largest early American cities.

◀ *Great Plains peoples, such as the Sioux, lived in temporary tepee villages.*

▶ *The Eastern Woodlands peoples lived in permanent, well-defended communities.*

■ California	□ Northwest Coast	■ Subarctic
□ Great Basin	■ Plateau	HOPI Tribal group
□ Great Plains	■ Southeast	
■ Northeast	□ Southwest	

KWAKIUTL
LILLOOET
THOMPSON
OKANAGAN
KAINAH (BLOOD)
PLAINS CREE
MICMAC
MALECITE
PASSAMAQUODDY
NOOTKA
SANPOIL
KUTENAI
KALISPEL
PIEGAN
ASSINIBOIN
HURON
ABENAKI
PENOBSCOT
PENNACOOK
MAKAH
SALISH
PUYALLUP
COLVILLE
SPOKANE
PALUS
COEUR D'ALENE
ATSINA (GROS VENTRE)
OTTAWA
HURON
MAHICAN
MASSACHUSET
WAMPANOAG
NIPMUC
NARRAGANSET
CHEHALIS
CHINOOK
NISQUALLY
COWLITZ
YAKIMA
KLIKITAT
WALLA WALLA
FLATHEAD
HIDATSA
MANDAN
MENOMINI
OJIBWA
MOHAWK
ONEIDA
ONONDAGA
CAYUGA
SENECA
PEQUOT
MOHEGAN
WAPPINGER
TILLAMOOK
MOLALA
KALAPUYA
NEZ PERCE
CROW
ARIKARA
SANTEE DAKOTA
SAUK FOX
WINNEBAGO
POTAWATOMI
TIONONTATI
SUSQUEHANNOCK (CONESTOGA)
DELAWARE (LENI LENAPE)
COOS UMPQUA CAYUSE
TAKELMA KLAMATH
KAROK
BANNOCK
TETON DAKOTA
YANKTON DAKOTA
ERIE
NANTICOKE
YUROK
WIYOT
HUPA
MATTOLE
MODOC
ACHOMAWI
ATSUGEWI
SHASTA
YANA
PAVIOTSO
SHOSHONE (SNAKE)
NORTHERN CHEYENNE
PONCA
IOWA
KICKAPOO
KASKASKIA
PEORIA
MIAMI
WEA
ILLINOIS
PAMUNKEY
POWHATAN
CHICKAHOMINY
MATTAPONI
MAIDU
YUKI
NORTHERN PAIUTE
GOSIUTE
WASHO
PAWNEE
OMAHA
OTO
MISSOURI
PIANKASHAW
TUTELO
PAMLICO
NOTTOWAY
POMO
WINTUN
MIWOK
KAWAIISU
ARAPAHO
KANSA
OSAGE
SHAWNEE
TUSCARORA
COSTANOAN
YOKUTS
SOUTHERN PAIUTE
UTE
SOUTHERN CHEYENNE
CHEROKEE
YUCHI
TUSKEGEE
CATAWBA
SALINAN
MONO
PANAMINT
HAVASUPAI
NAVAJO
JICARILLA APACHE
KIOWA
QUAPAW
CREEK
YAMASEE
CHUMASH
CHEMEHUEVI
WALAPAI
HOPI
ZUÑI
PUEBLO
KIOWA APACHE
TAWAKONI
CHICKASAW
HICHITI
GUALE
TIMUCUA
SERRANO
CAHUILLA
MOJAVE
YAVAPAI
PIMA
MESCALERO APACHE
WICHITA
CADDO
TUNICA
ALABAMA
APALACHEE
YUMA
MARICOPA
PAPAGO
WESTERN APACHE
COMANCHE
KICHAI
WACO
NATCHEZ
CHOCTAW
BILOXI MOBILE
OPATA
LIPAN APACHE
TONKAWA
ATAKAPA
CHITIMACHA
SEMINOLE
CONCHO
TARAHUMARA
CAHITA
KARANKAWA
CALUSA

PACIFIC OCEAN

ATLANTIC OCEAN

Gulf of Mexico

40°N
30°N
120°W
110°W
100°W
90°W
80°W

0 400 kilometers
0 400 miles
Lambert Azimuthal Equal-Area projection

◀ *The Cherokee established permanent settlements throughout the Southeast.*

▲ *Pueblo peoples of the Southwest built multistory complexes out of adobe.*

Analyzing GEOGRAPHY

1. **Movement** Why did some of the people of the Great Plains become nomadic?

2. **Human-Environment Interaction** How does the housing style of each group reflect its environment?

Native American Cultural Diversity

In the Eastern Woodlands, most Native Americans combined hunting and fishing with farming. Many different groups lived in the Eastern Woodlands, but most spoke either Algonquian or Iroquoian languages.

In the Southeast, the Cherokee were the largest group. They, along with the Creek, Choctaw, Natchez, and others, generally built wooden stockades around their villages for protection. Women did most of the farming, while men hunted deer, bear, and alligator.

In the Southwest, the Hohokam and the Anasazi eventually disappeared, but their descendants, including the Zuni and the Hopi, continued to farm corn, beans, and cotton. Around the 1500s, two other groups—the Apache and the Navajo—came to the Southwest. The Navajo settled in farming villages, but many of the Apache remained nomadic hunters.

Hunting also sustained the Sioux and other peoples who lived on the western Great Plains. They followed buffalo herds and camped in tepees that they could easily set up, dismantle, and carry.

Along the Pacific Coast, the Northwest was home to fishing peoples like the Kwakiutls and the Chinook. They caught the plentiful salmon, built wooden houses and canoes, and crafted ceremonial totem poles from the trunks of redwood and cedar trees. To the south, in what is today central California, groups such as the Pomo trapped small game and gathered acorns. Farther inland lived other hunter-gatherer groups like the Nez Perce, the Yakima, the Ute, and the Shoshone.

Meanwhile, in the Far North region from Alaska to Greenland, the Inuit and the Aleut hunted seals, walruses, whales, polar bears, and caribou. They adapted to their harsh environment by inventing tools such as the harpoon, kayak, dogsled, and oil lamp.

By the 1500s, Native Americans had established a wide array of cultures and languages. They had also developed economies and lifestyles suited to their particular environments.

For an example of Native American storytelling, read the selections on pages R64–R65 in the **American Literature Library.**

Reading Check **Explaining** How did climate and food sources help shape Native American lifestyles?

European Explorations

MAIN Idea European countries began to explore the world and established colonies in the Americas.

HISTORY AND YOU Have you tried new foods from other parts of the world? Read about the exchange of foods after European explorations.

As the people of Europe emerged from the Middle Ages, they became interested in Asia, the source of spices, perfumes, fine silks, and jewels. Rulers of Portugal, Spain, France, and England wanted to find a sailing route to Asia that would bypass the merchants and traders from Italy and the Middle East.

Columbus's Voyages

While Portugal took the lead in searching for a sea route around Africa to Asia in the early 1400s, Spain funded an expedition by Christopher Columbus, an Italian sea captain, to sail west across the Atlantic Ocean. In August 1492 Columbus and his crew set off in three ships—the *Niña*, the *Pinta*, and the *Santa Maria*. After a harrowing voyage, they landed on present-day San Salvador Island and then explored other islands in the Caribbean. Columbus claimed the new lands for Spain, believing all the time that he was in Asia.

When Columbus returned home to Europe with the news he had reached land on the other side of the Atlantic, he triggered a wave of European exploration and settlement of North and South America.

Continuing Expeditions

Europeans soon realized that Columbus had not reached Asia but a part of the globe unknown to Europeans. They named the new continent America in honor of Amerigo Vespucci, who explored the South American coastline for Portugal.

The 1494 Treaty of Tordesillas confirmed Spain's right to most of these newly discovered lands, and conquistadors began building a Spanish Empire in the Americas. With their superior weapons, the Spanish easily conquered the local peoples. Hernán Cortés defeated the Aztec in Mexico in 1521. Francisco Pizarro conquered the Inca in Peru eleven years later. The Spanish also explored parts of North America. Juan Ponce de León claimed

> ▶ Although no images of Christopher Columbus exist from his lifetime, this painting from about 1525 is considered to be the closest likeness.

Turning Point

Columbus Arrives in America

Columbus's first voyage to the Americas was a major turning point in world history. For Europeans, it opened up new areas of exploration and discovery and provided vast wealth through trade. The event was devastating, however, for native peoples of the Americas, whose cultures were changed or destroyed by war, disease, and enslavement.

ANALYZING HISTORY Describe one positive and one negative effect of Columbus's voyage to the Americas.

▲ The Landing of Columbus *was painted by American artist Albert Bierstadt in 1892, the year of the 400th anniversary of Columbus's arrival in North America. Note that the artist portrayed the indigenous people as shrouded in darkness and shadow, emerging to kneel worshipfully before the Europeans, who bring with them the "light" of civilization. Unfortunately, the arrival of Europeans did more to destroy the indigenous cultures than to enlighten them.*

Florida, Francisco Vásquez de Coronado explored the Southwest, and Hernando de Soto explored the Southeast.

The Spanish soon controlled an immense territory stretching from the Florida peninsula to California and into South America. Settlers farmed the land, established mines and ranches, and tried to spread the Catholic faith.

Cultural Changes

The arrival of Europeans in the Americas altered life for everyone. Native Americans introduced the Europeans to new farming methods and foods like corn, potatoes, squash, pumpkins, beans, and chocolate, as well as tobacco and chewing gum. Europeans also adopted many Native American inventions, including canoes, snowshoes, and ponchos.

Meanwhile, the Europeans introduced Native Americans to wheat, rice, coffee, bananas, citrus fruits, and domestic livestock such as chickens, cattle, pigs, sheep, and horses. In addition, Native Americans acquired new technologies, including better metalworking methods. Along with these beneficial imports, however, came deadly ones—germs that cause diseases. Native Americans had never before been exposed to influenza, measles, chicken pox, mumps, typhus, or smallpox. With no immunity, millions of Native Americans died in widespread epidemics. Military conquests also devastated Native Americans, costing them their lands and their traditional ways of life.

Reading Check **Identifying** Why did millions of Native Americans die after contact with Europeans?

Early French and English Settlement

MAIN Idea The French and English settled in North America, and English colonists began their own local governments.

HISTORY AND YOU Have you ever wanted to move somewhere new? Why do you think most people move today? Read to learn why the French and English settlers came to North America.

For the complete text of the Mayflower Compact, see page R39 in **Documents in American History.**

Soon after Columbus made his historic voyage, France and England began exploring the eastern part of North America. England sent John Cabot on expeditions in 1497 and 1498. France funded trips by Jacques Cartier and Giovanni da Verrazano in the early 1500s. Yet it was not until the 1600s that the countries succeeded in establishing colonies.

New France

In 1608 French geographer Samuel de Champlain founded the outpost of Quebec. The backers of New France sought profits from fur, and Frenchmen began a brisk trade with Native Americans. Quebec eventually became the capital of New France, a sparsely settled colony of fur traders and Jesuit missionaries.

In the late 1600s, France began expanding the colony. Explorers Louis Jolliet and Jacques Marquette reached the Mississippi River, and René-Robert Cavelier de La Salle followed it to the Gulf of Mexico. The French named the newly claimed region Louisiana. Settlers founded the towns of New Orleans, Biloxi, and Mobile, and they began growing sugar, rice, and tobacco. The French also began importing enslaved Africans to do the hard field work that these labor-intensive crops required.

Jamestown

A year before the French founded Quebec, the English established their first lasting settlement in Virginia. The colony, **Jamestown,** was funded by a **joint-stock company,** a group of private investors who pooled their money to support big projects. These investors, along with others in business and government, saw colonies as sources of raw materials and markets for English goods.

Despite early troubles, the settlers survived with the help of the Powhatan Confederacy, a group of local Native Americans. Within a few years, they began to prosper by growing tobacco. Newcomers arrived, attracted by the promise of land ownership. In 1619 colonists formed an assembly, the House of Burgesses, to make their own laws.

Encouraged by the Virginia Company, more than 4,500 settlers **immigrated** to Virginia by 1622. This expansion alarmed Native Americans, who attacked Jamestown in 1622. An English court blamed the Company's policies for the high death rate and revoked its charter. Virginia became a royal colony run by a governor appointed by the king.

Plymouth Colony

Not all settlers came for economic gain. King James was persecuting a group of Puritans who were called Separatists because they wanted to form their own congregations separate from the Anglican Church, the official church of England. These Separatists hoped to be able to worship freely in America.

In 1620 a small band of Separatists, who came to be known as **Pilgrims,** headed for Virginia on the *Mayflower*. A storm blew their ship off its course. The Pilgrims finally dropped anchor off the coast of Cape Cod, territory without an English government. The settlers drew up a plan for self-government called the Mayflower Compact. They quickly built homes and befriended the local Wampanoag people. The following autumn, the Pilgrims joined with the Wampanoag in a harvest celebration—the first Thanksgiving.

Ten years later, after increasing persecution of Puritans, another group of Puritans arrived in Massachusetts Bay with a charter for a new colony. They founded several towns, including Boston. A depression of England's wool industry drew more people to Massachusetts.

The people of Massachusetts set up a representative government, with an elected assembly to make laws. Government and religion were closely intertwined. The government collected taxes to support the church, and the Puritan leaders of the colony set strict rules for behavior.

Reading Check **Explaining** Why did English colonists come to America?

The Thirteen Colonies

MAIN Idea As English settlements grew, colonists developed different forms of government.

HISTORY AND YOU Have you ever been a part of a new organization? What rules did you draw up? Read how colonies established their governments.

The early colonies were only the beginning of English settlements. Over the next century, colonies grew all along the east coast.

The Growth of New England

Puritan efforts in the Massachusetts Bay Colony to suppress other religious beliefs led to other New England colonies. One early dissenter was a minister named Roger Williams. In 1636, after being banned from Massachusetts,

Williams headed south, purchased land from the Narraganset people, and founded the town of Providence. There the government had no authority in religious matters.

Like Roger Williams, Anne Hutchinson was exiled from Massachusetts because of her religious views. Hutchinson and a few followers settled near Providence, as did other free-thinking Puritans over the next years. In 1644 Providence joined with neighboring towns to become the colony of Rhode Island and Providence Plantations. Religious freedom, with a total separation of church and state, was a key feature of this new colony.

Some religious dissenters, along with fishers and fur traders, went north instead of south to Rhode Island. In 1679 a large area north of Massachusetts became the royal colony of New Hampshire.

PRIMARY SOURCE

The Causes of English Settlement in America

Three major factors led the English to found colonies in the Americas.

RELIGIOUS PERSECUTION

◄ English Puritans and non-Anglicans faced prejudice and legal harassment. Many fled to North America where they could worship as they wished.

ECONOMIC CHANGES

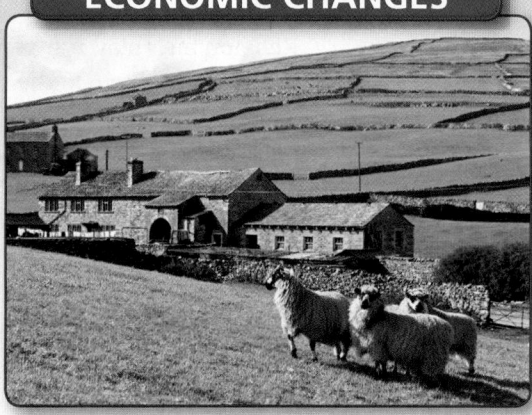

▲ The enclosure movement displaced thousands of tenant farmers. Many English leaders thought that having colonies would help absorb England's unemployed people.

RIVALRY WITH SPAIN

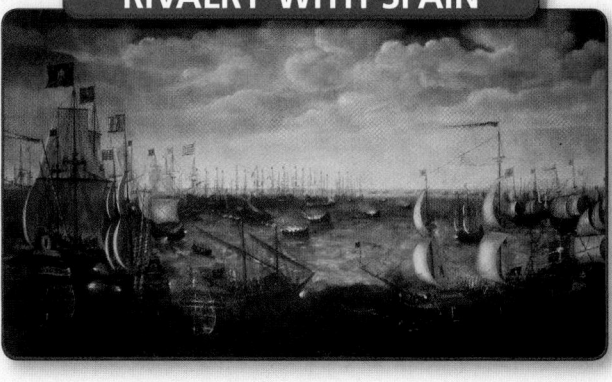

◄ The Protestant English wanted to share the riches of the Americas that Catholic Spain was monopolizing.

Analyzing VISUALS

1. **Determining Cause and Effect** How did England's rivalry with Spain drive the nation to establish new colonies in North America?

2. **Explaining** Why did religious groups found colonies?

People IN HISTORY

Roger Williams
1603?–1683

Shortly after his arrival in Boston in 1631, Roger Williams declared he was a Separatist and began criticizing Puritan leaders. He served as a minister in Salem, moved briefly to Plymouth Colony in 1632, and then returned to preach at Salem.

When Williams returned to Salem, he continued to criticize Puritan leaders for not making a complete break from the corrupt Anglican Church. He also insisted on greater separation of church and state. Finally, he denounced Massachusetts Bay's charter because it assumed the king had the right to give away land belonging to Native Americans. As Puritan leaders prepared to banish him, Williams fled.

In 1636 he founded Providence—later to be part of Rhode Island—on land he purchased from the Narragansets. In his new colony, Williams created a haven for Quakers, Separatists, Jews, and others whose religious practices or views were not tolerated elsewhere. Most important, Williams championed religious freedom, which later became an important American principle.

What significant contribution to civil rights did Roger Williams make?

Anne Hutchinson
1591–1643

Anne Hutchinson, an experienced midwife and the wife of a prosperous merchant, arrived in Boston in 1634. There, she began to hold meetings with other women to discuss sermons, express her own beliefs, and evaluate the ministers.

Hutchinson stirred up controversy with her discussions of how salvation could be obtained. To most Puritans, this was heresy. In 1637 Hutchinson was tried for sedition by the Massachusetts General Court. Hutchinson did not repent. She said that God "hath let me see which was the clear [correct] ministry and which the wrong. . . . " When asked how God let her know, she replied that God spoke to her "by an immediate revelation." The Court ordered her banished.

Hutchinson, her family, and some of her followers founded a settlement in what is today Rhode Island. After the death of her husband, she moved to Long Island. In 1643 she and all but one of her children were killed in an attack by Native Americans. Some Puritans viewed her tragic death as God's judgment against a heretic.

How did Hutchinson challenge Puritan authority in the Massachusetts Bay Colony?

For an excerpt of the Fundamental Orders of Connecticut, see R40 in **Documents in American History.**

Religion also played a part in the founding of Connecticut. In 1636 the Reverend Thomas Hooker moved his entire congregation from Massachusetts to the Connecticut River valley. Hooker disagreed with the political system that allowed only church members to vote. Three years later, the new colony adopted America's first written constitution, the Fundamental Orders of Connecticut. It allowed all adult men to vote and hold office.

Life in New England New England Puritans valued religious devotion, hard work, and obedience to strict rules regulating daily life. Puritan society revolved around town life. Towns included a meetinghouse (church), a school, and a marketplace around an open public area called the town common. At town meetings, New Englanders discussed local problems and issues. These meetings evolved into the local government, with landowners voting on laws and electing officials to oversee town matters. Yet even residents without property could attend meetings and express their opinions. The colonists grew used to managing their own affairs and came to believe in their right to self-government.

New England's thin and rocky soil was ill suited for cash crops. Instead, from Connecticut to Maine, colonists practiced **subsistence farming** on small farms, raising only enough food to feed their families. The main crop was wheat, but farmers also grew other grains, vegetables, apples, and berries, and they raised dairy cattle, sheep, and pigs.

It was maritime activity, however, that brought prosperity to New England. Fishers sold their catch of cod, mackerel, halibut, and herring to other colonists, people in the Caribbean, and Southern Europeans. Whaling providing blubber for candles and lamp oil.

A thriving lumber industry developed, too. Timber was plentiful, and lumber was in high demand for furniture, building materials, and the barrels that were used to store and ship almost everything in the colonial era. Equally successful was shipbuilding, which was quick and cheap because of forests and sawmills close to the coast. By the 1770s, one of every three British ships had been built in America.

King Philip's War In 1637 war broke out between the English settlers and the Pequot people of New England. This conflict ended with the near extermination of the Pequot people. In the following decades, however, English settlers and Native Americans lived in relative peace.

In the 1670s, colonial governments began to demand that Native Americans follow English laws and customs. Tensions peaked in 1675 when Plymouth Colony tried and executed three Wampanoag men for murder. This touched off King Philip's War, named after the Wampanoag leader Metacomet, whom the settlers called King Philip. By the time the war ended in 1678, few Native Americans were left in New England.

The Middle Colonies

While the English focused their early settlements on Virginia and New England, the Dutch had claimed much of the land south of Connecticut. In 1609 Henry Hudson, a navigator hired by Dutch merchants, had discovered what is now the Hudson River valley in New York. The Dutch called the region New Netherland and established their main settlement of New Amsterdam on Manhattan Island. Dutch policies encouraged immigration, and by 1664 New Netherland was England's main rival in North America.

New Settlements Charles II, who had become king of England in 1660 after the English Civil War, decided to act. He seized New Netherland from the Dutch and granted the land to his brother, James, the Duke of York. James held onto the largest portion of the land, renaming it New York. The rest of the land became New Jersey, a colony that offered generous land grants, religious freedom, and the right to have a legislative assembly.

In 1681 King Charles gave **William Penn** permission to create a new colony south of New York. Penn regarded Pennsylvania as a "holy experiment" where settlers would have religious freedom and a voice in government. He particularly wanted to help his fellow Quakers escape persecution in England. Quakers objected to obligatory taxes and military service. They also opposed war or violence as a means to settle disputes. A treaty Penn signed in 1682 assured peace with a local group

of Native Americans. To give his colony access to the Atlantic Ocean, Penn soon acquired coastal land to the southeast. This land later became the colony of Delaware.

Europe's population growth also brought a new wave of immigrants to America. Many of these newcomers settled particularly in the Middle Colonies, where land was still available.

The Economy The Middle Colonies were blessed with fertile land and a long growing season. Farmers produced bumper crops of rye, oats, barley, and potatoes. Wheat rapidly became the region's main cash crop. In the early and mid-1700s, the demand for wheat soared, thanks to population growth in Europe. Between 1720 and 1770, wheat prices more than doubled in the Middle Colonies. Some people who grew wealthy from the wheat boom invested in new businesses such as glass and pottery works and built large gristmills to produce flour for export.

The Southern Colonies

Farther south, tobacco helped Virginia to thrive. The colony had been joined by Maryland, a **proprietary colony** which began in the 1630s. A proprietary colony was one owned by an individual who could govern it any way he wanted, appointing officials, coining money, imposing taxes, and even raising an army. The owner of the colony was George Calvert, also known as Lord Baltimore. He hoped to make the colony a refuge for Catholics because they, like the Puritans, were persecuted in England. Most settlers, however, were Protestants. Maryland passed the Toleration Act in 1649, granting religious toleration to all Christians in the colony.

New Settlements After the end of the English Civil War, new colonies sprang up south of Virginia. In 1663 King Charles II gave eight friends and political allies a vast tract of land named Carolina. From the start, Carolina developed as two separate regions. A small and scattered population of farmers grew tobacco in North Carolina. North Carolina's coastline made the colony hard to reach, and many more settlers headed to South Carolina. There they established the community of Charles Towne (Charleston), exported deerskins, and grew rice in the tidal swamps.

Settled by 1660
Settled by 1700
Settled by 1760

New York
England took New York from the Dutch in 1664 and continued its focus on trade.

Pennsylvania
William Penn established Pennsylvania in 1681 as a place of religious freedom.

Virginia
The Virginia Company established its colony in 1607 as a money-making venture.

The Carolinas
The Carolina colony was chartered in 1663 as a proprietary colony; its proprietors hoped to make money growing cash crops.

Georgia
James Oglethorpe founded Georgia in 1733 as a refuge for England's poor.

Massachusetts
The Pilgrims arrived in Plymouth in 1620, and the Puritans arrived in Massachusetts Bay 10 years later; both groups fled religious persecution in England.

Rhode Island
Roger Williams founded Providence in 1636 as a place of religious toleration.

Connecticut
Thomas Hooker founded Hartford in 1636 to escape Massachusetts' Puritan political system.

Maryland
Lord Baltimore established Maryland in 1634 as a refuge for Catholics.

Maine (part of Mass.)
N.H. (1623)
Portsmouth
Boston
Plymouth
Providence
Hartford
New Haven
New Amsterdam
N.J. (1664)
Philadelphia
Del. (1638)
Baltimore
Williamsburg
Jamestown
Wilmington
Charles Towne
Savannah

St. Lawrence R.
Connecticut R.
Hudson R.
L. Huron
L. Ontario
L. Erie
Ohio R.
Tennessee R.
APPALACHIAN MOUNTAINS

ATLANTIC OCEAN

40°N
80°W
30°N

0   200 kilometers
0   200 miles
Lambert Azimuthal Equal-Area projection

Analyzing GEOGRAPHY

1. **Location** Why were the earliest settlements on the coast?
2. **Place** Which colony was founded as a haven for debtors?

Georgia arose south of the Carolinas in 1733, based on an idea of James Oglethorpe. A wealthy member of Parliament, Oglethorpe had been horrified to learn that many English prisoners were jailed simply because they could not pay their debts. Oglethorpe asked King George II for a colony where the poor could start over. The king agreed, realizing that a new Southern colony also would keep Spain from expanding north of Florida.

Life in the South Agriculture was the focus of the Southern economy. In early colonial days, there was plenty of land, but not enough labor to work it. England had the opposite problem—not enough land and high unemployment. The situation led many poor English people to come to America as **indentured servants.** They signed contracts with American colonists, agreeing to work for four or more years in return for paid passage to America

and free food, clothing, and shelter. Southern farmers also relied on the labor of enslaved Africans, a practice that grew dramatically as time passed.

The hard lives of enslaved workers and indentured servants contrasted sharply with the privileged lives of the elite. A small number of wealthy colonists bought most of the land along the rivers and established large plantations. These landholders had enormous economic and political influence. They served in the governing councils and assemblies, commanded the local militias (citizen armies), and became county judges. With few towns or roads in the region, their plantations functioned as self-contained communities.

Although they dominated Southern society, large landowners were few in number. Most Southerners were small farmers living inland in the backcountry. They owned modest plots devoted mostly to subsistence farming.

Another group of colonists were tenant farmers—landless settlers who worked fields that they rented.

By the 1660s, Virginia's government was dominated by wealthy planters led by the governor, Sir William Berkeley. Berkeley arranged to restrict voting to property owners, cutting the number of voters in half. He also exempted himself and his councillors from taxation. These actions angered the backcountry farmers and tenant farmers. Yet it was the governor's land policies toward Native Americans that led to a rebellion.

Crisis Over Land

Over time, acquiring land became an important issue for most colonists. Many indentured servants and tenant farmers wanted to own farms eventually. Backcountry farmers wanted to expand their holdings. By the 1670s, most land left was in areas claimed by Native Americans in the Piedmont, the region of rolling hills between the coastal plains and the Appalachians. Most wealthy planters, who lived near the coast, opposed expansion because they did not want to endanger their plantations by risking war with the Native Americans.

In 1675 war broke out between settlers and a Susquehannock group, but Governor Berkeley refused to support further military action. Nathaniel Bacon, a well-to-do but sympathetic planter, took up the cause of outraged backcountry farmers. After organizing a militia to attack the Native Americans, he ran for office and won a seat in the House of Burgesses. The assembly at once authorized another attack. It also restored the right to vote to all free men and took away tax exemptions Berkeley had granted to his supporters. Not satisfied with these reforms, Bacon challenged Berkeley, and a civil war erupted. Bacon's Rebellion ended suddenly the next month, when Bacon, hiding in a swamp, became sick and died. Without his leadership, his army rapidly disintegrated, and Berkeley returned to power.

Bacon's Rebellion convinced many wealthy planters that land should be made available to backcountry farmers. From the 1680s onward, Virginia's government generally supported expanding the colony westward, regardless of the impact on Native Americans.

The rebellion also helped increase Virginia's reliance on enslaved Africans rather than indentured servants. Enslaved workers did not have to be freed and, therefore, would never need their own land. In addition, in 1672 King Charles II granted a charter to the Royal African Company to engage in the slave trade. Planters now found it easier to acquire enslaved people because they no longer had to go through the Dutch or the Portuguese. Earlier purchases had been difficult because English laws limited trade between the English colonies and other countries. Planters also discovered another economic advantage to slavery. Because enslaved Africans, unlike indentured servants, were considered property, planters could use them as collateral to borrow money and expand their plantations.

Reading Check **Analyzing** How did the types of settlements influence the way each was governed?

Vocabulary
1. **Explain** the significance of: Jamestown, joint-stock company, Pilgrim, subsistence farming, William Penn, proprietary colony, indentured servant.

Main Ideas
2. **Describing** How did geography and climate affect the cultures and traditions of Native American groups?

3. **Explaining** How did the arrival of Europeans affect both Native American and European cultures?

4. **Identifying** How did the Jamestown colony finally prosper?

5. **Analyzing** What role did religion play in the founding of English colonies?

Critical Thinking
6. **Big Ideas** In what ways did early settlers in the English colonies develop new and unique forms of government?

7. **Categorizing** Use a graphic organizer to list the colonies and the reasons for their founding.

Colony	Reason for Founding

8. **Analyzing Visuals** Examine the images on page 9. Summarize the different reasons for English settlement in America.

Writing About History
9. **Descriptive Writing** Take on the role of a settler in Jamestown. Write a letter to someone back in England describing the hardships you faced.

History ONLINE

Study Central™ To review this section, go to glencoe.com and click on Study Central.

GEOGRAPHY & HISTORY

The Columbian Exchange

The arrival of Europeans in the Americas set in motion a series of complex interactions between peoples and environments. These interactions, called the Columbian Exchange, permanently altered the world's ecosystems and changed nearly every culture around the world.

Native Americans introduced Europeans to new crops. Corn, squash, pumpkins, beans, sweet potatoes, tomatoes, chili peppers, peanuts, chocolate, and potatoes all made their way to Europe, as did tobacco and chewing gum. Perhaps the most significant import for Europeans was the potato. European farmers learned that four times as many people could live off the same amount of land when potatoes were planted instead of grain.

The Europeans introduced Native Americans to wheat, oats, barley, rye, rice, onions, bananas, coffee, and citrus fruits such as lemons and oranges. They also brought over livestock such as cattle, pigs, sheep, and chickens. Perhaps the most important form of livestock was the horse—which dramatically changed life for many Native Americans on the Great Plains.

How Did Geography Shape the Exchange?

The isolation of the Americas from the rest of the world meant that Native Americans had no resistance to diseases that were common in other parts of the world, such as influenza, measles, chicken pox, mumps, typhus, and smallpox. The consequences were devastating. Epidemics killed millions of Native Americans. This catastrophe also reduced the labor supply available to Europeans, who then turned to the slave trade, eventually bringing millions of Africans to the Americas.

Horses

Horses allowed some Native Americans to become nomadic hunters.

Corn

Peppers

Cocoa

Analyzing GEOGRAPHY

1. **Movement** What new crops were introduced in Europe from the Americas? How did these crops improve the diet of Europeans?

2. **Human-Environment Interaction** How did geography play a role in the spread of diseases?

Pigs

European diseases decimated Native American populations.

Disease

Citrus Fruit

Grains

Sugarcane planters imported millions of enslaved Africans to the Americas.

Sugarcane

Cattle

Honeybees

Bananas

Coffee

Beans

Squash and Pumpkins

Potatoes increased northern Europe's population and changed Ireland's diet.

Potatoes

Peanuts improved people's health in West Africa by providing protein.

Peanuts

Tobacco use killed tens of millions in only a few hundred years.

Disease

Tobacco

Tomatoes became popular in Europe and greatly changed cuisine of Italy.

Tomatoes

A Diverse Society

Guide to Reading

Big Ideas
Culture and Beliefs Immigrants from Europe or those brought by force from Africa greatly increased the population of the American colonies in the 1700s.

Content Vocabulary
• triangular trade *(p. 16)*
• slave code *(p. 18)*

Academic Vocabulary
• hierarchy *(p. 16)*

People and Events to Identify
• John Locke *(p. 20)*
• Great Awakening *(p. 21)*

Reading Strategy
Taking Notes As you read about colonial society in the 1700s, complete a graphic organizer similar to the one below by identifying why immigrants settled in the colonies.

Group	Where They Settled	Reasons for Immigrating
Germans		
Scots-Irish		
Jews		

The American colonies experienced rapid population growth. The importation of enslaved Africans continued even as colonists engaged in philosophical and religious discussions about the rights of individuals.

Growth of Colonial America

MAIN Idea The different colonies created new social structures that were more open than those of aristocratic Europe.

HISTORY AND YOU Think about the social structure in your school, from the principal down to you, the student. Read on to learn about the social structure that developed in the growing English settlements.

The population of the American colonies grew rapidly in the eighteenth century. Between 1640 and 1700, the colonial population increased from 25,000 to more than 250,000, and it reached roughly 2.5 million by the time of the American Revolution. High birthrates as well as improved housing and sanitation contributed to this growth. Contagious diseases, however, such as typhoid fever, tuberculosis, cholera, diphtheria, and scarlet fever, remained a threat. The increasing population and a rise in trade changed colonial society. This brought a growth of cities, increased immigration, and changes in status for women and Africans.

Trade and the Rise of Cities

In the early colonial period, settlers produced few goods that England wanted in exchange for the goods they purchased. Instead, colonial merchants developed systems of **triangular trade** involving exchanges of goods among the colonies, England, Caribbean sugar planters, and Africa.

This trade brought great wealth for merchants, who began to build factories. It also fostered the growth of cities in the North. By 1760 the Middle Colonies boasted the two largest cities in America: Philadelphia, with 30,000 people, and New York with 25,000.

In these cities, a new society with distinct social classes developed. At the top of the **hierarchy** were a small number of wealthy merchants who controlled trade. Below them, artisans, or skilled workers, made up nearly half of the urban population in colonial times. Innkeepers and retailers with their own businesses held a similar status. The lower class consisted of people without skills or property. Below them in status were indentured servants and enslaved Africans. Although relatively few enslaved people lived in the North, they made up 10 to 20 percent of the urban population.

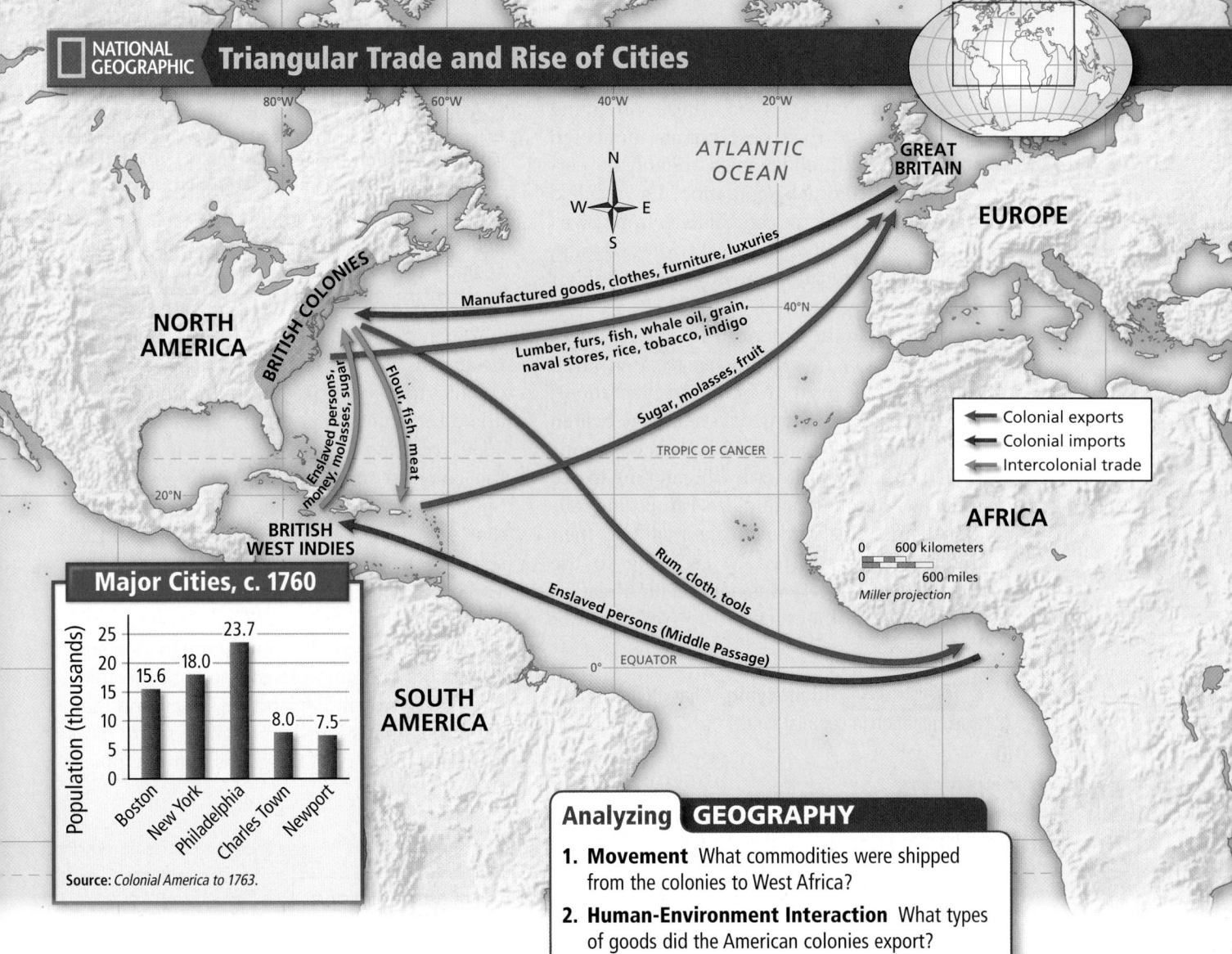

ATLANTIC OCEAN

GREAT BRITAIN

EUROPE

NORTH AMERICA

BRITISH COLONIES

Manufactured goods, clothes, furniture, luxuries

Lumber, furs, fish, whale oil, grain, naval stores, rice, tobacco, indigo

Sugar, molasses, fruit

Enslaved persons, money, molasses, sugar

Flour, fish, meat

TROPIC OF CANCER

AFRICA

BRITISH WEST INDIES

Rum, cloth, tools

Enslaved persons (Middle Passage)

EQUATOR

SOUTH AMERICA

← Colonial exports
← Colonial imports
← Intercolonial trade

0 600 kilometers
0 600 miles
Miller projection

Major Cities, c. 1760

City	Population (thousands)
Boston	15.6
New York	18.0
Philadelphia	23.7
Charles Town	8.0
Newport	7.5

Source: *Colonial America to 1763.*

Analyzing GEOGRAPHY

1. **Movement** What commodities were shipped from the colonies to West Africa?
2. **Human-Environment Interaction** What types of goods did the American colonies export?

Immigrants

Between 1700 and 1775, hundreds of thousands of free white immigrants streamed in. Most settled in the Middle Colonies, especially Pennsylvania. Among them were Germans fleeing religious wars back home and Scots-Irish escaping high taxes, poor harvests, and religious discrimination in Ireland. Jews migrated to America for religious reasons, too. By 1776 approximately 1,500 Jews lived in the colonies, mainly in the cities of New York, Philadelphia, Charleston, Savannah, and Newport. They were allowed to worship freely, but they could not vote or hold public office.

Women

Women did not have equal rights in colonial America. At first, married women could not legally own property or make contracts or wills. Husbands were the sole guardians of the children and were allowed to physically discipline both their children and their wives. Single women and widows had more rights and could own and manage property, file lawsuits, and run businesses. In the 1700s, the status of married women improved. Despite legal limitations, many women worked outside their homes.

Enslaved Africans

Historians estimate that some 10 to 12 million Africans were enslaved and sent to the Americas between 1450 and 1870. On the way, about 2 million died at sea. Of the 8 to 10 million Africans who reached the Americas, approximately 500,000 were transported to British North America.

Africans had arrived in Virginia as early as 1619, when they were regarded as "Christian servants." By about 1775, these unwilling immigrants and their descendants numbered about 540,000 in all colonies, roughly 20 percent of the colonial population. Laws called **slave codes** kept African captives from owning property, testifying against whites in court, receiving an education, moving about freely, or meeting in large groups.

No group in the American colonies endured lower status or more hardship than enslaved Africans. Most lived on Southern plantations, where they worked long days and were beaten and branded by planters. Planters also controlled enslaved Africans by threatening to sell them away from their families. Family and religion helped enslaved Africans maintain their dignity. Some resisted by escaping to the North, where slavery was not as widespread as in the South; others refused to work hard or lost their tools.

✔ Reading Check **Identifying** What groups faced discrimination in colonial times?

New Ideas

MAIN Idea The ideas of justified revolutions, the Enlightenment, and the Great Awakening made the colonists question their role as English subjects and their limited freedom under mercantilist policies.

HISTORY AND YOU What rights do you have under the Bill of Rights? Read on to learn about the English Bill of Rights.

When Charles II assumed the throne in 1660, he and his advisers were determined to use the colonies to generate wealth for England. Charles asked Parliament to pass the Navigation Acts of 1660, requiring all goods shipped to and from the colonies to be carried on English ships. Specific products, including the major products that earned money for the colonies, could be sold only to England or other English colonies. Three years later, in 1663, Parliament passed another navigation act, the Staple Act. It required all colonial imports to come through England. Merchants bringing foreign goods to the colonies had to stop in England, pay taxes, and then ship the goods out on English ships. This increased the price of the goods in the colonies.

The Atlantic Slave Trade 1500–1800

In 1619 the first Africans arrived in the English colonies, beginning the brutal African slave trade. After a nearly fatal voyage across the Atlantic, known as the Middle Passage, under stifling, dirty, and crowded conditions, those starved and exhausted Africans who managed to survive were sold in markets or at auction.

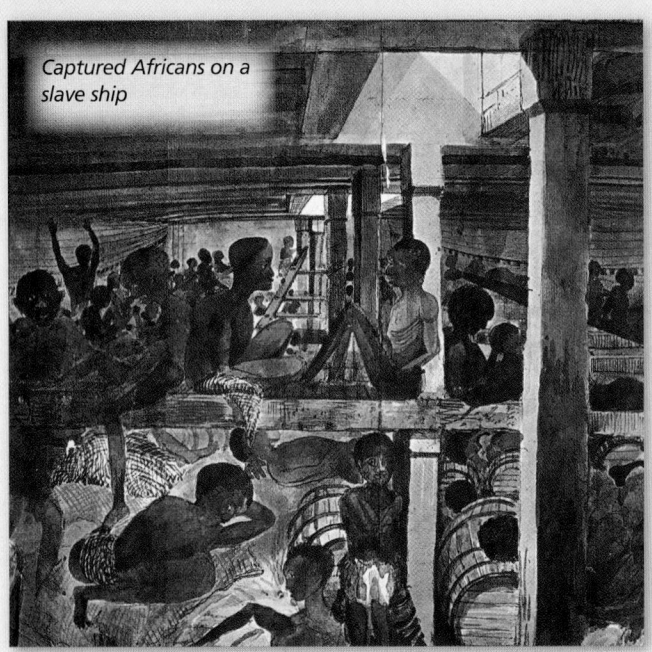

Captured Africans on a slave ship

People of African ancestry as a percentage of the population
- 90–100
- 40–50
- 30–39.9
- • Major slave-trade port

ATLANTIC OCEAN

40°N

NORTH AMERICA

New Orleans • Charleston

Gulf of Mexico

20°N

Santo Domingo

Cartagena

80°W SOUTH AMERICA

Pernambuco •

Bahia •

40°W

0°

SLAVE DESTINATIONS			
SOUTH AMERICA		**CENTRAL AMERICA**	
Brazil	3,650,000	Spanish	1,500,000
Dutch America	500,000	**NORTH AMERICA**	
WEST INDIES		British Colonies	500,000
British	1,660,000	**EUROPE**	175,000
French	1,660,000		
		TOTAL	9,645,000

Frustration with the Navigation Acts led to many colonial merchants routinely smuggling goods to Europe, the Caribbean, and Africa. To better enforce English law, Charles II deprived Massachusetts of its charter in 1684 and declared it a royal colony. James II, who succeeded his brother Charles to the throne in 1685, went even further by creating a new royal province called the Dominion of New England. At first it included Plymouth, Massachusetts, and Rhode Island, and later Connecticut, New Jersey, and New York. Sir Edmund Andros, the first governor-general of the dominion, quickly made himself unpopular by levying new taxes, rigorously enforcing the Navigation Acts, and attempting to undermine the authority of the Puritan Church.

The Glorious Revolution

While Andros was angering New England colonists, King James II was offending many in England by disregarding Parliament, revoking the charters of many English towns, and practicing Catholicism. The birth of James's son in 1688 led to protests against a Catholic heir. To prevent a Catholic dynasty, Parliament invited James's Protestant daughter Mary and her Dutch husband, William of Orange, to claim the throne. James fled, and William and Mary became the new rulers. This change of power is known as the Glorious Revolution.

Before assuming the throne, William and Mary had to accept the English Bill of Rights. This document, written in 1689, said monarchs could not suspend Parliament's laws or create their own courts, nor could they impose taxes or raise an army without Parliament's consent. The Bill of Rights also guaranteed freedom of speech within Parliament, banned excessive bail and cruel and unusual punishments, and guaranteed every English subject the right to an impartial jury in legal cases.

Almost immediately Boston colonists ousted Governor-General Andros. William and Mary then permitted Rhode Island and Connecticut to resume their previous forms of government, and they issued a new charter for Massachusetts in 1691, granting the right to assemble and freedom of worship.

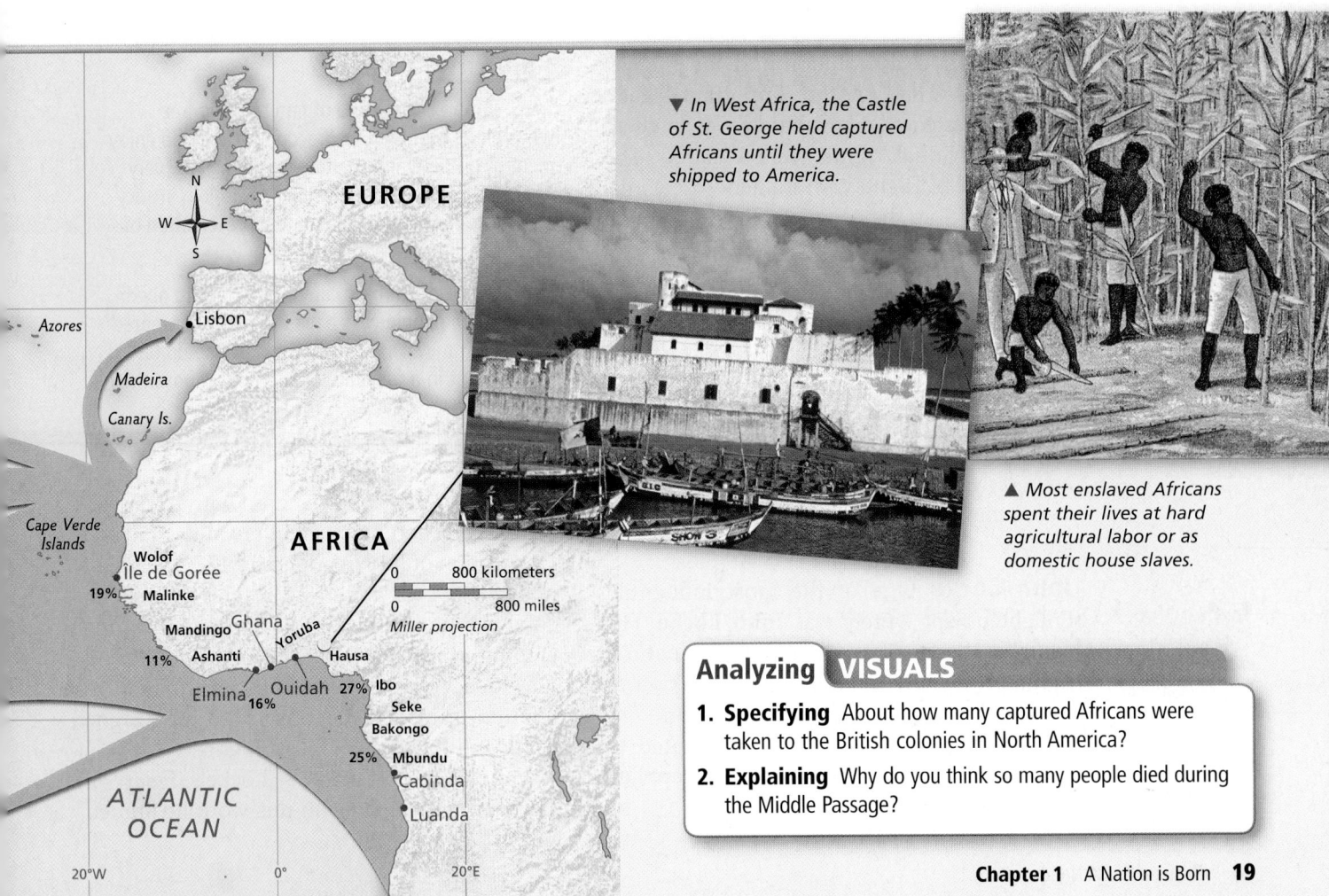

▼ In West Africa, the Castle of St. George held captured Africans until they were shipped to America.

▲ Most enslaved Africans spent their lives at hard agricultural labor or as domestic house slaves.

Analyzing VISUALS

1. **Specifying** About how many captured Africans were taken to the British colonies in North America?

2. **Explaining** Why do you think so many people died during the Middle Passage?

John Locke
1632–1704

The Glorious Revolution of 1688 importantly suggested that there were times when revolution was justified. In 1690, John Locke, a philosopher allied with those who had overthrown King James II, wrote *Two Treatises of Government* on this topic.

He argued that a government's right to rule came from the people, who were born with certain natural rights, including the right to life, liberty, and property. People created government to protect their rights, making a contract to obey the government's laws while the government protected their rights. If a ruler violated those rights, the people were justified in rebelling.

Locke's ideas greatly influenced the American colonists. The Mayflower Compact and the Fundamental Orders of Connecticut were agreements between the people and their government. The colonists saw Locke's "natural rights" as the specific rights of Englishmen set out in the Magna Carta and the English Bill of Rights. By the 1770s, the American colonies would put these ideas into practice when they launched their own revolution against Britain.

According to Locke, what is the source of a government's right to rule?

Benjamin Franklin
1706–1790

This famous patriot is an example of the social mobility ideal that has driven many Americans, while also demonstrating the Enlightenment ideal that one could unlock the laws of nature through rational exploration.

Franklin grew up humbly, the son of a Boston candle and soap maker. At sixteen, Franklin's passion for books and writing led him to Philadelphia: "I was dirty from my journey . . . and I knew no soul nor where to look for lodging . . . my whole stock of cash consisted of a Dutch dollar and about a shilling in copper." He eventually achieved success as a printer, writer, scientist, and philosopher. By the time he was 42, the man who popularized the proverb "Time is money" could afford to retire and devote himself to public life.

In this retirement, he began his scientific investigations. Most famously, his kite experiments proved that lightning was electrical in nature and gained him an international reputation as an Enlightenment thinker.

How did Franklin's life experiences demonstrate American social mobility?

For an excerpt from the English Bill of Rights, see page R41 in **Documents in American History.**

The Glorious Revolution and the English Bill of Rights had another important legacy. They suggested that revolution was justified when individual rights were violated. The English Bill of Rights also influenced colonial demands before the American Revolution and helped shape American government.

The Enlightenment

During the late 1600s and 1700s in Europe, a period known as the Age of Enlightenment, philosophers put forth the theory that both the physical world and human nature operated in an orderly way according to natural laws. They also believed anyone could figure out these laws by using reason and logic.

John Locke One of the most influential Enlightenment writers was **John Locke.** His contract theory of government and natural rights profoundly influenced the thinking of American political leaders. In his work *Two Treatises of Government,* Locke attempted to use reason to discover natural laws that applied to politics and society:

For an excerpt from the *Second Treatise of Government,* see page R42 in **Documents in American History.**

PRIMARY SOURCE

"123. If man in the state of nature be so free . . . why will he part with his freedom . . . ? [T]he enjoyment of property in this state is very unsafe, very insecure. This makes him willing . . . to join in society with others . . . for the mutual preservation of their lives, liberties and estates . . . .

192. For no government can have a right to obedience from a people who have not freely consented to it; which they can never be supposed to do till . . . they are put in a full state of liberty to choose their government. . . ."

—from *Two Treatises of Government*

Locke's ideas struck a chord with American colonists. When Thomas Jefferson drafted the Declaration of Independence in 1776, he relied upon the words and ideas of John Locke. The colonists understood Locke's "natural rights" to be the specific rights English people had developed over the centuries and that were referred to in documents such as the Magna Carta and the English Bill of Rights.

Equally important was Locke's *Essay on Human Understanding.* In this work he argued that contrary to what the Church taught, people were not born sinful. Instead their minds were blank slates that society and education could shape for the better. These ideas that all people have rights and that society can be improved became core beliefs in American society.

Rousseau and Montesquieu French thinker Jean-Jacques Rousseau carried Locke's ideas further. In *The Social Contract*, he argued that a government should be formed by the consent of the people, who would then make their own laws. Another influential Enlightenment writer was Baron Montesquieu. In his work *The Spirit of Laws*, published in 1748, Montesquieu suggested that there were three types of political power—executive, legislative, and judicial. These powers should be separated into different branches of the government to protect the liberty of the people. The different branches would provide checks and balances against each other and would prevent the government from abusing its authority.

The Great Awakening

While some Americans turned away from a religious worldview in the 1700s, others renewed their Christian faith. Throughout the colonies, ministers held revivals—large public meetings for preaching and prayer—where they stressed piety and being "born again," or emotionally uniting with God. This widespread resurgence of religious fervor is known as the **Great Awakening.**

The Great Awakening reached its height around 1740 with the fiery preaching of Jonathan Edwards and George Whitefield. Churches soon split into factions over a movement called pietism, which stressed an individual's devoutness. Those who embraced the new ideas—including Baptists, Presbyterians, and Methodists—won many converts, while older, more traditional churches lost members.

In the South, the Baptists gained a strong following among poor farmers. Baptists also welcomed enslaved Africans at their revivals and condemned the brutality of slavery. Hundreds of Africans joined Baptist congregations and listened to sermons that taught that all people were equal before God. Despite violent attempts by planters to break up Baptist meetings, about 20 percent of Virginia's whites and thousands of enslaved Africans had become Baptists by 1775.

A Powerful Legacy

Both the Enlightenment and the Great Awakening emphasized an individualism that inclined American colonists toward political independence. The Enlightenment, along with the Glorious Revolution, provided supporting arguments against British rule. The Great Awakening undermined allegiance to traditional authority.

Reading Check **Determining Cause and Effect** How did the Enlightenment and the Great Awakening affect the established order?

Section 2 REVIEW

Vocabulary

1. **Explain** the significance of: triangular trade, slave codes, John Locke, Great Awakening.

Main Ideas

2. **Describing** What was slavery like in the early colonies?

3. **Analyzing** In what ways did the Great Awakening contribute to the independent spirit of American colonists?

Critical Thinking

4. **Big Ideas** What factors and motivations brought people to the American colonies in the 1700s?

5. **Categorizing** Use a graphic organizer similar to the one below to explain the reasons for the population increase in the colonies in the 1700s.

Factors Contributing to Colonial Population Increase

6. **Analyzing Visuals** Study the map on pages 18–19. How did enslaved Africans come to the American colonies? Which destination received the most enslaved people?

Writing About History

7. **Persuasive Writing** Suppose that you are a German immigrant to the colonies in 1725. Write a letter to relatives in Germany explaining what your life in the colonies has been like and encouraging them to join you.

History ONLINE

Study Central™ To review this section, go to glencoe.com and click on Study Central.

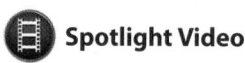
The American Revolution

Guide to Reading

Big Ideas
Struggles for Rights American colonists became dissatisfied with Britain's rule and fought to gain independence.

Content Vocabulary
- customs duty *(p. 23)*
- committee of correspondence *(p. 25)*
- minutemen *(p. 26)*

Academic Vocabulary
- communicate *(p. 25)*

People and Events to Identify
- Stamp Act *(p. 23)*
- Townshend Acts *(p. 24)*
- Intolerable Acts *(p. 26)*
- Lexington *(p. 26)*
- Concord *(p. 26)*
- George Washington *(p. 26)*
- Yorktown *(p. 29)*

Reading Strategy
Organizing Complete a graphic organizer like the one below to describe the causes that led the colonies to declare their independence.

Escalating tensions over British control of the colonies resulted in a true revolt against British rule. The colonists established a new government for themselves and won their independence.

Growing Rebelliousness

MAIN Idea Unpopular British laws and taxes led to colonial protests and violence.

HISTORY AND YOU Have you ever read letters to the editor of your local newspaper protesting some local policies? Read on to learn how the colonists began to protest against unpopular taxes.

Britain and France struggled for dominance on the North American continent. Whenever the two countries were at war, their colonies were as well. In 1754 such a conflict began in America.

The French and Indian War

In the 1740s, Great Britain became interested in the Ohio River valley. So did Britain's long-standing rivals, the French. Before long, fighting broke out, and the French, with help from their Native American allies, took temporary control of the region.

From 1754 to 1759, the French and Indian War raged along the North American frontier. The fighting between Great Britain and France also spread to Europe, where it was known as the Seven Years' War. In the end, the British triumphed. The Treaty of Paris of 1763 made Great Britain the dominant power in North America. Its empire now included all of New France east of the Mississippi, except New Orleans. Britain also gained Florida from Spain, which had allied itself with France. However, France gave Spain all of its territory west of the Mississippi and New Orleans.

Unpopular Regulations

Great Britain's victory left it with steep debts to repay and new territories to govern and defend. Many British leaders thought that the colonies should share in these costs. The American colonists did not like the policies Britain adopted to solve its financial problems.

The first troubles came with passage of the Proclamation Act of 1763. This act tried to halt colonial expansion into Native American lands west of the Appalachian Mountains. King George III wanted to avoid another costly war with the Native Americans, but the colonists who wanted access to the Ohio River valley were enraged.

JOIN, or DIE.

▲ After developing the Albany Plan, proposing a union of the colonies, Benjamin Franklin drew this cartoon urging the colonies to stand together. A popular legend at the time said that a snake could put itself back together and live if it did so before sunset.

0   200 kilometers
0   200 miles
Albers Equal-Area projection

NEWFOUNDLAND

Gulf of St. Lawrence

NEW FRANCE

Sept. 18, 1759: British forces led by Wolfe capture Quebec

July 26, 1758: French surrender Louisbourg

Sept. 8, 1760: French surrender Montreal

ALGONQUIN

July 26, 1759: British troops capture Fort Carillon (Ticonderoga)

Maine (part of Mass.)

Port Royal

NOVA SCOTIA

October, 1755: British deport 6,000 Acadian farmers and disperse them among the colonies

August 27, 1758: Fort Frontenac captured by the British

Lake Champlain

Fall of 1755: Colonial troops are defeated at Crown Point

Fort Oswego

Lake Ontario

N.H.

August 9, 1757: British surrender Fort William Henry

ATLANTIC OCEAN

60°W

Fort Niagara

IROQUOIS CONFEDERACY

New York

Albany

Boston

Mass.

40°N

Lake Erie

Conn. R.I.

70°W

65°W

July 9, 1755: Braddock defeated by French and Indian troops at Fort Duquesne

New York

- ◄── British advance
- ◄── French advance
- ✸ British victory
- ✸ French victory
- ☐ Fort

NEW FRANCE

Pennsylvania

New Jersey

Philadelphia

Ohio R.

Maryland

Virginia

Delaware

75°W

July 4, 1754: Washington surrenders at Fort Necessity

Analyzing GEOGRAPHY

1. **Location** Where did most of the British victories occur?
2. **Movement** From which colonial port did the British fleet sail to conquer Quebec?

▲ High cliffs protected Quebec, the capital of New France. As this painting depicts, British General James Wolfe found a path from the river up the steep cliffs. After defeating the French forces at Quebec, the British captured the city.

While western farmers denounced the Proclamation Act, eastern merchants objected to new tax policies. The British government had learned that the colonists were smuggling goods without paying **customs duties**—taxes on imports and exports. Britain tightened customs control and began introducing other unpopular measures. To bring in new revenue, the Sugar Act of 1764 raised taxes on imports of raw sugar and molasses. It also placed new taxes on silk, wine, coffee, and indigo. To make the colonists contribute to their own defense,

the Quartering Act of 1765 obligated them to provide shelter for British troops.

Nothing, however, outraged the colonists more than the **Stamp Act** of 1765. The act required stamps to be bought and placed on most printed materials, from newspapers to playing cards. This was a direct tax—the first Britain had ever placed on the colonists. Editorials, pamphlets, and speeches poured out against it. Groups calling themselves the Sons of Liberty organized protests and tried to intimidate stamp distributors.

In October 1765 representatives from nine colonies met for what became known as the Stamp Act Congress. They issued the Declaration of Rights and Grievances, arguing that only representatives elected by the colonists, not Parliament, had the right to tax them. "No taxation without representation" became a popular catch-phrase.

On November 1, when the Stamp Act took effect, the colonists ignored it and began to boycott all goods made in Britain. Merchants in England saw sales plunge, and thousands of workers lost their jobs. Under pressure, British lawmakers repealed the Stamp Act in 1766.

The Townshend Acts

With British financial problems worsening, Parliament passed new measures in 1767 to raise money from the colonies. These came to be called the **Townshend Acts,** after Charles Townshend, the head of Britain's treasury. The Townshend Acts put new customs duties on glass, lead, paper, paint, and tea imported into the colonies. They also gave customs officers new powers to arrest smugglers.

The Townshend Acts led to a great outcry. In Massachusetts, Sam Adams and James Otis led the resistance. In Virginia, Patrick Henry, George Washington, and Thomas Jefferson organized opposition. When both colonies passed statements challenging Britain's right to tax them, Parliament dissolved their assemblies.

On March 5, 1770, anger turned to violence in Boston. A crowd of colonists began taunting a British soldier guarding a customs house. He called for help, and during the commotion, the British troops opened fire on the crowd, killing five colonists. The Boston Massacre, as the incident became known, might well have initiated more violence. Within weeks, though, tensions were calmed by news that the British had repealed almost all of the Townshend Acts. Parliament kept one tax—on tea—to uphold its right to tax the colonies. At the same time, it allowed the colonial assemblies to resume meeting. Peace and stability returned to the colonies, at least temporarily.

✔ Reading Check **Summarizing** What disagreements arose between Britain and the colonies in the 1700s?

Countdown to Revolution, 1763–1776

1763
Proclamation of 1763 bans colonists from settling west of the Proclamation Line

1765
Stamp Act Congress issues Declaration of Rights and Grievances

1767
Townshend Acts impose new taxes on trade goods; violators to be tried in vice admiralty courts

1768
Colonial merchants begin nonimportation campaign, refusing to import British goods; Daughters of Liberty help by spinning cloth

1764 **1766** **1768** **1770**

1764
Sugar Act imposes new taxes on trade; James Otis argues that taxation without representation violates colonists' liberties

1765
The Stamp Act imposes taxes on printed materials; Sons of Liberty organize protests and boycotts

1770
British troops shoot colonists at Boston Massacre; most Townshend Acts are repealed

The Road to War

MAIN Idea When Britain introduced new laws to assert its authority, the colonists decided to declare their independence.

HISTORY AND YOU Have you ever wondered how the colonists must have felt as they decided to defy Parliament? Read on to learn about the growing discontent of the colonists.

The repeal of the Townshend Acts in 1770 brought calm to the colonies for a time. Soon, however, new British policies led American colonists to declare their independence.

The Colonists Defy Britain

After trade with England had resumed, so had smuggling. When some 150 colonists seized and burned the stranded customs ship *Gaspee*, the British gave investigators the authority to bring suspects back to England for trial. Colonists thought this denied them the right to a trial by a jury of their peers. Based on a suggestion by Thomas Jefferson, they created **committees of correspondence** to **communicate** with one another and coordinate strategy.

In May 1773, Parliament passed the Tea Act, which created favorable business terms for the struggling British East India Company. American merchants, who feared they would be squeezed out of business, were outraged. That fall, when new shipments of British tea arrived in American harbors, colonists in New York, Philadelphia, and Charleston blocked its delivery. Bostonians went one step further. On the night before the tea was to be unloaded, about 150 men boarded the ships. They dumped 342 chests of tea overboard as several thousand people on shore cheered. The raid came to be called the Boston Tea Party.

The Boston Tea Party outraged the British. In the spring of 1774, Parliament passed new laws known as the Coercive Acts to punish Massachusetts. One law shut down Boston's port until the city paid for the destroyed tea. Other laws banned most town meetings and expanded the powers of the royally appointed governor, General Thomas Gage. To enforce the acts, the king stationed 2,000 troops in New England.

1773
At Boston Tea Party, colonists toss British tea into Boston Harbor

1774
Britain imposes Coercive Acts; First Continental Congress meets, passes the Suffolk Resolves, and issues Declaration of Rights and Grievances

January 1776
Tom Paine publishes *Common Sense*, arguing for independence

July 4, 1776
Congress issues Declaration of Independence

1772   **1774**   **1776**

1775
British battle colonial militia at Lexington and Concord; Second Continental Congress meets, selects George Washington to head Continental Army

Analyzing TIME LINES

1. **Stating** When and under what circumstances did the concept of "taxation without representation" first appear?
2. **Specifying** Which occurred first—the Boston Tea Party or the battles at Lexington and Concord?

A few months later the British introduced the Quebec Act, which extended Quebec's boundaries to include much of what is today Ohio, Illinois, Michigan, Indiana, and Wisconsin. Colonists in that territory would have no elected assembly. The Quebec Act, coming so soon after the Coercive Acts, seemed to signal Britain's desire to seize control of colonial governments.

Colonists wasted no time in protesting the **Intolerable Acts,** as the Coercive Acts and the Quebec Act jointly came to be known. In June 1774, the Massachusetts Assembly suggested that representatives from all the colonies meet to discuss the next step. The First Continental Congress met in Philadelphia on September 5. The 55 delegates, who came from each of the 12 colonies except Georgia, debated a variety of ideas. Finally they approved a plan to boycott British goods. They also agreed to hold a second Continental Congress in May 1775 if the crisis remained unresolved.

The Revolution Begins

Meanwhile, Great Britain had suspended the Massachusetts assembly. Massachusetts lawmakers responded by regrouping and naming John Hancock as their leader. He became, in effect, a rival governor to General Gage. A full-scale rebellion was now under way. The Massachusetts militia began to drill. The town of Concord created a special unit of **minutemen** who were trained and ready to "stand at a minute's warning in case of alarm."

Although many colonists disagreed with Parliament's policies, some still felt a strong sense of loyalty to the king and believed British law should be upheld. These Americans came to be known as Loyalists, or Tories. On the other side were the Patriots, or Whigs, who believed the British had become tyrants. The Patriots dominated in New England and Virginia, while the Loyalists were strong in Georgia, the Carolinas, and New York.

In April 1775, General Gage decided to seize Patriot arms and ammunition being stored in Concord. On the night of April 18, about 700 British troops secretly set out from nearby Boston. Messengers, including Paul Revere, were sent to spread the alarm. When the British reached **Lexington,** a town on the way to Concord, 70 minutemen were waiting for them. No one knows who fired first,

but when the smoke cleared, 8 minutemen lay dead and 10 more were wounded.

The British then headed to **Concord,** only to find most of the military supplies already removed. Colonial militiamen and farmers in the area fired at them from behind trees, stone walls, barns, and houses as they retreated to Boston. As news of the fighting spread, militia raced from all over New England to help. By May 1775, militia troops had surrounded Boston, trapping the British inside.

Three weeks later, the Second Continental Congress met and voted to "adopt" the militia surrounding Boston. **George Washington** became general and commander in chief of this Continental Army. Before Washington could reach his troops, the militia was tested again. It turned back two British advances at the Battle of Bunker Hill before running out of ammunition. The resulting stalemate helped to

Debates IN HISTORY

Should the American Colonies Declare Independence?

Although it may seem like the only natural course today, in 1776 independence was not the obvious choice for the 13 British colonies. While many were fed up with British actions and thought that it was time to institute true self-rule, others felt loyalty to what they considered their mother country and wanted to pursue a resolution of their grievances through political and diplomatic, not military, means. British-born Thomas Paine was one who strongly supported independence, as he discussed in his famous pamphlet, *Common Sense.* American-born John Dickinson, while angered at the behavior of the British, expressed in a speech to the Congress his arguments against splitting from Great Britain.

build American confidence. It showed that the largely untrained colonial militia could stand up to one of the world's most feared armies.

Decision for Independence

Many colonists were still not prepared to break away from Great Britain. In July 1775, the Continental Congress sent King George III a document known as the Olive Branch Petition. The petition asserted the colonists' loyalty to the king and urged him to resolve their grievances peacefully. King George not only rejected the petition, but he declared the colonies to be "open and avowed enemies."

With no compromise likely, the fighting spread. The Continental Congress established a navy and began seizing British merchant ships. Patriots invaded Canada and faced off against British and Loyalist troops in Virginia and the Carolinas. More and more colonists now began to favor a break with Britain.

Thomas Paine helped sway public opinion with his pamphlet *Common Sense*, published in January 1776. Paine argued that King George III, and not Parliament, was responsible for British actions against the colonies. In his view, George III was a tyrant, and it was time to declare independence.

In early July, a committee of the Continental Congress approved a document that Thomas Jefferson had drafted in which the colonies dissolved ties with Britain. On July 4, 1776, the full Congress issued this Declaration of Independence. The colonies now proclaimed themselves the United States of America, and the American Revolution formally began.

History ONLINE Student Web Activity Visit glencoe.com and complete the activity on the American Revolution.

✓ Reading Check **Explaining** Why did the colonies declare their independence?

YES

Thomas Paine
Writer

PRIMARY SOURCE

"It is the good fortune of many to live distant from the scene of present sorrow; . . . But let our imaginations transport us for a few moments to Boston. . . . The inhabitants of that unfortunate city who but a few months ago were in ease and affluence, have now no other alternative than to stay and starve, or turn out to beg. . . .

Men of passive tempers look somewhat lightly over the offenses of Britain and, still hoping for the best, are apt to call out, *Come, come we shall be friends again for all this.* But examine the passions and feelings of mankind; Bring the doctrine of reconciliation to the touchstone of nature, and then tell me whether you can hereafter love, honour, and faithfully serve the power that hath carried fire and sword into your land?"

—from *Common Sense*

NO

John Dickinson
Delegate, Continental Congress

PRIMARY SOURCE

"Even those Delegates who are not restrained by Instructions [from their legislatures] have no Right to establish an independent separate Government for a Time of Peace. . . . without a full & free Consent of the People plainly exprest [sic]. . . . We are now acting on a principle of the English Constitution in resisting the assumption or Usurpation of an unjust power. We are now acting under that Constitution. Does that Circumstance [support] its Dissolution? But granting the present oppression to be a Dissolution, the Choice of . . . Restoring it, or forming a new one is vested in our Constituents, not in Us. They have not given it to Us. We may pursue measures that will force them into it. But that implies not a Right so to force them."

—from *Letters of Delegates to Congress, 1774–1789*

DBQ Document-Based Questions

1. **Finding the Main Idea** What are the main ideas in Paine's argument?
2. **Paraphrasing** Why does Dickinson believe that the Congress has no right to form a new government?
3. **Assessing** Which argument do you think is the most logical? Explain.

War for Independence

MAIN Idea With the help of allies, the Americans defeated the British in the Revolutionary War.

HISTORY AND YOU Can you think of wars in which the weaker side defeated a stronger power? Read to learn how the Americans managed to defeat Britain.

The Continental Army could not match the British Army in size, funding, discipline, or experience. However, the Continental Army was fighting on home ground and in every state had help from local militias that used unconventional tactics. Moreover, Britain already faced threats to other parts of its empire and could not afford a long and costly war.

The Northern Campaign

The British under the command of General William Howe were quickly able to seize New York City. Then, in October, Howe led his troops south toward Philadelphia, where the Continental Congress was meeting. George Washington raced to meet him, but both armies were surprised by the early onset of winter weather and set up camp. Nevertheless, Washington decided to try a surprise attack. On the night of December 25, 1776, he led some 2,400 men across the icy Delaware River from Pennsylvania to New Jersey. There they achieved two small victories before they camped for the winter.

By the spring of 1777, both sides were on the move again. General Howe revived his plan to capture Philadelphia and the Continental Congress. On September 11, 1777, he defeated Washington at the Battle of Brandywine Creek. Howe captured Philadelphia, but the Continental Congress escaped.

While General Howe remained in Philadelphia, another British force, led by General John Burgoyne, was marching south from Quebec. Burgoyne expected to link up with Howe in New York but failed to coordinate with him. When he and his 5,000 men reached Saratoga in upstate New York, they

NATIONAL GEOGRAPHIC

North America Following the Treaty of Paris, 1783

160°W
ARCTIC CIRCLE
60°N
Hudson Bay
BRITISH NORTH AMERICA
140°W
40°N
UNITED STATES
PACIFIC OCEAN
SPANISH LOUISIANA
ATLANTIC OCEAN
NEW SPAIN
Gulf of Mexico
TROPIC OF CANCER
60°W
20°N
80°W
100°W
120°W

0   800 kilometers
0   800 miles
Lambert Azimuthal Equal-Area projection

- British
- French
- Russian
- Spanish
- United States
- Disputed

▲ The British surrender at Yorktown. John Trumbull was not present at the surrender but did his best to depict true likenesses of those he knew personally, such as George Washington, shown on horseback in front of the flag.

Analyzing GEOGRAPHY

1. **Location** After the American Revolution, what were the borders of the United States in the north? In the south? In the west?

2. **Regions** Which foreign colonies shared a border with the United States in 1783?

were surrounded by a far bigger American army. On October 17, 1777, they surrendered—a stunning victory for the Americans. The victory improved morale and convinced the French to commit troops to the American cause.

While both Spain and France had been secretly aiding the Americans, the French now agreed to fight openly. On February 6, 1778, France signed an alliance, becoming the first country to recognize the United States as an independent nation. In 1779 Spain entered the war as an ally of France.

Fighting on Other Fronts

After losing the Battle of Saratoga, the British suffered other significant losses on the western frontier. In 1779 George Rogers Clark secured American control of the Ohio River valley. American troops also took control of western Pennsylvania, western New York, and Cherokee lands in western Virginia and North Carolina.

In the South, though, the British expected to find more Loyalist support and at first held the upper hand. In December 1778, they captured Savannah, Georgia, and seized control of Georgia's backcountry. Then a massive British force led by General Charles Cornwallis moved on to Charleston, South Carolina. On May 8, 1780, they forced the surrender of nearly 5,500 American troops, the greatest American defeat in the war. The tide finally turned on October 7, 1780, at the Battle of Kings Mountain. After defeating Loyalists, Patriot forces drove the British out of most of the South.

The Americans also fought the British at sea. Since they did not have the resources to assemble a large navy, Congress issued letters of marque, or licenses, to about 2,000 privately owned ships. In addition to winning some naval battles, the Americans were able to seriously harm British trade by attacking merchant ships.

The American Victory

The last major battle of the Revolutionary War was fought in **Yorktown,** Virginia, in the fall of 1781. General Cornwallis became trapped there, with George Washington closing in on land and the French navy blocking escape by sea. On October 19, 1781, Cornwallis and approximately 8,000 British troops surrendered.

After learning of the American victory at Yorktown, Parliament voted to end the war. Peace talks began in early April 1782, and the final settlement, the Treaty of Paris, was signed on September 3, 1783. In this treaty, Britain recognized the United States of America as an independent nation with the Mississippi River as its western border. The British kept Canada, but they gave Florida back to Spain and made other concessions to France. On November 24, 1783, the last British troops left New York City. The Revolutionary War was over, and a new nation began to take shape.

Reading Check **Analyzing** Which major battle during the war was a turning point for the Americans?

Section 3 REVIEW

Vocabulary

1. **Explain** the significance of: customs duties, Stamp Act, Townshend Acts, committees of correspondence, Intolerable Acts, minutemen, George Washington, Yorktown.

Main Ideas

2. **Explaining** Why did the British decide to raise taxes to bring in new revenue?

3. **Describing** In July 1775, how did the Continental Congress begin to act like an independent government?

4. **Summarizing** What event convinced the French to openly assist the Americans?

Critical Thinking

5. **Big Ideas** Why were the French at first reluctant to make an alliance with the colonies?

6. **Categorizing** Use a graphic organizer to indicate ways in which colonists defied Britain's attempts at regulation and taxation.

Colonists' Acts of Defiance

7. **Analyzing Visuals** Study the cartoon on page 23. What was the purpose of the cartoon? What did each section of the snake represent?

Writing About History

8. **Persuasive Writing** Suppose that you are a colonial leader during the American Revolution. Write a letter to convince the ruler of a European nation to support the Americans in the war.

History ONLINE

Study Central™ To review this section, go to glencoe.com and click on Study Central.

THE DECLARATION OF INDEPENDENCE

In Congress, July 4, 1776. The unanimous Declaration of the thirteen united States of America,

[Preamble]

When in the Course of human events, it becomes necessary for one people to dissolve the political bands which have connected them with another, and to assume among the Powers of the earth, the separate and equal station to which the Laws of Nature and of Nature's God entitle them, a decent respect to the opinions of mankind requires that they should declare the causes which **impel** them to the separation.

[Declaration of Natural Rights]

We hold these truths to be self-evident, that all men are created equal, that they are **endowed** by their Creator with certain unalienable Rights, that among these are Life, Liberty, and the pursuit of Happiness.

That to secure these rights, Governments are instituted among Men, deriving their just powers from the consent of the governed,

That whenever any Form of Government becomes destructive of these ends, it is the Right of the People to alter or to abolish it, and to institute new Government, laying its foundation on such principles and organizing its powers in such form, as to them shall seem most likely to effect their Safety and Happiness. Prudence, indeed, will dictate that Governments long established should not be changed for light and transient causes; and accordingly all experience hath shown, that mankind are more disposed to suffer, while evils are sufferable, than to right themselves by abolishing the forms to which they are accustomed. But when a long train of abuses and usurpations, pursuing invariably the same Object evinces a design to reduce them under absolute **Despotism,** it is their right, it is their duty, to throw off such Government, and to provide new Guards for their future security.

[List of Grievances]

Such has been the patient sufferance of these Colonies; and such is now the necessity which constrains them to alter their former Systems of Government. The history of the

---

What It Means
The Preamble The Declaration of Independence has four parts. The Preamble explains why the Continental Congress drew up the Declaration.

impel *force*

What It Means
Natural Rights The second part, the Declaration of Natural Rights, states that people have certain basic rights and that government should protect those rights. John Locke's ideas strongly influenced this part. In 1690 Locke wrote that government was based on the consent of the people and that people had the right to rebel if the government did not uphold their right to life, liberty, and property.

endowed *provided*

despotism *unlimited power*

What It Means
List of Grievances The third part of the Declaration lists the colonists' complaints against the British government. Notice that King George III is singled out for blame.

present King of Great Britain is a history of repeated injuries and **usurpations,** all having in direct object the establishment of an absolute Tyranny over these States. To prove this, let Facts be submitted to a candid world.

He has refused his Assent to Laws, the most wholesome and necessary for the public good.

He has forbidden his Governors to pass Laws of immediate and pressing importance, unless suspended in their operation till his Assent should be obtained; and when so suspended, he has utterly neglected to attend to them.

He has refused to pass other Laws for the accommodation of large districts of people, unless those people would **relinquish** the right of Representation in the Legislature, a right **inestimable** to them and formidable to tyrants only.

He has called together legislative bodies at places unusual, uncomfortable, and distant from the depository of their Public Records, for the sole purpose of fatiguing them into compliance with his measures.

He has dissolved Representative Houses repeatedly, for opposing with manly firmness his invasions on the rights of the people.

He has refused for a long time, after such dissolutions, to cause others to be elected; whereby the Legislative Powers, incapable of **Annihilation,** have returned to the People at large for their exercise; the State remaining in the mean time exposed to all the dangers of invasion from without, and **convulsions** within.

He has endeavoured to prevent the population of these States; for that purpose obstructing the Laws for **Naturalization of Foreigners;** refusing to pass others to encourage their migrations hither, and raising the conditions of new Appropriations of Lands.

He has obstructed the Administration of Justice, by refusing his Assent to Laws for establishing Judiciary Powers.

He has made Judges dependent on his Will alone, for the **tenure** of their offices, and the amount and payment of their salaries.

He has erected a multitude of New Offices, and sent hither swarms of Officers to harass our people, and eat out their substance.

He has kept among us, in times of peace, Standing Armies without the Consent of our legislature.

He has affected to render the Military independent of and superior to the Civil Power.

He has combined with others to subject us to a jurisdiction foreign to our constitution, and unacknowledged by our laws; giving his Assent to their acts of pretended legislation:

For **quartering** large bodies of troops among us:

For protecting them, by a mock Trial, from Punishment for any Murders which they should commit on the Inhabitants of these States:

usurpations *unjust uses of power*

relinquish *give up*
inestimable *priceless*

annihilation *destruction*

convulsions *violent disturbances*

Naturalization of Foreigners *process by which foreign-born persons become citizens*

tenure *term*

quartering *lodging*

For cutting off our Trade with all parts of the world:

For imposing taxes on us without our Consent:

For depriving us in many cases, of the benefits of Trial by Jury:

For transporting us beyond Seas to be tried for pretended offences:

For abolishing the free System of English Laws in a neighbouring Province, establishing therein an Arbitrary government, and enlarging its Boundaries so as to **render** it at once an example and fit instrument for introducing the same absolute rule into these Colonies:

For taking away our Charters, abolishing our most valuable Laws, and altering fundamentally the Forms of our Governments:

For suspending our own Legislature, and declaring themselves invested with Power to legislate for us in all cases whatsoever.

He has **abdicated** Government here, by declaring us out of his Protection and waging War against us.

He has plundered our seas, ravaged our Coasts, burnt our towns, and destroyed the lives of our people.

He is at this time transporting large armies of foreign mercenaries to compleat the works of death, desolation and tyranny, already begun with circumstances of Cruelty & **perfidy** scarcely paralleled in the most barbarous ages, and totally unworthy the Head of a civilized nation.

He has constrained our fellow Citizens taken Captive on the high Seas to bear Arms against their Country, to become the executioners of their friends and Brethren, or to fall themselves by their Hands.

He has excited domestic **insurrections** amongst us, and has endeavoured to bring on the inhabitants of our frontiers, the merciless Indian Savages, whose known rule of warfare, is an undistinguished destruction of all ages, sexes and conditions.

In every stage of these Oppressions We have **Petitioned for Redress** in the most humble terms: Our repeated Petitions have been answered only by repeated injury. A Prince, whose character is thus marked by every act which may define a Tyrant, is unfit to be the ruler of a free People.

Nor have We been wanting in attention to our British brethren. We have warned them from time to time of attempts by their legislature to extend an **unwarrantable jurisdiction** over us. We have reminded them of the circumstances of our emigration and settlement here. We have appealed to their native justice and magnanimity, and we have conjured them by the ties of our common kindred to disavow these usurpations, which, would inevitably interrupt our connections and correspondence. They too have been deaf to the voice of justice and of **consanguinity.** We must, therefore, acquiesce in the necessity, which denounces our Separation, and hold them, as we hold the rest of mankind, Enemies in War, in Peace Friends.

render *make*

abdicated *given up*

perfidy *violation of trust*

insurrections *rebellions*

petitioned for redress *asked formally for a correction of wrongs*

unwarrantable jurisdiction *unjustified authority*

consanguinity *originating from the same ancestor*

[Resolution of Independence by the United States]

We, therefore, the Representatives of the united States of America, in General Congress, Assembled, appealing to the Supreme Judge of the world for the **rectitude** of our intentions, do, in the Name, and by Authority of the good People of these Colonies, solemnly publish and declare, That these United Colonies are, and of Right ought to be Free and Independent States; that they are Absolved from all Allegiance to the British Crown, and that all political connection between them and the State of Great Britain, is and ought to be totally dissolved; and that as Free and Independent States, they have full Power to levy War, conclude Peace, contract Alliances, establish Commerce, and to do all other Acts and Things which Independent States may of right do.

And for the support of this Declaration, with a firm reliance on the Protection of Divine Providence, we mutually pledge to each other our Lives, our Fortunes and our sacred Honor.

What It Means
Resolution of Independence The final section declares that the colonies are "Free and Independent States" with the full power to make war, to form alliances, and to trade with other countries.

rectitude *rightness*

John Hancock
    President from
    Massachusetts

Georgia
Button Gwinnett
Lyman Hall
George Walton

North Carolina
William Hooper
Joseph Hewes
John Penn

South Carolina
Edward Rutledge
Thomas Heyward, Jr.
Thomas Lynch, Jr.
Arthur Middleton

Maryland
Samuel Chase
William Paca
Thomas Stone
Charles Carroll
    of Carrollton

Virginia
George Wythe
Richard Henry Lee
Thomas Jefferson
Benjamin Harrison
Thomas Nelson, Jr.
Francis Lightfoot Lee
Carter Braxton

Pennsylvania
Robert Morris
Benjamin Rush
Benjamin Franklin
John Morton
George Clymer
James Smith
George Taylor
James Wilson
George Ross

Delaware
Caesar Rodney
George Read
Thomas McKean

New York
William Floyd
Philip Livingston
Francis Lewis
Lewis Morris

New Jersey
Richard Stockton
John Witherspoon
Francis Hopkinson
John Hart
Abraham Clark

New Hampshire
Josiah Bartlett
William Whipple
Matthew Thornton

Massachusetts
Samuel Adams
John Adams
Robert Treat Paine
Elbridge Gerry

Rhode Island
Stephen Hopkins
William Ellery

Connecticut
Samuel Huntington
William Williams
Oliver Wolcott
Roger Sherman

What It Means
Signers of the Declaration The signers, as representatives of the American people, declared the colonies independent from Great Britain. Most members signed the document on August 2, 1776.

The Constitution

Guide to Reading

Big Ideas
Government and Society American leaders created a new Constitution based on compromise that promised a Bill of Rights.

Content Vocabulary
- popular sovereignty *(p. 37)*
- federalism *(p. 37)*
- separation of powers *(p. 38)*
- checks and balances *(p. 38)*
- veto *(p. 38)*
- ratification *(p. 39)*

Academic Vocabulary
- framework *(p. 35)*
- interpret *(p. 38)*
- revise *(p. 39)*

People and Events to Identify
- Federalist *(p. 39)*
- Anti-Federalist *(p. 39)*

Reading Strategy
Categorizing Complete a graphic organizer similar to the one below by listing the supporters and goals of the Federalists and Anti-Federalists.

	Federalists	Anti-Federalists
Source of Support		
Goals		

States adopted individual constitutions that called for government with powers divided among three different branches. They rejected the Articles of Confederation and ratified the national Constitution after many compromises and the promise of a Bill of Rights.

The Young Nation

MAIN Idea The states created constitutions that gave people more rights, but the national framework could not address all the problems of the new nation.

HISTORY AND YOU If you had lived in the colonies under British rule, what kind of government would you have created? Read on to learn how the American leaders at first created a weak central government.

When American leaders created the United States of America, they were very much aware that they were creating something new. They made a deliberate choice to replace royal rule with a republic. In a republic, power resides with citizens who are entitled to vote. The power is exercised by elected officials who are responsible to the citizens and must govern according to laws or a constitution.

In an ideal republic, all citizens are equal under the law, regardless of their wealth or social class. These ideas conflicted with many traditional beliefs, including ideas about slavery, about women not being allowed to vote or own property, and about certain families being "better" than others. Despite these contradictions, republican ideas began to change American society after the war.

New State Constitutions

Before the war ended, each state had drawn up its own written constitution. Virginia's, written in 1776, and Massachusetts's, drafted in 1780, became models for other states to follow. Their constitutions called for a separation of powers among the executive, legislative, and judicial branches of government. They set up bicameral, or two-house, legislatures, with a senate to represent people of property and an assembly to protect the rights of the common people. They also included a list of rights guaranteeing essential freedoms.

Other states varied in their constitutions. Perhaps most democratic was that of Pennsylvania. Rather than simply limiting the power of the governor, the Pennsylvania constitution eliminated the position entirely, along with the upper house. Instead, the state would be governed by a one-house legislature in which representatives would be elected annually.

The Revolution Changes Government

Wealth of Elected Officials

Northern States

1765–1775 / 1783–1790

Southern States

1765–1775 / 1783–1790

Over £ 5,000   £ 2,000–£ 5,000   Under £ 2,000

Source: "Government by the People: The American Revolution and the Democratization of the Legislatures."

Analyzing VISUALS

1. **Analyzing** In the North after the Revolution, how much did the percentage of wealthy officeholders increase?

2. **Specifying** In which region did the greater number of middle-class people enter public office after the Revolution?

▲ After the Revolution, voting rights expanded. The New Jersey constitution adopted in 1776 granted the right to vote to "all inhabitants" who owned a certain amount of wealth. This wording (probably unintentionally) allowed unmarried women who owned property to vote. Married women did not have property rights.

Changes in Society

The concern for individual liberty led, among other things, to greater separation of church and state. For example, the Virginia Statute for Religious Freedom, passed in 1786, declared that Virginia no longer had an official church and that the state could not collect taxes to support churches.

Voting rights also expanded. Many states allowed any white male taxpayer to vote, whether or not he owned property. Property restrictions on running for office were also relaxed, and more people of modest means became eligible to serve in government.

Women and African Americans continued to be denied political rights, but they made some advances. Women gained greater access to education and could more easily obtain a divorce. For African Americans, emancipation, or freedom from enslavement, became a major issue. Thousands of enslaved people achieved freedom during the Revolution in return for their military service. Several Northern states, such as Massachusetts, even took steps to abolish slavery gradually. In the South enslaved labor remained crucial to the economy, and little changed.

A Weak National Government

American leaders now worked to plan a central government for the new nation. On March 2, 1781, the **framework** they created took effect. The Articles of Confederation loosely unified the states under a single governing body, the Congress. There were no separate branches of government, and Congress had only limited powers. After fighting to free themselves from Britain's domineering rule, the states did not want to create a new government that might become tyrannical.

Under the Articles, each state had one vote in Congress. Congress could act only in certain arenas. It could negotiate with other nations, raise armies, and declare war, but it had no authority to regulate trade or impose taxes.

Despite its weaknesses, the Congress was able to pass the Northwest Ordinance of 1787, a plan for selling and then governing the new lands west of the Appalachian Mountains and north of the Ohio River. The ordinance spelled out how states would be created from the Northwest Territory. It also guaranteed residents certain rights, including freedom of religion and freedom from slavery.

Congress lacked the power to effectively handle other challenges. Trade problems arose because states did not have uniform trade policies, and Congress had no authority to intervene. Foreign relations suffered because Congress could not compel the states to honor its agreements with other countries. The country sank into a severe recession, or economic slowdown, because without the power to tax,

Congress could not raise enough money to pay its war debts or its expenses. It could not even stop the states from issuing their own currency, which rapidly lost value and further weakened the economy.

Among those hardest hit by the recession were poor farmers. Their discontent turned violent in January 1787, when a bankrupt Massachusetts farmer named Daniel Shays led some 1,200 followers in a protest of new taxes. Shays's Rebellion was put down by the state militia, but the incident showed the weakness of the Congress to solve the nation's problems. Increasingly, many people began to call for a stronger central government.

Reading Check **Explaining** In what ways was the Congress ineffective?

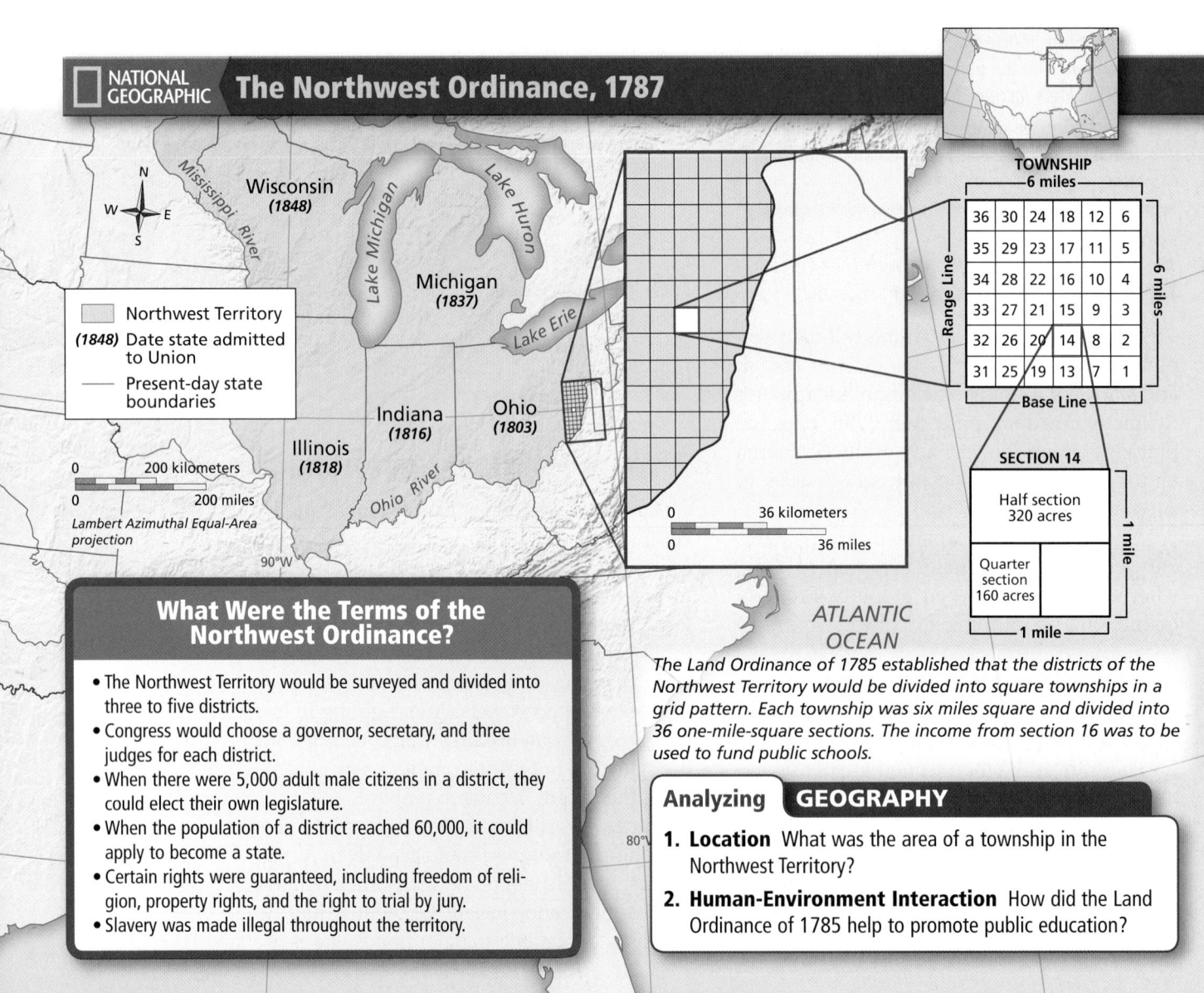

NATIONAL GEOGRAPHIC — The Northwest Ordinance, 1787

Legend:
- Northwest Territory
- *(1848)* Date state admitted to Union
- Present-day state boundaries

0 200 kilometers
0 200 miles
Lambert Azimuthal Equal-Area projection
90°W

Wisconsin *(1848)*
Michigan *(1837)*
Indiana *(1816)*
Ohio *(1803)*
Illinois *(1818)*
Mississippi River
Lake Michigan
Lake Huron
Lake Erie
Ohio River

0 36 kilometers
0 36 miles

TOWNSHIP
6 miles

36	30	24	18	12	6
35	29	23	17	11	5
34	28	22	16	10	4
33	27	21	15	9	3
32	26	20	14	8	2
31	25	19	13	7	1

Range Line — Base Line — 6 miles

SECTION 14

| Half section 320 acres | |
| Quarter section 160 acres | |

1 mile — 1 mile

ATLANTIC OCEAN
80°W

What Were the Terms of the Northwest Ordinance?

- The Northwest Territory would be surveyed and divided into three to five districts.
- Congress would choose a governor, secretary, and three judges for each district.
- When there were 5,000 adult male citizens in a district, they could elect their own legislature.
- When the population of a district reached 60,000, it could apply to become a state.
- Certain rights were guaranteed, including freedom of religion, property rights, and the right to trial by jury.
- Slavery was made illegal throughout the territory.

The Land Ordinance of 1785 established that the districts of the Northwest Territory would be divided into square townships in a grid pattern. Each township was six miles square and divided into 36 one-mile-square sections. The income from section 16 was to be used to fund public schools.

Analyzing GEOGRAPHY

1. **Location** What was the area of a township in the Northwest Territory?
2. **Human-Environment Interaction** How did the Land Ordinance of 1785 help to promote public education?

A New Constitution

MAIN Idea American leaders created a new constitution based on compromise.

HISTORY AND YOU Have you ever come up with new rules to a game because the old ones did not work? Read on to learn why the Constitution replaced the Articles of Confederation.

The political and economic problems facing the United States in 1787 worried many American leaders. They believed that the new nation would not survive without a strong national government and that the Articles of Confederation had to be revised.

In May 1787 every state except Rhode Island sent delegates to Philadelphia "for the sole purpose of revising the Articles of Confederation." Instead of changing the Articles, though, the delegates quickly decided to abandon the Articles and write a brand-new framework of government. The meeting, attended by 55 of America's most distinguished leaders, is therefore known as the Constitutional Convention. The majority were attorneys, and most of the others were planters or merchants. Most had experience in colonial, state, or national government. The delegates chose George Washington as their presiding officer. Other notable delegates included Benjamin Franklin, Alexander Hamilton, and James Madison.

Debate and Compromise

All the delegates supported a stronger national government with the power to levy taxes and make laws that would be binding upon the states. The delegates also accepted the idea of dividing the government into executive, legislative, and judicial branches.

On other points, the delegates found themselves split. One contentious question was how each state should be represented in Congress. The larger states insisted that representation in Congress should be based on population. The smaller states feared that the larger states would outvote them under such a system and instead wanted each state to have an equal vote. The convention appointed a special committee to find a compromise. Ben Franklin, one of the committee members, warned the delegates what would happen if they failed to agree:

"[You will] become a reproach and by-word down to future ages. And what is worse, mankind may hereafter, from this unfortunate instance, despair of establishing governments by human wisdom, and leave it to chance, war, and conquest."

—from *Debates on the Adoption of the Federal Constitution*

The committee's solution was based on a suggestion by Roger Sherman from Connecticut. Congress would be divided into two houses. In one, the House of Representatives, the number of a state's representatives would depend on its population. In the other, the Senate, each state would have equal representation. The voters in each state would elect members to the House of Representatives, but the state legislatures would choose senators. This proposal came to be known as the Great Compromise or the Connecticut Compromise.

The Connecticut Compromise sparked a fresh controversy: whether to count enslaved people when determining how many representatives each state would have in the House. The matter was settled by the Three-Fifths Compromise. Every five enslaved people would count as three free persons for determining both representation and taxation.

In another compromise, the delegates dealt with the power of Congress to regulate trade. Delegates agreed that the new Congress could not tax exports. They also agreed that it could not ban the slave trade until 1808 or impose high taxes on the import of enslaved persons.

Framework of Government

With the major disputes behind them, the delegates now focused on the details of the new government. The new Constitution they crafted was based on the principle of **popular sovereignty** (SAH·vuhrn· tee), or rule by the people. Rather than a direct democracy, it created a representative system of government in which elected officials speak for the people.

To strengthen the central government but still preserve the rights of the states, the Constitution created a system known as **federalism.** Under federalism, power is divided between the federal, or national, government and the state governments.

The Constitution also provided for a **separation of powers** in the new government by dividing power among three branches. The two houses of Congress would compose the legislative branch of the government. They would make the laws. The executive branch, headed by a president, would implement and enforce the laws Congress passed. The president would perform other duties as well, such as proposing legislation, appointing judges, putting down rebellions, and serving as commander in chief of the armed forces. The judicial branch—a system of federal courts—would hear all cases arising under federal law and the Constitution, **interpret** federal laws, and render judgment in cases involving those laws. To keep the branches separate, no one serving in one branch could serve in the other branches at the same time.

Checks and Balances

In addition to giving each of the three branches of government separate powers, the framers of the Constitution created a system of **checks and balances** to prevent any one of the three branches from becoming too powerful. Each branch would have some ability to limit the power of the other two.

The president could check Congress by deciding to **veto,** or reject, a proposed law. The legislature would need a two-thirds vote in both houses to override a veto. The Senate also had the power to approve or reject presidential

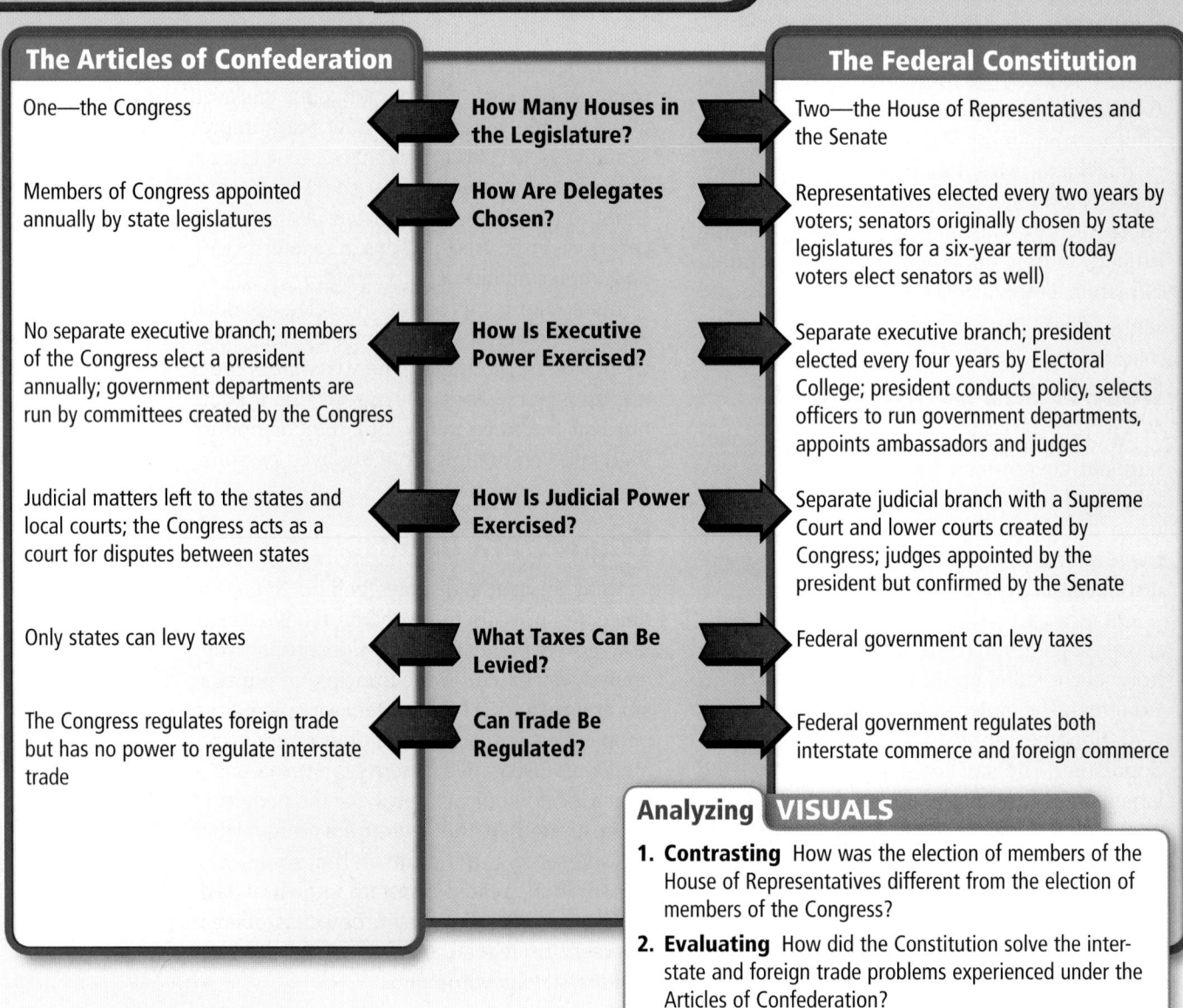

INFOGRAPHIC
Comparing Constitutions

The Articles of Confederation		The Federal Constitution
One—the Congress	**How Many Houses in the Legislature?**	Two—the House of Representatives and the Senate
Members of Congress appointed annually by state legislatures	**How Are Delegates Chosen?**	Representatives elected every two years by voters; senators originally chosen by state legislatures for a six-year term (today voters elect senators as well)
No separate executive branch; members of the Congress elect a president annually; government departments are run by committees created by the Congress	**How Is Executive Power Exercised?**	Separate executive branch; president elected every four years by Electoral College; president conducts policy, selects officers to run government departments, appoints ambassadors and judges
Judicial matters left to the states and local courts; the Congress acts as a court for disputes between states	**How Is Judicial Power Exercised?**	Separate judicial branch with a Supreme Court and lower courts created by Congress; judges appointed by the president but confirmed by the Senate
Only states can levy taxes	**What Taxes Can Be Levied?**	Federal government can levy taxes
The Congress regulates foreign trade but has no power to regulate interstate trade	**Can Trade Be Regulated?**	Federal government regulates both interstate commerce and foreign commerce

Analyzing VISUALS

1. **Contrasting** How was the election of members of the House of Representatives different from the election of members of the Congress?
2. **Evaluating** How did the Constitution solve the interstate and foreign trade problems experienced under the Articles of Confederation?

appointees to the executive branch and had to consent to any treaties the president negotiated. Congress also had the power of the purse. All bills involving taxes or the spending of government money had to originate in the House of Representatives. If any branch of government became too powerful, the House could always refuse to fund it. In addition, Congress could impeach, or formally accuse of misconduct, the president and other high-ranking officials in the executive or judicial branch and, if convicted, remove them from office.

Members of the judicial branch could hear all cases arising under federal laws and the Constitution. The powers of the judiciary were counterbalanced by the other two branches. The president had the power to nominate judges, including a chief justice of the United States, and the Senate had to confirm or reject such nominations. Once appointed, however, federal judges would serve for life to ensure their independence from the other branches.

Amending the Constitution

The delegates recognized that the Constitution they wrote in the summer of 1787 might need to be **revised** over time. To ensure this could happen, they created a clear system for making amendments, or changes, to the Constitution. To prevent the government from being changed constantly, they made it difficult for amendments to be adopted.

The delegates established a two-step process for amending the Constitution: proposal and ratification. An amendment could be proposed by a vote of two-thirds of the members of both houses of Congress. Alternatively, two-thirds of the states could call a constitutional convention to propose new amendments. To become effective, the proposed amendment would then have to be ratified by three-fourths of the state legislatures or by conventions in three-fourths of the states.

The success of the Philadelphia Convention in creating a government that reflected the country's many different viewpoints was, in Washington's words, "little short of a miracle." The convention, John Adams declared, was "the single greatest effort of national deliberation that the world has ever seen."

Reading Check **Summarizing** What compromises did the delegates agree on during the convention?

Ratification

MAIN Idea The promise of a Bill of Rights guaranteed the ratification of the Constitution.

HISTORY AND YOU Have you ever had to convince a friend to agree to something? Read on to learn how the states agreed to ratify the Constitution.

On September 28, Congress voted to submit the Constitution to the states. Each state would hold a convention to vote on it. To go into effect, the Constitution required the **ratification,** or approval, of 9 of the 13 states.

Delaware became the first state to ratify the new Constitution, on December 7, 1787. Pennsylvania, New Jersey, Georgia, and Connecticut quickly followed suit. However, the most important battles still lay ahead. Arguments broke out among Americans, who debated whether the Constitution should be ratified at all.

Debating the Constitution

In fact, debate over ratification began at once—in state legislatures, mass meetings, newspapers, and everyday conversations. Supporters of the new Constitution began calling themselves **Federalists.** They chose the name to emphasize that the Constitution would create a federal system—one with power divided between a central government and state governments.

Many Federalists were large landowners who wanted the property protection that a strong central government could provide. Supporters also included merchants and artisans in large coastal cities and farmers who depended on trade. They all believed it would help their businesses to have an effective federal government that could impose taxes on foreign goods or regulate interstate trade consistently.

Opponents of the Constitution were called **Anti-Federalists,** although they were not truly against federalism. They accepted the need for a national government, but they were determined to protect the powers of the states and concerned about whether the federal or state governments would be supreme. Some Anti-Federalists also believed that the new Constitution needed a bill of rights. Many Anti-Federalists were western farmers living far from the coast. These people considered themselves self-sufficient and were suspicious of the wealthy and powerful.

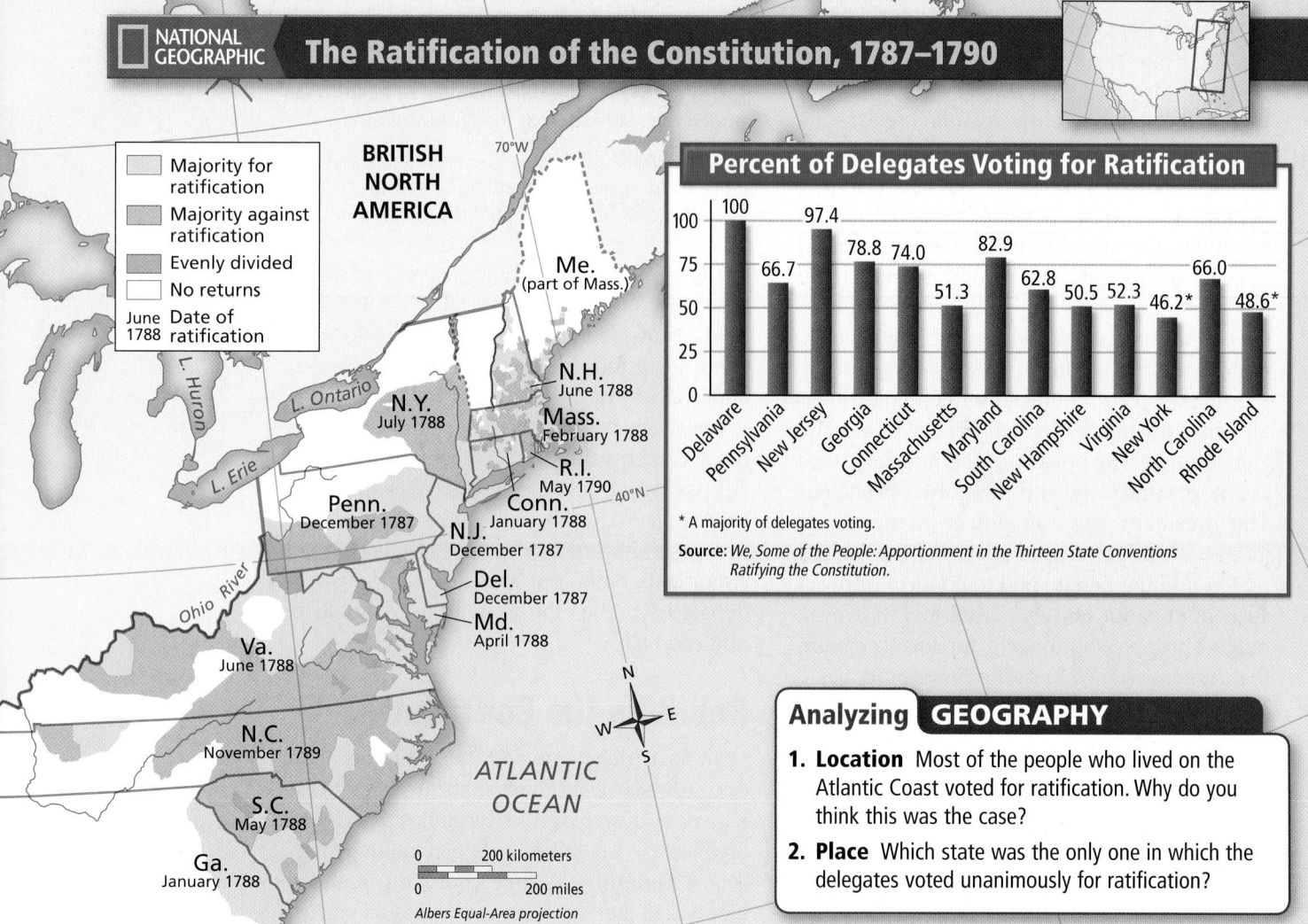

BRITISH NORTH AMERICA

Majority for ratification
Majority against ratification
Evenly divided
No returns
June 1788 Date of ratification

Me. (part of Mass.)

N.H. June 1788

N.Y. July 1788

Mass. February 1788

R.I. May 1790

Penn. December 1787

Conn. January 1788

N.J. December 1787

Del. December 1787

Md. April 1788

Va. June 1788

N.C. November 1789

S.C. May 1788

Ga. January 1788

ATLANTIC OCEAN

L. Huron
L. Ontario
L. Erie
Ohio River

0   200 kilometers
0   200 miles
Albers Equal-Area projection

Percent of Delegates Voting for Ratification

State	Percent
Delaware	100
Pennsylvania	66.7
New Jersey	97.4
Georgia	78.8
Connecticut	74.0
Massachusetts	51.3
Maryland	82.9
South Carolina	62.8
New Hampshire	50.5
Virginia	52.3
New York	46.2*
North Carolina	66.0
Rhode Island	48.6*

* A majority of delegates voting.

Source: *We, Some of the People: Apportionment in the Thirteen State Conventions Ratifying the Constitution.*

Analyzing GEOGRAPHY

1. **Location** Most of the people who lived on the Atlantic Coast voted for ratification. Why do you think this was the case?

2. **Place** Which state was the only one in which the delegates voted unanimously for ratification?

As the states prepared for ratification, both sides knew the decision could go either way. Those in favor of the Constitution summarized their arguments in *The Federalist*—a collection of 85 essays written by James Madison, Alexander Hamilton, and John Jay. Federalist No. 1, the first essay in the series, tried to set the framework for the debate:

PRIMARY SOURCE

"After an unequivocal experience of the inefficacy of the subsisting Foederal [sic] Government, you are called upon to deliberate on a new Constitution for the United States of America. . . . It has been frequently remarked that it seems to have been reserved to the people of this country, by their conduct and example, to decide the important question, whether societies of men are really capable or not of establishing good government from reflection and choice, or whether they are forever destined to depend for their political constitutions on accident and force."

—from *The Independent Journal,* October 27, 1787

The essays were extremely influential. Even today, judges, lawyers, legislators, and historians rely upon them to help interpret the intention of the framers of the Constitution.

Massachusetts

In Massachussetts opponents of the proposed Constitution held a clear majority. They included Samuel Adams, who had signed the Declaration of Independence but now strongly believed the Constitution endangered the independence of the states and failed to safeguard Americans' rights.

Federalists quickly promised to attach a bill of rights to the Constitution once it was ratified. They also agreed to support an amendment that would reserve for the states or the people all powers not specifically granted to the federal government. These Federalist promises and the support of artisans guaranteed Massachusetts's approval. In 1791 the promises led to the adoption of the first ten amendments to the Constitution, which came to be known as the Bill of Rights. The amendments guaranteed the freedoms of speech, press, and religion; protection from unreasonable searches and seizures; and the right to a trial by jury.

Maryland easily ratified the Constitution in April 1788, followed by South Carolina in May. On June 21, New Hampshire became the ninth state to ratify the Constitution. The Federalists had now reached the minimum number of states required to put the new Constitution into effect. Virginia and New York, however, still had not ratified. Together, Virginia and New York represented almost 30 percent of the nation's population. Without the support of these states, many feared the new government would not succeed.

Virginia and New York

At the Virginia convention in June, George Washington and James Madison presented strong arguments for ratification. Patrick Henry, Richard Henry Lee, and other Anti-Federalists argued against it. Madison's promise to add a bill of rights won the day for the Federalists—but barely. The Virginia convention voted 89 in favor of the Constitution and 79 against.

In New York, two-thirds of the members elected to the state convention were Anti-Federalists. The Federalists, led by Alexander Hamilton and John Jay, managed to delay the final vote until news arrived that New Hampshire and Virginia had voted to ratify the Constitution and that the new federal government was now in effect. If New York refused to ratify, it would have to operate independently of all of the surrounding states that had accepted the Constitution. This argument convinced enough Anti-Federalists to change sides. The vote was very close, 30 to 27, but the Federalists won.

By July 1788, all the states except Rhode Island and North Carolina had ratified the Constitution. Because ratification by nine states was all that the Constitution required, the members of the Confederation Congress prepared to proceed without them. In mid-September 1788, they established a timetable for electing the new government. The new Congress would hold its first meeting on March 4, 1789.

The two states that had held out finally ratified the Constitution after the new government was in place. North Carolina waited until November 1789 after a bill of rights had actually been proposed. Rhode Island, still nervous about losing its independence, did not ratify the Constitution until May 1790.

The United States now had a new government, but no one knew if the Constitution would work any better than the Articles of Confederation. Many expressed great confidence, however, because George Washington had been chosen as the first president under the new Constitution.

✔ **Reading Check** **Examining** Why was it important for Virginia and New York to ratify the Constitution, even after the required nine states had done so?

Vocabulary

1. **Explain** the significance of: popular sovereignty, federalism, separation of powers, checks and balances, veto, ratification, Federalist, Anti-Federalist.

Main Ideas

2. **Explaining** What did the Northwest Ordinance accomplish?

3. **Describing** How was the Constitution written as a flexible framework of government?

4. **Analyzing** How did the Federalists attempt to assure ratification of the Constitution?

Critical Thinking

5. **Big Ideas** What do you think was the most serious flaw of the Articles of Confederation? Explain.

6. **Categorizing** Use a graphic organizer to list the compromises reached at the Constitutional Convention.

Compromises Reached

7. **Analyzing Visuals** Study the map of the Northwest Ordinance on page 36. What significant provision of this law would contribute to dividing the nation?

Writing About History

8. **Persuasive Writing** Take on the role of a Federalist or an Anti-Federalist at a state ratifying convention. Write a speech in which you try to convince your audience to either accept or reject the new constitution.

History ONLINE

Study Central™ To review this section, go to glencoe.com and click on Study Central.

Causes of European Colonization

- The wealth Spain acquired from conquering the Aztec and mining gold encourages others to consider creating colonies.
- The Protestant Reformation in England leads to the rise of Puritans who are persecuted by the English government, as are Catholics and others who disagree with the Anglican Church.
- Puritans, Catholics, and other religious dissenters, such as the Quakers, seek religious freedom by migrating to America.
- The growth of trade and the rising demand for English wool leads to landowners evicting peasants so as to raise sheep. Some of the peasants migrate to America to escape poverty and obtain land.

▲ Trading ships like these vessels of the Dutch East India Company carried goods around the world.

▲ The British surrender at Saratoga. The victory at Saratoga boosted morale and helped Americans gain the support of France and Spain.

Causes of the American Revolution

- Defending the colonies in the French and Indian War costs Britain a great deal of money; Britain seeks ways to cover the costs incurred.
- Britain issues the Proclamation Act of 1763 banning colonists from moving west of the Proclamation line.
- The British crack down on smuggling by enforcing customs duties and creating a vice-admiralty court to try smugglers.
- The Sugar Act is attacked by colonists as taxation without representation.
- The Currency Act banning paper money angers farmer and artisans.
- The 1765 Stamp Act leads to widespread colonial protests.
- The 1767 Townshend Acts lead to further protests.
- The Boston Massacre convinces many that the British are tyrants.
- In 1773 British efforts to help the East India Company lead to the Boston Tea party and other protests against the tea shipments.
- Britain bans Massachusetts town meetings, closes Boston's port, and begins quartering troops in private homes.
- Neither King George nor British officials agree to compromise with the Continental Congress, and Congress orders a boycott of British goods.
- British troops fire on militia at Lexington and Concord; the revolution begins; and the Declaration of Independence is issued, July 4, 1776.

Reviewing Vocabulary

Directions: Choose the word or words that best complete the sentence.

1. Because Pennsylvania was owned by William Penn, it was considered

   A a charter colony.

   B a joint-stock company.

   C a proprietary colony.

   D part of the headright system.

2. Who signed individual contracts with American colonists agreeing to work for paid passage to America?

   A serfs

   B indentured servants

   C mercantilists

   D subsistence farmers

3. Massachusetts towns formed militia groups known as _____ in case of British aggression.

   A committees

   B minutemen

   C privateers

   D the Sons of Liberty

4. One of the president's checks against excessive congressional power is the

   A veto.

   B power to set taxes.

   C recession.

   D amendment.

5. Which Enlightenment writer influenced American political leaders with his contract theory of government and natural rights?

   A Baron Montesquieu

   B Jean-Jacques Rousseau

   C Thomas Paine

   D John Locke

Reviewing Main Ideas

Directions: Choose the best answer for each of the following questions.

Section 1 *(pp. 4–13)*

6. How was the Massachusetts Bay Colony similar to Jamestown?

   A Both were founded by individuals escaping religious persecution.

   B Tobacco was the primary source of income.

   C The earliest settlers were mainly single men.

   D Each established a local government for the area.

7. Bacon's Rebellion began because

   A farmers wanted to expand their land west into Native American territories.

   B farmers were tired of paying high taxes.

   C farmers were restricted from voting.

   D Virginia's governor was exempt from paying taxes.

Section 2 *(pp. 16–21)*

8. In the 1700s the English colonies were affected by a resurgence of religious zeal known as

   A the Enlightenment.

   B the Glorious Revolution.

   C the Renaissance.

   D the Great Awakening.

Section 3 *(pp. 22–29)*

9. King George III issued the Proclamation of 1763 to

   A make peace with the French and Spanish.

   B give more lands to the colonists.

   C make peace with Native Americans.

   D punish the port of Boston.

TEST-TAKING

As you read each question, be sure to look for main ideas. A main idea or a key word repeated in an answer choice may be a clue that it is the right answer.

Need Extra Help?									
If You Missed Questions . . .	1	2	3	4	5	6	7	8	9
Go to Page . . .	11	12	26	38	20	8	13	21	22

10. The First Continental Congress was formed in reaction to the

   A Intolerable Acts.

   B Tea Act.

   C Townshend Acts.

   D Stamp Act.

11. Which of the following was one disadvantage the British faced during the Revolution?

   A They did not have enough money to support the war effort.

   B They had a large, well-trained army.

   C They had few officers capable of leading.

   D They were in a strange land with long distances between supplies.

12. Under the Treaty of Paris, which ended the Revolution, the western boundary of the United States would become the

   A Appalachian Mountains.

   B Mississippi River.

   C Rocky Mountains.

   D Pacific Ocean.

Section 4 *(pp. 34–41)*

13. The Northwest Ordinance outlined the process for

   A ratifying the Constitution.

   B achieving statehood.

   C negotiating international treaties.

   D extending slavery north of the Ohio River.

14. The Framers ensured that the Constitution could evolve over time by

   A establishing a process for replacing it.

   B establishing a bill of rights.

   C establishing that the states could veto federal laws.

   D establishing a process for amending it.

Critical Thinking

Directions: Choose the best answers to the following questions.

Base your answers to questions 15 and 16 on the map below and on your knowledge of Chapter 1.

Settlement of the Colonies, 1587–1700

15. Which of the following colonies had the largest settled areas by 1660?

   A Massachusetts

   B North Carolina

   C New Hampshire

   D Virginia

16. Most colonial cities were located close to

   A the Appalachian Mountains.

   B the Great Lakes.

   C the Atlantic Ocean.

   D the Piedmont.

Need Extra Help?							
If You Missed Questions . . .	10	11	12	13	14	15	16
Go to Page . . .	26	28	29	36	39	R15	R15

17. The Framers provided for a separation of powers in the federal government by

A establishing executive, legislative, and judicial branches.

B giving the president the power to command the army.

C making the Supreme Court the most important court in the nation.

D establishing a process of changing the Constitution.

Analyze the cartoon and answer the questions that follow. Base your answers on the cartoon and on your knowledge of Chapter 1.

18. To what does the cartoonist compare the states that have ratified the Constitution?

A pillars supporting the nation

B storm clouds of controversy

C stepping-stones to ratification

D a woven basket of unity

19. Which state is the "ninth and sufficient" state?

A Massachusetts

B Virginia

C New York

D New Hampshire

Document-Based Questions

Directions: Analyze the document and answer the short-answer questions that follow the document.

In this excerpt from his 1789 textbook, *The American Geography,* the Reverend Jedediah Morse discusses the defects of the Articles of Confederation:

> "[The Articles of Confederation] were framed during the rage of war, when a principle of common safety supplied the place of a coercive power in the government. . . .
> When resolutions were passed in Congress, there was no power to compel obedience. . . . Had one State been invaded by its neighbour, the Union was not constitutionally bound to assist in repelling the invasion. . . ."
>
> —from *The American Geography*

20. What defects in the Articles does Morse mention?

21. Why does Morse think that the Articles were effective during the American Revolution, but not afterwards?

Extended Response

22. The Constitutional Convention met in 1787 to address weaknesses in the Articles of Confederation. Soon the delegates agreed that the Articles had failed and that the Confederation should be replaced with a new form of government. In an essay, explain the three most important changes that the delegates made from the Articles to the Constitution. Explain the change in detail and why it was an improvement. Your essay should include an introduction, at least three paragraphs, and a conclusion.

History ONLINE

For additional test practice, use Self-Check Quizzes—Chapter 1 at glencoe.com.

Need Extra Help?						
If You Missed Questions . . .	17	18	19	20	21	22
Go to Page . . .	38	R18	R18	45	R19	34–41

THE CONSTITUTION HANDBOOK

Guide to Reading

Big Ideas
Government and Society A written contract between the people and their government can preserve natural rights and allow for change over time.

Content Vocabulary
- popular sovereignty *(p. 46)*
- federalism *(p. 46)*
- enumerated powers *(p. 47)*
- reserved powers *(p. 47)*
- concurrent powers *(p. 48)*
- impeach *(p. 49)*
- bill *(p. 50)*
- cabinet *(p. 51)*
- judicial review *(p. 53)*
- due process *(p. 53)*

Academic Vocabulary
- grant *(p. 47)*
- responsive *(p. 55)*

Reading Strategy
Taking Notes As you read about the Constitution, use the major headings of the handbook to fill in an outline.

    I. Major Principles
       A.
       B.
       C.
       D.
       E.
       F.
    II.

Serving as the framework of national government and the source of American citizens' basic rights, the Constitution is the most important document of the United States. To preserve self-government, all citizens need to understand their rights and responsibilities.

Major Principles

MAIN Idea The Constitution's basic principles assure people's rights and provide for a balance among the different branches of government.

HISTORY AND YOU If you had to create the rules for a new organization, would you give all members an equal voice? Read on to learn how the Constitution reflects representative government.

The principles outlined in the Constitution were the Framers' solution to the complex problems of a representative government. The Constitution rests on seven major principles of government: (1) **popular sovereignty,** (2) republicanism, (3) limited government, (4) **federalism,** (5) separation of powers, (6) checks and balances, and (7) individual rights.

Popular Sovereignty and Republicanism

The opening words of the Constitution, "We the people," reinforce the idea of popular sovereignty, or "authority of the people." In the Constitution, the people consent to be governed and specify the powers and rules by which they shall be governed.

The Articles of Confederation's government had few powers, and it was unable to cope with the many challenges facing the nation. The new federal government had greater powers, but it also had specific limitations. A system of interlocking responsibilities kept any one branch of government from becoming too powerful.

Voters are sovereign, that is, they have ultimate authority in a republican system. They elect representatives and give them the responsibility to make laws and run the government. For most Americans today, the terms republic and representative democracy mean the same thing: a system of limited government where the people are the final source of authority.

Limited Government

Although the Framers agreed that the nation needed a stronger central authority, they feared misuse of power. They wanted to prevent the government from using its power to give one group special advantages or to deprive another group of its rights. By creating a limited government, they restricted the government's authority to specific powers **granted** by the people.

The delegates to the Constitutional Convention were very specific about the powers granted to the new government. Their decision to provide a written outline of the government's structure also served to show what they intended. Articles I, II and III of the Constitution describe the powers of the federal government and the limits on those powers. Other limits are set forth in the Bill of Rights, which guarantees certain rights to the people.

Federalism

In establishing a strong central government, the Framers did not deprive states of all authority. The states gave up some powers to the national government but retained others. This principle of shared power is called federalism. The federal system allows the people of each state to deal with their needs in their own way, but at the same time, it lets the states act together to deal with matters that affect all Americans.

The Constitution defines three types of government powers. Certain powers belong only to the federal government. These **enumerated powers** include the power to coin money, regulate interstate and foreign trade, maintain the armed forces, and create federal courts (Article I, Section 8).

The second kind of powers are those retained by the states, known as **reserved powers,** including the power to establish schools, set marriage and divorce laws, and regulate trade within the state. Although reserved powers are not specifically listed in the Constitution, the Tenth Amendment says that all powers not granted to the federal government "are reserved to the States."

The third set of powers defined by the Constitution is **concurrent powers**—powers the state and federal governments share. They include the right to raise taxes, borrow money, provide for public welfare, and administer criminal justice. Conflicts between state law and federal law must be settled in a federal court. The Constitution declares that it is "the supreme Law of the Land."

Separation of Powers

To prevent any single group or institution in government from gaining too much authority, the Framers divided the federal government into three branches: legislative, executive, and judicial. Each branch has its own functions and powers. The legislative branch, Congress, makes the laws. The executive branch, headed by the president, carries out the laws. The judicial branch, consisting of the Supreme Court and other federal courts, interprets and applies the laws.

In addition to giving separate responsibility to separate branches, the membership of each branch is chosen in different ways. The president nominates federal judges and the Senate confirms the appointments. People vote for members of Congress. Voters cast ballots for president, but the method of election is indirect. On Election Day the votes in each state are counted. Whatever candidate receives a majority receives that state's electoral votes, which total the number of senators and representatives the state has in Congress. Electors from all states meet to formally elect a president. A candidate must receive at least 270 of 538 electoral votes to win.

Checks and Balances

The Framers who wrote the Constitution deliberately created a system of checks and balances in which each branch of government can check, or limit, the power of the other branches. This system helps balance the power of the three branches and prevents any one branch from becoming too powerful. For example, imagine that Congress passes a law. The president can reject the law by vetoing it. However, Congress can override, or reverse, the president's veto if two-thirds of the members of both the Senate and the House of Representatives vote again to approve the law.

Individual Rights

Ten amendments to the Constitution were approved in 1791 to protect certain basic rights, including freedom of speech, religion, and the right to a trial by jury. These ten amendments are referred to as the Bill of Rights. Over the years, 17 more amendments were added to the Constitution. Some give additional rights to Americans and some modify how the government works. Included among them are amendments that abolish slavery, guarantee voting rights, authorize an income tax, and set a two-term limit on the presidency.

✔ Reading Check **Explaining** What are the three branches of government?

INFOGRAPHIC
The Federal Government

The Constitution divides power in three ways:

1. Between the federal and state governments
2. Between three branches of government
3. By providing checks and balances

The Federal System

Enumerated Powers
Powers *enumerated* to national government; for example, declaring war

Concurrent Powers
Powers *concurrent* to national and state governments; for example, the power to tax

Reserved Powers
Powers *reserved* for state governments; for example, setting up educational system

The Legislative Branch

MAIN Idea The Legislative branch makes the nation's laws and appropriates funds.

HISTORY AND YOU Have you ever written to your representative to support or oppose a bill? Read to find out how Congress makes laws.

The legislative branch includes the two houses of Congress: the Senate and the House of Representatives. Congress's two primary roles are to make the nation's laws and to decide how federal funds are spent.

The government cannot spend any money unless Congress appropriates, or sets aside, funds. All tax and spending bills must originate in the House of Representatives and be approved in both the House and the Senate before moving to the president for signature.

Congress also monitors the executive branch and investigates possible abuses of power. The House of Representatives can **impeach,** or bring formal charges against, any federal official it suspects of wrongdoing or misconduct. If an official is impeached, the Senate acts as a court and tries the accused official. Officials who are found guilty may be removed from office.

The Senate has certain additional powers. Two-thirds of the Senate must ratify treaties made by the president. The Senate must also confirm presidential appointments of federal officials such as department heads, ambassadors, and federal judges.

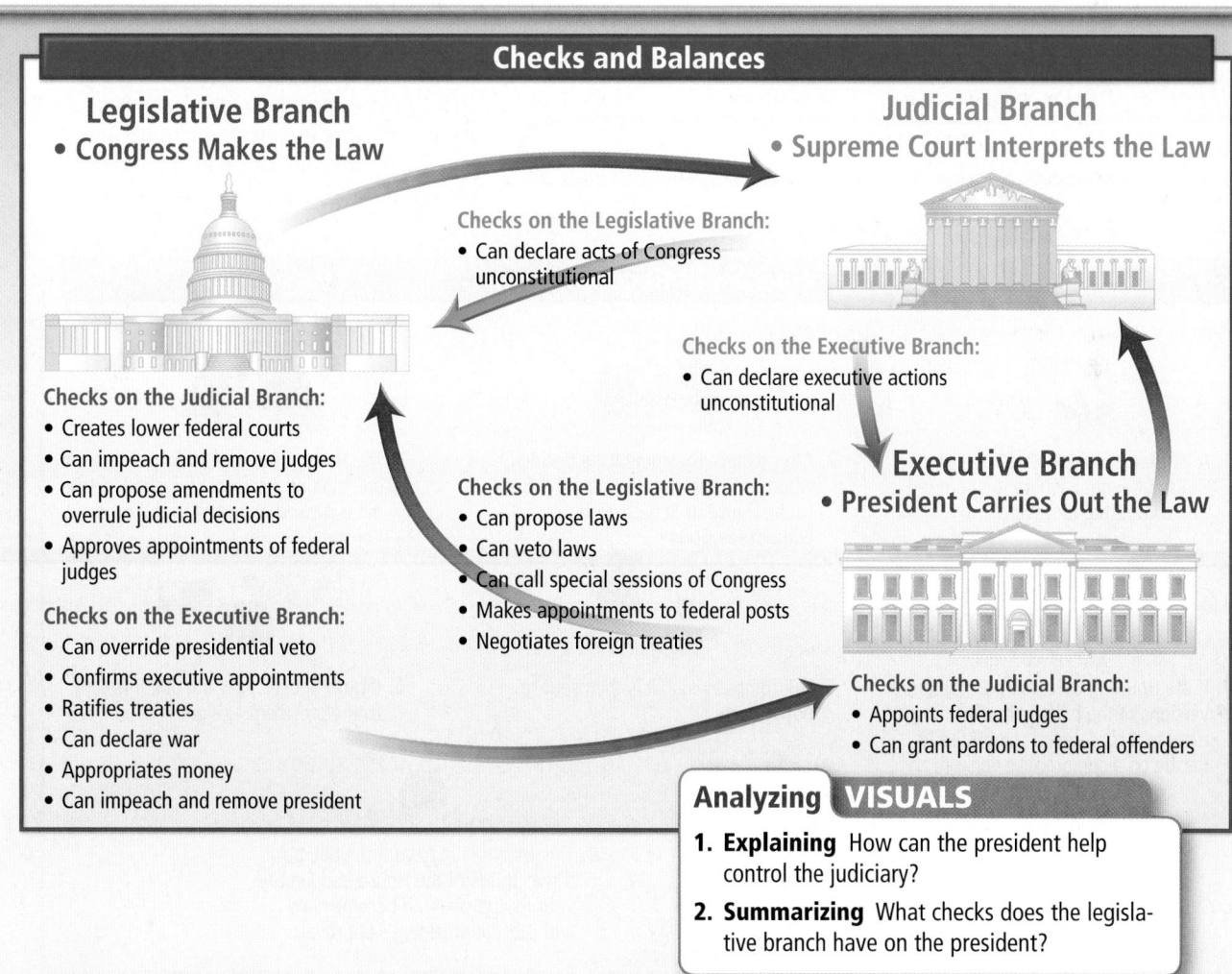

Checks and Balances

Legislative Branch
• **Congress Makes the Law**

Judicial Branch
• **Supreme Court Interprets the Law**

Checks on the Legislative Branch:
• Can declare acts of Congress unconstitutional

Checks on the Executive Branch:
• Can declare executive actions unconstitutional

Executive Branch
• **President Carries Out the Law**

Checks on the Judicial Branch:
• Creates lower federal courts
• Can impeach and remove judges
• Can propose amendments to overrule judicial decisions
• Approves appointments of federal judges

Checks on the Executive Branch:
• Can override presidential veto
• Confirms executive appointments
• Ratifies treaties
• Can declare war
• Appropriates money
• Can impeach and remove president

Checks on the Legislative Branch:
• Can propose laws
• Can veto laws
• Can call special sessions of Congress
• Makes appointments to federal posts
• Negotiates foreign treaties

Checks on the Judicial Branch:
• Appoints federal judges
• Can grant pardons to federal offenders

Analyzing VISUALS

1. **Explaining** How can the president help control the judiciary?

2. **Summarizing** What checks does the legislative branch have on the president?

All members of Congress have the responsibility to represent their constituents, the people of their home states and districts. As a constituent, you can expect your senators and representative to promote national and state interests. Thousands of **bills**—proposed laws—are introduced in Congress every year. Because individual members of Congress cannot possibly study all these bills carefully, both houses use committees of selected members to evaluate proposed legislation.

Standing committees are permanent committees in both the House and the Senate that specialize in a particular topic, such as agriculture, commerce, or veterans' affairs. These committees are usually divided into subcommittees that focus on a particular aspect of an issue. The House and the Senate also form temporary select committees to deal with issues requiring special attention. These committees meet only until they complete their task.

Occasionally the House and the Senate form joint committees with members from both houses. These committees meet to consider specific issues. One type of joint committee, a conference committee, has a special function. If the House and the Senate pass different versions of the same bill, a conference committee meets to work out a compromise bill acceptable to both houses.

Once a committee in either house of Congress approves a bill, it is sent to the full Senate or House for debate. After debate the bill may be passed, rejected, or returned to the committee for further changes. When both houses pass a bill, it goes to the president. If the president approves the bill and signs it, the bill becomes law. If the president vetoes the bill, it does not become law unless Congress takes it up again and votes to override the veto.

✔ Reading Check **Analyzing** What is the most important power of the legislative branch?

INFOGRAPHIC

How a Bill Becomes Law

The legislative process is complex. It begins with a representative in Congress introducing a bill and eventually works its way to the president who either signs the bill into law or vetoes it.

How a Bill Becomes Law

1. A legislator introduces a bill in the House or Senate, where it is referred to a committee for review.

2. After review, the committee decides whether to shelve it or to send it back to the House or Senate with or without revisions.

3. The House or Senate then debates the bill, making revisions if desired. If the bill is passed, it is sent to the other house.

4. If the House and Senate pass different versions of the bill, the houses must meet in a conference committee to decide on a compromise version.

5. The compromise bill is then sent to both houses.

6. If both houses pass the bill, it is sent to the president to sign.

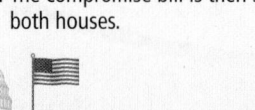

7. If the president signs the bill, it becomes law.

8. The president may veto the bill, but if two-thirds of the House and Senate vote to approve it, it becomes law without the president's approval.

The Executive Branch

MAIN Idea As the nation's leader, the president carries out laws with the help of executive offices, departments, and agencies.

HISTORY AND YOU What would you do if you were the student council president? Read on to learn about the roles of the U.S. president.

The executive branch of government includes the president, the vice president, and various executive offices, departments, and agencies. The executive branch executes, or carries out, the laws that Congress passes.

The President's Roles

The president plays a number of different roles in government. These roles include serving as the nation's chief executive, chief diplomat, commander in chief of the military, chief of state, and legislative leader.

▲ President Bush signs the Voting Rights Act of 2006.

Analyzing VISUALS

1. **Describing** What is the role of a conference committee?

2. **Analyzing** How can a bill become law without the approval of the president?

Chief Executive As chief executive, the president is responsible for carrying out the nation's laws. As chief diplomat, the president directs foreign policy, appoints ambassadors, and negotiates treaties with other nations.

Commander in Chief As commander in chief of the armed forces, the president can give orders to the military and direct its operations. The president cannot declare war; only Congress holds this power. The president can send troops to other parts of the world for up to 60 days but must notify Congress when doing so. The troops may remain longer only if Congress gives its approval or declares war.

Chief of State As chief of state, the president is symbolically the representative of all Americans. The president fulfills this role when receiving foreign ambassadors or heads of state, visiting foreign nations, or honoring Americans.

Legislative Leader The president serves as a legislative leader by proposing laws to Congress and working to see that they are passed. In the annual State of the Union address, the president presents his goals for legislation in the upcoming year.

The Executive at Work

Many executive offices, departments, and independent agencies help the president carry out and enforce the nation's laws. The Executive Office of the President (EOP) is made up of individuals and agencies that directly assist the president. Presidents rely on the EOP for advice and for gathering information needed for decision making.

The executive branch has 15 executive departments, each responsible for a different area of government. For example, the Department of State carries out foreign policy, and the Department of the Treasury manages the nation's finances. The department heads have the title of secretary, and are members of the president's **cabinet.** The cabinet helps the president set policies and make decisions.

✓ Reading Check **Explaining** What are the major roles of the president?

The Judicial Branch

MAIN Idea The judicial branch consists of different federal courts that review and evaluate laws and interpret the Constitution.

HISTORY AND YOU The Constitution did not specifically give the judicial branch the power to review laws. Do you think it is a reasonable task? Read to learn about the role of federal judges and the Supreme Court.

Article III of the Constitution calls for the creation of a Supreme Court and "such inferior [lower] courts as Congress may from time to time ordain and establish." Today the judicial branch consists of three main categories of courts, including:

District and Appellate Courts

United States district courts are the lowest level of the federal court system. These courts consider criminal and civil cases that come under federal authority, such as kidnapping, federal tax evasion, claims against the federal government, and cases involving constitutional rights, such as free speech. There are 94 district courts, with at least one in every state.

The appellate courts, or appeals courts, consider district court decisions in which the losing side has asked for a review of the verdict. If an appeals court disagrees with the lower court's decision, it can overturn the verdict or order a retrial. There are 14 appeals courts, one for each of 12 federal districts, one military appeals court, and an appellate court for the federal circuit.

The Supreme Court

The Supreme Court is the final authority in the federal court system. It consists of a chief justice and eight associate justices. Most of the Supreme Court's cases come from appeals of lower court decisions. Only cases involving foreign ambassadors or disputes between states can begin in the Supreme Court.

INFOGRAPHIC
The Federal Court System

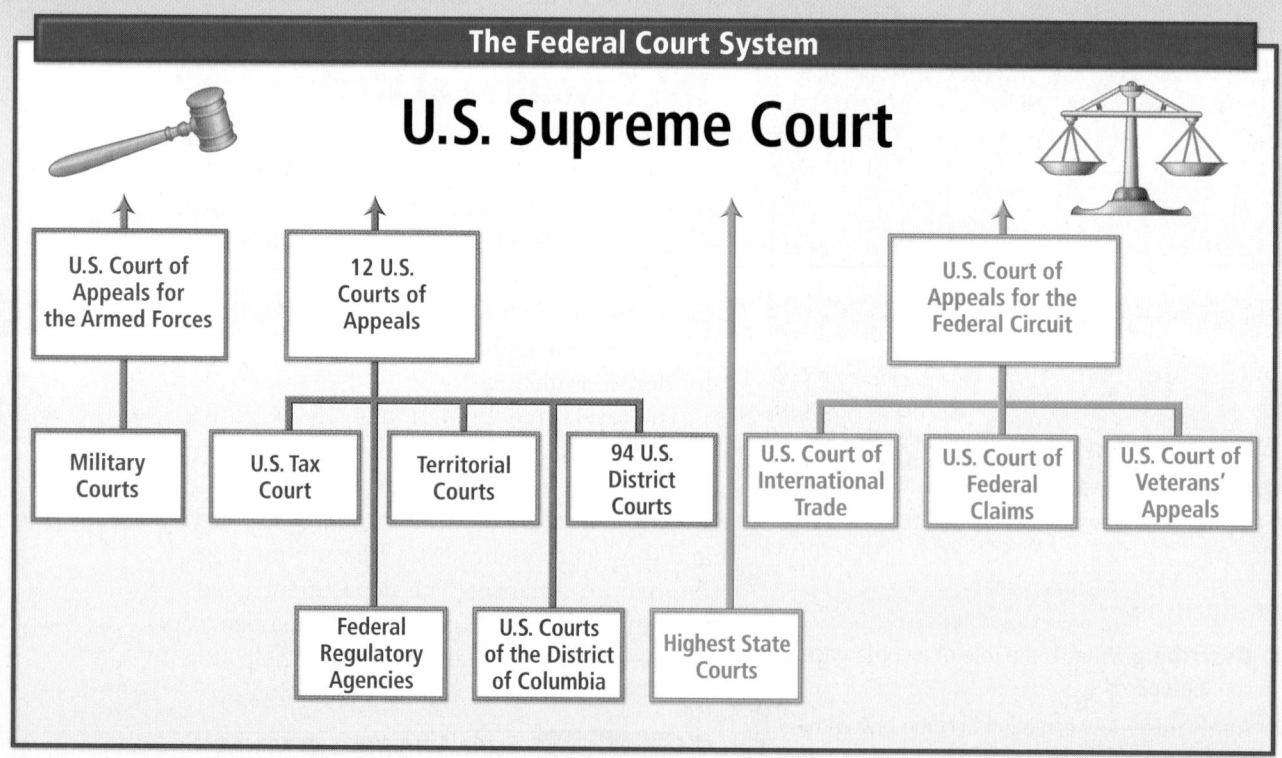

The Federal Court System

- U.S. Supreme Court
  - U.S. Court of Appeals for the Armed Forces
    - Military Courts
  - 12 U.S. Courts of Appeals
    - U.S. Tax Court
    - Territorial Courts
    - 94 U.S. District Courts
      - Federal Regulatory Agencies
      - U.S. Courts of the District of Columbia
  - Highest State Courts
  - U.S. Court of Appeals for the Federal Circuit
    - U.S. Court of International Trade
    - U.S. Court of Federal Claims
    - U.S. Court of Veterans' Appeals

Supreme Court Independence The president appoints the Court's justices for life, and the Senate confirms the appointments. The public has no input. The Framers hoped that by appointing judges, they would be free to evaluate the law with no concern for pleasing voters.

Judicial Review The role of the judicial branch is not described in detail in the Constitution, but the role of the courts has grown as powers implied in the Constitution have been put into practice. In 1803 Chief Justice John Marshall expanded the power of the Supreme Court by striking down an act of Congress in the case of *Marbury* v. *Madison*. Although not mentioned in the Constitution, judicial review has become a major power of the judicial branch. **Judicial review** gives the Supreme Court the ultimate authority to interpret the meaning of the Constitution.

> ☑ Reading Check **Analyzing** How does the Supreme Court protect the Constitution?

▲ The U.S. Supreme Court, front row, left to right, Justices Anthony Kennedy and John Paul Stevens, Chief Justice John Roberts, Justices Antonin Scalia and David Souter; back row, left to right, Justices Stephen Breyer, Clarence Thomas, Ruth Bader Ginsburg, Samuel Alito

Analyzing VISUALS

1. **Interpreting** How many routes to the U.S. Supreme Court are depicted in the chart?

2. **Analyzing** How would a case originating in Puerto Rico be appealed to the U.S. Supreme Court?

Rights and Responsibilities

MAIN Idea The Constitution and the Bill of Rights provide Americans with protection and freedoms.

HISTORY AND YOU How do you think the Constitution protects your rights as a student? Read on to find out about the major rights of Americans.

All American citizens have certain basic rights, but they also have specific responsibilities. Living in a system of self-government means ultimately that every citizen is partly responsible for how their society is governed and for the actions the government takes on their behalf.

The Rights of Americans

The rights of Americans fall into three broad categories: the right to be protected from unfair actions of the government, to receive equal treatment under the law, and to retain certain basic freedoms.

Protection from Unfair Actions Parts of the Constitution and the Bill of Rights protect all Americans from unfair treatment by the government or the law. Among these rights are the right to a lawyer when accused of a crime and the right to trial by jury when charged with a crime. In addition, the Fourth Amendment protects us from unreasonable searches and seizures. This provision requires police to have a court order before searching a person's home for criminal evidence. To obtain this, the police must have a very strong reason to suspect the person of committing a crime.

Equal Treatment All Americans, regardless of race, religion, or political beliefs, have the right to be treated the same under the law. The Fifth Amendment states that no person shall "be deprived of life, liberty, or property, without due process of law." **Due process** means that the government must follow procedures established by law and guaranteed by the Constitution, treating all people equally. The Fourteenth Amendment requires every state to grant its citizens "equal protection of the laws."

Basic Freedoms The basic freedoms are described in the First Amendment—freedom of speech, freedom of religion, freedom of the press, freedom of assembly, and the right to petition. In a democracy, power rests in the hands of the people. Therefore, citizens in a democratic society must be able to exchange ideas freely. The First Amendment allows citizens to criticize the government, in speech or in the press, without fear of punishment.

In addition, the Ninth Amendment states that the rights of Americans are not limited to those in the Constitution. This has allowed Americans to assert other basic rights over the years that have been upheld in court, or assured by amending the Constitution.

Limits on Rights The rights of Americans are not absolute. They are limited based on the principle of respecting everyone's rights equally. For example, many cities and towns require groups to obtain a permit to march on city streets. Such laws do limit free speech, but they also protect the community by ensuring that the march will not endanger other people.

In this and other cases, the government balances an individual's rights, the rights of others, and the community's health and safety. Most Americans are willing to accept some limitations on their rights to gain these protections as long as the restrictions are reasonable and apply equally to all. A law banning all marches would violate the First Amendment rights of free speech and assembly and be unacceptable. Similarly, a law preventing only certain groups from marching would be unfair because it would not apply equally to everyone.

Citizens' Responsibilities

Citizens in a democratic society have both duties and responsibilities. Duties are actions required by law. Responsibilities are voluntary actions. Fulfilling both your duties and your responsibilities helps ensure good government and protects your rights.

Duties One basic duty of all Americans is to obey the law. Laws serve three important functions. They help maintain order; they protect

INFOGRAPHIC
Amending the Constitution

Article V of the Constitution enables Congress and the states to amend, or change, the Constitution.

The Amendment Process

Proposal

Amendment proposed by a vote of two-thirds of both houses of Congress

or

Amendment proposed by a national convention requested by two-thirds of states

Ratification

After approval by three-fourths of state legislatures

or

After approval by three-fourths of state ratifying conventions

New amendment to the Constitution

Analyzing VISUALS

1. **Summarizing** What role do the states play in the amendment process?
2. **Explaining** How many approvals by state legislatures are required for an amendment to the Constitution?

the health, safety, and property of all citizens; and they make it possible for people to live together peacefully. If you believe a law is wrong, you can work through your representatives to change it.

Americans also have a duty to pay taxes. The government uses tax money to defend the nation, to build roads and bridges, and to assist people in need. Americans benefit from services provided by the government. Another duty of citizens is to defend the nation. All males aged 18 and older must register with the government in case the nation needs to call on them for military service. Military service is not automatic, but a war could make it necessary.

The Constitution guarantees all Americans the right to a trial by a jury of their equals. For this reason, you may be called to jury duty when you reach the age of 18. Having a large group of jurors on hand is necessary to guarantee the right to a fair and speedy trial. You also have a duty to serve as a trial witness if called to do so.

Most states require you to attend school until a certain age. School is where you gain the knowledge and skills needed to be a good citizen. In school you learn to think more clearly, to express your opinions more accurately, and to analyze the ideas of others. These skills will help you make informed choices when you vote.

Responsibilities The responsibilities of citizens are not as clear-cut as their duties, but they are as important because they help maintain the quality of government and society. One important responsibility is to be well informed. You need to know what is happening in your community, your state, your country, and the world. Knowing what your government is doing and expressing your thoughts about its actions helps to keep it **responsive** to the wishes of the people. You also need to be informed about your rights and to assert them when necessary. Knowing your rights helps preserve them. Other responsibilities include accepting responsibility for your actions, and supporting your family.

To enjoy your rights to the fullest, you must be prepared to respect the rights of others. Respecting the rights of others also means respecting the rights of people with whom you disagree. Respecting and accepting others regardless of race, religion, beliefs, or other differences is essential in a democracy.

Vote, Vote, Vote! Perhaps the most important responsibility of American citizens is to vote when they reach the age of 18. Voting allows you to participate in government and to guide its direction. When you vote for people to represent you in government, you will be exercising your right of self-government. If you disapprove of the job your representatives are doing, it will be your responsibility to help elect other people in the next election. You can also let your representatives know what you think about issues through letters, telephone calls, and petitions and by taking part in public meetings or political rallies.

Reading Check **Describing** What are the major rights and responsibilities of an American citizen?

Vocabulary

1. **Explain** the significance of: popular sovereignty, federalism, enumerated powers, reserved powers, concurrent powers, impeach, bill, cabinet, judicial review, due process.

Main Ideas

2. **Explaining** What are the provisions of the First Amendment?

3. **Summarizing** How are popular sovereignty and voting connected?

Critical Thinking

4. **Big Ideas** What is the difference between a duty and a responsibility?

5. **Organizing** Use a graphic organizer similar to the one below to list reasons why the framers of the Constitution provided for separation of powers.

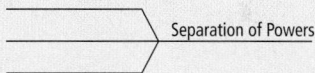
Separation of Powers

6. **Analyzing Visuals** Study the photograph on page 53. How has the composition of the Supreme Court changed over time?

Writing About History

7. **Expository Writing** Working with a partner, choose one of the constitutional rights listed below. Write a report that traces the right's historical development, from the time the Constitution was ratified to the present.

suffrage
freedom of speech
freedom of religion
equal protection of law

History ONLINE

Study Central™ To review this section, go to glencoe.com and click on Study Central.

THE CONSTITUTION
OF THE UNITED STATES

The Constitution of the United States is a truly remarkable document. It was one of the first written constitutions in modern history. The entire text of the Constitution and its amendments follow. For easier study, those passages that have been set aside or changed by the adoption of amendments are printed in blue. Also included are explanatory notes that will help clarify the meaning of important ideas presented in the Constitution.

A burst of fireworks over the Lincoln Memorial in Washington, D.C.

Preamble

We the People of the United States, in Order to form a more perfect Union, establish Justice, insure domestic Tranquility, provide for the common defence, promote the general Welfare, and secure the Blessings of Liberty to ourselves and our Posterity, do ordain and establish this **Constitution** for the United States of America.

Article I

Section 1

All legislative Powers herein granted shall be vested in a Congress of the United States, which shall consist of a Senate and House of Representatives.

Section 2

[1.] The House of Representatives shall be composed of Members chosen every second Year by the People of the several States, and the Electors in each State shall have the Qualifications requisite for Electors of the most numerous Branch of the State Legislature.

[2.] No person shall be a Representative who shall not have attained to the Age of twenty five Years, and been seven Years a Citizen of the United States, and who shall not, when elected, be an Inhabitant of that State in which he shall be chosen.

[3.] Representatives and direct Taxes shall be apportioned among the several States which may be included within this Union, according to their respective Numbers, which shall be determined by adding to the whole Number of free Persons, including those bound to Service for a Term of Years, and excluding Indians not taxed, three fifths of all other Persons. The actual **Enumeration** shall be made within three Years after the first Meeting of the Congress of the United States, and within every subsequent Term of ten Years, in such Manner as they shall by Law direct. The Number of Representatives shall not exceed one for every thirty Thousand, but each State shall have at Least one Representative; and until such enumeration shall be made, the State of New Hampshire shall be entitled to chuse three; Massachusetts eight, Rhode-Island and Providence Plantations one, Connecticut five, New-York six, New Jersey four, Pennsylvania eight, Delaware one, Maryland six, Virginia ten, North Carolina five, South Carolina five, and Georgia three.

[4.] When vacancies happen in the Representation from any State, the Executive Authority thereof shall issue Writs of Election to fill such Vacancies.

[5.] The House of Representatives shall chuse their Speaker and other Officers; and shall have the sole Power of **Impeachment.**

The Preamble introduces the Constitution and sets forth the general purposes for which the government was established. The Preamble also declares that the power of the government comes from the people.

The printed text of the document shows the spelling and punctuation of the parchment original.

Article I. The Legislative Branch

The Constitution contains seven divisions called articles. Each article covers a general topic. For example, Articles I, II, and III create the three branches of the national government—the legislative, executive, and judicial branches. Most of the articles are divided into sections.

> **Section 1. Congress**
> **Lawmaking** The power to make laws is given to a Congress made up of two chambers to represent different interests: the Senate to represent the states and the House to be more responsive to the people's will.

> **Section 2.**
> **House of Representatives**
> **Division of Representatives Among the States** The number of representatives from each state is based on the size of the state's population. Each state is entitled to at least one representative. The Constitution states that each state may specify who can vote, but the Fifteenth, Nineteenth, Twenty-fourth, and Twenty-sixth Amendments have established guidelines that all states must follow regarding the right to vote. What are the qualifications for members of the House of Representatives?

Vocabulary

preamble: *introduction*
constitution: *principles and laws of a nation*
enumeration: *census or population count*
impeachment: *bringing charges against an official*

Section 3. The Senate

Voting Procedure Originally, senators were chosen by the legislators of their own states. The Seventeenth Amendment changed this, so that senators are now elected by their state's people. There are 100 senators, 2 from each state.

What Might Have Been

Electing Senators South Carolina delegate Charles Pinckney suggested during the Convention that the members of the Senate come from four equally proportioned districts within the United States and that the legislature elect the executive every seven years.

Section 3. The Senate

Trial of Impeachments One of Congress's powers is the power to impeach—to accuse government officials of wrongdoing, put them on trial, and, if necessary, remove them from office. The House decides if the offense is impeachable. The Senate acts as a jury, and when the president is impeached, the Chief Justice of the United States serves as the judge. A two-thirds vote of the members present is needed to convict impeached officials. What punishment can the Senate give if an impeached official is convicted?

Vocabulary

president pro tempore: *presiding officer of Senate who serves when the vice president is absent*

quorum: *minimum number of members that must be present to conduct sessions*

adjourn: *to suspend a session*

Section 3

[1.] The Senate of the United States shall be composed of two Senators from each State, chosen by the Legislature thereof, for six Years; and each Senator shall have one Vote.

[2.] Immediately after they shall be assembled in Consequence of the first Election, they shall be divided as equally as may be into three Classes. The Seats of the Senators of the first Class shall be vacated at the Expiration of the second Year, of the second Class at the Expiration of the fourth Year, and of the third Class at the Expiration of the sixth Year, so that one third may be chosen every second Year; and if Vacancies happen by Resignation, or otherwise, during the Recess of the Legislature of any State, the Executive thereof may make temporary Appointments until the next Meeting of the Legislature, which shall then fill such Vacancies.

[3.] No Person shall be a Senator who shall not have attained to the Age of thirty Years, and been nine Years a Citizen of the United States, and who shall not, when elected, be an Inhabitant of that State for which he shall be chosen.

[4.] The Vice President of the United States shall be President of the Senate, but shall have no Vote, unless they be equally divided.

[5.] The Senate shall chuse their other Officers, and also a **President pro tempore,** in the Absence of the Vice-President, or when he shall exercise the Office of the President of the United States.

[6.] The Senate shall have the sole Power to try all Impeachments. When sitting for that Purpose, they shall be on Oath or Affirmation. When the President of the United States is tried, the Chief Justice shall preside: And no Person shall be convicted without the Concurrence of two thirds of the Members present.

[7.] Judgment in Cases of Impeachment shall not extend further than to removal from Office, and disqualification to hold and enjoy any Office of honor, Trust or Profit under the United States: but the Party convicted shall nevertheless be liable and subject to Indictment, Trial, Judgment and Punishment, according to Law.

Section 4

[1.] The Times, Places and Manner of holding Elections for Senators and Representatives, shall be prescribed in each State by the Legislature thereof; but the Congress may at any time by Law make or alter such Regulations, except as to the Places of chusing Senators.

[2.] The Congress shall assemble at least once in every Year, and such Meeting shall be on the first Monday in December, unless they shall by Law appoint a different Day.

Section 5

[1.] Each House shall be the Judge of the Elections, Returns and Qualifications of its own Members, and a Majority of each shall constitute a **Quorum** to do Business; but a smaller Number may **adjourn** from day to day, and may be authorized to compel the Attendance of absent Members, in such Manner, and under such Penalties as each House may provide.

[2.] Each House may determine the Rules of its Proceedings, punish its Members for disorderly Behaviour, and, with the **Concurrence** of two thirds, expel a Member.

[3.] Each House shall keep a Journal of its Proceedings, and from time to time publish the same, excepting such Parts as may in their Judgment require Secrecy; and the Yeas and Nays of the Members of either House on any question shall, at the Desire of one fifth of those Present, be entered on the Journal.

[4.] Neither House, during the Session of Congress, shall, without the Consent of the other, adjourn for more than three days, nor to any other Place than that in which the two Houses shall be sitting.

Section 6

[1.] The Senators and Representatives shall receive a Compensation for their Services, to be ascertained by Law, and paid out of the Treasury of the United States. They shall in all Cases, except Treason, Felony and Breach of the Peace, be privileged from Arrest during their Attendance at the Session of their respective Houses, and in going to and returning from the same; and for any Speech or Debate in either House, they shall not be questioned in any other Place.

[2.] No Senator or Representative shall, during the Time for which he was elected, be appointed to any civil Office under the Authority of the United States, which shall have been created, or the **Emoluments** whereof shall have been encreased during such time; and no Person holding any Office under the United States, shall be a Member of either House during his Continuance in Office.

Section 7

[1.] All Bills for raising **Revenue** shall originate in the House of Representatives; but the Senate may propose or concur with Amendments as on other **Bills.**

[2.] Every Bill which shall have passed the House of Representatives and the Senate, shall, before it become a Law, be presented to the President of the United States; If he approve he shall sign it, but if not he shall return it, with his Objections to that House in which it shall have originated, who shall enter the Objections at large on their Journal, and proceed to reconsider it. If after such Reconsideration two thirds of that House shall agree to pass the Bill, it shall be sent, together with the Objections, to the other House, by which it shall likewise be reconsidered, and if approved by two thirds of that House, it shall become a Law. But in all such Cases the Votes of both Houses shall be determined by yeas and Nays, and the Names of the Persons voting for and against the Bill shall be entered on the Journal of each House respectively. If any Bill shall not be returned by the President within ten Days (Sundays excepted) after it shall have been presented to him, the Same shall be a Law, in like Manner as if he had signed it, unless the Congress by their Adjournment prevent its Return, in which Case it shall not be a Law.

Section 6. Privileges and Restrictions

Pay and Privileges To strengthen the federal government, the Founders set congressional salaries to be paid by the United States Treasury rather than by members' respective states. Originally, members were paid $6 per day. In 2002, all members of Congress received a base salary of $150,000.

Section 7. Passing Laws

Revenue Bill All tax laws must originate in the House of Representatives. This ensures that the branch of Congress that is elected by the people every two years has the major role in determining taxes.

Section 7. Passing Laws

How Bills Become Laws A bill may become a law only by passing both houses of Congress and by being signed by the president. The president can check Congress by rejecting—vetoing—its legislation. How can Congress override the president's veto?

Section 8.
Powers Granted to Congress

Expressed Powers Expressed powers are those powers directly stated in the Constitution. Most of the expressed powers of Congress are itemized in Article I, Section 8. These powers are also called enumerated powers because they are numbered 1 to 18. Which clause gives Congress the power to declare war?

Vocabulary

resolution: *legislature's formal expression of opinion*
naturalization: *procedure by which a citizen of a foreign nation becomes a citizen of the United States*

[3.] Every Order, **Resolution,** or Vote to which the Concurrence of the Senate and House of Representatives may be necessary (except on a question of Adjournment) shall be presented to the President of the United States; and before the Same shall take Effect, shall be approved by him, or being disapproved by him, shall be repassed by two thirds of the Senate and House of Representatives, according to the Rules and Limitations prescribed in the Case of a Bill.

Section 8

[1.] The Congress shall have the Power to lay and collect Taxes, Duties, Imposts and Excises, to pay the Debts and provide for the common Defence and general Welfare of the United States; but all Duties, Imposts and Excises shall be uniform throughout the United States;

[2.] To borrow Money on the credit of the United States;

[3.] To regulate Commerce with foreign Nations, and among the several States, and with the Indian Tribes;

[4.] To establish an uniform Rule of **Naturalization,** and uniform Laws on the subject of Bankruptcies throughout the United States;

[5.] To coin Money, regulate the Value thereof, and of foreign Coin, and fix the Standard of Weights and Measures;

[6.] To provide for the Punishment of counterfeiting the Securities and current Coin of the United States;

[7.] To establish Post Offices and post Roads;

[8.] To promote the Progress of Science and useful Arts, by securing for limited Times to Authors and Inventors the exclusive Right to their respective Writings and Discoveries;

[9.] To constitute Tribunals inferior to the supreme Court;

[10.] To define and punish Piracies and Felonies committed on the high Seas, and Offences against the Law of Nations;

[11.] To declare War, grant Letters of Marque and Reprisal, and make Rules concerning Captures on Land and Water;

[12.] To raise and support Armies, but no Appropriation of Money to that Use shall be for a longer Term than two Years;

[13.] To provide and maintain a Navy;

[14.] To make Rules for the Government and Regulation of the land and naval Forces;

[15.] To provide for calling forth the Militia to execute the Laws of the Union, suppress Insurrections and repel Invasions;

[16.] To provide for organizing, arming, and disciplining, the Militia, and for governing such Part of them as may be employed in the Service of the United States, reserving to the States respectively, the Appointment of the Officers, and the Authority of training the Militia according to the discipline prescribed by Congress;

[17.] To exercise exclusive Legislation in all Cases whatsoever, over such District (not exceeding ten Miles square) as may, by Cession of particular States, and the Acceptance of Congress, become the Seat of Government of the United States, and to exercise like Authority over all Places purchased by the Consent of the Legislature of the State in which the Same shall be, for the Erection of Forts, Magazines, Arsenals, dock-Yards, and other needful Buildings; And

[18.] To make all Laws which shall be necessary and proper for carrying into Execution the foregoing Powers, and all other Powers vested by this Constitution in the Government of the United States, or in any Department or Officer thereof.

Section 9

[1.] The Migration or Importation of such Persons as any of the States now existing shall think proper to admit, shall not be prohibited by the Congress prior to the Year one thousand eight hundred and eight, but a Tax or duty may be imposed on such Importation, not exceeding ten dollars for each Person.

[2.] The Privilege of the Writ of Habeas Corpus shall not be suspended, unless when in Cases of Rebellion or Invasion the public Safety may require it.

[3.] No Bill of Attainder or ex post facto Law shall be passed.

[4.] No Capitation, or other direct, Tax shall be laid, unless in Proportion to the Census or Enumeration herein before directed to be taken.

[5.] No Tax or Duty shall be laid on Articles exported from any State.

[6.] No Preference shall be given by any Regulation of Commerce or Revenue to the Ports of one State over those of another: nor shall Vessels bound to, or from, one State, be obliged to enter, clear, or pay Duties in another.

[7.] No Money shall be drawn from the Treasury, but in Consequence of Appropriations made by Law; and a regular Statement and Account of the Receipts and Expenditures of all public Money shall be published from time to time.

[8.] No Title of Nobility shall be granted by the United States:And no Person holding any Office of Profit or Trust under them, shall, without the Consent of the Congress, accept of any present, Emolument, Office, or Title, of any kind whatever, from any King, Prince, or foreign State.

Section 10

[1.] No State shall enter into any Treaty, Alliance, or Confederation; grant Letters of Marque and Reprisal; coin Money; emit Bills of Credit; make any Thing but gold and silver Coin a Tender in Payment of Debts; pass any Bill of Attainder, ex post facto Law, or Law impairing the Obligation of Contracts, or grant any Title of Nobility.

[2.] No State shall, without the Consent of the Congress, lay any Imposts or Duties on Imports or Exports, except what may be absolutely necessary for executing it's inspection Laws: and the net Produce of all Duties and Imposts, laid by any State on Imports and Exports, shall be for the Use of the Treasury of the United States; and all such Laws shall be subject to the Revision and Controul of the Congress.

[3.] No State shall, without the Consent of Congress, lay any Duty of Tonnage, keep Troops, or Ships of War in time of Peace, enter into any Agreement or Compact with another State, or with a foreign Power, or engage in War, unless actually invaded, or in such imminent Danger as will not admit of delay.

Section 8.
Powers Granted to Congress

Elastic Clause The final enumerated power is often called the "elastic clause." This clause gives Congress the right to make all laws "necessary and proper" to carry out the powers expressed in the other clauses of Article I. It is called the elastic clause because it lets Congress "stretch" its powers to meet situations the Founders could not have anticipated.

What does the phrase "necessary and proper" in the elastic clause mean? It was a subject of dispute from the beginning. The issue was whether a strict or a broad interpretation of the Constitution should be applied. The dispute was first addressed in 1819, in the case of *McCulloch* v. *Maryland,* when the Supreme Court ruled in favor of a broad interpretation. The Court stated that the elastic clause allowed Congress to use its powers in any way that was not specifically prohibited by the Constitution.

Section 9. Powers Denied to the Federal Government

Original Rights A writ of habeas corpus issued by a judge requires a law official to bring a prisoner to court and show cause for holding the prisoner. A bill of attainder is a bill that punishes a person without a jury trial. An "ex post facto" law is one that makes an act a crime after the act has been committed. What does the Constitution say about bills of attainder?

Section 10.
Powers Denied to the States

Limitations on Powers Section 10 lists limits on the states. These restrictions were designed, in part, to prevent an overlapping in functions and authority with the federal government.

Article II. The Executive Branch

Article II creates an executive branch to carry out laws passed by Congress. Article II lists the powers and duties of the president, describes qualifications for office and procedures for electing the president, and provides for a vice president.

What Might Have Been

Term of Office Alexander Hamilton also provided his own governmental outline at the Constitutional Convention. Some of its most distinctive elements were that both the executive and the members of the Senate were "elected to serve during good behaviour," meaning there was no specified limit on their time in office.

Section 1.
President and Vice President
Former Method of Election In the election of 1800, the top two candidates received the same number of electoral votes, making it necessary for the House of Representatives to decide the election. To eliminate this problem, the Twelfth Amendment, added in 1804, changed the method of electing the president stated in Article II, Section 3. The Twelfth Amendment requires that the electors cast separate ballots for president and vice president.

Section 1.
President and Vice President
Qualifications The president must be a citizen of the United States by birth, at least 35 years of age, and a resident of the United States for 14 years.

What Might Have Been

Qualifications At the Constitutional Convention, the New Jersey Amendments, sponsored by the smaller states, raised the possibility of making the executive a committee of people rather than a single individual. Also, executives were not allowed to run for a second term of office under this plan.

Article II
Section 1

[1.] The executive Power shall be vested in a President of the United States of America. He shall hold his Office during the Term of four Years, and, together with the Vice-President, chosen for the same Term, be elected, as follows

[2.] Each State shall appoint, in such Manner as the Legislature thereof may direct, a Number of Electors, equal to the whole Number of Senators and Representatives to which the State may be entitled in the Congress: but no Senator or Representative, or Person holding an Office of Trust or Profit under the United States, shall be appointed an Elector.

[3.] The Electors shall meet in their respective States, and vote by Ballot for two Persons, of whom one at least shall not be an Inhabitant of the same State with themselves. And they shall make a List of all the Persons voted for, and of the Number of Votes for each; which List they shall sign and certify, and transmit sealed to the Seat of the Government of the United States, directed to the President of the Senate. The President of the Senate shall, in the Presence of the Senate and House of Representatives, open all the Certificates, and the Votes shall then be counted. The Person having the greatest Number of Votes shall be the President, if such Number be a Majority of the whole Number of Electors appointed; and if there be more than one who have such Majority, and have an equal Number of Votes, then the House of Representatives shall immediately chuse by Ballot one of them for President; and if no person have a Majority, then from the five highest on the List the said House shall in like Manner chuse the president. But in chusing the President, the Votes shall be taken by States, the Representation from each State having one Vote; A quorum for this Purpose shall consist of a Member or Members from two thirds of the States, and a Majority of all the States shall be necessary to a Choice. In every Case, after the Choice of the President, the Person having the greatest Number of Votes of the Electors shall be the Vice-President. But if there should remain two or more who have equal Votes, the Senate shall chuse from them by Ballot the Vice President.

[4.] The Congress may determine the Time of chusing the Electors, and the Day on which they shall give their Votes; which Day shall be the same throughout the United States.

[5.] No Person except a natural born Citizen, or a Citizen of the United States, at the time of the Adoption of this Constitution, shall be eligible to the Office of President; neither shall any Person be eligible to that Office who shall not have attained to the Age of thirty five Years, and been fourteen Years a Resident within the United States.

[6.] In Case of the Removal of the President from Office, or of his Death, Resignation, or Inability to discharge the Powers and Duties of the said Office, the Same shall devolve on the Vice-President, and the Congress may by Law provide for the Case of Removal, Death, Resignation or Inability, both of the President and Vice-President, declaring what Officer shall then act as President, and such Officer shall act accordingly, until the Disability be removed, or a President shall be elected.

[7.] The President shall, at stated Times, receive for his Services, a Compensation, which shall neither be encreased nor diminished during the Period for which he shall have been elected, and he shall not receive within that Period any other Emolument from the United States, or any of them.

[8.] Before he enter on the Execution of his Office, he shall take the following Oath or Affirmation—"I do solemnly swear (or affirm) that I will faithfully execute the Office of President of the United States, and will to the best of my Ability, preserve, protect and defend the Constitution of the United States."

Section 2

[1.] The President shall be Commander in Chief of the Army and Navy of the United States, and of the Militia of the several States, when called into the actual Service of the United States; he may require the Opinion, in writing, of the principal Officer in each of the executive Departments, upon any Subject relating to the Duties of their respective Offices, and he shall have Power to grant Reprieves and Pardons for Offences against the United States, except in Cases of Impeachment.

[2.] He shall have Power, by and with the Advice and Consent of the Senate, to make Treaties, provided two thirds of the Senators present concur; and he shall nominate, and by and with the Advice and Consent of the Senate, shall appoint Ambassadors, other public Ministers and Consuls, Judges of the supreme Court, and all other Officers of the United States, whose Appointments are not herein otherwise provided for, and which shall be established by Law: but the Congress may by Law vest the Appointment of such inferior Officers, as they think proper, in the President alone, in the Courts of Law, or in the Heads of Departments.

[3.] The President shall have Power to fill up all Vacancies that may happen during the Recess of the Senate, by granting Commissions which shall expire at the End of their next Session.

Section 3

He shall from time to time give to the Congress Information of the State of the Union, and recommend to their Consideration such Measures as he shall judge necessary and expedient; he may, on extraordinary Occasions, convene both Houses, or either of them, and in Case of Disagreement between them, with Respect to the Time of Adjournment, he may adjourn them to such Time as he shall think proper; he shall receive Ambassadors and other public Ministers; he shall take Care that the Laws be faithfully executed, and shall Commission all the Officers of the United States.

Section 1.
President and Vice President
Vacancies If the president dies, resigns, is removed from office by impeachment, or is unable to carry out the duties of the office, the vice president becomes president.

Section 1.
President and Vice President
Salary Originally, the president's salary was $25,000 per year. The president's current salary is $400,000 plus a $50,000 expense account per year. The president also receives living accommodations in the White House and Camp David.

Section 2.
Powers of the President
Cabinet Mention of "the principal officer in each of the executive departments" is the only suggestion of the president's cabinet to be found in the Constitution. The cabinet is an advisory body, and its power depends on the president. Section 2, Clause 1 also makes the president the head of the armed forces. This established the principle of civilian control of the military.

Section 2.
Powers of the President
Treaties The president is responsible for the conduct of relations with foreign countries. What role does the Senate have in approving treaties?

Section 3.
Duties of the President
Executive Orders An important presidential power is the ability to issue executive orders. An executive order is a rule or command the president issues that has the force of law. Only Congress can make laws under the Constitution, but executive orders are considered part of the president's duty to "take care that the laws be faithfully executed." This power is often used during emergencies. Over time the scope of executive orders has expanded. Decisions by federal agencies and departments are also considered to be executive orders.

Section 4. Impeachment
Reasons for Removal From Office This section states the reasons for which the president and vice president may be impeached and removed from office. Only Andrew Johnson and Bill Clinton have been impeached by the House. Richard Nixon resigned before the House could vote on possible impeachment.

Article III. The Judicial Branch
The term *judicial* refers to courts. The Constitution set up only the Supreme Court but provided for the establishment of other federal courts. The judiciary of the United States has two different systems of courts. One system consists of the federal courts, whose powers derive from the Constitution and federal laws. The other includes the courts of each of the 50 states, whose powers derive from state constitutions and laws.

Section 2. Jurisdiction
General Jurisdiction Federal courts deal mostly with "statute law," or laws passed by Congress, treaties, and cases involving the Constitution itself.

Section 2. Jurisdiction
The Supreme Court A court with "original jurisdiction" has the authority to be the first court to hear a case. The Supreme Court generally has "appellate jurisdiction" in that it mostly hears cases appealed from lower courts.

Section 2. Jurisdiction
Jury Trial Except in cases of impeachment, anyone accused of a crime has the right to a trial by jury. The trial must be held in the state where the crime was committed. Jury trial guarantees were strengthened in the Sixth, Seventh, Eighth, and Ninth Amendments.

Vocabulary
original jurisdiction: *authority to be the first court to hear a case*

appellate jurisdiction: *authority to hear cases that have been appealed from lower courts*

Section 4
The President, Vice-President and all civil Officers of the United States, shall be removed from Office on Impeachment for, and Conviction of, Treason, Bribery, or other high Crimes and Misdemeanors.

Article III
Section 1
The judicial Power of the United States, shall be vested in one supreme Court, and in such inferior Courts as the Congress may from time to time ordain and establish. The Judges, both of the supreme and inferior Courts, shall hold their Offices during good Behaviour, and shall, at stated Times, receive for their Services, a Compensation, which shall not be diminished during their Continuance in Office.

Section 2
[1.] The judicial Power shall extend to all Cases, in Law and Equity, arising under this Constitution, the Laws of the United States, and Treaties made, or which shall be made, under their Authority;—to all Cases affecting Ambassadors, other public Ministers and Consuls;—to all Cases of admiralty and maritime Jurisdiction;—to Controversies to which the United States shall be a Party;—to Controversies between two or more States;—between a State and Citizens of another State;—between Citizens of different States,—between Citizens of the same State claiming Lands under Grants of different States, and between a State, or the Citizens thereof, and foreign States, Citizens or Subjects.
[2.] In all Cases affecting Ambassadors, other public Ministers and Consuls, and those in which a State shall be Party, the supreme Court shall have **original Jurisdiction.** In all the other Cases before mentioned, the supreme Court shall have **appellate Jurisdiction,** both as to Law and Fact, with such Exceptions, and under such Regulations as the Congress shall make.
[3.] The Trial of all Crimes, except in Cases of Impeachment, shall be by Jury; and such Trial shall be held in the State where the said Crimes shall have been committed; but when not committed within any State, the Trial shall be at such Place or Places as the Congress may by Law have directed.

Section 3
[1.] Treason against the United States, shall consist only in levying War against them, or in adhering to their Enemies, giving them Aid and Comfort. No Person shall be convicted of Treason unless on the Testimony of two Witnesses to the same overt Act, or on Confession in open Court.
[2.] The Congress shall have Power to declare the Punishment of Treason, but no Attainder of Treason shall work Corruption of Blood, or Forfeiture except during the Life of the Person attainted.

Article IV

Section 1

Full Faith and Credit shall be given in each State to the public Acts, Records, and judicial Proceedings of every other State. And the Congress may by general Laws prescribe the Manner in which such Acts, Records and Proceedings shall be proved, and the Effect thereof.

Section 2

[1.] The Citizens of each State shall be entitled to all Privileges and Immunities of Citizens in the several States. [2.] A Person charged in any State with **Treason,** Felony, or other Crime, who shall flee from Justice, and be found in another State, shall on Demand of the executive Authority of the State from which he fled, be delivered up, to be removed to the State having Jurisdiction of the Crime. [3.] No Person held to Service of Labour in one State, under the Laws thereof, escaping into another, shall, in Consequence of any Law or Regulation therein, be discharged from such Service or Labour, but shall be delivered up on Claim of the Party to whom such Service or Labour may be due.

Section 3

[1.] New States may be admitted by the Congress into this Union; but no new State shall be formed or erected within the Jurisdiction of any other State; nor any State be formed by the Junction of two or more States, or Parts of States, without the Consent of the Legislatures of the States concerned as well as of the Congress. [2.] The Congress shall have Power to dispose of and make all needful Rules and Regulations respecting the Territory or other Property belonging to the United States; and nothing in this Constitution shall be so construed as to Prejudice any Claims of the United States, or of any particular State.

Section 4

The United States shall guarantee to every State in this Union a Republican Form of Government, and shall protect each of them against Invasion; and on Application of the Legislature, or of the Executive (when the Legislature cannot be convened) against domestic Violence.

Article V

The Congress, whenever two thirds of both Houses shall deem it necessary, shall propose **Amendments** to this Constitution, or, on the Application of the Legislatures of two thirds of the several States, shall call a Convention for proposing Amendments, which, in either Case, shall be valid to all Intents and Purposes, as Part of this Constitution, when ratified by the Legislatures of three fourths of the several States, or by Conventions in three fourths thereof, as the one or the other Mode of **Ratification** may be proposed by the Congress; Provided

Article IV. Relations Among the States

Article IV explains the relationship of the states to one another and to the national government. This article requires each state to give citizens of other states the same rights as its own citizens, addresses the admission of new states, and guarantees that the national government will protect the states.

Section 1. Official Acts Recognition by States This provision ensures that each state recognizes the laws, court decisions, and records of all other states. For example, a marriage license issued by one state must be accepted by all states.

Vocabulary

treason: *violation of the allegiance owed by a person to his or her own country, for example, by aiding an enemy*

amendment: *a change to the Constitution*

ratification: *process by which an amendment is approved*

**Section 3.
New States and Territories
New States** Congress has the power to admit new states. It also determines the basic guidelines for applying for statehood. Two states, Maine and West Virginia, were created within the boundaries of another state. In the case of West Virginia, President Lincoln recognized the West Virginia government as the legal government of Virginia during the Civil War. This allowed West Virginia to secede from Virginia without obtaining approval from the Virginia legislature.

Article V. The Amendment Process

Article V explains how the Constitution can be amended, or changed. All of the 27 amendments were proposed by a two-thirds vote of both houses of Congress. Only the Twenty-first Amendment was ratified by constitutional conventions of the states. All other amendments have been ratified by state legislatures. 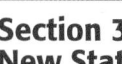 What is an amendment?

Article VI. Constitutional Supremacy

Article VI contains the "supremacy clause." This clause establishes that the Constitution, laws passed by Congress, and treaties of the United States "shall be the supreme Law of the Land." The "supremacy clause" recognizes the Constitution and federal laws as supreme when in conflict with those of the states.

Article VII. Ratification

Article VII addresses ratification and states that, unlike the Articles of Confederation, which required approval of all thirteen states for adoption, the Constitution would take effect after it was ratified by nine states.

that no Amendment which may be made prior to the Year One thousand eight hundred and eight shall in any Manner affect the first and fourth Clauses in the Ninth Section of the first Article; and that no State, without its Consent, shall be deprived of its equal Suffrage in the Senate.

Article VI

[1.] All Debts contracted and Engagements entered into, before the Adoption of this Constitution, shall be as valid against the United States under this Constitution, as under the Confederation.

[2.] This Constitution, and the Laws of the United States which shall be made in Pursuance thereof; and all Treaties made, or which shall be made, under the Authority of the United States, shall be the supreme Law of the Land; and the Judges in every State shall be bound thereby, any Thing in the Constitution or Laws of any State to the Contrary notwithstanding.

[3.] The Senators and Representatives before mentioned, and the Members of the several State Legislatures, and all executive and judicial Officers, both of the United States and of the several States, shall be bound by Oath or Affirmation, to support this Constitution; but no religious Test shall ever be required as a Qualification to any Office or public Trust under the United States.

Article VII

The Ratification of the Conventions of nine States, shall be sufficient for the Establishment of this Constitution between the States so ratifying the same.

Done in Convention by the Unanimous Consent of the States present the Seventeenth Day of September in the Year of our Lord one thousand seven hundred and Eighty seven and of the Independence of the United States of America the Twelfth. In witness whereof We have hereunto subscribed our Names,

Signers

George Washington,
President and Deputy
from Virginia

New Hampshire
John Langdon
Nicholas Gilman

Massachusetts
Nathaniel Gorham
Rufus King

Connecticut
William Samuel Johnson
Roger Sherman

New York
Alexander Hamilton

New Jersey
William Livingston
David Brearley
William Paterson
Jonathan Dayton

Pennsylvania
Benjamin Franklin
Thomas Mifflin
Robert Morris
George Clymer
Thomas FitzSimons
Jared Ingersoll
James Wilson
Gouverneur Morris

Delaware
George Read
Gunning Bedford, Jr.
John Dickinson
Richard Bassett
Jacob Broom

Maryland
James McHenry
Daniel of St. Thomas
Jenifer
Daniel Carroll

Virginia
John Blair
James Madison, Jr.

North Carolina
William Blount
Richard Dobbs Spaight
Hugh Williamson

South Carolina
John Rutledge
Charles Cotesworth
Pinckney
Charles Pinckney
Pierce Butler

Georgia
William Few
Abraham Baldwin

Attest:
William Jackson,
Secretary

Amendment I

Congress shall make no law respecting an establishment of religion, or prohibiting the free exercise thereof; or abridging the freedom of speech, or of the press; or the right of the people peaceably to assemble, and to petition the Government for a redress of grievances.

Amendment II

A well regulated Militia, being necessary to the security of a free State, the right of the people to keep and bear Arms, shall not be infringed.

Amendment III

No Soldier shall, in time of peace be **quartered** in any house, without the consent of the Owner, nor in time of war, but in a manner to be prescribed by law.

Amendment IV

The right of the people to be secure in their persons, houses, papers, and effects, against unreasonable searches and seizures, shall not be violated, and no **Warrants** shall issue, but upon **probable cause,** supported by Oath or affirmation, and particularly describing the place to be searched, and the persons or things to be seized.

Amendment V

No person shall be held to answer for a capital, or otherwise infamous crime, unless on a presentment or indictment of a Grand Jury, except in cases arising in the land or naval forces, or in the Militia, when in actual service in time of War or public danger; nor shall any person be subject for the same offence to be twice put in jeopardy of life or limb; nor shall be compelled in any criminal case to be a witness against himself, nor be deprived of life, liberty, or property, without due process of law; nor shall private property be taken for public use without just compensation.

Amendment VI

In all criminal prosecutions, the accused shall enjoy the right to a speedy and public trial, by an impartial jury of the State and district wherein the crime shall have been committed, which district shall have been previously ascertained by law, and to be informed of the nature and cause of the accusation; to be confronted with the witnesses against him; to have compulsory process for obtaining Witnesses in his favor, and to have the assistance of counsel for his defence.

Amendment VII

In Suits at common law, where the value in controversy shall exceed twenty dollars, the right of trial by jury shall be preserved, and no fact tried by a jury, shall be otherwise reexamined in any Court of the United States, than according to the rules of **common law.**

The Amendments

This part of the Constitution consists of changes and additions. The Constitution has been amended 27 times throughout the nation's history.

The Bill of Rights

The first 10 amendments are known as the Bill of Rights (1791). These amendments limit the powers of the federal government. The First Amendment protects the civil liberties of individuals in the United States. The amendment freedoms are not absolute, however. They are limited by the rights of other individuals. What freedoms does the First Amendment protect?

Vocabulary

quarter: *to provide living accommodations*

warrant: *document that gives police particular rights or powers*

probable cause: *police must have a reasonable basis to believe a person is linked to a crime*

Amendment 5
Rights of the Accused

This amendment contains important protections for people accused of crimes. One of the protections is that government may not deprive any person of life, liberty, or property without due process of law. This means that the government must follow proper constitutional procedures in trials and in other actions it takes against individuals. According to Amendment V, what is the function of a grand jury?

Amendment 6
Right to Speedy and Fair Trial

A basic protection is the right to a speedy, public trial. The jury must hear witnesses and evidence on both sides before deciding the guilt or innocence of a person charged with a crime. This amendment also provides that legal counsel must be provided to a defendant. In 1963, in *Gideon* v. *Wainwright*, the Supreme Court ruled that if a defendant cannot afford a lawyer, the government must provide one to defend him or her. Why is the right to a "speedy" trial important?

Vocabulary

common law: *law established by previous court decisions*

Vocabulary

bail: *money that an accused person provides to the court as a guarantee that he or she will be present for a trial*

> ### Amendment 9
> **Powers Reserved to the People** This amendment prevents government from claiming that the only rights people have are those listed in the Bill of Rights.

> ### Amendment 10
> **Powers Reserved to the States** This amendment protects the states and the people from the federal government. It establishes that powers not given to the national government and not denied to the states by the Constitution belong to the states or to the people. These are checks on the "necessary and proper" power of the federal government, which is provided for in Article I, Section 8, Clause 18.

> ### Amendment 11
> **Suits Against States** The Eleventh Amendment (1795) provides that a lawsuit brought by a citizen of the United States or a foreign nation against a state must be tried in a state court, not in a federal court. The Supreme Court had ruled in *Chisholm* v. *Georgia* (1793) that a federal court could try a lawsuit brought by citizens of South Carolina against a citizen of Georgia.

Vocabulary

majority: *more than half*

> ### Amendment 12
> **Election of President and Vice President** The Twelfth Amendment (1804) corrects a problem that had arisen in the method of electing the president and vice president, which is described in Article II, Section 1, Clause 3. This amendment provides for the Electoral College to use separate ballots in voting for president and vice president. If no candidate receives a majority of the electoral votes, who elects the president?

Amendment VIII

Excessive **bail** shall not be required, nor excessive fines imposed, nor cruel and unusual punishments inflicted.

Amendment IX

The enumeration in the Constitution, of certain rights, shall not be construed to deny or disparage others retained by the people.

Amendment X

The powers not delegated to the United States by the Constitution, nor prohibited by it to the States, are reserved to the States respectively, or to the people.

Amendment XI

The Judicial power of the United States shall not be construed to extend to any suit in law or equity, commenced or prosecuted against one of the United States by Citizens of another State, or by Citizens or Subjects of any Foreign State.

Amendment XII

The electors shall meet in their respective states and vote by ballot for President and Vice-President, one of whom, at least, shall not be an inhabitant of the same state with themselves; they shall name in their ballots the person voted for as President, and in distinct ballots the person voted for as Vice-President, and they shall make distinct lists of all persons voted for as President, and of all persons voted for as Vice-President, and of the number of votes for each, which lists they shall sign and certify, and transmit sealed to the seat of the government of the United States, directed to the President of the Senate;—The President of the Senate shall, in the presence of the Senate and House of Representatives, open all the certificates and the votes shall then be counted;—The person having the greatest number of votes for President, shall be the President, if such number be a **majority** of the whole number of Electors appointed; and if no person have such majority, then from the persons having the highest numbers not exceeding three on the list of those voted for as President, the House of Representatives shall choose immediately, by ballot, the President. But in choosing the President, the votes shall be taken by states, the representation from each state having one vote; a quorum for this purpose shall consist of a member or members from two-thirds of the states, and a majority of all the states shall be necessary to a choice. And if the House of Representatives shall not choose a President whenever the right of choice shall devolve upon them, before the fourth day of March next following, then the Vice-President shall act as President, as in the case of the death or other constitutional disability of the President. The person having the greatest number of votes as Vice-President, shall be the Vice-President, if such number be a majority of the whole number of Electors appointed, and if no person have a majority, then from the two highest numbers on the list, the Senate shall choose the Vice-President; a quorum for the purpose shall consist of two-thirds of the whole number of Senators, and a majority of the whole number shall be necessary to a choice. But no person constitutionally ineligible to the office of President shall be eligible to that of Vice-President of the United States.

Amendment XIII
Section 1
Neither slavery nor involuntary servitude, except as a punishment for crime whereof the party shall have been duly convicted, shall exist within the United States, or any place subject to their jurisdiction.

Section 2
Congress shall have power to enforce this article by appropriate legislation.

Amendment XIV
Section 1
All persons born or naturalized in the United States, and subject to the jurisdiction thereof, are citizens of the United States and of the State wherein they reside. No State shall make or enforce any law which shall **abridge** the privileges or immunities of citizens of the United States; nor shall any State deprive any person of life, liberty, or property, without due process of law; nor deny to any person within its jurisdiction the equal protection of the laws.

Section 2
Representatives shall be apportioned among the several States according to their respective numbers, counting the whole number of persons in each State, excluding Indians not taxed. But when the right to vote at any election for the choice of electors for President and Vice-President of the United States, Representatives in Congress, the Executive and Judicial officers of a State, or the members of the Legislature thereof, is denied to any of the male inhabitants of such State, being twenty-one years of age, and citizens of the United States, or in any way abridged, except for participation in rebellion, or other crime, the basis of representation therein shall be reduced in the proportion which the number of such male citizens shall bear to the whole number of male citizens twenty-one years of age in such State.

Section 3
No person shall be a Senator or Representative in Congress, or elector of President and Vice-President, or hold any office, civil or military, under the United States, or under any State, who, having previously taken an oath, as a member of Congress, or as an officer of the United States, or as a member of any State legislature, or as an executive or judicial officer of any State, to support the Constitution

Amendment 13
Abolition of Slavery Amendments Thirteen (1865), Fourteen, and Fifteen often are called the Civil War amendments because they grew out of that conflict. The Thirteenth Amendment outlaws slavery.

Amendment 14
Rights of Citizens The Fourteenth Amendment (1868) originally was intended to protect the legal rights of the freed slaves. Its interpretation has been extended to protect the rights of citizenship in general by prohibiting a state from depriving any person of life, liberty, or property without "due process of law." In addition, it states that all citizens have the right to equal protection of the laws in all states.

Amendment 14. Section 2
Representation in Congress This section reduced the number of members a state had in the House of Representatives if it denied its citizens the right to vote. Later civil rights laws and the Twenty-fourth Amendment guaranteed the vote to African Americans.

Vocabulary
abridge: *to reduce*

Amendment 14. Section 3
Penalty for Engaging in Insurrection The leaders of the Confederacy were barred from state or federal offices unless Congress agreed to remove this ban. By the end of Reconstruction, all but a few Confederate leaders were allowed to return to public service.

Amendment 14. Section 4
Public Debt The public debt acquired by the federal government during the Civil War was valid and could not be questioned by the South. However, the debts of the Confederacy were declared to be illegal. Could former slaveholders collect payment for the loss of their slaves?

Amendment 15
Voting Rights The Fifteenth Amendment (1870) prohibits the government from denying a person's right to vote on the basis of race. Despite the law, many states denied African Americans the right to vote by such means as poll taxes, literacy tests, and white primaries.

Amendment 16
Income Tax The origins of the Sixteenth Amendment (1913) date back to 1895, when the Supreme Court declared a federal income tax unconstitutional. To overturn this decision, this amendment authorizes an income tax that is levied on a direct basis.

Amendment 17
Direct Election of Senators The Seventeenth Amendment (1913) states that the people, instead of state legislatures, elect United States senators. How many years are in a Senate term?

Vocabulary

insurrection: *rebellion against the government*
apportionment: *distribution of seats in House based on population*
vacancy: *an office or position that is unfilled or unoccupied*

of the United States, shall have engaged in insurrection or rebellion against the same, or given aid or comfort to the enemies thereof. But Congress may by a vote of two-thirds of each House, remove such disability.

Section 4
The validity of the public debt of the United States, authorized by law, including debts incurred for payment of pensions and bounties for service, in suppressing insurrection or rebellion, shall not be questioned. But neither the United States nor any State shall assume or pay any debt or obligation incurred in aid of **insurrection** or rebellion against the United States, or any claim for the loss or emancipation of any slave; but all such debts, obligations and claims shall be held illegal and void.

Section 5
The Congress shall have power to enforce, by appropriate legislation, the provisions of this article.

Amendment XV
Section 1
The right of citizens of the United States to vote shall not be denied or abridged by the United States or by any State on account of race, color, or previous condition of servitude.

Section 2
The Congress shall have power to enforce this article by appropriate legislation.

Amendment XVI
The Congress shall have power to lay and collect taxes on incomes, from whatever source derived, without **apportionment** among the several States and without regard to any census or enumeration.

Amendment XVII
Section 1
The Senate of the United States shall be composed of two Senators from each State, elected by the people thereof, for six years; and each Senator shall have one vote. The electors in each State shall have the qualifications requisite for electors of the most numerous branch of the State legislatures.

Section 2
When **vacancies** happen in the representation of any State in the Senate, the executive authority of such State shall issue writs of election to fill such vacancies: *Provided*, That the legislature of any State may empower the executive thereof to make temporary appointments until the people fill the vacancies by election as the legislature may direct.

Section 3

This amendment shall not be so construed as to affect the election or term of any Senator chosen before it becomes valid as part of the Constitution.

Amendment XVIII
Section 1

After one year from ratification of this article, the manufacture, sale, or transportation of intoxicating liquors within, the importation thereof into, or the exportation thereof from the United States and all territory subject to the jurisdiction thereof for beverage purposes is hereby prohibited.

Section 2

The Congress and the several States shall have concurrent power to enforce this article by appropriate legislation.

Section 3

This article shall be inoperative unless it shall have been ratified as an amendment to the Constitution by the legislatures of the several States, as provided in the Constitution, within seven years from the date of the submission hereof to the States by the Congress.

Amendment XIX
Section 1

The right of citizens of the United States to vote shall not be denied or abridged by the United States or by any state on account of sex.

Section 2

Congress shall have power by appropriate legislation to enforce the provisions of this article.

Amendment XX
Section 1

The terms of the President and Vice President shall end at noon on the 20th day of January, and the terms of the Senators and Representatives at noon on the 3rd day of January, of the years in which such terms would have ended if this article had not been ratified; and the terms of their successors shall then begin.

Section 2

The Congress shall assemble at least once in every year, and such meeting shall begin at noon on the 3rd day of January, unless they shall by law appoint a different day.

Amendment 18
Prohibition The Eighteenth Amendment (1919) prohibited the production, sale, or transportation of alcoholic beverages in the United States. Prohibition proved to be difficult to enforce. This amendment was later repealed by the Twenty-first Amendment.

Amendment 19
Woman Suffrage The Nineteenth Amendment (1920) guaranteed women the right to vote. By then women had already won the right to vote in many state elections, but the amendment made their right to vote in all state and national elections constitutional.

Amendment 20
"Lame Duck" The Twentieth Amendment (1933) sets new dates for Congress to begin its term and for the inauguration of the president and vice president. Under the original Constitution, elected officials who retired or who had been defeated remained in office for several months. For the outgoing president, this period ran from November until March. Such outgoing officials, referred to as "lame ducks," could accomplish little. What date was fixed as Inauguration Day?

**Amendment 20. Section 3
Succession of President and
Vice President** This section provides
that if the president-elect dies before
taking office, the vice president-elect
becomes president.

Vocabulary

president-elect: *individual who is elected president
but has not yet begun serving his or her term*

**Amendment 21
Repeal of Prohibition** The
Twenty-first Amendment (1933) repeals
the Eighteenth Amendment. It is the only
amendment ever passed to overturn an
earlier amendment. It is also the only
amendment ratified by special state conventions instead of state legislatures.

Section 3

If, at the time fixed for the beginning of the term of the
President, the President elect shall have died, the Vice
President elect shall become President. If a President
shall not have been chosen before the time fixed for the
beginning of his term, or if the **President elect** shall have
failed to qualify, then the Vice President elect shall act as
President until a President shall have qualified; and the
Congress may by law provide for the case wherein neither a President elect nor a Vice President elect shall have
qualified, declaring who shall then act as President, or the
manner in which one who is to act shall be selected, and
such person shall act accordingly until a President or Vice
President shall have qualified.

Section 4

The Congress may by law provide for the case of the
death of any of the persons from whom the House of
Representatives may choose a President whenever the right
of choice shall have devolved upon them, and for the case
of the death of any of the persons from whom the Senate
may choose a Vice President whenever the right of choice
shall have devolved upon them.

Section 5

Sections 1 and 2 shall take effect on the 15th day of
October following the ratification of this article.

Section 6

This article shall be inoperative unless it shall have been
ratified as an amendment to the Constitution by the legislatures of three-fourths of the several States within seven
years from the date of its submission.

Amendment XXI
Section 1

The eighteenth article of amendment to the Constitution
of the United States is hereby repealed.

Section 2

The transportation or importation into any State,
Territory, or possession of the United States for delivery or
use therein of intoxicating liquors, in violation of the laws
thereof, is hereby prohibited.

Section 3

This article shall be inoperative unless it shall have been
ratified as an amendment to the Constitution by conventions in the several States, as provided in the Constitution,
within seven years from the date of the submission hereof
to the States by the Congress.

Amendment XXII

Section 1

No person shall be elected to the office of the President more than twice, and no person who had held the office of President, or acted as President, for more than two years of a term to which some other person was elected President shall be elected to the office of the President more than once. But this Article shall not apply to any person holding the office of President when this Article was proposed by the Congress, and shall not prevent any person who may be holding the office of President, or acting as President, during the term within which this Article becomes operative from holding the office of President or acting as President during the remainder of such term.

Section 2

This article shall be inoperative unless it shall have been ratified as an amendment to the Constitution by the legislatures of three-fourths of the several States within seven years from the date of its submission to the States by the Congress.

Amendment XXIII

Section 1

The District constituting the seat of Government of the United States shall appoint in such manner as the Congress may direct:

A number of electors of President and Vice President equal to the whole number of Senators and Representatives in Congress to which the District would be entitled if it were a State, but in no event more than the least populous State; they shall be in addition to those appointed by the States, but they shall be considered, for the purposes of the election of President and Vice President, to be electors appointed by a State; and they shall meet in the District and perform such duties as provided by the twelfth article of amendment.

Section 2

The Congress shall have power to enforce this article by appropriate legislation.

Amendment XXIV

Section 1

The right of citizens of the United States to vote in any primary or other election for President or Vice President, for electors for President or Vice President, or for Senator or Representative in Congress, shall not be denied or abridged by the United States or any State by reason of failure to pay any poll tax or other tax.

Amendment 22
Presidential Term Limit The Twenty-second Amendment (1951) limits presidents to a maximum of two elected terms. The amendment wrote into the Constitution a custom started by George Washington. It was passed largely as a reaction to Franklin D. Roosevelt's election to four terms between 1933 and 1945. It also provides that anyone who succeeds to the presidency and serves for more than two years of the term may not be elected more than one more time.

Amendment 23
D.C. Electors The Twenty-third Amendment (1961) allows citizens living in Washington, D.C., to vote for president and vice president, a right previously denied residents of the nation's capital. The District of Columbia now has three presidential electors, the number to which it would be entitled if it were a state.

Amendment 24
Abolition of the Poll Tax The Twenty-fourth Amendment (1964) prohibits poll taxes in federal elections. Prior to the passage of this amendment, some states had used such taxes to keep low-income African Americans from voting. In 1966 the Supreme Court banned poll taxes in state elections as well.

Section 2

The Congress shall have power to enforce this article by appropriate legislation.

Amendment XXV

Section 1

In case of the removal of the President from office or his death or resignation, the Vice President shall become President.

Section 2

Whenever there is a vacancy in the office of the Vice President, the President shall nominate a Vice President who shall take the office upon confirmation by a majority vote of both Houses of Congress.

Section 3

Whenever the President transmits to the President pro tempore of the Senate and the Speaker of the House of Representatives his written declaration that he is unable to discharge the powers and duties of his office, and until he transmits to them a written declaration to the contrary, such powers and duties shall be discharged by the Vice President as Acting President.

Section 4

Whenever the Vice President and a majority of either the principal officers of the executive departments or of such other body as Congress may by law provide, transmit to the President pro tempore of the Senate and the Speaker of the House of Representatives their written declaration that the President is unable to discharge the powers and duties of his office, the Vice President shall immediately assume the power and duties of the office of Acting President.

Thereafter, when the President transmits to the President pro tempore of the Senate and the Speaker of the House of Representatives his written declaration that no inability exists, he shall resume the powers and duties of his office unless the Vice President and a majority of either the principal officers of the executive department or of such other body as Congress may by law provide, transmit within four days to the President pro tempore of the Senate and the Speaker of the House of Representatives their written declaration that the President is unable to discharge the powers and duties of his office. Thereupon Congress shall decide the issue, assembling within forty-eight hours for that purpose if not in session. If the Congress, within twenty-one days after receipt of the latter written declaration, or, if Congress is not in session, within twenty-one days after Congress is required to assemble, determines by two-thirds vote of both Houses that the President is unable to discharge the powers and duties of his office, the Vice President shall continue to discharge the same as Acting President; otherwise, the President shall resume the power and duties of his office.

Amendment XXVI

Section 1

The right of citizens of the United States, who are eighteen years of age or older, to vote shall not be denied or abridged by the United States or by any State on account of age.

Section 2

The Congress shall have power to enforce this article by appropriate legislation.

Amendment XXVII

No law, varying the compensation for the services of Senators and Representatives, shall take effect, until an election of representatives shall have intervened.

Amendment 26
Voting Age of 18 The Twenty-sixth Amendment (1971) lowered the voting age in both federal and state elections to 18.

Amendment 27
Congressional Salary Restraints The Twenty-seventh Amendment (1992) makes congressional pay raises effective during the term following their passage. James Madison offered the amendment in 1789, but it was never adopted. In 1982 Gregory Watson, then a student at the University of Texas, discovered the forgotten amendment while doing research for a school paper. Watson made the amendment's passage his crusade.

Chapter 2

The Young Republic
1789–1850

SECTION 1 **The New Republic**

SECTION 2 **The Growth of a Nation**

SECTION 3 **Growing Division and Reform**

SECTION 4 **Manifest Destiny and Crisis**

1789
• Washington elected president

1808
• Congress bans international slave trade

1820
• Missouri Compromise proposed by Henry Clay

Washington 1789–1797

J. Adams 1797–1801

Jefferson 1801–1809

Madison 1809–1817

Monroe 1817–1825

J.Q. Adams 1825–1829

U.S. PRESIDENTS

U.S. EVENTS

1790

WORLD EVENTS

1810

1794
• Polish rebellion suppressed by Russians

1812
• Napoleon's invasion and retreat from Russia

1821
• Mexico and Greece declare independence

MAKING CONNECTIONS
How Do Nations Grow?

The young republic saw the growth of the federal government and nationalism. Sectional disputes began as industry developed in the North while Southern agriculture depended on slavery. As the nation expanded west, sectional conflict continued to escalate.

- *How did economic differences between North and South cause tensions?*

- *How do you think the migration of settlers to the West affected the North and South?*

FOLDABLES™

Analyzing Events Create a Trifold Book Foldable listing what happened, how it influenced events leading to the Civil War, and what might have happened if the event had turned out differently. Choose one of the following events to complete the Foldable: the Fugitive Slave Act, the Dred Scott Decision, the Lincoln-Douglas Debates, the Missouri Compromise, the Kansas-Nebraska Act, or John Brown's Raid.

1832
- Democrats hold their first presidential nominating convention

1846
- United States begins war with Mexico

1850
- Compromise of 1850 adopted in an attempt to ease sectional tensions

Jackson 1829–1837

Van Buren 1837–1841

W. Harrison 1841

Tyler 1841–1845

Polk 1845–1849

Taylor 1849–1850

1830

1850

1832
- Male voting rights expanded in England

1842
- China opened by force to foreign trade

1848
- Karl Marx and Friedrich Engels's *The Communist Manifesto* published

1859
- Darwin's *Origin of Species* published

History ONLINE Visit glencoe.com and enter **QuickPass**™ code TAVMT5147c2 for Chapter 2 resources.

The New Republic

D ifferences over how to make the government function effectively became the basis for two new political parties. The growth of the nation, along with the War of 1812, gave Americans a strong sense of national pride.

The Early Years of the Republic

MAIN Idea The United States established a federal government, created a Bill of Rights, and witnessed the first political parties.

HISTORY AND YOU Of all the freedoms that are granted to Americans, which do you consider most precious, and why? Read on to learn about the ratification of the Bill of Rights, which guarantees basic freedoms to all Americans.

The newly elected members of Congress met even before the Constitution had been ratified. Americans were confident, though, because they knew George Washington would be the first president.

One of the first tasks of President Washington and Congress was to organize the government itself. In the summer of 1789, Congress created three executive departments: the Department of State, the Department of the Treasury, and the Department of War, along with the Office of the Attorney General. Washington then chose his **cabinet**—the individuals who would head these departments and advise him. His appointments included Thomas Jefferson as Secretary of State and Alexander Hamilton as Treasury Secretary.

Congress also organized the judicial branch. The Judiciary Act of 1789 outlined the makeup of the Supreme Court and established lower federal courts. Washington chose John Jay as the first Chief Justice of the United States.

The Bill of Rights

One of the most important acts of Congress in 1789 was to propose amendments to the Constitution. During the campaign to ratify the Constitution, the Federalists had promised to add a bill of rights detailing the rights of American citizens.

In September 1789, Congress agreed on 12 **constitutional** amendments. They were then sent to the states, but only 10 were approved. These 10 went into effect and are generally referred to as the **Bill of Rights.** Eight of the amendments protect the rights of individuals against the government. The Ninth Amendment states that the people have other rights not listed in the Constitution. The Tenth Amendment adds that any powers not specifically given to the federal government are reserved for the states.

Guide to Reading

Big Ideas
Government and Society An important Supreme Court decision asserted that the Court had the power to decide whether laws passed by Congress are constitutional.

Content Vocabulary
• cabinet *(p. 78)*
• Bill of Rights *(p. 78)*
• enumerated powers *(p. 79)*
• implied powers *(p. 79)*
• judicial review *(p. 83)*

Academic Vocabulary
• constitutional *(p. 78)*

People and Events to Identify
• District of Columbia *(p. 80)*
• Louisiana Territory *(p. 83)*
• Louisiana Purchase *(p. 83)*

Reading Strategy
Sequencing Complete a graphic organizer similar to the one below by indicating the tasks completed by the first Congress under the Constitution.

Tasks of Congress

Origins of the Bill of Rights

Basic Rights	Magna Carta (1215)	English Bill of Rights (1689)	Virginia Declaration of Rights (1776)	Virginia Statute for Religious Freedom (1786)	American Bill of Rights (1791)
No state religion				●	●
Freedom of worship		● limited	●	●	●
Freedom of speech		●	●		●
Right to petition		● limited			●
Right to bear arms					●
No quartering troops in private homes without permission					●
No searches and seizures without a specific search warrant	●		●		●
Government cannot take away life, liberty, or property unless it follows proper court procedures (due process)	●	●	●		●
Right to a speedy public trial by jury and to a lawyer	●	●	●	●	●
No excessive bail, fines, or cruel and unusual punishment	●	●	●		●

Steps to the Bill of Rights

In creating the Bill of Rights, the first ten amendments to the Constitution, James Madison drew on the great founding documents of English legal history and tradition: the Magna Carta, the English Bill of Rights, the Virginia Declaration of Rights, and the Virginia Statute for Religious Freedom. Beginning in 1215, these and other documents had established protections of individual rights and freedoms designed to safeguard citizens from oppression and tyrannical government.

Analyzing VISUALS

1. **Specifying** Which right was established in the Magna Carta and appears in all subsequent documents?

2. **Explaining** Which two rights are the only ones unique to the American Bill of Rights, and why do you think that is?

Tackling Financial Troubles

With the bureaucracy up and running, the most pressing concerns involved the economy. The federal government had inherited a huge debt from the Continental Congress. Secretary of the Treasury Alexander Hamilton proposed a plan to pay off all debts. He also wanted the federal government to accept responsibility for the states' outstanding debts. Hamilton called for the creation of a national bank to manage the country's finances.

Thomas Jefferson, James Madison, and others favored less government interference in the economy. They also pointed out that establish-ing a bank was not one of the federal government's **enumerated powers**—the powers specifically mentioned in the Constitution. Hamilton rebuffed this criticism by citing Article I, Section 8, which gives the federal government the power "to make all laws which shall be necessary and proper" to fulfill its responsibilities. The "necessary and proper" clause, he said, created **implied powers**—powers not explicitly listed in the Constitution but necessary for the government to do its job. A national bank, Hamilton argued, was indeed necessary so that the government could collect taxes, regulate trade, and provide for the common defense.

Hamilton eventually won approval for his financial program after promises to Southern congressmen that the nation's capital would be moved to the **District of Columbia** on land donated by Virginia and Maryland. With that settled, the Bank of the United States was established in 1791 for a 20-year period.

The same year, Congress enacted a high tax on whiskey. The new tax brought in needed revenue, but it proved extremely unpopular among Western farmers who resisted the tax by terrorizing tax collectors, robbing mail, and destroying whiskey-making stills of those who paid the tax. In August 1794, President Washington sent nearly 13,000 troops to crush the Whiskey Rebellion.

History ONLINE
Student Web Activity Visit glencoe.com and complete the activity on political parties.

The Rise of Political Parties

The handling of the Whiskey Rebellion intensified the tensions that had arisen over Hamilton's financial program. By 1794 the factions in Congress had solidified into rival political parties.

Hamilton's supporters called themselves Federalists. They favored a strong national government led by the "rich, well born, and able." The Federalist Party included many manufacturers, merchants, and bankers, especially in the urban Northeast who believed that manufacturing and trade were the basis of national wealth and power.

Their opponents, led by Madison and Jefferson, took the name Democratic-Republicans, although most people at the time referred to them as Republicans. They favored strict limits on the federal government's power and protection of states' rights. They also believed that the strength of the United States was its independent, land-owning farmers and thus supported agriculture over commerce and trade. The party had a strong base among farmers in the rural South and West.

Tough Times for Adams

For an excerpt from "Washington's Farewell Address," see page R46 in **Documents in American History.**

After two terms as president, a weary George Washington left office. His Farewell Address to the American people warned of the dangers of party politics and sectionalism—pitting North against South, or East against West. Washington also urged Americans "to steer clear of permanent alliances with any portion of the foreign world."

Washington's successor as president was a fellow Federalist, John Adams. One of Adams's most urgent challenges was averting war with France. France was enraged by a treaty between the United States and Britain and had begun seizing American ships at sea. The two nations soon were fighting an undeclared war at sea until negotiations finally brought an end to hostilities in 1800.

Meanwhile, the division between the two political parties had been deepening. The Federalists resented the harsh Republican criticism. Using their majority in Congress, they passed the Alien and Sedition Acts in 1798. One of these laws made it a crime to utter or print anything "false, scandalous, and malicious" against the federal government or any federal official. The other laws were directed at aliens—foreigners living in the country—who often were anti-British and tended to vote Republican once they became citizens. The new laws made it harder for them to gain citizenship and left them vulnerable to deportation without trial.

Many Americans denounced the Alien and Sedition Acts as an infringement on people's freedoms. In 1798 and 1799, Kentucky and Virginia passed resolutions challenging the laws' constitutionality. At the time, few states accepted the premise behind the resolutions that states had a right to decide on the validity of federal laws. Many years later, states used these ideas to defend their interests.

The Election of 1800

Although John Adams hoped to win reelection in 1800, he faced an uphill battle. The Alien and Sedition Acts had angered many people, as had new taxes on houses, land, and enslaved Africans. The Republican nominees, Thomas Jefferson for president and Aaron Burr for vice president, campaigned against the taxes and the national bank. They accused the Federalists of favoring monarchy and discouraging political participation.

The election was very close, and it revealed a flaw in the system for selecting the president. The Constitution does not let citizens vote directly for the chief executive. Instead, each state chooses electors—the same number as it has senators and representatives. This group, known as the Electoral College, then votes for the president.

Turning Points

The Election of 1800

The election of 1800 was a major turning point in American political history. This is because it was the first transfer of power between parties under the federal Constitution, and, despite the enormous political and personal hatred between the party members, it was accomplished peacefully. It demonstrated the commitment on all sides to the Constitution and to a democratic republic despite partisan passions.

ANALYZING HISTORY What made the election of 1800 so significant in American political history?

▲ This cartoon reveals the emotions in American politics and the divisive nature of the relationship between the parties in the early years of the nation. The scene depicts a fight in the House of Representatives in 1798, begun when Federalist Roger Griswold of Connecticut assaulted Republican Matthew Lyon of Vermont.

Presidential Election of 1800

Map showing electoral votes by state:
NH 6, VT 4, NY 12, MA 16, RI 4, PA 8, CT 9, NJ 7, DE 3, MD 3, KY 4, VA 21, NC 4, TN 3, SC 8, GA 4

Presidential Candidate	Popular Votes	% of Popular Vote	Electoral Votes
Jefferson	*	*	73
Adams	*	*	65

*Electors were not chosen by popular vote, but by state legislatures.

According to the original terms of the Constitution, each elector in the Electoral College voted for two people in a presidential election. The person receiving the most votes became president, and the person receiving the second-highest number of votes became vice president. Under this system a tie was possible, as happened in the case of the tie between Thomas Jefferson and Aaron Burr in 1800. The House of Representatives then elected Jefferson after 35 rounds of voting in which there was no clear winner. To prevent such confusion in the future, the Twelfth Amendment was added to the Constitution in 1804. The amendment stipulates that electoral votes for president and vice president are counted and listed separately.

The Constitution called for each elector in the Electoral College to vote for two people. The normal practice was for an elector to cast one vote for his party's presidential candidate and another for the vice presidential candidate. To avoid a tie between Jefferson and Burr, the Republicans had intended for one elector to refrain from voting for Burr, but when the votes were counted, Jefferson and Burr each had 73. Since no candidate had a majority, the Federalist-controlled House of Representatives had to choose a president.

The divided House took days to reach a decision. Many Federalists distrusted Jefferson and refused to vote for him. Historians think Jefferson may have promised he would not dis-

mantle Hamilton's financial system because eventually one Federalist cast a blank ballot enabling Jefferson to become president. The election of 1800 was an important turning point in American history. At the time, the Federalists controlled the army and the government, and were powerful enough to overthrow the Constitution. Instead they stepped down, establishing that power could be peacefully transferred despite strong disagreements. The election also led to the Twelfth Amendment in 1804, providing for separate ballots for the president and vice president.

✔ Reading Check **Examining** What is the difference between enumerated powers and implied powers?

Republicans in Power

MAIN Idea During the Jefferson administration, the Supreme Court established judicial review, and the country doubled in size.

HISTORY AND YOU Are there times when you feel especially patriotic? Read on to learn about the War of 1812, which generated a new spirit of patriotism.

President Jefferson attempted to limit federal powers, while the country expanded in size and faced a war with Great Britain.

Jefferson in Office

Thomas Jefferson took office committed to limiting the scope of government. He began paying off the federal debt, cut government spending, eliminated the hated whiskey tax, and trimmed the armed forces.

Weakening the Federalists' control of the judiciary was another aim of the new administration. On his last day in office, President Adams had appointed dozens of new Federalist judges and court officers. Jefferson asked the incoming Republican Congress to abolish some of the new positions and to withhold the paperwork confirming other appointments. One of those who didn't receive his documents, William Marbury, took the matter to the Supreme Court. The Court sympathized with Marbury but ruled in 1803 that it could not issue an enforcement order. According to Chief Justice John Marshall and his colleagues, the law that authorized the Court to write such orders actually was unconstitutional and invalid.

NATIONAL GEOGRAPHIC The Louisiana Purchase, 1803

0   200 kilometers
0   200 miles
Lambert Azimuthal Equal-Area projection

Ft. Clatsop, winter quarters 1805–1806

OREGON TERRITORY

BRITISH TERRITORY

Columbia R.

Lewis
Clark

Ft. Mandan, winter quarters 1804–1805

Snake R.

LOUISIANA PURCHASE

Missouri R.

Indiana Territory

Ohio

Pa.

Colorado R.

Pikes Peak

St. Louis

Ohio R.

Va.

Kentucky

Santa Fe

Arkansas R.

Tenn.

N.C.

S.C.

ATLANTIC OCEAN

Mississippi Territory

Ga.

Red R.

SPANISH TERRITORY

Brazos R.

Natchitoches

Rio Grande

Chihuahua

New Orleans

Spanish Florida

Gulf of Mexico

← Lewis and Clark's expedition
← Zebulon Pike's expedition
  United States, 1803

▲ Meriwether Lewis and William Clark with their Native American guide, Sacagawea.

Analyzing GEOGRAPHY

1. **Location** Where did Lewis and Clark begin their expedition?

2. **Movement** What two rivers in Spanish territory did Pike cross during his explorations?

With the case of *Marbury* v. *Madison,* the Court asserted its right of **judicial review,** the power to decide whether laws are constitutional and to strike down those that are not. During more than 30 years as Chief Justice, John Marshall continued to build the Supreme Court into a powerful, independent branch of government.

Westward Expansion

Under Jefferson, the size of the country increased considerably. The Treaty of Paris of 1783 had already established the Mississippi River as the western border of the United States. After the defeat of Native Americans in the Northwest Territory and the Treaty of Greenville in 1795, more settlers poured into the region. During Washington's term, Kentucky and Tennessee had become new states, and Ohio followed suit in 1803.

In 1800 Spain had given Louisiana back to France. To finance his plans for European conquest, the French leader, Napoleon Bonaparte, now offered to sell all of the **Louisiana Territory,** as well as New Orleans, to the United States. Congress overwhelmingly approved the **Louisiana Purchase** of April 30, 1803. The United States paid $11.25 million and also agreed to take on French debts of about $3.75 million owed to American citizens. With the purchase, the United States had more than doubled its size.

The War of 1812

A foreign relations crisis loomed when Republican James Madison became president in 1809. The British regularly seized American ships at sea and often practiced impressment, kidnapping sailors to serve in the British navy. Americans in the West also accused Britain of inciting Native Americans to attack white settlers. President Jefferson had tried economic sanctions with the Embargo Act of 1807, but the actions mostly hurt the United States.

Like Jefferson, President Madison first responded with economic measures. After several attempts, the measures finally began to have the desired effect; unfortunately, word of British cooperation came too late—Congress had already declared war.

At the beginning of the War of 1812, conquering Canada was the primary objective of the United States. American forces on Lake Erie and Lake Champlain were victorious but could not prevent the British from setting fire to both the White House and the Capitol in Washington, D.C. The British, however, had to abandon their attack on Baltimore after bombarding the city's harbor throughout the night of September 13. The sight of the American flag still flying at dawn inspired Francis Scott Key to pen "The Star-Spangled Banner," which later became the national anthem.

With battles still raging, peace talks began in the European city of Ghent. The Treaty of Ghent, signed on December 24, 1814, restored prewar boundaries but did not mention neutral rights or impressment. Still, it increased the nation's prestige overseas and generated a new spirit of patriotism. The American victory also destroyed the Federalist Party, which had strongly opposed the war.

Reading Check **Explaining** Why is the Supreme Court decision *Marbury* v. *Madison* important?

Section 1 REVIEW

Vocabulary

1. **Explain** the significance of: cabinet, Bill of Rights, enumerated powers, implied powers, judicial review, District of Columbia, Louisiana Territory, Louisiana Purchase.

Main Ideas

2. **Summarizing** How was the election of 1800 different from previous elections? What resulted from the election?

3. **Explaining** Why did Napoleon sell Louisiana to the United States?

Critical Thinking

4. **Big Ideas** How did the Supreme Court decision in *Marbury* v. *Madison* strengthen the federal judiciary?

5. **Categorizing** Use a graphic organizer similar to the one below to list the first political parties in the United States, their supporters, and the issues they promoted.

Political Party	Supporters	Issues Supported

6. **Analyzing Visuals** Study the map of the Louisiana Purchase on page 82. In what territory did Lewis and Clark make their 1805–1806 winter camp during their expedition?

Writing About History

7. **Persuasive Writing** Take on the role of an American citizen in 1798. Write a speech to persuade others not to support Alexander Hamilton's financial program.

History ONLINE

Study Central™ To review this section, go to glencoe.com and click on Study Central.

Profile

HULTON GETTY

GEORGE WASHINGTON *At the age of 16, George Washington carefully transcribed in his own hand the* Rules of Civility and Decent Behaviour in Company and Conversation. *Among the rules our first president lived by:*

- Every action done in company ought to be with some sign of respect to those that are present.

- When in company, put not your hands to any part of the body, not usually [un]covered.

- Put not off your clothes in the presence of others, nor go out your chamber half dressed.

- Sleep not when others speak.

- Spit not in the fire, nor stoop low before it. Neither put your hands into the flames to warm them, nor set your feet upon the fire, especially if there is meat before it.

- Shake not the head, feet or legs. Roll not the eyes. Lift not one eyebrow higher than the other. Wry not the mouth, and bedew no man's face with your spittle, by approaching too near him when you speak.

- Show not yourself glad at the misfortune of another though he were your enemy.

- Be not hasty to believe flying reports to the disparagement of any.

- Think before you speak.

- Cleanse not your teeth with the Table Cloth.

VERBATIM

WAR'S END

❝I hope you will not consider yourself as commander-in-chief of your own house, but be convinced, that there is such a thing as equal command.❞

> **LUCY FLUCKER KNOX,**
> *to her husband Henry Knox, upon his return as a hero from the Revolutionary War*

❝The American war is over, but this is far from being the case with the American Revolution. Nothing but the first act of the drama is closed.❞

> **BENJAMIN RUSH,**
> *signer of the Declaration of Independence and member of the Constitutional Convention*

❝You could not have found a person to whom your schemes were more disagreeable.❞

> **GEORGE WASHINGTON,**
> *to Colonel Lewis Nicola, in response to his letter urging Washington to seize power and proclaim himself king*

❝It appears to me, then, little short of a miracle that the delegates from so many states . . . should unite in forming a system of national government.❞

> **GEORGE WASHINGTON,**
> *in a letter to the Marquis de Lafayette at the close of the Constitutional Convention*

❝It astonishes me to find this system approaching to near perfection as it does; and I think it will astonish our enemies.❞

LEONARD DESELVA/CORBIS

> **BENJAMIN FRANKLIN,**
> *remarking on the structure of the new United States government*

Annual Salaries

Annual federal employee salaries, 1789

President (he refused it)	$25,000
Vice President	$5,000
Secretary of State	$3,500
Chief Justice	$4,000
Senator	$6 per day
Representative	$6 per day
Army Captain	$420
Army Private	$48

CORBIS

1780s WORD PLAY

Dressing the "Little Pudding Heads"

Can you match these common items of Early American clothing with their descriptions?

1. clout

2. stays

3. surcingle

4. pilch

5. pudding cap

a. a band of strong fabric wrapped around a baby to suppress the navel

b. a diaper

c. the wool cover worn over a diaper

d. a head covering for a child learning to walk to protect its brain from falls

e. a garment worn by children to foster good posture, made from linen and wood or baleen splints

answers: 1. b; 2. e; 3. a; 4. c; 5. d

Milestones

SETTLED, 1781. LOS ANGELES, by a group of 46 men and women, most of whom are of Native American and African descent.

CALLED, 1785. LEMUEL HAYNES, as minister to a church in Torrington, Connecticut. Haynes, who fought at Lexington during the Revolutionary War, is the first African American to minister to a white congregation. A parishioner insulted Haynes by refusing to remove his hat in church, but minutes into the sermon, the parishioner was so moved that the hat came off. He is now a prayerful and loyal member of the congregation.

PUBLISHED, 1788. *THE ELEMENTARY SPELLING BOOK,* by Noah Webster, a 25-year-old teacher from Goshen, N.Y. The book standardizes American spelling and usage that differs from the British.

PIX/FPG

CRITICAL THINKING

1. *Contrasting* Benjamin Rush made a distinction between the American war and the American Revolution. What do you think he meant by his statement?

2. *Making Inferences* Based on the rules George Washington lived by, how would you describe his character?

The Growth of a Nation

Guide to Reading

Big Ideas
Science and Technology New technologies reshaped American industry.

Content Vocabulary
- revenue tariff *(p. 87)*
- protective tariff *(p. 87)*
- labor union *(p. 92)*

Academic Vocabulary
- transportation *(p. 86)*

People and Events to Identify
- "Era of Good Feelings" *(p. 86)*
- John C. Calhoun *(p. 87)*
- *McCulloch* v. *Maryland (p. 88)*
- Monroe Doctrine *(p. 88)*
- Industrial Revolution *(p. 90)*

Reading Strategy
Organizing Complete a graphic organizer similar to the one below by listing actions that strengthened the federal government after the War of 1812.

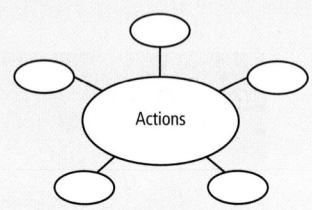

The United States entered an "Era of Good Feelings" after the War of 1812. The national government began building the national road, defended its authority to regulate interstate commerce, and declared the Western Hemisphere off-limits for future colonization.

Growth of American Nationalism

MAIN Idea The surge of nationalism and the survival of only one political party made it possible to make economic and judicial decisions that strengthened the national government.

HISTORY AND YOU Do you know of any Supreme Court decisions that had a significant national impact? Read on to learn about Supreme Court decisions that strengthened the power of the federal government.

After the War of 1812, a sense of nationalism swept the United States. More and more Americans began to consider themselves to be part of a whole, rather than **identifying** with a state or region. The *Columbian Centinel,* a Boston newspaper, called this time the **"Era of Good Feelings."** Riding this wave of nationalism was Republican James Monroe, the nation's fifth president.

Partisan infighting had largely ended in national politics because only one major political party—the Republicans—remained. The Federalist Party rapidly lost political influence after the War of 1812. At the same time, the war taught Republican leaders that a stronger federal government was necessary. This new perspective allowed many who might have been Federalists in the past to now join the Republicans instead. As a result, James Monroe won the presidency in 1816 with 83 percent of the electoral vote. By the election of 1820, the Federalist Party was gone. All the presidential candidates were members of the Republican Party.

Economic Nationalism

As Monroe's presidency began, focus shifted from world affairs to national growth. The Republicans quickly set out to strengthen the American financial system, protect manufacturers, and to improve the **transportation** system.

The Second Bank Republicans traditionally had opposed the idea of a national bank. They had blocked the charter renewal of the First Bank of the United States in 1811 and offered nothing in its place. The results were disastrous. State-chartered banks and other private banks greatly expanded their lending with bank notes that were used

National Road
1820 boundary

▶ Conestoga wagons carried pioneers west

CANADA

Michigan Territory
Lake Michigan
Lake Erie

Illinois

Indiana

Ohio

Pennsylvania

Wabash River

Richmond
Springfield
Wheeling
Uniontown

Indianapolis
Terre Haute
Zanesville
Columbus
Cumberland

Effingham
Vandalia

St. Louis

Kentucky

Virginia

Maryland

Del.

District of Columbia

Ohio River
Potomac River

0   100 kilometers
0   100 miles
Albers Equal-Area projection

In 1806 Congress funded the building of a major east-west highway to connect the eastern United States to St. Louis and the Missouri River, the gateway to the territory of the new Louisiana Purchase. In 1811 laborers started cutting the roadbed westward from Cumberland, Maryland. The 32-foot-wide bed had a surface of sand and gravel. By the 1820s the National Road was a heavily traveled superhighway for its time. It was completed to Vandalia, Illinois, when funding ceased. The National Road turned out to be the only great federally funded transportation project of its time. President Madison vetoed a bill to fund further roads and canals. He did not think the Constitution gave the federal government the authority to make "internal improvements."

Analyzing GEOGRAPHY

1. **Location** Where did the National Road begin and end?
2. **Movement** How long was the stretch of National Road that was federally funded?

---

as money. Without a national bank to regulate currency, prices rose rapidly during the War of 1812. When the government borrowed money to pay for the war, it had to pay high interest rates on the loans.

Because of these problems, many Republicans changed their minds after the war. In 1816 Representative **John C. Calhoun** of South Carolina introduced a bill proposing the Second Bank of the United States. With the support of Henry Clay of Kentucky and Daniel Webster of Massachusetts, the bill passed in 1816. This legislation gave the bank the power to issue notes that would serve as a national currency and to control state banks.

The Protective Tariff Protection of manufacturers from foreign competition was another part of the Republican program. During the War of 1812, an embargo had prevented Americans from buying British goods. American manufacturers had increased their output to meet the demand. Once the war was over, however, British goods flowed into the United States at

such low prices that they threatened to put American manufacturers out of business.

Congress responded with the Tariff of 1816. Unlike earlier **revenue tariffs,** which provided income for the federal government, this tariff was a **protective tariff,** designed to protect American manufacturers by taxing imports to drive up their prices. New England shippers and Southern farmers opposed the tariff and the higher prices it caused, but they could not block its passage.

Transportation The Republicans also wanted to improve the nation's transportation system. In 1816 Calhoun sponsored a federal internal improvement plan that included building roads and canals, but President Madison vetoed it, arguing that spending money to improve transportation was not expressly granted in the Constitution. Nevertheless, road and canal construction soon began, with private businesses and state and local governments funding much of the work.

Judicial Nationalism

The judicial philosophy of the Chief Justice of the United States, John Marshall, provided another boost to postwar nationalism. In several important cases between 1816 and 1824, Marshall interpreted the Constitution broadly to support federal power.

🏛 For further information on the cases of *Martin* v. *Hunter's Lessee* and *Gibbons* v. *Ogden*, see page R59 in **Supreme Court Case Summaries.**

Martin* v. *Hunter's Lessee In 1816 the Court decided in *Martin* v. *Hunter's Lessee* that it had the authority to hear all appeals of state court decisions in cases involving federal statutes and treaties. In this case, Denny Martin, a British subject, tried to sell land in Virginia inherited from his uncle, Lord Fairfax, a British Loyalist during the war. However, Virginia law stated that no "enemy" could inherit land. The Supreme Court ruled that Virginia's law conflicted with Jay's Treaty, which protected land belonging to Loyalists before the war. The decision helped establish the Supreme Court as the nation's court of final appeal.

McCulloch* v. *Maryland The 1819 case of **McCulloch v. Maryland** involved Maryland's attempt to tax the Baltimore branch of the Second Bank of the United States. Before addressing Maryland's right to tax the national bank, the Supreme Court first ruled on the federal government's right to create a national bank in the first place. In the Court's opinion, written by John Marshall, the Constitution gave the federal government the power to collect taxes, to borrow money, to regulate commerce, and to raise armies and navies. The national bank helped the federal government exercise these powers. Marshall concluded that the "necessary and proper" clause allowed the federal government to use its powers in any way not specifically prohibited by the Constitution.

Marshall went on to argue that the federal government was "supreme in its own sphere of action." This meant that a state government could not interfere with an agency of the federal government exercising its specific constitutional powers within a state's borders.

📜 For the text of the Monroe Doctrine, see page R48 in **Documents in American History.**

Gibbons* v. *Ogden The Court ruled in another case, *Gibbons* v. *Ogden,* that states could regulate commerce only within their borders, but that control of interstate commerce was a federal right. Defenders of states' rights attacked many of Marshall's decisions, which helped make the "necessary and proper" clause and the interstate commerce clause vehicles for expanding federal power.

Nationalist Diplomacy

Postwar nationalism also influenced foreign affairs. During the early 1800s, Spanish-held Florida was a source of frustration for Southerners. Many runaway slaves hid there, and the Seminole, a Native American group, often clashed with American settlers across the border in Georgia. When Spain was unable to control the border, Secretary of War John C. Calhoun sent troops under the command of Andrew Jackson into Florida. Secretary of State John Quincy Adams then put pressure on Spain concerning ongoing border questions. Occupied with problems throughout its Latin American empire, Spain gave in and ceded all of Florida to the United States in the Adams-Onís Treaty of 1819.

Spain had good reason to worry about Latin America. In 1809 rebellions began to erupt in Spain's colonies, and by 1824 all of Spain's colonies on the American mainland had declared independence. Meanwhile, some European monarchies expressed their interest in helping Spain suppress these Latin American revolutions. However, neither Great Britain nor the United States wanted Spain to regain control of its colonies.

At the same time, Russia's growing presence on North America's Pacific Coast also worried the American government. Russia already claimed Alaska, and in 1821 it announced that its empire extended south into the Oregon Country between Russian Alaska and the western United States.

Under these circumstances, Monroe decided to issue a statement in December 1823. In the **Monroe Doctrine,** the president declared that the American continents were "henceforth not to be considered as subjects for future colonization by any European powers." He specifically advised Europe to respect the sovereignty of new Latin American nations.

✔ **Reading Check** **Analyzing** How did the decisions of the Marshall Court strengthen the federal government?

ANALYZING SUPREME COURT CASES

What Does "Necessary and Proper" Mean?

★ *McCulloch v. Maryland,* 1819

Background to the Case

In 1816, President James Madison and Congress worked to establish the Second Bank of the United States. Two years later, the state of Maryland passed legislation imposing a tax on the Second Bank. The cashier at the Second Bank's branch in Baltimore, Maryland, James McCulloch, refused to pay the tax, and the matter went to the Supreme Court.

How the Court Ruled

In a unanimous decision the Court found that, under the "necessary and proper" clause, the federal government did have the unenumerated power to establish a national bank and that, while the states had the power to tax, they could not interfere with instruments of the federal government, and the tax was construed to be interference. This established the supremacy of the federal government over the governments of the states.

▲ *The Second Bank of the United States was located in Philadelphia. The Supreme Court held with the* McCulloch v. Maryland *ruling that the federal government had the right to establish a national bank and that the states could not tax it or otherwise interfere in any federal enterprise.*

PRIMARY SOURCE

The Court's Opinion

Can the Federal Government Create a Bank?

" . . . Although, among the enumerated powers of government, we do not find the word 'bank' or 'incorporation,' we find the great powers, to lay and collect taxes; to borrow money; to regulate commerce; to declare and conduct a war; and to raise and support armies and navies. . . . But it may with great reason be contended, that a government, entrusted with such ample powers . . . must also be entrusted with ample means for their execution.

. . . To its enumeration of powers is added, that of making 'all laws which shall be necessary and proper, for carrying into execution the foregoing powers, and all other powers vested by this constitution, in the government of the United States, or in any department thereof.'. . . [I]t is the unanimous and decided opinion of this Court, that the act to incorporate the Bank of the United States is . . . constitutional."

Can a State Tax a Federal Agency or Activity?

" . . . the power to tax involves the power to destroy. . . . If the states may tax one instrument, employed by the government . . . they may tax all the means employed by the government, to an excess which would defeat all the ends of government. . . . The result is a conviction that the states have no power, by taxation or otherwise, to retard, impede, burden, or in any manner control, the operations of the constitutional laws enacted by congress to carry into execution the powers vested in the general government. This is, we think, the unavoidable consequence of that supremacy which the constitution has declared."

—Chief Justice John Marshall writing for the Court in *McCulloch v. Maryland*

DBQ Document-Based Questions

1. **Specifying** What two questions did the decision in *McCulloch v. Maryland* address?
2. **Describing** How did Marshall interpret the "necessary and proper" clause in this case?
3. **Summarizing** How did Marshall's decision establish the authority of the federal government over the states?

A Growing Nation

MAIN Idea New industries and railroads transformed the North in the early 1800s, while slavery expanded in the South.

HISTORY AND YOU What kinds of businesses generate the most wealth in the United States today? Read on to learn about the critical role that farming and industry played during the early 1800s.

The early 1800s were a time of rapid change in the United States. Transportation greatly improved access to different regions, while the Industrial Revolution began transforming the North into a manufacturing center. The South, meanwhile, continued to rely on agriculture.

Transportation Revolution

With the United States expanding rapidly, Americans sought new ways to connect the distant regions of the country. The first steps came in 1806, when Congress funded the National Road. Soon afterward, states, localities, and private businesses began laying hundreds of miles of toll roads.

Rivers offered a more efficient and cheaper way to move goods than did early roads. Loaded boats and barges, however, could usually travel only downstream, as trips against the current with heavy cargoes were impractical. The invention of the steamboat changed all that. The first successful steamboat was the *Clermont,* developed by Robert Fulton and promoted by Robert R. Livingston. By 1850 more than 700 steamboats, also called riverboats, traveled the Mississippi, the Great Lakes, and other waterways.

Railroads also appeared in the early 1800s. A wealthy, self-educated industrialist named Peter Cooper built the *Tom Thumb,* a tiny but powerful locomotive based on engines originally developed in Great Britain. Perhaps more than any other kind of transportation, trains helped settle the West and expand trade among the nation's different regions.

Industrialization

Along with changes in transportation, a revolution occurred in industry. The **Industrial Revolution,** which began in Britain in the middle 1700s, spread to the United States. Businesses began large-scale manufacturing using complex machines and organized workforces in factories. Manufacturers sold their wares nationwide or abroad instead of just

TECHNOLOGY & HISTORY

New technologies in the early 1800s revolutionized transportation, communications, manufacturing, and agriculture. They began transforming the North into an industrial society and contributed to the spread of the cotton plantation in the South.

▲ **The Railroad Locomotive**
The *Tom Thumb* was the first American locomotive. Railroads transformed the nation, allowing people and goods to move quickly from city to city and helping to encourage settlement in the West.

▲ **The Steamboat**
Paddle-wheeled steamboats, such as Robert Fulton's *Clermont*, made river travel easier and more reliable.

locally. These developments transformed not only the economy, but society as well.

The United States industrialized quickly for several reasons. Perhaps the key factor was the American system of free enterprise based on private property rights. People could acquire and use capital without strict governmental controls. At the same time, competition between companies encouraged them to try new technologies. The era's low taxes also meant that entrepreneurs had more money to invest. In addition, beginning in the 1830s, many states promoted industrialization by passing general incorporation laws that made it much easier to form businesses.

Industrialization began in the Northeast, where many swift-flowing streams provided factories with waterpower. The region was also home to many entrepreneurs who were willing to invest in British technology. Soon textile mills sprung up throughout the Northeast. The use of interchangeable parts, or standard components, popularized by a New Englander named Eli Whitney, led to factories producing lumber, shoes, leather, wagons, and other products. The sewing machine allowed inexpensive clothes to be mass produced, and canning allowed foods to be stored and transported without fear of spoilage.

In 1832 a major improvement in communications took place when Samuel F.B. Morse began perfecting the telegraph and developing Morse code. Journalists began using the telegraph to speedily relay news. By 1860 more than 50,000 miles of telegraph wire connected most parts of the country.

Immigration

Between 1815 and 1860, over 5 million foreigners journeyed to America. While thousands of newcomers, particularly Germans, became farmers in the rural West, many others settled in cities, providing a steady source of cheap labor. A large number of Irish—over 44,000—arrived in 1845, after a devastating potato blight caused widespread famine in their homeland.

Not all Americans welcomed the new immigrants. Some had feelings of nativism, a preference for native-born people and a desire to limit immigration. Several societies sprang up to keep foreign-born persons and Catholics—the main religion of the Irish and many Germans—from holding public office. In 1854 delegates from some of these groups formed the American Party. This party came to be called the Know-Nothings.

◄ **The Water Frame**
The water frame allowed cotton fibers to be easily spun into cotton thread.

The Telegraph ▶
The first modern breakthrough in communications was the telegraph and Morse code. Suddenly, news and other information could be sent via telegraph keys over long distances nearly instantly.

▲ **The Cotton Gin**
In 1793, Eli Whitney built a device that removed the seeds of cotton and increased the profitability of cotton and the need for enslaved laborers.

Analyzing VISUALS

1. **Making Connections** What were the advantages to traveling by railroad rather than steamboat?
2. **Discussing** Which invention do you think was the most significant? Why?

Rise of Labor Unions

By 1860, factory workers numbered roughly 1.3 million. They included many women and children, who would accept lower wages than men. Not even men were well paid, however, and factory workers typically toiled for 12 or more drudgery-filled hours a day. Hoping to gain higher wages or shorter workdays, some workers began to organize in **labor unions**—groups of workers who press for better working conditions and member benefits. During the late 1820s and early 1830s, about 300,000 men and women belonged to these organizations. Early labor unions had little power. Most employers refused to bargain with them, and the courts often saw them as unlawful conspiracies that limited free enterprise.

Importance of Agriculture

Despite the trend toward urban and industrial growth, agriculture remained the country's leading economic activity. Until the late 1800s, farming employed more people and produced more wealth than any other kind of work. Northern farmers produced enough to sell their surplus in the growing eastern cities and towns.

Farming was even more important in the South, which had few cities and less industry. The South thrived on the production of several major cash crops, including tobacco, rice, and sugarcane. No crop, however, played a greater role in the South's fortunes during this period than cotton, which was grown in a wide belt stretching from inland South Carolina west into Texas.

Removing cotton seeds by hand from the fluffy bolls was so tedious that it took a worker an entire day to separate a pound of cotton lint. In 1793 Eli Whitney invented the cotton gin—"gin" being short for engine—that quickly and efficiently removed cotton seeds from bolls, or cotton pods. Cotton production soared, and by 1860 Southern cotton accounted for nearly two-thirds of the total export trade of the United States. Southerners began saying, rightly, "Cotton is King."

NATIONAL GEOGRAPHIC — An Economy Built on Enslaved Labor, c. 1850

Distribution of Slave Labor

- Rice, Sugar, Hemp 10%
- Tobacco 10%
- Cotton 55%
- Mining, Lumbering, Industry, Construction 10%
- Domestic Servants 15%

Legend:
- Cotton
- Rice
- Sugarcane
- Tobacco
- Coal
- Iron
- Lumber

0 — 200 kilometers
0 — 200 miles
Albers Equal-Area projection

Analyzing GEOGRAPHY

1. **Regions** Why do you think the use of enslaved miners was more common in Virginia and Kentucky?

2. **Human-Environment Interaction** How does the information on the map relate to the percentage of slave labor used in farming?

Maps In Motion See *StudentWorks™ Plus* or glencoe.com.

While agriculture brought prosperity to Southern states, they lagged behind the North in industrialization. Compared to the many textile mills and factories in the North, the Southern region had only scattered iron works, textile mills, and coal, iron, salt, and copper mines. Together, these accounted for only 16 percent of the nation's total manufacturing.

Enslaved and Free African Americans

The spread of cotton plantations boosted the Southern economy, but it also made the demand for slave labor skyrocket. Congress had outlawed the foreign slave trade in 1808, but a high birthrate among enslaved women—encouraged by slaveholders—kept the population growing. Between 1820 and 1850, the number of enslaved persons in the South rose from about 1.5 million to nearly 3.2 million, to account for almost 37 percent of the total Southern population.

The overwhelming majority of enslaved African Americans toiled in the fields on small farms. Some became house servants, while others worked in trades. All enslaved persons, no matter how well treated, suffered indignities. State slave codes forbade enslaved men and women from owning property, leaving a slaveholder's premises without permission, or testifying in court against a white person. Laws even banned them from learning to read and write. Frederick Douglass, who rose from slavery to become a prominent leader of the antislavery movement, recalled how life as an enslaved person affected him:

PRIMARY SOURCE

"My natural elasticity was crushed; my intellect languished; the disposition to read departed; the cheerful spark that lingered about my eye died; the dark night of slavery closed in upon me, and behold a man transformed to a brute."

—from *Narrative of the Life of Frederick Douglass*

Music helped many African Americans endure the horrors of slavery. Songs also played a key role in religion, one of the most important parts of African American culture.

Many enslaved men and women found ways to actively resist the dreadful lifestyle forced on them. Some quietly staged work slowdowns. Others broke tools or set fire to houses and barns. Still others risked beatings or mutilations by running away. Some enslaved persons turned to violence, killing their owners or plotting revolts.

Free African Americans occupied an ambiguous position in Southern society. In cities like Charleston and New Orleans, some were successful enough to become slaveholders themselves. Almost 200,000 free African Americans lived in the North, where slavery had been outlawed, but they were not embraced there either. Still, in the North free African Americans could organize their own churches and voluntary associations. They also were able to earn money from the jobs they held.

Reading Check **Describing** How did the Industrial Revolution change American society?

Section 2 REVIEW

Vocabulary

1. **Explain** the significance of: "Era of Good Feelings," John C. Calhoun, revenue tariff, protective tariff, *McCulloch* v. *Maryland*, Monroe Doctrine, Industrial Revolution, labor union.

Main Ideas

2. **Summarizing** What did the Marshall Court interpret the "necessary and proper" clause to mean?

3. **Determining Cause and Effect** How did the invention of the cotton gin help to increase the importance of cotton as a cash crop in the South?

Critical Thinking

4. **Big Ideas** How did interchangeable parts revolutionize the manufacturing process?

5. **Organizing** Use a graphic organizer similar to the one below to list the effects of some of the technological advances of the early 1800s.

6. **Analyzing Visuals** Study the circle graph on the distribution of slave labor on page 92. After those who worked to produce cotton, what was the next largest group of enslaved workers?

Writing About History

7. **Expository Writing** Suppose that you are a European visitor to the South in 1830. Write a newspaper article explaining your impressions of life in this region.

History ONLINE

Study Central™ To review this section, go to glencoe.com and click on Study Central.

Growing Division and Reform

S ectional differences continued to divide free and slave states as new states joined the Union. While Native Americans were forced to move west, reform movements focused on social issues and the rights of women and African Americans.

Guide to Reading

Big Ideas
Government and Society The American political system became more democratic during the Jacksonian era.

Content Vocabulary
- spoils system *(p. 97)*
- secede *(p. 97)*
- benevolent societies *(p. 100)*
- temperance *(p. 100)*
- emancipation *(p. 102)*

Academic Vocabulary
- controversy *(p. 95)*
- exposure *(p. 99)*

People and Events to Identify
- Missouri Compromise *(p. 95)*
- Tariff of Abominations *(p. 97)*
- Trail of Tears *(p. 99)*
- Whigs *(p. 99)*
- Second Great Awakening *(p. 100)*
- Frederick Douglass *(p. 103)*

Reading Strategy
Organizing Complete a graphic organizer similar to the one below by listing the divisive political issues of the 1820s.

Divisive Issues of the 1820s

The Resurgence of Sectionalism

MAIN Idea Sectionalism increased after the War of 1812, while voting rights expanded for American citizens.

HISTORY AND YOU What do you see as the defining characteristics of your state and region? Read on to learn why conflicts between different sections of the United States arose in the early and mid-1800s.

The Louisiana Purchase and improved transportation spurred new settlement in the West. Soon some of the territories grew large enough to apply for statehood. The matter of statehood for Missouri stirred up passionate disagreements. Increasingly, sectional disputes came to divide Americans.

The Missouri Compromise

The Monroe administration's Era of Good Feelings could not ward off the nation's growing sectional disputes and the passionately differing opinions over slavery. Tensions rose to the boiling point in 1819, when Missouri's application for statehood stirred up the country's most divisive issue: whether slavery should expand westward.

In 1819 the Union consisted of 11 free and 11 slave states. While the House of Representatives already had a majority of Northerners, admitting any new state, either slave or free, would upset the balance of political power in the Senate and touch off a bitter struggle over political power. Many Northerners opposed extending slavery into the western territories because they believed that human bondage was morally wrong. The South feared that if slavery could not expand, new free states would eventually give the North enough votes in the Senate to outlaw slaveholding.

Missouri's territorial government requested admission into the Union as a slave state in 1819. The House of Representatives then passed a resolution banning slaveholders from bringing enslaved people into Missouri as a condition of statehood. Southern Senators angrily blocked the proposal. The next year, Maine, then a part of Massachusetts, sought statehood. The Senate decided to combine Maine's request with Missouri's, and it voted to admit Maine as a free state and Missouri as a slave state. The Senate added an

The Missouri Compromise

Slave state/territory

Free state/territory

Territory opened to slavery by the Missouri Compromise

Closed to slavery by the Missouri Compromise

0   400 kilometers
0   400 miles
Albers Equal-Area projection

Maine
Admitted as free state in 1820

CANADA

N.H.

Vt.

N.Y.

Michigan Territory

Conn.

Mass.

R.I.

Unorganized Territory

Pa.

40°N

N.J.

Ill. Ind. Ohio

Del.

Md.

Mo.
Admitted as slave state in 1821

Va.

Ky.

Missouri Compromise Line 36°30'N

Tenn.

N.C.

Arkansas Territory

S.C.

ATLANTIC OCEAN

Miss. Ala. Ga.

30°N

NEW SPAIN

La.

Fla.

Gulf of Mexico

N
W   E
S

90°W   80°W

Voting for the Compromise

Maine

Missouri

House of Representatives, 1820

Vote yes to Missouri as slave state and Maine as free state and for compromise line

Vote yes to Missouri and Maine, but no for compromise line

Votes no on Missouri and Maine, but yes on compromise line

Votes no on Missouri and Maine, and no to compromise line

Analyzing GEOGRAPHY

1. **Regions** Most representatives from which region of the country voted for both provisions of the Missouri Compromise?

2. **Place** Which state came into the Union as a slave state, and which came in as a free state?

amendment to prohibit slavery in the rest of the Louisiana Territory north of Missouri's southern boundary. This would allow slavery to expand into Arkansas territory south of Missouri, but it would keep it out of the rest of the Louisiana Purchase. Southerners agreed, viewing this Northern region as unsuitable for farming anyway.

Henry Clay carefully steered the **Missouri Compromise** through the House of Representatives, which passed it by a close vote in March 1820. The next year, Missouri became the twenty-fourth state, and the Missouri Compromise temporarily settled the dispute over the westward expansion of slavery. Like Jefferson, however, many leaders feared more trouble ahead.

Once the issue was settled, a new problem developed. Pro-slavery members of the Missouri constitutional convention added a clause to the proposed state constitution prohibiting free African Americans from entering the state. This new **controversy** threatened final approval of Missouri's admission to the Union. Clay again engineered a solution by getting the Missouri legislature to state that they would not honor the spirit of the clause's wording.

Despite Clay's efforts, many leaders feared that the Missouri Compromise was only a temporary solution. "I take it for granted," John Quincy Adams wrote, "that the present question is a mere preamble—a title page to a great tragic volume." The Compromise merely postponed a debate over the future of slavery.

A Disputed Election

Although the Republicans remained the only official political party, sectional tensions were strong in the election campaign of 1824. On Election Day, four Republicans ran for president. Andrew Jackson of Tennessee led in the popular vote and in the Electoral College, but he did not win the necessary majority of electoral votes. In accordance with constitutional procedure, the decision went to the House of Representatives, whose members would select the president from the top three with the most votes.

Henry Clay of Kentucky, who had placed fourth, was eliminated. As the Speaker of the House, Clay enjoyed tremendous influence, and he threw his support to John Quincy Adams of Massachusetts. On February 9, 1825, Adams won the House election easily, with 13 votes to Jackson's 7 and William Crawford's 4.

Upon taking office, the new president named Clay as his secretary of state. Jackson's supporters immediately accused the pair of striking a "corrupt bargain," whereby Clay had secured votes for Adams in return for a cabinet post. Adams and Clay denied any wrongdoing, and no evidence of a deal ever emerged. Still, Jackson's outraged supporters decided to break with the faction of the party allied with Adams. The Jacksonians called themselves Democratic Republicans, later shortened to Democrats. Adams and his followers became known as National Republicans.

A New Era in Politics

Throughout the first decades of the 1800s, hundreds of thousands of white males gained the right to vote. This was largely because many states lowered or eliminated property ownership as a voting qualification. They did so partly to reflect the ideals of the Declaration of Independence and the social equality of frontier life. In addition, as cities and towns grew, the percentage of working people who did not own property increased. These people paid taxes and had an interest in the political affairs of their communities, so they wanted a say in electing those who represented them. The expansion of voting rights was very much in evidence by 1828. That year, more than 1.13 million citizens voted for president, compared with about 355,000 in 1824.

The campaign that year pitted John Quincy Adams against Andrew Jackson, who believed

PAST & PRESENT

Choosing a President

Today, nearly all American citizens age 18 and older are eligible to vote. This was not the case in the early 1800s. Under the state constitutions adopted at the time of the American Revolution, the right to vote was usually limited to white males who owned property. Over the next few decades, however, states began lowering or eliminating property requirements for voters. Women could not vote, nor could the overwhelming majority of African American men, even those living in the North who met other requirements for voting. Still, changes in the Jacksonian era meant many more Americans could participate in presidential elections.

The rise of national nominating conventions also changed the process of choosing a president. Rather than congressional party leaders deciding on the party's candidate, delegates from the states could participate in the decision at a nominating convention.

Today, parties still hold national conventions in presidential election years, but voting to choose the party's nominee for president has become largely symbolic. The party's nominee has generally been decided in advance, through state primaries and state caucuses.

1844

▲ Men crowd around the ballot boxes at a New York City polling station, waiting for their chance to vote in the presidential election of 1844.

that the presidency had been unjustly denied him four years earlier. The candidates resorted to mudslinging, attacking each other's personalities and morals. When the results came in, Jackson had 56 percent of the popular vote and 178 of the 261 electoral votes, a clear victory. Much of his support came from the West and South, where rural and small-town residents, many voting for the first time, saw Jackson as the candidate most likely to represent their interests.

As president, Jackson actively tried to make the government more inclusive. In an effort to strengthen democracy, he vigorously utilized the **spoils system,** the practice of appointing people to government jobs based on party loyalty and support. In his view, he was getting rid of a permanent office-holding class and opening up the government to more ordinary citizens.

Jackson's supporters also moved to make the political system—specifically, the way in which presidential candidates were chosen—more democratic. At that time, political parties used the caucus system to select presidential candidates. The members of the party who served in Congress would hold a closed meeting, or caucus, to choose the party's nominee.

Jackson's supporters believed that such a method restricted access to office to mainly the elite and well connected. The Jacksonians replaced the caucus with the national nominating convention, where delegates from the states gathered to decide on the party's presidential nominee.

The Nullification Crisis

Jackson had not been in office long before he had to focus on a national crisis. It centered on South Carolina, but it also highlighted the growing rift between the nation's Northern and Southern regions.

In the early 1800s, South Carolina's economy began to decline. Many of the state's residents blamed this situation on the nation's tariffs—the taxes the United States charged other countries to bring their goods into the country. Because it had few industries, South Carolina purchased many of its manufactured goods from England, but tariffs made them extremely expensive. When Congress levied yet another new tariff in 1828—which critics called the **Tariff of Abominations**—many South Carolinians threatened to **secede,** or withdraw, from the Union.

2004

▲ George W. Bush accepts the presidential nomination at the Republican National Convention in 2004.

▲ Today, electronic voting is becoming common. Nearly all U.S. citizens older than 18 years of age may vote.

MAKING CONNECTIONS

1. **Contrasting** How is the electorate different today than it was in the early 1800s?

2. **Synthesizing** How have national party conventions changed since the early 1800s?

The growing turmoil particularly troubled Vice President John C. Calhoun, who was from South Carolina. Calhoun felt torn between upholding the country's policies and helping his fellow Carolinians. Rather than support secession, Calhoun put forth the idea of nullification. He argued that because the states had created the federal union, they had the right to declare a federal law null, or not valid.

The issue of nullification intensified in January 1830, when Senators Robert Hayne of South Carolina and Daniel Webster of Massachusetts confronted each other on the Senate floor. Hayne, asserting that the Union was no more than a voluntary association of states, advocated "liberty first and Union afterward." Webster countered that neither liberty nor the Union could survive without binding federal laws. He ended his speech with a stirring call: "Liberty *and* Union, now and for ever, one and inseparable!"

The war of words intensified in 1832 when Congress passed yet another tariff law. Enraged, a special session of South Carolina's legislature voted to nullify the law. President Jackson considered nullification an act of treason and sent a warship to Charleston. As tensions rose, Senator Henry Clay managed to defuse the crisis. At Clay's insistence, Congress passed a bill that would lower tariffs gradually until 1842. South Carolina then repealed its nullification of the tariff law.

NATIONAL GEOGRAPHIC — Effects of the Indian Removal Act, 1831–1842

In 1832 Sauk and Fox warriors led by Chief Black Hawk fought to reclaim territory east of the Mississippi River, but were defeated.

▲ Cherokee travel the Trail of Tears.

The Cherokee took their refusal to move to the Supreme Court—and won. Federal troops forced them to leave in 1838.

Chief Osceola led the Seminole in rebellion.

Multi-group removal route
Trail of Tears
■ Fort
1840 border

0 400 kilometers
0 400 miles
Albers Equal-Area projection

Analyzing GEOGRAPHY

1. **Movement** Name two Native American groups in the northern half of the United States that were forced to relocate.

2. **Location** Where did the Trail of Tears end?

Maps In MOtion See *StudentWorks*™ *Plus* or glencoe.com.

Native American Removal

Although slavery remained a divisive question, President Jackson decided to focus on other matters, including Native Americans. While Jackson wanted to ensure the survival of Native American peoples, he accelerated the effort of moving them out of the way of white settlers. In 1830 Jackson signed the Indian Removal Act, which helped the states relocate Native Americans to largely uninhabited regions west of the Mississippi River.

The Cherokee in Georgia fought back by appealing to the Supreme Court, hoping to gain legal recognition of their territorial rights. Chief Justice Marshall supported this right in two decisions, *Cherokee Nation* v. *Georgia* (1831) and *Worcester* v. *Georgia* (1832). Jackson refused to carry out the decision. "Marshall has made his opinion," the president reportedly said, "now let him enforce it."

In 1838 Martin Van Buren, Jackson's successor, sent in the army to forcibly move the Cherokee. Roughly 2,000 Cherokee died in camps while waiting for the westward march. On the journey, known to the Cherokee as the **Trail of Tears,** about 2,000 others died of starvation, disease, and **exposure.**

Missionary-minded religious groups and a few members of Congress, like Henry Clay, declared that Jackson's policies toward Native Americans stained the nation's honor. Most citizens, however, supported them. By 1838 the majority of Native Americans still living east of the Mississippi had been forced onto government reservations.

A New Party Emerges

President Jackson also decided to dismantle the Second Bank of the United States. He resented the power of its wealthy stockholders. Jackson vetoed a bill that would have extended the Bank's charter for 20 years. Then, by withdrawing the federal government's deposits, he forced the Bank to end.

Opposition to Jackson By the mid-1830s, those who criticized Jackson's decision had formed a new political party, the **Whigs.** Led by former National Republicans like Henry Clay, John Quincy Adams, and Daniel Webster, the Whigs wanted to expand the federal government, encourage industrial and commercial development, and create a centralized economy. Such policies differed from those of the Democrats, who favored a limited federal government. The Whigs ran three candidates for president in the election of 1836. Jackson's continuing popularity, however, helped assure victory for his handpicked successor, Democrat Martin Van Buren.

Economic Crisis Shortly after Van Buren took office, a crippling economic crisis hit the nation. The roots of the crisis stretched back to the end of Jackson's term, a period in which investment in roads, canals, and railroads boomed, prompting a wave of land speculation and bank lending. This heavy spending pushed up inflation, which Jackson feared eventually would render the nation's paper currency worthless. Just before leaving office, therefore, Jackson issued the Specie Circular, which ordered that all payments for public lands must be made in the form of silver or gold.

Jackson's directive set off the Panic of 1837. With easy paper credit no longer available, land sales plummeted and economic growth slowed. In addition, the National Bank, which could have helped stabilize the economy, no longer existed. As a result, many banks and businesses failed, and thousands of farmers lost their land through foreclosures. Van Buren, a firm believer in his party's philosophy of limited federal government, did little to ease the crisis.

The Whigs and Tyler With Van Buren clearly vulnerable, the Whigs easily won the 1840 election by nominating General William Henry Harrison, a hero of the battle against Native Americans at Tippecanoe in 1811. Harrison, who spoke at his inauguration for two hours in bitter cold without coat or hat, died one month later of pneumonia. Vice President John Tyler, a Southerner and former Democrat who had left his party in protest over the nullification issue, then took over.

Tyler's ascension to the presidency dismayed Whig leaders. Tyler sided with the Democrats on numerous key issues, refusing to support a higher tariff or a new national bank. The new president did win praise, however, for the 1842 Webster-Ashburton Treaty, which established a firm boundary between the United States and Canada.

✔ Reading Check **Summarizing** What caused the nullification crisis?

The Reform Spirit

MAIN Idea The Second Great Awakening brought an era of reform.

HISTORY AND YOU Identify an issue you believe citizens and lawmakers need to address. Read on to learn about reformers during the mid-1800s.

During the mid-1800s, many citizens worked to reform various aspects of American society. The reform movement stemmed in large part from a revival of religion.

The Second Great Awakening

Many church leaders sensed that the growth of scientific knowledge and rationalism were challenging the doctrine of faith. In the early 1800s, religious leaders organized to revive Americans' commitment to religion. The resulting movement came to be called the **Second Great Awakening.** Various Protestant denominations—most often the Methodists, Baptists, and Presbyterians—held camp meetings where thousands of followers sang, prayed, and participated in emotional outpourings of faith. One of the most successful ministers was Charles G. Finney, who pioneered many methods of revivalism evangelists still use today.

Growth of Churches As membership in many Protestant churches swelled, other religious groups also flourished. Among them were Unitarianism, Universalism, and the Church of Jesus Christ of Latter-day Saints, whose followers are commonly known as Mormons. Joseph Smith began preaching the Mormon faith in New York in the 1820s. After enduring much harassment in New York, Ohio, Missouri, and elsewhere, Mormons across the Midwest moved to the settlement of Nauvoo in Illinois. However, persecution continued, and following the murder of Joseph Smith, the Mormons headed west, and settled in the Utah Territory.

Revivalists preached that individuals could improve themselves and the world. Lyman Beecher, one of the nation's most prominent Presbyterian ministers, insisted that the nation's citizenry, more than its government, was responsible for building a better society.

Benevolent Societies Associations known as **benevolent societies** sprang up everywhere. At first, they focused on spreading the word of God and attempting to convert non-believers. Soon, they sought to combat a number of social problems. One of the most striking features of the reform effort was the overwhelming presence of women. Young women in particular had joined the revivalist movement in much larger numbers than men. One reason was that many unmarried women with uncertain futures discovered in religion a foundation on which to build their lives. As more women turned to the church, many also joined religious-based reform groups.

Social Reform

The optimism and emphasis on the individual in religion gave rise to dozens of utopian communities in which people wanted to find a better life. While only a few chose that path, many more attempted to reform society instead. A number of these reformers, many of them women, argued that no social vice caused more crime, poverty, or family damage than the excessive use of alcohol.

Although advocates of **temperance,** or moderation in the consumption of alcohol, had been active since the late 1700s, the new reformers energized the campaign. Temperance groups formed across the country, preaching the evils of alcohol and urging heavy drinkers to give up liquor. In 1833 a number of groups formed a national organization, the American Temperance Union, to strengthen the movement.

While persuading people not to drink, temperance societies pushed to halt the sale of liquor. In 1851 Maine passed the first state prohibition law, an example a dozen other states followed by 1855. Other states passed "local option" laws, which allowed towns and villages to prohibit liquor sales within their boundaries.

Other reformers focused on prisons and education. Around 1816 many states began replacing overcrowded prisons with new penitentiaries where prisoners were to be rehabilitated rather than simply locked up. States also began to establish a system of public education—government-funded schools open to all citizens. Reformers focused on creating elementary schools to teach all children the basics of reading, writing, and arithmetic, and to instill a work ethic. The schools were open to all and supported by local and state taxes and tuition fees.

The Seneca Falls Declaration

▲ Susan B. Anthony (left) and Elizabeth Cady Stanton (right) were two of the most prominent women's suffrage advocates. Stanton attended the Seneca Falls Convention that issued the Declaration of Sentiments.

PRIMARY SOURCE

Declaration of Sentiments

". . . We hold these truths to be self-evident: that all men and women are created equal; that they are endowed by their Creator with certain inalienable rights. . . .

The history of mankind is a history of repeated injuries and usurpations on the part of man toward woman, having in direct object the establishment of an absolute tyranny over her. . . .

Resolutions

Resolved, That all laws which prevent woman from occupying such a station in society as her conscience shall dictate, or which place her in a position inferior to that of man, are contrary to the great precept of nature, and therefore of no force or authority.

Resolved, That woman is man's equal—was intended to be so by the Creator, and the highest good of the race demands that she should be recognized as such.

. . . *Resolved,* That it is the duty of women of this country to secure to themselves their sacred right to the elective franchise.

. . . *Resolved,* therefore, That, being invested by the Creator with the same capabilities, and the same consciousness of responsibility for their exercise, it is demonstrably the right and duty of woman, equally with man, to promote every righteous cause by every righteous means . . . both in private and in public, by writing and by speaking, by any instrumentalities proper to be used, and in any assemblies proper to be held. . . ."

—from The Seneca Falls Declaration

DBQ **Document-Based Questions**

1. **Identifying** According to the third resolution, what is the duty of American women?

2. **Paraphrasing** What does the Declaration ask all women to do?

The Women's Movement

Women did not have the right to vote in the 1800s. Most people believed the home was the proper place for women, partly because the outside world was seen as dangerous and partly because of the era's ideas about the family. Many parents treated raising children as a solemn responsibility because it prepared young people for a proper Christian life. Women were viewed as better able to serve as models of piety and virtue for their families. The ideas of the era implied that wives were partners with their husbands and, in some ways, morally superior.

As the reform movements of the 1830s got underway, some women set out to create more educational opportunities for girls and women. The early 1800s saw the funding of schools for girls that taught academic subjects. In 1837 the first higher education institution for women, Mount Holyoke Female Seminary in Massachusetts, opened.

The idea that women had an important role in building a virtuous home was soon expanded to society. As women became involved in reform movements, some argued for the right to promote their ideas. In 1848 activists Lucretia Mott and Elizabeth Cady Stanton organized the Seneca Falls Convention in New York. This gathering of women reformers marked the beginning of an organized woman's movement. The convention issued the Declaration of Sentiments and Resolutions, better known as the Seneca Falls Declaration. It began with words expanding the Declaration of Independence: "We hold these truths to be self-evident: that all men and women are created equal. . . ."

Although Stanton shocked the women present when she proposed a focus on suffrage, or the right to vote, the convention narrowly passed her proposal. Throughout the 1850s, women organized conventions to promote greater rights for themselves.

The Abolitionist Movement Begins

Since colonial times many Americans had believed slavery was immoral. The Second Great Awakening and the general spirit of reform in the period of the 1830s, however, created an environment in which abolition began to gain widespread support. William Lloyd Garrison sparked the movement by publishing *The Liberator,* through which he spread his ideas, and by founding the American Anti-Slavery Society. Garrison's energy, moral certitude, and strong rhetoric attracted fellow activists, as well as new converts, and gave the movement momentum on a national scale.

ANALYZING HISTORY How did William Lloyd Garrison start the abolitionist movement of the 1830s?

▶ *Major leaders of the early abolitionist movement included William Lloyd Garrison (above left), sisters Angelina Grimké (above center) and Sarah Grimké (above right), as well as Frederick Douglass (shown seated left of the table) and Theodore Weld (seated in front).*

The Abolitionist Movement

Of all the reform movements that began in the early 1800s, the movement calling for abolition, or the immediate end to slavery, was the most divisive. It polarized the nation and helped bring about the Civil War.

Early Opposition Many of the country's founders knew that the nation would have difficulty remaining true to its ideals of liberty and equality if it continued to enslave human beings. Quakers and Baptists in both North and South argued that slavery was a sin. After the Revolution, Baptists in Virginia called for "every legal measure to [wipe out] this horrid evil from the land."

Early antislavery societies advocated gradualism, the idea that slavery should be ended gradually. First they would stop slave traders. Then they would end slavery in phases, first in the North, then in the upper South, and finally in the lower South. They believed this strategy would give the South time to adjust.

One example of antislavery efforts in the early 1800s was the formation of the American Colonization Society (ACS) in 1816. This group, supported by such prominent figures as President James Monroe and Chief Justice John Marshall, encouraged African Americans to resettle in Africa. The privately funded ACS chartered ships and helped relocate between 12,000 and 20,000 African Americans along the west coast of Africa in what became the nation of Liberia. Still, there were more than 1.5 million enslaved persons in the United States in 1820. Many of them, already two or three generations removed from Africa, strongly objected to the idea of resettlement.

New Abolitionists The antislavery movement gained new momentum in the 1830s, thanks largely to William Lloyd Garrison. In his newspaper, the *Liberator,* Garrison called for the immediate **emancipation,** or freeing, of enslaved persons. Garrison went on to found the New England Antislavery Society in 1832 and the American Antislavery Society in 1833.

Many women supported abolitionism. Lucretia Mott, a strong advocate of women's rights, spoke out in favor of abolition. Some Southern women, such as the South Carolina sisters Sarah and Angelina Grimké, also joined the crusade.

African American Abolitionists Not surprisingly, free African Americans took a prominent role in the abolitionist movement. The most famous was **Frederick Douglass,** who had escaped from slavery in Maryland. He published his own anti-slavery newspaper, the *North Star,* and an autobiography. Another important African American abolitionist was Sojourner Truth. She gained freedom in 1827 when New York freed all remaining enslaved persons in the state. Although she lacked a formal education, her eloquent and deeply religious antislavery speeches attracted huge crowds.

Northern Opposition Some Northerners objected to abolitionism because they considered it a dangerous threat to the existing social system. Some whites, including many prominent businesspeople, warned that it would produce a destructive war between the North and the South. Others feared it might bring a great influx of freed African Americans to the North, overwhelming the labor and housing markets. Many Northerners also had no desire to see the South's economy crumble. If that happened, they might lose the huge sums Southern planters owed to Northern banks as well as the Southern cotton that fed Northern textile mills.

Southern Reaction To most Southerners, slavery was a "peculiar institution," one that was distinctive and vital to the Southern way of life. The South had remained mostly agricultural, becoming increasingly tied to cotton and the enslaved people who planted and picked it. Southerners responded to the growing attacks against slavery by vehemently defending the institution. South Carolina's governor called it a "national benefit," while Thomas Dew, a leading academic of the South, claimed that most enslaved persons had no desire for freedom, as they enjoyed a close and beneficial relationship with their slaveholders. "We have no hesitation in affirming," he declared, "that . . . the slaves of good [slaveholders] are his warmest, most constant, and most devoted friends."

In 1831, when a slave rebellion left more than 50 white Virginians dead, Southerners were outraged. They cracked down on enslaved persons throughout the region and railed against the North. Further, they demanded the suppression of abolitionist material as a condition for remaining in the Union. Southern postal workers refused to deliver abolitionist newspapers. In 1836, under Southern pressure, the House of Representatives passed a "gag rule" providing that all abolitionist petitions be shelved without debate. Such measures did not deter abolitionists. While their movement was still relatively small, it continued to cause an uproar.

Reading Check **Comparing** How did Northerners' views on abolition differ from those of Southerners?

Section 3 REVIEW

Vocabulary

1. **Explain** the significance of: Missouri Compromise, spoils system, Tariff of Abominations, secede, Trail of Tears, Whigs, Second Great Awakening, benevolent societies, temperance, emancipation, Frederick Douglass.

Main Ideas

2. **Describing** How was the nullification crisis resolved?

3. **Explaining** On what document did the Seneca Falls Convention base the "Declaration of Sentiments"?

Critical Thinking

4. **Big Ideas** In what ways did the United States become more democratic during Jackson's administration?

5. **Categorizing** Use a graphic organizer similar to the one below to list the major areas of reform in the mid-1800s.

Areas of Reform

6. **Analyzing Visuals** Study the map of the effects of Indian removal on page 98. Which groups tried to keep their lands through armed resistance?

Writing About History

7. **Persuasive Writing** Think of one social reform you think is needed in the United States today. Write a letter to a legislator expressing reasons why the reform is needed and how it might be achieved. Give examples of specific problems in your community or state to support your argument.

History ONLINE

Study Central™ To review this section, go to glencoe.com and click on Study Central.

Manifest Destiny and Crisis

Guide to Reading

Big Ideas

War, Trade, and Migration War with Mexico brought new territories under the control of the United States and increasing discord about slavery.

Content Vocabulary

• popular sovereignty *(p. 107)*
• secession *(p. 108)*

Academic Vocabulary

• resolution *(p. 106)*
• civil *(p. 109)*

People and Events to Identify

• Manifest Destiny *(p. 104)*
• James K. Polk *(p. 105)*
• Treaty of Guadalupe Hidalgo *(p. 107)*
• Compromise of 1850 *(p. 109)*
• Underground Railroad *(p. 110)*
• Harriet Tubman *(p. 110)*
• Kansas-Nebraska Act *(p. 111)*
• Dred Scott *(p. 112)*

Reading Strategy

Taking Notes Use the major headings in this section to record main ideas about the United States' westward expansion and its results.

Manifest Destiny and Crisis
I. Manifest Destiny
  A. Pushing West
  B. Texas and Oregon
  C. War with Mexico
    a. Onset of War

Sectionalism and disagreements over slavery in the new territories intensified as the United States continued to expand west. The friction led to the breakdown and formation of political parties.

Manifest Destiny

MAIN Idea In the 1840s, the nation expanded as settlers moved west.

HISTORY AND YOU To which country did California and Texas belong before they became part of the United States? Read on to learn how the two states entered the Union.

With the Louisiana Purchase opening up the West, thousands of people began pushing west, journeying all the way to California and the Oregon Territory. Between the late 1830s and early 1860s, more than 250,000 Americans braved great obstacles on overland trails.

Pushing West

The opportunity to farm fertile soil, enter the fur trade, or trade with foreign nations across the Pacific lured farmers, adventurers, and merchants alike. Most emigrants, like the majority of Americans, believed in **Manifest Destiny.** Manifest Destiny was the idea that the nation was meant to spread to the Pacific.

Latecomers to the Midwest set their sights on California and Oregon, although other nations had already claimed parts of these lands. The United States and Great Britain had agreed in 1818 to occupy the Oregon land jointly. The British dominated the region until about 1840, when the enthusiastic reports of American missionaries began to attract large numbers of settlers.

California was a frontier province of Mexico. Because few Mexicans wanted to live in California, the local government welcomed foreign settlers. By 1845 more than 700 Americans lived in California. Although the Mexican government relied on these American settlers, it was suspicious about their national loyalties.

By the 1840s, several east-to-west routes had been carved, including the Oregon Trail, the California Trail, and the Santa Fe Trail. As the overland traffic increased, the Plains Indians came to resent the threat it posed to their way of life. They feared that the buffalo herds, on which they relied for food, shelter, clothing, and tools, would die off or migrate elsewhere. In 1851, the federal government negotiated the Treaty of Fort Laramie to ensure peace. Eight Plains Indian groups agreed to specific geographic boundaries, while the United States promised that the defined territories would belong to the Native Americans forever.

Analyzing GEOGRAPHY

1. **Location** Name three Missouri cities that served as starting points for western emigrants.

2. **Regions** Why did emigrants bypass the Great Plains and travel all the way to the Far West?

Maps In Motion See *StudentWorks™ Plus* or glencoe.com.

White settlers still streamed across the plains, however, provoking Native American hostility.

Texas and Oregon

At first, Mexico had encouraged Americans to settle the Mexican region of Texas, which at the time was part of the state of Coahuila. Tensions developed, however, when the American settlers refused to follow Mexico's conditions for settling the region. When Mexico closed its borders in 1830 to further immigration, the settlers, under the leadership of Stephen Austin and Sam Houston, tried to negotiate policy changes. When repeated attempts failed, they decided to separate from Texas and create their own government. Devastating losses at the Alamo and Goliad galvanized the Americans, who were able to defeat Mexican forces at the Battle of San Jacinto on April 21, 1836.

Five months later, the citizens of Texas voted in favor of joining the United States. However, Texas wished to enter the Union as a slave state, which antislavery leaders in Congress opposed. In addition, Mexico continued to claim ownership of Texas. To avoid conflict, President Andrew Jackson made no move toward annexation.

Texas statehood became a key issue in the presidential race of 1844. The Democratic nominee, **James K. Polk** of Tennessee, promised to annex not only Texas but also the contested Oregon Territory in the Northwest. He also vowed to buy California from Mexico. This platform promised to further Manifest Destiny while maintaining the delicate balance between free and slave states. Henry Clay, the Whig nominee, originally opposed annexing Texas but later announced his support if it would not cause a war with Mexico.

Many Whigs opposed to slavery felt so betrayed by Clay's actions that they voted for James G. Birney of the pro-abolition Liberty Party. With the Whig vote split, Polk won the election. In February 1845, Congress passed a joint **resolution** to annex Texas, and in December 1845 Texas became a state. Six months later, Britain and the United States agreed to divide Oregon along the 49th parallel. Britain took the Canadian province of British Columbia, and the Americans received the land that later became the states of Oregon, Washington, and Idaho.

War With Mexico

Texas's entry into the Union outraged the Mexican government, which promptly broke diplomatic relations with the United States. Matters worsened when the two countries disputed Texas's southwestern border.

President Polk's designs on California added to the conflict. In November 1845, he sent John Slidell as an envoy to Mexico City to try to purchase California and resolve other differences. Mexico's new president, José Joaquín Herrera, refused to meet with Slidell.

NATIONAL GEOGRAPHIC — The War With Mexico, 1846–1848

General Winfield Scott leads American troops into Mexico City in September 1847.

Legend:
- ← American troops
- ✹ American victory
- ← Mexican troops
- ✹ Mexican victory
- ⛵ U.S. naval blockade

0 — 400 kilometers
0 — 400 miles
Lambert Azimuthal Equal-Area projection

Oregon Country
Unorganized Terr.
Iowa Terr.
UNITED STATES
Mo.
Ark.
La.
Texas
MEXICO
PACIFIC OCEAN
Gulf of California
Gulf of Mexico

FRÉMONT
Bear Flag Revolt, June 1846
San Francisco
Monterey, July 1846
STOCKTON
Los Angeles
San Gabriel, Jan. 1847
San Pasqual, Dec. 1846
San Diego
SLOAT
KEARNY
Santa Fe, Aug. 1846
DONIPHAN
El Brazito, Dec. 1846
Sacramento, Feb. 1847
Mazatlán
WOOL
TAYLOR
Buena Vista Feb. 1847
SANTA ANNA
Tampico
Cerro Gordo April 1847
Mexico City, Sept. 1847
Veracruz
SCOTT
San Antonio
Corpus Christi
Monterrey, Sept. 1846
Ft. Leavenworth
Platte R.
Colorado R.
Rio Grande
Red R.
Arkansas R.
Disputed Terr.
TROPIC OF CANCER
30°N
20°N
120°W
110°W

Analyzing GEOGRAPHY

1. **Movement** Which commanders led the invasion of California?
2. **Location** Where did Scott fight his first battle?

Maps In MOtion — See *StudentWorks™ Plus* or glencoe.com.

Onset of War With no realistic chance of a diplomatic solution, in January 1846 Polk ordered General Zachary Taylor to lead troops across the Nueces River into territory claimed by both the United States and Mexico. He wanted Mexican troops to fire the first shot, because then he could more easily win support for a war. On May 9, news arrived that a Mexican force had attacked Taylor's men. Four days later, the Senate and House both overwhelmingly voted in favor of the war.

California Even before war with Mexico was officially declared, settlers in northern California, led by American general John C. Frémont, had begun an uprising. The settlers had little trouble overcoming the weak official Mexican presence in the territory. On June 14, 1846, they declared California independent and renamed the region the Bear Flag Republic. Within a month, American naval forces arrived to occupy the ports of San Francisco and San Diego and to claim the republic for the United States.

Despite the loss of California and defeat in several battles, Mexico refused to surrender. Then Polk sent General Winfield Scott to seize Mexico City. After a 6-month campaign beginning in the Gulf Coast city of Veracruz, Scott's forces captured Mexico's capital in September 1847.

Peace Terms Defeated, on February 2, 1848, Mexico's leaders signed the **Treaty of Guadalupe Hidalgo.** Mexico gave the United States more than 500,000 square miles (1,295,000 sq. km) of territory—what are now the states of California, Nevada, and Utah, as well as most of Arizona and New Mexico and parts of Colorado and Wyoming. Mexico accepted the Rio Grande as the southern border of Texas. In return, the United States paid Mexico $15 million and took over $3.25 million in debts the Mexican government owed to American citizens.

With Oregon and the former Mexican territories under the American flag, the dream of Manifest Destiny had been realized. The question of whether the new lands should allow slavery, however, would soon lead the country into another bloody conflict.

Reading Check **Explaining** What is the idea of Manifest Destiny?

Slavery and Western Expansion

MAIN Idea Continuing disagreements over the westward expansion of slavery increased sectional tensions between the North and South.

HISTORY AND YOU Under what circumstances, if any, do you believe that citizens are justified in disobeying a law? Read on to learn how some Northerners responded to the Fugitive Slave Act of 1850, which required them to aid in the capture of runaway slaves.

When California applied for statehood, attempts by Congress to find a compromise further heightened opposing viewpoints on slavery.

The Impact of the War With Mexico

In mid-1846, Representative David Wilmot, a Democrat from Pennsylvania, proposed that in any territory the United States had gained from Mexico, "neither slavery nor involuntary servitude shall ever exist."

Wilmot's proposal outraged Southerners. They believed that any antislavery policy about the territories endangered slavery everywhere. Despite fierce Southern opposition, a coalition of Northern Democrats and Whigs passed the Wilmot Proviso in the House of Representatives. The Senate, however, refused to vote on it. During the debate, Senator John C. Calhoun of South Carolina argued that Americans settling in the territories had the right to bring along their property, including enslaved laborers, and that Congress had no power to ban slavery in the territories.

Senator Lewis Cass of Michigan suggested that the citizens of each new territory should be allowed to decide for themselves if they wanted to permit slavery. This idea, which came to be called **popular sovereignty,** appealed strongly to many members of Congress because it removed the slavery issue from national politics. It also appeared democratic, since the settlers themselves would make the decision. Abolitionists, however, argued that it still denied African Americans their right to be free.

As the 1848 presidential election approached, both major candidates—Democrat Lewis Cass and General Zachary Taylor, the Whig nominee—sidestepped the slavery issue. Many Northern opponents of slavery decided to join with members of the abolitionist Liberty Party to form the Free-Soil Party, which opposed the spread of slavery onto the "free soil" of the western territories. Adopting the slogan "Free soil, free speech, free labor, and free men," they chose former president Martin Van Buren as their candidate. On Election Day, support for the Free-Soilers pulled votes away from the Democrats. When the ballots were counted, the Whig candidate, Zachary Taylor, had won a narrow victory.

Struggle for a Compromise

Within a year of President Taylor's inauguration, the issue of slavery took center stage. A year earlier, in January 1848, a carpenter named James Marshall found traces of gold in a stream near a sawmill in Sacramento, California. Word of the find leaked out, and San Franciscans abandoned their homes and businesses to pile into wagons and head to the mountains in search of gold. During the summer, news of the find swept all the way to the East Coast and beyond, and the California Gold Rush was on.

By the end of 1849, over 80,000 "Forty-Niners" had arrived in California hoping to make their fortunes. Mining towns sprang up overnight, and the frenzy for gold led to chaos and violence. In need of a strong government to maintain order, Californians decided to seek statehood. With the encouragement of President Taylor, California applied to enter the Union as a free state in December 1849.

At the time, the union consisted of 15 free states and 15 slave states. If California tipped the balance, the slaveholding states would become a minority in the Senate. Southerners dreaded losing power in national politics, fearful that this would lead to limits on slavery. A few Southern politicians began to talk of **secession**—taking their states out of the Union.

In early 1850, one of the most senior and influential leaders in the Senate, Henry Clay of Kentucky, tried to find a compromise that would enable California to join the Union and resolve other sectional disputes. Among other resolutions, Clay proposed allowing California to come in as a free state and organizing the rest of the Mexican cession without any restric-

The Compromise of 1850

Leaders in the California Territory submitted their request to become a state in 1849. Debate in Congress over California's entry into the Union as a free state ended in the Compromise of 1850. California joined the Union in September 1850 as part of the Compromise.

". . . [I]t is this circumstance, Sir, the prohibition of slavery . . . which has contributed to raise . . . the dispute as to the propriety of the admission of California into the Union under this constitution."

—Daniel Webster, speech in the Senate, March 7, 1850

► Daniel Webster, Henry Clay, and John Calhoun were the main participants in the 1850 debate over the slavery issue and California's entry into the Union.

◄ As word of the discovery of gold in California spread through the nation, Americans rushed to the mountains in search of gold.

tions on slavery. Clay further proposed that Congress would be prohibited from interfering with the domestic slave trade and would pass a stronger law to help Southerners recover African American runaways. These measures were intended to assure the South that the North would not try to abolish slavery after California joined the Union.

Clay's proposal triggered a massive debate in Congress. When President Taylor, who opposed the compromise, died unexpectedly of cholera in July 1850, Vice President Millard Fillmore succeeded him and quickly threw his support behind the measure. By September, Congress had passed all parts of the **Compromise of 1850,** which had been divided into several smaller bills.

The Fugitive Slave Act

As part of the Compromise of 1850, Henry Clay had convinced Congress to pass the Fugitive Slave Act as a benefit to slaveholders. However, the law actually hurt the southern cause by creating active hostility toward slavery among many Northerners. Under this law, a slaveholder or slave catcher had only to point out alleged run-aways to have them taken into custody. The accused would then be brought before a federal commissioner. With no right to testify on their own behalf, even those who had earned their freedom years earlier had no way to prove their case. An affidavit asserting that the captive had escaped from a slaveholder, or testimony by white witnesses, was all a court needed to order the person sent South. Furthermore, federal commissioners had a financial incentive to rule in favor of slaveholders: such judgments earned them a $10 fee, while judgments in favor of the accused paid only $5.

Defiance In addition, the act required federal marshals to assist slave catchers. Marshals could even deputize citizens to help them. It was this requirement that drove many Northerners into active defiance. The abolitionist Frederick Douglass, himself an escapee from slavery, would work crowds into a furor over this part of the law. Northerners justified their defiance of the Fugitive Slave Act on moral grounds. In his 1849 essay "**Civil** Disobedience," Henry David Thoreau wrote that if the law "requires you to be the agent of injustice to another, then I say, break the law."

Harriet Tubman
1820–1913

Known as "Moses" for her courage in leading enslaved people to freedom as Moses had led the Hebrews out of slavery in Egypt, Harriet Tubman was a heroine of the antislavery movement. Tubman was born into slavery in Maryland and struggled early against the system's brutality. At age 13, she tried to save another enslaved person from punishment, and an overseer fractured her skull. Miraculously, she recovered, but she suffered from occasional blackouts for the rest of her life.

Tubman escaped to freedom in 1849. About crossing into Pennsylvania, she later wrote, "I looked at my hands to see if I was the same person. There was such a glory over everything. The sun came up like gold through the trees, and I felt like I was in Heaven."

Her joy inspired others. After Congress passed the Fugitive Slave Act, Tubman returned to the South 19 times to guide enslaved people along the Underground Railroad to freedom.

Tubman became notorious in the eyes of slaveholders, but despite a large reward offered for her capture, no one ever betrayed her whereabouts. Furthermore, in all her rescues, she never lost a "passenger." Tubman's bravery and determination made her one of the most important figures in the antislavery movement.

What do you think Tubman meant when she wrote, "I looked at my hands to see if I was the same person?"

Harriet Beecher Stowe
1811–1896

Daughter of reformer-minister Lyman Beecher, Harriet Beecher Stowe was born into a family of high achievers. Unlike many young women of the time, Stowe received a good education, including teacher training in Hartford, Connecticut. In 1832 Stowe moved to Cincinnati, Ohio. There, Stowe began writing and teaching. She spent 18 years in Ohio—right across the river from the slave state of Kentucky. During this period, she met fugitive slaves, employed a former enslaved woman, and learned about slavery from Southern friends.

In 1850 Stowe moved with her husband to Maine. There, in reaction to the Fugitive Slave Law, she began writing *Uncle Tom's Cabin*, based on what she had learned while in Ohio and antislavery materials she had read. The novel, which humanized the plight of the enslaved, was an instant sensation and further hardened the positions of both abolitionists and slaveholders. When President Lincoln met Stowe, so the story goes, he exclaimed, "So you're the little woman who wrote the book that started this Great War!"

Stowe went on to write many more novels, stories, and articles but is today best known for the novel that so fanned the sectional flames over slavery that it contributed to the start of the Civil War.

What was the effect of Uncle Tom's Cabin on the slavery debate?

The Underground Railroad One reason why so many African Americans could escape from the South was the **Underground Railroad.** This informal but well-organized network of abolitionists helped thousands of enslaved persons flee north. "Conductors" transported runaways in secret, gave them shelter and food along the way, and saw them to freedom in the Northern states or Canada. The most famous conductor was **Harriet Tubman,** herself a runaway. Again and again, she journeyed into the slave states to bring out men, women, and children.

Another important conductor was Levi Coffin, who allowed runaways to stay at his homes in Indiana and Ohio where several Underground Railroad routes converged. Some 3,300 African Americans stayed with Coffin while traveling north to freedom.

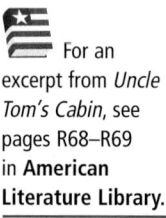 For an excerpt from *Uncle Tom's Cabin*, see pages R68–R69 in **American Literature Library.**

Uncle Tom's Cabin A major stop on the railroad was Cincinnati, Ohio, where author Harriett Beecher Stowe resided. Her exposure to runaway slaves and the tragic reports she heard later about victims of the Fugitive Slave Law inspired her to "write something that would make this whole nation feel what an accursed thing slavery is."

Stowe's book, *Uncle Tom's Cabin,* was first published in 1852. Stowe's depiction of the enslaved hero, Tom, and the villainous overseer, Simon Legree, aroused passionate antislavery sentiment in the North. Despite Southern outrage, the book eventually sold millions of copies. It had such a dramatic impact on public opinion that many historians consider it a cause of the Civil War.

New Territorial Troubles

The opening of the Oregon country and the admission of California to the Union brought further problems as the nation expanded.

Many people became convinced of the need for a transcontinental railroad to promote growth in the territories along the route. The choice of the railroad's eastern starting point was contentious. Many Southerners favored the southern route, from New Orleans to San Diego. Since part of that route would lead through northern Mexico, the United States purchased the necessary land for $10 million.

Democratic Senator Stephen A. Douglas of Illinois wanted the eastern starting point to be in Chicago. He knew that any route from the north would run through the unsettled lands west of Missouri and Iowa and prepared a bill to organize the region into a new territory to be called Nebraska. Key Southern committee leaders prevented this bill from coming to a vote in the Senate. They made it clear that before Nebraska could be organized, Congress had to repeal part of the Missouri Compromise and allow slavery in the new territory.

Kansas-Nebraska Act At first, Douglas tried to gain Southern support for his bill by saying that any states organized in the new Nebraska territory would be allowed to exercise popular sovereignty with regard to slavery. When this failed, Douglas agreed to repeal the antislavery provision of the Missouri Compromise and to divide the region into two territories. Nebraska, adjacent to the free state of Iowa, appeared to become a free state, while Kansas, located west of the slave state of Missouri, would become a slave state. Warned that the South might secede without such concessions, President Pierce eventually gave his support to the bill. Despite opposition, Congress passed the **Kansas-Nebraska Act** in May 1854.

"Bleeding Kansas" Hordes of Northerners hurried into Kansas to create an antislavery majority. Before the March elections of 1855, however, thousands of armed Missourians—called "border ruffians" in the press—crossed the border to vote illegally, helping to elect a pro-slavery legislature. Furious antislavery settlers countered by drafting their own constitution that prohibited slavery. By March 1856, Kansas had two governments, one opposed to slavery and the other supporting it. As more Northern settlers arrived, border ruffians began attacks. "Bleeding Kansas," as newspapers dubbed the territory, had become the scene of a territorial civil war.

Reading Check **Analyzing** Why did the Compromise of 1850 fail to end sectional division?

The Crisis Deepens

MAIN Idea The slavery controversy shook up political parties and accelerated the crisis between North and South.

HISTORY AND YOU Do you know of Supreme Court cases that have sparked major debates? Read to learn how the Dred Scott case divided the nation.

The Kansas-Nebraska Act enraged many opponents of slavery because it reopened the territories to slavery and made obsolete the delicate balance previously maintained by the Missouri Compromise. While a few people struck back with violence, others worked for change through the political system.

Changes in Political Parties

The repeal of the Missouri Compromise had a dramatic effect on the political system. Pro-slavery Southern Whigs and antislavery Northern Whigs had long battled for control of their party, but now the party began to fall apart.

During the congressional elections of 1854, many Northern Whigs joined forces with Free-Soilers and a few antislavery Democrats to organize the Republican Party. Their main goal was to stop Southern planters from becoming an aristocracy that controlled the government. Republicans did not agree on whether slavery should be abolished, but they did agree that it had to be kept out of the territories. A large majority of Northern voters shared this view, enabling the Republicans to make great strides in the elections.

At the same time, public anger against the Northern Democrats enabled the American Party—also known as the Know-Nothings—to make gains. The American Party was an anti-Catholic and nativist party. It opposed immigration. Prejudice and fears that immigrants would take away jobs enabled the Know-Nothings to win many seats in Congress and the state legislatures in 1854. The party began to come apart when Know-Nothings from the Upper South split with Know-Nothings from the North over their support for the Kansas-Nebraska Act. Most Americans considered slavery a far more important issue than immigration. Eventually, the Republican Party absorbed the Northern Know-Nothings.

John Brown Becomes a Martyr

Issued in the North in 1863, in the middle of the Civil War, this print depicts John Brown being led to his execution. The symbols in the print show how John Brown had become a martyr to many Northerners.

The flag says *Sic Semper Tyrannis*—Latin for "as always with tyrants" and refers to the idea that tyrants must be killed.

Brown is shown standing upright, unhurt, and uncowed as he is led to his death.

A figure wearing a tri-cornered hat of the American Revolution with the number *76* emblazoned on it looks on with concern.

Brown's jailers look malevolent, with angry snarls and hands on weapons.

A statue of Justice is shown with her arms and scales broken.

According to tradition, Brown kissed an enslaved child as he was led to the scaffold. This enslaved child and its mother are portrayed in a way that would remind viewers of paintings of Jesus and his mother Mary.

Analyzing VISUALS

1. **Identifying Central Issues** How is John Brown portrayed in this image?
2. **Drawing Conclusions** Why do you think that the statue of Justice is depicted as broken?

The 1856 Election The presidential campaign pitted Republican John C. Frémont, Democrat James Buchanan, and former president Millard Fillmore, the Know-Nothing candidate, against each other. Buchanan had not taken a public stand on the Kansas-Nebraska Act and campaigned on the idea that only he could save the Union. When the votes were counted, Buchanan had won.

Sectional Divisions Grow

Just two days after Buchanan's inauguration, the Supreme Court ruled in a landmark case involving slavery, *Dred Scott* v. *Sandford*. **Dred Scott** was a Missouri slave who had been taken north to work in free territory for several years. After he returned with his slaveholder to Missouri, Scott sued to end his slavery, arguing that living in free territory had made him a free man. His case went all the way to the Supreme Court. On March 6, 1857, Chief Justice Roger B. Taney delivered the majority opinion. Taney ruled against Scott because, he claimed, African Americans were not citizens and therefore could not sue in the courts. Taney then addressed the Missouri Compromise's ban on slavery in territory north of Missouri's southern border:

PRIMARY SOURCE

"It is the opinion of the court that the Act of Congress which prohibited a citizen from holding and owning [enslaved persons] in the territory of the United States north of the line therein mentioned is not warranted by the Constitution and is therefore void."

—from *Dred Scott* v. *Sandford*

While Democrats cheered the *Dred Scott* decision, Republicans called it a "willful perversion" of the Constitution. They argued that if Dred Scott could not legally bring suit, then the Supreme Court should have dismissed the case without considering the constitutionality of the Missouri Compromise.

After the *Dred Scott* decision, the conflict in "Bleeding Kansas" intensified. Hoping to end the troubles, Buchanan urged the territory to apply for statehood. The pro-slavery legislature scheduled an election for delegates to a constitutional convention, but antislavery Kansans boycotted it. The resulting constitution, drafted in 1857 in the town of Lecompton, legalized slavery in the territory.

An antislavery majority then voted down the Lecompton constitution in a territory-wide referendum, or popular vote on an issue. Although the Senate approved the vote, Republicans and Northern Democrats in the House blocked the measure, arguing that it ignored the people's will. Finally, in 1858, President Buchanan and Southern leaders in Congress agreed to allow another referendum in Kansas. Again the voters in Kansas overwhelmingly rejected the Lecompton constitution. Not until 1861 did Kansas become a state—a free one.

John Brown's Raid

About a year after the second rejection of the Lecompton constitution, national attention shifted to John Brown, a fervent abolitionist who opposed slavery not with words but with violence. After pro-slavery forces sacked the town of Lawrence in the Kansas Territory, Brown took revenge by abducting and murdering five pro-slavery settlers living near Pottawatomie Creek.

In 1859 Brown decided to seize the federal arsenal at Harpers Ferry, Virginia (today in West Virginia), free and arm the enslaved people of the area, and begin an insurrection, or rebellion, against slaveholders. On the night of October 16, 1859, Brown and 18 followers seized the arsenal. To the terrified night watchman, he announced, "I have possession now of the United States armory, and if the citizens interfere with me I must only burn the town and have blood." A contingent of U.S. Marines, commanded by Colonel Robert E. Lee, rushed from Washington, D.C., to Harpers Ferry. Outnumbered, Brown surrendered, and a Virginia court sentenced him to death. In his last words, Brown, repenting nothing, declared:

PRIMARY SOURCE

"I believe that to have interfered as I have done, as I have always freely admitted I have done in behalf of [God's] despised poor, I did no wrong, but right. Now if it is deemed necessary that I should forfeit my life for the furtherance of the ends of justice and mingle my blood . . . with the blood of millions in this slave country whose rights are disregarded by wicked, cruel and unjust enactments, I say, let it be done!"

—from *The Life and Letters of Captain John Brown*

Many Northerners saw Brown as a martyr in a noble cause. The execution, Henry David Thoreau predicted, would strengthen abolitionism in the North. "He is not old Brown any longer," Thoreau declared, "he is an angel of light." For most Southerners, however, Brown's raid proved that Northerners were actively plotting the murder of slaveholders. "Defend yourselves!" cried Georgia senator Robert Toombs. "The enemy is at your door!"

Reading Check **Evaluating** How did the issue of Kansas statehood reflect the growing division between North and South?

Section 4 REVIEW

Vocabulary

1. **Explain** the significance of: Manifest Destiny, James K. Polk, Treaty of Guadalupe Hidalgo, popular sovereignty, secession, Compromise of 1850, Underground Railroad, Harriet Tubman, Kansas-Nebraska Act, Dred Scott.

Main Ideas

2. **Identifying** How did Britain and the United States divide the Oregon Territory?

3. **Explaining** Why did Kansas become an area of civil war?

4. **Synthesizing** How did the ruling in *Dred Scott* v. *Sandford* increase sectional division?

Critical Thinking

5. **Big Ideas** What new problem did the additional territories cause for the United States?

6. **Categorizing** Use a graphic organizer similar to the one below to list the provisions of the Treaty of Guadalupe Hidalgo.

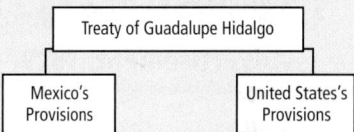

Treaty of Guadalupe Hidalgo

Mexico's Provisions | United States's Provisions

7. **Analyzing Visuals** Study the image of John Brown's martyrdom on page 112. What do you think is the significance of the figure in the tri-cornered hat?

Writing About History

8. **Expository Writing** Suppose that you are a reporter for a Southern or Northern newspaper in the 1850s. Write an article on the reaction to *Uncle Tom's Cabin*.

History ONLINE

Study Central™ To review this section, go to glencoe.com and click on Study Central.

ANALYZING PRIMARY SOURCES

Living Under Slavery

Enslaved persons were not free. That fundamental fact meant they could be sold and separated from their families. They could not legally marry or leave their slaveholder's property without permission. Slaveholders held such power that they controlled access to basic life necessities and could physically punish, even kill, the people they held in slavery without breaking the law.

Study these primary sources and answer the questions that follow.

Autobiography, 1845

"The men and women slaves received, as their monthly allowance of food, eight pounds of pork, or its equivalent in fish, and one bushel of corn meal. Their yearly clothing consisted of two coarse linen shirts, one pair of linen trousers, like the shirts, one jacket, one pair of trousers for winter, made of coarse negro cloth, one pair of stockings, and one pair of shoes; the whole of which could not have cost more than seven dollars. The allowance of the slave children was given to their mothers, or the old women having the care of them. The children unable to work in the field had neither shoes, stockings, jackets, nor trousers, given to them; their clothing consisted of two coarse linen shirts per year. When these failed them, they went naked until the next allowance-day. Children from seven to ten years old, of both sexes, almost naked, might be seen at all seasons of the year.

There were no beds given the slaves, unless one coarse blanket be considered such, and none but the men and women had these. This, however, is not considered a very great privation. They find less difficulty from the want of beds, than from the want of time to sleep; for when their day's work in the field is done, the most of them having their washing, mending, and cooking to do, and having few or none of the ordinary facilities for doing either of these, very many of their sleeping hours are consumed in preparing for the field the coming day; and when this is done, old and young, male and female, married and single, drop down side by side, on one common bed,—the cold, damp floor,—each covering himself or herself with their miserable blankets; and here they sleep till they are summoned to the field by the driver's horn."

—from *Narrative of the Life of Frederick Douglass, an American Slave*

Advertisement, 1829

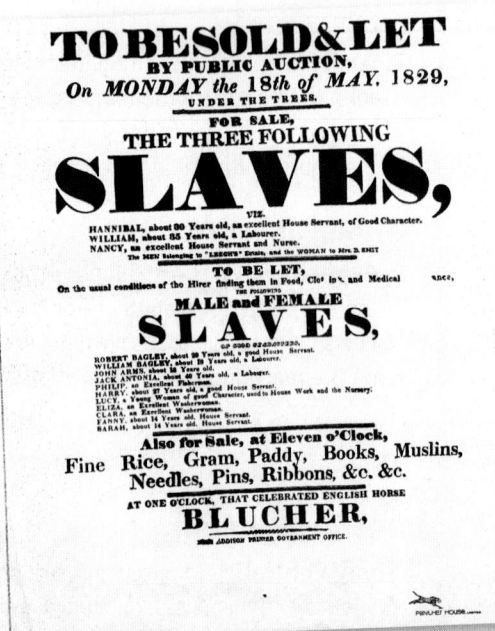

Photograph, 1863

▼ *Gordon escaped from his slaveholder in Mississippi during the Civil War. In this photograph, he shows the scars from a brutal whipping.*

PRIMARY SOURCE 4

Autobiography, 1861

"I once saw two beautiful children playing together. One was a fair white child; the other was her slave, and also her sister. When I saw them embracing each other, and heard their joyous laughter, I turned sadly away from the lovely sight. I foresaw the inevitable blight that would fall on the little slave's heart. I knew how soon her laughter would be changed to sighs. The fair child grew up to be a still fairer woman. From childhood to womanhood her pathway was blooming with flowers, and overarched by a sunny sky. Scarcely one day of her life had been clouded when the sun rose on her happy bridal morning.

How had those years dealt with her slave sister, the little playmate of her childhood? She, also, was very beautiful; but the flowers and sunshine of love were not for her. She drank the cup of sin, and shame, and misery, whereof her persecuted race are compelled to drink."

—from *Incidents in the Life of a Slave Girl*

PRIMARY SOURCE 5

Painting, c. 1852

Slave Auction of African Family

PRIMARY SOURCE 6

Photograph, 1858

▶ *Louisa, an enslaved teenager from St. Louis, Missouri, is shown photographed with her slaveholders' son.*

DBQ   Document-Based Questions

1. **Analyzing** What does Source 1 reveal about the daily lives of enslaved persons?

2. **Interpreting** Examine Sources 2 and 3. What do these images demonstrate about the status and treatment of enslaved persons?

3. **Comparing and Contrasting** Read Source 4. How were the lives of the two girls similar when they were young but different when they became young women?

4. **Analyzing Visuals** Look at Source 5 and examine the people in the painting. Write a paragraph describing what you see going on in this scene.

5. **Speculating** Study Source 6. How do you think Louisa felt about taking care of this young boy? How might slavery complicate personal relationships?

A Growing Nation

Political Developments

- Washington creates the first cabinet; Supreme Court is established.
- The Bill of Rights is added to the Constitution.
- The first political parties develop; the convention system emerges.
- Voting rights are widely extended to free adult men.
- Women begin to seek voting rights.
- United States fights the War of 1812 against Britain.
- Supreme Court asserts power to overturn laws in *Marbury* v. *Madison*.
- The U.S. issues the Monroe Doctrine.

Economic Change

- Canals, railroads, and roads are built linking the nation together.
- Factories open in the North; cotton farming spreads across the South.

Territorial Growth

- The Louisiana Purchase doubles size of the nation.
- United States obtains Florida from Spain.
- The U.S. annexes Texas and divides Oregon with Britain.
- U.S. acquires the Southwest and California after the War with Mexico.

An Emerging National Culture

- Religious revivalism triggers movements to reform education, prisons, asylums, and reduce alcohol consumption.
- New American literature is written.

The U.S. experienced rapid economic growth in the 1800s as new industries opened in the North and cotton farming spread across the South.

135,000 SETS, 270,000 VOLUMES SOLD.

UNCLE TOM'S CABIN

FOR SALE HERE.

AN EDITION FOR THE MILLION, COMPLETE IN 1 Vol., PRICE 37 1-2 CENTS.
" " IN GERMAN, IN 1 Vol., PRICE 50 CENTS.
" " IN 2 Vols., CLOTH, 6 PLATES, PRICE $1.50.
SUPERB ILLUSTRATED EDITION, IN 1 Vol., WITH 153 ENGRAVINGS,
PRICES FROM $2.50 TO $5.00.

The Greatest Book of the Age.

The Dred Scott decision and the publication of Uncle Tom's Cabin fueled the bitter section struggle over slavery.

A Divided Nation

Economic Differences

- North's economy is based on small family farms, trade, and small-scale industrial production.
- South's economy is based on enslaved labor on plantations and farms.

Political Conflict

- Missouri Compromise divides territories into areas where slavery is and is not permitted.
- Jackson threatens to use force to ensure federal authority over South Carolina in the Nullification Crisis.
- Abolitionism emerges in the North; Southern anxiety grows.
- Underground Railway develops to help enslaved people escape North.
- *Uncle Tom's Cabin* builds support for abolition but enrages the South.
- Compromise of 1850 angers both North and South.
- Northerners openly defy the Fugitive Slave Law.
- Kansas-Nebraska Act leads to fighting between proslavery and anti-slavery settlers.
- Dred Scott ruling allows slavery in territories, angering Northerners.
- John Brown's Raid terrifies and angers Southerners.

Reviewing Vocabulary

Directions: Choose the word or words that best complete the sentence.

1. Washington set a precedent when he met regularly with his _____ to review issues within the executive departments.

A secretary

B speculators

C cabinet

D generals

2. The Constitution's "necessary and proper" clause created _____. These powers expanded the potential power of the federal government.

A implied powers

B speculator powers

C enumerated powers

D creditor powers

3. The Tariff of 1816 was a _____, unlike earlier measures.

A promotional tariff

B protective tariff

C revenue tariff

D state tariff

4. Under the guidance of religious leaders, associations known as _____ began to address social problems.

A benevolent societies

B penitentiaries

C asylums

D seminaries

5. To spare Congress from continued fighting over slavery, Senator Lewis Cass proposed the idea of _____, which would allow each territory to decide if it wanted to allow slavery or not.

A martial law

B popular sovereignty

C abolition

D insurrection

Reviewing Main Ideas

Directions: Choose the best answer for each of the following questions.

Section 1 *(pp. 78–83)*

6. One of the most important acts of the first U.S. Congress under the Constitution was to

A elect George Washington as the first president.

B establish a federal banking system.

C pass the Tariff of 1789.

D add a Bill of Rights to the Constitution.

7. The Supreme Court decision in *Marbury* v. *Madison* established the principle of

A judicial review.

B democratic republicanism.

C nullification.

D constitutionality.

Section 2 *(pp. 86–93)*

8. Which of the following cases established the Supreme Court as the final court of appeal?

A *Commonwealth* v. *Hunt*

B *Martin* v. *Hunter's Lessee*

C *McCulloch* v. *Maryland*

D *Gibbons* v. *Ogden*

9. What began the United States's long-term policy of opposing European intervention in Latin America?

A Monroe Doctrine

B Adams-Onís Treaty

C The Missouri Compromise

D The "corrupt bargain"

TEST-TAKING

When a question stem contains a negative, try to reword the sentence or phrase to make it positive.

Need Extra Help?									
If You Missed Questions . . .	1	2	3	4	5	6	7	8	9
Go to Page . . .	78	79	87	100	107	78	83	88	88

Section 3 *(pp. 94–103)*

10. In 1828, passage of which piece of legislation caused South Carolinians to threaten to secede from the Union?

  A the charter for the Second Bank of the United States

  B the Tariff of Abominations

  C the Force Bill

  D the Indian Removal Act

11. At the Seneca Falls Convention in 1848, attendees were shocked when Elizabeth Cady Stanton

  A wore pants to all the meetings.

  B proposed that women seek the right to vote.

  C insisted that African Americans be admitted.

  D announced that she would run for Congress.

Section 4 *(pp. 104–113)*

12. The term "Manifest Destiny" describes the idea that

  A European nations have no right to establish new colonies in the Western Hemisphere.

  B Protestantism should be the official religion of the United States.

  C the United States should control all of North America.

  D Native Americans should be allowed to retain all their original lands.

13. Which of the following best describes the party called the Know-Nothings?

  A proslavery and antigovernment

  B antislavery and pro-immigration

  C pro-Catholic and pro-immigration

  D anti-immigration and anti-Catholic

14. In the *Dred Scott* decision, the Supreme Court determined that it was unconstitutional to

  A allow slavery in the territories.

  B prohibit slavery in the territories.

  C free slaves in the United States.

  D bring enslaved people from one state to another.

Critical Thinking

Directions: Choose the best answers to the following questions.

15. Which of the following was a characteristic of the Era of Good Feelings?

  A a decrease in national pride

  B a one-party political system

  C a decrease in urban populations

  D an increase in state power

Base your answers to questions 16 and 17 on the graph below and your knowledge of Chapter 2.

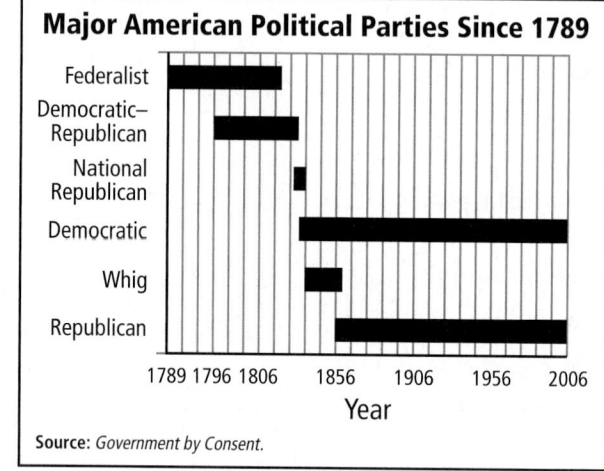

Major American Political Parties Since 1789

Source: *Government by Consent.*

16. What party shown had the shortest life span?

  A Federalist

  B Democratic-Republican

  C Whig

  D National Republican

17. Which party emerged to oppose Andrew Jackson and his policies?

  A Democratic

  B Federalist

  C Whig

  D Republican

Need Extra Help?								
If You Missed Questions . . .	10	11	12	13	14	15	16	17
Go to Page . . .	97	101–102	104	111	112	86	R16	R16

18. Which of the following was an element of the Compromise of 1850?

   A The Fugitive Slave Act was passed.

   B California was admitted as a slave state.

   C Slavery was banned in Washington, D.C.

   D Slavery was permitted in Oregon.

Analyze the cartoon and answer the question that follows. Base your answer on the cartoon and on your knowledge of Chapter 2.

19. What does Jackson appear to be trampling underfoot?

   A Presidential veto orders

   B Declaration of Independence

   C Articles of Confederation

   D United States Constitution

Document-Based Questions

Directions: Analyze the document and answer the short-answer questions that follow the document.

In her 1861 memoir, Harriet Ann Jacobs recounted what life was like under enslavement. In the excerpt below, she describes circumstances experienced by her enslaved maternal grandmother:

> "She was the daughter of a planter . . . who, at his death, left her mother and his three children free, with money to go to St. Augustine. . . . It was during the Revolutionary War; and they were captured. . . . She was a little girl when she was captured and sold to the keeper of a large hotel. . . . But as she grew older she evinced so much intelligence, and was so faithful, that her master and mistress could not help seeing it was for their interest to take care of such a valuable piece of property. She became an indispensable personage in the household, officiating in all capacities, from cook and wet nurse to seamstress. She was much praised for her cooking; . . . In consequence of numerous requests . . . she asked permission of her mistress to bake crackers at night, after all the household work was done; and she obtained leave to do it, provided she would clothe herself and her children from the profits."
>
> —from *Incidents in the Life of a Slave Girl*

20. In what ways was Jacobs's grandmother treated like property and not a person?

21. Why does the grandmother's mistress give her permission to bake crackers at night?

Extended Response

22. Even at the time, many Americans questioned the motives and goals of the war with Mexico, while others felt it was necessary to fulfill America's Manifest Destiny and the needs of the developing nation. Do you think that the war was justified or not? Choose to support or oppose the war with Mexico. Write a persuasive essay that includes an introduction and at least three paragraphs that support your position.

STOP

History ONLINE

For additional test practice, use Self-Check Quizzes—Chapter 2 at glencoe.com.

Need Extra Help?					
If You Missed Questions . . .	18	19	20	21	22
Go to Page . . .	108–109	R18	119	119	R10

The Civil War and Reconstruction

1848–1877

SECTION 1 The Civil War Begins

SECTION 2 Fighting the Civil War

SECTION 3 Reconstruction

1862
- Lincoln presents Emancipation Proclamation

Lincoln 1861–1865

1865
- Lee surrenders to Grant
- Lincoln assassinated

A. Johnson 1865–1869

1866
- Congress passes the Fourteenth Amendment

1861
- Fort Sumter fired upon

1863
- Battle of Gettysburg

1867
- Congress passes the Military Reconstruction Act

U.S. PRESIDENTS

U.S. EVENTS

1860

1863

1866

1869

WORLD EVENTS

1861
- Russian serfs emancipated by Czar Alexander II

1862
- British firm builds the warship *Alabama* for the Confederacy

1864
- Karl Marx founds First International to promote socialism

1866
- Completion of transatlantic cable

1868
- Meiji Restoration begins Japanese modernization

1869
- First ships pass through Suez Canal

MAKING CONNECTIONS

How Do Nations Fight and Recover From War?

The Civil War was in many respects the first modern war. Both sides fielded large armies, and hundreds of thousands of soldiers were killed. Following the war, the nation faced major problems. American leaders had to find a way to reconcile Northerners and Southerners, restore Southern governments, and protect the rights of the formerly enslaved.

- *Why was the North able to defeat the South?*
- *What did the United States do to reconstruct the South?*

FOLDABLES™

Outlining Compromise Efforts Create a Half-Book Foldable that lists the failure of compromise efforts before the Civil War. Complete the chart by showing the series of compromises attempted. Describe each compromise effort on the left-hand column. In the right-hand column, describe the outcome of each compromise.

Compromise Efforts / *Outcomes*

1870
- Fifteenth Amendment ratified

Grant 1869–1877

1875
- "Whiskey Ring" scandal breaks

1877
- Compromise of 1877 ends Reconstruction efforts

Hayes 1877–1881

1872   1875   1878

1871
- Germany is unified; the German Empire proclaimed

1874
- First Impressionist art exhibit opens in Paris

History ONLINE Visit glencoe.com and enter *QuickPass*™ code TAVMT5147c3 for Chapter 3 resources.

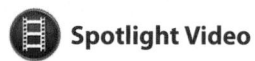
The Civil War Begins

In the end, all attempts at compromise between the North and South over slavery failed. The outcome of the 1860 election triggered the first shots of the long, bloody Civil War.

The Union Dissolves

MAIN Idea The election of Abraham Lincoln led the Southern states to secede from the Union.

HISTORY AND YOU Think of a time when you were unable to compromise over an issue. Read on to learn why Southern states refused to compromise in 1861 and instead decided to secede from the Union, sparking a bloody civil war.

John Brown's raid on Harpers Ferry became a turning point for the South. Many Southerners were terrified and enraged by the idea that Northerners would deliberately try to arm enslaved people and encourage them to rebel. Although Republican leaders quickly denounced Brown's raid, many Southern newspapers and politicians blamed Republicans for the attack. To many Southerners, the key point was that both the Republicans and Brown opposed slavery.

The Election of 1860

In April 1860, with the South still in an uproar, Democrats from across the United States gathered in Charleston, South Carolina, to choose their nominee for president.

The Democrats Split Southern Democrats wanted their party to uphold the *Dred Scott* decision and defend slaveholders' rights in the territories. Northern Democrats, led by Stephen Douglas, preferred to continue supporting popular sovereignty. When Northerners also rebuffed the idea of a federal slave code in the territories, 50 Southern delegates stormed out of the convention. The walkout meant that neither Douglas nor anyone else could muster the two-thirds majority needed to become the party's nominee.

In June 1860, the Democrats reconvened in Baltimore. Again, Southern delegates walked out. The remaining Democrats then chose Stephen Douglas as their candidate. The Southerners who had bolted organized their own convention in Richmond and nominated John C. Breckinridge of Kentucky, the sitting vice president.

Meanwhile, many former Whigs and others were alarmed at the prospect of Southern secession. They created a new party, the Constitutional Union Party, and chose former Tennessee senator John Bell to run for president. The party took no position on issues dividing

The Election of 1860

After the slavery issue split the Democratic Party, the election of 1860 evolved into a four-way race. In the cartoon, the artist implies that Lincoln won because he had the best bat, which is labeled "equal rights and free territories," while the other candidates were for compromise or the extension of slavery.

Stephen Douglas holds a bat labeled "Non-intervention" and blames Lincoln's rail for his loss.

John Breckinridge's bat is labeled "slavery extension" and his belt says Disunion Club.

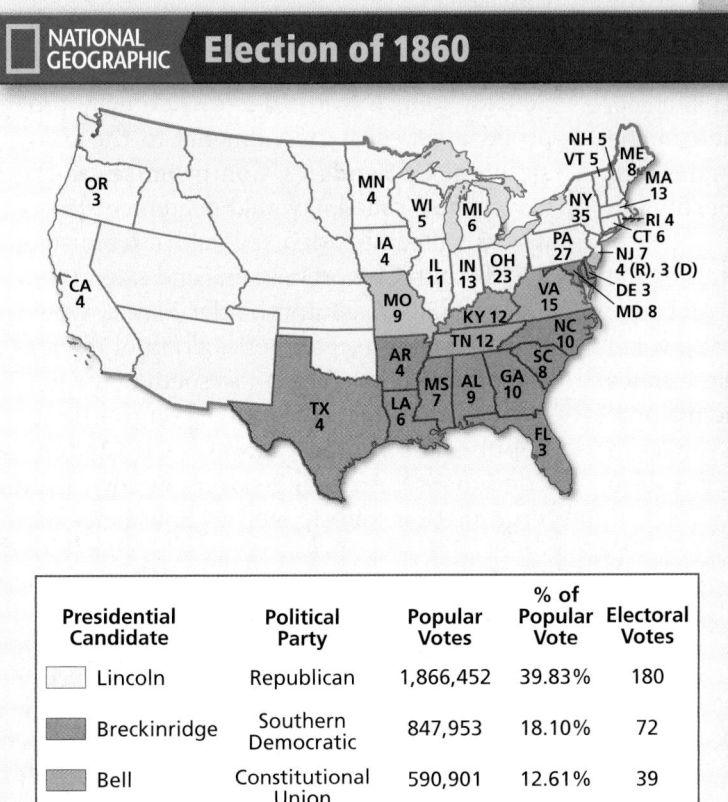

NATIONAL GEOGRAPHIC Election of 1860

Presidential Candidate	Political Party	Popular Votes	% of Popular Vote	Electoral Votes
Lincoln	Republican	1,866,452	39.83%	180
Breckinridge	Southern Democratic	847,953	18.10%	72
Bell	Constitutional Union	590,901	12.61%	39
Douglas	Democratic	1,380,202	29.46%	12

John Bell's bat is labeled "Fusion" and his belt says Union Club.

Abraham Lincoln, the winner, stands on home base holding a rail labeled "Equal Rights and Free Territory."

Analyzing VISUALS   DBQ

1. **Interpreting** How does the map show that Lincoln was a sectional candidate?
2. **Identifying Points of View** Do you think that the artist was sympathetic to abolition or not? Explain.

North and South. Their purpose, they said, was to uphold the Constitution and the Union.

Lincoln Is Elected The Republicans, realizing they stood no chance in the South, needed a candidate who could sweep most of the North. The most prominent Republican at the time was Senator William Seward from New York, but many Republicans did not think Seward had a wide enough appeal. Instead, they nominated Abraham Lincoln, who had gained a national reputation during his debates

with Douglas. Although he was not an abolitionist, Lincoln believed that slavery was morally wrong, and he opposed its spread into the western territories.

During the campaign the Republicans remained true to their free-soil principles, but they reaffirmed the right of the Southern states to preserve slavery within their borders. They also supported higher tariffs to protect manufacturers and workers, a new homestead law for settlers in the West, and federal funds for a transcontinental railroad.

The Republican proposals angered many Southerners, but with the Democrats divided, Lincoln won the election by winning the electoral votes of all the free states except New Jersey, whose votes he split with Douglas.

Secession Begins Many Southerners viewed Lincoln's election as a threat to their society and culture, even their lives. They saw no choice but to secede. The dissolution of the Union began with South Carolina. Shortly after Lincoln's election, the state legislature called for a convention. On December 20, 1860, amid marching bands, fireworks, and militia drills, the convention voted unanimously to repeal the state's ratification of the Constitution and dissolve its ties to the Union.

By February 1, 1861, six more states in the Lower South—Mississippi, Florida, Alabama, Georgia, Louisiana, and Texas—had also voted to secede. Although a minority in these states did not want to leave the Union, the majority of Southerners viewed secession as similar to the American Revolution—a necessary course of action to uphold people's rights.

Compromise Fails

Although Lincoln was elected president in November 1860, he would not be inaugurated until the following March. The Union's initial response to secession was the responsibility of President Buchanan. Declaring that the government had no authority to forcibly preserve the Union, Buchanan urged Congress to be conciliatory.

Crittenden's Compromise In December, Senator John J. Crittenden of Kentucky proposed a series of amendments to the Constitution. **Crittenden's Compromise,** as the newspapers called it, would guarantee slavery where it already existed. It would also reinstate the Missouri Compromise line and extend it all the way to the California border. Slavery would be prohibited in all territories north of the line and protected in all territories south of the line.

At Lincoln's request, congressional Republicans voted against Crittenden's Compromise. Accepting slavery in any of the territories, Lincoln argued, "acknowledges that

Steps to Civil War, 1846–1860

▲ David Wilmot

1846
Wilmot Proviso proposing to ban slavery in Mexican cession enrages Southerners

1848
Free-Soil Party is founded by Northern antislavery Whigs, Democrats, and members of the Liberty Party

1850
Compromise of 1850 allows California to enter Union as a free state, giving free states a Senate majority, but the new Fugitive Slave law enrages Northerners

1846 **1848** **1850** **1852**

1847
Vice President George Dallas proposes popular sovereignty; Democrat Lewis Cass popularizes the idea, angering Northern antislavery Democrats

1849
California Gold Rush brings flood of settlers; California applies for statehood

1852
Uncle Tom's Cabin is published

slavery has equal rights with liberty, and surrenders all we have contended for."

Founding the Confederacy On February 8, 1861, delegates from the seceding states met in Montgomery, Alabama, where they declared themselves to be a new nation—the Confederate States of America. They drafted a constitution similar to the U.S. Constitution but with major changes. The Confederate Constitution acknowledged the independence of each state, guaranteed slavery in Confederate territory, banned tariffs, and limited the president to a single six-year term.

The convention delegates chose former Mississippi senator **Jefferson Davis** to be president. In his inaugural address, Davis declared, "The time for compromise has now passed." He then called on the remaining Southern states to join the **Confederacy.**

The Civil War Begins

In his inaugural address on March 4, 1861, President Lincoln again promised not to interfere with slavery where it existed but insisted that "the Union of these States is perpetual." Lincoln encouraged reconciliation:

PRIMARY SOURCE

"In your hands, my dissatisfied countrymen, and not in mine is the momentous issue of civil war. The government will not assail you. You can have no conflict, without yourselves being the aggressors. . . . We must not be enemies. Though passion may have strained, it must not break our bonds of affection."

—from Lincoln's First Inaugural Address

Fort Sumter Falls In April Lincoln announced that he intended to resupply **Fort Sumter** in Charleston Harbor, one of the few federal military bases that Southerners had not already seized. Confederate President Jefferson Davis now faced a problem. To tolerate U.S. troops in the South's most vital Atlantic harbor seemed unacceptable for a sovereign nation. However, firing on the supply ship would undoubtedly provoke war. Jefferson decided to demand the surrender of Fort Sumter before the supply ship arrived.

1854
Kansas-Nebraska Act crafted by Stephen Douglas repeals Missouri Compromise; Republican Party is founded

1856
Charles Sumner is caned in the Senate

1858
Abraham Lincoln wins national attention during Lincoln-Douglas debates

1859
John Brown raids Harpers Ferry

1860
Lincoln is elected; secession begins

1854   **1856**   **1858**   **1860**

1856
Border ruffians attack antislavery settlers in Lawrence, Kansas; John Brown leads attack on pro-slavery settlers in Pottawatomie Creek, Kansas

1857
Dred Scott decision allowing slavery in all federal territories enrages Northerners

▲ *Antislavery settlers in Kansas*

Analyzing TIME LINES

1. **Specifying** How many years elapsed between the Compromise of 1850 and the beginning of the Civil War?
2. **Identifying** Which came first—the *Dred Scott* decision or the Wilmot Proviso?

The fort's commander, U.S. Army Major Robert Anderson, refused. Confederate forces then bombarded Fort Sumter for 33 hours on April 12 and 13, until Anderson and his exhausted men gave up.

The Upper South Secedes After the fall of Fort Sumter, President Lincoln called for 75,000 volunteers to serve in the military for 90 days. This created a crisis in the Upper South. Many people in those states did not want to secede, but they were not willing to take up arms against fellow Southerners. Between April 17 and June 8, 1861, four more states chose to leave the Union—Virginia, Arkansas, North Carolina, and Tennessee. The Confederate Congress then established Richmond, Virginia, as the capital.

Holding the Border States With the Upper South gone, Lincoln could not afford to lose the slaveholding border states as well. Delaware seemed safe, but Lincoln worried about Kentucky, Missouri, and particularly Maryland. Virginia's secession had placed a Confederate state across the Potomac River from the nation's capital. If Maryland joined the South, Washington, D.C., would be surrounded by Confederate territory. To prevent Maryland's secession, Lincoln imposed **martial law**—military rule—in Baltimore, where angry mobs had already attacked federal troops. Fearing that Confederate agents in Washington, D.C., were plotting against the Union government, Lincoln suspended the right of habeas corpus, which protects citizens from illegal imprisonment without evidence. Dozens of suspected secessionist leaders were imprisoned. Chief Justice Robert Taney ruled against the suspension, but Lincoln ignored this in the face of impending war.

Kentucky initially declared neutrality in the conflict, but when Confederate troops occupied part of Kentucky, the state declared war on the Confederacy, and Lincoln sent troops to help. In Missouri, despite strong public support for the Confederacy, the state convention voted to stay in the Union. Federal troops then ended fights between the pro-Union government and secessionists.

✓ **Reading Check** **Explaining** Why did Southern Democrats walk out of the Democratic Convention?

The Opposing Sides

MAIN Idea The North and South each had distinct advantages and disadvantages at the beginning of the Civil War.

HISTORY AND YOU Do you believe limiting civil liberties during wartime is justified? Read on to learn how President Lincoln decided to suspend writs of habeas corpus during the Civil War.

On the same day that he learned his home state of Virginia had voted to secede from the Union, **Robert E. Lee**—one of the best senior officers in the United States Army—received an offer from General Winfield Scott to command Union troops. Although Lee had spoken against secession and considered slavery "a moral and political evil," he refused to fight against the South. Instead, he offered his services to the Confederacy.

Lee was one of hundreds of military officers who resigned to join the Confederacy. In 1860 seven of the nation's eight military colleges were in the South. These colleges provided the region with a large number of trained officers to quickly organize an effective fighting force.

Just as the South had a strong military tradition, the North had a strong naval tradition. More than three-quarters of the Navy's officers came from the North, and the crews of American merchant ships were almost entirely from the North. They provided a large pool of trained sailors for the Union navy as it expanded.

The Opposing Economies

Although the South had many experienced officers to lead its troops in battle, the North had several economic advantages. In 1860 the population of the North was about 22 million, while the South had about 9 million people. The North's larger population gave it a great advantage in raising an army and in supporting the war effort.

Industry The North's industries also gave the region an important economic advantage over the South. In 1860 almost 90 percent of the nation's factories were located in the Northern states. The North could provide its troops with ammunition and other supplies more easily. In addition, the South had only half as many miles of railroad track as the North and had only one line—from Memphis

The Opposing Sides

▲ Confederate soldiers of the 3rd Georgia Infantry (above) fought under Lee's command during the Peninsula campaign. The Confederacy had fewer soldiers but many of the nation's best officers.

▲ Men of the 110th Pennsylvania Infantry Regiment at Falmouth, Virginia, April 1863. Union troops were generally better equipped than Confederate forces.

Analyzing VISUALS

1. **Interpreting** Based on the graph, what were the North's greatest advantages over the South?

2. **Assessing** Which of the North's advantages do you think were most important in winning the war? Why?

Resources of the Union and of the Confederacy

Union / Confederacy

- Population: 71% / 29%
- Manufactured goods: 92% / 8%
- Exports: 56% / 44%
- Merchant ships: 90% / 10%
- Miles of railroad track: 72% / 28%
- Number of farms: 67% / 33%
- Iron production: 94% / 6%
- Banking capital: 82% / 18%

Source: *Historical Statistics of the United States.*

to Chattanooga—connecting the western states of the Confederacy to the east. This made it much easier for Northern troops to disrupt the Southern rail system and prevent the movement of supplies and troops.

Financing the War The Union also controlled the national treasury and could expect continued revenue from tariffs. Many Northern banks also held large reserves of cash, which they lent the government by purchasing bonds.

In order to make more money available for emergency use, Congress also passed the Legal Tender Act, creating a national currency and allowing the government to issue paper money. The paper money came to be known as greenbacks, because of its color.

In contrast to the Union, the Confederacy's financial situation was poor, and it became worse over time. Most Southern planters were in debt and unable to buy bonds. Southern banks were small and had few cash reserves; as a result, they could not buy many bonds either. The best hope for the South to raise money was by taxing trade. Then, shortly after the war began, the Union Navy blockaded Southern ports, which reduced trade and, as a result, tax revenues. The Confederacy had to resort to direct taxation of its people, but many Southerners refused to pay.

Lacking **sufficient** money from taxes or bonds, the Confederacy was forced to print paper money to pay its bills. This caused rapid inflation in the South, and Confederate paper money eventually became almost worthless. By the end of the war, the South had experienced 9,000 percent inflation, compared to only 80 percent in the North.

The Political Situation

Although many Republicans wanted to end slavery, Lincoln wanted to preserve the Union, even if it meant allowing slavery to continue. The president also had to contend with the Democrats. A faction known as the War Democrats supported a war to save the Union but opposed ending slavery. Peace Democrats wanted to negotiate instead of fighting a war.

One major disagreement between Republicans and Democrats concerned conscription—or forcing people through a draft into military service. In 1862, Congress passed a militia law requiring states to use conscription if they could not recruit enough volunteers, but many Democrats opposed it.

Criticism also greeted President Lincoln's decision to suspend writs of **habeas corpus.** A writ of habeas corpus is a court order that requires the government to charge an imprisoned person with a crime or let the person go free. When writs of habeas corpus are suspended, a person can be imprisoned indefinitely without trial. In this case, President Lincoln suspended the writ for anyone who openly supported the rebels or encouraged others to resist the militia draft. "Must I shoot a simple-minded soldier boy who deserts," the president asked, "while I must not touch a hair of a wily agitator who induces him to desert?

Although the South had no organized opposition party, Confederate president Jefferson Davis also faced political problems. The Confederate constitution protected states' rights and limited the central government's power. This interfered with Davis's ability to conduct the war. Some Southern leaders opposed Davis when he supported conscription and established martial law early in 1862. They also opposed the suspension of writs of habeas corpus, which the South, like the North, had introduced.

TECHNOLOGY & HISTORY

Civil War Technology Military conflict often leads to the use of new technologies. The Civil War was no exception. New weapons, ships and means of communication greatly changed the nature of warfare.

▲ **Conoidal Bullets**

These new bullets made gunfire more accurate at greater ranges and increased the number of casualties.

▲ **Telegraph**

Invented before the war, the telegraph let generals learn the results of battles almost immediately, and change their strategy and give new orders quickly.

▲ **Balloons**

The Civil War marked the first time aerial reconnaissance was used in war. Both sides used balloons to observe enemy troops.

◄ **Ironclads**

To operate on enemy rivers and coast lines guarded by shore-based cannon, both sides built armor-plated steamships. Ironclads marked the beginning of the shift from wooden ships to steel ships.

Analyzing VISUALS

1. **Explaining** How did balloons change warfare?
2. **Describing** How did the telegraph help both sides fight the war?

The outbreak of the Civil War put the major governments of Europe in a difficult situation. The Union government did not want the Europeans interfering in the war, but Southern leaders wanted them to recognize the Confederacy and provide it with military aid. Southern leaders knew that European textile factories depended on Southern cotton. To pressure the British and French, many Southern planters agreed to stop selling their cotton in these markets until the Europeans recognized the Confederacy. Despite these efforts, both countries chose not to go to war against the United States.

The First Modern War

The North and South were about to embark on what was, in many respects, the first modern war. Unlike earlier European wars, the Civil War involved huge armies that consisted mostly of civilian volunteers and required vast amounts of supplies.

Military Technology By the 1850s, French and American inventors had developed an inexpensive conoidal—or cone-shaped—bullet that was accurate at much greater distances. At the same time, instead of standing in a line, troops defending positions began to use trenches and barricades to protect themselves. This resulted in much higher casualties. **Attrition**—the wearing down of one side by the other through exhaustion of soldiers and resources—also played a critical role as the war dragged on.

The South's Strategy Early in the war, Jefferson Davis imagined a struggle similar to the American war for independence. Southern generals would pick their battles carefully, attacking and retreating when necessary to avoid heavy losses. By waging a defensive war of attrition, Davis believed the South could force the Union to spend its resources until it became tired of the war and agreed to negotiate. Although this strategy made sense, Davis felt great pressure to strike for a quick victory. Many Southerners believed that their military traditions made them superior fighters. In the war, Southern troops went on the offensive in eight battles, suffering 20,000 more casualties than the Union by charging enemy lines. These were heavy losses the South could not afford.

The Union's Anaconda Plan The general in chief of the United States, Winfield Scott, suggested that the Union blockade Confederate ports and send gunboats down the Mississippi River to divide the Confederacy in two. The South, thus separated, would gradually run out of resources and surrender. Many Northerners rejected the strategy, which they called the **Anaconda Plan,** after a snake that slowly strangles its prey to death. They thought it was too slow and indirect for certain victory. Lincoln eventually agreed to **implement** Scott's suggestions and imposed a blockade of Southern ports. He and other Union leaders realized that only a long war that focused on destroying the South's armies had any chance of success.

Reading Check **Comparing** In what areas did the opposing sides have advantages and disadvantages?

Section 1 REVIEW

Vocabulary

1. **Explain** the significance of: Crittenden's Compromise, Jefferson Davis, Confederacy, Fort Sumter, martial law, Robert E. Lee, habeas corpus, attrition, Anaconda Plan.

Main Ideas

2. **Identifying** Where and under what circumstances did the American Civil War begin?

3. **Explaining** Why did the South resort to using paper money during the war?

Critical Thinking

4. **Big Ideas** How did the Southerners' belief in states' rights hamper the Confederate government during the war?

5. **Organizing** Using a graphic organizer similar to the one below, list the military innovations of the Civil War era.

Military Innovations

6. **Analyzing Visuals** Examine the conoidal bullets shown on page 128. How did conoidal bullets affect the war effort? What other innovations made the Civil War the first "modern" war?

Writing About History

7. **Persuasive Writing** Suppose you are living in one of the border states at the beginning of the Civil War. Write a letter to a relative explaining why you are planning to join either the Union or Confederate army.

History ONLINE
Study Central™ To review this section, go to glencoe.com and click on Study Central.

Fighting the Civil War

Guide to Reading

Big Ideas
Individual Action In the final year of the war, Grant refused to let up the pressure the Union forces were putting on Lee's weary troops.

Content Vocabulary
• blockade runner *(p. 130)*
• siege *(p. 134)*
• mandate *(p. 137)*

Academic Vocabulary
• crucial *(p. 133)*
• guarantee *(p. 137)*

People and Events to Identify
• "Stonewall" Jackson *(p. 130)*
• Ulysses S. Grant *(p. 131)*
• Battle of Antietam *(p. 133)*
• Emancipation Proclamation *(p. 133)*
• Gettysburg *(p. 134)*
• William Tecumseh Sherman *(p. 136)*
• Thirteenth Amendment *(p. 137)*

Reading Strategy
Categorizing Complete a graphic organizer similar to the one below by filling in the results of each battle listed.

Battle	Results
First Battle of Bull Run	
Battle of Shiloh	
Seven Days' Battle	
Second Battle of Bull Run	
Antietam	

Despite early losses, with the help of key victories at Vicksburg and Gettysburg, the North defeated the South after four long years of fighting. Debate over slavery continued until President Lincoln decided that the time was right for emancipation.

The Early Stages

MAIN Idea With Union casualties rising, President Lincoln issued the Emancipation Proclamation.

HISTORY AND YOU Do you know someone who experienced rationing during World War II? Read on to learn how the war affected daily life.

Soon after the Civil War began, President Lincoln approved an assault on Confederate troops gathered near Manassas Junction, Virginia, only 25 miles (40 km) south of Washington, D.C. The First Battle of Bull Run, as it came to be called, started well for the Union as it forced Confederate troops to retreat. Then the tide turned when reinforcements under the command of **Thomas J. "Stonewall" Jackson** helped the Confederates defeat the Union forces. This outcome made it clear that the North would need a large, well-trained army to prevail against the South.

Lincoln had originally called for 75,000 men to serve for three months. The day after Bull Run, he signed a bill for the enlistment of 500,000 men for three years. The North initially tried to encourage voluntary enlistment by offering a bounty—a sum of money given as a bonus—to individuals who promised three years of military service. Eventually both the Union and the Confederacy instituted the draft.

The Naval War

While the Union and Confederacy mobilized their armies, President Lincoln proclaimed a blockade of all Confederate ports in an effort to cut Confederate trade with the world. Although the blockade became increasingly effective as the war dragged on, Union vessels were thinly spread and found it difficult to stop all the **blockade runners**—small, fast vessels the South used to smuggle goods past the blockade. The South could ship at least some of its cotton to Europe in exchange for shoes, rifles, and other supplies.

As part of its effort to close Southern ports, the Union navy decided to seize New Orleans—the South's largest city and a center of the cotton trade. In April 1862, forty-two warships under the command of Admiral David G. Farragut fought their way up the Mississippi to New Orleans and unloaded some 15,000 Union troops. Six days later, the troops took control of the city.

	Union states
	Confederate states
	Union blockade
	Union forces
	Confederate forces
	Union victory
	Confederate victory
	Inconclusive battle

▲ The Battle of Shiloh resulted in enormous casualties.

N.Y.

Pa.

Ohio

Gettysburg July 1–3, 1863

Antietam Sept. 17, 1862

N.J.

Bull Run July 21, 1861, Aug. 29–30, 1862

Md. Del.

Washington, D.C.

Fredericksburg Dec. 13, 1862

70°W

40°N

W.Va. (admitted to Union, 1863)

Chancellorsville May 1–5, 1863

Richmond

Seven Days June 25–July 1, 1862

Va.

Hampton Roads March 8–9, 1862

Ohio R.

Mo.

Ill.

Ind.

Louisville

Ky.

Perryville Oct. 8, 1862

Roanoke Island Feb. 8, 1862

35°N

Kans.

Wilson's Creek Aug. 10, 1861

Paducah

Ft. Donelson Feb. 16, 1862

Ft. Henry Feb. 6, 1862

Nashville

Tenn.

Murfreesboro Dec. 31, 1862–Jan. 2, 1863

N.C.

Cape Hatteras Aug. 27–28, 1862

Arkansas R.

Pea Ridge March 7–8, 1862

Shiloh April 6–7, 1862

Chattanooga Nov. 23–25, 1863

ATLANTIC OCEAN

Indian Territory

Memphis

Corinth

Chickamauga Sept. 19–20, 1863

S.C.

Ark.

Red R.

Corinth Oct. 3–4, 1862

Birmingham

Atlanta

Ft. Sumter April 12–14, 1861

0   200 kilometers

Mansfield (Sabine Cross Roads) April 8, 1864

Miss.

Ala.

Ga.

Ft. Pulaski April 10–11, 1862

Port Royal Nov. 7, 1861

0   200 miles

Albers Equal-Area projection

Tex.

Vicksburg May 19–July 4, 1863

Jackson

Natchez

30°N

Sabine R.

Sabine Pass Sept. 24–25, 1862

La.

Baton Rouge

Mobile

Fla.

Galveston Oct. 4, 1862

Port Hudson May 8–July 9, 1863

New Orleans April 24–25, 1862

80°W

75°W

New Orleans

95°W

90°W

85°W

Analyzing GEOGRAPHY

1. **Location** Name four battles that occurred along the eastern seaboard.

2. **Movement** What purpose did the North have in fighting so many battles along the coasts?

The War in the West

In February 1862, as Farragut prepared for his attack on New Orleans, Union general **Ulysses S. Grant** began a campaign to seize control of the Cumberland and Tennessee Rivers. Control of these rivers would cut Tennessee in two and provide the Union with a river route deep into Confederate territory.

All of Kentucky and most of western Tennessee fell into Union hands. Grant next headed up the Tennessee River to attack

Corinth, Mississippi. Seizing Corinth would cut the Confederacy's only rail line connecting Mississippi and western Tennessee to the east. Early on April 6, 1862, Confederate forces launched a surprise attack on Grant's troops, near a small church named Shiloh. The Union won the Battle of Shiloh the following day, but both sides paid an enormous cost. Twenty thousand troops had been killed or wounded. When newspapers demanded Grant be fired because of the high casualties, Lincoln refused, saying, "I can't spare this man; he fights."

Turning Point

▲ President Lincoln meets General George McClellan (left center, facing Lincoln) after the Battle of Antietam.

◄ With their backs to Antietam Creek, Union troops under the command of General McClellan attack Confederate positions, September 17, 1862.

The Battle of Antietam and the Emancipation Proclamation

The Battle of Antietam marked an important turning point in the war. The Union's victory kept Britain from recognizing the Confederacy as a separate nation. If Britain had taken this action, the balance in the struggle might have tipped in favor of the Confederacy. Also, the victory at Antietam and the terribly high casualties brought President Lincoln to the decision that the time had come to end slavery in the South by issuing the Emancipation Proclamation. The Proclamation was the first step toward finally outlawing slavery throughout the United States.

ANALYZING HISTORY How did emancipation change the war? Write a brief essay explaining your opinion.

▲ Lincoln reads the Emancipation Proclamation to members of his cabinet. Left of Lincoln are Secretary of War Edwin M. Stanton and Secretary of the Treasury Salmon P. Chase. In front of the table sits Secretary of State William Seward.

For the text of the Emancipation Proclamation, see page R49 in **Documents in American History.**

The War in the East

While Grant fought in the West, Union General George B. McClellan's forces set out to capture Richmond, Virginia, the Confederate capital. In late June 1862, Confederate General Robert E. Lee began a series of attacks on McClellan's forces that became known as the Seven Days' Battle. Lee's attacks forced the Union troops to retreat. Together the two sides suffered over 30,000 casualties.

As McClellan's forces withdrew, Lee marched toward Union forces defending Washington. The maneuver led to another battle at Bull Run.

The South again forced the North to retreat, leaving the Confederates only 20 miles (32 km) from Washington, D.C. Soon after, Lee's forces invaded Maryland.

Both Lee and Jefferson Davis believed that an invasion would convince the North to accept the South's independence. They also thought that a victory on Northern soil might help the South win recognition from the British and help the Peace Democrats gain control of Congress in the upcoming elections. Lee could also feed his troops from Northern farms and draw Union troops out of Virginia during harvest season.

On September 17, 1862, Lee's forces met Union troops under the command of General McClellan at Antietam (an·TEE·tuhm) Creek. The fight was the bloodiest one-day battle in American history, ending with over 6,000 men killed and another 16,000 wounded. McClellan did not break Lee's lines, but he inflicted so many casualties that Lee decided to retreat to Virginia.

The **Battle of Antietam** was a **crucial** victory for the Union. The British government had been ready to intervene in the war as a mediator if Lee's invasion had succeeded. Britain also had begun making plans to recognize the Confederacy should the North reject mediation. Now the British decided to wait and see how the war progressed. With this decision, the South lost its best chance at gaining international recognition and support. The South's defeat at Antietam had an even more important political impact in the United States. It convinced Lincoln that the time had come to end slavery in the South.

Proclaiming Emancipation

Most Democrats opposed any move to end slavery, while Republicans were divided on the issue. With Northern casualties rising, however, many Northerners began to agree that slavery had to end, in part to punish the South and in part to make the soldiers' sacrifices worthwhile. On September 22, 1862, encouraged by the Union victory at Antietam, Lincoln publicly announced that he would issue the **Emancipation Proclamation**—a decree freeing all enslaved persons in states still in rebellion after January 1, 1863.

Because the Proclamation freed enslaved African Americans only in states at war with the Union, it did not address slavery in the border states. Short of a constitutional amendment, Lincoln could not end slavery in the border states, nor did he want to endanger their loyalty. The Proclamation, by its very existence, transformed the conflict over preserving the Union into a war of liberation.

Life During the Civil War

As the war intensified, the economies of the North and South went in different directions. By the end of 1862, the South's economy had begun to suffer greatly. The collapse of its transportation system and the presence of Union troops in several important agricultural regions led to severe food shortages in the winter of 1862. In several communities, food shortages led to riots. Hearing of such hardships, many Confederate soldiers deserted to return home to help their families.

In contrast, the North actually experienced an economic boom because of the war. With its large, well-established banking industry, the North raised money for the war more easily than the South. Its growing industries also supplied Union troops with clothes, munitions, and other necessities.

Daily Life Both Union and Confederate soldiers endured a hard life with few comforts. They faced the constant threat of disease and extreme medical procedures if injured in battle. Life for prisoners of war was just as difficult, especially in Southern prisons that faced food shortages.

Innovations in agriculture helped minimize the loss of labor as men left to fight. Greater use of mechanical reapers and mowers made farming possible with fewer workers, many of whom were women. Women also filled labor shortages in various industries, particularly in clothing and shoemaking factories.

African Americans While the war brought hardship to many Americans, it offered new opportunities for African Americans. The Emancipation Proclamation officially permitted African Americans to enlist in the Union army and navy. Almost immediately, thousands of African Americans rushed to join the military.

Women Women helped in the war effort at home by managing family farms and businesses. Perhaps their most important contribution to the Civil War was in serving as nurses to the wounded. One of the most prominent war nurses was Clara Barton, who left her job in a Washington patent office to aid soldiers on the battlefield. The Civil War was a turning point for the American nursing profession. The courage shown by women helped break down the belief that women were emotionally weaker than men.

History ONLINE Student Web Activity Visit glencoe.com and complete the activity on Civil War letters.

✓ Reading Check **Analyzing** Why do you think African Americans were willing to volunteer to fight?

The Turning Point

MAIN Idea Key victories at Vicksburg and Gettysburg helped the North defeat the South.

HISTORY AND YOU Recall a time when you faced a situation you had been dreading. Did the outcome surprise you? Read on to learn about Confederate General Robert E. Lee's surrender to Ulysses S. Grant.

As 1863 began, there was no end to the war in sight. More than two years of battle lay ahead for Americans, and the casualties would continue to rise steeply. Still, 1863 marked the turning point of the war. Three major Union victories put the Confederacy on the defensive and set the stage for its surrender.

Vicksburg

Gaining control of the Mississippi River was a vital element of the Union strategy for winning the Civil War. If the Union could capture Vicksburg, Mississippi, the last major Confederate stronghold on the river, then the North could cut the South in two.

In May 1863, Grant launched two assaults on Vicksburg, but the city's defenders repulsed both attacks and inflicted high casualties. Grant decided to put the city under **siege**—to cut off its food and supplies and bombard it until its defenders gave up. On July 4, 1863, with his troops starving, the Confederate commander at Vicksburg surrendered.

Gettysburg

Meanwhile, in Virginia, Lee had been able to defeat Union forces at Fredericksburg and Chancellorsville. Emboldened by these victories, Lee decided in June 1863 to launch another invasion of the North. At the end of June, as Lee's army foraged in the Pennsylvania countryside, some of his troops headed into **Gettysburg,** hoping to seize a supply of shoes. When they arrived near the town, they discovered two brigades of Union cavalry. On July 1,

PRIMARY SOURCE
The Gettysburg Address

The bloody victory at Gettysburg was a major turning point in the Civil War. It kept Britain out of the war, inflicted serious losses on the Confederacy and helped restore Union morale. In November 1863 Lincoln went to Gettysburg to dedicate part of the battlefield as a cemetery. His speech, the Gettysburg Address, became one of the best-known orations in American history.

▼ On July 3, 1863, the Confederate forces launched an attack known later as Pickett's Charge. Charging up Cemetery Ridge into withering cannon fire, the Confederates suffered nearly 7,000 casualties in less than two hours. Soon after the attack failed, General Lee ordered Southern forces to withdraw.

1863, as Confederates pushed the Union troops out of the town, the main forces of both armies hurried to the scene of the fighting.

On July 2, Lee attacked, but the Union troops held their ground. The following day, Lee ordered nearly 15,000 men under the command of General George E. Pickett and General A.P. Hill to make a massive assault. The attack, known as Pickett's Charge, caused 7,000 casualties in less than half an hour, but failed to break the Union lines. "It is all my fault," said Lee. "It is I who have lost this fight." Lee's troops retreated to Virginia. At Gettysburg, the Union suffered 23,000 casualties, the South an estimated 28,000, more than one-third of Lee's entire force.

The disaster at Gettysburg proved to be the turning point of the war in the East. The Union's victory strengthened the Republicans politically and ensured once again that the British would not recognize the Confederacy. For the remainder of the war, Lee's forces remained on the defensive, slowly giving ground to the advancing Union army.

Grant Secures Tennessee

After the Union's major victories at Vicksburg and Gettysburg, fierce fighting erupted in Tennessee near Chattanooga. Chattanooga was a vital railroad junction. Both sides knew that if the Union forces captured Chattanooga, they would control a major railroad running south to Atlanta. Following several battles, Union forces under the command of General Grant succeeded in scattering the Confederate soldiers who blocked the way to the city.

By the spring of 1864, Grant's capture of Vicksburg had given the Union control of the Mississippi River, while his victory at Chattanooga had secured eastern Tennessee and cleared the way for an invasion of Georgia. Lincoln rewarded Grant by appointing him general in chief of the Union forces and promoting him to lieutenant general, a rank no one had held since George Washington. The president had finally found a general he trusted to win the war.

▲ More than 50,000 Americans were killed or wounded during the Battle of Gettysburg.

PRIMARY SOURCE

"Four score and seven years ago our fathers brought forth on this continent a new nation, conceived in Liberty, and dedicated to the proposition that all men are created equal.

Now we are engaged in a great civil war, testing whether that nation, or any nation so conceived and so dedicated, can long endure. We are met on a great battle-field of that war. We have come to dedicate a portion of that field, as a final resting place for those who here gave their lives that that nation might live. It is altogether fitting and proper that we should do this.

But, in a larger sense, we cannot dedicate—we cannot consecrate—we cannot hallow—this ground. The brave men, living and dead, who struggled here, have consecrated it, far above our poor power to add or detract. The world will little note, nor long remember what we say here, but it can never forget what they did here. It is for us the living, rather, to be dedicated here to the unfinished work which they who fought here have thus far so nobly advanced. It is rather for us to be here dedicated to the great task remaining before us—that from these honored dead we take increased devotion to that cause for which they gave the last full measure of devotion—that we here highly resolve that these dead shall not have died in vain—that this nation, under God, shall have a new birth of freedom—and that government of the people, by the people, for the people, shall not perish from the earth."

—The Gettysburg Address, November 19, 1863

DBQ Document-Based Questions

1. **Specifying** To what event is Lincoln referring that occurred "fourscore and seven years ago"?

2. **Identifying Central Issues** What does Lincoln say is the main purpose of the Civil War and the reason for the sacrifices at Gettysburg?

▲ Robert E. Lee surrenders to General Grant at Appomattox Courthouse on April 9, 1865.

Casualties of the Civil War

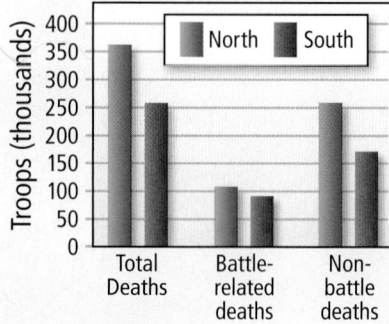

Troops (thousands)

■ North ■ South

| | Total Deaths | Battle-related deaths | Non-battle deaths |

Source: *For the Common Defense.*

American War Deaths*

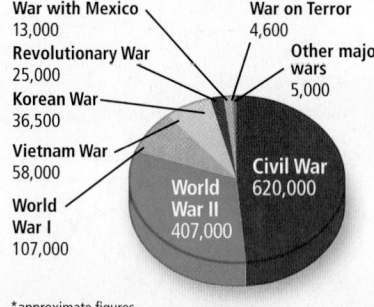

War with Mexico 13,000
War on Terror 4,600
Revolutionary War 25,000
Other major wars 5,000
Korean War 36,500
Vietnam War 58,000
World War I 107,000
World War II 407,000
Civil War 620,000

*approximate figures
Sources: United States Civil War Center; *For the Common Defense*

▲ The war devastated the South. Hundreds of thousands of people were dead, and several major cities, including Richmond (above), lay in ruins.

Analyzing VISUALS

1. **Identifying** The Civil War cost more American lives than any other conflict. What were the next two most deadly wars?

2. **Specifying** Which region suffered the highest number of battle-related deaths?

Grant Versus Lee

"Whatever happens, there will be no turning back," Grant promised Lincoln. He was determined to march southward, attacking Lee's forces relentlessly, regardless of the cost, until the South surrendered.

Grant kept his forces on the move and gave Lee's troops no time to recover. He attacked them first in the Wilderness, a densely forested area near Fredericksburg, Virginia, then at Spotsylvania Courthouse, then at Cold Harbor, a strategic crossroads northeast of Richmond. He then put the town of Petersburg under siege knowing that once it fell, Richmond, Virginia, would be cut off from supplies.

Sherman's March to the Sea

General Grant had put his most trusted subordinate, **William Tecumseh Sherman,** in charge of Union operations in the west while he headed east to fight Lee. In early August 1864, Sherman marched into Georgia, heading toward the city of Atlanta. After capturing the city, Sherman's troops set fires to destroy its railroads, warehouses, mills, and factories. The fires spread, however, destroying more than one-third of Atlanta.

On November 15, 1864, Sherman led his troops east across Georgia in what became known as the March to the Sea. The purpose of the march was to make Southern civilians understand the horrors of war and to pressure them into giving up the struggle. Sherman's troops cut a path of destruction through Georgia that was at times 60 miles (97 km) wide. By December 21, 1864, they had reached the coast and seized the city of Savannah. Sherman now turned north and headed into South Carolina, the state that many people believed had started the Civil War.

The South Surrenders

The capture of Atlanta revitalized Northern support for the war and for Lincoln, who was elected president to another term. Lincoln interpreted his reelection as a **mandate** to end slavery permanently by amending the Constitution. On January 31, 1865, with the help of Democrats opposed to slavery, the **Thirteenth Amendment** to the Constitution, banning slavery in the United States, passed the House of Representatives and was sent to the states for ratification.

Appomattox Courthouse Meanwhile, Lee knew that time was running out. On April 1, 1865, Union troops led by Philip Sheridan cut the last rail line into Petersburg at the Battle of Five Forks. The following night, Lee's troops withdrew from their positions near the city and raced west.

Lee's desperate attempt to escape Grant's forces failed when Sheridan's cavalry got ahead of Lee's troops and blocked the road at Appomattox Courthouse. With his ragged and battered troops surrounded and outnumbered, Lee surrendered to Grant on April 9, 1865. Grant's generous terms of surrender **guaranteed** that the United States would not prosecute Confederate soldiers for treason. When Grant agreed to let Confederates take their horses home "to put in a crop to carry themselves and their families through the next winter," Lee thanked him, adding that the kindness would "do much toward conciliating our people."

Lincoln's Assassination With the war over, Lincoln delivered a speech describing his plan to restore the Southern states to the Union. In the speech, he mentioned including African Americans in Southern state governments. One listener, actor John Wilkes Booth, sneered to a friend, "That is the last speech he will ever make."

Although his advisers had repeatedly warned him not to appear unescorted in public, Lincoln went to Ford's Theater with his wife to see a play on the evening of April 14, 1865. Just after 10 P.M., Booth slipped quietly behind the president and shot him in the back of the head. Lincoln died the next morning.

The North's victory in the Civil War saved the Union and strengthened the power of the federal government over the states. It transformed American society by ending slavery, but it also left the South socially and economically devastated, and many questions unresolved. Americans from the North and the South tried to answer these questions in the years following the Civil War—an era known as Reconstruction.

Reading Check **Examining** Why did General Sherman march his army to the sea?

Section 2 REVIEW

Vocabulary

1. **Explain** the significance of: "Stonewall" Jackson, blockade runner, Ulysses S. Grant, Battle of Antietam, Emancipation Proclamation, siege, Gettysburg, William Tecumseh Sherman, mandate, Thirteenth Amendment.

Main Ideas

2. **Identifying Central Issues** What was the significance of the Battle of Antietam for the South?

3. **Explaining** Why was capturing Vicksburg important to the Union?

Critical Thinking

4. **Big Ideas** How did northern military strategy change after Ulysses S. Grant took command of the Union Army.

5. **Organizing** Using a graphic organizer, list the results of the Battle of Gettysburg. Make sure that you consider both the Union and the Confederacy.

Battle of Gettysburg

6. **Analyzing Visuals** Examine the graphs of war deaths on page 136. What would account for the thousands of noncombat deaths?

Writing About History

7. **Descriptive Writing** Take on the role of a reporter living in Georgia during Sherman's March to the Sea. Write a brief article describing the Union's actions and their effects on the people.

History ONLINE

Study Central™ To review this section, go to glencoe.com and click on Study Central.

GEOGRAPHY & HISTORY

The Battle of Gettysburg

The Confederate invasion of the North in 1863 was a bold stroke. By moving north, General Robert E. Lee gained access to the rich farms and other resources of Pennsylvania. When his troops arrived in Gettysburg on July 1, they forced Union troops to flee to the hills south of the town. Had Confederate forces attacked the Union troops in the hills immediately, they might have won. The decision not to attack enabled Union troops to reinforce their position and build a formidable defensive line.

How Did Geography Shape the Battle?

The Union line stretched from Culp's Hill and Cemetery Hill in the north, south along Cemetery Ridge to another hill called Little Round Top. The Union forces controlled the high ground and were deployed in such a way that troops could easily be moved from one part of the line to another depending on where the enemy attacked.

On July 2, Lee tried to seize Little Round Top. Controlling the hill would have let his artillery fire down the length of the Union line. After savage fighting, his attack was repulsed, but Lee believed the Union had shifted so many troops south to hold Little Round Top that it had left its line on Cemetery Ridge vulnerable to attack.

On July 3, Lee ordered some 12,500 troops to attack Cemetery Ridge in what became known as Pickett's Charge. Union artillery ripped holes in the Confederate line as it advanced. When the Confederates neared the crest of the ridge, Union troops, protected by trenches and barricades they had built, unleashed volley after volley. Firing at point-blank rage, stabbing with bayonets, and battering with rifle butts, the Union soldiers drove the Confederates back. Lee knew he had been beaten. The next day he began his retreat to Virginia.

Town of Gettysburg

Culp's Hill

Seminary Ridge

Army of Northern Virginia
General Robert E. Lee

Analyzing GEOGRAPHY

1. **Place** Why was the Union army in such a strong position in the Battle of Gettysburg?

2. **Movement** What made Pickett's charge so difficult? Why did Lee think it would succeed?

On July 3, Lee ordered some 12,500 men to attack Cemetery Ridge. The Confederates marched three-quarters of a mile across open fields and then uphill toward Union lines. Although the attack is known as Pickett's Charge, General Pickett's troops made up only about one-third of the Confederate force that attacked.

Union advance
Confederate advance

0   40 kilometers
0   40 miles
Albers Equal-Area projection

Pennsylvania
Carlisle
Wrightsville
Chambersburg
Gettysburg
Frederick
Baltimore
Maryland
West Virginia
Winchester
Front Royal
Washington, D.C.
Virginia
Fredericksburg
Chancellorsville
Richmond

Cemetery Ridge

Army of the Potomac
General George G. Meade

Little Round Top

The Devil's Den

Peach Orchard

On July 2, Lee ordered Longstreet to attack the Union lines near the hill named Little Round Top. Savage fighting erupted in the Peach Orchard, on the slopes of Little Round Top, and near a jumble of boulders called the Devil's Den. The Union forces held Little Round Top and drove back the Confederates.

Chapter 3 The Civil War and Reconstruction **139**

Reconstruction

Guide to Reading

Big Ideas
Economics and Society After Reconstruction, the South tried to build a new economy, but many problems remained.

Content Vocabulary
- amnesty *(p. 140)*
- pocket veto *(p. 142)*
- black codes *(p. 143)*
- carpetbagger *(p. 145)*
- scalawag *(p. 145)*
- sharecropper *(p. 149)*

Academic Vocabulary
- commissioner *(p. 145)*
- infrastructure *(p. 147)*

People and Events to Identify
- Reconstruction *(p. 140)*
- Radical Republicans *(p. 140)*
- Freedmen's Bureau *(p. 142)*
- Fourteenth Amendment *(p. 143)*
- Fifteenth Amendment *(p. 145)*
- Compromise of 1877 *(p. 148)*

Reading Strategy
Organizing Complete a graphic organizer similar to the one below to explain how each piece of legislation listed affected African Americans.

Legislation	Effect
black codes	
Civil Rights Act of 1866	
Fourteenth Amendment	
Fifteenth Amendment	

President Lincoln, moderate Republicans, and Radical Republicans had different ideas about how to rebuild the South and to secure the rights of African Americans. As Democrats regained power in the South, Reconstruction ended.

Reconstruction Begins

MAIN Idea In the months after the Civil War, the nation began the effort to rebuild and reunite.

HISTORY AND YOU Think of a war you have studied in a history course. What were the terms of the peace treaty, and who benefited? Read on to learn about President Lincoln's policies after Union victory in the Civil War.

Helping freed African Americans find their way as citizens of the United States was only one of a myriad of problems the nation faced. At the end of the Civil War, the South was a defeated region with a devastated economy. While some Southerners were bitter over the Union military victory, for many rebuilding their land and their lives was more important. Meanwhile, the president and Congress grappled with the difficult task of **Reconstruction,** or rebuilding the nation after the war.

Lincoln and the Radical Republicans

In December 1863, President Lincoln offered a general **amnesty,** or pardon, to all Southerners who took an oath of loyalty to the United States and accepted the Union's proclamations concerning slavery. When 10 percent of a state's voters in the 1860 presidential election had taken this oath, they could organize a new state government. Certain people, such as Confederate government officials and military officers, could not take the oath or be pardoned. In March 1865, in his Second Inaugural Address, President Lincoln spoke of ending the war "with malice toward none, with charity for all." Therefore, President Lincoln wanted a moderate plan to reconcile the South with the Union instead of punishing it for treason.

Resistance to Lincoln's plan surfaced at once among a group of Republicans in Congress known as **Radical Republicans.** Led by Representative Thaddeus Stevens of Pennsylvania and Senator Charles Sumner of Massachusetts, the radicals wanted to prevent the leaders of the Confederacy from returning to power after the war. They also wanted the Republican Party to become a powerful institution in the South. Finally, and perhaps most importantly, they wanted the federal government to help African Americans achieve political equality by guaranteeing their right to vote in the South.

Three Plans for Reconstruction

After the Civil War, three plans were proposed to restore the South to the Union. The political struggle that resulted revealed that sectional tensions had not ended with the Civil War.

1. Lincoln's Plan for Reconstruction

- Amnesty to all but a few Southerners who took an oath of loyalty to the United States and accepted its proclamations concerning slavery
- When 10 percent of a state's voters in the 1860 presidential election had taken the oath, they could organize a new state government
- Members of the former Confederate government, officers of the Confederate army, and former federal judges, members of Congress, and military officers who had left their posts to help the Confederacy would not receive amnesty

2. Congressional Reconstruction

- Passed the Fourteenth and Fifteenth Amendments
- Military Reconstruction Act divided the South into five military districts
- New state constitutions required to guarantee voting rights
- Military rule protected voting rights for African Americans
- Empowered African Americans in government and supported their education

▲ Thaddeus Stevens

▶ Charles Sumner

3. Johnson's Plan for Reconstruction

- Amnesty for those taking an oath of loyalty to the United States; excluded high-ranking Confederates and those with property over $20,000, but they could apply for pardons individually
- Required states to ratify the Thirteenth Amendment abolishing slavery

Analyzing VISUALS

1. **Identifying** Which plan made the most provisions for formerly enslaved African Americans?
2. **Specifying** Which plan was most forgiving of former Confederate political and military leaders?

Congressional Republicans knew that the abolition of slavery would give the South more seats in the House of Representatives. Before the Civil War, enslaved people had only counted in Congress as three-fifths of a free person. Now that African Americans were free, the South was entitled to more seats in Congress. This would endanger Republican control of Congress unless Republicans could find a way to protect African American voting rights in the South.

Although the radicals knew that giving African Americans in the South the right to vote would help the Republican Party win elections, most were not acting cynically. Many of them had been abolitionists before the Civil War and had pushed Lincoln into making emancipation a goal of the war. They believed in a right to political equality for all Americans, regardless of their race.

The Wade-Davis Bill

Many moderate Republicans considered Lincoln too lenient, but they also thought the radicals were going too far in their support for African American equality and voting rights. By the summer of 1864, the moderates and radicals had come up with a plan for Reconstruction that they could both support.

This alternative to Lincoln's plan was the Wade-Davis Bill of 1864, which required the majority of the adult white males in a former Confederate state to take an oath of allegiance to the Union. The state could then hold a constitutional convention to create a new state government. The people chosen to attend the constitutional convention had to take an "iron-clad" oath asserting that they had never fought against the Union or supported the Confederacy in any way. Each state's convention would then have to abolish slavery, reject all debts the state had acquired as part of the Confederacy, and deprive all former Confederate government officials and military officers of the right to vote or hold office.

Although Congress passed the Wade-Davis Bill, Lincoln blocked it with a **pocket veto.** Although Lincoln sympathized with some of the radicals' goals, he believed that imposing a harsh peace would only alienate many whites in the South.

History ONLINE
Student Web Activity Visit glencoe.com and complete the activity on Southern Reconstruction.

The Freedmen's Bureau

Lincoln realized that the South was already in chaos, with thousands unemployed, homeless, and hungry. At the same time, the victorious Union armies had to try to help the large numbers of African Americans who flocked to Union lines as the war progressed. As Sherman marched through Georgia and South Carolina, thousands of freed African Americans—now known as freedmen—began following his troops seeking food and shelter.

In March 1865, Congress established the Bureau of Refugees, Freedmen, and Abandoned Lands, better known as the **Freedmen's Bureau.** The Bureau was directed to feeding and clothing war refugees in the South using surplus army supplies. Beginning in September 1865, it issued nearly 30,000 rations a day for the next year.

The Bureau helped formerly enslaved people find work on plantations and negotiated labor contracts with planters. Many Northerners argued that people who had been enslaved should receive land to support themselves now that they were free. To others, however, taking land from plantation owners and giving it to freedmen seemed to violate the nation's commitment to individual property rights. As a result, Congress refused to confirm the right of African Americans to own the lands that had

been seized from plantation owners and given to them.

Johnson Takes Office

Shortly after Congress established the Freedmen's Bureau, Lincoln was assassinated. Although his successor, Vice President Andrew Johnson, was a Democrat from Tennessee, he had remained loyal to the Union. Like Lincoln, he believed in a moderate policy to bring the South back into the Union.

In the summer of 1865, with Congress in recess, Johnson began implementing his reconstruction plan. He offered to pardon all former citizens of the Confederacy who took an oath of loyalty to the Union and to return their property. He excluded from the pardon the same people Lincoln had excluded. Like Lincoln, Johnson required Southern states to ratify the Thirteenth Amendment.

The former Confederate states, for the most part, met Johnson's conditions. They then organized new governments and held elections. By the time Congress gathered for its next session in December 1865, Johnson's plan was well underway. Many members of

◀ Turning Point ▶

The Fourteenth Amendment

The passage of the Fourteenth Amendment was a turning point in American political and legal history. Since its ratification, the amendment has been used to expand federal power over the states and to extend civil rights through its equal protection clause. It also provided the foundation for the doctrine of incorporation—the concept that the rights and protections in the Bill of Rights apply to the states. This doctrine was first upheld by the Supreme Court in *Gitlow* v. *New York* in 1925. In the 1950s and 1960s, the Warren Court used the clause extensively to extend civil rights in cases such as *Brown* v. *Board of Education*, *Gideon* v. *Wainwright*, and *Reynolds* v. *Sims*, among others.

ANALYZING HISTORY What is significant about the ratification of the Fourteenth Amendment? Write a brief essay to explain your answer.

Congress were astonished and angered when they realized that Southern voters had elected dozens of Confederate leaders to Congress. Moderate Republicans joined with the Radical Republicans and voted to reject the new Southern members of Congress.

Congressional Republicans were also angry that the new Southern legislatures had passed laws, known as **black codes,** which seemed to be intended to keep African Americans in a condition similar to slavery. They required African Americans to enter into annual labor contracts. Those who did not could be arrested for vagrancy and forced into involuntary servitude. Several codes established specific hours of labor and also required them to get licenses to work in nonagricultural jobs.

Radical Reconstruction

With the election of former Confederates to office and the introduction of the black codes, more and more moderate Republicans joined the radicals. Finally, in late 1865, House and Senate leaders created a Joint Committee on Reconstruction to develop their own program for rebuilding the Union.

The Fourteenth Amendment In March 1866, congressional Reconstruction began with the passage of an act intended to override the black codes. The Civil Rights Act of 1866 granted citizenship to all persons born in the United States except for Native Americans. The act guaranteed the rights of African Americans to own property and stated that they were to be treated equally in court. It also gave the federal government the power to sue people who violated those rights. Johnson vetoed the act, arguing it was unconstitutional and would "[cause] discord among the races." The veto convinced the remaining moderate Republicans to join the radicals in overriding Johnson's veto, and the act became law.

Fearing that the Civil Rights Act might later be overturned in court, however, the radicals introduced the **Fourteenth Amendment** to the Constitution. This amendment granted citizenship to all persons born or naturalized in the United States and declared that no state could deprive any person of life, liberty, or property "without due process of law." It also declared that no state could deny any person "equal protection of the laws." In 1868, the amendment was ratified.

The Fourteenth Amendment

"No State shall make or enforce any law which shall abridge the privileges or immunities of citizens of the United States; nor shall any State deprive any person of life, liberty, or property, without due process of law; nor deny to any person within its jurisdiction the equal protection of the laws."

▲ In 1964, in Reynolds v. Sims, the Court used the Fourteenth Amendment's equal protection clause to ensure that state voting districts were of equal size.

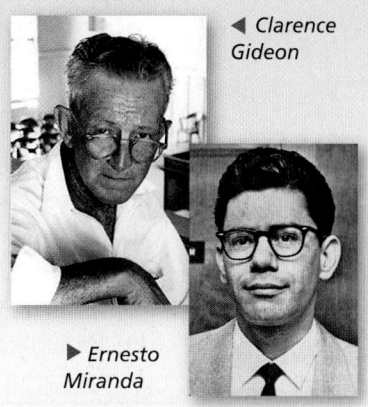

◄ Clarence Gideon

► Ernesto Miranda

▲ In two major cases, Gideon v. Wainwright in 1963 and Miranda v. Arizona in 1966, the Court clarified that the Fifth and Sixth Amendments of the Bill of Rights had to be upheld by the states.

► In 1925, in Gitlow v. New York, the Supreme Court began using the Fourteenth Amendment to apply the Bill of Rights to the states. In this case, it held that state laws had to protect free speech.

▲ Benjamin Gitlow

◄ In 1954 the Supreme Court based its decision ending school segregation, Brown v. Board of Education, on the Fourteenth Amendment's equal protection clause.

What Are the Provisions of the Reconstruction Amendments?

The 13th Amendment (1865)
- Slavery is illegal.

The 14th Amendment (1868)
- All people born or naturalized in the United States are citizens.
- The states may not deny anyone the equal protection of the laws.
- Leaders of the Confederacy cannot serve in the U.S. government or military without a two-thirds vote by Congress.

The 15th Amendment (1870)
- The rights of citizens to vote shall not be denied on account of race, color, or previous condition of servitude.

Military Districts and Commanders

1	General John Schofield
2	General Daniel Sickles
3	General John Pope
4	General Edward Ord
5	General Philip Sheridan

1868 Date of readmission to Union

Analyzing GEOGRAPHY

1. **Location** Which former Confederate state was not part of a military district?
2. **Movement** How many years after the war ended was the last Southern state readmitted to the United States?

Maps In Motion See *StudentWorks™ Plus* or glencoe.com.

President Johnson attacked the Fourteenth Amendment and made it the major issue of the 1866 congressional elections. He hoped Northerners would vote out the Radical Republicans and elect representatives who supported his plan for Reconstruction. Instead, the Republicans won approximately a three-to-one majority in Congress. They now could override any presidential veto and could claim that they had a mandate, or command, to enact their own Reconstruction program in place of Johnson's plan.

Military Reconstruction Begins In March 1867, Congress passed the Military Reconstruction Act, which essentially nullified Johnson's programs. The act divided the former Confederacy, except for Tennessee—which had ratified the Fourteenth Amendment in 1866—into five military districts. A Union general was placed in charge of each district with orders

to maintain peace and "protect the rights of persons and property."

In the meantime, each former Confederate state had to hold another constitutional convention to design a constitution acceptable to Congress. The new state constitutions had to give the right to vote to all adult male citizens, regardless of race. Each state also had to ratify the Fourteenth Amendment before it would be allowed to elect people to Congress.

Johnson's Impeachment Republicans knew that they had the votes to override presidential vetoes, but they also knew that President Johnson could still refuse to enforce the laws they passed. To restrict Johnson, Congress passed two new laws: the Command of the Army Act and the Tenure of Office Act. The Command of the Army Act required all orders from the president to go through the headquarters of the General of the Army. This was the headquarters of General Grant, whom the Republicans trusted. The Tenure of Office Act required the Senate to approve the removal of any official whose appointment had required the Senate's consent.

In order to challenge the Tenure of Office Act, Johnson fired Secretary of War Edwin M. Stanton, who supported the Radical Republicans. Three days later, the House of Representatives voted to impeach Johnson, meaning that they charged him with "high crimes and misdemeanors" in office. They accused Johnson of breaking the law by refusing to uphold the Tenure of Office Act.

As provided in the Constitution, the Senate then put the president on trial. If two-thirds of the senators found the president guilty of the charges, he would be removed from office. In May 1868, the Senate voted 35 to 19 that Johnson was guilty of high crimes and misdemeanors. This was just one vote short of the votes needed for conviction.

Although Johnson remained in office, he finished his term quietly and did not run for election in 1868. That year, the Republicans nominated Ulysses S. Grant. During the campaign, Union troops in the South enabled African Americans to vote in large numbers. As a result, Grant won six Southern states and most Northern states. The Republicans also retained large majorities in Congress.

The Fifteenth Amendment With their majority secure, and a trusted president in office, congressional Republicans moved rapidly to expand their Reconstruction program. Recognizing the importance of African American suffrage, Congress passed the **Fifteenth Amendment.** This amendment declared that the right to vote "shall not be denied . . . on account of race, color, or previous condition of servitude." By March 1870, the amendment had been ratified.

Radical Reconstruction had a dramatic impact on the South, particularly in the short term. It brought hundreds of thousands of African Americans into the political process for the first time. It also began to change Southern society. As it did so, it angered many white Southerners, who began to fight back against the federal government's policies.

Reading Check **Analyzing** Why did congressional Republicans pass amendments to the Constitution?

Republican Rule

MAIN Idea As African Americans entered politics, some white Southerners began to resist Republican reforms.

HISTORY AND YOU Have you heard of recent activities of the Ku Klux Klan? Read on to find out when and why the KKK was founded.

By late 1870, all former Confederate states had rejoined the Union. With many issues unresolved, reunification did little to restore harmony between the North and South.

Carpetbags and Scalawags

During Reconstruction, a large number of Northerners traveled to the South. Many were eventually elected or appointed to positions in the new state governments. Southerners, particularly supporters of the Democratic Party, called these newcomers **carpetbaggers** because some arrived with their belongings in suitcases made of carpet fabric. Local residents saw them as intruders seeking to exploit the South for their own gain.

Some white Southerners did work with the Republicans and supported Reconstruction. Other Southerners called them **scalawags**— an old Scots-Irish term for weak, underfed, worthless animals. The scalawags were a diverse group. Some were former Whigs who had grudgingly joined the Democratic Party before the war. Others were owners of small farms who did not want the wealthy planters to regain power. Some were business people who favored Republican economic plans.

African Americans

Having gained the right to vote, African American men entered into politics with great enthusiasm. They served as legislators and administrators for nearly all levels of government. Hundreds served as delegates to the conventions that created the new state constitutions. They also won election to many local offices, from mayor to police chief to school **commissioner.** Dozens served in the South's state legislatures, 14 were elected to the House of Representatives, and two, Hiram Revels and Blanche K. Bruce, were elected to the Senate.

African Americans Enter Politics

Reconstruction provided African Americans with new opportunities to participate in politics. Many took part in the state constitutional conventions and were elected to state legislatures—achieving a majority in South Carolina's state assembly—and to local offices.

▲ This drawing from 1867 depicts the primary groups that became political leaders of the South's African American community—artisans (shown with tools), the middle class, and Union soldiers.

▲ This sketch from 1868 shows African Americans campaigning. African Americans were excited to participate in politics. The sketch shows women and children as well, suggesting that the entire community regarded political issues as important, even though only adult males could vote.

Analyzing VISUALS

1. **Identifying Central Issues** Why do you think African Americans were so enthusiastic about participating in politics?
2. **Explaining** What about the illustration above indicates the political position of women?

▲ The sketch above from the 1870s shows South Carolina's legislature—the only state legislature with an African American majority during Reconstruction.

As formerly enslaved people entered Southern politics, many white Southerners claimed that "Black Republicanism" ruled the South. Such claims were greatly exaggerated. No African American ever served as governor. In South Carolina, where African Americans were a majority of the population, they did gain control of the legislature, but it lasted for only one term. African Americans participated in government, but they did not control it.

Many African Americans wanted an education, something they had been denied under slavery. As Reconstruction began, the Freedmen's Bureau, with the help of Northern charities, established schools for African Americans across the South. In the 1870s, Reconstruction governments built a public school system in the South, and by 1876 about 40 percent of all African American children (roughly 600,000 students) attended school.

Formerly enslaved people across the South also began building their own churches. Churches frequently served as the center of many African American communities, as they housed schools and hosted social events and political gatherings.

Republican Reforms

Because of past disloyalty, some Southern whites were barred from participating in the new Southern governments, and many others simply refused to do so. Republicans did have the support of many poor white farmers, who resented the planters and Democratic Party that had dominated the South before the war. This enabled a coalition of poor Southern-born whites, African Americans, and Northern carpetbaggers to elect Republican candidates.

The Republican governments in the South instituted a number of reforms. They repealed the black codes, and established state hospitals and institutions for orphans. To improve the **infrastructure,** they rebuilt roads, railways, and bridges damaged during the Civil War and provided funds for the construction of new railroads and industries in the South.

Many white Southerners scorned these reforms, which did not come without cost. Many state governments had to borrow money and impose high property taxes to pay for the repairs and new programs. Many landowners, unable to pay these new taxes, lost their land.

Southern Resistance

Unable to strike openly at the Republicans running their states, some Southern opponents of Reconstruction organized secret societies to undermine Republican rule. The largest of these groups was the Ku Klux Klan. Started in 1866 by former Confederate soldiers in Pulaski, Tennessee, the Klan spread rapidly throughout the South. Hooded, white-robed Klan members rode in bands at night terrorizing African Americans, white Republicans, carpetbaggers, teachers in African American schools, and others who supported the Republican governments. Republicans and African Americans responded by organizing their own militias to fight back.

As the violence increased, Congress passed three Enforcement Acts in 1870 and 1871, one of which outlawed the activities of the Klan. Although local authorities and federal agents arrested more than 3,000 Klan members, only about 600 were convicted, and fewer still served any time in prison.

✔ **Reading Check** **Explaining** Why did only some Southerners support Republican reforms?

Reconstruction Ends

MAIN Idea Reconstruction ended as Democrats regained power in the South and in Congress.

HISTORY AND YOU What values and policies do you associate with the Republican and Democratic parties? Read to learn about the roles these parties played during the Reconstruction period.

As commander of the Union forces, Ulysses S. Grant had led the North to victory in the Civil War. His reputation had then carried him into the White House in the election of 1868. Unfortunately, Grant had little experience in politics. He believed that the president's role was to carry out the laws and leave the development of policy to Congress. This approach pleased the Radical Republicans in Congress, but it left the president weak and ineffective when dealing with other issues. Eventually, Grant's lack of political experience helped to divide the Republican Party and to undermine public support for Reconstruction.

During his first term, Ulysses S. Grant faced a growing number of Republicans who were concerned that interests in making money and selling influence were beginning to dominate the Republican Party. These critics also argued that the economic policies most Republicans supported, such as high tariffs, favored the rich over the poor. In 1872, these critics, known as Liberal Republicans, split from the Republican Party and nominated their own candidate, the influential newspaper publisher Horace Greeley. Despite this split, Grant easily won reelection to a second term.

During Grant's second term, a series of scandals damaged his reputation. In addition, the nation endured a staggering and long-lasting economic crisis that began during Grant's second term. After a powerful banking firm declared bankruptcy, a wave of fear known as the Panic of 1873 quickly spread through the nation's financial community. The panic soon set off a full-fledged depression that lasted until almost the end of the decade.

The scandals in the Grant administration and the nation's deepening economic depression hurt the Republicans politically. In the 1874 midterm elections, the Democrats won back control of the House of Representatives and made gains in the Senate.

The New South was a blend of the old and the new. Industry began to develop, but agriculture remained vital to the economy. By the 1890s, the South was exporting more cotton, rice, and tobacco than before the Civil War. Although slavery had ended, many African Americans were poor sharecroppers who harvested crops for landowners.

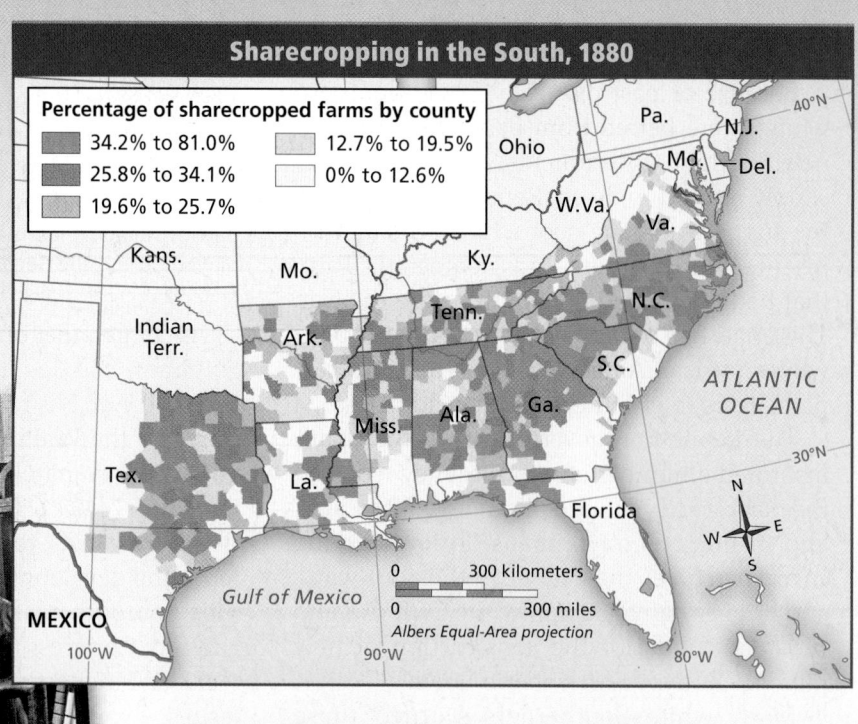

Sharecropping in the South, 1880

Percentage of sharecropped farms by county
- 34.2% to 81.0%
- 25.8% to 34.1%
- 19.6% to 25.7%
- 12.7% to 19.5%
- 0% to 12.6%

▲ The industry of the "New South" was still driven by agricultural products, such as tobacco. The workers shown above are processing tobacco in a Richmond tobacco factory in 1899.

Analyzing VISUALS

1. **Specifying** In which three states was sharecropping most common?

2. **Explaining** Why do you think the South's economy remained so dependent on agriculture after Reconstruction?

▲ Sharecroppers harvest cotton in Georgia in 1898.

The Compromise of 1877

The rising power of the Democrats in Congress and Republican concerns over scandals made enforcing Reconstruction more difficult. At the same time, many Northerners were becoming more concerned about the economy than the situation in the South.

In the 1870s, Democrats began to regain power in the South. They did so in part through intimidation and fraud, and in part by defining elections as a struggle between whites and African Americans. They also won back support by promising to cut the high taxes the Republicans had imposed and by accusing

Republicans of corruption. Southern Democrats viewed their efforts to regain power as a crusade to help save the South from Republican rule. By 1876, the Democrats had taken control of all but three Southern state legislatures.

That year, the nation's presidential election pitted Republican Rutherford B. Hayes, a former governor of Ohio, against Democrat Samuel Tilden, a wealthy corporate lawyer and former governor of New York. On Election Day, twenty electoral votes were disputed. Nineteen of the votes were in the three Southern states controlled by Republicans. As a result, congressional leaders worked out a deal known as the **Compromise of 1877.**

Historians are not sure if a deal really took place or what its exact terms were. The Compromise of 1877 reportedly included a promise by the Republicans to pull federal troops out of the South, if Hayes was elected, and that is in fact what happened within a month of Hayes taking office. However, it is also true that the nation was tired of the politics of Reconstruction and that Republican leaders were ready to end Reconstruction. Indeed, President Grant had pulled troops out of Florida even before Hayes took office.

A "New South" Arises

Many Southern leaders realized the South could never return to the pre–Civil War agricultural economy dominated by the planter elite. Instead, they called for the creation of a "New South"—a phrase coined by Henry Grady, editor of the *Atlanta Constitution*. They believed the region had to develop a strong industrial economy.

An alliance between powerful white Southerners and Northern financiers brought great economic changes to some parts of the South. Northern capital helped to build railroads, and by 1890, almost 40,000 miles of railroad track crisscrossed the South—nearly four times the amount there in 1860. Southern industry also grew. A thriving iron and steel industry developed around Birmingham, Alabama. In North Carolina, tobacco processing became big business, and cotton mills appeared in numerous small towns.

In other ways, however, the South changed little. Despite its industrial growth, the region remained agrarian. As late as 1900, only 6 percent of the Southern labor force worked in manufacturing. For many African Americans in particular, the end of Reconstruction meant a return to the "Old South," where they had little political power and were forced to labor under difficult and unfair conditions.

The collapse of Reconstruction ended African American hopes of being granted their own land in the South. Instead, many returned to plantations owned by whites, where they either worked for wages or became tenant farmers, paying rent for the land they farmed. Most tenant farmers eventually became **sharecroppers.** Sharecroppers did not pay their rent in cash. Instead, they paid a share of their crops—often as much as one-half to two-thirds—to cover their rent as well as the cost of the seed, fertilizer, tools, and animals they needed.

Many sharecroppers needed more seed and supplies than their landlords could provide. Local suppliers, known as furnishing merchants, provided the supplies on credit, but at interest rates as high as 40 percent. To make sure sharecroppers paid their debts, laws allowed merchants to put liens on their crops. This meant the merchant could take crops to cover the debts. The crop lien system and high interest rates trapped sharecroppers on the land because they could not pay off their debts and leave, nor could they declare bankruptcy. Failure to pay off debts could lead to imprisonment or forced labor. The Civil War had ended slavery, but Reconstruction had left many African Americans trapped in poverty.

Reading Check **Explaining** What major issue was settled by the Compromise of 1877?

Section 3 REVIEW

Vocabulary

1. **Explain** the significance of: Reconstruction, amnesty, Radical Republicans, pocket veto, Freedmen's Bureau, black codes, Fourteenth Amendment, Fifteenth Amendment, carpet-baggers, scalawags, Compromise of 1877, sharecroppers.

Main Ideas

2. **Identifying Points of View** What was President Lincoln's attitude toward the Reconstruction goals of the Radical Republicans?

3. **Explaining** What was the goal of one of the Enforcement Acts, passed in 1870–1871?

4. **Determining Cause and Effect** What was the cause and effect of the Panic of 1873?

Critical Thinking

5. **Big Ideas** What factors contributed to the improving economy of the South after Reconstruction?

6. **Organizing** Use a graphic organizer similar to the one below to identify the problems faced by Grant's administration.

Problems Faced by Grant's Administration

7. **Analyzing Visuals** Review the map on page 144. In what year were most southern states readmitted to the Union, and which states were they?

Writing About History

8. **Expository Writing** Write a short essay explaining what you consider to be the three most important events of Reconstruction and why you chose them.

History ONLINE

Study Central™ To review this section, go to glencoe.com and click on Study Central.

STUDY TO GO You can study anywhere, anytime by downloading quizzes and flashcards to your PDA from glencoe.com.

▲ *Jefferson Davis meets with his cabinet and General Lee.*

▲ *After the Battle of Antietam (above), Lincoln issued the Emancipation Proclamation.*

▲ *Grant's forces wore down Lee's troops in a series of battles in northern Virginia. At Cold Harbor (above), the Union suffered heavy losses.*

North v. South

1861
- Lincoln orders a blockade of Southern ports.
- The Confederacy organizes its government.
- The South wins the First Battle of Bull Run.
- Both sides begin building up their forces.

1862
- Farragut captures New Orleans.
- After the Battles of Shiloh and Murfreesboro, the Union gains control of western Tennessee.
- Led by McClellan, Union troops land in Virginia to begin the Peninsula Campaign; after a series of battles with Lee's forces, McClellan's forces withdraw.
- Lee invades the North but is defeated at the Battle of Antietam.

1863: The Turning Point
- Lincoln issues the Emancipation Proclamation.
- Grant captures Vicksburg after a long siege and cuts the Confederacy in two.
- After winning the battles of Fredericksburg and Chancellorsville, Lee invades the north but is defeated at the Battle of Gettysburg.
- After losing the Battle of Chickamauga, Union forces drive back Southern forces at the Battle of Chattanooga.
- Grant is given command of all Union forces.

1864
- Grant battles Lee's forces in northern Virginia; Lee retreats into Petersburg, which Grant puts under siege.
- Sherman captures Atlanta, then begins his March to the Sea across Georgia.

1865
- Lee attempts to escape from Petersburg but is surrounded by Grant's forces and surrenders at Appomattox Courthouse; other Confederate forces surrender as well.
- Lincoln is assassinated.

▼ *The capture of New Orleans (below) gave the Union control of the mouth of the Mississippi River.*

▼ *The failure of Pickett's Charge convinced Lee to withdraw from Gettysburg. It was the turning point of the war.*

▼ *Mourners surround Lincoln's hearse in Philadelphia in April 1865.*

Reviewing Vocabulary

Directions: Choose the word or words that best complete the sentence.

1. Abraham Lincoln declared _____ in Baltimore to prevent Maryland's secession.

   A martial law

   B abolition

   C habeas corpus

   D popular sovereignty

2. Because of the effectiveness of the Union Navy, the Confederacy often used _____ to get needed supplies.

   A ironclads

   B blockade runners

   C cavalry

   D British warships

3. General Ulysses S. Grant employed a strategy known as a _____ to capture the city of Vicksburg.

   A battle

   B blockade

   C siege

   D charge

4. Part of President Lincoln's plan for Reconstruction was to offer _____ to Southerners who would take an oath of loyalty to the United States.

   A imprisonment

   B amnesty

   C debt peonage

   D exile

5. Northerners who came to the South during Reconstruction were called _____ by Southerners who believed the Northerners were exploiting the South's misfortune for personal gain.

   A scalawags

   B sharecroppers

   C carpetbaggers

   D furnishing merchants

Reviewing Main Ideas

Directions: Choose the best answer for each of the following questions.

Section 1 (pp. 122–129)

6. The Civil War began when

   A Lincoln refused to send troops into Kentucky.

   B Fort Sumter fell to the Confederacy.

   C Virginia seceded from the Union.

   D Army officers imprisoned many suspected secessionists.

7. Which of the following was part of the Union's Anaconda Plan for defeating the Confederacy?

   A a blockade of Southern ports

   B a quick ground offensive

   C the assassination of Jefferson Davis

   D a defensive war of attrition

Section 2 (pp. 130–137)

8. One result of the Battle of Antietam was that

   A Lincoln issued the Emancipation Proclamation.

   B the Confederacy was split in two.

   C Great Britain decided to support the Confederacy.

   D David Farragut became a hero in the North.

9. The institution of slavery was formally abolished in the United States by the

   A Compromise of 1850.

   B Emancipation Proclamation of 1863.

   C ratification of the Thirteenth Amendment.

   D creation of the Freedmen's Bureau in 1865.

TEST-TAKING

Be sure to read each question carefully to identify any key words that may help you to either choose the correct answer choice or eliminate incorrect answer choices.

Need Extra Help?									
If You Missed Questions . . .	1	2	3	4	5	6	7	8	9
Go to Page . . .	126	130	134	140	145	125	129	133	137

10. After the successful capture of Chattanooga, Lincoln

    A recalled General Sherman to Washington, D.C.

    B issued the Emancipation Proclamation.

    C began negotiations for peace with the Confederacy.

    D made General Grant general in chief of the Union.

Section 3 (pp. 140–149)

11. Which of the following was a provision of the Wade-Davis Bill for readmitting Southern states to the Union?

    A The majority of white men in the state had to take an oath of allegiance to the United States.

    B States could not hold constitutional conventions.

    C All former Confederate political and military leaders would be given the right to vote.

    D Freed African Americans had to be provided with "forty acres and a mule."

12. In the Compromise of 1877, supposedly Rutherford B. Hayes would be made president if he would do which of the following once in office?

    A free all enslaved African Americans in the Southern states

    B ensure the passage of the Enforcement Acts

    C pardon members of President Grant's administration

    D remove all federal troops from the Southern states

13. Following the Civil War, many Southern states enacted Black Codes to

    A provide free farmland for African Americans.

    B guarantee equal civil rights for African Americans.

    C restrict the rights of formerly enslaved persons.

    D support the creation of the Freedmen's Bureau.

14. One way in which Reconstruction failed was that, in the end, it

    A did not reunite the Confederate states with the Union.

    B led to much corruption in the Grant administration.

    C gave the Democrats complete control of every level of government.

    D allowed African Americans to lose many of their new rights.

Critical Thinking

Directions: Choose the best answers to the following questions.

15. One advantage that the Confederacy held during the Civil War was that

    A it received military and financial support from the British and French.

    B many battles occurred on lands with which Southerners were more familiar.

    C the largest weapons factories were located in the South.

    D most people in the country agreed with the position of the Southern states.

Base your answers to questions 16 and 17 on the map below and your knowledge of Chapter 3.

Peninsula Campaign, April–May 1862

16. How did General McClellan move his troops to Virginia?

    A by railroad

    B by wagon

    C by land

    D by water

17. The object of the Peninsula Campaign for the Union was to

    A capture Richmond.

    B capture Yorktown.

    C beat Magruder to Fredericksburg.

    D blockade Chesapeake Bay.

Need Extra Help?								
If You Missed Questions . . .	10	11	12	13	14	15	16	17
Go to Page . . .	135	141–142	148–149	143	147–149	132–133	R15	R15

18. After the Civil War, many formerly enslaved African Americans earned a living by becoming

   A railroad workers in the West.

   B sharecroppers on Southern farms.

   C workers in Northern factories.

   D gold miners in California.

Analyze the cartoon and answer the question that follows. Base your answer on the cartoon and on your knowledge of Chapter 3.

19. This cartoon features Peace Democrats, called "Copperheads," and the main idea is that they are

   A helpful to the Union cause.

   B a threat to the Union cause.

   C frightening to many people.

   D peaceful and caring.

20. Which of the following statements best describes the aims of the Peace Democrats?

   A They wished to join with the seceding Southern states.

   B They wished to remove Abraham Lincoln from office.

   C They wanted to avoid war by negotiating with the Confederacy.

   D They wanted Jefferson Davis to replace Lincoln as president.

Document-Based Questions

Directions: Analyze the document and answer the short-answer questions that follow the document.

At the beginning of the Civil War, Robert E. Lee wrote a letter to his sister, Anne Marshall, explaining his decision to resign from the U.S. Army. Below is an excerpt from that letter:

> "My Dear Sister:
>
> . . . With all my devotion to the Union and the feeling of loyalty and duty of an American citizen, I have not been able to make up my mind to raise my hand against my relatives, my children, my home. I have, therefore, resigned my commission in the Army, and, save in defense of my native state . . . I hope I may never be called on to draw my sword. I know you will blame me; but you must think as kindly of me as you can. . . ."
>
> —from *Personal Reminiscences, Anecdotes, and Letters of General Robert E. Lee*

21. Why did Robert E. Lee think it was necessary to resign from the U.S. Army at the start of the war?

22. What do you think Lee's feelings were about the war?

Extended Response

23. President Lincoln suspended writs of habeas corpus during the Civil War to prevent interference with the draft. In a persuasive essay, explain your views on the suspension of civil liberties in this case, and in general. Do you think that the suspension of civil liberties is justified in some situations? In your essay, include an introduction and at least three paragraphs with details from the chapter to support your views.

STOP

History ONLINE

For additional test practice, use Self-Check Quizzes—Chapter 3 at glencoe.com.

Need Extra Help?						
If You Missed Questions . . .	18	19	20	21	22	23
Go to Page . . .	149	R18	128	R19	R19	R12

The Birth of Modern America
1865–1901

Why It Matters

Following the turmoil of the Civil War and Reconstruction, the United States began its transformation from a rural nation to an industrial, urban nation linked together by railroads. New inventions and scientific discoveries fundamentally altered how Americans lived and worked. New factories employed thousands of workers; cities grew dramatically in size, and tens of millions of new immigrants flooded into the country.

Wabash Avenue and the elevated railroad in downtown Chicago, 1900

155

Chapter 4

Settling the West

1865–1890

SECTION 1 Miners and Ranchers

SECTION 2 Farming the Plains

SECTION 3 Native Americans

Cattle ranching in the American West has changed little in 140 years. Here an Apache cowboy herds cattle into a corral during spring roundup on an Arizona ranch.

U.S. PRESIDENTS

U.S. EVENTS

WORLD EVENTS

1862
• Homestead Act makes cheap land available to settlers

1864
• Sand Creek Massacre takes place

Johnson
1865–1869

1867
• Chisholm Trail cattle drive begins

Grant
1869–1877

1876
• Battle of the Little Bighorn

Hayes
1877–1881

Garfield
1881

1860

1870

1880

1867
• British colonies unite to form Canada

1871
• Prussia unites German states to create Germany

1876
• Porfirio Diaz becomes dictator of Mexico

1879
• Zulu launch war against British settlers

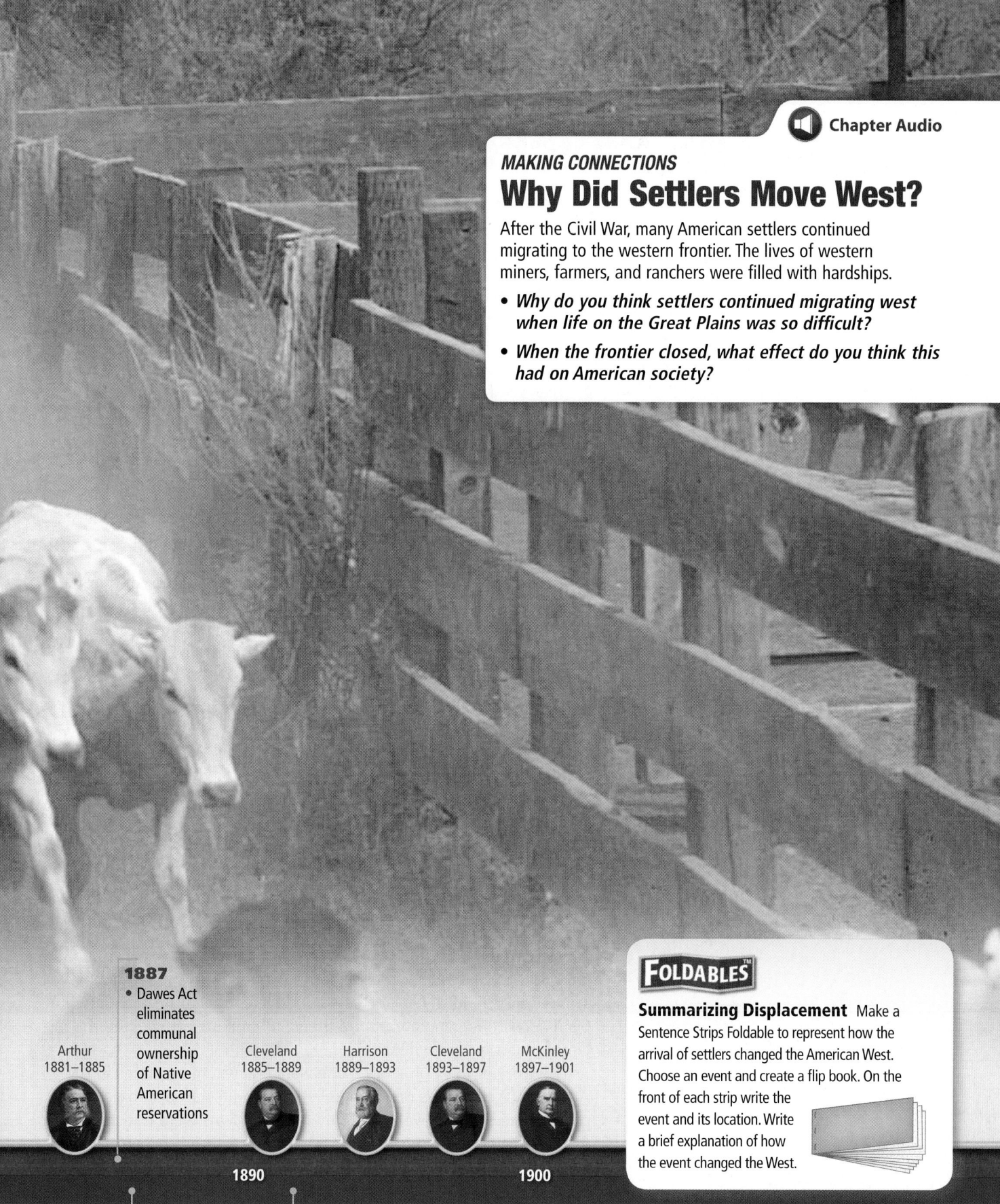

MAKING CONNECTIONS

Why Did Settlers Move West?

After the Civil War, many American settlers continued migrating to the western frontier. The lives of western miners, farmers, and ranchers were filled with hardships.

- *Why do you think settlers continued migrating west when life on the Great Plains was so difficult?*

- *When the frontier closed, what effect do you think this had on American society?*

1887
- Dawes Act eliminates communal ownership of Native American reservations

Arthur
1881–1885

Cleveland
1885–1889

Harrison
1889–1893

Cleveland
1893–1897

McKinley
1897–1901

1890

1900

1886
- Gold is discovered in South Africa

1891
- Russia begins Trans-Siberian railway and many settlers head east to Siberia

FOLDABLES™

Summarizing Displacement Make a Sentence Strips Foldable to represent how the arrival of settlers changed the American West. Choose an event and create a flip book. On the front of each strip write the event and its location. Write a brief explanation of how the event changed the West.

History ONLINE Visit glencoe.com and enter *QuickPass*™ code TAVMT5147c4 for Chapter 4 resources.

Miners and Ranchers

Mining and ranching attracted settlers to western territories that soon had populations large enough to qualify for statehood. People mined for gold, silver, and lead, or shipped longhorn cattle to the East.

Growth of the Mining Industry

MAIN Idea The discovery of gold, silver, and other minerals attracted thousands of settlers who established new states on the frontier.

HISTORY AND YOU Do you remember reading about the 1849 California gold rush? Read on to learn how mineral discoveries shaped the settlement of the West.

Mining played an important role in the settling of the American West. Beginning with the California gold rush, and continuing throughout the late 1800s, wave after wave of prospectors came to the region hoping to strike it rich mining gold, silver, and other minerals. Demand for minerals rose dramatically after the Civil War as the United States changed from a farming nation to an industrial nation. Mining in the West also encouraged the building of railroads to connect the mines to factories back east.

Boomtowns

In 1859 a prospector named **Henry Comstock** staked a claim in Six-Mile Canyon, near Virginia City, Nevada. Frustrated by his failure to find any gold, Comstock sold his claim a few months later. He had not realized that the sticky, blue-gray clay that made mining in the area difficult was in fact nearly pure silver ore.

News of the Comstock Lode, as the strike came to be called, brought a flood of eager prospectors to Virginia City. So many people arrived that, in 1864, Nevada was admitted as the 36th state. The Comstock Lode generated more than $230 million and helped the Union finance the Civil War.

The story of the Comstock Lode was replayed many times in the American West. News of a mineral strike would start a stampede of prospectors. Almost overnight, tiny frontier towns were transformed into small cities. Virginia City, for example, grew from a town of a few hundred people to nearly 30,000 in just a few months. It had an opera house, shops with furniture and fashions from Europe, several newspapers, and a six-story hotel.

These quickly growing towns were called **boomtowns.** Using the word "boom" this way began in the late 1800s. It refers to a time of rapid economic growth.

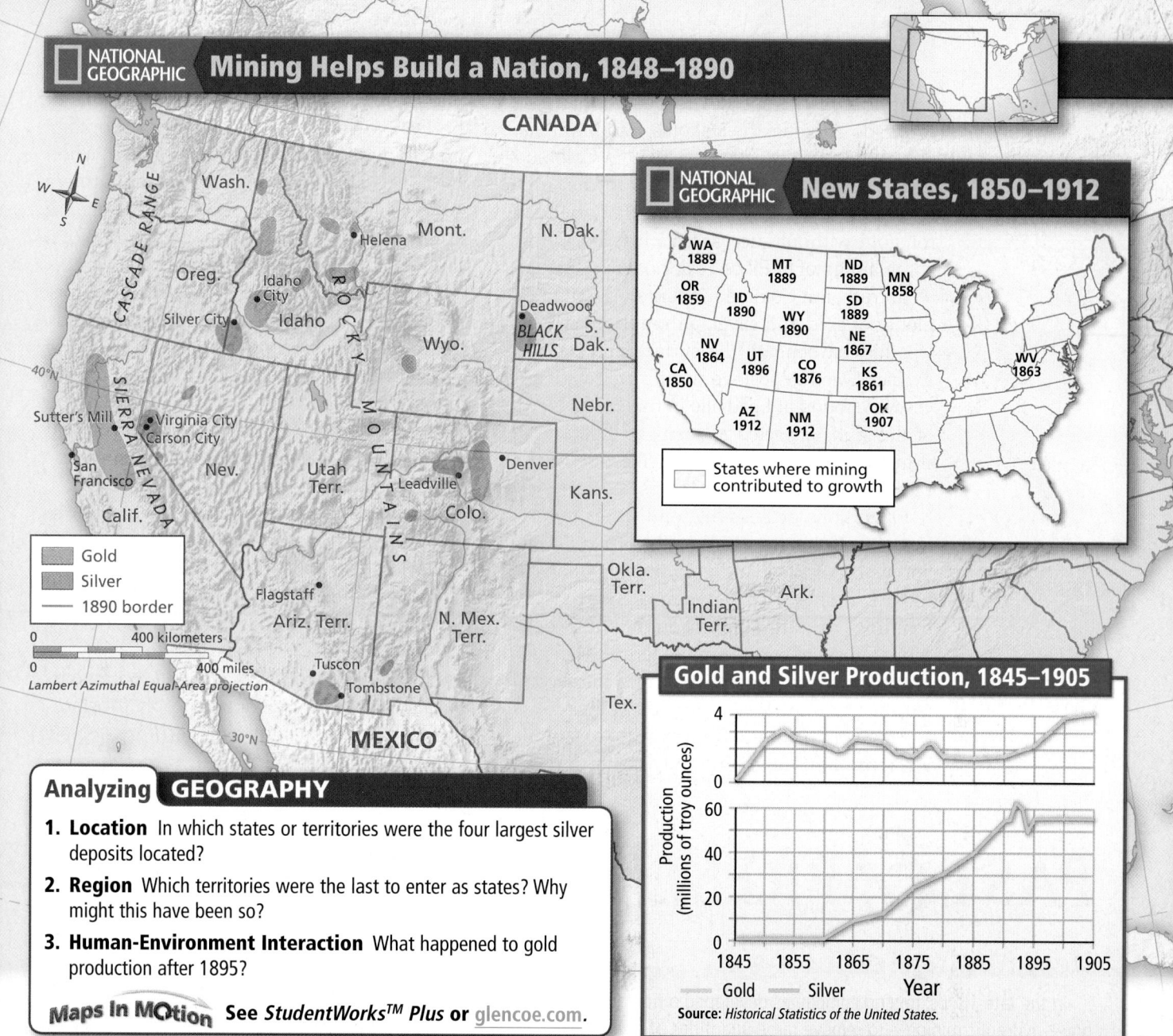

NATIONAL GEOGRAPHIC — Mining Helps Build a Nation, 1848–1890

CANADA

Wash.
Oreg.
Mont.
N. Dak.
Helena
Idaho
Idaho City
Silver City
Wyo.
Deadwood
BLACK HILLS
S. Dak.
Sutter's Mill
Virginia City
Carson City
San Francisco
Nev.
Utah Terr.
Leadville
Denver
Nebr.
Calif.
Colo.
Kans.
Flagstaff
Ariz. Terr.
N. Mex. Terr.
Tuscon
Tombstone
Okla. Terr.
Indian Terr.
Ark.
Tex.
MEXICO

Legend:
- Gold
- Silver
- 1890 border

0 — 400 kilometers
0 — 400 miles
Lambert Azimuthal Equal-Area projection

NATIONAL GEOGRAPHIC — New States, 1850–1912

WA 1889	MT 1889	ND 1889
OR 1859	ID 1890	MN 1858
	WY 1890	SD 1889
NV 1864	UT 1896	NE 1867
CA 1850	CO 1876	KS 1861
		WV 1863
AZ 1912	NM 1912	OK 1907

States where mining contributed to growth

Analyzing GEOGRAPHY

1. **Location** In which states or territories were the four largest silver deposits located?

2. **Region** Which territories were the last to enter as states? Why might this have been so?

3. **Human-Environment Interaction** What happened to gold production after 1895?

Maps In Motion See StudentWorks™ Plus or glencoe.com.

Gold and Silver Production, 1845–1905

Production (millions of troy ounces)

Gold chart (top): values 0 to 4
Silver chart (bottom): values 0, 20, 40, 60

Year: 1845, 1855, 1865, 1875, 1885, 1895, 1905

— Gold   — Silver

Source: *Historical Statistics of the United States.*

Boomtowns were rowdy places. Prospectors fought over claims, and thieves haunted the streets and trails. Often, "law and order" was enforced by **vigilance committees**—self-appointed volunteers who would track down and punish wrongdoers. In some cases, they punished the innocent or let the guilty go free, but most people respected the law and tried to deal firmly but fairly with the accused.

Men were usually first to arrive at a mining site, but women soon followed. Many found work in laundries or as cooks. Others worked at "hurdy-gurdy" houses (named after the mechanical violin), where they waited on tables and danced with men for the price of a drink. Some women became property owners and community leaders.

Boomtowns could not last forever because, eventually, the mines that supported the economy would be used up. A few boomtowns were able to survive when the mines closed, but many did not. Instead, they went "bust"—a term borrowed from card games that refers to players losing all of their money. In Virginia City, for example, the mines were exhausted by the late 1870s, and the economy collapsed. Most residents moved on; by 1930, Virginia City had only 500 residents. Other towns were completely abandoned, becoming "ghost-towns."

Mining Leads to Statehood

Mining also spurred the development of Colorado, Arizona, the Dakotas, and Montana. After gold was discovered in 1858 in Colorado near Pikes Peak, miners rushed to the area, declaring "Pikes Peak or Bust." Many panned for gold without success and headed home, complaining of a "Pikes Peak hoax."

In truth, the Colorado mountains contained plenty of gold and silver, although much of it was hidden beneath the surface and hard to **extract.** Deep deposits of lead mixed with silver were found at Leadville in the 1870s. News of the strike attracted as many as 1,000 new-comers a week, making Leadville one of the West's most famous boomtowns.

Operations at Leadville and other mining towns in Colorado yielded more than $1 billion worth of silver and gold (many billions in today's money). This bonanza spurred the building of railroads through the Rocky Mountains and transformed Denver, the supply point for the mining areas, into the second largest city in the West, after San Francisco.

Three railroads, the Denver and Rio Grande Western, the South Park and Pacific, and the Colorado Midland all made stops at towns in the mining region.

The discovery of gold in the Black Hills of the Dakota Territory and copper in Montana drew miners to the region in the 1870s. When the railroads were completed, many farmers and ranchers settled the area. In 1889 Congress admitted three new states: North Dakota, South Dakota, and Montana.

In the Southwest, the Arizona Territory followed a similar pattern. Miners had already begun moving to Arizona in the 1860s and 1870s to work one of the nation's largest copper deposits. When silver was found at the town of Tombstone in 1877, however, it set off a boom that attracted a huge wave of prospectors to the territory.

The boom lasted less than 10 years, but in that time, Tombstone became famous for its lawlessness. Marshall Wyatt Earp and his brothers gained their reputations during the famous gunfight at the O. K. Corral there in 1881. Although Arizona did not grow as quickly as Colorado, Nevada, or Montana, by 1912 it had enough people to apply for statehood, as did the neighboring territory of New Mexico.

PAST & PRESENT

New Mining Technology

In the late 1800s, mining companies developed a new technology—hydraulic mining—to remove large quantities of earth and process it for minerals. Miners generated a high-pressure spray by directing water from nearby rivers into narrower and narrower channels, through a large canvas hose and out a giant iron nozzle called a monitor. Using a powerful high-pressure blast of water, "a handful of men," as one journalist wrote, "took out the very heart of a mountain."

Although hydraulic mining is no longer used in the United States, the invention of earth-moving machines such as bulldozers and excavators has made it possible to continue to dig for minerals by removing large quantities of earth. This kind of mining is called open-pit mining or strip mining. It has many of the same problems faced by hydraulic miners. Specifically, something has to be done with the leftovers. The processed ore is usually pumped to a pond, where the water evaporates. These ponds can often be toxic because of the chemicals and minerals that are left after the ore is removed.

1866

▲ The high-pressure water washed the loose earth into large sluices, or ditches that carried the water and earth into riffle boxes. The boxes agitated the water, causing the silver or gold to settle out. The leftover debris, called tailings or "slickens," was then washed into a nearby stream.

Mining Technology

Extracting minerals from the rugged mountains of the American West required ingenuity and patience. Early prospectors extracted shallow deposits of ore in a process called placer mining, using simple tools like picks, shovels, and pans.

Other prospectors used sluice mining. Sluices were used to search riverbeds more quickly than the panning method. A sluice diverted the current of a river into trenches. The water was directed to a box with metal "riffle" bars that caused heavier minerals to settle to the bottom of the box. A screen at the end of the box prevented the minerals from escaping with the water and sediment.

When deposits near the surface ran out, miners began **hydraulic mining** to remove large quantities of earth and process it for minerals. Miners sprayed water at very high pressure against the hill or mountain they were mining. The water pressure washed away the dirt, gravel, and rock, and exposed the minerals beneath the surface.

Hydraulic mining began in California, near Nevada City. It effectively removed large quantities of minerals and generated a lot of tax money for local and state governments. Unfortunately, it also had a devastating effect on the local environment. Millions of tons of silt, sand, and gravel were washed into local rivers. The sediment raised the riverbed, and the rivers began overflowing their banks, causing major floods that wrecked fences, destroyed orchards, and deposited rocks and gravel on what had been good farm soil.

In the 1880s farmers fought back by suing the mining companies. In 1884 federal judge Lorenzo Sawyer ruled in favor of the farmers. He declared hydraulic mining a "public and private nuisance" and issued an injunction stopping the practice.

Congress eventually passed a law in 1893 allowing hydraulic mining if the mining company created a place to store the sediment. By then most mining companies had moved to quartz mining—the kind of mining familiar to people today—in which deep mine shafts are dug, and miners go underground to extract the minerals.

Reading Check **Explaining** What role did mining play in the development of the American West?

August 1995

▼ Mining is still very important to the western economy. The Kennecott Copper Mine in Bingham Canyon, Utah, is the largest human-made excavation in the world. The mine is 2½ miles wide and ¾ mile deep. It supplies approximately 15% of all copper used in the United States.

▲ An example of the problems of open-pit mining can be seen at the Berkeley Pit copper mine in Montana (above). When the mine closed, groundwater flooded the pit. The water passed through mineral deposits and became very acidic and contaminated with chemicals. Cleanup is scheduled for 2018 once a treatment plant has been built.

MAKING CONNECTIONS

1. **Comparing** How was mining in the 1880s similar to mining today?
2. **Problem-Solving** How might mining companies avoid damaging the environment and still extract the minerals they need?

Ranching and Cattle Drives

MAIN Idea Ranchers built vast cattle ranches on the Great Plains and shipped their cattle on railroads to eastern markets.

HISTORY AND YOU What images come to mind when you think of cowboys? Read on to learn about the realities of life as a cowboy in the West.

While many Americans headed to the Rocky Mountains to mine gold and silver, others began herding cattle on the Great Plains. Americans had long believed it was impossible to raise cattle in the region. Water was scarce, and cattle from the East could not survive on the tough prairie grasses. In Texas, however, lived a breed of cattle that had **adapted** to the Great Plains—the Texas longhorn.

The longhorn was descended from Spanish cattle introduced two centuries earlier. These cattle had been allowed to run wild and, slowly, a new breed—the longhorn—had emerged.

Lean and rangy, the longhorn could easily survive the harsh climate of the Plains. By 1865, some 5 million roamed the Texas grasslands.

Cattle ranching also prospered on the Plains because of the **open range,** a vast area of grassland that the federal government owned. The open range covered much of the Great Plains and provided land where ranchers could graze their herds free of charge and unrestricted by private property.

The Long Drive Begins

Prior to the Civil War, ranchers had little incentive to round up the longhorns. Beef prices were low, and moving cattle to eastern markets was not practical. The Civil War and the coming of the railroads changed this situation. During the Civil War, eastern cattle were slaughtered in huge numbers to feed the armies of the Union and the Confederacy. After the war, beef prices soared and ranchers looked for a way to round up the longhorns and sell them to eastern businesses.

NATIONAL GEOGRAPHIC

Cattle Ranching and the Long Drive, c. 1870

Cattle trails
Railroads
1890 border

0   200 kilometers
0   200 miles
Lambert Azimuthal Equal-Area projection

PRIMARY SOURCE

Charles Goodnight and Oliver Loving carved out the Goodnight-Loving Trail from Texas to Colorado, New Mexico, and Wyoming. Goodnight spoke of the dangers of a night stampede:

"The cattle were nervous and easily frightened, and the slightest noise might startle them into running. The heat developed by a large drove of cattle during a stampede was surprising .... Animal heat seems to attract electricity, especially when the cattle are wet, and after a storm I have seen the faces of men riding with a herd scorched as if some furnace blast had blazed against them."

—from *The West*

By the 1860s, railroads had reached the Great Plains. Lines ended at Abilene and Dodge City in Kansas and at Sedalia in Missouri. Ranchers and livestock dealers realized that if they could move the cattle as far as the railroad, the longhorns could be sold for a huge profit and shipped east to market.

In 1866 ranchers began rounding up the longhorns and drove about 260,000 of them to Sedalia, Missouri. Most of the cattle did not survive this first **long drive,** but those that survived sold for 10 times the price they would have brought in Texas. Other trails soon opened. The route to Abilene, Kansas, became the major route north. Between 1867 and 1871, cowboys drove nearly 1.5 million head of cattle up the Chisholm Trail from southern Texas to Abilene. As the railroads expanded in the West, other trails reached from Texas to more towns in Kansas, Nebraska, Montana, and Wyoming.

A long drive was a spectacular sight. In the spring, ranchers met with their cowboys to round up cattle from the open range. Stock from many different owners made up these herds. Cowboys from major ranches went north with the herds. The only way to tell them apart was by the brands burned onto their hides by branding irons. Stray calves without brands were called mavericks. These were divided and branded. The herds could number anywhere from 2,000 to 5,000 cattle.

Ranching Becomes Big Business

Cowboys drove millions of cattle north from Texas to Kansas and points beyond. Some of the longhorns went straight to slaughterhouses, but others were sold to ranchers who were building up herds in Wyoming, Montana, and other territories. Sheep herders moved their flocks onto the range and farmers settled there, blocking the trails. "Range wars" broke out among groups competing for land. Eventually, after much loss of life, hundreds of square miles were fenced cheaply and easily with a new invention—barbed wire.

At first, ranchers did not want to abandon open grazing and complained when farmers put up barriers that prevented the ranchers' livestock from roaming. Soon, however, ranchers used barbed wire to shut out those competing with them for land and to keep their animals closer to sources of food and water. For cowboys, however, barbed wire ended the adventure of the long cattle drive.

The fencing of the range was not the only reason the long drives ended. Investors from the East and from Britain had poured money into the booming cattle business, causing an oversupply of animals on the market. Prices plummeted in the mid-1880s and many ranchers went bankrupt. Then, in the winter of 1886–1887, blizzards buried the Plains in deep snow, and temperatures dropped as low as 40 degrees below zero. Massive numbers of cattle froze or starved to death.

The cattle industry survived this terrible blow, but it was changed forever. The day of the open range had ended. From that point on, herds were raised on fenced-in ranches. New European breeds replaced longhorns, and the cowboy became a ranch hand.

▼ Women help rope and brand cattle at the J. W. Lough ranch in Kansas, 1891.

Analyzing VISUALS **DBQ**

1. **Explaining** What were two by-products of a cattle stampede?
2. **Analyzing** Why did the cattle trails north stop where they did?

✔ Reading Check **Analyzing** How did heavy investment in the cattle industry affect the industry as a whole?

Settling the Hispanic Southwest

MAIN Idea The arrival of new settlers changed life for Hispanics in the Southwest.

HISTORY AND YOU Do you remember reading about New Spain? Read on to learn how the Hispanic community changed when the Southwest became part of the United States.

For centuries, much of what is today the American Southwest belonged to Spain's empire. After Mexico won its independence, the region became the northern territories of the Republic of Mexico. When the United States defeated Mexico in 1848 and took control of the region, it acquired the Spanish-speaking population living there. According to the Treaty of Guadalupe Hidalgo ending the war, the region's residents retained their property rights and became American citizens.

In California, the Spanish mission system had collapsed by the early 1800s. In its place, a society dominated by a landholding elite had emerged. These landowners owned vast **haciendas**—huge ranches that covered thousands of acres. The heavy influx of "Forty-Niners" during the California gold rush, however, changed this society dramatically. California's population grew from 14,000 to 100,000 in two years. Suddenly, Hispanic Californians were vastly outnumbered.

Some Hispanic Californians welcomed the newcomers and the economic growth that resulted. Others distrusted the English-speaking prospectors, who tried to exclude them from the mines. When California achieved statehood in 1850, Hispanics served in many state and local offices. Increasingly, however, the original Hispanic population found their status diminished and, frequently, they were relegated to lower-paying and less desirable jobs.

As they had done with Native Americans, settlers from the East clashed with Mexican Americans over land. Across the region, many Hispanics lost their land to the new settlers.

PRIMARY SOURCE
Hispanics in the Southwest

In the mid-19th century, most Hispanics in the Southwest lived on large haciendas where they worked in the fields harvesting crops or helped tend cattle.

A fancily dressed vaquero, known as a *charro*, poses for a photo in 1890.

PRIMARY SOURCE

"As a horseman, [the vaquero] has no superiors, and it is mounted that he operates with such sure effect against the wild animals. The sport of 'lassoing' wild bulls and other cattle is highly exciting, and one of which all Spanish Americans are passionately fond. To catch the animal by his horns or neck requires much skill, yet to seize him with certainty by the leg, when at the top of his speed, requires greater practice and dexterity. "

—from *Gleason's Pictorial Drawing-Room Companion*, 1852

▲ Hispanic farmworkers harvest grapes in southern California in 1905.

Analyzing VISUALS

1. **Making Generalizations** Based on the appearance of the vaquero in the photo at left, what generalizations can you make about the man?

2. **Analyzing** What do you notice about the types of people who were farmworkers? Why might this be so?

Mexican American claims to the land often dated back to Spanish land grants. These grants were hundreds of years old and defined the boundaries of property in vague terms. When ownership of a property was claimed by more than one person, American courts frequently held that the old land grants were insufficient proof of ownership. This allowed others to stake claim to the property. In some instances, outright fraud was used to take land illegally from Mexican Americans.

The cattle boom of the 1870s and 1880s had a tremendous impact on Hispanics in the Southwest, where many had long worked as vaqueros (the Spanish word for "cowboys"). Vaqueros developed the tools and techniques for managing cattle. They taught American cowboys their trade and enriched the English language with words of Spanish origin, including "lariat," "lasso," and "stampede."

With the increasing demand for beef in the eastern United States, English-speaking ranchers wanted to expand their herds and claimed large tracts of land of Mexican origin. In some cases, the Hispanic population fought back. In New Mexico, residents of the town of Las Vegas were outraged when English-speaking ranchers tried to fence in land that had long been used by the community to graze livestock. In 1889 a group of Hispanic New Mexicans calling themselves *Las Gorras Blancas* (white caps) raided ranches owned by English-speakers, tore down their fences, and burned their barns and houses. The raids finally ended in 1890 when the governor threatened to call in federal troops.

Despite the influx of English-speaking settlers, Hispanics in New Mexico remained more influential in public affairs than did their counterparts in California and Texas. Hispanics remained the majority, both in population and in the territorial legislature. In addition, a Hispanic frequently served as New Mexico's territorial delegate to Congress.

As more railroads were built in the 1880s and 1890s, the population of the Southwest continued to swell. The region not only attracted Americans and European immigrants, but also immigrants from Mexico. Mexican immigrants worked mainly in agriculture and on the railroads. In the growing cities of the Southwest—such as El Paso, Albuquerque, and Los Angeles—Hispanics settled in neighborhoods called **barrios.** Barrios had Spanish-speaking businesses and Spanish-language newspapers and they helped keep Hispanic cultural and religious traditions alive. As native Californian Mariano Guadalupe Vallejo explained in 1890:

PRIMARY SOURCE

"No class of American citizens is more loyal than the Spanish Californians, but we shall always be especially proud ... to honor the founders of our ancient families, and the saints and heroes of our history since the days when Father Junipero planted the cross at Monterey."

—quoted in *Foreigners in Their Native Land*

Reading Check **Describing** How did vaqueros contribute to the cattle industry in the West?

Section 1 REVIEW

Vocabulary

1. **Explain** the significance of: Henry Comstock, boomtown, vigilance committee, hydraulic mining, open range, long drive, hacienda, barrios.

Main Ideas

2. **Explaining** How did hydraulic mining affect the environment?

3. **Stating** What caused the decline of the cattle business in the late 1800s?

4. **Describing** How did the gold rush change society in California?

Critical Thinking

5. **Big Ideas** How did mining contribute to the development of the West?

6. **Organizing** Use a graphic organizer similar to the one below to list the ways barbed wire was used and the result of using barbed wire on the Great Plains.

7. **Analyzing Visuals** Sketch a map of the western cattle trails. Then compare your map to the one on page 162, and list the differences between the two maps.

Writing About History

8. **Descriptive Writing** Write a summary for a story line for a Hollywood movie. Your script should realistically portray the life of either a miner or rancher in the West in the mid- to late 1800s.

History ONLINE

Study Central™ To review this section, go to glencoe.com and click on Study Central.

Farming the Plains

Guide to Reading

Big Ideas
Group Action After 1865 settlers staked out homesteads and began farming the Great Plains.

Content Vocabulary
- homestead *(p. 167)*
- dry farming *(p. 168)*
- sodbuster *(p. 168)*
- bonanza farm *(p. 169)*

Academic Vocabulary
- prospective *(p. 166)*
- innovation *(p. 168)*

People and Events to Identify
- Great Plains *(p. 166)*
- Stephen Long *(p. 166)*
- Homestead Act *(p. 167)*
- Wheat Belt *(p. 169)*

Reading Strategy
Organizing As you read about the settlement of the Great Plains, complete a graphic organizer similar to the one below by listing the ways the government encouraged settlement.

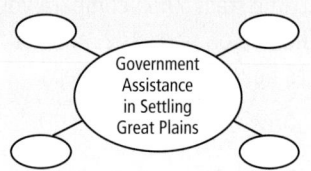

Government Assistance in Settling Great Plains

The Homestead Act encouraged settlers to move to the Great Plains. Although life was difficult, settlers discovered that wheat could be grown on the Great Plains using new technologies. By 1890 there was no longer a true frontier in the United States.

The Beginnings of Settlement

MAIN Idea Settlers staked out homesteads and began farming the region.

HISTORY AND YOU Would you move to a region with extreme weather such as drought and blizzards? Read on to learn how settlers coped with the harsh environment of the Great Plains.

The population of the **Great Plains** grew steadily in the decades after the Civil War. Land once thought to be worthless for farming was transformed into America's wheat belt. Homesteaders faced many challenges. Without trees to use as timber, many early settlers built their homes from chunks of sod, densely packed soil held together by grass roots. To obtain water, they had to drill wells more than 100 feet deep and operate the pump by hand. Nothing was wasted. Homesteader Charley O'Kieffe recalled eating weeds from the garden, as well as the vegetables, joking that he was obeying the rule, "If you can't beat 'em, eat 'em."

O'Kieffe and his neighbors were early settlers on the Great Plains. This region extends westward to the Rocky Mountains from around the 100th meridian—a line of longitude running north and south from the central Dakotas through western Texas. It is dry grassland where trees grow naturally only along rivers and streams. For centuries this open country had been home to vast herds of buffalo that grazed on the prairie grasses. Nomadic Native American groups had hunted the buffalo for food and used buffalo hides for clothing and shelter.

Major **Stephen Long,** who explored the region with an army expedition in 1819, called it the "Great American Desert" and concluded that it was "almost wholly unfit for cultivation." He predicted that the scarcity of wood and water would prove to be "an insuperable obstacle in . . . settling the country."

During the late 1800s, several developments undermined the assumption that the region was uninhabitable. One important factor was the construction of the railroads. Railroad companies sold land along the rail lines at low prices and provided credit to **prospective** settlers. Pamphlets and posters spread the news to city dwellers across Europe and America that cheap farm land was theirs to claim if they were willing to move.

Corn
Cotton
Wheat
Cattle

0 200 kilometers
0 200 miles
Lambert Azimuthal Equal-Area projection

▲ *A family stands outside their sod house on the Great Plains in 1880. There were very few trees on the Great Plains, and wood was expensive because it had to be shipped to the region. So settlers cut chunks of earth from the ground to build their homes.*

What Was the Homestead Act?

The Homestead Act of 1862 created a procedure for people who wanted to settle on federal land in the West.

Requirements of the Act
- Settlers had to be 21 years of age.
- Settlers had to be head of a household.
- Settlers had to pay a $10 filing fee and $2 commission to the land agent to be given 160 acres of land.
- To gain title to the land, settlers had to live on it for five years, and make improvements such as building a house and clearing land for farming.
- Alternatively, settlers could buy the land for $1.25 per acre after six months.

Analyzing GEOGRAPHY

1. **Human-Environment Interaction** What were the similarities and differences in land use between Iowa and California?
2. **Region** In what region of the country were both cattle raised and cotton grown?

A Nebraskan coined the slogan "Rain follows the plow" to sell the idea that cultivating the Plains would increase rainfall. The weather seemed to cooperate. For more than a decade beginning in the 1870s, rainfall on the Plains was well above average. The lush green of the plains contradicted assertions that the region was a desert.

In 1862 the government encouraged settlement on the Great Plains by passing the **Homestead Act.** For a $10 registration fee, an individual could file for a **homestead**—a tract of public land available for settlement. A homesteader could claim up to 160 acres of land and could receive title to that land after living there for five years. Later government legislation increased the size of the tracts available. With their property rights assured, more settlers moved to the Plains.

Settlers often found life very difficult on the Plains. In addition to building sod houses and drilling deep wells for water, they faced summer temperatures greater than 100°F. Prairie fires were a frequent danger. Sometimes swarms of grasshoppers swept over farms and destroyed the crops. In winter there were terrible blizzards and extreme cold. Despite these challenges and hardships, most homesteaders persisted and gradually learned how to live in the difficult environment.

☑ Reading Check **Analyzing** What is the relationship between private property rights and the settlement of the Great Plains?

The Wheat Belt

MAIN Idea As a result of new farming methods and machinery, settlers on the Great Plains were able to produce large amounts of wheat.

HISTORY AND YOU Do you remember learning about the way the cotton gin changed Southern life? Read on to learn how agricultural practices changed life on the Plains.

History ONLINE
Student Web Activity Visit glencoe.com and complete the activity on settling the West.

Many new farming methods and inventions in the nineteenth century revolutionized agriculture. One approach, called **dry farming,** was to plant seeds deep in the ground, where there was enough moisture for them to grow. By the 1860s farmers on the Plains were using plows, seed drills, reapers, and threshing machines. These new steel machines made dry farming possible. Unfortunately, soil on the plains could blow away during a dry season. Many **sodbusters,** as those who plowed the Plains were called, eventually lost their homesteads through the combined effects of drought, wind erosion, and overuse of the land.

Large landholders could invest in mechanical reapers and steam tractors that made it easier to harvest a large crop. Threshing machines knocked kernels loose from the stalks. Mechanical binders tied the stalks into bundles for collection. These **innovations** were well suited for harvesting wheat, a crop that could endure the dry conditions of the Great Plains.

During the 1880s many farmers from the Midwest moved to the Great Plains to take advantage of the inexpensive land and the new

TECHNOLOGY & HISTORY

Farm Machinery Farmers are indebted to the inventions of John Deere and Cyrus McCormick. Deere's steel plow broke through the hard ground. McCormick's mechanical reaper did the work of five men. Later inventions included a mechanical harrow to help prepare the ground for seeds and a grain drill to plant seeds.

The tail keeps the rotor oriented into the wind.

▼ Windmills were vital to settling the Great Plains where farmers faced one major problem: a lack of water. There were few rivers, and it rarely rained. To get water, settlers drilled deep wells and used windmills to pump the water to the surface. The strong winds on the flat, treeless plains were an ideal power source.

In the 1870s, the rotor was made of wooden blades. In high winds, the sections could tilt open to let wind through and protect the rotor from damage.

The pump is run by a crank in the gear box that is connected to a shaft in the tower.

▼ Technology made farming the vast open plains of America feasible. Here, horse-drawn binders are being used to gather hay in the late 1800s.

Analyzing VISUALS

1. **Identifying** What was used to power the windmill?
2. **Analyzing Visuals** In addition to field hands, what else did farmers using mechanical harvesting machines need?

farming technology. The **Wheat Belt** began at the eastern edge of the Great Plains and encompassed much of the Dakotas and parts of Nebraska and Kansas. The new machines allowed a single family to bring in a substantial harvest on a wheat farm covering several hundred acres. Some wheat farms covered up to 50,000 acres. These were called **bonanza farms** because they yielded big profits. Like mine owners, bonanza farmers formed companies, invested in property and equipment, and hired laborers as needed.

Farmers Fall on Hard Times

The bountiful harvests in the Wheat Belt helped the United States become the world's leading exporter of wheat by the 1880s. Then things began to go wrong. A severe drought struck the Plains in the late 1880s, destroying crops and turning the soil to dust. In addition, competition from farmers in other countries began to increase. By the 1890s a glut of wheat on the world market caused prices to drop. Some farmers tried to make it through these difficult times by mortgaging their land—that is, they borrowed money based on the value of their land. If they failed to meet their mortgage payments, they forfeited the land to the bank. Some who lost their land continued to work it as tenant farmers, renting the land from its new owners. By 1900 tenants cultivated about one-third of the farms on the Plains.

Closing the Frontier

On April 22, 1889, the government opened one of the last large territories for settlement. Within hours, more than 10,000 people raced to stake claims in an event known as the Oklahoma Land Rush. The next year, the Census Bureau reported that there was no longer a true frontier left in America. In reality, there was still a lot of unoccupied land, and new settlement continued into the 1900s, but the "closing of the frontier" marked the end of an era. It worried many people, including historian Frederick Jackson Turner. Turner believed that the frontier had provided a "safety-valve of social discontent." It was a place where Americans could always make a fresh start.

Most settlers did indeed make a fresh start, adapting to the difficult environment of the Plains. Water from their deep wells enabled them to plant trees and gardens. Railroads brought lumber and brick to replace sod as a building material, as well as coal for fuel. They also brought manufactured goods from the East, such as clothes and household goods. Small-scale farmers rarely became wealthy, but they could be self-sufficient. Typical homesteaders raised cattle, chickens, and a few crops. The real story of the West was not one of limitless opportunity, nor one in which heroes rode off into the sunset. It was about ordinary people who settled down and built homes and communities through great effort.

Reading Check **Identifying** What technological innovations helped farmers cultivate the Plains?

Section 2 REVIEW

Vocabulary

1. **Explain** the significance of: Great Plains, Stephen Long, Homestead Act, homestead, dry farming, sodbuster, Wheat Belt, bonanza farm.

Main Ideas

2. **Identifying** How did the Homestead Act encourage settlement of the Plains?

3. **Explaining** What factors contributed to the making of the Wheat Belt in the Great Plains and then to troubled times for wheat farmers in the 1890s?

Critical Thinking

4. **Big Ideas** What challenges did Plains farmers face?

5. **Organizing** Make a graphic organizer similar to the one below that lists the effects of technology on farming in the Great Plains.

Invention	Advantage for Farmers

6. **Analyzing Visuals** Examine the photograph on page 168 of farmers using machinery. Based on the terrain and the type of work they needed to do, what other types of technology would have helped farmers on the Plains?

Writing About History

7. **Persuasive Writing** Write an advertisement to persuade people from the East and Europe to establish homesteads on the Great Plains.

History ONLINE

Study Central™ To review this section, go to glencoe.com and click on Study Central.

Native Americans

Guide to Reading

Big Ideas
Culture and Beliefs Settling the West dramatically changed the way of life of the Plains Indians.

Content Vocabulary
• nomad (p. 170)
• annuity (p. 170)
• assimilate (p. 175)
• allotment (p. 175)

Academic Vocabulary
• relocate (p. 170)
• ensure (p. 172)
• approximately (p. 175)

People and Events to Identify
• Sand Creek Massacre (p. 172)
• Indian Peace Commission (p. 172)
• George A. Custer (p. 173)
• Chief Joseph (p. 174)
• Dawes Act (p. 175)

Reading Strategy
Sequencing As you read about the crises facing Native Americans during the late 1800s, complete a time line to record the battles between Native Americans and the United States government and the results of each.

As settlers entered Native American lands on the Great Plains, clashes grew more common. Conflicts continued as the government tried to force Native Americans onto reservations and encouraged them to assimilate into the culture of the United States.

Struggles of the Plains Indians

MAIN Idea The settlement of the West dramatically altered the way of life of the Plains Indians.

HISTORY AND YOU Can you recall a situation in which someone broke a promise to you? Do you remember your reaction? Read on to learn how Native Americans responded when the federal government broke treaties.

For centuries the Great Plains were home to many groups of Native Americans. Some lived in communities as farmers and hunters, but many were **nomads** who roamed vast distances, following their main source of food—the buffalo.

The groups of Plains Indians were similar in many ways. Plains Indian nations were divided into bands consisting of up to 500 people. A governing council headed each band, but most members participated in making decisions. Most lived in extended family groups and believed in the spiritual power of the natural world.

The ranchers, miners, and farmers who moved onto the Plains deprived Native Americans of their hunting grounds, broke treaties guaranteeing certain lands to the Plains Indians, and often forced them to **relocate** to new territory. Native Americans resisted by attacking wagon trains, stagecoaches, and ranches. Occasionally, an entire group would go to war against nearby settlers and troops.

The Dakota Sioux Uprising

The first major clash began in 1862, when the Dakota people (also known as the Sioux) launched a major uprising in Minnesota. The Sioux had agreed to live on a reservation in exchange for **annuities**, or annual payments from the government. The annuities, however, frequently got caught up in bureaucracy and corruption and never reached them. By 1862 many lived in desperate poverty and faced possible starvation. When Chief Little Crow asked local traders to provide food on credit, one replied, "If they are hungry, let them eat grass or their own dung." Two weeks later, when the Dakota took up arms, that trader was found dead with his mouth stuffed with grass.

Little Crow reluctantly agreed to lead this uprising. He wanted to wage war against soldiers, not civilians, but he was unable to keep

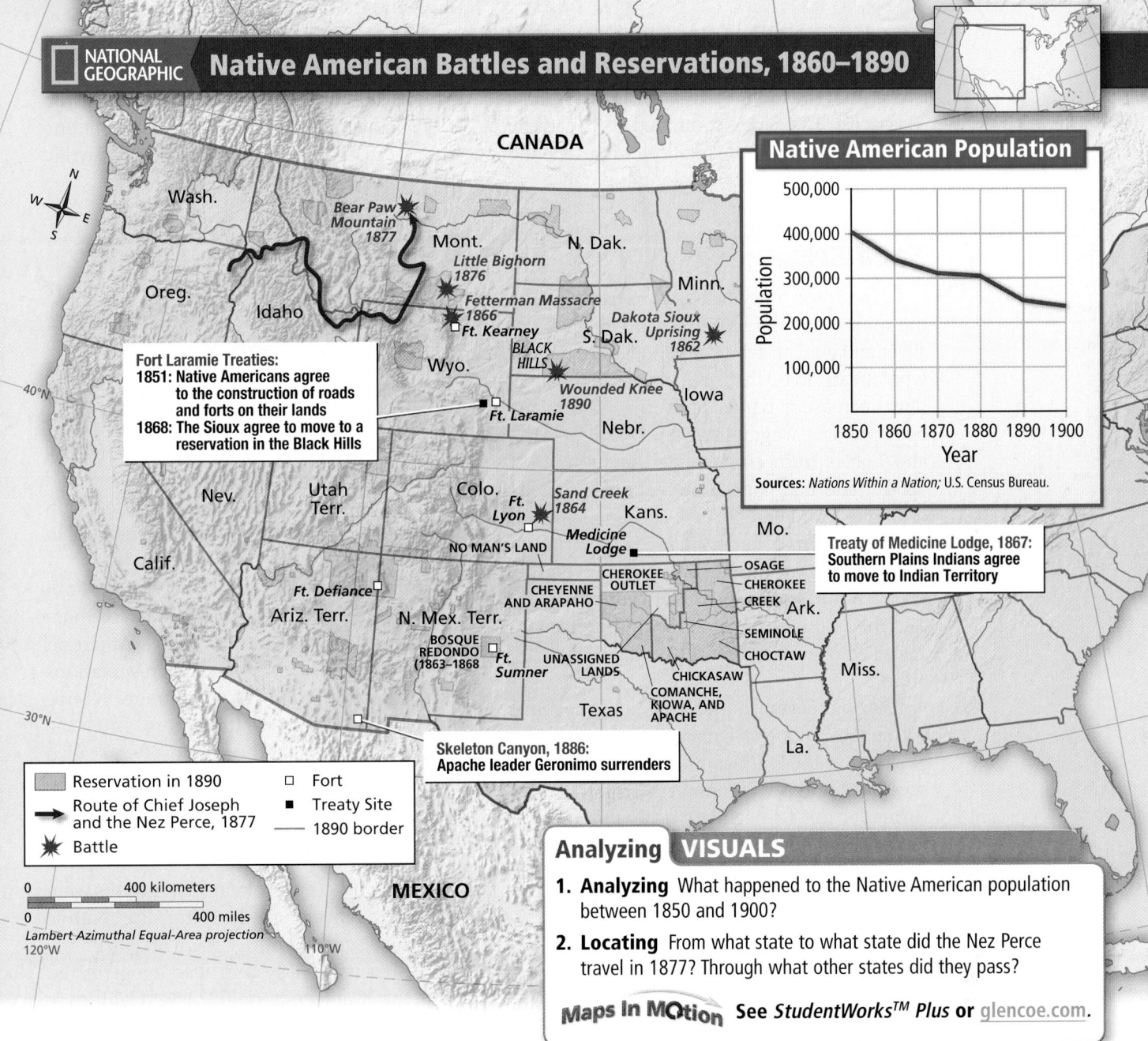

Native American Population

CANADA

Wash.

Bear Paw Mountain 1877

Mont.

N. Dak.

Little Bighorn 1876

Minn.

Fetterman Massacre 1866

Oreg.

Idaho

Ft. Kearney

Dakota Sioux Uprising 1862

S. Dak.

BLACK HILLS

Fort Laramie Treaties:
1851: Native Americans agree to the construction of roads and forts on their lands
1868: The Sioux agree to move to a reservation in the Black Hills

Wyo.

Wounded Knee 1890

Iowa

Ft. Laramie

Nebr.

Nev.

Utah Terr.

Colo.

Ft. Lyon

Sand Creek 1864

Kans.

Mo.

NO MAN'S LAND

Medicine Lodge

Treaty of Medicine Lodge, 1867:
Southern Plains Indians agree to move to Indian Territory

Calif.

Ft. Defiance

Ariz. Terr.

CHEYENNE AND ARAPAHO

CHEROKEE OUTLET

OSAGE

CHEROKEE

CREEK

Ark.

N. Mex. Terr.

BOSQUE REDONDO (1863–1868)

Ft. Sumner

UNASSIGNED LANDS

SEMINOLE

CHOCTAW

Miss.

CHICKASAW

Texas

COMANCHE, KIOWA, AND APACHE

La.

Skeleton Canyon, 1886:
Apache leader Geronimo surrenders

Reservation in 1890

Route of Chief Joseph and the Nez Perce, 1877

Battle

Fort

Treaty Site

1890 border

0   400 kilometers
0   400 miles

Lambert Azimuthal Equal-Area projection
120°W   110°W

MEXICO

Sources: *Nations Within a Nation;* U.S. Census Bureau.

Analyzing VISUALS

1. **Analyzing** What happened to the Native American population between 1850 and 1900?

2. **Locating** From what state to what state did the Nez Perce travel in 1877? Through what other states did they pass?

Maps In MOtion See *StudentWorks*™ *Plus* or glencoe.com.

angry Dakota from slaughtering hundreds of settlers in the area.

After the rebellion was suppressed, a military tribunal sentenced 307 Dakota to death. After reviewing the evidence, President Lincoln reduced the number to 38. Others fled the reservation when federal troops arrived and became exiles in a region that bore their name—the Dakota Territory.

Red Cloud's War

The Dakota Territory was home to another Sioux tribe, the Lakota. The Lakota were a nomadic tribe who fought hard to keep control

of their hunting grounds, which extended from the Black Hills westward to the Bighorn Mountains. They had battled rival groups for this country and did not intend to let settlers have it. Leading them were chiefs Red Cloud, Crazy Horse, and Sitting Bull.

The army suffered a major defeat during "Red Cloud's War" of 1866–1868. The army was constructing forts along the Bozeman Trail, the path used to reach the Montana gold mines. In December 1866, Crazy Horse, a religious leader and war chief, tricked the fort's commander into sending Captain William Fetterman and about 80 soldiers out to pursue what they thought was a small raiding party.

Hundreds of warriors were waiting in ambush and wiped out the entire unit (an event that became known as Fetterman's Massacre). The Sioux continued to resist any military presence in the region, and in 1868 the army abandoned its posts along the trail.

Sand Creek

In the 1860s tensions began to rise between the miners coming into Colorado in search of silver and gold and the Cheyenne and Arapaho who already lived there. As the number of settlers increased, bands of Native Americans began raiding wagon trains and stealing cattle and horses from ranches. By the summer of 1864, trade had come to a standstill, dozens of homes had been burned, and an estimated 200 settlers had been killed. The territorial governor, John Evans, ordered the Native Americans to surrender at Fort Lyon, where he said they would be given food and protection. Those who failed to report would be subject to attack.

Although several hundred Native Americans surrendered at the fort, many others did not. In November 1864, Chief Black Kettle brought several hundred Cheyenne to the fort, not to surrender but to negotiate a peace deal. The fort's commander did not have the authority to negotiate, and he told Black Kettle to make camp at Sand Creek while he waited for orders. Shortly afterward, Colonel John Chivington of the Colorado Volunteers was ordered to attack the Cheyenne at Sand Creek.

When Chivington stopped at Fort Lyon, he was told that the Native Americans at Sand Creek were waiting to negotiate. Chivington replied that, since the Cheyenne had been attacking settlers, including women and children, there could be no peace. The events that followed became known as the **Sand Creek Massacre.**

What actually happened at Sand Creek is unclear. Some witnesses stated afterward that Black Kettle had been flying both an American flag and a white flag of truce, which Chivington ignored. Others reported that the American troops fired on the unsuspecting Native Americans and then brutally murdered hundreds of women and children. Still others described a savage battle in which both sides fought ferociously for two days. Fourteen sol-diers died, but the number of Native Americans reported killed varied from 69 to 600. One general later called Chivington's attack "the foulest and most unjustifiable crime in the annals of America." The truth of what really happened is still debated.

A Doomed Plan for Peace

In light of escalating conflict with Native Americans on the Great Plains, Congress took action. In 1867 Congress formed an **Indian Peace Commission,** which proposed creating two large reservations on the Plains, one for the Sioux and another for Native Americans of the southern Plains. Agents from the federal government's Bureau of Indian Affairs would run the reservations. The army would deal with any groups that refused to report or remain there.

Reservations were not a new idea. Both Puritan and Jesuit missionaries had used them in colonial days to separate Native American nations from one another. The reservations were also intended to encourage Native Americans to adopt white culture. After the American Revolution, the Iroquois (who called themselves the Haudenosaunee) were placed on reservations in western New York. These reservations, however, existed to separate Native Americans and citizens of the United States. Nearly a century later, reservations were based exclusively on keeping the Native Americans separate from American citizens.

The reservation system was again tested after the California gold rush. California, Oregon, and Washington all tried reservations as a way to minimize conflicts between Native Americans and settlers.

The Indian Peace Commission's plan was doomed to failure. Pressuring Native American leaders into signing treaties, as negotiators did at Medicine Lodge Creek in 1867, did not **ensure** that chiefs or their followers would abide by them, nor could they prevent settlers from violating their terms. Those who did move to reservations faced much the same conditions that drove the Dakota Sioux to violence—poverty, despair, and the corrupt practices of American traders.

> **Reading Check** **Explaining** What proposal did the Indian Peace Commission present to the Plains Indians?

The Last Native American Wars

MAIN Idea Settlers and Native Americans fought for land and cultural traditions.

HISTORY AND YOU Can you identify parts of the world where development is destroying local cultures? Read how the destruction of the buffalo changed some Native American cultures.

By the 1870s many Native Americans on the southern Plains had left the reservations in disgust. They preferred hunting buffalo on the open plains, so they joined others who had also shunned the reservations. Buffalo, however, were rapidly disappearing as settlers killed off thousands of the animals.

Following the Civil War, professional buffalo hunters invaded the area, seeking buffalo hides for markets in the East. Other hunters killed merely for sport, leaving carcasses to rot. Then railroad companies hired sharpshooters to kill large numbers of buffalo that were obstructing rail traffic and used them to feed the workers.

The army, determined to force Native Americans onto reservations, encouraged buffalo killing. By 1889 very few of the animals remained.

Battle of the Little Bighorn

In 1876 prospectors overran the Lakota Sioux reservation in the Dakota Territory to mine gold in the Black Hills. The Lakota saw no reason they should abide by a treaty that American settlers were violating, so many left the reservation that spring to hunt near the Bighorn Mountains in southeastern Montana.

The government responded by sending an expedition commanded by General Alfred H. Terry. Lieutenant Colonel **George A. Custer** and the Seventh Cavalry were with the expedition. Custer underestimated the fighting capabilities of the Lakota and Cheyenne. On June 25, 1876, ignoring orders, and acting on his own initiative, he launched a three-pronged attack in broad daylight on one of the largest groups of Native American warriors ever assembled on the Great Plains.

POLITICAL CARTOONS PRIMARY SOURCE
Government Native American Policies

▲ This cartoon from 1878 shows Secretary of the Interior Carl Schurz investigating the Indian "bureau."

▲ This cartoon is labeled "The Reason of the Indian Outbreak" and quotes General Miles who said the "Indians are starved into rebellion."

Analyzing VISUALS — DBQ

1. **Examining** Who does the cartoon on the right blame for the problems of Native Americans?

2. **Analyzing** According to the cartoon on the left, why was the Indian Bureau unable to help Native Americans?

People IN HISTORY

George Custer
1839–1876

George Custer, who graduated at the bottom of his West Point class, became an unlikely hero during the Civil War. During the many cavalry charges he led, 11 horses were shot out from under him. At the age of 23, he became the youngest Union Army general. When Custer later commanded the Seventh Cavalry in the West, the Cheyenne called him "Yellow Hair," because he wore his curly blond hair to his shoulders. Custer wore buckskins for battle, though he wore velveteen uniforms in the camp. He spent many hours studying military tactics and reading military history. He risked his own career to testify against the corruption of the Indian Bureau. In anger at his testimony, President Grant removed him from command. However, the public outcry in favor of Custer led to his return to command, a decision that cost the lives of Custer and all his troops.

How did Custer's actions in the Civil War indicate what he might do in other combat situations?

Sitting Bull
c. 1831–1890

The great Lakota chief Sitting Bull faced his first battle at age 14, in a raid against the Crow tribe. As a young man he joined two groups, a warrior society known as Strong Heart and a group that worked for tribal welfare, Silent Eaters. Sitting Bull became chief when he was 37 years old. A holy man as well as a warrior, Sitting Bull led Native Americans in sun dances and prayers to the Great Spirit. After his victory at the Little Bighorn, Sitting Bull led his people to Canada to avoid the reservation system. In 1881, with his people facing starvation, Sitting Bull led them to Montana. He asked his son to hand the commanding officer of Fort Buford his rifle, hoping to show that "he has become a friend of the Americans." Sitting Bull also asked it to be remembered that "I was the last man of my tribe to surrender my rifle." Four years later, he briefly joined Buffalo Bill's Wild West show. He was killed by a Lakota, as he had seen in a vision five years before: A Lakota policeman shot him in a scuffle trying to keep the great chief from joining a Ghost Dance, which had been outlawed.

How did Sitting Bull wish to be remembered?

The Native American forces first repulsed a cavalry charge from the south. Then they turned on Custer and his 210 soldiers and killed all but one of them. One Lakota warrior recalled the scene afterward: "The soldiers were piled one on top of another, dead, with here and there, an Indian among the soldiers. Horses lay on top of men, and men on top of horses."

Newspaper accounts portraying Custer as a victim of a massacre produced a public outcry in the East, and the army stepped up its campaign against Native Americans on the Plains. Sitting Bull fled with his followers to Canada, but the other Lakota were forced to return to the reservation and give up the Black Hills.

Flight of the Nez Perce

Farther west, the Nez Perce people, led by **Chief Joseph,** refused to be moved to a smaller reservation in Idaho in 1877. When the army came to relocate them, they fled their homes and embarked on a journey of more than 1,300 miles. Finally, in October 1877, Chief Joseph surrendered, and he and his followers were exiled to Oklahoma. His speech summarized the hopelessness of their cause:

PRIMARY SOURCE

"Our chiefs are killed. . . . The little children are freezing to death. My people . . . have no blankets, no food. . . . Hear me, my chiefs; I am tired; my heart is sick and sad. From where the sun now stands I will fight no more forever."

—quoted in *Bury My Heart at Wounded Knee*

Tragedy at Wounded Knee

Native American resistance came to a final and tragic end on the Lakota Sioux reservation in 1890. Defying the orders of the government, the Lakota continued to perform the Ghost Dance, a ritual that celebrated a hoped-for day of reckoning when settlers would disappear, the buffalo would return, and Native Americans would reunite with their dead ancestors.

Federal authorities had banned the ceremony fearing it would lead to violence. They blamed the latest defiance on Chief Sitting Bull, who had returned from Canada, and sent police to arrest the chief. Sitting Bull's supporters tried to stop the arrest. In the exchange of gunfire that followed, the chief himself was killed.

A group of Ghost Dancers then fled the reservation, and the army went after them. On December 29, 1890, as troops tried to disarm them at Wounded Knee Creek, gunfire broke out. A deadly battle ensued, taking the lives of 25 U.S. soldiers and **approximately** 200 Lakota men, women, and children.

The Dawes Act

Some Americans had long opposed the treatment of Native Americans. In her 1881 book *A Century of Dishonor*, Helen Hunt Jackson detailed the years of broken promises and injustices. Her descriptions of events such as the massacre at Sand Creek sparked new debate on the issue. Some Americans believed the solution was to encourage Native Americans to **assimilate,** or be absorbed, into American society as landowners and citizens. This meant dividing reservations into individual **allotments,** where families could become self-supporting.

This policy became law in 1887 when Congress passed the **Dawes Act.** This act allotted to each head of household 160 acres of reservation land for farming; single adults received 80 acres, and 40 acres were allotted for children. The land that remained after all members had received allotments would be sold to American settlers, with the proceeds going into a trust for Native Americans.

This plan failed to achieve its goals. Some Native Americans succeeded as farmers or ranchers, but many had little training or enthusiasm for either pursuit. Like homesteaders, they often found their allotments too small to be profitable, so they sold them. Some Native American groups had grown attached to their reservations and hated to see them transformed into homesteads for settlers as well as Native Americans.

In the end, the assimilation policy proved a dismal failure. No legislation could provide a satisfactory solution to the Native American issue, because there was no entirely satisfactory solution to be had. The Native Americans were doomed because they were dependent on buffalo for food, clothing, fuel, and shelter. When the herds were wiped out, Native Americans on the Plains had no way to sustain their way of life, and few adopted American settlers' lifestyles in place of their traditional cultures.

The Dawes Act granted citizenship to Native Americans who stayed on their allotments for 25 years. Few qualified, and it was not until 1924 that Congress passed the Citizenship Act, granting all Native Americans citizenship. Some states—Arizona, Maine, and New Mexico—did not grant Native Americans the right to vote until after World War II.

Under Franklin Roosevelt's New Deal, the policies of assimilation and allotments finally ended in 1934. The Indian Reorganization Act reversed the Dawes Act's policy of assimilation. It restored some reservation lands, gave Native American tribes control over those lands, and permitted them to elect tribal governments.

Reading Check **Cause and Effect** What effect did Helen Hunt Jackson's book *A Century of Dishonor* have?

Section 3 REVIEW

Vocabulary

1. **Explain** the significance of: nomad, annuity, Sand Creek Massacre, Indian Peace Commission, George A. Custer, Chief Joseph, assimilate, allotment, Dawes Act.

Main Ideas

2. **Comparing** In what ways were the different groups of the Plains Indians similar?

3. **Discussing** Why do you think the government's policy of assimilation of Native Americans was a failure?

Critical Thinking

4. **Big Ideas** How did Native Americans respond to the loss of land from white settlement of the Great Plains?

5. **Organizing** Use a graphic organizer similar to the one below to list the reasons the government's plans to move the Plains Indians onto reservations failed.

6. **Analyzing Visuals** Examine the map of battle sites and reservations on page 171. Then, from the point of view of a historian, explain the actions taken against Native Americans within the historical context of the time.

Writing About History

7. **Descriptive Writing** Assume the role of a Plains Indian. Write a journal entry describing how you feel about the Dawes Act and how it has affected your life.

Study Central™ To review this section, go to glencoe.com and click on Study Central.

Causes of Settlers Moving West to the Great Plains

Mining

- Deposits of gold, silver, and copper are discovered.
- New technologies, such as hydraulic mining, make it possible to remove vast quantities of ore.

Ranching

- Wild longhorn cattle, found to survive well on the Plains, are available in large numbers to be rounded up.
- Railroads provide an easy way to ship cattle to eastern markets.

Farming

- Congress passes the Homestead Act in 1862.
- New farming technologies, including new plows, reapers, and drills, make it possible to farm on the Plains.
- Railroads advertise for settlers and bring necessities such as lumber and coal to the Plains.

▶ *Tens of thousands of settlers headed west, lured by the possibility of striking it rich mining gold or silver. This photo shows miners standing beside a stack of silver ingots in Leadville, Colorado, c. 1880.*

▶ *A Plains family stands atop their reaper on their Nebraska farm in the 1890s. Technology such as the reaper made farming the Great Plains practical.*

▲ *Although the Dawes Act was intended to assimilate Native Americans, traditional ways of life persisted. Above, a Cheyenne woman uses a stone mortar and pestle to grind wild cherries outside her home in the 1890s.*

Effects of Settling the Great Plains

- Miners arrive in such large numbers that Colorado, the Dakotas, Nevada, and Montana are able to become states.
- Hydraulic mining damages the environment in some areas and interferes with farming.
- The Great Plains becomes the nation's Wheat Belt, growing tens of thousands of acres of wheat.
- The arrival of miners, ranchers, and farmers leads to conflict with Native Americans.
- The federal government fights several wars with the Native Americans, establishes reservations, and passes the Dawes Act to assimilate Native Americans.

Reviewing Vocabulary

Directions: Choose the word or words that best completes the sentence.

1. Cattle ranching developed on the Great Plains as a result of the _____, which was a vast area of grassland owned by the government.

    A open range

    B long drive

    C barbed wire

    D Chisholm Trail

2. The government promoted settlement in the Great Plains by allowing individuals to file for a _____, which let people claim public land as their own.

    A bonanza farm

    B mine permit

    C homestead

    D reservation

3. The challenges of farming on the Great Plains led to new agricultural techniques and technologies. _____ required the invention of seed drills to place crop seeds deep in the ground where moisture was more plentiful.

    A Sodbusting

    B Bonanza farming

    C Reservations

    D Dry farming

4. _____ were yearly payments made by the United States government to Native Americans on reservations.

    A Nomads

    B Allotments

    C Sodbusters

    D Annuities

5. In the early 1800s, society in California was dominated by landowners who lived on large

    A barrios.

    B haciendas.

    C bonanza farms.

    D homesteads.

Reviewing Main Ideas

Directions: Choose the best answers to the following questions.

Section 1 *(pp. 158–165)*

6. In 1889 the discovery of gold and copper led to the rapid development of the northern Great Plains with the following states being formed:

    A Montana, North Dakota, South Dakota.

    B Montana, Wyoming, Idaho.

    C North Dakota, South Dakota, Iowa.

    D North Dakota, South Dakota, Nebraska.

7. The open range was closed to grazing with the use of

    A the long drive.

    B barbed wire.

    C hydraulic mining.

    D placer mining.

8. Why did *Las Gorras Blancas* carry out night raids in New Mexico?

    A The English-speaking ranchers claimed land used by the community to graze livestock.

    B Vaqueros were outlawed by the English-speaking ranchers.

    C The English-speaking majority in the legislature closed the barrios.

    D The Hispanic minority did not want New Mexico to join the United States.

TEST-TAKING TIP

Look at each question to find clues to support your answer. Try not to get confused by the wording of the question. Then look for an answer that best fits the question.

Need Extra Help?								
If You Missed Questions . . .	1	2	3	4	5	6	7	8
Go to Page . . .	162–163	166–167	168	170	164	160	162–163	164–165

 GO ON

Section 2 (pp. 166–169)

9. Which of the following factors provided an incentive for people to farm the Great Plains?

A long cattle drives

B large amounts of rainfall

C the Homestead Act

D dry, windy weather

10. Why was wheat a suitable crop to grow on the Great Plains?

A The environment was windy.

B Wheat needs more water than corn.

C Wheat requires large amounts of rainfall.

D New innovations were suited for harvesting wheat.

11. Why were some Americans concerned about the closing of the frontier?

A People were worried that Native Americans might revolt.

B People were worried that the idea of Americans traveling west to make a new start had come to an end.

C Some farmers wanted more land to increase their political power with the federal government.

D Settlers worried about the cost of supplies with the increased number of homesteaders.

Section 3 (pp. 170–175)

12. The Indian Peace Commission was formed to end the conflict with Native Americans on the Great Plains. They proposed

A a treaty to end the Battle of the Little Bighorn.

B federal regulations for hunting buffalo.

C creating two large reservations for the Plains Indians.

D removing Sitting Bull from power.

13. The aim of the Dawes Act of 1887 was to

A restore previously taken land to Native American tribes.

B maintain traditional Native American cultures.

C end all governmental contact with Native Americans.

D assimilate Native Americans into American culture.

Critical Thinking

Directions: Choose the best answers to the following questions.

14. The Native American wars that occurred between 1860 and 1890 were mainly the result of

A disputes over the spread of slavery.

B conflict with Mexico over Texas and California.

C the search for gold in California.

D the movement of settlers onto the Great Plains.

Base your answers to questions 15 and 16 on the chart below and your knowledge of Chapter 4.

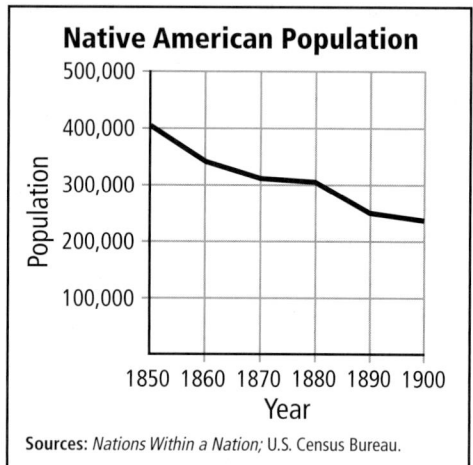

Native American Population

Sources: *Nations Within a Nation;* U.S. Census Bureau.

15. What does the graph indicate about the Native American population between 1850 and 1900?

A The Native American population was over 400,000 in 1860.

B The Native American population increased over 50 years.

C The Native American population declined between 1840 and 1850.

D The Native American population was less than 300,000 in 1890.

16. What factor caused the Native American population to decline sharply between 1880 and 1890?

A increase in reservation land

B conflict with American settlers from the East

C increase in the number of wild buffalo

D conflict with Hispanic settlers

Need Extra Help?								
If You Missed Questions . . .	9	10	11	12	13	14	15	16
Go to Page . . .	166–167	168–169	169	172	174–175	173–175	170–175	173–175

GO ON

17. Placer mining is a process by which

   A deep mine shafts are dug and miners go underground to extract the minerals.

   B miners use simple tools like picks, shovels, and pans to extract shallow deposits of minerals.

   C a number of men use a high-pressure blast of water to loosen large quantities of earth and remove the minerals.

   D earth-moving machines remove large quantities of earth to remove the minerals.

18. Vigilance committees performed what function?

   A found new lodes

   B ensured that mining companies did not harm the environment

   C supervised the building of western railroads

   D enforced law and order in boomtowns

19. What type of mining allowed sediment into the local rivers, causing them to overflow and flood the area?

   A placer mining

   B quartz mining

   C hydraulic mining

   D panning mining

20. Why did the Dakota Sioux clash with local traders and settlers in 1862?

   A Annuity payments never reached them, resulting in poverty.

   B Other Native American tribes claimed the area as their own.

   C Settlers began to increase in the area, disregarding the local treaties.

   D Buffalo hunters invaded the area and killed the remaining buffalo.

Document-Based Questions

Directions: Analyze the document and answer the short-answer questions that follow the document.

In the late 1860s, the U.S. government adopted a policy of forcing Native Americans onto small reservations. Many Native Americans refused to move and fought to maintain their traditional way of life. In the excerpt that follows, Satanta, a chief of the Kiowa, responds to the government's policy:

> *"I have heard that you intend to settle us on a reservation near the mountains. I don't want to settle. I love to roam over the prairies. There I feel free and happy, but when we settle down we grow pale and die. I have laid aside my lance, bow, and shield, and yet I feel safe in your presence. I have told you the truth. I have no little lies hid about me, but I don't know how it is with the commissioners. Are they as clear as I am? A long time ago this land belonged to our fathers; but when I go up to the river I see camps of soldiers on its banks. These soldiers cut down my timber; they kill my buffalo; and when I see that, my heart feels like bursting; I feel sorry . . . . Has the white man become a child that he should recklessly kill and not eat? When the red men slay game, they do so that they may live and not starve."*
>
> —quoted in *Bury My Heart at Wounded Knee*

21. What reasons does Satanta give for not wanting to settle on a reservation?

22. How does Satanta view the white settlers' approach to the land and the resources on it?

Extended Response

23. Write an essay comparing two different perspectives of the settlement of the West. Analyze how the views of Native Americans and white settlers differed on settling the Great Plains. How did each group view the government's involvement and the environment? The essay should include an introduction, at least three paragraphs, and a conclusion that supports your position.

STOP

History ONLINE

For additional test practice, use Self-Check Quizzes—Chapter 4 at glencoe.com.

Need Extra Help?							
If You Missed Questions . . .	17	18	19	20	21	22	23
Go to Page . . .	160–161	159	160–161	170–171	179	R19	166–175

Industrialization
1865–1901

A steel-mill worker gathers a ball of molten iron at the U.S. Steel plant in Gary, Indiana. At the time of this photo, steelworkers were planning to strike for higher wages.

U.S. PRESIDENTS

U.S. EVENTS

WORLD EVENTS

1879
• Thomas Edison perfects lightbulb

1876
• Alexander Graham Bell invents telephone

1882
• Standard Oil forms trust

1869
• Transcontinental railroad is completed

Hayes 1877–1881

Garfield 1881

Arthur 1881–1885

Cleveland 1885–1889

1865

1875

1885

1865
• Dmitri Mendeleyev creates periodic table of elements

1876
• Nicholas Otto builds first practical gasoline engine

1880
• John Milne develops seismograph

1885
• Canada's transcontinental railway is completed

MAKING CONNECTIONS
Did Industry Improve Society?

Many factors promoted industrialization, including cheap labor, new inventions and technology, and plentiful raw materials. Railroads rapidly expanded, while government policies encouraged economic growth.

- *What changes in lifestyle do you think occurred because of industrialization?*

- *How do you think industrialization changed American politics?*

1886
- Haymarket riot occurs

1892
- Homestead strike occurs

B. Harrison
1889–1893

Cleveland
1893–1897

1894
- Pullman strike begins

McKinley
1897–1901

1901
- J.P. Morgan forms U.S. Steel

1895

1892
- Rudolf Diesel patents diesel engine

1895
- Louis and Auguste Lumière introduce motion pictures

FOLDABLES™

Analyzing Organizations Make a Three-Tab Book Foldable to help you analyze how the Civil War transformed the nature of industry.
As you read the chapter, write details under the corresponding tab.

Before the Civil war | Both | After the Civil war

INDUSTRIALIZATION

History 🖱 **ONLINE** Visit glencoe.com and enter *QuickPass*™ code TAVMT5147c5 for Chapter 5 resources.

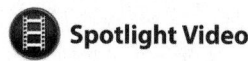
The Rise of Industry

A merican business and industry grew rapidly after the end of the Civil War. Industrialization changed the way people lived and worked.

Guide to Reading

Big Ideas
Government and Society The United States government adopted a policy of laissez-faire economics, allowing business to expand.

Content Vocabulary
- gross national product *(p. 182)*
- laissez-faire *(p. 186)*
- entrepreneur *(p. 187)*

Academic Vocabulary
- resource *(p. 182)*
- practice *(p. 187)*

People and Events to Identify
- Edwin Drake *(p. 182)*
- Alexander Graham Bell *(p. 184)*
- Thomas Alva Edison *(p. 184)*
- Morrill Tariff *(p. 187)*

Reading Strategy
Organizing As you read about the changes brought about by industrialization, complete a graphic organizer similar to the one below, listing the causes of industrialization.

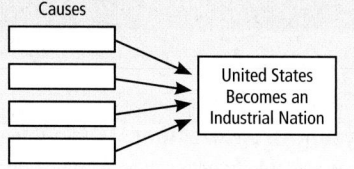

Causes → United States Becomes an Industrial Nation

The United States Industrializes

MAIN Idea Natural resources and a large labor force allowed the United States to industrialize rapidly.

HISTORY AND YOU What natural resources are located in your area? Read to learn how the availability of raw materials encouraged industrialization.

Although the Industrial Revolution reached the United States in the early 1800s, most Americans still lived on farms. Out of a population of over 30 million, only 1.3 million Americans worked in industry when the Civil War began in 1861. After the war, industry rapidly expanded, and millions of Americans left their farms to work in mines and factories. Factories began to replace smaller workshops as complex machinery began to substitute for simpler hand tools.

By the late 1800s, the United States was the world's leading industrial nation. By 1914 the nation's **gross national product** (GNP)—the total value of all goods and services that a country produces—was eight times greater than it had been in 1865 when the Civil War came to an end.

Natural Resources

An abundance of raw materials was one reason for the nation's industrial success. The United States had vast natural **resources,** including timber, coal, iron, and copper. This meant that American companies could obtain them cheaply and did not have to import them from other countries. Many of these resources were located in the American West. The settlement of this region helped accelerate industrialization, as did the transcontinental railroad. Railroads took settlers and miners to the region and carried resources back to factories in the East.

At the same time, people began using a new resource, petroleum. Even before the automotive age, petroleum was in high demand because it could be turned into kerosene. The American oil industry was built on the demand for kerosene, a fuel used in lanterns and stoves. The industry began in western Pennsylvania, where residents had long noticed oil bubbling to the surface of area springs and streams. In 1859 **Edwin Drake** drilled the first oil well near Titusville, Pennsylvania. By 1900 oil fields from Pennsylvania to Texas had been drilled. As oil production rose, it led to economic expansion.

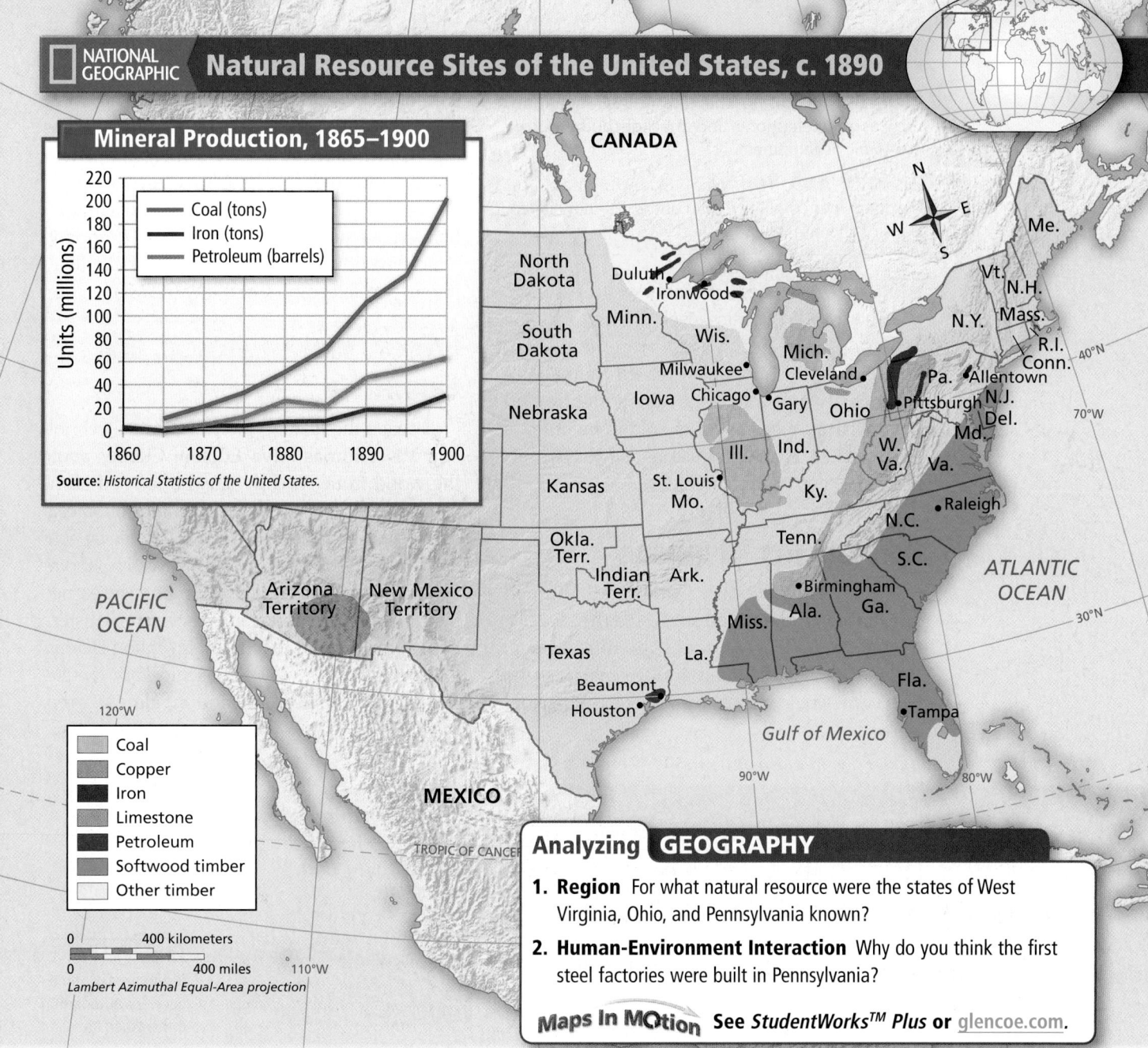

Mineral Production, 1865–1900

Coal (tons)
Iron (tons)
Petroleum (barrels)

Units (millions)

220 200 180 160 140 120 100 80 60 40 20 0

1860 1870 1880 1890 1900

Source: *Historical Statistics of the United States.*

Map Labels:

CANADA

Duluth
Ironwood
North Dakota
Minn.
South Dakota
Wis.
Milwaukee
Mich.
Cleveland
Iowa
Chicago
Gary
Ohio
Nebraska
Ill.
Ind.
Kansas
St. Louis
Mo.
Ky.
Okla. Terr.
Indian Terr.
Ark.
Tenn.
N.C.
Raleigh
S.C.
Birmingham
Ala.
Ga.
Miss.
Texas
La.
Beaumont
Houston
Fla.
Tampa
Me.
Vt.
N.H.
N.Y.
Mass.
R.I.
Conn.
Pa.
Allentown
Pittsburgh
N.J.
Del.
Md.
W. Va.
Va.

PACIFIC OCEAN
ATLANTIC OCEAN
Gulf of Mexico
MEXICO

Arizona Territory
New Mexico Territory

120°W 110°W 90°W 80°W 70°W 40°N 30°N

TROPIC OF CANCER

Legend:
- Coal
- Copper
- Iron
- Limestone
- Petroleum
- Softwood timber
- Other timber

0 400 kilometers
0 400 miles
Lambert Azimuthal Equal-Area projection

Analyzing GEOGRAPHY

1. **Region** For what natural resource were the states of West Virginia, Ohio, and Pennsylvania known?

2. **Human-Environment Interaction** Why do you think the first steel factories were built in Pennsylvania?

Maps In Motion See *StudentWorks*™ *Plus* or glencoe.com.

A Large Workforce

The human resources available to American industry were as important as natural resources in enabling the nation to industrialize rapidly. Between 1860 and 1910 the population of the United States nearly tripled. This population growth provided industry with an abundant workforce and also created greater demand for the consumer goods manufactured by factories.

Population growth stemmed from two causes—large families and a flood of immigrants. Because of better living conditions, more children survived and grew to adulthood. American industry began to grow at a time when social and economic conditions in eastern Europe and China convinced many people to immigrate to the United States in search of a better life. Many were also seeking to escape oppressive governments and religious persecution. Between 1870 and 1910, more than 17 million immigrants arrived in the United States. These multitudes entered the growing industrial workforce, helped factories increase production, and became consumers of industrial products.

Reading Check **Explaining** How did oil production affect the American economy?

New Inventions

MAIN Idea During the late 1800s, inventions such as the telephone and the lightbulb spurred economic development.

HISTORY AND YOU What invention has most changed your daily life? Read about the new inventions of the late 1800s.

Natural resources and labor were essential to America's economic development, but new inventions and technology were important as well. New technology increased the nation's productivity and improved transportation and communications networks. New inventions also resulted in new industries, which in turn produced more wealth and jobs.

Bell and the Telephone

In 1874 a Scottish immigrant named **Alexander Graham Bell** suggested the idea of a telephone to his assistant, Thomas Watson. Watson recalled, "He had an idea by which he believed it would be possible to talk by telegraph."

Bell began experimenting with ways to transmit sound via an electrical current of varying intensity. In 1876 he succeeded. Picking up the crude telephone, he placed a call to the next room, saying, "Come here, Watson, I want you." Watson heard and came. The telephone revolutionized business and personal communication. In 1877 Bell organized the Bell Telephone Company, which eventually became the American Telephone and Telegraph Company (AT&T).

Edison, Westinghouse, and Electricity

Perhaps the leading pioneer in new technology was **Thomas Alva Edison.** Curious about the world from an early age, he learned all he could about the mechanical workings of objects. His laboratory at Menlo Park, New Jersey, was the forerunner of the modern research laboratory. Edison set up his lab with money he earned by improving the telegraph system for Western Union. He referred to it as an "invention factory." During the first five years Menlo Park existed, Edison patented an invention almost every

American Inventions, 1865–1895

1872
Elijah McCoy invents automatic lubricator for steam engines, allowing trains to run faster with less maintenance

1877
Thomas Edison develops phonograph

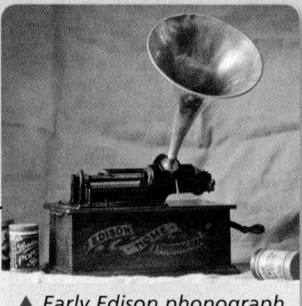
▲ Early Edison phonograph

1886
Josephine Cochrane develops automatic dishwasher; its basic design is still used today

1870 ▶ **1875** ▶ **1880** ▶ **1885** ▶

1873
Christopher Sholes develops typewriter and sells it to Remington and Sons

1876
Alexander Graham Bell invents telephone

▲ Bell's first telephone

1882
Lewis Latimer invents the carbon filament for lightbulbs, allowing them to last much longer

▲ Alexander Graham Bell

▲ Edison's first commercial lightbulb

month. By the time he died, Edison held more than one thousand patents.

Edison first achieved international fame in 1877 with the invention of the phonograph. Two years later he perfected the electric generator and the lightbulb. Although Edison had expected to produce an inexpensive lightbulb in six weeks, the task took more than a year. His laboratory then went on to invent or improve several other major devices, including the battery, the dictaphone, and the motion picture.

An Edison company began to transform American society in 1882 when it started supplying electric power to New York City. In 1889 several Edison companies merged to form the Edison General Electric Company (today known as GE).

Engineer and industrialist George Westinghouse invented an air-brake system for railroads. Unlike earlier manual systems that required brakes to be applied to each car, Westinghouse's invention provided a continuous braking system, so that all the cars' brakes were applied at the same time. Because the trains could brake rapidly and smoothly, they could safely travel at higher speeds.

Westinghouse also developed an alternating current (AC) system to distribute electricity using transformers and generators. Working with inventor Nikola Tesla, Westinghouse further improved his system. His Westinghouse Electric Company lit Chicago's Columbia Exhibition in 1893. It was also the first to use the hydroelectric power of Niagara Falls to generate electricity for streetcars and lights in Buffalo, New York, 22 miles away.

Technology's Impact

In ways big and small, technology changed the way people lived. Shortly after the Civil War, Thaddeus Lowe invented the ice machine, the basis of the refrigerator. In the early 1870s Gustavus Swift, founder of Swift Meatpacking, hired an engineer to develop a refrigerated railroad car. Swift shipped the first refrigerated load of fresh meat in 1877. The widespread use of refrigeration kept food fresh longer and reduced the risk of food poisoning.

1893
Charles and Frank Duryea invent gasoline-powered automobile

1903
Wilbur and Orville Wright make first successful powered flight at Kitty Hawk, North Carolina

▲ The Wright Flyer lifts off, December 17, 1903.

1890 1895 1900 1905

1888
George Eastman patents first hand-held camera, the Kodak

Analyzing TIME LINES

1. **Sequencing** Did the invention of the phonograph occur before or after the invention of the typewriter?

2. **Calculating** How much time elapsed between the invention of a gasoline-powered automobile and the first flight of the Wright brothers?

3. **Identifying** For what invention is Josephine Cochrane known?

The textile industry had long depended on machines to turn fibers into cloth. By the mid-1800s, the introduction of the Northrop automatic loom allowed cloth to be made at a much faster rate. Bobbins, which had to be changed by hand, could now be changed automatically.

Changes also took place in the clothing industry. Standard sizes were used in making ready-made clothes. Power-driven sewing machines and cloth cutters rapidly moved the clothing business from small tailor shops to large factories. Similar changes took place in shoemaking. By 1900 cobblers had nearly disappeared.

Technology's impact also included improved communications. Cyrus Field laid a telegraph cable across the Atlantic Ocean in 1866. This cable provided instant contact between the United States and Europe.

✔ **Reading Check** **Explaining** How did the use of electric power affect economic development?

Free Enterprise

MAIN Idea Laissez-faire economics promoted industrialization, but tariffs protected American companies from competition.

HISTORY AND YOU Do you remember how Americans objected to British taxes on trade before the American Revolution? Read how tariffs affected American industries in the late 1800s.

Another important reason the United States was able to industrialize rapidly was its free enterprise system. In the late 1800s, many Americans embraced the idea of **laissez-faire** (leh•say•FARE), a French phrase meaning "let people do as they choose." Supporters of laissez-faire believe the government should not interfere in the economy other than to protect private property rights and maintain peace. They argue that if the government regulates the economy, it increases costs and eventually hurts society more than it helps.

POLITICAL CARTOONS PRIMARY SOURCE
Should Government Regulate the Economy?

◀ Entitled "The Consumer Consumed," this cartoon shows a shopper being told that if he buys domestic goods, he has to pay extra money to trusts (monopolies), and if he buys foreign goods, he has to pay extra money (duties) to the government.

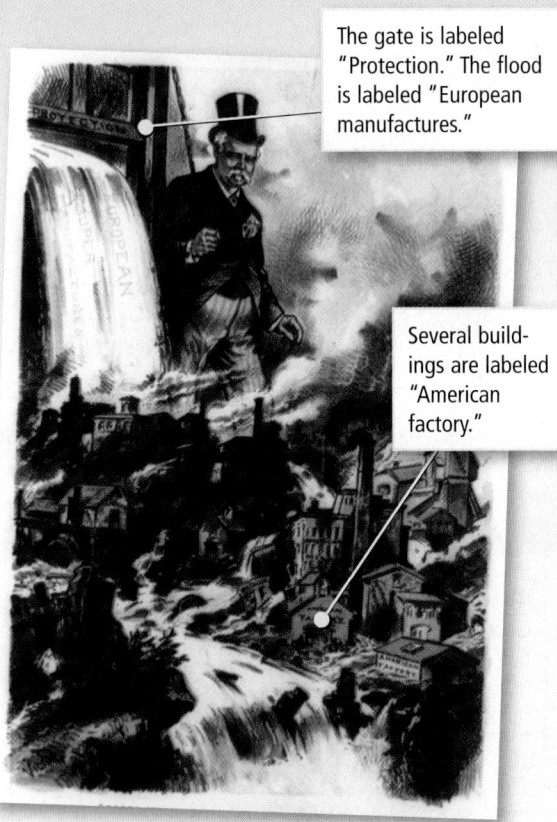

The gate is labeled "Protection." The flood is labeled "European manufactures."

Several buildings are labeled "American factory."

▲ The original caption for this cartoon read "Goods will be so much cheaper—Democratic argument. But what will happen to all the American factories?"

Analyzing VISUALS   DBQ

1. **Interpreting** What is happening to American factories after the protection gate is opened?

2. **Analyzing** What argument does the cartoon on the left give in favor of free trade?

Laissez-faire relies on supply and demand, rather than the government, to regulate wages and prices. Supporters believe a free market with competing companies leads to greater efficiency and creates more wealth for everyone. Laissez-faire advocates also support low taxes and limited government debt to ensure that private individuals, not the government, will make most of the decisions about how the nation's wealth is spent.

In the late 1800s, the profit motive attracted many capable and ambitious people into business. **Entrepreneurs**—people who risk their capital to organize and run businesses—were attracted by the prospect of making money in manufacturing and transportation. Many entrepreneurs from New England, who had accumulated money by investing in trade, fishing, and textile mills, now invested in factories and railroads. An equally important source of private capital was Europe, especially Great Britain. Foreign investors saw great opportunities for profit in the United States.

In many ways, the United States **practiced** laissez-faire economics in the late 1800s. State and federal governments kept taxes and spending low. They did not impose costly regulations on industry or try to control wages and prices. In other ways, however, the government went beyond laissez-faire and introduced policies intended to promote business.

Since the early 1800s, leaders in the Northeast and the South had different ideas about the proper role of the government in the economy. Northern leaders wanted high tariffs to protect manufacturers from foreign competition and also supported federal subsidies for companies building roads, canals, and railroads. Southern leaders opposed subsidies and favored low tariffs to promote trade and to keep the cost of imported goods low.

The Civil War ended the debate. After the Southern states seceded, the Republican-controlled Congress passed the **Morrill Tariff,** which greatly increased tariff rates. By 1865 tariffs had nearly tripled. Congress also gave vast tracts of Western land and nearly $65 million in loans to Western railroads, and sold public lands with mineral resources for much less than their market value.

In the late 1800s, the United States was one of the largest free trade areas in the world. The Constitution bans states from imposing tariffs, and there were few regulations on commerce or immigration. Supporters of laissez-faire say these factors played a major role in the country's tremendous economic growth.

High tariffs, however, contradicted laissez-faire ideas. When the nation raised tariffs on foreign goods, other countries raised their tariffs on American goods. This hurt American companies trying to sell goods abroad, particularly farmers who sold their products overseas. Despite these problems, many business leaders and members of Congress believed tariffs were necessary. Few believed that new American industries could compete with established European factories without tariffs to protect them. Later, in the early 1900s, after American companies had become large and efficient, business leaders began to push for free trade. They believed they could now compete internationally and win sales in foreign markets.

✓ Reading Check **Analyzing** Do you think government policies at this time helped or hindered industrialization? Why?

Section 1 REVIEW

Vocabulary

1. **Explain** the significance of: gross national product, Edwin Drake, Alexander Graham Bell, Thomas Alva Edison, laissez-faire, entrepreneur, Morrill Tariff.

Main Ideas

2. **Explaining** How did an abundance of natural resources contribute to economic growth in the United States in the late 1800s?

3. **Organizing** Use a graphic organizer similar to the one below to indicate how the inventions listed affected the nature of American work and business.

Invention	Effects
telephone	
lightbulb	
automatic loom	

4. **Describing** How did the principles of the free enterprise system, laissez-faire, and profit motive encourage the rise of industry?

Critical Thinking

5. **Big Ideas** What role did the federal government play in increasing industrialization after the Civil War?

6. **Analyzing Visuals** Examine the time line on pages 184–185. Choose one invention and explain how it changed society.

Writing About History

7. **Descriptive Writing** Imagine you are a young person living in this country in the late 1800s. Choose one of the inventions discussed in the section and write a journal entry describing its impact on your life.

History ONLINE

Study Central™ To review this section, go to glencoe.com and click on Study Central.

The Railroads

Major railroads, including the transcontinental railroad, were constructed rapidly after the Civil War ended. Railroads required major capital investment and government land grants. The huge profits to be made, however, led to some corruption as well.

Linking the Nation

MAIN Idea After the Civil War, the rapid construction of railroads accelerated the nation's industrialization and linked the country together.

HISTORY AND YOU How has technology helped unify the United States in recent years? Read to learn how railroads helped connect the nation.

In 1865 the United States had about 35,000 miles of railroad track, almost all of it east of the Mississippi River. After the Civil War, railroad construction expanded dramatically, linking the distant regions of the nation in a transportation network. By 1900 the United States, now a booming industrial power, had more than 200,000 miles of track.

The Transcontinental Railroad

The railroad boom began in 1862, when President Abraham Lincoln signed the **Pacific Railway Act.** This act provided for the construction of a transcontinental railroad by two corporations. To encourage rapid construction, the government offered each company land along its right-of-way. A competition between the two companies developed, as each raced to obtain as much land and money as possible.

The Union Pacific Under the direction of engineer **Grenville Dodge,** a former Union general, the Union Pacific began pushing westward from Omaha, Nebraska, in 1865. The laborers faced blizzards in the mountains, scorching heat in the desert, and, sometimes, angry Native Americans. Labor, money, and engineering problems plagued the supervisors of the project. As Dodge observed:

PRIMARY SOURCE

"Everything—rails, ties, bridging, fastenings, all railway supplies, fuel for locomotives and trains, and supplies for men and animals on the entire work—had to be transported from the Missouri River."

—quoted in *The Growth of the American Republic*

The railroad workers of the Union Pacific included Civil War veterans, newly recruited Irish immigrants, frustrated miners and farmers, cooks, adventurers, and ex-convicts. At the height of the project, the Union

NATIONAL GEOGRAPHIC

The two railroads join at Promontory Summit, Utah, 1869.

▲ Led by Grenville Dodge (top right), workers built the Union Pacific Railroad from Omaha, across the Great Plains, to Utah. Many Irish immigrants worked on the railroad.

▲ The Union Pacific and Central Pacific met in Utah, where a ceremonial gold spike was driven, joining the two lines.

▲ Led by Theodore Judah (above, left), workers built the Central Pacific Railroad eastward from Sacramento, through the Rocky Mountains to Utah. Many Chinese immigrants worked on the railroad.

Analyzing VISUALS

1. **Analyzing** Based on the map and photos, why do you think Union Pacific workers were able to lay so many more miles of track than Central Pacific workers?

2. **Describing** Based on the photos, why do you think life as a railroad worker was so difficult?

Pacific employed about 10,000 workers. Camp life was rough, dirty, and dangerous, with lots of gambling, hard drinking, and fighting.

The Central Pacific The Central Pacific Railroad began as the dream of engineer Theodore Judah. He sold stock in his fledgling Central Pacific Railroad Company to four Sacramento merchants: grocer **Leland Stanford,** shop owner Charley Crocker, and hardware store owners Mark Hopkins and Collis P. Huntington. These "Big Four" eventually made huge fortunes, and Stanford became governor of California, served as a United States senator, and founded Stanford University.

Because of a shortage of labor in California, the Central Pacific Railroad hired about 10,000 workers from China and paid them about $1.00 a day. All the equipment—rails, cars, locomotives, and machinery—was shipped from the eastern United States, either around Cape Horn at the tip of South America or over the isthmus of Panama in Central America.

Railroads and the Economy Building the railroad system led to the creation of new technologies and jobs. Economists refer to this as the "multiplier effect." Whenever a new technology becomes widely used, it creates many new jobs in other industries that are needed to support it.

Railroads greatly increased the demand for coal, both to power locomotives and to melt iron in steel refineries. This created a huge coal-mining industry in Pennsylvania and West Virginia. In 1860, some 36,000 people were coal miners; by 1889, there were more than 290,000.

Building railroad engines and cars created many jobs in other industries. For example, textile workers made fabric for seats in passenger cars, glassworkers made the lenses for the lamps, and metalworkers cast the bronze bells.

Railroads created many new jobs. Engineers, firemen, and brakemen were needed to run the trains; mechanics, machinists, oilers, dispatchers, track workers, loaders, and many others were needed to keep the railway running. By 1900, more than 1 million people worked for the railroads.

In 1860 the nation had 30,000 miles of railroad track. By 1890, another 130,000 miles had been laid. Track-laying crews employed thousands of workers. In addition, the lumber industry needed tens of thousands of workers to make railroad ties. Thousands of others worked in iron mines and in the steel industry, helping make rails, engine boilers, and other steel components.

The Last Spike Workers completed the Transcontinental Railroad in only four years, despite the physical challenges. Each mile of track required 400 rails; each rail took 10 spikes. The Central Pacific, starting from the west, laid a total of 688 miles of track. The Union Pacific laid 1,086 miles.

On May 10, 1869, hundreds of spectators gathered at Promontory Summit, Utah, to watch dignitaries hammer five gold and silver spikes into the final rails that would join the Union Pacific and Central Pacific. General Grenville Dodge was at the ceremony:

PRIMARY SOURCE

"The trains pulled up facing each other, each crowded with workmen. . . . The officers and invited guests formed on each side of the track. . . . Prayer was offered; a number of spikes were driven in the two adjoining rails . . . and thus the two roads were welded into one great trunk line from the Atlantic to the Pacific."

—from *Mine Eyes Have Seen*

After Leland Stanford hammered in the last spike, telegraph operators sent the news across the nation. Cannons blasted in New York City, Chicago held a parade, and citizens in Philadelphia rang the Liberty Bell.

Railroads Spur Growth

The transcontinental railroad was the first of many lines that began crisscrossing the nation after the Civil War. By linking the nation, railroads increased the markets for many products, spurring American industrial growth. Railroads also stimulated the economy by spending huge amounts of money on steel, coal, timber, and other materials.

Hundreds of small, unconnected railroads had been built before the Civil War. Gradually, however, large rail lines took them over. By 1890, for example, the Pennsylvania Railroad had consolidated 73 smaller companies. Eventually, seven giant systems with terminals in major cities and scores of branches

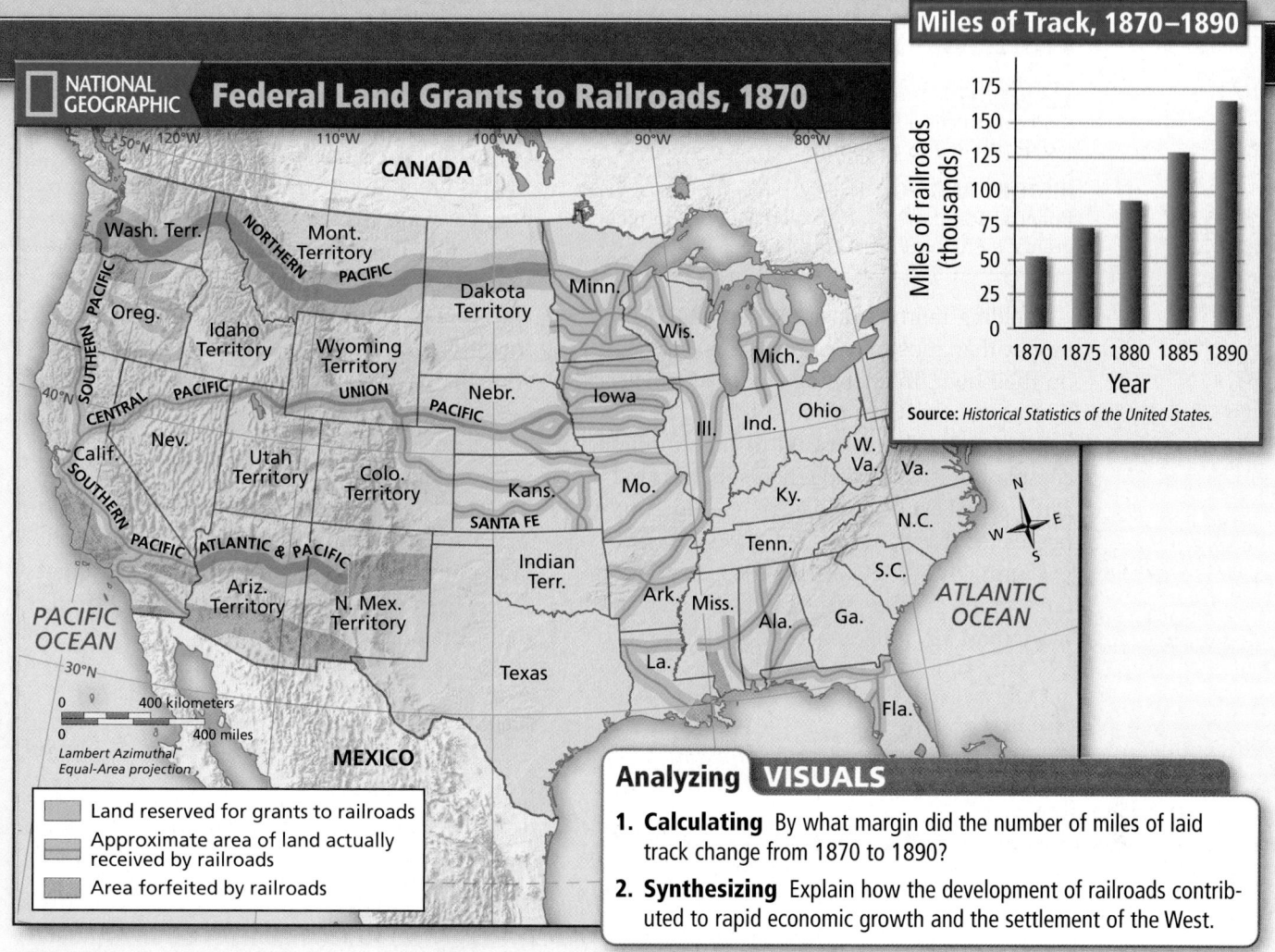

NATIONAL GEOGRAPHIC Federal Land Grants to Railroads, 1870

Miles of Track, 1870–1890

Source: *Historical Statistics of the United States.*

Land reserved for grants to railroads

Approximate area of land actually received by railroads

Area forfeited by railroads

Lambert Azimuthal Equal-Area projection

Analyzing VISUALS

1. **Calculating** By what margin did the number of miles of laid track change from 1870 to 1890?

2. **Synthesizing** Explain how the development of railroads contributed to rapid economic growth and the settlement of the West.

reaching into the countryside controlled most rail traffic.

One of the most successful railroad consolidators was **Cornelius Vanderbilt.** By 1869, Vanderbilt had purchased and merged three short New York railroads to form the New York Central, running from New York City to Buffalo. Within four years he had extended his control over lines all the way to Chicago, which enabled him to offer the first direct rail service between New York City and Chicago. In 1871 Vanderbilt began building New York's Grand Central Terminal.

Before the 1880s each community set its clocks by the sun's position at noon. Having many local time zones interfered with train scheduling, however, and at times even threatened passenger safety. When two trains traveled on the same track, collisions could result from scheduling errors caused by variations in time. To make rail service safer and more reliable, the American Railway Association divided the country into four **time zones** in

1883. The federal government ratified this change in 1918.

Meanwhile, new locomotive technology and the invention of air brakes enabled railroads to put longer and heavier trains on their lines. When combined with large, **integrated** railroad systems, operations became so efficient that the average rate per mile for a ton of freight dropped from two cents in 1860 to three-quarters of a cent in 1900.

The nationwide rail network also helped unite Americans in different regions. The *Omaha Daily Republican* observed in 1883 that railroads had "made the people of the country homogeneous, breaking through the peculiarities and provincialisms which marked separate and unmingling sections." This was a bit of an overstatement, but it recognized that railroads were changing American society.

Reading Check **Explaining** Why was the country divided into four time zones?

Robber Barons

MAIN Idea The government helped finance railroad construction by providing land grants, but this system also led to corruption.

HISTORY AND YOU Have you heard of any recent financial scandals? Read to learn how government grants led to large-scale corruption.

Building railroad lines often required more money than most private **investors** could raise on their own. To encourage railroad construction across the Great Plains, the federal government gave **land grants** to many railroad companies. The railroads then sold the land to settlers, real estate companies, and other businesses to raise money to build the railroad.

During the 1850s and 1860s, the federal land grant system gave railroad companies more than 120 million acres of public land, an area larger than New England, New York, and Pennsylvania combined. Several railroads, including the Union Pacific and Central Pacific, received enough land to cover most of the cost of building their lines.

The great wealth many railroad entrepreneurs acquired in the late 1800s led to accusations that they had built their fortunes by swindling investors and taxpayers, bribing officials, and cheating on their contracts and debts. Infamous for manipulating stock, **Jay Gould** was the most notoriously corrupt railroad owner.

Bribery occurred frequently, partly because government helped fund the railroads. Some investors quickly discovered that they could make more money by acquiring government land grants than by operating a railroad. To get more grants, some investors began bribing members of Congress.

POLITICAL CARTOONS PRIMARY SOURCE
The Robber Barons

▲ Jay Gould bowls on Wall Street with balls labeled "Trickery," and "False Reports." The pins are labeled "Banker," "Inexperienced Investor," "Small Operator," and "Stock Broker."

▲ Railroad owners Jay Gould (lower left), Cornelius Vanderbilt (upper left), Russell Sage (upper right), and Cyrus W. Field (lower right) carve up the United States. The figure in back is lowering an envelope to European royalty labeled "Sealed proposals for the purchase of Europe."

Analyzing VISUALS DBQ

1. **Analyzing Visuals** What "pins" has Jay Gould managed to knock down, and what does this suggest?

2. **Interpreting** What do the faces and actions of the five men in the cartoon suggest?

The Crédit Mobilier Scandal

Corruption in the railroad industry became public in 1872, when the **Crédit Mobilier** scandal erupted. Crédit Mobilier was a construction company set up by several stockholders of the Union Pacific Railroad, including Oakes Ames, a member of Congress. Acting for both the Union Pacific and Crédit Mobilier, the investors signed contracts with themselves. Crédit Mobilier greatly overcharged Union Pacific and added miles to the railroad construction. Because the same investors controlled both companies, the railroad agreed to pay the inflated bills without questions.

By the time the Union Pacific railroad was completed, these investors had made millions of dollars, but the railroad itself had used up its federal grants and was almost bankrupt. To convince Congress to give the railroad more grants, Ames sold other members of Congress shares in the Union Pacific at a price well below their market value.

During the election campaign of 1872, an angry associate of Ames sent a letter to the *New York Sun* listing the members of Congress who had accepted shares. The scandal led to an investigation that implicated several members of Congress, including Speaker of the House James G. Blaine and Representative James Garfield, who later became president. It also revealed that Vice President Schuyler Colfax had accepted stock from the railroad. Neither criminal nor civil charges were filed against anyone involved with Crédit Mobilier, however, nor did the scandal affect the outcome of the elections.

The Great Northern Railroad

The Crédit Mobilier scandal created the impression that all railroad entrepreneurs were "robber barons"—people who loot an industry and give nothing back. Some, like Jay Gould, deserved this reputation, but others did not.

James J. Hill was clearly no robber baron. Hill built and operated the Great Northern Railroad from Wisconsin and Minnesota in the East to Washington in the West, without any federal land grants or subsidies. He had carefully planned the railroad's route to pass close to established towns in the region.

To increase business, he offered low fares to settlers who homesteaded along his route. Later, he sold homesteads to the Norwegian and Swedish immigrants coming to the region. He then identified American products that were in demand in China, including cotton, textiles, and flour, and arranged to haul those goods to Washington for shipment to Asia. This enabled the railroad to earn money by hauling goods both east and west, instead of simply sending lumber and farm products east and coming back empty, as many other railroads did at that time. The Great Northern became the most successful transcontinental railroad and the only one that was not eventually forced into bankruptcy.

✔ **Reading Check** **Describing** How was the Great Northern different from other railroads of its time?

Section 2 REVIEW

Vocabulary

1. **Explain** the significance of: Pacific Railway Act, Grenville Dodge, Leland Stanford, Cornelius Vanderbilt, time zone, land grant, Jay Gould, Crédit Mobilier, James J. Hill.

Main Ideas

2. **Describing** How did Grenville Dodge contribute to the economic growth of the United States in the late 1800s?

3. **Listing** Use a graphic organizer similar to the one below to list the different ways by which railroads were financed.

Ways Railroads Were Financed

Critical Thinking

4. **Big Ideas** How did railroad expansion lead to industrial growth?

5. **Theorizing** Why might politicians be tempted to accept gifts of railroad stock? Why did Crédit Mobilier become a scandal?

6. **Analyzing Visuals** Examine the map and graph on page 191. Then make up a quiz of at least five questions based on the information presented.

Writing About History

7. **Persuasive Writing** Take on the role of an employee of a major railroad corporation. Your job is to write an advertisement to recruit workers for your corporation. After writing the advertisement, present it to your class.

History ONLINE

Study Central™ To review this section, go to glencoe.com and click on Study Central.

Big Business

Guide to Reading

Big Ideas
Economics and Society Business people such as Andrew Carnegie developed new ways to expand business.

Content Vocabulary
- corporation *(p. 194)*
- stock *(p. 194)*
- economies of scale *(p. 194)*
- pool *(p. 196)*
- vertical integration *(p. 197)*
- horizontal integration *(p. 197)*
- monopoly *(p. 197)*
- trust *(p. 198)*
- holding company *(p. 198)*

Academic Vocabulary
- distribution *(p. 194)*
- consumer *(p. 196)*

People and Events to Identify
- Andrew Carnegie *(p. 196)*
- John D. Rockefeller *(p. 197)*

Reading Strategy
Organizing As you read about the rise of corporations in the United States, complete a graphic organizer showing the steps large business owners took to weaken or eliminate competition.

Following the Civil War, large corporations developed that could consolidate various business functions and produce goods more efficiently. Retail stores began using advertising and mail-order catalogs to attract new consumers.

The Rise of Big Business

MAIN Idea Corporations could produce goods more efficiently, which allowed the rise of big business.

HISTORY AND YOU Do you own stock in a corporation or know someone who does? Read to learn why corporations issue stock.

Before the Civil War, most manufacturing enterprises were owned by just a few people working in partnership. Everything had changed by 1900. Big businesses dominated the economy, operating vast complexes of factories, warehouses, and **distribution** facilities.

Big business would not have been possible without the **corporation.** A corporation is an organization owned by many people but treated by law as though it were a person. It can own property, pay taxes, make contracts, and sue and be sued. The people who own the corporation are called stockholders because they own shares of ownership called **stock.** Issuing stock allows a corporation to raise large amounts of money for big projects while spreading out the financial risk.

Before the 1830s there were few corporations, because entrepreneurs had to convince a state legislature to issue them a charter. In the 1830s, however, states began passing general incorporation laws, allowing companies to become corporations and issue stock without charters from the legislature.

With the money they raised from the sale of stock, corporations could invest in new technologies, hire large workforces, and purchase many machines, greatly increasing their efficiency. This enabled them to achieve **economies of scale:** the cost of manufacturing is decreased by producing goods quickly in large quantities.

All businesses have two kinds of costs, fixed costs and operating costs. Fixed costs are costs a company has to pay, whether or not it is operating. For example, a company has to pay its loans, mortgages, and taxes, regardless of whether it is operating. Operating costs are costs that occur when running a company, such as paying wages and shipping costs and buying raw materials and supplies.

The small manufacturers that were common before the Civil War usually had low fixed costs but high operating costs. If sales dropped, it was cheaper to shut down temporarily. Big manufacturers,

Types of Business Organizations

	Sole proprietorship	Partnership	Corporation
Who owns the business?	One person owns the business and often manages it	Two or more people own and manage the business	All investors who own its stock; managers are hired
How is money raised?	Owner uses savings and borrows money from a bank	Partners each invest some of their own money and borrow money from a bank	Shares of stock are sold to finance business; bank loans are also used
Advantages	Easy to start Low fixed costs, as facilities are usually small and inexpensive to maintain	Partners share responsibility for running the business Low fixed costs	Limited liability for investors Low operating costs; can stay open if economy slows
Disadvantages	Difficult to raise money; limited opportunities for growth; owner has unlimited liability; high operating costs may force business to shut down if the economy is weak	Partners may disagree on direction the company should take; owners have unlimited liability High operating costs	Often have high fixed costs because of size of facilities and equipment needed

▶ The rise of corporations whose stock could be sold publicly also led to the rise of stock exchanges, where stockbrokers bought and sold stock for investors. The photo shows the trading floor of the New York Stock Exchange (NYSE) in 1908. By the late 1800s, the NYSE was the nation's most important stock exchange.

U.S. Businesses, 1870–1900

Businesses (thousands)

Source: *Historical Statistics of the United States.*

Analyzing VISUALS

1. **Making Inferences** After comparing proprietorships and corporations, why do you think both still exist today?
2. **Making Generalizations** Based on the chart, what generalization can you make about the growth of U.S. businesses during those three decades? What explanation can you offer?

however, had the high fixed costs of building and maintaining a factory. Compared to their fixed costs, the operating costs of big businesses were low. Operating costs, such as wages, were such a small part of a corporation's costs that it made sense to continue operating, even in a recession.

In these circumstances, big corporations had several advantages. They could produce more goods cheaply and efficiently. They could continue to operate in poor economic times by cutting prices to increase sales rather than shutting down. Many were also able to negotiate rebates from the railroads, further lowering their operating costs.

Small businesses with high operating costs found it difficult to compete with large corporations, and many were forced out of business. At the time, many people criticized corporations for cutting prices and negotiating rebates. They believed the corporations were behaving unethically by driving small companies out of business. In many cases, it was the changing nature of business organization and the new importance of fixed costs that caused competition to become so severe and led to so many small companies going out of business.

Reading Check **Describing** What factors led to the rise of big business in the United States?

Consolidating Industry

MAIN Idea Business leaders devised new and larger forms of business organizations and new ways to promote their products.

HISTORY AND YOU How does advertising reach you today? How has technology created new ways to market and sell goods? Read to learn how an increase in new products led to new selling methods.

Many business leaders did not like the intense competition that had been forced on them. Although falling prices benefited **consumers,** they cut into profits. To stop prices from falling, many companies organized **pools,** or agreements, to keep prices at a certain level.

American courts and legislatures were suspicious of pools because they interfered with competition and property rights. As a result, companies that formed pools had no legal protection and could not enforce their agreements in court. Pools generally did not last long anyway. They broke apart whenever one member cut prices to steal the market share from another. By the 1870s, competition had reduced many industries to a few large and highly efficient corporations.

Andrew Carnegie and Steel

The remarkable life of **Andrew Carnegie** illustrates many of the factors that led to the rise of big business in the United States. Born in Scotland, Carnegie was the son of a poor hand weaver who moved to the United States in 1848. At age 12, Carnegie went to work as a bobbin boy in a textile factory earning $1.20 per week. After two years, he became a messenger in a telegraph office, then worked as secretary to Thomas Scott, a superintendent and, later, president of the Pennsylvania Railroad. Carnegie's energy impressed Scott, and when Scott was promoted, Carnegie became the new superintendent.

As a railroad supervisor, Carnegie knew that he could make a lot of money by investing in companies that served the railroad industry. He bought shares in iron mills and factories that made sleeping cars and locomotives. He also invested in a company that built railroad bridges. By his early 30s, he was earning $50,000 per year and decided to quit his job to concentrate on his own business investments.

As part of his business activities, Carnegie frequently traveled to Europe. On one trip, he

INFOGRAPHIC
The Rise of the Steel Industry

Several factors led to the rise of big business in the late 1800s: the use of new technology, the advantages of economies of scale, and the process of vertical and horizontal integration.

Coke, iron ore, and limestone are hoisted to the top of the blast furnace and sprinkled into the furnace. Blasts of super-hot air melt the ore as it falls.

Impurities rise to the top of the molten iron and are skimmed off. The iron drains out the bottom of the furnace and is carried to the Bessemer converter.

Carnegie's use of a Bessemer converter enabled his steel mills to make large quantities of inexpensive steel. Molten iron is poured into the converter and then air is blown in, separating the impurities, and leaving high grade steel to pour out.

Blast furnace

Bessemer converter

Coke (from coal)   Iron ore   Limestone

met Sir Henry Bessemer, who had invented a new process for making high-quality steel efficiently and cheaply. After meeting Bessemer, Carnegie opened a steel company in Pittsburgh in 1875 and began using the Bessemer process. Carnegie often boasted about how cheaply he could produce steel:

PRIMARY SOURCE

"Two pounds of iron stone mined upon Lake Superior and transported nine hundred miles to Pittsburgh; one pound and one-half of coal mined and manufactured into coke, and transported to Pittsburgh; one-half pound of lime, mined and transported to Pittsburgh; a small amount of manganese ore mined in Virginia and brought to Pittsburgh—and these four pounds of materials manufactured into one pound of steel, for which the consumer pays one cent."

—quoted in *The Growth of the American Republic*

To make his company more efficient, Carnegie began the **vertical integration** of the steel industry. A vertically integrated company owns all of the different businesses on which it depends for its operation. Instead of paying companies for coal, lime, and iron, Carnegie's steel company bought coal mines, limestone quarries, and iron ore fields. Vertical integration saved money and enabled many companies to become even bigger.

Rockefeller and Standard Oil

Successful business leaders also pushed for **horizontal integration,** or combining firms in the same business into one large corporation. Horizontal integration took place as companies competed. When a company began to lose market share, it would often sell out to competitors to create a larger organization.

Perhaps the most famous industrialist who achieved almost complete horizontal integration of his industry is **John D. Rockefeller.** When oil was discovered in Pennsylvania, many entrepreneurs started drilling for oil, hoping to strike it rich. Rockefeller decided to build oil refineries instead. By 1870, his company, Standard Oil, was the nation's largest oil refiner. He then began buying out his competitors. By 1880, the company controlled about 90 percent of the oil-refining industry in the United States. When a single company achieves control of an entire market, it becomes a **monopoly.**

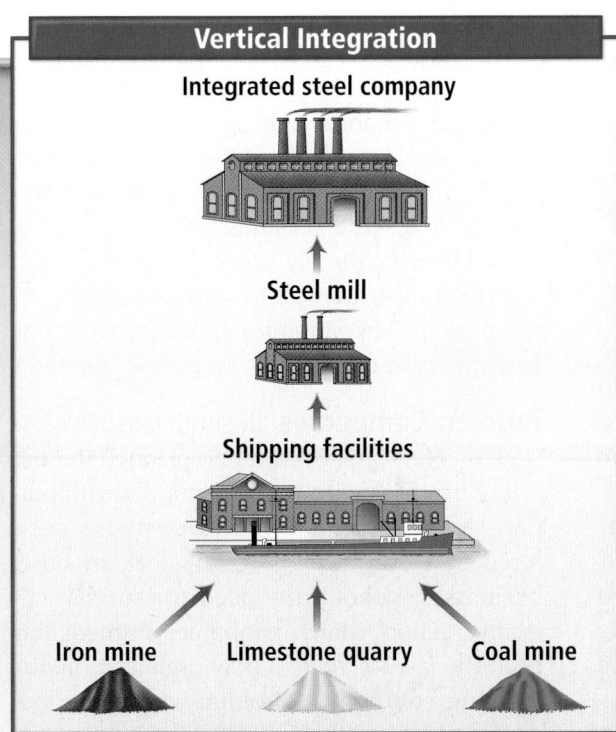

▲ *In a vertically integrated industry, a company owns all parts of the industrial process. In this case, a steel company owns the iron and coal mines, the limestone quarries, and the ships and trains that move the materials, as well as the steel mills.*

▲ *When one company grows by buying up its competitors, it is using horizontal integration to expand.*

Analyzing VISUALS

1. **Analyzing Visuals** What enabled entrepreneurs such as Andrew Carnegie to build large steel factories?

2. **Explaining** Why did business owners want to vertically integrate their companies?

John D. Rockefeller
1839–1937

John Davison Rockefeller was one of the foremost industrialists of the late 1800s. Born in upstate New York, Rockefeller moved with his family to Cleveland, Ohio, as a teenager. As a young man, he established a grain and livestock business that made huge profits during the Civil War.

Meanwhile, Cleveland had emerged as a center for refining the oil extracted from the oil fields of western Pennsylvania. In 1863 Rockefeller used his wartime profits to start an oil-refining company. He then began buying up other oil refineries. In 1870 Rockefeller and some associates founded the Standard Oil Company. Rockefeller invested in the newest and most efficient refining technology. He also became known for using ruthless tactics to get preferential shipping rates from railroad companies and acquire competing oil refineries.

By the early 1880s, Rockefeller had created the Standard Oil Trust. With a near-monopoly on American oil refining, Standard Oil made Rockefeller one of the richest men in the world. Rockefeller later donated much of his wealth to philanthropic causes, most notably funding colleges and universities.

What made Standard Oil so successful?

J. P. Morgan
1837–1913

John Pierpont Morgan, the most powerful and influential financier of his era, built a financial empire that became known as the "House of Morgan." The son of a successful Boston banker, Morgan began his career working in the New York City branch of his father's bank.

Morgan soon developed a reputation for shrewd business sense. He specialized in financing railroads, an industry plagued by cutthroat competition and instability. Before Morgan would agree to rescue a troubled railroad company, he insisted the company reorganize to become more efficient, combine smaller railway lines to create a larger coordinated railroad system, and agree to have a representative from Morgan's firm oversee future decisions.

During the depression of the 1890s, Morgan used his immense fortune to finance a bond to rescue the federal government's depleted gold reserve. In 1901 Morgan made history when he organized the first billion-dollar corporation, U.S. Steel, by merging the Carnegie Steel Company and several other steel companies.

How did Morgan try to help the railroad industry?

New Business Organizations

Many Americans feared monopolies because they believed that a monopoly could charge whatever it wanted for its products. Others, however, believed that monopolies had to keep prices low because raising prices would encourage competitors to reappear and offer the products for a lower price. In some industries, one company had a near-monopoly in the United States but was competing on a global scale. Standard Oil, for example, came very close to having a monopoly in the United States, but international competition forced the company to keep its prices low in the late 1800s and early 1900s.

In the late 1800s, in an effort to stop horizontal integration and the rise of monopolies, many states made it illegal for one company to own stock in another company. It did not take long, however, for companies to discover ways around the laws.

Trusts In 1882 Standard Oil formed the first **trust,** a new way of merging businesses that did not violate such laws. A trust is a legal arrangement that allows one person to manage another person's property. The person who manages that property is called a trustee.

Instead of buying a company outright, Standard Oil had stockholders give their stocks to a group of Standard Oil trustees. In exchange, the stockholders received shares in the trust, which entitled them to a portion of the trust's profits. Since the trustees did not own the stock but were merely managing it, they were not violating any laws. The trustees could control a group of companies as if they were one large, merged company.

Holding Companies Beginning in 1889, the state of New Jersey further accelerated the rise of big business with a new general incorporation law. This law allowed corporations chartered in New Jersey to own stock in other businesses without any need for special legislative action. Many companies immediately used the law to create a new organization, the **holding company.** A holding company does not produce anything itself. Instead, it owns the stock of companies that do produce goods. The holding company manages the companies it owns, effectively merging them into one large enterprise.

Investment Banking Another increase in the size of corporations began in the mid-1890s, when investment bankers began to help put new holding companies together. Perhaps the most famous and successful investment banker of the era was J. P. Morgan. John Pierpont Morgan began his career in 1857 as an agent for his father's banking company in New York, America's financial capital. Investment bankers like Morgan specialized in helping companies issue stock. Companies would sell large blocks of stock to investment bankers at a discount. The bankers would then find people willing to buy the stock and sell it for a profit.

In the mid-1890s, investment bankers became interested in selling stock in holding companies that merged many of America's already large corporations. In 1901, J. P. Morgan bought out Andrew Carnegie. Morgan then merged Carnegie Steel with other large steel companies into an enormous holding company called the United States Steel Company. U.S. Steel, worth $1.4 billion, was the first billion-dollar company in American history. By 1904, the United States had 318 holding companies. Together, these giant corporations controlled over 5,300 factories and were worth more than $7 billion.

Selling the Product

The creation of giant manufacturing companies in the United States forced retailers—companies that sell products directly to consumers—to expand in size as well. The vast array of products that American industries produced led retailers to look for new ways to attract consumers. N. W. Ayer and Son, the first advertising company, began creating large illustrated ads instead of relying on the old small print line ads previously used in newspapers. By 1900, retailers were spending over $90 million a year on advertising in newspapers and magazines.

Advertising attracted readers to the newest retail business, the department store. In 1877 advertisements billed John Wanamaker's new Philadelphia department store, the Grand Depot, as the "largest space in the world devoted to retail selling on a single floor." When it opened, only a handful of department stores existed in the United States; soon hundreds sprang up. Department stores provided a huge selection of products in one large, elegant building. The store atmosphere made shopping seem glamorous and exciting.

Chain stores, a group of retail outlets owned by the same company, first appeared in the mid-1800s. In contrast to department stores, which offered many services, chain stores focused on offering low prices. Woolworth's, which opened in 1879, became one of the most successful retail chains in American history.

To reach the millions of people who lived in rural areas far from chain stores or department stores, retailers began issuing mail-order catalogs. Two of the largest mail-order retailers were Montgomery Ward and Sears, Roebuck and Co. Their huge catalogs, widely distributed through the mail, used attractive illustrations and appealing descriptions to advertise thousands of items for sale.

✔ Reading Check **Explaining** What techniques did corporations use to consolidate their industries?

Section 3 REVIEW

Vocabulary

1. **Explain** the significance of: corporation, stock, economies of scale, pool, Andrew Carnegie, vertical integration, horizontal integration, John D. Rockefeller, monopoly, trust, holding company.

Main Ideas

2. **Stating** Why did the number of corporations increase in the late 1800s?

3. **Comparing** Use a graphic organizer to list ways business leaders in the 1800s tried to eliminate competition.

Attempts to Eliminate Competition

Critical Thinking

4. **Big Ideas** What techniques were used by Carnegie and others to consolidate their industries? How did state governments respond?

5. **Forming an Opinion** Do you think an individual today can rise from "rags to riches" like Andrew Carnegie did? Why or why not?

6. **Analyzing Visuals** Look again at the chart on page 195. During which decade did the number of U.S. businesses increase the most? By how many?

Writing About History

7. **Expository Writing** Write a newspaper editorial in which you explain why entrepreneurs were a positive or a negative force on the U.S. economy in the late 1800s.

History ONLINE

Study Central™ To review this section, go to glencoe.com and click on Study Central.

Unions

Guide to Reading

Big Ideas
Struggles for Rights Unions grew and labor unrest intensified as workers fought for more rights.

Content Vocabulary
- deflation *(p. 200)*
- trade union *(p. 201)*
- industrial union *(p. 201)*
- blacklist *(p. 201)*
- lockout *(p. 202)*
- arbitration *(p. 204)*
- injunction *(p. 205)*
- closed shop *(p. 206)*

Academic Vocabulary
- restraint *(p. 202)*
- constitute *(p. 207)*

People and Events to Identify
- Marxism *(p. 202)*
- Knights of Labor *(p. 204)*
- American Federation of Labor *(p. 206)*
- Samuel Gompers *(p. 206)*

Reading Strategy
Sequencing As you read about the increase of American labor unions in the late 1800s, complete a time line similar to the one below by filling in the incidents of labor unrest discussed and the results of each incident.

Workers tried to form unions in the late 1800s, hoping to improve wages, hours, and working conditions. Business leaders were willing to deal with some trade unions but generally opposed industrial unions. Many strikes in this era led to violence, which hurt the image of unions and slowed their growth.

Working in the United States

MAIN Idea Low wages, long hours, and difficult working conditions caused resentment among workers and led to efforts to organize unions.

HISTORY AND YOU Have you ever felt that you were underpaid for an after-school job? Read about the conditions that made workers want to organize.

Life for workers in industrial America was difficult. Many workers had to perform dull, repetitive tasks in working conditions that were often unhealthy and dangerous. Workers breathed in lint, dust, and toxic fumes. Heavy machines lacking safety devices caused many injuries. Despite the difficult working conditions, industrialism led to a dramatic rise in the standard of living. The average worker's wages rose by 50 percent between 1860 and 1890. Nonetheless, the uneven division of income between the wealthy and the working class caused resentment among workers. In 1900 the average industrial worker made 22¢ per hour and worked 59 hours per week.

Deflation, or a rise in the value of money, added to tensions between workers and employers. Between 1865 and 1897, deflation caused prices to fall, which increased the buying power of workers' wages. Although companies cut wages regularly in the late 1800s, prices fell even faster, so that wages were actually still going up in buying power. Workers, however, resented getting less money. Eventually, many concluded that they needed a union to bargain for them in order to get higher wages and better working conditions.

Early Unions

There were two basic types of industrial workers in the United States in the 1800s—craft workers and common laborers. Craft workers had special skills and training. They included machinists, iron molders, stonecutters, shoemakers, printers, and many others. Craft workers received higher wages and had more control over how they organized their time. Common laborers had few skills and received lower wages.

Why Did Workers Want to Organize?

In 1893 a recession hit the United States; by 1894, millions of workers were unemployed and over 750,000 were on strike. A former quarry foreman named Jacob Coxey organized unemployed workers and began a march on Washington to demand jobs on public works projects. The marchers were known as "Coxey's Army."

▲ *Whether they were working in Western silver mines (top photo) or handling hot steel at a Pittsburgh foundry (above), workers toiled in unsafe conditions for very little money.*

Annual Nonfarm Earnings

Earnings (dollars)

600
500
400
300
200
100
0

1865 1870 1875 1880 1885 1890 1895 1900

Year

— Real wages
— Not adjusted for inflation

Source: *Historical Statistics of the United States.*

Analyzing VISUALS

1. **Analyzing** What do you observe about the working conditions and equipment of the men in both of the inset photos?

2. **Contrasting** What happened to real wages and those not adjusted for inflation between 1865 and 1900? Given this fact, why do you think workers wanted to organize?

In the 1830s, as industrialization began to spread, craft workers began to form **trade unions.** By 1873 there were 32 national trade unions in the United States. Among the largest and most successful were the Iron Molders' International Union, the International Typographical Union, and the Knights of St. Crispin—the shoemakers' union.

Industry Opposes Unions Employers often had to negotiate with trade unions because they represented workers whose skills they needed. However, employers generally viewed unions as conspiracies that interfered with property rights. Business leaders particularly opposed **industrial unions,** which united all workers in a particular industry.

Companies used several techniques to stop workers from forming unions. They required workers to take oaths or sign contracts promising not to join a union. They hired detectives to identify union organizers. Workers who tried to organize a union or strike were fired and placed on a **blacklist**—a list of "troublemakers"—so that no company would hire them.

When workers formed a union, companies used **"lockouts"** to break it. They locked workers out of the property and refused to pay them. If the union called a strike, employers would hire replacements, or strikebreakers.

Political and Social Opposition Efforts to break unions often succeeded because there were no laws giving workers the right to form unions or requiring owners to negotiate with them. Courts frequently ruled that strikes were "conspiracies in **restraint** of trade," for which labor leaders might be fined or jailed.

Unions also suffered from the perception that they were un-American. In the 1800s, the ideas of Karl Marx, called **Marxism,** became very influential in Europe. Marx argued that the basic force shaping capitalist society was the class struggle between workers and owners. He believed that workers would eventually revolt, seize control of the factories, and overthrow the government.

Marxists claimed that after the revolution the government would seize all private property and create a socialist society where wealth was evenly divided. Eventually, Marx thought, the state would disappear, leaving a communist society where classes did not exist.

While many labor supporters agreed with Marx, a few supported anarchism. Anarchists believe that society does not need any government. At the time, some believed that with only a few acts of violence they could ignite a revolution to topple the government. In the late 1800s, anarchists assassinated government officials and set off bombs all across Europe, hoping to trigger a revolution.

During the same period, tens of thousands of European immigrants headed to America. Anti-immigrant feelings were already strong in the United States and, as people began to associate immigrant workers with radical ideas, they became suspicious of unions. These fears, and concerns for law and order, often led officials to use the courts, the police, and even the army to crush strikes and break up unions.

Reading Check **Identifying** Why were some Americans suspicious of unions?

INFOGRAPHIC
Working in the United States, 1870–1900

The status of the American economy played an important role in the development of unions. Although union membership rose dramatically by 1900, the willingness of people to join unions at any given time varied depending on how well the economy was doing.

Union Membership, 1880–1900

Members (thousands)

Sources: *New Estimates of Union Membership; The Growth of American Trade Unions.*

The U.S. Economy, 1870–1900

Level of business activity

— Business activity — Wholesale prices   **Year**

Source: *The Great Republic.*

Struggling to Organize

MAIN Idea Workers began to form unions to fight for better wages and working conditions but had few successes.

HISTORY AND YOU Do you sometimes feel that you spend too many hours a day in school? Read to learn how workers sought an eight-hour workday.

Although workers attempted on many occasions to create large industrial unions, they rarely succeeded. In many cases the confrontations with owners and the government led to violence and bloodshed. In 1868 William Sylvis, president of the Iron Molders' Union, wrote to Karl Marx in support of his work and to express his own beliefs:

PRIMARY SOURCE

"... monied power is fast eating up the substance of the people. We have made war upon it, and we mean to win it. If we can we will win through the ballot box; if not, we will resort to sterner means. A little bloodletting is sometimes necessary in desperate causes."

—quoted in *Industrialism and the American Worker*

The Great Railroad Strike

The panic of 1873 was a severe recession that struck the American economy and forced many companies to cut wages. The economy had still not recovered when, in July 1877, the Baltimore and Ohio Railroad announced it was cutting wages, for the third time. In Martinsburg, West Virginia, workers walked off the job and blocked the tracks.

As word spread, railroad workers across the country walked off the job. The strike eventually involved 80,000 railroad workers and affected two-thirds of the nation's railways. Angry strikers smashed equipment, tore up tracks, and blocked rail service in New York, Baltimore, Pittsburgh, St. Louis, and Chicago. The governors of several states called out their militias. In many places, gun battles erupted between the militia and the strikers.

Declaring a state of "insurrection," President Hayes sent federal troops to Martinsburg, Baltimore, Pittsburgh, and elsewhere. It took 12 bloody days for police, state militias, and

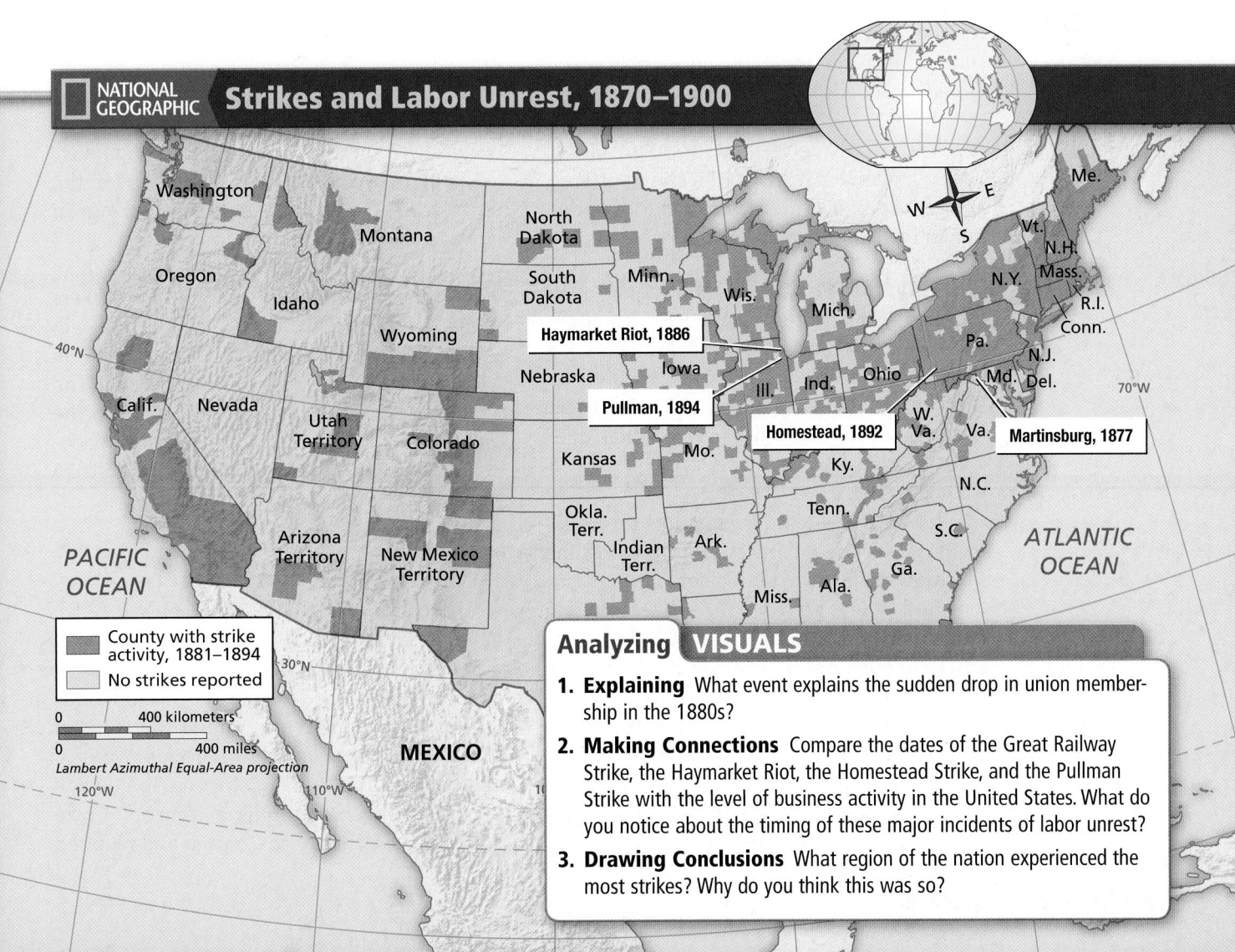

NATIONAL GEOGRAPHIC Strikes and Labor Unrest, 1870–1900

Haymarket Riot, 1886

Pullman, 1894

Homestead, 1892

Martinsburg, 1877

PACIFIC OCEAN

ATLANTIC OCEAN

MEXICO

- County with strike activity, 1881–1894
- No strikes reported

0   400 kilometers
0   400 miles
Lambert Azimuthal Equal-Area projection

Analyzing VISUALS

1. **Explaining** What event explains the sudden drop in union membership in the 1880s?

2. **Making Connections** Compare the dates of the Great Railway Strike, the Haymarket Riot, the Homestead Strike, and the Pullman Strike with the level of business activity in the United States. What do you notice about the timing of these major incidents of labor unrest?

3. **Drawing Conclusions** What region of the nation experienced the most strikes? Why do you think this was so?

federal troops to restore order. By the time the strike collapsed, more than 100 people lay dead, and over $10 million in railroad property had been destroyed. The violence of this strike alarmed many Americans and pointed to the need for more peaceful means to settle labor disputes.

The Knights of Labor

The **Knights of Labor,** founded in 1869, took a different approach to labor issues. Its leader, Terence Powderly, opposed strikes, preferring to use boycotts to pressure employers. The Knights of Labor also supported **arbitration,** a process in which a third party helps workers and employers reach an agreement. The Knights called for an eight-hour workday and supported equal pay for women, the abolition of child labor, and the creation of worker-owned factories. Unlike many organizations of the era, the Knights welcomed women and African Americans as members.

History ONLINE
Student Web Activity Visit glencoe.com and complete the activity on the Homestead Strike.

Early Successes In the early 1880s, the Knights began to use strikes and were initially successful. After they convinced one of Jay Gould's railroads to reverse wage cuts in 1885, membership in the union soared. In less than one year, the Knights grew from 100,000 to 700,000 members. Then, in the spring of 1886, an event known as the Haymarket Riot undermined the Knights' reputation.

The Haymarket Riot In 1886 supporters of the eight-hour workday called for a nationwide strike on May 1st. On that date, strikes took place in many cities. In Chicago, the local Knights of Labor led a march of 80,000 people through the center of the city on that date. Over the next few days, nearly 70,000 workers went on strike across the city.

On May 3, police intervened to stop a fight on the picket line at the McCormick Harvesting Machine Company. The incident turned violent and police fired on the strikers, killing four. Afterward, a local anarchist group organized a meeting in Chicago's Haymarket Square to protest the shooting of the strikers.

On the evening of May 4, about 3,000 people gathered to hear the speeches. As the meeting began to break up, the police moved in to keep order. Someone threw a bomb, killing one officer and wounding six others. The police opened fire, and workers shot back. About 100 people, including nearly 70 police officers, were injured.

The police arrested eight people for the bombing. Seven were German immigrants and advocates of anarchism. The incident horrified people across the country. Although the evidence was weak, all eight men were convicted, and four were executed.

Critics long opposed to the union movement pointed to the Haymarket riot to claim that unions were dominated by dangerous radicals. One of the men arrested was a member of the Knights of Labor. This association hurt the Knights' reputation and, coupled with lost strikes, led to a steady decline in membership and influence.

The Homestead Strike

In the summer of 1892, another labor dispute led to bloodshed. A steel mill owned by Andrew Carnegie in Homestead, Pennsylvania, was managed by an anti-union business partner, Henry Clay Frick. The mill's employees belonged to the Amalgamated Association of Iron, Steel, and Tin Workers, the largest craft union in the country. When the union's contract was about to expire, Frick proposed to cut wages by 20 percent. He then locked employees out of the plant and arranged for the Pinkerton Detective Agency to bring in replacement workers.

When the Pinkertons and strikebreakers approached the plant on barges, the strikers refused to let them land. Gunfire followed. After 14 hours, several Pinkertons and strikers were dead, and dozens more were injured. The governor of Pennsylvania then ordered the militia to take control and protect the replacement workers. After four months, the strike collapsed.

The Pullman Strike

Under the leadership of Eugene V. Debs, railroad employees organized the American Railway Union (ARU) in 1893. As an industrial union, the ARU tried to organize all employees of the railroad industry. Among the workers the union organized were the employees of the Pullman Palace Car Company. The owner, George Pullman, had built a company town, Pullman, just outside of Chicago and required

Comparing Major Strikes

	Homestead Steel Strike, 1892	Pullman Railroad Strike, 1894	Lawrence Textile Strike, 1912
Conditions	Seeking to break the union, the Carnegie Steel Company rejects wage increase and proposes a 20% wage cut	Deep wage cuts without cuts in rent and food prices at company housing and company stores	Very low wages; high mortality among workers (many workers are young girls); extreme poverty among workers; strike begins after new wage cuts
Union	Amalgamated Association of Iron, Steel, and Tin Workers	American Railway Union	International Workers of the World (IWW); strikers mostly female, immigrant textile workers
Tactics	**Workers:** Surround factory with pickets and armed workers to keep it shut down and keep strikebreakers out **Employer:** Locks workers out of the plant; hires Pinkertons to break strike	**Workers:** Refuse to handle any railcars built by Pullman; railroads are tied up nationwide **Employer:** Locks workers out of factory	**Workers:** Picketing; union provides food and money to strikers; gains support by touring child workers around country **Employer:** Uses firehoses on picketing workers
Role of Government	State government sends in militia to end violence between strikers and Pinkertons	Federal government gets court injunction to end strike because it interferes with shipment of U.S. mail; federal troops end strike	Local police and state and local militia make mass arrests, attack picketers; after attack on women and children, strike is publicized; Congress and President Taft investigate
Outcome	Company hires strikebreakers; strike collapses after anarchist tries to kill plant manager	ARU leaders are jailed, strike ends unsuccessfully; ARU membership declines	Employers give in, grant workers' demands

Analyzing VISUALS

1. **Contrasting** How does the Lawrence Textile Strike differ from the others?
2. **Analyzing Visuals** In which instance do federal troops break the strike, and on what grounds?

his workers to live there and to buy goods from company stores. In 1893 the Pullman Company laid off workers and slashed wages. The wage cuts made it difficult for workers to pay their rent and the high prices at the company stores. After the company refused to discuss workers' grievances, a strike began on May 11, 1894. To show support for the Pullman strikers, other ARU members across the United States refused to handle Pullman cars.

This boycott tied up the railroads and threatened to paralyze the economy. Determined to break the strike, railroad managers arranged for U.S. mail cars to be attached to the Pullman cars. If the strikers refused to handle the Pullman cars, they would be interfering with the U.S. mail, a violation of federal law. President Grover Cleveland then sent in troops, claiming it was his responsibility to keep the mail running. Then a federal court issued an **injunction,** or formal court order, directing the union to halt the boycott. Debs went to jail for violating the injunction, but both the strike at Pullman and the ARU strike collapsed. In the case *In re Debs* (1895), the Supreme Court upheld the right to issue such an injunction. This gave business a powerful tool for dealing with labor unrest.

Reading Check **Summarizing** Why was it difficult for unions to succeed in the 1800s?

New Unions Emerge

MAIN Idea The AFL fought for skilled workers; new unions tried to organize unskilled workers.

HISTORY AND YOU Do you know anyone who belongs to a union? Read on to learn about the different types of unions and how they tried to help their members.

Although workers often shared the same complaints about wage rates and working hours, unions took very different approaches to how they tried to improve workers' lives. Trade unions remained the most common type of labor organization. Of course, most workers were unskilled and unrepresented by trade unions. Thus, new types of unions emerged that tried to reach out to those workers and had different ideas about how to help them.

The Rise of the AFL

The **American Federation of Labor** (AFL) was the dominant union of the late 1800s. In 1886 leaders of several national trade unions came together to create the AFL. From its beginning, the AFL focused on promoting the interests of skilled workers.

Samuel Gompers was the first president of the AFL, a position he held until 1924 (with the exception of one year). While other unions became involved in politics, Gompers tried to steer away from controversy and stay focused on "pure and simple" unionism. That is, he thought it best that the AFL stay focused on "bread and butter" issues—wages, working hours, and working conditions. He was willing to use the strike but preferred to negotiate.

The AFL had three main goals. First, it tried to convince companies to recognize unions and to agree to collective bargaining. Second, it pushed for **closed shops,** meaning that companies could only hire union members. Third, it promoted an eight-hour workday.

The AFL grew slowly, but by 1900 it was the biggest union in the country, with over 500,000 members. Still, at that time, the AFL represented less than 15 percent of all nonfarm workers. Most AFL members were white men, because the unions discriminated against African Americans, and only a few would admit women.

The IWW

In 1905 a group of labor radicals, many of them socialists, created the Industrial

People IN HISTORY

Samuel Gompers
1850–1924

Samuel Gompers was the longest-serving president of the American Federation of Labor. Born in London to a Dutch Jewish family, Gompers quit school at 10 to earn money for his family, working as a cigarmaker. He and his family moved to the United States in 1863.

In 1877 Gompers became president of the Cigarmakers' Union. In 1886 he persuaded other craft unions to form the American Federation of Labor and became its first president. Within four years, the AFL had a quarter of a million members. That number grew to one million during the next two years.

A practical man who distrusted socialism, Gompers avoided political ideas and concentrated on improving working conditions. He believed that a just society was built on a fair labor policy. "Show me the country in which there are no strikes and I will show you that country in which there is no liberty," he said.

Do you agree that a union can try to improve working conditions without becoming involved in politics? Explain your answer.

Eugene V. Debs
1855–1926

Eugene Victor Debs was a prominent labor leader and member of the American Socialist Party. Born in Terre Haute, Indiana, Debs went to work at age 15 as a railroad fireman. He helped found the Brotherhood of Locomotive Firemen.

In 1893 Debs helped organize the American Railway Union (ARU). At the time, railway engineers, firemen, conductors, and switchmen all had separate unions. The ARU tried to organize all railroad employees into one union. Debs was arrested for interfering with the U.S. mail during the ARU's unsuccessful Pullman strike. While in prison, Debs read works by Karl Marx and became very critical of capitalism.

Debs ran for president five times between 1900 and 1920 as the nominee of the American Socialist Party. He waged his last campaign from prison while serving time for speaking against America's involvement in World War I.

What did Debs think about combining politics with union activities? How does this differ from Gompers's approach?

Workers of the World (IWW). Nicknamed "the Wobblies," the IWW wanted to organize all workers according to industry, without making distinctions between skilled and unskilled workers. The IWW endorsed using strikes and believed "The working class and the employing class have nothing in common."

The IWW believed all workers should be organized into "One Big Union." In particular, the IWW tried to organize the unskilled workers who were ignored by most unions.

In 1912 the IWW led a successful strike of textile workers in Lawrence, Massachusetts. After textile companies cut wages, 25,000 workers went on strike. During the strike, the children of strikers were sent out of town—in case things became violent. The companies reversed the wage cuts after ten weeks. The Lawrence strike was the IWW's greatest victory. Most IWW strikes failed.

The IWW never gained a large membership, but its radical philosophy and controversial strikes led many to condemn the organization as subversive.

Working Women

After the Civil War, the number of women wage earners began to increase. By 1900 women made up more than 18 percent of the labor force. The type of jobs women did outside the home reflected society's ideas about what **constituted** "women's work." About one-third of women wage earners worked as domestic servants. Another third worked as teachers, nurses, and sales clerks. The remaining third were industrial workers. Many worked in the garment industry and food-processing plants.

Regardless of the job, women were paid less than men even when they performed the same jobs. It was assumed that a woman had a man helping to support her, and that a man needed higher wages to support a family. Most unions excluded women.

One of the most famous labor leaders of the era was Mary Harris Jones, also known as "Mother Jones." An Irish immigrant, Jones began as a labor organizer for the Knights of Labor, then helped to organize mine workers. Her persuasiveness as a public speaker made her a very successful organizer, leading John D. Rockefeller to label her "the most dangerous woman in America."

In 1900 Jewish and Italian immigrants who worked in the clothing business in New York City founded the International Ladies' Garment Workers Union. The membership, composed mostly of female workers, expanded rapidly in a few years. In 1909 a strike of 20,000 garment workers won union recognition in the industry and better wages and benefits for employees.

In 1903 Mary Kenney O'Sullivan and Leonora O'Reilly decided to establish a separate union for women. With the help of Jane Addams and Lillian Wald, they established the Women's Trade Union League (WTUL), the first national association dedicated to promoting women's labor issues. The WTUL pushed for an eight-hour workday, the creation of a minimum wage, an end to evening work for women, and the abolition of child labor.

Reading Check **Comparing** How were female industrial workers treated differently from male workers in the late 1800s?

Vocabulary

1. **Explain** the significance of: deflation, trade union, industrial unions, blacklist, lockout, Marxism, Knights of Labor, arbitration, injunction, American Federation of Labor, Samuel Gompers, closed shop.

Main Ideas

2. **Identifying** Use a graphic organizer similar to the one below to list the factors that led to an increase in unions in the late 1800s.

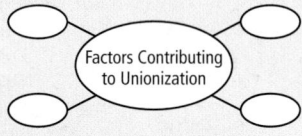

Factors Contributing to Unionization

3. **Describing** What groups of workers were represented by the Knights of Labor?

4. **Discussing** How did employers and unions treat women differently from men? What reasons were given for the differences?

Critical Thinking

5. **Big Ideas** Why did industrial unions frequently fail in the late 1800s?

6. **Determining Cause and Effect** Why do you think the rise of unions might have led to increased opposition to immigrants in the United States?

7. **Analyzing Visuals** Look at the map on page 203. In what state did two major disturbances occur? How do you explain this?

Writing About History

8. **Persuasive Writing** Imagine that you are an American worker living in one of the nation's large cities. Write a letter to a friend explaining why you support or oppose the work of labor unions.

History ONLINE

Study Central™ To review this section, go to glencoe.com and click on Study Central.

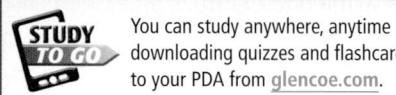
Causes of Industrialization

- Abundant natural resources
- Cheap immigrant labor force
- High tariffs reduce the import of foreign goods
- National transportation and communication networks

▶ The Central Pacific Railroad Company changed the way companies did business and helped link the nation together.

▲ Blast furnaces of a U.S. Steel plant line the Monongahela River east of Pittsburgh in Braddock, Pennsylvania, in 1905. New technology and new forms of business organization made possible the rise of large-scale industrial factories in the late 1800s.

Causes of the Growth of Big Business

- Little or no government intervention
- Development of pools, trusts, holding companies, and monopolies
- Small businesses could not compete with economies of scale of larger businesses
- Practices of some big businesses sometimes limited competition

Effects on the Workplace

- Rural migration and immigration created large, concentrated workforce
- Low wages, long hours, and dangerous working conditions were common in large-scale industries
- First large unions formed but had little bargaining power against larger companies

▶ Workers fill molds with molten steel at a foundry in 1905. Working conditions of the era led to many industrial accidents and contributed to the rise of unions.

Reviewing Vocabulary

Directions: Choose the word or words that best completes the sentence.

1. _____ are formed by a legal agreement in which one person manages another person's property.

   A Trusts

   B Pools

   C Corporations

   D Monopolies

2. The American Railway Association created _____ to make the railroads run more safely and more reliably.

   A fixed costs

   B time zones

   C land grants

   D holding companies

3. _____ united all craft workers and common laborers in a particular industry.

   A Closed shops

   B Trade unions

   C Industrial unions

   D Blacklists

4. Costs a company has to pay, such as loans, mortgages, and taxes, whether or not it is operating, are called

   A investment funds.

   B economies of scale.

   C fixed costs.

   D operating costs.

5. Supporters of _____ believe that the government should not interfere in the economy other than to protect private property rights.

   A high tariffs

   B laissez-faire

   C industrial regulations

   D high taxes for private individuals

Reviewing Main Ideas

Directions: Choose the best answers to the following questions.

Section 1 *(pp. 182–187)*

6. What factors contributed to industrialization?

   A lack of natural resources

   B free enterprise system

   C limited workforce

   D deteriorating railroad system

7. Laissez-faire relies on

   A the government to regulate wages and prices.

   B high taxes and government debt to fund businesses.

   C high tariffs on foreign goods.

   D supply and demand to regulate wages and prices.

Section 2 *(pp. 188–193)*

8. How did the federal government aid railroad construction in the 1850s and 1860s?

   A advertised overseas to attract immigrants to help build tracks

   B used tax dollars to fund many railroad projects

   C passed laws to legalize railroad monopolies

   D granted public lands to railroads to sell to raise funds

9. The Pacific Railway Act provided for the construction of a railway

   A by offering right-of-way land grants to railroad companies.

   B along the Pacific coast from California north to Canada.

   C solely by the Union Pacific Railroad company.

   D solely by the Central Pacific Railroad company.

TEST-TAKING TIP

Be sure to pay close attention to specific words in a question. Words can change the meaning of the sentence and of the correct answer.

Need Extra Help?									
If You Missed Questions . . .	1	2	3	4	5	6	7	8	9
Go to Page . . .	198	191	201–202	194–195	186–187	186–187	186–187	192	188

 GO ON

Section 3 *(pp. 194–199)*

10. Corporations are organizations that

  A receive federal funding.

  B sell stock to the public.

  C have a monopoly on a product or service.

  D earn profits for their workers.

11. In the late 1800s, which of the following helped business leaders eliminate competition?

  A strikes

  B labor unions

  C closed shops

  D monopolies

Section 4 *(pp. 200–207)*

12. Labor unions were formed to

  A protect factory owners and improve workers' wages.

  B improve workers' wages and make factories safer.

  C make factories safer and prevent lockouts.

  D prevent lockouts and fight deflation.

13. Which of the following events reduced membership in the Knights of Labor?

  A the Pullman Strike

  B the panic of 1873

  C the Haymarket Riot

  D the Great Railroad Strike of 1877

14. In the last half of the 1800s, which development led to the other three?

  A expansion of the middle class

  B growth of industrialization

  C formation of trusts

  D creation of labor unions

Critical Thinking

Directions: Choose the best answers to the following questions.

15. The slogan "Eight hours for work, eight hours for sleep, eight hours for what we will" was used in the late 1800s to promote a major goal of

  A farmers.

  B politicians.

  C industrialists.

  D organized labor.

Base your answers to questions 16 and 17 on the chart below and your knowledge of Chapter 5.

Steel Production, 1865–1895

Source: *Historical Statistics of the United States.*

16. Between what years did steel production increase the most?

  A 1865–1870

  B 1885–1890

  C 1890–1895

  D 1895–1900

17. How did increased steel production contribute to American industrialization?

  A decreased the number of jobs available for workers

  B discouraged the consolidation of industry

  C improved transportation methods such as railroads

  D encouraged immigration by providing a safe work environment

Need Extra Help?								
If You Missed Questions . . .	10	11	12	13	14	15	16	17
Go to Page . . .	194	197–199	200–202	204	200–204	200–207	194–199	196–197

GO ON

18. Which of the following statements about labor unions in the late 1800s is accurate?

  A Strikes by labor unions usually gained public support.

  B Labor union activities were frequently opposed by the government.

  C Demands by labor unions were usually met.

  D Arbitration was commonly used to end labor unrest.

19. The immigrants who came to the United States between 1870 and 1910 came primarily from

  A eastern Europe and China.

  B northern and western Europe.

  C East Asia.

  D Latin America.

Analyze the cartoon and answer the question that follows. Base your answer on the cartoon and on your knowledge of Chapter 5.

Source: Bernhard Gillam, *Puck*, February 7, 1883

20. What does this cartoon say about Gould and Vanderbilt?

  A They are giving money to the hard-working laborers.

  B They are getting rich at the expense of others' back-breaking work.

  C The ship is slowly crumbling like their empires.

  D The workers are determined to overthrow them.

Document-Based Questions

Directions: Analyze the document and answer the short-answer questions that follow the document.

In the following excerpt from *History of the Standard Oil Company*, Ida Tarbell warns of the effects of Rockefeller's business practices on the nation's morality. Read the excerpt and answer the questions that follow:

> "*Very often people who admit the facts, who are willing to see that Mr. Rockefeller has employed force and fraud to secure his ends, justify him by declaring, 'It's business.' That is, 'It's business' has come to be a legitimate excuse for hard dealing, sly tricks, special privileges. It is a common enough thing to hear men arguing that the ordinary laws of morality do not apply in business.*
>
> *As for the ethical side, there is no cure but in an increasing scorn of unfair play. . . . When the businessman who fights to secure special privileges, to crowd his competitor off the track by other than fair competitive methods, receives the same summary disdainful ostracism by his fellows that the doctor or lawyer who is 'unprofessional,' . . . we shall have gone a long way toward making commerce a fit pursuit for our young men.*"
>
> —from *History of the Standard Oil Company*

21. According to Tarbell, what practices had Rockefeller used to establish Standard Oil Company?

22. In what way did Tarbell believe the attitudes of the American people contributed to Rockefeller's business practices?

Extended Response

23. Identify labor unions formed during the late 1800s and early 1900s. Discuss the different views, goals, and activities of each organization. How were these organizations similar to or different from each other? What roles did unions and union members play in industrialization? Write an expository essay that supports your position with relevant facts and details.

History ONLINE

For additional test practice, use Self-Check Quizzes— Chapter 5 at glencoe.com.

Need Extra Help?						
If You Missed Questions . . .	18	19	20	21	22	23
Go to Page . . .	201–207	182–187	197–199	211	211	200–207

Urban America

1865–1896

Immigrants look toward New York City while waiting on a dock at Ellis Island in the early 1900s.

U.S. PRESIDENTS

U.S. EVENTS

WORLD EVENTS

1870
- Fifteenth Amendment ratified
- Farmers' Alliance founded

Hayes 1877–1881

1881
- President Garfield assassinated

1883
- Brooklyn Bridge completed
- Civil Service Act adopted

Garfield 1881

Arthur 1881–1885

Cleveland 1885–1889

1870

1875

1880

1885

1872
- Ballot Act makes voting secret in Britain

1876
- Porfirio Diaz becomes dictator of Mexico

1881
- Anti-Jewish pogroms erupt in Russia

1884
- First subway in London opens

🔊 **Chapter Audio**

MAKING CONNECTIONS
Why Do People Migrate?

European and Asian immigrants arrived in the United States in great numbers during the late 1800s. Providing cheap labor, they made rapid industrial growth possible. They also helped populate the growing cities.

- *How do you think life in big cities was different from life on farms and in small towns?*
- *How do you think the immigrants of the late 1800s changed American society?*

FOLDABLES™

Analyzing Information Make a Folded Table Foldable to clarify your understanding of how immigration and urbanization are related. As you read the chapter, list the causes and effects of immigration and urbanization. In each cell, list as many causes and effects as possible and include approximate dates where appropriate.

1888
- First electric trolley line opens in Richmond, Virginia

Harrison
1889–1893

1890
- Sherman Antitrust Act passed

1895
- Booker T. Washington gives Atlanta Compromise speech

Cleveland
1893–1897

1896
- *Plessy* v. *Ferguson* establishes "separate but equal" doctrine

1890

1895

1888
- Brazil ends slavery

1889
- Eiffel Tower completed for Paris World Exhibit

1896
- Athens hosts first modern Olympic games

History ONLINE Visit glencoe.com and enter *QuickPass*™ code TAVMT5147c6 for Chapter 6 resources.

Immigration

Guide to Reading

Big Ideas
Trade, War, and Migration Many people from Europe came to the United States to escape war, famine, or persecution or to find better jobs.

Content Vocabulary
• steerage *(p. 215)*
• nativism *(p. 218)*

Academic Vocabulary
• immigrant *(p. 214)*
• ethnic *(p. 216)*

People and Events to Identify
• Ellis Island *(p. 215)*
• Jacob Riis *(p. 216)*
• Angel Island *(p. 217)*
• Chinese Exclusion Act *(p. 219)*

Reading Strategy
Categorizing Complete a graphic organizer similar to the one below by filling in the reasons people left their homelands to immigrate to the United States.

Reasons for Immigrating	
Push Factors	Pull Factors

In the late nineteenth century, a major wave of immigration began. Most immigrants settled in cities, where distinctive ethnic neighborhoods emerged. Some Americans, however, feared that the new immigrants would not adapt to American culture or might be harmful to American society.

Europeans Flood Into America

MAIN Idea Immigrants from Europe came to the United States for many reasons and entered the country through Ellis Island.

HISTORY AND YOU Have you ever been to an ethnic neighborhood where residents have re-created aspects of their homeland? Read on to learn how immigrants adjusted to life in the United States.

Between 1865—the year the Civil War ended—and 1914—the year World War I began—nearly 25 million Europeans immigrated to the United States. By the late 1890s, more than half of all **immigrants** in the United States were from eastern and southern Europe, including Italy, Greece, Austria-Hungary, Russia, and Serbia. This period of immigration is known as "new" immigration. The "old" immigration, which occurred before 1890, had been primarily of people from northern and western Europe. More than 70 percent of these new immigrants were men; they were working either to be able to afford to purchase land in Europe or to bring family members to America.

Europeans immigrated to the United States for many reasons. Many came because American industries had plenty of jobs available. Europe's industrial cities, however, also offered plenty of jobs, so economic factors do not entirely explain why people migrated. Many came in the hope of finding better jobs that would let them escape poverty and the restrictions of social class in Europe. Some moved to avoid forced military service, which in some nations lasted for many years. In some cases, as in Italy, high food prices encouraged people to leave. In Poland and Russia, population pressure led to emigration. Others, especially Jews living in Russia and the Austro-Hungarian Empire, fled to escape religious persecution.

In addition, most European states had made moving to the United States easy. Immigrants were allowed to take their savings with them, and most countries had repealed old laws forcing peasants to stay in their villages and banning skilled workers from leaving the country. At the same time, moving to the United States offered a chance to break away from Europe's class system and move to a democratic nation where people had the opportunity to move up the social ladder.

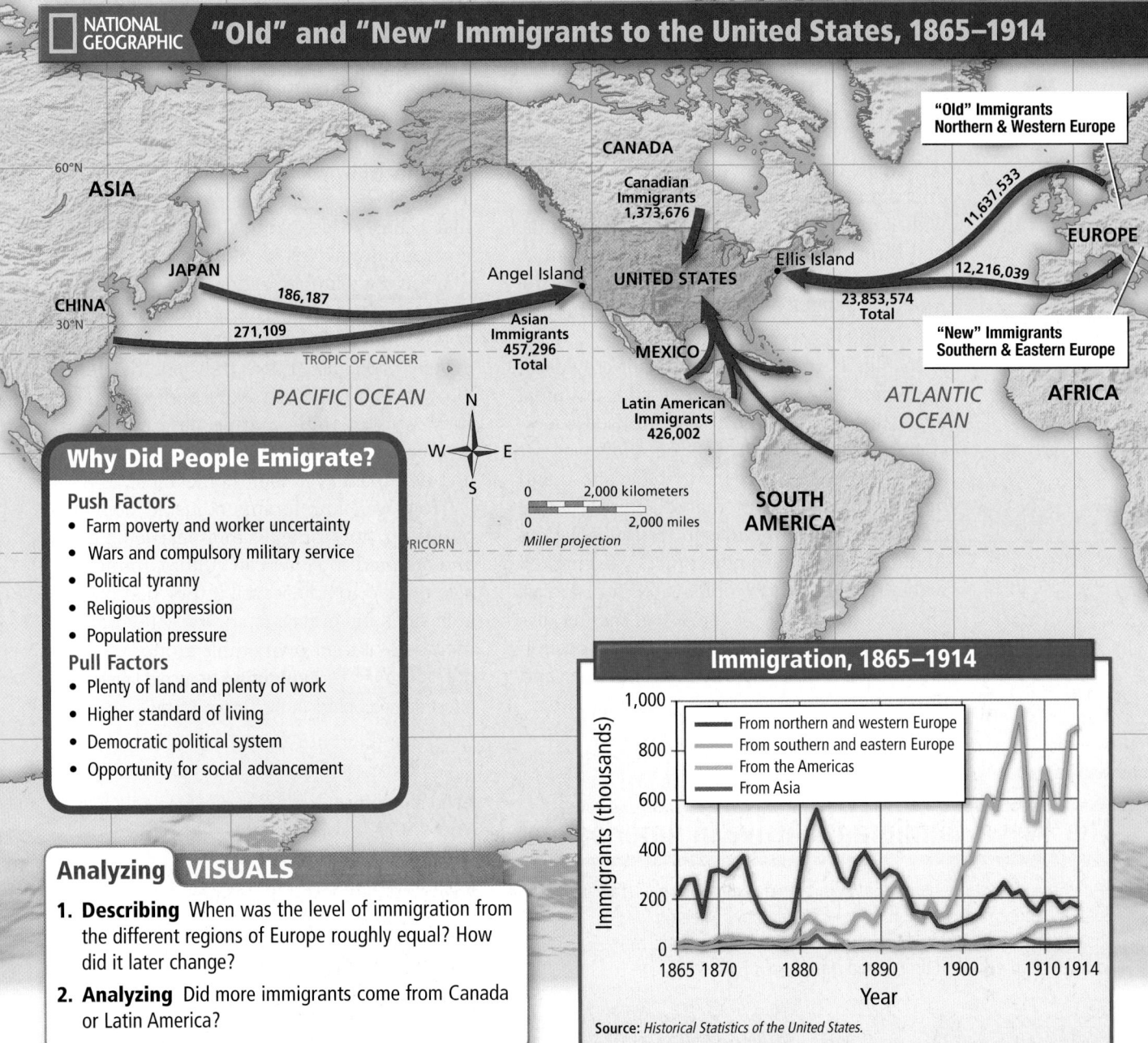

"Old" and "New" Immigrants to the United States, 1865–1914

NATIONAL GEOGRAPHIC

ASIA

JAPAN 186,187

CHINA 271,109

Angel Island

Asian Immigrants 457,296 Total

PACIFIC OCEAN

CANADA

Canadian Immigrants 1,373,676

UNITED STATES

Ellis Island

MEXICO

Latin American Immigrants 426,002

SOUTH AMERICA

"Old" Immigrants Northern & Western Europe

EUROPE

11,637,533

12,216,039

23,853,574 Total

"New" Immigrants Southern & Eastern Europe

ATLANTIC OCEAN

AFRICA

TROPIC OF CANCER

N W E S

0   2,000 kilometers
0   2,000 miles
Miller projection

Why Did People Emigrate?

Push Factors
- Farm poverty and worker uncertainty
- Wars and compulsory military service
- Political tyranny
- Religious oppression
- Population pressure

Pull Factors
- Plenty of land and plenty of work
- Higher standard of living
- Democratic political system
- Opportunity for social advancement

Analyzing VISUALS

1. **Describing** When was the level of immigration from the different regions of Europe roughly equal? How did it later change?

2. **Analyzing** Did more immigrants come from Canada or Latin America?

Immigration, 1865–1914

Immigrants (thousands) vs. Year

- From northern and western Europe
- From southern and eastern Europe
- From the Americas
- From Asia

Source: *Historical Statistics of the United States.*

The Atlantic Voyage

The voyage to the United States was often very difficult. Most immigrants booked passage in **steerage,** the cheapest accommodations on a steamship. Edward Steiner, an Iowa clergyman who posed as an immigrant in order to write a book on immigration, described the miserable quarters:

PRIMARY SOURCE

"Narrow, steep and slippery stairways lead to it. Crowds everywhere, ill smelling bunks, uninviting washrooms—this is steerage. The odors of scat- tered orange peelings, tobacco, garlic and disinfec- tants meeting but not blending. No lounge or chairs for comfort, and a continual babble of tongues—this is steerage. The food, which is miserable, is dealt out of huge kettles into the dinner pails provided by the steamship company."

—quoted in *World of Our Fathers*

At the end of a 14-day journey, the passengers usually disembarked at **Ellis Island,** a tiny island in New York Harbor. There, a huge three-story building served as the processing center for many of the immigrants arriving from Europe after 1892.

Ellis Island

Most immigrants passed through Ellis Island in about a day. They would not soon forget their hectic introduction to the United States. A medical examiner who worked there later described how "hour after hour, ship load after ship load ... the stream of human beings with its kaleidoscopic variations was ... hurried through Ellis Island by the equivalent of 'step lively' in every language of the earth." About 12 million immigrants passed through Ellis Island between 1892 and 1954.

In Ellis Island's enormous hall, crowds of immigrants filed past the doctor for an initial inspection. "Whenever a case aroused suspicion," an inspector wrote, "the alien was set aside in a cage apart from the rest ... and his coat lapel or shirt marked with colored chalk" to indicate the reason for the isolation. About one out of five newcomers was marked with an "H" for heart problems, "K" for hernias, "Sc" for scalp problems, or "X" for mental disability. Newcomers who failed the inspection might be separated from their families and returned to Europe.

Ethnic Cities

Many of those who passed these inspections settled in the nation's cities. By the 1890s, immigrants made up a large percentage of the population of major cities, including New York, Chicago, Milwaukee, and Detroit. **Jacob Riis,** a Danish-born journalist, observed in 1890 that a map of New York City, "colored to designate nationalities, would show more stripes than on the skin of a zebra."

In the cities, immigrants lived in neighborhoods that were often separated into **ethnic** groups, such as "Little Italy" or the Jewish "Lower East Side" in New York City. There they spoke their native languages and re-created the churches, synagogues, clubs, and newspapers of their homelands.

How well immigrants adjusted depended partly on how quickly they learned English and adapted to American culture. Immigrants also tended to adjust well if they had marketable skills or money, or if they settled among members of their own ethnic group.

✔ Reading Check **Explaining** How did immigration affect demographics in the United States?

PRIMARY SOURCE
The "New" Immigrants Arrive in America

In the late 1800s, the number of immigrants coming from northwest Europe began to decline, while "new immigrants," fleeing war, poverty, and persecution, began to arrive in large numbers from southern and eastern Europe, and from Asia.

▲ Many Italian immigrants took jobs as construction workers, bricklayers, and dockworkers in urban areas, but this group is building a railroad, c. 1900.

▲ Jewish people migrated to the United States from all across Europe seeking an opportunity to better their lives. Many Jews from Eastern Europe (such as those above) were also fleeing religious persecution.

◄ Many Chinese came to America to escape poverty and civil war. Many helped build railroads. Others set up small businesses. These children were photographed in San Francisco's Chinatown, c. 1900.

Asian Immigration

MAIN Idea Asian immigrants arrived on the West Coast, where they settled mainly in cities.

HISTORY AND YOU Do you know someone who has moved to the United States from Asia? What motivated that person to come here? Read on to learn about the experiences of earlier generations of Asian immigrants.

In the mid-1800s, China's population reached about 430 million, and the country was suffering from severe unemployment, poverty, and famine. Then, in 1850, the Taiping Rebellion erupted in China. This insurrection caused such suffering that thousands of Chinese left for the United States. In the early 1860s, as construction began on the Central Pacific Railroad, the demand for railroad workers led to further Chinese immigration.

Chinese immigrants settled mainly in western cities, where they often worked as laborers or servants or in skilled trades. Others became merchants. Because native-born Americans kept them out of many businesses, some Chinese immigrants opened their own.

Japanese also began immigrating to the United States. Although some came earlier, the number of Japanese immigrants soared upward between 1900 and 1910. As Japan industrialized, economic problems caused many Japanese to leave their homeland for new economic opportunities.

Until 1910 Asian immigrants arriving in San Francisco first stopped at a two-story shed at the wharf. As many as 500 people at a time were often squeezed into this structure, which Chinese immigrants from Canton called *muk uk,* or "wooden house." In January 1910 California opened a barracks on **Angel Island** for Asian immigrants. Most were young men in their teens or twenties, who nervously awaited the results of their immigration hearings. The wait could last for months. On the walls of the barracks, several immigrants wrote anonymous poems in pencil or ink.

Reading Check **Making Generalizations** Why did Chinese immigrants come to the United States?

Why Did Immigrants Come to America? / Typical Occupations in America

Italians
- cholera epidemic in 1880s
- land shortage for peasants; landlords charge high rent
- food shortages
- poverty, unemployment

Italians
- unskilled labor— dock work, construction, railroads
- some skilled labor, such as bricklayers, stonemasons, and other trades

East Europeans
- Russians, Poles: land shortages for peasants, unemployment, high taxes; long military draft
- Jews: discrimination, poverty, and recurring pogroms

East Europeans
- Poles: farmers, coal miners, steel and textile millworkers; meatpacking
- Jews: laborers, garment workers, merchants

Chinese
- famine
- land shortage for peasants
- civil war (Taiping rebellion)

Chinese
- railroad and construction workers; some skilled labor
- merchants, small businesses

NATIONAL GEOGRAPHIC — Immigration Settlement Patterns

Legend: China, Germany, Ireland, Italy, Japan, Mexico, Poland, Russia, Scandinavia

Settlement figures in thousands

New York: 480 425 182 165 66 42 7
Massachusetts: 249 32 28 26
Wisconsin: 242 61 30 23
Illinois: 332 129 114 64 28 23
California: 72 44 40 10 8
Texas: 72 48
Ohio: 204 55
Pennsylvania: 212 205 72 66 50

Analyzing VISUALS

1. **Analyzing Visuals** To which state did most Russian immigrants come to live?

2. **Contrasting** How would you contrast the immigration settlement patterns of Texas and Ohio?

Nativism Resurges

MAIN Idea Economic concerns and religious and ethnic prejudices led some Americans to push for laws restricting immigration.

HISTORY AND YOU In what ways does immigration affect the area in which you live? Read on to learn why nativists tried to stop immigration.

Eventually the wave of immigration led to increased feelings of nativism on the part of many Americans. **Nativism** is an extreme dislike of immigrants by native-born people. It had surfaced during the heavy wave of Irish immigration in the 1840s and 1850s. In the late 1800s, anti-immigrant feelings focused mainly on Asians, Jews, and eastern Europeans.

Nativists opposed immigration for many reasons. Some feared that the influx of Catholics from countries such as Ireland, Italy, and Poland would swamp the mostly Protestant United States. Many labor unions also opposed immigration, arguing that immigrants undermined American workers because they would work for low wages and accept jobs as strikebreakers.

Prejudice Against Catholics

Increased feelings of nativism led to the founding of anti-immigrant organizations. The American Protective Association, founded by Henry Bowers in 1887, was an anti-Catholic organization. Its members vowed not to hire or vote for Catholics.

The Irish were among the immigrants who suffered most from the anti-Catholic feeling. Arriving to escape famine and other hardships, many were illiterate and found only the lowest-paying work as miners, dockhands, ditch-diggers, and factory workers. Irish women worked as cooks, servants, and millworkers. The dominant Protestant, British culture in America, which considered Irish poverty to be the result of laziness, superstition, and ignorance, had no use for the Catholic Irish.

Although several presidents vetoed legislation that would have limited immigration, prejudice

POLITICAL CARTOONS PRIMARY SOURCE
Prejudice Against Catholic Immigrants

Anti-Catholic prejudice was strong in the United States for most of the 1800s. Many Americans tried to prevent Catholic immigration to the United States, fearing Catholic beliefs were incompatible with American values.

THE AMERICAN RIVER GANGES.

▲ Catholic priests crawl ashore as children are tossed to them by New York politicians in this 1871 cartoon criticizing New York's decision to fund Catholic schools.

PRIMARY SOURCE

"We unite to protect our country and its free institutions against the secret, intolerant, and aggressive efforts . . . by a certain religious political organization to control the government of the United States. . . .

. . . We have men born in several countries remote from this that are as loyal as any native, but they are not Romanists [Catholics]. American loyalty consists in devotion to our Constitution, laws, institutions, flag, and, above all, our public schools, for without intelligence this representative republic will go to pieces. . . . We are opposed to priests and prelates as such 'taking part in elections' and voting their laity as a unit in the interests of a foreign corporation . . ."

—from the platform of the American Protective Association, 1894

DBQ Document-Based Questions

1. **Explaining** What does the American Protective Association believe is incompatible with American citizenship? To what power does the statement refer?

2. **Detecting Bias** How does the cartoon express hostility toward Catholicism? Why might the cartoonist have depicted the public school on the hill in ruins?

against immigrants stimulated the passage of a new federal law. Enacted in 1882, the law banned convicts, paupers, and the mentally disabled from immigrating to the United States. The law also placed a 50¢ per head tax on each newcomer.

Restrictions on Asian Immigration

In the West, anti-Chinese sentiment sometimes led to racial violence. Denis Kearney, himself an Irish immigrant, organized the Workingman's Party of California in the 1870s to fight Chinese immigration. The party won seats in California's legislature and pushed to cut off Chinese immigration.

In 1882 Congress passed the **Chinese Exclusion Act.** The law barred Chinese immigration for 10 years and prevented the Chinese already in the country from becoming citizens. The Chinese in the United States organized letter-writing campaigns, petitioned the president, and even filed suit in federal court, but their efforts failed. Congress renewed the law in 1892 and made it permanent in 1902. It was not repealed until 1943.

On October 11, 1906, in response to rising Japanese immigration, the San Francisco Board of Education ordered "all Chinese, Japanese and Korean children" to attend the racially segregated "Oriental School" in the city's Chinatown neighborhood. (Students of Chinese heritage had been forced to attend racially segregated schools since 1859.) The directive caused an international incident. Japan took great offense at the insulting treatment of its people.

In response, Theodore Roosevelt invited school board leaders to the White House. He proposed a deal. He would limit Japanese immigration, if the school board would rescind its segregation order. Roosevelt then carried out his end of the deal. He began talks with Japan, and negotiated an agreement whereby Japan agreed to curtail the emigration of Japanese to the continental United States. The San Francisco school board then revoked its segregation order. This deal became known as the "Gentleman's Agreement" because it was not a formal treaty and depended on the leaders of both countries to uphold the agreement.

The Literacy Debate

In 1905 Theodore Roosevelt commissioned a study on how immigrants were admitted to the nation. The commission recommended an English literacy test. Two years later, another commission suggested literacy tests—in any language—for immigration. These recommendations reflected the bias of people against the "new immigrants," who were thought to be less intelligent than the "old immigrants." Although Presidents Taft and Wilson both vetoed legislation to require literacy from immigrants, the legislation eventually passed in 1917 over Wilson's second veto. The purpose of the law was to reduce immigration from southeastern European nations.

✔ Reading Check **Explaining** Why did the federal government pass the Chinese Exclusion Act?

Section 1 REVIEW

Vocabulary

1. **Explain** the significance of: steerage, Ellis Island, Jacob Riis, Angel Island, nativism, Chinese Exclusion Act.

Main Ideas

2. **Listing** Why did European immigrants come to the United States?

3. **Describing** What caused the increase in Chinese immigration in the 1860s?

4. **Organizing** Complete a graphic organizer by listing the reasons nativists opposed immigration to the United States.

Reasons Nativists Opposed Immigration

Critical Thinking

5. **Big Ideas** Where did most immigrants settle in the late 1800s? How did this benefit ethnic groups?

6. **Interpreting** Why did some Americans blame immigrants for the nation's problems?

7. **Analyzing Visuals** Select one of the people featured in any photo in this section. Write a journal entry about his or her experience, based on what you see in the photo.

Writing About History

8. **Descriptive Writing** Imagine that you are an immigrant who arrived in the United States in the 1800s. Write a letter to a relative in your home country describing your feelings during processing at either Ellis Island or Angel Island.

History ONLINE

Study Central™ To review this section, go to glencoe.com and click on Study Central.

ANALYZING PRIMARY SOURCES

Immigration

The United States is a nation of immigrants. In the late nineteenth century, more immigrants arrived on American shores than ever before. Some came from places such as the British Isles and Germany, from which many earlier immigrants had arrived. Others came from southern and eastern Europe, Asia, and other parts of the Americas. As the United States welcomed this mixture of ethnicities, religions, and languages, immigration became a subject of heated political debate.

Study these primary sources and answer the questions that follow.

PRIMARY SOURCE 2

Photograph, 1905

▼ *Immigrants are checked for trachoma and other contagious eye diseases at Ellis Island. The inspector is using a buttonhook, normally used to fasten ladies' gloves, to lift this woman's eyelid. The instrument was "cleaned" between inspections by wiping it on the towel hanging nearby.*

PRIMARY SOURCE 1

Political Cartoon, 1880

▼ *"Welcome to All," by J. Keppler, Puck (1880)*

PRIMARY SOURCE 3

Memoir Reflecting on Arrival at Ellis Island

"A group of Slovenian immigrants, of which this writer was one, arrived in New York from . . . Austria. . . . It was a beautiful morning in May 1906. After leaving the French ship LA TOURAINE, we were transported to Ellis Island for landing and inspection. There we were 'sorted out' as to the country we came from and placed in a 'stall' with the letter 'A' above us. ('A' was for Austria.)

There were at least a hundred Slovenian immigrants. We separated ourselves, as was the custom at home—men on the right and women and children on the left. All of us were waiting to leave for all parts of the United States.

The day was warm and we were very thirsty. An English-speaking immigrant asked the near-by guard where we could get a drink of water. The guard withdrew and returned shortly with a pail of water, which he set before the group of women. Some men stepped forward quickly to have a drink, but the guard pushed them back saying: 'Ladies first!' When the women learned what the guard had said, they were dumbfounded, for in Slovenia . . . women always were second to men. . . . Happy at the sudden turn of events, one elderly lady stepped forward, holding a dipper of water, and proposed this toast:

'Živijo Amerika, kjer so ženske prve!'
(Long live America, where women are first!)"

—Marie Priesland, recalling her arrival in the United States

Magazine Article, 1903

"When I went to work for that American family I could not speak a word of English, and I did not know anything about housework. The family consisted of husband, wife and two children. They were very good to me and paid me $3.50 a week, of which I could save $3.

"I did not understand what the lady said to me, but she showed me how to cook, wash, iron, sweep, dust, make beds, wash dishes, clean windows, paint and brass, polish the knives and forks, etc., by doing the things herself and then overseeing my efforts to imitate her. . . . In six months I had learned how to do the work of our house quite well, and . . . I had also learned English. . . . I worked for two years as a servant . . . . and I was now ready to start in business."

—Chinese immigrant Lee Chew, reflecting on his first years in America

Questions Asked Immigrants, c. 1907

	U.S. IMMIGRATION SERVICE	
1	Calling or Occupation?	farmer
2	Able to Read?	yes
3	Able to Write?	yes
4	Nationality?	Germany
5	Whether having a ticket to final destination?	yes
6	By whom was passage paid?	father
7	Whether in possession of $50, and if less, how much?	$20
8	Whether going to join a relative or friend?	friend
9	Ever in prison or almshouse or institution for care or treatment of the insane or supported by charity?	no
10	Whether a Polygamist?	no
11	Whether an Anarchist?	no
12	Whether coming by reason of any offcr. solicitation, promise, or agreement, express or implied, to labor in the United States? Condition of Health, Mental and Physical.	no, no health problem
13	Deformed or Crippled. Nature, length of time and cause.	no

Political Cartoon, 1896

"The Immigrant: The Stranger at Our Gate,"
The Ram's Horn *(April 25, 1896)*
Emigrant: "Can I come in?"
Uncle Sam: "I 'spose you can; there's no law to keep you out."

THE STRANGER AT OUR GATE.
EMIGRANT.—Can I come in?   UNCLE SAM.—I 'spose you can; there's no law to keep you out.

DBQ Document-Based Questions

1. **Analyzing Visuals** Compare the political cartoons in Sources 1 and 6. How do the two depictions differ on the reasons why immigrants left their homeland and why they came to the United States?

2. **Making Inferences** Why did immigrants have to undergo health inspections? What do you suppose happened when an immigrant was found to have a contagious illness?

3. **Interpreting** Why do you think the author of Source 3 remembered Ellis Island so clearly decades later?

4. **Evaluating** According to Lee Chew in Source 4, what were some factors that helped him adapt as an immigrant and become a small business owner?

5. **Making Inferences** Study the questions listed in Source 5. Why do you think immigrants were required to answer these questions?

Urbanization

Guide to Reading

Big Ideas
Government and Society The growth of and problems in major cities led to political machines that controlled local politics.

Content Vocabulary
- skyscraper *(p. 222)*
- tenement *(p. 225)*
- political machine *(p. 227)*
- party boss *(p. 227)*
- graft *(p. 227)*

Academic Vocabulary
- incentive *(p. 222)*
- trigger *(p. 227)*

People and Events to Identify
- Louis Sullivan *(p. 223)*
- George Plunkitt *(p. 227)*
- William "Boss" Tweed *(p. 227)*

Reading Strategy
Organizing As you read about urbanization in the United States in the late 1800s, complete a graphic organizer similar to the one below by filling in the problems the nation's cities faced.

Native-born Americans and immigrants were drawn to cities by the jobs available in America's growing industries. The new, modern cities had skyscrapers, public transportation systems, and neighborhoods divided by social class. In many cities, political machines controlled city government.

Americans Migrate to the Cities

MAIN Idea Rural Americans and immigrants moved to the cities where skyscrapers and mass transit were developed to deal with congestion.

HISTORY AND YOU Have you ever ridden the bus, subway, or railway system? How do you think your ride to school or the store would be different without mass transportation? Read on to learn why cities developed mass transportation systems.

After the Civil War, the urban population of the United States grew from around 10 million in 1870 to more than 30 million in 1900. New York City, which had more than 800,000 inhabitants in 1860, grew to almost 3.5 million by 1900. During the same period, Chicago swelled from 109,000 residents to more than 1.6 million. The United States had only 131 cities with populations of 2,500 or more residents in 1840; by 1900, there were more than 1,700 such urban areas.

Most of the immigrants who poured into the United States in the late 1800s lacked both the money to buy farms and the education to obtain higher-paying jobs. Thus, they settled in the nation's growing cities, where they toiled long hours for little pay in the rapidly expanding factories of the United States. Despite the harshness of their new lives, most immigrants found that the move had improved their standard of living.

Rural Americans also began moving to the cities at this time. Farmers moved to cities because urban areas offered more and better-paying jobs than did rural areas. Cities had much to offer, too—bright lights, running water, and modern plumbing, plus attractions such as museums, libraries, and theaters.

The physical appearance of cities also changed dramatically. As city populations grew, demand raised the price of land, creating the **incentive** to build upward rather than outward. Soon, tall, steel frame buildings called **skyscrapers** began to appear. Chicago's ten-story Home Insurance Building, built in 1885, was the first skyscraper, but other buildings quickly dwarfed it. New York City, with its business district on the narrow island of Manhattan, boasted more skyscrapers than any other city in the world. With limited space, New Yorkers had to build up, not out.

TECHNOLOGY & HISTORY

The Technology of Urbanization

Before the mid-1800s, few buildings exceeded four or five stories. To make wooden and stone buildings taller required enormously thick walls in the lower levels. This changed when steel companies began mass-producing cheap steel girders and steel cable.

Completed in 1913, the Wool-worth Building is 792 feet high. It was the tallest building in the world until 1930.

A steel frame carries the weight, allowing the building to be much taller than stone or wood structures.

▲ Steel Cable

Steel also changed the way bridges were built. Engineers could now suspend bridges from steel towers using thick steel cables. Using this technique, engineer John Roebling designed New York's Brooklyn Bridge—the world's largest suspension bridge at the time. It was completed in 1883.

With steel beams instead of walls supporting the building, windows could be larger.

▶ Elevators

Elisha Otis invented the safety elevator in 1852. By the late 1880s, the first electric elevators had been installed, making tall buildings practical.

Analyzing VISUALS

1. **Theorizing** What other technologies were necessary in order to build modern skyscrapers?
2. **Predicting** What long-term effects do you think the new building technologies had on cities?

No one contributed more to the design of skyscrapers than Chicago's **Louis Sullivan.** "What people are within, the buildings express without," explained Sullivan, whose lofty structures featured simple lines and spacious windows using new, durable plate glass.

To move people around cities quickly, various kinds of mass transit developed. At first, almost all cities relied on the horsecar, a railroad car pulled by horses. In 1890 horsecars moved about 70 percent of urban traffic in the United States.

More than 20 cities, beginning with San Francisco in 1873, installed cable cars, which were pulled along tracks by underground cables. Then, in 1887, engineer Frank J. Sprague developed the electric trolley car. The country's first electric trolley line opened the following year in Richmond, Virginia.

In the largest cities, congestion became so bad that engineers began looking for ways to move mass transit off the streets. Chicago responded by building an elevated railroad, while Boston, followed by New York, built the first subway systems.

✔ Reading Check **Summarizing** What new technologies helped people in the late 1800s get to and from work?

Separation by Class

MAIN Idea In the cities, society was separated by classes, with the upper, middle, and working classes living in different neighborhoods.

HISTORY AND YOU Do you know the history of certain neighborhoods in your city or town? Can you see where the classes were divided? Read on to learn how each class lived in the cities.

In the growing cities, the wealthy people and the working class lived in different parts of town. So, too, did members of the middle class. The boundaries between neighborhoods were quite definite and can still be seen in many American cities today.

High Society

During the last half of the 1800s, the wealthiest families established fashionable districts in the heart of a city. Americans with enough money could choose to construct homes in the style of a feudal castle, an English manor house, a French château, a Tuscan villa, or a Persian pavilion. In Chicago, merchant and real estate developer Potter Palmer chose a castle. In New York, Cornelius Vanderbilt's grandson commissioned a $3 million French château with a two-story dining room, a gymnasium, and a marble bathroom.

As their homes grew larger, wealthy women managed an increasing number of servants, such as cooks, maids, butlers, coachmen, nannies, and chauffeurs, and spent a great deal of money on social activities. In an age in which many New Yorkers lived on $500 a year, socialite hostess Cornelia Sherman Martin spent $360,000 on a dance.

Middle-Class Gentility

American industrialization also helped expand the middle class. The nation's rising middle class included doctors, lawyers, engineers, managers, social workers, architects, and teachers. Many people in the middle class moved away from the central city so as to escape the crime and pollution and be able to afford larger homes. Some took advantage of the new commuter rail lines to move to "streetcar suburbs."

Urban industrial society in the late 1800s was divided into social classes. The upper class and middle class lived well, but conditions for the working class and poor were often abysmal.

THE MIDDLE CLASS

▲ Middle class families could generally afford their own homes and better quality clothing. Women rarely worked—and if they did it was usually because they wanted a career, not out of necessity. Many families had at least one servant (shown above in back holding the baby) and enough money left over to buy luxuries, such as the new gramophone shown above.

THE UPPER CLASS

▲ The upper class could afford elaborate mansions and many servants. Men typically owned or managed large businesses. Women almost never worked. Clothing was elaborate and expensive. Events, such as afternoon tea in their garden (above), required formal dress and shows they had substantial leisure time.

In the late nineteenth century, most middle class families had at least one live-in servant. This gave the woman of the house more time to pursue activities outside the home. "Women's clubs" became popular. At first, these clubs focused on social and educational activities. Over time, however, "club women" became very active in charitable and reform activities. In Chicago, for example, the Women's Club helped establish juvenile courts and exposed the terrible conditions at the Cook County Insane Asylum.

The Working Class

Few families in the urban working class could hope to own a home. Most spent their lives in crowded **tenements,** or apartment buildings. The first tenement in the United States was built in 1839. In New York, three out of four residents squeezed into tenements, dark and crowded multi-family apartments. To supplement the average industrial worker's annual income of $445, many families rented precious space to a boarder. Zalmen Yoffeh, a journalist, lived in a New York tenement as a child. He recalled:

PRIMARY SOURCE

"With . . . one dollar a day [our mother] fed and clothed an ever-growing family. She took in boarders. Sometimes this helped; at other times it added to the burden of living. Boarders were often out of work and penniless; how could one turn a hungry man out? She made all our clothes. She walked blocks to reach a place where meat was a penny cheaper, where bread was a half cent less. She collected boxes and old wood to burn in the stove."

—quoted in *How We Lived*

History ONLINE
Student Web Activity Visit glencoe.com and complete the activity on tenement life.

The Family Economy

Within the working class, some people were better off than others. White native-born men earned higher wages than African American men, immigrants, and women.

One economist estimated that 64 percent of working class families relied on more than one wage earner in 1900. In some cases, the whole family worked, including the children. The dangerous working conditions faced by child workers, and the fact that they were not in school, alarmed many reformers.

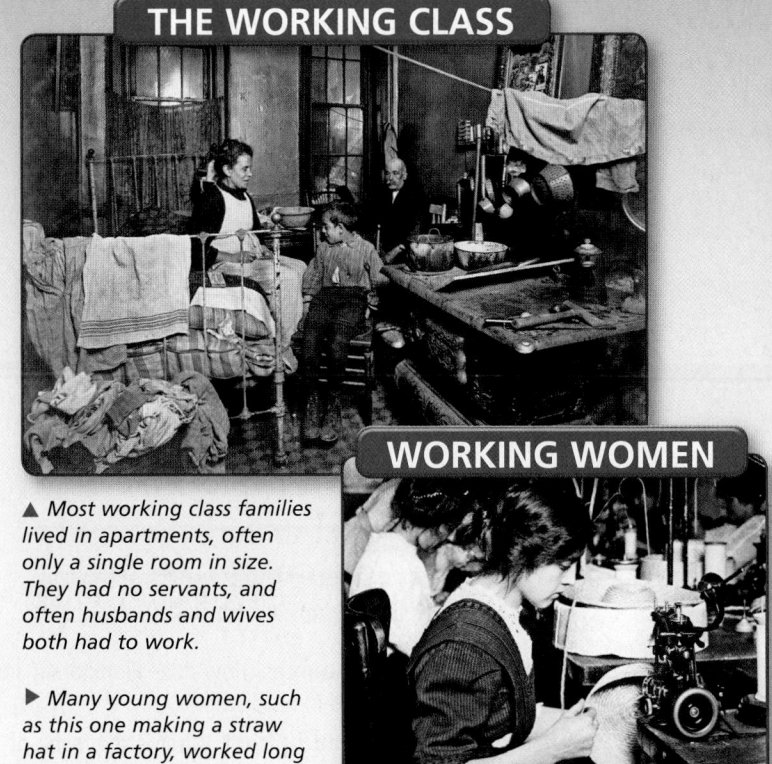

THE WORKING CLASS

▲ Most working class families lived in apartments, often only a single room in size. They had no servants, and often husbands and wives both had to work.

WORKING WOMEN

▶ Many young women, such as this one making a straw hat in a factory, worked long hours for little pay.

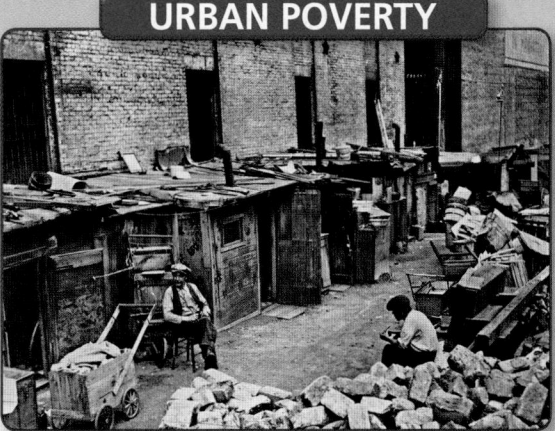

URBAN POVERTY

▲ Unable to afford homes, the urban poor slept on the street or built shacks in back alleys like these in New York City in the early 1900s.

Analyzing VISUALS

1. **Comparing and Contrasting** What do the upper class and middle class have in common compared to the working class and poor?
2. **Drawing Conclusions** How effective was industrial society at meeting people's needs?

A growing number of women took jobs outside the home. Native-born white women typically had more years of education than other women. Thus, many used their literacy to work as teachers or do clerical work.

The largest source of employment for women, however, remained domestic service. Immigrant women often worked as domestic servants in the North; African American women usually worked as domestic servants in the South. Such work involved long hours, low wages, and social isolation.

When people were physically unable to work, they had to rely on family members or charity. When a worker was maimed or killed on the job, there was usually no compensation. Most older Americans lived with family members. Nearly 70 percent of those 65 or older lived with their grown children. A growing number, however, lived independently or in homes for the aged.

✔ Reading Check **Explaining** Who was in the "middle class" in the late 1800s? Where did they live?

Urban Problems

MAIN Idea Major problems plagued the cities; political machines provided help for some residents but were frequently corrupt.

HISTORY AND YOU What kinds of programs are used in your area to deal with urban problems? Read about political machines and how they ran city government.

City living posed the risks of crime, violence, fire, disease, and pollution. The rapid growth of cities only made these problems worse and complicated the ability of urban governments to respond to these problems.

Crime and Pollution

Crime was a growing problem in American cities. Minor criminals, such as pickpockets, swindlers, and thieves, thrived in crowded urban living conditions. Major crimes multiplied as well. From 1880 to 1900, the murder rate jumped sharply from 25 per million people to more than 100 per million people.

POLITICAL CARTOONS PRIMARY SOURCE
Were Political Machines Bad for Cities?

Critics of political machines said that they took bribes and gave contracts to friends, robbing cities of resources. Defenders argued that they provided services and kept the city running.

EMPTY. "WHAT ARE YOU GOING TO DO ABOUT IT?" FULL.

EMPTY TO THE WORKMEN. THE FOUR MASTERS THAT EMPTIED IT.

▲ Workers in New York find the city treasury empty, while behind the scenes, Boss Tweed and other city politicians enjoy a sumptuous feast.

PRIMARY SOURCE

New York "Boss" George W. Plunkitt explains the benefits of the political machines:

"The poor are the most grateful people in the world, and, let me tell you, they have more friends in their neighborhoods than the rich have in theirs.

If there's a family in my district in want I know it before the charitable societies do, and me and my men are first on the ground.... The consequence is that the poor look up to George W. Plunkitt ... and don't forget him on election day.

Another thing, I can always get a job for a deservin' man.... I know every big employer in the district and in the whole city, for that matter, and they ain't in the habit of sayin' no to me when I ask them for a job."

—quoted in William L. Riordan, *Plunkitt of Tammany Hall*

DBQ Document-Based Questions

1. **Analyzing Primary Sources** How does Plunkitt say he learns of people in need in his district?

2. **Determining Cause and Effect** What is the result of Plunkitt's care for the needy in his district?

Alcohol contributed to violent crime, both inside and outside the home. Danish immigrant Jacob Riis, who documented slum life in his 1890 book *How the Other Half Lives,* accused saloons of "breeding poverty," corrupting politics, bringing suffering to the wives and children of drunkards, and fostering "the corruption of the child" by selling beer to minors.

Disease and pollution posed even bigger threats. Improper sewage disposal contaminated city drinking water and **triggered** epidemics of typhoid fever and cholera. Though flush toilets and sewer systems existed in the 1870s, pollution remained a severe problem as horse manure was left in the streets, smoke belched from chimneys, and soot and ash accumulated from coal and wood fires.

Machine Politics

The **political machine,** an informal political group designed to gain and keep power, came about partly because cities had grown much faster than their governments. New city dwellers needed jobs, housing, food, heat, and police protection. In exchange for votes, political machines and the **party bosses** who ran them eagerly provided these necessities.

Graft and Fraud The party bosses who ran the political machines also controlled the city's finances. Many machine politicians grew rich as the result of fraud or **graft**—getting money through dishonest or questionable means. **George Plunkitt,** one of New York City's most powerful party bosses, defended what he called "honest graft." For example, a politician might find out in advance where a new park was to be built and buy the land near the site. The politician would then sell the land to the city for a profit. As Plunkitt stated, "I see my opportunity, and I take it."

Outright fraud occurred when party bosses accepted bribes from contractors who were supposed to compete fairly to win contracts to build streets, sewers, and buildings. Corrupt bosses also sold permits to their friends to operate public utilities, such as railroads, waterworks, and power systems.

Tammany Hall Tammany Hall, the New York City Democratic political machine, was the most infamous such organization. **William "Boss" Tweed** was its leader during the 1860s and 1870s. Tweed's corruptness led to a prison sentence in 1874.

City machines often controlled all the city services, including the police department. In St. Louis, the "boss" never feared arrest when he called out to his supporters at the police-supervised voting booth, "Are there any more repeaters out here that want to vote again?"

Opponents of political machines, such as political cartoonist Thomas Nast, blasted bosses for their corruption. Defenders, though, argued that machines provided necessary services and helped to assimilate the masses of new city dwellers.

Reading Check **Evaluating** Why did political machines help city dwellers in the late 1800s?

Vocabulary

1. **Explain** the significance of: skyscraper, Louis Sullivan, tenement, political machine, party boss, graft, George Plunkitt, William "Boss" Tweed.

Main Ideas

2. **Identifying** What technologies made the building of skyscrapers possible?

3. **Comparing** How did the living conditions of the upper, middle, and the working classes in the late 1800s compare?

4. **Organizing** Complete the graphic organizer below by listing the effects of many Americans moving from rural to urban areas in the late 1800s.

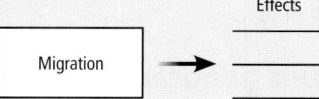

Critical Thinking

5. **Big Ideas** How did political machines respond to the needs of the people?

6. **Synthesizing** Why were pollution and sewage a problem in American cities in the late 1800s?

7. **Analyzing Visuals** Look at the photos on pages 224–225. How did industrialization affect the class structure in the United States?

Writing About History

8. **Persuasive Writing** Take on the role of an urban planner in a major city in the late 1800s. Write a letter to members of the city government listing specific reasons for the importance of setting aside city land for parks and recreational areas.

History ONLINE

Study Central™ To review this section, go to glencoe.com and click on Study Central.

GEOGRAPHY & HISTORY

Italian Immigration to America

Italians from southern Italy were among the largest group of the "new immigrants"—the peoples who flooded American shores between 1880 and 1920. In Italy, most were poor peasants who worked for absentee landlords and lived in extreme poverty. They were often illiterate and had never traveled even as far as the next village. Leaving for America was daunting. "Make yourself courage"—those were the last words one boy heard his father say as they said goodbye in Naples.

How Did Geography Shape Urban Life?

In New York City, these peasant-immigrants congregated in Little Italy in lower Manhattan. They would find an apartment on the street where people from their village in Italy lived. In 1910, as many as 40,000 people were packed in a 17-block area of Little Italy. As they mingled with other Italians, they began thinking of themselves as Italians, not Neapolitans (from Naples) or Sicilians (from Sicily).

New York's Little Italy bustled with peddlers, bakers, and laborers, but also with immigrants moving in or out of the area. Italian families were hardworking and thrifty. As soon as possible, they moved to cleaner, sunnier places, such as Brooklyn or Long Island. By 1914, one reformer said there were at least 1500 lawyers, 500 physicians, and a growing number of merchants, bankers, and businessmen in New York City who were of Italian heritage. It was a very American success story.

Women worked long hours. They went out once or even twice a day to shop from pushcarts for their meals. They often cooked and did the washing for their family and for male boarders, too.

Analyzing GEOGRAPHY

1. **Place** What drew Italian immigrants to specific areas of New York City?

2. **Movement** What years represented the peak period for the new immigrants to the United States?

Mulberry Street was the heart of Little Italy. Neapolitans (people from Naples) tended to settle on Mulberry Street, while Sicilians crowded the tenements on Elizabeth Street two blocks away.

Around 1900, roughly 4,300 tenement apartments were occupied with large families who lived in just a few rooms.

Street vendors often sold foods that were popular in Italy. They were very busy during holidays. In Little Italy, one of the biggest holidays was the feast of Saint Gennaro, patron saint of Naples—still celebrated in Little Italy in New York today.

Bread was often sold on the streets because tenement ovens could not produce the traditional Italian crust. Young children ran many errands, like buying food and gathering wood for fuel.

Section 3

The Gilded Age

Guide to Reading

Big Ideas
Past and Present Ideas about wealth during the last part of the 1800s continue to affect society today.

Content Vocabulary
- individualism *(p. 230)*
- Social Darwinism *(p. 231)*
- philanthropy *(p. 232)*
- settlement house *(p. 239)*
- Americanization *(p. 239)*

Academic Vocabulary
- evolution *(p. 231)*
- publish *(p. 233)*

People and Events to Identify
- Gilded Age *(p. 230)*
- Gospel of Wealth *(p. 232)*
- Mark Twain *(p. 233)*
- Social Gospel *(p. 238)*
- Jane Addams *(p. 239)*

Reading Strategy
Categorizing Complete a graphic organizer similar to the one below by filling in the main idea of each of the theories and movements listed.

Theory or Movement	Main Idea
Social Darwinism	
Laissez-Faire	
Gospel of Wealth	
Realism	

The industrialization of the United States led to new art and literature and new ideas about government's role in society. Social Darwinists believed society developed through "survival of the fittest." Other Americans thought steps needed to be taken to help the less fortunate.

Social Darwinism

MAIN Idea Individualism and Social Darwinism shaped Americans' attitudes toward industrial society.

HISTORY AND YOU Do you think each individual person should be left on his or her own to succeed, or should people help those who fall behind? Read to learn about people who applied the notion of "survival of the fittest" to human society.

In 1873 Mark Twain and Charles Warner wrote a novel entitled *The Gilded Age: A Tale of Today.* Historians later adopted the term and applied it to the era in American history that began about 1870 and ended around 1900. The era was in many ways a time of marvels. Amazing new inventions led to rapid industrial growth. Cities expanded to sizes never seen before. Masses of workers thronged the streets. Skyscrapers reached to the sky, electric lights banished the darkness, and wealthy entrepreneurs built spectacular mansions.

By calling this era the **Gilded Age,** Twain and Warner were sounding an alarm. Something is gilded if it is covered with gold on the outside but made of cheaper material inside. A gilded age might appear to sparkle, but critics pointed to corruption, poverty, crime, and great disparities in wealth between the rich and the poor.

Whether the era was golden or merely gilded, it was certainly a time of great cultural activity. Industrialism and urbanization altered the way Americans looked at themselves and their society, and these changes gave rise to new values, new art, and new entertainment.

The Idea of Individualism

One of the strongest beliefs of the era—and one that remains strong today—was the idea of **individualism.** Many Americans firmly believed that no matter how humble their origins, they could rise in society and go as far as their talents and commitment would take them. No one expressed the idea of individualism better than Horatio Alger, who wrote more than 100 "rags-to-riches" novels. In his books, a poor person goes to the big city and, through a combination of hard work and luck,

The Gospel of Wealth

"In bestowing charity, the main consideration should be to help those who will help themselves; to provide part of the means by which those who desire to improve may do so; to give those who desire to rise the aids by which they may rise; to assist, but rarely or never to do all. Neither the individual nor the race is improved by almsgiving. Those worthy of assistance, except in rare cases, seldom require assistance. The really valuable men of the race never do, except in cases of accident or sudden change.... He is the only true reformer who is as careful and as anxious not to aid the unworthy as he is to aid the worthy, and, perhaps, even more so, for in almsgiving more injury is probably done by rewarding vice than by relieving virtue.... "

—Andrew Carnegie, quoted in *The North American Review*, June 1889

"Robert was very different. He inherited from his father an unusual amount of courage and self-reliance, and if one avenue was closed to him, he at once set out to find another. It is of this class that successful men are made, and we have hopes that Robert will develop into a prosperous and successful man."

—from Horatio Alger, *Brave and Bold*

DBQ Document-Based Questions

1. **Analyzing Primary Sources** What does Carnegie believe is the way to dignify the lives of rich people?

2. **Describing** On what does Alger base Robert's chances of success? Do you agree with his criteria? Why or why not?

becomes successful. His popular books convinced many young people that no matter how many obstacles they faced, success was possible.

Social Darwinism

Another powerful idea of the era was **Social Darwinism.** This philosophy, loosely derived from Darwin's theories, strongly reinforced the idea of individualism.

Herbert Spencer British philosopher Herbert Spencer applied Charles Darwin's theory of **evolution** and natural selection to human society. In his 1859 book *On the Origin of Species by Means of Natural Selection,* Darwin argued that plant and animal life had evolved over the years by a process he called natural selection. In this process, those species that cannot adapt to the environment in which they live gradually die out, while those that do adapt thrive and live on.

Spencer took this theory intended to explain developments over millions of years and argued that human society also evolved through competition and natural selection. He argued that society progressed and became better because only the fittest people survived. Spencer and others, such as American scholar William Graham Sumner, who shared his views, became known as Social Darwinists, and their ideas became known as Social Darwinism. "Survival of the fittest" became the catchphrase of their philosophy.

Social Darwinism also paralleled the economic doctrine of laissez-faire that opposed any government programs that interfered with business. Not surprisingly, industrial leaders heartily embraced the theory. John D. Rockefeller maintained that survival of the fittest, as demonstrated by the growth of huge businesses like his own Standard Oil, was "merely the working out of the law of nature and the law of God."

Darwinism and the Church For many devout Christians, however, Darwin's conclusions were upsetting and offensive. They rejected the theory of evolution because they believed it contradicted the Bible's account of creation. Some ministers, however, concluded that evolution may have been God's way of creating the world. One of the most famous ministers of the era, Henry Ward Beecher, called himself a "Christian evolutionist."

Carnegie's Gospel of Wealth Andrew Carnegie advocated a gentler version of Social Darwinism that he called the **Gospel of Wealth.** This philosophy held that wealthy Americans should engage in **philanthropy** and use their great fortunes to create the conditions that would help people help themselves. Building schools and hospitals, for example, was better than giving handouts to the poor. Carnegie himself helped fund the creation of public libraries in cities across the nation because libraries provided the information people needed to get ahead in life.

✔ **Reading Check** **Summarizing** What was the main idea of Social Darwinism?

A Changing Culture

MAIN Idea Artists and writers began portraying life in America more realistically, and cities offered new forms of entertainment.

HISTORY AND YOU Have you read Mark Twain's *The Adventures of Huckleberry Finn*? Read to learn about how Twain portrayed American life in a realistic way.

The late 1800s was a period of great cultural change for writers and artists, and for many urban Americans who sought new forms of entertainment.

Realism

A new movement in art and literature called realism began in the 1800s. Just as Darwin tried to explain the natural world scientifically, artists and writers tried to portray the world realistically. European realists included Edgar Degas and Edouard Manet. Perhaps the best known American realist painter was Thomas Eakins. In realistic detail, he painted young men rowing and athletes playing baseball, and he showed surgeons and scientists in action.

PRIMARY SOURCE
Realism in Art and Literature

Realist writers and artists did not want to portray people and the world idealistically. Instead they sought to present things as accurately as possible.

> ### PRIMARY SOURCE
>
> "'Say, who is you? Whar is you? Dog my cats ef I didn' hear sumf'n. Well, I know what I's gwyne to do: I's gwyne to set down here and listen tell I hears it agin.'"
>
> So he set down on the ground betwixt me and Tom. He leaned his back up against a tree, and stretched his legs out till one of them most touched one of mine. My nose begun to itch. It itched till the tears come into my eyes. But I dasn't scratch. Then it begun to itch on the inside. Next I got to itching underneath. I didn't know how I was going to set still. This miserableness went on as much as six or seven minutes; but it seemed a sight longer than that."
>
> —from *The Adventures of Huckleberry Finn* by Mark Twain

▲ *Realist painters did not generally choose heroic or historical topics for their art. Instead they preferred to depict ordinary people doing ordinary things. Thomas Eakins, perhaps the best-known American realist, depicted various aspects of American life, including a carriage ride by the wealthy (above) or a professional baseball game (right).*

Writers also attempted to capture the world as they saw it. In several novels, William Dean Howells presented realistic descriptions of American life. For example, his novel *The Rise of Silas Lapham* (1885) described the attempts of a self-made man to enter Boston society. Also an influential literary critic, Howells was the first to declare **Mark Twain** an incomparable American genius.

Twain, whose real name was Samuel Clemens, **published** his masterpiece, *The Adventures of Huckleberry Finn,* in 1884. In this novel, the title character and his friend Jim, an escaped slave, float down the Mississippi River on a raft. Twain wrote in local dialect with a lively sense of humor. He had written a true American novel, in which the setting, subject, characters, and style were clearly American.

Popular Culture

Popular culture changed considerably in the late 1800s. Industrialization improved the standard of living for many people, enabling them to spend money on entertainment and recreation. Increasingly, urban Americans divided their lives into separate units—that of work and that of home. People began "going out" to public entertainment.

The Saloon In cities, saloons often outnumbered groceries and meat markets. As a place for social gathering, saloons played a major role in the lives of male workers. Saloons offered drinks, free toilets, water for horses, and free newspapers for customers. They even offered the first "free lunch": salty food that made patrons thirsty and eager to drink more. Saloons also served as political centers and saloonkeepers were often key figures in political machines.

Amusement Parks and Sports Working-class families and single adults could find entertainment at new amusement parks such as New York's Coney Island. Amusements such as water slides and railroad rides cost only a nickel or dime.

Watching professional sports also became popular during the late 1800s. Formed in 1869, the first professional baseball team was the Cincinnati Red Stockings. Other cities soon fielded their own teams. In 1903 the first official World Series was played between the Boston Red Sox and the Pittsburgh Pirates. Football also gained in popularity and by the late 1800s had spread to public colleges.

As work became less strenuous, many people looked for activities involving physical exercise. Tennis, golf, and croquet became popular. In 1891 James Naismith, athletic director for a college in Massachusetts, invented a new indoor game called basketball.

Vaudeville and Ragtime Adapted from French theater, vaudeville took on an American flavor in the early 1880s with its hodgepodge of animal acts, acrobats, and dancers. The fast-paced shows went on continuously all day and night.

Like vaudeville, ragtime music echoed the hectic pace of city life. Its syncopated rhythms grew out of the music of riverside honky-tonks, saloon pianists, and banjo players, using the patterns of African American music. Scott Joplin, one of the most important African American ragtime composers, became known as the "King of Ragtime." He wrote his most famous piece, "The Maple Leaf Rag," in 1899.

Analyzing VISUALS DBQ

1. **Analyzing** How does Twain's writing reflect a realist approach to writing?
2. **Making Inferences** Why might Realist art have become popular in the late 1800s?

✔ Reading Check **Describing** What was the importance of the saloon in city life?

For examples of literature from the Gilded Age, read excerpts from the writings of Mark Twain and Carl Sandburg on pages R70–71 in **American Literature Library.**

Politics in Washington

MAIN Idea The two major parties were closely competitive in the late 1800s; tariff rates and big business regulation were hotly debated political issues.

HISTORY AND YOU Have you ever considered getting a job working for the government once you graduate? Read to learn why you will have to take an examination if you want a government job.

After President James A. Garfield was elected in 1880, many of his supporters tried to claim the "spoils of office"—the government jobs that are handed out following an election victory. President Garfield did not believe in the spoils system. One of these job seekers made daily trips to the White House in the spring of 1881 asking for a job. He was repeatedly rejected. Reasoning that he would have a better chance for a job if Vice President Chester A. Arthur were president, this man shot President Garfield on July 2, 1881. Weeks later, Garfield died from his wounds.

Civil Service Reform

For many, Garfield's assassination highlighted the need to reform the political system. Traditionally, under the spoils system, elected politicians extended patronage—the power to reward supporters by giving them government jobs. Many Americans believed the system made government inefficient and corrupt. In the late 1870s, reformers had begun pushing him for an end to patronage.

When Rutherford B. Hayes became president in 1877, he tried to end patronage by firing officials who had been given their jobs because of their support of the party and replacing them with reformers. His actions divided the Republican Party between "Stalwarts" (who supported patronage) and the "Halfbreeds" (who opposed it), and no reforms were passed. In 1880 the Republicans nominated James Garfield, a "Halfbreed," for president and Chester A. Arthur, a "Stalwart," for vice president. Despite the internal feud over patronage, the Republicans managed to win the election, only to have Garfield assassinated a few months later.

Garfield's assassination turned public opinion against the spoils system. In 1883 Congress responded by passing the Pendleton Act. This law required that some jobs be filled by competitive written examinations, rather than through patronage. This marked the beginning of professional civil service—a system where most government workers are given jobs based on their qualifications rather than on their political affiliation. Although only about 10 percent of federal jobs were made civil service positions in 1883, the percentage steadily increased over time.

The Election of 1884

In 1884 the Democratic Party nominated Grover Cleveland, the governor of New York, for president. Cleveland was a reformer with a reputation for honesty. The Republican Party nominated James G. Blaine, a former Speaker of the House rumored to have accepted bribes. Some Republican reformers were so unhappy with Blaine that they supported Cleveland. They became known as "Mugwumps," from an Algonquian word meaning "great chief." If Blaine was their party's candidate, declared the Mugwumps, they would vote for Cleveland, "an honest Democrat."

Blaine hoped to make up for the loss of the Mugwumps by courting Catholic voters. Shortly before the election, however, Blaine met with a Protestant minister who denounced the Democrats for having ties to Catholicism. When Blaine was slow to condemn the remark, he lost many Catholic votes. Cleveland narrowly won the election.

As the first elected Democratic president since 1856, Grover Cleveland faced a horde of supporters who expected him to reward them with jobs. Mugwumps, on the other hand, expected him to increase the number of jobs protected by the civil service system. Cleveland chose a middle course and angered both sides. Economic issues, however, soon replaced the debate about patronage reform.

The Interstate Commerce Commission

Many Americans were concerned by the power of large corporations. Small businesses and farmers had become particularly angry at the railroads. While large corporations such as Standard Oil were able to negotiate rebates and lower rates because of the volume of goods they shipped, others were forced to pay much higher rates. Although the high fixed costs and low operating costs of railroads caused much

▲ Senator Pendleton is congratulated for his civil service bill; behind him a trash bin overflows with papers saying reform is impossible.

▲ John Bull, symbol of Britain, thanks Grover Cleveland for free trade because it keeps British workers employed even if everyone else starves.

Analyzing VISUALS

1. **Analyzing** Does the cartoon on the right say free trade is a good idea? How do you know?

2. **Explaining** Did the artist who drew the cartoon on the left favor civil service reform? How does he indicate his opinion?

of this problem, many Americans believed railroads were gouging customers.

Neither party moved quickly at the federal level to address these problems. Both believed that government should not interfere with corporations' property rights, which courts had held to be the same as those of individuals. Many states, however, passed laws regulating railroad rates; in 1886 the Supreme Court ruled in the case of *Wabash, St. Louis, and Pacific Railway* v. *Illinois* that states could not regulate railroad rates for traffic between states because only the federal government could regulate interstate commerce.

Public pressure forced Congress to respond to the Wabash ruling. In 1887 Cleveland signed the Interstate Commerce Act. This act, which created the Interstate Commerce Commission (ICC), was the first federal law to regulate interstate commerce. The legislation limited railroad rates to what was "reasonable and just," forbade rebates to high-volume users, and made it illegal to charge higher rates for shorter hauls. The commission was not very

effective in regulating the industry, however, because it had to rely on the courts to enforce its rulings.

Debating Tariffs Another major economic issue concerned tariffs. Many Democrats thought that Congress should cut tariffs because these taxes had the effect of raising the price of manufactured goods. Although it may have made sense to protect weak domestic manufacturing after the Civil War, many questioned the need to maintain high tariffs in the 1880s, when large American companies were fully capable of competing internationally. High tariffs also forced other nations to respond in kind, making it difficult for farmers to export their surpluses.

In December 1887 President Cleveland proposed lowering tariffs. The House, with a Democratic majority, passed moderate tariff reductions, but the Republican-controlled Senate rejected the bill. With Congress deadlocked, tariff reduction became a major issue in the election of 1888.

Republicans Regain Power

The Republicans and their presidential candidate, Benjamin Harrison, received large campaign contributions in 1888 from industrialists who benefited from high tariffs. Cleveland and the Democrats campaigned against high tariff rates. In one of the closest races in American history, Harrison lost the popular vote but won the electoral vote.

The McKinley Tariff The election of 1888 gave the Republicans control of both houses of Congress as well as the White House. Using this power, the party passed legislation to address points of national concern. In 1890 Representative William McKinley of Ohio pushed through a tariff bill that cut tobacco taxes and tariff rates on raw sugar but greatly increased rates on other goods, such as textiles, to discourage people from buying those imports.

The McKinley Tariff was intended to protect American industry from foreign competition and encourage consumers to buy American goods. Instead, it helped to trigger a steep rise in the price of all goods that angered many Americans and may have contributed to President Harrison's defeat in the 1892 election.

The Sherman Antitrust Act Congress also responded to popular pressure to do something about the power of the large business combinations known as trusts. In 1890 Congress passed the Sherman Antitrust Act, which prohibited any "combination . . . or conspiracy, in restraint of trade or commerce among the several States." The law, however, was vaguely worded, poorly enforced, and weakened by judicial interpretation. Most significantly, the Supreme Court ruled the law did not apply to manufacturing, holding that manufacturing was not interstate commerce. Thus the law had little impact. In the 1890s businesses formed trusts and combinations at a great rate. Like the ICC, the Sherman Antitrust Act was more important for establishing a precedent than for its immediate impact.

✔ Reading Check) **Summarizing** What actions did Congress take to regulate big business?

The Rebirth of Reform

MAIN Idea Reformers developed new methods and philosophies for helping the urban poor.

HISTORY AND YOU Have you ever been to a YMCA? What activities can you do there? Read on to find out the origin of the YMCA and other community centers.

The tremendous changes that industrialism and urbanization brought triggered a debate over how best to address society's problems. While many Americans embraced the ideas of individualism and Social Darwinism, others disagreed, arguing that society's problems could be fixed only if Americans and their government began to take a more active role in regulating the economy and helping those in need.

Debates
IN HISTORY

Is Social Darwinism the Best Approach for Ensuring Progress and Economic Growth?

The social problems that came with industrialization led to a debate over government's role in the economy. Some believed that government should intervene to help the poor and solve problems while others argued that leaving things alone was the best solution.

Challenging Social Darwinism

In 1879 journalist Henry George published *Progress and Poverty,* a discussion of the American economy that quickly became a national bestseller. In his book George observed, "The present century has been marked by a prodigious increase in wealth-producing power." This should, he asserted, have made poverty "a thing of the past." Instead, he claimed, the "gulf between the employed and the employer is growing wider; social contrasts are becoming sharper." In other words, laissez-faire economics was making society worse—the opposite of what Social Darwinists believed.

Most economists now argue that George's analysis was flawed. Industrialism did make some Americans very wealthy, but it also improved the standard of living for most others as well. At the time, however, in the midst of poverty, crime, and harsh working conditions, many Americans did not believe things were improving. George's economic theories encouraged other reformers to challenge the assumptions of the era.

Lester Frank Ward In 1883 Lester Frank Ward published *Dynamic Sociology,* in which he argued that humans were different from animals because they had the ability to make plans to produce the future outcomes they desired.

Ward's ideas came to be known as Reform Darwinism. People, he insisted, had succeeded in the world because of their ability to cooperate; competition was wasteful and time-consuming. Government, he argued, could regulate the economy, cure poverty, and promote education more efficiently than competition in the marketplace could.

YES

William Graham Sumner

Professor

PRIMARY SOURCE

"The moment that government provided work for one, it would have to provide work for all, and there would be no end whatever possible. Society does not owe any man a living. In all the cases that I have ever known of young men who claimed that society owed them a living, it has turned out that society paid them—in the State prison . . . The fact that a man is here is no demand upon other people that they shall keep him alive and sustain him. He has got to fight the battle with nature as every other man has; and if he fights it with the same energy and enterprise and skill and industry as any other man, I cannot imagine his failing—that is, misfortune apart."

—testimony before the U.S. House of Representatives, 1879

NO

Lester Frank Ward

Sociologist

PRIMARY SOURCE

"The actions of men are a reflex of their mental characteristics. Where these differ so widely the acts of their possessors will correspondingly differ. Instead of all doing the same thing they will do a thousand different things. The natural and necessary effect of this is to give breadth to human activity. Every subject will be looked at from all conceivable points of view, and no aspect will be overlooked or neglected. It is due to this multiplicity of viewpoints, growing out of natural inequalities in the minds of men, that civilization and culture have moved forward along so many lines and swept the whole field of possible achievement."

—from "Social Classes in the Light of Modern Sociological Theory," 1908

 DBQ **Document-Based Questions**

1. **Summarizing** What argument does Professor Sumner make against government assisting people?

2. **Paraphrasing** How does Professor Ward believe that different abilities aid society?

3. **Contrasting** How can you contrast the ideas of the two men?

4. **Evaluating** Which opinion do you agree with? Write a brief essay explaining your ideas.

People IN HISTORY

Jane Addams
1860–1935

After visiting a settlement house in London, England, Jane Addams decided to open Hull House in 1889 to assist poor immigrants in Chicago.

That assistance took on many forms: day care, kindergartens, libraries, an art gallery, an employment agency, and a meeting place for trade unions. The women who worked at Hull House, many of them college-educated in social work, pushed for protective legislation for children and women, which was enacted first in Illinois and then nationally.

Addams wrote books about her experiences at Hull House, giving an example to many others throughout the nation who also founded settlement houses. She favored woman suffrage and supported the founding of the American Civil Liberties Union and the National Association for the Advancement of Colored People. She was active in the peace movement, serving as first president of the organization that became the Women's International League for Peace and Freedom. For her efforts, she was awarded the Nobel Peace Prize in 1931.

What kind of assistance did Hull House provide immigrants?

▲ *Children stand in front of Hull House in 1905.*

Looking Backward Writer Edward Bellamy promoted another alternative to Social Darwinism and laissez-faire economics. In 1888 he published *Looking Backward,* a novel about a man who falls asleep in 1887 and awakens in the year 2000 to find that the nation has become a perfect society with no crime, poverty, or politics. In this fictional society, the government owns all industry and shares the wealth equally with all Americans. Bellamy's ideas were essentially a form of socialism. His book became a bestseller and helped to shape the thinking of some American reformers.

Naturalism in Literature Criticism of industrial society also appeared in literature in a new style of writing known as naturalism. Social Darwinists argued that people could make choices to improve their situation. Naturalists challenged this idea by suggesting that some people failed in life simply because they were caught up in circumstances they could not control. Sometimes people's lives were destroyed through no fault of their own.

Among the most prominent naturalist writers were Stephen Crane, Jack London, and Theodore Dreiser. Stephen Crane's novel

Maggie, A Girl of the Streets (1893), told the story of a girl's descent into prostitution and death. Jack London's tales of the Alaskan wilderness demonstrated the power of nature over civilization. Theodore Dreiser's novels, such as *Sister Carrie* (1900), painted a world where people sinned without punishment and where the pursuit of wealth and power often destroyed their character.

Helping the Urban Poor

The plight of the urban poor prompted some reformers to find new ways to help. Their efforts gave rise to the Social Gospel movement, the Salvation Army, the YMCA, and settlement houses.

The Social Gospel The **Social Gospel** movement worked to better conditions in cities according to the biblical ideals of charity and justice. Washington Gladden, a minister, was an early advocate who popularized the movement in writings such as *Applied Christianity* (1887). Walter Rauschenbusch, a Baptist minister from New York, became the leading voice in the Social Gospel movement.

The Church, he argued, must "demand protection for the moral safety of the people." The Social Gospel movement inspired many churches to take on new community functions. Some churches built gyms and provided social programs and child care. Others focused exclusively on helping the poor.

The Salvation Army and the YMCA The Salvation Army and the YMCA also combined faith and an interest in reform. The Salvation Army offered practical aid and religious counseling to the urban poor. The Young Men's Christian Association (YMCA) tried to help industrial workers and the urban poor by organizing Bible studies, citizenship training, and group activities. YMCAs, or "Ys," offered libraries, gymnasiums, auditoriums, and low-cost hotel rooms available on a temporary basis to those in need.

The head of the Chicago YMCA, Dwight L. Moody, was a gifted preacher who founded his own church, today known as Moody Memorial Church. By 1867, Moody had begun to organize revival meetings in other American cities, which drew thousands of people. Moody rejected both the Social Gospel and Social Darwinism. He believed the way to help the poor was not by providing them with services but by redeeming their souls and reforming their character.

The Settlement House Movement The **settlement house** movement began as an offshoot of the Social Gospel movement. In the late 1800s idealistic reformers—including many college-educated women—established settlement houses in poor, often heavily immigrant neighborhoods. A settlement house was a community center where reformers resided and offered everything from medical care and English classes to kindergartens and recreational programs. **Jane Addams** opened the famous Hull House in Chicago in 1889. Her work inspired others, including Lillian Wald, who founded the Henry Street Settlement in New York City.

Public Education As the United States became increasingly industrialized and urbanized, it needed more workers who were trained and educated. The number of public schools increased dramatically after the Civil War. The number of children attending school rose from 6,500,000 in 1870 to 17,300,000 in 1900. Public schools were often crucial to the success of immigrant children. At public schools, immigrant children were taught English and learned about American history and culture, a process known as **Americanization.**

Schools also tried to instill discipline and a strong work ethic. Grammar schools divided students into grades and drilled them in punctuality, neatness, and efficiency—necessary habits for the workplace. At the same time, vocational education in high schools taught skills required in specific trades.

Not everyone had access to school. Cities were far ahead of rural areas. Many African Americans also did not have equal educational opportunities. Some African Americans started their own schools, following the example of Booker T. Washington, who founded the Tuskegee Institute in 1881.

✔ **Reading Check** **Explaining** What was the purpose of a settlement house?

Section 3 REVIEW

Vocabulary

1. **Explain** the significance of Gilded Age, individualism, Social Darwinism, Gospel of Wealth, philanthropy, Mark Twain, Social Gospel, settlement house, Jane Addams, Americanization.

Main Ideas

2. **Defining** What were the defining characteristics of the Gilded Age?

3. **Describing** How did changes in art and literature reflect the issues and characteristics of the late 1800s?

4. **Explaining** Why was the Sherman Antitrust Act ineffective?

5. **Categorizing** Complete a chart like the one below by listing the names and goals of reform movements that arose in the late 1800s to help the urban poor.

Reform Movement	Goals

Critical Thinking

6. **Big Ideas** Do you think the idea of the Gospel of Wealth is still alive today? Why or why not?

7. **Analyzing Visuals** Look at the cartoon on the right on page 235. What do the figures in the background suggest?

Writing About History

8. **Descriptive Writing** Imagine that you are a newspaper editor in the late 1800s. Write an editorial in which you support or oppose the philosophy of Social Darwinism.

History ONLINE

Study Central™ To review this section, go to glencoe.com and click on Study Central.

Eyewitness

BROWN BROTHERS

In his exposé of urban poverty, How the Other Half Lives *(1890),* **JACOB RIIS** *documented the living conditions in New York City tenements:*

"The statement once made a sensation that between seventy and eighty children had been found in one tenement. It no longer excites even passing attention, when the sanitary police report counting 101 adults and 91 children in a Crosby Street house, one of twins, built together. The children in the others, if I am not mistaken, numbered 89, a total of 180 for two tenements! Or when midnight inspection in Mulberry Street unearths a hundred and fifty "lodgers" sleeping on filthy floors in two buildings. In spite of brown-stone fittings, plate-glass and mosaic vestibule floors, the water does not rise in summer to the second story, while the beer flows unchecked to the all-night picnics on the roof. The saloon with the side-door and the landlord divide the prosperity of the place between them, and the tenant, in sullen submission, foots the bill."

VERBATIM

❝Tell 'em quick, and tell 'em often.❞

WILLIAM WRIGLEY,
soap salesman and promoter of chewing gum,
on his marketing philosophy

❝A pushing, energetic, ingenious person, always awake and trying to get ahead of his neighbors.❞

HENRY ADAMS,
historian, describing the average New Yorker or Chicagoan

❝We cannot all live in cities, yet nearly all seem determined to do so.❞
HORACE GREELEY,
newspaper editor

INDICATORS:
Livin' in the City

Moving off the farm for a factory job? Sharpen your pencil. You'll need to budget carefully to buy all you will need.

Here are the numbers for a Georgia family of four in 1890. The husband is a textile worker, and the wife works at home. There is one child, age 4, and a boarder. They share a two-room, wood-heated, oil-lighted apartment.

INCOME: (annual)

husband's income	$312.00
boarder's rent	10.00
TOTAL INCOME.	**$322.00**

EXPENSES: (annual)

medical	$65.00
furniture	46.90
clothing	46.00
rent	21.00
flour/meal	25.00
hog products	17.00
other meat	13.00
vegetables	13.00
lard	6.50
potatoes	6.40
butter	5.00
sugar	4.00
charitable donations	6.10
vacation	3.25
alcohol	3.25
tobacco	3.00
molasses	2.00
other food	27.80
miscellaneous	68.20
TOTAL EXPENSES.	**$382.40**

Milestones

ON THE RUN, 1881. THE JESSE JAMES GANG, after robbing a Chicago, Rock Island, and Pacific train near Winston, Missouri, and killing the conductor and a passenger.

OVERTURNED, 1878. BY THE SUPREME COURT, a Louisiana court decision that awarded damages to an African American woman who had been refused admission to a steamship stateroom reserved for whites.

PLAGUED BY GRASSHOPPERS, 1874. THE AMERICAN GREAT PLAINS. Insect swarms a mile wide blot out the midday sun. Two inches deep on the ground, they leave "nothing but the mortgage," as one farmer put it.

CELEBRATED IN EUROPE, 1887. ANNIE OAKLEY, star of Buffalo Bill's Wild West Show. Oakley shot a cigarette from the lips of Crown Prince Wilhelm of Germany. Years later, when the U.S. goes to war against Kaiser Wilhelm, Oakley will quip: "I wish I'd missed that day!"

Susan B. Anthony

Jesse James

REMOVED, 1884. IDA B. WELLS, journalist and former slave, from a ladies coach on a train. Wells refused to move to the smoking car where African Americans were to be seated.

ARRESTED, 1872. SUSAN B. ANTHONY, for casting a ballot in Rochester, New York. Anthony argued that the Fourteenth and Fifteenth Amendments applied to women.

NUMBERS

1 in 12 Americans living in cities of 100,000 or more in 1865

A crowded New York City street

1 in 5 Americans living in cities in 1896

- -

522 Inhabitants in a one-acre area in the Bowery, New York City

- -

$2 Daily wage for a farm laborer, New York, 1869

- -

$4 Daily wage for a plumber, New York City, 1869

- -

50¢ Price of a pair of boy's knee pants, a parasol, button boots, or a necktie (1870s)

- -

$8 Price of a "Fine All-Wool Suit," 1875

- -

25¢ Admission to "Barnum's American Museum" (featuring the smallest pair of human beings ever seen!), 1896

CRITICAL THINKING

1. *Analyzing Visuals* Look at the Jacob Riis photo of an urban family and the photo of a New York City street. What do the pictures tell you about urban life in the 1890s?

2. *Comparing* What character traits do you think Ida B. Wells and Susan B. Anthony may have shared?

Populism

Guide to Reading

Big Ideas
Economics and Society The Populist movement and its presidential candidate William Jennings Bryan strongly supported silver as the basis for currency.

Content Vocabulary
- populism *(p. 242)*
- greenbacks *(p. 242)*
- inflation *(p. 242)*
- deflation *(p. 242)*
- cooperatives *(p. 243)*
- graduated income tax *(p. 245)*

Academic Vocabulary
- bond *(p. 242)*
- currency *(p. 243)*
- strategy *(p. 244)*

People and Events to Identify
- Farmers' Alliance *(p. 244)*
- People's Party *(p. 245)*
- William Jennings Bryan *(p. 246)*
- William McKinley *(p. 247)*

Reading Strategy
Taking Notes As you read about the emergence of populism in the 1890s, use the major headings of the section to create an outline similar to the one below.

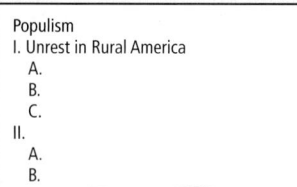

Populism
I. Unrest in Rural America
    A.
    B.
    C.
II.
    A.
    B.

After the Civil War, falling crop prices and deflation made it hard for farmers to make a living. Farmers tried to overcome these problems by forming organizations such as the Grange and the Farmers' Alliance. In the 1890s, many farmers joined the Populist Party.

Unrest in Rural America

MAIN Idea Deflation, low crop prices, and tariffs hurt farmers economically.

HISTORY AND YOU What can you buy for a dollar today? Read on to learn how the value of a dollar has changed over time.

Populism was a movement to increase farmers' political power and to work for legislation in their interest. Farmers joined the Populist movement because they were in the midst of an economic crisis. New technology enabled farmers to produce more crops, but the greater supply had caused prices to fall. High tariffs also made it hard for farmers to sell their goods overseas. Farmers also felt they were victimized by large and faraway entities: the banks from which they obtained loans and the railroads that set their shipping rates.

The Money Supply
Some farmers thought adjusting the money supply would solve their economic problems. During the Civil War, the federal government had expanded the money supply by issuing millions of dollars in **greenbacks**—paper currency that could not be exchanged for gold or silver coins. This increase in the money supply without an increase in goods for sale caused **inflation,** or a decline in the value of money. As the paper money lost value, the prices of goods soared.

After the Civil War ended, the United States had three types of currency in circulation—greenbacks, gold and silver coins, and national bank notes backed by government **bonds.** To get inflation under control, the federal government stopped printing greenbacks and began paying off its bonds. In 1873 Congress also decided to stop making silver into coins. These decisions meant that the money supply was not large enough for the country's growing economy. In 1865, for example, there was about $30 in circulation for each person. By 1895, there was only about $23. As the economy expanded, **deflation**—or an increase in the value of money and a decrease in prices—began. As money increased in value, prices fell.

Deflation hit farmers especially hard. Most farmers had to borrow money for seed and other supplies to plant their crops. Because

Why Were Farmers Having Problems?

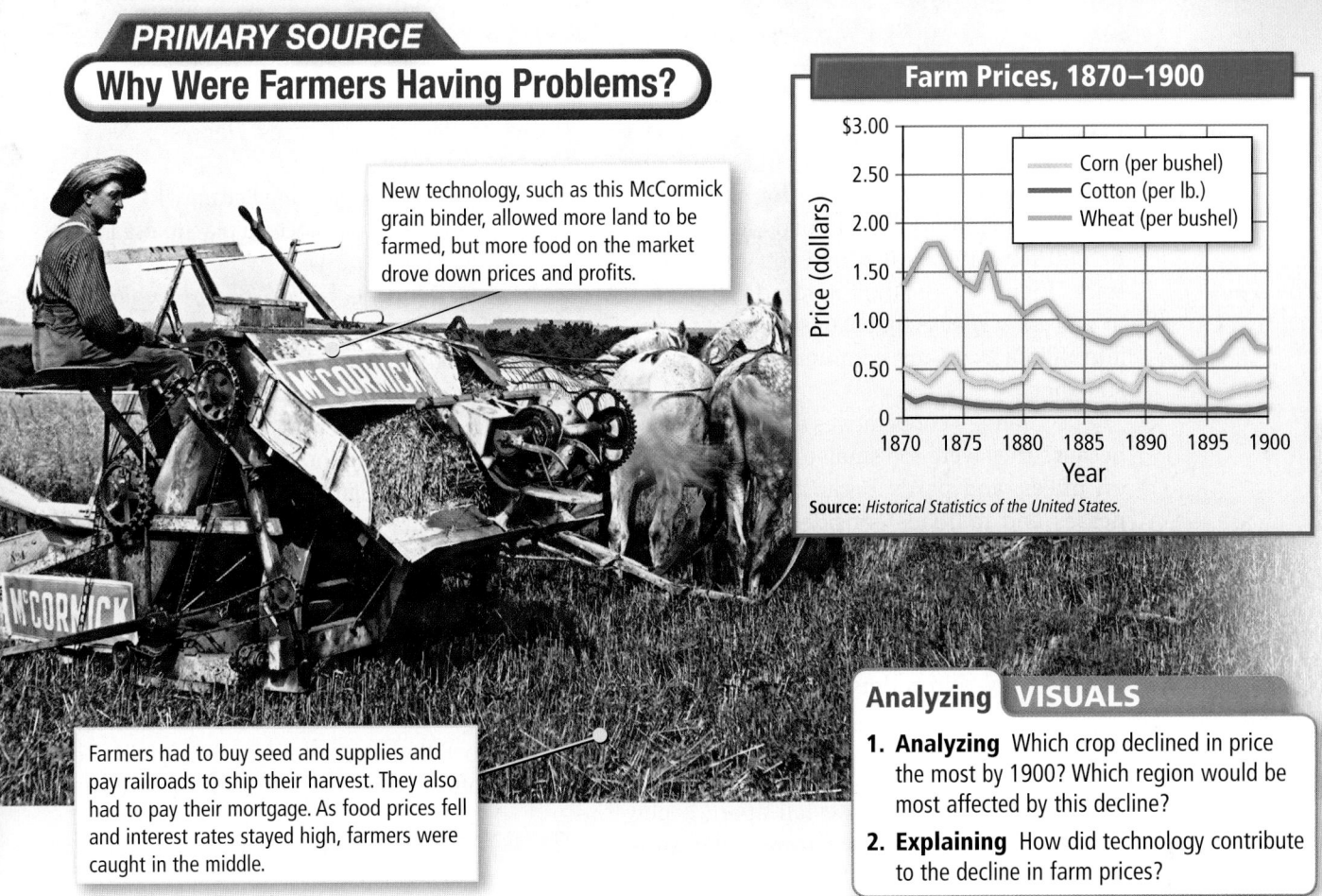

New technology, such as this McCormick grain binder, allowed more land to be farmed, but more food on the market drove down prices and profits.

Farm Prices, 1870–1900

Corn (per bushel)
Cotton (per lb.)
Wheat (per bushel)

Source: *Historical Statistics of the United States.*

Farmers had to buy seed and supplies and pay railroads to ship their harvest. They also had to pay their mortgage. As food prices fell and interest rates stayed high, farmers were caught in the middle.

Analyzing VISUALS

1. **Analyzing** Which crop declined in price the most by 1900? Which region would be most affected by this decline?

2. **Explaining** How did technology contribute to the decline in farm prices?

---

money was in short supply, interest rates began to rise, which increased the amount farmers owed. Rising interest rates also made mortgages more expensive, but falling prices meant the farmers sold their crops for less, and they still had to make the same mortgage payments to the banks.

Realizing that their problems were partly caused by a shortage of **currency,** many farmers concluded that Eastern bankers had pressured Congress into reducing the money supply. Some farmers called for the printing of more greenbacks. Others, particularly those in the West where new silver mines had been found, wanted the government to mint silver coins. They referred to the decision to stop minting silver as "The Crime of '73."

The Grange Takes Action

In 1866 the Department of Agriculture sent Oliver H. Kelley to tour the rural South and report on the condition of the region's farmers. Realizing how isolated farmers were from each other, Kelley founded the first national farm organization, the Patrons of Husbandry, better known as the Grange, in 1867.

At first Grangers met largely for social and educational purposes. Then, in 1873, the nation plunged into a severe recession, and farm income fell sharply. Farmers looking for help joined the Grange in large numbers. By 1874, the Grange had between 800,000 and 1.5 million members.

Grangers responded to the crisis by pressuring state legislatures to regulate railroad and warehouse rates. They also tried to create **cooperatives**—marketing organizations that try to increase prices and lower costs for their members.

One of the reasons farmers could not charge higher prices for their crops was that there were so many farmers in competition. If a farmer raised prices, a buyer could always go elsewhere and pay less. Cooperatives pooled farmers' crops and held them off the market in order to force up prices. Because a cooperative controlled a large quantity of farm products, it could also negotiate better shipping rates with the railroads.

None of the **strategies** the Grangers employed improved farmers' economic conditions. Several Western states passed "Granger laws" that set maximum rates and prohibited railroads from charging more for short hauls than for long ones. The railroads fought back by cutting services and refusing to lay new track. Then, in 1886, the Supreme Court ruled in *Wabash* v. *Illinois* that states could not regulate railroads or any commerce that crossed state lines.

The Grange's cooperatives also failed, partly because they were too small to have any effect on prices, and partly because Eastern businesses and railroads considered them to be similar to unions—illegitimate conspiracies that restricted trade—so they refused to do business with them. By the late 1870s, farmers began to leave the Grange for organizations they hoped would address their problems.

The Farmers' Alliance

As the Grange began to fall apart, a new organization, known as the **Farmers' Alliance,** began to form. By 1890, the Alliance had between 1.5 and 3 million members, with strong support in the South and on the Great Plains, particularly in Kansas, Nebraska, North Dakota, and South Dakota.

When Charles W. Macune became the leader of the Alliance, he announced a plan to organize very large cooperatives, which he called exchanges. Macune hoped these exchanges would be big enough to force farm prices up and to make loans to farmers at low interest rates. The exchanges had some success. The Texas Exchange successfully marketed cotton at prices slightly higher than those paid to individual farmers, while the Illinois Exchange negotiated slightly better railroad rates for wheat farmers.

Ultimately, the large cooperatives failed. Many overextended themselves by lending too much money at low interest rates that was never repaid. In many cases, wholesalers, railroads, and bankers discriminated against them, making it difficult for them to stay in business. They also failed because they were still too small to affect world prices for farm products.

✔**Reading Check** **Explaining** How did the Farmers' Alliance try to help farmers?

Who Is to Blame for Farmers' Problems?

▲ A farmer wearing a Granger hat tries to warn people about the railroad.

THE POLITICAL POOR RELATION.—AN UNWELCOME GUEST.

▲ A thin farmer is an unwelcome guest at the Congressional kitchen, where businessmen are enjoying their meals.

Analyzing VISUALS

1. **Analyzing** What is the cartoon on the left implying about the railroad's relationship to farmers?

2. **Explaining** Who does the cartoon on the right blame for the problems facing farmers?

The Rise of Populism

MAIN Idea Farmers started the People's Party to fight for their interests and attracted many supporters when a depression hit in the 1890s.

HISTORY AND YOU Do you remember reading about the creation of the Republican Party in the 1850s? Read how another new party, the Populists, shook up politics in the 1890s.

By 1890 the Alliance's lack of success had started a debate in the organization. Some Alliance leaders, particularly in the western states, wanted to form a new party and push for political reforms. Members of the Kansas Alliance formed the **People's Party,** also known as the Populists, and nominated candidates to run for Congress and the state legislature. Alliances in Nebraska, South Dakota, and Minnesota quickly followed Kansas's example.

Most Southern leaders of the Alliance opposed the idea of a third party. They did not want to undermine the Democrats' control of the South. Instead, they suggested that the Alliance produce a list of demands and promise to vote for candidates who supported those demands. They hoped this would force Democrats to adopt the Alliance program.

The Subtreasury Plan

To get Southern Democrats to support the Alliance, Charles Macune introduced the subtreasury plan, which called for the government to set up warehouses called subtreasuries. Farmers would store their crops in the warehouses, and the government would provide low-interest loans to the farmers.

Macune believed the plan would enable farmers to hold their crops off the market in large enough quantities to force prices up. The Alliance also called for the free coinage of silver, an end to protective tariffs and national banks, tighter regulation of the railroads, and direct election of senators by voters.

Macune's strategy seemed to work at first. In 1890 the South elected four governors, all Democrats, who had pledged to support the Alliance program. Several Southern legislatures now had pro-Alliance majorities, and more than 40 Democrats who supported the Alliance program were elected to Congress.

A Populist Runs for President

Meanwhile, the new People's Party did equally well in the West. Populists took control of the Kansas and Nebraska legislatures. Populists also held the balance of power in Minnesota and South Dakota. Eight Populist representatives and two Populist senators were elected to the United States Congress.

At first, Southern members of the Alliance were excited over their success in electing so many pro-Alliance Democrats to Congress and to Southern state legislatures, but over the next two years, their excitement turned into frustration. Despite their promises, few Democrats followed through in their support of the Alliance program.

In May 1891 Western populists met with some labor and reform groups in Cincinnati. There, they endorsed the creation of a new national People's Party to run candidates for president. The following year, many Southern farmers had reached the point where they were willing to break with the Democratic Party and join the People's Party.

In July 1892 the People's Party held its first national convention in Omaha, Nebraska. James B. Weaver was nominated to run for president. The Omaha convention endorsed a platform that denounced the government's refusal to coin silver as a "vast conspiracy against mankind" and called for a return to unlimited coinage of silver at a ratio that gave 16 ounces of silver the same value as one ounce of gold. It also called for federal ownership of railroads and a **graduated income tax,** one that taxed higher earnings more heavily.

Populists also adopted proposals designed to appeal to organized labor. The Omaha platform also called for an eight-hour workday and immigration restrictions, but workers found it hard to identify with a party focused on rural problems and the coinage of silver. The Populists had close ties to the Knights of Labor, but that organization was in decline, and the fast-growing American Federation of Labor had steered clear of an alliance with them. As a result, most urban workers continued to vote for the Democrats, whose candidate, Grover Cleveland, won the election.

Reading Check **Summarizing** What was the main outcome of the Populist campaign in the elections of 1892?

The Election of 1896

MAIN Idea Although William Jennings Bryan had the support of the Populists and the Democrats, Republican William McKinley defeated him.

HISTORY AND YOU What was the best speech you have ever heard? How did the speaker draw you in? Read on to learn how a powerful speech won the presidential nomination for William Jennings Bryan.

As the election of 1896 approached, leaders of the People's Party decided to make the free coinage of silver the focus of their campaign. They also decided to hold their convention after the Republican and Democratic conventions. They believed the Republicans would endorse a gold standard, and they did. They also expected the Democrats to nominate Grover Cleveland, even though Cleveland also strongly favored a gold standard. The People's Party hoped that when they endorsed silver, pro-silver Democrats would abandon their party and vote for the Populists.

Unfortunately for the Populists, their strategy failed. The Democrats did not waiver on the silver issue. Instead, they nominated **William Jennings Bryan,** a strong supporter of silver. When the Populists gathered in St. Louis for their own convention, they faced a difficult choice: endorse Bryan and risk undermining their identity as a separate party, or nominate their own candidate and risk splitting the silver vote. They eventually decided to support Bryan as well.

Bryan's Campaign

William Jennings Bryan, a former member of Congress from Nebraska, was only 36 years old when the Democrats and the Populists nominated him for president. Bryan had served in Congress as a representative from Nebraska. He was a powerful speaker and he won the Democratic nomination by delivering an electrifying address in defense of silver—one of the most famous in American political history.

Turning Point

The Election of 1896

Before the Civil War, farmers of the West and the South determined the outcome of elections. As industrialization caused Eastern cities to grow, the balance of political power shifted. From the 1870s to the 1890s, elections became very close, and power swung back and forth between the parties. The election of 1896 marked a turning point. Political power shifted from voters in the rural parts of the country to those in urban areas in the Northeast and industrial Midwest. Never again would farm votes determine the winner of a presidential election. The South and West did not regain their political importance until their urban areas grew to match those in the Northeast and Midwest.

MAKING CONNECTIONS Does the pattern of 1896's election resemble recent elections? Write an essay comparing a recent election to the 1896 election.

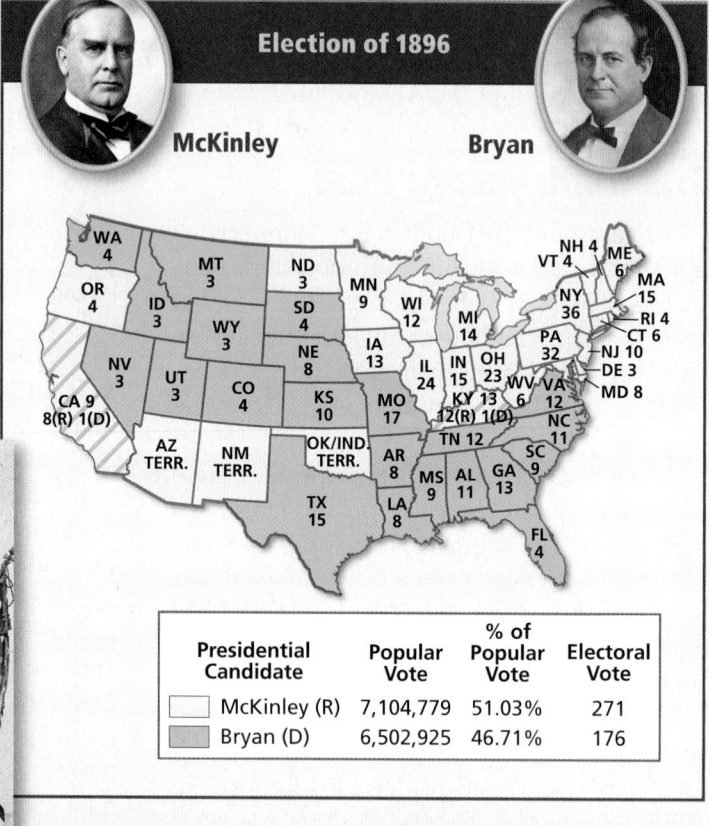

Election of 1896

McKinley   Bryan

Presidential Candidate	Popular Vote	% of Popular Vote	Electoral Vote
McKinley (R)	7,104,779	51.03%	271
Bryan (D)	6,502,925	46.71%	176

◀ For many, the campaign to elect William Jennings Bryan was viewed as both a crusade and a revolution, as the symbols and slogans on this 1896 poster show.

With a few well-chosen words, Bryan transformed the campaign for silver into a crusade:

PRIMARY SOURCE

"Having behind us the producing masses of this nation and the world, supported by the commercial interests, the laboring interests and the toilers everywhere, we will answer their demand for a gold standard by saying to them: You shall not press down upon the brow of labor this crown of thorns; you shall not crucify mankind upon a cross of gold."

—quoted in *America in the Gilded Age*

Bryan waged an energetic campaign, traveling thousands of miles and delivering 600 speeches in 14 weeks. Some found his relentless campaigning undignified, and Catholic immigrants and other city dwellers cared little for the silver issue. They did not like Bryan's speaking style either. It reminded them of rural Protestant preachers, who were sometimes anti-Catholic. Republicans knew that Democrats and Populists would be hard to beat in the South and the West. To regain the White House, they had to sweep the Northeast and the Midwest. They decided on **William McKinley,** the governor of Ohio, as their candidate.

The Front Porch Campaign

Unlike Bryan, McKinley launched a "Front Porch Campaign," greeting delegates who came to his home in Canton, Ohio. The Republicans campaigned against the Democrats by promising workers that McKinley would provide a "full dinner pail." This meant more to urban workers than the issue of silver money because the economy was in a severe recession following the Panic of 1893. At the same time, most business leaders supported the Republicans, convinced that unlimited silver coinage would ruin the country. Many employers warned workers that if Bryan won, businesses would fail and unemployment would rise further.

McKinley's reputation as a moderate on labor issues and as tolerant toward ethnic groups helped improve the Republican Party's image with urban workers and immigrants. When the votes were counted, McKinley had won with a decisive victory. He captured 51 percent of the popular vote and had a winning margin of 95 electoral votes—hefty numbers in an era of tight elections. As expected, Bryan won the South and most of the West, but few of the states he carried had large populations or delivered many electoral votes. By embracing populism and its rural base, Bryan and the Democrats lost the northeastern industrial areas, where votes were concentrated.

The Populist Party declined after 1896. Their efforts to ease the economic hardships of farmers and to regulate big business had not worked. Some of the reforms they favored, including the graduated income tax and some governmental regulation of the economy—however, came about in the subsequent decades.

Reading Check **Evaluating** What were the results of the 1896 presidential election?

Section 4 REVIEW

Vocabulary

1. **Explain** the significance of: populism, greenbacks, inflation, deflation, cooperatives, Farmers' Alliance, People's Party, graduated income tax, William Jennings Bryan, William McKinley.

Main Ideas

2. **Organizing** Use a graphic organizer that lists the factors that contributed to and the results of farmers' unrest in the 1890s.

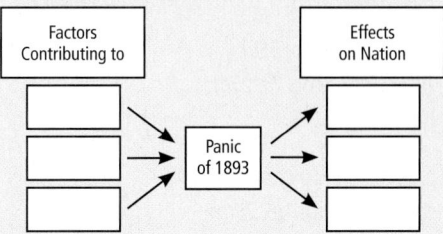

3. **Describing** What economic factors caused farmers to support populism?

4. **Listing** What issues did the Democrats endorse in the 1896 presidential election?

Critical Thinking

5. **Big Ideas** Why did the Populists support William Jennings Bryan?

6. **Synthesizing** How did the Farmers' Alliance contribute to the rise of a new political party?

7. **Analyzing Visuals** Look at the campaign poster on page 246. Choose one of the symbols or slogans and explain its meaning to Bryan's campaign.

Writing About History

8. **Persuasive Writing** Imagine you support the Populist Party and that you have been asked to write copy for a campaign poster. Include a slogan that provides reasons for people to support the Populists.

History **ONLINE**

Study Central™ To review this section, go to glencoe.com and click on Study Central.

The Rise of Segregation

Guide to Reading

Big Ideas
Individual Action Several prominent African Americans led the fight against racial discrimination.

Content Vocabulary
- poll tax *(p. 250)*
- segregation *(p. 250)*
- Jim Crow laws *(p. 250)*
- lynching *(p. 252)*

Academic Vocabulary
- discrimination *(p. 250)*

People and Events to Identify
- Ida B. Wells *(p. 252)*
- Booker T. Washington *(p. 253)*
- W. E. B. Du Bois *(p. 253)*

Reading Strategy
Organizing As you read, complete a web diagram listing ways that states disenfranchised African Americans and legalized discrimination.

Factors Contributing to Discrimination

After Reconstruction ended, Southern states began passing laws that eroded the rights of African Americans by introducing segregation and denying voting rights. African American leaders struggled to protect civil rights and improve quality of life but could not always agree on the most effective strategy.

Resistance and Repression

MAIN Idea Many African Americans fled the South, but some stayed and joined the Populist Party.

HISTORY AND YOU Do you remember reading about the rise of sharecropping after the Civil War? Read how African American farmers tried to work together in the late 1800s.

After Reconstruction, many African Americans in the rural South lived in conditions of grinding poverty. Most were sharecroppers, landless farmers who gave their landlords a large portion of their crops as rent, rather than paying cash. Sharecropping usually left farmers in chronic debt. Many eventually left farming and sought jobs in Southern towns or headed west to claim homesteads.

The Exodusters Head to Kansas

In the mid-1870s, Benjamin "Pap" Singleton, a former slave, became convinced that African Americans would never be given a chance to get ahead in the South. He began urging African Americans to move west, specifically to Kansas, and form their own independent communities where they could help each other get ahead. His ideas soon set in motion a mass migration. In the spring of 1879, African American communities in Louisiana, Mississippi, and Texas were swept with a religious enthusiasm for moving to Kansas—seeing it as a new promised land. In less than two months, approximately 6,000 African Americans left their homes in the rural South and headed to Kansas. The newspapers called it "an Exodus," like the Hebrews' escape from Egyptian bondage. The migrants themselves came to be known as "Exodusters."

One of the migrants to Kansas later explained why they went: "The whole South—every State in the South—had got into the hands of the very men that held us as slaves." The first Exodusters, many possessing little more than hope and the clothes on their backs, arrived in Kansas in the spring of 1879. A journalist named Henry King described the scene:

The Exodusters

NATIONAL GEOGRAPHIC **The Exodus to Kansas**

Legend:
- State abandoned by Exodusters
- State where Exodusters settled
- ← Route of migration

▲ *In 1879, soon after Reconstruction ended, an estimated 6,000–15,000 African Americans left the rural South and headed to Kansas where they hoped to build a better life for themselves.*

Analyzing VISUALS

1. **Analyzing** According to the map, which states were departure points for the Exodusters?
2. **Making Connections** What earlier events in American history would have made the Exodusters think Kansas was a good place to settle?

PRIMARY SOURCE

"One morning in April, 1879, a Missouri steamboat arrived at Wyandotte, Kansas, and discharged a load of negro men, women and children, with . . . barrels, boxes, and bundles of household effects. . . . [T]heir garments were incredibly patched and tattered . . . and there was not probably a dollar in money in the pockets of the entire party. . . . They looked like persons coming out of a dream. And, indeed, such they were . . . . for this was the advance guard of the Exodus."

—quoted in *Eyewitness: The Negro in History*

Forming a Separate Alliance

While some African Americans fled the South, others joined with poor white farmers who had created the Farmers' Alliance. Alliance leaders urged African Americans to form a similar organization. In 1886 African American farmers established the Colored Farmers' National Alliance. By 1890, the organization had about 1.2 million members.

When the Populist Party formed in 1891, many African American farmers joined the new organization. This posed a major challenge to the Democratic Party in the South. If poor whites left the party and joined with African Americans in voting for the Populists, the coalition might be unbeatable.

To win back the poor white vote, Democratic leaders began appealing to racism, warning whites that support for Populism would return the South to "Black Republican" rule, similar to Reconstruction. In addition, election officials began using various methods to make it harder and harder for African Americans to vote. As one Democratic leader in the South told a reporter, "Some of our people, some editors especially, deny that [African Americans] are hindered from voting; but what is the good of lying? They are interfered with, and we are obliged to do it, and we may as well tell the truth."

✔ **Reading Check** **Examining** Who were the Exodusters, and why did they migrate to Kansas?

Imposing Segregation

MAIN Idea Southern states passed laws that imposed segregation and denied African American men their voting rights.

HISTORY AND YOU Can you think of a rule that is unfairly or unevenly enforced? Read about the tactics used to disfranchise African Americans.

After Reconstruction ended in 1877, the rights of African Americans were gradually undermined. Attempts to unify whites and African Americans politically and economically failed. Instead, a movement to diminish the civil rights of African Americans gained momentum as the century ended.

Taking Away the Vote

The Fifteenth Amendment prohibits states from denying citizens the right to vote on the basis of "race, color, or previous condition of servitude," but it does not bar states from denying the right to vote on other grounds. In the late 1800s, Southern states began imposing restrictions that, while not mentioning race, were designed to make it difficult or impossible for African Americans to vote.

In 1890 Mississippi began requiring all citizens registering to vote to pay a **poll tax** of $2, a sum beyond the means of most poor African Americans. Mississippi also instituted a literacy test, requiring voters to read and understand the state constitution. Few African Americans born after the Civil War had been able to attend school and those who had grown up under slavery were largely illiterate. Even those who knew how to read often failed the test because officials deliberately picked passages that few people could understand.

Other Southern states adopted similar restrictions. In Louisiana the number of African Americans registered to vote fell from about 130,000 in 1890 to around 5,300 in 1900. In Alabama the number fell from about 181,000 to about 3,700.

Election officials were far less strict in applying the poll tax and literacy requirements to whites, but the number of white voters also fell significantly. To let more whites vote, Louisiana introduced the "grandfather clause," which allowed any man to vote if he had an ancestor who could vote in 1867. This provision, which was adopted in several Southern states, exempted most whites from voting restrictions such as literacy tests.

Legalizing Segregation

African Americans in the North were often barred from public places, but **segregation,** or the separation of the races, was different in the South. Southern states passed laws that enforced **discrimination**. These laws became known as **Jim Crow laws.** The term probably refers to the song "Jump Jim Crow," which was popular in minstrel shows of the day.

Civil Rights Cases In 1883 the Supreme Court set the stage for legalized segregation when it overturned the Civil Rights Act of 1875. That law had prohibited keeping people out of public places on the basis of race and barred racial **discrimination** in selecting jurors. The 1883 Supreme Court decision, however, said that the Fourteenth Amendment provided only that "no state" could deny citizens equal protection under the law. Private organizations—such as hotels, theaters, and railroads—were free to practice segregation.

Encouraged by the Supreme Court's ruling and by the decline of congressional support for civil rights, Southern states passed a series of laws that established racial segregation in virtually all public places. Southern whites and African Americans could no longer ride together in the same railroad cars, eat in the same dining halls, or even drink from the same fountains.

Plessy* v. *Ferguson In 1892 an African American named Homer Plessy challenged a Louisiana law that forced him to ride in a separate railroad car from whites. He was arrested for riding in a "whites-only" car. In 1896 the Supreme Court, in *Plessy* v. *Ferguson*, upheld the Louisiana law and set out a new doctrine of "separate but equal" facilities for African Americans. The ruling established the legal basis for discrimination in the South for more than 50 years. While public facilities for African Americans in the South were always separate, they were far from equal. In many cases, they were inferior.

Reading Check **Summarizing** How did the Supreme Court help to legalize segregation?

ANALYZING SUPREME COURT CASES

Do states have the right to segregate citizens by race?

★ *Plessy v. Ferguson*, 1896

Background to the Case

When Homer Adolph Plessy, a light-skinned man who was one-eighth African American, took a seat in the whites-only section of an East Louisiana Railway train and refused to move, he was arrested. Convicted of breaking a Louisiana law enacted in 1890, Plessy appealed his case to the Louisiana Supreme Court, then to federal Supreme Court. The incident was planned in advance to test the statute, using Plessy, who appeared to be white, to show the folly of the law. Although the words "separate but equal" do not appear in the court responses, the term came to describe a condition that persisted until 1954.

How the Court Ruled

The Court upheld the right of states to make laws that sustained segregation. The majority of justices wanted to distinguish between political rights guaranteed by the Fourteenth and Fifteenth Amendments and social rights.

PRIMARY SOURCE

The Court's Opinion

"The object of the [Fourteenth] amendment was undoubtedly to enforce the absolute equality of the two races before the law, but . . . it could not have been intended to abolish distinctions based upon color, or to enforce social, as distinguished from political equality, or a commingling of the two races upon terms unsatisfactory to either. Laws permitting, and even requiring, their separation in places where they are liable to be brought into contact do not necessarily imply the inferiority of either race to the other . . . We cannot say that a law which authorizes or even requires the separation of the two races in public conveyances is unreasonable."

—Justice Henry Billings Brown writing for the Court in *Plessy* v. *Ferguson*

▲ *A conductor orders Homer Plessy to leave the white section of the railroad car.*

PRIMARY SOURCE

Other Views

"Our constitution is color-blind, and neither knows nor tolerates classes among citizens. In respect of civil rights, all citizens are equal before the law. . . . We boast of the freedom enjoyed by our people above all other peoples. But it is difficult to reconcile that boast with a state of law which, practically, puts the brand of servitude and degradation upon a large class of our fellow citizens—our equals before the law. The thin disguise of 'equal' accommodations for passengers in railroad coaches will not mislead any one, nor atone for the wrong this day done."

—Justice John Marshall Harlan writing the lone dissent in *Plessy* v. *Ferguson*

DBQ Document-Based Questions

1. **Analyzing Primary Sources** What distinction does Justice Brown make about the rights of citizens?

2. **Identifying Points of View** How does Justice Harlan regard the Court's decision?

3. **Evaluating** What rights do you think all states should extend to their citizens? Why do you think so?

The African American Response

MAIN Idea Some African American leaders focused on practical vocational education, while others pushed for full civil rights and educational opportunities.

HISTORY AND YOU How would your life be different without an education? Read on to learn why some early civil rights leaders focused on access to education.

The African American community responded to violence and discrimination in several ways. Ida B. Wells used the press to end violence, while Mary Church Terrell worked in education. Booker T. Washington proposed that African Americans focus on achieving economic goals, rather than political goals. W. E. B. Du Bois argued African Americans should demand equal rights immediately.

Ida B. Wells

In the late 1800s, mob violence increased in the United States, particularly in the South. Between 1890 and 1899, there was an average of 187 **lynchings**—hangings without proper court proceedings—each year.

In 1892 **Ida B. Wells,** a fiery young African American woman from Tennessee, launched a fearless crusade against lynching. After a mob drove Wells out of town, she settled in Chicago and continued her campaign. In 1895 she published a book denouncing mob violence and demanding "a fair trial by law for those accused of crime, and punishment by law after honest conviction." Although Congress rejected an anti-lynching bill, the number of lynchings decreased significantly in the 1900s, due in great part to the efforts of activists such as Wells.

Mary Church Terrell

One lynching victim had been a close friend of Mary Church Terrell, a college-educated woman who'd been born during the Civil War. This death, and President Harrison's refusal to publicly condemn lynching, started Terrell on her lifelong battle against lynching, racism, and sexism.

Terrell also worked with woman suffrage workers such as Jane Addams and Susan B. Anthony. In addition to helping found the

---

People IN HISTORY

Booker T. Washington
1856–1915

Born into slavery on a plantation in Virginia, Booker T. Washington spent his childhood working in the coal mines of West Virginia. At age 16, he heard about the Hampton Institute in Virginia, where African Americans could learn farming or a trade. With little money in his pockets, Washington left home and walked nearly 500 miles to the school, where he was able to work as a janitor to pay for his education.

When the Alabama legislature decided in 1881 to begin a school to train black leaders, Washington was recommended for the job. He borrowed money to buy an abandoned plantation; the students built classrooms, a chapel, and dormitories. The Tuskegee Institute became well-known, attracting prominent scholars such as George Washington Carver to the faculty.

Washington used his influence with white businessmen to raise money for the school. He encouraged the development of black-owned businesses, and he organized the National Negro Business League in 1900. He was a nationally known spokesperson for the African American community and advised presidents William Howard Taft and Theodore Roosevelt on political appointments.
What were Booker T. Washington's most important achievements?

W. E. B. Du Bois
1868–1963

W. E. B. Du Bois was born in Massachusetts a few years after the end of the Civil War. After graduating from Fisk University, Du Bois earned a Ph.D. from Harvard. As a professor at Atlanta University, Du Bois focused his research on race relations in the United States.

The Souls of Black Folk, Du Bois's 1903 collection of essays, had a major impact on its readers. In them, Du Bois directly criticized Booker T. Washington for being too cautious and conservative on civil rights issues. Du Bois believed African Americans needed to insist upon equal treatment and voting rights. He also helped to found the Niagara Movement, the forerunner of the NAACP. In 1910 he began publishing *The Crisis,* the official magazine of the NAACP.

In his later years, Du Bois turned to socialism and became active in the peace movement. This led to political censure and the State Department's refusal to allow Du Bois to travel outside the country. When he was permitted to leave, he went to Ghana, where he became a citizen the year he died.
How did W. E. B. Du Bois's approach to civil rights differ from Washington's approach?

National Association of Colored Women and the National Association for the Advancement of Colored People, Terrell formed the Women Wage-Earners Association, which assisted African American nurses, waitresses, and domestic workers.

Terrell led a boycott against department stores in Washington, D.C., that refused to serve African Americans. In an address to the National American Women's Suffrage Association Terrell said, "With courage, born of success achieved in the past, with a keen sense of the responsibility which we shall continue to assume, we look forward to a future large with promise and hope. Seeking no favors because of our color, nor patronage because of our needs, we knock at the bar of justice, asking an equal chance."

Calls for Compromise

The most famous African American of the late nineteenth century was the influential educator **Booker T. Washington.** He proposed that African Americans concentrate on achieving economic goals rather than political ones. In 1895 Washington summed up his views in a speech before a mostly white audience in Atlanta. Known as the Atlanta Compromise, the speech urged African Americans to postpone the fight for civil rights and instead concentrate on preparing themselves educationally and vocationally for full equality:

PRIMARY SOURCE

"The wisest among my race understand that the agitation of questions of social equality is the extremest folly, and that the enjoyment of all the privileges that will come to us must be the result of severe and constant struggle rather than of artificial forcing. . . . It is important and right that all privileges of the law be ours, but it is vastly more important that we be prepared for the exercise of these privileges. The opportunity to earn a dollar in a factory just now is worth infinitely more than the opportunity to spend a dollar in an opera-house."

—adapted from *Up From Slavery*

Du Bois Rejects Compromise

The Atlanta Compromise speech provoked a strong challenge from **W. E. B. Du Bois,** the leader of a new generation of African American activists. In his 1903 book *The Souls of Black Folk,* Du Bois explained why he saw no advantage in giving up civil rights, even temporarily. He was particularly concerned with protecting and exercising voting rights. "Negroes must insist continually, in season and out of season," he wrote, "that voting is necessary to proper manhood, that color discrimination is barbarism." In the years that followed, many African Americans worked to win the vote and end discrimination. The struggle, however, would prove to be a long one.

Reading Check **Describing** How did Ida B. Wells try to stop the practice of lynching?

Section 5 REVIEW

Vocabulary

1. **Explain** the significance of: poll tax, segregation, Jim Crow laws, lynching, Ida B. Wells, Booker T. Washington, W. E. B. Du Bois.

Main Ideas

2. **Describing** Under what kind of conditions did many African Americans in the South live in after Reconstruction?

3. **Identifying** How did Southern states restrict African American voting in the 1890s?

4. **Organizing** Use a graphic organizer similar to the one below to list the responses of some prominent African Americans to racial discrimination.

African American	Response to Discrimination
Ida B. Wells	
Booker T. Washington	
W.E.B. Du Bois	

Critical Thinking

5. **Big Ideas** How did Booker T. Washington's answer to racial discrimination differ from that of W. E. B. Du Bois?

6. **Analyzing Visuals** Look at the cartoon on page 251. How does the cartoonist play into white fears?

Writing About History

7. **Expository Writing** Imagine that you are living in the 1890s. Write a letter to the editor of the local newspaper explaining your view of the Supreme Court ruling in *Plessy* v. *Ferguson.*

History ONLINE

Study Central™ To review this section, go to glencoe.com and click on Study Central.

Effects of Industrialization:

1. Immigration and Urbanization

- Rise of large factories greatly increases the demand for labor in the United States, encouraging immigrants to move to America in large numbers.

- The increase in industrial jobs encourages large numbers of Americans and immigrants to settle in cities.

- As cities grow large, pollution, crime, disease, and fire become serious problems.

- New industrial technology allows cities to grow even larger with the development of the skyscraper, the elevator, and the trolley car.

- Large urban areas change the nature of politics creating corrupt urban political "machines" such as Tammany Hall in New York.

▲ A crowded immigrant community in New York in the early 1900s

▲ Sharecroppers in the South were often trapped in poverty and debt.

Effects of Industrialization:

2. Farm Problems

- Industrialization and new technology increases farm production and creates the ability to ship farm products across the country.

- Farmers produce huge surpluses, driving down food prices, while a money shortage leads to high interest rates; farmers grow deeper in debt while income falls.

- High railroad rates in the West combine with high rents for tenant farmers in the South to create a crisis for farmers.

- Farmers form the Grange, the Alliance, and the Populist Party to help address their concerns.

Effects of Industrialization:

3. Changes in Culture

- Industrial society initially leads to a strong belief in individualism; Social Darwinism emerges as the idea that government should not interfere in society.

- Ongoing social problems caused by industrialization lead to Reform Darwinism and the emergence of reformers who want to use government to help solve society's problems and regulate the economy.

- New forms of realist and naturalist art and literature depict industrial life in serious and realistic ways.

▲ Settlement houses, such as Hull House (above), helped poor immigrants educate their children and adapt to life in the United States.

Reviewing Vocabulary

Directions: Choose the word or words that best completes the sentence.

1. _____ was a philosophy that believed wealthy Americans bore the responsibility of using their fortunes to further social progress.

A Social Darwinism

B Realism

C Gospel of Wealth

D Individualism

2. Immigrant children became knowledgeable about American culture at public schools—a process known as

A Americanization.

B nativism.

C Social Darwinism.

D individualism.

3. The rapid increase in the money supply without an increase in the amount of goods for sale caused _____, or the decline in the value of money.

A goldbugs

B silverites

C deflation

D inflation

4. The _____ was an informal political group that provided city services in return for votes and political power.

A party bosses

B political machine

C Populists

D Grange

5. The _____ was one method of segregation used in the South after the Civil War.

A cooperative

B poll tax

C tenement

D graft

Reviewing Main Ideas

Directions: Choose the best answers to the following questions.

Section 1 *(pp. 214–219)*

6. In the late nineteenth century, many labor unions opposed immigration, arguing that immigrants

A would work for higher wages.

B eased financial drains on social services.

C assimilated into American culture.

D would accept jobs as strikebreakers.

7. What was the major reason for Chinese immigration to the United States in the early nineteenth century?

A Many Chinese were escaping severe unemployment and famine.

B Many Chinese were escaping religious persecution.

C Many Chinese left to avoid required military service.

D Many Chinese left to escape the class system and move up the social ladder.

Section 2 *(pp. 222–227)*

8. Working class individuals residing in cities usually lived

A in the streetcar suburbs.

B in tenements.

C in fashionable downtown districts.

D away from the central city.

9. Who was the leader of Tammany Hall during the 1860s and 1870s?

A Thomas Nast

B James Pendergast

C William Tweed

D Thomas Pendergast

TEST-TAKING

Read the questions carefully. From the wording of each question, you can see that some have two or three concepts in common. Find the one choice that best answers each question.

Need Extra Help?									
If You Missed Questions . . .	1	2	3	4	5	6	7	8	9
Go to Page . . .	231–232	239	242–243	227	250	218	217	225	227

Section 3 *(pp. 230–239)*

10. The nineteenth-century philosophy of Social Darwinism maintained that

  A the government should have control over the means of production and the marketplace.

  B all social class distinctions in American society should be eliminated.

  C economic success comes to those who are the hardest working and most competent.

  D wealth and income should be more equally distributed.

11. The Interstate Commerce Act (1887) was designed to regulate interstate commerce by requiring

  A railroads to increase rebates to high-volume users.

  B railroads to charge higher rates for short hauls.

  C states to regulate interstate railroad traffic.

  D the federal government to regulate railroad rates.

Section 4 *(pp. 242–247)*

12. Populists supported federal ownership of railroads because they thought the government would

  A increase access to railroads in rural areas.

  B make the trains run on time.

  C manage the railroads in the public interest.

  D collect enough revenue to allow it to eliminate the graduated income tax.

Section 5 *(pp. 248–253)*

13. The ruling from *Plessy* v. *Ferguson* (1896) was based on the Supreme Court's interpretation of the

  A necessary and proper clause from Article I, Section 8 of the U.S. Constitution.

  B free speech provision of the First Amendment.

  C equal protection clause in the Fourteenth Amendment.

  D voting rights provision in the Fifteenth Amendment.

Critical Thinking

Directions: Choose the best answers to the following questions.

14. In 1890 the Populists formed the People's Party and supported

  A the subtreasury plan where farmers could store crops in warehouses to force prices up.

  B limited governmental regulations for the railroad companies.

  C the election of senators by state legislatures.

  D the free coinage of gold.

Base your answer to question 15 on the chart below and your knowledge of Chapter 6.

Farm Prices, 1870–1900

Source: *Historical Statistics of the United States.*

15. What happened to crop prices between 1870 and 1880?

  A The price of cotton increased as the price of wheat and corn decreased.

  B The price of wheat, corn, and cotton increased.

  C The price of cotton, wheat, and corn stayed the same following an initial increase.

  D The price of wheat significantly decreased as the price of cotton decreased steadily.

Need Extra Help?						
If You Missed Questions . . .	10	11	12	13	14	15
Go to Page . . .	230–231	234–235	245	250	245	243

16. Which of the following concepts is associated with the Gospel of Wealth?

  A survival of the fittest

  B laissez-faire

  C unregulated competition

  D philanthropy

Analyze the cartoon and answer the question that follows. Base your answer on the cartoon and on your knowledge of Chapter 6.

17. What does the cartoon express about immigrants coming to the United States?

  A Immigrants were welcome to the United States.

  B Immigrants had to pass by dogs to gain entry.

  C Anarchists, Socialists, and Communists were welcome.

  D Anarchists, Socialists, and Communists were not welcome.

18. The "new immigrants" to the United States between 1890 and 1915 came primarily from

  A southern and eastern Europe.

  B northern and western Europe.

  C East Asia.

  D Latin America.

Document-Based Questions

Directions: Analyze the document and answer the short-answer questions that follow the document.

Reaction in the United States to "old" immigration was generally more favorable than reaction to "new" immigration. The following excerpt from an 1882 editorial in the *Commercial and Financial Chronicle* addresses the effects of immigration on the nation:

> "In the very act of coming and traveling to reach his destination, he [the immigrant] adds . . . to the immediate prosperity and success of certain lines of business. Not only do the ocean steamers . . . get very large returns in carrying passengers of this description, but in forwarding them to the places chosen by the immigrants as their future homes the railroad companies also derive great benefit and their passenger traffic is greatly swelled. . . .
>
> . . . These immigrants not only produce largely, . . . but, having wants which they cannot supply themselves, create a demand for outside supplies. . . . Thus it is that the Eastern manufacturer finds the call upon him for his wares and goods growing more urgent all the time, thus the consumption of coal keeps on expanding notwithstanding the check to new railroad enterprises, and thus there is a more active and larger interchange of all commodities."
>
> —from *Commercial and Financial Chronicle*

19. According to the editorial, what effect did immigration have on the nation's economy?

20. How is the editorial's view of the effects of immigration different from that of the nativists?

Extended Response

21. Identify how events during the late 1800s and early 1900s, such as urbanization and immigration, influenced social change, and evaluate the extent to which reform movements were successful in bringing about change. Write an expository essay that supports your answer with relevant facts, examples, and details.

STOP

History ONLINE

For additional test practice, use Self-Check Quizzes—Chapter 6 at glencoe.com.

Need Extra Help?						
If You Missed Questions . . .	16	17	18	19	20	21
Go to Page . . .	231–232	230–233	214–215	257	218–219	236–239

Imperialism and Progressivism

1890–1920

Why It Matters

Between 1890 and 1920 two very important developments took place in American history. First, the United States began its rise to the global superpower it is today. Second, reformers began changing the government to solve problems caused by industrialism. Government became more involved in society than ever before.

U.S. warships battle the Spanish off the coast of Cuba, 1898.

Chapter 7

Becoming a World Power

1872–1917

SECTION 1 The Imperialist Vision

SECTION 2 The Spanish-American War

SECTION 3 New American Diplomacy

A tugboat tows the battleship USS Ohio through the recently completed Panama Canal, July 1915.

1878
- U.S. signs treaty with Samoa to use Pago Pago harbor

1893
- Americans overthrow Queen Liliuokalani of Hawaii

Hayes
1877–1881

Garfield
1881

Arthur
1881–1885

Cleveland
1885–1889

B. Harrison
1889–1893

Cleveland
1893–1897

U.S. PRESIDENTS

U.S. EVENTS
WORLD EVENTS

1872

1882

1892

1874
- Britain annexes Fiji Islands

1882
- Germany, Austria, and Italy form Triple Alliance

1889
- First Pan-American conference is held

1894
- Sino-Japanese War breaks out

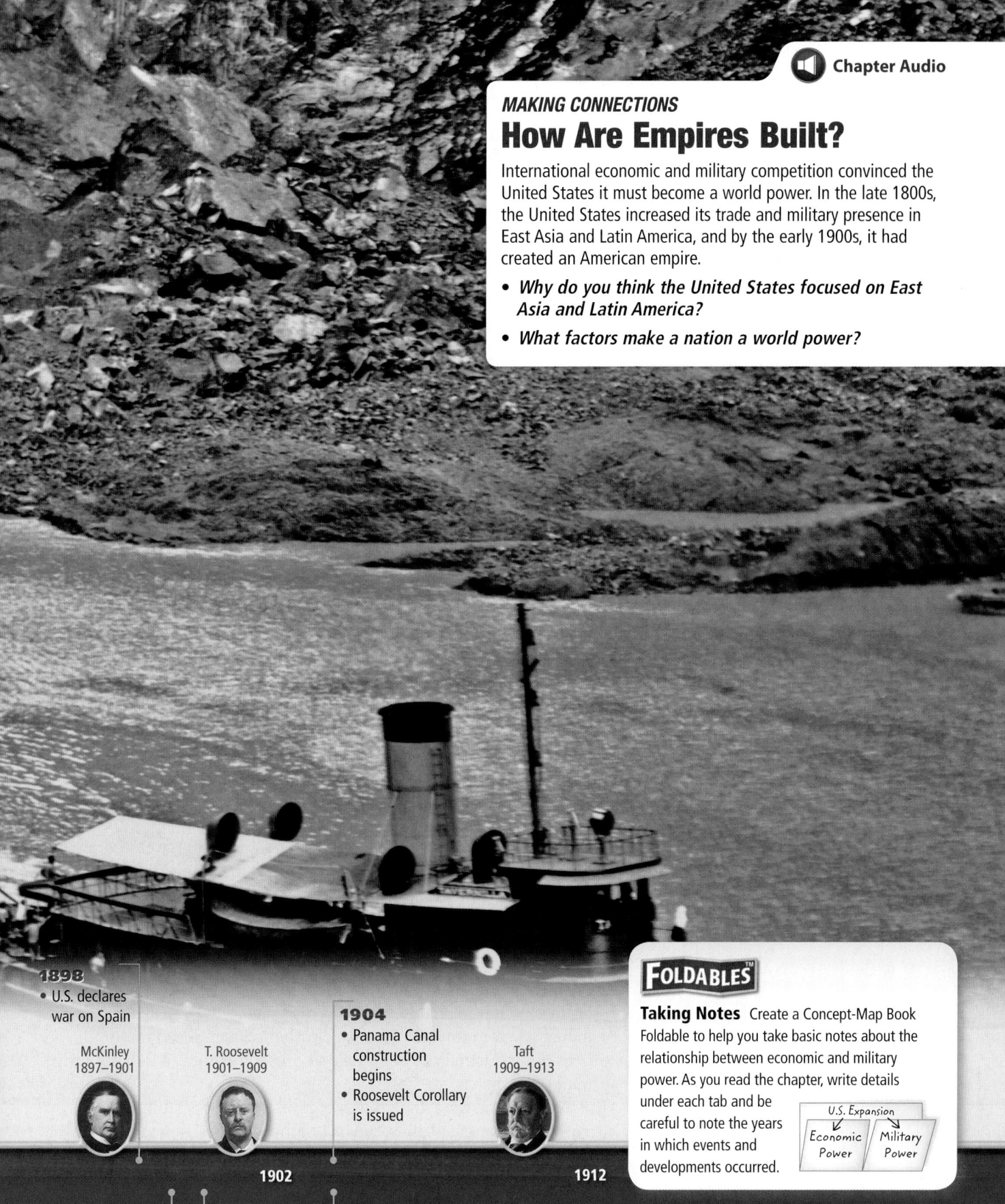
MAKING CONNECTIONS

How Are Empires Built?

International economic and military competition convinced the United States it must become a world power. In the late 1800s, the United States increased its trade and military presence in East Asia and Latin America, and by the early 1900s, it had created an American empire.

- *Why do you think the United States focused on East Asia and Latin America?*
- *What factors make a nation a world power?*

1898
- U.S. declares war on Spain

McKinley
1897–1901

T. Roosevelt
1901–1909

1904
- Panama Canal construction begins
- Roosevelt Corollary is issued

Taft
1909–1913

1902

1912

1899
- John Hay sends Open Door notes

1900
- Boxer Rebellion begins in China

1904
- Russo-Japanese War begins

FOLDABLES™

Taking Notes Create a Concept-Map Book Foldable to help you take basic notes about the relationship between economic and military power. As you read the chapter, write details under each tab and be careful to note the years in which events and developments occurred.

U.S. Expansion
Economic Power / *Military Power*

History 🖱 **ONLINE** Visit glencoe.com
and enter *QuickPass*™ code TAVMT5147c7 for Chapter 7 resources.

The Imperialist Vision

Guide to Reading

Big Ideas

Economics and Society In the late 1800s, many Americans wanted the United States to expand its military and economic power overseas.

Content Vocabulary

- imperialism *(p. 262)*
- protectorate *(p. 262)*

Academic Vocabulary

- expansion *(p. 263)*
- conference *(p. 267)*

People and Events to Identify

- Anglo-Saxonism *(p. 264)*
- Matthew C. Perry *(p. 265)*
- Queen Liliuokalani *(p. 266)*
- Pan-Americanism *(p. 267)*

Reading Strategy

Organizing As you read about the development of the United States as a world power, use the major headings of the section to create an outline similar to the one below.

> The Imperialist Vision
> I. Building Support for Imperialism
>   A.
>   B.
>   C.
> II.
>   A.
>   B.

During the late 1800s, the desire to find new markets, increase trade, and build a powerful navy caused the United States to become more involved in international affairs.

Building Support for Imperialism

MAIN Idea A desire for world markets and belief in the superiority of Anglo-Saxon culture led the United States to assert itself as a world power.

HISTORY AND YOU Do you remember what role George Washington thought the United States should play in world affairs? Read to learn why Americans' opinions changed in the 1880s.

In the years immediately following the Civil War, most Americans showed little interest in expanding their nation's territory outside the United States or increasing its international influence. Instead, they focused on reconstructing the South, building up the nation's industries, and settling the West. Beginning in the 1880s, however, economic and military competition from other nations, as well as a growing feeling of cultural superiority, convinced many Americans that the United States should become a world power.

A Desire for New Markets

Several European nations were already expanding overseas, a development known as the New Imperialism. **Imperialism** is the economic and political domination of a strong nation over weaker ones. Europeans expanded their power overseas for many reasons. Factories depended on raw materials from all over the world. No country had all of the resources its economy needed. In addition, by the late 1800s, most industrialized countries had placed high tariffs against each other. These tariffs were intended to protect a nation's industries from foreign competition. The tariffs reduced trade between industrialized countries, forcing companies to look for other markets overseas.

At the same time, the growth of investment opportunities in Western Europe had slowed. Most of the factories, railroads, and mines that Europe's economy needed had been built. Increasingly, Europeans began looking overseas for places to invest their capital. They started to invest in industries located in other countries, particularly in Africa and Asia.

To protect their investments, European nations began exerting control over those territories. Some areas became colonies. Many others became protectorates. In a **protectorate,** the imperial power

Causes of American Imperialism

American imperialism had three main causes:

1. The belief in the superiority of American culture
2. The belief that the nation needed a large navy for security, with bases overseas
3. The belief that the economy needed overseas markets

1. ANGLO-SAXONISM

"The work which the English race began when it colonized North America is destined to go on until every land . . . that is not already the seat of an old civilization shall become English in its language, in its religion, in political habits and traditions, and to a predominant extent in the blood of its people."
—John Fiske, quoted in *The Expansionists of 1898*

2. MILITARY BASES

". . . [T]he ships of war of the United States, in war, will be like land birds, unable to fly far from their own shores. To provide resting-places for them, where they can coal and repair, would be one of the first duties of a government proposing to itself the development of the power of the nation at sea."
—Alfred Thayer Mahan, *The Influence of Sea Power Upon History*

3. OVERSEAS MARKETS

"[W]e are raising more than we can consume, . . . making more than we can use. Therefore we must find new markets for our produce..."
—Albert Beveridge, quoted in *The Meaning of the Times and Other Speeches*

Exports and Imports, 1865–1900

Source: *Historical Statistics of the United States.*

DBQ Document-Based Questions

1. **Interpreting** Based on the quote above, how do you think Albert Beveridge would use the data shown in the graph to support his argument?
2. **Comparing** What is the difference between Fiske's support for expanding American power overseas and Mahan's support for establishing military bases overseas?

allowed the local rulers to stay in control and protected them against rebellions and invasion. In exchange, the local rulers usually had to accept advice from the Europeans on how to govern their countries.

The United States noticed the **expansion** of European power overseas. As the United States industrialized, many Americans took an interest in the new imperialism. Until the late 1800s, the United States had expanded by settling more territory in North America. Now, with settlers finally filling up the western frontier, many Americans concluded that the nation

needed new overseas markets to keep its economy strong.

A Feeling of Superiority

In addition to economic concerns, certain other key ideas convinced many Americans to encourage their nation's expansion overseas. Many supporters of Social Darwinism argued that nations competed with each other politically, economically, and militarily, and that only the strongest would survive. To them, this idea justified increasing American influence abroad.

Many Americans, such as the well-known writer and historian John Fiske, took this idea even further. Fiske argued that English-speaking nations had superior character, ideas, and systems of government.

Fiske's ideas, known as **Anglo-Saxonism,** were popular in Britain and the United States. Many Americans linked it with the idea of Manifest Destiny. They believed the nation's destiny had been to expand westward to the Pacific Ocean. Now they believed the United States was destined to expand overseas and spread its civilization to other people.

Another influential advocate of Anglo-Saxonism was Josiah Strong, a popular American minister in the late 1800s. Strong linked Anglo-Saxonism to Christian missionary ideas. His ideas influenced many Americans. "The Anglo-Saxon," Strong declared, "[is] divinely commissioned to be, in a peculiar sense, his brother's keeper." By linking missionary work with Anglo-Saxonism, Strong convinced many Americans to support an expansion of American power overseas.

Building a Modern Navy

As imperialism and Anglo-Saxonism gained support, the United States became increasingly assertive in foreign affairs. Three international crises illustrated this new approach. In 1888 the country risked war to prevent Germany from taking control of Samoa in the South Pacific. Three years later, when a mob in Chile attacked American sailors in the port of Valparaíso, the United States threatened to go to war unless Chile paid reparations. Then, in 1895, the United States backed Venezuela against Great Britain in a border dispute with British Guiana. After Britain rejected an American ultimatum, many newspapers and members of Congress called for war. All three crises were eventually resolved peacefully.

As Americans became increasingly willing to risk war to defend American interests overseas, support for building a large modern navy began to grow. Supporters argued that if the United States did not build up its navy and acquire bases overseas, European nations would shut it out of foreign markets.

Captain Alfred T. Mahan, an officer in the U.S. Navy who taught at the Naval War College, best expressed this argument. In 1890 Mahan published his lectures in a book called *The*

Influence of Sea Power upon History, 1660–1783. In this book Mahan pointed out that many prosperous peoples in the past, such as the British and Dutch, had built large fleets of merchant ships to trade with the world. He then suggested that a nation also needed a large navy to protect its merchant ships and to defend its right to trade with other countries.

Mahan's book became a best-seller, helping to build public support for a big navy. Two powerful senators, Henry Cabot Lodge and Albert J. Beveridge, pushed for constructing a new navy. In the executive branch, Benjamin Tracy, secretary of the navy under President Harrison, and John D. Long, secretary of the navy under President McKinley, strongly supported Mahan's ideas.

By the 1890s, several different ideas had come together in the United States. Business leaders wanted new markets overseas. Anglo-Saxonism had convinced many Americans of their destiny to dominate the world. Growing European imperialism threatened America's security. Combined with Mahan's theories, these ideas convinced Congress to authorize the construction of a large, modern navy.

✓ Reading Check **Summarizing** How did Americans' opinions about overseas expansion change in the late 1800s?

PRIMARY SOURCE
Perry Arrives in Japan

In 1853 Japan was a closed society. Its rulers had deliberately ended contact with the outside world, permitting only a small amount of trade with the Dutch and the Chinese. They were largely unaware of the changes the industrial revolution had brought to Europe and the United States. Perry's black steamships, belching smoke, and moving without any visible sails, were something the Japanese had never seen before.

The Japanese had cannons and guns, but Perry's ships carried 65 large cannons—a staggering number that represented immense power—and a direct threat to Japan's many coastal castles and towns. Perry's arrival carried different meanings for people living in the two countries, as shown in the two images to the right—one from Japan and the other from the United States.

American Expansion in the Pacific

MAIN Idea The desire for new markets led to trade with Japan and the annexation of Hawaii.

HISTORY AND YOU What products do you use that are made in Japan? Read how the United States and Japan first became trading partners.

From the earliest days of the Republic, Americans had expanded their nation by moving westward. When Americans began looking overseas for new markets in the 1800s, therefore, they naturally tended to look toward the Pacific. Even before imperialist ideas became popular, American businesses had begun sending ships to trade in East Asia.

Perry Opens Japan

Many American business leaders believed that the United States would benefit from trade with Japan, as well as with China. Japan's rulers, however, who believed that excessive contact with the West would destroy their culture, allowed only the Chinese and Dutch to trade with their nation. In 1852, after receiving several petitions from Congress, President Millard Fillmore decided to force Japan to trade with the United States. He ordered Commodore **Matthew C. Perry** to take a naval expedition to Japan to negotiate a trade treaty.

On July 8, 1853, four American warships under Perry's command entered Edo Bay (today known as Tokyo Bay). The display of American technology and firepower impressed the Japanese, who had never before seen steamships. Realizing that they could not resist modern Western technology and weapons, the Japanese agreed to sign the Treaty of Kanagawa. In addition to granting the United States permission to trade at two ports in Japan, the treaty called for peace between the two countries; promised help for any American ships and sailors shipwrecked off the Japanese coast; and gave American ships permission to buy supplies such as wood, water, food, and coal in the Japanese ports.

The American decision forcing Japan to open trade played an important role in Japanese history. Japanese leaders concluded that it was time to remake their society. They adopted Western technology and launched their own industrial revolution. By the 1890s, the Japanese had a powerful navy and had begun building their own empire in Asia.

▶ American painter James Evans entitled his work "Commodore Perry Carrying the Gospel of God to the Heathen, 1853."

▼ This Japanese color print depicts one artist's perspective of Perry's "black ships" that arrived in Japan in 1853.

Analyzing VISUALS

1. **Comparing** What elements did both the American and Japanese artists depict the same way? Which were different?

2. **Making Inferences** What impression of the Americans does the Japanese image convey? What is the American painting communicating about Perry's mission?

People IN HISTORY

Queen Liliuokalani
1838–1917

Queen Liliuokalani was the last ruling monarch of the Hawaiian Islands. A group of white sugar planters had forced her predecessor to accept a new constitution that minimized the power of the monarchy, gave voting rights to Americans and Europeans, and denied voting rights to most Hawaiians and all Asians.

As queen, Liliuokalani was determined to regain royal power and reduce the power of foreigners. On January 14, 1893, she issued a new constitution, which restored the power of the monarchy and the rights of the Hawaiian people. In response, a group of planters led by Sanford B. Dole launched a revolt. Under protest, Liliuokalani surrendered her throne on January 17. After supporters led a revolt in an attempt to restore her to power in 1895, Liliuokalani was placed under house arrest for several months. After her release, she lived out her days in Washington Place in Honolulu.

Why did sugar planters lead a revolt against Queen Liliuokalani?

▲ *Sanford B. Dole gives Hawaii, represented as the bride, to Uncle Sam.*

Annexing Hawaii

For an example of American views on annexing Hawaii read "President Harrison on Hawaiian Annexation" on page R51 in **Documents in American History.**

As trade with Asia grew during the 1800s, Americans began seeking ports where they could refuel and resupply while crossing the Pacific Ocean. Pago Pago, in the Samoan Islands, had one of the finest harbors in the South Pacific. In 1878 the United States negotiated permission to open a base there.

More important was Hawaii. Whaling ships and merchant vessels crossing the Pacific often stopped there to rest and to take on supplies. In 1820 missionaries from New England arrived in Hawaii. American settlers found that sugarcane grew well in Hawaii's climate and soil. By the mid-1800s, businessmen had established many plantations on the islands.

A severe recession struck Hawaii in 1872. Three years later, worried that the economic crisis might force the Hawaiians to turn to the British or French for help, the United States signed a treaty exempting Hawaiian sugar from tariffs. When the treaty came up for renewal several years later, the Senate insisted that Hawaii grant the United States exclusive rights to a naval base at Pearl Harbor.

The treaty led to a boom in the Hawaiian sugar industry and wealth for the planters. In 1887 prominent planters pressured the Hawaiian king into accepting a constitution that limited the king's authority. As tensions mounted between the planters and Hawaiians, Congress passed a new tariff in 1890 that gave subsidies to sugar producers in the United States. The subsidies made Hawaiian sugar more expensive than American sugar. Unable to sell much sugar, planters concluded that the only way to increase sales was to have Hawaii become part of the United States.

In 1891 **Queen Liliuokalani** ascended the Hawaiian throne. Liliuokalani disliked the influence that American settlers had gained in Hawaii. In January 1893 she tried to impose a new constitution reasserting her authority as ruler of Hawaii. In response, a group of planters tried to overthrow the monarchy. Supported by the marines from the *USS Boston*, they forced the queen to step down. Then they set up a provisional government and asked the United States to annex Hawaii.

President Cleveland strongly opposed imperialism. He withdrew the annexation treaty from the Senate and tried to return Liliuokalani to power. Hawaii's new leaders refused to restore the queen and decided to wait until Cleveland left office. Five years later, the United States annexed Hawaii.

✓ **Reading Check** **Explaining** How did the search for new markets push the United States to become a world power?

Diplomacy in Latin America

MAIN Idea The United States worked to increase trade with Latin America.

HISTORY AND YOU What products have you used that come from Latin America? Read to learn how the United States tried to expand its trade relations with Latin America.

The Pacific was not the only region where the United States sought to increase its influence in the 1800s. It also focused on Latin America. Although the United States bought raw materials from this region, Latin Americans bought most of their manufactured goods from Europe. American business leaders and government officials wanted to increase the sale of American products to the region. They also wanted the Europeans to understand that the United States was the dominant power in the region.

James G. Blaine, who served as secretary of state in three administrations in the 1880s, led early efforts to expand American influence in Latin America. "What we want," Blaine explained, "are the markets of these neighbors of ours that lie to the south of us. . . . With these markets secured new life would be given to our manufacturers, the product of the western farmer would be in demand, the reasons for and inducements to strikers, with all their attendant evils, would cease." Blaine proposed that the United States invite the Latin American nations to a **conference** in Washington, D.C. The conference would discuss ways in which the American nations could work together to support peace and to increase trade. The idea that the United States and Latin America should work together came to be called **Pan-Americanism.**

On October 2, 1889, Washington, D.C., hosted the first modern Pan-American conference, which all Latin American nations except the Dominican Republic attended. Blaine had two goals for the conference. First, he wanted to create a customs union between Latin America and the United States. He also wanted to create a system for American nations to work out their disputes peacefully.

A customs union would require all of the American nations to reduce their tariffs against each other and to treat each other equally in trade. Blaine hoped that a customs union would turn the Latin Americans away from European products and toward American products. He also hoped that a common system for settling disputes would keep the Europeans from meddling in American affairs.

Although the warm reception they received in the United States impressed the Latin American delegates to the conference, they rejected both of Blaine's ideas. They did agree, however, to create the Commercial Bureau of the American Republics, an organization that worked to promote cooperation among the nations of the Western Hemisphere. In 1902 the name was changed to the International Bureau of the American Republics. This organization was later known as the Pan-American Union and is today called the Organization of American States (OAS).

✔ **Reading Check** **Summarizing** How did Secretary of State Blaine attempt to increase American influence in Latin America?

Section 1 REVIEW

Vocabulary

1. **Explain** the significance of: imperialism, protectorate, Anglo-Saxonism, Matthew C. Perry, Queen Liliuokalani, Pan-Americanism.

Main Ideas

2. **Listing** Use a graphic organizer to list the factors that led the United States to adopt an imperialist policy in the 1890s.

Factors Leading to U.S. Imperialist Policy

3. **Describing** Why and how did the Americans force the Japanese to trade with the United States?

4. **Explaining** Why did Secretary of State James G. Blaine convene the Pan-American conference in 1889?

Critical Thinking

5. **Big Ideas** Do you think the United States should have supported the planters in their attempt to overthrow Queen Liliuokalani of Hawaii? Why or why not?

6. **Evaluating** How did trade with the United States change Japanese society?

7. **Analyzing Visuals** Study the two images of Perry's ship on page 265. How do the artists' perspectives vary? Do you think the artists show any bias in their representations? Why or why not?

Writing About History

8. **Persuasive Writing** Imagine that you are living in the United States in the 1890s. Write a letter to the president persuading him to support or oppose an imperialist policy for the United States.

History ONLINE

Study Central™ To review this section, go to glencoe.com and click on Study Central.

The Spanish-American War

Guide to Reading

Big Ideas
Trade, War, and Migration The United States defeated Spain in a war, acquired new overseas territories, and became an imperial power.

Content Vocabulary
• yellow journalism *(p. 269)*
• autonomy *(p. 270)*
• jingoism *(p. 271)*

Academic Vocabulary
• intervene *(p. 270)*
• volunteer *(p. 272)*

People and Events to Identify
• José Martí *(p. 268)*
• William Randolph Hearst *(p. 269)*
• Joseph Pulitzer *(p. 269)*
• Emilio Aguinaldo *(p. 272)*
• Platt Amendment *(p. 274)*
• Foraker Act *(p. 275)*

Reading Strategy
Organizing As you read about the Spanish-American War, complete a graphic organizer like the one below by listing the circumstances that contributed to war with Spain.

D uring the Spanish-American War, the United States defeated Spanish troops in Cuba and the Philippines. Afterward, the United States annexed the Philippines and became an imperial power.

The Coming of War

MAIN Idea In support of the Cuban rebellion and in retaliation for the loss of the USS *Maine*, the United States declared war on Spain.

HISTORY AND YOU Do you remember what led the American colonists to declare their independence from Britain? Read about another colony that fought for independence from a colonial ruler.

By 1898 Cuba and Puerto Rico were Spain's last remaining colonies in the Western Hemisphere. Cubans had periodically revolted against Spanish rule, and many Americans regarded the Spanish as tyrants. Ultimately, the United States issued a declaration of war. Although the fighting lasted only a few months, the "splendid little war," as Secretary of State John Hay described it, dramatically altered the position of the United States on the world stage.

The Cuban Rebellion Begins

Cuba was one of Spain's oldest colonies in the Americas. Its sugar-cane plantations generated considerable wealth for Spain and produced nearly one-third of the world's sugar in the mid-1800s. Until Spain abolished slavery in 1886, about one-third of the Cuban population was enslaved and forced to work for wealthy landowners on the plantations.

In 1868 Cuban rebels declared independence and launched a guerrilla war against Spanish authorities. Lacking internal support, the rebellion collapsed a decade later. Many Cuban rebels then fled to the United States. One of the exiled leaders was **José Martí,** a writer and poet. While living in New York City in the 1880s, Martí brought together Cuban exile groups living in the United States. The groups raised funds, purchased weapons, and trained troops in preparation for an invasion of Cuba.

By the early 1890s, the United States and Cuba had become closely linked economically. Cuba exported much of its sugar to the United States, and Americans had invested approximately $50 million in Cuba's sugar plantations, mines, and railroads. These economic ties created a crisis in 1894, when the United States imposed a new tariff on sugar that devastated Cuba's economy. With Cuba in financial

Causes of the Spanish-American War

The Spanish-American War had four main causes:

1. The Cuban Rebellion against Spain
2. American desire to protect its investments in Cuba
3. Yellow journalism that intensified public anger at Spain
4. The explosion of the USS *Maine*

CUBANS REBEL AGAINST SPAIN

◀ Spanish oppression of the Cuban people triggered a rebellion that earned the sympathy of many Americans, some of whom began providing arms and money to the rebels.

U.S. Investment in Cuba, 1897

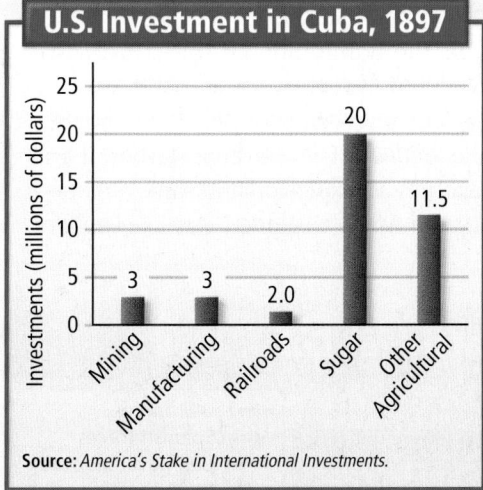

Source: *America's Stake in International Investments.*

◀ With $30 to $50 million invested in Cuba and nearly $100 million in annual trade, American business leaders wanted Spain out of Cuba and an end to the rebellion.

YELLOW JOURNALISM

▲ Dramatic and emotional stories in newspapers owned by Hearst and Pulitzer described Spanish atrocities in Cuba and enraged the American people, some of whom began to call for war.

THE *MAINE* EXPLODES, 1898

▲ President McKinley sent the battleship Maine to Cuba to help Americans evacuate. When the ship exploded, an enraged nation blamed Spain, and "Remember the Maine!" became the battle cry for war.

Analyzing VISUALS

1. **Interpreting** What do you think contributed to American sympathy with the Cubans?
2. **Identifying Central Issues** What role did economics play in the lead-up to war with Spain?

---

distress, Martí's followers launched a new rebellion in February 1895. Although Martí died during the fighting, the rebels seized control of eastern Cuba, declared independence, and formally established the Republic of Cuba in September 1895.

America Supports Cuba

When the uprising in Cuba began, President Grover Cleveland declared the United States neutral. Outside the White House, however, many people openly supported the rebels. Some citizens compared the Cubans' struggle to the American Revolution. A few sympathetic Americans even began smuggling guns from Florida to the Cuban rebels.

What caused most Americans to support the rebels were the stories of Spanish atrocities reported in two of the nation's major newspapers, the *New York Journal* and the *New York World*. The *Journal*, owned by **William Randolph Hearst,** and *The World*, owned by **Joseph Pulitzer,** competed with each other to increase their circulation. The *Journal* reported outrageous stories of the Spanish feeding Cuban prisoners to sharks and dogs. Not to be outdone, *The World* described Cuba as a place with "blood on the roadsides, blood in the fields, blood on the doorsteps, blood, blood, blood!" This kind of sensationalist reporting, in which writers often exaggerated and even made up stories to attract readers, became known as **yellow journalism.**

Although the press invented sensational stories, Cubans indeed suffered horribly. The Spanish sent nearly 200,000 troops to the island to put down the rebellion and appointed General Valeriano Weyler as governor. Weyler's harsh policies quickly earned him the nickname "El Carnicero" ("The Butcher").

The Cuban rebels staged hit-and-run raids, burned plantations and sugar mills, tore up railroad tracks, and attacked supply depots. Knowing that many American businesses had investments in Cuba, the rebels hoped that the destruction of American property would lead to American intervention in the war.

To prevent Cuban villagers from helping the rebels, Weyler herded hundreds of thousands of rural men, women, and children into "reconcentration camps," where tens of thousands died of starvation and disease. News reports of these camps enraged Americans.

Calls for War

In 1897 Republican William McKinley became president of the United States. The new president did not want to **intervene** in the war, believing it would cost too many lives and hurt the economy. In September 1897, he asked the Spanish if the United States could help negotiate an end to the conflict. He made it clear that if the war did not end soon, the United States might have to intervene.

Spain removed Weyler from power and offered the Cubans **autonomy**—the right to their own government—but only if Cuba remained part of the Spanish empire. The Cuban rebels refused to negotiate.

Spain's concessions enraged many Spanish loyalists in Cuba. In January 1898, the loyalists rioted in Havana. Worried that Americans in Cuba might be attacked, McKinley sent the battleship USS *Maine* to Havana in case the Americans had to be evacuated.

On February 9, 1898, the *New York Journal* printed a letter intercepted by a Cuban agent. Written by Enrique Dupuy de Lôme, the Spanish ambassador to the United States, the letter described McKinley as "weak and a bidder for the admiration of the crowd." The nation erupted in fury over the insult.

Then, on the evening of February 15, 1898, while the *Maine* sat in Havana Harbor, it was ripped apart by an explosion and sank. No one is sure why the *Maine* exploded. An investigation

The Spanish-American War

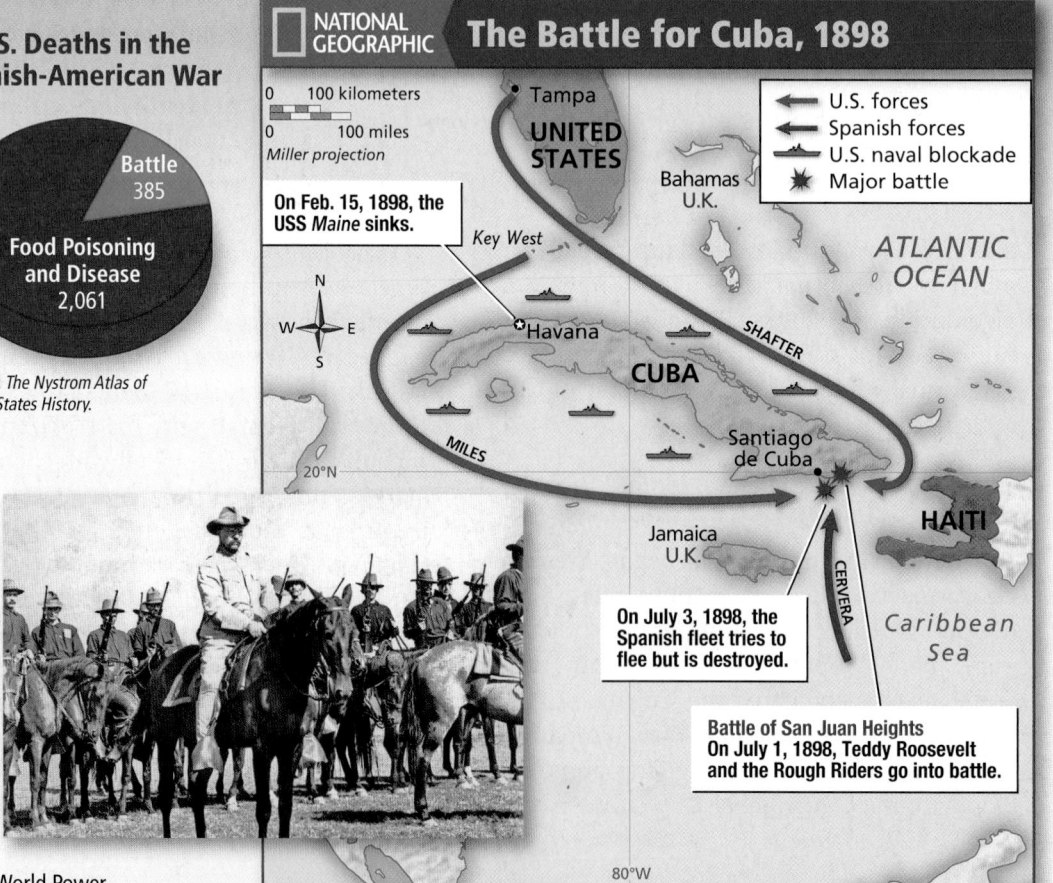

When the United States declared war on Spain, the U.S. Army had approximately 25,000 soldiers. Spain had roughly 200,000 in Cuba alone. To expand its forces, the government called into service soldiers from the state militias and also enlisted some 180,000 volunteers in the army. Among those volunteers was the First Volunteer Cavalry, nicknamed the Rough Riders, under the command of Colonels Leonard Wood and Theodore Roosevelt.

U.S. Deaths in the Spanish-American War

Battle 385

Food Poisoning and Disease 2,061

Source: *The Nystrom Atlas of United States History.*

NATIONAL GEOGRAPHIC **The Battle for Cuba, 1898**

0   100 kilometers
0   100 miles
Miller projection

On Feb. 15, 1898, the USS *Maine* sinks.

UNITED STATES

Tampa

Key West

Havana

CUBA

Bahamas U.K.

ATLANTIC OCEAN

SHAFTER

Santiago de Cuba

Jamaica U.K.

CERVERA

HAITI

Caribbean Sea

20°N

MILES

80°W

- ← U.S. forces
- ← Spanish forces
- U.S. naval blockade
- ★ Major battle

On July 3, 1898, the Spanish fleet tries to flee but is destroyed.

Battle of San Juan Heights On July 1, 1898, Teddy Roosevelt and the Rough Riders go into battle.

in the 1970s suggested that the spontaneous combustion of a coal bunker aboard the ship caused the explosion, but a study in the 1990s concluded that a mine could have done the damage. In 1898, however, many Americans believed it was an act of sabotage by Spanish agents. "Remember the *Maine!*" became the rallying cry for those demanding a declaration of war against Spain.

In response, Congress authorized McKinley to spend $50 million for war preparations. McKinley faced tremendous pressure to go to war. Within the Republican Party, **jingoism**—aggressive nationalism—was very strong. Many Democrats also demanded war, and Republicans feared that if McKinley did not go to war, the Democrats would win the elections in 1900. Finally, on April 11, 1898, McKinley asked Congress to authorize the use of force.

On April 19, Congress proclaimed Cuba independent, demanded that Spain withdraw from the island, and authorized the president to use armed force if necessary. In response, on April 24, Spain declared war on the United States. For the first time in 50 years, the United States was at war with another nation.

Reading Check **Examining** What conditions led to the Cuban rebellion in 1895?

A War on Two Fronts

MAIN Idea The United States fought and defeated Spain in both the Caribbean and the Pacific.

HISTORY AND YOU Have you ever had to plan a trip or an event? Read to learn about the problems American troops encountered in the war of 1898.

The United States Navy was ready for war with Spain. The navy's North Atlantic Squadron blockaded Cuba, and Commodore George Dewey, commander of the American naval squadron based in Hong Kong, was ordered to attack the Spanish fleet based in the Philippines. The Philippines was a Spanish colony, and American naval planners wanted to prevent the Spanish fleet based there from sailing east to attack the United States.

The Battle of Manila Bay

A short time after midnight, on May 1, 1898, Dewey's squadron entered Manila Bay in the Philippines. As dawn broke, four American ships in the squadron opened fire and rapidly destroyed all eight of the severely outgunned Spanish warships.

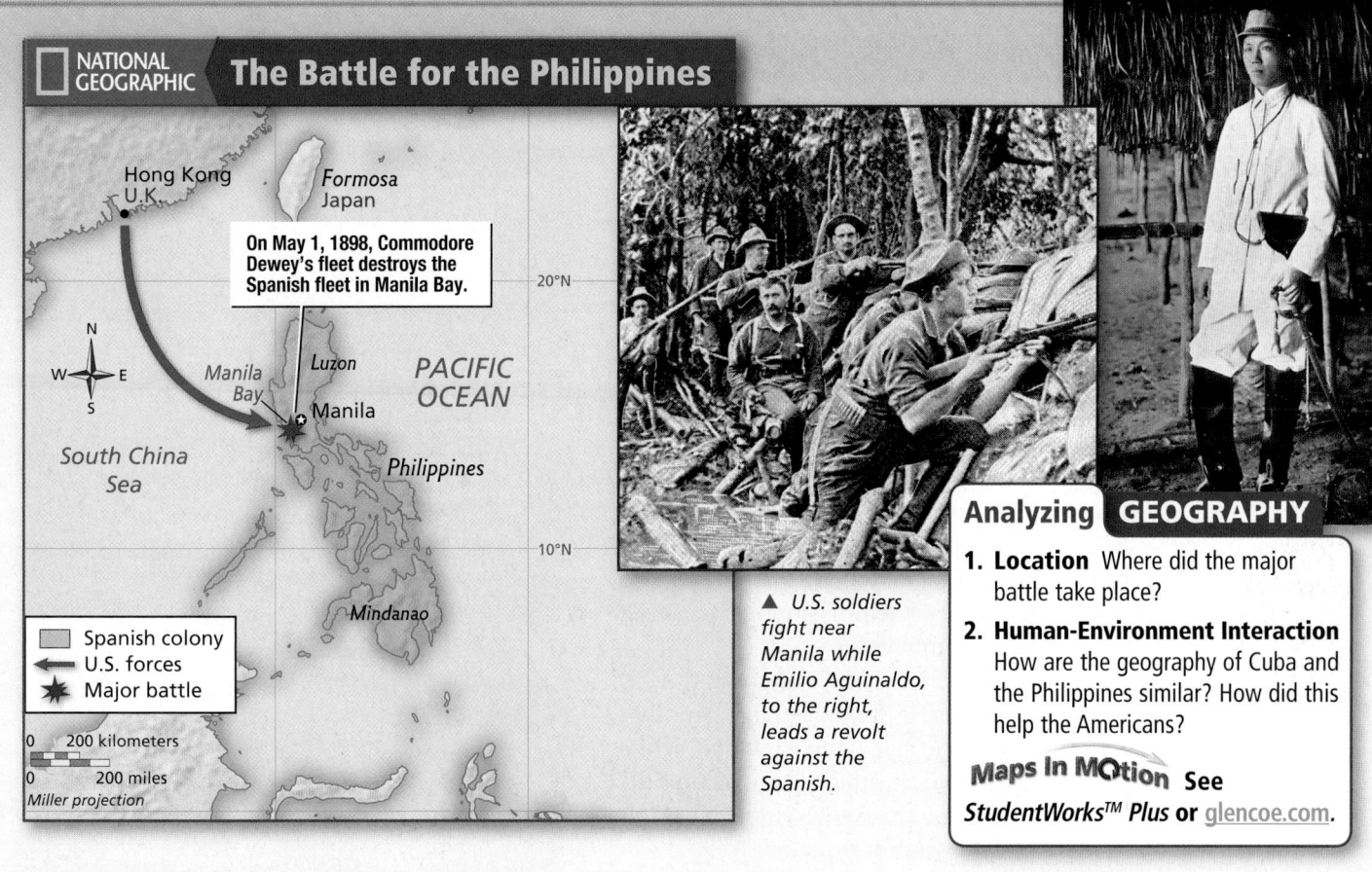

NATIONAL GEOGRAPHIC **The Battle for the Philippines**

On May 1, 1898, Commodore Dewey's fleet destroys the Spanish fleet in Manila Bay.

Hong Kong U.K. — Formosa Japan — PACIFIC OCEAN — Manila Bay — Luzon — Manila — South China Sea — Philippines — Mindanao — 20°N — 10°N

- Spanish colony
- U.S. forces
- Major battle

0   200 kilometers
0   200 miles
Miller projection

▲ U.S. soldiers fight near Manila while Emilio Aguinaldo, to the right, leads a revolt against the Spanish.

Analyzing GEOGRAPHY

1. **Location** Where did the major battle take place?

2. **Human-Environment Interaction** How are the geography of Cuba and the Philippines similar? How did this help the Americans?

Maps In Motion See *StudentWorks™ Plus* or glencoe.com.

Dewey's quick victory took McKinley and his advisers by surprise. The army was not yet ready to send troops to help Dewey. Hastily, the army assembled 20,000 troops to sail from San Francisco to the Philippines. On the way, the Americans also seized the island of Guam, another Spanish possession in the Pacific.

While waiting for the American troops to arrive, Dewey contacted **Emilio Aguinaldo,** a Filipino revolutionary leader who had staged an unsuccessful uprising against the Spanish in 1896. Aguinaldo quickly launched a new rebellion against the Spanish. While the rebels took control of most of the islands, American troops seized the Philippine capital of Manila.

American Forces in Cuba

The Spanish in Cuba were not prepared for war. Tropical diseases and months of fighting rebels had weakened their soldiers. Their warships were old and their crews poorly trained. Both sides knew that the war would ultimately be decided at sea. If the United States could defeat the Spanish fleet, Spain would not be able to supply its troops in Cuba. Eventually, they would have to surrender.

The United States Army was not prepared for war either. Although there were many **volunteers,** the army lacked the resources to train and equip them. In many training camps, conditions were so unsanitary that epidemics broke out, and hundreds died—far more than would be killed in battle with the Spanish.

Finally, on June 22, 1898, a force of about 17,000 troops landed east of the city of Santiago, Cuba. The Spanish fleet, well-protected by powerful shore-based guns, occupied Santiago Harbor. American military planners wanted to capture those guns to drive the Spanish fleet out of the harbor and into battle with the American fleet waiting nearby.

Among the American troops advancing toward Santiago was a volunteer cavalry unit from the American west. They were a flamboyant mix of cowboys, miners, and law officers known as the "Rough Riders." Colonel Leonard Wood commanded them. Theodore Roosevelt was second in command.

On July 1, American troops attacked the village of El Caney northeast of Santiago. Another force attacked the San Juan Heights. While one group of soldiers attacked San Juan Hill, the Rough Riders attacked Kettle Hill. After seizing Kettle Hill, Roosevelt and his men assisted in the capture of San Juan Hill.

The all-black 9th and 10th Cavalry Regiments accompanied the Rough Riders up Kettle Hill. Roughly one-fourth of the American troops fighting in Cuba were African Americans, four of whom received the Medal of Honor for their bravery during the war.

The Spanish commander in Santiago panicked after the American victories at El Caney and the San Juan Heights and ordered the Spanish fleet in the harbor to flee. As they exited the harbor on July 3, American warships attacked them, sinking or beaching every Spanish vessel. Two weeks later, the Spanish troops in Santiago surrendered. Soon afterwards, American troops occupied the nearby Spanish colony of Puerto Rico as well.

✔Reading Check **Comparing** How prepared was the U.S. Army as compared to the U.S. Navy to fight a war against Spain?

Debates IN HISTORY

Should the United States Annex the Philippines?

In the Treaty of Paris of 1898, Spain ceded control of the Philippine Islands to the United States. Americans were divided over whether the United States should give the Filipinos their independence or become an imperial power by annexing the Philippines. Supporters of annexation argued the United States would benefit economically and the Filipinos would benefit from exposure to American values and principles. Opponents, however, considered it hypocritical for the United States, with its own colonial past, to become an imperial nation.

An American Empire

MAIN Idea In defeating Spain, the United States acquired an overseas empire.

HISTORY AND YOU Do you think Puerto Rico should become the 51st state? Read how Puerto Rico became an American territory.

As American and Spanish leaders met to discuss the terms for a peace treaty, Americans debated what to do about their newly acquired lands. Cuba would receive its independence as promised, and Spain had agreed to the U.S. annexation of Guam and Puerto Rico. The big question was what to do with the Philippines. The United States faced a difficult choice—remain true to its republican ideals or become an imperial power that ruled a foreign country without the consent of its people. The issue sparked an intense political debate.

The Debate Over Annexation

Many people who supported annexing the Philippines emphasized the economic and military benefits of taking the islands. They would provide the United States with another Pacific naval base, a stopover on the way to China, and a large market for American goods.

Other supporters believed America had a duty to help "less civilized" peoples. "Surely this Spanish war has not been a grab for empire," commented a New England minister, "but a heroic effort [to] free the oppressed and to teach the millions of ignorant, debased human beings thus freed how to live."

Not all Americans supported annexation. Anti-imperialists included William Jennings Bryan, industrialist Andrew Carnegie, social worker Jane Addams, writer Samuel Clemens (Mark Twain), and Samuel Gompers, leader of the American Federation of Labor.

YES

Albert J. Beveridge
United States Senator

PRIMARY SOURCE

"The Opposition tells us that we ought not to govern a people without their consent. I answer, The rule of liberty that all just government derives its authority from the consent of the governed, applies only to those who are capable of self-government. We govern the Indians without their consent, we govern our territories without their consent, we govern our children without their consent. . . . Would not the people of the Philippines prefer the just, humane, civilizing government of this Republic to the savage, bloody rule of pillage and extortion from which we have rescued them?"

—from *The Meaning of the Times*

NO

William Jennings Bryan
Presidential Candidate

PRIMARY SOURCE

"It is not necessary to own people in order to trade with them. We carry on trade today with every part of the world, and our commerce has expanded more rapidly than the commerce of any European empire. . . . A harbor and coaling station in the Philippines would answer every trade and military necessity and such a concession could have been secured at any time without difficulty.

. . . Imperialism finds no warrant in the Bible. The command 'Go ye into all the world and preach the gospel to every creature' has no Gatling gun attachment. . . ."

—from *Speeches of William Jennings Bryan*

DBQ Document-Based Questions

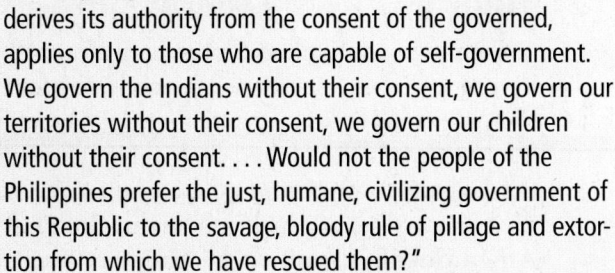

1. **Making Inferences** According to Albert Beveridge, why is annexation of the Philippines an honorable decision?

2. **Recognizing Bias** What does Beveridge think of the people of the Philippines?

3. **Analyzing** What are William Jennings Bryan's two main criticisms of imperialism?

4. **Drawing Conclusions** After studying both sides of the issue, who do you think was right? Explain.

The Debate Over Empire

▲ President McKinley (the waiter) prepares to take Uncle Sam's order. The menu posted on the wall shows three regions of choice: the Cuba steak, the Porto [Puerto] Rico pig; and the Philippines and Sandwich Islands (Hawaii) in the Pacific.

▲ President McKinley raises the American flag over the Philippines while William Jennings Bryan tries to chop it down.

Analyzing VISUALS

1. **Identifying Central Issues** Based on the cartoon on the left, what do you think McKinley is trying to accomplish? What about Bryan?

2. **Making Inferences** What does the cartoon on the right suggest that Uncle Sam is going to do? On what basis do you infer that?

History ONLINE Student Web Activity Visit glencoe.com and complete the activity on American imperialism.

Andrew Carnegie argued that the cost of an empire far outweighed the economic benefits it provided. Gompers worried that competition from cheap Filipino labor would drive down American wages. Addams, Clemens, and others believed imperialism violated American principles. Despite the objections of the anti-imperialists, President McKinley ultimately decided to annex the islands. He later explained his reasoning as follows:

PRIMARY SOURCE

"And one night late it came to me this way. . . (1) that we could not give them back to Spain— that would be cowardly and dishonorable; (2) that we could not turn them over to France or Germany. . . that would be bad for business and discreditable; (3) that we could not leave them to themselves—they were unfit for self-government. . . and (4) that there was nothing left for us to do but to take them all, and to educate the Filipinos, and uplift and civilize and Christianize them."

—*A Diplomatic History of the American People*

On December 10, 1898, the United States and Spain signed the Treaty of Paris. Under the treaty, Cuba became an independent nation, and the United States acquired Puerto Rico and Guam and agreed to pay Spain $20 million for the Philippines. After an intense debate, the Senate ratified the treaty in February 1899. The United States had become an imperial power.

The Platt Amendment

Although the United States had promised to grant Cuba its independence, President McKinley took steps to ensure that Cuba would remain tied to the United States. He allowed the Cubans to prepare a new constitution for their country but attached conditions. The **Platt Amendment,** submitted by Senator Orville Platt, specified the following: (1) Cuba could not make any treaty with another nation that would weaken its independence; (2) Cuba had to allow the United States to buy or lease naval stations in Cuba; (3) Cuba's debts had to be kept low to prevent foreign countries from landing troops to enforce payment; and (4) the United States would have the right to intervene to protect Cuban independence and keep order.

Reluctantly, the Cubans added the amendment to their constitution. The Platt Amendment, which effectively made Cuba an American protectorate, remained in effect until its repeal in 1934.

Governing Puerto Rico

Another pressing question was how to govern Puerto Rico. In 1900 Congress passed the **Foraker Act,** establishing a civil government for the island. The law provided for an elected legislature, but also called for a governor and executive council, to be appointed by the president, who held final authority. Supreme Court rulings subsequently held that Puerto Ricans were not American citizens and so did not possess the constitutional rights of citizens.

Congress gradually allowed Puerto Ricans greater self-government. In 1917 it granted Puerto Ricans American citizenship. Thirty years later, islanders were allowed to elect their own governor. At this time a debate began over whether Puerto Rico should become a state, become independent, or continue as a self-governing commonwealth of the United States. This debate over Puerto Rico's status continues today.

Rebellion in the Philippines

The United States quickly learned that controlling its new empire would not be easy. Emilio Aguinaldo called the American decision to annex his homeland a "violent and aggressive seizure" and ordered his troops to attack American soldiers. The Philippine-American war, or Philippine Insurrection as it was referred to at the time, lasted for more than three years. Approximately 126,000 American soldiers were sent to the Philippines to fight the insurgency. More than 4,300 American soldiers died, either from combat or disease, as did an estimated 50,000–200,000 Filipinos.

To fight the Filipino guerrillas, the United States military adopted many of the same policies that America had condemned Spain for using in Cuba. Reconcentration camps were established to separate Filipino guerrillas from civilians. Consequently, thousands of people died from disease and starvation, just as they had in Cuba.

While American troops fought the guerrillas, the first U.S. civilian governor of the islands, William Howard Taft, tried to win over the Filipinos by improving education, transportation, and health care. Railroads and bridges were built. Public schools were set up, and new health-care policies virtually eliminated diseases such as cholera and smallpox. These reforms slowly reduced Filipino hostility.

In March 1901, American troops captured Aguinaldo. A month later, Aguinaldo called on the guerrillas to surrender. On July 4, 1902, the United States declared the war over. Eventually the United States allowed the Filipinos a greater role in governing their own country. By the mid-1930s, they were permitted to elect their own congress and president. Finally, in 1946, the United States granted independence to the Philippines.

Reading Check **Explaining** What were the arguments for and against establishing an American empire?

Section 2 REVIEW

Vocabulary
1. **Explain** the significance of: José Martí, William Randolph Hearst, Joseph Pulitzer, yellow journalism, autonomy, jingoism, Emilio Aguinaldo, Platt Amendment, Foraker Act.

Main Ideas
2. **Explaining** Why did many Americans blame Spain for the explosion of the USS *Maine*?

3. **Identifying** How did the U.S. fight the Spanish-American War on two fronts?

4. **Categorizing** Complete the table by summarizing the effects of the United States annexing lands obtained after the Spanish-American War.

Lands Annexed	Effects

Critical Thinking
5. **Big Ideas** How has the government of Puerto Rico changed since the Foraker Act was passed in 1900?

6. **Evaluating** Why did Filipinos feel betrayed by the U.S. government after the Spanish-American War?

7. **Analyzing Visuals** Study the circle graph on page 270. What caused the most casualties during the war? Explain.

Writing About History
8. **Descriptive Writing** Imagine that you are a Filipino living during the time of the U.S. annexation of the Philippine Islands. Write a journal entry in which you describe your feelings about American control of the islands.

History ONLINE
Study Central™ To review this section, go to glencoe.com and click on Study Central.

New American Diplomacy

Guide to Reading

Big Ideas

Trade, War, and Migration Under President Theodore Roosevelt, the United States increased its power on the world stage.

Content Vocabulary
- sphere of influence *(p. 276)*
- Open Door policy *(p. 277)*
- dollar diplomacy *(p. 281)*
- guerrilla *(p. 283)*

Academic Vocabulary
- access *(p. 277)*
- tension *(p. 280)*

People and Events to Identify
- Boxer Rebellion *(p. 278)*
- Hay-Pauncefote Treaty *(p. 280)*
- Roosevelt Corollary *(p. 280)*
- Victoriano Huerta *(p. 283)*
- Pancho Villa *(p. 283)*

Reading Strategy

Organizing As you read about American diplomacy complete a graphic organizer by listing the reasons the U.S. wanted a canal through Central America.

Reasons to Build Canal

Succeeding President McKinley, President Theodore Roosevelt mediated disputes in Asia and Latin America and acquired the Panama Canal Zone. Presidents Taft and Wilson worked to increase American trade and influence in Latin America.

American Diplomacy in Asia

MAIN Idea The United States pursued an Open Door policy to allow all nations access to China's markets.

HISTORY AND YOU Do you remember reading about a trade agreement with Japan in the 1850s? Read to learn about America's efforts to keep trade open with China in the 1900s.

In 1899 the United States was a major power in Asia, with naval bases all across the Pacific. Operating from those bases, the United States Navy—by then the third-largest navy in the world—could exert American power anywhere in East Asia. The nation's primary interest in Asia, however, was not conquest but commerce. Between 1895 and 1900, American exports to China increased fourfold. Although China bought only about two percent of American exports, the vast Chinese markets excited American business leaders, especially those in the textile, oil, and steel industries.

The Open Door Policy

In 1894 war erupted between China and Japan over Korea, which at that time was a client state of China. Western observers were astonished when Japan easily defeated China's massive military. In the peace treaty, China recognized the independence of Korea and gave Japan territory in Manchuria. The war showed that Japan had mastered Western technology and industry. It also demonstrated that China was far weaker than anyone had thought.

The Russians were concerned about Japan's rising power. They did not want Japan to acquire the territory in Manchuria, because it bordered Russia. Backed by France and Germany, Russia forced Japan to return the Manchurian territory it had acquired. Then, in 1898, Russia demanded China lease the territory to Russia instead.

Leasing a territory meant that it would still belong to China, even though a foreign government would maintain overall control. Soon Germany, France, and Britain demanded "leaseholds" in China as well. Each "leasehold" became the center of a country's **sphere of influence,** an area where a foreign nation controlled economic development such as railroad construction and mining.

In June 1900, Boxer rebels attack foreign compounds in Peking and Tientsin.

What Was the Open Door Policy?

1. Within its sphere of influence, each power agreed not to interfere with any existing business interests or port treaties of other powers.

2. Existing Chinese tariffs would remain unchanged in all spheres of influence and would be collected by the Chinese government.

3. Within each sphere of influence, harbor fees and railroad charges would be the same for all countries, giving no special rates to the countries whose businesses owned and operated the harbors and railroads.

▲ Secretary of State John Hay

Empire / Sphere of Influence
- British
- French
- Japanese
- Russian
- German

0   1000 kilometers
0   1000 miles
Miller projection

Analyzing VISUALS

1. **Interpreting** What do you think Britain was attempting with the locations of their spheres of influence?

2. **Analyzing** Based on the map, which country do you believe had the most influence?

▲ International soldiers pose in Tianjin after rescuing their besieged delegations during the Boxer Rebellion. The American is second from left.

Politicians and businessmen in the United States worried about these events. President McKinley and Secretary of State John Hay both supported what they called an **Open Door policy,** in which all countries would be allowed to trade with China. In 1899 Hay sent notes to countries with leaseholds in China asking them not to discriminate against other nations wanting to do business in their sphere of influence. Each of the nations responded by saying they accepted the Open Door policy but would not act on it unless all of the others agreed. Once Hay had received assurances from all of the nations with leaseholds, he declared that the United States expected the other powers to uphold the policy.

The Boxer Rebellion

While foreign countries debated **access** to China's market, secret Chinese societies organized to fight foreign control. Westerners referred to one such group, the Society of Harmonious Fists, as the Boxers. In 1900 the group decided to destroy both the "foreign devils" and their Chinese Christian converts, whom they believed were corrupting Chinese society.

In what became known as the **Boxer Rebellion,** the Boxers, supported by some Chinese troops, besieged foreign embassies in Peking and Tientsin, killing more than 200 foreigners and taking others prisoner. After the German ambassador to China was killed, eight nations—Germany, Austria-Hungary, Britain, France, Italy, Japan, Russia, and the United States—decided to intervene. A large international force of nearly 50,000 troops, including 3,400 Americans, landed in China to rescue the foreigners and smash the rebellion.

During the crisis, Secretary of State John Hay worked with British diplomats to persuade the other powers not to partition China. In a second set of Open Door notes, Hay convinced the participating powers to accept compensation from China for damages caused by the rebellion. After some discussion, the powers agreed not to break up China into European-controlled colonies. The United States retained access to China's lucrative trade in tea, spices, and silk and maintained an increasingly larger market for its own goods.

Reading Check **Explaining** What was the purpose of the Open Door policy?

Roosevelt's Diplomacy

MAIN Idea Presidents Roosevelt and Taft continued to support a policy of expanding United States influence in foreign countries.

HISTORY AND YOU Do you know of a country that is trying to expand its influence today? Read to find out about expansion of United States influence in the early 1900s.

The election of 1900 once again pitted President McKinley against William Jennings Bryan. Bryan, an anti-imperialist, attacked the Republicans for their support of imperialism in Asia. McKinley, who chose war hero Theodore Roosevelt as his running mate, focused on the country's increased prosperity and ran on the slogan "Four Years More of the Full Dinner Pail." He won the election by a wide margin.

On September 6, 1901, while visiting Buffalo, New York, President McKinley was attacked by Leon Czolgosz, an anarchist who opposed all forms of government. Czolgosz fired two shots and hit the president. A few days later, McKinley died from his wounds. Theodore Roosevelt took over the presidency.

PAST & PRESENT

The Great White Fleet

In 1907 President Theodore Roosevelt sent 16 new battleships on a voyage around the world to showcase the nation's ability to project power to any place in the world. Painted white, the ships became known as the "Great White Fleet." The tour made a stop in Japan to demonstrate that the United States would uphold its interests in Asia. The visit did not help ease the growing tensions between the United States and Japan.

The use of naval power to send a diplomatic message continues today. Just as the battleship symbolized naval power in 1900, so too today does the aircraft carrier symbolize the power and global reach of the United States Navy. In March 1996, for example, a strike force led by the aircraft carrier *Kitty Hawk* was sent to the Taiwan Straits. This show of force came after China tested missiles in the area. The carrier sent the message to China that the United States would protect Taiwan from aggression.

1907

Great White Fleet

▲ *The Great White Fleet gets underway in December 1907.*

◄ *The Great White Fleet circumnavigated the globe.*

Theodore Roosevelt, just 42 years old at the time, was the youngest person ever to become president. Republican leaders had asked him to run for vice president because his charisma and status as a war hero would win votes, but they had hoped the relatively powerless position of vice president would keep him from causing political problems. Now they cringed at the thought of him in the White House. Ohio Republican senator Mark Hanna exclaimed, "Now look, that . . . cowboy is president of the United States!"

Roosevelt favored increasing American power on the world stage. He warned Americans not to become "an assemblage of well-to-do hucksters who care nothing for what happens beyond." Roosevelt also accepted some of Anglo-Saxonism's ideas. He believed that the United States had a duty to shape the "less civilized" corners of the earth.

Balancing Power in East Asia

As president, Theodore Roosevelt supported the Open Door policy in China and worked to prevent any single nation from monopolizing trade there. This concern prompted Roosevelt to help negotiate an end to the war between Japan and Russia that had broken out in 1905. At a peace conference in Portsmouth, New Hampshire, Roosevelt convinced the Russians to recognize Japan's territorial gains and persuaded the Japanese to stop fighting and to seek no further territory. For his efforts in ending the war, Roosevelt won the Nobel Peace Prize in 1906.

In the years after the peace treaty, relations between the United States and Japan grew steadily worse. As the two nations vied for greater influence in Asia, they held each other in check through a series of agreements. They pledged to respect each other's territorial possessions, to uphold the Open Door policy, and to support China's independence.

The Panama Canal

Theodore Roosevelt believed in a strong global military presence. He insisted that displaying American power to the world would make nations think twice about fighting, and thus promote peace. He often expressed this belief with a West African saying, "Speak softly and carry a big stick."

2003

▼ *The aircraft carrier USS* Kitty Hawk *leaves Yokosuka Naval Base in Japan en route to monitor North Korea.*

MAKING CONNECTIONS

1. **Comparing** In what ways are the missions of the Great White Fleet and a modern carrier force similar?

2. **Making Generalizations** Do you think a large navy is a useful tool in diplomacy? Explain your answer. What problems can it cause? What benefits does it bring?

Roosevelt's "big stick" policy was perhaps most evident in the Caribbean. There the world witnessed one of the most dramatic acts of his presidency—the acquisition and construction of the Panama Canal. Roosevelt and others believed that having a canal through Central America was vital to American power in the world. A canal would save time and money for both commercial and military shipping.

Acquiring the Canal Zone As early as 1850, the United States and Great Britain had agreed not to build a canal without the other's participation. In 1901 the United States and Great Britain signed the **Hay-Pauncefote Treaty,** which gave the United States the exclusive right to build any proposed canal through Central America.

A French company had begun digging a canal through Panama in 1881. By 1889, however, it abandoned its efforts because of bankruptcy and terrible losses from disease among the workers. The company was reorganized in 1894, but it hoped only to sell its rights to dig the canal.

The United States had long considered two possible canal sites, one through Nicaragua and one through Panama. The French company eased this choice by offering to sell its rights and property in Panama to the United States.

In 1903 Panama was Colombia's most northern province. Secretary of State Hay offered Colombia $10 million and a yearly rent of $250,000 for the right to construct the canal and to control a narrow strip of land on either side of it. Considering the price too low and afraid of losing control of Panama, the Colombian government refused the offer.

Panama Revolts Some Panamanians feared losing the commercial benefits of the canal. Panama had opposed Colombian rule since the mid-1800s, and the canal issue added to the **tension.** In addition, the French company remained concerned that the United States would build the canal in Nicaragua instead. The French company's agent, Philippe Bunau-Varilla, and Panamanian officials decided that the only way to ensure the canal would be built was to make their own deal with the United States. Bunau-Varilla arranged for a small army to stage an uprising in Panama.

Meanwhile, to prevent Colombian interference, President Roosevelt ordered U.S. warships to the area.

On November 3, 1903, with ten U.S. warships looming offshore, Bunau-Varilla's forces revolted. Within a few days, the United States recognized Panama's independence, and the two nations soon signed a treaty allowing the canal to be built.

Protesters in the United States and throughout Latin America condemned Roosevelt's actions as unjustifiable aggression. The president countered that he had advanced "the needs of collective civilization" by building a canal that shortened the distance between the Atlantic and the Pacific by about 8,000 nautical miles (14,816 km).

The Roosevelt Corollary

By the early 1900s, American officials had become very concerned about the size of the debts Latin American nations owed to European banks. In 1902, after Venezuela defaulted on its debts, Great Britain, Germany, and Italy blockaded Venezuelan ports. The crisis was resolved peacefully after the United States intervened and put pressure on both sides to reach an agreement.

To address the problem, Roosevelt gave an address to Congress in which he declared what came to be known as the **Roosevelt Corollary** to the Monroe Doctrine. The corollary stated that the United States would intervene in Latin American affairs when necessary to maintain economic and political stability in the Western Hemisphere:

PRIMARY SOURCE

"Chronic wrongdoing . . . may, in America, as elsewhere, ultimately require intervention by some civilized nation, and in the Western Hemisphere the adherence of the United States to the Monroe Doctrine may force the United States, however reluctantly, in flagrant cases of such wrongdoing or impotence, to the exercise of an international police power."

—quoted in *The Growth of the United States*

The goal of the Roosevelt Corollary was to prevent European powers from using the debt problems of Latin America to justify intervening in the region. The United States first applied the Roosevelt Corollary in the

1916: U.S. forces enter Mexico to capture Pancho Villa and end raids on U.S. towns

UNITED STATES

ATLANTIC OCEAN

1915–1934: Marines deployed to put down revolt and limit French and German influence

1906–1922: U.S. repeatedly intervenes in Cuba to prevent revolution and protect U.S. interests

1905: Marines land to enforce tariff collections and debt payments

MEXICO

Gulf of Mexico

Bahamas Br.

1914: U.S. troops occupy Veracruz to force Huerta from power

Havana

CUBA

1916–1924: U.S. troops occupy the country to maintain order

Mexico City · Veracruz

Guantanamo

HAITI DOM. REP.

Puerto Rico Virgin Is. Antigua Br.

British Honduras Br.

1903: U.S. leases base at Guantanamo, Cuba

Caribbean Sea

Guadeloupe Fr.
Dominica Br.
Martinique Fr. St. Lucia Br.

GUATEMALA HONDURAS

EL SALVADOR NICARAGUA

Barbados Br.

Grenada Br.

Trinidad Br.

1909: U.S. troops support rebels and force regime change

COSTA RICA

PANAMA

1903: U.S. supports Panama's independence; work begins on Panama Canal

1912–1933: U.S. troops put down revolts and enforce tariff collection

1906: U.S. troops intervene to stop war with Guatemala

PACIFIC OCEAN

0 400 kilometers
0 400 miles
Miller projection

U.S. Investments Central America, 1911

Haiti and Dominican Republic	7.5	
Cuba	220	
Costa Rica	7	
Guatemala	20	
Honduras	3	
Nicaragua	2.5	
Panama	5	
El Salvador	2.5	

Investments (millions of dollars): 250, 200, 150, 100, 50, 0

Source: *America's Stake in International Investments.*

Analyzing VISUALS

1. **Analyzing** Based on the map, what are the main reasons the United States intervened in Latin American states?

2. **Inferring** Where did the United States invest the most money in Latin America? Why do you think this happened?

Dominican Republic, which had fallen behind on its debt payments to European nations. In 1905 the United States assumed the responsibility of collecting customs tariffs in the Dominican Republic, using the United States Marine Corps as its agent.

Dollar Diplomacy

Latin American nations resented the growing American influence in the region, but Roosevelt's successor, William Howard Taft, continued his policies. Taft placed much less emphasis on military force and more on helping Latin American industry. He believed that if American business leaders supported Latin American development, everyone would benefit. American businesses would increase their trade and profits, and countries in Latin America would rise out of poverty and social disorder. Taft's policy came to be called **dollar diplomacy.**

Administration officials also worked hard to replace European loans with loans from American banks. The goal of this policy was to give the Europeans fewer reasons to intervene in Latin American affairs. During Taft's administration, American bankers took over debts that Honduras owed to Britain and took control of Haiti's national bank.

Although Taft described his brand of diplomacy as "substituting dollars for bullets," in Nicaragua he used both. American bankers began making loans to Nicaragua to support its shaky government in 1911. The following year, civil unrest forced the Nicaraguan president to appeal for greater assistance. American marines entered the country, replaced the collector of customs with an American agent, and formed a committee of two Americans and one Nicaraguan to control the customs commissions. American troops stayed to support both the government and customs until 1925.

✔ **Reading Check** **Summarizing** What was Roosevelt's view of the role of the United States in the world and how did he implement it?

POLITICAL CARTOONS PRIMARY SOURCE
Wilson and Mexico

▲ *President Wilson (who had a Ph.D.) is shown teaching Venezuela, Nicaragua, and Mexico that revolution for personal gain is wrong, while Mexico is shown hiding a note labeled "How to create a revolution."*

Analyzing VISUALS

1. **Analyzing** In what ways is the cartoon making fun of President Wilson?

2. **Inferring** What is the cartoon implying about Mexico?

Woodrow Wilson's Diplomacy in Mexico

MAIN Idea Wilson believed in "moral diplomacy" and tried to encourage democracy in Latin America.

HISTORY AND YOU Can you think of a country today that is going through a long civil war? Read how the United States became involved in the Mexican Revolution.

"It would be the irony of fate," remarked Woodrow Wilson just before he was inaugurated in 1913, "if my administration had to deal chiefly with foreign affairs." Wilson had written books on state government, Congress, and George Washington, as well as a five-volume history of the nation. His experience and interest were in domestic policy. He was a university professor before entering politics. He also was a committed progressive. However, foreign affairs did absorb much of Wilson's time and energy as president.

Wilson opposed imperialism and resolved to "strike a new note in international affairs" and see that "sheer honesty and even unselfishness . . . should prevail over nationalistic self-seeking in American foreign policy." He also believed that democracy was essential to a nation's stability and prosperity. To ensure a world free of revolution and war, the United States should promote democracy. During Wilson's presidency, however, other forces frustrated his hope to lead the world by moral example. In fact, Wilson's first international crisis was awaiting him when he took office.

The Mexican Revolution

For more than 30 years, Porfirio Díaz ruled Mexico as a dictator. During his reign, Mexico became much more industrialized, but foreign investors owned and financed the new railroads and factories that were built. Most Mexican citizens remained poor and landless. In 1911 widespread discontent erupted into revolution.

Francisco Madero, a reformer who appeared to support democracy, constitutional government, and land reform, led the revolution. Madero, however, proved to be an unskilled administrator. Worried about Madero's plans for land reform, conservative forces plotted against him. In February 1913, General **Victoriano Huerta** seized power; Madero was murdered, presumably on Huerta's orders.

Huerta's brutality repulsed Wilson, who refused to recognize the new government. Instead, Wilson announced a new policy. Groups that seized power in Latin America would have to set up "a just government based upon law, not upon arbitrary or irregular force," in order to win American recognition. Wilson was convinced that, without the support of the United States, Huerta soon would be overthrown. Meanwhile, Wilson ordered the navy to intercept arms shipments to Huerta's government. He also permitted Americans to arm Huerta's opponents.

Wilson Sends Troops Into Mexico

In April 1914, American sailors visiting the city of Tampico were arrested after entering a restricted area. Although they were quickly released, their American commander demanded an apology. The Mexicans refused. Wilson saw the refusal as an opportunity to overthrow Huerta. He asked Congress to authorize the use of force, and shortly after Congress passed the resolution, he learned that a German ship was unloading weapons at the Mexican port of Veracruz. Wilson immediately ordered American warships to shell the Veracruz harbor and then sent marines to seize the city.

Although the president expected the Mexican people to welcome his action, anti-American riots broke out. Wilson then accepted international mediation to settle the dispute. Venustiano Carranza, whose forces had acquired arms from the United States, became Mexico's president.

Mexican forces opposed to Carranza were not appeased, and they conducted raids into the United States, hoping to force Wilson to intervene. In March 1916, **Pancho Villa** (VEE•yah) and a group of **guerrillas**—an armed band that uses surprise attacks and sabotage rather than open warfare—burned the town of Columbus, New Mexico, and killed 16 Americans. Wilson responded by sending 6,000 troops under General John J. Pershing across the border to find and capture Villa. The expedition dragged on with no success. Wilson's growing concern over the war raging in Europe finally caused him to recall Pershing's troops in 1917.

Wilson's Mexican policy damaged U.S. foreign relations. The British ridiculed the president's attempt to "shoot the Mexicans into self-government." Latin Americans regarded his "moral imperialism" as no improvement over Theodore Roosevelt's "big stick" diplomacy. In fact, Wilson followed Roosevelt's example in the Caribbean. In 1914 he negotiated exclusive rights for naval bases and a canal with Nicaragua. In 1915 he sent marines into Haiti to put down a rebellion. The marines remained there until 1934. In 1916 he sent troops into the Dominican Republic to preserve order and to set up a government he hoped would be more stable and democratic than the current regime.

Reading Check **Examining** Why did President Wilson intervene in Mexico?

Section 3 REVIEW

Vocabulary

1. **Explain** the significance of: sphere of influence, Open Door policy, Boxer Rebellion, Hay-Pauncefote Treaty, Roosevelt Corollary, dollar diplomacy, Victoriano Huerta, Pancho Villa, guerrilla.

Main Ideas

2. **Summarizing** Use a graphic organizer to list the results of the Open Door policy.

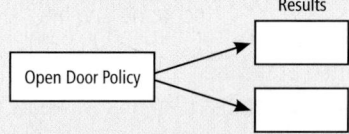

3. **Identifying** Why did President Theodore Roosevelt want to increase U.S. influence overseas?

4. **Specifying** How did Latin Americans view Wilson's "moral imperialism"?

Critical Thinking

5. **Big Ideas** Why did the United States decide to build a canal through Panama? How did Roosevelt assist Panama in becoming independent?

6. **Analyzing** How did the Roosevelt Corollary and dollar diplomacy affect U.S. relations with other countries?

7. **Analyzing Visuals** Study the map on page 281. To which countries did the U.S. send troops most often?

Writing About History

8. **Expository Writing** Imagine that you are a Mexican citizen during Wilson's presidency. Write a radio news broadcast expressing your feelings about American actions in Mexico.

History ONLINE

Study Central™ To review this section, go to **glencoe.com** and click on Study Central.

GEOGRAPHY & HISTORY

The Panama Canal

The idea of a canal connecting the Atlantic and Pacific oceans had been around for a long time before a French company began digging a canal across Panama in 1882. Disease and mud slides killed more than 20,000 workers before financial setbacks halted construction. In the early 1900s, the United States negotiated rights to build the canal with Colombia (Panama was part of Colombia at that time), but Colombia's Senate refused to ratify the treaty. With the support of the United States, Panama declared independence from Colombia and signed a treaty giving the United States a perpetual lease on the canal site in exchange for $10 million and annual payments. Construction resumed in 1904, and the canal was opened in 1914.

How Does Geography Affect the Canal?

Before the canal opened, ships sailing from New York to San Francisco traveled 12,600 miles (20,277 km) around the treacherous tip of South America. Afterwards, the trip was only 4,900 miles (7,886 km) and could be completed in less than half the time. Panama's geography made building the canal a challenge because the center of the country was much higher than sea level. Engineers built a series of lakes and concrete locks to raise and lower ships as they traveled the 51-mile canal. In each chamber of the locks, some 26 million gallons of water are pumped in or drained out in only 7 minutes to raise or lower a ship. At the artificial Gatun Lake, a dam generates electricity that powers the locks while gravity adjusts the water level.

Ships transit the canal more than 14,000 times each year, generating over $1 billion in tolls.

Analyzing GEOGRAPHY

1. **Human-Environment Interaction** How were the geographical features of Panama used or overcome in order to build the canal?

2. **Location** Why do you think the Panama site was ultimately selected for the canal?

Pacific Ocean

Panama City •

Atlantic
Ocean

Pacific
Ocean

**Miraflores
Locks**

**Pedro Miguel
Lock**

Lake Gatún

**Gatún
Locks**

Atlantic
Ocean

Cross Section of the Panama Canal

Gatún Dam created Lake Gatún—one of the largest artificial lakes in the world. A hydroelectric station at the dam generates power to run the pumps and gates of the locks.

Gatún Locks has 3 chambers for each direction. Together they raise ships at sea level up 86 feet to the level of Lake Gatún.

Lake Gatún

• Colón

▲ The Miraflores locks (above) are one of three sets of locks on the Panama Canal, and the first set for ships entering from the Pacific. After a ship enters a lock chamber, water is pumped in raising the ship up 27 feet to the next level. The ship then moves to the next chamber and is raised another 27 feet.

Causes of American Imperialism

- The United States wanted new markets for its products, particularly its manufactured goods.
- Many Americans believed it was the destiny of the United States to spread its power and civilization to other parts of the world.
- American leaders believed that having a powerful navy and controlling trade were key to being a world power.

▶ *USS* Texas *docks in port in 1896*

▲ *American soldiers in Cuba cheer the news that the city of Santiago, Cuba, has surrendered during the Spanish-American War, 1898.*

Effects of the Spanish-American War

- Cuba officially became an independent nation, although the United States claimed control over its foreign relations and exerted influence over internal politics.
- The United States acquired Puerto Rico, Guam, and the Philippines.
- Americans debated the morality and wisdom of becoming an imperial nation.
- The United States fought a three-year war to secure control over the Philippines.

The United States Acts As a World Power

- The United States used diplomatic means to establish the Open Door policy in China.
- President Theodore Roosevelt negotiated a peace agreement between Russia and Japan.
- The United States completed construction of the Panama Canal.
- The United States intervened, with the intent to provide stability, in the affairs of several Caribbean nations.
- The United States twice intervened in the lengthy Mexican Revolution.

▲ *After supporting a revolution in Panama, the United States begins construction of the Panama Canal.*

Reviewing Vocabulary

Directions: Choose the word or words that best complete the sentence.

1. The major European powers each had a(n) _____ in China.

 A protectorate

 B sphere of influence

 C Open Door policy

 D tariff policy

2. Taft's policies in Latin America were called

 A "big stick" diplomacy.

 B open door diplomacy.

 C missionary diplomacy.

 D dollar diplomacy.

3. Congress's authorization of $50 million for war preparation after the destruction of the U.S.S. *Maine* was an example of

 A Anglo-Saxonism.

 B imperialism.

 C jingoism.

 D dollar diplomacy.

4. Support for the war against Spain came in part from the _____ practiced by some newspapers.

 A anti-Americanism

 B objectivity

 C yellow journalism

 D sphere of influence

5. Local rulers are permitted to retain some power in a

 A protectorate.

 B monarchy.

 C republic.

 D dictatorship.

Reviewing Main Ideas

Directions: Choose the best answers to the following questions.

Section 1 *(pp. 262–267)*

6. Which of the following was a major contributor to the growth of American imperialism in the late 1800s?

 A curiosity about other cultures

 B need for spices from the East Indies

 C the end of the Civil War

 D desire for new markets for American goods

7. What effect did Commodore Matthew C. Perry have on Japan?

 A Japan began building an army.

 B Japan began to westernize.

 C Japan ended its trade with China.

 D Japan refused to negotiate with the United States.

8. A major goal of the Pan-American conference in 1889 was to

 A create a customs union for nations in the Americas.

 B end trade with the nations of Europe.

 C free Cuba from Spanish control.

 D decide on a route for a canal through Central America.

Section 2 *(pp. 268–275)*

9. The effect of yellow journalism on the Cuban rebellion was

 A unimportant to people in the United States.

 B helpful in changing McKinley's mind about going to war with Spain.

 C critical to raising public support for war against Spain.

 D harmful to American businesses in Cuba.

TEST-TAKING

Note that in some cases you are asked to choose the BEST answer. This means that in some instances there will be more than one possible answer. Be sure to read all the choices carefully before selecting your answer.

Need Extra Help?									
If You Missed Questions . . .	1	2	3	4	5	6	7	8	9
Go to Page . . .	276	281	271	269	262–263	262–264	265	267	269

10. Spanish resistance in Cuba ended with the surrender of

A San Juan Hill.

B Kettle Hill.

C Guam.

D Santiago.

11. What effect did the Platt Amendment have on Cuba?

A It made Cuba a virtual protectorate of the United States.

B It cut sugarcane production so Cuba could not compete with production in the United States.

C It guaranteed all the freedoms of the Bill of Rights to Cubans.

D It gave Cuba the right to allow European countries to buy or lease naval stations in Cuba.

Section 3 (pp. 276–283)

12. The purpose of the Open Door policy in China was to

A end the Boxer Rebellion.

B gain leaseholds.

C establish spheres of influence.

D ensure trading rights for all nations.

13. What was the Roosevelt Corollary to the Monroe Doctrine?

A It provided for the purchase of land to build a canal across Panama.

B It warned the nations of Europe not to impose high tariffs on goods from the Americas.

C It stated that the United States would intervene in Latin American affairs as needed for political and economic stability.

D It reinforced the policy of isolationism of the United States in world affairs.

Critical Thinking

Directions: Choose the best answers to the following questions.

Base your answers to questions 14 and 15 on the map below and your knowledge of Chapter 7.

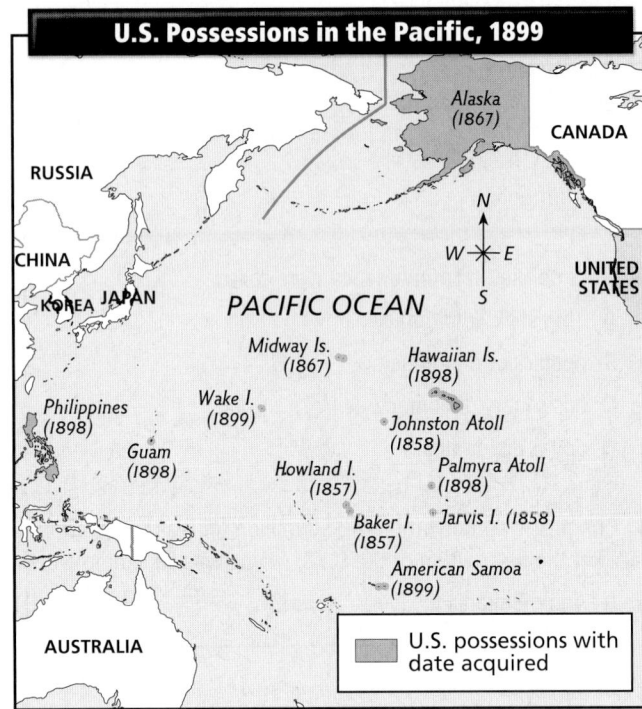

U.S. Possessions in the Pacific, 1899

14. Which of the following became a U.S. possession before the Spanish-American War?

A Wake Island

B Howland Island

C American Samoa

D Guam

15. Which U.S. possession are the Philippines nearest to?

A Alaska

B Hawaii

C Midway Islands

D Guam

Need Extra Help?

If You Missed Questions . . .	10	11	12	13	14	15
Go to Page . . .	272	274–275	276–277	280–281	271–274	271–274

GO ON

16. The "big stick" policy and dollar diplomacy were attempts to

A increase the United States's power in Latin America.

B contain the spread of communism in eastern Europe.

C protect free trade on the Asian continent.

D strengthen political ties with Western Europe.

Analyze the cartoon and answer the question that follows. Base your answer on the cartoon and on your knowledge of chapter 7.

17. What does the cartoon demonstrate?

A It disagrees with Taft's dollar diplomacy.

B It shows Theodore Roosevelt's "big stick" policy in the Caribbean.

C It shows the effect of John Jay's Open Door policy.

D It demonstrates the difficulty of finding land for a canal.

18. The sugarcane planters in Hawaii revolted against Queen Liliuokalani because

A she taxed the sugarcane plantations too heavily.

B she wanted a constitution that returned her to power as the ruler of Hawaii.

C they wanted to overturn the McKinley Tariff.

D they hoped to open Asian markets to sugarcane from Hawaii.

Document-Based Questions

Directions: Analyze the document and answer the short-answer questions that follow the document.

After the Spanish-American War, Carl Schurz, the leader of the liberal wing of the Republican Party, opposed American expansion abroad. In the following excerpt, Schurz attacks the arguments for taking over the Philippine Islands:

> "Many imperialists admit that our trade with the Philippines themselves will not nearly be worth its cost; but they say that we must have the Philippines as a foothold, a sort of power station, for the expansion of our trade on the Asiatic continent, especially in China. Admitting this, for argument's sake, I ask what kind of a foothold we should really need. Coaling stations and docks for our fleet, and facilities for the establishment of commercial houses and depots. That is all. And now I ask further, whether we could not easily have had these things if we had, instead of making war upon the Filipinos, favored the independence of the islands. Everybody knows that we could. We might have those things now for the mere asking if we stopped the war and came to a friendly understanding with the Filipinos tomorrow. . . ."
> —quoted in *The Policy of Imperialism*

19. What does Schurz believe is necessary to establish a foothold in trade with Asia?

20. What action other than annexation does Schurz suggest the United States could have taken to obtain trade with Asia?

Extended Response

21. Discuss U.S. foreign policy during the late 1800s and early 1900s. How were the various countries and regions of the world changed by the policies of the United States? Write an expository essay that includes an introduction, several paragraphs, and a conclusion that supports your position.

History ONLINE

For additional test practice, use Self-Check Quizzes—Chapter 7 at glencoe.com.

Need Extra Help?						
If You Missed Questions . . .	16	17	18	19	20	21
Go to Page . . .	276–283	278–281	266	289	289	262–263

Chapter 8

The Progressive Movement

1890–1920

SECTION 1 The Roots of Progressivism

SECTION 2 Roosevelt and Taft

SECTION 3 The Wilson Years

Women wearing academic dress march in a New York City parade for woman suffrage in 1910.

1889
- Hull House opens in Chicago

1890
- Jacob Riis's *How the Other Half Lives* is published

1902
- Maryland passes first U.S. workers' compensation laws

1906
- Pure Food and Drug Act passed

B. Harrison
1889–1893

Cleveland
1893–1897

McKinley
1897–1901

T. Roosevelt
1901–1909

U.S. PRESIDENTS

U.S. EVENTS

1890

1900

WORLD EVENTS

1884
- Toynbee Hall, first settlement house, is established in London

1903
- Russian Bolshevik Party is established by Lenin

1906
- British pass workers' compensation law

MAKING CONNECTIONS

Can Politics Fix Social Problems?

Industrialization changed American society. Cities were crowded, working conditions were often bad, and the old political system was breaking down. These conditions gave rise to the Progressive movement. Progressives campaigned for both political and social reforms.

- *What reforms do you think progressives wanted to achieve?*
- *Which of these reforms can you see in today's society?*

Taft
1909–1913

1910
- Mann-Elkins Act passed

Wilson
1913–1921

1913
- Seventeenth Amendment requires direct election of senators

1920
- Nineteenth Amendment gives women voting rights

1910

1920

1908
- Germany limits working hours for children and women

1911
- British create national health insurance program

1914
- World War I begins in Europe

1917
- Russian Revolution begins

FOLDABLES™

Analyzing Reform Programs Create a Pocket Book Foldable that divides the Progressive agenda into political reforms and social reforms. Take notes on a wide range of reforms, placing each one in the proper column of the Foldable.

Progressive Political Reform

Progressive Social Reforms

History ONLINE Visit glencoe.com and enter *QuickPass*™ code TAVMT5147c8 for Chapter 8 resources.

The Roots of Progressivism

The Progressive Era was a time when many Americans tried to improve their society. They tried to make government honest, efficient, and more democratic. The movement for women's suffrage gained more support, as did efforts to limit child labor and reduce alcohol abuse.

The Rise of Progressivism

MAIN Idea Progressives tried to solve the social problems that arose as the United States became an urban, industrialized nation.

HISTORY AND YOU What areas of public life do you believe need to be reformed? Read on to learn about a movement that tried to fix many of society's problems.

Progressivism was a collection of different ideas and activities. It was not a tightly organized political movement with a specific set of reforms. Rather, it was a series of responses to problems in American society that had emerged from the growth of industry. Progressives had many different ideas about how to fix the problems they saw in American society.

Who Were the Progressives?

Progressivism was partly a reaction against laissez-faire economics and its emphasis on an unregulated market. Progressives generally believed that industrialization and urbanization had created many social problems. After seeing the poverty of the working class and the filth and crime of urban society, reformers began doubting the free market's ability to address those problems.

Progressives belonged to both major political parties. Most were urban, educated, middle-class Americans. Among their leaders were journalists, social workers, educators, politicians, and members of the clergy. Most agreed that government should take a more active role in solving society's problems. At the same time, they doubted that the government in its present form could fix those problems. They concluded that government had to be fixed before it could be used to fix other problems.

One reason progressives thought they could improve society was their strong faith in science and technology. The application of scientific knowledge had produced the lightbulb, the telephone, and the automobile. It had built skyscrapers and railroads. Science and technology had benefited people; thus, progressives believed using scientific principles could also produce solutions for society.

The Photojournalism of Jacob Riis

Photography offered a new tool in combating injustice. One of the most famous early photojournalists was Jacob Riis, whose book, *How the Other Half Lives*, helped stir progressives to action:

PRIMARY SOURCE

"Look into any of these houses, everywhere the same piles of rags, of malodorous bones and musty paper. . . . Here is a 'flat' or 'parlor' and two pitch-dark coops called bedrooms. Truly, the bed is all there is room for. The family teakettle is on the stove, doing duty for the time being as a wash-boiler. By night it will have returned to its proper use again, a practical illustration of how poverty in 'the Bend' makes both ends meet. One, two, three beds are there, if the old boxes and heaps of foul straw can be called by that name; a broken stove with crazy pipe from which the smoke leaks at every joint, a table of rough boards propped up on boxes, piles of rubbish in the corner. The closeness and smell are appalling. How many people sleep here? The woman with the red bandanna shakes her head sullenly, but the bare-legged girl with the bright face counts on her fingers—five, six!"

—from *How the Other Half Lives*

▲ *New York slum dwellers in this Jacob Riis photograph, taken about 1890, lived in wooden shacks in a city alley.*

DBQ Document-Based Questions

1. **Analyzing Visuals** What effect do Riis's photos convey?
2. **Making Inferences** Based on the quotation above, how could you summarize Riis's views on changing life in the slums?

▲ *Riis took this photograph of a crowded one-room apartment in a New York tenement in 1885.*

The Muckrakers

Among the first people to articulate progressive ideas was a group of crusading journalists who investigated social conditions and political corruption. President Theodore Roosevelt nicknamed these writers "**muckrakers.**" The term referred to a character in John Bunyan's book *Pilgrim's Progress*, who single-mindedly scraped up the filth on the ground, ignoring everything else. These journalists, according to Roosevelt, were obsessed with scandal and corruption. Widely circulated, cheap newspapers and magazines helped to spread the muckrakers' ideas.

Muckrakers uncovered corruption in many areas. Some concentrated on exposing the unfair practices of large corporations. In *Everybody's Magazine*, Charles Edward Russell attacked the beef industry. In *McClure's*, Ida Tarbell published a series of articles critical of the Standard Oil Company. Other muckrakers targeted government and social problems. Lincoln Steffens reported on vote stealing and other corrupt practices of urban political machines. These articles were later collected into a book, *The Shame of the Cities*.

Still other muckrakers concentrated on social problems. In his influential book, *How the Other Half Lives* (1890), **Jacob Riis** published photographs and descriptions of the poverty, disease, and crime that afflicted many immigrant neighborhoods in New York City. By raising public awareness of these problems, the muckrakers stimulated calls for reform.

Read literature from the era on pages R72–R73 in the **American Literature Library.**

✓ Reading Check **Describing** How did the muckrakers help spark the Progressive movement?

History ONLINE

Student Web Activity Visit glencoe.com and complete the activity on the Progressive movement.

Reforming Government

MAIN Idea Progressives tried to make government more efficient and more responsive to citizens.

HISTORY AND YOU How do you use your time and resources wisely? Read on to learn how progressives tried to make the government more efficient.

Progressivism included a wide range of reform activities. Different issues led to different approaches, and progressives even took opposing positions on how to address some problems. They condemned corruption in government but did not always agree on the best way to fix the problem.

Making Government Efficient

One group of progressives focused on making government more efficient by using ideas from business. Theories of business efficiency first became popular in the 1890s. Books such as Frederick W. Taylor's *The Principles of Scientific Management* (1911) described how a company could increase efficiency by managing time, breaking tasks down into small parts, and using standardized tools. In his book, Taylor argued that this "scientific method" of managing businesses optimized productivity and provided more job opportunities for unskilled workers. Many progressives argued that managing a modern city required the use of business management techniques.

Progressives saw corruption and inefficiency in municipal government where, in most cities, the mayor or city council chose the heads of city departments. Traditionally, they gave these jobs to political supporters and friends, who often knew little about managing city services.

Progressives supported two proposals to reform city government. The first, a commission plan, divided city government into several departments, each one under an expert commissioner's control. The second approach was a council-manager system. The city council would hire a city manager to run the city instead of the mayor. In both systems, experts play a major role in managing the city. Galveston, Texas, adopted the commission system in 1901. Other cities soon followed.

Democratic Reforms

Another group of progressives focused on making the political system more democratic and more responsive to citizens. Many believed that the key to improving government was to make elected officials more responsive and accountable to the voters.

La Follette's Laboratory of Democracy Led by Republican governor **Robert M. La Follette,** Wisconsin became a model of progressive reform. La Follette attacked the way political parties ran their conventions. Party bosses controlled the selection of convention delegates, which meant they also controlled the nomination of candidates. La Follette pressured the state legislature to pass a law requiring parties to hold a **direct primary,** in which all party members could vote for a candidate to run in the general election. This and other successes earned Wisconsin a reputation as the "laboratory of democracy." La Follette later recalled:

PRIMARY SOURCE
New Types of Government

The most deadly hurricane in United States history slammed into Galveston, Texas, on September 8, 1900, killing about 6,000 people. Because the political machine running the city was incapable of responding to the disaster, local business leaders convinced the state to allow them to take control. The following April, Galveston introduced the commission system of local government, which replaced the mayor and city council with five commissioners. Sometimes referred to as the Galveston Plan, its constitutionality was confirmed and took effect.

Four of those commissioners were local business leaders. Reformers in other cities were impressed by the city's rapid recovery. Clearly, the city benefited from dividing the government into departments under the supervision of an expert commissioner. Soon, other cities adopted either the commission or council-manager systems of government.

▶ *A house sits on its side after a hurricane ripped through Galveston, Texas, in September 1900.*

PRIMARY SOURCE

"It was clear to me that the only way to beat boss and ring rule was to keep the people thoroughly informed. Machine control is based upon misrepresentation and ignorance. Democracy is based upon knowledge. It is of first importance that the people shall know about their government and the work of their public servants."

—from La Follette's *Autobiography*

Wisconsin's use of the direct primary soon spread to other states, but to force legislators to listen to the voters, progressives also pushed for three additional reforms: the initiative, the referendum, and the recall. The **initiative** permitted a group of citizens to introduce **legislation** and required the legislature to vote on it. The **referendum** allowed citizens to vote on proposed laws directly without going to the legislature. The **recall** provided voters an option to demand a special election to remove an elected official from office before his or her term had expired.

Direct Election of Senators Progressives also targeted the Senate. As originally written, the federal constitution directed each state legislature to elect two senators. Political machines and business interests often influenced these elections. Some senators, once elected, repaid their supporters with federal contracts and jobs.

To counter Senate corruption, progressives called for direct election of senators by the state's voters. In 1912, Congress passed a direct-election amendment. Although the direct election of senators was intended to end corruption, it also removed one of the state legislatures' checks on federal power. In 1913 the amendment was ratified and became the Seventeenth Amendment to the Constitution.

✔ **Reading Check** **Evaluating** What was the impact of the Seventeenth Amendment? What problem was it intended to solve?

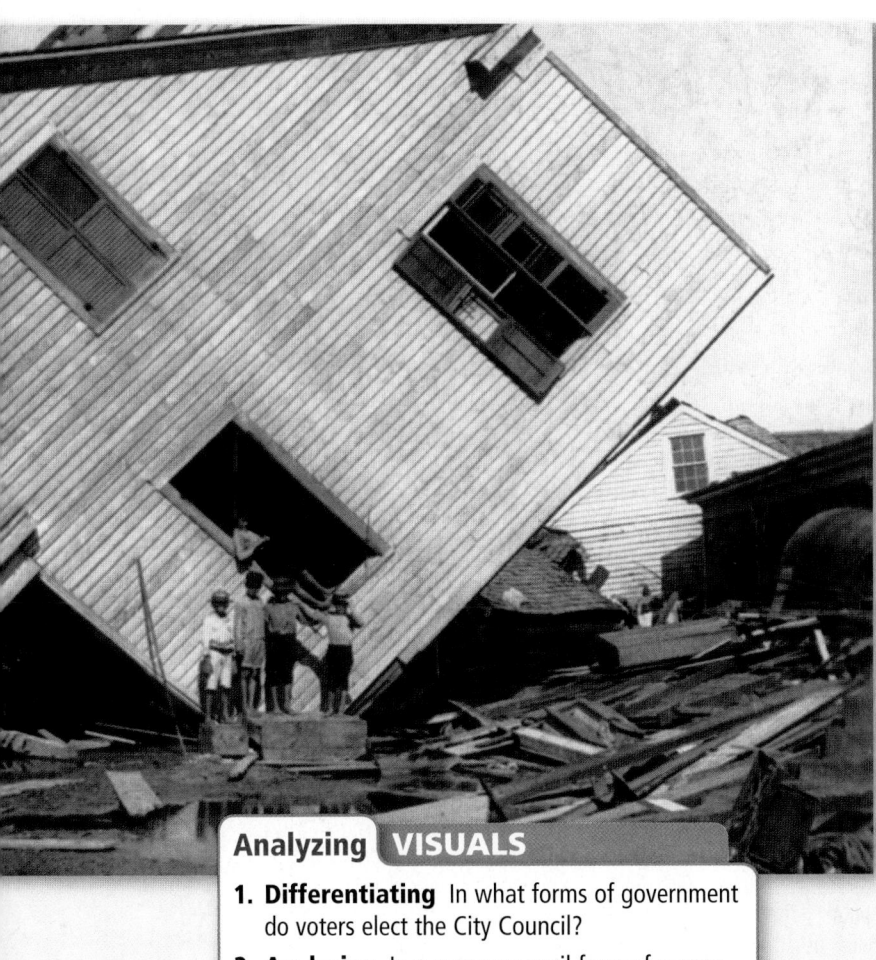

Analyzing VISUALS

1. **Differentiating** In what forms of government do voters elect the City Council?
2. **Analyzing** In a mayor-council form of government, who is responsible to carry out policy?

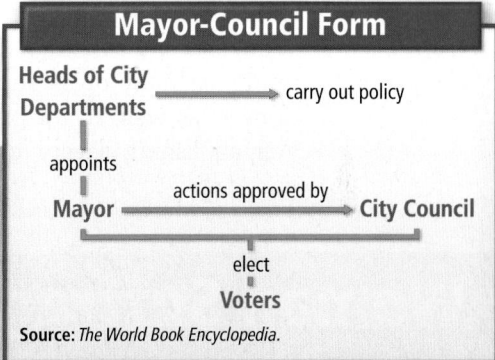

Mayor-Council Form

Heads of City Departments → carry out policy

appoints

Mayor —— actions approved by —→ City Council

elect

Voters

Source: *The World Book Encyclopedia.*

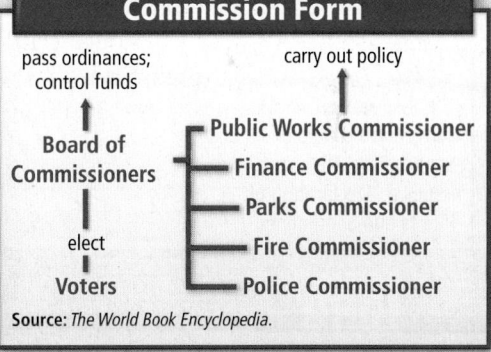

Commission Form

pass ordinances; control funds   carry out policy

Board of Commissioners
- Public Works Commissioner
- Finance Commissioner
- Parks Commissioner
- Fire Commissioner
- Police Commissioner

elect

Voters

Source: *The World Book Encyclopedia.*

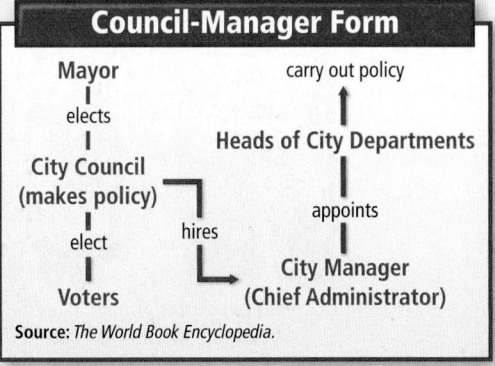

Council-Manager Form

Mayor   carry out policy

elects

City Council (makes policy)   Heads of City Departments

elect   hires   appoints

Voters   City Manager (Chief Administrator)

Source: *The World Book Encyclopedia.*

For an example of the early woman suffrage movement read "The Seneca Falls Declaration" on page R48 in **Documents in American History.**

Suffrage

MAIN Idea Many progressives joined the movement to win voting rights for women.

HISTORY AND YOU Do you remember reading about the Seneca Falls Convention in 1848? Read about the momentum of the women's rights movement in the 1910s.

At the first women's rights convention in Seneca Falls, New York, in 1848, Elizabeth Cady Stanton convinced the delegates that their first priority should be the right to vote. Decades later, universal woman **suffrage**—the right to vote—still had not been granted. It became a major goal for women progressives.

Early Problems

The woman suffrage movement got off to a slow start. Some people threatened women suffragists and said they were unfeminine and immoral. Many of its supporters were abolitionists, as well. In the years before the Civil War, abolishing slavery took priority.

After the Civil War, Congress introduced the Fourteenth and Fifteenth Amendments to grant citizenship to African Americans and voting rights to African American men. Leaders of the woman suffrage movement wanted these amendments to give women the right to vote, as well. They were disappointed when Republicans refused.

The debate over the Fourteenth and Fifteenth Amendments split the suffrage movement into two groups: the New York City–based National Woman Suffrage Association, which Elizabeth Cady Stanton and Susan B. Anthony founded in 1869, and the Boston-based American Woman Suffrage Association, which Lucy Stone and Julia Ward Howe led.

The first group wanted to focus on passing a constitutional amendment. The second group believed that the best strategy was convincing state governments to give women voting rights before trying to amend the Constitution. This split weakened the movement, and by 1900 only Wyoming, Idaho, Utah, and Colorado had granted women full voting rights.

THE **Woman Suffrage Movement**

1848
The first women's rights convention is held in Seneca Falls, New York, and issues a "Declaration of Rights and Sentiments"

1872
Susan B. Anthony votes illegally in the presidential election in Rochester, New York, claiming the Fourteenth Amendment gives her that right; she is arrested and found guilty

▲ Susan B. Anthony

 1850

 1870

1890

▲ Women voting in Cheyenne, Wyoming, 1869

1869
Territory of Wyoming becomes the first state or territory to grant women the right to vote

▲ Elizabeth Cady Stanton

1890
Elizabeth Cady Stanton becomes president of the National American Woman Suffrage Association

Building Support

In 1890 the two groups united to form the National American Woman Suffrage Association (NAWSA) but still had trouble convincing women to become politically active. As the Progressive movement gained momentum, however, many middle-class women concluded that they needed the vote to promote the reforms they favored. Many working-class women also wanted the vote to pass labor laws protecting women.

As the movement grew, women began lobbying lawmakers, organizing marches, and delivering speeches on street corners. On March 3, 1913, the day before President Wilson's inauguration, suffragists marched on Washington, D.C.

Alice Paul, a Quaker social worker who headed NAWSA's congressional committee, had organized the march. Paul wanted to use protests to confront Wilson on suffrage. Other members of NAWSA who wanted to negotiate with Wilson were alarmed. Paul left NAWSA and formed the National Woman's Party. Her supporters picketed the White House, blocked sidewalks, chained themselves to lampposts, and went on hunger strikes if arrested.

In 1915 **Carrie Chapman Catt** became NAWSA's leader and tried to mobilize the suffrage movement in one final nationwide push. She also threw NAWSA's support behind Wilson's reelection campaign.

As more states granted women the right to vote, Congress began to favor a constitutional amendment. In 1918 the House of Representatives passed a women's suffrage amendment. The Senate voted on the amendment, but it failed by two votes.

During the midterm elections of 1918, Catt used NAWSA's resources to defeat two antisuffrage senators. In June 1919 the Senate passed the amendment by slightly more than the two-thirds vote needed. On August 26, 1920, after three-fourths of the states had ratified it, the Nineteenth Amendment, guaranteeing women the right to vote, went into effect.

Reading Check **Evaluating** How successful were women in lobbying for the Nineteenth Amendment?

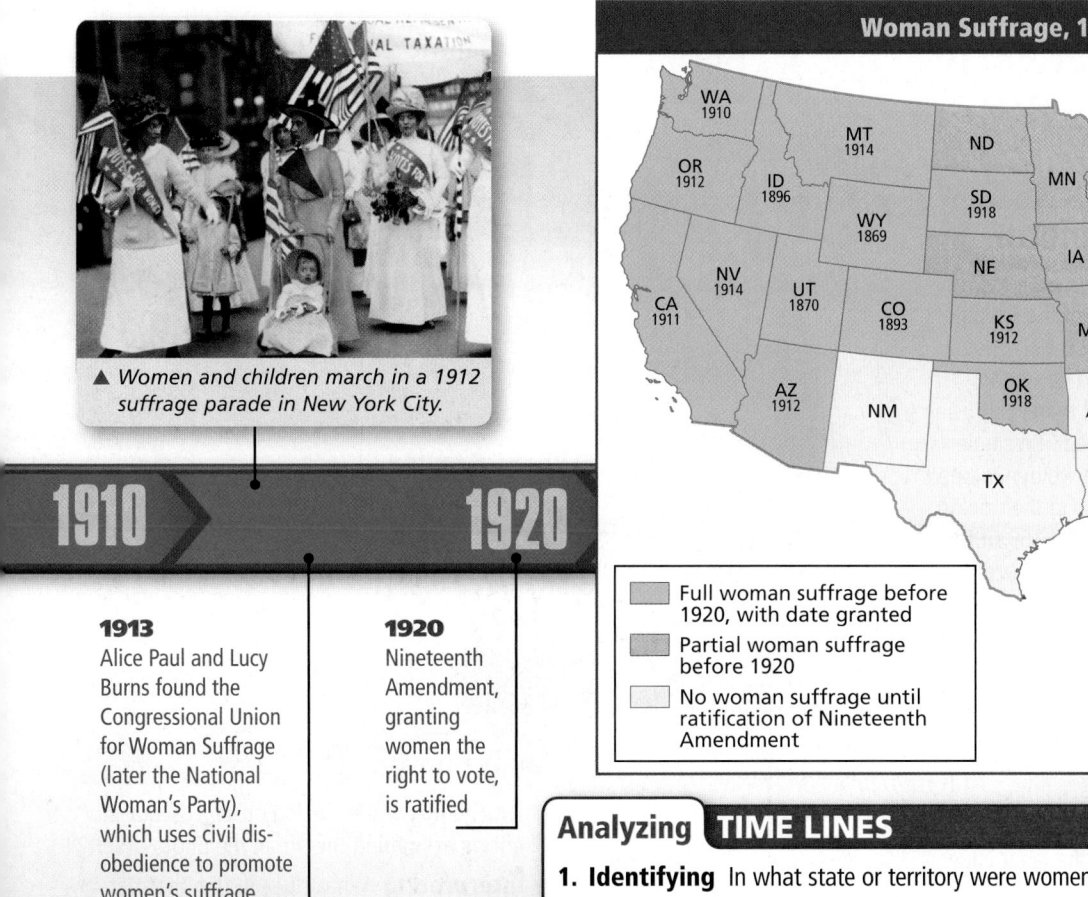

▲ Women and children march in a 1912 suffrage parade in New York City.

1910 ▶ **1920**

1913
Alice Paul and Lucy Burns found the Congressional Union for Woman Suffrage (later the National Woman's Party), which uses civil disobedience to promote women's suffrage

1920
Nineteenth Amendment, granting women the right to vote, is ratified

Woman Suffrage, 1869–1920

- Full woman suffrage before 1920, with date granted
- Partial woman suffrage before 1920
- No woman suffrage until ratification of Nineteenth Amendment

WA 1910
OR 1912
ID 1896
MT 1914
ND
SD 1918
WY 1869
MN
WI
MI 1918
VT
NH
ME
NY 1917
MA
RI
CT
NV 1914
UT 1870
CO 1893
NE
IA
IL
IN
OH
PA
NJ
DE
MD
CA 1911
AZ 1912
NM
KS 1912
MO
KY
WV
VA
NC
OK 1918
AR
TN
SC
TX
LA
MS
AL
GA
FL

Analyzing **TIME LINES**

1. **Identifying** In what state or territory were women first granted the right to vote?
2. **Analyzing** What region of the nation seemed most willing to grant woman suffrage without a national amendment?

Reforming Society

MAIN Idea Many progressives focused on social welfare problems such as child labor, unsafe working conditions, and alcohol abuse.

History ONLINE
Student Skill Activity To learn how to create and modify a database, visit glencoe.com and complete the skill activity.

HISTORY AND YOU Have you heard of companies using "sweatshop" labor in foreign countries? Read on to learn how progressives tried to ban child labor and make factories safer for workers.

While many progressives focused on reforming the political system, others focused on social problems. These social-welfare progressives created charities to help the poor and disadvantaged. They also pushed for new laws they hoped would fix social problems.

Child Labor

Probably the most emotional progressive issue was the campaign against child labor. Children had always worked on family farms, but mines and factories presented more dangerous and unhealthy working conditions. Muckraker John Spargo's 1906 book, *The Bitter Cry of the Children,* presented detailed evidence of child labor conditions. It told of coal mines that hired thousands of 9- or 10-year-old

"breaker boys" to pick slag out of coal, paying them 60 cents for a 10-hour day. It described the way that the work bent their backs permanently and often crippled their hands.

Reports like these convinced states to pass laws that set a minimum age for employment and established other limits on child labor, such as maximum hours children could work.

Health and Safety Codes

Many adult workers also labored in difficult conditions. When workers were injured or killed on the job, they and their families received little or no compensation. Progressives joined union leaders to pressure states for workers' compensation laws. These laws established insurance funds that employers financed. Workers injured in accidents received payments from the funds.

In two cases, *Lochner* v. *New York* (1905) and *Muller* v. *Oregon* (1908), the Supreme Court addressed government's authority to regulate business to protect workers. In the Lochner case, the Court ruled that a New York law forbidding bakers to work more than 10 hours a day was unconstitutional. The state did not have the right to interfere with the liberty of

PRIMARY SOURCE
A Tragedy Brings Reform

Fire broke out on the top floors of the Triangle Shirtwaist Company on March 25, 1911. Young women struggled against locked doors to escape. A few women managed to get out using the fire escape before it collapsed. The single elevator stopped running. Some women jumped from windows on the ninth floor to their death, while others died in the fire. Nearly 150 of the 500 employees lost their lives in the blaze.

The Triangle factory was a nonunion shop. Health and safety issues were a major concern for unions. The disaster illustrated that fire precautions and inspections were inadequate. Exit doors were kept locked, supposedly to prevent theft. As a result of the fire and loss of life, New York created a Factory Investigating Commission. Between 1911 and 1914, the state passed 36 new laws reforming the labor code.

▲ Firemen fight Triangle Shirtwaist fire, March 25, 1911.

▲ Trade union members march in support of the women who died.

Analyzing VISUALS

1. **Analyzing** What do you observe about the efforts at fighting the fire in the photo at left?

2. **Interpreting** What clues in the photo at right suggest that at least some of the women who died were immigrants?

employers and employees. In the case of women working in laundries in Oregon, however, the Court upheld the state's right to limit hours. The different judgments were based on gender differences. The Court stated that healthy mothers were the state's concern and, therefore, the limits on women's working hours did not violate their Fourteenth Amendment rights.

Some progressives also favored zoning laws as a method of protecting the public. These laws divided a town or city into zones for commercial, residential, or other development, thereby regulating how land and buildings could be used. Building codes set minimum standards for light, air, room size, and sanitation, and required buildings to have fire escapes. Health codes required restaurants and other facilities to maintain clean environments for their patrons.

The Prohibition Movement

Many progressives believed alcohol explained many of society's problems. Settlement house workers knew that hard-earned wages were often spent on alcohol and that drunkenness often led to physical abuse and sickness. Some employers believed drinking hurt workers' efficiency. The temperance movement—which **advocated** that people stop, or at least moderate, their alcohol consumption—emerged from these concerns.

For the most part, women led the temperance movement. In 1874 a group of women formed the Woman's Christian Temperance Union (WCTU). By 1911 the WCTU had nearly 250,000 members. In 1893 evangelical Protestant ministers formed another group, the Anti-Saloon League. When the temperance movement began, it concentrated on reducing alcohol consumption. Later it pressed for **prohibition**—laws banning the manufacture, sale, and consumption of alcohol.

Progressives Versus Big Business

Many progressives agreed that big business needed regulation. Some believed the government should break up big companies to restore competition. This led to the Sherman Antitrust Act in 1890. Others argued that big business was the most efficient way to organize the economy. They pushed for government to regulate big companies and prevent them from abusing their power. The Interstate Commerce Commission (ICC), created in 1887, was an early example of this kind of thinking.

Some progressives went even further and advocated socialism—the idea that the government should own and operate industry for the community. They wanted the government to buy up large companies, especially industries that affected everyone, such as utilities. At its peak, socialism had some national support. Eugene V. Debs, the former American Railway Union leader, won nearly a million votes as the American Socialist Party candidate for president in 1912. Most progressives and most Americans, however, believed the American system of free enterprise was superior.

Reading Check **Comparing** In what ways were progressive efforts to end child labor and impose safety codes similar?

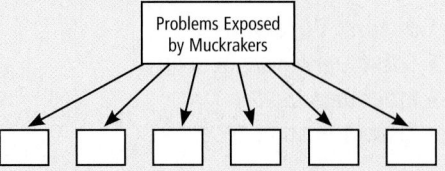
Section 1 REVIEW

Vocabulary
1. **Explain** the significance of: muckraker, Jacob Riis, Robert M. La Follette, direct primary, initiative, referendum, recall, suffrage, Carrie Chapman Catt, prohibition.

Main Ideas
2. **Organizing** Use a graphic organizer similar to the one below to list the kinds of problems that muckrakers exposed.

Problems Exposed by Muckrakers

3. **Summarizing** How did initiative, referendum, and recall change democracy in the United States?

4. **Stating** What key provision did the Nineteenth Amendment make?

5. **Describing** Explain the various zoning laws and codes favored by progressives.

Critical Thinking
6. **Big Ideas** Identify the different social issues associated with progressives. How do these ideals influence society today?

7. **Analyzing Visuals** Study the charts on page 295. Which system gives voters the most control over department heads? How?

Writing About History
8. **Expository Writing** Create a database of progressive ideas of the period. Then write a one-page report using a word processor to summarize the progressive ideals.

History ONLINE

Study Central™ To review this section, go to glencoe.com and click on Study Central.

Roosevelt and Taft

Guide to Reading

Big Ideas
Individual Action Presidents Theodore Roosevelt and William Taft worked to improve labor conditions, control big business, and support conservation.

Content Vocabulary
- Social Darwinism (p. 300)
- arbitration (p. 301)
- insubordination (p. 307)

Academic Vocabulary
- regulate (p. 302)
- environmental (p. 304)

People and Events to Identify
- Square Deal (p. 300)
- United Mine Workers (p. 301)
- Hepburn Act (p. 302)
- Upton Sinclair (p. 302)
- Meat Inspection Act (p. 302)
- Pure Food and Drug Act (p. 302)
- Gifford Pinchot (p. 304)
- Richard A. Ballinger (p. 306)
- Children's Bureau (p. 307)

Reading Strategy
Notes As you read about the Roosevelt and Taft administrations, use the headings of the section to create an outline similar to the one below.

```
Roosevelt and Taft
I. Roosevelt Revives the Presidency
   A.
   B.
   C.
   D.
II.
```

A s president, Theodore Roosevelt extended the federal government's ability to curb the power of big business and to conserve natural resources. His successor, William Howard Taft, was less popular with progressives.

Roosevelt Revives the Presidency

MAIN Idea Theodore Roosevelt, who believed in progressive ideals for the nation, took on big business.

HISTORY AND YOU How much do you think a president's personal beliefs should shape national policy? Read on to learn how Theodore Roosevelt used his ideas to change trusts and big business.

Theodore Roosevelt became president at age 42—the youngest person ever to take office. Roosevelt was intensely competitive, strong-willed, and extremely energetic. In international affairs, Roosevelt was a Social Darwinist. He believed the United States was in competition with the other nations of the world and that only the fittest would survive. Domestically, however, Roosevelt was a committed progressive, who believed that government should actively balance the needs of competing groups in American society.

"I shall see to it," Roosevelt declared in 1904, "that every man has a square deal, no less and no more." His reform programs soon became known as the **Square Deal.** To Roosevelt, it was not inconsistent to believe in **Social Darwinism** and progressivism at the same time.

Roosevelt Takes on the Trusts

Roosevelt believed that trusts and other large business organizations were very efficient and part of the reason for America's prosperity. Yet Roosevelt remained concerned that the monopoly power of some trusts hurt the public interest. His goal was to ensure that trusts did not abuse their power. When the *New York Sun* declared that Roosevelt was "bringing wealth to its knees," the president disagreed. "We draw the line against misconduct," he declared, "not against wealth."

Roosevelt decided to make an example out of major trusts that he believed were abusing their power. His first target was J. P. Morgan's railroad holding company, Northern Securities. Established in 1901, the company proposed, through an exchange of stock, to merge existing railroad systems to create a monopoly on railroad traffic in the Northwest. As a monopoly, Northern Securities would have no competition. Farmers and business owners feared it would raise rates and hurt their profits. In 1902 the president ordered the attorney

Roosevelt Versus the Trusts

Jay Gould was a well-known railroad speculator who had been involved in many scandals. At one point, he controlled the four largest western railroads, including the Union Pacific.

John D. Rockefeller, founder of Standard Oil, which controlled most oil production in the United States

James J. Hill, founder of the Great Northern Railway Company and a partner with J. P. Morgan in Northern Securities

J. P. Morgan controlled a huge banking and financial empire. He also created the U.S. Steel Corporation and helped finance several railroads.

Theodore Roosevelt, shown standing in the middle of Wall Street carrying a sword labeled "Public Service"

Analyzing VISUALS DBQ

1. **Inferring** Why do you think the scene is set on Wall Street?
2. **Analyzing** What do the giants represent?

general to file suit under the Sherman Antitrust Act, charging the company was a "combination in restraint of trade."

Roosevelt's action baffled J. P. Morgan. Expecting to resolve the suit without legal action, he inquired what could be done to "fix it up." Unmoved, Roosevelt proceeded with the case. In 1904, in *Northern Securities* v. *United States*, the Supreme Court ruled that Northern Securities had indeed violated the Sherman Antitrust Act. Roosevelt proclaimed, "The most powerful men in the country were held to accountability before the law." Newspapers hailed Roosevelt as a "trustbuster," and his popularity with the American public soared.

The Coal Strike of 1902

As president, Roosevelt regarded himself as the nation's head manager. He believed it was his job to keep society operating efficiently by mediating conflicts between different groups and their interests. In the fall of 1902, he put these beliefs into practice.

The previous spring, the **United Mine Workers** (UMW) had launched a strike by the anthracite (hard coal) miners of eastern Pennsylvania. Nearly 150,000 workers walked out, demanding increased pay, reduced work hours, and union recognition. Coal prices began to rise. Roosevelt viewed it as another example of groups pursuing their private interests at the nation's expense. If the strike dragged on too long, the country would face a coal shortage that could shut down factories and leave many homes unheated.

Roosevelt urged the union and the owners to accept **arbitration**—a settlement negotiated by an outside party. The union agreed; the mine owners did not. The mine owners' stubbornness infuriated Roosevelt, as well as the public. Roosevelt threatened to order the army to run the mines. Fearful of this, the mine owners finally accepted arbitration. By intervening in the dispute, Roosevelt took the first step toward establishing the federal government as an honest broker between powerful groups in society.

Regulating Big Business

Despite his lawsuit against Northern Securities and his role in the coal strike, Roosevelt believed most trusts benefited the economy and that breaking them up would do more harm than good. Instead, he proposed creating a new federal agency to investigate corporations and publicize the results. He believed the most effective way to keep big business from abusing its power was to keep the public informed.

In 1903 Roosevelt convinced Congress to create the Department of Commerce and Labor. The following year, this department began investigating U.S. Steel, a gigantic holding company that had been created in 1901. Worried about a possible antitrust lawsuit, the company's leaders met privately with Roosevelt and offered a deal. They would open their account books and records for examination. In exchange, if any problems were found, the company would be advised privately and allowed to correct them without having to go to court.

Roosevelt accepted this "gentlemen's agreement," as he called it, and soon made similar deals with other companies. These arrangements gave Roosevelt the ability to **regulate** big business without having to sacrifice economic efficiency by breaking up the trusts.

In keeping with his belief in regulation, Roosevelt pushed the **Hepburn Act** through Congress in 1906. This act was intended to strengthen the Interstate Commerce Commission (ICC) by giving it the power to set railroad rates. At first, railroad companies were suspicious of the ICC and tied up its decisions by challenging them in court. Eventually, the railroads realized that they could work with the ICC to set rates and regulations that limited competition and prevented new competitors from entering the industry. Over time, the ICC became a supporter of the railroads' interests, and by 1920 it had begun setting rates at levels intended to ensure the industry's profits.

Consumer Protection

By 1905 consumer protection had become a national issue. That year, a journalist named Samuel Hopkins Adams published a series of articles in *Collier's* magazine describing the patent medicine business.

Many companies patented and marketed potions they claimed would cure a variety of ills. Many of these medicines were little more than alcohol, colored water, and sugar. Others contained caffeine, opium, cocaine, and other dangerous compounds. Consumers had no way to know what they were taking, nor did they receive any assurance that the medicines worked as claimed. Adams's articles pointed out that these supposed cures could cause health problems. The articles in *Collier's* outraged many Americans.

Many Americans were equally concerned about the food they ate. Dr. W. H. Wiley, chief chemist at the United States Department of Agriculture, had issued reports documenting the dangerous preservatives being used in what he called "embalmed meat." Then, in 1906, **Upton Sinclair** published his novel *The Jungle.* Based on Sinclair's close observations of the slaughterhouses of Chicago, the powerful book featured appalling descriptions of conditions in the meatpacking industry:

PRIMARY SOURCE

"[T]here would come all the way back from Europe old sausage that had been rejected, and that was [moldy] and white—it would be dosed with borax and glycerine, and dumped into the hoppers, and made over again for home consumption. . . . There would be meat stored in great piles in rooms; and the water from leaky roofs would drip over it, and thousands of rats would race about [upon] it."

—from *The Jungle*

Sinclair's book was a best-seller. It made consumers ill—and angry. Many became vegetarians after reading the book. Roosevelt and Congress responded with the **Meat Inspection Act,** passed in 1906. It required federal inspection of meat sold through interstate commerce and required the Agriculture Department to set standards of cleanliness in meatpacking plants. The **Pure Food and Drug Act,** passed on the same day in 1906, prohibited the manufacture, sale, or shipment of impure or falsely labeled food and drugs.

Reading Check **Identifying** What term was used to describe Roosevelt's policies and how accurate was it?

ANALYZING SUPREME COURT CASES

Can Government Regulate Business Activity?

★ *Northern Securities* v. *United States,* 1904

Background to the Case

In 1901 three powerful businessmen, J. P. Morgan, James J. Hill, and Edward H. Harriman, created Northern Securities—a holding company that owned the majority of the stock in several major railroads. The government sued the company for violating the Sherman Antitrust Act, and a court ordered the company broken up.

How the Court Ruled

The Constitution gives the federal government the power to regulate interstate commerce—but did "commerce" mean all business activity, or just the movement of goods across state lines? The owners of Northern Securities argued that their company was a holding company set up to buy stock. It had been created legally under New Jersey law, and federal laws should not apply because the company itself did not engage in interstate commerce. In a 5-4 decision, the Court concluded that the commerce clause allows the federal government to regulate the ownership of companies.

NO MOLLY-CODDLING HERE

▲ *President Roosevelt once said "Speak softly and carry a big stick." This cartoon shows Roosevelt swinging his stick and knocking down the trusts—and everything else, as well.*

PRIMARY SOURCE

The Court's Opinion

"No state can, by merely creating a corporation . . . project its authority into other states, and across the continent, so as to prevent Congress from exerting the power it possesses under the Constitution over interstate and international commerce. . . .

. . . Every corporation created by a state is necessarily subject to the supreme law of the land. . . . In short, the court may make any order necessary to bring about the dissolution or suppression of an illegal combination that restrains interstate commerce. All this can be done without infringing in any degree upon the just authority of the states.

—Justice John Marshall Harlan, writing for the Court

PRIMARY SOURCE

Dissenting Views

"Commerce depends upon population, but Congress could not, on that ground, undertake to regulate marriage and divorce. If the act before us is to be carried out according to what seems to me the logic of the argument . . . I can see no part of the conduct of life with which . . . Congress might not interfere.

. . . This act is construed by the Government to affect the purchasers of shares in two railroad companies because of the effect it may have . . . upon the competition of these roads. If such a remote result of the exercise of an ordinary incident of property and personal freedom is enough to make that exercise unlawful, there is hardly any transaction concerning commerce between the States that may not be made a crime by the finding of a jury or a court."

—Justice Oliver Wendell Holmes, dissenting

DBQ Document-Based Questions

1. **Interpreting** How does Justice Harlan view the rights of states and the authority of Congress?
2. **Defining** How does Justice Harlan refer to the Sherman Antitrust Act?
3. **Analyzing** What does Justice Holmes fear in narrowly applying a law?

Conservation

MAIN Idea New legislation gave the federal government the power to conserve natural resources.

HISTORY AND YOU Have you ever visited a national park or forest? Read on to find out how Roosevelt made some national parks and forests possible.

Roosevelt put his stamp on the presidency most clearly in the area of **environmental** conservation. Realizing that the nation's bountiful natural resources were being used up at an alarming rate, Roosevelt urged Americans to conserve those resources.

An enthusiastic outdoorsman, Roosevelt valued the country's minerals, animals, and rugged terrain. He cautioned against unregulated exploitation of public lands and believed in conservation to manage the nation's resources. Roosevelt argued that the government must distinguish "between the man who skins the land and the man who develops the country. I am going to work with, and only with, the man who develops the country."

Western Land Development

Roosevelt quickly applied his philosophy in the dry Western states, where farmers and city dwellers competed for scarce water. In 1902 Roosevelt supported passage of the Newlands Reclamation Act, authorizing the use of federal funds from public land sales to pay for irrigation and land development projects. The federal government thus began transforming the West's landscape and economy on a large scale.

Gifford Pinchot

Roosevelt also backed efforts to save the nation's forests through careful management of the timber resources of the West. He appointed his close friend **Gifford Pinchot** to head the United States Forest Service established in 1905. "The natural resources," Pinchot said, "must be developed and preserved for the benefit of the many and not merely for the profit of a few."

As progressives, Roosevelt and Pinchot both believed that trained experts in forestry and resource management should apply the same scientific standards to the landscape that others were applying to managing cities and industry. They rejected the laissez-faire argument that the best way to preserve public land was to sell it to lumber companies, who would then carefully conserve it because it was the source of their profits. With the president's support, Pinchot's department drew up regulations controlling lumbering on federal lands. Roosevelt also added over 100 million acres to the protected national forests and established five new national parks and 51 federal wildlife reservations.

Roosevelt's Legacy

President Theodore Roosevelt changed the role of the federal government and the nature of the presidency. He used his power in the

Debates IN HISTORY

Should Resources Be Preserved?

The origins of the environmentalist movement can be traced back to the Progressive Era. Then, as now, people disagreed over the best approach to the environment. Their disagreements were represented in the differing views of John Muir, founder of the Sierra Club, who worked with Roosevelt to create Yosemite National Park, and Gifford Pinchot, head of the U.S. Forest Service under Theodore Roosevelt. Muir was a preservationist, hoping that wild places could be left as they were. Pinchot was a conservationist who believed in managing the use of land for the benefit of the nation's citizens.

White House to present his views, calling it his "bully pulpit." Increasingly, Americans began looking to the federal government to solve the nation's economic and social problems.

Under Roosevelt, the power of the executive branch of government had dramatically increased. The Hepburn Act gave the Interstate Commerce Commission the power to set rates, the Meat Inspection Act stated that the Agriculture Department could inspect food, the Department of Commerce and Labor could monitor business, the Bureau of Corporations could investigate corporations and issue reports, and the attorney general could rapidly bring antitrust lawsuits under the Expedition Act.

Reading Check **Examining** How did Roosevelt's policies help the conservation of natural resources?

Taft's Reforms

MAIN Idea William Howard Taft broke with progressives on tariff and conservation issues.

HISTORY AND YOU Have you ever been judged in comparison with the accomplishments of a sibling or friend? Read on to learn how Taft had to deal with comparisons with Roosevelt.

Roosevelt believed William Howard Taft to be the ideal person to continue his policies. Taft had worked closely with Roosevelt. He had served as a judge, as governor of the Philippines, and as Roosevelt's secretary of war. Taft easily received his party's nomination. His victory in the general election in November 1908 was a foregone conclusion. The Democratic candidate, William Jennings Bryan, lost for a third time.

YES

John Muir
Sierra Club Founder

PRIMARY SOURCE

"The making of gardens and parks goes on with civilization all over the world, and they increase both in size and number as their value is recognized.

Everybody needs beauty as well as bread, places to play in and pray in, where Nature may heal and cheer and give strength to body and soul alike. . . . Nevertheless, like anything else worth while . . . they have always been subject to attack by despoiling gainseekers . . . eagerly trying to make everything immediately and selfishly commercial, with schemes disguised in smug-smiling philanthropy, industriously, shampiously crying, 'Conservation, conservation, panutilization,' that man and beast may be fed and the dear Nation made great."

—from *The Yosemite*

NO

Gifford Pinchot
Chief of U.S. Forest Service

PRIMARY SOURCE

"The first principle of conservation is development, the use of the natural resources now existing on this continent for the benefit of the people who live here now. There may be just as much waste in neglecting the development and use of certain natural resources as there is in their destruction. . . .

Conservation stands emphatically for the development and use of water-power now, without delay. It stands for the immediate construction of navigable waterways . . . as assistants to the railroads. . . .

In addition . . . natural resources must be developed and preserved for the benefit of the many, and not merely for the profit of the few."

—from *The Fight for Conservation*

DBQ Document-Based Questions

1. **Contrasting** How do the two men differ in their views about nature?

2. **Making Connections** Which view do you think is more common today? Why do you think so?

3. **Speculating** Which viewpoint do you think was more likely to be held by ranchers and farmers in California in the early twentieth century?

Campaigning Against Child Labor

In 1900, 18 percent of children were employed. Mary Harris Jones, "Mother" Jones, as she was called, campaigned against child labor. After working with children in an Alabama cotton mill, she wrote, "Little girls and boys . . . reaching thin little hands into the machinery to repair snapped threads. They replaced spindles all day long; all night through . . . six-year-olds with faces of sixty did an eight-hour shift for ten cents a day . . ."

Using posters like the one shown at right to build public support, the campaign against child labor made steady progress. Between 1880 and 1910, 36 states passed laws on the minimum age for manufacturing workers.

Analyzing VISUALS

1. **Analyzing** What in the photo indicates that the children could easily be injured?
2. **Hypothesizing** What effect do you think the images on the inset poster may have had on people in the early 1900s?

▲ At a Georgia cotton mill in 1909, two boys keep a spinning machine running by repairing broken thread and replacing bobbins as they are filled.

The Payne-Aldrich Tariff

Like many progressives, Taft believed high tariffs limited competition, hurt consumers, and protected trusts. Roosevelt had warned him to stay away from tariff reform because it would divide the Republican Party. Taft, however, called Congress into special session to lower tariff rates.

As Roosevelt predicted, the tariff debate divided progressives, who favored tariff reduction, and conservative Republicans who wanted to maintain high tariffs. In the prolonged negotiations on the bill, Taft's support for tariff reductions wavered, and then collapsed. In the end, Taft signed into law the Payne-Aldrich Tariff, which cut tariffs hardly at all and actually raised them on some goods.

Progressives felt outraged by Taft's decision:"I knew the fire had gone out of [the progressive movement]," recalled the head of the U.S. Forest Service, Gifford Pinchot, after Roosevelt left office. "Washington was a dead town. Its leader was gone, and in his place [was] a man whose fundamental desire was to keep out of trouble."

Ballinger Versus Pinchot

With Taft's standing among Republican progressives deteriorating, a sensational controversy broke out late in 1909 that helped permanently destroy Taft's popularity with reformers. Many progressives were unhappy when Taft replaced Roosevelt's secretary of the interior, James R. Garfield, an aggressive conservationist, with **Richard A. Ballinger,** a more conservative corporate lawyer. Suspicion of Ballinger grew when he tried to make nearly a million acres of public forests and mineral reserves available for private development.

In the midst of this mounting concern, Gifford Pinchot charged the new secretary with having once plotted to turn over valuable public lands in Alaska to a private business group for personal profit. Taft's attorney general investigated the charges and decided they were groundless. Not satisfied, Pinchot leaked the story to the press and asked Congress to investigate. Taft fired Pinchot for **insubordination,** or disobedience to authority. The congressional investigation cleared Ballinger.

By the second half of his term of office, many Americans believed that Taft had "sold the Square Deal down the river." Popular indignation was so great that the congressional elections of 1910 resulted in a sweeping Democratic victory, with Democrats taking the majority in the House, and Democrats and progressive Republicans grabbing control of the Senate from conservative Republicans.

Taft's Achievements

Despite his political problems, Taft also had several successes. Although Roosevelt was nicknamed the "trustbuster," Taft was a strong opponent of monopoly and actually brought twice as many antitrust cases in four years as his predecessor had in seven. In other areas, too, Taft pursued progressive policies. Taft established the **Children's Bureau** in 1912, an agency that investigated and publicized the problems of child labor. The agency exists today, and deals with issues such as child abuse prevention, adoption, and foster care.

The Ballinger-Pinchot controversy aside, Taft was also a dedicated conservationist. His contributions in this area actually equaled or surpassed those of Roosevelt. He set up the Bureau of Mines in 1910 to monitor the activities of mining companies, expand the national forests, and protect waterpower sites from private development. Most of the new and emerging technologies in the minerals field were partly made possible by the existence of the Bureau of Mines.

After Taft took office in 1909, Roosevelt left for a big-game hunt in Africa, followed by a tour of Europe. He did not return to the United States until June 1910. Although disturbed by stories of Taft's "betrayal" of progressivism, Roosevelt at first refused to criticize the president.

In October 1911 Taft announced an antitrust lawsuit against U.S. Steel, claiming that the company's decision to buy the Tennessee Coal and Iron Company in 1907 had violated the Sherman Antitrust Act. The lawsuit was the final straw for Roosevelt. As president, he had approved U.S. Steel's plan to buy the company.

Roosevelt believed Taft's focus on breaking up trusts was destroying the carefully crafted system of cooperation and regulation that Roosevelt had established with big business. In November 1911 Roosevelt publicly criticized Taft's decision. Roosevelt argued that the best way to deal with the trusts was to allow them to exist while continuing to regulate them.

After Roosevelt broke with Taft, it was only a matter of time before progressives convinced him to reenter politics. In late February 1912, Roosevelt announced that he would enter the presidential campaign of 1912 and attempt to replace Taft as the Republican nominee for president.

Reading Check **Evaluating** How did Taft's accomplishments regarding conservation and trust-busting compare to Roosevelt's?

Section 2 REVIEW

Vocabulary
1. **Explain** the significance of: Square Deal, Social Darwinism, United Mine Workers, arbitration, Hepburn Act, Upton Sinclair, Meat Inspection Act, Pure Food and Drug Act, Gifford Pinchot, Richard A. Ballinger, insubordination, Children's Bureau.

Main Ideas
2. **Explaining** What was the intent of the Hepburn Act?

3. **Describing** How did Roosevelt's policies change the Western landscape?

4. **Discussing** How did Taft help conservation efforts and child labor problems?

Critical Thinking
5. **Big Ideas** How did Upton Sinclair contribute to involving the federal government in protecting consumers?

6. **Organizing** Use a graphic organizer to list Taft's progressive reforms.

Taft's Progressive Reforms

7. **Analyzing Visuals** Study the photo on page 306. Could this photo be used to rally the cause against child labor? Explain the dangerous elements of the job.

Writing About History
8. **Expository Writing** Suppose that you are living in the early 1900s and have just read Sinclair's *The Jungle*. Write a letter to a friend summarizing the plot and how it characterizes the Progressive Era.

History ONLINE
Study Central™ To review this section, go to glencoe.com and click on Study Central.

The Wilson Years

Guide to Reading

Big Ideas
Individual Action Woodrow Wilson increased the control of the government over business.

Content Vocabulary
• income tax *(p. 310)*
• unfair trade practices *(p. 311)*

Academic Vocabulary
• academic *(p. 308)*
• unconstitutional *(p. 312)*

People and Events to Identify
• Progressive Party *(p. 308)*
• New Nationalism *(p. 309)*
• New Freedom *(p. 309)*
• Federal Reserve Act *(p. 311)*
• Federal Trade Commission *(p. 311)*
• Clayton Antitrust Act *(p. 311)*
• National Association for the Advancement of Colored People *(p. 313)*

Reading Strategy
Organizing As you read about progressivism during the Wilson administration, complete a chart similar to the one below by listing Wilson's progressive economic and social reforms.

Economic Reforms	Social Reforms

Woodrow Wilson, a progressive Democrat, won the election of 1912. While in office, he supported lower tariffs, more regulation of business, and creation of a federal reserve banking system.

The Election of 1912

MAIN Idea Woodrow Wilson was elected after Republican voters split between Taft and Roosevelt.

HISTORY AND YOU Do you remember a catchy slogan from a political campaign? Read about the competing slogans and platforms in the 1912 election.

The 1912 presidential campaign featured a current president, a former president, and an **academic** who had entered politics only two years earlier. The election's outcome determined the path of the Progressive movement.

Picking the Candidates

Believing that President Taft had failed to live up to progressive ideals, Theodore Roosevelt informed seven state governors that he was willing to accept the Republican nomination. "My hat is in the ring!" he declared. "The fight is on."

The struggle for control of the Republican Party reached its climax at the national convention in Chicago in June 1912. Conservatives rallied behind Taft. Most of the progressives supported Roosevelt. When it became clear that Taft's delegates controlled the nomination, Roosevelt decided to leave the party and campaign as an independent.

Declaring himself "fit as a bull moose," Roosevelt became the presidential candidate for the newly formed **Progressive Party,** which quickly became known as the Bull Moose Party. Because Taft had alienated so many groups, the election of 1912 became a contest between two progressives: Roosevelt and the Democratic candidate, Woodrow Wilson.

After a university teaching career that ended in his becoming the president of Princeton University, Woodrow Wilson entered politics as a firm progressive. As governor of New Jersey, he pushed through one progressive reform after another. He signed laws that introduced the direct primary, established utility regulatory boards, and allowed cities to adopt the commissioner form of government. In less than two years, New Jersey became a model of progressive reform.

New Nationalism Versus New Freedom

WILSON'S NEW FREEDOM

Presidential Election of 1912

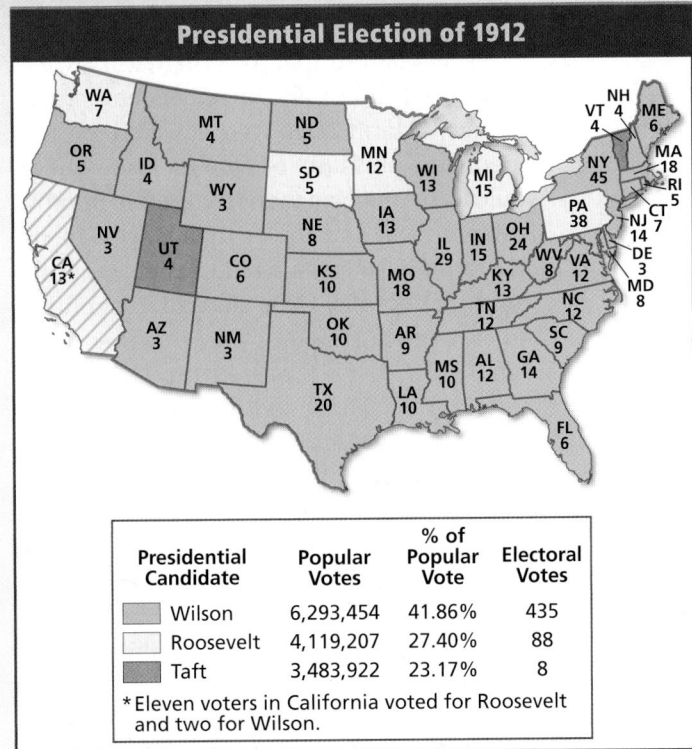

Presidential Candidate	Popular Votes	% of Popular Vote	Electoral Votes
Wilson	6,293,454	41.86%	435
Roosevelt	4,119,207	27.40%	88
Taft	3,483,922	23.17%	8

*Eleven voters in California voted for Roosevelt and two for Wilson.

"I am perfectly willing that [a business] should beat any competitor by fair means . . . But there must be no squeezing out the beginner . . . no secret arrangements against him. All the fair competition you choose, but no unfair competition of any kind. . . . A trust is an arrangement to get rid of competition. . . . A trust does not bring efficiency . . . it *buys efficiency out of business*. I am for big business, and I am against the trusts . . . any man who can put others out of business by making the thing cheaper to the consumer . . . I take off my hat to . . . "

—from *The New Freedom*

ROOSEVELT'S NEW NATIONALISM

"Combinations in industry [trusts] are the result of an imperative economic law which cannot be repealed by political legislation. . . . The way out lies, not in attempting to prevent such combinations, but in completely controlling them in the interest of the public welfare. . . . The absence of an effective state, and, especially national, restraint upon unfair money getting has tended to create a small class of enormously wealthy and economically powerful men. . . . The prime need is to change the conditions which enable these men to accumulate power."

—from *The New Nationalism*

DBQ Document-Based Questions

1. **Analyzing Visuals** From which state did Roosevelt gain the most Electoral College votes?

2. **Analyzing Primary Sources** How do Wilson and Roosevelt differ on trusts?

3. **Making Generalizations** What can you generalize about the two men based solely on their appearance in giving a speech?

Maps In Motion See *StudentWorks™ Plus* or glencoe.com.

Wilson Versus Roosevelt

The election of 1912 was a contest between two progressives with different approaches to reform. Roosevelt accepted the large trusts as a fact of life and set out proposals to increase regulation. Roosevelt also outlined a complete program of reforms. He favored legislation to protect women and children in the labor force and supported workers' compensation for those injured on the job. Roosevelt called his program the **New Nationalism.**

Wilson countered with what he called the **New Freedom.** He criticized Roosevelt's New Nationalism for supporting "regulated monopoly." Monopolies, he believed, should be destroyed, not regulated. Wilson argued that Roosevelt's approach gave the federal government too much power in the economy and did nothing to restore competition. Freedom, in Wilson's opinion, was more important than efficiency. "The history of liberty," Wilson declared, "is the history of the limitation of governmental power. . . . If America is not to have free enterprise, then she can have freedom of no sort whatever."

As expected, Roosevelt and Taft split the Republican voters, enabling Wilson to win the Electoral College with 435 votes and the election, even though he received less than 42 percent of the popular vote.

Reading Check **Summarizing** Who were the major candidates in the election of 1912?

Wilson's Reforms

MAIN Idea President Wilson reformed tariffs and banks and oversaw the creation of the Federal Trade Commission.

HISTORY AND YOU Are you aware of recent economic concerns and presidential responses to them? Read to learn of Wilson's economic actions after his election.

The new chief executive lost no time in embarking on his program of reform. "The president is at liberty, both in law and conscience, to be as big a man as he can," Wilson had once written. "His capacity will set the limit." During his eight years as president, Wilson demonstrated his executive power as he crafted reforms affecting tariffs, the banking system, trusts, and workers' rights.

Reforming Tariffs

Five weeks after taking office, Wilson appeared before Congress, the first president to do so since John Adams. He had come to present his bill to reduce tariffs. Wilson personally lobbied members of Congress to support the tariff reduction bill. Not even Roosevelt had taken such an active role in promoting legislation.

Wilson believed that lowering tariffs would benefit both American consumers and manufacturers. If tariff rates were lowered, he reasoned, the pressure of foreign competition would lead American manufacturers to improve their products and lower their prices. In the long term, businesses would benefit from the "constant necessity to be efficient, economical, and enterprising."

In 1913 Congress passed the Underwood Tariff, and Wilson signed it into law. This law reduced the average tariff on imported goods to about 30 percent of the value of the goods, or about half the tariff rate of the 1890s.

An important section of the Underwood Tariff Act provided for levying an **income tax,** or a direct tax on the earnings of individuals. The Constitution originally prohibited direct taxes on individuals. Ratification of the Sixteenth Amendment in 1913, however, gave the federal government the power to tax the income of individuals directly.

INFOGRAPHIC
Progressives Reform the Economic System

During Wilson's presidency, Congress passed several major reforms affecting the nation's economy. The Federal Reserve and the Federal Trade Commission were created, federal income tax was introduced, and unions were legalized.

The Federal Reserve

Why Was the Federal Reserve Created?
- to create national supervision of the banking industry
- to decentralize banking institutions and access to credit
- to prevent recurring "panics," such as the Panic of 1907
- to allow the demands of business to control the expanding and contracting of currency

What Does the Federal Reserve Do?
- controls the money supply and credit policies
- raises interest rates to member banks in times of plenty so that people won't borrow or spend too much money
- lowers interest rates to member banks during recessions so that people can more easily obtain needed credit
- supervises and supports Federal Reserve banks in twelve regions
- buys and sells government bonds and other securities

NATIONAL GEOGRAPHIC Federal Reserve System

- **6** Federal Reserve District
- ★ Federal Reserve Bank
- • Federal Reserve Branch Bank

Reforming the Banks

The United States had not had a central bank since the 1830s. During the economic depressions that hit the country periodically after that time, hundreds of small banks collapsed, wiping out the life savings of many of their customers.

To restore public confidence in the banking system, President Wilson supported the establishment of a federal reserve system. Banks would have to keep a portion of their deposits in a regional reserve bank, which would provide a financial cushion against unanticipated losses. The **Federal Reserve Act** of 1913 created 12 regional banks to be supervised by a Board of Governors, appointed by the president. This allowed national supervision of the banking system. The Board could set the interest rates the reserve banks charged other banks, thereby indirectly controlling the interest rates of the entire nation and the amount of money in circulation. The Federal Reserve Act became one of the most significant pieces of legislation in American history.

Other Reforms

Why Was the Federal Trade Commission Created?
- to advise business people on the legality of their actions
- to protect consumers from false advertising
- to investigate unfair trade practices

What Was the Clayton Antitrust Act?
- outlawed unfair trade practices
- made it illegal for a company to hold stock in another, if by doing so, it reduced competition
- made owners and directors of businesses guilty of violating antitrust laws criminally liable
- allowed private parties who had been injured by trusts to collect any damages in legal suits
- banned use of injunctions against strikes
- farm and labor organizations could no longer be considered illegal combinations in restraint of trade

Analyzing **VISUALS**

1. **Analyzing** What do the Federal Trade Commission and the Clayton Antitrust Act have in common?
2. **Identifying** What do you notice about the Western states and the locations of the Federal Reserve Banks? Why do you think this pattern exists?

Antitrust Action

During his campaign, Wilson had promised to restore competition to the economy by breaking up monopolies. Roosevelt had argued this was unrealistic, because big businesses were more efficient and unlikely to be replaced by smaller, more competitive firms. Once in office, Wilson's opinion shifted and he came to agree with Roosevelt. Progressives in Congress, however, continued to demand action against big business.

In the summer of 1914, at Wilson's request, Congress created the **Federal Trade Commission** (FTC) to monitor American business. The FTC had the power to investigate companies and issue "cease and desist" orders against companies engaging in **unfair trade practices,** or those that hurt competition. The FTC could be taken to court if a business disagreed with its rulings.

Wilson did not want the FTC to break up big business. Instead, it was to work toward limiting business activities that unfairly limited competition. He deliberately appointed conservative business leaders to serve as the FTC's first commissioners.

Unsatisfied by Wilson's approach, progressives in Congress responded by passing the **Clayton Antitrust Act** in 1914. The act outlawed certain practices that restricted competition. For example, it forbade agreements that required retailers who bought from one company to stop selling a competitor's products. It also banned price discrimination. Businesses could not charge different customers different prices. Manufacturers could no longer give discounts to some retailers who bought a large volume of goods, but not to others. Farm and labor organizations could no longer be considered illegal combinations in restraint of trade. The passing of the Clayton Antitrust Act corrected deficiencies in the Sherman Antitrust Act of 1890, which was the first federal antitrust law.

Before the Clayton act passed, labor unions lobbied Congress to exempt unions from antitrust legislation. The Clayton Antitrust Act specifically declared that its provisions did not apply to labor organizations or agricultural organizations. When the bill became law, Samuel Gompers, the head of the American Federation of Labor, called the act the workers' "Magna Carta" because it gave unions the right to exist.

Regulating Business

Despite his accomplishments, Wilson was not guaranteed reelection. In the congressional elections of 1914, Democrats suffered major losses. The Republican Party was also not likely to be divided as it had been in the election of 1912.

In 1916 Wilson signed the first federal law regulating child labor. The Keating-Owen Child Labor Act prohibited the employment of children under the age of 14 in factories producing goods for interstate commerce. In 1918 the Supreme Court declared the law **unconstitutional** on the grounds that child labor was not interstate commerce and therefore only states could regulate it. Wilson's effort, however, helped his reputation with progressive voters. Wilson also supported the Adamson Act, which established the eight-hour workday for railroad workers, and the Federal Farm Loan Act, which helped provide farmers with loans at low interest rates.

Reading Check **Evaluating** What was the impact of the passage of the Sixteenth Amendment?

Progressivism's Legacy and Limits

MAIN Idea Progressivism changed many people's ideas about the government's role in social issues.

HISTORY AND YOU Do you believe that groups of people have been left out of "the American dream"? Read on to find out about progressivism's failures and successes.

During his presidency, Wilson had built upon Roosevelt's foundation. He expanded the role of the federal government and the power of the president.

A New Kind of Government

Progressivism made important changes in the political life of the United States. Before this era, most Americans did not expect the government to pass laws protecting workers or regulating big business. In fact, many courts had previously ruled the passage of such laws unconstitutional.

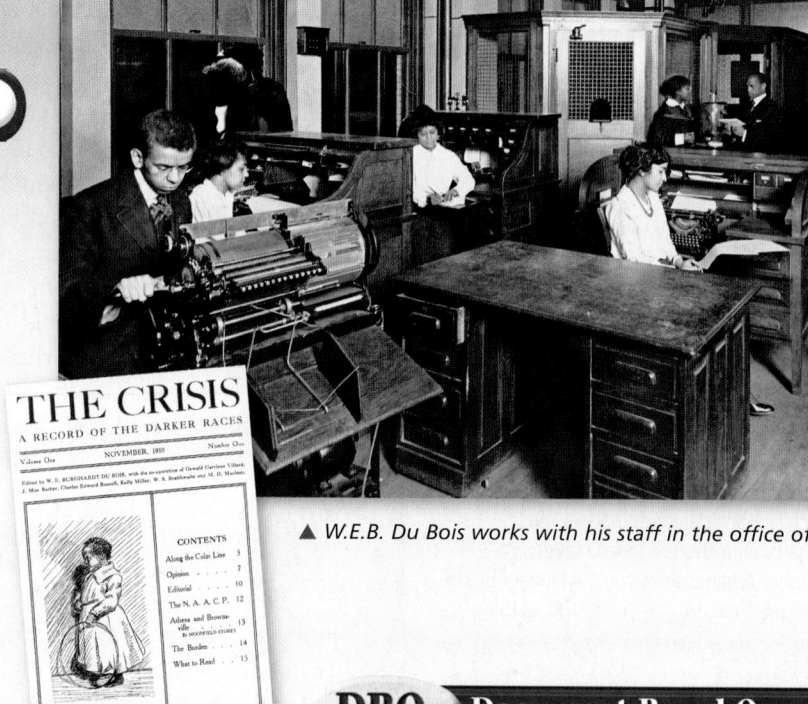

PRIMARY SOURCE
Founding of the NAACP

W.E.B. Du Bois was one of six founders of the NAACP. In *The Crisis*, the journal of the NAACP, Du Bois wrote:

PRIMARY SOURCE

"The object of this publication is to set forth those facts and arguments which show the danger of race prejudice. . . . It takes its name from the fact that the editors believe that this is a critical time in the history. . . . Catholicity and tolerance, reason and forbearance can today make the world-old dream of human brotherhood approach realization: while bigotry and prejudice, emphasized race consciousness and force can repeat the awful history of the contact of nations and groups in the past. We strive for this higher and broader vision of Peace and Good Will."

—from *The Crisis*, November 1910

▲ *The first issue of* The Crisis, *November 1910*

▲ *W.E.B. Du Bois works with his staff in the office of* The Crisis.

DBQ **Document-Based Questions**

1. **Analyzing** According to Du Bois, why was the magazine given its name?

2. **Analyzing Primary Sources** What "vision" does Du Bois recommend to his readers?

By the end of the Progressive Era, however, both legal and public opinion had shifted. Increasingly, Americans expected the government, particularly the federal government, to play a more active role in regulating the economy and solving social problems.

The Limits of Progressivism

The most conspicuous limit to progressivism was its failure to address racial and religious discrimination. African Americans themselves, however, were absorbing the reform spirit, which fueled their longstanding desire for advancement.

In 1905 W.E.B. Du Bois and 28 other African American leaders met at Niagara Falls to demand full rights for African Americans. They met on the Canadian side of the falls because no hotel on the American side would accept them. There, they launched what became known as the Niagara Movement. This meeting was one of many steps leading to the founding of the **National Association for the Advancement of Colored People** (NAACP) in 1909. Du Bois and other NAACP founders believed that voting rights were essential to end lynching and racial discrimination. "The power of the ballot we need in sheer self-defense," Du Bois said, "else what shall save us from a second slavery? Freedom too, the long-sought we still seek,—the freedom of life and limb, the freedom to work and think, the freedom to love and aspire. Work, culture, liberty,—all these we need, not singly, but together."

In 1908 race riots in Springfield, Illinois, shocked many people, including Mary White Ovington, a settlement house worker. She had been studying African Americans in New York, determined to do something to improve their situation. Other progressives, including Jane Addams of Hull House, and muckrakers Ida Wells-Barnett and Lincoln Steffens, joined Ovington in calling for change. Capitalizing on Springfield as Lincoln's hometown and his centennial birthday on February 12, 1909, they organized a national conference to take stock of the progress in emancipation. At a second conference the following year, the NAACP was born. Through Du Bois, the members learned of the Niagara Movement, and the two groups eventually merged.

African Americans were not the only minority group facing discrimination. Jewish people also lived in fear of mob violence. In 1913 Leo Frank, a Jew being tried in Atlanta for a murder he did not commit, was sentenced to death. Although his sentence was changed to life imprisonment, a mob lynched him two years later.

In this context, lawyer Sigmund Livingston started the Anti-Defamation League (ADL) to combat stereotypes and discrimination. The ADL worked to remove negative portrayals of Jews in movies, in print, and on stage. For example, the League protested an army manual published during World War I that targeted Jews as likely to pretend to be sick to escape work or battle. When the ADL complained, President Wilson had the manual recalled.

Reading Check **Evaluating** How did progressivism change American beliefs about the federal government?

Section 3 REVIEW

Vocabulary

1. **Explain** the significance of: Progressive Party, New Nationalism, New Freedom, income tax, Federal Reserve Act, Federal Trade Commission, unfair trade practices, Clayton Antitrust Act, National Association for the Advancement of Colored People.

Main Ideas

2. **Discussing** Explain how Wilson won the presidency without winning the popular vote.

3. **Identifying** Why did Wilson propose the Federal Reserve system?

4. **Organizing** Use a graphic organizer similar to the one below to list the effects progressivism had on American society.

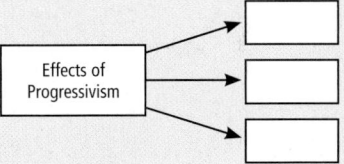

Critical Thinking

5. **Big Ideas** What new federal agencies increased the government's power to regulate the economy?

6. **Forming an Opinion** Which of Wilson's reforms do you consider to be most important? Why?

7. **Analyzing Visuals** Study the chart on page 310. What was the purpose of the Federal Reserve?

Writing About History

8. **Expository Writing** Suppose that you are a newspaper editor during Wilson's administration. Write an article about the failure of Progressives to address African American reform issues.

History ONLINE

Study Central™ To review this section, go to glencoe.com and click on Study Central.

Causes of the Progressive Movement

- People thought progress in science and knowledge could improve society.
- People thought immigration, urbanization, and industrialization had created social problems.
- People thought laissez-faire economics and an unregulated market led to social problems and that government could fix them.
- Political corruption prevented the government from helping its citizens.

▶ In 1910 a young boy works in a glass factory, an example of the type of child labor progressive reformers wanted to end.

Effects on Business and Society

- Interstate Commerce Commission is strengthened.
- Consumer protection laws are passed.
- Federal Trade Commission is created.
- Federal Reserve System is created to regulate the money supply.
- Clayton Antitrust Act grants labor unions more rights.
- Zoning laws and building codes improve urban housing.
- Child labor laws are passed, regulating time and conditions for minors to work.
- Workers' compensation laws are passed.
- Temperance movement begins seeking limitations on the production and consumption of alcohol.

▲ Trade unions begin their march honoring victims of the Triangle Shirtwaist Factory fire.

Effects on Politics

- Cities begin adopting commission and city-manager forms of government.
- States begin to adopt the direct primary system, allowing voters to choose candidates for office.
- States begin to allow initiatives, referendums, and recall votes.
- Seventeenth Amendment is ratified, requiring direct election of senators.
- Nineteenth Amendment is ratified, guaranteeing women the right to vote.

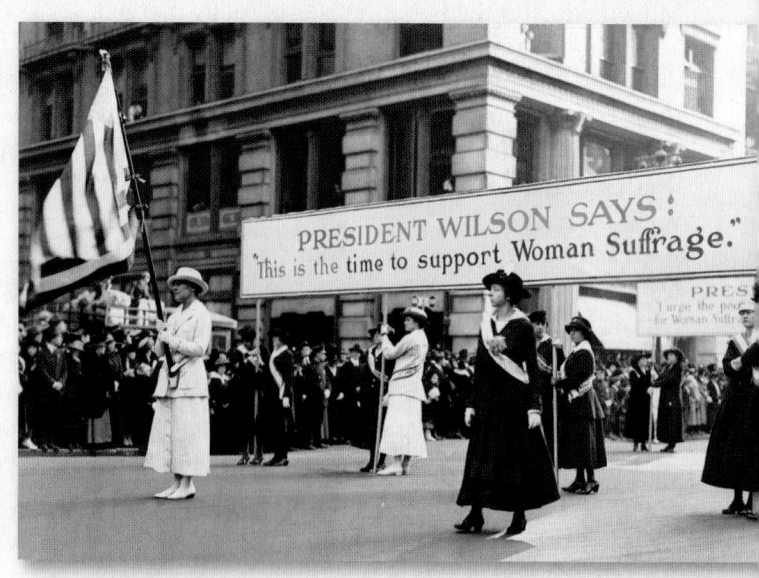

PRESIDENT WILSON SAYS: "This is the time to support Woman Suffrage."

▶ Women march in 1916 in support of Woodrow Wilson's efforts to grant women the right to vote.

Reviewing Vocabulary

Directions: Choose the word or words that best complete each sentence.

1. The term "muckraker" was used in the early 1900s to describe

   A street sweepers.

   B investigative journalists.

   C farmers.

   D garden designers.

2. Women spent more than 70 years actively seeking _____, or the right to vote.

   A initiative

   B petition

   C recall

   D suffrage

3. The temperance movement was linked to the _____ of alcohol.

   A prohibition

   B production

   C reduction

   D requisition

4. When Gifford Pinchot leaked a story to the press against William Taft's will, the president fired him for

   A arbitration.

   B prohibition.

   C insubordination.

   D initiation.

5. The Federal Trade Commission was created to combat monopolies and trusts. It did this, in part, by preventing

   A unfair trade practices.

   B Social Darwinism.

   C insubordination.

   D regulation.

Reviewing Main Ideas

Directions: Choose the best answers to the following questions.

Section 1 *(pp. 292–299)*

6. Progressivism used the principles of science to solve problems resulting from

   A industrialization and urbanization.

   B global warming and fossil fuel use.

   C the outbreak of war and proliferation of weapons.

   D epidemic diseases and plagues.

7. Which of the following allowed proposed legislation to be placed on the ballot for voter approval?

   A direct primary

   B referendum

   C initiative

   D veto

8. What did the Nineteenth Amendment accomplish?

   A It required colleges to accept women.

   B It guaranteed child care for workers' children.

   C It granted women the right to vote.

   D It guaranteed equal pay for equal work.

Section 2 *(pp. 300–307)*

9. Theodore Roosevelt became known as a trustbuster for his actions against

   A the Northern Securities company.

   B the United Mine Workers.

   C the automobile industry.

   D national parks.

TEST-TAKING

You can eliminate some answers by using your own knowledge and common sense. Read through each option and decide if it fits with what you know; if it does not, discard it.

Need Extra Help?									
If You Missed Questions . . .	1	2	3	4	5	6	7	8	9
Go to Page . . .	293	296–297	299	306–307	311	304	295	296–297	300–301

10. Upton Sinclair's novel *The Jungle* was instrumental in exposing which industry?

A steel

B meatpacking

C oil

D alcohol

11. President Taft broke with Roosevelt and progressives over

A unions.

B child labor.

C trust-busting.

D tariffs.

Section 3 *(pp. 308–313)*

12. How did President Wilson attempt to reform the banking industry?

A He created the Federal Reserve System.

B He vetoed the Underwood Tariff Act.

C He opposed the Sixteenth Amendment.

D He refused to break up monopolies.

13. What did Du Bois and other NAACP founders believe was essential to end racial violence?

A establishment of African American colleges

B higher-paying jobs for low-income citizens

C voting rights for African Americans

D private schools for African American children

Critical Thinking

Directions: Choose the best answers to the following questions.

14. How did Wisconsin governor Robert M. La Follette help to expand democracy in the United States?

A by favoring women's suffrage

B by requiring political parties to hold a direct primary

C by allowing recall elections to remove elected officials from office before the end of his or her term

D by providing for absentee ballots to voters

Base your answers to questions 15 and 16 on the map below and on your knowledge of Chapter 8.

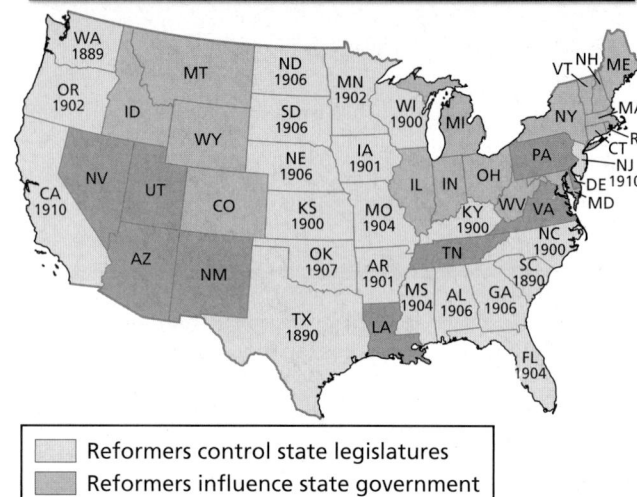

Progressives and State Governments, 1889–1912

☐ Reformers control state legislatures
☐ Reformers influence state government
■ Reformers not effective
1900 Date reformers came to power

15. Which state came under the control of reformers before Wisconsin?

A Florida

B Oregon

C Washington

D Nebraska

16. According to the map, what generalization can you make about progressives in state governments?

A Progressives were most active in the Pacific Northwest, the Great Plains, and the South.

B They had no influence in the New England states.

C Reformers controlled few state legislatures by 1910.

D Reformers had little success in the Deep South.

Need Extra Help?							
If You Missed Questions . . .	10	11	12	13	14	15	16
Go to Page . . .	302	306	311	313	294–295	294–295	294–295

GO ON

17. The Progressive movement strengthened the cause of women's suffrage by

   A drawing attention to child labor.

   B encouraging trustbusting.

   C making government more efficient.

   D showing women they needed the vote to get the reforms they wanted.

Analyze the cartoon and answer the question that follows. Base your answer on the cartoon and on your knowledge of Chapter 8.

Source: S.D. Ehrhart, *Puck*, February 24, 1909

18. How does the cartoon portray William Howard Taft?

   A as eager to see Roosevelt leave the White House

   B as Roosevelt's equal in every way

   C as a servant walking off with Roosevelt's big stick

   D as a nursemaid to the baby, Roosevelt's policies

Document-Based Questions

Directions: Analyze the document and answer the short-answer questions that follow the document.

Lucy Haessler writes of her childhood memories surrounding the woman suffrage movement:

> "The suffragettes had a big headquarters in downtown Washington. My mother would take me up there on Saturdays when she volunteered to help out with mailings. The backbone of the suffrage movement was composed of well-to-do, middle-class women, both Republicans and Democrats. There weren't many working-class women in the movement. . . .
>
> The suffragettes organized pickets and marches and rallies. I was only ten years old the first time I went to a march with my mother. She told me, 'Oh, you're too young, you can't go.' But I said, 'I am going, because you're going to win the right to vote and I'm going to vote when I'm grown-up.' So she let me march. . . . The more marches that were held, the more you could feel the movement just building and building. . . ."
>
> —quoted in *The Century for Young People*

19. Who does Haessler say were the backbone of the movement? Why do you think working-class women were not involved?

20. Why did Haessler want to march when she was only ten years old?

Extended Response

21. Upton Sinclair and other muckrakers took on the social ills of their day, forcing passage of legislation such as the Pure Food and Drug Act. Select one social problem of modern life and write a persuasive essay that suggests legislation to address the issue. The essay should include an introduction, several paragraphs, and a conclusion that supports your position.

History ONLINE

For additional test practice, use Self-Check Quizzes—Chapter 8 at glencoe.com.

Need Extra Help?					
If You Missed Questions . . .	17	18	19	20	21
Go to Page . . .	294–297	305–307	296–297	296–297	293–299

World War I and Its Aftermath

1914–1920

American soldiers fire on German positions during the Battle of the Argonne Forest, 1918

U.S. PRESIDENTS

Wilson 1913–1921

1915
- German submarine sinks the *Lusitania*

1917
- U.S. enters the war
- Selective Service Act passed

U.S. EVENTS

WORLD EVENTS

1914

1916

1914
- Franz Ferdinand assassinated; war begins in Europe

1916
- Battle of Verdun begins in February
- Battle of the Somme begins in July

1917
- Bolshevik Revolution begins in October

MAKING CONNECTIONS
Why Do Nations Go to War?

World War I was the first time in American history that the United States sent troops to fight in Europe. This decision ended the long-standing policy of remaining neutral in Europe's wars.

- *Why do you think the United States changed its policy and sent troops to Europe?*
- *Do you think it was a difficult decision?*

FOLDABLES™

Organizing Information As you read the chapter, write information under each tab, listing which country is in the alliance, why it joined the alliance, or what reasons it had for disagreeing with the countries in the opposing alliance.

Central Powers	Allied Powers
World War I	

1918
- Congress passes Sedition Act
- Armistice ends fighting on November 11

1919
- Race riots and strikes take place in Northern cities

1920
- Red Scare and Palmer Raids

1918   1920

1918
- Treaty of Brest-Litovsk ends Russian-German war

1919
- Versailles Peace Conference begins

History ONLINE Visit glencoe.com and enter *QuickPass*™ code TAVMT5147c9 for Chapter 9 resources.

The United States Enters World War I

Guide to Reading

Big Ideas
Trade, War, and Migration Although the United States tried to stay neutral, events pushed the nation into war.

Content Vocabulary
- militarism (p. 321)
- nationalism (p. 322)
- propaganda (p. 324)
- contraband (p. 326)

Academic Vocabulary
- emphasis (p. 322)
- erode (p. 326)

People and Events to Identify
- Balkans (p. 322)
- Franz Ferdinand (p. 322)
- Sussex pledge (p. 327)
- Zimmermann telegram (p. 327)

Reading Strategy
Organizing Complete the graphic organizer shown below by identifying the factors that contributed to the conflict.

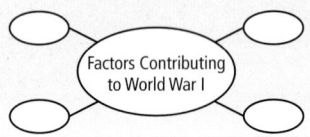

Factors Contributing to World War I

Militarism, alliances, imperialism, and nationalism led to World War I in Europe. Attacks on U.S. ships and American support for the Allies eventually caused the United States to enter the war.

World War I Begins

MAIN Idea Old alliances and nationalist sentiments among European nations set the stage for World War I.

HISTORY AND YOU Does your school have a long-standing rivalry with another school? Read how European nations formed political alliances that brought most of the continent into war.

Despite more than 40 years of general peace, tensions among European nations were building in 1914. Throughout the late 1800s and early 1900s, a number of factors created problems among the powers of Europe and set the stage for a monumental war.

Militarism and Alliances

The roots of World War I date back to the 1860s. In 1864, while Americans fought the Civil War, the German kingdom of Prussia launched the first of a series of wars to unite the various German states into one nation. By 1871 Prussia had united Germany and proclaimed the birth of the German Empire. The new German nation rapidly industrialized and quickly became one of the most powerful nations in the world.

The creation of Germany transformed European politics. In 1870, as part of their plan to unify Germany, the Prussians had attacked and defeated France. They then forced the French to give up territory along the German border. From that point forward, France and Germany were enemies. To protect itself, Germany signed alliances with Italy and with Austria-Hungary, a huge empire that controlled much of southeastern Europe. This became known as the Triple Alliance.

The new alliance alarmed Russian leaders, who feared that Germany intended to expand eastward into Russia. Russia and Austria-Hungary were also competing for influence in southeastern Europe. Many of the people of southeastern Europe were Slavs—the same ethnic group as the Russians—and the Russians wanted to support them against Austria-Hungary. As a result, Russia and France had a common interest in opposing Germany and Austria-Hungary. In 1894 they signed the Franco-Russian Alliance, promising to come to each other's aid in a war with the Triple Alliance.

In 1839, Britain gave Belgium a guarantee that it would protect Belgium's neutrality.

Triple Entente
Triple Alliance
Other European states

Germany took Alsace-Lorraine from France in 1870. The French were determined to recover the territory.

Russia and Serbia were both Slavic countries. Russia did not have an alliance with Serbia but was determined to help Serbia against Austria-Hungary.

Balkan Nationalism
Southeastern Europe is known as the Balkans. In the 1800s, two empires controlled this region—Austria-Hungary and the Turkish Ottoman Empire. As the ideas of nationalism spread across Europe, the people in the region fought a series of wars to gain their independence. By 1914, most of the Balkans were free, except for the Slavs living in Bosnia.

The Growth of Armies, 1870–1914

1870   1914

Thousands of Troops — Russia, France, Germany, Austria-Hungary, Britain

0 400 kilometers
0 400 miles
Lambert Azimuthal Equal-Area projection

Analyzing VISUALS

1. **Interpreting** Study the map and chart above. Why might Britain think it had to have the strongest navy in Europe?

2. **Analyzing** Germany feared France might go to war with them. Based on the map and chart, why would German leaders have reached this conclusion?

Maps In Motion See *StudentWorks™ Plus* or glencoe.com.

The system of alliances in Europe encouraged **militarism**—the aggressive build-up of armed forces to intimidate and threaten other nations. German militarism eventually forced Britain to become involved in the alliance system. Britain's policy was to support weaker countries against stronger ones so as to make sure no country conquered all of Europe. By the late 1800s, it was clear that Germany had become the strongest nation in Europe.

In 1898 Germany began building a large modern navy as well. A strong German navy threatened the British, who depended on their naval strength to protect their island from invasion. By the early 1900s, an arms race had begun between Great Britain and Germany, as both nations raced to build warships.

The naval race greatly increased tensions between Germany and Britain and convinced the British to establish closer relations with France and Russia. The British still refused to sign a formal alliance, so their new relationship with the French and Russians became known as an entente cordiale—a friendly understanding. Britain, France, and Russia became known as the Triple Entente.

Causes of World War I

Use the acronym MAIN to remember the four main causes of World War I: Militarism, Alliances, Imperialism, Nationalism.

MILITARISM

▲ *Warships of the German Imperial fleet are shown anchored near Kiel, Germany in 1911. The naval race between Britain and Germany caused tension in Europe prior to World War I.*

ALLIANCES

France

Austria-Hungary

Germany   Italy

▲ *An 1883 British cartoon illustrates the Triple Alliance.*

IMPERIALISM

▲ *Franz Joseph, Emperor of Austria-Hungary, and Wilhelm II, Emperor of Germany, salute during a parade in Berlin in 1889.*

Imperialism and Nationalism

By the late 1800s, **nationalism,** or a feeling of intense pride in one's homeland, had become a powerful idea in Europe. Nationalists place primary **emphasis** on promoting their homeland's culture and interests above those of other countries. Nationalism was one of the reasons for the tensions among the European powers. Each nation viewed the others as competitors, and many people were willing to go to war to expand their nation at the expense of others.

One of the basic ideas of nationalism is the right to self-determination—the idea that people who share a national identity should have their own country and government. In the 1800s nationalism led to a crisis in southeastern Europe in the region known as the **Balkans.** Historically, the Ottoman Empire and the Austro-Hungarian Empire had ruled the Balkans. Both of these empires were made up of many different nations.

Imperialism—the idea that a country can increase its power and wealth by controlling other peoples—had convinced the major European powers to build empires in the 1700s and 1800s. Nationalism ran counter to imperialism. As the idea of nationalism spread in the late 1800s and early 1900s, the different national groups within Europe's empires began to press for independence.

Among the groups pushing for independence were the Serbs, Bosnians, Croats, and Slovenes. These people all spoke similar languages and had come to see themselves as one people. They called themselves South Slavs, or Yugoslavs. The first of these people to obtain independence were the Serbs, who formed a nation called Serbia between the Ottoman and Austro-Hungarian Empires. Serbs believed their nation's mission was to unite the South Slavs.

Russia supported the Serbs, while Austria-Hungary did what it could to limit Serbia's growth. In 1908 Austria-Hungary annexed Bosnia, which had belonged to the Ottoman Empire. The Serbs were furious. They wanted Bosnia to be part of their nation. The annexation demonstrated to the Serbs that Austria-Hungary had no intention of letting the Slavic people in its empire become independent.

A Terrorist Attack Brings War

In late June 1914 the heir to the Austro-Hungarian throne, the Archduke **Franz Ferdinand,** visited the Bosnian capital of Sarajevo. As he and his wife rode through the city, a Bosnian revolutionary named Gavrilo

NATIONALISM

▲ Serbian nationalist Gavrilo Princip is dragged into police headquarters in Sarajevo shortly after killing Archduke Franz Ferdinand, heir to the Austro-Hungarian throne.

Analyzing VISUALS

1. **Interpreting** What point is the cartoonist trying to make about the Triple Alliance?

2. **Explaining** How did Austrian imperialism and Balkan nationalism contribute to the outbreak of World War I?

Princip rushed their open car and shot the couple to death. The assassin was a member of a Serbian nationalist group nicknamed the "Black Hand." The assassination took place with the knowledge of Serbian officials who hoped to start a war that would bring down the Austro-Hungarian Empire.

The Alliances Are Triggered The Austro-Hungarian government blamed Serbia for the attack and decided the time had come to crush Serbia in order to prevent Slavic nationalism from undermining its empire. Knowing an attack on Serbia might trigger a war with Russia, the Austrians asked their German allies for support. Germany promised to support Austria-Hungary if war erupted.

Austria-Hungary then issued an ultimatum to the Serbian government. The Serbs counted on Russia to back them up, and the Russians, in turn, counted on France. French leaders were worried that they might someday be caught alone in a war with Germany, so they promised to support Russia if war began.

On July 28 Austria-Hungary declared war on Serbia. Russia immediately mobilized its army, including troops stationed on the German border. On August 1 Germany declared war on Russia. Two days later, it declared war on France. World War I had begun.

Germany's Plan Fails Germany had long been prepared for war against France and Russia. It immediately launched a massive invasion of France, hoping to knock the French out of the war. It would then be able to send its troops east to deal with the Russians.

The German plan had one major problem. It required the German forces to advance through neutral Belgium in order to encircle the French troops. The British had guaranteed Belgium's neutrality. When German troops crossed the Belgian frontier, Britain declared war on Germany.

Those fighting for the Triple Entente were called the Allies. France, Russia, and Great Britain formed the backbone of the Allies along with Italy, which joined them in 1915 after the other Allies promised to cede Austro-Hungarian territory to Italy after the war. What remained of the Triple Alliance—Germany and Austria-Hungary—joined with the Ottoman Empire and Bulgaria to form the Central Powers.

The German plan seemed to work at first. German troops swept through Belgium and headed into France, driving back the French and British forces. Then, to the great surprise of the Germans, Russian troops invaded Germany. The Germans had not expected Russia to mobilize so quickly. They were forced to pull some of their troops away from the attack on France and send them east to stop the Russians. This weakened the German forces just enough to give the Allies a chance to stop them. The Germans drove to within 30 miles (48 km) of Paris, but stubborn resistance by British and French troops at the Battle of the Marne finally stopped the German advance. Because the swift German attack had failed to defeat the French, both sides became locked in a bloody stalemate along hundreds of miles of trenches that would barely change position for the next three years.

The Central Powers had greater success on the Eastern Front. German and Austro-Hungarian forces stopped the Russian attack and then went on the offensive. They swept across hundreds of miles of territory and took hundreds of thousands of prisoners. Russia suffered 2 million killed, wounded, or captured in 1915 alone, but it kept fighting.

✔ **Reading Check** **Explaining** What incident triggered the beginning of World War I?

America Declares War

MAIN Idea British propaganda and business interests led most Americans to a pro-British stance on the war.

HISTORY AND YOU Do you recall a time when you tried to remain neutral in a fight between friends? Read how the United States tried to stay out of World War I.

When the fighting began, President Wilson was determined to keep the country out of a European war. He immediately declared the United States to be neutral in the conflict. "We must be impartial in thought as well as in action," Wilson stated. For many Americans that proved difficult to do.

Americans Take Sides

Despite the president's plea, many Americans supported one side or the other. Many of the country's 8 million German Americans, for example, supported their homeland. Many of the nation's 4.5 million Irish Americans, whose homeland endured centuries of British rule, also sympathized with the Central Powers.

In general, however, American public opinion favored the Allied cause. Many Americans valued the heritage, language, and political ideals they shared with Britain. Others treasured America's links with France, a great friend to America during the Revolutionary War.

For more than two years, the United States officially remained neutral. During this time a great debate began over whether the United States should prepare for war. Supporters of the "preparedness" movement believed that preparing for war was the best way to stay out of the conflict. They also argued that if the United States was pulled into the war, it was better to be prepared.

Other Americans disagreed. In 1915 Carrie Chapman Catt and Jane Addams—leaders of the woman suffrage movement—founded the Women's Peace Party (later known as the International League for Peace and Freedom). This organization, along with others such as the League to Limit Armament, worked to keep America out of the war by urging the president not to build up the military.

Government Officials Back Britain One select group of Americans was decidedly pro-British: President Wilson's cabinet. Only Secretary of State William Jennings Bryan favored neutrality. The other cabinet members, as well as Bryan's chief adviser, Robert Lansing, and Walter Hines Page, the American ambassador to London, argued forcefully on behalf of Britain. Many American military leaders also backed the British. They believed that an Allied victory was the only way to preserve the international balance of power.

British officials worked diligently to win American support. One method they used was **propaganda,** or information designed to influence opinion. Both sides used propaganda, but German propaganda was mostly anti-Russian and did not appeal to most Americans. British propaganda, on the other hand, was extremely skillful.

Debates IN HISTORY

Should America Stay Neutral in World War I?

Americans were deeply divided about whether the United States should remain neutral in World War I. Despite President Wilson's pronouncement that Americans should remain neutral in thought as well as action, many Americans, including those working for the government, had very definite opinions as to whether or not the United States should enter the war.

To control the flow of news to the United States, the British cut the transatlantic telegraph cable from Europe to the United States. This meant that most war news would be based on British reports. The American ambassador to Britain, Walter Hines Page, himself strongly pro-British, gave the reports legitimacy by endorsing many of them. When stories arrived describing German atrocities, enough Americans believed them to help sway American support in favor of the Allies.

Business Supports Britain American business interests also leaned toward the Allies. Companies in the United States, particularly on the East Coast, had strong ties with businesses in the Allied countries. As business leader Thomas W. Lamont stated, "Our firm had never for one moment been neutral: we did not know how to be. From the very start we did everything that we could to contribute to the cause of the Allies."

Many American banks began to invest heavily in an Allied victory. American loans to the cash-hungry Allies skyrocketed. By 1917 such loans would total over $2 billion. Other American banks, particularly in the Midwest, where pro-German feelings were strongest, also lent some $27 million to Germany.

More money might have been lent to Germany, but most foreign loans required the approval of William McAdoo, the secretary of the Treasury. McAdoo was strongly pro-British and did what he could to limit loans to Germany. As a result, the country's prosperity was intertwined with the military fortunes of Britain, France, and Russia. If the Allies won, the money would be paid back; if not, the money might be lost forever.

YES

John Works
Civil War Veteran and U.S. Senator

PRIMARY SOURCE

"Germany is not moving against this country. She has not been guilty of any aggression against us. She has taken the lives of a few of our citizens, because they got in the way when she was prosecuting a war against another nation and fighting to preserve her existence. If the German Government should make aggressive warfare against the United States you would not need any exhortation in the Senate of the United States to arouse the patriotism of the American people. You would not be holding open your enlisting stations without getting any soldiers."

—from *The Congressional Record*, March 4, 1917

NO

Robert Lansing
Secretary of State

PRIMARY SOURCE

"I have come to the conclusion that the German Government is utterly hostile to all nations with democratic institutions because those who compose it see in democracy a menace to absolutism and the defeat of the German ambition for world domination....

... Germany must not be permitted to win this war and to break even, though to prevent it this country is forced to take an active part. This ultimate necessity must be constantly in our minds in all our controversies with the belligerents. American public opinion must be prepared for the time, which may come, when we will have to cast aside our neutrality and become one of the champions of democracy."

—from *War Memoirs of Robert Lansing*

DBQ **Document-Based Questions**

1. **Summarizing** When does Senator Works believe war is justified?

2. **Explaining** Why does Secretary of State Lansing believe Germany is a threat to the United States?

3. **Comparing** Based on these sources, what is the focus of the neutrality debate? What is not being discussed?

4. **Evaluating** Which position do you agree with? Write an essay explaining why the other side is wrong.

Moving Toward War

Although most Americans supported the Allies and hoped for their victory, they did not want to join the conflict. However, a series of events gradually **eroded** American neutrality and drew the nation into the war.

German Submarines Go Into Action

Shortly after the war began, the British declared a blockade of German ports and began intercepting neutral merchant ships sailing to Europe. They forced the ships to land at British ports where they were inspected for **contraband,** or goods prohibited from shipment to Germany and its allies.

Although Britain's decision to intercept neutral ships, including American ships, led to protests from the U.S. government, the German response angered Americans even more. Britain and France depended on food, equipment, and other supplies from both the United States and their overseas empires. To stop those shipments, Germany deployed submarines known as U-boats—from the German word *Unterseeboot* ("underwater boat"). In February 1915, the Germans announced that they would sink without warning any ship they found in the waters around Britain.

Germany's announcement triggered outrage in the United States and elsewhere. Germany had signed an international treaty that banned attacks on civilian ships without warning. The Germans claimed that their U-boats would be placed at great risk if they had to surface and give a warning before firing.

The Germans Sink the *Lusitania*

The issue reached a crisis on May 7, 1915, when the British passenger ship *Lusitania* entered the war zone. A German submarine sunk the ship, killing nearly 1,200 passengers—including 128 Americans. The attack outraged Americans who saw the sinking as a terrorist attack on civilians, including women and children, not as a legitimate act of war.

Wilson tried to defuse the crisis. He refused to threaten Germany with war saying that the United States was "too proud to fight." Instead, he sent several official protests to Germany insisting that it stop endangering the lives of noncombatants in the war zone.

Late in March 1916, Wilson's policy was tested when a U-boat torpedoed the French passenger ship *Sussex*, injuring several Americans on board. Although Wilson's closest advisers favored breaking off diplomatic relations with Germany, the president chose

Turning Points

The Sinking of the *Lusitania*

When World War I began, many Americans supported one side or the other, but most agreed the United States should stay out of the war. Eight months later, when the German submarine U-20 sank the *Lusitania*, killing 1,195 people, including 128 Americans, attitudes began to shift.

The attack seemed to prove that Germany was acting in an uncivilized way and it gave credibility to British propaganda. Even though the United States would not enter the war for nearly two more years, the attack on the *Lusitania* marked a turning point in the war because it changed American attitudes and set the stage for the American entry into the war.

ANALYZING HISTORY Do you think the use of submarines in World War I was justified? Write a brief essay explaining your opinion.

▲ A mass funeral for Lusitania *victims was held in Queenston, Ireland, on May 23, 1915.* **How do you think people reacted when they saw photos like this in the newspaper?**

▲ After the sinking, the Boston Committee of Public Safety issued this poster showing a drowning woman and baby and urging Americans to prepare for war by building up the military.

to issue one last warning. He demanded that the German government abandon its methods of submarine warfare or risk war with the United States.

Germany did not want to strengthen the Allies by drawing the United States into the war. It promised with certain conditions to sink no more merchant ships without warning. The **Sussex Pledge,** as it was called, met the foreign-policy goals of both Germany and President Wilson by keeping the United States out of the war a little longer.

Wilson's efforts to keep American soldiers at home played an important part in his reelection bid in 1916. Campaigning as the "peace" candidate, his campaign slogan, "He kept us out of the war," helped Wilson win a narrow victory over the Republican nominee, Charles Evans Hughes.

The United States Declares War

Following Wilson's reelection, events quickly brought the country to the brink of war. In January 1917, a German official named Arthur Zimmermann sent a telegram to the German ambassador in Mexico asking him to make an offer to the Mexican government: If Mexico agreed to become an ally of Germany in a war with the United States, Germany promised Mexico would regain its "lost territory in Texas, New Mexico, and Arizona" after the war. British intelligence intercepted the **Zimmermann telegram.** Shortly afterward, it was leaked to American newspapers. Furious, many Americans now concluded war with Germany was necessary.

Then, on February 1, 1917, Germany resumed unrestricted submarine warfare. German military leaders believed that they could starve Britain into submission in four to six months if their U-boats began sinking all ships on sight. Although they knew this decision might draw the United States into the war, they did not believe the Americans could raise an army and transport it to Europe in time. Between February 3 and March 21, German U-boats sank six American ships. Finally roused to action, President Wilson appeared before a special session of Congress on April 2, 1917. Declaring that "the world must be made safe for democracy," Wilson asked Congress to declare war on Germany.

PRIMARY SOURCE

"It is a fearful thing to lead this great peaceful people into war. . . . But the right is more precious than peace, and we shall fight for the things which we have always carried nearest to our hearts—for democracy, for the right of those who submit to authority to have a voice in their own governments, for the rights and liberties of small nations. . . ."

—quoted in the Congressional Record, 1917

After a debate, the Senate passed the resolution on April 4 by a vote of 82 to 6. The House concurred 373 to 50 on April 6, and Wilson signed the resolution. America was at war.

Reading Check **Summarizing** How did Germany's use of unrestricted submarine warfare bring America into World War I?

Section 1 REVIEW

Vocabulary
1. **Explain** the significance of: militarism, nationalism, Balkans, Franz Ferdinand, propaganda, contraband, Sussex Pledge, Zimmermann telegram.

Main Ideas
2. **Identifying** Name the two alliances in Europe at the start of World War I, and list the members of each alliance.

3. **Explaining** Why did many Americans support the British in the war even though the United States was officially neutral?

Critical Thinking
4. **Big Ideas** How did trade and economics contribute to America's entry into World War I?

5. **Organizing** Use a graphic organizer similar to the one below to identify the events that led the United States to enter World War I.

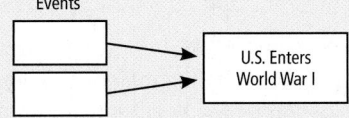

6. **Analyzing Visuals** Examine the images on page 326. How did images like these contribute to America's eventual entry into the war?

Writing About History
7. **Expository Writing** Imagine you are an American survivor of the sinking of the *Lusitania.* Write a letter to President Wilson about what you think he should do.

History ONLINE
Study Central™ To review this section, go to glencoe.com and click on Study Central.

The Home Front

Guide to Reading

Big Ideas
Government and Society To successfully fight the war, the United States government had to mobilize the entire nation.

Content Vocabulary
• victory garden *(p. 328)*
• espionage *(p. 330)*

Academic Vocabulary
• migrate *(p. 330)*
• draft *(p. 332)*

People and Events to Identify
• War Industries Board *(p. 328)*
• National War Labor Board *(p. 329)*
• Committee on Public Information *(p. 330)*
• selective service *(p. 332)*

Reading Strategy
Taking Notes Use the major headings of this section to create an outline similar to the one below.

> The Home Front
> I. Organizing the Economy
>   A.
>   B.
>   C.
> II.
>   A.
>   B.

To fight World War I, the American government used progressive ideas and new government agencies to mobilize the population and organize the economy.

Organizing the Economy

MAIN Idea The government used progressive ideas to manage the economy and pay for the war.

HISTORY AND YOU How do you help conserve food or fuel resources? Read how Americans made sacrifices to aid the war effort.

When the United States entered the war in April 1917, progressives controlled the federal government. Rather than abandon their ideas during wartime, they applied progressive ideas to fighting the war. Their ideas about planning and scientific management shaped how the American government organized the war effort.

Wartime Agencies

To efficiently manage the relationship between the federal government and private companies, Congress created new agencies to coordinate mobilization and ensure the efficient use of national resources. These agencies emphasized cooperation between big business and government, not direct government control. Business executives, managers, and government officials staffed the new agencies.

Managing the Economy Perhaps the most important of the new agencies was the **War Industries Board** (WIB), established in July 1917 to coordinate the production of war materials. At first, the WIB's authority was limited, but problems with production convinced Wilson to expand its powers and appoint Bernard Baruch, a Wall Street stockbroker, to run it. The WIB told manufacturers what they could produce, allocated raw materials, ordered the construction of new factories, and, in a few instances, set prices.

Perhaps the most successful agency was the Food Administration, run by Herbert Hoover. This agency was responsible for increasing food production while reducing civilian consumption. Using the slogan "Food Will Win the War—Don't Waste It," it encouraged families to conserve food and grow their own vegetables in **victory gardens.** By having Wheatless Mondays, Meatless Tuesdays, and Porkless Thursdays, families would leave more food for the troops.

While Hoover managed food production, the Fuel Administration, run by Harry Garfield, tried to manage the nation's use of coal and oil.

"SHALL WE BE MORE TENDER WITH OUR DOLLARS THAN WITH THE LIVES OF OUR SONS?"

McAdoo

WE DEPEND ON YOU

BUY A UNITED STATES GOVERNMENT BOND OF THE

2ND LIBERTY LOAN OF 1917

REMEMBER! THE FLAG OF LIBERTY SUPPORT IT!

BUY U.S. Government Bonds 3rd. LIBERTY LOAN

▶ The actor Douglas Fairbanks urges Americans to buy Liberty Bonds at a rally held in New York City in 1918.

Paying for World War I

Billions of dollars (y-axis: 0 to 8.0)

Categories: First Liberty Loan, Second Liberty Loan, Third Liberty Loan, Fourth Liberty Loan, Victory Loan, Other Loans, Taxation

Analyzing VISUALS

To pay for World War I, the U.S. government increased taxes and issued bonds. Progressives liked bonds because they were voluntary and Americans could buy them based on their financial situation. Officials worried, however, that the war had so divided Americans that few would buy them. To get people to buy bonds, the government printed posters, organized parades, and asked movie stars to promote them.

1. **Analyzing** What was the total revenue raised by loans? What percentage of the cost of the war was paid by taxes?

2. **Interpreting** What point is the poster for the 2nd Liberty Loan making? What group of people does the poster for the 3rd Liberty Loan address?

To conserve energy, Garfield introduced daylight savings time and shortened workweeks for factories that did not make war materials. He also encouraged Americans to observe Heatless Mondays.

Paying for the War By the end of the war, the United States had spent about $32 billion. To fund the war effort, Congress raised income tax rates, placed new taxes on corporate profits, and imposed an extra tax on the profits of arms factories.

Taxes, however, did not cover the entire cost of the war. The government also borrowed over $20 billion through the sale of Liberty Bonds and Victory Bonds. Americans who bought bonds were lending money to the government that would be repaid with interest in a specified number of years.

Mobilizing the Workforce

The success of the war effort also required the cooperation of workers. To prevent strikes from disrupting the war effort, the government established the **National War Labor Board** (NWLB) in March 1918. Chaired by William Howard Taft and Frank Walsh, a prominent labor attorney, the NWLB attempted to mediate labor disputes that might otherwise lead to strikes.

The NWLB often pressured industry to improve wages, adopt an eight-hour workday, and allow unions the right to organize and bargain collectively. In exchange, labor leaders agreed not to disrupt war production with strikes or other disturbances. As a result, membership in unions increased by just over one million between 1917 and 1919.

History ONLINE
Student Web Activity Visit glencoe.com and complete the activity on wartime propaganda.

For an example of government efforts to promote patriotism, read "The American's Creed" on page R51 in **Documents in American History.**

Women Support Industry With large numbers of men in the military, employers were willing to hire women for jobs that had traditionally been limited to men. Some one million women joined the workforce for the first time during the war, and another 8 million switched to higher paying industrial jobs. Women worked in factories, shipyards, and railroad yards and served as police officers, mail carriers, and train engineers.

The wartime changes in female employment were not permanent. When the war ended, most women returned to their previous jobs or stopped working. Although the changes were temporary, they demonstrated that women were capable of holding jobs that many had believed only men could do.

The Great Migration Begins Women were not the only group in American society to benefit economically. Desperate for workers, Henry Ford sent company agents to the South to recruit African Americans. Other companies quickly followed Ford's example. Their promises of high wages and plentiful work convinced between 300,000 and 500,000 African Americans to leave the South and move to northern cities.

This massive population movement became known as the "Great Migration." It greatly altered the racial makeup of such cities as Chicago, New York, Cleveland, and Detroit. It would also, eventually, change American politics. In the South, African Americans were generally denied the right to vote, but in the northern cities they were able to vote and affect the policies of northern politicians.

Mexican Americans Head North The war also encouraged other groups to **migrate.** Continuing political turmoil in Mexico and the wartime labor shortage in the United States convinced many Mexicans to head north. Between 1917 and 1920, over 100,000 Mexicans migrated into the Southwest, providing labor for farmers and ranchers.

Meanwhile, Mexican Americans found new opportunities in factory jobs in Chicago, St. Louis, Omaha, and other cities. Many faced hostility and discrimination when they arrived in American cities. Like other immigrant groups before them, they tended to settle in their own separate neighborhoods, called barrios, where they could support each other.

Shaping Public Opinion

Progressives did not think that organizing the economy was enough to ensure the success of the war effort. They also believed the government needed to shape public opinion.

Selling the War Eleven days after asking Congress to declare war, President Wilson created the **Committee on Public Information** (CPI) to "sell" the war to the American people. Headed by George Creel, a journalist, the CPI recruited advertising executives, artists, authors, songwriters, entertainers, public speakers, and motion picture companies to help sway public opinion in favor of the war.

The CPI distributed pamphlets and arranged for thousands of short patriotic talks, called "four-minute speeches," to be delivered at movie theaters and other public places. Some 75,000 speakers, known as Four-Minute Men, urged audiences to support the war in various ways, from buying war bonds to reporting draft dodgers to the authorities.

Civil Liberties Curtailed Besides using propaganda, the government also passed legislation to limit opposition to the war and fight **espionage,** or spying to acquire government information. The Espionage Act of 1917 made it illegal to aid the enemy, give false reports, or interfere with the war effort. The Sedition Act of 1918 made it illegal to speak against the war publicly. In practice, it allowed officials to prosecute anyone who criticized the government. These two laws led to over 1,000 convictions.

Wartime fears also led to attacks on German Americans, labor activists, socialists, and pacifists. Ads urged Americans to monitor their fellow citizens. Americans even formed private groups, such as the American Protective League and the Boy Spies of America, to spy on neighbors and coworkers.

Despite protests, the Espionage and Sedition Acts were upheld in court. Although the First Amendment specifically states that "Congress shall make no law . . . abridging the freedom of speech, or of the press," the Supreme Court departed from a strict literal interpretation of the Constitution. The Court ruled that the government could restrict speech when the words constitute a "clear and present danger."

Reading Check **Explaining** Why did Congress pass the Espionage Act in 1917?

ANALYZING SUPREME COURT CASES

Can Government Limit Free Speech?

★ *Schenck* v. *United States,* 1919
★ *Abrams* v. *United States,* 1919

Background to the Cases

In the fall of 1917, Charles Schenck mailed pamphlets to draftees telling them the draft was wrong and urging them to write protest letters. In August 1918, Jacob Abrams wrote pamphlets denouncing the war and criticizing the decision to send troops to Russia to fight communist forces. Both men were convicted of violating the Espionage Act. Both appealed their convictions all the way to the Supreme Court.

How the Court Ruled

The Schenck and Abrams cases raised the question: Are there some circumstances in which the First Amendment's protection of free speech no longer applies? In both cases, the Supreme Court upheld the Espionage Act, concluding that under certain circumstances, the government can indeed limit free speech. In the Schenck case, the Supreme Court decision was unanimous, but in the Abrams case, the Court split 7-2 in their decision.

▲ Eugene Debs, leader of the American Socialist Party, delivers a speech protesting the war in Canton, Ohio, in 1918. Debs was arrested for making the speech and convicted under the Espionage Act. He appealed to the Supreme Court, but the Court upheld his conviction, citing the *Schenck* case as the precedent.

PRIMARY SOURCE

The Court's Opinion

"The most stringent protection of free speech would not protect a man in falsely shouting fire in a theatre and causing a panic. . . . The question in every case is whether the words used are used in such circumstances and are of such a nature as to create a clear and present danger that they will bring about the substantive evils that Congress has a right to prevent. It is a question of proximity and degree. When a nation is at war, many things that might be said in time of peace are such a hindrance to its effort that their utterance will not be endured so long as men fight, and that no Court could regard them as protected by any constitutional right."

—Justice Oliver Wendell Holmes writing for the Court in *Schenck* v. *U.S.*

PRIMARY SOURCE

Dissenting Views

"It is only the present danger of immediate evil or an intent to bring it about that warrants Congress in setting a limit to the expression of opinion where private rights are not concerned. . . . Now nobody can suppose that the surreptitious publishing of a silly leaflet by an unknown man, without more, would present any immediate danger that its opinions would hinder the success of the government arms. . . .

. . . the ultimate good desired is better reached by free trade in ideas—that the best test of truth is the power of the thought to get itself accepted in the competition of the market . . ."

—Justice Oliver Wendell Holmes dissenting in *Abrams* v. *U.S.*

DBQ   Document-Based Questions

1. **Explaining** When does Holmes think the government can restrict speech?

2. **Analyzing** What does Holmes mean by referring to the "free trade in ideas?"
   Do you think the government should ever be allowed to restrict free speech? Why or why not?

3. **Making Inferences** Why do you think Holmes regarded *Schenck* as a much more immediate danger than *Abrams*? What was the difference between their actions?

Building the Military

MAIN Idea The United States instituted a draft for military service, and African Americans and women took on new roles.

HISTORY AND YOU Describe a time you were required to do something that you might not have done otherwise. Read on to learn about the selective service system.

Progressives did not abandon their ideas when it came to building up the military. Instead, they applied their ideas and developed a new system for recruiting a large army.

Volunteers and Conscripts

When the United States entered the war in 1917, the army and National Guard together had slightly more than 300,000 troops. Many men volunteered after war was declared, but many more were still needed.

Selective Service Many progressives believed that conscription—forced military service—was a violation of democratic and republican principles. Believing a **draft** was necessary, however, Congress, with Wilson's support, created a new conscription system called **selective service.**

Instead of having the military run the draft from Washington, D.C., the Selective Service Act of 1917 required all men between 21 and 30 to register for the draft. A lottery randomly determined the order in which they were called before a local draft board in charge of selecting or exempting people from military service.

The thousands of local boards were the heart of the system. The members of the draft boards were civilians from local communities. Progressives believed local people, understanding community needs, would know which men to draft and would do a far better job than a centralized government bureaucracy. Eventually about 2.8 million Americans were drafted.

Volunteers for War Not all American soldiers were drafted. Approximately 2 million men volunteered for military service. Some had heard stories of German atrocities and wanted to fight back. Others believed democracy was at stake. Many believed they had a duty to respond to their nation's call. They had

PRIMARY SOURCE
African Americans in World War I

During World War I, the U.S. Army kept most African American soldiers out of combat, assigning them to work as cooks, laborers, and laundrymen. The 369th Regiment, however, was assigned to the French Army and was sent to frontline trenches almost immediately. Nicknamed the "Harlem Hell-Fighters," the entire 369th was awarded the French Croix de Guerre ("war cross"), for gallantry in combat. The regiment spent 191 days in the trenches, much longer than many other units, and suffered 1,500 casualties.

▼ African American soldiers march near Verdun, France, November 1918.

"Liberty And Freedom Shall Not Perish" A. Lincoln

COLORED MEN The First Americans Who Planted Our Flag on the Firing Line

▲ A 1918 poster commemorates the 369th Regiment—the first Americans to see combat in World War I.

Analyzing VISUALS

1. **Theorizing** Why do you think the French were willing to use African Americans in combat?

2. **Analyzing** Why do you think the poster includes a quote from Abraham Lincoln?

grown up listening to stories of the Civil War and the Spanish-American War. They saw World War I as a great adventure and wanted to fight for their country.

Although the horrors of war soon became apparent to the American troops, their morale remained high, helping to ensure victory. More than 50,000 Americans died in combat and over 200,000 were wounded. Another 60,000 soldiers died from disease, mostly from the influenza epidemic of 1918 and 1919.

The flu epidemic was not limited to the battlefield. It spread around the world and made more than a quarter of all Americans sick. The disease killed an estimated 25–50 million people worldwide, including more than 500,000 Americans.

African Americans in the War Of the nearly 400,000 African Americans who were drafted, about 42,000 served overseas as combat troops. African American soldiers encountered discrimination and prejudice in the army, where they served in racially segregated units, almost always under the supervision of white officers.

Despite these challenges, many African American soldiers fought with distinction. For example, the African American 92nd and 93rd Infantry Divisions fought in bitter battles along the Western Front. Many of them won praise from both the French commander, Marshal Henri Pétain, and the United States commander, General John Pershing.

Women Join the Military

World War I was the first war in which women officially served in the armed forces, although only in noncombat positions. As the military prepared for war in 1917, it faced a severe shortage of clerical workers because so many men were assigned to active duty. Early in 1917, the navy authorized the enlistment of women to meet its clerical needs.

Women serving in the navy wore a standard uniform and were assigned the rank of yeoman. By the end of the war, over 11,000 women had served in the navy. Although most performed clerical duties, others served as radio operators, electricians, pharmacists, chemists, and photographers.

Unlike the navy, the army refused to enlist women. Instead, it began hiring women as temporary employees to fill clerical jobs. The only women to actually serve in the army were in the Army Nursing Corps.

Women nurses had served in both the army and navy since the early 1900s, but as auxiliaries. They were not assigned ranks, and were not technically enlisted in the army or navy. Army nurses were the only women in the military sent overseas during the war. More than 20,000 nurses served in the Army Nursing Corps during the war, including more than 10,000 overseas.

Reading Check **Describing** How did Congress ensure that the United States would have enough troops to serve in World War I?

Section 2 REVIEW

Vocabulary

1. **Explain** the significance of: War Industries Board, victory gardens, National War Labor Board, Committee on Public Information, espionage, selective service.

Main Ideas

2. **Examining** How did government efforts to ensure public support for the war conflict with ideas about civil rights?

3. **Describing** What were the contributions of African Americans during the war?

Critical Thinking

4. **Big Ideas** How did progressives use their ideas to mobilize both the economy and the American people during the war?

5. **Organizing** Use a graphic organizer similar to the one below to identify the effects of the war on the American workforce.

U.S. Groups	Effects
Women	
African Americans	
Hispanics	

6. **Analyzing Visuals** Examine the graph on page 329. How much did World War I cost? Do you think the government should rely on taxes or loans to fund a war? Explain.

Writing About History

7. **Persuasive Writing** Imagine that you are working for the Committee on Public Information. Write text for an advertisement or lyrics to a song in which you attempt to sway public opinion in favor of the war.

History ONLINE

Study Central™ To review this section, go to glencoe.com and click on Study Central.

ANALYZING PRIMARY SOURCES

Propaganda in World War I

All of the warring nations in World War I used propaganda to boost support for their side. Many Americans believed the propaganda coming from Europe, particularly from the British government and press. When the United States entered the war, the American government also began using propaganda in an attempt to unite Americans behind the war effort.

Read the passages and study the posters. Then answer the questions that follow.

PRIMARY SOURCE 1

Movie Poster, 1918

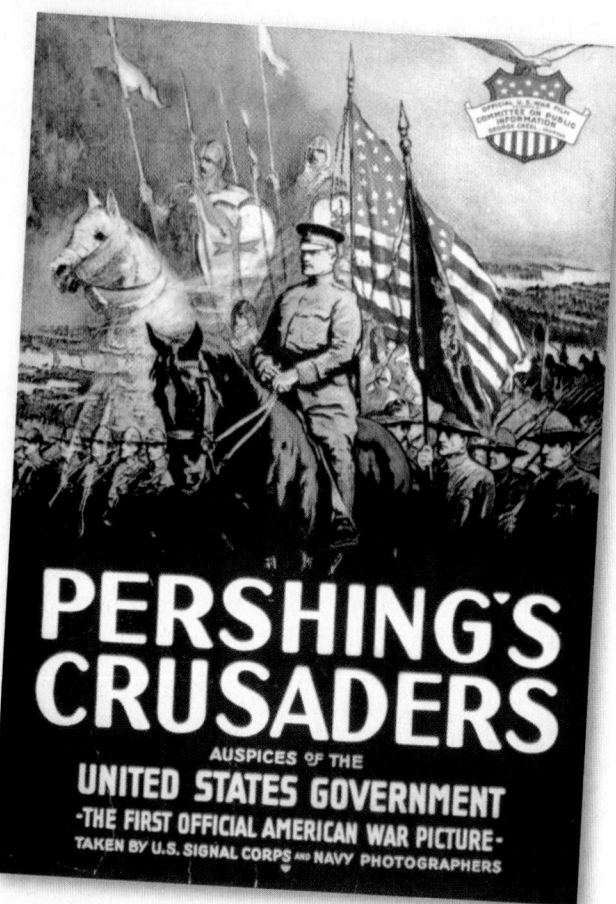

PRIMARY SOURCE 2

Government War Bond Advertisement, 1918

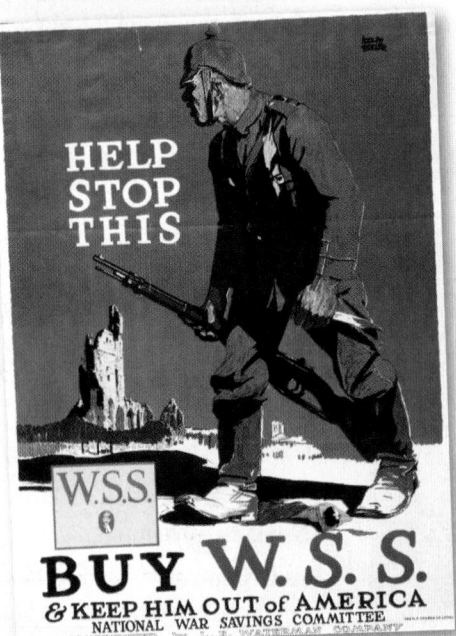

PRIMARY SOURCE 3

American Soldier's Diary, 1918

"Germans, and a German—so different. Fishing through the poor torn pockets of shabby German body, drooped over wreck of machine gun, to find well-thumbed photograph of woman and little boy and little girl—so like one's own . . . impossible to hate what had been that body.

Nothing so revolting as bitter, pitiless cruelty of those who know nothing of reality of it all. Those . . . Germano-baiters at home, so much more cruel than those who have the right— and are not."

—Diary of Lieutenant Howard V. O'Brien,
October 6, 1918

PRIMARY SOURCE 4

Newspaper Column, *New York Times*, May 1915

▼ *Great Britain established the Bryce Committee to investigate German atrocities in Belgium. Its findings, released just five days after the sinking of the Lusitania, increased anti-German sentiment in the United States. Investigations after the war, however, found that many of the stories were false or gross exaggerations.*

GERMAN ATROCITIES ARE PROVED, FINDS BRYCE COMMITTEE

Not Only Individual Crimes, but Premeditated Slaughter in Belgium.

YOUNG AND OLD MUTILATED

Women Attacked, Children Brutally Slain, Arson and Pillage Systematic.

COUNTENANCED BY OFFICERS

Wanton Firing on Red Cross and White Flag; Prisoners and Wounded Shot.

CIVILIANS USED AS SHIELDS

Proof That Belgians Did Not Fire on Germans at Louvain—Germans Received Kindness.

PRIMARY SOURCE 5

U.S. Government Pamphlet, 1918

"Fear, perhaps, is rather an important element to be bred in the civilian population. It is difficult to unite a people by talking only on the highest ethical plane. To fight for an ideal, perhaps, must be coupled with thoughts of self-preservation. So a truthful appeal to the fear of men, the recognition of the terrible things that would happen if the German Government were permitted to retain its prestige, may be necessary in order that all people unite in the support of the needed sacrifices."

—Pamphlet for speakers from the Committee on Public Information, quoted in the *New York Times,* February 4, 1918

PRIMARY SOURCE 6

American Red Cross Poster

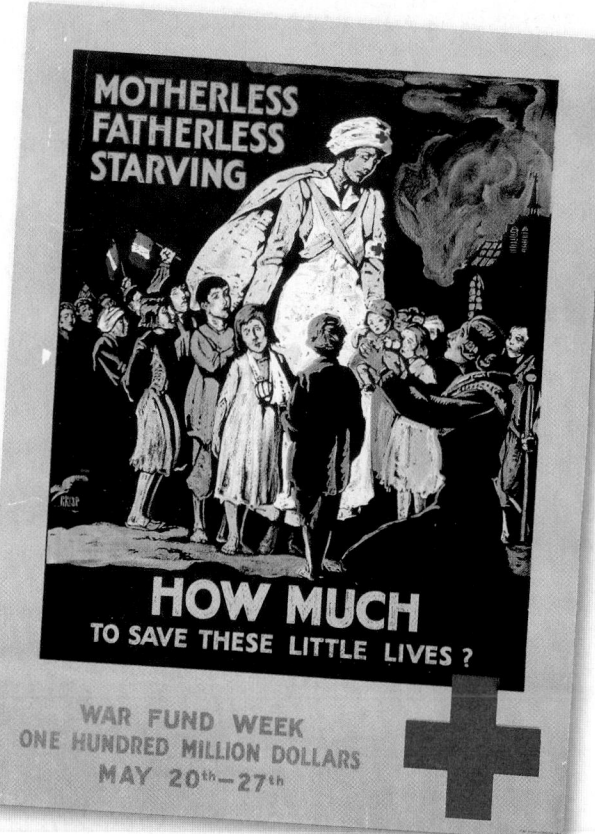

MOTHERLESS FATHERLESS STARVING

HOW MUCH TO SAVE THESE LITTLE LIVES?

WAR FUND WEEK
ONE HUNDRED MILLION DOLLARS
MAY 20th—27th

DBQ Document-Based Questions

1. **Explaining** Examine Primary Source 1. What is the underlying message behind the poster for "Pershing's Crusaders"?

2. **Identifying** What images of the Germans do Primary Sources 2 and 6 promote?

3. **Analyzing** Study Primary Source 4. How do you think stories of German atrocities affected American neutrality?

4. **Making Connections** Read Primary Sources 3 and 5. Why do you think the government used propaganda? Do you think propaganda is a good idea in wartime?

5. **Evaluating** According to Primary Sources 2, 5, and 6, what is at stake in the war? What should citizens do to help the war effort?

A Bloody Conflict

Guide to Reading

Big Ideas
Individual Action American troops played a major role in helping end the war.

Content Vocabulary
- convoy (p. 339)
- armistice (p. 341)
- national self-determination (p. 342)
- reparations (p. 344)

Academic Vocabulary
- network (p. 336)
- adequately (p. 339)
- resolve (p. 342)

People and Events to Identify
- no-man's-land (p. 336)
- John J. Pershing (p. 340)
- Treaty of Versailles (p. 342)
- Fourteen Points (p. 342)
- League of Nations (p. 343)

Reading Strategy
Organizing Complete a graphic organizer similar to the one below by listing the kinds of warfare and technology used in the fighting.

Warfare and Technology Used in World War I

Technology caused both sides to lose millions of men during World War I. The arrival of American troops helped the Allies win, but the peace treaty set the stage for another war to come.

Combat in World War I

MAIN Idea New technologies made World War I the first modern war.

HISTORY AND YOU What new technologies have been developed or proposed in your lifetime? Read on to learn about the weapons that World War I personnel faced.

By the spring of 1917, World War I had devastated Europe. Old-fashioned strategies and new technologies resulted in terrible destruction. Many Americans believed, however, that their troops would make a difference and quickly bring the war to an end.

Trench Warfare

Early offensives in 1914 demonstrated that warfare had changed. Powerful artillery guns were placed several miles behind the front lines. From there, they hurled huge explosive shells onto the battlefield. More people were killed by artillery fire than by any other weapon in World War I. Artillery fire produced horrific scenes of death and destruction, as one American noted in his diary:

PRIMARY SOURCE

"Many dead Germans along the road. One heap on a manure pile. . . . Devastation everywhere. Our barrage has rooted up the entire territory like a ploughed field. Dead horses galore, many of them have a hind quarter cut off—the Huns [Germans] need food. Dead men here and there."

—quoted in *The American Spirit*

To protect themselves from artillery, troops began digging trenches. On the Western Front—where German troops confronted French, British, and Belgian forces—the troops dug a **network** of trenches that stretched from the English Channel to the Swiss border. To prevent the enemy from overrunning the trenches, troops relied upon a new weapon, the machine gun, to hold off the attackers. The space between opposing trenches was called **no-man's-land.** It was a rough barren landscape filled with craters from artillery fire. To prevent troops from crossing no-man's-land, both sides built barbed wire entanglements and obstacles in front of their trenches.

Major Battles

1 **Tannenberg,** Aug. 1914. Germans stop Russian invasion.

2 **Marne,** Sept. 1914. French stop German advance on Paris; trench warfare begins.

3 **1st Ypres,** Oct.–Nov. 1914. British stop German advance on French ports.

4 **Gallipoli,** Feb.–Dec. 1915. Turks block British and French effort to secure a supply route to Russia.

5 **2nd Ypres,** April–May 1915. Germans use poison gas for the first time, but British lines hold.

6 **Isonzo,** June–Dec. 1915. Austrians block Italian efforts to take Trieste.

7 **Somme,** July–Nov. 1916. British and French push back German lines. British use tanks for the first time.

8 **Verdun,** Feb.–Dec. 1916. Massive German attack, but French lines hold.

Map legend:
- Allied Powers
- Central Powers
- Neutral Powers
- Line of trench warfare, 1915–1917
- Allied victory
- Central Powers victory

0 400 kilometers
0 400 miles
Lambert Azimuthal Equal-Area projection

Trench Warfare

Labels: Machine gun nests, Reserve trench, Support trench, Front-line trench, Barbed wire, No-man's-land, Artillery guns several miles behind the lines

Analyzing GEOGRAPHY

1. **Location** Along what nations' boundaries did the Western Front lie?

2. **Human-Environment Interaction** In addition to weapons, what other dangers did troops in the trenches face?

To break through enemy lines, the attacker would begin with a massive artillery barrage. Soldiers would then scramble out of their trenches, race across no-man's-land while enemy machine guns fired at them, and try to capture the enemy's trenches.

Before charging enemy trenches, troops fixed bayonets—long knives—to their rifles. For those troops that made it across no-man's-land, fighting in the trenches was brutal. Troops threw grenades—small bombs—at each other, and used bayonets, rifle butts, knives, axes, pistols and even rocks and fists to kill the enemy.

The results of this kind of warfare were horrific. In major battles, both sides often lost hundreds of thousands of men, yet neither side was able to break through the other's lines.

New Technology

New technologies were needed to break through enemy lines. In April 1915, the Germans first used poison gas near Ypres. The fumes caused vomiting, blindness, and suffocation. Soon afterward the Allies also began using poison gas. To counter gas attacks, both sides developed gas masks.

In late 1915, the British introduced the armored tank into battle. These tanks were slow and mechanically unreliable, but they could crush barbed wire and cross trenches. Unfortunately, there were not enough of them. The tanks could support the troops, but they did not revolutionize warfare in World War I. By the time World War II broke out, however, tanks had replaced cavalry in most modern armies and made trench warfare obsolete.

World War I also marked the first use of aircraft in war. In addition, it was the first and last time that zeppelins were used in combat. Zeppelins are giant rigid balloons, also known as blimps or dirigibles. Early in the war, the Germans sent squadrons of zeppelins to drop bombs on British warships in the North Sea.

At first, airplanes were used as scouts. They flew over enemy territory, as well as the English Channel and the North Sea, spying on enemy troops and ships. Before long, however, the Allies equipped them with machine guns to attack the German zeppelin fleet. The machine guns were timed to fire through the aircraft's propeller as it spun so that the bullets did not hit the propeller. A few airplanes even carried rockets to destroy the zeppelins. Others carried small bombs to drop on enemy lines.

As technology advanced, aircraft were used to shoot down other aircraft. Battles between aircraft became known as dogfights. Early military aircraft were difficult to fly and easy to destroy. The wings and body frame were covered in cloth and easily caught fire. Pilots did not carry parachutes. The average life expectancy of a combat pilot in World War I was about two weeks.

Reading Check **Describing** What new technologies were introduced in World War I?

The Americans Arrive

MAIN Idea The arrival of Americans changed the course of the war and helped the Allies win.

HISTORY AND YOU Have you ever had to boost someone's morale? Read on to learn about Americans who helped the Allies win World War I.

Waves of American troops marched into this bloody stalemate—nearly 2 million before the war's end. Although the "doughboys," as American soldiers were nicknamed, were inexperienced, they were fresh and eager to fight. Their presence boosted the morale of Allied forces. It also demoralized the German soldiers, who now faced large numbers of fresh troops. As the Americans began to arrive, many in Germany concluded that the war was lost.

Winning the War at Sea

No American troopships were sunk on their way to Europe thanks to the efforts of American Admiral William S. Sims. The British preferred to fight German submarines by sending warships to find them, while merchant ships would race across the Atlantic individually. This approach enabled German submarines to inflict heavy losses on British shipping. Sims

TECHNOLOGY & HISTORY

New Weapons World War I is often called the first modern war because troops used new technology that is still widely used in warfare today. Much of this new technology developed in response to trench warfare.

◀ **Artillery Forces Troops into Trenches**
Australian soldiers load an artillery shell during the Battle of Passchendaele in 1917. Powerful long-range artillery fire from guns like this forced troops to build trenches for protection.

▲ **Machine Guns Defend Trenches**
Machine guns made it very difficult to capture enemy trenches. They could fire thousands of bullets per minute. A small team with a machine gun could down hundreds of troops crossing open terrain. This photo shows a German machine gun crew.

proposed that merchant ships and troop transports be gathered into groups, called **convoys.** Small highly maneuverable warships called destroyers would protect and escort the convoys across the Atlantic.

Convoys also saved lives. If a ship was sunk, other ships in the convoy could rescue survivors. The system worked. Convoys greatly reduced shipping losses and ensured that a large number of American troops arrived safely in Europe in time to help stop Germany's last great offensive on the Western Front.

Russia Leaves the War

In March 1917, riots broke out in Russia over the government's handling of the war and the scarcity of food and fuel. Czar Nicholas II, the leader of the Russian Empire, abdicated his throne. This marked the beginning of the Russian Revolution.

Political leadership in Russia passed to a provisional, or temporary, government. The leaders of the provisional government wanted Russia to stay in the war. However, the government was unable to deal **adequately** with the major problems afflicting the nation, such as food shortages. The Bolshevik Party, led by Vladimir Lenin, overthrew the provisional government and established a Communist government in November 1917.

Germany's military fortunes improved with the Bolshevik takeover of Russia. Lenin's first act after seizing power was to pull Russia out of the war and concentrate on establishing a Communist state. Lenin agreed to the Treaty of Brest-Litovsk with Germany on March 3, 1918. Under this treaty, Russia lost substantial territory. It gave up the Ukraine, its Polish and Baltic territories, and Finland.

With the Eastern Front settled, Germany could now concentrate its forces in the west. German leaders knew this was their last chance to win. If the troops transferred from Russia could not break Allied lines, it was only a matter of time before Germany would have to surrender.

Americans Enter Combat

At the time World War I began, many Americans knew that the French had helped the United States during the American Revolution. American school children still learned the story of the Marquis de Lafayette, who had brought French officers to America to help train American soldiers and who had served on George Washington's staff during the Revolutionary War. Many Americans regarded the French people as friends and believed the nation owed the French a debt for their help in the revolution.

◀ **Poison Gas vs. Trenches**
To break through trench lines, both sides began using poison gas. To protect against gas attacks, troops were forced to carry gas masks similar to those shown here worn by American soldiers in France in 1917.

▲ **Airplanes Bomb Trenches**
Airplanes offered both sides a way to counter trench warfare. Several types of aircraft, including the British Sopwith Camel shown above, could carry 4–5 small bombs to drop on enemy artillery and trenches. They also attacked troops using their machine guns.

Tanks vs. Trenches ▶
To help capture trenches, the Allies built tanks that were immune to machine gun fire and able to smash through barbed wire. Tanks had tracks instead of wheels, enabling them to cross the mud and craters of no-man's-land.

Analyzing VISUALS

1. **Analyzing** Modern militaries do not use trench warfare. Which weapons pictured eventually ended the use of trenches?

2. **Synthesizing** Explain how the different technologies of World War I worked together to kill so many people.

When General **John J. Pershing,** commander of the American Expeditionary Force (AEF), arrived in Paris on July 4, 1917, he and his officers headed to Picpus Cemetery where Lafayette was buried. One of Pershing's officers, Colonel Charles E. Stanton, raised his hand in salute and proclaimed, "Lafayette, we are here!" France had helped the United States gain its freedom. Now American soldiers would help the French to preserve theirs.

When American troops began arriving in France, the British and French commanders wanted to integrate them into their armies under British and French command. Pershing refused, and President Wilson supported him. Pershing insisted that American soldiers fight in American units under American command.

Despite French and British pleas that they needed American soldiers to replace their own losses, Pershing held firm with one exception. The 93rd Infantry Division—an African American unit—was transferred to the French. Its soldiers became the first Americans to enter combat.

Germany's Last Offensive

On March 21, 1918, the Germans launched a massive attack along the Western Front, beginning with gas attacks and a huge artillery bombardment. German forces, strengthened by reinforcements from the Russian front, pushed deep into Allied lines. By early June, they were less than 40 miles (64 km) from Paris.

American troops played an important role in containing the German offensive. In late May, as the German offensive continued, the Americans launched their first major attack, quickly capturing the village of Cantigny. On June 1, American and French troops blocked the German drive on Paris at the town of Château-Thierry. On July 15, the Germans launched one last massive attack in an attempt to take Paris, but American and French troops held their ground.

The Battle of the Argonne Forest

With the German drive stalled, French Marshal Ferdinand Foch, supreme commander of the Allied forces, ordered massive counterattacks. In mid-September, American troops drove back German forces at the battle of Saint-Mihiel. Next, an American offensive was launched in the region between the Meuse River and the Argonne Forest. General Pershing

assembled over 600,000 American troops, 40,000 tons of supplies, and roughly 4,000 artillery pieces for the most massive attack in American history.

The attack began on September 26, 1918. German positions slowly fell to the advancing American troops. The Germans inflicted heavy casualties, but by early November the Americans had shattered German defenses and opened a hole on the eastern flank of the German lines. Soon after, all across the Western Front, the Germans began to retreat.

American Heroes

Although the brutal trench warfare of World War I led to many acts of astonishing bravery, the actions of two Americans, Corporal Alvin York and Captain Eddie Rickenbacker, captured the nation's imagination.

Alvin York

Born in 1887, Alvin York grew up poor in the mountains of Tennessee, where he learned to shoot by hunting wild game. Opposed to war, he initially tried to avoid the draft as a conscientious objector—a person who refuses to obey the law because of his moral or religious beliefs. As a Christian, York

Alvin York and the Battle of the Argonne Forest

October 8th 1918, Argonne Forest, France.

"So on the morning of the 8th, just before daylight, we started for the hill of Chattel Chehery. So before we got there it got light, and the Germans sent over a heavy barrage and also gas, and we put on our gas masks and just pressed right on through those shells and got to the top of hill 223.... [A]t the zero hour ... we done went over the top.... The Germans ... jes stopped us in our tracks. Their machine guns were up there on the heights overlooking us and well hidden, and we couldn't tell for certain where the terrible heavy fire was coming from.... So we decided to try and get them by a surprise attack in the rear.... So there was 17 of us boys went around on the left flank to see if we couldn't put those guns out of action."

—from *Sergeant York*

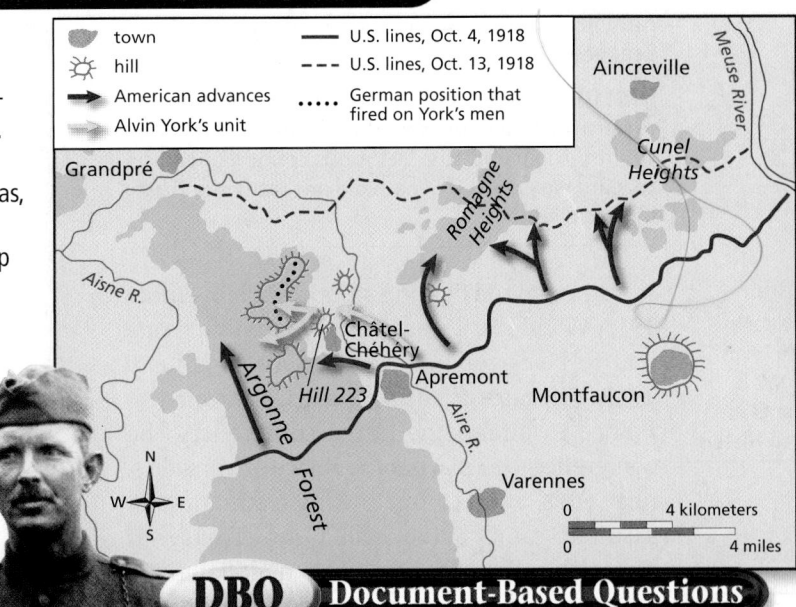

DBQ — Document-Based Questions

1. **Extrapolating** Why was the American victory in the Argonne Forest important?

2. **Explaining** What made capturing enemy positions in the Argonne Forest so difficult?

Maps In MOtion See *StudentWorks™ Plus* or glencoe.com.

believed he was not allowed to kill anyone. Eventually, he decided that he could fight in a war if the cause was just.

On October 8, 1918, during the Battle of the Argonne Forest, German machine guns on a fortified hill fired on York's platoon and killed nine men. York took command and charged the machine guns. By the end of the battle, York had killed between 9 and 25 Germans, captured the machine guns, and taken 132 prisoners. For his actions, he received the Medal of Honor and the French Croix de Guerre. After returning home, he used his fame to raise money for the Alvin York Institute—a school for poor Tennessee children.

Eddie Rickenbacker Born in Columbus, Ohio, Eddie Rickenbacker was a famous race car driver before the war. Rickenbacker's car-racing reflexes served him well as a combat pilot. He was named commander of the 94th Aero Squadron, the first all-American squadron to enter combat. In all, he fought in 134 air battles and shot down 26 aircraft, becoming the top American combat pilot. In one battle, he single-handedly fought seven German aircraft—a feat for which he was later awarded the Congressional Medal of Honor.

The War Ends

While fighting raged along the Western Front, a revolution engulfed Austria-Hungary. In October 1918, Poland, Hungary, and Czechoslovakia declared independence. By early November, the governments of the Austro-Hungarian Empire and the Ottoman Empire had surrendered to the allies.

On November 3, sailors in Kiel, the main base of the German fleet, mutinied. Within days, groups of workers and soldiers seized power in other German towns. As the revolution spread, the German emperor decided to step down. On November 9, Germany became a republic. Two days later the government signed an **armistice**—a truce, or an agreement to stop fighting. At the 11th hour on the 11th day of the 11th month, 1918, the fighting stopped.

✓ **Reading Check** **Interpreting** Why would Pershing want to keep U.S. soldiers in their own units?

A Flawed Peace

MAIN Idea The United States Senate refused to ratify the Treaty of Versailles and rejected the League of Nations.

HISTORY AND YOU How might your feelings toward a peace plan differ if you lived in a defeated country compared to a victorious country? Read on to learn why the U.S. Senate did not ratify the Treaty of Versailles.

Read Wilson's "Fourteen Points" on page R52 in **Documents in American History.**

Although the fighting stopped in November 1918, World War I was not over. A peace treaty had to be negotiated and signed. In January 1919, delegates from 27 countries traveled to France to attend the peace conference. The conference took place at the Palace of Versailles, near Paris, and the treaty with Germany that resulted came to be called the **Treaty of Versailles.** The conference also negotiated the Treaty of Saint-Germain, ending the war with Austria-Hungary.

Negotiations on the Treaty of Versailles lasted five months. The most important participants were the so-called "Big Four" of the Allies: President Wilson of the United States, British Prime Minister David Lloyd George, French Premier Georges Clemenceau, and Italian Prime Minister Vittorio Orlando.

Representatives from Russia were not invited to the conference. Wilson and the other Allied leaders refused to recognize Lenin's government as legitimate. At the time of the peace conference, a civil war was raging in Russia between communist and non-communist forces. In mid-1918, the United States, Great Britain, and Japan had sent troops to Russia to help the anti-communist forces. Nearly 15,000 American troops remained in Russia—which had been renamed the Soviet Union by the Bolsheviks—until the spring of 1920. By that time, it had become clear that the Bolsheviks had won the civil war.

The Fourteen Points

When President Wilson arrived in Paris in January 1919, he brought with him a peace plan known as the **Fourteen Points.** Wilson had presented the plan to Congress in January 1918 to explain the goals of the United States in the war. The president believed that if the Fourteen Points were implemented, they would establish the conditions for a lasting peace in Europe.

The Paris Peace Conference

What Did President Wilson Want?

The Fourteen Points

1. End secret treaties and secret diplomacy among nations.
2. Guarantee freedom of navigation on the seas for all nations.
3. Create free trade among nations.
4. Reduce armed forces as much as possible consistent with domestic safety.
5. Settle all colonial claims fairly taking into account the views of both the colonial peoples and the imperial nations.
6. Evacuate German troops from Russia and restore all conquered territory.
7. Restore Belgium's independence.
8. Restore all French territory occupied by Germany, including Alsace-Lorraine.
9. Adjust Italy's borders based on where Italians live.
10. Divide Austria-Hungary into new nations for each ethnic group.
11. Base borders of the Balkan states on nationality.
12. Break up the Ottoman Empire and make Turkey a separate country.
13. Create an independent Poland.
14. Create a League of Nations.

The Fourteen Points were based on "the principle of justice to all peoples and nationalities." In the first five points, Wilson proposed to eliminate the causes of the war through free trade, freedom of the seas, disarmament, an impartial adjustment of colonial claims, and open diplomacy instead of secret agreements.

The next eight points addressed the right of **national self-determination.** This is the idea that the borders of countries should be based on ethnicity and national identity. A group of people who feel that they are a nation should be allowed to have their own country. Wilson and other supporters of national self-determination believed that when borders are not based on national identity, border disputes will occur and nations are more likely to go to war to **resolve** them.

The principle of national self-determination also meant that no nation should be allowed to keep territory taken from another nation. Wilson's Fourteen Points required the Central Powers to evacuate all of the countries invaded during the war. Wilson also wanted the territory

NATIONAL GEOGRAPHIC **Changes in Europe, 1919**

Former Austria-Hungary boundary
Former German boundary
Former Russian boundary

Analyzing VISUALS

1. **Comparing** How many of the Fourteen Points were accepted at the Paris Peace Conference?
2. **Analyzing** What nations received territory from the Austro-Hungarian Empire?

Maps In MOtion See *StudentWorks™ Plus* or glencoe.com.

of Alsace-Lorraine that Germany had taken in 1871 restored to France.

The fourteenth point was most important to Wilson. It called for the creation of a "general association of nations" that would later be called the **League of Nations.** The League's member nations would help preserve peace by pledging to respect and protect each other's territory and political independence. Wilson was so determined to get agreement on the League of Nations that he was willing to give up other goals in the Fourteen Points in exchange for support for the League.

The Treaty of Versailles

Wilson received an enthusiastic reception from crowds in Paris and other national capitals that he visited. Wilson's popularity in Europe put him in a strong negotiating position. He was delighted when the peace conference decided to use the Fourteen Points as the basis for negotiations.

Not everyone was impressed by President Wilson's ideas. Premier Clemenceau of France and British Prime Minister Lloyd George wanted the Germans punished for the suffering they had inflicted on the rest of Europe. Additionally, Great Britain refused to give up its sizable naval advantage by agreeing to Wilson's call for freedom of the seas. Clemenceau, in particular, was determined to end the German threat once and for all. Other Allied governments tended to agree.

Despite Wilson's hopes, the peace terms were harsh. The Treaty of Versailles, reluctantly signed by Germany on June 28, 1919, included many terms designed to punish and weaken Germany. Germany's armed forces were greatly reduced in size and Germany was not allowed to put troops west of the Rhine River—the region near the French border. The treaty also specifically blamed Germany for the war, stating that it had been caused by "the aggression of Germany."

When the German government signed the treaty, it, in effect, acknowledged that Germany was guilty of causing the war. This allowed the Allies to demand that Germany pay **reparations**—monetary compensation for all of the war damage it had caused. A commission set up after the treaty was signed decided that Germany owed the Allies approximately $33 billion. This sum was far more than Germany could pay all at once and was intended to keep Germany's economy weak for a long time.

Wilson had somewhat better success in promoting national self-determination. Four empires were dismantled as a result of World War I and the peace negotiations: the Austro-Hungarian Empire, the Russian Empire, the German Empire, and the Ottoman Empire. The various peace treaties signed after the war created nine new nations in Europe: Austria, Czechoslovakia, Estonia, Finland, Hungary, Latvia, Lithuania, Poland and Yugoslavia. In general, the majority of people in these new countries were from one ethnic group.

National self-determination was not, however, applied to Germany. Both Poland and Czechoslovakia were given territory where the majority of the people were German. Germany was even split in two in order to give Poland access to the Baltic Sea. By leaving a large number of Germans living outside Germany, the Treaty of Versailles helped set the stage for a new series of crises in the 1930s.

The Treaty of Versailles did not address several of Wilson's Fourteen Points. It did not mention freedom of the seas or free trade. It also ignored Wilson's goal of a fair settlement of colonial claims. No colonial people in Asia or Africa were granted independence. Germany's colonies in Africa and the Middle East were placed under the supervision of Britain and France. Japan was given responsibility for Germany's colonies in East Asia.

The treaty also stated that new countries were to be created from the Ottoman Empire. In 1920 the Ottoman Empire was divided into the state of Turkey, the French Mandate of Syria and Lebanon, and the British Mandates of Iraq and Palestine. In 1921 the Palestine Mandate was divided to create the kingdom of Transjordan.

Although disappointed with many parts of the Treaty of Versailles, Wilson achieved his

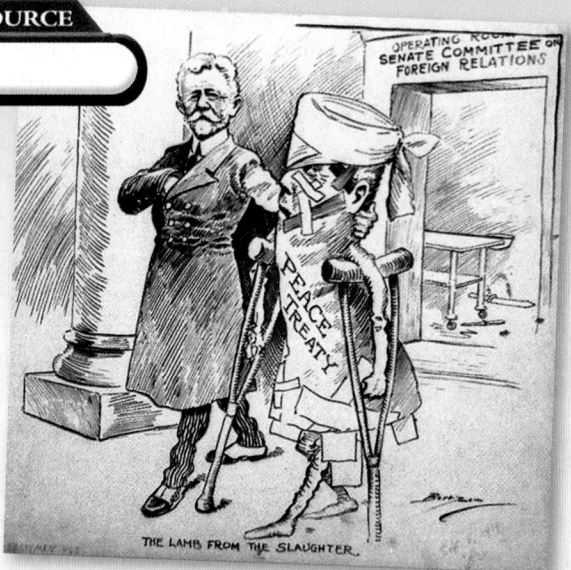

◄ Senator Henry Cabot Lodge escorts the peace treaty out of the Senate.

◄ In the original caption of this cartoon, President Wilson is saying: "Build your house up there where it can't be washed away."

Analyzing VISUALS DBQ

1. **Identifying** What point is the cartoon on the right trying to make?

2. **Interpreting** Why does the cartoon on the left suggest that international agreement on a peace treaty is important?

primary goal. The treaty called for the creation of a League of Nations. League members promised to reduce armaments, to submit all disputes that endangered the peace to arbitration, and to come to the aid of any member who was threatened with aggression by another state.

The U.S. Senate Rejects the Treaty

President Wilson was confident the American people would support the Treaty of Versailles, but he had badly underestimated the opposition in Congress. All treaties signed by the United States must be ratified by two-thirds of the Senate, and in November 1918, the Democratic Party had lost control of the Senate. Even though he needed Republican support to ratify the treaty, Wilson refused to take any Republican leaders with him to the peace conference. This ensured that Wilson's views prevailed, but it also meant that Republican concerns were not addressed.

Opposition in the Senate focused on the League of Nations. One group of senators, nicknamed the "Irreconcilables," refused to support the treaty under any circumstances. They assailed the League as the kind of "entangling alliance" that the Founders had warned against. A larger group of senators, known as the "Reservationists," was led by the powerful chairman of the Foreign Relations committee, Henry Cabot Lodge. The Reservationists were willing to support the treaty if certain amendments were made to the League of Nations.

The Reservationists pointed out that the Constitution requires Congress to declare war. Yet the League of Nations could require member states to aid any member who was attacked. The Reservationists argued that this might force the United States into a war without Congressional approval. They agreed to ratify the treaty if it was amended to say that any military action by the United States required the approval of Congress. Wilson refused, fearing the change would undermine the League's effectiveness.

To overcome Senate opposition, Wilson decided to take his case directly to the American people. If public support for the treaty was strong enough, the senators would back down. Starting in September 1919, Wilson traveled 8,000 miles and made over 30 major speeches in three weeks. On September 25, the president collapsed from the physical strain and soon afterward suffered a stroke. Bedridden, Wilson ignored the advice of his wife and Democratic leaders and refused to compromise on the treaty.

The Senate finally voted in November 1919. It voted again in March 1920. Both times it refused to ratify the treaty. After Wilson left office in 1921, the United States negotiated separate peace treaties with each of the Central Powers. The League of Nations, the foundation of President Wilson's plan for lasting world peace, took shape without the United States.

Reading Check **Examining** What was national self-determination and why did Wilson think it would help prevent war?

Section 3 REVIEW

Vocabulary

1. **Explain** the significance of: no-man's-land, convoy, John J. Pershing, armistice, Treaty of Versailles, Fourteen Points, national self-determination, League of Nations, reparations.

Main Ideas

2. **Explaining** How did technology change the way World War I was fought?

3. **Analyzing** What impact did John J. Pershing and the Battle of the Argonne Forest have on World War I?

4. **Organizing** Use a graphic organizer to list the results of World War I.

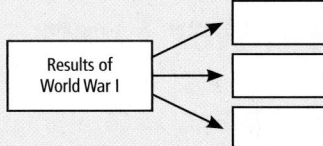

Results of World War I

Critical Thinking

5. **Big Ideas** Why did President Wilson propose his Fourteen Points?

6. **Analyzing** What countries were involved in the Paris peace conference in 1919? Which country was not invited to participate? Why?

7. **Analyzing Maps and Charts** Examine the map and chart on page 343. Prepare a quiz with questions based on information from both. Give the quiz to some of your classmates.

Writing About History

8. **Descriptive Writing** Imagine that you are an American soldier fighting in Europe during World War I. Write a letter home describing your situation and how you feel about fighting there.

History ONLINE
Study Central™ To review this section, go to glencoe.com and click on Study Central.

TIME NOTEBOOK

American soldiers set sail for Europe.

World War Firsts

Human ingenuity goes to work in the service of war:

AERIAL COMBAT, 1914. War takes to the air. Two Allied aircraft chase two German planes across Britain.

GAS ATTACKS, 1915. The German High Command admits to using chlorine gas bombs and shells on the field of combat. Deadly mustard gas is used in 1917.

GAS MASKS. Issued to Allied soldiers in 1915.

DONKEY'S EARS. A new trench periscope enables soldiers to observe the battleground from the relative safety of a trench without risking sniper fire.

BIG BERTHA. Enormous howitzer gun bombards Paris. "Big Bertha," named after the wife of its manufacturer, is thought to be located nearly 63 miles behind German lines. Moving at night on railroad tracks, the gun is difficult for the Allies to locate.

Color My World

Some bright spots in a dark decade:

- Color newspaper supplements (1914)
- 3-D films (1915)
- Nail polish (1916)
- Three-color traffic lights (1918)
- Color photography introduced by Eastman Kodak (1914)

One of the first color photographs

VERBATIM

❝ My message was one of death for young men. How odd to applaud that. **❞**

> **WOODROW WILSON,**
> *on returning to the White House after asking Congress for a declaration of war, 1917*

❝ Food is Ammunition—Don't Waste It **❞**

> **POSTER FROM U.S. FOOD ADMINISTRATION,**
> *administered by Herbert Hoover*

❝ I have had a hard time getting over this war. My old world died. **❞**

> **RAY STANNARD BAKER,**
> *journalist*

❝ Let us, while this war lasts, forget our special grievances and close our ranks shoulder to shoulder with our own white fellow citizens and the allied nations that are fighting for democracy. **❞**

> **W.E.B. DU BOIS,**
> *African American scholar and leader, 1918*

❝ America has at one bound become a world power in a sense she never was before. **❞**

> **BRITISH PRIME MINISTER DAVID LLOYD GEORGE,**
> *on the U.S. entry into World War I, 1917*

❝ In the camps I saw barrels mounted on sticks on which zealous captains were endeavoring to teach their men how to ride a horse. **❞**

> **THEODORE ROOSEVELT,**
> *on touring U.S. military training facilities, 1917*

❝ The war was over, and it seemed as if everything in the world were possible, and everything was new, and that peace was going to be all we dreamed about. **❞**

> **FLORENCE HARRIMAN,**
> *Red Cross volunteer, in Paris on Armistice Day, 1918*

How to Make a Doughboy

Take one American infantryman.

1. Arm with 107 pieces of fighting equipment, including:
   - rifle
   - rifle cartridges
   - cartridge belt
   - steel helmet
   - clubs
   - knives
   - gas mask
   - wire cutters
   - trench tool
   - bayonet and scabbard
   - grenades

2. Add 50 articles of clothing, including 3 wool blankets and a bedsack.

3. Equip with eating utensils and 11 cooking implements.

4. Train well.

TOTAL COST: $156.30

(not including training and transportation to Europe)

Milestones

SHOT DOWN AND KILLED, APRIL 22, 1918. "THE RED BARON," Manfred von Richthofen, Germany's ace pilot. Von Richthofen destroyed more than 80 Allied aircraft. The English fighter pilot Edward Mannock said, "I hope he roasted all the way down."

Vladimir Lenin

REPATRIATED, APRIL 10, 1917. VLADIMIR ILYICH LENIN, to Russia, after an 11-year absence. The leader of the leftist Bolshevik party hopes to reorganize his revolutionary group.

Jeannette Rankin

ELECTED, NOVEMBER 7, 1916. JEANNETTE RANKIN of Montana, to the U.S. Congress. The first woman congressional representative explained her victory by saying that women "got the vote in Montana because the spirit of pioneer days was still alive."

NUMBERS 1915

$1,040 Average annual income for workers in finance, insurance, and real estate

$687 Average income for industrial workers (higher for union workers, lower for nonunion workers)

$510 Average income for retail trade workers

$355 Average income for farm laborers

$342 Average income for domestic servants

$328 Average income for public school teachers

$11.95 Cost of a bicycle

$1.15 Cost of a baseball

$1 Average cost of a hotel room

39¢ Cost of one dozen eggs

5¢ Cost of a glass of cola

7¢ Cost of a large roll of toilet paper

CRITICAL THINKING

1. Analyzing What pioneer qualities was Jeannette Rankin referring to when she said women "got the vote in Montana because the spirit of pioneer days was still alive"?

2. Drawing Conclusions How do you think the inventions in "Color My World" kept up spirits on the home front during World War I? Why was this important?

The War's Impact

Guide to Reading

Big Ideas

Economics and Society The change from wartime to peacetime caused many economic and social problems.

Content Vocabulary
- cost of living (p. 348)
- general strike (p. 349)
- deport (p. 352)

Academic Vocabulary
- widespread (p. 349)
- authorities (p. 352)

People and Events to Identify
- Calvin Coolidge (p. 349)
- Red Scare (p. 351)
- A. Mitchell Palmer (p. 351)
- J. Edgar Hoover (p. 352)

Reading Strategy

Organizing Complete a graphic organizer similar to the one below to list the effects of the end of World War I on the American economy.

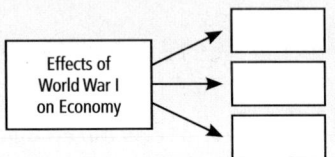

America's victory overseas led to turmoil at home. The end of the wartime economy led to a depression and fears of communism, as strikes, riots, and bombings took place.

An Economy in Turmoil

MAIN Idea The country suffered economic uncertainty, strikes, and riots in the year after the war.

HISTORY AND YOU Do you know anyone who has participated in a strike? Read why millions of workers went on strike in 1919.

With the war over, Americans welcomed the soldiers back as heroes. Parades were thrown in their honor, and a new organization, the American Legion, was created to support the veterans. But their arrival home was also bittersweet. Two million men now needed to find jobs in an economy that was shutting down its production of war materials and sliding into recession.

When the war ended, government agencies removed their controls from the economy. People raced to buy goods that had been rationed, while businesses rapidly raised prices they had been forced to keep low during the war. The result was rapid inflation. In 1919 prices rose more than 15 percent. Inflation greatly increased the **cost of living**—the cost of food, clothing, shelter, and other essentials that people need to survive. Orders for war materials evaporated, so factories laid off workers. Soldiers returned home looking for civilian employment but found jobs scarce. In short, 1919 was a year of economic turmoil.

Inflation Leads to Strikes

Many companies had been forced to raise wages during the war, but inflation now threatened to wipe out the gains workers had made. While workers wanted higher wages to keep up with inflation, companies resisted because inflation was also driving up their operating costs.

During the war, the number of workers in unions had increased dramatically. By the time the war ended, workers were better organized and much more capable of implementing strikes. Many business leaders, on the other hand, were determined to break the power of the unions and roll back the gains labor had made. These circumstances led to an enormous wave of strikes in 1919. By the end of the year, more than 3,600 strikes involving more than 4 million workers had taken place.

▲ *National Guard troops get rioting under control in Boston during the Police Strike of 1919*

Workers on Strike, 1916–1921

Thousands of Workers

4,500
4,000
3,500
3,000
2,500
2,000
1,500
1,000

1916 1917 1918 1919 1920 1921

Year

Analyzing VISUALS

1. **Evaluating** Why do you think strikes in 1919 worried the government more than strikes in previous years?

2. **Making Inferences** Why do you think the Boston Police Strike received so much attention? Why were officials willing to use military force in Boston so quickly?

The Seattle General Strike The first major strike took place in Seattle, where some 35,000 shipyard workers walked off the job demanding higher wages and shorter hours. Other unions in Seattle soon joined the shipyard workers and organized a general strike.

A **general strike** is a strike that involves all workers in a community, not just workers in a particular industry. The Seattle general strike involved more than 60,000 people and paralyzed the city for five days. Although the strikers returned to work without making any gains, their actions worried many Americans because the general strike was a common tactic used in Europe by communists and other radical groups.

The Boston Police Strike Perhaps the most famous strike of 1919 took place in Boston, where roughly 75 percent of the police force walked off the job. Riots and looting soon erupted in the city, forcing the governor, **Calvin Coolidge,** to call in the National Guard. When the strikers tried to return to work, the police commissioner then fired the strikers and hired a new police force instead.

Despite protests, Coolidge agreed that the men should be fired, declaring: "There is no right to strike against the public safety by anybody, anywhere, anytime." Coolidge's response earned him **widespread** public support and convinced the Republicans to make him their vice presidential candidate in the 1920 election.

The Steel Strike Shortly after the police strike ended, one of the largest strikes in American history began when an estimated 350,000 steelworkers went on strike for higher pay, shorter hours, and recognition of their union. Elbert H. Gary, the head of U.S. Steel, refused even to talk to union leaders. Instead, he set out to break the union by using anti-immigrant feelings to divide the workers.

Many steelworkers were immigrants. The company blamed the strike on foreign radicals and called for loyal Americans to return to work. Meanwhile, to keep the mills running, the company hired African Americans and Mexicans as replacement workers. Clashes between company guards and strikers were frequent. In Gary, Indiana, a riot left 18 strikers dead. The strike collapsed in early 1920 and its failure set back the union cause in the steel industry. Steel workers remained unorganized until 1941.

Racial Unrest

The economic turmoil after the war also contributed to widespread racial unrest. Many African Americans had moved north during the war to take factory jobs. As people began to be laid off and returning soldiers found it hard to find work and affordable housing, many gave in to feelings of racism and blamed African Americans for taking their jobs. Frustration and racism combined to produce violence.

In the summer of 1919, 25 race riots broke out across the nation. African American leader James Weldon Johnson called the summer of 1919, "the red summer" because of the amount of blood that was spilled. The riots began in July, when a mob of angry white people burned shops and homes in an African American neighborhood in Longview, Texas. A week later, in Washington, D.C., gangs of African Americans and whites fought each other for four days before troops got the riots under control.

The worst violence occurred in Chicago. On a hot July day, African Americans went to a whites-only beach. Both sides began throwing stones at each other. Whites also threw stones at an African American teenager swimming near the beach to prevent him from coming ashore, and he drowned. A full-scale riot then erupted in the city.

Angry African Americans attacked white neighborhoods while whites attacked African American neighborhoods. The Chicago riot lasted for almost two weeks and the government was forced to send in National Guard troops to impose order. By the time the rioting ended, 38 people had been killed—15 white and 23 black—and over 500 had been injured.

The race riots of 1919 disillusioned some African Americans who felt their wartime contributions had been for nothing. For others, however, the wartime struggle for democracy encouraged them to fight for their rights at home.

The race riots of 1919 were different in one respect. For the first time, African Americans organized and fought back against the white mobs. Many African Americans also dedicated themselves to fighting for their rights politically. The NAACP surged in membership after the war, and in 1919, it launched a new campaign for a federal law against lynching.

Reading Check **Analyzing** Why did the end of the war lead to race riots?

PAST & PRESENT

Terrorists Attack America

When terrorists attacked the United States on September 11, 2001, many Americans believed the United States was experiencing something new—multiple attacks by a terrorist organization.

It is almost forgotten by the American people that in June 1919, eight bombs exploded in eight American cities within minutes of each other, and another 30 bombs sent through the mail were intercepted before they exploded. In September 1920 an even larger bomb exploded in New York. As it did after 9/11, the United States government created a new federal agency to protect the American people. In 1919 the government created the General Intelligence Division, headed by J. Edgar Hoover, who later headed the FBI. In 2002 the government created the Department of Homeland Security.

June 1919 Bombings

Boston
Newton
Paterson
New York
East Orange
Philadelphia
Pittsburgh
Washington, D.C.

September, 1920

▲ In September 1920, a bomb made of 100 lbs. of dynamite and 500 lbs. of steel fragments exploded in New York City, killing 38 people and injuring 300 others.

The Red Scare

MAIN Idea Fear of a Communist revolution caused a nationwide panic.

HISTORY AND YOU Many Americans believed the country was in danger in 1919. Read on to see similarities with today's concerns about security.

The wave of strikes in 1919 helped to fuel fears that Communists were conspiring to start a revolution in the United States. Americans had been stunned when Communists seized power in Russia and negotiated a separate peace agreement with Germany. Many Americans viewed this as a betrayal, and hostility toward Communists increased. Communism became associated with disloyalty and treachery.

Americans had long been suspicious of communist ideas. Since the late 1800s, many Americans had accused immigrants of importing radical socialist and communist ideas and blamed them for labor unrest and violence. Events in Russia seemed to justify fears of a Communist revolution. The Soviet establishment of the Communist International in 1919—an organization for coordinating Communist parties in other countries—appeared to be further proof of a growing threat.

The strikes of 1919 fueled fears that Communists, or "reds," as they were called, might seize power. This led to a nationwide panic known as the **Red Scare.** Many people were particularly concerned about workers using strikes to start a revolution. Seattle's mayor, Ole Hanson, for example, claimed that the Seattle general strike was part of an attempt to "take possession of our American government and try to duplicate the anarchy of Russia."

In April, the postal service intercepted more than 30 parcels containing homemade bombs addressed to prominent Americans. In May, union members, socialists, and communists organized a parade in Cleveland to protest the jailing of American Socialist Party leader Eugene Debs. The parade turned into a series of riots. By the time police and army units got the violence under control, two people were dead and another 40 were injured.

In June, eight bombs in eight cities exploded within minutes of one another, suggesting a nationwide conspiracy. One of them damaged the home of United States Attorney General **A. Mitchell Palmer.** Most people believed the bombings were the work of radicals trying to destroy the American way of life.

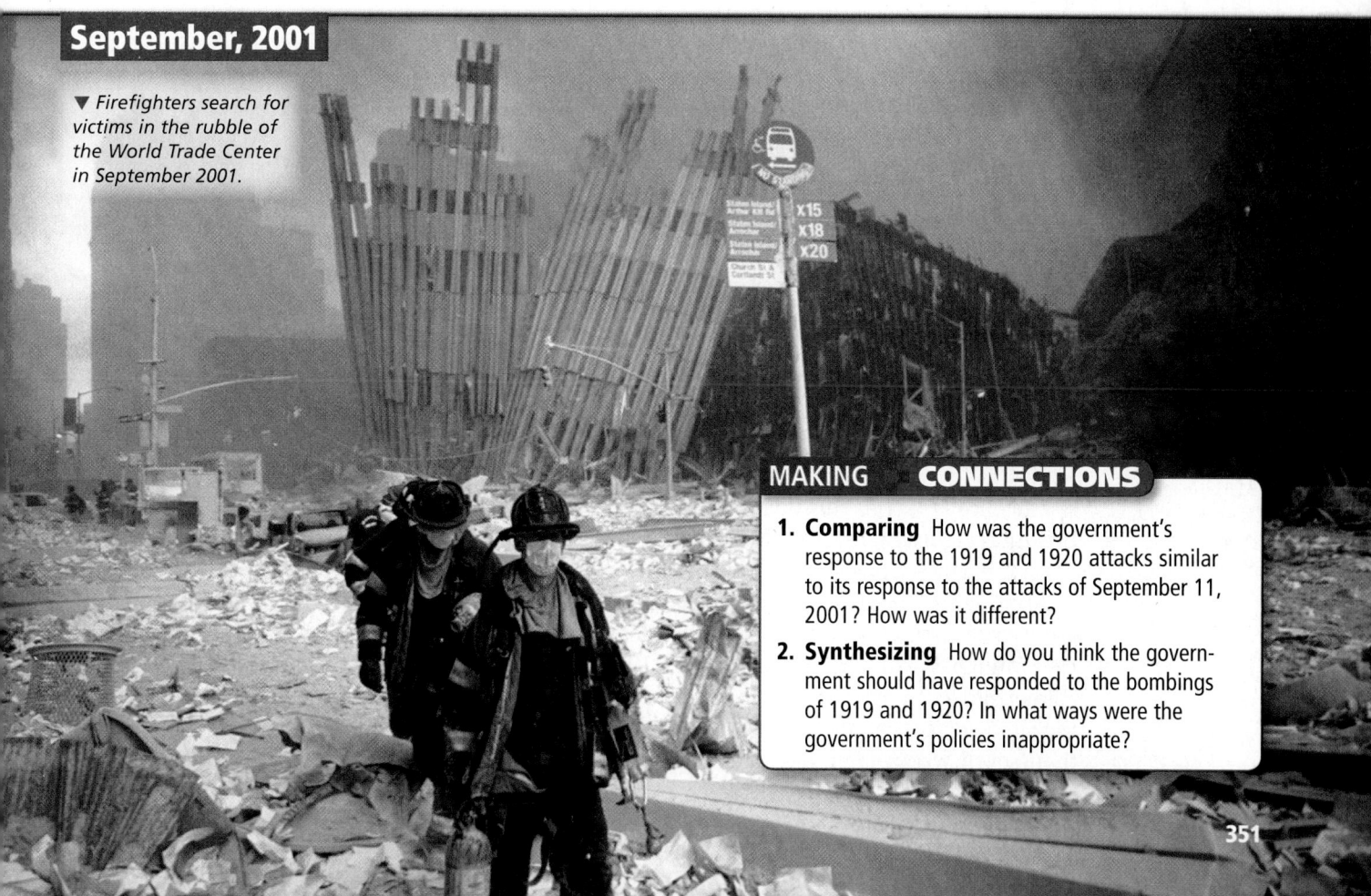

September, 2001

▼ Firefighters search for victims in the rubble of the World Trade Center in September 2001.

MAKING CONNECTIONS

1. **Comparing** How was the government's response to the 1919 and 1920 attacks similar to its response to the attacks of September 11, 2001? How was it different?

2. **Synthesizing** How do you think the government should have responded to the bombings of 1919 and 1920? In what ways were the government's policies inappropriate?

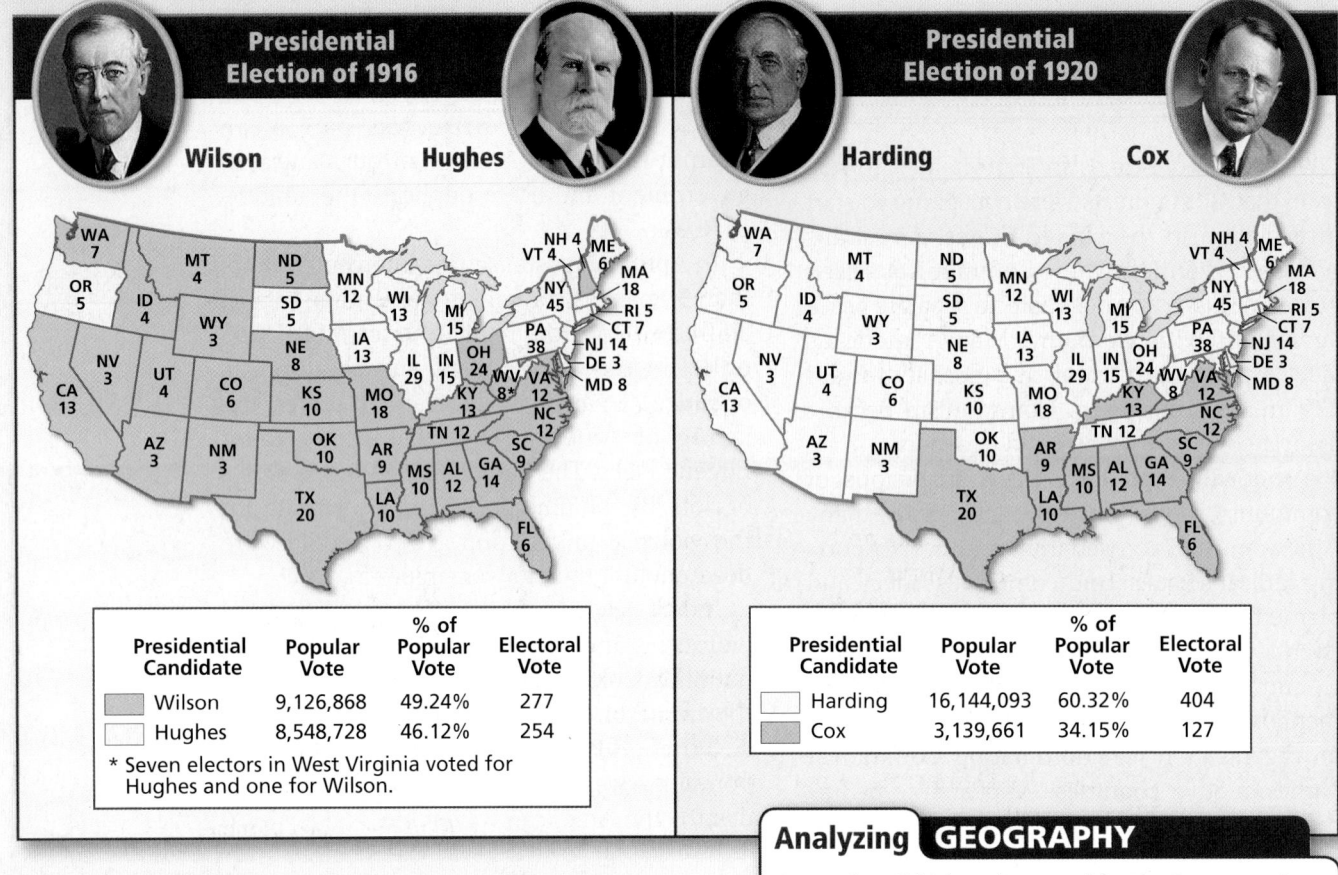

Presidential Election of 1916

Wilson — Hughes

Presidential Election of 1920

Harding — Cox

Presidential Candidate	Popular Vote	% of Popular Vote	Electoral Vote
Wilson	9,126,868	49.24%	277
Hughes	8,548,728	46.12%	254

* Seven electors in West Virginia voted for Hughes and one for Wilson.

Presidential Candidate	Popular Vote	% of Popular Vote	Electoral Vote
Harding	16,144,093	60.32%	404
Cox	3,139,661	34.15%	127

Many political historians used to think of the election of 1920 as the end of the Progressive Era. It is true that the 1920 election represented a dramatic shift from the progressive Woodrow Wilson to the much more traditionally conservative Warren Harding. But did the election really show a great change in voting habits throughout the country?

Analyzing GEOGRAPHY

1. **Region** Which region voted for the Democrats in both elections? Which region voted Republican in both elections?

2. **Region** What region of the country changed its vote between 1916 and 1920? Why do you think this happened? Does this change suggest people's views of progressivism had changed?

The Palmer Raids

Declaring that a "blaze of revolution" was "burning up the foundations of society," Palmer took action. He established a special division within the Justice Department, the General Intelligence Division. This division, headed by **J. Edgar Hoover,** eventually became the Federal Bureau of Investigation (FBI).

Although evidence pointed to no single group as the bombers, Palmer's agents targeted the foreign-born. On November 7, 1919, Palmer ordered a series of raids on offices of the Union of Russian Workers in 12 cities. Less than seven weeks later, a transport ship left New York for Russia carrying 249 immigrants who had been deported, or expelled from the country.

In January 1920, Palmer ordered another series of raids, this time on the headquarters of various radical organizations. Nearly 6,000 people were arrested. That same month, the New York state legislature expelled five members of the Socialist Party who had been elected to the legislature. Over the next few months, 32 states passed sedition laws making it illegal to join groups advocating revolution. Palmer's raids continued until the spring of 1920. **Authorities** detained thousands of suspects and nearly 600 people were **deported.**

Palmer's agents often ignored the civil liberties of the suspects. Officers entered homes and offices without search warrants. People were mistreated. Some were jailed for indefinite periods of time and were not allowed to talk to their attorneys. Many of the immigrants who were deported were never granted a court hearing to challenge the evidence against them or to contest the deportation order.

For a while, Palmer was regarded as a national hero. His raids, however, failed to turn up any hard evidence of revolutionary conspiracy. When his prediction that violence would rock the nation on May Day 1920—a celebration of workers in Europe—proved wrong, Palmer lost much of his credibility and support.

The Red Scare greatly influenced people's attitudes during the 1920s. Americans often linked radicalism with immigrants, and that attitude led to a call for Congress to limit immigration.

The Election of 1920

Economic problems, labor unrest, and racial tensions, as well as the fresh memories of World War I, all combined to create a general sense of disillusionment in the United States. By 1920 Americans wanted an end to the upheaval.

During the 1920 campaign, Ohio governor James M. Cox and his running mate, Assistant Secretary of the Navy Franklin D. Roosevelt, ran on a platform of progressive ideals. President Wilson tried to convince the Democrats to make the campaign a referendum on the Treaty of Versailles and the League of Nations, but the party chose not to take a strong stand on the issue for fear of alienating voters.

The Republican candidate, Warren G. Harding, called for a return to "normalcy." His vice-presidential running mate, Calvin Coolidge, was chosen because people admired the way he had handled the Boston police strike. Harding argued that what the United States needed was a return to simpler days before the Progressive Era reforms:

PRIMARY SOURCE

"[Our] present need is not heroics, but healing; not nostrums, but normalcy; not revolution, but [bold] restoration; not agitation, but adjustment; not surgery, but serenity; not the dramatic, but the dispassionate; ... not submergence in internationality, but sustainment in triumphant nationality."

—quoted in *Portrait of a Nation*

Harding's sentiments struck a chord with voters, and he won the election by a landslide margin of over 7 million votes. Many Americans were weary of more crusades to reform society and the world. They hoped to put the country's racial and labor unrest and economic troubles behind them and build a more prosperous and stable society.

Reading Check **Examining** After World War I, why were Americans suspicious of some union leaders?

Section 4 REVIEW

Vocabulary

1. **Explain** the significance of: cost of living, general strike, Calvin Coolidge, Red Scare, A. Mitchell Palmer, J. Edgar Hoover, deport.

Main Ideas

2. **Identifying** Use a chart like the one below to list the various causes of labor unrest in 1919.

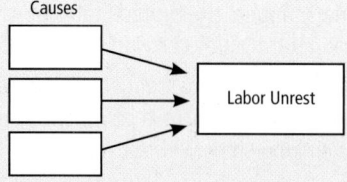

3. **Describing** What events made many Americans believe a revolution was imminent in 1919?

Critical Thinking

4. **Big Ideas** Why did the end of World War I bring such turmoil to the United States?

5. **Analyzing** Provide evidence to explain whether or not the Palmer raids deprived some people of their civil rights.

6. **Analyzing Visuals** Examine the photograph on page 349. What do you notice about the rioters? What does this tell you about the riots?

Writing About History

7. **Persuasive Writing** Imagine that you are a European immigrant working in a factory in the United States in 1919. Write a letter to a relative in Europe describing the feelings of Americans toward you and other immigrants.

History ONLINE

Study Central™ To review this section, go to glencoe.com and click on Study Central.

Causes of America's Entry Into World War I

- Americans hear stories of German atrocities and many become anti-German.
- Many of President Wilson's advisors support the Allies.
- American banks lend the Allies large amounts of money and American companies sell the Allies food, weapons, and military supplies.
- Germany angers the United States by ordering submarines to attack neutral ships carrying goods to the Allies.
- Germany sinks the passenger ships *Lusitania* and *Sussex*, enraging Americans. To keep America out of the war, Germany stops sinking ships without warning in 1916.
- Germany tries to make an alliance with Mexico, further angering Americans.
- In a last attempt to win the war, Germany orders submarines to attack ships without warning in 1917; six American ships are sunk.
- The United States declares war, April 1917.

NEW YORK JOURNAL

House by a Vote of 373 to 50 Passes Joint Resolution

WAR IS DECLARED BY U.S.

Interned German Ships Seized by Customs Authorities

Washington, April 6.—After a debate of nearly seventeen hours, the House early to-day passed the resolution previously adopted in the Senate, declaring a state of war against the Government of Germany. The vote was 373 to 50.

The resolution now goes to Vice-President Marshall, who must sign it in formal session of the Senate...

▶ *German U-boats helped cause the United States to enter the war.*

▲ *World War I enabled women to take jobs traditionally reserved for men.*

Social and Cultural Effects of World War I

- Northern factories recruit African Americans from the rural South; African Americans migrate to northern cities in large numbers, improving their standard of living and changing politics in northern cities.
- In search of workers, companies also hire large numbers of women for jobs traditionally reserved for men.
- Labor shortages cause many Mexicans to migrate north to take work in the United States. Many Hispanic Americans leave farmwork for factory work.
- Laws limiting civil rights in wartime are upheld by the Supreme Court in the cases of *Schenck* v. *U.S.* and *Abrams* v. *U.S.*
- During the war, anti-German feelings are widespread.
- The end of the war leads to economic and social tensions; many workers go on strike; race riots erupt in many cities.
- After the war, many Americans become anti-immigrant, anti-communist, and anti-union.

Reviewing Vocabulary

Directions: Choose the word or words that best complete the sentence.

1. The British used _____ to convince Americans to support the Allied war effort.

   A espionage

   B armistice

   C conscription

   D propaganda

2. The _____ system ensured that American troops arrived safely in Europe.

   A nationalism

   B convoy

   C reparations

   D cost of living

3. British officials ordered a naval blockade to prevent _____, or prohibited materials, from entering Germany.

   A contraband

   B cost of living

   C conscription

   D self-determination

4. Soldiers in World War I dug a complex _____ of trenches to protect themselves.

   A emphasis

   B stability

   C restoration

   D network

5. During the war, the federal government tried to shape opinions about the war and to prevent _____, spying to acquire government information.

   A espionage

   B propaganda

   C reparations

   D militarism

Reviewing Main Ideas

Directions: Choose the best answers to the following questions.

Section 1 *(pp. 320–327)*

6. Which of the following was one of the primary causes of World War I?

   A a complex set of alliances among European nations

   B the exile of Mexican General Victoriano Huerta

   C the dissatisfaction of Russian peasants

   D the breakup of the Austro-Hungarian Empire

7. The event that triggered the American entry into World War I was

   A the sinking of the *Lusitania*.

   B the resumption of unrestricted submarine warfare.

   C the invasion of neutral Belgium.

   D the interception of the Zimmermann telegram.

Section 2 *(pp. 328–333)*

8. During World War I, which federal mobilization agency introduced daylight savings time and shortened the work week for some factories?

   A War Industries Board

   B Committee on Public Information

   C National War Labor Board

   D Fuel Administration

9. Both the Espionage Act and the Sedition Act of 1918 were designed to

   A provide plans for rebuilding Germany after the war.

   B help the British and French economies during the war.

   C limit opposition to the war in the United States.

   D protect the rights of German Americans.

TEST-TAKING

> Eliminate answers that do not make sense. For instance, if an answer refers to World War II, you know it cannot be correct.

Need Extra Help?									
If You Missed Questions . . .	1	2	3	4	5	6	7	8	9
Go to Page . . .	324	338–339	326	336	330	320–322	326–327	328–329	330

Section 3 *(pp. 336–345)*

10. Which of the following technologies was first used during World War I?

   A tanks

   B cannons

   C aircraft carriers

   D hot air balloons

11. Why did the Senate reject the Treaty of Versailles?

   A to keep the United States free from foreign entanglements

   B to express opposition to the harsh sanctions imposed on Germany

   C to avoid the dues for membership in the League of Nations

   D to reduce United States military forces in Europe

Section 4 *(pp. 348–353)*

12. The Red Scare was a fear that

   A nuclear power would result in widespread destruction in the United States.

   B Communists would seize power in the United States.

   C fire would spread quickly through overcrowded American cities.

   D the Soviet Union would develop an atomic bomb.

13. The organization that eventually became the Federal Bureau of Investigation was originally formed to

   A uncover German spies during World War I.

   B spread propaganda within the United States in support of World War I.

   C infiltrate unions to head off strikes.

   D raid the headquarters of radical organizations in order to look for evidence of a Communist conspiracy.

Critical Thinking

Directions: Choose the best answers to the following questions.

14. How did Congress ensure that the United States would have enough troops to serve in World War I?

   A Congress allowed women to serve in the armed forces.

   B The Selective Service Act of 1917 required all men ages 21 to 30 to register for the draft.

   C Congress allowed African Americans to serve in the armed forces.

   D Congress offered a free education and cheap land to anyone willing to serve.

Base your answer to question 15 on the map below and your knowledge of Chapter 9.

Europe after WWI

15. Which countries lost territory as a result of World War I?

   A Germany, Russia, France

   B Germany, France, England

   C Germany, Italy, Austria-Hungary

   D Germany, Austria-Hungary, Russia

Need Extra Help?						
If You Missed Questions . . .	10	11	12	13	14	15
Go to Page . . .	337–339	343–345	351	352	332–333	342–343

16. President Wilson's Fourteen Points plan called for

A Germany to pay war reparations to the Allies.

B Germany to acknowledge guilt for the outbreak of World War I.

C the creation of the United Nations.

D the creation of the League of Nations.

Analyze the cartoon and answer the question that follows. Base your answers on the cartoon and on your knowledge of Chapter 9.

17. The cartoonist is expressing the opinion that

A England's blockade of Germany was beneficial for neutral shipping.

B England's blockade of the United States hurt neutral shipping.

C England's blockade of the United States hurt American shipping.

D England's blockade of Germany hurt American shipping.

Document-Based Questions

Directions: Analyze the document and answer the short-answer questions that follow the document.

On September 12, 1918, Socialist leader Eugene V. Debs was convicted of violating the Espionage Act. Debs later spoke to the court at his sentencing. The document below is an excerpt from that speech:

> "I look upon the Espionage laws as a despotic enactment in flagrant conflict with democratic principles and with the spirit of free institutions. . . . I am opposed to the social system in which we live. . . . I believe in fundamental change, but if possible by peaceful and orderly means. . . .
>
> I am thinking this morning of the men in the mills and factories, . . . of the women who for a paltry wage are compelled to work out their barren lives; of the little children who in this system are robbed of their childhood and . . . forced into industrial dungeons. . . . In this high noon of our twentieth century Christian civilization, money is still so much more important than the flesh and blood of childhood. In very truth gold is god. . . . "
>
> —from Eugene Debs in *Echoes of Distant Thunder*

18. According to Debs, what were some problems in American society at this time? How did he believe change should be brought about?

19. How did Debs seem to feel about the Espionage Act? Do you agree with him? Why or why not?

Extended Response

20. After World War I, the United States Senate refused to ratify the Treaty of Versailles despite the intense efforts of Woodrow Wilson to convince Americans that ratification would help ensure that the peace would be an enduring one. Choose to either support or oppose the United States's ratification of the Treaty of Versailles. Write a persuasive essay that includes an introduction and at least three paragraphs that support your position.

STOP

History ONLINE

For additional test practice, use Self-Check Quizzes—Chapter 9 at glencoe.com.

Need Extra Help?

If You Missed Questions . . .	16	17	18	19	20
Go to Page . . .	342–343	324–327	357	R19	342–345

Unit 4

Boom and Bust
1920–1941

Why It Matters

In the 1920s, new technology, including automobiles, airplanes, radios, and electric appliances helped create a booming economy with rising stock prices and increased consumer spending. In 1929, economic problems triggered the Great Depression. This led to increased federal regulation of the economy and several new programs, such as Social Security as the federal government took on the task of protecting people from economic hardship.

The Great White Way, Times Square, New York, 1925

The Jazz Age
1921–1929

Joe "King" Oliver's jazz band plays in San Francisco in 1921, with singer Lil Hardin.

U.S. PRESIDENTS

1921
- Washington Conference convenes

Harding 1921–1923

1922
- Claude McKay's *Harlem Shadows* is published

1923
- Teapot Dome scandal erupts

Coolidge 1923–1929

1924
- Congress passes National Origins Act

1925
- Scopes trial begins

U.S. EVENTS

1921

1923

1925

WORLD EVENTS

1921
- Ireland becomes independent country

1922
- Mussolini and Fascists take power in Italy

1923
- France invades Ruhr
- Hitler writes *Mein Kampf*

1924
- Vladimir Lenin dies

Making Connections
Why Does Culture Change?

In the 1920s, technology spurred economic growth and cultural change. Although not everyone approved, young people adopted new styles of dress, listened to jazz music, and had more independence than earlier generations.

- *What technologies changed life in the 1920s?*
- *How do you think the invention of radio and movies changed popular culture?*

1927
- Lindbergh completes first solo transatlantic flight

1928
- Kellogg-Briand Pact signed

Hoover
1929–1933

1927

1929

1926
- British General Strike paralyzes British economy

1927
- Stalin gains control of Soviet Union

1928
- Chiang Kai-shek becomes leader of China

FOLDABLES

Categorizing the Harlem Renaissance
Create a Trifold Book Foldable to present a brief biography, with artistic works, of major figures in the Harlem Renaissance under the category of writers, poets, and musicians. You may want to expand on your entries by using the Internet.

Writers	Poets	Musicians

History ONLINE Visit glencoe.com and enter *QuickPass*™ code TAVMT5147c10 for Chapter 10 resources.

The Politics of the 1920s

Guide to Reading

Big Ideas
Economics and Society Government policies helped create prosperity in the 1920s.

Content Vocabulary
- supply-side economics *(p. 365)*
- cooperative individualism *(p. 365)*
- isolationism *(p. 366)*

Academic Vocabulary
- investigation *(p. 363)*
- revelation *(p. 364)*

People and Events to Identify
- Teapot Dome *(p. 363)*
- Charles G. Dawes *(p. 367)*
- Charles Evans Hughes *(p. 367)*
- Kellogg-Briand Pact *(p. 367)*

Reading Strategy
Taking Notes As you read about Presidents Harding and Coolidge, create an outline similar to the one below.

```
The Politics of the 1920s
I. The Harding Administration
    A.
    B.
II.
III.
    A.
    B.
```

Warren G. Harding's administration suffered from corruption and scandals. His successor, Calvin Coolidge, worked hard to restore the American public's faith in their government and to promote a healthy economy.

The Harding Administration

MAIN Idea President Harding staffed his administration with political friends from Ohio; his presidency was marred by many scandals.

HISTORY AND YOU If you were choosing teammates, would you pick a friend or a better player? Read on to learn about the problems Harding created by making poor choices for government appointments.

Warren G. Harding was born in 1865 in Corsica, Ohio. In 1898 voters elected Harding to the Ohio General Assembly, where he fit in comfortably with the powerful Ohio Republican political machine. Voters elected him as Ohio's lieutenant governor in 1903 and United States senator in 1914. After serving one term in the Senate, Harding ran for and won the presidency in 1920.

Harding's political philosophy fit in well with the times. In his campaign, he had promised "a return to normalcy," by which he meant "normal" life after the war. His charm and genial manner endeared him to the nation, and people applauded when the open, easygoing atmosphere of the Harding administration replaced the quiet gloom of President Wilson's last years.

Teapot Dome and Other Scandals

Harding made several distinguished appointments to the cabinet, including former Supreme Court Justice Charles Evans Hughes as secretary of state, former Food Administrator Herbert Hoover as secretary of commerce, and business tycoon Andrew Mellon as secretary of the treasury. All three men would play an important role in supporting and shaping the economic prosperity of the 1920s.

Many of Harding's other appointments, however, were disastrous. He gave cabinet posts and other high-level jobs to friends and political allies from Ohio. Harding named Harry M. Daugherty, his campaign manager and boss of the Ohio Republican Party, attorney general. He made his boyhood friend Daniel Crissinger chairman of the Federal Reserve Board and selected Colonel Charles R. Forbes—another Ohio acquaintance—to head the Veterans Bureau.

Harding felt more comfortable among his old poker-playing friends, known as the Ohio Gang, than he did around such sober and

▲ *"Bargain Day in Washington"* shows the U.S. Capitol, the Washington Monument, the army, the White House, and the navy as having been *"sold"* to the highest bidder.

▲ This cartoon shows politicians on the slippery *"White House Highway"* trying to outrun the scandal of Teapot Dome.

Analyzing VISUALS DBQ

1. **Drawing Conclusions** What does the cartoon on the left suggest about politicians?

2. **Analyzing** What does the cartoon on the right imply about corruption in the federal government?

serious people as Herbert Hoover. According to Alice Roosevelt Longworth, the White House study resembled a speakeasy.

PRIMARY SOURCE

"The air [would be] heavy with tobacco smoke, trays with bottles containing every imaginable brand of whiskey . . . cards and poker chips at hand—a general atmosphere of waistcoat unbuttoned, feet on desk, and spittoons alongside."

—quoted in *The Perils of Prosperity, 1914–1932*

The Ohio Gang did more than drink, smoke, and play poker with the president. Some members used their positions to sell government jobs, pardons, and protection from prosecution. Forbes sold scarce medical supplies from veterans' hospitals and kept the money for himself, costing the taxpayers about $250 million. When Harding learned what was going on, he complained privately that he had been betrayed. He said that he had no troubles with his enemies, but his friends were a different story: "They're the ones that keep me walking the floor nights!"

In June 1923 Harding left to tour the West. En route from Alaska to California, he became ill with what was probably a heart attack. He died in San Francisco on August 2, shortly before the news of the Forbes scandal broke. Early the next morning, the vice president, Calvin Coolidge, took the oath of office and became president.

The Forbes scandal was only the latest in a series of scandals and accusations that had marked the Harding administration. The most famous scandal, known as **Teapot Dome,** began in early 1922 when Harding's secretary of the interior, Albert B. Fall, secretly allowed private interests to lease lands containing U.S. Navy oil reserves at Teapot Dome, Wyoming, and Elk Hills, California. In return, Fall received bribes from these private interests totaling more than $300,000.

After the *Wall Street Journal* broke the story, the Senate launched an **investigation** that took most of the 1920s to complete. Trials followed; the Supreme Court invalidated the leases in 1927, and in 1929 Secretary Fall became the first cabinet officer in American history to go to prison.

Another Harding administration scandal involved Attorney General Harry Daugherty. During World War I, the federal government had seized a German-owned company in the United States as enemy property. To acquire the company and its valuable chemical patents, a German agent bribed a "go-between" politician, and a portion of the bribe ended up in a bank account that Daugherty controlled.

Under investigation by his own Justice Department, Daugherty refused to turn over requested files and bank records. He also refused to testify under oath, claiming immunity, or freedom from prosecution, on the grounds that he had had confidential dealings with the president. Daugherty's actions disgusted the new president, Calvin Coolidge, who demanded his resignation.

"Silent Cal" Takes Over

Calvin Coolidge was very different from Harding. Harding had enjoyed the easy conversation and company of old friends. Coolidge, joked a critic, could be "silent in five languages." Although he quickly distanced himself from the Harding administration, Coolidge asked the most capable cabinet members—Hughes, Mellon, and Hoover—to remain in the cabinet. Coolidge's philosophy of government was simple. He believed that prosperity rested on business leadership and that part of his job as president was to make sure that government interfered with business and industry as little as possible.

In the year following Harding's death and the **revelations** of the scandals, Coolidge avoided crises and adopted policies to help keep the nation prosperous. He easily won the Republican nomination for president in 1924.

The Republicans campaigned using the slogan "Keep Cool with Coolidge." They promised the American people that the policies that had brought prosperity would continue. Coolidge won the election easily, winning more than half the popular vote and 382 electoral votes.

✔ Reading Check **Analyzing** What do the scandals of the Harding administration have in common with each other?

PRIMARY SOURCE
Coolidge and Prosperity

Critics have accused Calvin Coolidge of catering to big business and cite his comment that the "business of the American people is business." This quote comes from his 1925 speech to the American Society of Newspaper Editors. Examine the graphs and the speech to assess if his policies benefited business at the expense of the public.

PRIMARY SOURCE

"After all, the chief business of the American people is business. They are profoundly concerned with producing, buying, selling, investing and prospering in the world. . . . In all experience, the accumulation of wealth means the multiplication of schools, the increase of knowledge, the dissemination of intelligence, the encouragement of science, the broadening of outlook, the expansion of liberties, the widening of culture. . . . We make no concealment of the fact that we want wealth, but there are many other things that we want very much more. We want peace and honor, and that charity which is so strong an element of all civilization.

The chief ideal of the American people is idealism. I cannot repeat too often that America is a nation of idealists."

—*New York Times*, January 18, 1925

U.S. Budget, 1919–1928

Expenditures (billions of dollars) / Year

Source: *Historical Statistics of the United States.*

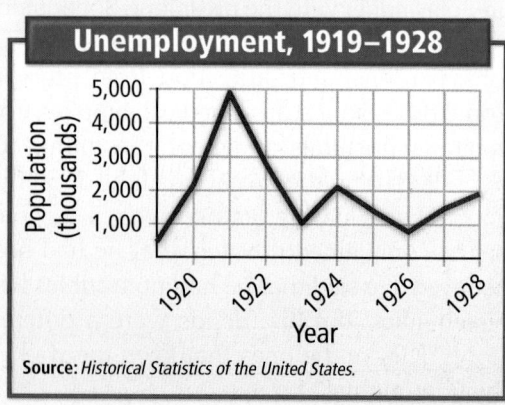

Unemployment, 1919–1928

Population (thousands) / Year

Source: *Historical Statistics of the United States.*

Policies of Prosperity

MAIN Idea During the 1920s, the government cut taxes and spending to encourage economic growth.

HISTORY AND YOU Do you have a sales tax in your state? Do you think taxes are too high? How do you know? Read to learn about changes to American taxes in the 1920s.

Although Harding gave many corrupt friends government jobs, he also selected several highly qualified individuals for his cabinet. Among them were Andrew Mellon and Herbert Hoover. Both of these men were responsible for policies that contributed to the economic growth and prosperity of the 1920s.

At the beginning of the 1920s, the nation had a large national debt, and many people were worried that it would not recover from the postwar recession. Harding chose Andrew Mellon, a successful banker and industrialist, to be secretary of the treasury. Mellon became the chief architect of economic policy and served as secretary of the treasury for three Republican presidents.

When Mellon took office, he had three major goals: to balance the budget, to reduce the government's debt, and to cut taxes. He was convinced these policies would promote economic growth and prosperity. He also firmly believed that the government should apply business principles to its operations.

In 1921 Mellon convinced Congress to create both the Bureau of the Budget to prepare a unified federal budget, and the General Accounting Office to track spending. He then began cutting spending. The federal budget fell from $6.4 billion to less than $3 billion in seven years. He also cut tax rates.

Mellon argued that high tax rates actually reduced the amount of tax money the government collected. If taxes were lower, businesses and consumers would spend and invest their extra money, causing the economy to grow. As the economy grew, Americans would earn more money, and the government would actually collect more taxes at a lower rate than it would if it kept tax rates high. This idea is known today as **supply-side economics,** or "trickle-down" economics.

At Mellon's urging, Congress dramatically reduced tax rates. When Mellon took office, most taxpayers paid 4 percent federal income tax, while wealthy Americans in the highest bracket paid 73 percent. By 1928, Congress had reduced the rate most Americans paid to 0.5 percent and cut the rate for the wealthiest Americans to 25 percent.

Secretary of Commerce Herbert Hoover also sought to promote economic growth. He tried to balance government regulation with his own philosophy of **cooperative individualism.** This idea involved encouraging businesses to form trade associations that would voluntarily share information with the federal government. Hoover believed this system would reduce costs and promote economic efficiency.

To assist businesses, Hoover directed the Bureau of Foreign and Domestic Commerce to find new markets for companies. He also established the Bureau of Aviation to regulate and promote the growth of the airline industry and the Federal Radio Commission to help the young radio industry by regulating radio frequencies and the power of transmitters.

✔ Reading Check **Summarizing** What strategies did Mellon use to promote economic growth?

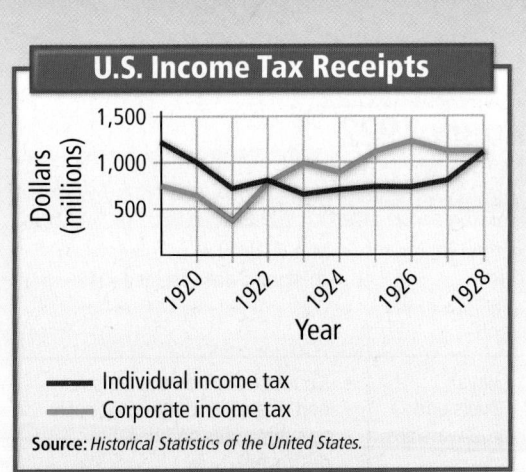

U.S. Income Tax Receipts

Dollars (millions) vs. Year (1920–1928)

— Individual income tax
— Corporate income tax

Source: *Historical Statistics of the United States.*

Analyzing VISUALS *DBQ*

1. **Analyzing Primary Sources** What does Coolidge believe is the point of accumulating wealth? Do you believe that the United States has achieved Coolidge's goals? Explain.

2. **Evaluating** Based on the graphs, what did Coolidge's economic policies achieve in the 1920s?

Trade and Arms Control

MAIN Idea During the 1920s, the United States tried to promote peace and stability through economic policies and arms control agreements.

HISTORY AND YOU Do you remember reading about the Treaty of Versailles and how the United States never ratified it? Read to learn how America initiated other treaties in the 1920s.

Before World War I the United States was a debtor nation. By the end of the war, the situation was reversed. Wartime allies owed the United States more than $10 billion in war debts. By the 1920s, the United States was the dominant economic power in the world. Under the leadership of Secretary of State Charles Evan Hughes, the nation tried to use its economic power to promote peace and stability.

The Myth of Isolationism

The majority of Americans—tired of being entangled in the baffling, hostile, and dangerous politics of Europe—favored **isolationism.** This is the idea that the United States will be safer and more prosperous if it stays out of world affairs.

To many people at the time, it appeared that the United States had become isolationist. The United States had not ratified the Treaty of Versailles and had not joined the League of Nations. The Permanent Court of International Justice, better known as the World Court, opened in 1921, but the United States refused to join it as well.

Despite appearances, the United States was too powerful and too interconnected with other countries economically to be truly isolationist. Instead of relying on armed force and the collective security of the League of Nations, the United States tried to promote peace by using economic policies and arms control agreements.

The Dawes Plan

America's former allies had difficulty making the payments on their immense war debts. High American tariffs hampered their economic

INFOGRAPHIC

The Washington Conference, November 1921–February 1922

Treaty	Signers	Terms	Weaknesses
Four-Power Treaty	United States, Great Britain, France, Japan	• All agreed to respect the others' territory in the Pacific • Full and open negotiations in the event of disagreements	• Mutual defense of other co-signers not specified
Five-Power Treaty	United States, Great Britain, France, Japan, Italy	• All agreed to freeze naval production at 1921 levels and halt production of large warships for 10 years • U.S. and Great Britain agreed not to build new naval bases in the western Pacific	• No restrictions on the construction of smaller battle craft such as submarines and naval destroyers • Did not place restrictions on the ground forces
Nine-Power Treaty	United States, Great Britain, France, Japan, Italy, Belgium, China, the Netherlands, Portugal	• All agreed to preserve equal commercial rights to China—a reassertion of the Open Door policy	• No enforcement of the terms of the Open Door policy specified

Analyzing VISUALS

1. **Interpreting Charts** Which countries signed the Five-Power Treaty?

2. **Analyzing** Why do you think the terms of the treaties focused on the Pacific region?

recovery by making it difficult to sell their products in the United States. This meant they could not acquire the money to pay off their war debts. These countries also were receiving reparations—huge cash payments Germany was required to make as punishment for starting the war. These payments, however, were crippling the German economy.

It was vital for the United States that European economies be healthy so that the Europeans could buy American exports and repay their debts. Thus, in 1924, American diplomat **Charles G. Dawes** negotiated an agreement with France, Britain, and Germany by which American banks would make loans to Germany that would enable it to make reparations payments. In exchange, Britain and France would accept less in reparations and pay back more on their war debts.

The Washington Conference

Despite their debts, the major powers were involved in a costly postwar naval arms race. To end the weapons race, the United States invited representatives from eight major countries—Great Britain, France, Italy, China, Japan, Belgium, the Netherlands, and Portugal—to Washington, D.C., to discuss disarmament. The Washington Conference opened on November 12, 1921.

In his address to the delegates, Secretary of State **Charles Evans Hughes** proposed a 10-year moratorium, or halt, on the construction of new warships. He also proposed a list of warships in each country's navy to be destroyed, beginning with some American battleships. The discussions that followed produced the Five-Power Naval Limitation Treaty in which Britain, France, Italy, Japan, and the United States essentially formalized Hughes's proposal.

As a long-term effort to prevent war, the conference had some serious shortcomings. It did nothing to limit land forces. It also angered the Japanese because it required Japan to maintain a smaller navy than either the United States or Great Britain. It did, however, give Americans cause to look forward to a period of peace, recovery, and prosperity.

Abolishing War

The apparent success of the Washington Conference boosted hopes that written agreements could end war altogether. Perhaps the highest expression of that idea occurred when U.S. Secretary of State Frank Kellogg and French Foreign Minister Aristide Briand proposed a treaty to outlaw war. On August 27, 1928, the United States and 14 other nations signed the **Kellogg-Briand Pact.** Although it had no binding force, the pact was hailed as a victory for peace. It stated that all signing nations agreed to abandon war and to settle all disputes by peaceful means. The Kellogg-Briand Pact and the Dawes Plan were perhaps the most notable foreign policy achievements of the Coolidge administration.

Reading Check **Identifying** What problem was the Dawes Plan intended to solve?

Vocabulary

1. **Explain** the significance of: Teapot Dome, supply-side economics, cooperative individualism, isolationism, Charles G. Dawes, Charles Evans Hughes, Kellogg-Briand Pact.

Main Ideas

2. **Summarizing** What scandals marred Harding's presidency?

3. **Explaining** What strategies did Andrew Mellon and Herbert Hoover use to stimulate economic growth?

4. **Describing** In what two ways did the United States try to promote peace during the 1920s?

Critical Thinking

5. **Big Ideas** What efforts did the United States make to promote worldwide economic recovery?

6. **Categorizing** Use a graphic organizer like the one below to list the major terms of the treaties resulting from the Washington Conference.

Major Terms of Treaties	

7. **Analyzing Visuals** Examine the charts on page 364. What explanation can you offer for the drop in the United States's budget from 1919 to 1928?

Writing About History

8. **Persuasive Writing** Imagine that you are an American business owner or farmer in the 1920s. Write a letter to your representatives in Congress explaining why you think cutting taxes is a good or bad idea.

History ONLINE

Study Central™ To review this section, go to glencoe.com and click on Study Central.

A Growing Economy

Guide to Reading

Big Ideas
Economics and Society The United States experienced stunning economic growth during the 1920s.

Content Vocabulary
- mass production *(p. 368)*
- assembly line *(p. 368)*
- Model T *(p. 368)*
- welfare capitalism *(p. 374)*
- open shop *(p. 374)*

Academic Vocabulary
- disposable *(p. 370)*
- credit *(p. 372)*

People and Events to Identify
- Charles Lindbergh *(p. 372)*

Reading Strategy
Organizing As you read about the booming era of the 1920s, complete a graphic organizer to analyze the causes of economic growth and prosperity in the 1920s.

Industry

Society

In the 1920s widespread ownership of automobiles, radios, and other innovations changed how Americans lived. The Coolidge administration encouraged business growth and tried to promote stability in international affairs.

The Rise of New Industries

MAIN Idea Mass production and the assembly line allowed new industries, such as automobile and airplane manufacturing, to grow.

HISTORY AND YOU How would businesses, governments, and your family be affected if air travel did not exist? Read to learn how the transportation industry changed during the 1920s and 1930s.

By the 1920s, the automobile had become an accepted part of American life. In a 1925 survey conducted in Muncie, Indiana, 21 out of 26 families who owned cars did not have bathtubs with running water. When asked why her family decided a car was more important than indoor plumbing, a farm wife explained, "You can't ride to town in a bathtub."

The automobile was just one part of a rising standard of living that Americans experienced in the 1920s. Real per capita earnings soared 22 percent between 1923 and 1929. Meanwhile, as Americans' wages increased, their work hours decreased. In 1923 U.S. Steel cut its daily work shift from 12 hours to 8 hours. In 1926 Henry Ford cut the workweek for his employees from six days to five, and International Harvester, a maker of farm machinery, instituted an annual two-week paid vacation for employees. These changes took place because **mass production,** or large-scale manufacturing done with machinery, increased supply and reduced costs. Workers could be paid more and the consumer goods they bought cost less.

The Assembly Line and the Model T

First adopted by carmaker Henry Ford, the moving **assembly line** divided operations into simple tasks and cut unnecessary motion to a minimum. In 1913 Ford installed the first moving assembly line at his plant in Highland Park, Michigan. By the following year, workers were building an automobile every 93 minutes. Before, the task had taken 12 hours. By 1925 a Ford car was rolling off the line every 10 seconds.

Ford's assembly-line product, the **Model T**—affectionately called the "Tin Lizzie" or "Flivver"—demonstrated the economic concept of elasticity, or how sensitive product demand is to price. In 1908, the

The Car Changes America

Many industries that were needed to build cars prospered. Car manufacturers needed steel for the car body, glass for the windows, and rubber for the tires. The automobile also led to changes in society. People moved to the suburbs, but were less isolated from the benefits of the city. At the same time, there was a decline in mass transportation such as railroads and trolleys.

▲ Cars allowed people greater mobility and freedom. These young women drove to the country to have a picnic.

▲ The car let people live further out in the suburbs and commute to jobs in the city.

▲ Cars greatly increased the demand for oil, leading to a boom in the oil business, as shown by the forest of oil wells in Signal Hills, California in 1930. To keep cars refueled, roadside gas stations sprang up across the country.

▶ The auto industry spurred a boom in other industries, as well. These workers at Goodyear Tire and Rubber in Akron, Ohio, are removing car tires from curing pits.

Analyzing VISUALS — DBQ

1. **Determining Cause and Effect** How did the automobile help other industries grow? Which industries were most affected?

2. **Drawing Conclusions** Based on the images above, how did the car change people's lives?

Model T's first year, it sold for $850. In 1914 mass production reduced the price to $490. Three years later, improved assembly-line methods and a high volume of sales brought the price down to $360. By 1924 Model Ts were selling for $295, and Ford sold millions of them. His business philosophy was: lower the cost per car and thereby increase the volume of sales.

The low prices made possible by Ford's mass-production methods not only created an immense market for his cars but also spawned imitators. By the mid-1920s, other car manufacturers, notably General Motors and Chrysler, competed successfully with Ford. The auto industry also spurred growth in other industries, such as rubber, plate glass, nickel, and lead. The auto industry alone consumed 15 percent of the nation's steel and led to a huge expansion of the petroleum industry.

High Wages for Workers Ford also increased his workers' wages in 1914 to $5 a day (doubling their pay) and reduced the workday to eight-hour shifts. Ford took these dramatic steps to build up workers' loyalty and to undercut union organizers.

There were strings attached, however. Ford created a "Sociological Department," which set requirements workers had to meet. For example, renting space in one's home to nonfamily members was strictly forbidden. Investigators visited employees' homes to verify their eligibility and workers who broke the rules could be disqualified from extra pay, suspended, or even fired.

The Social Impact of the Automobile

Cars revolutionized American life. They eased the isolation of rural life and enabled more people to live farther from work. An entirely new kind of worker, the auto commuter, appeared. Since commuters could drive from their homes in suburbia to their workplaces, other forms of urban transportation, such as the trolley, became less popular.

Consumer Goods

In response to rising **disposable** income, many other new goods came on the market. Americans bought such innovations as electric razors, facial tissues, frozen foods, and home hair color.

Companies created many new products for the home. As indoor plumbing became more common, Americans' concern for hygiene led to the development of numerous household cleaning products. By appealing to people's health concerns, advertisers convinced homemakers to buy cleansers in hopes of protecting their families from disease.

New appliances advertised as labor-savers changed the home. Electric irons, vacuum cleaners, washing machines, and refrigerators changed the way people cleaned their homes and prepared meals.

Another lucrative category of consumer products focused on Americans' concern with fashion and youthful appearance. Mouthwash, deodorants, cosmetics, and perfumes became popular products in the 1920s.

Birth of the Airline Industry

In the early 1900s, many people were trying to build the first powered airplane that could

TECHNOLOGY & HISTORY

Labor- and Time-saving Machines The technology of the 1920s changed the way many people lived. Applying electric motors to items such as washers, dryers, food mixers, and refrigerators revolutionized household tasks. Improved technology helped raise many Americans' standard of living.

◄ **Assembly Lines Reduce Prices**

The moving assembly line and standardized parts made auto assembly fast, efficient and cheap. As a result, most Americans could afford to buy a car.

Electric Appliances Save Time and Labor

New electrical appliances changed life for the growing middle class that could afford them. Refrigerators, such as the 1926 Kelvinator (above left) made it practical to buy and store larger quantities of food. The electric washer with hand wringer (above center) and the vacuum cleaner saved cleaning time. The Air-Way Sanitizor vacuum cleaner (above right) was the first to have a disposable bag.

carry a human being. Samuel Langley, secretary of the Smithsonian Institution, was perhaps best known for his attempts at the time. Langley had built small model airplanes powered by steam engines, and the War Department had awarded him $50,000 to build an airplane that could carry a person. On December 8, 1903, Langley demonstrated his plane to government officials in Washington, D.C. Unfortunately, his plane broke apart on takeoff and crashed into the Potomac River.

The War Department, in its final report on the Langley project, concluded that "[W]e are still far from the ultimate goal, and it would seem as if years of constant work and study by experts, together with the expenditure of thousands of dollars, would still be necessary before we can hope to produce an apparatus of practical utility on these lines."

Nine days later, Wilbur and Orville Wright, two inventors from Dayton, Ohio, tested the airplane they had built using only $1,000 of their personal savings. The Wright brothers had carefully studied the problems of earlier airplanes and had designed one with better wings, a more efficient propeller, and a strong but very light engine. On December 17, 1903, at Kitty Hawk, North Carolina, Orville made the first crewed, powered flight in history.

After the Wright brothers' successful flight, the aviation industry began developing rapidly. Leading the way was American inventor Glenn Curtiss. Curtiss owned a motorcycle company in Hammondsport, New York. Fascinated by airplanes, he agreed in 1907 to become director of experiments at the Aerial Experiment Association, an organization that Alexander Graham Bell founded. Within a year, Curtiss had invented ailerons—surfaces attached to wings that can be tilted to steer the plane. Ailerons made it possible to build rigid wings and much larger aircraft. They are still used today.

Curtiss's company began building aircraft and sold the first airplanes in the United States. The company grew from a single factory to a huge industrial enterprise during World War I, as orders for his biplanes and engines flooded in from Allied governments. Although Curtiss retired in 1920, his inventions made possible the airline industry that emerged in the 1920s.

Radio Links the Nation Together ▶
Commercial radio grew rapidly in the 1920s. It helped create a national community as people across the country could listen to the same music, sports, news, and entertainment programs. The technicians shown at right are preparing for the first NBC radio show, which was broadcast in 1926.

Airlines Speed Travel
The aviation industry developed quickly after the Wright brothers' first successful flight in 1903 (above). Below, passengers are shown boarding a Northwest Orient Airlines Ford Tri-motor. Although seating was cramped (right), passenger airlines carried increasing numbers of people in the 1920s.

Analyzing VISUALS **DBQ**

1. **Making Connections** Which of the inventions pictured is most important to your life? Which do you think is most important to the nation as a whole?

2. **Making Generalizations** How have advances in transportation and communication changed life in the United States in the past 100 years?

After Curtiss and other entrepreneurs started building practical aircraft, the federal government began to support the airline industry. President Wilson's postmaster general introduced the world's first regular airmail service in 1918 by hiring pilots to fly mail between Washington, D.C., and New York. In 1919 the Post Office expanded airmail service across the continent.

The aviation industry received an economic boost in 1925 when Congress passed the Kelly Act, authorizing postal officials to contract with private airplane operators to carry mail. The following year Congress passed the Air Commerce Act, which provided federal aid for building airports. Former airmail pilot **Charles Lindbergh** made an amazing transatlantic solo flight in 1927, showing the possibilities of commercial aviation. By the end of 1928, 48 airlines were serving 355 American cities.

The Radio Industry

In 1913 Edwin Armstrong, an American engineer, invented a special circuit that made it practical to transmit sound via long-range radio. The radio industry began a few years later. In November 1920 the Westinghouse Company broadcast the news of Harding's landslide election victory from station KDKA in Pittsburgh—one of the first public broadcasts in history. That success persuaded Westinghouse to open other stations.

In 1926 the National Broadcasting Company (NBC) set up a network of stations to broadcast daily programs. By 1927, almost 700 stations dotted the country. Sales of radio equipment grew from $12.2 million in 1921 to $842.5 million in 1929, by which time 10 million radios were in use across the country.

In 1928 the Columbia Broadcasting System (CBS) assembled a coast-to-coast network of stations to rival NBC. The two networks sold advertising time and hired musicians, actors, and comedians from vaudeville, movies, and the nightclub circuit to appear on their shows. Americans experienced the first presidential election campaign to use radio broadcasts in 1928, when the radio networks sold more than $1 million in advertising time to the Republican and Democratic Parties.

✔ Reading Check **Analyzing** How did the automobile change the way people lived?

The Consumer Society

MAIN Idea Consumer credit and advertising helped to create a nation of consumers.

HISTORY AND YOU Have you ever purchased something on credit or bought an item because of advertising? Read to discover the beginnings of the widespread consumer culture in America.

Higher wages and shorter workdays resulted in a decade-long buying spree that kept the economy booming. Shifting from traditional attitudes of thrift and prudence, Americans in the 1920s enthusiastically accepted their new role as consumers.

Easy Consumer Credit

One notable aspect of the economic boom was the growth of individual borrowing. **Credit** had been available before the 1920s, but most Americans had considered debt shameful. Now, however, attitudes toward debt started changing as people began believing in their ability to pay their debts over time. Many

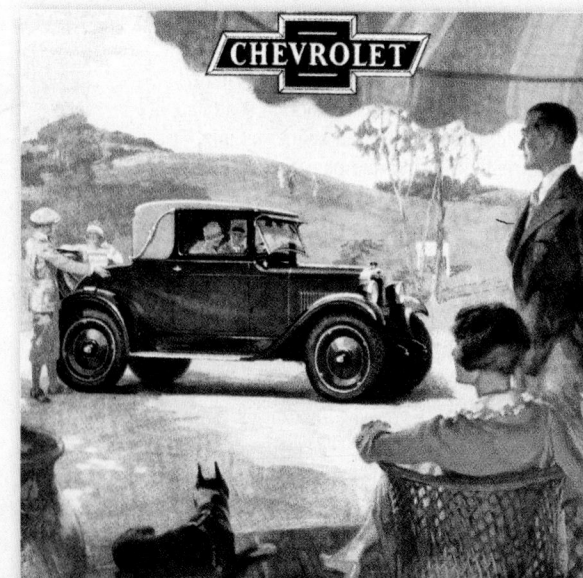

PRIMARY SOURCE
Advertising to Consumers

The early advertising age used techniques that continue to persuade consumers today. Easy credit terms and installment plans, envy of peers and neighbors, and the link of a product with a famous, attractive person all convinced people that they needed the flood of newly available consumer goods.

listened to the sales pitch "Buy now and pay in easy installments," and racked up debts. Americans bought 75 percent of their radios and 60 percent of their automobiles on the installment plan. Some started buying on credit at a faster rate than their incomes increased.

Mass Advertising

When inventor Otto Rohwedder developed a commercial bread slicer in 1928, he faced a problem common to new inventions: the invention—sliced bread—was something no one knew was needed. To attract consumers, manufacturers turned to advertising, another booming industry in the 1920s.

Advertisers linked products with qualities associated with the modern era, such as progress, convenience, leisure, success, and style. In a 1924 magazine advertisement for deodorant, the headline read, "Flappers they may be—but they know the art of feminine appeal!" An advertisement for a spaghetti product told homemakers that heating is the same as cooking: "Just one thing to do and it's ready to serve." Advertisers also preyed on consumers' fears and anxieties, such as jarred nerves due to the hectic pace of modern life or insecurities about one's status or weight.

The Managerial Revolution

By the early 1920s, many industries had begun to create modern organizational structures. Companies were split into divisions with different functions, such as sales, marketing, and accounting. To run these divisions, businesses needed to hire managers. Managers freed executives and owners from the day-to-day running of the companies.

The managerial revolution in companies created a new career—the professional manager. The large numbers of new managers helped expand the size of the middle class, which in turn added to the nation's prosperity. Similarly, so many companies relied on new technology that engineers were also in very high demand. They, too, joined the ranks of the growing middle class.

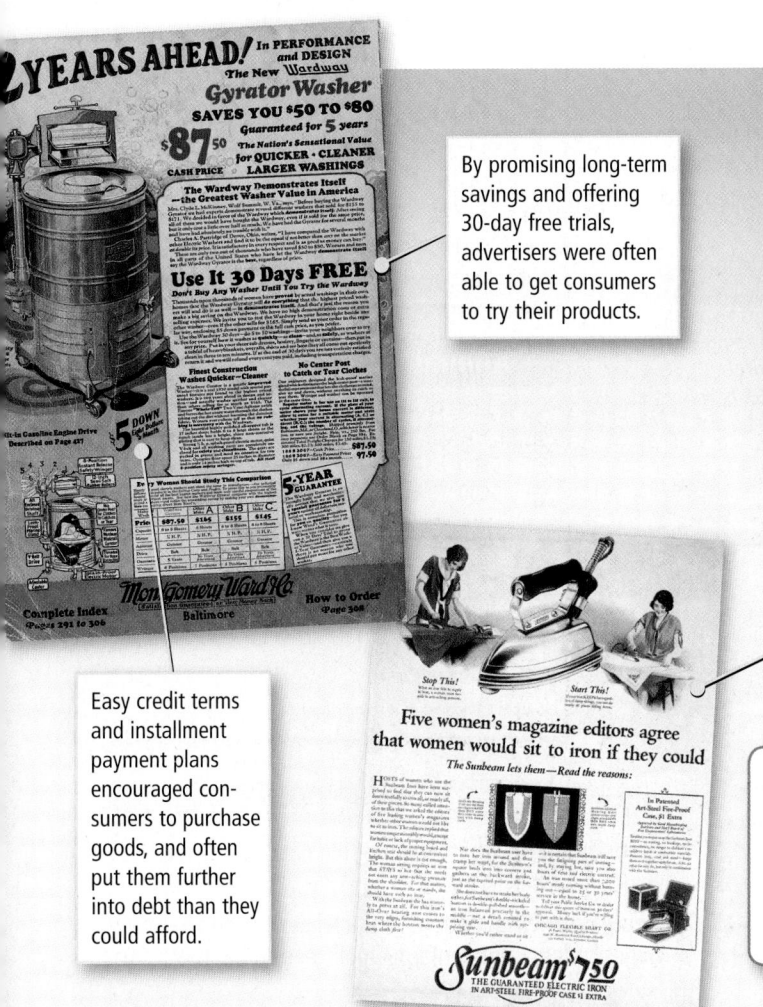

By promising long-term savings and offering 30-day free trials, advertisers were often able to get consumers to try their products.

Easy credit terms and installment payment plans encouraged consumers to purchase goods, and often put them further into debt than they could afford.

This 1928 advertisement appeals to "expert opinion" to sell the product. It also shows that 1920s advertisers believed ironing to be a woman's job.

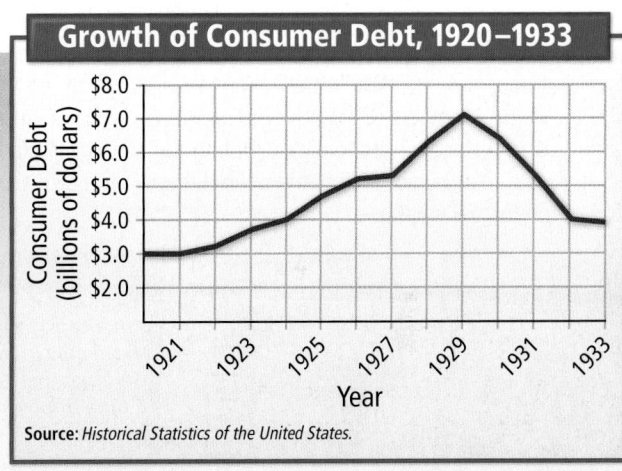

Growth of Consumer Debt, 1920–1933

Source: *Historical Statistics of the United States.*

Analyzing VISUALS

1. **Making Connections** What techniques do advertisers use today to sell automobiles?

2. **Analyzing Visuals** What happened to consumer debt between 1921 and 1929? Why might this have happened?

Welfare Capitalism

Middle-class Americans were not the only members of the new consumer society. Industrial workers also had more disposable income, partly due to rising wages and partly because many corporations introduced what came to be called **welfare capitalism.** Companies allowed workers to buy stock, participate in profit sharing, and receive medical care and pensions.

The Decline of Unions Benefits programs also made unions seem unnecessary to many workers. During the 1920s, unions lost both influence and membership. Employers promoted the **open shop**—a workplace where employees were not required to join a union. With benefits covering some of their basic needs, workers were able to spend more of their income to improve their quality of life. Many purchased consumer goods they previously could not afford.

Uneven Prosperity Not all Americans shared in this economic boom. Thousands of African Americans had factory jobs during World War I. When servicemen returned from the war, they replaced both African Americans and women.

Native Americans were also excluded from prosperity. Although granted citizenship in 1924, they were often isolated on reservations, where there was little productive work.

The majority of immigrants to the United States continued to come from Europe. Even these people often found it difficult to find work; most of them were farmers and factory workers whose wages were pitifully low.

Many people in the Deep South were also left out of the economic boom. The traditional agricultural economic base eroded after the war ended. Farmers in general failed to benefit from the growing economy.

✔ **Reading Check** **Analyzing** How did advertisers try to convince Americans to buy their products?

PRIMARY SOURCE
Prosperity for Whom?

Although many people benefited from the economic boom of the 1920s, several groups did not share in the general prosperity, nor did all regions of the country. Members of minority groups, newly arrived immigrants, and farmers often struggled economically. During the 1920s, for example, laborers in manufacturing not only outnumbered farmers but also acquired three times more actual wealth.

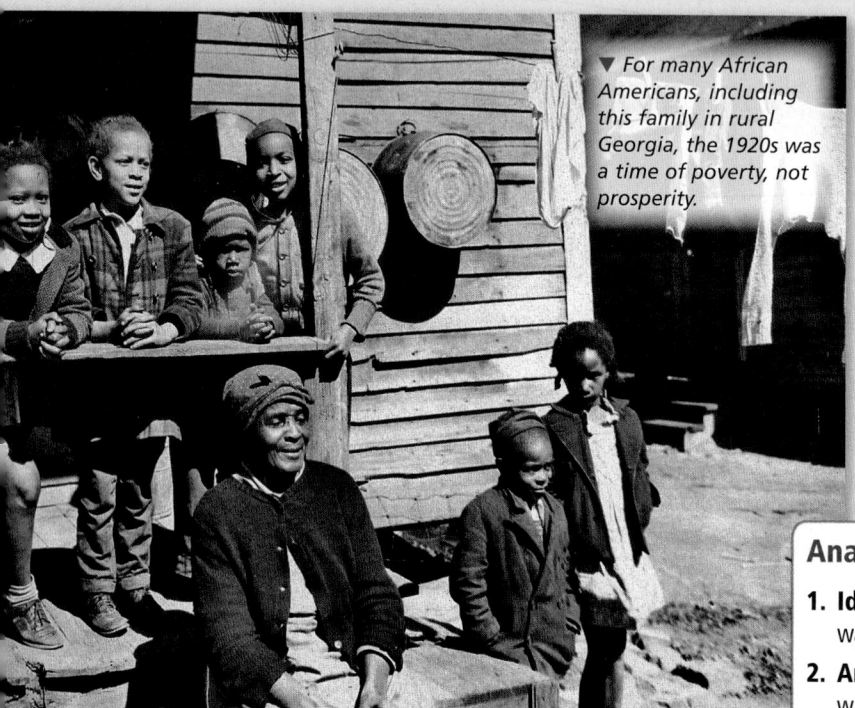

▼ For many African Americans, including this family in rural Georgia, the 1920s was a time of poverty, not prosperity.

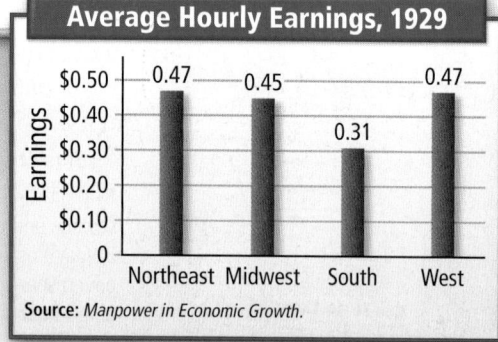

Average Hourly Earnings, 1929

Region	Earnings
Northeast	0.47
Midwest	0.45
South	0.31
West	0.47

Source: *Manpower in Economic Growth.*

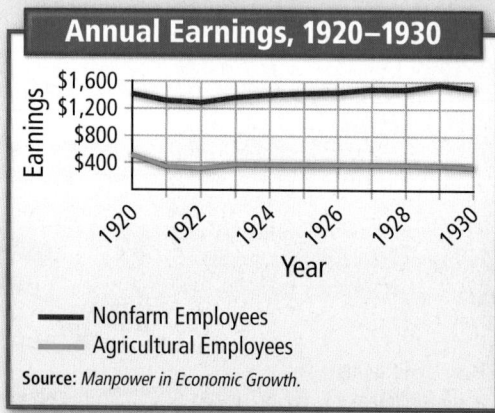

Annual Earnings, 1920–1930

— Nonfarm Employees
— Agricultural Employees

Source: *Manpower in Economic Growth.*

Analyzing VISUALS

1. **Identifying** In what region of the nation were hourly wages lowest in 1929?

2. **Analyzing** What pattern characterizes the gap between wages of farm and nonfarm employees during the 1920s?

The Farm Crisis

MAIN Idea Increases in farm productivity and decreases in foreign markets led to lower prices for farmers.

HISTORY AND YOU Do you remember reading about the platform of the Populist Party in the 1890s? Read to learn about farmers' troubles in the 1920s.

American farmers did not share in the prosperity of the 1920s. On average, they earned less than one-third of the income of workers in the rest of the economy. Technological advances in fertilizers, seed varieties, and farm machinery allowed them to produce more, but higher yields without a corresponding increase in demand meant that they received lower prices. Between 1920 and 1921, corn prices dropped almost 19 percent, and wheat went from $1.83 a bushel to $1.03. The cost of the improved farming technology, meanwhile, continued to increase.

Changing Market Conditions

Many factors contributed to this "quiet depression" in American agriculture. During the war, the government had urged farmers to produce more to meet the great need for food supplies in Europe. Many farmers borrowed heavily to buy new land and new machinery to raise more crops. Sales were strong, prices were high, and farmers prospered. After the war, however, European farm output rose, and the debt-ridden countries of Europe had little money to spend on American farm products. Congress had unintentionally made matters worse when it passed the Fordney-McCumber Act in 1922. This act raised tariffs dramatically in an effort to protect American industry from foreign competition. By dampening the American market for foreign goods, however, it provoked a reaction in foreign markets against American agricultural products. Farmers in the United States could no longer sell as much of their crops overseas, and prices tumbled.

Helping Farmers

Some members of Congress tried to help the farmers sell their surplus. Every year from 1924 to 1928, Senator Charles McNary of Oregon and Representative Gilbert Haugen of Iowa proposed the McNary-Haugen Bill, a plan in which the government would boost farm prices by buying up surpluses and selling them, at a loss, overseas.

Congress passed the bill twice, but President Coolidge vetoed it both times. He argued that with money flowing to farmers under this law, they would be encouraged to produce even greater surpluses. American farmers remained mired in a recession throughout the 1920s.

✓ Reading Check **Synthesizing** What factors led to the growing economic crisis in farming?

Section 2 REVIEW

Vocabulary

1. **Explain** the significance of: mass production, assembly line, Model T, Charles Lindbergh, welfare capitalism, open shop.

Main Ideas

2. **Evaluating** How did the automobile affect American society?

3. **Summarizing** What factors led to the new consumer society in the United States during the 1920s?

4. **Analyzing** What conditions contributed to the tough times farmers faced in the early 1920s?

Critical Thinking

5. **Big Ideas** How did the availability of credit change society?

6. **Organizing** Use a graphic organizer like the one below to list some of the new industries that grew in importance during the 1920s.

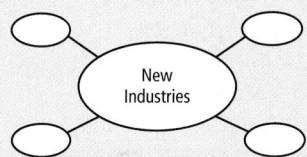

New Industries

7. **Analyzing Visuals** Study the Technology & History on pages 370–371. How do appliances, cars, and airplanes differ today? How do you think new products change society today?

Writing About History

8. Write an article for a contemporary newspaper analyzing the impact of Charles Lindbergh's transatlantic flight on the development of aviation in the United States and the world.

History ONLINE
Study Central™ To review this section, go to glencoe.com and click on Study Central.

A Clash of Values

Guide to Reading

Big Ideas
Past and Present The struggles of the 1920s regarding immigration and proper behavior continue to affect current events.

Content Vocabulary
• nativism *(p. 376)*
• anarchist *(p. 376)*
• evolution *(p. 380)*
• creationism *(p. 380)*
• speakeasy *(p. 381)*

Academic Vocabulary
• source *(p. 378)*
• deny *(p. 380)*

People and Events to Identify
• Emergency Quota Act *(p. 378)*
• National Origins Act *(p. 378)*
• Fundamentalism *(p. 380)*

Reading Strategy
Organizing As you read about Americans' reactions to immigrants during the 1920s, complete a graphic organizer similar to the one below by filling in the causes and effects of anti-immigrant prejudices.

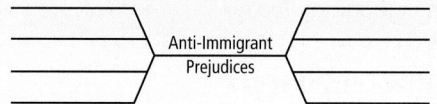

The 1920s are often called the "Roaring Twenties" because to many the decade seemed to be one long party. Urban Americans celebrated the new "modern" culture, but not everyone agreed that the new trends were a good thing. Rural Americans believed traditional society and morality were under attack.

Nativism Resurges

MAIN Idea Nativism and racism increased in the 1920s and led to changes in immigration laws.

HISTORY AND YOU In your school, is there a limit to the number of students in each class? Read to learn why the United States imposed new rules in the 1920s limiting the number of immigrants admitted each year.

The 1920s was a time of economic growth, but it was also a time of cultural turmoil. When the 1920s began, an economic recession, an influx of immigrants, and cultural tensions combined to create an atmosphere of disillusionment and intolerance. The fear and prejudice many felt toward Germans and communists during and after World War I expanded to include all immigrants. This triggered a general rise in racism and **nativism**—a belief that one's native land needs to be protected against immigrants.

During World War I, immigration to the United States had dropped sharply. By 1921, however, it had returned to prewar levels, with the majority of immigrants coming from southern and eastern Europe. Many Americans reacted to the bombings, strikes, and recession of the postwar years by blaming immigrants. Many believed immigrants were taking jobs that would otherwise have gone to soldiers returning home from the war.

The Sacco-Vanzetti Case

The controversial Sacco-Vanzetti case reflected the prejudices and fears of the era. On April 15, 1920, two men robbed and murdered two employees of a shoe factory in Massachusetts. Police subsequently arrested two Italian immigrants, Nicola Sacco and Bartolomeo Vanzetti, for the crime.

The case created a furor when newspapers revealed that the two men were **anarchists,** or people who oppose all forms of government. They also reported that Sacco owned a gun similar to the murder weapon and that the bullets used in the murders matched those in Sacco's gun. The evidence was questionable, but the fact that the accused men were anarchists and foreigners led many people to assume they were guilty, including the jury. On July 14, 1921,

Hostility Toward Immigrants

In the 1920s, many Americans believed that immigrants from southern and eastern Europe would not assimilate into American culture. These concerns led to the rise of a new Ku Klux Klan and efforts in Congress to pass legislation that would keep "undesirable" immigrants out.

Men, women, and children participate in a Klan march in Cincinnati, Ohio, in 1925 (left). Membership in the KKK soared in the early 1920s because of its opposition to immigrants. Not everyone agreed with the Klan, however; the cartoon above mocks a proposal to impose a literacy test on immigrants.

European Immigration, 1900–1924

Immigrants (millions)

United Kingdom · Germany · Eastern Europe · Southern Europe

Source: *Historical Statistics of the United States.*

Analyzing VISUALS   DBQ

1. **Making Inferences** What does the presence and membership of children in the Klan suggest to others?

2. **Analyzing Visuals** What is the "wall" made of in the cartoon?

3. **Making Connections** From which two regions did the majority of immigrants come? Why were so many people from these regions willing to leave their homelands and come to the United States?

Sacco and Vanzetti were found guilty and sentenced to death. After six years of appeals, Sacco and Vanzetti were executed on August 23, 1927.

Return of the Ku Klux Klan

At the forefront of the movement to restrict immigration was the Ku Klux Klan, or KKK. The old KKK had flourished in the South after the Civil War and used threats and violence to intimidate newly freed African Americans. The new Klan had other targets as well: Catholics, Jews, immigrants, and other groups said to be "un-American." In the 1920s, the Klan claimed it was fighting for "Americanism."

William J. Simmons founded the new Ku Klux Klan in Georgia, in 1915. A former preacher, Simmons pledged to preserve America's white, Protestant civilization. The Klan attracted few members until 1920, when Simmons began using professional promoters to sell Klan memberships. By 1924 membership had reached nearly 4 million as it spread beyond the South into Northern cities.

The Klan began to decline in the late 1920s, however, largely as a result of scandals and power struggles between its leaders. Membership shrank, and politicians backed by the Klan were voted out of office. In addition, new restrictions on immigration deprived the Klan of one of its major issues.

Read "Sacco and Vanzetti Must Die" by John Dos Passos on pages R74–R75 of the **American Literature Library.**

Controlling Immigration

American immigration policies changed in response to the postwar recession and nativist pleas to "Keep America American." Even some business leaders, who had favored immigration as a **source** of cheap labor, now saw the new immigrants as radicals.

In 1921 President Harding signed the **Emergency Quota Act.** The act restricted annual admission to the United States to only 3 percent of the total number of people in any ethnic group already living in the nation. Ethnic identity and national origin thus determined admission to the United States.

In 1924 the **National Origins Act** made immigration restriction a permanent policy. The law set quotas at 2 percent of each national group represented in the U.S. Census of 1890. Thus, immigration quotas were based on the ethnic composition of the country more than 30 years earlier—before the heavy wave of immigration from southern and eastern Europe. The new quotas deliberately favored immigrants from northwestern Europe. Although subsequent legislation made some changes in immigration laws, the National Origins Act set the framework for immigration for the next four decades.

Hispanic Immigration

While workers and unions rejoiced at the reduction in competition with European immigrants for jobs, employers desperately needed laborers for agriculture, mining, and railroad work. Mexican immigrants were able to fill this need because the National Origins Act of 1924 exempted natives of the Western Hemisphere from the quota system.

Large numbers of Mexican immigrants had already begun moving to the United States after the passage of the Newlands Reclamation Act of 1902. The act funded irrigation projects in the Southwest and led to the creation of large factory farms that needed thousands of farmworkers. As the demand for cheap farm labor steadily increased, Mexican immigrants crossed the border in record numbers. By the end of the 1920s, nearly 700,000 had migrated to the United States.

Reading Check **Explaining** How was the Ku Klux Klan of the 1920s different from the earlier Klan?

A Clash of Cultures

MAIN Idea Supporters of the new morality in the 1920s clashed with those who supported more traditional values.

HISTORY AND YOU How do you think older generations view your generation? Read about the changes in morality during the 1920s.

Many groups that wanted to restrict immigration also wanted to preserve what they considered to be traditional values. They feared that a "new morality" was taking over the nation. Challenging traditional ways of behaving, the new morality glorified youth and personal freedom and changed American society—particularly the status of women.

Women in the 1920s

Having won the right to vote in 1920, many women sought to break free of the traditional roles and behaviors that were expected of them. Attitudes toward marriage—popularized by magazines and other media—changed considerably. As the loving and emotional aspects of marriage grew in importance, the

PRIMARY SOURCE
Changing Roles for Women

As women achieved greater independence, access to higher education, and professional opportunities in the 1920s, they adopted new clothing styles that expressed their identities.

▶ *Many young women adopted the flapper style in the 1920s. They stopped wearing corsets, bobbed their hair, and wore short skirts, high heels, and rounded hats with almost no brim. The style expressed the sense of freedom many women felt in the 1920s.*

ideas of romance, pleasure, and friendship became linked to successful marriages.

The popularizing of Sigmund Freud's psychological theories also changed people's ideas about relationships. Freudian psychology emphasized human sexuality and his theories (often oversimplified) became acceptable subjects of public conversation.

The automobile played a role in encouraging the new morality. Cars allowed young people to escape the careful watch of their parents. Instead of socializing at home with the family, many youths could now use cars to "go out" with their friends.

Women in the workforce began to define the new morality. Many working-class women took jobs because they or their families needed the wages but for some young, single women, work was a way to break away from parental authority and establish financial independence. Earning money also allowed women to participate in the consumer culture.

Fashion, too, changed during the 1920s, particularly for women, who "bobbed," or shortened, their hair, wore flesh-colored silk stockings, and copied the glamorous look of movie stars. The flapper personified these changes, even though she was not typical of most women. The flapper smoked cigarettes, drank prohibited liquor, and wore makeup and sleeveless dresses with short skirts.

Women who attended college in the 1920s often found support for their emerging sense of independence. Women's colleges, in particular, encouraged their students to pursue careers and to challenge traditional ideas about women's role in society.

Many professional women made major contributions in science, medicine, law, and literature in the 1920s. In medicine, Florence Sabin's research led to a dramatic drop in death rates from tuberculosis while Edith Wharton, Willa Cather, and Edna Ferber each won a Pulitzer Prize in fiction for their novels.

Public health nurse Margaret Sanger believed that families could improve their standard of living by limiting the number of children they had. She founded the American Birth Control League in 1921 to promote knowledge about birth control. This organization became Planned Parenthood in the 1940s. During the 1920s and 1930s, the use of birth control increased dramatically, particularly among middle-class couples.

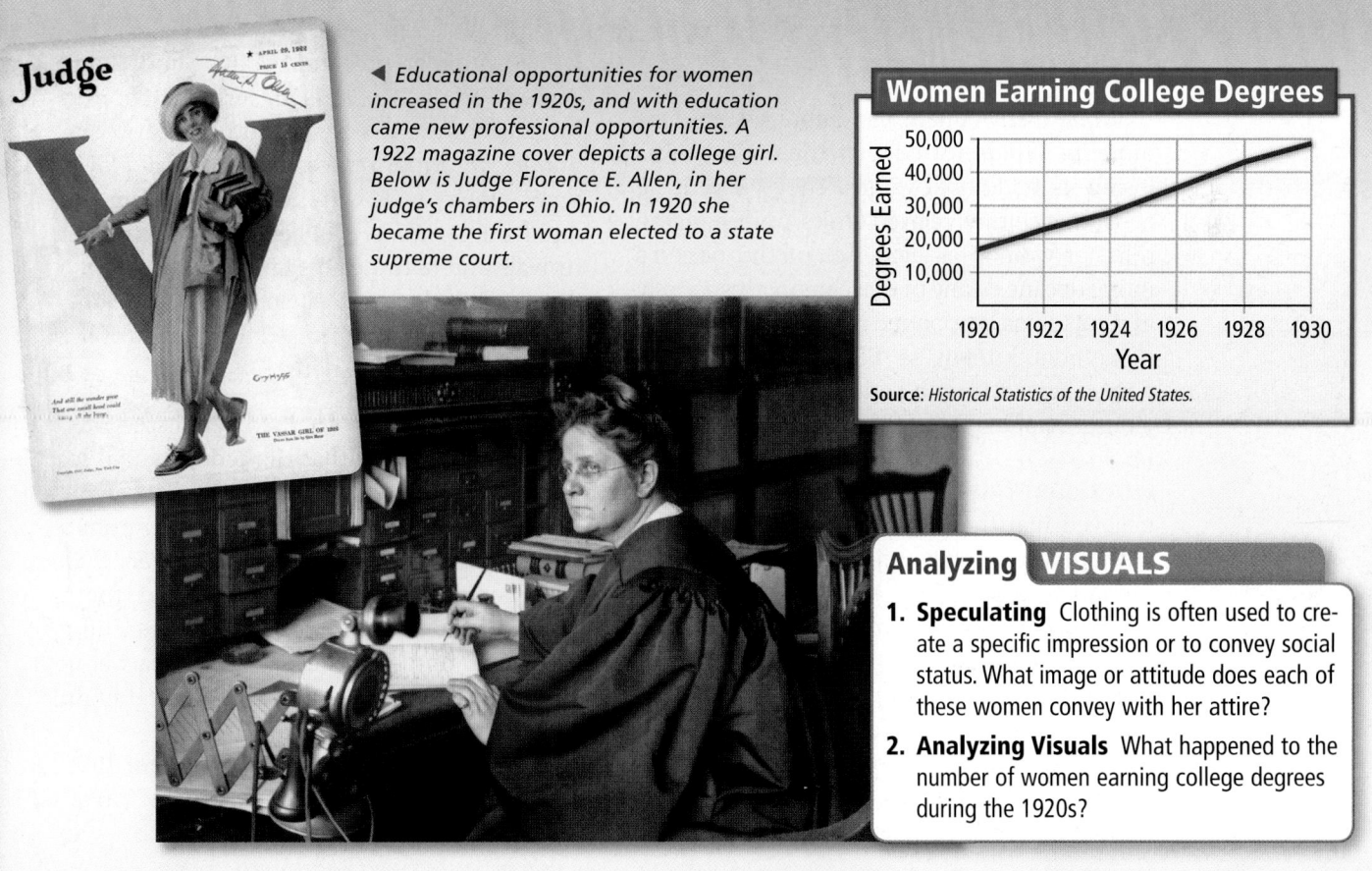

◀ Educational opportunities for women increased in the 1920s, and with education came new professional opportunities. A 1922 magazine cover depicts a college girl. Below is Judge Florence E. Allen, in her judge's chambers in Ohio. In 1920 she became the first woman elected to a state supreme court.

Women Earning College Degrees

Source: *Historical Statistics of the United States.*

Analyzing VISUALS

1. **Speculating** Clothing is often used to create a specific impression or to convey social status. What image or attitude does each of these women convey with her attire?

2. **Analyzing Visuals** What happened to the number of women earning college degrees during the 1920s?

The War Against Alcohol

Prohibition supporters argued that it reduced violence, illness, and poverty. Critics argued that it increased violence because gangs fought to control the sale of illegal alcohol, and that it led to illness because many people drank unsafe "moonshine."

The Shadow of Danger

U.S. MELLOW WHISKEY

If you believe that the traffic in Alcohol does more harm than good—help stop it!

Strengthen America Campaign
Strengthen America Campaign · 105 East Twenty-Second Street, New York City, N.Y.

▲ Supporters of Prohibition portrayed the sale of alcohol as a danger to mothers and children.

◀ Prohibition led to the creation of a special federal bureau charged with stopping the sale of illegal alcohol. In this photo, a federal agent cracks open barrels of illegal rum in San Francisco in 1927.

Murder Rate, 1920–1940

Number of Murders*

10.0
9.0
8.0
7.0
6.0

1920 1925 1930 1935 1940

Year

*per 100,000 residents

Source: *Historical Statistics of the United States.*

Analyzing VISUALS DBQ

1. **Theorizing** How might opponents of Prohibition use the murder rate in the 1920s and 1930s to support their argument? Can you think of other reasons the murder rate might have fallen in the 1930s?

2. **Analyzing Visuals** How does the poster use emotional appeal to strengthen its argument?

Fundamentalism

While many Americans embraced the new morality, others feared that the country was losing its traditional values. They viewed the consumer culture, relaxed ethics, and changing roles of women as evidence of the nation's moral decline. Many of these people, especially in rural towns, responded by joining a religious movement known as **Fundamentalism,** a name derived from a series of Christian religious pamphlets titled "The Fundamentals."

Fundamentalist Beliefs Fundamentalists believed that the Bible was literally true and without error. They rejected the idea that human beings derived their moral behavior from society and nature, not God. In particular, they rejected Charles Darwin's theory of **evolution,** which said that human beings had developed from lower forms of life over the course of millions of years. Instead, they believed in **creationism**—the belief that God created the world as described in the Bible.

Two popular preachers, Billy Sunday and Aimee Semple McPherson, stirred supporters by preaching in very nontraditional ways. Sunday, a former professional baseball player, drew huge crowds with his showmanship and rapid-fire sermons. McPherson conducted her revivals and faith healings in Los Angeles in a flamboyant theatrical style, using stage sets and costumes that expressed the themes of her highly emotional sermons.

The Scopes Trial In 1925 Tennessee outlawed any teaching that **denied** "the story of the Divine Creation of man as taught in the Bible," or taught that "man descended from a lower order of animals." The American Civil Liberties Union (ACLU) advertised for a teacher willing to be arrested for teaching evolution. John T. Scopes, a biology teacher in Dayton, Tennessee, volunteered. He taught evolution and was arrested.

The trial took place in the summer of 1925. William Jennings Bryan, a three-time presidential candidate, was the prosecutor who represented the creationists. Clarence Darrow, one of the country's most celebrated trial lawyers, defended Scopes. After eight days of trial, Scopes was found guilty and fined $100, although the conviction was later overturned on a technicality. The trial had been broadcast over the radio, and Darrow's blistering cross-examination of Bryan hurt the Fundamentalist cause. Increasingly, Fundamentalists felt isolated and their commitment to political activism declined.

Prohibition

The movement to ban alcohol grew stronger in the early 1900s. People supported the prohibition of alcohol sales for many reasons. Some opposed alcohol consumption for religious reasons; others thought prohibition would reduce unemployment, domestic violence, and poverty. Prohibition supporters achieved their goal when the Eighteenth Amendment went into effect in January 1920.

Congress passed the Volstead Act, making the U.S. Treasury Department responsible for enforcing Prohibition. Treasury agents had enforced federal tax laws for many years, but police powers—a government's power to control people and property in the interest of public safety, health, welfare, and morals—had generally been reserved for state governments. The Eighteenth Amendment granted federal and state governments the power to enforce Prohibition, marking a dramatic increase in federal police powers.

The Treasury Department struggled to enforce Prohibition. During the 1920s, treasury agents made more than 540,000 arrests, but Americans persisted in blatantly ignoring the law. People flocked to secret bars called **speakeasies,** where they could purchase alcohol. In New York City alone, an estimated 32,000 speakeasies sold liquor illegally. Liquor also was readily available in rural areas, where bootlegging—the illegal production and distribution of liquor—was common.

Organized crime thrived on the illegal trade in alcohol. Huge profits could be made smuggling liquor from Canada and the Caribbean. Crime became big business, and some gangsters had enough money to corrupt local politicians. Al Capone, one of the most successful and violent gangsters of the era, had many police officers, judges, and other officials on his payroll. Capone dominated organized crime in Chicago. Finally, Eliot Ness, the leader of a special Treasury Department task force, brought Capone to justice. More than 70 federal agents were killed while enforcing Prohibition in the 1920s.

The battle to repeal Prohibition began almost as soon as the Eighteenth Amendment was ratified. The Twenty-first Amendment, ratified in 1933, repealed the Eighteenth Amendment and ended Prohibition. Prohibition had reduced alcohol consumption, but it had not improved society in the ways its supporters had hoped.

✔ **Reading Check** **Identifying** What political, social, and economic contributions did women make to American society in the 1920s?

Vocabulary

1. **Explain** the significance of: nativism, anarchist, Emergency Quota Act, National Origins Act, Fundamentalism, evolution, creationism, speakeasy.

Main Ideas

2. **Identifying** What two factors influenced the limits on immigration?

3. **Summarizing** What issues caused clashes between traditional and new moralities?

Critical Thinking

4. **Big Ideas** Why did many Americans oppose immigration after World War I? What connections can you make with immigration policies today?

5. **Categorizing** Use a graphic organizer similar to the one below to list the provisions of the immigration acts passed in the 1920s.

Act	Provisions

6. **Analyzing Visuals** Look at the chart on page 377 showing European immigration. How would these figures have affected someone who was a nativist? Why?

Writing About History

7. **Persuasive Writing** Imagine it is the 1920s. Write a letter to your senator persuading him or her either to continue supporting Prohibition or to work for its repeal.

History ONLINE

Study Central™ To review this section, go to glencoe.com and click on Study Central.

Cultural Innovations

Guide to Reading

Big Ideas
Culture and Beliefs Through sharing in the arts and sports of the time, Americans embraced new ways of thinking.

Content Vocabulary
• bohemian (p. 382)
• mass media (p. 385)

Academic Vocabulary
• diverse (p. 382)
• unify (p. 385)

People and Events to Identify
• Carl Sandburg (p. 383)
• Willa Cather (p. 383)
• Ernest Hemingway (p. 384)
• F. Scott Fitzgerald (p. 384)
• Edith Wharton (p. 384)

Reading Strategy
Organizing As you read about the 1920s, complete a graphic organizer like the one below by filling in the main characteristics of art, literature, and popular culture that reflect the era.

Cultural Movement	Main Characteristics
Art	
Literature	
Popular Culture	

The 1920s was an era of great artistic innovation. Artists and writers experimented with new techniques. Popular culture also changed. Broadcast radio introduced Americans around the country to the latest trends in music and entertainment, and motion pictures became a major leisure-time activity.

Art and Literature

MAIN Idea New York City's Greenwich Village and Chicago's South Side became known as centers for new artistic work.

HISTORY AND YOU Is there a neighborhood with many art galleries in your community? Read about the flowering of the arts during the 1920s in the United States.

During the 1920s, American artists and writers challenged traditional ideas. These artists explored what it meant to be "modern," and they searched for meaning in the emerging challenges of the modern world. Many artists, writers, and intellectuals of the era flocked to Manhattan's Greenwich Village and Chicago's South Side. The artistic and unconventional, or **bohemian,** lifestyle of these neighborhoods allowed young artists, musicians, and writers greater freedom to express themselves.

Modern American Art

European art movements greatly influenced the modernists of American art. Perhaps most striking was the **diverse** range of artistic styles, each attempting to express the individual, modern experience. American painter John Marin drew on nature as well as the urban dynamics of New York for inspiration, explaining, "the whole city is alive; buildings, people, all are alive; and the more they move me the more I feel them to be alive." Painter Charles Scheeler applied the influences of photography and the geometric forms of Cubism to urban and rural American landscapes. Edward Hopper revived the visual accuracy of realism in his haunting scenes. His paintings conveyed a modern sense of disenchantment and isolation. Georgia O'Keeffe's landscapes and flowers were admired in many museums throughout her long life.

Poets and Writers

Poets and writers of the 1920s varied greatly in their styles and subject matter. Chicago poet, historian, folklorist, and novelist **Carl**

Ashcan Realists and the Lost Generation

Many artists and writers focused on the isolation and alienation of modern society. A group of artists who painted urban life became known as the Ashcan Realists. The writers who described modern life as spiritually empty and materialistic became known as the "Lost Generation."

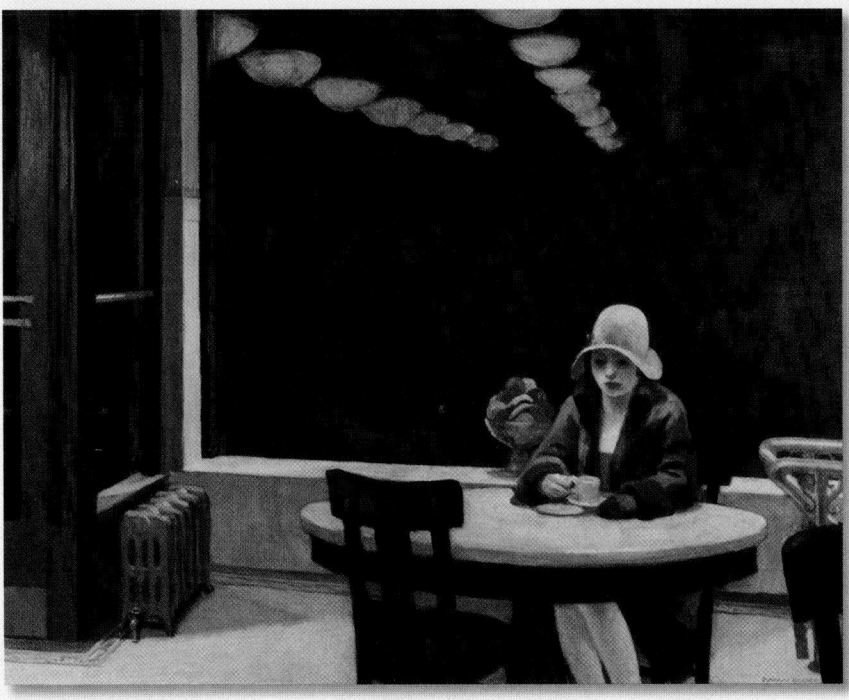

Excerpt from
"The Hollow Men" (1925)
by T.S. Eliot

We are the hollow men
We are the stuffed men
Leaning together
Headpiece filled with straw. Alas!
Our dried voices, when
We whisper together
Are quiet and meaningless
As wind in dry grass
Or rats' feet over broken glass
In our dry cellar
Shape without form, shade without colour,
Paralysed force, gesture without motion;
Those who have crossed
With direct eyes, to death's other
Kingdom
Remember us—if at all—not as lost
Violent souls, but only
As the hollow men
The stuffed men.

◀ *Edward Hopper studied with one of the founders of the Ashcan Realist movement. His painting,* Automat, *(left) expresses the loneliness and isolation many young people felt during the 1920s. An automat was a place where a person could buy food or drinks from vending machines.*

Excerpt from *The Great Gatsby* (1925)
by F. Scott Fitzgerald

"They were careless people, Tom and Daisy—they smashed up things and creatures and then retreated back into their money or their vast carelessness, or whatever it was that kept them together, and let other people clean up the mess they had made. . . .

I shook hands with him; it seemed silly not to, for I felt suddenly as though I were talking to a child. Then he went into the jewelry store to buy a pearl necklace—or perhaps only a pair of cuff buttons—rid of my provincial squeamishness forever."

DBQ · Document-Based Questions

1. **Analyzing Primary Sources** How does Fitzgerald characterize Tom and Daisy? What does their attitude say about the culture of the 1920s?

2. **Explaining** Eliot uses the adjectives *hollow* and *stuffed* to describe contemporary people. How can both be true?

3. **Analyzing Primary Sources** How is Hopper's painting similar to Eliot's poem and Fitzgerald's novel?

Sandburg used common speech to glorify the Midwest, as did Pulitzer Prize–winner **Willa Cather,** who wrote about life on the Great Plains. In Greenwich Village, another Pulitzer Prize winner, Edna St. Vincent Millay, expressed women's equality and praised a life intensely lived.

Several poets had an important impact on the literary culture. Gertrude Stein, an avant-garde poet of the era, was a mentor to many writers, including Ernest Hemingway. Some poets, including Ezra Pound, Amy Lowell, and William Carlos Williams, used clear, concise images to express moments in time. Others concentrated on portraying what they perceived to be the negative effects of modernism. In "The Hollow Men," for example, T.S. Eliot described a world filled with empty dreams that would end "not with a bang but a whimper."

Among playwrights, one of the most innovative was Eugene O'Neill. His plays, filled with bold artistry and modern themes, portrayed realistic characters and situations, offering a vision of life that sometimes touched on the tragic.

Many American writers wrote about their disillusionment with World War I. Some, known as the "Lost Generation," moved to Paris or other cities in Europe. There, they often wrote about "heroic antiheroes"—flawed individuals who still had heroic qualities. **Ernest Hemingway** was one such writer. In direct simple prose, he described the experience of war in such novels as *For Whom the Bell Tolls* and *A Farewell to Arms*.

Sinclair Lewis wrote about the absurdities of small-town life in *Main Street* and *Babbitt*. **F. Scott Fitzgerald's** colorful characters chased futile dreams in *The Great Gatsby*, a novel critical of modern society's superficiality. Similarly, **Edith Wharton** used irony and humor to criticize upper-class ignorance and pretensions. Her 1920 novel, *The Age of Innocence*, won the Pulitzer Prize.

✔ Reading Check **Examining** Why did many creative people flock to Greenwich Village during the 1920s?

Popular Culture

MAIN Idea Broadcast radio and "talking" pictures were new forms of popular entertainment.

HISTORY AND YOU What forms of entertainment make up today's popular culture? Read how Americans spent their leisure time in the 1920s.

The economic prosperity of the 1920s provided many Americans with more leisure time and more spending money, which they devoted to making their lives more enjoyable. Millions of Americans eagerly watched sports and enjoyed music, theater, and other forms of popular entertainment. They also fell in love with motion pictures and radio programs.

Movies and Radio Shows

For many Americans in the 1920s, nothing quite matched the allure of motion pictures. Before technology made sound possible in films, theaters hired piano players to provide music during the feature, while subtitles explained the plot. Audiences thronged to see such stars as Mary Pickford, Charlie Chaplin, Tom Mix, Douglas Fairbanks, Sr., Rudolph Valentino, and Clara Bow. In 1927 the golden age of Hollywood began when the first "talking" picture—*The Jazz Singer*—was produced.

Irving Berlin was one of the famous songwriters of the 1920s. He worked in an area of New York City known as Tin Pan Alley, where composers wrote the popular music of the era. Berlin's famous songs include "Puttin' on the Ritz" and "White Christmas." Radio broadcasts such as *The Eveready Hour* offered everything from classical music to comedy. In one of the most popular shows, *Amos 'n' Andy*, the troubles of two African American characters (portrayed by white actors) captured the nation's attention every evening.

The **mass media**—radio, movies, newspapers, and magazines aimed at a broad audience—did more than just entertain. Their easy availability to millions helped break down patterns of provincialism, or narrow focus on local interests. They fostered a sense of shared experience that helped **unify** the nation and spread new ideas and attitudes.

Sports

Thanks to motion pictures and radio, sports such as baseball and boxing reached new heights of popularity in the 1920s. Baseball star Babe Ruth became a national hero, famous for hitting hundreds of home runs. As one broadcaster remarked, "He wasn't a baseball player. He was a worldwide celebrity, an international star, the likes of which baseball has never seen since."

Sports fans also idolized boxer Jack Dempsey. Dempsey held the title of world heavyweight champion from 1919 until 1926, when he lost it to Gene Tunney. When Dempsey attempted to win back the title in 1927, fans' enthusiasm for the rematch reached such a frenzy that one store sold $90,000 worth of radios—an incredible sum at that time—in the two weeks before the event.

Americans eagerly followed other sports and sports figures, too. Newspaper coverage helped generate enthusiasm for college football. One of the most famous players of the 1920s was Red Grange of the University of Illinois. Grange was known as the "Galloping Ghost" because of his speed and ability to evade members of opposing teams.

The triumphs of Bobby Jones, the best golfer of the decade, and tennis players Bill Tilden and Helen Wills, who dominated world tennis, also thrilled sports fans. In 1926 Jones became the first golfer to win the U.S. Open and the British Open in the same year. When swimmer Gertrude Ederle shattered records by swimming the English Channel in a little over 14 hours in 1927, Americans were enchanted.

Reading Check **Summarizing** How did the economy of the 1920s affect popular culture?

Section 4 REVIEW

Vocabulary

1. **Explain** the significance of: bohemian, Carl Sandburg, Willa Cather, Ernest Hemingway, F. Scott Fitzgerald, Edith Wharton, mass media.

Main Ideas

2. **Describing** What were the main themes of artists and writers during the 1920s?

3. **Discussing** How did Americans enjoy their leisure time in the 1920s? What made these activities possible?

Critical Thinking

4. **Big Ideas** How did writers, artists, and popular culture of the 1920s affect traditional ideas in the United States?

5. **Organizing** Use a graphic organizer similar to the one below to list the effects of mass media on American culture.

Effects

Mass Media of 1920s

6. **Analyzing Visuals** Look at the painting on page 383. How does Edward Hopper create a sense of alienation in this painting?

Writing About History

7. **Descriptive Writing** Imagine that you have moved to New York's Greenwich Village in the 1920s. Write a letter to a friend describing the atmosphere in your neighborhood.

History ONLINE

Study Central™ To review this section, go to glencoe.com and click on Study Central.

BETTMANN/CORBIS

Appreciation

LOUIS DANIEL ARMSTRONG *Writer Stanley Crouch remembers Louis Armstrong, a Jazz Age great.*

Pops. Sweet Papa Dip. Satchmo. He had perfect pitch and perfect rhythm. His improvised melodies and singing could be as lofty as a moon flight or as low-down as the blood drops of a street thug dying in the gutter. The extent of his influence across jazz and across American music continues to this day.

Not only do we hear Armstrong in trumpet players who represent the present renaissance in jazz, we can also detect his influence in certain rhythms that sweep from country-and-western music to rap.

Louis Daniel Armstrong was born in New Orleans on August 4, 1901. It was at a home for troubled kids that young Louis first put his lips to the mouthpiece of a cornet and, later, a trumpet.

In 1922 Armstrong went to Chicago, where he joined King Oliver and his Creole Jazz Band. The band brought out the people and all the musicians, black and white, who wanted to know how it was truly done.

When he first played in New York City in 1924, his improvisations set the city on its head. The stiff rhythms of the time were slashed away by his combination of the percussive and the soaring. He soon returned to Chicago, perfected what he was doing, and made one record after another.

Louis Armstrong was so much, in fact, that every school of jazz since has had to address how he interpreted the basics of the idiom—swing, blues, ballads, and Afro-Hispanic rhythms. His freedom, his wit, and his discipline give his music a perpetual position in the wave of the future that is the station of all great art.

VERBATIM

❝The great creators of the government . . . thought of America as a light to the world, as created to lead the world in the assertion of the right of peoples and the rights of free nations.❞

WOODROW WILSON,
in defense of the League of Nations, 1920

❝We seek no part in directing the destinies of the Old World.❞

WARREN G. HARDING,
Inaugural Address, 1921

❝Here was a new generation, . . . dedicated more than the last to the fear of poverty and the worship of success; grown up to find . . . all wars fought, all faiths in man shaken.❞

F. Scott Fitzgerald

CULVER PICTURES

F. SCOTT FITZGERALD,
author, This Side of Paradise

❝There has been a change for the worse during the past year in feminine dress, dancing, manners and general moral standards. [One should] realize the serious ethical consequences of immodesty in girls' dress.❞

from the **PITTSBURGH OBSERVER,** *1922*

❝[In New York] I saw 7,000,000 two-legged animals penned in an evil smelling cage, . . . streets as unkempt as a Russian steppe, . . . rubbish, waste paper, cigar butts. . . . One glance and you know no master hand directs.❞

article in Soviet newspaper **PRAVDA**
describing New York City in 1925

WHAT'S NEW

Invented This Decade

How did we live without . . .

- push-button elevators
- neon signs
- oven thermostats
- electric razors
- tissues
- spiral-bound notebooks
- motels
- dry ice
- zippers
- pop-up toasters
- flavored yogurt
- car radios
- adhesive tape
- food disposals
- water skiing
- automatic potato peeler
- self-winding wristwatch

Milestones

EMBARRASSED, 1920. TEXAS SENATOR MORRIS SHEPPARD, a leading proponent of the Eighteenth Amendment, when a large whiskey still is found on his farm.

ERASED, 1922. THE WORD "OBEY," from the Episcopal marriage ceremony, by a vote of American Episcopal bishops.

DIED, 1923. HOMER MOREHOUSE, 27, in the 87th hour of a record-setting 90-hour, 10-minute dance marathon.

EXONERATED, 1921. EIGHT CHICAGO WHITE SOX PLAYERS charged with taking bribes to throw the 1919 World Series. The players were found "not guilty" when grand jury testimony disappeared. Newly appointed commissioner of baseball Kenesaw Mountain Landis banned the "Black Sox" from baseball.

MAKING A COMEBACK, 1926. SANTA CLAUS, after falling into low favor in the last decade. Aiming at children, advertisers are marketing St. Nick heavily.

NUMBERS

60,000
Families with radios in 1922

9,000,000
Motor vehicles registered in U.S. in 1920

33.5 Number of hours Charles Lindbergh spent in his nonstop flight from New York to Paris on May 20, 1927

1,800 Tons of ticker tape and shredded paper dropped on Charles Lindbergh in his parade in New York City

$16,000 Cost of cleaning up after the parade

7,000 Job offers received by Lindbergh

3.5 million
Number of letters received by Lindbergh

Charles Lindbergh

CRITICAL THINKING

1. Recognizing Bias How does the communist newspaper *Pravda* describe New York City? Why do you think the writer described the city in such negative terms?

2. Making Connections Why do you think Charles Lindbergh's flight caused such excitement among Americans in 1927?

African American Culture

Guide to Reading

Big Ideas
Group Action The artistic and political contributions of African Americans changed American society.

Content Vocabulary
- jazz (p. 389)
- blues (p. 390)

Academic Vocabulary
- symbolize (p. 390)
- impact (p. 392)
- ongoing (p. 393)

People and Events to Identify
- Great Migration (p. 388)
- Harlem Renaissance (p. 388)
- Claude McKay (p. 388)
- Langston Hughes (p. 388)
- Zora Neale Hurston (p. 388)
- Cotton Club (p. 390)
- Marcus Garvey (p. 393)

Reading Strategy
Organizing As you read about the African American experience in the 1920s, complete a graphic organizer similar to the one below by filling in the causes and effects of the Harlem Renaissance.

Causes   Effects

Harlem Renaissance

The Harlem Renaissance was a creative era for African American artists and writers. The growing African American population in the North meant an increasing number of African Americans had meaningful political power to continue the struggle for civil rights.

The Harlem Renaissance

MAIN Idea The Harlem Renaissance sparked new trends in literature, music, and art.

HISTORY AND YOU Can you think of any examples of integrating different cultures in today's music and visual arts? Read to learn about the contributions of African Americans to the arts during the 1920s.

During World War I and the 1920s, hundreds of thousands of African Americans joined in the **Great Migration** from the rural South to industrial cities in the North. By moving north, African Americans sought to escape Southern segregation, find economic opportunities, and build better lives. Although job discrimination and economic inequality remained the norm in Northern cities, the North still offered much greater economic opportunities for African Americans compared to the South. After World War I, African American populations swelled in large Northern cities. The cities were full of nightclubs and music, particularly in the New York City neighborhood of Harlem—the heart and soul of the African American renaissance. It was there that African American artistic development, racial pride, and political organization thrived. The result was a flowering of African American arts that became known as the **Harlem Renaissance.**

The Writers

Claude McKay was the first important writer of the Harlem Renaissance. McKay translated the shock of American racism into *Harlem Shadows,* a collection of poetry published in 1922. In such poems as "The Lynching" and "If We Must Die," McKay's eloquent verse expressed a proud defiance and bitter contempt of racism—two striking characteristics of Harlem Renaissance writing. **Langston Hughes** was a prolific, original, and versatile writer. He became a leading voice of the African American experience in America.

Another important Harlem Renaissance author was **Zora Neale Hurston.** Hurston published her first novels, *Jonah's Gourd Vine* and *Their Eyes Were Watching God,* in the 1930s. Hurston's personal and spirited portrayals of rural African American culture were also the

Voices From the Harlem Renaissance

▲ Zora Neale Hurston

Excerpt from
Dust Tracks on a Road
by Zora Neale Hurston

"I can look back and see sharp shadows, high lights, and smudgy inbetweens. I have been in Sorrow's kitchen and licked out all the pots. Then I have stood on the peaky mountain wrapped in rainbows, with a harp and a sword in my hands.

"What I had to swallow in the kitchen has not made me less glad to have lived, nor made me want to low-rate the human race . . . It is the graceless acknowledgment of defeat . . . I am in the struggle with the sword in my hands, and I don't intend to run until you run me [away]."

I, Too, Sing America
by Langston Hughes

I, too, sing America.

I am the darker brother.
They send me to eat in the kitchen
When company comes,
But I laugh,
And eat well,
And grow strong.

Tomorrow,
I'll be at the table
When company comes.
Nobody'll dare
Say to me,
"Eat in the kitchen,"
Then.

Besides,
They'll see how
beautiful I am
And be ashamed—

I, too, am America.

▲ Langston Hughes stressed racial pride in his poetry. He reminded African Americans that they had their own history and achievements which were in every way as worthy of celebration as those of white people.

If We Must Die
By Claude McKay

If we must die—let it not be like hogs
Hunted and penned in an inglorious spot,
While round us bark the mad and hungry dogs,Making their mock at our accursed lot. If we must die—oh, let us nobly die,
So that our precious blood may not be shed
In vain; then even the monsters we defy
Shall be constrained to honor us though dead!
Oh, Kinsmen! We must meet the common foe;
Though far outnumbered, let us show us brave,
And for their thousand blows deal one deathblow!
What though before us lies the open grave?
Like men we'll face the murderous, cowardly pack,
Pressed to the wall, dying, but fighting back!

◀ Originally from Jamaica, Claude McKay wrote both poems and novels. "If We Must Die" was written shortly after World War I when race riots were erupting across the nation.

DBQ Document-Based Questions

1. **Speculating** What might have been some of the "pots" in Sorrow's kitchen for a woman in the Harlem Renaissance?

2. **Comparing and Contrasting** What does McKay's poem have in common with Hurston's excerpt and the poem by Hughes?

first major stories featuring African American women as central characters. Other notable writers of the Harlem Renaissance include Countee Cullen, Alain Locke, Dorothy West, and Nella Larsen.

Jazz, Blues, and the Theater

When New Orleans native Louis Armstrong moved to Chicago in 1922, he introduced an improvisational early form of **jazz,** a style of music influenced by Dixieland blues and ragtime, with its syncopated rhythms and improvisational elements. Three years later, Armstrong awed fellow musicians with a series of recordings made with his group, the Hot Five. In these recordings, especially in the song "Cornet Chop Suey," Armstrong broke away from the New Orleans tradition of ensemble or group playing by performing highly imaginative solos. He became the first great cornet and trumpet soloist in jazz music. The artistic freedom of Chicago's South Side gave Armstrong the courage to create his own type of jazz.

History ONLINE
Student Web Activity Visit glencoe.com and complete the activity on the Jazz Age.

Ragtime also influenced the composer, pianist, and bandleader Edward "Duke" Ellington, who listened as a teenager to ragtime piano players in Washington, D.C. In 1923 Ellington, also known simply as "Duke," formed a small band, moved to New York, and began playing in speakeasies and clubs. He soon created his own sound, a blend of improvisation and orchestration using different combinations of instruments. In fact, Ellington often did not like to use the word "jazz," since he believed it put a restriction on the general concept of his music. The Ellington style appeared in such hits as "Mood Indigo" and "Sophisticated Lady." Ellington, who had to be forced to practice piano as a child, eventually composed nearly 6,000 musical pieces, about a third of them jazz numbers. He also wrote religious music, the scores for five movies, and a ballet.

Like many other African American entertainers, Ellington got his start at the **Cotton Club,** the most famous nightclub in Harlem (but one that served only white customers). Years later, reflecting on the music of this era, Ellington said, "Everything, and I repeat, every-thing had to swing. And that was just it, those cats really had it; they had that soul. And you know you can't just play some of this music without soul. Soul is very important."

Bessie Smith seemed to **symbolize** soul. Her emotional singing style and commanding voice earned her the title "the Empress of the Blues." Smith sang of unfulfilled love, poverty, and oppression—the classic themes of the **blues,** a soulful style of music that evolved from African American spirituals. Born in Tennessee, Smith started performing in tent shows, saloons, and small theaters in the South. Discovered by Ma Rainey, one of the early great blues singers, Smith later performed with many of the greatest jazz bands of the era, including those of Louis Armstrong, Fletcher Henderson, and Benny Goodman. Her first recorded song, "Down Hearted Blues," became a major hit in 1923.

While jazz and blues filled the air during the Harlem Renaissance, the theater arts were also flourishing. *Shuffle Along,* the first musical written, produced, and performed by African Americans, made its Broadway debut in 1921. The show's success helped launch a number of

Scenes From the Harlem Renaissance

The Harlem Renaissance made both jazz and blues music popular and enabled African American entertainers to reach a wide audience.

▲ Louis Armstrong and his band, the Hot Five

▲ Many famous acts got their start at Harlem's Cotton Club. Patrons flocked there to hear the latest jazz music—African American music played by African American musicians—but the audience was limited to whites.

▶ Duke Ellington and his band at a Chicago nightclub

careers, including those of Florence Mills and Paul Robeson.

Robeson first gained recognition as an athlete at Rutgers University, where he was valedictorian of his class. After graduating from law school, he focused on an acting career. A celebrated singer and actor, Robeson received wide acclaim in the title role of a 1924 New York production of *Emperor Jones,* a play by Eugene O'Neill. Four years later, Robeson gained fame for his work in the musical, *Show Boat.* He also often appeared at the Apollo Theater, another famous club in Harlem.

Perhaps the most daring performer of the era, Josephine Baker transformed a childhood knack for flamboyance into a career as a well-known singer and dancer. Baker performed on Broadway but later moved to Paris and launched an international career.

The Harlem Renaissance succeeded in bringing international fame to African American arts. It also sparked a political transformation in the United States.

Reading Check **Analyzing** How did African Americans help shape the national identity through the use of music?

African Americans and 1920s Politics

MAIN Idea While the NAACP pursued racial equality through the courts, black nationalists supported independence and separation from whites.

HISTORY AND YOU How does a sense of positive self-esteem help you perform better? Read how African Americans developed a new sense of pride.

In 1919, 1,300 African American veterans of World War I marched through Manhattan to Harlem. The march symbolized the new aspirations of African Americans in the 1920s. W. E. B. Du Bois captured the new sense of dignity and defiance of African Americans:

PRIMARY SOURCE

"We return. We return from fighting. We return fighting. Make way for democracy! We saved it in France, and by the Great Jehovah, we will save it in the United States of America, or know the reason why."

—quoted in *When Harlem Was in Vogue*

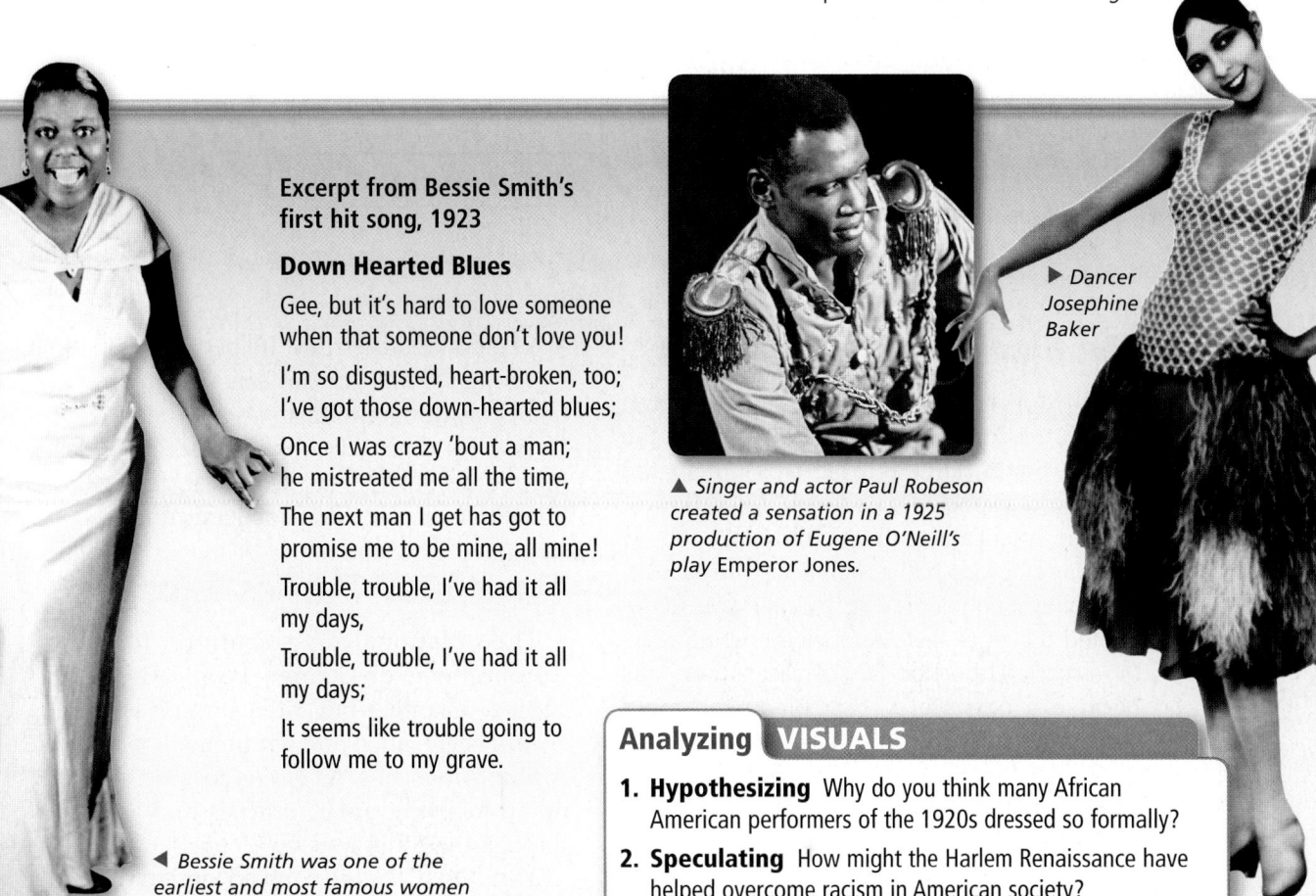

Excerpt from Bessie Smith's first hit song, 1923

Down Hearted Blues

Gee, but it's hard to love someone when that someone don't love you!

I'm so disgusted, heart-broken, too; I've got those down-hearted blues;

Once I was crazy 'bout a man; he mistreated me all the time,

The next man I get has got to promise me to be mine, all mine!

Trouble, trouble, I've had it all my days,

Trouble, trouble, I've had it all my days;

It seems like trouble going to follow me to my grave.

◀ Bessie Smith was one of the earliest and most famous women blues singers.

▲ Singer and actor Paul Robeson created a sensation in a 1925 production of Eugene O'Neill's play Emperor Jones.

▶ Dancer Josephine Baker

Analyzing **VISUALS**

1. **Hypothesizing** Why do you think many African American performers of the 1920s dressed so formally?

2. **Speculating** How might the Harlem Renaissance have helped overcome racism in American society?

The Great Migration, 1917–1930

During World War I, thousands of African Americans began the Great Migration from the rural South to the industrial cities of the North. Many African American neighborhoods, including Harlem in New York City, developed at this time.

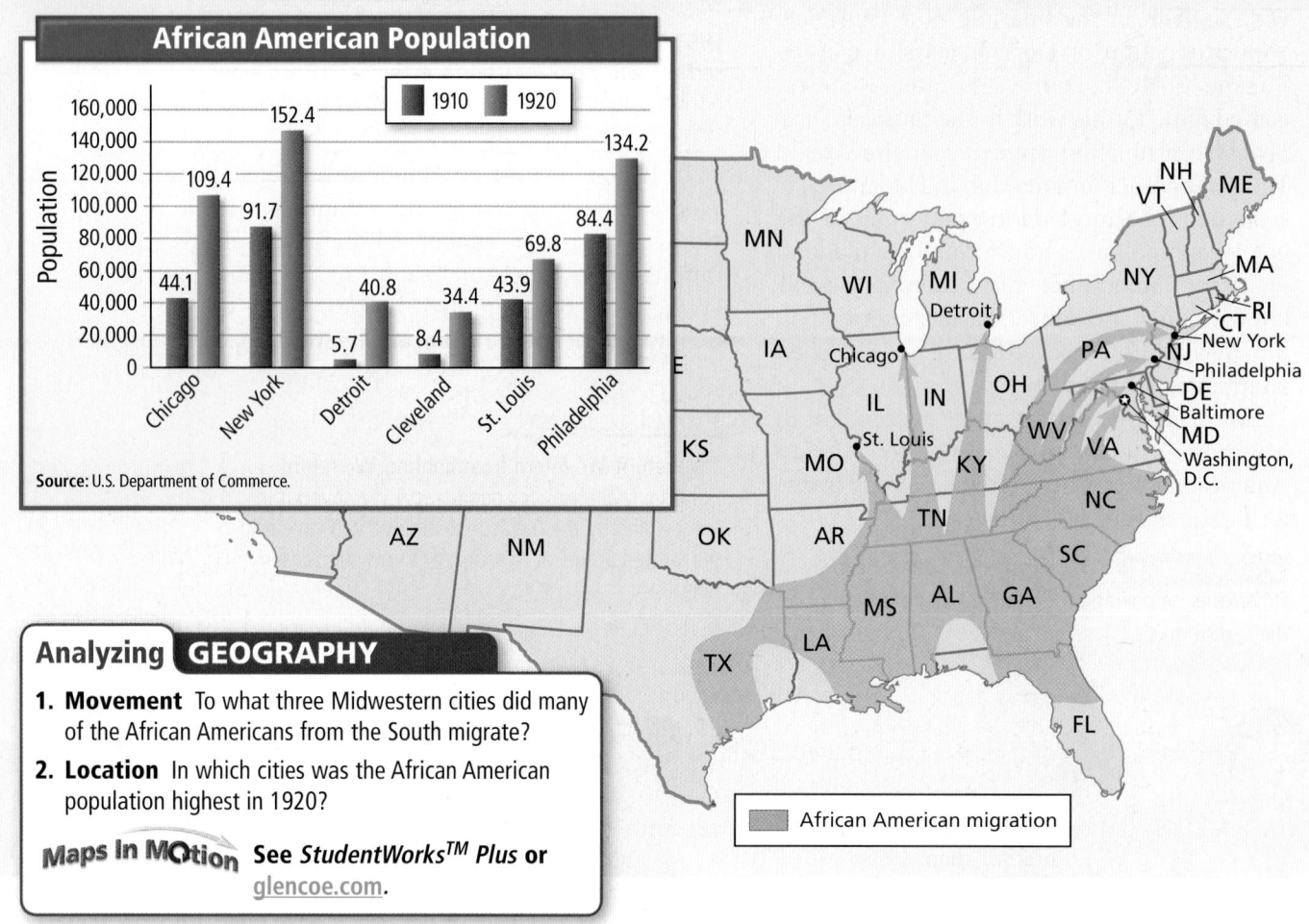

African American Population

Source: U.S. Department of Commerce.

Analyzing GEOGRAPHY

1. **Movement** To what three Midwestern cities did many of the African Americans from the South migrate?

2. **Location** In which cities was the African American population highest in 1920?

Maps In MOtion See *StudentWorks™ Plus* or glencoe.com.

African American migration

The Black Vote in the North

World War I set the stage for African Americans to reenter federal politics in the United States, although perhaps not in the way many expected. The Great Migration of African Americans to the North to take jobs in the war factories had a significant **impact** on the political power of African Americans in the United States as well. As their numbers grew in city neighborhoods, African Americans became a powerful voting bloc that could sometimes sway the outcome of elections.

At election time, most African American voters in the North cast their votes for Republicans, the party of Abraham Lincoln. In 1928 African American voters in Chicago achieved a significant political breakthrough.

Voting as a bloc, they helped elect Oscar DePriest, the first African American representative in Congress from a Northern state. During his three terms in Congress, DePriest introduced laws to oppose racial discrimination and make lynching a federal crime.

The NAACP Battles Injustice

The National Association for the Advancement of Colored People (NAACP) battled valiantly—but often unsuccessfully—against segregation and discrimination against African Americans. Its efforts focused primarily on lobbying public officials and working through the court system.

The NAACP also lobbied and protested against the horrors of lynching. The NAACP's persistent efforts led to the passage of antilynching legislation in the House of Representatives in 1922. The Senate defeated the bill, but the NAACP continued the fight. Its **ongoing** efforts to end lynching kept the issue in the news and probably helped to reduce the number of lynchings that took place.

One of the NAACP's greatest political triumphs occurred in 1930 with the defeat of Judge John J. Parker's nomination to the U.S. Supreme Court. The NAACP joined with labor unions to launch a highly organized national campaign against the North Carolina judge, who allegedly was racist and antilabor. By a narrow margin, the Senate refused to confirm Parker's nomination. His defeat demonstrated that African American voters and lobby groups had finally achieved enough influence to affect national politics and change decisions in Congress.

Black Nationalism and Marcus Garvey

While the NAACP fought for integration and improvement in the economic and political position of African Americans, other groups began to emphasize black nationalism and black pride. Eventually, some began calling for black separation from white society.

A dynamic black leader from Jamaica, **Marcus Garvey,** captured the imagination of millions of African Americans with his "Negro Nationalism," which glorified the black culture and traditions. Inspired by Booker T. Washington's call for self-reliance, Garvey founded the Universal Negro Improvement Association (UNIA), an organization aimed at promoting black pride and unity. The central message of Garvey's Harlem-based movement was that African Americans could gain economic and political power by educating themselves. Garvey also advocated separation and independence from whites. In 1920, at the height of his power, Garvey told his followers they would never find justice or freedom in America, and he proposed leading them to Africa.

The emerging African American middle class and intellectuals distanced themselves from Garvey and his push for racial separation. FBI officials saw UNIA as a dangerous catalyst for black uprisings in urban areas. Garvey also alienated key figures in the Harlem Renaissance by characterizing them as "weak-kneed and cringing . . . [flatterers of] the white man." Convicted of mail fraud in 1923, Garvey served time in prison. In 1927 President Coolidge commuted Garvey's sentence and used Garvey's immigrant status to have him deported to Jamaica.

Despite Garvey's failure to keep his movement alive, he instilled millions of African Americans with a sense of pride in their heritage and inspired hope for the future. That sense of pride and hope survived long after Garvey and his "back to Africa" movement was gone. This pride and hope reemerged strongly during the 1950s and played a vital role in the civil rights movement of the 1960s.

Reading Check **Summarizing** How did World War I change attitudes among African Americans toward themselves and their country?

Section 5 REVIEW

Vocabulary

1. **Explain** the significance of: Great Migration, Harlem Renaissance, Claude McKay, Langston Hughes, Zora Neale Hurston, jazz, Cotton Club, blues, Marcus Garvey.

Main Ideas

2. **Analyzing** What musical style did Duke Ellington create? How was it different from other styles of music?

3. **Synthesizing** How did the Great Migration affect the political power of African Americans in the North?

Critical Thinking

4. **Big Ideas** What actions did the NAACP take to expand political rights for African Americans?

5. **Organizing** Use a graphic organizer similar to the one below to describe the impact of the Harlem Renaissance on U.S. society.

Impact of Harlem Renaissance

6. **Analyzing Visuals** Look at the photographs of Harlem Renaissance writers on page 389. Select one person and write a description of him or her, based only on what you see in the photo.

Writing About History

7. **Descriptive Writing** Imagine that you witnessed the African American men of the 369th Infantry, who had come back from the war, march through Manhattan and home to Harlem. Write a paragraph describing your feelings upon seeing these men.

History ONLINE

Study Central™ To review this section, go to glencoe.com and click on Study Central.

Causes of Prosperity

Government's Role

- Limits interference with business
- Cuts taxes, debt, and government spending
- Imposes higher tariffs to protect young industries

Business Innovation and Technology

- Mass production creates a wide range of consumer goods sold at low prices.
- Technology such as autos, airplanes, and radio leads to new industries and economic growth.
- Business pays high wages.

New Consumer Society

- People have more disposable income and leisure time
- Credit is more readily available
- Mass advertising begins

▲ The moving assembly line, pioneered by Henry Ford, made building automobiles efficient and greatly reduced prices.

▲ Joe "King" Oliver's band, with Louis Armstrong on slide trumpet, performs in Chicago in 1923, introducing the sound of jazz to America.

A Changing Society

Cultural Changes

- A new youth culture with a "new morality" develops.
- Young people and women gain more independence.
- The working class enjoys more leisure time.
- New mass media in radio, movies, and sports develops.

Changes for African Americans

- Harlem Renaissance begins.
- Literature reveals racial pride and contempt of racism.
- Jazz and blues are popularized.
- Great Migration during the war creates strong African American voting blocs in Northern cities.
- First African American from the North is elected to Congress.
- NAACP battles segregation and discrimination.

Opposition to Change

- Nativists and a new Ku Klux Klan target immigrants, Catholics, Jews, and African Americans.
- Government imposes new quotas on immigration.
- Fundamentalists push for traditional values.
- Prohibition is implemented.

◀ A federal agent enforces Prohibition by dumping barrels of illegal alcohol as neighborhood children watch.

Reviewing Vocabulary

Directions: Choose the word or words that best complete each sentence.

1. What economic philosophy encouraged businesses to form trade associations?

   A monopolies

   B cooperative individualism

   C moratorium

   D supply-side economics

2. Companies introduced _____, which were programs that benefited workers by allowing them to participate in profit-sharing and to receive health benefits and pensions.

   A normalcy

   B open shop system

   C supply-side economics

   D welfare capitalism

3. Sacco and Vanzetti were _____, or people who opposed all forms of government.

   A anarchists

   B Communists

   C bohemians

   D creationists

4. Prohibition led to an increase in _____, or bars where people sold liquor illegally.

   A mass media

   B speakeasies

   C police powers

   D bootlegging

5. The artistic and unconventional, or _____ lifestyles of some urban neighborhoods spurred 1920s cultural innovations.

   A bohemian

   B anarchistic

   C nativist

   D open shop

Reviewing Main Ideas

Directions: Choose the best answers to the following questions.

Section 1 *(pp. 362–367)*

6. Teapot Dome is an example of a scandal during the administration of

   A Calvin Coolidge.

   B Warren G. Harding.

   C Woodrow Wilson.

   D William Howard Taft.

7. What agreement involved American banks giving loans to Germany to pay war reparations to France and Britain?

   A the Washington Conference

   B Kellogg-Briand Pact

   C the Dawes Plan

   D Four-Power Treaty

Section 2 *(pp. 368–375)*

8. Henry Ford's contribution to manufacturing was the

   A expansion of the petroleum industry.

   B requirement of open shop.

   C idea of mass marketing.

   D adoption of the assembly line.

9. The change in Americans' ideas about _____ resulted in more spending on what had once been luxury goods.

   A mass production

   B consumer credit

   C advertising

   D welfare capitalism

TEST-TAKING

Make sure that you can define the chapter's vocabulary terms. You will see these words in questions on standardized tests. By understanding their meanings you can omit incorrect answers through the process of elimination.

Need Extra Help?									
If You Missed Questions . . .	1	2	3	4	5	6	7	8	9
Go to Page . . .	365	374	376–377	381	382	362–364	366–367	368–370	372–373

Section 3 *(pp. 376–381)*

10. The passage of the Eighteenth Amendment was seen as a victory for

   A opponents of alcohol consumption.

   B supporters of women's suffrage.

   C nativists.

   D Sacco and Vanzetti.

11. What act restricted immigration to 2 percent of each national group represented in the 1890 U.S. Census?

   A Emergency Quota Act

   B National Origins Act

   C Reclamation Act

   D Clayton Antitrust Act

Section 4 *(pp. 382–385)*

12. Chicago's South Side and New York's Greenwich Village were centers for

   A the arts.

   B industry.

   C politics.

   D banking.

Section 5 *(pp. 388–393)*

13. The artistic developments of African Americans in the 1920s were known as the

   A Great Migration.

   B Saint Louis blues.

   C New Orleans sound.

   D Harlem Renaissance.

14. What was an idea of black nationalism?

   A integration and political improvement in society

   B separation and independence from whites

   C emigration from the United States to Jamaica

   D support for the arts as a way to improve African American society

Critical Thinking

Directions: Choose the best answers to the following questions.

15. What effect did greater education and job opportunities for women create?

   A Many women began earning as much money as men did.

   B Women contributed to both scientific and artistic knowledge.

   C More women preferred to remain at home.

   D Most women working outside the home gained leadership positions.

Base your answer to question 16 on the map below and on your knowledge of Chapter 10.

European Immigration Totals, 1890–1920

Number of People Immigrating to U.S. by Region, 1890–1920

488,099	2,135,312
672,223	3,060,151
1,130,656	3,695,828
1,195,628	3,859,297
1914 border	

16. Which nation or empire sent the greatest number of immigrants to the United States between 1890 and 1920?

   A Italy

   B Russian Empire

   C German Empire

   D Spain

Need Extra Help?

If You Missed Questions . . .	10	11	12	13	14	15	16
Go to Page . . .	381	378	382–384	388	393	378–379	377–378

GO ON

17. What written agreement declared war illegal?

A the Washington Conference

B the Dawes Plan

C the Kellogg-Briand Pact

D the League of Nations Charter

18. What was a principal reason for rapid economic growth in the United States during the 1920s?

A prosperity of American agriculture

B increase of American imports

C development of many new consumer goods

D increased spending on defense

Analyze the cartoon and answer the question that follows. Base your answer on the cartoon and your knowledge of Chapter 10.

19. What does the cartoon imply about Coolidge?

A He was trying to select which party to support in the next election.

B He wanted to control the congressional leadership.

C He wanted to cut back on unnecessary government expenditures.

D He wanted to increase taxes and government spending.

Document-Based Questions

Directions: Analyze the document and answer the short-answer questions that follow the document.

Charles Lindbergh, who made the first transatlantic flight from New York to Paris in 1927, later wrote a book about the experience. He titled the book after the plane he flew, *The Spirit of St. Louis.* The following excerpt is from that book:

> *"What endless hours I worked over this chart in California, measuring, drawing, rechecking each 100-mile segment of its great-circle route, each theoretical hour of my flight. . . . A few lines and figures on a strip of paper, a few ounces of weight, this [map] strip is my key to Europe. With it, I can fly the ocean. With it, that black dot at the other end marked 'Paris' will turn into a famous French city with an aerodrome where I can land. But without this chart, all my years of training, all that went into preparing for this flight, no matter how perfectly the engine runs or how long the fuel lasts, all would be as directionless as those columns of smoke in the New England valleys behind me."*
> —from *The Spirit of St. Louis*

20. What does Lindbergh believe is the most valuable tool he has?

21. What conclusions can you draw about Lindbergh as a person, based on this excerpt?

Extended Response

22. The Harding and Coolidge administrations promoted economic prosperity and world peace. Consider how both administrations attempted this difficult task. Write an essay that explains the methods used to accomplish the goal of economic and political stability worldwide. How successful was each administration? Your essay should include an introduction, several paragraphs, and a conclusion. Use relevant facts and details to support your conclusion.

History ONLINE

For additional test practice, use Self-Check Quizzes—Chapter 10 at glencoe.com.

Need Extra Help?						
If You Missed Questions . . .	17	18	19	20	21	22
Go to Page . . .	367	367–372	R18	397	R19	362–365

The Great Depression Begins

1929–1932

Women and children wait in a bread line at New York City's New Hope Mission in the early 1930s.

U.S. PRESIDENTS

Hoover
1929–1933

U.S. EVENTS

1929

WORLD EVENTS

1929
- Stock market crashes on Black Tuesday

1930
- Congress passes Hawley-Smoot Tariff

1930

1931

1928
- Soviets introduce First Five-Year Plan to industrialize the country

1929
- Mexico passes 8-hour day, right to strike, and unemployment insurance

1930
- France creates a health and old age insurance plan

1931
- Collapse of large Austrian bank triggers bank failures across Europe

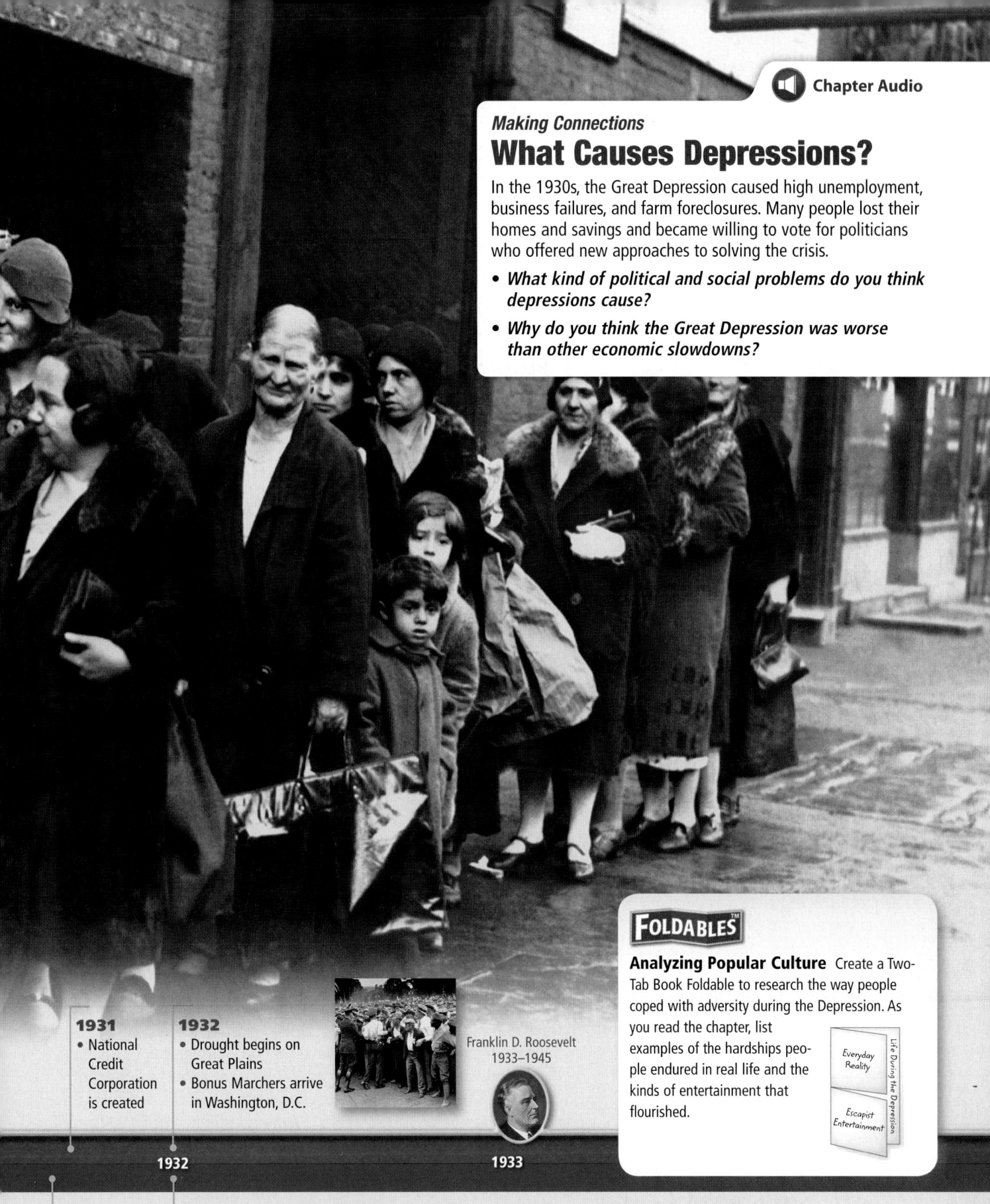

Making Connections

What Causes Depressions?

In the 1930s, the Great Depression caused high unemployment, business failures, and farm foreclosures. Many people lost their homes and savings and became willing to vote for politicians who offered new approaches to solving the crisis.

- *What kind of political and social problems do you think depressions cause?*
- *Why do you think the Great Depression was worse than other economic slowdowns?*

FOLDABLES

Analyzing Popular Culture Create a Two-Tab Book Foldable to research the way people coped with adversity during the Depression. As you read the chapter, list examples of the hardships people endured in real life and the kinds of entertainment that flourished.

Everyday Reality

Escapist Entertainment

Life During the Depression

1931
- National Credit Corporation is created

1932
- Drought begins on Great Plains
- Bonus Marchers arrive in Washington, D.C.

Franklin D. Roosevelt 1933–1945

1932

1933

1931
- Japan invades Manchuria

1932
- Government-induced famine begins in USSR, killing millions
- Unemployment in Germany reaches 6 million

History ONLINE Visit glencoe.com and enter *QuickPass*™ code TAVMT5147c11 for Chapter 11 resources.

The Causes of the Great Depression

Guide to Reading

Big Ideas
Economics and Society Stock speculation on an unregulated stock market put investors and banks at risk in the 1920s.

Content Vocabulary
- stock market *(p. 400)*
- bull market *(p. 401)*
- margin *(p. 401)*
- margin call *(p. 401)*
- speculation *(p. 401)*
- bank run *(p. 403)*
- installment *(p. 405)*

Academic Vocabulary
- collapse *(p. 400)*
- invest *(p. 401)*
- sum *(p. 403)*

People and Events to Identify
- Alfred E. Smith *(p. 400)*
- Black Tuesday *(p. 402)*
- Hawley-Smoot Tariff *(p. 405)*

Reading Strategy
Categorizing As you read about the election of 1928, complete a graphic organizer similar to the one below comparing the backgrounds and issues of the presidential candidates.

1928 Presidential Campaign		
Candidate	Background	Issues

Although the 1920s were prosperous, speculation in the stock market, risky lending policies, overproduction, and uneven income distribution eventually undermined the economy and led to the Great Depression.

The Long Bull Market

MAIN Idea A strong economy helped Herbert Hoover win the 1928 election, but increasing speculation in the stock market set the stage for a crash.

HISTORY AND YOU Have you ever taken a risk while playing a game or sport? How did you decide if the risk was worth it? Read on to learn about the risks people were willing to take in the stock market in the 1920s.

The economic **collapse** that began in 1929 seemed unimaginable only a year earlier. In the 1928 election, both presidential candidates tried to paint a rosy picture of the future. Republican Herbert Hoover declared, "We are nearer to the final triumph over poverty than ever before in the history of any land."

The Election of 1928

When Calvin Coolidge declined to run for reelection in 1928, the Republicans nominated his secretary of commerce, Herbert Hoover. Hoover was well-known to Americans because he had run the Food Administration during World War I. The Democrats chose **Alfred E. Smith,** four-time governor of New York. Smith was the first Roman Catholic to win a major party's nomination for president.

Smith's beliefs became a campaign issue. Some Protestants claimed that the Catholic Church financed the Democratic Party and would rule the United States if Smith became president. These slurs embarrassed Hoover, a Quaker, and he tried to quash them, but the charges damaged Smith's candidacy.

Smith's biggest challenge, however, was the prosperity of the 1920s, for which the Republicans took full credit. Hoover defeated Smith by more than 6 million votes and won the Electoral College in a landslide, 444 to 87. On March 4, 1929, an audience of 50,000 stood in the rain to hear Hoover's inaugural speech. "I have no fears for the future of our country," Hoover said. "It is bright with hope."

The Stock Market Soars

The optimism that swept Hoover into the White House also drove stock prices to new highs. Sometimes the **stock market** experiences

Hoover and "Rugged Individualism"

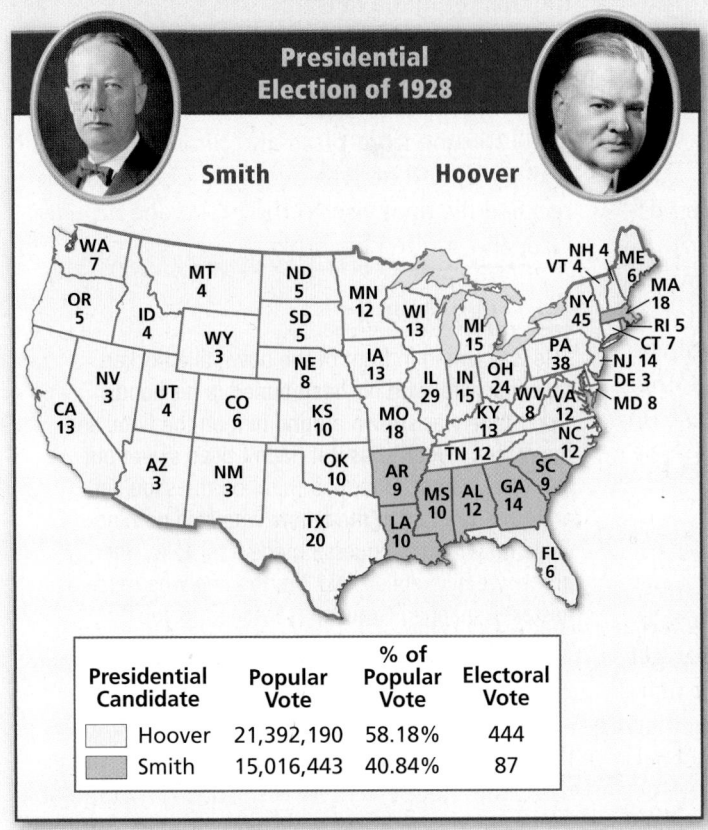

Presidential Election of 1928

Smith   Hoover

Presidential Candidate	Popular Vote	% of Popular Vote	Electoral Vote
Hoover	21,392,190	58.18%	444
Smith	15,016,443	40.84%	87

"We were challenged with a peacetime choice between the American system of rugged individualism and a European philosophy of diametrically opposed doctrines—doctrines of paternalism and state socialism. . . . [T]hese ideas would have meant the destruction of self-government through centralization of government. It would have meant the undermining of . . . individual initiative and enterprise . . .

". . . You cannot extend the mastery of the government over the daily working life of a people without at the same time making it the master of the people's souls and thoughts. . . . Free speech does not live many hours after free industry and free commerce die. . . . Every step of bureaucratizing of the business of our country poisons the very roots of liberalism—that is, political equality, free speech, free assembly, free press, and equality of opportunity. It is the road not to more liberty, but to less liberty."

—Herbert Hoover, speech delivered October 22, 1928

DBQ Document-Based Questions

1. **Contrasting** Against what other system does Hoover contrast "rugged individualism"?

2. **Analyzing Primary Sources** What does Hoover believe is at stake if free industry and free commerce die? Do you agree or disagree? Explain your position.

a long period of rising stock prices, or a **bull market.** In the late 1920s a prolonged bull market convinced many people to **invest** in stocks. By 1929 approximately 10 percent of American households owned stocks.

As the market continued to soar, many investors began buying stocks on **margin,** making only a small cash down payment (as low as 10 percent of the price). With $1,000, an investor could buy $10,000 worth of stock. The other $9,000 would come as a loan from a stockbroker, who earned both a commission on the sale and interest on the loan. The broker held the stock as collateral.

If the price of the stock kept rising, the investor could make a profit. For example, the investor who borrowed to buy $10,000 worth of stock had only to wait for it to rise to $11,000 in value. The investor could then sell the stock, repay the loan, and make $1,000 in profit. The problem came if the stock price began to fall.

To protect the loan, a broker could issue a **margin call,** demanding the investor repay the loan at once. As a result, many investors were very sensitive to any fall in stock prices. If prices fell, they had to sell quickly, or they might not be able to repay their loans.

Before the late 1920s, the prices investors paid for stocks had generally reflected the stocks' true value. If a company made a profit or had good future sales prospects, its stock price rose; prices fell when earnings dropped. In the late 1920s, however, many investors bid prices up without considering a company's earnings and profits. Buyers, hoping for a quick windfall, engaged in **speculation.** They bet the market would continue to climb, thus enabling them to sell the stock and make money quickly.

Reading Check **Summarizing** What was the stock market like in the 1920s?

The Great Crash

MAIN Idea Rising stock prices led to risky investment practices; when the stock market crashed, banks were in trouble.

HISTORY AND YOU Have you ever paid more for something than it was worth? Read on to learn why the stock market collapsed in 1929.

The bull market lasted only as long as investors continued putting new money into it. By the latter half of 1929, the market was running out of new customers. In September, professional investors sensed danger and began to sell off their holdings. Prices slipped. Other investors sold shares to pay the interest on their brokerage loans. Prices fell further.

The Stock Market Crash

On Monday, October 21, 1929, the comedian Groucho Marx was awakened by a telephone call from his broker. "You'd better get down here with some cash to cover your margin," the broker said. The stock market had plunged. The dazed comedian had to pay back the money he had borrowed to buy stocks, which were now selling for far less than he had paid for them. Other brokers made similar margin calls. Nervous customers put their stocks up for sale at a frenzied pace, driving the market into a tailspin.

On October 24, a day that came to be called Black Thursday, the market plummeted further. Marx was wiped out. He had earned a small fortune from plays and films, but now it was gone, and he was deeply in debt. His son recalled his final visit to the brokerage firm, as Groucho spotted his broker:

PRIMARY SOURCE

"He was sitting in front of the now-stilled ticker-tape machine, with his head buried in his hands. Ticker tape was strewn around him on the floor, and the place . . . looked as if it hadn't been swept out in a week. Groucho tapped [him] on the shoulder and said, 'Aren't you the fellow who said nothing could go wrong?' 'I guess I made a mistake,' the broker wearily replied. 'No, I'm the one who made a mistake,' snapped Groucho. 'I listened to you.'"

—quoted in *1929: The Year of the Great Crash*

The following week, on October 29, a day that was later dubbed **Black Tuesday,** prices took the steepest dive yet. That day, almost 16 million shares of stock were sold; the stock

---

Turning Point

A Crash Becomes a Depression

When the stock market crashed in October 1929, it exposed many weaknesses in the American economy. By 1932 over 25 percent of American workers were unemployed. Charities could not help all who were in need. Many cities had gone bankrupt and newly created state relief agencies had insufficient funds to help.

The Great Depression prompted major political changes. When Franklin D. Roosevelt ran for president in 1932, he had offered few details about how he would save the economy. Once in office, however, he launched a massive program to rescue the banking system, stabilize industry, and aid the unemployed. By the late 1930s, the federal government had taken on huge new responsibilities for the health of the economy and welfare of American families.

ANALYZING HISTORY Do you think the Great Depression required government intervention to resolve? Write a brief essay explaining your opinion.

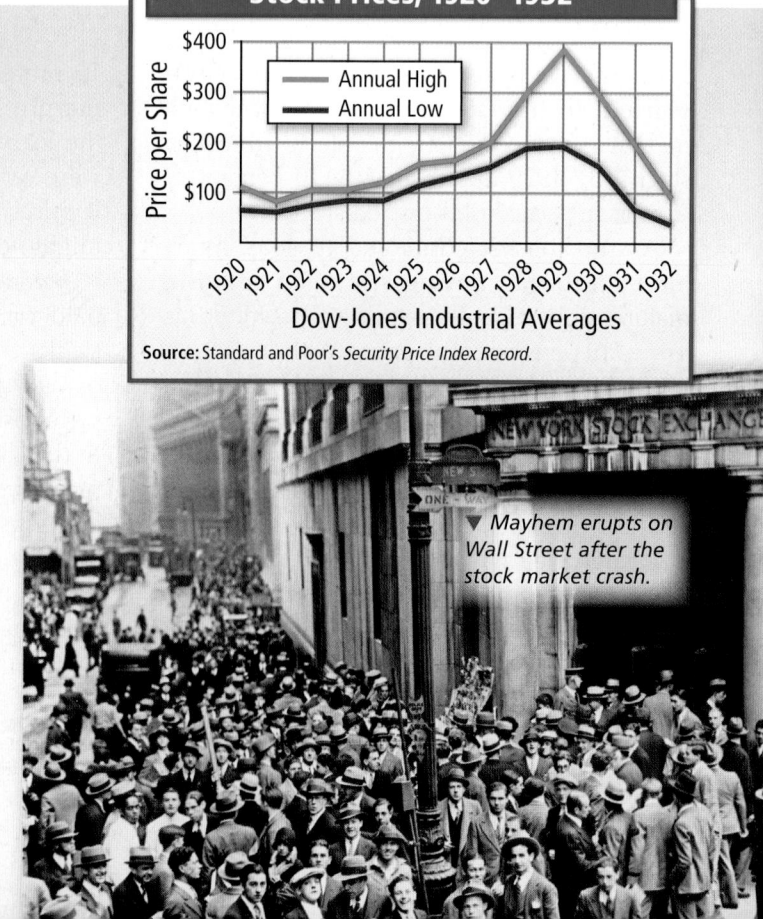

Stock Prices, 1920–1932

Price per Share — $400, $300, $200, $100

— Annual High
— Annual Low

Dow-Jones Industrial Averages

Source: Standard and Poor's *Security Price Index Record.*

▼ *Mayhem erupts on Wall Street after the stock market crash.*

market lost between $10 billion and $15 billion in value. By mid-November, stock prices had dropped by more than one-third. Some $30 billion was lost, a **sum** roughly equal to the total wages Americans earned in 1929. Although the stock market crash was not the major cause of the Great Depression, it undermined the economy's ability to overcome other weaknesses.

Banks Begin to Close

The market crash severely weakened the nation's banks in two ways. First, by 1929 banks had loaned nearly $6 billion to stock speculators. Second, many banks had invested depositors' money in the stock market, hoping for higher returns than they could get by using the money for loans.

When stock values collapsed, banks lost money on their investments, and speculators defaulted on their loans. Having suffered serious losses, many banks cut back drastically on the loans they made. With less credit available, consumers and businesses were not able to borrow as much money. This helped to send the economy into a recession.

Some banks could not absorb the losses they suffered and were forced to close. The government did not insure bank deposits, so if a bank collapsed, customers, including those who did not invest in the stock market, lost their savings. Bank failures in 1929 and 1930 created a crisis of confidence in the banking system.

News of bank failures worried Americans. Some depositors made runs on banks, causing the banks to collapse. A **bank run** takes place when many depositors decide to withdraw their money at one time, usually because of fear that the bank is going to collapse.

Most banks make a profit by lending money received from depositors and collecting interest on the loans. The bank keeps only a fraction of depositors' money in reserve to cover daily business and withdrawals. Usually, that reserve is enough to meet the bank's needs. If too many people withdraw their money, however, the bank will collapse. More than 10 percent of the nation's banks—nearly 3,500—had closed by 1932.

Reading Check **Determining Cause and Effect** What chain of events led to the economic crash of 1929?

Bank Failures, 1928–1933

Number of Failures (0 to 4,000): 1928, 1929, 1930, 1931, 1932, 1933

Source: *Historical Statistics of the United States.*

◀ Depositors at a New York bank line up to withdraw their money in 1930.

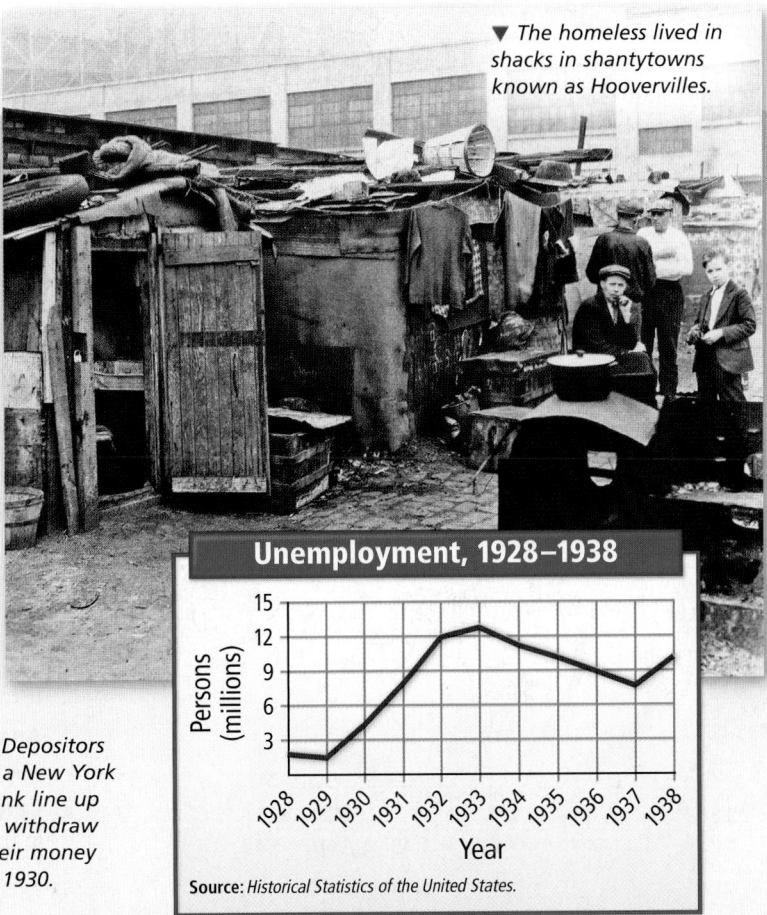

▼ The homeless lived in shacks in shantytowns known as Hoovervilles.

Unemployment, 1928–1938

Persons (millions) (3 to 15): 1928, 1929, 1930, 1931, 1932, 1933, 1934, 1935, 1936, 1937, 1938

Year

Source: *Historical Statistics of the United States.*

The Roots of the Great Depression

MAIN Idea An uneven distribution of income, tariff policies, and the Federal Reserve Board's mistakes contributed to the Great Depression.

HISTORY AND YOU How evenly is wealth distributed in your community? Read about the uneven distribution of income in the late 1920s.

The stock market crash played a major role in putting the economy into a recession. Yet the crash would not have led to a long-lasting depression if other forces had not been at work. The roots of the Great Depression were deeply entangled in the economy of the 1920s.

The Uneven Distribution of Income

Overproduction was one factor contributing to the onset of the Great Depression. More efficient machinery increased the production capacity of both factories and farms. Most Americans, however, did not earn enough to buy up the flood of goods they helped produce. While manufacturing output per person-hour rose 32 percent, the average worker's wage increased only 8 percent. In 1929 the top 5 percent of all American households earned 30 percent of the nation's income. In contrast, about two-thirds of families earned less than $2,500 a year, leaving them with little disposable income.

INFOGRAPHIC
Causes of the Great Depression

What Caused the Economy to Collapse?

- **Low Interest Rates** Federal Reserve kept interest rates low; companies borrowed money and expanded more than necessary.
- **Overproduction** Companies made more goods than could be sold.
- **Uneven Distribution of Wealth** Not everyone who wanted consumer goods could afford them.
- **High Tariffs** Tariffs restricted foreign demand for American goods.
- **Falling Demand** With too many goods unsold, production was cut back and employees were laid off.
- **Stock Market Speculation** Low interest rates encouraged borrowing money to speculate, endangering bank solvency.

Cyclical Effect

Automobile sales declined. This loss of demand meant less demand for:

Textiles

Oil

Steel

Rubber

Industry slowed, which caused:

Lower wages

Unemployment

Which helped contribute further to:

Income and Spending

Source: *Historical Statistics of the United States.*

Value of Exports, 1929–1932

Source: *Historical Statistics of the United States.*

Analyzing VISUALS · DBQ

1. **Analyzing** What effect did the decline in automobile sales have on the steel industry?
2. **Calculating** Between what two years was the decrease in the value of exports the greatest?

During the 1920s many Americans had purchased high-cost items, such as refrigerators and cars, on the **installment** plan. Purchasers could make small down payments and pay the remainder of the item's price in monthly installments. Paying off such debts eventually forced some buyers to stop making new purchases. Because of the decrease in sales, manufacturers in turn cut production and laid off employees.

The slowdown in retail sales reverberated throughout the economy. When radio sales slumped, for example, makers cut back on orders for copper wire, wood cabinets, and glass radio tubes. Montana copper miners, Minnesota lumberjacks, and Ohio glass-workers, in turn, lost their jobs. Jobless workers cut back on purchases, further cutting sales. This kind of chain reaction put more and more Americans out of work. Many families had little or no savings. They had nothing to support themselves when they lost their jobs. In 1930 alone, about 26,000 businesses collapsed.

The Loss of Export Sales

Many jobs might have been saved if American manufacturers had sold more goods abroad. As the bull market of the 1920s sped up, U.S. banks made loans to speculators rather than loans to foreign companies. Foreign countries were also facing a recession after World War I. Many nations did not have the money to buy American-manufactured goods or crops.

In 1929 Hoover wanted to encourage overseas trade by lowering tariffs. Conservative Republicans, however, wanted to protect American industry from foreign competition by raising tariffs. The resulting legislation, the **Hawley-Smoot Tariff,** raised the average tariff rate to the highest level in American history. In the end, it failed to help American businesses, because foreign countries responded by raising their own tariffs. This meant fewer American products were sold overseas. By 1932 exports had fallen to about one-fifth of what they had been in 1929, which hurt both American companies and farmers.

Mistakes by the Federal Reserve

Just as consumers were able to buy more goods on credit, access to easy money propelled the stock market. Instead of raising interest rates to curb excessive speculation, the Federal Reserve Board kept its rates very low throughout the 1920s.

The Board's failure to raise interest rates significantly helped cause the Depression in two ways. First, by keeping rates low, it encouraged member banks to make risky loans. Second, its low interest rates led business leaders to think the economy was still expanding. As a result, they borrowed more money to expand production, a serious mistake because it led to overproduction when sales were falling. When the Depression finally hit, companies had to lay off workers to cut costs. Then the Federal Reserve made another mistake. It raised interest rates, tightening credit. The economy continued to spiral downward.

✔ Reading Check **Listing** What were three factors that contributed to the Great Depression?

Section 1 REVIEW

Vocabulary

1. **Explain** the significance of: Alfred E. Smith, stock market, bull market, margin, margin call, speculation, Black Tuesday, bank run, installment, Hawley-Smoot Tariff.

Main Ideas

2. **Identifying** What factors contributed to Herbert Hoover's election in 1928?

3. **Examining** How did the stock market collapse affect banks?

4. **Explaining** What effect did tariff policies have on the Great Depression?

Critical Thinking

5. **Big Ideas** How did the practice of buying on margin and speculation cause the stock market to rise?

6. **Organizing** Use a graphic organizer similar to the one below to list the causes of the Great Depression.

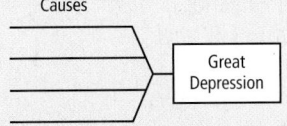

Causes

Great Depression

7. **Analyzing Visuals** Look at the graph on page 402. What generalization can you make about the variation in highs and lows of the stock market from 1920 to 1932?

Writing About History

8. **Expository Writing** Write an article for a financial magazine explaining the stock market's rapid decline in 1929 and the reasons for the crash on Black Tuesday.

History ONLINE

Study Central™ To review this section, go to glencoe.com and click on Study Central.

Life During the Depression

The Great Depression caused large numbers of people to lose their jobs and property. To help people escape their misery, popular entertainment offered humorous and optimistic movies and radio programs. Novelists and photographers created more realistic portrayals of American life.

The Depression Worsens

MAIN Idea Hunger and homelessness became severe problems by the early 1930s; then, a terrible drought devastated the Great Plains.

HISTORY AND YOU Have you ever been caught outside in a thunderstorm? Read about the deadly dust storms of the 1930s.

The Depression grew steadily worse during Hoover's administration. In 1930, 1,352 banks **suspended** operations across the nation, more than twice the number of bank failures in 1929. More than 9,000 banks had failed by 1933. In 1932 alone, some 30,000 companies went out of business. By 1933 more than 12 million workers, or roughly one-fourth of the workforce, were unemployed.

Struggling to Get By

People without jobs often went hungry. Whenever possible they stood in bread lines—sometimes blocks long—for free food or lined up outside soup kitchens, which private organizations set up to give the poor meals. New York City's YMCA fed up to 12,000 people daily.

Families or individuals who could not pay their rent or mortgage lost their homes. Some of them, paralyzed by fear and humiliation over their sudden misfortune, simply would not or could not move. Their landlord would then ask the court for an eviction notice. Court officers known as **bailiffs** then ejected the nonpaying tenants, piling their belongings in the street.

Throughout the country, newly homeless people put up shacks on unused or public lands, forming communities called shantytowns. Blaming the president for their plight, people referred to such places as Hoovervilles.

In search of work or a better life, many homeless and unemployed Americans began to wander around the country—walking, hitchhiking, or, most often, "riding the rails." These wanderers, called **hobos,** would sneak past railroad police to slip into open boxcars on freight trains. Hundreds of thousands of people, mostly boys and young men, wandered from place to place in this fashion.

Fleeing the Dustbowl

The fierce dust storms of the 1930s destroyed farms and caused many to flee the Great Plains. Below, girls pump water during a dust storm in Springfield, Colorado.

About 40 percent of migrant farmers who fled the Dust Bowl went to California's San Joaquin Valley to pick cotton and grapes. In his novel *The Grapes of Wrath*, John Steinbeck describes what these migrants found when they arrived to harvest crops:

PRIMARY SOURCE

"Maybe he [the owner of the fields] needs two hunderd men, so he talks to five hunderd, an' they tell other folks, an' when you get to the place, they's a thousan' men. This here fella says, 'I'm payin' twenty cents an hour.' An' maybe half the men walk off. But they's still five hunderd that's so . . . hungry they'll work for nothin' but biscuits. Well, this here fella's got a contract to pick them peaches or—chop that cotton. You see now? The more fellas he can get, an' the hungrier, less he's gonna pay. An' he'll get a fella with kids if he can."

—from *The Grapes of Wrath*

DBQ Document-Based Questions

1. **Analyzing Primary Sources** What advantage does the owner of the fields have when it comes to paying people to work?

2. **Drawing Conclusions** Why might the owners of the fields prefer to get "a fella with kids"?

The Dust Bowl

Farmers soon faced a new disaster. Since homesteading had begun on the Great Plains, farmers' plows had uprooted the wild grasses that held the soil's moisture. When crop prices dropped in the 1920s, farmers left many of their fields uncultivated. Then, a terrible drought struck the Great Plains. With neither grass nor wheat to hold the scant rainfall, the soil dried to dust. From the Dakotas to Texas, America's wheat fields became a vast **"Dust Bowl."**

Winds whipped the arid earth, blowing it aloft and blackening the sky for hundreds of miles. When the dust settled, it buried crops and livestock. Humans and animals caught outdoors sometimes died of suffocation when the dust filled their lungs. The number of yearly dust storms grew, from 22 in 1934 to 72 in 1937. Will and Carolyn Henderson farmed in western Oklahoma. Carolyn wrote a series of articles for the *Atlantic Monthly* about their life during the drought.

PRIMARY SOURCE

"At the little country store, after one of the worst of these storms, the candies in the show case all looked alike and equally brown. Dust to eat and dust to breathe and dust to drink. Dust in the beds and in the flour bin, on dishes and walls and windows, in hair and eyes and ears and teeth and throats. . . ."

—from *Dust to Eat: Drought and Depression in the 1930s*

Some Great Plains farmers managed to hold on to their land, but many had no chance. If their withered fields were mortgaged, they had to turn them over to the banks. Then, nearly penniless, many families headed west, hoping for a better life in California. Because many migrants were from Oklahoma, they became known as "Okies." In California, they lived in roadside camps and remained homeless and impoverished.

✔ Reading Check **Explaining** What chain of events turned the once-fertile Great Plains into the Dust Bowl?

History ONLINE
Student Web Activity Visit glencoe.com and complete the activity on hobo life during the Depression.

Art and Entertainment

MAIN Idea Movies and radio shows were very popular during the 1930s, a period that also produced new art and literature.

HISTORY AND YOU Has a movie ever helped you get through a difficult time? Read to learn ways that people coped with the Great Depression.

The hard times of the 1930s led many Americans to prefer entertainment that let them escape their worries. For this reason, movies and radio plays grew increasingly popular. Also, in the 1930s, comic books grew rapidly in popularity. The first comic books cheered people by reprinting newspaper comics, but in the late 1930s, the "superhero" genre was born with the printing of the first tales of *Superman* in 1938 and *Batman* in 1939.

Hollywood

During the 1930s more than 60 million Americans went to the movies each week. Child stars such as Shirley Temple and Jackie Coogan delighted viewers. Groucho Marx wisecracked while his brothers amused audiences in such films as *Animal Crackers,* and comedies became very popular because they provided a release from daily worries.

King Kong, first released in 1933, showcased new special effects. Moviegoers also loved cartoons. **Walt Disney,** who brought Mickey Mouse to life in 1928, produced the first feature-length animated film, *Snow White and the Seven Dwarfs,* in 1937.

Even serious films were optimistic. In *Mr. Smith Goes to Washington,* Jimmy Stewart played a naïve scout leader who becomes a senator. He exposes the corruption of some of his **colleagues** and calls upon senators to view American government as a high achievement.

In 1939 MGM produced *The Wizard of Oz,* a colorful musical that lifted viewers' spirits. That same year, Vivien Leigh and Clark Gable thrilled audiences in *Gone with the Wind,* a Civil War epic that won nine Academy Awards. Hattie McDaniel, who won the award for Best Supporting Actress, was the first African American to win an Academy Award.

On the Air

While movies captured the imagination, radio offered information and entertainment as near as the living room. Tens of millions of people listened to the radio daily, and radio comedians such as Jack Benny, George Burns, and Gracie Allen were popular, as were the radio adventures of superheroes such as the Green Hornet and the Lone Ranger.

People IN HISTORY

Margaret Bourke-White
1904–1971

While a student at Columbia University, Margaret Bourke-White took a course on photography. She went on to become one of the leading photographers of her time. In 1927 she began photographing architectural and industrial subjects. Her originality led to jobs at major magazines such as *Fortune* and *Life.* During World War II she became the first woman photographer attached to the U.S. armed forces. She covered the Italian campaign and the siege of Moscow. She was among those who photographed concentration camp survivors. Bourke-White traveled to India after the war to document Gandhi's efforts to gain that nation's independence from Great Britain. During the Korean War, she traveled with South Korean troops.

What made Margaret Bourke-White's career and photography unusual for the time?

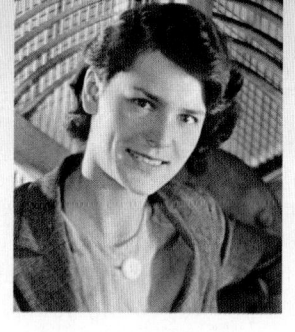

▲ *African American flood victims wait for food and clothing from the Red Cross in 1937 in one of Margaret Bourke-White's most famous photos. The people contrast sharply with the billboard.*

Daytime radio dramas carried over their story lines from day to day. Programs such as *The Guiding Light* presented middle-class families confronting illness, conflict, and other problems. The shows' sponsors were often makers of laundry soaps, so the shows were nicknamed **soap operas.** Radio created a new type of community. Even strangers found common ground in discussing the lives of radio characters.

Literature and Art

Literature and art also flourished during the 1930s. Writers and artists tried to portray life around them, using the homeless and unemployed as their subjects in stories and pictures.

Novelist **John Steinbeck** added flesh and blood to journalists' reports of poverty and misfortune. His writing evoked both sympathy for his characters and indignation at social injustice. In *The Grapes of Wrath* (1939), which was awarded the Pulitzer Prize and was made into a movie, Steinbeck tells the story of the Joad family fleeing the Dust Bowl to find a new life in California after losing their farm. The novel was based on Steinbeck's visits to migrant camps and his interviews with migrant families. In one article he described typical housing for the migrants, for which they paid the growers as much as $2.00 daily:

PRIMARY SOURCE

"[They have] one-room shacks usually about 10 by 12 feet, have no rug, no water, no bed. In one corner there is a little iron wood stove. Water must be carried from the faucet at the end of the street."

—from *Dust to Eat: Drought and Depression*

Other novelists developed new writing techniques. In *The Sound and the Fury,* **William Faulkner,** who later won the Nobel Prize for Literature, shows what his characters are thinking and feeling before they speak. Using this stream of consciousness **technique,** he exposes hidden attitudes of Southern whites and African Americans in a fictional Mississippi county.

Although written words remained powerful, images were growing more influential. Photographers roamed the nation with the new 35-millimeter cameras, seeking new subjects. In 1936, *Time* magazine publisher Henry Luce introduced *Life,* a weekly photojournalism magazine that enjoyed instant success. The striking pictures of photojournalists Dorothea Lange and Margaret Bourke-White showed how the Great Depression had affected average Americans.

Painters in the 1930s included Thomas Hart Benton and **Grant Wood,** whose styles were referred to as the regionalist school. Their work emphasized traditional American values, especially those of the rural Midwest and South. Wood's painting that is best-known today is *American Gothic.* The portrait pays tribute to no-nonsense Midwesterners while gently making fun of their severity.

Reading Check **Examining** What subjects did artists, photographers, and writers emphasize during the 1930s?

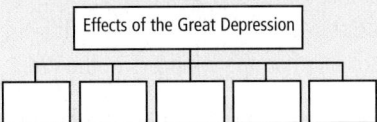

Section 2 REVIEW

Vocabulary

1. **Explain** the significance of: bailiff, hobo, Dust Bowl, Walt Disney, soap opera, John Steinbeck, William Faulkner, Grant Wood.

Main Ideas

2. **Analyzing** What environmental event of the 1930s worsened the Great Depression?

3. **Explaining** How did people try to escape the realities of life during the Great Depression?

Critical Thinking

4. **Big Ideas** How did some Great Plains farmers respond to the loss of their fields to the banks?

5. **Organizing** Use a graphic organizer such as the one below to identify the effects of the Great Depression.

Effects of the Great Depression				

6. **Analyzing Visuals** Look at the photo on page 407. What details indicate that this is a severe dust storm?

Writing About History

7. **Descriptive Writing** Imagine you are writing the catalogue for an art show of photographs by Dorothea Lange or Margaret Bourke-White. Write a paragraph describing one of the images in this section or discussing their photographic skill.

History ONLINE

Study Central™ To review this section, go to glencoe.com and click on Study Central.

GEOGRAPHY & HISTORY

The Dust Bowl

In the late nineteenth century, settlers on the Great Plains turned the semiarid region into the breadbasket of America, growing vast fields of wheat and other crops. Intensive farming destroyed the region's native grasses and loosened the soil. At first, this was not a problem, as the Great Plains experienced higher than normal rainfall in the late 1800s. Over time, however, farmers exhausted the soil. When rainfall began to decline and temperatures rose in the 1920s, the soil began to dry out. In 1932, a full-scale drought hit. The fierce heat dried the exhausted soil into fine dustlike particles. The high winds of the open plains easily lifted the dirt into the air creating "dust storms." In 1932 alone, 14 dust storms struck the Great Plains. These storms carried the soil of the Great Plains hundreds of miles. In May 1934, a huge storm dumped piles of dirt in Chicago. Further east, silt from the storm collected on the windows of the White House.

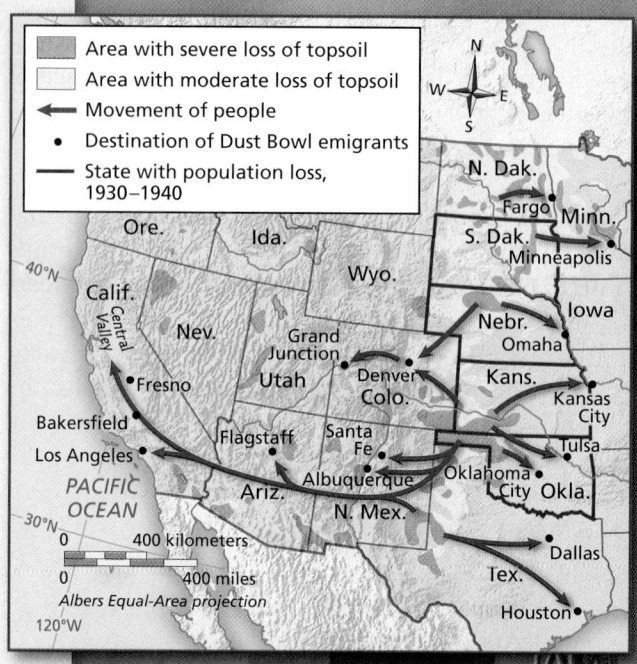

Area with severe loss of topsoil
Area with moderate loss of topsoil
Movement of people
Destination of Dust Bowl emigrants
State with population loss, 1930–1940

How Did the Dust Bowl Affect Americans?

The "Dust Bowl" is sometimes called a human-made natural disaster. The drought and rising temperatures of the 1930s were a natural disaster. But the dust storms were human-made, the result of decades of overcultivation. These "black blizzards" scoured and buried homes, ruined vehicle engines, and diminished visibility. The blowing dirt could injure eyes and damage lungs; it even suffocated people. As the drought destroyed their livelihood, and the dust storms destroyed their belongings, many farmers abandoned the land, packed up their families, and fled the region in search of work elsewhere.

The drought on the Great Plains in the 1930s was the worst ever recorded in U.S. history. Summer temperatures soared above 110 degrees in many locations, setting records that still stand. The lack of water and fierce heat dried the soil to a fine dust. An estimated 200 million acres of land lost some or all of its topsoil.

Analyzing GEOGRAPHY

1. **Movement** Which states lost population in the 1930s? In which direction did most people fleeing the Dust Bowl move?

2. **Human-Environment Interaction** Study the image at right. What problems and dangers does the dust storm create?

Dust storms towered thousands of feet in the air and moved rapidly across the open plains. When a storm hit, it became dark outside, and visibility often dropped to only a few feet.

▲ Many farmers in the Dust Bowl, such as Elmer Thomas and his family of Muskogee, Oklahoma (above), decided to leave the region. Many became migrant workers, traveling from across the west in search of short-term employment.

The fine grit of dust storms could clog car engines and other mechanical devices beyond repair.

People raced for cover when a storm hit. The grit stung the skin and eyes. Breathing the dust could cause dust pneumonia. Many people, especially children and senior citizens, became sick, and many died.

Hoover Responds to the Depression

Guide to Reading

Big Ideas
Government and Society President Hoover's ideas about government shaped his response to the Great Depression, making the government slow to respond.

Content Vocabulary
- public works *(p. 412)*
- relief *(p. 414)*
- foreclose *(p. 415)*

Academic Vocabulary
- series *(p. 412)*
- community *(p. 413)*

People and Events to Identify
- Reconstruction Finance Corporation *(p. 413)*
- Bonus Army *(p. 415)*

Reading Strategy
Categorizing As you read about Herbert Hoover's response to the Depression, create a graphic organizer listing his major initiatives and their results.

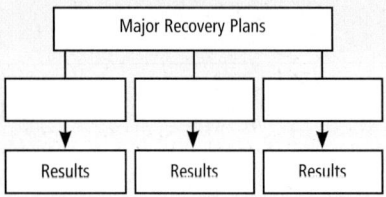

President Hoover tried to fix the economy by providing loans to banks and corporations and by starting public works projects. Later, he reluctantly supported direct aid to impoverished families. By the early 1930s, more Americans were demanding the government's help.

Promoting Recovery

MAIN Idea Hoover encouraged businesses to stop laying off workers and created public works projects.

HISTORY AND YOU What efforts would you have taken to help the economy if you had been president? Read about the public works efforts of the early 1930s.

On Friday, October 25, 1929, the day after Black Thursday, President Herbert Hoover declared that "the fundamental business of the country . . . is on a sound and prosperous basis." On March 7, 1930, he told the press that "the worst effects of the crash upon employment will have passed during the next sixty days." Critics derided his optimism as conditions worsened. Hoover, however, hoped to downplay the public's fears. He wanted to avoid more bank runs and layoffs by urging consumers and business leaders to make rational decisions. In the end, Hoover's efforts failed to inspire the public's confidence, and the economy continued its downward slide.

President Hoover believed that the American system of "rugged individualism" would keep the economy moving. He felt that the government should not step in to help individuals out. After World War I, many European countries had implemented a form of socialism, which Hoover felt contributed to their lack of economic recovery. In 1922 Hoover had written a book, *American Individualism,* which presented arguments for why the American system of individualism was the best social, political, spiritual, and economic system in the world. Thus, it was difficult for Hoover to propose policies that had the government taking more control.

Despite his public statements that the economy was not in trouble, Hoover was worried. To devise strategies for improving the economy, he organized a **series** of conferences, bringing together the heads of banks, railroads, and other big businesses, as well as labor leaders and government officials.

Industry leaders pledged to keep factories open and to stop slashing wages. By 1931, however, they had broken those pledges. Hoover then increased the funding for **public works,** or government-financed building projects. The resulting construction jobs were intended to replace some of those lost in the private sector.

Can Hoover Fight the Depression?

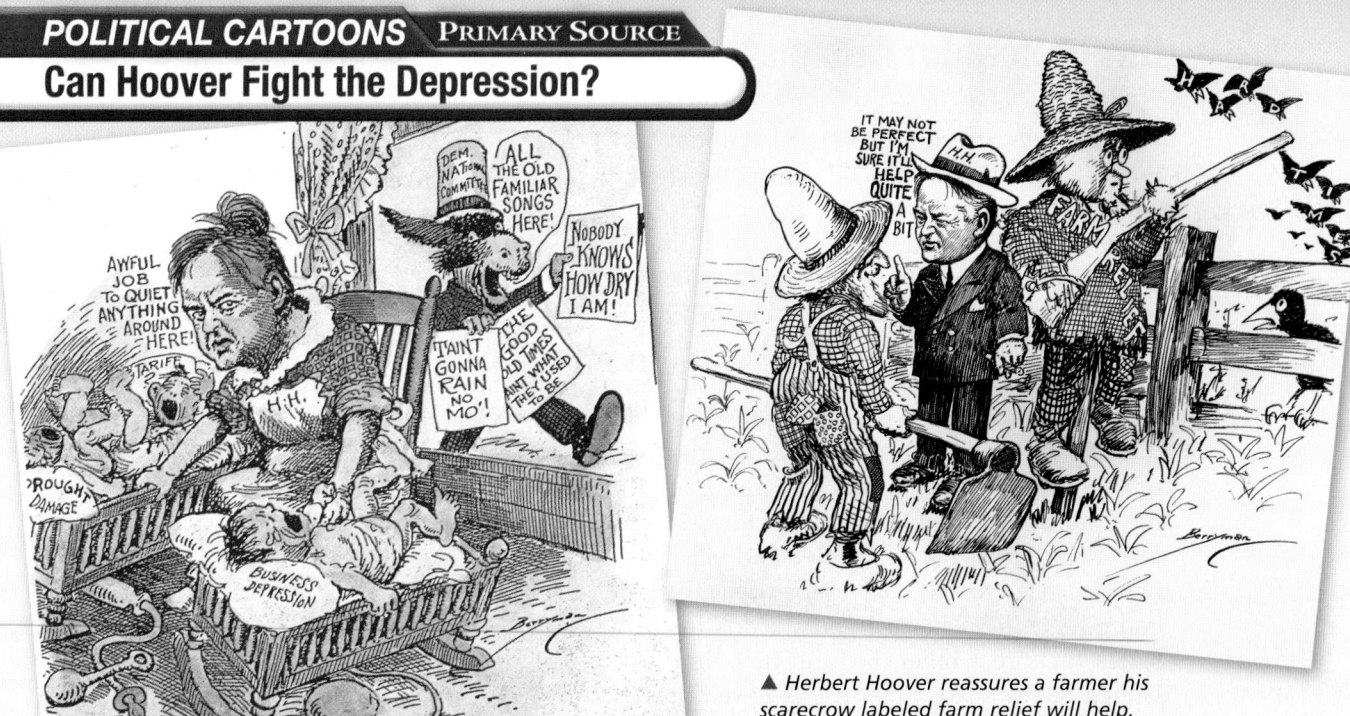

▲ While the Democratic Party donkey marches outside singing old songs, Hoover tries to deal with economic problems caused by high tariffs, depression and drought.

▲ Herbert Hoover reassures a farmer his scarecrow labeled farm relief will help.

Analyzing VISUALS **DBQ**

1. **Analyzing** What does the cartoon on the right suggest about Hoover's plan to help farmers?

2. **Analyzing** How are Hoover and the Democrats portrayed in the cartoon on the left?

Public works projects did create some jobs but for only a small fraction of the millions who were unemployed. The government could create enough new jobs only by massively increasing government spending, which Hoover refused to do.

Someone had to pay for public works projects. If the government raised taxes to pay for them, consumers would have less money to spend, further hurting already struggling businesses. If the government kept taxes low and ran a budget deficit instead—spending more money than it collected in taxes—it would have to borrow the money. Borrowing would mean less money available for businesses to expand and for consumer loans. Hoover feared that deficit spending would actually delay an economic recovery.

As the 1930 congressional elections approached, most Americans felt threatened by rising unemployment. Citizens blamed the party in power for the ailing economy. The Republicans lost 49 seats and their majority in the House of Representatives; they held on to the Senate by a single vote.

Trying to Rescue the Banks

To get the economy growing again, Hoover focused on expanding the money supply. The government, he believed, had to help banks make loans to corporations, which could then expand production and rehire workers.

The president asked the Federal Reserve Board to put more currency into circulation, but the Board refused. In an attempt to ease the money shortage, Hoover set up the National Credit Corporation (NCC) in October 1931. The NCC created a pool of money that allowed troubled banks to continue lending money in their **communities.** This program, however, failed to meet the nation's needs.

In 1932 Hoover requested Congress to set up the **Reconstruction Finance Corporation** (RFC) to make loans to businesses. By early 1932 the RFC had lent about $238 million to approximately 160 banks, 60 railroads, and 18 building-and-loan organizations. The RFC was overly cautious, however. It failed to increase its lending sufficiently to meet the need, and the economy continued its decline.

Direct Help for Citizens

From the start, Hoover strongly opposed the federal government's participation in **relief**—money given directly to impoverished families. He believed that only state and local governments should dole out relief. Any other needs should be met by private charity, not by the federal government. By the spring of 1932, however, state and local governments were running out of money, and private charities lacked the resources to handle the crisis.

That year, political support for a federal relief measure increased, and Congress passed the Emergency Relief and Construction Act in July. Reluctantly, Hoover signed the bill. The new act called for $1.5 billion for public works and $300 million in emergency loans to the states for direct relief. For the first time in United States history, the federal government was supplying direct relief funds, although governors of the states had to apply for the loans. By this time, however, the new program could not reverse the accelerating collapse.

✔ Reading Check **Summarizing** Why did Hoover oppose a federal relief program?

In an Angry Mood

MAIN Idea Farmers, veterans, and others who were suffering grew frustrated and demanded the government do something to help.

HISTORY AND YOU Have you ever felt strongly enough about an issue to take part in a protest? Read what happened when veterans of World War I demonstrated in Washington, D.C., in 1932.

In the months after the Wall Street crash, most Americans were resigned to bad economic news. By 1931, however, many people were becoming increasingly discontent.

Hunger Marches and Protests by Farmers

In January 1931 about 500 residents of Oklahoma City looted a grocery store. Crowds began showing up at rallies and "hunger marches" organized by the American Communist Party. On December 5, 1932, in Washington, D.C., a group of about 1,200 hunger marchers chanted, "Feed the hungry, tax the rich." Police herded them into a cul-de-sac

An Angry Nation

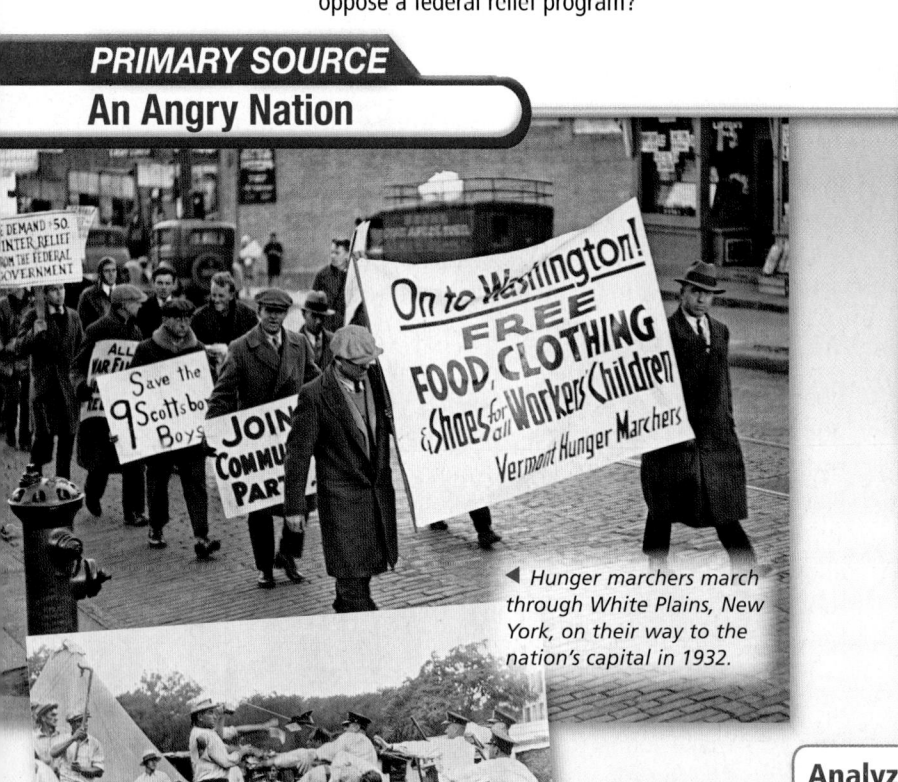

◄ Hunger marchers march through White Plains, New York, on their way to the nation's capital in 1932.

◄ On July 29, 1932, armed guards use tear gas and clubs to move Bonus Army marchers.

▲ Angry at low prices, dairy farmers dump milk in an attempt to drive up prices and draw attention to their problems.

Analyzing VISUALS   DBQ

1. **Analyzing Visuals** What do you observe about the Bonus Army's attempt to defend itself?

2. **Speculating** How do you think poor and hungry people would have responded to the photo at top right?

and denied them food and water, until some members of Congress insisted on the marchers' right to petition their government. They were then permitted to march to Capitol Hill.

The hungry poor were not the only people who began to protest conditions during the Depression. During World War I's agricultural boom, many farmers had heavily mortgaged their land to pay for seed, feed, and equipment. After the war, prices sank so low that farmers began losing money. Creditors **foreclosed** on nearly one million farms between 1930 and 1934, taking ownership of the land and evicting the families. Some farmers began destroying their crops, desperately trying to raise prices by reducing the supply. In Nebraska, farmers burned corn to heat their homes. Georgia dairy farmers blocked highways and stopped milk trucks, dumping the milk into ditches.

The Bonus Marchers

After World War I, Congress had enacted a $1,000 bonus for each veteran, to be distributed in 1945. In 1931 Texas congressman Wright Patman introduced a bill that would authorize early payment of these bonuses. In May 1932 several hundred Oregon veterans began marching to Washington to lobby for passage of the legislation. As they moved east, other veterans joined them until they numbered about 1,000. Wearing ragged military uniforms, they trudged along the highways or rode the rails, singing old war songs. The press termed the marchers the **"Bonus Army."**

Once in Washington, the marchers camped in Hoovervilles. More veterans joined them until the Bonus Army swelled to 15,000. President Hoover acknowledged the veterans' right to petition but refused to meet with them. When the Senate voted down the bonus bill, veterans outside the Capitol began to grumble. Many returned home, but some marchers stayed on. Some squatted in vacant buildings downtown.

In late July, Hoover ordered the buildings cleared. The police tried, but when an officer panicked and fired into a crowd, killing two veterans, the city government called in the army. General Douglas MacArthur ignored Hoover's orders to clear the buildings but to leave the camps alone. MacArthur sent in cavalry, infantry, and tanks to clear the camps.

Soon unarmed veterans were running away, pursued by 700 soldiers. The soldiers tear-gassed stragglers and burned the shacks. National press coverage of troops assaulting veterans further harmed Hoover's reputation and hounded the president throughout the 1932 campaign.

Although Hoover failed to resolve the economic crisis, he did more than any prior president to expand the federal government's economic role. The Reconstruction Finance Corporation was the first federal agency created to stimulate the economy during peacetime. The rout of the Bonus Army marchers and the lingering Depression, however, tarnished Hoover's public image.

✔ Reading Check Evaluating How did Americans react as the Depression continued?

Section 3 REVIEW

Vocabulary

1. **Explain** the significance of: public works, Reconstruction Finance Corporation, relief, foreclose, Bonus Army.

Main Ideas

2. **Identifying** What two major strategies did President Hoover use to promote economic recovery?

3. **Explaining** What did World War I veterans do to try to get their service bonuses early?

Critical Thinking

4. **Big Ideas** How did President Hoover's philosophy of government guide his response to the Depression?

5. **Organizing** Use a graphic organizer similar to the one below to list American reactions to the Great Depression.

American Reactions

6. **Analyzing Visuals** Look at the photo of the Hunger Marchers on page 414. How would you compare their approach and style to protestors today?

Writing About History

7. **Persuasive Writing** Imagine that you are a World War I veteran in 1931. Write a persuasive letter to your congressperson explaining why you need your bonus now, not in 1945.

History ONLINE

Study Central™ To review this section, go to glencoe.com and click on Study Central.

Chapter 11 VISUAL SUMMARY

You can study anywhere, anytime by downloading quizzes and flashcards to your PDA from glencoe.com.

Causes of the Depression

Long-Range Causes

- Uneven distribution of wealth ensures that many consumers do not have enough income to purchase the goods being produced.

- Interest rates are kept too low by the Federal Reserve, which encourages businesses to borrow money and to expand production beyond market demand.

- Overproduction by business eventually floods the market with goods that cannot be sold. Businesses begin laying off workers and shutting down production.

Immediate Causes

- People and businesses borrow money to invest in the stock market; speculation drives stock prices too high and when they collapse, many people lose all of their money, and many banks collapse when loans are not repaid.

- As companies lay off workers, demand for goods falls as workers lack the income to purchase goods being produced. This in turn causes even more layoffs and a cyclical effect sets in, driving up unemployment.

- In order to protect American companies from competition, Congress raises tariffs. When other countries respond in kind, foreign demand for American goods falls, further hurting American companies.

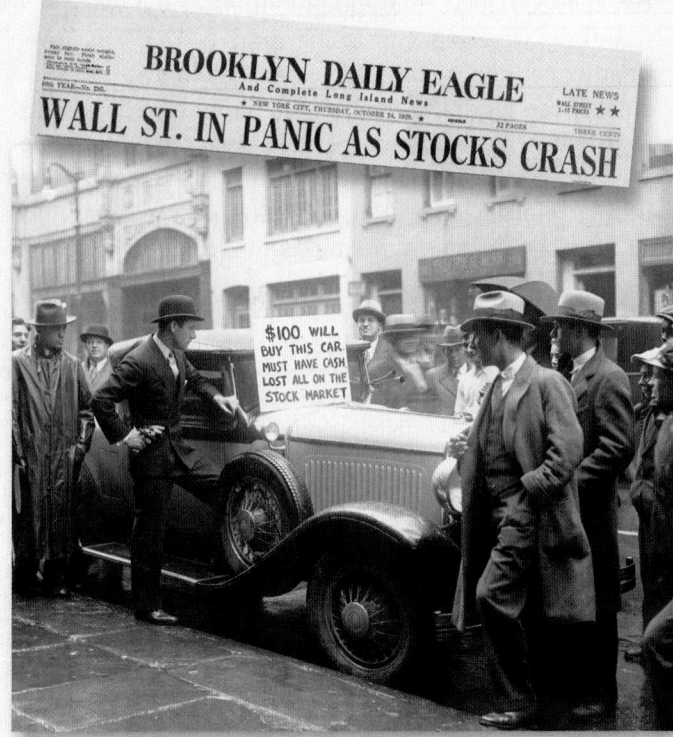

▲ A New York paper trumpets the stock crash. To raise cash to pay their stock debts, people began selling anything of value, including this car.

▲ Shantytowns appeared in many cities during the Depression as homelessness and unemployment rose.

Effects of the Depression

- Unemployment rises to record levels.

- Many people, unable to pay their debts, lose their homes and farms; the homeless create shantytowns, nicknamed Hoovervilles, on the edges of cities.

- Hunger marches, protests by farmers, and marches by veterans seeking their bonuses indicate growing anger among the population at economic conditions.

- The Republican Party rapidly loses political support, enabling the Democrats to take control of Congress.

- The federal government, for the first time, begins providing direct relief to citizens in need.

- Forms of entertainment, including movies, radio shows, and comic books, focus on distracting people from their daily lives.

Reviewing Vocabulary

Directions: Choose the word or words that best complete the sentence.

1. In the late 1920s, many investors engaged in speculation, or purchasing stock

 A after considering a company's earnings and profits.

 B and quickly selling the stock for a profit.

 C by borrowing money from a stockbroker.

 D to invest long-term in the future of the company.

2. The Democratic Party's first Roman Catholic candidate for president was

 A Alfred E. Smith.

 B Franklin Delano Roosevelt.

 C Herbert Hoover.

 D Calvin Coolidge.

3. A _____ most often traveled by hopping a railroad car.

 A photographer

 B journalist

 C novelist

 D hobo

4. Which popular radio style of the 1930s gained its description from its sponsor?

 A *Amos 'n' Andy*

 B soap operas

 C *Animal Crackers*

 D *American Gothic*

5. President Hoover opposed _____, or giving money directly to needy families.

 A foreclosure

 B relief

 C public works

 D unionization

Reviewing Main Ideas

Directions: Choose the best answers to the following questions.

Section 1 *(pp. 400–405)*

6. One of the major problems with the stock market in the late 1920s was the number of people who bought stocks

 A on margin, with borrowed money.

 B in companies that they supported.

 C only after carefully studying a company's history.

 D without knowing their stockbroker's reputation.

7. Which of the following was a root cause of the Great Depression?

 A prohibiting the sale of alcohol

 B giving women the right to vote

 C uneven distribution of income

 D the end of federal control of banks

8. Herbert Hoover won the 1928 election in a landslide, in part because of

 A fears of another world war.

 B prosperity under Calvin Coolidge.

 C having been vice president.

 D his support for unions.

Section 2 *(pp. 406–409)*

9. Drought and _____ brought about the conditions that caused the Dust Bowl.

 A overgrazing at large cattle farms

 B the near-extinction of the buffalo

 C famine

 D poor farming practices

TEST-TAKING

If you are not sure of the answer, try to narrow the options. First, eliminate any choices that you know are clearly wrong. Then, if necessary, make a guess among the remaining choices.

Need Extra Help?									
If You Missed Questions . . .	1	2	3	4	5	6	7	8	9
Go to Page . . .	401	400	406	409	414	400–401	404–405	400	407

10. The people who lost their homes in the Great Depression sometimes lived

   A in shantytowns.

   B in roadside motels.

   C on the lawn of the U.S. Capitol.

   D in public libraries opened to them.

11. Despite the poverty of the 1930s, more than 60 million people went to the movies weekly. Why were movies so popular?

   A The special effects used in movies then were amazing.

   B People could not get over the fact that actors talked.

   C Movies offered an escape from viewers' hard lives.

   D Theaters were air conditioned and offered free popcorn.

Section 3 *(pp. 412–415)*

12. Hoover was slow to respond to the economic crisis because he opposed

   A all public works projects.

   B deficit spending.

   C investing in stocks.

   D private charities.

13. How did American citizens respond to the Great Depression in the 1930 midterm election?

   A by reelecting Hoover

   B by electing socialist candidates

   C by staying away from the polls

   D by electing Democrats

14. What was Hoover's response to the Bonus Army marchers who came to Washington, D.C.?

   A He ordered them to be paid their bonuses.

   B He had the army remove them.

   C He visited them and listened to them.

   D He set up soup kitchens to feed them.

Critical Thinking

Base your answers to questions 15 and 16 on the map below and on your knowledge of Chapter 11.

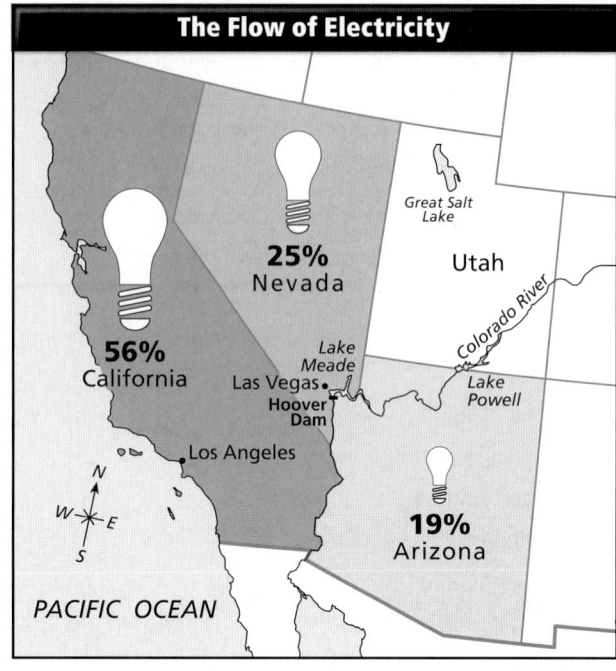

The Flow of Electricity

Directions: Choose the best answers to the following questions.

15. The federal government began building Hoover Dam in 1931. What body of water was it designed to control?

   A the Pacific Ocean

   B Lake Powell

   C the Great Salt Lake

   D the Colorado River

16. Which state benefited most from the hydroelectric power of Hoover Dam?

   A Utah

   B California

   C Nevada

   D Arizona

Need Extra Help?							
If You Missed Questions . . .	10	11	12	13	14	15	16
Go to Page . . .	406	408–409	413	413	415	R15	R15

GO ON

17. Why did writers such as John Steinbeck use fiction to draw attention to the Great Depression?

A Readers could be sympathetic to the characters' situations.

B Writing fiction meant the authors didn't have to do any research.

C Nonfiction sales had dropped during the 1920s.

D Publishers weren't interested in true accounts of national events.

Analyze the cartoon and answer the question that follows. Base your answer on the cartoon and on your knowledge of Chapter 11.

18. What does the cartoon reveal about the character?

A The man was careless with his money.

B He saved his money so it would be there in hard times but lost it through no fault of his own.

C The man should have purchased stocks and bonds rather than put his money in the bank.

D The man should be more prepared by storing his money under his mattress.

Document-Based Questions

Directions: Analyze the document and answer the short-answer questions that follow the document.

Gordon Parks, who later became a famous photographer, was a young man when the stock market crashed in 1929:

> "The newspapers were full of it, and I read everything I could get my hands on, gathering in the full meaning of such terms as Black Thursday, deflation and depression. I couldn't imagine such financial disaster touching my small world; it surely concerned only the rich. But by the first week of November I too knew differently; along with millions of others across the nation, I was without a job. All that next week I searched for any kind of work that would prevent my leaving school. Again it was, 'We're firing, not hiring.' 'Sorry, sonny, nothing doing here.' Finally, on the seventh of November I went to school and cleaned out my locker, knowing it was impossible to stay on. A piercing chill was in the air as I walked back to the rooming house. The hawk had come. I could already feel his wings shadowing me."
>
> —from *A Choice of Weapons*

19. Why did Parks at first think he was safe from the effects of the stock market crash? What changed his mind?

20. Why do you think Parks used the image of a hawk to express his feelings about the Great Depression?

Extended Response

21. Write an essay that analyzes the following quote from John Steinbeck's novel *The Grapes of Wrath*. "If you're in trouble or hurt or need—go to poor people. They're the only ones that'll help." Based on your knowledge of the Great Depression, indicate whether you believe the quote to be true or false and why. Support your answer with relevant facts and details.

For additional test practice, use Self-Check Quizzes—Chapter 11 at glencoe.com.

Need Extra Help?					
If You Missed Questions . . .	17	18	19	20	21
Go to Page . . .	409	R18	419	R19	406–409

Chapter 12

Roosevelt and the New Deal

1933–1941

SECTION 1 The First New Deal

SECTION 2 The Second New Deal

SECTION 3 The New Deal Coalition

During the 1932 presidential campaign, New York governor Franklin D. Roosevelt greets a coal miner in West Virginia.

NRA
MEMBER
U.S.
WE DO OUR PART

U.S. PRESIDENTS			
Hoover 1929–1933	Franklin D. Roosevelt 1933–1945		

1933
- Unemployment peaks at 24.9%
- FDR's "100 Days" results in 9 new federal programs

1934
- Securities and Exchange Commission is created

1935
- Social Security Act and Wagner Act are passed
- Supreme Court strikes down NIRA

U.S. EVENTS

WORLD EVENTS

1931   1933   1935

1933
- Hitler becomes German chancellor
- World Economic Conference fails to reduce tariffs

1935
- Hitler denounces Treaty of Versailles
- Canada creates minimum wage and unemployment insurance

🔊 **Chapter Audio**

MAKING CONNECTIONS

Can Government Fix the Economy?

During the 1930s, New Deal programs increased government regulation of banking, industry, and farming; gave greater rights to workers; and provided government aid to the unemployed and senior citizens.

- *What kind of problems do you think government can solve?*

- *What difficulties can result when the government tries to regulate the economy?*

FOLDABLES™

Analyzing Long-Term Effects Make a Folded Chart Foldable showing major New Deal programs and their long-term effects. In one column, describe the program's original purpose. In the second column, identify how those programs still influence government and society today.

New Deal Measures	Purpose in the 1930s	Effects Today
Social Security		
National Labor Relations Board		
Federal Deposit Insurance Corporation		

1936
- "Court-packing" plan creates controversy

1937
- Sit-down strikes force General Motors to recognize UAW

1938
- Fair Labor Standards Act sets minimum wage and 40-hour workweek

1937 — 1939

1936
- Wave of sit-down strikes in France leads to 40-hour workweek
- Spanish Civil War begins

1938
- Germany annexes Austria
- Mexico takes control of U.S. oil companies in Mexico

1939
- World War II begins

History ONLINE Visit glencoe.com and enter *QuickPass*™ code TAVMT5147c12 for Chapter 12 resources.

The First New Deal

Franklin Delano Roosevelt was elected president in 1932, following his promise of a "new deal" for Americans. In his first 100 days in office, he let loose a flood of legislation designed to rescue banks, industry, and agriculture and provide jobs for the unemployed.

Roosevelt's Rise to Power

MAIN Idea Franklin D. Roosevelt was governor of New York when he was elected president in 1932, promising a New Deal for the American people.

HISTORY AND YOU Do you believe your past experiences can make you stronger? Read how FDR's experiences helped prepare him to be president.

A distant cousin of Theodore Roosevelt, Franklin Delano Roosevelt grew up in Hyde Park, New York. In his youth he learned to hunt, ride horses, and sail; he also developed a lifelong commitment to conservation and a love of rural America. Roosevelt was educated at Harvard and Columbia Law School. While at Harvard, he became friends with Theodore Roosevelt's niece Eleanor, whom he later married.

Intensely competitive, Roosevelt liked to be in control. He also liked being around people. His charming personality, deep rich voice, and wide smile expressed confidence and optimism. In short, his personality seemed made for a life in politics.

Roosevelt began his political career in 1910, when he was elected to the New York State Senate. Three years later, having earned a reputation as a progressive reformer, he became assistant secretary of the navy in the Wilson administration. In 1920 his reputation (and famous surname) helped him win the vice presidential nomination on the unsuccessful Democratic ticket.

After losing the election, Roosevelt temporarily withdrew from politics. The next year he caught the dreaded paralyzing disease **polio.** Although there was no cure, Roosevelt refused to give in. He began a vigorous exercise program to restore muscle control. Eventually, by wearing heavy steel braces on his legs, he was able to walk short distances by leaning on a cane and someone's arm and swinging his legs forward from his hips.

While recovering from polio, Roosevelt depended on his wife and his aide Louis Howe to keep his name prominent in the New York Democratic Party. Eleanor Roosevelt became an effective public speaker, and her efforts kept her husband's political career alive.

By the mid-1920s, Roosevelt was again active in the Democratic Party. In 1928 he ran for governor of New York. He campaigned hard

March 4, 1933

"This is preeminently the time to speak the truth, the whole truth, frankly and boldly. Nor need we shrink from honestly facing conditions in our country today. This great Nation will endure as it has endured, will revive and will prosper. So, first of all, let me assert my firm belief that the only thing we have to fear is fear itself—nameless, unreasoning, unjustified terror which paralyzes needed efforts to convert retreat into advance.

. . . Restoration calls, however, not for changes in ethics alone. This Nation asks for action, and action now.

. . . Our greatest primary task is to put people to work. This is no unsolvable problem if we face it wisely and courageously. It can be accomplished in part by direct recruiting by the Government itself, treating the task as we would treat the emergency of a war.

. . . Action in this image and to this end is feasible under the form of government which we have inherited from our ancestors. Our Constitution is so simple and practical that it is possible always to meet extraordinary needs by changes in emphasis and arrangement without loss of essential form.

We do not distrust the future of essential democracy. The people of the United States have not failed. In their need they have registered a mandate that they want direct, vigorous action."

—from *The Public Papers and Addresses of Franklin D. Roosevelt*

▲ *Franklin Roosevelt delivers his First Inaugural Address.*

DBQ Document-Based Questions

1. **Analyzing Primary Sources** Why does Roosevelt think that "nameless, unreasoning, unjustified terror" is such a big problem?

2. **Identifying Central Issues** What unspoken fear does Roosevelt address in the final two paragraphs?

---

to demonstrate that his illness had not slowed him down, and he narrowly won the election. Two years later he was reelected in a landslide. As governor, Roosevelt oversaw the creation of the first state relief agency to aid the unemployed.

Roosevelt's popularity in New York paved the way for his presidential nomination in 1932. Americans saw in him an energy and optimism that gave them hope despite the tough economic times. After Roosevelt became president, his serenity and confidence amazed people. When one aide commented on his attitude, Roosevelt replied, "If you had spent two years in bed trying to wiggle your big toe, after that anything else would seem easy."

In mid-June 1932, with the country deep in the Depression, Republicans gathered in Chicago and nominated Herbert Hoover to run for a second term as president. Later that month, the Democrats also held their national convention in Chicago. When Roosevelt won the nomination, he broke with tradition by flying to Chicago to accept it in person. His speech set the tone for his campaign:

PRIMARY SOURCE

"Let it be from now on the task of our Party to break foolish traditions. . . . It is inevitable that the main issue of this campaign should revolve about . . . a depression so deep that it is without precedent. . . . Republican leaders not only have failed in material things, they have failed in national vision, because in disaster they have held out no hope. . . . I pledge you, I pledge myself, to a new deal for the American people."

—from *The Public Papers and Addresses of Franklin D. Roosevelt*

From that point forward, Roosevelt's policies for ending the Depression became known as the **New Deal.** Roosevelt's confidence that he could make things better contrasted sharply with Herbert Hoover's **apparent** failure to do anything effective. On Election Day, Roosevelt won in a landslide, receiving the electoral vote of all but six states.

✔ Reading Check) **Interpreting** What events in Roosevelt's life shaped his ideas and character?

The Hundred Days

MAIN Idea Upon taking office, FDR launched the New Deal by sending 15 major pieces of legislation to Congress.

HISTORY AND YOU Do you remember reading about the "New Nationalism" and "New Freedom"? Read how those ideas influenced New Deal legislation.

Although Roosevelt won the presidency in November 1932, the country's unemployed and homeless had to endure another winter as they waited for his inauguration on March 4, 1933. All through the winter, unemployment continued to rise and bank runs increased, further threatening the banking system.

Some of the bank runs occurred because people feared that Roosevelt would abandon the **gold standard** and reduce the value of the dollar in order to fight the Depression. Under the gold standard, one ounce of gold equaled a set number of dollars. To reduce the value of the dollar, the United States would have to stop exchanging dollars for gold. Many Americans, and many foreign investors with deposits in American banks, decided to take their money out of the banks and convert it to gold before it lost its value.

Across the nation, people stood in long lines with paper bags and suitcases, waiting to withdraw their money from banks. By March 1933, more than 4,000 banks had collapsed, wiping out nine million savings accounts. In 38 states, governors declared **bank holidays**—closing the remaining banks before bank runs could put them out of business.

By the day of Roosevelt's inauguration, most of the nation's banks were closed. One in four workers was unemployed. The economy seemed paralyzed. Roosevelt knew he had to restore the nation's confidence. "First of all," the president declared in his Inaugural Address, "let me assert my firm belief that the only thing we have to fear is fear itself. . . . This nation asks for action, and action now!"

The New Deal Begins

Roosevelt and his advisers, sometimes called the "brain trust," came into office bursting with ideas about how to end the Depression. Roosevelt had no clear agenda, nor did he have a strong political **ideology.** The previous spring, during his campaign for the presidential nomination, Roosevelt had revealed the approach he would take as president. "The country needs," Roosevelt explained, "bold, persistent experimentation . . . . Above all, try something."

The new president began to send bill after bill to Congress. Between March 9 and June 16, 1933—which came to be called the **Hundred Days**—Congress passed 15 major acts to resolve the economic crisis, setting a pace for new legislation that has never been equaled. Together, these programs made up what would later be called the First New Deal.

A Divided Administration

To generate new ideas and programs, Roosevelt deliberately chose advisers who disagreed with each other. He wanted to hear many different points of view, and by setting his advisers against one another, Roosevelt ensured that he alone made the final decision on what policies to pursue.

Despite their disagreements, Roosevelt's advisers generally favored some form of government intervention in the economy—although they disagreed over what the government's role should be.

One influential group during the early years of Roosevelt's administration supported the "New Nationalism" of Theodore Roosevelt. These advisers believed that if government agencies worked with businesses to regulate wages, prices, and production, they could lift the economy out of the Depression.

A second group of Roosevelt's advisers went even further. They distrusted big business and blamed business leaders for causing the Depression. These advisers wanted government planners to run key parts of the economy.

A third group in Roosevelt's administration supported the "New Freedom" of Woodrow Wilson. These advisers wanted Roosevelt to support "trust busting" by breaking up big companies and allowing competition to set wages, prices, and production levels. They also thought the government should impose regulations to keep economic competition fair.

Reading Check **Summarizing** What ideas did Roosevelt's advisers support?

Eleanor Roosevelt
1884–1962

Orphaned at age 10, Eleanor Roosevelt was raised by relatives and later attended boarding school in England. When she returned home as a young woman, she devoted time to a settlement house on Manhattan's Lower East Side. During this time, she became engaged to Franklin D. Roosevelt, a distant cousin. They were married in 1905. At their wedding, Eleanor's uncle, President Theodore Roosevelt, gave her away.

During FDR's presidency, Eleanor Roosevelt transformed the role of First Lady. Rather than restricting herself to traditional hostess functions, she became an important figure in his administration. She traveled extensively, toured factories and coal mines, and met with factory workers and farmers. She then told her husband what people were thinking. In doing so, she became FDR's "eyes and ears" when his disability made travel difficult.

Eleanor was also a strong supporter of civil rights and prodded her husband to stop discrimination in New Deal programs. When the Daughters of the American Revolution barred African American singer Marian Anderson from performing in its auditorium, Eleanor intervened and arranged for Anderson to perform at the Lincoln Memorial instead.

After FDR's death, Eleanor remained politically active. She continued to write her syndicated newspaper column, "My Day," which she began in 1936, and became a delegate to the United Nations where she helped draft the Universal Declaration of Human Rights.

How might Franklin Roosevelt's political career have been different if Eleanor had not been his wife?

▲ In this 1935 photo, Eleanor Roosevelt speaks to Geraldine Walker, a five-year-old from Detroit, Michigan, as slums in that city were about to be cleared.

Banks and Debt Relief

MAIN Idea President Roosevelt took steps to strengthen banks and the stock market and to help farmers and homeowners keep their property.

HISTORY AND YOU Have you ever watched a presidential address? Read about Roosevelt's "fireside chats" and how they encouraged optimism that the economy would get better.

As the debate over policies and programs swirled around him, President Roosevelt took office with one thing clear in his mind. Very few of the proposed solutions would work as long as the nation's banks remained closed. The first thing he had to do was restore confidence in the banking system.

On his very first night in office, Roosevelt told Secretary of the Treasury William H. Woodin that he wanted an emergency banking bill ready for Congress in less than five days. The following afternoon, Roosevelt declared a national bank holiday, temporarily closing all banks, and called Congress into a special session scheduled to begin on March 9, 1933.

When Congress convened, the House of Representatives unanimously passed the Emergency Banking Relief Act after only 38 minutes of debate. The Senate approved the bill that evening, and Roosevelt signed it into law shortly afterward. The new law required federal examiners to survey the nation's banks and issue Treasury Department licenses to those that were financially sound.

On March 12 President Roosevelt addressed the nation by radio. Sixty million people listened to this first of many "**fireside chats,**" direct talks in which Roosevelt let the American people know what he was trying to accomplish. He told people that their money would be secure if they put it back into the banks: "I assure you that it is safer to keep your money in a reopened bank than under the mattress." When banks opened the day after the speech, deposits far outweighed withdrawals. The banking crisis was over.

The FDIC and SEC

Although President Roosevelt had restored confidence in the banking system, many of his advisers urged him to go further. They pushed for new regulations for both banks and the stock market. Roosevelt agreed with their ideas and supported the Securities Act of 1933 and the Glass-Steagall Banking Act.

The Securities Act required companies that sold stocks and bonds to provide complete and truthful information to investors. The following year, Congress created a government agency, the Securities and Exchange Commission (SEC), to regulate the stock market and prevent fraud.

The Glass-Steagall Act separated commercial banking from investment banking. Commercial banks handle everyday transactions. They take deposits, pay interest, cash checks, and lend money for mortgages. Under the Glass-Steagall Act, these banks were no longer allowed to risk depositors' money by using it to speculate on the stock market.

To further protect depositors, the Glass-Steagall Act also created the Federal Deposit Insurance Corporation (FDIC) to provide government insurance for bank deposits up to a certain amount. By protecting depositors in this way, the FDIC greatly increased public confidence in the banking system.

Mortgage and Debt Relief

While some of Roosevelt's advisers believed low prices had caused the Depression, others believed that debt was the main obstacle to economic recovery. With incomes falling, people had to use most of their money to pay their debts and had little left over to buy goods or services. Many Americans, terrified of losing their homes and farms, cut back on their spending to make sure they could pay their mortgages. Roosevelt responded to the crisis by introducing several policies intended to assist Americans with their debts.

The Home Owners' Loan Corporation To help homeowners make their mortgage payments, Roosevelt asked Congress to establish the Home Owners' Loan Corporation (HOLC). The HOLC bought the mortgages of many

THE First Hundred Days

March 9
Roosevelt signs the Emergency Banking Relief Act and 3 days later delivers his first fireside chat

▲ Farmers in Texas receive their AAA checks.

May 12
The Agricultural Adjustment Act is signed, and farmers soon begin receiving payments to destroy their crops in an effort to push up prices

April 1933   **May 1933**

March 31
The Civilian Conservation Corps is created and soon afterward begins hiring 3 million young men to work in the nation's forests

May 12
The Federal Emergency Relief Administration begins making grants to states to help the unemployed

homeowners who were behind in their payments. It then restructured them with longer terms of repayment and lower interest rates. Roughly 10 percent of homeowners received HOLC loans.

The HOLC did not help everyone. It made loans only to homeowners who were not farm owners and who were still employed. When people lost their jobs and could no longer make their mortgage payments, the HOLC foreclosed on their property, just as a bank would have done. Between 1933 and 1936, the three years during which it functioned as a loan source, the HOLC made loans to cover one million mortgages—one out of every ten in the United States.

The Farm Credit Administration Three days after Congress authorized the creation of the HOLC, it authorized the Farm Credit Administration (FCA) to help farmers refinance their mortgages. Over the next seven months, the FCA lent four times as much money to farmers as the entire banking system had the year before. It was also able to push interest rates substantially lower. These loans saved millions of farms from foreclosure.

Although FCA loans helped many farmers in the short term, their long-term value can be questioned. FCA loans helped less efficient farmers keep their land, but giving loans to poor farmers meant that the money was not available to lend to more efficient businesses in the economy. Although FCA loans may have slowed the overall economic recovery, they did help many desperate and impoverished people hold onto their land.

✔ Reading Check **Explaining** How did the government restore confidence in the banking system?

▲ *Workers of the Grand Coulee Dam in Washington.*

May 18
Congress creates the Tennessee Valley Authority

June 13
The Home Owners' Loan Corporation is authorized to make low interest mortgage loans to homeowners

June 16
The Public Works Administration is created. Under the leadership of Harold Ickes, it begins spending over $3 billion on public works such as new highways, dams, and public buildings. The agency begins spending.

June 1933

June 16
The National Recovery Administration is authorized to begin setting codes and regulations for industry

Analyzing TIME LINES

1. **Analyzing** What groups of people were targeted for help in the first hundred days of Roosevelt's first term?
2. **Drawing Conclusions** What was Roosevelt's first act after becoming president? Why do you think he chose this as a first step?

Farms and Industry

MAIN Idea New Deal legislation tried to raise crop prices and stabilize industry.

HISTORY AND YOU Can you think of a product that gets more expensive when less of it is available? Read to learn how some New Deal programs tried to raise prices.

Many of Roosevelt's advisers believed that both farmers and businesses were suffering because prices were too low and production too high. Several advisers believed competition was inefficient and bad for the economy. They favored creating federal agencies to manage the economy.

The AAA

To further help the nation's farmers, Secretary of Agriculture Henry Wallace drafted the Agricultural Adjustment Act. President Roosevelt asked Congress to pass the act. This legislation was based on a simple idea—that prices for farm goods were low because farmers grew too much food. Under Roosevelt's program, the government would pay some farmers *not* to raise certain livestock, and *not* to grow certain crops. Some farmers were also asked *not* to produce dairy products. As the program went into effect, farmers slaughtered 6 million piglets and 200,000 sows and plowed under 10 million acres of cotton—all in an effort to raise prices. The program was administered by the Agricultural Adjustment Administration (AAA).

Over the next two years, farmers withdrew millions more acres from cultivation and received more than $1 billion in support payments. The program accomplished its goal: the farm surplus fell greatly by 1936. Food prices then rose, as did total farm income, which quickly increased by more than 50 percent.

In a nation caught in a Depression, however, raising food prices drew harsh criticism. Furthermore, not all farmers benefited. Large commercial farmers who concentrated on one crop profited more than smaller farmers who raised several products. Worse, thousands of poor tenant farmers, many of them African Americans, became homeless and jobless when landlords took their fields out of production.

PAST & PRESENT

The TVA

The Tennessee Valley Authority (TVA) was a New Deal project that produced visible benefits. The TVA built dams to control floods, conserve forest lands, and bring electricity to rural areas.

Today, TVA power facilities include 17,000 miles of transmission lines, 29 hydroelectric dams, 11 fossil-fuel plants, 4 combustion-turbine plants, 3 nuclear power plants, and a pumped-storage facility. These combine to bring power to nearly 8 million people in a seven-state region.

Since 1998, the TVA has been working to reduce air pollution. Projects are designed to cut harmful emissions released into the air. The TVA is committed to developing programs that protect the environment.

The TVA, 1940

Legend:
- Area served by TVA
- Major dam
- Power plant

0   100 kilometers
0   100 miles
Albers Equal-Area projection

The NRA

The government turned its attention to manufacturing in June 1933, when Roosevelt and Congress enacted the National Industrial Recovery Act (NIRA). The NIRA suspended antitrust laws and allowed business, labor, and government to cooperate in setting up voluntary rules for each industry.

These rules were known as codes of fair competition. Some codes set prices, established minimum wages, and limited factories to two shifts per day so that production could be spread to as many firms as possible. Other codes shortened workers' hours, with the goal of creating additional jobs. Another provision in the law guaranteed workers the right to form unions. The codes also helped businesses develop codes of fair competition within industries.

Under the leadership of Hugh Johnson, the National Recovery Administration (NRA) ran the entire program. Business owners who signed code agreements received signs displaying the National Recovery Administration's symbol—a blue eagle—and the slogan, "We Do Our Part." The NRA had limited power to enforce the codes, but urged consumers to buy goods only from companies that displayed the blue eagle.

The NRA did revive a few American industries, but its gains proved short-lived. Small companies complained, justifiably, that large corporations wrote the codes to favor themselves. American employers disliked codes that gave workers the right to form unions and bargain collectively over wages and hours. They also argued that paying high minimum wages forced them to charge higher prices to cover their costs.

The codes were also difficult to administer, and business leaders often ignored them. Furthermore, businesses could choose not to sign code agreements and thus not be bound by their rules. It became obvious that the NRA was failing when industrial production actually fell after the organization was established. By the time the Supreme Court declared the NRA unconstitutional in 1935, it had already lost much of its political support.

✔ Reading Check **Examining** What were the goals of the Agricultural Adjustment Act and the National Industrial Recovery Act?

2006

▲ *This photo shows the completed Cherokee Hydroelectric Dam.*

▲ *Tennessee's Cherokee Dam is today part of the TVA. Workers (upper right) built it in the late 1930s.*

MAKING CONNECTIONS

1. **Listing** Look at the map on the previous page. What states other than Tennessee benefited from the TVA projects?

2. **Examining** Where were most of the projects located?

Maps In MOtion See *StudentWorks™ Plus* or glencoe.com.

Relief Programs

MAIN Idea Programs such as the CCC, the PWA, and the WPA provided jobs for some unemployed workers.

HISTORY AND YOU Do you know who built your school, post office, or playground? Read about the projects completed by the New Deal workers.

History ONLINE
Student Skill Activity To learn how to use a word processor, visit glencoe.com and complete the Skill activity.

While many of President Roosevelt's advisers emphasized tinkering with prices and providing debt relief to solve the Depression, others maintained that its **fundamental** cause was low consumption. They thought getting money into the hands of needy individuals would be the fastest remedy. Because neither Roosevelt nor his advisers wanted simply to give money to the unemployed, they supported work programs for the unemployed.

The CCC

The most highly praised New Deal work relief program was the **Civilian Conservation Corps** (CCC). The CCC offered unemployed young men 18 to 25 years old the opportunity to work under the direction of the forestry service planting trees, fighting forest fires, and building reservoirs. To prevent a repeat of the Dust Bowl, the workers planted a line of more than 200 million trees, known as a Shelter Belt, from north Texas to North Dakota.

The young men lived in camps near their work areas and earned $30 a month, $25 of which was sent directly to their families. The average CCC worker returned home after six to twelve months, better nourished and with greater self-respect. CCC programs also taught more than 40,000 of its recruits to read and write. By the time the CCC closed down in 1942, it had put 3 million young men to work outdoors—including 80,000 Native Americans, who helped to reclaim land they had once owned. After a second Bonus Army March on Washington in 1933, Roosevelt added some 250,000 veterans to the CCC as well.

FERA and the PWA

A few weeks after authorizing the CCC, Congress established the Federal Emergency Relief Administration (FERA). Roosevelt chose

---

POLITICAL CARTOONS · PRIMARY SOURCE
Did the New Deal Help Americans?

▲ This cartoon, entitled "How Much More Do We Need?" shows Uncle Sam grasping New Deal lifesavers to stay afloat.

▶ This 1935 cartoon shows FDR as a doctor with a variety of medicines to help ailing Uncle Sam.

Analyzing VISUALS — DBQ

1. **Interpeting** In the cartoon at the left, what is happening to the dock, and why?

2. **Analyzing** With whom is President Roosevelt conferring in the cartoon at right?

Harry Hopkins, a former social worker, to run the agency. FERA did not initially create projects for the unemployed. Instead, it channeled money to state and local agencies to fund their relief projects.

Half an hour after meeting with Roosevelt to discuss his new job, Hopkins set up a desk in the hallway outside of his office. In the next two hours, he spent $5 million on relief projects. When critics charged that some of the projects did not make sense in the long run, Hopkins replied, "People don't eat in the long run—they eat every day."

In June 1933 Congress authorized another relief agency, the Public Works Administration (PWA). One-third of the nation's unemployed were in the construction industry. To put them back to work, the PWA began building highways, dams, sewer systems, schools, and other government facilities. In most cases, the PWA did not hire workers directly but instead awarded contracts to construction companies. By insisting that contractors not discriminate against African Americans, the agency broke down some of the long-standing racial barriers in the construction trades.

The CWA

By the fall of 1933 neither FERA nor the PWA had reduced unemployment significantly. Hopkins realized that unless the federal government acted quickly, a huge number of unemployed citizens would be in severe distress once winter began. After Hopkins explained the situation, President Roosevelt authorized him to set up the Civil Works Administration (CWA).

Unlike the PWA, the CWA hired workers directly. That winter the CWA employed 4 million people, including 300,000 women. Under Hopkins's direction, the agency built or improved 1,000 airports, 500,000 miles of roads, 40,000 school buildings, and 3,500 playgrounds and parks. The cost of the CWA was huge—the program spent nearly $1 billion in just five months.

Although the CWA helped many people get through the winter, President Roosevelt was alarmed by how quickly the agency was spending money. He did not want Americans to get used to the federal government providing them with jobs. Warning that the CWA would "become a habit with the country," Roosevelt insisted that it be shut down the following spring.

Success of the First New Deal

During his first year in office, Roosevelt convinced Congress to pass an astonishing array of legislation. The programs enacted during the first New Deal did not restore prosperity, but they reflected Roosevelt's zeal for action and his willingness to experiment. Banks were reopened, many more people retained their homes and farms, and more people were employed. Perhaps the most important result of the first New Deal was a noticeable change in the spirit of the American people. Roosevelt's actions had inspired hope and restored Americans' faith in their nation.

✔ Reading Check Identifying What types of projects did public works programs undertake?

Section 1 REVIEW

Vocabulary

1. **Explain** the significance of: polio, New Deal, gold standard, bank holiday, Hundred Days, fireside chats, Civilian Conservation Corps.

Main Ideas

2. **Describing** What actions did Roosevelt take during the Hundred Days?

3. **Explaining** How did government regulate banks and the stock market in the first Roosevelt administration?

4. **Interpreting** How did the AAA affect farm prices?

5. **Organizing** Use a graphic organizer to list the major organizations of the First New Deal.

Roosevelt's New Agencies

Critical Thinking

6. **Big Ideas** In what ways did FDR's early experiences shape his political ideology?

7. **Analyzing Charts** Look at the time line on pages 426–427. How did the various agencies listed change the role of government?

Writing About History

8. **Expository Writing** Interview a member of your community who lived during the Great Depression. How did the New Deal programs affect your community? Create a one-page report using a word processor to summarize your findings.

History ONLINE

Study Central™ To review this section, go to glencoe.com and click on Study Central.

ANALYZING PRIMARY SOURCES

The First New Deal

When FDR took office in 1933, the economy had been getting worse for more than three years. During the first one hundred days of his presidency, he oversaw 15 major pieces of legislation that attempted to revive the nation's economy and provide relief to the unemployed. Never before had the federal government intervened so directly in the economy. Key to stopping the economic downslide was FDR's ability to inspire confidence that the nation's economic problems could be solved.

Study these primary sources and answer the questions that follow.

PRIMARY SOURCE 1

Inaugural Address, 1933

"I am certain that my fellow Americans expect that on my induction into the Presidency I will address them with a candor and a decision which the present situation of our nation impels. This is pre-eminently the time to speak the truth, the whole truth, frankly and boldly. . . .

"So, first of all, let me assert my firm belief that the only thing we have to fear is fear itself—nameless, unreasoning, unjustified terror which paralyzes needed efforts to convert retreat into advance. In every dark hour of our national life a leadership of frankness and vigor has met with that understanding and support of the people themselves which is essential to victory. I am convinced that you will again give that support to leadership in these critical days. . . .

"This Nation asks for action, and action now.

"Our greatest primary task is to put people to work. This is no unsolvable problem if we face it wisely and courageously. It can be accomplished in part by direct recruiting by the Government itself, treating the task as we would treat the emergency of a war, but at the same time, through this employment, accomplishing greatly needed projects to stimulate and reorganize the use of our natural resources."

—President Franklin D. Roosevelt, first inaugural address, delivered March 4, 1933

Excerpted from *The Public Papers and Addresses of Franklin D. Roosevelt*

PRIMARY SOURCE 2

Oral History Interview

"During the whole '33 one-hundred days' Congress, people didn't know what was going on, the public. Couldn't understand these things that were being passed so fast. They knew something was happening, something good for them. They began investing and working and hoping again. . . .

"A Depression is much like a run on a bank. It's a crisis of confidence. People panic and grab their money."

—Raymond Moley, original member of FDR's "brains trust"

Excerpted from *Hard Times: An Oral History of the Great Depression (1970)*

PRIMARY SOURCE 3

Magazine Cover, 1933

▶ *"The Faces of Victory and Defeat," portrayal of Herbert Hoover and Roosevelt on inauguration day, March 4, 1933*

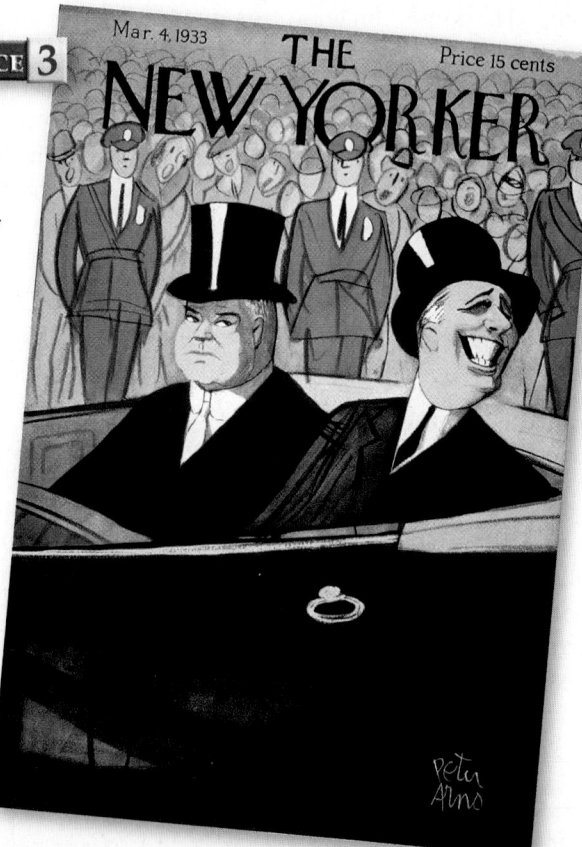

PRIMARY SOURCE 4

New Deal poster for the CCC, c. 1935 ▼

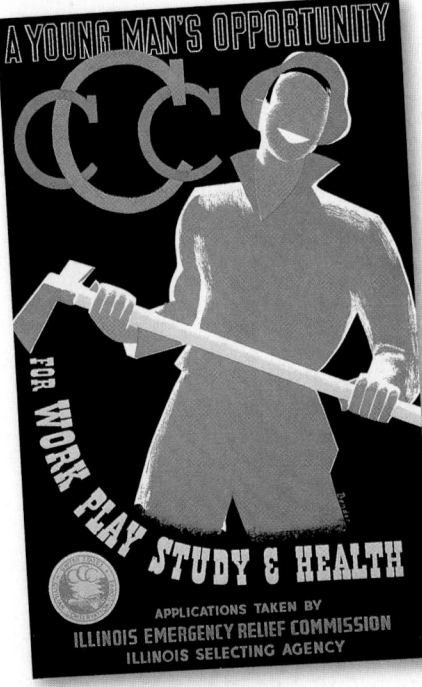

PRIMARY SOURCE 5

Oral History Interview

"What Roosevelt and the New Deal did was to turn about and face the realities. . . . A hundred years from now, when historians look back on it, they will say a big corner was turned. People agreed that old things didn't work. What ran through the whole New Deal was finding a way to make things work.

"Before that, Hoover would loan money to farmers to keep their mules alive, but wouldn't loan money to keep their children alive. This was perfectly right within the framework of classical thinking. If an individual couldn't get enough to eat, it was because he wasn't on the ball. It was his responsibility. The New Deal said: Anybody who is unemployed isn't necessarily unemployed because he's shiftless."

—Economist Gardiner C. Means, economic adviser in the Roosevelt administration

Excerpted from *Hard Times: An Oral History of the Great Depression* (1970)

PRIMARY SOURCE 7

Political Cartoon, 1933

▶ *President Roosevelt tries to "prime" the economic pump with government spending.*

PRIMARY SOURCE 6

Contemporary Book, 1934

"Even if the government conduct of business could give us the maximum of efficiency instead of least efficiency, it would be purchased at the cost of freedom. It would increase rather than decrease abuse and corruption, stifle initiative and invention, undermine the development of leadership, cripple the mental and spiritual energies of our people and the forces which make progress."

—Former president Herbert Hoover in his book, *The Challenge to Liberty* (1934)

Excerpted from *The Era of Franklin D. Roosevelt, 1933–1945*

DBQ Document-Based Questions

1. **Evaluating** What themes did Roosevelt emphasize in his inaugural address? How would you have responded to this speech if you had been an unemployed worker?

2. **Explaining** Study Sources 2 and 3. How did FDR inspire confidence and optimism? What effect did this have on the economy?

3. **Describing** In Source 4, the poster highlights four opportunities offered by the CCC. Describe some specific ways the CCC provided such opportunities.

4. **Paraphrasing** In Source 5, how does the author define Roosevelt's attitude toward unemployment and Hoover's approach to unemployment?

5. **Evaluating** In Source 6, why does Herbert Hoover object to the New Deal? What programs do you think he found most objectionable?

6. **Speculating** Study the picture in Source 7. How does the artist feel about the New Deal? What symbols are used to convey that message?

The Second New Deal

In response to criticisms of the New Deal, President Roosevelt introduced several major pieces of legislation in 1935. These laws created the Works Progress Administration, the National Labor Relations Board, and the Social Security Administration.

Launching the Second New Deal

MAIN Idea By 1935, the New Deal faced political and legal challenges, as well as growing concern that it was not ending the Depression.

HISTORY AND YOU Do you know anyone who can easily convince others to follow his or her ideas? Read about several people who used this power against Roosevelt and his New Deal policies.

Harry Hopkins, head of the Federal Emergency Relief Administration, worked long hours in his Washington office, a bare, dingy room with exposed water pipes. Hopkins also took to the road to explain the New Deal. Once in Iowa, where he was discussing spending programs, someone called out, "Who's going to pay for it?" Hopkins peeled off his jacket, loosened his tie, and rolled up his sleeves, before roaring his response: "You are!"

President Roosevelt appreciated Harry Hopkins's feistiness. He needed effective speakers who were willing to contend with his adversaries. Although Roosevelt had been tremendously popular during his first two years in office, opposition to his policies had begun to grow.

The economy had shown only a slight improvement, even though the New Deal had been in effect for two years. Although the programs had created more than 2 million new jobs, more than 10 million workers remained unemployed, and the nation's total income was about half of what it had been in 1929.

Criticism From Left and Right

Hostility toward Roosevelt came from both the political right and the left. People on the right generally believed the New Deal regulated business too tightly. The right wing also included many Southern Democrats who believed the New Deal had expanded the federal government's power at the expense of states' rights.

The right wing, which had opposed the New Deal from the beginning, increased that opposition by late 1934. To pay for his programs, Roosevelt had started **deficit spending,** abandoning a balanced budget and borrowing money. Many business leaders became greatly alarmed at the government's growing deficit.

Opposition to the New Deal

By 1935 some Americans had grown impatient with the New Deal economic recovery. They believed that the reforms did not go far enough and called for wider-ranging change.

THE TOWNSEND PLAN
$200. PER MONTH FOR THOSE OVER 60 YRS OF AGE -THE SPENDING OF THIS MONEY WILL PUT THE CONTROL OF CREDIT IN THE HANDS OF THE PEOPLE- PREVENTING ECONOMIC CHAOS

◀ Dr. Francis Townsend explains his ideas to offer pensions to business leaders at a 1936 luncheon in Philadelphia.

▶ Huey Long, who served Louisiana in the U.S. Senate, looked for ways to redistribute wealth.

▲ Father Coughlin speaks to a crowd of 6,000 members of the National Union for Social Justice at the Hippodrome in Detroit shortly after the stock market collapse in 1929. By the mid-1930s, Coughlin favored massive taxes.

Analyzing VISUALS

1. **Comparing and Contrasting** What strikes you as the same and different about these three men?
2. **Assessing** Which man do you think would have the largest audience, and why?

In August 1934 business leaders and anti–New Deal politicians from both parties joined together to create the **American Liberty League.** Its purpose was to organize opposition to the New Deal and "teach the necessity of respect for the rights of person and property."

While criticisms from the right threatened to split the Democratic Party and reduce business support for Roosevelt, another serious challenge to the New Deal came from the political left. People on the left believed Roosevelt had not gone far enough. They wanted even more dramatic government economic intervention to shift wealth from the rich to middle-income and poor Americans.

Huey Long Perhaps the most serious threat came from Huey Long of Louisiana. As governor of Louisiana, Long had championed the poor and downtrodden. He had improved schools, colleges, and hospitals, and built roads and bridges. These **benefits** made Long popular, enabling him to build a powerful—but corrupt—political machine. In 1930 Long was elected to the U.S. Senate.

Long's attacks on the rich were popular in the midst of the Great Depression. He captivated audiences with folksy humor and fiery oratory. By 1934, he had established a national organization, the Share Our Wealth Society, to promote his plan for massive redistribution of wealth. Long announced he would run for president in 1936.

Father Coughlin Roosevelt also faced a challenge from Father Charles Coughlin, a Catholic priest in Detroit. About 30 to 45 million listeners heard his weekly radio show.

Originally an ardent New Deal supporter, Coughlin had become impatient with its moderate reforms. He called instead for inflating the currency and nationalizing the banking system. In 1935 Coughlin organized the National Union for Social Justice, which some Democrats feared would become a new political party.

History ONLINE
Student Web Activity Visit glencoe.com and complete the activity on the New Deal.

The Townsend Plan A third challenge came from Francis Townsend, a California physician. Townsend proposed that the federal government pay citizens over age 60 a pension of $200 a month. Recipients would have to retire and spend their entire pension check each month. He believed the plan would increase spending and remove people from the workforce, freeing up jobs for the unemployed.

Townsend's proposal attracted millions of supporters, especially among older Americans, who mobilized as a political force for the first time. Townsend's program was particularly popular in the West. When combined with Long's support in the Midwest and South, and Coughlin's support among urban Catholics in the Northeast, Roosevelt faced the possibility of a coalition that would draw enough votes to prevent his reelection.

The WPA

Roosevelt was also disturbed by the failure of the New Deal to generate a rapid economic recovery. In 1935 he launched a series of programs now known as the Second New Deal.

Among these new programs was the **Works Progress Administration** (WPA). Headed by Harry Hopkins, the WPA was the largest public works program of the New Deal. Between 1935 and 1941, the WPA spent $11 billion. Its 8.5 million workers constructed about 650,000 miles of highways, roads, and streets, 125,000 public buildings, and more than 8,000 parks. It built or improved more than 124,000 bridges and 853 airports.

The WPA's most controversial program was Federal Number One, a program for artists, musicians, theater people, and writers. The artists created thousands of murals and sculptures for public buildings. Musicians established 30 symphony orchestras, as well as hundreds of smaller musical groups. The Federal Theater Project **financed** playwrights, actors, and directors. It also funded writers who recorded the stories of former slaves and others whose voices were not often heard.

The Supreme Court's Role

In May 1935, in *Schechter Poultry Company* v. *United States*, the Supreme Court unanimously struck down the authority of the National Recovery Administration. The Schechter broth-

ers had been convicted of violating the NRA's poultry code.

The Court ruled that the Constitution did not allow Congress to delegate its legislative powers to the executive branch. Thus, it declared the NRA's codes unconstitutional. Although relieved to be rid of that "awful headache," the NRA, Roosevelt still worried about the ruling. It suggested that the Court could strike down the rest of the New Deal.

Roosevelt knew he needed a new series of programs to keep voters' support. He called congressional leaders to a White House conference. Pounding his desk, he thundered that Congress could not go home until it passed his new bills. That summer, Congress worked busily to pass Roosevelt's programs.

✔ Reading Check **Identifying Points of View** What criticisms prompted the Second New Deal?

Debates IN HISTORY

Was the New Deal Socialistic?

Franklin Roosevelt took extraordinary measures to stimulate the economy with his New Deal programs. Many Americans were divided on the issue of increased government intervention in the economy. Some claimed the New Deal was socialistic and a violation of American values. Others thought the New Deal did not do enough to help Americans.

Reforms for Workers and Senior Citizens

MAIN Idea Roosevelt asked Congress to pass the Wagner Act and Social Security to build support among workers and older Americans.

HISTORY AND YOU Do you have an older relative who has retired from his or her job? Read about benefits created by the Social Security Act.

When the Supreme Court struck down the NRA, it also invalidated the section of the NIRA that gave workers the right to organize. President Roosevelt and the Democrats in Congress knew that the working-class vote was very important in winning reelection in 1936. They also believed that unions could help end the Depression. They thought that high union wages would give workers more money to spend, **thereby** boosting the economy. Opponents disagreed, arguing that high wages forced companies to charge higher prices and hire fewer people. Despite these concerns, Congress pushed ahead with new labor legislation.

The Wagner Act

In July 1935 Congress passed the National Labor Relations Act (also called the Wagner Act after its author, Senator Robert Wagner of New York). The act guaranteed workers the right to organize unions and to bargain collectively. It also set up the **National Labor Relations Board** (NLRB), which organized factory elections by secret ballot to determine whether workers wanted a union.

YES

Alfred E. Smith
Former Democratic Candidate

PRIMARY SOURCE

"Now what would I have my party do? I would have them re-declare the principles that they put forth in that 1932 platform [reduce the size of government, balance the federal budget] . . .

Just get the platform of the Democratic party and get the platform of the Socialist party and . . . make your mind up to pick up the platform that more nearly squares with the record, and you will have your hand on the Socialist platform. . . .

[I]t is all right with me, if they want to disguise themselves as Karl Marx or Lenin or any of the rest of that bunch, but I won't stand for their allowing them to march under the banner of Jackson or Cleveland."
—speech delivered January 25, 1936

NO

Norman Thomas
Socialist Party Candidate

PRIMARY SOURCE

"All of these leaders or would-be leaders out of our wilderness, however they may abuse one another, however loosely they may fling around the charge of socialism or communism—still accept the basic institutions and loyalties of the present system. A true Socialist is resolved to replace that system. . . .

The New Deal did not say, as socialism would have said, 'Here are so many millions of American people who need to be well fed and well clothed. How much food and cotton do we require?' We should require more, not less. What Mr. Roosevelt said was 'How much food and cotton can be produced for which the exploited masses must pay a higher price?'"
—speech delivered February 2, 1936

DBQ Document-Based Questions

1. **Distinguishing Fact From Opinion** Compare Smith's attack on the New Deal with what you have read about it elsewhere. Does he make any valid points?

2. **Contrasting** According to Thomas, how are the principles of the New Deal and those of the Socialist Party different?

3. **Evaluating** Which speaker do you find more persuasive? Why?

4. **Hypothesizing** Do you think either speaker would be able to persuade someone who did not agree with him to reconsider his or her attitudes?

The Wagner Act also set up a process called **binding arbitration** whereby dissatisfied union members could take their complaints to a neutral party who would listen to both sides and decide on the issues. The NLRB could investigate employers' actions and stop unfair practices, such as spying on workers.

The CIO Is Formed The Wagner Act led to a burst of labor activity. John L. Lewis led the United Mine Workers union. He worked with several other unions to organize industrial workers. They formed the Committee for Industrial Organization (CIO) in 1935.

The CIO set out to organize unions that included all workers, skilled and unskilled, in a particular industry. It focused first on the automobile and steel industries—two of the largest industries in which workers were not yet unionized.

Sit-Down Strikes Union organizers used new tactics, such as the **sit-down strike,** in which employees stopped work inside the factory and refused to leave. (This technique prevented management from sending in replacement workers.) First used effectively to organize rubber workers, the sit-down strike became a common CIO tactic for several years.

The United Auto Workers (UAW), a CIO union, initiated a series of sit-down strikes against General Motors. On December 31, 1936, the workers at General Motor's plant in Flint, Michigan, began a sit-down strike. The UAW strikers held the factory for weeks, while spouses, friends, and other supporters passed them food and other provisions through windows. A journalist who was allowed to enter the plant reported on conditions in the factory:

PRIMARY SOURCE

"Beds were made up on the floor of each car, the seats being removed if necessary. . . . I could not see—and I looked for it carefully—the slightest damage done anywhere to the General Motors Corporation. The nearly completed car bodies, for example, were as clean as they would be in the salesroom, their glass and metal shining."

—quoted in *The Great Depression*

Violence broke out in Flint when police launched a tear gas assault on one of the plants. The police wounded 13 strikers, but the strike held. On February 11, 1937, the company gave in and recognized the UAW as its employees' sole bargaining agent. The UAW became one of the most powerful unions in the United States.

PRIMARY SOURCE
The CIO Uses Sit-Down Strikes

▲ *Sit-down strikers at the GM Fisher Body plant in Flint, Michigan, take over the plant on December 30, 1936. Their action led to a national strike that lasted until February 11, 1937.*

Union Membership, 1933–1940

Members (thousands): 10,000 / 8,000 / 6,000 / 4,000 / 2,000 / 0

1933 1934 1935 1936 1937 1938 1939 1940

Source: *Historical Statistics of the United States.*

Analyzing VISUALS

1. **Analyzing** How can you tell from the men's appearance and activities that they intend to stay?

2. **Summarizing** When did union membership increase the most? How can you account for this jump?

U.S. Steel, the nation's largest steel producer and a long-standing opponent of unionizing, decided it did not want to repeat the General Motors experience. In March 1937 the company recognized the CIO's steelworkers union. Smaller steel producers did not follow suit and suffered bitter strikes. By 1941, however, the steelworkers union had won contracts throughout the industry.

In the late 1930s, workers in other industries worked hard to gain union recognition from their employers. Union membership tripled from roughly 3 million in 1933 to about 9 million in 1939. In 1938 the CIO changed its name to the **Congress of Industrial Organizations** and became a federation of industrial unions.

Social Security

After passing the Wagner Act, Congress began work on one of America's most important pieces of legislation. This was the **Social Security Act.** Its major goal was to provide some security for older Americans and unemployed workers.

Roosevelt and his advisers spent months preparing the bill, which they viewed primarily as an insurance measure. Workers earned the right to receive benefits because they paid premiums, just as they did in buying a life insurance policy. The premiums were a tax paid to the federal government. The legislation also provided modest welfare payments to other needy people, including those with disabilities and poor mothers with dependent children.

The core of Social Security was the monthly retirement benefit, which people could collect when they stopped working at age 65. Another important benefit, unemployment insurance, supplied a temporary income to unemployed workers looking for new jobs. Some critics did not like the fact that the money came from payroll taxes imposed on workers and employers, but to Roosevelt these taxes were crucial: "We put those payroll contributions there so as to give the contributors a legal, moral, and political right to collect their pensions and their unemployment benefits."

Since the people receiving benefits had already paid for them, he explained, "no . . . politician can ever scrap my social security program." What Roosevelt did not anticipate was that, in the future, Congress would borrow money from the Social Security fund to pay for other programs while failing to raise payroll deductions enough to pay for the benefits.

Although Social Security helped many people, initially it left out many of the neediest—farm and domestic workers. Some 65 percent of all African American workers in the 1930s fell into these two categories. Nevertheless, Social Security established the principle that the federal government should be responsible for those who, through no fault of their own, were unable to work.

Reading Check **Explaining** How did the Social Security Act protect workers?

Section 2 REVIEW

Vocabulary

1. **Explain** the significance of: deficit spending, American Liberty League, Works Progress Administration, National Labor Relations Board, binding arbitration, sit-down strike, Congress of Industrial Organizations, Social Security Act.

Main Ideas

2. **Summarizing** How did the ideas of Father Coughlin, Senator Long, and Dr. Townsend differ?

3. **Analyzing** Why was the Social Security Act an important piece of legislation?

Critical Thinking

4. **Big Ideas** How did the New Deal contribute to the growth of industrial unions?

5. **Organizing** Use a graphic organizer similar to the one below to list the political challenges Roosevelt faced in his first term.

Political Challenges

6. **Analyzing Visuals** Look again at the photo of Dr. Townsend on page 435. How does he intend to prevent economic chaos?

Writing About History

7. **Persuasive Writing** Choose one of the figures who criticized the New Deal. Write an editorial to the local newspaper expressing why people should be in favor of or opposed to that person's ideas.

History ONLINE

Study Central™ To review this section, go to glencoe.com and click on Study Central.

The New Deal Coalition

Guide to Reading

Big Ideas
Group Action Backed by a new coalition of voters FDR easily won reelection, but conservative opposition prevented the passage of additional reforms.

Content Vocabulary
• court-packing (p. 442)
• broker state (p. 445)
• safety net (p. 445)

Academic Vocabulary
• recovery (p. 442)
• mediate (p. 445)

People and Events to Identify
• Frances Perkins (p. 441)
• Henry Morgenthau (p. 442)
• John Maynard Keynes (p. 442)

Reading Strategy
Taking Notes As you read, create an outline similar to the one below.

The New Deal Coalition
I. Roosevelt's Second Term
   A.
   B.
   C.
II.
   A.
   B.

President Roosevelt won a landslide reelection victory in 1936. Early in his second term, however, his court-packing plan and a new recession hurt him politically. The Fair Labor Standards Act, the last significant piece of New Deal legislation, provided new protections for workers.

Roosevelt's Second Term

MAIN Idea Roosevelt was easily reelected, but the New Deal lost momentum during his second term due to his court-packing plan and a new recession.

HISTORY AND YOU Does your family rent or own your home? Read how the New Deal started programs that tried to make home ownership more affordable.

Since the Civil War, African Americans had been reliable Republican voters. The Republican Party was the party of both Abraham Lincoln and emancipation. In the 1930s, however, this allegiance unraveled. The Great Depression had hit African Americans hard, and the Republican Party had done little to help. To many African Americans, it seemed their votes were taken for granted. That was certainly the sentiment of Robert L. Vann, editor of the *Pittsburgh Courier,* Pennsylvania's leading African American newspaper. Vann decided it was time for a change and started a campaign to persuade African Americans to join the Democratic Party. "My friends, go turn Lincoln's picture to the wall," he told audiences. "That debt has been paid in full."

The dramatic shift in party allegiance by African Americans was part of a historic political realignment the New Deal triggered. As the election of 1936 approached, millions of voters owed their jobs, mortgages, and bank accounts to the New Deal, and they knew it.

The white South, which had been the core of the Democratic Party, now became just one part of a new coalition that included farmers, industrial workers, African Americans, new immigrants, ethnic minorities, women, progressives, and intellectuals. First Lady Eleanor Roosevelt helped bring about the change in the African American and women's vote. She had demonstrated strong sympathies toward African Americans in her many tours of the country. She recounted her experiences to her husband and persuaded him to address at least some of their problems in his New Deal programs.

African Americans made some modest gains during the New Deal. The president appointed several African Americans to positions in his administration, where they informally became known as the Black Cabinet. FDR also tried to see that public works projects included African Americans.

Building the New Deal Coalition

By creating programs that addressed the needs of different groups in American society, the New Deal created a new voting coalition: African Americans, women, and laborers.

▲ **New Deal Raises African American Hopes**
Mary McLeod Bethune, shown with Eleanor Roosevelt, was appointed in 1936 as director of the Office of Minority Affairs within the National Youth Association. Bethune became the first black woman to head a federal agency. Roosevelt also relied on an informal advisory group, the "Black Cabinet," also known as the "Black Brain Trust." FDR failed in some areas of civil rights, such as not opposing poll taxes for fear of causing Southern Democrats to block New Deal programs.

▲ **Appealing to Women and Workers**
The appointment of Secretary of Labor Frances Perkins, shown surveying work on the Golden Gate Bridge in 1935, was one example of Roosevelt's effort to bring women voters into the New Deal coalition. Perkins headed the team that designed the Social Security program and the Fair Labor Standards Act. Social Security, along with the New Deal's labor programs, helped bring many workers into the New Deal coalition.

Analyzing VISUALS

1. **Analyzing** Look at the photo of Frances Perkins and the workers. What clues do you get that she took her job seriously?
2. **Evaluating** What mood does the photograph of Mary McLeod Bethune and Eleanor Roosevelt convey?

▲ **A New Deal for Native Americans**
Commissioner of Indian Affairs John Collier, shown here consulting with Native American leaders in South Dakota, helped create the Indian Reorganization Act of 1934. The act reversed the Dawes Act's policy of assimilation. It restored some reservation lands, gave Native Americans control over those lands, and permitted them to elect their own governments.

A similar policy guided FDR's approach to women. He appointed the first woman to a cabinet post, Secretary of Labor **Frances Perkins,** and appointed many other women to lower-level posts. He also appointed two female diplomats and a female federal judge. Despite these gains, New Deal programs paid women lower wages than men.

The Election of 1936

To challenge President Roosevelt's reelection bid, the Republicans nominated Alfred Landon, the governor of Kansas. Although Landon favored some New Deal policies, he declared it was time "to unshackle initiative and free the spirit of American enterprise." Landon was unable to convince the majority of American voters it was time for a change. Roosevelt and the New Deal that he represented remained very popular, and on Election Day, Roosevelt swept to victory in one of the largest landslides in American history. He won more than 60 percent of the popular vote and carried every state except Maine and Vermont.

The Court-Packing Plan

Although many people supported the New Deal, the Supreme Court saw things differently. In January 1936, in *United States* v. *Butler,* the Court had declared the Agricultural Adjustment Act unconstitutional. With cases pending on Social Security and the Wagner Act, it was possible that the Court would strike down most of the major New Deal programs.

Roosevelt was furious that a handful of jurists, "nine old men" as he called them, were blocking the wishes of a majority of the people. After winning reelection, he decided to try to change the political balance on the Court. In March 1937 he sent Congress a bill to increase the number of justices. It proposed that if any justice had served for 10 years and did not retire within six months after reaching the age of 70, the president could appoint an additional justice to the Court. Since four justices were in their 70s and two more were in their late 60s, the bill, if passed, would allow Roosevelt to quickly appoint as many as six new justices.

The **court-packing** plan, as the press called it, was Roosevelt's first serious political mistake. Although Congress had the power to change the Court's size, the scheme created the impression that the president was trying to undermine the Court's independence.

The issue split the Democratic Party. Many Southern Democrats feared Roosevelt's plan would put justices on the Court who would overturn segregation. At the same time, African American leaders worried that once Roosevelt set the precedent of changing the Court's makeup, a future president might pack the Court with justices opposed to civil rights. Many Americans believed the plan would give the president too much power.

Despite the uproar, Roosevelt's actions appeared to force the Supreme Court to back down. In April 1937, the Court upheld the constitutionality of the Wagner Act by a vote of 5-4 in the case *National Labor Relations Board* v. *Jones and Laughlin Steel Corporation.* In May the Court narrowly upheld the Social Security Act in *Steward Machine Company* v. *Davis.* Shortly afterward, a conservative justice resigned, enabling Roosevelt to appoint a New Deal supporter to the Court.

In mid-July the Senate quietly killed the court-packing bill without bringing it to a vote.

Roosevelt achieved his goal of changing the Court's view of the New Deal. The fight over the court-packing plan, however, hurt his reputation and encouraged conservative Democrats to work with Republicans to block any further New Deal proposals.

The Recession of 1937

In late 1937 Roosevelt's reputation again suffered when unemployment suddenly surged. Early in the year, the economy had seemed on the verge of full **recovery.** Industrial output was almost back to pre-Depression levels, and many people believed the worst was over. Roosevelt decided it was time to balance the budget. Concerned about the dangers of too much debt, Roosevelt ordered the WPA and the PWA to be cut significantly. Unfortunately, Roosevelt cut spending just as the first Social Security payroll taxes removed $2 billion from the economy, which plummeted. By the end of 1937, about 2 million people had been thrown out of work.

The recession of 1937 led to a debate inside Roosevelt's administration. Treasury Secretary **Henry Morgenthau** favored balancing the budget and cutting spending. This would encourage business leaders to invest in the economy. Harry Hopkins, head of the WPA, and Harold Ickes, head of the PWA, both disagreed. They pushed for more government spending using a new theory called Keynesianism to support their arguments.

Keynesianism was based on the theories of an influential British economist named **John Maynard Keynes.** In 1936 Keynes published a book arguing that government should spend heavily in a recession, even if it required deficit spending, to jump-start the economy.

According to Keynesian economics, Roosevelt had done the wrong thing when he cut back programs in 1937. At first, Roosevelt was reluctant to begin deficit spending again. Many critics believed the recession proved the public was becoming too dependent on government spending. Finally, in the spring of 1938, with no recovery in sight, Roosevelt asked Congress for $3.75 billion for the PWA, the WPA, and other programs.

Reading Check **Summarizing** What events weakened Roosevelt's reputation in 1937?

ANALYZING SUPREME COURT CASES

Can Government Regulate Business?

★ *Schechter Poultry v. United States* (1935)

★ *NLRB v. Jones & Laughlin Steel Corp.* (1937)

Background to the Cases

These two cases look at the federal government's right to regulate interstate commerce. In the *Schechter* case, the Court overturned the NIRA and the industrial codes that regulated business. In the *Jones & Laughlin* case, Chief Justice Hughes switched sides from the *Schechter* case and upheld the Wagner Act's labor regulations. The case marks the Supreme Court's shift toward upholding New Deal legislation.

How the Court Ruled

Both cases addressed the question of federal power to regulate interstate commerce. In the *Schechter* case, the Court ruled that the federal government could regulate only business activity that was *directly* related to interstate commerce. In the *NLRB* case, the Court extended congressional power to regulate commerce and upheld the constitutionality of the Wagner Act.

▲ In this 1937 cartoon, the donkey, a symbol of the Democratic Party, kicks up a storm and the dove of peace flies off, dropping the olive branch, in response to FDR's court-packing plan.

PRIMARY SOURCE

The Court's Opinion

"The persons employed in slaughtering and selling in local trade are not employed in interstate commerce. Their hours and wages have no direct relation to interstate commerce. The question of how many hours these employees should work and what they should be paid differs in no essential respect from similar questions in other local businesses which handle commodities brought into a state and there dealt in as a part of its internal commerce. . . .

On both the grounds we have discussed, the attempted delegation of legislative power and the attempted regulation of intrastate transactions which affect interstate commerce only indirectly, we hold the code provisions here in question to be invalid."

—Chief Justice Charles E. Hughes
writing for the Court in *Schechter* v. *U.S.*

PRIMARY SOURCE

Dissenting Views

"The fundamental principle is that the power to regulate commerce is the power to enact 'all appropriate legislation' for its 'protection or advancement' . . . Although activities may be intrastate in character when separately considered, if they have such a close and substantial relation to interstate commerce that their control is essential or appropriate to protect that commerce from burdens and obstructions, Congress cannot be denied the power to exercise that control.

When industries organize themselves on a national scale . . . . how can it be maintained that their industrial labor relations constitute a forbidden field into which Congress may not enter when it is necessary to protect interstate commerce from the paralyzing consequences of industrial war?"

—Chief Justice Charles E. Hughes
writing for the Court in *NLRB* v. *Jones & Laughlin Steel Corporation*

DBQ Document-Based Questions

1. **Explaining** In *Schechter,* why does the Court assert that poultry workers are not engaged in interstate commerce?

2. **Analyzing** In the *NLRB* decision, how has the Court's reasoning changed?

3. **Drawing Conclusions** How would you explain the shift in the Court's attitude toward federal labor regulations?

The New Deal Ends

MAIN Idea The New Deal expanded federal power over the economy and established a social safety net.

HISTORY AND YOU Do you think the government should help those in need? Read how people felt about the government as the New Deal came to an end.

In his second Inaugural Address, Roosevelt had pointed out that despite the nation's progress in climbing out of the Depression, many Americans were still poor:

PRIMARY SOURCE

"I see one-third of a nation ill-housed, ill-clad, ill-nourished. . . . The test of our progress is not whether we add more to the abundance of those who have much; it is whether we provide enough for those who have too little."

—from *The Public Papers and Addresses of Franklin D. Roosevelt*

The Last New Deal Reforms

One of the president's goals for his second term was to provide better housing for the nation's poor. Eleanor Roosevelt, who had toured poverty-stricken Appalachia and the rural South, strongly urged the president to do something. Roosevelt responded with the National Housing Act, establishing the United States Housing Authority. This organization received $500 million to subsidize loans for builders willing to provide low-cost housing.

Roosevelt also sought to help the nation's tenant farmers. Before being shut down, the AAA had paid farmers to take land out of production. In doing so, it had inadvertently hurt tenant farmers. Landowners had expelled tenants from the land to take it out of production. As a result, some 150,000 white and 195,000 African American tenants left farming during the 1930s. To stop this trend, Congress created the Farm Security Administration to give loans to tenants so they could purchase farms.

INFOGRAPHIC
What New Deal Programs Still Exist Today?

▲ All workers are required to have a Social Security card, printed on bank paper to decrease forgeries.

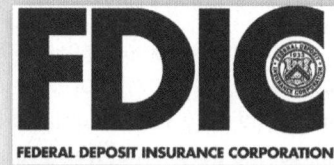

▶ The Federal Deposit Insurance Corporation sign is posted at most banks.

Program	Purpose Today
Social Security	The Social Security Administration provides old age pensions, unemployment insurance, and disability insurance.
National Labor Relations Board	The NLRB oversees union elections, investigates complaints of unfair labor practices, and mediates labor disputes.
Securities and Exchange Commission	The SEC regulates and polices the stock market.
Federal Deposit Insurance Corporation	The FDIC insures deposits up to $100,000.
Tennessee Valley Authority	The TVA provides electrical power to more than 8 million consumers.
Federal Housing Authority	Renamed the Department of Housing and Urban Development (HUD) in 1965, it insures mortgage loans, assists low-income renters, and fights housing discrimination.

◀ The Federal Housing Administration Web site uses this logo.

Analyzing VISUALS

1. **Identifying** Which organization regulates and oversees the stock market policies?
2. **Listing** What is the new name for the Federal Housing Authority?

To further help workers, Roosevelt pushed through Congress the Fair Labor Standards Act, which abolished child labor, limited the workweek to 44 hours for most workers, and set the first federal minimum wage at 25 cents an hour. The Fair Labor Standards Act was the last major piece of New Deal legislation. The recession of 1937 enabled the Republicans to win seats in Congress in the midterm elections of 1938. Together with conservative Southern Democrats, they began blocking further New Deal legislation. By 1939, the New Deal era had come to an end.

The New Deal's Legacy

The New Deal had only limited success in ending the Depression. Unemployment remained high, and economic recovery was not complete until after World War II. Even so, the New Deal gave many Americans a stronger sense of security and stability.

As a whole, the New Deal tended to balance competing economic interests. Business leaders, farmers, workers, homeowners, and others now looked to government to protect their interests. The federal government's ability to take on this new role was enhanced by two important Supreme Court decisions. In 1937, in *NLRB* v. *Jones and Laughlin Steel,* the Court ruled that the federal government had the authority to regulate production within a state. Later, in 1942, in *Wickard* v. *Filburn,* the Court used a similar argument to allow the federal government to regulate consumption in the states. These decisions increased federal power over the economy and allowed it to **mediate** between competing groups.

In taking on this mediating role, the New Deal established what some have called the **broker state,** in which the government works out conflicts among different interests. This broker role has continued under the administrations of both parties ever since. The New Deal also brought about a new public attitude toward government. Roosevelt's programs had succeeded in creating a **safety net** for Americans—safeguards and relief programs that protected them against economic disaster. By the end of the 1930s, many Americans felt that the government had a duty to maintain this safety net, even though doing so required a larger, more expensive federal government.

Critics continue to argue that the New Deal made the government too powerful. Thus, another legacy of the New Deal is a continuing debate over how much the government should intervene in the economy or support the disadvantaged. Throughout the hard times of the Depression, most Americans maintained a surprising degree of confidence in the American system. Journalist Dorothy Thompson expressed this feeling in 1940:

PRIMARY SOURCE

"We have behind us eight terrible years of a crisis. . . . Here we are, and our basic institutions are still intact, our people relatively prosperous and most important of all, our society relatively affectionate. . . . No country is so well off."

—from the *Washington Post,* October 9, 1940

Reading Check **Summarizing** What was the legacy of Roosevelt's New Deal?

Section 3 REVIEW

Vocabulary

1. **Explain** the significance of: Frances Perkins, court-packing, Henry Morgenthau, John Maynard Keynes, broker state, safety net.

Main Ideas

2. What caused a recession early in Roosevelt's second term?

3. How did the New Deal expand federal power over the economy?

Critical Thinking

4. **Big Ideas** What groups made up the New Deal coalition?

5. **Organizing** Use a chart like the one below to list the achievements and defeats of Roosevelt's second term.

Achievements	Defeats

6. **Analyzing Visuals** Choose one of the photos on page 441 and write a brief account of the day's activities from the viewpoint of one of the people in the photograph.

Writing About History

7. **Persuasive Writing** Imagine that you are a staff member in Roosevelt's cabinet. Write a short paper criticizing or defending FDR's court-packing plan.

History ONLINE

Study Central™ To review this section, go to glencoe.com and click on Study Central.

The New Deal in Action

Banking and Finances

- Emergency Banking Relief Act regulated banks.
- Federal Deposit Insurance Corporation insured bank deposits.
- Farm Credit Administration refinanced farm mortgages.
- Home Owners' Loan Corporation financed homeowners' mortgages.

Agriculture and Industry

- Agricultural Adjustment Administration paid farmers to limit surplus production.
- National Industrial Recovery Act limited industrial production and set prices.
- National Labor Relations Act gave workers the right to organize unions and bargain collectively.
- Tennessee Valley Authority financed rural electrification and helped develop the economy of a seven-state region.

▲ A steel worker labors on the Grand Coulee Dam on the Columbia River in eastern Washington.

Work and Relief

- Civilian Conservation Corps created forestry jobs for young men.
- Federal Emergency Relief Administration funded city and state relief programs.
- Public Works Administration created work programs to build public projects, such as roads, bridges, and schools.

◄ A Civilian Conservation Corps member plants trees.

Social "Safety Net"

- Social Security Act provided
  - income for senior citizens, handicapped, and unemployed
  - monthly retirement benefit for people over 65

▶ In 1935 President Roosevelt signs the Social Security Bill while Secretary of Labor Perkins and legislators observe.

Reviewing Vocabulary

Directions: Choose the word or words that best complete the sentence.

1. The purpose of a _____ was to prevent banks from being closed completely because of bank runs.

  A New Deal

  B bank holiday

  C gold standard

  D fireside chat

2. The period of intense congressional activity after FDR took office was known as the

  A Square Deal.

  B Securities and Exchange Commission.

  C New Deal.

  D Hundred Days.

3. _____ involves borrowing money to pay for programs.

  A Deficit spending

  B The gold standard

  C States' rights

  D Binding arbitration

4. Roosevelt ran into major opposition to his _____ plan.

  A broker state

  B gold standard

  C recovery

  D court-packing

5. The New Deal created a new public attitude toward government, by imagining the federal government used a _____ to protect citizens from economic disasters.

  A broker state

  B deficit nation

  C safety net

  D gold standard

Reviewing Main Ideas

Directions: Choose the best answers to the following questions.

Section 1 *(pp. 422–431)*

6. One of the ways in which Franklin Roosevelt gained political experience before being president was by serving as the

  A U.S. senator for Maine.

  B mayor of Boston.

  C governor of New York.

  D congressional representative from Connecticut.

7. The _____ was created to protect bank deposits.

  A Agricultural Adjustment Act

  B Home Owners' Loan Corporation

  C Securities and Exchange Commission

  D Federal Deposit Insurance Corporation

8. To _____, the Agricultural Adjustment Act paid farmers not to grow certain crops.

  A raise farm prices

  B lower farm prices

  C feed the homeless

  D let farmers relax

9. The _____ provided work for unemployed young men, who planted trees and built reservoirs.

  A Civil Works Administration

  B Public Works Administration

  C Civilian Conservation Corps

  D Federal Emergency Relief Administration

TEST-TAKING TIP

Questions sometimes ask for the exception, rather than the one right answer. Be sure to read through the question carefully, as well as each response, to see which one does not fit.

Need Extra Help?									
If You Missed Questions . . .	1	2	3	4	5	6	7	8	9
Go to Page . . .	424	424	434–435	442	445	422–423	426	428	430

 GO ON

Section 2 *(pp. 434–439)*

10. By 1935 the New Deal was criticized because it

A had created too many new programs.

B was focusing only on the Midwest.

C had spent too much money on the stock market.

D had not ended the Great Depression.

11. Benefits for older Americans were guaranteed by the

A Congress of Industrial Organizations.

B Works Progress Administration.

C Social Security Act.

D Wagner Act.

Section 3 *(pp. 440–445)*

12. Roosevelt split his own party by suggesting the need to

A appoint additional Supreme Court judges.

B include African Americans in New Deal programs.

C appoint women to his cabinet.

D follow Keynesian economics.

13. Part of the New Deal's legacy was an expansion of

A state power over the courts.

B federal power over the economy.

C federal power over the Constitution.

D state power over social safety nets.

14. The New Deal changed American attitudes toward government and

A the desire for easy wealth.

B the challenge of unionization.

C the duty to regulate industry.

D the need to provide a safety net.

Critical Thinking

Directions: Choose the best answers to the following questions.

Base your answers to questions 15 and 16 on the map below and on your knowledge of Chapter 12.

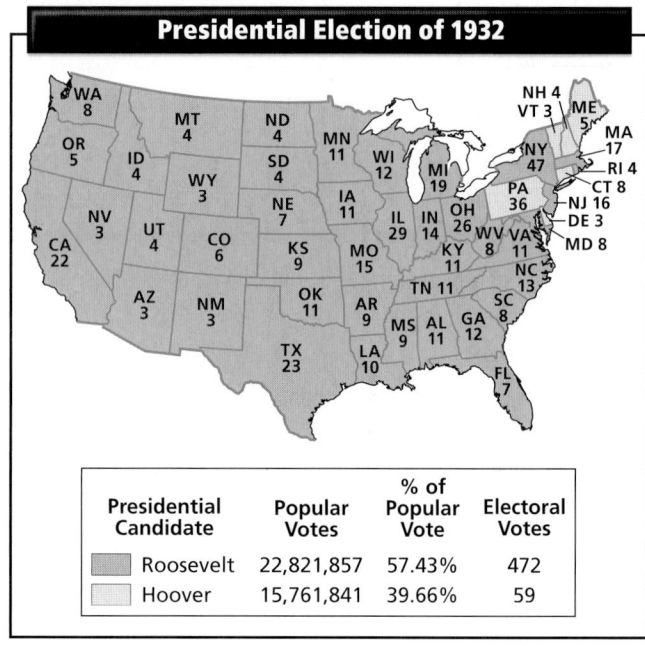

Presidential Election of 1932

Presidential Candidate	Popular Votes	% of Popular Vote	Electoral Votes
Roosevelt	22,821,857	57.43%	472
Hoover	15,761,841	39.66%	59

15. Which of the following regions remained supportive of Republican President Hoover?

A Midwest

B South

C Northeast

D West

16. Which state gave Hoover the largest number of votes in the Electoral College?

A Pennsylvania

B New York

C Connecticut

D Texas

Need Extra Help?							
If You Missed Questions . . .	10	11	12	13	14	15	16
Go to Page . . .	434–436	439	442	445	440–444	R15	R15

17. Social Security was an important piece of legislation because it

   A provided monthly retirement benefits.

   B encouraged state governments to improve schools.

   C forced the federal government to hire the unemployed.

   D mandated that workers be issued safety equipment.

Analyze the cartoon and answer the question that follows. Base your answer on the cartoon and your knowledge of Chapter 12.

18. This cartoon was published just after FDR took office. What message does it send?

   A Republicans are not very happy about the new legislation.

   B Congress is slow and stubborn as a donkey.

   C The new president is not slowed down by being in a wheelchair.

   D The Congress and many people are happy to follow Roosevelt.

Document-Based Questions

Directions: Analyze the document and answer the short-answer questions that follow the document.

Eleanor Roosevelt wrote in her autobiography of her experiences with people around the country:

> "This trip to the mining areas was my first contact with the work being done by the Quakers. I liked the idea of trying to put people to work to help themselves. The men were started on projects and taught to use their abilities to develop new skills. The women were encouraged to revive any household arts they might once have known but which they had neglected in the drab life of the mining village.
>
> This was only the first of many trips into the mining districts but it was the one that started the homestead idea [placing people in communities with homes, farms, and jobs] . . . . It was all experimental work, but it was designed to get people off relief, to put them to work building their own homes and to give them enough land to start growing food."
>
> —from *The Autobiography of Eleanor Roosevelt*

19. Why did Eleanor Roosevelt like the Quaker project?

20. Based on this excerpt, how do you think Eleanor Roosevelt felt about New Deal programs? Explain your answer.

Extended Response

21. Review the various New Deal programs discussed in the chapter. Select one that you think could be used or adapted to a current situation. Explain what group or groups it would help and how it would do so.

History ONLINE

For additional test practice, use Self-Check Quizzes— Chapter 12 at glencoe.com.

Need Extra Help?					
If You Missed Questions . . .	17	18	19	20	21
Go to Page . . .	439	R18	449	R19	422–431

Global Struggles
1931–1960

Why It Matters

The rise of dictatorships in the 1930s led to World War II, the most destructive war in world history. The United States played a major role in the war, fighting in Europe, Africa, and Asia. Afterwards, the United States emerged as a global superpower, abandoned isolationism, and began building alliances around the world. Confrontation with the Soviet Union led to the Cold War, as the United States sought to contain the spread of communism.

Despite the fog, American soldiers march in Belgium during the winter of 1944–1945.

A World in Flames

1931–1941

Italian dictator Benito Mussolini, at left, walks in Munich, Germany, with German dictator Adolf Hitler, center, in 1938.

Roosevelt
1933–1945

1934
- Nye Committee holds hearings on causes of World War I

1935
- First Neutrality Act bars sale of weapons to warring nations

1937
- Neutrality Act limits trade with all warring nations

U.S. PRESIDENTS

U.S. EVENTS

WORLD EVENTS

| 1931 | 1933 | 1935 | 1937 |

1931
- Japan invades Manchuria

1933
- Hitler becomes chancellor of Germany

1935
- Hitler denounces Treaty of Versailles
- Italy invades Ethiopia

1936
- Spanish Civil War begins
- Hitler reoccupies the Rhineland

1937
- Japan invades China

MAKING CONNECTIONS

Could World War II Have Been Prevented?

In the 1930s, global economic problems brought dictators to power in Europe and Japan, and another world war erupted. Many Americans, disillusioned by World War I, wanted to remain neutral, but when Japan attacked Pearl Harbor, the United States was forced to join the war.

- *What problems do you think World War I created that contributed to the outbreak of World War II?*

- *Do you think different American policies in the 1920s and 1930s could have prevented World War II?*

FOLDABLES™

Comparing Totalitarian Dictators Make a Trifold Book Foldable to compare and contrast the dictatorships of Benito Mussolini, Joseph Stalin, and Adolf Hitler. As you read the chapter, add details about each ruler under his name. Use your list as a helpful study guide on their differences and similarities.

Mussolini	Stalin	Hitler
Totalitarian Dictators		

1938
- Munich Conference gives Sudetenland to Hitler

1939
- United States denies SS *St. Louis* permission to dock
- Poland invaded; World War II begins

1940
- Roosevelt makes "destroyers-for-bases" deal with Britain
- France surrenders to Germany; Britain wins Battle of Britain

1941
- Congress passes Lend Lease Act
- Japan attacks Pearl Harbor

1939 1941

History ONLINE Visit glencoe.com and enter *QuickPass*™ code TAVMT5147c13 for Chapter 13 resources.

Section 1

America and the World

Guide to Reading

Big Ideas
Government and Society In the years following World War I, aggressive and expansionistic governments took power in both Europe and Asia.

Content Vocabulary
- fascism (p. 454)
- collective (p. 455)
- internationalism (p. 459)

Academic Vocabulary
- exploit (p. 454)
- dominate (p. 457)

People and Events to Identify
- Benito Mussolini (p. 454)
- Vladimir Lenin (p. 455)
- Joseph Stalin (p. 455)
- Adolf Hitler (p. 456)
- Manchuria (p. 457)
- Neutrality Act of 1935 (p. 458)
- Axis Powers (p. 459)

Reading Strategy
Taking Notes As you read about the events in Europe and Asia after World War I, use the major headings of the section to create an outline similar to the one below.

America and the World
I. The Rise of Dictators
   A.
   B.
   C.
   D.
II.

In the years following World War I, aggressive and expansionist governments took power in Europe and Asia. Meanwhile, most Americans did not want to get involved in another foreign war.

The Rise of Dictators

MAIN Idea Dictators took control of the governments of Italy, the Soviet Union, Germany, and Japan.

HISTORY AND YOU Can you think of a country today that is ruled by a dictator? Read about the repressive governments that arose during the 1920s and 1930s.

When World War I ended, President Wilson had hoped that the United States could "aid in the establishment of just democracy throughout the world." Instead, the treaty that ended the war, along with the economic depression that followed, contributed to the rise of antidemocratic governments in both Europe and Asia.

Mussolini and Fascism in Italy

One of Europe's first dictatorships arose in Italy. In 1919 **Benito Mussolini** founded Italy's Fascist Party. **Fascism** was an aggressive nationalistic movement that considered the nation more important than the individual. Fascists believed that order in society would come only through a dictator who led a strong government. They also thought nations became great by building an empire.

Fascism was also strongly anticommunist. After the Russian Revolution, many Europeans feared that communists, allied with labor unions, were trying to bring down their governments. Mussolini **exploited** these fears by portraying fascism as a bulwark against communism. Fascism began to stand for the protection of private property and the middle class. Mussolini also promised the working class full employment and social security. He pledged to return Italy to the glories of the Roman Empire.

Backed by the Fascist militia known as the Blackshirts, Mussolini threatened to march on Rome in 1922, claiming he was coming to defend Italy against a communist revolution. Liberal members of the Italian parliament insisted that the king declare martial law. When he refused, the cabinet resigned. Conservative advisers then persuaded the king to appoint Mussolini as the premier.

Once in office, Mussolini worked quickly to set up a dictatorship. Weary of strikes and riots, many Italians welcomed Mussolini's leadership. With the support of industrialists, landowners, and the Roman

0   1,000 kilometers
0   1,000 miles
Lambert Equal-Area projection

ARCTIC OCEAN

ATLANTIC OCEAN

PACIFIC OCEAN

In 1926 Joseph Stalin becomes dictator of the Soviet Union and begins to collectivize agriculture and industrialize the economy. His policies kill millions of rural peasants.

In 1933, high unemployment and fears of communism enable Adolf Hitler and the Nazi Party to take power. Hitler imposed a dictatorship, enacted anti-Jewish policies, and began rebuilding the military.

In 1936 General Francisco Franco launches a military revolt that overthrows Spain's democratic government; Franco then establishes a dictatorship.

Sea of Okhotsk

GERMANY

SPAIN

EUROPE

ITALY

SOVIET UNION

JAPANESE EMPIRE

Black Sea

Caspian Sea

ASIA

In 1922 fears of communism and economic chaos enable Benito Mussolini to lead the Fascists to power in Italy.

In 1931, the militarist Empire of Japan invades Manchuria; six years later, Japan attacks China. In 1941 General Hideki Tōjō becomes prime minister and led the nation into war with the United States.

Red Sea

AFRICA

Arabian Sea

Analyzing GEOGRAPHY

1. **Region** In which region of the world did a dictator first come to power, and when?

2. **Human-Environment Interactions** What effect did Stalin's policies have on the Soviet Union?

Catholic Church, Mussolini—who took the title of Il Duce, or "The Leader"—embarked on an ambitious program of bringing order to Italy.

Stalin Takes Over the USSR

After the Russian Revolution, the Communist Party, led by **Vladimir Lenin,** established communist governments throughout the Russian Empire. In 1922 they renamed these territories the Union of Soviet Socialist Republics (USSR). The Communists instituted one-party rule, suppressed individual liberties, and punished opponents.

After Lenin died in 1924, a power struggle began between Leon Trotsky and **Joseph Stalin.** Born with the surname of Dzuhgashvili, Stalin replaced his last name with the Russian word *stal,* meaning "steel." Between 1902 and 1913, he had been imprisoned or exiled seven times, but he always escaped.

By 1926, Stalin had become the new Soviet dictator. He began a massive effort to industrialize his country, using Five-Year Plans. During the first two of these Five-Year Plans, from 1928 to 1937, steel production increased from 4 million to 18 million tons (3.628 to 16.326 million t). At the same time, however, industrial wages declined by 43 percent from 1928 to 1940. Family farms were combined and turned into **collectives,** or government-owned farms. Peasants who resisted by killing livestock or hoarding crops faced show trials or death from starvation. As many as 10 million peasants died in famines during 1932 and 1933.

Stalin tolerated no opposition, targeting not only political enemies but also artists and intellectuals. During the late 1930s, the USSR was a nation of internal terrorism, with public trials that featured forced confessions. A new constitution, passed in 1936, promised many freedoms but was never enforced.

Stalin also used concentration camps; by 1935 some 2 million people were in camps, most of which were located in the Arctic. Prisoners were used as slave labor. Between 8 and 10 million people died as a result of Stalin's rule, which lasted until his death in 1953.

Hitler and Nazi Germany

Adolf Hitler was a fervent anticommunist and an admirer of Mussolini. A native Austrian, Hitler had fought for Germany in World War I. Germany's surrender and the subsequent Treaty of Versailles caused him and many other Germans to hate both the victorious Allies and the German government that had accepted the peace terms.

Postwar Germany's political and economic chaos led to the rise of new political parties. One of these was the National Socialist German Workers' Party, or the Nazi Party. The party was nationalistic and anticommunist, calling for Germany to expand its territory and not abide by the terms of the Treaty of Versailles. It also was anti-Semitic. Using the words *Socialist* and *Workers* in its name, the party

hoped to attract unhappy workers. Adolf Hitler was one of the party's first recruits.

In November 1923, the Nazis tried to seize power by marching on city hall in Munich, Germany. Hitler intended to seize power locally and then march on Berlin, the German capital, but the plan failed. The Nazi Party was banned for a time, and Hitler was arrested.

While in prison, Hitler wrote *Mein Kampf* ("My Struggle"), in which he called for the unification of all Germans under one government. He claimed that Germans, particularly blond, blue-eyed Germans, belonged to a "master race" called Aryans. He argued that Germans needed more space and called for Germany to expand east into Poland and Russia. According to Hitler, the Slavic peoples of eastern Europe belonged to an inferior race, which Germans should enslave. Hitler's racism was strongest, however, toward Jews. Hitler blamed the Jews for many of the world's problems, especially for Germany's defeat in World War I.

After his release, Hitler changed his tactics. Instead of trying to seize power violently, he focused on getting Nazis elected to the

NATIONAL GEOGRAPHIC   War and Civil War in the 1930s

▼ *Japanese officers targeted resource-rich Manchuria as the first goal in their drive to build an empire.*

Japan Invades Manchuria, 1931

Japanese invasion of Manchuria

Italy Invades Ethiopia, 1935

Italian-held territory
Ethiopia (Abyssinia)
Italian invasion route

▲ *Mussolini, the dictator of Italy, wanted to build a new Roman Empire in Africa. In 1935 the Italian army invaded Ethiopia, then known as Abyssinia. The emperor, Haile Selassie, went into exile.*

Reichstag, the lower house of the German parliament. When the Great Depression struck Germany, many desperate Germans began to vote for radical parties, including the Nazis and Communists. By 1932, the Nazis were the largest party in the Reichstag. The following year, the German president appointed Hitler as chancellor, or prime minister.

After taking office, Hitler called for new elections. He then ordered the police to crack down on the Socialist and Communist Parties. Storm troopers, as the Nazi paramilitary units were called, began intimidating voters. After the election, the Reichstag, dominated by the Nazis and other right-wing parties, voted to give Hitler dictatorial powers. In 1934 Hitler became president, which gave him control of the army. He then gave himself the new title of Der Führer, or "The Leader."

Militarists Control Japan

In Japan, as in Germany, difficult economic times helped undermine the political system. Japanese industries had to import nearly all of the resources they needed to produce goods.

During the 1920s Japan did not earn enough money from its exports to pay for its imports, which limited economic growth. When the Depression struck, other countries raised their tariffs. This made the situation even worse.

Many Japanese military officers blamed the country's problems on corrupt politicians. Most officers believed that Japan was destined to **dominate** East Asia and saw democracy as "un-Japanese" and bad for the country.

Japanese military leaders and their civilian supporters argued that seizing territory was the only way Japan could get the resources it needed. In September 1931, the Japanese army invaded **Manchuria,** a resource-rich region of northern China. When the Japanese prime minister tried to stop the war by negotiating with China, officers assassinated him. From that point forward, the military controlled the country. Japan's civilian government supported the nationalist policy of expanding the empire and appointed a military officer to serve as prime minister.

Reading Check **Examining** How did postwar conditions contribute to the rise of dictatorships in Europe?

The Spanish Civil War, 1936–1939

In 1936 a civil war broke out in Spain when Fascist General Francisco Franco attempted a military coup. With aid from Hitler and Mussolini, Spain became a testing ground for new military ideas such as air strikes. On April 26, 1937, planes released 100,000 pounds of bombs, destroying 70% of Guernica, shown at left after the bombing. A mere 15 days after the bombing, the artist Pablo Picasso began painting Guernica (above).

Analyzing VISUALS

1. **Comparing** In what way were the three wars shown on the map all a prelude to World War II?

2. **Analyzing** How does Picasso show the terror of the Guernica bombing?

American Neutrality

MAIN Idea Most Americans did not want to get involved in another European war, despite Franklin Roosevelt's emphasis on internationalism.

HISTORY AND YOU Do you think the United States should become involved in the wars of other nations even when it is not under attack? Read to learn about American attitudes during the 1930s.

The rise of dictatorships and militarism discouraged many Americans. The sacrifices they had made during World War I seemed pointless. Once again, Americans began supporting isolationism and trying to avoid involvement in international conflicts.

The Nye Committee

Isolationist ideas became stronger in the early 1930s for two reasons. When the Depression began, many European nations found it difficult to repay money they had borrowed during World War I. In 1934 all of the debtor nations except Finland announced they would no longer repay their war debts.

Meanwhile, dozens of books and articles appeared arguing that arms manufacturers had tricked the United States into entering World War I. In 1934 Senator Gerald P. Nye of North Dakota held hearings to investigate these allegations. The Nye Committee documented the huge profits that arms factories had made during the war. The report created the impression that these businesses influenced the decision to go to war. Coupled with the European refusal to repay their loans, the Nye Committee's findings turned even more Americans toward isolationism.

Legislating Neutrality

Italian and German aggression increased under Mussolini and Hitler. Worried that the actions of these nations might lead to war, Congress passed the **Neutrality Act of 1935.** This legislation—reflecting the belief that arms sales had helped bring the United States into World War I—made it illegal for Americans to sell arms to any country at war.

In 1936 a rebellion erupted in Spain after voters elected a coalition of Republicans, Socialists, and Communists. General Francisco Franco led the rebellion, backed by Spanish Fascists, army officers, landowners, and Catholic Church leaders. The revolt became a civil war and attracted

INFOGRAPHIC
The Neutrality Acts, 1935–1937

Causes
- Nye Senate Committee report suggesting that the American arms industry had pushed the nation into World War I for its own profit
- growing belief that America should have stayed out of World War I

The Neutrality Act of 1935
- mandatory embargo on selling or exporting arms, ammunition, or implements of war to nations at war
- discretionary travel restrictions
- set to expire after 6 months

Causes
- Italy's invasion of Ethiopia; FDR encourages a moral embargo against Italy, which he could not enforce

The Neutrality Act of 1936
- arms embargo with countries at war
- discretionary travel restrictions
- ban on loans to nations fighting, but short-term credits exempted
- republics in the Americas exempted

Causes
- Spanish Civil War
- sale of aviation parts to rebels in Spain, which FDR thought unpatriotic
- agreements creating the Axis alliance

The Neutrality Act of 1937
- arms embargo against nations at war
- travel ban on warring nations' ships
- trade with countries at war on a cash-and-carry basis allowed if goods were not contraband or sent on foreign ships

▲ Republican Senator Gerald Nye headed the Senate Munitions Committee, whose findings convinced many that arms makers were "merchants of death" and that the United States should remain neutral.

Analyzing VISUALS

1. **Analyzing** What impact did the Nye Committee's findings have on public opinion?

2. **Evaluating** Why did so many Americans support neutrality?

worldwide attention. Congress passed a second neutrality act, banning the sale of arms to either side in a civil war.

Shortly after the Spanish Civil War began, Hitler and Mussolini pledged to cooperate on several international issues. Mussolini termed this new relationship the Rome-Berlin Axis. The following month, Japan aligned itself with Germany and Italy when it signed the Anti-Comintern Pact with Germany. The pact required the two countries to exchange information about communist groups. Together, Germany, Italy, and Japan became known as the **Axis Powers,** although they did not formally become military allies until September 1940.

With tensions in Europe worsening, Congress passed the Neutrality Act of 1937. This act not only continued the ban on selling arms to warring nations, but also required them to buy all nonmilitary supplies from the United States on a "cash-and-carry" basis. Countries at war had to send their own ships to the United States to pick up the goods, and they had to pay cash. Loans were not allowed. Isolationists knew that attacks on American ships carrying supplies to Europe had helped bring the country into World War I. They wanted to prevent such attacks from involving the nation in another European war.

Roosevelt's Internationalism

When he took office in 1933, President Roosevelt knew that ending the Great Depression was his first priority. He was not, however, an isolationist. He supported **internationalism,** the idea that trade between nations creates prosperity and helps prevent war. Internationalists also believed that the United States should try to preserve peace in the world. Roosevelt warned that the neutrality acts "might drag us into war instead of keeping us out," but he did not veto the bills.

In July 1937, Japanese forces in Manchuria launched a full-scale attack on China. Roosevelt decided to help the Chinese. Because neither China nor Japan had actually declared war, Roosevelt claimed the Neutrality Act of 1937 did not apply, and he authorized the sale of weapons to China. He warned that the nation should not stand by and let an "epidemic of lawlessness" infect the world:

PRIMARY SOURCE

"When an epidemic of physical disease starts to spread, the community ... joins in a quarantine of the patients in order to protect the health of the community against the spread of the disease. . . . War is a contagion, whether it be declared or undeclared. . . . There is no escape through mere isolation or neutrality. . . . "

—quoted in *Freedom From Fear*

Despite his words, Americans were still not willing to risk another war. "It is a terrible thing," the president said, "to look over your shoulder when you are trying to lead—and find no one there."

Reading Check **Evaluating** Why did many Americans support isolationism?

Section 1 REVIEW

Vocabulary

1. **Explain** the significance of: Benito Mussolini, fascism, Vladimir Lenin, Joseph Stalin, collectives, Adolf Hitler, Manchuria, Neutrality Act of 1935, Axis Powers, internationalism.

Main Ideas

2. **Identifying** Which nations did dictators govern during the years after World War I?

3. **Analyzing** What events caused Roosevelt to become more of an internationalist?

Critical Thinking

4. **Big Ideas** Why did antidemocratic governments rise to power in postwar Europe and Asia?

5. **Organizing** Use a graphic organizer similar to the one below to compare the governments opposed to democracy in Europe and Asia.

Country	Dictator	Ideology

6. **Analyzing Visuals** Look at the photograph on page 457 of Guernica after it was destroyed. How might both isolationists and internationalists have used the image to win support for their cause?

Writing About History

7. **Persuasive Writing** Write a newspaper editorial supporting either isolationism or internationalism after World War I. Include reasons that support your ideas and that help convince others to embrace your position.

History ONLINE

Study Central™ To review this section, go to glencoe.com and click on Study Central.

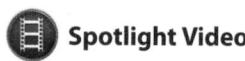
World War II Begins

Guide to Reading

Big Ideas
Trade, War, and Migration World War II officially began with the Nazi invasion of Poland and the French and British declarations of war on Germany in September 1939.

Content Vocabulary
- appeasement *(p. 461)*
- blitzkrieg *(p. 462)*

Academic Vocabulary
- violation *(p. 460)*
- regime *(p. 460)*
- concentrate *(p. 462)*
- transport *(p. 465)*

People and Events to Identify
- *Anschluss (p. 460)*
- Munich Conference *(p. 461)*
- Maginot Line *(p. 462)*
- Winston Churchill *(p. 465)*
- Battle of Britain *(p. 465)*

Reading Strategy
Sequencing As you read about the events leading up to World War II, record them by completing a time line similar to the one below.

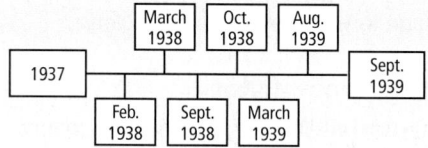

The shadow of World War I loomed large in the minds of European leaders in the late 1930s. Although Nazi Germany appeared increasingly aggressive, Britain and France wanted to avoid another bloody conflict. Efforts to negotiate peaceful agreements with Nazi Germany ultimately failed.

Path to War

MAIN Idea European nations tried to prevent war by giving in to Adolf Hitler's demands.

HISTORY AND YOU Do you remember reading how Europe was divided after World War I? Read to learn how German demands for more territory started World War II.

In 1935 Hitler began to defy the Treaty of Versailles that had ended World War I. He announced that Germany would build a new air force and begin a military draft that would greatly expand its army—actions in direct **violation** of the treaty. Rather than enforce the treaty by going to war, European leaders tried to negotiate with Hitler. At the time, the Nazi **regime** was weaker than it later would become. If European leaders had responded more aggressively, could war have been avoided? Historians still debate this question today.

Europe's leaders had several reasons for believing—or wanting to believe—that a deal could be reached with Hitler and that war could be avoided. First, they wanted to avoid a repeat of the bloodshed of World War I. Second, some thought most of Hitler's demands were reasonable, including his demand that all German-speaking regions be united. Third, many people assumed that the Nazis would be more interested in peace once they gained more territory.

The Austrian *Anschluss*

In late 1937 Hitler again called for the unification of all German-speaking people, including those in Austria and Czechoslovakia. He believed that Germany could expand its territory only by "resort[ing] to force with its attendant risks."

In February 1938 Hitler threatened to invade German-speaking Austria unless Austrian Nazis were given important government posts. Austria's chancellor gave in to this demand, but then tried to put the matter of unification with Germany to a democratic vote. Fearing the outcome, Hitler sent troops into Austria in March and announced the *Anschluss,* or unification, of Austria and Germany.

0   200 kilometers
0   200 miles
Lambert Azimuthal
Equal-Area projection

Hitler demands the return of Danzig to Germany, October 1938.

In August 1939, the Nazi-Soviet Pact is signed. One week later, on Sept. 1, Germany invades Poland.

In March 1936, Germany sends troops into the Rhineland, defying the Treaty of Versailles.

Austrian *Anschluss*, 1938— Germany annexes Austria.

NORWAY SWEDEN FINLAND
Oslo Helsinki
IRELAND UNITED DEN. ESTONIA
Dublin KINGDOM Copenhagen Tallinn
North LATVIA Moscow
Sea Riga
LITHUANIA SOVIET UNION
Danzig Kaunas
London NETH. Berlin
Amsterdam Warsaw
ATLANTIC Brussels GERMANY POLAND
OCEAN BEL. LUX.
Paris Prague
Bern CZECH.
Munich Vienna
FRANCE SWITZ. AUSTRIA Budapest
ANDORRA HUNGARY ROMANIA
PORT. SPAIN Belgrade Bucharest Black
Madrid ITALY YUGOSLAVIA Sea
Rome BULGARIA
Tiranë Sofia
ALBANIA
GREECE TURKEY
Athens

▲ At Munich in 1938, Britain's Neville Chamberlain (third from left), Mussolini (center), and Hitler (third from right) agreed to prevent war but required Czechoslovakia to give up the Sudetenland (brown area on the Czech border above) to Germany. Six months later, Germany occupied all of Czechoslovakia.

Analyzing GEOGRAPHY

1. **Region** Why do you think Hitler's first military action was in the Rhineland?

2. **Region** Why might Hitler have welcomed a nonaggression pact with the Soviets?

Maps In Motion See *StudentWorks™ Plus* or glencoe.com.

The Munich Crisis

Hitler next announced German claims to the Sudetenland, an area of Czechoslovakia with a large German-speaking population. The Czechs strongly resisted Germany's demands for the Sudetenland. France threatened to fight if Germany attacked Czechoslovakia, and the Soviet Union also promised aid. Prime Minister Neville Chamberlain pledged Britain's support to France, its ally.

Representatives of Britain, France, Italy, and Germany agreed to meet in Munich to decide Czechoslovakia's fate. At the **Munich Conference,** on September 29, 1938, Britain and France agreed to Hitler's demands, a policy that came to be known as **appeasement.** In other words, they made concessions in exchange for peace. Supporters of appeasement believed that Hitler had a few limited demands. They felt that if they gave him what he wanted, they could avoid war. Czechoslovakia was told to give up the Sudetenland or fight Germany on its own. When Chamberlain returned home, he promised "a peace with honor . . . peace in our time," but he also began to speed up British rearmament— in case appeasement failed.

Appeasement did fail to preserve the fragile peace. In March 1939 Germany sent troops into Czechoslovakia and divided the country. Slovakia became independent in name, but it was actually under German control. The Czech lands became a German protectorate.

Hitler Demands Danzig

A month after the Munich Conference, Hitler demanded that the city of Danzig be returned to German control. Although Danzig was more than 90 percent German, it had been part of Poland since World War I. Hitler also requested a highway and railroad across the Polish Corridor, an area that separated western Germany from the German state of East Prussia.

Hitler's new demands convinced Britain and France that war was inevitable. On March 31, 1939, Britain announced that if Poland went to war to defend its territory, Britain and France would come to its aid. This declaration encouraged Poland to refuse Hitler's demands. In May 1939, Hitler ordered the German army to prepare to invade Poland. He also ordered his foreign minister to begin negotiations with the USSR. If Germany was going to fight Britain and France, Hitler did not want to have to fight the Soviets, too.

The Nazi-Soviet Pact

When German officials proposed a nonaggression treaty to the Soviets, Stalin agreed. He believed the best way to protect the USSR was to turn the capitalist nations against each other. If the treaty worked, Germany would go to war against Britain and France, and the USSR would be safe.

The nonaggression pact, signed by Germany and the USSR on August 23, 1939, shocked the world. Communism and Nazism were supposed to be totally opposed to each other. Leaders in Britain and France understood, however, that Hitler had made the deal to free himself for war against their countries and Poland. They did not know that the treaty also contained a secret deal to divide Poland between Germany and the Soviet Union.

✓ **Reading Check** **Identifying** What regions did Hitler take or demand in the lead-up to the war?

The War Begins

MAIN Idea After Poland and France fell to the Nazis, the British evacuated thousands of trapped troops from Dunkirk.

HISTORY AND YOU Can you think of a contemporary situation in which people acted heroically to save others in danger? Read to learn about the heroism of civilians and soldiers in World War II.

On September 1, 1939, Germany invaded Poland. Two days later, Britain and France declared war on Germany. World War II had begun.

Poland resisted, but its army was outdated. The Polish army rode horses and carried lances against German tanks. The Germans used a new type of warfare called **blitzkrieg,** or "lightning war." Blitzkrieg used large numbers of massed tanks to break through and encircle enemy positions. To support the tanks, waves of aircraft bombed enemy positions and dropped paratroopers to cut their supply lines. Warsaw, the Polish capital, fell to the Germans on September 27. By October 5, 1939, the Germans had defeated the Polish military.

The Fall of France

Meanwhile, western Europe remained eerily quiet. The British had sent troops to France, and both countries remained on the defensive, waiting for the Germans to attack.

After World War I, the French had built a line of concrete bunkers and fortifications called the **Maginot Line** along the German border. The French preferred to wait behind the Maginot Line for the Germans to approach. This decision proved to be disastrous for two reasons. First, it allowed Germany to **concentrate** on Poland first before facing the British and French. Second, Hitler decided to go around the Maginot Line, which protected France's border with Germany but not France's border with Belgium.

On May 10, Hitler launched a new blitzkrieg. While German troops parachuted into the Netherlands, tanks rolled into Belgium and Luxembourg. Expecting the attack, British and French forces raced north into Belgium. This was a mistake. Instead of sending their tanks through the open countryside of central Belgium, the Germans sent their main force through the Ardennes Mountains of Luxembourg and eastern Belgium. The French did not think that large numbers of tanks could move through the mountains, and had left only a few troops to defend that part of the border. The Germans smashed through the French lines, and then turned west across northern France to the English Channel. The British and French armies could not move back into France quickly enough and were trapped in Belgium.

The Miracle at Dunkirk

After trapping the Allied forces in Belgium, the Germans began to drive them toward the English Channel. The only hope for Britain and France was to evacuate their surviving troops by sea, but the Germans had captured all but one port, Dunkirk, in northern France near the Belgian border.

As German forces closed in on Dunkirk, Hitler suddenly ordered them to stop. No one is sure why he gave this order. Historians know that Hitler was nervous about risking his tank forces, and he wanted to wait until more infantry arrived. Hermann Goering, the head of the German air force, also assured Hitler that aircraft alone could destroy the trapped soldiers.

Whatever Hitler's reasons, his order provided a three-day delay. This gave the British time to strengthen their lines and begin the evacuation. Some 850 ships of all sizes—from navy warships to small sailboats operated by civilian volunteers—headed to Dunkirk from

TECHNOLOGY & HISTORY

Blitzkrieg In 1939 Germany unleashed blitzkrieg—lightning war—on Europe. Blitzkrieg combined several technologies—aircraft, tanks, parachutes, and radios—to produce a highly mobile, fast-moving army that could coordinate multiple attacks, break through lines, and rapidly encircle enemy positions.

◄ A superior air force led to Germany's defeat of western Europe by summer 1940. The aircraft could drop paratroopers behind enemy lines as well as bomb targets.

▲ German tanks rolled into Poland in 1939, ahead of the infantry, which followed to end any resistance. The bombers supported the swift-moving tanks from the air. The armored tanks, known as Panzers, often moved so rapidly that they had to wait for the infantry to catch up.

Analyzing VISUALS

1. **Drawing Conclusions** What do you observe about the advance of the Panzer tanks in the photo on the left?

2. **Evaluating** What dangers do you think the paratroopers in the center photo may have faced?

England, many of them making the 48-mile trip multiple times. French, Dutch, and Belgian ships joined British ones in "Operation Dynamo." The British had hoped to rescue about 45,000 troops. Instead, when the evacuation ended on June 4, an estimated 338,000 British and French troops had been saved. This became known as the "Miracle at Dunkirk."

The evacuation had its price, however. Almost all of the British army's equipment remained at Dunkirk—90,000 rifles, 7,000 tons of ammunition, and 120,000 vehicles. If Hitler invaded Britain, it would be almost impossible to stop him from conquering the country.

Three weeks later, on June 22, 1940, Hitler accepted the French surrender in the same railway car in which the Germans had surrendered at the end of World War I. Germany now occupied much of northern France and its Atlantic coastline. To govern the rest of France, Germany installed a puppet government at the town of Vichy and made Marshal Philippe Pétain the new government's figurehead leader. Though

Vichy France was officially a neutral party in the war, its powerless leaders collaborated with the Nazis to repress the people of France.

During the war, the United States recognized Vichy France as the official French government, but General Charles de Gaulle and his Free French resistance forces challenged the legitimacy of Vichy France. De Gaulle argued that he represented the continuity of the pre-invasion French government, that the Vichy government was illegal, and that the Vichy government leadership were traitors. From England and the French colony of Algiers, de Gaulle cooperated with Allied political leaders to fight against the Germans and to bring about the liberation of France. De Gaulle refused to concede the defeat of France. Similarly, the leaders and citizens of Great Britain were not ready to give up the fight against Germany's advancing troops.

Reading Check **Explaining** By what means did Hitler overtake both Poland and France?

PRIMARY SOURCE
The Battle of Britain, 1940

During the Battle of Britain, bombs fell around London's St. Paul's Cathedral, a famous architectural treasure as well as a place of worship. Some of the subways no longer ran but were converted to air-raid shelters where people could sleep.

PRIMARY SOURCE

"Even though large tracts of Europe and many old and famous States have fallen or may fall into the grip of the Gestapo and all the odious apparatus of Nazi rule, we shall not flag or fail, we shall go on to the end, we shall fight in France, we shall fight on the seas and oceans, we shall fight with growing confidence and growing strength in the air, we shall defend our island, whatever the cost may be, we shall fight on the beaches, we shall fight on the landing grounds, we shall fight in the fields and in the streets, we shall fight in the hills; we shall never surrender. . . ."

—Winston Churchill, Speech to Parliament, June 4, 1940

▲ Winston Churchill

DBQ   Document-Based Questions

1. **Identifying Points of View** What effect does Churchill suggest the fall of other European states will have on Britain?

2. **Analyzing Primary Sources** What does Churchill expect to grow as the Allied forces fight the Nazis?

3. **Hypothesizing** What effect do you think Churchill's words had on those who heard or read the speech?

Britain Remains Defiant

MAIN Idea Despite the bombing of London and other major cities, Britain's Winston Churchill stood firm against the threat of Nazi invasion.

HISTORY AND YOU Think of a time when the odds were against you. How did you react? Read about British resolve when faced with Nazi air raids.

Neither Pétain nor Hitler anticipated the bravery of the British people or the spirit of their leader, **Winston Churchill,** who had replaced Neville Chamberlain as prime minister. Hitler expected Britain to negotiate peace after France surrendered, but on June 4, 1940, Churchill delivered a defiant speech in Parliament, vowing that Britain would never surrender. The speech was intended to rally the British people and to alert the isolationist United States to Britain's plight.

Realizing Britain would not surrender, Hitler ordered his commanders to prepare to invade. Getting across the English Channel, however, posed a major challenge. Germany had few **transport** ships, and the British air force would sink them if they tried to land troops in England. To invade, therefore, Germany first had to defeat the British Royal Air Force.

In June 1940, the German air force, called the *Luftwaffe,* began to attack British shipping in the English Channel. Then, in mid-August, the *Luftwaffe* launched an all-out air battle to destroy the Royal Air Force. This air battle, which lasted into the fall of 1940, became known as the **Battle of Britain.**

On August 23, German bombers accidentally bombed London, the British capital. This attack on civilians enraged the British, who responded by bombing Berlin the following night. For the first time in the war, bombs fell on the German capital. Infuriated, Hitler ordered the *Luftwaffe* to stop its attacks on British military targets and to concentrate on bombing London.

Hitler's goal was to terrorize the British people into surrendering. The British endured, however, taking refuge in cellars and subway stations whenever German bombers appeared.

Although the Royal Air Force was greatly outnumbered, the British had one major advantage. They had developed a new technology called radar. Using radar stations placed along their coast, the British were able to detect incoming German aircraft and direct British fighters to intercept them.

Day after day, the British fighters inflicted more losses on the Germans than they suffered. During the long battle, Germany lost 1,733 aircraft while the British lost 915 fighter planes, along with 449 pilots. The skill of more than 2,000 British and 500 foreign pilots—including many Poles, Canadians, Frenchmen, and a few Americans—successfully thwarted Hitler's plan to invade Britain. These pilots flew as often as five times a day. Praising them, Churchill told Parliament, "Never in the field of human conflict was so much owed by so many to so few." On October 12, 1940, Hitler canceled the invasion of Britain.

Reading Check **Evaluating** How was Britain able to resist Hitler and the Nazis?

Section 2 REVIEW

Vocabulary

1. **Explain** the significance of: *Anschluss*, Munich Conference, appeasement, blitz-krieg, Maginot Line, Winston Churchill, Battle of Britain.

Main Ideas

2. **Explaining** Why did Europe's leaders first try to deal with Hitler through appeasement?

3. **Analyzing** Why was the decision to leave French forces behind the Maginot Line disastrous for Europe?

4. **Summarizing** In what ways did Winston Churchill prove to be an effective leader for Britain as the war began?

Critical Thinking

5. **Big Ideas** What was the new type of warfare used by Germany against Poland? Explain the technique.

6. **Organizing** Use a graphic organizer similar to the one below to list early events of the war in Poland and western Europe.

Events

7. **Analyzing Visuals** Look again at the photograph on page 461. What do you observe about the participants at the Munich Conference?

Writing About History

8. **Expository Writing** Choose one dramatic incident from the beginnings of World War II and write a news story explaining what happened.

History ONLINE

Study Central™ To review this section, go to glencoe.com and click on Study Central.

Section 3

 Section Audio　　 **Spotlight Video**

The Holocaust

Guide to Reading

Big Ideas
Group Action The Nazis believed Jews to be subhuman. They steadily increased their persecution of Jews and eventually set up death camps and tried to kill all the Jews in Europe.

Content Vocabulary
• concentration camp *(p. 470)*
• extermination camp *(p. 470)*

Academic Vocabulary
• prohibit *(p. 466)*
• assume *(p. 468)*
• virtually *(p. 471)*

People and Events to Identify
• *Shoah (p. 466)*
• Nuremberg Laws *(p. 466)*
• Gestapo *(p. 468)*
• Wannsee Conference *(p. 470)*

Reading Strategy
Organizing As you read about the Holocaust, complete a graphic organizer similar to the one below by listing examples of Nazi persecution of European Jews.

Examples of Persecution

Nazis first acted upon their racist ideology when they imposed restrictions on Jews and stripped them of basic rights. Eventually, Nazi Germany created concentration camps and systematically attempted to kill all European Jews and others whom they regarded as inferior.

Nazi Persecution of the Jews

MAIN Idea Nazi laws stripped Jews of citizenship and all fundamental rights; immigration restrictions in other countries made leaving Germany difficult.

HISTORY AND YOU Do you know anyone who came to the United States as a refugee? Read how Jewish refugees were turned away in the late 1930s.

During the Holocaust, the Nazis killed nearly 6 million European Jews. The Nazis also killed millions of people from other groups they considered inferior. The Hebrew term for the Holocaust is *Shoah,* meaning "catastrophe," but it is often used specifically to refer to the Nazi campaign to exterminate the Jews during World War II.

The Nuremberg Laws

Although the Nazis persecuted anyone who dared oppose them, as well as the disabled, Gypsies, homosexuals, and Slavic peoples, they reserved their strongest hatred for the Jews. This loathing went far beyond the European anti-Semitism that was common at the time. Over the centuries, people who were prejudiced against Jews had discriminated against them in many ways. For example, Jews had sometimes been segregated in ghettos or **prohibited** from owning land.

After the Nazis took power, they quickly moved to deprive German Jews of many established rights. In September 1935, the **Nuremberg Laws** took citizenship away from Jewish Germans and banned marriage between Jews and other Germans. Two months later, another decree defined a Jew as a person with at least one Jewish grandparent and barred Jews from holding public office or voting. Another law compelled Jews with German-sounding names to adopt "Jewish" names. Soon the passports of Jews were marked with a red *J* to identify them as Jewish.

By the summer of 1936, at least half of Germany's Jews were jobless, having lost the right to work as civil servants, journalists, farmers, teachers, and actors. In 1938 the Nazis also banned Jews from practicing law and medicine and from operating businesses. With no source of income, life became very difficult.

The Persecution Begins, 1935–1938

▼ Nazi storm troopers place warning signs encouraging a boycott on Jewish-owned businesses in 1933.

▲ On Kristallnacht, November 7, 1938, roaming bands of Nazi storm troopers destroyed Jewish property and terrorized Jewish families across the Third Reich.

Analyzing VISUALS

1. **Hypothesizing** What effect do you think the signs might have had on the woman in the photograph on the left?

2. **Making Connections** How do you think publication of the photograph of the synagogue would have affected world opinion toward the Nazis?

Despite worsening conditions, many Jews chose to remain in Germany during the early years of Nazi rule. Well integrated into German society before this time, they were reluctant to leave and give up the lives they had built there. Many also thought that conditions would surely improve after a time. In fact, conditions soon became worse.

Kristallnacht

On November 7, 1938, a young Jewish refugee named Herschel Grynszpan shot and killed a German diplomat in Paris. Grynszpan's father and 10,000 other Jews had been deported from Germany to Poland, and the distraught young man was seeking revenge for this act and for the persecution of the Jews in general.

In retaliation, an infuriated Hitler ordered his minister of propaganda, Joseph Goebbels, to stage attacks against the Jews that would seem like a spontaneous popular reaction to news of the murder. On the night of November 9, this plan played out in a spree of destruction. In Vienna, a Jewish child named Frederic Morton watched in terror that night as Nazi storm troopers broke into his family's apartment:

PRIMARY SOURCE

"They yanked out every drawer in every one of our chests and cupboards, and tossed each in the air. They let the cutlery jangle across the floor, the clothes scatter, and stepped over the mess to fling the next drawer.... 'We might be back,' the leader said. On the way out he threw our mother-of-pearl ashtray over his shoulder, like confetti. We did not speak or move or breathe until we heard their boots against the pavement."

—quoted in *Facing History and Ourselves*

The anti-Jewish violence that erupted throughout Germany and Austria that night came to be called *Kristallnacht*, or "night of broken glass," because broken glass littered the streets afterward. By the following morning, more than 90 Jews were dead, hundreds were badly injured, and thousands more were terrorized. The Nazis had forbidden police to interfere while roving bands of thugs destroyed 7,500 Jewish businesses and hundreds of synagogues.

The lawlessness of *Kristallnacht* persisted. Following that night of violence, the **Gestapo,** the government's secret police, arrested about 30,000 Jewish men, releasing them only if they agreed to emigrate and surrender all their possessions. The state also confiscated insurance payments owed to Jewish owners of ruined businesses.

Jewish Refugees Try to Flee

Kristallnacht and its aftermath marked a significant escalation of Nazi persecution against the Jews. Many Jews, including Frederic Morton's family, decided that it was time to leave and fled to the United States. Between 1933, when Hitler took power, and the start of

World War II in 1939, some 350,000 Jews escaped Nazi-controlled Germany. These emigrants included prominent scientists, such as Albert Einstein, and business owners like Otto Frank, who resettled his family in Amsterdam in 1933. Otto's daughter Anne kept a diary of her family's life in hiding after the Nazis overran the Netherlands. The "secret annex," as she called their hiding place, has become a museum.

Limits on Jewish Immigration By 1938, one American consulate in Germany had a backlog of more than 100,000 visa applications from Jews trying to leave for the United States. Following the Nazi *Anschluss,* some 3,000 Austrian Jews applied for American visas each day. Most never received visas to the United States or to the other countries where they applied. As a result, millions of Jews remained trapped in Nazi-dominated Europe.

Several factors limited Jewish immigration to the United States. Nazi orders prohibited Jews from taking more than about four dollars out of Germany. American immigration law, however, forbade granting a visa to anyone "likely to become a public charge." Customs officials tended to **assume** that this description

PRIMARY SOURCE
The Holocaust

▼ After World War II broke out, the Nazis methodically deprived Jews of their rights, confining many to overcrowded ghettos. After weeks of fierce resistance, Jews in the Warsaw ghetto in Poland (below) were rounded up for deportation to concentration camps in May 1943.

▲ By 1943, the Nazis had started to implement their plans to exterminate the Jews. The system of ghettos was abandoned in favor of herding men, women, and children onto cattle cars for transport to death camps.

applied to Jews, because Germany had forced them to leave behind any wealth. High unemployment rates in the 1930s also made immigration unpopular. Few Americans wanted to raise immigration quotas, even to accommodate European refugees. Others did not want to admit Jews because they held anti-Semitic attitudes. The existing immigration policy allowed only 150,000 immigrants annually, with a fixed quota from each country. The law permitted no exceptions for refugees or victims of persecution.

International Response At an international conference on refugees in 1938, several European countries, the United States, and Latin America stated their regret that they could not take in more of Germany's Jews without raising their immigration quotas. Meanwhile, Nazi propaganda chief Joseph Goebbels announced that "if there is any country that believes it has not enough Jews, I shall gladly turn over to it all our Jews." Hitler also declared himself "ready to put all these criminals at the disposal of these countries . . . even on luxury ships."

As war loomed in 1939, many ships departed from Germany crammed with Jews desperate to escape. Some of their visas, however, had been forged or sold illegally, and Mexico, Paraguay, Argentina, and Costa Rica all denied access to Jews with such documents. So, too, did the United States.

The *St. Louis* Affair On May 27, 1939, the SS *St. Louis* entered the harbor in Havana, Cuba, with 930 Jewish refugees on board. Most of these passengers hoped to go to the United States eventually, but they had certificates improperly issued by Cuba's director of immigration giving them permission to land in Cuba. When the ships arrived in Havana, the Cuban government revoked the certificates and refused to let the refugees come ashore. For several days, the ship's captain steered his ship in circles off the coast of Florida, awaiting official permission to dock at an American port. Denied permission, the ship turned back toward Europe. The passengers finally disembarked in France, Holland, Belgium, and Great Britain. Within two years, the first three of these countries fell under Nazi domination. Many of the refugees brought to these countries perished in the Nazis' "final solution."

✔ **Reading Check** **Analyzing** Why did many Jews stay in Germany despite being persecuted?

To read more of *Night* by Elie Wiesel, see page R76 in the **American Literature Library**.

In 1944 Elie Wiesel was taken to a concentration camp. In the excerpt below, he describes his wait during a move from one camp to another in 1944:

PRIMARY SOURCE

"The snow fell thickly. We were forbidden to sit down or even to move. The snow began to form a thick layer over our blankets. They brought us bread—the usual ration. We threw ourselves upon it. Someone had the idea of appeasing his thirst by eating the snow. Soon the others were imitating him. As we were not allowed to bend down, everyone took out his spoon and ate the accumulated snow off his neighbor's back. A mouthful of bread and a spoonful of snow. The SS [guards] who were watching laughed at the spectacle."

—Elie Wiesel, *Night*

▲ When the war ended, Allied troops managed to liberate the few surviving inmates of the death camps—many of whom were too shocked to believe they were being freed.

DBQ Document-Based Questions

1. **Explaining** How did the prisoners in Weisel's account try to quench their thirst?
2. **Describing** How did the guards react?

The Final Solution

MAIN Idea Nazi atrocities included sending millions of Jews, Gypsies, Slavs, the disabled, and others to concentration camps and extermination camps.

HISTORY AND YOU Can you think of a conflict today where violence is motivated by ethnic or religious hatred? Read to learn how prejudice led to mass murder in Nazi Germany.

On January 20, 1942, Nazi leaders met at the **Wannsee Conference** to determine the "final solution of the Jewish question." Previous "solutions" had included rounding up Jews, Gypsies, Slavs, and others from conquered areas, shooting them, and piling them into mass graves. Another method forced Jews and other "undesirables" into trucks and then piped in exhaust fumes to kill them. These methods, however, had proven too slow and inefficient for the Nazis.

At Wannsee, the Nazis made plans to round up Jews from the vast areas of Nazi-controlled Europe and take them to detention centers known as **concentration camps.** There, healthy individuals would work as slave laborers until they dropped dead of exhaustion, disease, or malnutrition. Most others, including the elderly, the infirm, and young children, would be sent to **extermination camps,** attached to many of the concentration camps, to be executed in massive gas chambers.

NATIONAL GEOGRAPHIC The Holocaust, 1939–1945

0 400 kilometers
0 400 miles
Lambert Azimuthal Equal-Area projection

Legend:
- ■ Concentration camp
- ■ Extermination camp
- □ Location of *Einsatzgruppen*
- — International boundary, January 1938

Jewish Losses, 1939–1945	
Baltic States	228,000
Belgium	40,000
Bulgaria	14,000
Byelorusian SSR	245,000
Czechoslovakia	155,000
Denmark	500
France	90,000
Germany and Austria	210,000
Greece	54,000
Hungary	450,000
Italy	8,000
Netherlands	195,000
Poland	3,000,000
Romania	300,000
Russian SSR	107,000
Ukrainian SSR	900,000
Yugoslavia	26,000

◄ A survivor of the Buchenwald camp drinks water outside the camp barracks, April 1945

Analyzing GEOGRAPHY

1. **Place** Where were most of the extermination camps located?
2. **Region** Which three nations had the highest number of Jewish losses?

Maps In MOtion See *StudentWorks™ Plus* or glencoe.com.

Concentration Camps

The Nazis had established their first concentration camps in 1933 to jail political opponents. After the war began, the Nazis built concentration camps throughout Europe.

Buchenwald, one of the largest concentration camps, was built near the town of Weimar in Germany in 1937. During its operation, more than 200,000 prisoners worked 12-hour shifts as slave laborers in nearby factories. Although Buchenwald had no gas chambers, hundreds of prisoners died there every month from exhaustion and horrible living conditions.

Leon Bass, a young American soldier, saw Buchenwald at the end of the war. A room built to hold 50 people had housed more than 150, with bunk beds built almost to the ceiling. Bass recalled:

PRIMARY SOURCE

"I looked at a bottom bunk and there I saw one man. He was too weak to get up; he could just barely turn his head. He was skin and bones. He looked like a skeleton; and his eyes were deep set. He didn't utter a sound; he just looked at me with those eyes, and they still haunt me today."

—quoted in *Facing History and Ourselves*

Extermination Camps

After the Wannsee Conference, the Nazis built extermination facilities in a number of the concentration camps, mostly in Poland, to kill Jews more efficiently. At these camps, including the infamous Treblinka and Auschwitz, Jews were the Nazis' main victims. Auschwitz alone housed about 100,000 people in 300 prison barracks. Its gas chambers, built to kill 2,000 people at a time, sometimes gassed 12,000 people in a day. Of the estimated 1,600,000 people who died at Auschwitz, about 1,300,000 were Jews. The other 300,000 were Poles, Soviet prisoners of war, and Gypsies.

Upon arrival at Auschwitz, healthy prisoners were selected for slave labor. Elderly or disabled people, the sick, and mothers and children went immediately to the gas chambers, after which their bodies were burned in giant crematoriums.

In only a few years, Jewish culture, which had existed in Europe for over 1,000 years, had been **virtually** obliterated by the Nazis in the lands they conquered. Despite exhaustive debate, there is still great controversy about why and how an event so horrifying as the Holocaust could have occurred. No consensus has been reached, but most historians point to a number of factors: the German people's sense of injury after World War I; severe economic problems; Hitler's control over the German nation; the lack of a strong tradition of representative government in Germany; German fear of Hitler's secret police; and a long history of anti-Jewish prejudice and discrimination in Europe.

Reading Check **Summarizing** How did Hitler try to exterminate Europe's Jewish population?

Section 3 REVIEW

Vocabulary

1. **Explain** the significance of: *Shoah*, Nuremberg Laws, Gestapo, Wannsee Conference, concentration camp, extermination camp.

Main Ideas

2. **Listing** What early steps did Germany take in persecution of Jewish people?

3. **Analyzing** What was the purpose of the Wannsee Conference?

Critical Thinking

4. **Big Ideas** Do you think the German people or other nations could have prevented the Holocaust? Why or why not?

5. **Organizing** Use a graphic organizer similar to the one below to list the methods the Nazis used to try to destroy the Jewish population.

Extermination Methods

6. **Analyzing Visuals** Study the photos on pages 467–468. How do the images show the destruction of Jewish life?

Writing About History

7. **Persuasive Writing** Imagine that you are living in the United States during the 1930s. You believe that more Jewish immigrants should be allowed to come into the country. Write a letter to your representative or senator in Congress to express your point of view.

History ONLINE

Study Central™ To review this section, go to glencoe.com and click on Study Central.

ANALYZING PRIMARY SOURCES

The Holocaust

As the Allies liberated areas from German control in the spring of 1945, they discovered horrifying scenes in Nazi concentration camps. The Nazi regime had systematically murdered six million Jews and killed another six million Poles, Slavs, Gypsies, homosexuals, communists, and mentally disabled persons. Photographs of the newly liberated camps shocked the American public, although the Roosevelt administration and the State Department had evidence of the death camps as early as 1942.

Study these primary sources and answer the questions that follow.

PRIMARY SOURCE 1

Eyewitness Account

"[There] were two barracks: the men stood on one side, the women on the other. They were addressed in a very polite and friendly way: 'You have been on a journey. You are dirty. You will take a bath. Get undressed quickly.' Towels and soap were handed out, and then suddenly the brutes woke up and showed their true faces: this horde of people, these men and women were driven outside with hard blows and forced both summer and winters to go the few hundred metres to the 'Shower Room.' Above the entry door was the word 'Shower'. One could even see shower heads on the ceiling which were cemented in but never had water flowing through them.

These poor innocents were crammed together, pressed against each other. Then panic broke out, for at last they realized the fate in store for them. But blows with rifle butts and revolver shots soon restored order and finally they all entered the death chamber. The doors were shut and, ten minutes later, the temperature was high enough to facilitate the condensation of the hydrogen cyanide for the condemned were gassed with hydrogen cyanide. This was the so-called 'Zyklon B'... which was used by the German barbarians.... One could hear fearful screams, but a few moments later there was complete silence."

—André Lettich, Jewish prisoner assigned to remove bodies from the gas chambers at Birkenau from *Nazism 1919–1945, Volume 3: Foreign Policy, War and Racial Extermination—A Documentary Reader*

PRIMARY SOURCE 2

Photograph, 1945

▼ *Newly liberated survivors at Dachau concentration camp, May 4, 1945*

PRIMARY SOURCE 3

Nazi Decree, 1941

I (1) Jews over six years of age are prohibited from appearing in public without wearing a Jewish star.
   (2) The Jewish star is a yellow piece of cloth with a black border, in the form of a six-pointed star the size of the palm of the hand. The inscription reads "JEW" in black letters. It shall be worn visibly, sewn on the left chest side of the garment.

II Jews are forbidden:
   (a) to leave their area of residence without written permission of the local police, carried on their person.
   (b) to wear medals, decorations or other insignia.

—Nazi decree issued September 1, 1941 from *Nazism 1919–1945, Volume 3: Foreign Policy, War and Racial Extermination—A Documentary Reader*

American Soldier's Diary, 1945

"One thousand Weimar citizens toured the Buchenwald camp in groups of 100. They saw blackened skeletons and skulls in the ovens of the crematorium. In the yard outside, they saw a heap of white human ashes and bones. . . .

The living actually looked worse than the dead. Those who lived wore striped uniforms, with the stripes running up and down. Those who were dead were stripped of their clothing and lay naked, many stacked like cordwood waiting to be burned in the crematory. At one time, 5,000 had been stacked on the vacant lot next to the crematory.

Often . . . the SS wished to make an example of someone in killing him. They hung him on the lot adjacent to the crematory, and all the three sections of the camp witnessed the sight—some 30,000 prisoners. They used what I call hay hooks, catching him under the chin and the other in the back of his neck. He hung in this manner until he died."

—diary of Captain Luther D. Fletcher, from *World War II: From the Battle Front to the Home Front*

Photograph, April 17, 1945

Painting

Unable to Work, *by Auschwitz survivor David Olère*

◄ *American soldiers force German civilians to view bodies after the liberation of the Buchenwald concentration camp.*

DBQ Document-Based Questions

1. **Speculating** How do you suppose soldiers could participate in such barbaric acts?

2. **Analyzing Visuals** What does the appearance of these survivors tell you about conditions in the camps?

3. **Drawing Conclusions** What purpose did the restrictions listed in Source 3 serve?

4. **Drawing Conclusions** Study Sources 5 and 6. How do you think American troops reacted to the horrifying scenes they found in the concentration camps? Why do you think American troops made Germans tour the liberated concentration camps?

5. **Analyzing Visuals** Study the painting in Source 6. What symbols does the artist use to illustrate the fate of those too weak to work?

America Enters the War

Guide to Reading

Big Ideas
Government and Society After World War II began, the United States attempted to continue its prewar policy of neutrality.

Content Vocabulary
- hemispheric defense zone *(p. 476)*
- strategic materials *(p. 478)*

Academic Vocabulary
- revise *(p. 474)*
- purchase *(p. 474)*
- underestimate *(p. 479)*

People and Events to Identify
- America First Committee *(p. 475)*
- Lend-Lease Act *(p. 476)*
- Atlantic Charter *(p. 477)*

Reading Strategy
Organizing As you read about America's efforts to stay neutral, complete a graphic organizer similar to the one below by naming events that shifted American opinion toward helping the Allies.

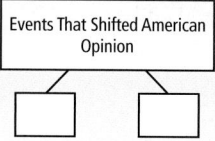

As World War II began, the United States remained officially neutral but aided Great Britain considerably in its fight against Germany. In the Pacific, Japan's territorial expansion led to growing tensions with the United States, which peaked when Japan attacked Pearl Harbor.

FDR Supports England

MAIN Idea President Roosevelt favored changes in American neutrality laws, although Americans remained divided about the war and American involvement.

HISTORY AND YOU Have you ever been drawn into an argument when you just wanted to be left alone? Read about the increasing difficulties that the United States faced in trying to stay out of World War II.

President Roosevelt officially proclaimed the United States neutral two days after Britain and France declared war on Germany. Despite this proclamation, however, he was determined to help the two countries as much as possible in their struggle against Hitler.

Destroyers-for-Bases Deal

Soon after the war began, Roosevelt called Congress into a special session to **revise** the neutrality laws. He asked Congress to eliminate the ban on arms sales to nations at war. Public opinion strongly supported the president. Congress passed the new law, but isolationists demanded a price for the revision. Under the Neutrality Act of 1939, warring nations could buy weapons from the United States only on a "cash-and-carry" basis. This law was similar to the 1937 Neutrality Act governing the sale of nonmilitary items to countries that were at war.

In the spring of 1940, the United States faced its first test in remaining neutral. In May, Prime Minister Winston Churchill asked Roosevelt to transfer old American destroyers to Britain, which had lost nearly half its destroyers. To protect its cargo ships from German submarines and to block any German attempt to invade Britain, the nation needed more destroyers.

Determined to give Churchill the destroyers, Roosevelt used a loophole in the neutrality act that required cash for **purchases.** In exchange for the right to build American bases on British-controlled Newfoundland, Bermuda, and islands in the Caribbean, Roosevelt sent 50 old American destroyers to Britain. Because the deal did not involve an actual sale, the neutrality act did not apply.

The Only Way We Can Save Her

" STAY OUT! STAY OUT FOR MY SAKE, AS WELL AS YOUR OWN!"

WAR MAD EUROPE

DEMOCRACY

AMERICA, THE LAST REFUGE OF DEMOCRACY

▲ This 1939 cartoon shows Uncle Sam standing guard over Democracy, whose only refuge is America.

ISOLATION POLICY

▲ Nazi bullets whiz past Uncle Sam and his isolationist policies.

Analyzing VISUALS DBQ

1. **Analyzing Visuals** According to the cartoon at left, what message is Democracy sending to Uncle Sam?

2. **Analyzing Visuals** What do you observe about Uncle Sam's perch in the cartoon above?

The Isolationist Debate

Widespread acceptance of the destroyers-for-bases deal reflected a change in public opinion. By July 1940, most Americans favored offering limited aid to the Allies. That spirit was hardly unanimous, however. In fact, people who wanted greater American involvement in the war and those who felt that the United States should remain neutral began debating the issue in the spring of 1940.

At one extreme was the Fight for Freedom Committee, a group that urged the repeal of all neutrality laws and stronger action against Germany. At the other extreme was the **America First Committee.** It was a staunchly isolationist group opposed to any American intervention or aid to the Allies. The committee's members included aviator Charles Lindbergh and Senator Gerald Nye.

Closer to the center, the Committee to Defend America by Aiding the Allies, which journalist William Allen White headed, pressed for increased American aid to the Allies but opposed armed intervention.

The heated neutrality debate took place during the 1940 presidential election campaign. For months, Americans had wondered whether President Roosevelt would follow the tradition George Washington had set and retire after a second term. With the United States in a precarious position, however, many believed a change of leaders might not be in the country's best interest. Roosevelt decided to run for an unprecedented third term.

During the campaign, FDR steered a careful course between neutrality and intervention. The Republican nominee, Wendell Willkie, did the same, promising he too would assist the Allies but stay out of the war. The voters reelected Roosevelt by a wide margin, preferring to keep a president they knew during this crisis period.

✓ Reading Check **Identifying** Identify different groups and their positions on U.S. neutrality in the late 1930s.

Edging Toward War

MAIN Idea In 1940 and 1941, the United States took more steps to provide aid to Great Britain.

HISTORY AND YOU What kinds of aid does America provide other countries today? Why? Read why FDR thought it was important to "lend" Britain some help.

Read "The Four Freedoms" on page R53 in **Documents in American History.**

With the election over, Roosevelt expanded the nation's role in the war. Britain was fighting for democracy, he said, and the United States had to help. Speaking to Congress, he listed the "Four Freedoms" for which both the United States and Britain stood: freedom of speech, freedom of worship, freedom from want, and freedom from fear.

The Lend-Lease Act

By December 1940, Great Britain had run out of funds to wage its war against Germany. Roosevelt came up with a way to remove the cash requirement of the most recent neutrality act. He proposed the **Lend-Lease Act,** which allowed the United States to lend or lease arms to any country considered "vital to the defense of the United States." The act allowed Roosevelt to send weapons to Britain if the British government promised to return or pay rent for them after the war.

Roosevelt warned that, if Britain fell, an "unholy alliance" of Germany, Japan, and Italy would keep trying to conquer the world. The president argued that the United States should become the "great arsenal of democracy" to keep the British fighting and make it unnecessary for Americans to go to war.

The America First Committee disagreed, but Congress passed the Lend-Lease Act by a wide margin. By the time the program ended, the United States had "lent" more than $40 billion in weapons, vehicles, and other supplies to the Allied war effort.

While shipments of supplies to Britain began at once, lend-lease aid eventually went to the Soviet Union, as well. In June 1941, violating the Nazi-Soviet pact, Hitler invaded the Soviet Union. Although Churchill detested communism and considered Stalin a harsh dictator, he vowed that any person or state "who fights against Nazism will have our aid." Roosevelt, too, supported this policy.

A Hemispheric Defense Zone

Congressional approval of the Lend-Lease Act did not solve the problem of getting American arms and supplies to Britain. German submarines patrolling the Atlantic Ocean were sinking hundreds of thousands of tons of shipments each month; the British Navy did not have enough ships to stop them.

Because the United States was still technically neutral, Roosevelt could not order the U.S. Navy to protect British cargo ships. Instead, he developed the idea of a **hemispheric defense zone.** Roosevelt declared that the entire western half of the Atlantic was part of the Western Hemisphere and, therefore, neutral. He then ordered the U.S. Navy to patrol the western Atlantic and reveal the location of German submarines to the British.

The Atlantic Charter

In August 1941, Roosevelt and Churchill met on board American and British warships anchored near Newfoundland. During these meetings, the two men agreed on the text of

---

PRIMARY SOURCE

Aiding Britain, 1939–1941

The Four Freedoms

"In the future days, which we seek to make secure, we look forward to a world founded upon four essential human freedoms.

The first is freedom of speech and expression—everywhere in the world.

The second is freedom of every person to worship God in his own way—everywhere in the world.

The third is freedom from want—which . . . will secure to every nation a healthy peacetime life for its inhabitants—everywhere in the world.

The fourth is freedom from fear—which, translated into world terms, means a world-wide reduction of armaments to such a point and in such a thorough fashion that no nation will be in a position to commit an act of physical aggression against any neighbor—anywhere in the world."

—Address to Congress, January 6, 1941

the **Atlantic Charter.** This agreement committed both nations to a postwar world of democracy, nonaggression, free trade, economic advancement, and freedom of the seas. By late September, an additional 15 anti-Axis nations had signed the charter. Churchill later said that FDR pledged to "force an 'incident' . . . which would justify him in opening hostilities" with Germany.

An incident quickly presented itself. In early September, a German submarine, or U-boat, fired on an American destroyer that had been radioing the U-boat's position to the British. Roosevelt promptly responded by ordering American ships to follow a "shoot-on-sight" policy toward German submarines.

The Germans escalated hostilities the following month, targeting two American destroyers. One of them, the *Reuben James,* sank after being torpedoed, killing 115 sailors. As the end of 1941 drew near, Germany and the United States continued a tense standoff.

Reading Check **Evaluating** How did the Lend-Lease Act help the Allied war effort?

Japan Attacks

MAIN Idea The Japanese attack on Pearl Harbor led the United States to declare war on Japan.

HISTORY AND YOU Do you remember how the United States acquired territory in the Pacific? Read about the threats to American interests as Japan expanded its empire.

Despite the growing tensions in the Atlantic, the Japanese attack on Pearl Harbor finally brought the United States into World War II. Ironically, Roosevelt's efforts to help Britain fight Germany resulted in Japan's decision to attack the United States.

America Embargoes Japan

Roosevelt knew that Britain needed much of its navy in Asia to protect its territories there from Japanese attack. As German submarines sank British ships in the Atlantic, however, the British began moving warships from Southeast Asia, leaving India and other colonial possessions vulnerable.

How Did FDR Help Britain While the U.S. Remained Neutral?

- Neutrality Act of 1939 allowed warring nations to buy weapons from the United States if they paid cash and transported arms on their own ships
- Destroyers-for-bases provided old American destroyers in exchange for the right to build U.S. defense bases in British-controlled Bermuda, Caribbean Islands, and Newfoundland
- Lend-Lease Act permitted U.S. to lend or lease arms to any country "vital to the defense of the United States"
- Hemispheric defense zone established the entire western half of the Atlantic as part of the Western Hemisphere and, therefore, neutral

What Did the Atlantic Charter Declare?

1. The U.S. and Britain do not seek to expand their territories.
2. Neither seeks territorial changes against the wishes of the people involved.
3. Both respect people's right to select their own government.
4. All nations should have access to trade and raw materials.
5. Improved labor standards and economic advances are vital.
6. Both nations hope people will be free from want and fear.
7. Everyone should be able to freely travel the high seas.
8. All nations must abandon the use of force; disarmament is necessary after the war.

NATIONAL GEOGRAPHIC **Sending Aid to Britain, 1939–1941**

September 4, 1941: Attack on the *Greer* prompts FDR's "shoot-on-sight" policy.

NORTH AMERICA

SOUTH AMERICA

ATLANTIC OCEAN

EUROPE

AFRICA

0   800 kilometers
0   800 miles
Miller projection

····· Hemispheric Defense Zone
→ Lend-Lease convoy route
⊶ Area with German submarines

DBQ **Document-Based Questions**

1. **Drawing Conclusions** Why do you think it was important to begin the Atlantic Charter with the first three points?

2. **Analyzing Primary Sources** How does the Atlantic Charter echo FDR's Four Freedoms speech?

Turning Point

Japan Attacks Pearl Harbor

Pearl Harbor was an important turning point because it not only brought the United States into the war but also decisively marked an end to U.S. isolationism. After the war ended, the nation did not withdraw from its role in international affairs, as it had done following World War I. Involvement in the war signaled the beginning of a global role for the United States that has continued to the present day. With the decision to support the United Nations and efforts to rebuild Europe, the nation became actively involved in international events.

HYPOTHESIZING Do you believe the United States would have entered the war regardless of the attack on Pearl Harbor? Support your ideas with reasons.

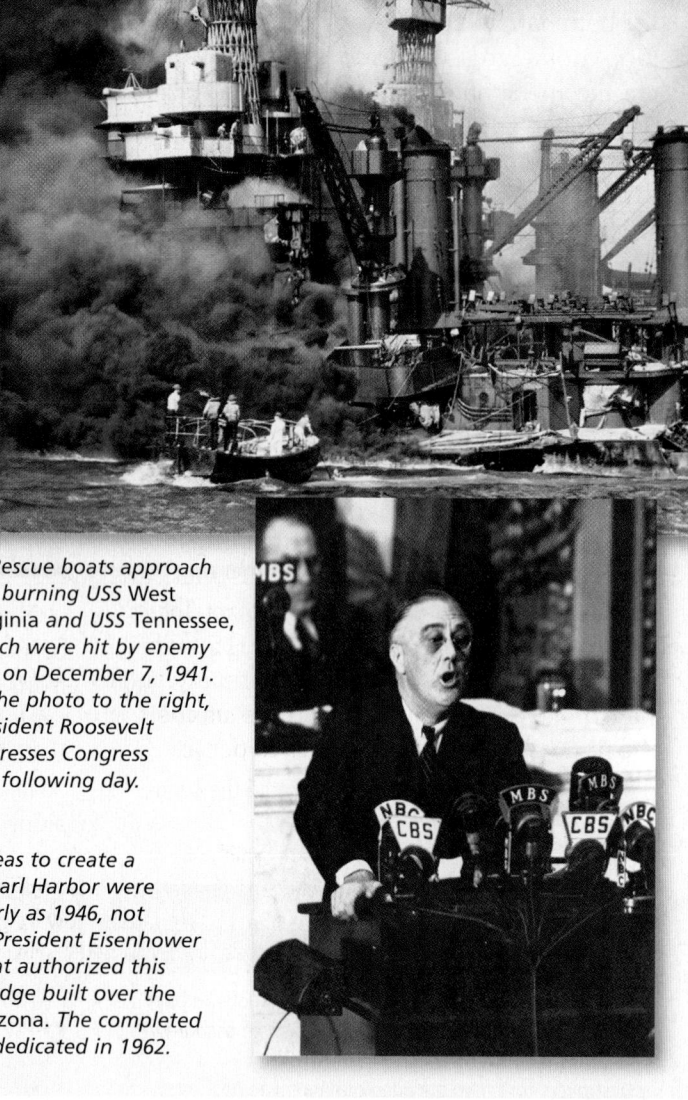

▲ Rescue boats approach the burning USS West Virginia and USS Tennessee, which were hit by enemy fire on December 7, 1941. In the photo to the right, President Roosevelt addresses Congress the following day.

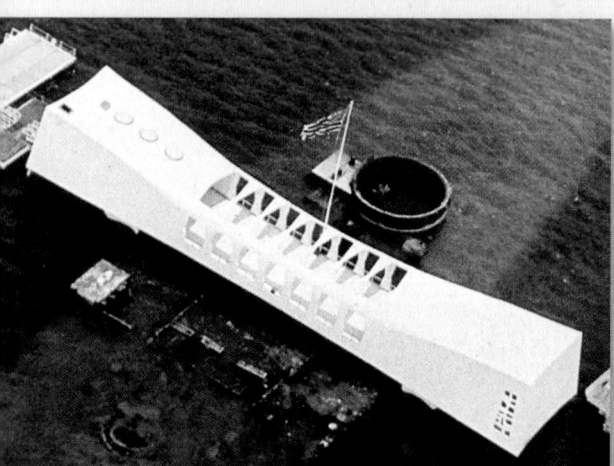

◄ Although ideas to create a memorial of Pearl Harbor were put forth as early as 1946, not until 1958 did President Eisenhower sign the bill that authorized this memorial, a bridge built over the sunken USS Arizona. The completed memorial was dedicated in 1962.

History ONLINE
Student Web Activity Visit glencoe.com and complete the activity on Pearl Harbor.

History ONLINE
Student Skill Activity To learn how to create multimedia presentations, visit glencoe.com and complete the skill activity.

To hinder Japanese aggression, Roosevelt began applying economic pressure. Japan depended on the United States for many key materials, including scrap iron, steel, and especially oil. At that time, the United States supplied roughly 80 percent of Japan's oil. In July 1940 Congress gave the president the power to restrict the sale of **strategic materials** (materials important for fighting a war). Roosevelt immediately blocked the sale of airplane fuel and scrap iron to Japan. Furious, the Japanese signed an alliance with Germany and Italy, becoming a member of the Axis.

In 1941 Roosevelt began sending lend-lease aid to China. Japan, which had invaded China in 1937, controlled much of the Chinese coast by 1941. Roosevelt hoped that lend-lease aid would enable the Chinese to tie down the Japanese and prevent them from attacking elsewhere. The strategy failed. By July 1941,

Japan had sent military forces into southern Indochina, posing a direct threat to the British Empire.

Roosevelt responded. He froze all Japanese assets in the United States, reduced the amount of oil being shipped to Japan, and sent General Douglas MacArthur to the Philippines to build up American defenses there.

Roosevelt made it clear that the oil embargo would end only if Japan withdrew from Indochina and made peace with China. With its war against China in jeopardy because of a lack of oil and other resources, the Japanese military planned to attack the resource-rich British and Dutch colonies in Southeast Asia. They also decided to seize the Philippines and to attack the American fleet at Pearl Harbor. While the Japanese prepared for war, negotiations with the Americans continued, but neither side would back down. In late November

1941, six Japanese aircraft carriers, two battleships, and several other warships set out for Hawaii.

Japan Attacks Pearl Harbor

The Japanese government appeared to be continuing negotiations with the United States in good faith. American intelligence, however, had decoded Japanese communications that made it clear that Japan was preparing to go to war against the United States.

On November 27, American commanders at the Pearl Harbor naval base received a war warning from Washington, but it did not mention Hawaii as a possible target. Because of the great distance from Japan to Hawaii, officials doubted that Japan would attempt such a long-range attack.

The U.S. military's inability to correctly interpret the information they were receiving left Pearl Harbor an open target. The result was devastating. Japan's surprise attack on December 7, 1941, sank or damaged eight battleships, three cruisers, four destroyers, and six other vessels. The attack also destroyed 188 airplanes and killed 2,403 Americans. Another 1,178 were injured.

That night, a gray-faced Roosevelt met with his cabinet, telling them the country faced the most serious crisis since the Civil War. The next day, he asked Congress to declare war:

PRIMARY SOURCE

"Yesterday, December 7, 1941—a date which will live in infamy—the United States of America was suddenly and deliberately attacked by naval and air forces of the Empire of Japan.... No matter how long it may take us . . . the American people in their righteous might will win through to absolute victory."

—from *The Public Papers and Addresses of Franklin D. Roosevelt*

The Senate voted 82 to 0 and the House 388 to 1 to declare war on Japan.

Germany Declares War

Although Japan and Germany were allies, Hitler was not bound to declare war against the United States. The terms of the alliance specified that Germany had to come to Japan's aid only if Japan was attacked, not if it attacked another country. Hitler had grown frustrated with the American navy's attacks on German submarines, however, and he believed the time had come to declare war.

Hitler greatly **underestimated** the strength of the United States. He expected the Japanese to easily defeat the Americans in the Pacific. By helping Japan, he hoped for Japanese support against the Soviet Union after they had defeated the Americans. On December 11, Germany and Italy both declared war on the United States.

☑ Reading Check **Examining** Why did military officials not expect an attack on Pearl Harbor?

Section 4 REVIEW

Vocabulary

1. **Explain** the significance of: America First Committee, Lend-Lease Act, hemispheric defense zone, Atlantic Charter, strategic materials.

Main Ideas

2. **Analyzing** What early efforts did Roosevelt make to help the British?

3. **Explaining** What was the hemispheric defense zone? Why was it developed?

4. **Summarizing** Why was the United States unprepared for Japan's attack on Pearl Harbor?

Critical Thinking

5. **Big Ideas** After Roosevelt's efforts to help Britain, some people accused him of being a dictator. Do you agree or disagree with this label? Explain your answer.

6. **Organizing** Use a graphic organizer similar to the one below to show how Roosevelt helped Britain while remaining officially neutral.

7. **Analyzing Visuals** Study the images on page 478. Then create a multimedia presentation that traces the Japanese attack on Pearl Harbor.

Writing About History

8. **Expository Writing** Write a letter to the editor of your newspaper explaining why you think the United States should either remain neutral or become involved in World War II.

History ONLINE

Study Central™ To review this section, go to glencoe.com and click on Study Central.

Chapter 13 VISUAL SUMMARY

STUDY TO GO — You can study anywhere, anytime by downloading quizzes and flashcards to your PDA from glencoe.com.

Causes of the Rise of Dictators

Italy

- Mussolini's Fascist Party believed in the supreme power of the state.
- In 1922 Mussolini threatened to march on Rome; the king appointed Mussolini as the premier.

Germany

- Hitler's Nazi Party believed in an all-powerful state, territorial expansion, and ethnic purity.
- Hitler believed that Germans needed more living space and called for Germany to expand east into Poland and Russia.
- Germany invaded Poland in 1939, France in 1940, and the USSR in 1941.

Japan

- Military leaders pushed for territorial expansion.
- Japan attacked Manchuria in 1931.
- Japan invaded China in 1937.
- Japan attacked Pearl Harbor in 1941.

▲ German tanks move down a highway near Soissons, France in May 1940.

▲ These survivors of Buchenwald, liberated in 1945, show the horrifying conditions under which they lived.

Effects

Holocaust

- During the Holocaust, the Nazis killed an estimated 6 million Jews.
- Jews were targeted and sent to concentration or extermination camps throughout Europe.

World War II

- Leaders of France and Britain tried to appease Hitler by allowing territorial growth.
- Britain and France declared war on Germany following the invasion of Poland.
- The United States sent aid to the Allied forces through the lend-lease program and cash-and-carry provision.
- France was defeated by the Nazis, who occupied the country in 1940.
- The United States declared war on Japan in 1941, after the bombing of Pearl Harbor.

Reviewing Vocabulary

Directions: Choose the word or words that best complete the sentence.

1. What type of government considered the nation more important than the individual?

   A dictatorship

   B monarchy

   C fascism

   D democracy

2. What did Hitler call Germany's quick air strikes?

   A blitzkrieg

   B *Kristallnacht*

   C *Anschluss*

   D gestapo

3. What were the Nuremberg Laws?

   A regulations passed by Congress that explained when the United States could go to war against Germany

   B regulations passed by Congress that restricted the number of Jewish immigrants allowed into the U.S.

   C regulations passed by the United Nations that outlawed World War II

   D regulations passed by Germany that deprived German Jews of certain rights such as citizenship

4. Buchenwald was a _____ built in 1937. Throughout its years of operation, over 200,000 prisoners worked there to the point of exhaustion and death.

   A ghetto

   B appeasement

   C Gestapo

   D concentration camp

5. _____, such as oil, steel, and iron supplies, were used by the United States to put pressure on Japan.

   A Rationed items

   B Strategic materials

   C Lend-Lease goods

   D Cash-and-carry materials

Reviewing Main Ideas

Directions: Choose the best answers to the following questions.

Section 1 *(pp. 454–459)*

6. Which factor encouraged an American policy of neutrality during the 1930s?

   A disillusionment with World War I and its results

   B decline in the military readiness of other nations

   C repeal of Prohibition

   D economic prosperity of the period

7. In the 1930s the United States responded to the rise of fascism in Europe by

   A invading Germany and Italy.

   B forming military alliances.

   C passing a series of neutrality laws.

   D joining the League of Nations.

Section 2 *(pp. 460–465)*

8. What term refers to the German annexation of Austria?

   A *Kristallnacht*

   B *Anschluss*

   C Munich Conference

   D Nazi-Soviet Nonaggression Pact

9. When France fell to the Nazis, the French and British evacuated thousands of troops from

   A Dunkirk.

   B Danzig.

   C Buchenwald.

   D Poland.

TEST-TAKING **TIP**

Look at each question to find clues to support your answer. Try not to get confused by the wording of the question. Then look for an answer that best fits the question.

Need Extra Help?

If You Missed Questions . . .	1	2	3	4	5	6	7	8	9
Go to Page . . .	454	462	466	470–471	478	458–459	458	460	462–464

 GO ON

Section 3 *(pp. 466–471)*

10. Concentration camps and extermination camps were part of what Nazis called

A justice for all.

B the "final solution."

C population control.

D the last straw.

Section 4 *(pp. 474–479)*

11. In 1939 the immediate response of the United States to the start of World War II in Europe was to

A modify its neutrality policy by providing aid to the Allies.

B declare war on Germany and Italy.

C strengthen its isolationist position by ending trade with Britain.

D send troops to the Allied nations to act as advisers.

12. What was one step that America took to aid Great Britain?

A created a hemispheric defense zone

B founded the America First Committee

C called for the Wannsee Conference

D attended the Munich Conference

13. Why did the United States enter the war in 1941?

A blitzkrieg over Poland

B bombing of Pearl Harbor

C embargo on Japan

D sinking of the *Lusitania*

Critical Thinking

Directions: Choose the best answers to the following questions.

14. When Roosevelt signed the Lend-Lease Act, he said America must become the "arsenal of democracy" in order to

A end the Depression. **C** remain neutral.

B help the Axis Powers. **D** help Britain.

Base your answers to questions 15 and 16 on the map below and on your knowledge of Chapter 13.

Nazi Concentration and Extermination Camps

(Map showing Europe with locations: Bergen-Belsen, Ravensbrück, Buchenwald, Dachau, Chelmno, Treblinka, Sobibor, Majdanek, Auschwitz-Birkenau)

□ Concentration camp
■ Extermination camp
— International boundary, Jan. 1938

0 ——— 400 kilometers
0 ——— 400 miles
Lambert Azimuthal Equal-Area projection

15. In which two countries were most of the concentration and extermination camps located?

A Germany and France

B Germany and Poland

C Germany and the Soviet Union

D Germany and Austria

16. What can you conclude about the extent of the Nazis' concentration and extermination camps?

A The Nazis constructed camps in every European country.

B The Nazis constructed camps in countries that Germany conquered.

C The Nazis constructed camps in Britain.

D The Nazis constructed camps in the Soviet Union.

Need Extra Help?

If You Missed Questions . . .	10	11	12	13	14	15	16
Go to Page . . .	470–471	474–476	476–477	477–479	476	R15	R15

GO ON

17. Why were the British able to prevent the Germans from invading their country?

   A The United States joined the Allied forces.

   B Germany could not penetrate the Maginot Line.

   C France defeated Germany and pushed them back into Belgium.

   D Britain had developed radar stations to detect German aircraft.

Analyze the cartoon and answer the question that follows. Base your answer on the cartoon and on your knowledge of Chapter 13.

HANDS ACROSS THE SEA —YES—

—BUT ARMS ACROSS THE SEA NO!

18. According to the cartoon, how did Americans feel about assisting the Allies?

   A They sent troops to help make the world safe for democracy.

   B Many Americans were willing to help the British but did not want to sell them arms.

   C Many Americans did not want to help the British fight the Germans.

   D The United States sold arms to Britain and France.

Document-Based Questions

Directions: Analyze the document and answer the short-answer questions that follow the document.

Daniel Inouye earned a Medal of Honor for his service in World War II and later became a United States senator. In 1941, however, he was a teenager living in Hawaii. This is his account of Pearl Harbor:

> "As soon as I finished brushing my teeth and pulled on my trousers, I automatically clicked on the little radio that stood on the shelf above my bed. I remember that I was buttoning my shirt and looking out the window . . . when the hum of the warming set gave way to a frenzied voice. 'This is no test,' the voice cried out. 'Pearl Harbor is being bombed by the Japanese!'"
>
> [The family ran outside to look toward the naval base at Pearl Harbor.]
>
> "And then we saw the planes. They came zooming up out of that sea of gray smoke, flying north toward where we stood and climbing into the bluest part of the sky, and they came in twos and threes, in neat formations, and if it hadn't been for that red ball on their wings, the rising sun of the Japanese Empire, you could easily believe that they were Americans, flying over in precise military salute."
>
> —quoted in *Eyewitness to America*

19. How did Inouye find out about the attack on Pearl Harbor?

20. What made him certain that the planes were Japanese, not American?

Extended Response

21. Could the Holocaust have been avoided if the Allies had intervened? Write an essay that takes a position and defends it. Your essay should include an introduction, several paragraphs, and a conclusion. Use relevant facts and details to support your conclusion.

For additional test practice, use Self-Check Quizzes—Chapter 13 at glencoe.com.

Need Extra Help?					
If You Missed Questions . . .	17	18	19	20	21
Go to Page . . .	465	R18	483	483	R6

Chapter 14

America and World War II

1941–1945

SECTION 1 Mobilizing for War

SECTION 2 The Early Battles

SECTION 3 Life on the Home Front

SECTION 4 Pushing Back the Axis

SECTION 5 The War Ends

Allied troops land in Normandy on D-Day, 1944.

1941
- United States enters World War II
- Roosevelt bans discrimination in defense industries

Franklin D. Roosevelt 1933–1945

1942
- Women's Army Auxiliary Corps established
- Japanese American relocation ordered

1943
- Detroit race riots
- Zoot-suit riots in Los Angeles

U.S. PRESIDENTS

U.S. EVENTS 1941 1942 1943

WORLD EVENTS

1941
- Japan attacks Pearl Harbor

1942
- Japan captures the Philippines
- Americans win Battle of Midway

1943
- Germans defeated at Stalingrad
- Allied forces land in Italy

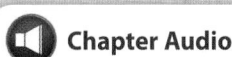

MAKING CONNECTIONS

What Kinds of Sacrifices Does War Require?

During World War II, millions of Americans enlisted in the armed forces, risking their lives in the struggle. On the home front, Americans also helped the war effort by giving up goods needed by the military and buying war bonds.

- *Why do you think so many Americans volunteered to fight in World War II?*

- *Should civilians have to make sacrifices in wartime?*

1944
- Supreme Court rules in *Korematsu* v. *United States* that Japanese American relocation is constitutional

Harry Truman
1945–1953

1945
- Franklin Roosevelt dies in office; Harry S. Truman becomes president

1944

1945

1944
- Eisenhower leads D-Day invasion
- MacArthur's forces land in the Philippines

1945
- U.S. Marines capture Iwo Jima
- United States drops atomic bomb on Japan

FOLDABLES

Summarizing American Life During World War II Make a Pocket Book Foldable to summarize various aspects of daily life that World War II affected. Label the two pockets as Economic and Social. Include general effects as well as specific programs under each pocket.

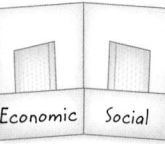

History ONLINE Visit glencoe.com and enter *QuickPass*™ code TAVMT5147c14 for Chapter 14 resources.

Mobilizing for War

Guide to Reading

Big Ideas
Economics and Society Americans quickly converted to a wartime economy to support the war effort.

Content Vocabulary
• cost-plus *(p. 488)*
• disenfranchised *(p. 491)*

Academic Vocabulary
• vehicle *(p. 489)*
• draft *(p. 490)*

People and Events to Identify
• War Production Board *(p. 489)*
• Office of War Mobilization *(p. 489)*
• "Double V" campaign *(p. 492)*
• Tuskegee Airmen *(p. 492)*
• Oveta Culp Hobby *(p. 493)*
• Women's Army Corps *(p. 493)*

Reading Strategy
Organizing Complete a graphic organizer similar to the one below by filling in the agencies that the U.S. government created to mobilize the nation for war.

Government Agencies Created to Mobilize the Economy

A fter World War I, America returned to isolationism. When the nation entered World War II in 1941, its armed forces ranked nineteenth in might, behind the tiny European nation of Belgium. Three years later, the United States was producing 40 percent of the world's arms.

Converting the Economy

MAIN Idea The United States quickly mobilized the economy to fight the war.

HISTORY AND YOU Have you ever changed the way you performed a task in order to do it faster or more efficiently? What steps did you take to speed things up? Read on to learn how the United States changed the way factories produced goods during World War II.

Shortly after 1:30 P.M. on December 7, 1941, Secretary of the Navy Frank Knox phoned President Roosevelt at the White House. "Mr. President," Knox said, "it looks like the Japanese have attacked Pearl Harbor." A few minutes later, Admiral Harold Stark, chief of naval operations, phoned and confirmed the attack.

Although President Roosevelt remained calm when he heard the news, he later expressed his concerns to his wife Eleanor: "I never wanted to have to fight this war on two fronts. We haven't got the Navy to fight in both the Atlantic and Pacific. . . . We will have to build up the Navy and the Air Force and that will mean we will have to take a good many defeats before we can have a victory."

Although the difficulties of fighting a global war troubled the president, British prime minister Winston Churchill was not worried. Churchill knew that victory in modern war depended on a nation's industrial power. He compared the American economy to a gigantic boiler: "Once the fire is lighted under it there is no limit to the power it can generate."

Churchill was right. The industrial output of the United States during the war astounded the rest of the world. American workers were twice as productive as German workers and five times more productive than Japanese workers. In 1943 the Soviet leader Joseph Stalin toasted "American production, without which this war would have been lost." American war production turned the tide in favor of the Allies. In less than four years, the United States and its allies achieved what no other group of nations had ever done—they fought and won a two-front war against two powerful military empires, forcing each to surrender.

The Arsenal of Democracy

U.S. Output of Military Products

Products

80,000
60,000
40,000
20,000

1941   1942   1943   1944   1945
Year

— Combat aircraft   — Ships   — Tanks

Source: *The Big 'L': American Logistics in World War II.*

Analyzing VISUALS

1. **Determining Cause and Effect** When did tank production begin to drop? Why might this be so?
2. **Making Connections** How do you think the workers felt as they watched the tanks rolling out of the factory?

The United States rapidly increased its war production after the attack on Pearl Harbor. The expansion was possible in part because the government had already begun mobilizing the economy before the country entered the war. When the German blitzkrieg swept into France in May 1940, President Roosevelt declared a national emergency and announced a plan to build 50,000 warplanes a year. Two months later he asked Congress for $4 billion to build a "Two-Ocean" Navy.

Shocked by the success of the German attack, many Americans were willing to build up the country's defenses. By October 1940, Congress had increased the defense budget to more than $17 billion. The Army-Navy Munitions Board—the military agency in charge of buying equipment—began signing contracts with American companies for new aircraft, ships, and equipment.

Roosevelt believed that government and business had to work together to prepare for war. He created the National Defense Advisory Committee to help mobilize the economy and asked several business leaders to serve on the committee. The president and his advisers believed that giving industry an incentive to move quickly was the best way to rapidly mobilize the economy. As Henry Stimson, the new secretary of war, wrote in his diary: "If you are going to try and go to war, or to prepare for war, in a capitalist country, you have got to let business make money out of the process or business won't work."

Normally when the government needed military equipment, it would ask companies to bid for the contract, but that system was too slow in wartime. Instead of asking for bids, the government signed **cost-plus** contracts. The government agreed to pay a company whatever it cost to make a product plus a guaranteed percentage of the costs as profit.

Under the cost-plus system, the more a company produced and the faster it did the work, the more money it would make. The system was not cheap, but it did get war materials produced quickly and in quantity.

Cost-plus convinced many companies to convert to war production. Other firms, however, could not afford to reequip their factories to make military goods. To convince more companies to convert, Congress gave new authority to the Reconstruction Finance Corporation (RFC). That government agency, set up during the Depression, could make loans to companies wanting to convert their factories to war production.

✓ **Reading Check** **Analyzing** What government policies helped American industry to produce large quantities of war materials?

American Industry Gets the Job Done

MAIN Idea Factories built tanks, airplanes, trucks, and jeeps for military use, as well as safer ships.

HISTORY AND YOU Has a coach or an instructor ever challenged you to improve your speed or efficiency at a task? Read on to learn how American industry helped the war effort.

By the fall of 1941, much had already been done to prepare the economy for war, but it was still only partially mobilized. Although many companies were producing military equipment, most still preferred to make consumer goods. The Great Depression was ending, demand was up, and sales were rising. The Japanese attack on Pearl Harbor, however, changed everything. A flood of orders by the government for war materials began, and by the summer of 1942, almost all major industries and some 200,000 companies had converted to war production. Together they made the nation's wartime "miracle" possible.

Building the Liberty Ships

▲ In this 1942 photograph, workers construct a Liberty ship in San Francisco.

PRIMARY SOURCE

"I took classes on how to weld. I had leather gloves, leather pants, a big hood, goggles and a leather jacket. . . .
They put me forty feet down in the bottom of the ship to be a tacker. I filled the long seams of the cracks in the ship corners full of hot lead and then brushed them good and you could see how pretty it was. The welders would come along and weld it so it would take the strong waves and deep water and heavy weight."

—Katie Grant, World War II riveter at
Kaiser Richmond Shipyard, California

DBQ **Document-Based Questions**

1. **Interpreting** Why would Katie Grant have had to wear leather clothing?

2. **Summarizing** What was her job?

Tanks Replace Cars

The automobile industry was uniquely suited to the mass production of military equipment. Automobile factories began producing trucks, jeeps, and tanks. Mass production was critical in modern warfare, because the country that could move troops and supplies most quickly usually won the battle. As General George C. Marshall, chief of staff for the United States Army, observed:

PRIMARY SOURCE

"The greatest advantage . . . the United States enjoyed on the ground in the fighting was . . . the jeep and the two-and-a-half ton truck. These are the instruments that moved and supplied United States troops in battle, while the German army . . . depended heavily on animal transport. . . . The United States, profiting from the mass production achievements of its automotive industry . . . had mobility that completely outclassed the enemy."

—quoted in *Miracle of World War II*

Automobile factories did not just produce **vehicles.** They also built artillery, rifles, mines, helmets, pontoon bridges, and dozens of other pieces of military equipment. Henry Ford created an assembly line for the enormous B-24 bomber known as the "Liberator" at Willow Run Airport near Detroit. By the end of the war, the factory had built more than 8,600 aircraft. Overall, the auto industry produced nearly one-third of all military equipment manufactured during the war.

Building the Liberty Ships

Ford's remarkable achievement in aircraft production was more than matched by Henry Kaiser's shipyards. Henry Kaiser started in the construction industry, but when World War II began, Kaiser shifted from the construction industry to shipbuilding.

German submarines were sinking American cargo ships at a terrifying rate. The United States had to find a way to build cargo ships as quickly as possible. Kaiser believed that speed was more important than quality and that cost was less important than results. He spent whatever it took to get the job done quickly. To save time, he applied techniques from the construction industry to shipbuilding. Instead of building an entire ship in one place from the keel up, parts were prefabricated and brought to the shipyard for assembly.

Kaiser's shipyards built many different kinds of ships, but they were best known for Liberty ships. The Liberty ship was the basic cargo ship used during the war. Liberty ships were welded instead of riveted. Although welded ships tended to crack, Vice Admiral Emory Land, head of the U.S. Maritime Commission, preferred the Liberty ships:

PRIMARY SOURCE

"Every time a riveted ship goes into dock you have a lot of repairs to do. You do not have them in welded ships. . . . On combat damage, comparing the welded Liberty ships and others, everything is in favor of the Liberty. . . . riveted ships are apt to go to the bottom if they are bombed or mined or torpedoed. . . . Never mind about the fractures or the cracks—[the Liberty ships] get into port."

—quoted in *Miracle of World War II*

When the war began, it took 244 days to build the first Liberty ship. After Kaiser shipyards applied their mass-production techniques, average production time dropped to 41 days. Kaiser's shipyards built 30 percent of all American ships constructed during the war, including nearly 3,000 Liberty ships.

The War Production Board

As American companies converted to war production, many business leaders became frustrated with the mobilization process. Government agencies argued constantly about supplies and contracts and whose orders had the highest priority.

After Pearl Harbor, President Roosevelt tried to improve the system by creating the **War Production Board** (WPB). He gave the WPB the authority to set priorities and production goals and to control the distribution of raw materials and supplies. Almost immediately, the WPB clashed with the military. Military agencies continued to sign contracts without consulting with the WPB. Finally, in 1943, Roosevelt established the **Office of War Mobilization** (OWM) to settle arguments among the different agencies.

Reading Check **Explaining** What military need led to the production of Liberty ships?

Building an Army

MAIN Idea Minorities and women played an important role in the United States armed forces during World War II.

HISTORY AND YOU Do you think the United States should have a military draft? Read to learn about the first peacetime draft in American history.

Converting factories to war production was only part of the mobilization process. To fight and win the war, the United States also needed to build up its armed forces.

Creating an Army

Within days of Germany's attack on Poland in 1939, President Roosevelt expanded the army to 227,000 soldiers. Before the spring of 1940, college students, unions, isolationists, and most members of Congress had opposed a peacetime **draft.** Opinions changed after France surrendered to Germany in June 1940. Two members of Congress introduced the Selective Service and Training Act, a plan for the first peacetime draft in American history. In September, Congress approved the draft by a wide margin.

You're in the Army Now

More than 60,000 men enlisted in the month after the attack on Pearl Harbor. At first, the flood of recruits overwhelmed the army's training facilities. Many recruits had to live in tents rather than barracks. The army also experienced equipment shortages. Troops carried sticks representing guns, threw stones simulating grenades, and practiced maneuvers with trucks labeled "TANK."

New recruits were initially sent to a reception center, where they were given physical exams and injections against smallpox and typhoid. The draftees were then issued uniforms, boots, and whatever equipment was available. The clothing bore the label "G.I.," meaning "Government Issue," which is why American soldiers were called GIs.

After taking aptitude tests, recruits went to basic training for eight weeks. They learned

PRIMARY SOURCE
Creating an American Army

▲ *Soldiers from a Mexican-American platoon train at Fort Benning in 1943.*

U.S. Armed Forces, 1939–1946

Military personnel (millions)

— Army
— Navy
— Marines

Year: 1939, 1940, 1941, 1942, 1943, 1944, 1945, 1946

Source: *Historical Statistics of the United States.*

PRIMARY SOURCE

For many Americans, entering the army changed their perspective, as historian Carl Degler recalls:

"Entrance into the Army in August, 1942, widened my horizons literally as well as experientially: for the first time I travelled beyond a 200 mile radius from Newark. I marvelled at the flatness of the prairie in Illinois . . . . Stops at posts in Miami Beach, Florida, and Richmond, Virginia, were my introduction to the American South."

—from *The History Teacher,* vol. 23, 1990

how to handle weapons, load backpacks, read maps, pitch tents, and dig trenches. Trainees drilled and exercised constantly and learned how to work as a team.

Basic training helped to break down barriers between soldiers. Recruits came from all over the country, and training together created a "special sense of kinship," as one soldier noted. "The reason you storm the beaches is not patriotism or bravery. It's that sense of not wanting to fail your buddies."

A Segregated Army

Although basic training promoted unity, most recruits did not encounter Americans from every part of society. At the start of the war, the U.S. military was segregated. White recruits did not train alongside African Americans. African Americans had separate barracks, latrines, mess halls, and recreational facilities. Once trained, African Americans were organized into their own military units, but white officers generally commanded them. Most military leaders also wanted to keep African American soldiers out of combat and assigned them to construction and supply units.

Some African Americans did not want to support the war. As one student at a black college noted: "The Army Jim Crows us. . . . Employers and labor unions shut us out. Lynchings continue. We are **disenfranchised** . . . and spat upon. What more could Hitler do to us than that?" Despite the bitterness, most African Americans agreed with African American writer Saunders Redding that they should support their country:

PRIMARY SOURCE

"There are many things about this war that I do not like . . . yet I believe in the war. . . . [W]e know that whatever the mad logic of [Hitler's] New Order there is no hope for us under it. The ethnic theories of the Hitler 'master folk' admit of no chance of freedom. . . . This is a war to keep [people] free. The struggle to broaden and lengthen the road of freedom—our own private and important war to enlarge freedom here in America—will come later. . . . I believe in this war because I believe in America. I believe in what America professes to stand for."

—from "A Negro Looks at This War"

A Segregated Army

Although the U.S. armed forces were segregated, discrimination did not prevent minority groups from performing with courage. Two of the best-known examples are the Tuskegee Airmen (right), comprised of African American volunteers, and the 442nd Regimental Combat Team (below), made up of Japanese American volunteers. The 450 Tuskegee Airmen fought in North Africa, Sicily, and Italy. The 442nd Regimental Combat Team became the most decorated unit in U.S. history.

Analyzing VISUALS

1. **Identifying** In what year did the army experience the most rapid growth? Why do you think that is the case?

2. **Evaluating** What do the expressions on the faces of the Tuskegee Airmen convey?

History ONLINE
Student Skill Activity To learn how to conduct an interview, visit glencoe.com and complete the Skill activity.

Pushing for "Double V" Many African American leaders combined patriotism with protest. In 1941 the National Urban League asked its members to encourage African Americans to join the war effort. It also asked them to make plans for building a better society in the United States after the war. The *Pittsburgh Courier*, a leading African American newspaper, launched the **"Double V" campaign.** The campaign urged African Americans to support the war to achieve a double victory—over both Hitler's racism abroad and the racism at home.

African Americans in Combat Under pressure from African American leaders, President Roosevelt ordered the army, air force, navy, and marines to recruit African Americans, and he told the army to put African Americans into combat. He also promoted Colonel Benjamin O. Davis, Sr., the highest-ranking African American officer, to the rank of brigadier general.

In early 1941 the air force created its first African American unit, the 99th Pursuit Squadron. The pilots trained in Tuskegee, Alabama, and became known as the **Tuskegee Airmen.** In April 1943, after General Davis urged the military to put African Americans into combat as soon as possible, the squadron was sent to the Mediterranean. Lieutenant Colonel Benjamin O. Davis, Jr., General Davis's son, commanded the squadron and helped win the battle of Anzio in Italy.

In late 1943 Colonel Davis took command of three new squadrons that had trained at Tuskegee. Known as the 332nd Fighter Group, these squadrons were ordered to protect American bombers as they flew to their targets. The 332nd Fighter Group flew 200 such missions and did not lose a single member to enemy aircraft.

African Americans also performed well in the army. The all–African American 761st Tank Battalion was commended for its service during the Battle of the Bulge. Although the

PRIMARY SOURCE
Women in World War II

About 400,000 American women played a major role in the military side of the war effort, if not in direct combat. Sixteen American women were awarded the Purple Heart for being injured as a result of enemy action. More than 400 American military women lost their lives.

▲ A doctor and an army nurse tend to a patient at a U.S. Army hospital in Leyte in the Philippines.

◄ *In this 1943 photo, Nancy Nesbit checks with the control tower from her plane at Avenger Field in Sweetwater, Texas, where the Women's Auxiliary Ferrying Squadron of the U.S. Army trained.*

Analyzing VISUALS

1. **Inferring** Why might the military have been reluctant to allow women in combat?

2. **Evaluating** What does the photo above suggest about conditions in military hospitals?

military did not end all segregation during the war, it did integrate military bases in 1943 and steadily expanded the role of African Americans within the armed forces. These successes paved the way for President Truman's decision to fully integrate the military in 1948.

Other Minorities in the Military Japanese Americans were not allowed to serve in the military at first. As the war progressed, however, second-generation Japanese Americans served in the 100th Infantry Battalion and the 442nd Regimental Combat Team. Almost half had been in internment camps in the American Southwest. Together these units became the most decorated in the history of the United States military. Many Mexican Americans had joined the National Guard during the 1930s and served on the front lines. Most minorities were allowed only in noncombat positions, such as kitchen workers. Native Americans, who were regarded as fierce warriors, were an exception to that policy. One-third of all healthy Native American men aged 18–50 served during the war.

Women Join the Armed Forces

Women joined the armed forces, as they had done during World War I. The army enlisted women for the first time, although they were barred from combat. Many jobs in the army were administrative and clerical. Assigning women to these jobs made more men available for combat.

Congress first allowed women in the military in May 1942, when it established the Women's Army Auxiliary Corps (WAAC) and appointed **Oveta Culp Hobby,** an official with the War Department, to serve as its first director. Although pleased about the establishment of the WAAC, many women were unhappy that it was an auxiliary corps and not part of the regular army. A little over a year later, the army replaced the WAAC with the **Women's Army Corps** (WAC). Director Hobby was assigned the rank of colonel. "You have a debt and a date," Hobby explained to those training to be the nation's first women officers. "A debt to democracy, a date with destiny."

As early as 1939, pilot Jackie Cochran had written to Eleanor Roosevelt suggesting that women pilots could aid the war effort. The following year, Nancy Love wrote to army officials to suggest that women be allowed to deliver planes. (The air force was not yet a separate branch of the military.) Training programs began in 1942; the Women Airforce Service Pilots (WASPs) began the next year. Although the WASPs were no longer needed after 1944, about 300 women pilots made more than 12,000 deliveries of 77 different kinds of planes.

The Coast Guard, the navy, and the marines quickly followed the army and set up their own women's units. In addition to serving in these new organizations, another 68,000 women served as nurses in the army and navy.

Reading Check **Summarizing** How did the status of women and African Americans in the armed forces change during the war?

Vocabulary

1. **Explain** the significance of: cost-plus, War Production Board, Office of War Mobilization, disenfranchised, "Double V" campaign, Tuskegee Airmen, Oveta Culp Hobby, Women's Army Corps.

Main Ideas

2. **Describing** How did Congress support factories that converted to war production?

3. **Analyzing** What role did the OWM play in the war production effort?

4. **Explaining** How were minorities discriminated against in the military?

Critical Thinking

5. **Big Ideas** How did American industry rally behind the war effort?

6. **Organizing** Use a graphic organizer like the one below to list the challenges facing the United States as it mobilized for war.

Challenges to Mobilization

7. **Analyzing Visuals** Look again at the photograph on page 488. What do you observe about the construction process?

Writing About History

8. **Expository Writing** Interview a World War II veteran or research your community during the war. How did industry rally behind the war effort? Write a one-page report to summarize your findings.

History ONLINE

Study Central™ To review this section, go to glencoe.com and click on Study Central.

Section Audio   **Spotlight Video**

The Early Battles

Guide to Reading

Big Ideas
Individual Action Several key people made decisions that changed the course of the war.

Content Vocabulary
• periphery (p. 497)
• convoy system (p. 499)

Academic Vocabulary
• code (p. 496)
• target (p. 498)

People and Events to Identify
• Chester Nimitz (p. 494)
• Douglas MacArthur (p. 494)
• Bataan Death March (p. 495)
• Corregidor (p. 495)
• James Doolittle (p. 495)

Reading Strategy
Organizing Complete a time line similar to the one below to record the major battles discussed and the victor in each.

The early battles of the war on both fronts required changes in strategy from all sides. In the Pacific, the Battle of Midway was a major turning point against the Japanese, while the Battle of the Atlantic and the Battle of Stalingrad made it clear that Germany would not win the war.

Holding the Line Against Japan

MAIN Idea The Japanese continued to win victories in the Pacific until the Battle of Midway.

HISTORY AND YOU Have you ever continued toward a goal even though the odds were against you? Read on to learn about the early battles in the Pacific.

Admiral **Chester Nimitz,** the commander of the United States Navy in the Pacific, began planning operations against the Japanese Navy. Although the Japanese had badly damaged the American fleet at Pearl Harbor, the American aircraft carriers, which were on a mission at sea, were safe. The United States had several carriers in the Pacific, and Nimitz was determined to use them. In the days just after Pearl Harbor, however, he could do little to stop Japan's advance into Southeast Asia.

The Fall of the Philippines

A few hours after bombing Pearl Harbor, the Japanese attacked American airfields in the Philippines. Two days later, they landed troops. The American and Filipino forces defending the Philippines were badly outnumbered. Their commander, General **Douglas MacArthur,** retreated to the Bataan Peninsula. Using the peninsula's rugged terrain, the troops held out for more than three months.

By March, in desperation, the troops ate cavalry horses and mules. The lack of food and supplies, along with diseases such as malaria, scurvy, and dysentery, took their toll. The women of the Army Nurse Corps worked on Bataan in primitive conditions. Patients slept in the open air. One nurse, Rose Meier, reported, "If we needed more room, we got our axes and chopped some bamboo trees down."

Realizing MacArthur's capture would demoralize the American people, President Roosevelt ordered the general to evacuate to Australia. MacArthur promised, "I came through, and I shall return."

On April 9, 1942, the weary defenders of the Bataan Peninsula finally surrendered. Nearly 78,000 prisoners of war were forced

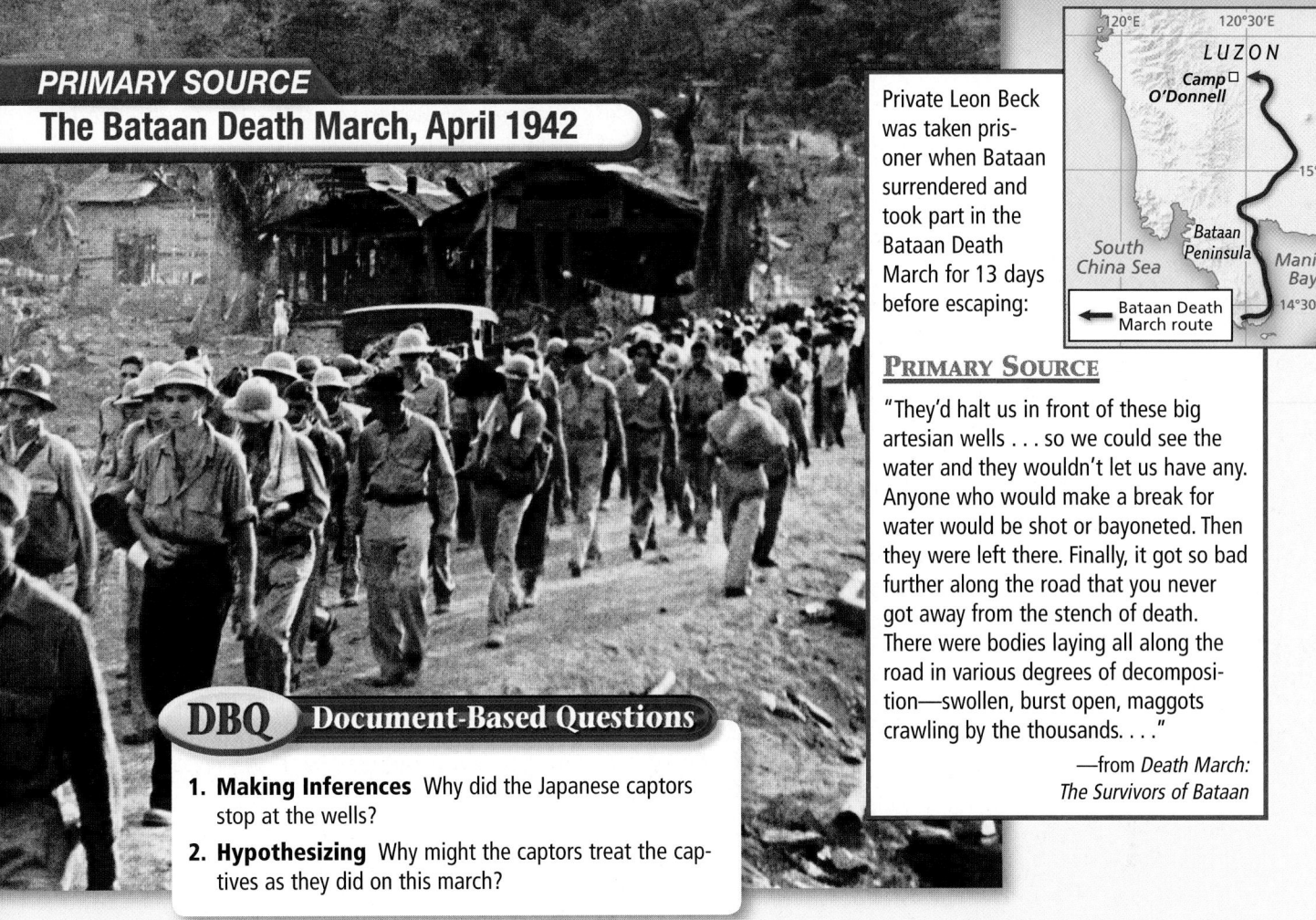

Private Leon Beck was taken prisoner when Bataan surrendered and took part in the Bataan Death March for 13 days before escaping:

PRIMARY SOURCE

"They'd halt us in front of these big artesian wells . . . so we could see the water and they wouldn't let us have any. Anyone who would make a break for water would be shot or bayoneted. Then they were left there. Finally, it got so bad further along the road that you never got away from the stench of death. There were bodies laying all along the road in various degrees of decomposition—swollen, burst open, maggots crawling by the thousands. . . ."

—from *Death March: The Survivors of Bataan*

DBQ **Document-Based Questions**

1. **Making Inferences** Why did the Japanese captors stop at the wells?

2. **Hypothesizing** Why might the captors treat the captives as they did on this march?

---

to march—sick, exhausted, and starving—65 miles (105 km) to a Japanese prison camp. Almost ten thousand troops died on this march, which was later called the **Bataan Death March.** Sixty-six women nurses were also captured and sent to the University of Santo Tomas in Manila. They remained there—with 11 navy nurses and some 3,000 Allied civilians—until early in 1945.

Although the troops in the Bataan Peninsula surrendered, a small force held out on the island of **Corregidor** in Manila Bay. Finally, in May 1942, Corregidor surrendered. The Philippines had fallen to the Japanese.

The Doolittle Raid on Tokyo

Even before the Philippines fell, President Roosevelt was searching for a way to raise the morale of the American people. He wanted to bomb Tokyo, but American planes could reach Tokyo only if an aircraft carrier brought them close enough. Unfortunately, Japanese ships in the North Pacific prevented carriers from getting near Japan.

In early 1942, a military planner suggested replacing the carrier's usual short-range bombers with long-range B-25 bombers that could attack from farther away. The only problem was that, although B-25s could take off from a carrier, the bombers could not land on its short deck. After attacking Japan, they would have to land in China.

President Roosevelt put Lieutenant Colonel **James Doolittle** in command of the mission to bomb Tokyo. At the end of March, a crane loaded sixteen B-25s onto the aircraft carrier *Hornet.* The next day, the *Hornet* headed west across the Pacific. On April 18, American bombs fell on Japan for the first time.

Japan Changes Strategy

While Americans rejoiced in the air force's success, Japanese leaders were aghast at the raid. Those bombs could have killed the emperor, who was revered as a god. The Doolittle raid convinced Japanese leaders to change their strategy.

Before the raid, the Japanese navy had disagreed about the next step. The officers in charge of the navy's planning wanted to cut American supply lines to Australia by capturing the south coast of New Guinea. The commander of the fleet, Admiral Yamamoto, wanted to attack Midway Island—the last American base in the North Pacific west of Hawaii. Yamamoto believed that attacking Midway would lure the American fleet into battle and enable his fleet to destroy it.

After Doolittle's raid, the Japanese war planners dropped their opposition to Yamamoto's idea. The American fleet had to be destroyed to protect Tokyo from bombing. The attack on New Guinea would still go ahead, but only three aircraft carriers were assigned to the mission. All of the other carriers were ordered to assault Midway.

The Battle of the Coral Sea

The Japanese believed that they could safely proceed with two attacks at once because they thought their operations were secret. What the Japanese did not know was that an American team of code breakers based in Hawaii had already broken the Japanese navy's secret **code** for conducting operations.

In March 1942, decoded Japanese messages alerted the United States to the Japanese attack on New Guinea. In response, Admiral Nimitz sent two carriers, the *Yorktown* and the *Lexington,* to intercept the Japanese in the Coral Sea. There, in early May, carriers from both sides launched all-out airstrikes against each other. Although the Japanese sank the *Lexington* and badly damaged the *Yorktown,* the American attacks prevented the Japanese from landing on New Guinea's south coast and kept the supply lines to Australia open.

The Battle of Midway

Back at Pearl Harbor, the code-breaking team now learned of the plan to attack Midway. With so many ships at sea, Admiral Yamamoto transmitted the plans for the Midway attack by radio, using the same code the Americans had already cracked.

Admiral Nimitz had been waiting for the opportunity to ambush the Japanese fleet. He

NATIONAL GEOGRAPHIC

The Battle of Midway, 1942

8 June 4, 5:01 P.M. *Yorktown* fliers join *Enterprise* attack on the *Hiryu,* setting it ablaze.

Course of Yorktown

Course of *Enterprise* and *Hornet*

9 June 6, 1:31 P.M. Japanese submarine *I-168* torpedoes the *Yorktown,* which sinks the next morning.

Hiryu sinks ✕

Course of Japanese fleet

Akagi sinks   *Soryu* sinks
Kaga sinks

Yorktown sinks

7 June 4, noon. Planes from the *Hiryu* attack U.S. carriers. *Yorktown* hit. The ship is abandoned but remains afloat.

6 June 4, 10:22-10:28 A.M. U.S. Dive-bombers score direct hits on *Kaga, Akagi,* and *Soryu.*

1 June 4, 4:30 A.M. Japanese carriers launch 108 warplanes to strike U.S. base at Midway.

2 June 4, 6:16 A.M. U.S. fighters clash with attackers.

5 June 4, 9:17 A.M. Japanese planes return. Fleet turns to engage U.S. carriers.

4 June 4, 7:08 A.M. U.S. fliers from Midway begin attacking Japanese fleet.

Line of U.S. submarines stationed 170 miles from Midway.

3 June 4, 6:30 A.M. Japanese begin bombing Midway.

Midway Islands (U.S.)

Kure Atoll (U.S.)

PACIFIC OCEAN

N W E S

U.S. Dauntless dive-bomber

● U.S. actions
● Japanese actions

immediately ordered carriers to take up positions near Midway. Unaware that they were heading into an ambush, the Japanese launched their aircraft against Midway on June 4, 1942. The Americans were ready. The Japanese ran into a blizzard of antiaircraft fire, and 38 planes were shot down. As the Japanese prepared a second wave to attack Midway, aircraft from the American carriers *Hornet, Yorktown,* and *Enterprise* then launched a counterattack. The American planes caught the Japanese carriers with fuel, bombs, and aircraft exposed on their flight decks. Within minutes, three Japanese carriers were reduced to burning wrecks. A fourth was sunk a few hours later, and Admiral Yamamoto ordered his remaining ships to retreat.

The Battle of Midway was a turning point in the war. The Japanese navy lost four large carriers—the heart of its fleet. Just six months after Pearl Harbor, the United States had stopped the Japanese advance. The victory was not without cost, however. The battle killed 362 Americans and 3,057 Japanese.

✔ **Reading Check** **Explaining** Why was the United States able to ambush the Japanese at Midway?

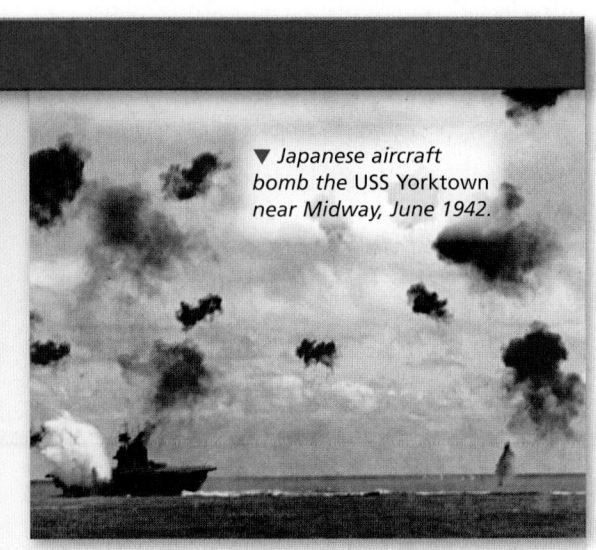

▼ *Japanese aircraft bomb the USS Yorktown near Midway, June 1942.*

Analyzing VISUALS

1. **Interpreting** When did Japan launch the attack on Midway?

2. **Drawing Conclusions** Why were aircraft carriers so vital to the war in the Pacific?

Maps In MOtion See *StudentWorks™ Plus* **or** glencoe.com.

Stopping the Germans

MAIN Idea The Allies defeated Germany in Africa and in the Atlantic. The Soviet victory at Stalingrad was a turning point of the war.

HISTORY AND YOU Have you ever tried something simple before attempting a more challenging problem? Read on to learn about the Allied strategy for attacking the Germans.

In 1942 Allied forces began to win victories in Europe as well. Almost from the moment the United States declared war in 1941, Joseph Stalin, the leader of the Soviet Union, urged President Roosevelt to open a second front in Europe. Stalin appreciated the lend-lease supplies that the United States had sent, but the Soviets were doing most of the fighting. If British and American troops opened a second front against Germany, it would take pressure off the Soviet Union.

Since 1940, U.S. military strategists had discussed with President Roosevelt the pressures of a two-front war. "Plan Dog" argued that the European theater must be the main focus because losing Great Britain would severely weaken any chance of regaining lost European territory. The shocking reality of Pearl Harbor put an end to theory. The United States carried out a two-front war, fighting both in the Pacific and in Europe.

Roosevelt wanted to get U.S. troops into battle in Europe, but Prime Minister Churchill did not believe the United States and Great Britain were ready to invade Europe. Instead, Churchill wanted to attack the **periphery,** or edges, of the German empire. Roosevelt agreed, and in July 1942, he ordered the invasion of Morocco and Algeria—two French territories indirectly under German control.

The Battle for North Africa

Roosevelt decided to invade Morocco and Algeria for two reasons. The invasion would give the army some experience without requiring a lot of troops. More important, it would help the British troops fight the Germans in Egypt. Great Britain needed Egypt because the Suez Canal was located there. Most of Britain's empire, including India, Hong Kong, Singapore, Malaya, and Australia, sent supplies to Britain through the canal.

History ONLINE **Student Web Activity** Visit glencoe.com and complete the activity on America and World War II.

El Alamein and Stalingrad, November 1942

Just as the Battle of Midway was a turning point in the war in the Pacific, so too were the battles of El Alamein in North Africa and Stalingrad in Europe. The British victory over German General Rommel at El Alamein secured the Suez Canal and kept the Germans away from the oil resources of the Middle East. Germany's defeat at the Battle of Stalingrad was a major turning point by ending Hitler's plans to dominate Europe.

◀ A British tank successfully navigates a wide ditch outside a town in North Africa.

▲ A Soviet gun crew fights against Nazi forces in Stalingrad. Only one day after the Nazis publicly boasted that the city would fall to them, the Red Army turned the tide of battle.

Analyzing VISUALS

1. **Assessing** How do you think the environment made combat at El Alamein and Stalingrad challenging?
2. **Evaluating** Why were the battles shown so important to the Allies?

General Erwin Rommel, whose success earned him the nickname "Desert Fox," commanded the "Afrika Korps." Although the British forced him to retreat in November 1942, after a 12-day battle against the coastal city of El Alamein, German forces remained a serious threat. Later that month, Americans commanded by General Dwight D. Eisenhower invaded North Africa. American general George Patton's forces in Morocco captured the city of Casablanca, while those in Algeria seized the cities of Oran and Algiers. The Americans then headed east into Tunisia, while British forces headed west into Libya.

When the American troops advanced into the mountains of western Tunisia, they had to fight the German army for the first time. At the Battle of Kasserine Pass, the Americans were outmaneuvered and outfought. They suffered roughly 7,000 casualties and lost nearly 200 tanks. Eisenhower fired the general who led the attack and put Patton in command. Together, the American and British forces finally pushed the Germans back. On May 13, 1943, the last German troops in North Africa surrendered.

The Battle of the Atlantic

As American and British troops fought the German army in North Africa, the war against German submarines in the Atlantic Ocean intensified. After Germany declared war on the United States, German submarines entered American coastal waters. American cargo ships were easy **targets,** especially at night when the glow from the cities in the night sky silhouetted the vessels. To protect the ships, cities on the East Coast dimmed their lights every evening. People also put up special "blackout curtains" and, if they had to drive at night, did so with their headlights off.

By August 1942, German submarines had sunk about 360 American ships along the East Coast. So many oil tankers were sunk that gasoline and fuel oil had to be rationed. To keep oil flowing, the government built the first long-distance oil pipeline, stretching some 1,250 miles (2,010 km) from Texas to Pennsylvania.

The loss of so many ships convinced the U.S. Navy to set up a **convoy system.** Under this system, cargo ships traveled in groups escorted by navy warships. The convoy system improved the situation dramatically. It made it much more difficult for a submarine to torpedo a cargo ship and escape without being attacked.

The spring of 1942 marked the high point of the German submarine campaign. In May and June alone, over 1.2 million tons of shipping were sunk. Yet in those same two months, American and British shipyards built more than 1.1 million tons of new shipping. From July 1942 onward, American shipyards produced more ships than German submarines managed to sink. At the same time, American airplanes and warships began to use new technology, including radar, sonar, and depth charges, to locate and attack submarines. As the new technology began to take its toll on German submarines, the Battle of the Atlantic turned in favor of the Allies.

The Battle of Stalingrad

In the spring of 1942, before the Battle of the Atlantic turned against Germany, Adolf Hitler was very confident that he would win the war. The German army was ready to launch a new offensive to knock the Soviets out of the war.

Hitler was convinced that only by destroying the Soviet economy could he defeat the Soviet Union. In May 1942, he ordered his army to capture strategic oil fields, factories, and farmlands in southern Russia and Ukraine. The city of Stalingrad, which controlled the Volga River and was a major railroad junction, was the key to the attack. If the German army captured Stalingrad, they would cut off the Soviets from the resources they needed to stay in the war.

When German troops entered Stalingrad in mid-September, Stalin ordered his troops to hold the city at all costs. Retreat was forbidden. The Germans were forced to fight from house to house, losing thousands of soldiers in the process. They were not equipped to fight in the bitter cold, but Soviet troops had quilted undersuits, felt boots, fur hats, and white camouflaged oversuits.

On November 23, Soviet reinforcements arrived and surrounded Stalingrad, trapping almost 250,000 German troops. When the battle ended in February 1943, some 91,000 Germans had surrendered, although only 5,000 of them survived the Soviet prison camps and returned home after the war. Each side lost nearly half a million soldiers. The Battle of Stalingrad was a major turning point in the war. Just as the Battle of Midway put the Japanese on the defensive for the rest of the war, the Battle of Stalingrad put the Germans on the defensive as well.

Reading Check **Describing** How did the United States begin winning the Battle of the Atlantic?

Section 2 REVIEW

Vocabulary

1. **Explain** the significance of: Chester Nimitz, Douglas MacArthur, Bataan Death March, Corregidor, James Doolittle, periphery, convoy system.

Main Ideas

2. **Explaining** Briefly explain the causes and effects of the effort to defeat the Japanese in 1942.

3. **Analyzing** Why did Churchill want to defeat the Germans in Africa before staging a European invasion?

Critical Thinking

4. **Big Ideas** Explain the significance of one person whose actions made a difference in the war.

5. **Organizing** Use a graphic organizer like the one below to list the reasons that the Battle of Midway is considered a turning point of the war.

Battle of Midway

6. **Analyzing Visuals** Look again at the map on page 496. How long did the Battle of Midway last?

Writing About History

7. **Expository Writing** Much of the course of wars is determined by the need for supply lines to remain open. Write a brief essay explaining how this need shaped early battles in which the United States was involved.

History ONLINE

Study Central™ To review this section, go to <u>glencoe.com</u> and click on Study Central.

Life on the Home Front

Although women and African Americans gained new work opportunities, Latinos and Japanese Americans faced violence in American cities. To assist with the war effort, the government controlled wages and prices, rationed goods, encouraged recycling, and sold bonds.

Women and Minorities Gain Ground

MAIN Idea With many men on active military duty, women and minorities found factory and other jobs open to them.

HISTORY AND YOU Do you remember reading about the unequal treatment of African American soldiers in World War I? Read on to learn how desegregation of the military began in World War II.

As American troops fought their first battles against the Germans and Japanese, the war began dramatically changing American society at home. In contrast to the devastation that large parts of Europe and Asia experienced, American society gained some benefits from World War II. The war finally ended the Great Depression. Mobilizing the economy created almost 19 million new jobs and nearly doubled the average family's income. For Robert Montgomery, a worker at an Ohio machine tool plant, "one of the most important things that came out of World War II was the arrival of the working class at a new status level in this society. . . . The war integrated into the mainstream a whole chunk of society that had been living on the edge."

The improvement in the economy did not come without cost. American families had to move to where the defense factories were located. Housing conditions were terrible. The pressures and prejudices of the era led to strikes, race riots, and rising juvenile delinquency. Goods were rationed and taxes were higher than ever before. Workers were earning more money, but they were also working an average of 90 hours per week. Despite the hardships, James Covert, whose mother owned a grocery store during the war, was probably right when he said that the war "changed our lifestyle and more important, our outlook. . . . There was a feeling toward the end of the war that we were moving into a new age of prosperity."

When the war began, American defense factories wanted to hire white men. With so many men in the military, however, there simply were not enough white men to fill all of the jobs. Under pressure to produce, employers began to recruit women and minorities.

We Can Do It!

At left, a riveter works on a bomber in Fort Worth, Texas. Posters such as those above and to the right encouraged women to participate in the war effort.

"THE GIRL HE LEFT BEHIND" IS STILL BEHIND HIM
She's a **WOW**
WOMAN ORDNANCE WORKER

Women Working

Labor force (millions)

Source: *Historical Statistics of the United States.*

Analyzing VISUALS

1. **Listing** During what years did women's employment outside the home hit its highest levels?

2. **Analyzing** How are the women portrayed in the posters?

Women in the Defense Plants

During the Great Depression, many people believed married women should not work outside the home, especially if they took jobs that could go to men trying to support their families. Most working women were young, single, and employed in traditional female jobs such as domestic work or teaching. The wartime labor shortage, however, forced factories to recruit married women for industrial jobs traditionally reserved for men.

Although the government hired nearly 4 million women, primarily for clerical jobs, the women working in the factories captured the public's imagination. The great symbol of the campaign to hire women was "Rosie the Riveter," a character from a popular song by the Four Vagabonds. The lyrics told of Rosie, who worked in a factory while her boyfriend served in the marines. Images of Rosie appeared on posters, in newspapers, and in magazines. Eventually 2.5 million women worked in shipyards, aircraft factories, and other manufacturing plants. Working in a factory changed the perspectives of many middle-class women like Inez Sauer:

PRIMARY SOURCE

"I learned that just because you're a woman and have never worked is no reason you can't learn. The job really broadened me. . . . I had always been in a shell; I'd always been protected. But at Boeing I found a freedom and an independence I had never known. After the war I could never go back to playing bridge again, being a club woman. . . . when I knew there were things you could use your mind for. The war changed my life completely."

—quoted in *The Homefront*

By the end of the war, the number of working women had increased from 12.9 million to 18.8 million. Although most women were laid off or left their jobs voluntarily after the war, their success permanently changed American attitudes about women in the workplace.

African Americans Demand War Work

Although factories were hiring women, they resisted hiring African Americans. Frustrated by the situation, **A. Philip Randolph,** the head of the Brotherhood of Sleeping Car Porters—a major union for African American railroad workers—decided to take action. He informed President Roosevelt that he was organizing "from ten to fifty thousand [African Americans] to march on Washington in the interest of securing jobs . . . in national defense and . . . integration into the military and naval forces."

In response, Roosevelt issued Executive Order 8802, on June 25, 1941. The order declared, "there shall be no discrimination in the employment of workers in defense industries or government because of race, creed, color, or national origin." To enforce the order, the president created the Fair Employment Practices Commission—the first civil rights agency the federal government had established since the Reconstruction Era.

Mexican Farmworkers

American citizens were not the only ones who gained in the wartime economy. In 1942 the federal government arranged for Mexican farmworkers to help with the harvest in the Southwest. The laborers were part of the **Bracero Program.** *Bracero* is a Spanish word meaning "worker." More than 200,000 Mexicans came to help harvest fruit and vegetables. Many also helped to build and maintain railroads. The Bracero Program continued until 1964. Migrant farmworkers thus became an important part of the Southwest's agricultural system.

✔ **Reading Check** **Describing** How did mobilizing the economy help end the Depression?

A Nation on the Move

MAIN Idea Millions of Americans relocated during the war to take factory jobs or to settle in less prejudiced areas.

HISTORY AND YOU Has someone in your family moved because of a job transfer? Read on to find out about relocations that resulted from the war.

The wartime economy created millions of new jobs, but the Americans who wanted these jobs did not always live near the factories. To get to the jobs, 15 million Americans moved during the war. The Midwest assembly plants and Northeast and Northwest shipyards attracted many workers. Most Americans, however, headed west and south in search of jobs.

The growth of southern California and the expansion of cities in the Deep South created a new industrial region—the **Sunbelt.** For the first time since the Industrial Revolution began

PRIMARY SOURCE
A Nation on the Move

During the war, millions of Americans flocked to the cities to work in factories. Many immigrants stayed on after the war to become citizens. As a result, the populations of Northern cities became more ethnically diverse, and these cities remained more populous after the war.

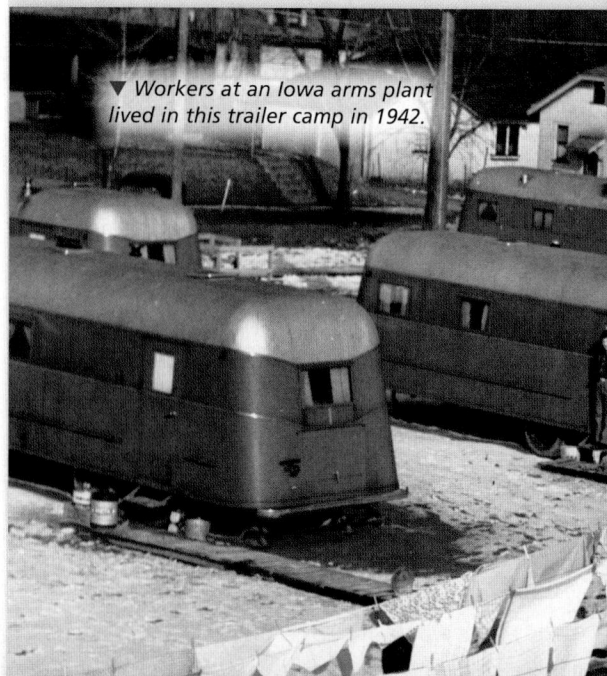

▼ *Workers at an Iowa arms plant lived in this trailer camp in 1942.*

in the United States, the South and West led the way in manufacturing and urbanization.

The Housing Crisis

The most difficult task facing cities with war industries was where to put the thousands of workers arriving in their communities. Tent cities and parks filled with tiny trailers sprang up. Anticipating the housing crisis, Congress had passed the Lanham Act in 1940. The act provided $150 million for housing. In 1942 President Roosevelt created the National Housing Agency (NHA) to **coordinate** all government housing programs. By 1943, those programs had been allocated over $1.2 billion. Although prefabricated public housing had tiny rooms, thin walls, poor heating, and almost no privacy, it was better than no housing at all. Nearly 2 million people lived in government-built housing during the war.

Racism Leads to Violence

African Americans left the South in large numbers during World War I in what became known to historians as the "**Great Migration.**" The migration slowed during the Great Depression but resumed when jobs in war factories opened up for African Americans during World War II. In the crowded cities of the North and West, however, African Americans were often met with suspicion and intolerance.

The worst racial violence of the war erupted in Detroit on Sunday, June 20, 1943. Nearly 100,000 people crowded into Belle Isle, a park on the Detroit River, to cool off. Gangs of white and African American teenage girls began fighting. These fights triggered others, and a riot erupted across the city. Twenty-five African Americans and 9 whites were killed.

The Zoot Suit Riots

Wartime prejudice boiled over elsewhere as well. In southern California, racial tensions became entangled with juvenile delinquency. Across the nation, the number of crimes committed by young people rose dramatically. In Los Angeles, racism against Mexican Americans and the fear of juvenile crime became linked because of the "zoot suit."

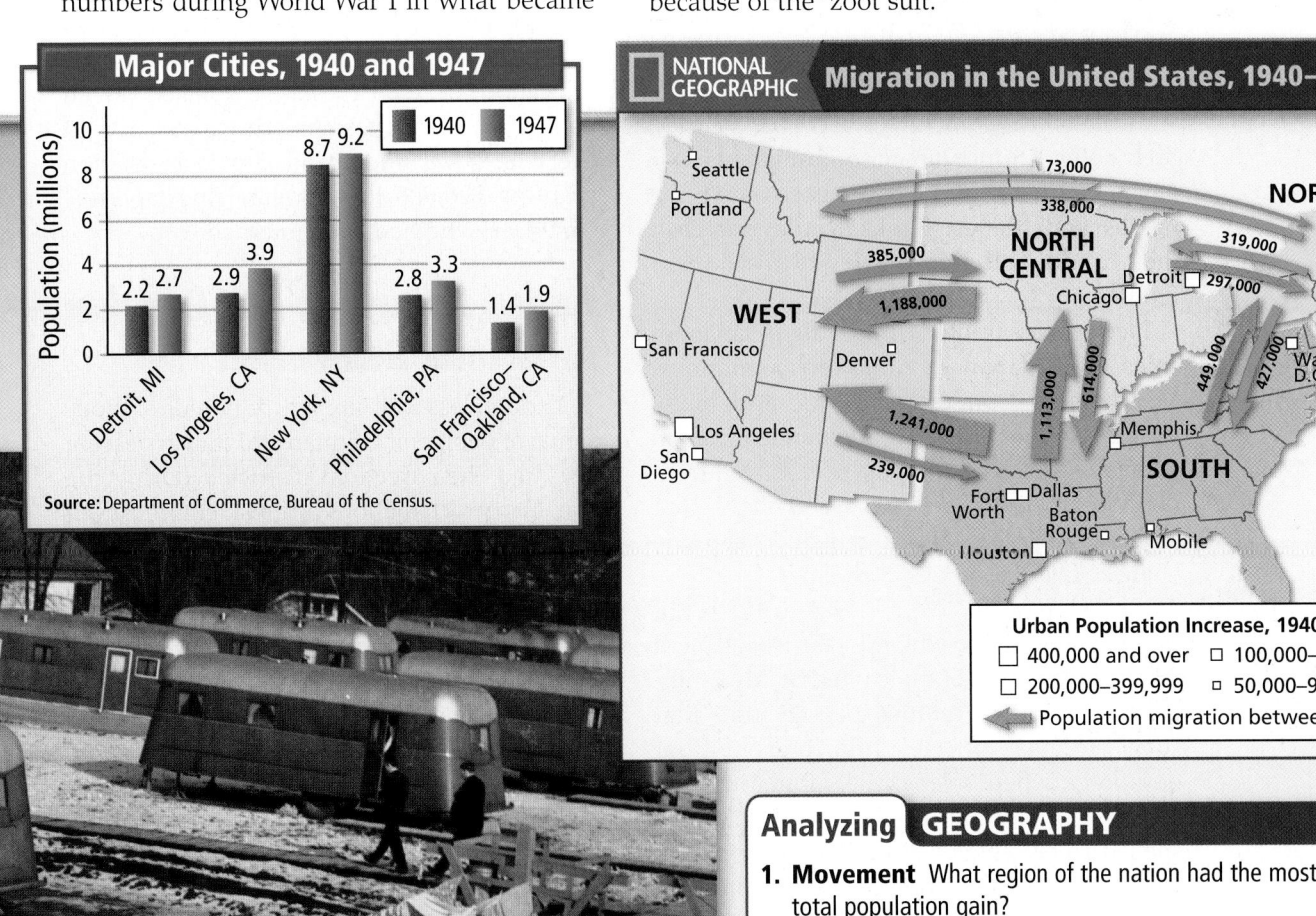

Major Cities, 1940 and 1947

Population (millions) — 1940 / 1947:
- Detroit, MI: 2.2 / 2.7
- Los Angeles, CA: 2.9 / 3.9
- New York, NY: 8.7 / 9.2
- Philadelphia, PA: 2.8 / 3.3
- San Francisco–Oakland, CA: 1.4 / 1.9

Source: Department of Commerce, Bureau of the Census.

NATIONAL GEOGRAPHIC   Migration in the United States, 1940–1950

Seattle
Portland
73,000
338,000
385,000
NORTH CENTRAL
NORTHEAST
319,000
1,188,000
Detroit 297,000
Chicago
New York City
WEST
San Francisco
Denver
1,241,000
614,000
1,113,000
449,000
427,000
Washington, D.C.
Los Angeles
San Diego
239,000
Memphis
SOUTH
Fort Worth Dallas
Baton Rouge
Houston
Mobile

Urban Population Increase, 1940–1947
- ☐ 400,000 and over
- ☐ 100,000–199,999
- ☐ 200,000–399,999
- ☐ 50,000–99,999
- ⬅ Population migration between regions

Analyzing GEOGRAPHY

1. **Movement** What region of the nation had the most total population gain?

2. **Movement** What region of the nation had the largest population loss?

A **zoot suit** had very baggy, pleated pants and an overstuffed, knee-length jacket with wide lapels, and sometimes a wide-brimmed hat. In order to save fabric for the war, most men wore a "**victory suit**"—a suit with no vest, no cuffs, a short jacket, and narrow lapels.

In California, Mexican American teenagers adopted the zoot suit. In June 1943, after hearing rumors that zoot-suiters had attacked several sailors, some 2,500 soldiers and sailors attacked Mexican American neighborhoods in Los Angeles. The police did not intervene, and the violence continued for several days.

Racial hostility against Mexican Americans did not deter them from joining the war effort. Approximately 500,000 Hispanic Americans served in the armed forces during the war. Most—about 400,000—were Mexican American. Another 65,000 were from Puerto Rico. By the end of the war, 17 Mexican Americans had received the Medal of Honor.

Japanese American Relocation

When Japan attacked Pearl Harbor, many Americans living on the West Coast turned their anger against Japanese immigrants and Japanese Americans. Mobs attacked their businesses and homes. Banks would not cash their checks, and grocers refused to sell them food.

Newspapers printed rumors about Japanese spies in the Japanese American community. Members of Congress, mayors, and many business and labor leaders demanded that all people of Japanese ancestry be removed from the West Coast. They did not believe that Japanese Americans would remain loyal to the United States in the war with Japan.

On February 19, 1942, President Roosevelt signed an order allowing the War Department to declare any part of the United States a military zone and to remove people from that zone. He must have felt **justified** only four days later, when a Japanese submarine surfaced north of Santa Barbara, California, and shelled an oil refinery, or in September of that year, when Japanese bombers twice dropped bombs on an Oregon forest. Secretary of War Henry Stimson declared most of the West

Coast a military zone and ordered all people of Japanese ancestry to evacuate to 10 internment camps further inland.

Not all Japanese Americans accepted the relocation without protest. Fred Korematsu argued that his rights had been violated and took his case to the Supreme Court. In December 1944, in *Korematsu* v. *United States,* the Supreme Court ruled that the relocation was constitutional because it was based not on race, but on "military urgency." Shortly afterward, the Court did rule in *Ex parte Endo* that loyal American citizens could not be held against their will. In early 1945, therefore, the government began to release the Japanese Americans from the camps.

Despite the fears and rumors, no Japanese American was ever tried for espionage or sabotage. Japanese Americans served as translators for the army during the war in the Pacific. The all-Japanese 100th Battalion, later integrated into the 442nd Regimental Combat Team, was the most highly decorated unit in World War II.

After the war, the Japanese American Citizens League (JACL) tried to help Japanese Americans who had lost property during the relocation. In 1988 President Ronald Reagan apologized to Japanese Americans on behalf of the U.S. government and signed legislation granting $20,000 to each surviving Japanese American who had been interned.

Italian American and German American Relocation

Though less well-known, hundreds of thousands of people of German and Italian descent also had their freedom restricted during the war. Two proclamations by President Roosevelt on December 8, 1941, stated that all unnaturalized residents of German and Italian descent, fourteen years of age or over, were designated as enemy aliens and were subject to government regulations such as travel restrictions, being forced to carry identification cards, and the seizure of personal property. Over 5000 were arrested and forced to live in military internment camps, primarily in Montana and North Dakota.

Reading Check **Comparing** Why did millions of people relocate during the war?

ANALYZING SUPREME COURT CASES

Can the Government Limit Civil Liberties in Wartime?

Korematsu v. *United States,* 1944
Background to the Case

During World War II, President Roosevelt's Executive Order 9066 and other legislation gave the military the power to exclude people of Japanese descent from areas that were deemed important to U.S. national defense and security. In 1942, Toyosaburo Korematsu refused to leave San Leandro, California, which had been designated as a "military area," based on Executive Order 9066. Korematsu was found guilty in federal district court of violating Civilian Exclusion Order No. 34. Korematsu petitioned the Supreme Court to review the federal court's decision.

How the Court Ruled

In their decision, the majority of the Supreme Court, with three dissenting, found that, although exclusion orders based on race are constitutionally suspect, the government is justified in time of "emergency and peril" to suspend citizens' civil rights. A request for a rehearing of the case in 1945 was denied.

▲ *Japanese American women and their children talk together at the Heart Mountain Relocation Camp.*

The Court's Opinion

"It should be noted, to begin with, that all legal restrictions which curtail the civil rights of a single racial group are immediately suspect. That is not to say that all such restrictions are unconstitutional. It is to say that courts must subject them to the most rigid scrutiny. Pressing public necessity may sometimes justify the existence of such restrictions; racial antagonism never can. . . . Korematsu was not excluded from the Military Area because of hostility to him or his race. He was excluded because . . . the properly constituted military authorities feared an invasion of our West Coast [by Japan] and felt constrained to take proper security measures, because they decided that the military urgency of the situation demanded that all citizens of Japanese ancestry be segregated from the West Coast temporarily, and finally, because Congress . . . determined that they should have the power to do just this."

—Justice Hugo Black
writing for the court in
Korematsu v. *United States*

Dissenting View

"I dissent, because I think the indisputable facts exhibit a clear violation of Constitutional rights. This is not . . . a case of temporary exclusion of a citizen from an area for his own safety or that of the community, nor a case of offering him an opportunity to go temporarily out of an area where his presence might cause danger to himself or to his fellows. On the contrary, it is the case of convicting a citizen as a punishment for not submitting to imprisonment in a concentration camp, based on his ancestry, and solely because of his ancestry, without evidence or inquiry concerning his loyalty and good disposition towards the United States. If this be a correct statement of the facts disclosed by this record, and facts of which we take judicial notice, I need hardly labor the conclusion that Constitutional rights have been violated."

—Justice Owen J. Roberts, dissenting in
Korematsu v. *United States*

DBQ Document-Based Questions

1. **Explaining** Why did the Supreme Court find in favor of the government in this case, even though the justices were suspicious of exclusion based on race?

2. **Contrasting** Why did Justice Roberts disagree with the majority opinion?

3. **Analyzing** Under what circumstances, if any, do you think the government should be able to suspend civil liberties of all or specific groups of American citizens?

Daily Life in Wartime

MAIN Idea The federal government took steps to stabilize wages and prices, as well as to prevent strikes. Americans supported the war through rationing, growing food, recycling, and buying bonds.

HISTORY AND YOU Have you ever given up something you enjoyed for a short period of time to gain something greater? Read on to learn how Americans sacrificed during the war.

Housing shortages and racial tensions were serious difficulties during the war, but mobilization strained society in other ways as well. Prices rose, materials were in short supply, and the question of how to pay for the war loomed ominously over the war effort.

Wage and Price Controls

Both wages and prices began to rise quickly during the war because of the high demand for workers and raw materials. The president worried about inflation. To stabilize both wages and prices, Roosevelt created the **Office of Price Administration** (OPA) and the Office of Economic Stabilization (OES). The OES regulated wages and the price of farm products. The OPA regulated all other prices. Despite some problems with labor unions, the OPA and OES kept inflation under control. At the end of the war, prices had risen only about half as much as they had during World War I.

While the OPA and OES worked to control inflation, the War Labor Board (WLB) tried to prevent strikes. In support, most American unions issued a "no strike pledge." Instead of striking, unions asked the WLB to mediate wage disputes. By the end of the war, the WLB had helped to settle more than 17,000 disputes involving more than 12 million workers.

Blue Points, Red Points

The demand for raw materials and supplies created shortages. The OPA began **rationing,** or limiting the purchase of, many products to make sure enough were available for military use. Meat and sugar were rationed. Gasoline was rationed, driving distances were restricted, and the speed limit was set at 35 miles per hour to save gas and rubber.

Hollywood Goes to War

In 1942 President Roosevelt created the Office of War Information (OWI). The OWI's role was to improve the public's understanding of the war and to act as a liaison office with the various media. The OWI established detailed guidelines for filmmakers, including a set of questions to be considered before making a movie, such as, "Will this picture help win the war?"

▲ Movies ranged from a comic Donald Duck cartoon to a serious portrayal of a bombing raid on Germany.

◄ Chaplin, noted as a comic and a director, made this movie in 1940, before the United States entered the war.

Analyzing VISUALS

1. **Interpreting** How would heroic movies like *The Memphis Belle* help win the war?

2. **Analyzing** Why do you think so many movies about Hitler were comedies?

A person from each household picked up a book of ration coupons every month. Blue coupons, called blue points, controlled processed foods. Red coupons, or red points, controlled meats, fats, and oils. Other coupons controlled items such as coffee, shoes, and sugar. Thirteen rationing programs were in effect at the height of the program. When people bought food, they also had to give enough coupon points to cover their purchases. Most rationing ended before the war was over. Sugar and rubber rationing continued after the war; sugar was rationed until 1947.

Victory Gardens and Scrap Drives

Americans also planted gardens to produce more food for the war effort. Any area of land might become a garden—backyards, school yards, city parks, and empty lots. The government encouraged **victory gardens** by praising them in film reels, pamphlets, and official statements.

Certain raw materials were so vital to the war effort that the government organized scrap drives. Volunteers collected spare rubber, tin, aluminum, and steel. They donated pots, tires, tin cans, car bumpers, broken radiators, and rusting bicycles. Oils and fats were so important to the production of explosives that the WPB set up fat-collecting stations. Americans would exchange bacon grease and meat drippings for extra ration coupons. The scrap drives boosted morale and did contribute to the success of American industry during the war.

Paying for the War

The federal government spent more than $300 billion during World War II—more money than it had spent from Washington's administration to the end of Franklin Roosevelt's second term. To raise money, the government raised taxes. Because most Americans opposed large tax increases, Congress refused to raise taxes as high as Roosevelt requested. As a result, the extra taxes collected covered only 45 percent of the war's cost.

The government issued war bonds to make up the difference between what was needed and what taxes supplied. Buying bonds is a way to lend money to the government. In exchange for the money, the government promises to repay the bonds' purchase price plus interest at some future date. The most common bonds during World War II were E bonds, which sold for $18.75 and could be redeemed for $25.00 after 10 years. Individuals bought nearly $50 billion worth of war bonds. Banks, insurance companies, and other financial institutions bought the rest—more than $100 billion worth of bonds.

Despite the hardships, the overwhelming majority of Americans believed the war had to be fought. Although the war brought many changes to the United States, most Americans remained united behind one goal—winning the war.

Reading Check **Evaluating** How did rationing affect daily life in the United States? How did it affect the economy?

Section 3 REVIEW

Vocabulary

1. **Explain** the significance of: A. Philip Randolph, Bracero Program, Sunbelt, Great Migration, zoot suit, victory suit, Office of Price Administration, rationing, victory garden.

Main Ideas

2. **Assessing** Why were jobs suddenly available to women and minorities?

3. **Evaluating** For what reasons did Americans relocate during the war?

4. **Explaining** How did the federal government control the economy during the war?

Critical Thinking

5. **Big Ideas** What challenges did Americans at home face during the war?

6. **Organizing** Use a graphic organizer like the one below to list the results of increased racial tensions during the war.

| Racial Tensions |
| Result | Result | Result |

7. **Analyzing Visuals** Look again at the photograph on pages 502–503. How does the photographer capture the feeling of people settling into a new area?

Writing About History

8. **Persuasive Writing** Write a newspaper editorial urging fellow citizens to conserve resources so that those resources can be used in the war effort.

History ONLINE

Study Central™ To review this section, go to glencoe.com and click on Study Central.

Pushing Back the Axis

Guide to Reading

Big Ideas
Geography and History The Allies slowly pushed back the German and Japanese forces during 1943 and 1944.

Content Vocabulary
• amphtrac (p. 514)
• kamikaze (p. 515)

Academic Vocabulary
• briefly (p. 512)
• intense (p. 512)

People and Events to Identify
• Casablanca Conference (p. 508)
• D-Day (p. 512)
• Omar Bradley (p. 512)
• Guadalcanal (p. 515)

Reading Strategy
Organizing Complete a graphic organizer similar to the one below by filling in the names and battles fought. Indicate whether Allied or Axis forces won the battle.

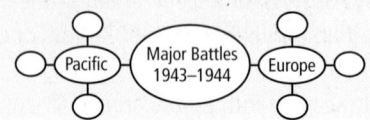

After British and American troops won victories over the Axis in North Africa and Italy, Allied leaders made plans for an invasion of Europe. Led by Admiral Nimitz and General MacArthur, American forces steadily advanced across the Pacific.

Striking Germany and Italy

MAIN Idea The Allies stepped up bombing of Germany and invaded Sicily and Italy.

HISTORY AND YOU Have you ever talked over your ideas with a good friend whose opinion you value? Read on to learn about FDR's meetings with Churchill and Stalin.

The Allied invasion of North Africa in November 1942 had shown that a large-scale invasion from the sea was possible. The success of the landings convinced Roosevelt to meet again with Churchill to plan the next stage of the war. In January 1943, FDR headed to Casablanca, Morocco, to meet the prime minister.

At the **Casablanca Conference,** Roosevelt and Churchill agreed to step up the bombing of Germany. The goal of this new campaign was "the progressive destruction of the German military, industrial, and economic system, and the undermining of the morale of the German people." The Allies also agreed to attack the Axis on the island of Sicily. Churchill called Italy the "soft underbelly" of Europe. He was convinced that the Italians would quit the war if the Allies invaded their homeland.

Strategic Bombing

The Allies had been bombing Germany even before the Casablanca Conference. Britain's Royal Air Force had dropped an average of 2,300 tons (2,093 t) of explosives on Germany every month for more than three years. The United States Eighth Army Air Force had dropped an additional 1,500 tons (1,365 t) of bombs during the last six months of 1942. These numbers were small, however, compared to the massive new campaign. Between January 1943 and May 1945, the Royal Air Force and the United States Eighth Army Air Force dropped approximately 53,000 tons (48,230 t) of explosives on Germany every month.

The bombing campaign did not destroy Germany's economy or undermine German morale, but it did cause a severe oil shortage and wrecked the railroad system. It also destroyed so many aircraft factories that Germany's air force could not replace its losses. By the time

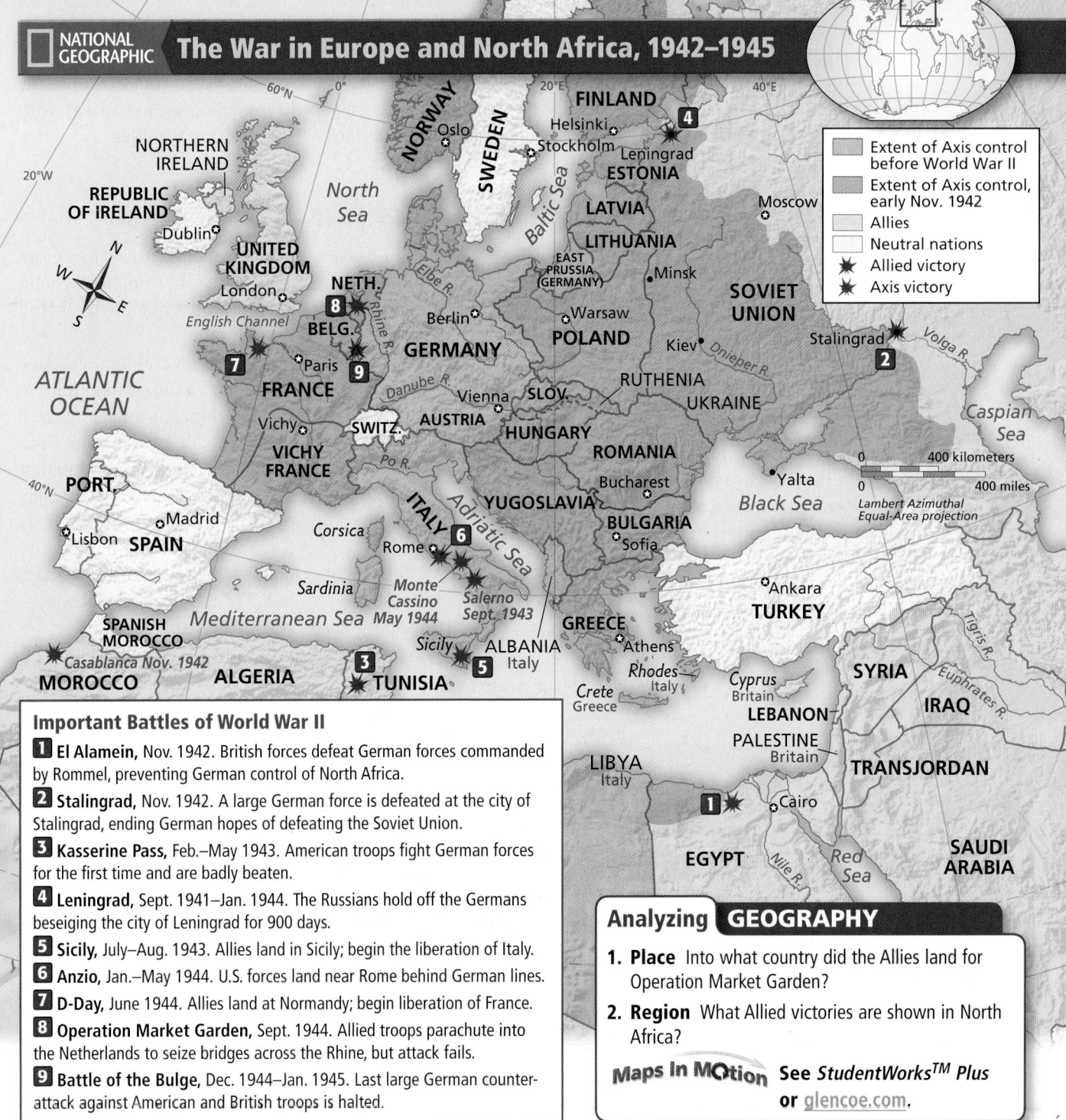

Extent of Axis control before World War II
Extent of Axis control, early Nov. 1942
Allies
Neutral nations
★ Allied victory
✸ Axis victory

400 kilometers
400 miles
Lambert Azimuthal Equal-Area projection

Important Battles of World War II

1 El Alamein, Nov. 1942. British forces defeat German forces commanded by Rommel, preventing German control of North Africa.

2 Stalingrad, Nov. 1942. A large German force is defeated at the city of Stalingrad, ending German hopes of defeating the Soviet Union.

3 Kasserine Pass, Feb.–May 1943. American troops fight German forces for the first time and are badly beaten.

4 Leningrad, Sept. 1941–Jan. 1944. The Russians hold off the Germans beseiging the city of Leningrad for 900 days.

5 Sicily, July–Aug. 1943. Allies land in Sicily; begin the liberation of Italy.

6 Anzio, Jan.–May 1944. U.S. forces land near Rome behind German lines.

7 D-Day, June 1944. Allies land at Normandy; begin liberation of France.

8 Operation Market Garden, Sept. 1944. Allied troops parachute into the Netherlands to seize bridges across the Rhine, but attack fails.

9 Battle of the Bulge, Dec. 1944–Jan. 1945. Last large German counter-attack against American and British troops is halted.

Analyzing GEOGRAPHY

1. **Place** Into what country did the Allies land for Operation Market Garden?

2. **Region** What Allied victories are shown in North Africa?

Maps In MOtion See *StudentWorks™ Plus* or glencoe.com.

the Allies landed in France, they had control of the air, ensuring that their troops would not be bombed.

Striking the Soft Underbelly

As the bombing campaign against Germany intensified, plans to invade Sicily also moved ahead. General Dwight D. Eisenhower commanded the invasion, with General Patton and the British General Bernard Montgomery head-

ing the ground forces. The invasion began before dawn on July 10, 1943. Despite bad weather, the Allied troops made it ashore with few casualties. A new amphibious truck delivered supplies and artillery to the soldiers on the beach.

Eight days after the troops came ashore, American tanks smashed through enemy lines and captured the western half of the island. Patton's troops then headed east, while the British attacked from the south. By August 18, the Germans had evacuated the island.

The attack on Sicily created a crisis within the Italian government. The king of Italy, Victor Emmanuel, and a group of Italian generals decided that it was time to depose Mussolini. On July 25, 1943, the king invited the dictator to his palace. "My dear Duce," the king began, "it's no longer any good. Italy has gone to bits. The soldiers don't want to fight anymore. At this moment, you are the most hated man in Italy." The king then arrested Mussolini, and the new Italian government began negotiating a surrender to the Allies.

Following Italy's surrender, however, German troops seized control of northern Italy, including Rome, and returned Mussolini to power. The Germans then took up positions near the heavily fortified town of Cassino. The terrain near Cassino was steep, barren, and rocky. Rather than attack such difficult terrain, the Allies landed at Anzio, behind German lines. Instead of retreating, however, as the Allies had hoped, the Germans surrounded the Allied troops near Anzio.

It took the Allies five months to break through the German lines at Cassino and Anzio. Finally, in late May 1944, the Germans retreated. Less than two weeks later, the Allies captured Rome. Fighting in Italy continued, however, for another year. The Italian campaign was one of the bloodiest in the war, with more than 300,000 Allied casualties.

The Tehran Conference

Roosevelt wanted to meet with Stalin before the Allies invaded France. In late 1943, Stalin agreed, proposing that Roosevelt and Churchill meet him in Tehran, Iran.

The leaders reached several agreements. Stalin promised to launch a full-scale offensive against the Germans when the Allies invaded France in 1944. Roosevelt and Stalin then agreed to divide Germany after the war so that it would never again threaten world peace. Stalin promised that once Germany was defeated, the Soviet Union would help the United States against Japan. He also accepted Roosevelt's proposal of an international peace-keeping organization after the war.

✓ Reading Check **Explaining** What effect did the Allied victory in Sicily have on Italy?

Driving Back the Germans, 1943–1944

November 28, 1943
Stalin, Roosevelt, and Churchill meet at the Tehran Conference

January 1943
The British and American air forces begin massive strategic bombing of German industry and infrastructure

Jan. 1943 ❯ **March 1943** ❯ **July 1943** ❯ **Dec. 1943**

July 10, 1943
Patton and Montgomery land forces on Sicily, beginning the invasion of Italy

July 25, 1943
The king of Italy puts Mussolini under arrest and the new Italian government negotiates surrender with the Allies

December 4–6, 1943
Roosevelt and Churchill meet in Cairo to plan D-Day. Roosevelt selects Eisenhower to command the invasion

Landing in France

MAIN Idea The Allies landed a massive force on France's beaches on June 6, 1944, known as D-Day.

HISTORY AND YOU What has been the biggest surprise you ever planned? Read on to find out how the Allies made a surprise landing in France.

After the conference in Tehran, Roosevelt headed to Cairo, Egypt, where he and Churchill continued planning the invasion of France. One major decision still had to be made. The president had to choose the commander for Operation Overlord—the code name for the invasion. Roosevelt selected General Eisenhower.

Planning Operation Overlord

Hitler had fortified the French coast along the English Channel, but he did not know when or where the Allies would land. The Germans believed the landing would be in Pas-de-Calais—the area of France closest to Britain. The Allies encouraged this belief by placing dummy equipment along the coast across from Calais. The real target was further south, a 60-mile stretch of five beaches along the Normandy coast.

Planners also discussed who should lead France after the invasion. General Eisenhower had informed Charles de Gaulle that the French Resistance forces would assist in the liberation of Paris, but President Roosevelt was not sure he trusted de Gaulle and refused to recognize him as the official French leader.

By the spring of 1944, more than 1.5 million American soldiers, 12,000 airplanes, and 5 million tons (4.6 million t) of equipment had been sent to England. Only setting the invasion date and giving the command to go remained. The invasion had to begin at night to hide the ships crossing the English Channel. The ships had to arrive at low tide so that they could see the beach obstacles. The low tide had to come at dawn so that gunners bombarding the coast could see their targets. Paratroopers, who would be dropped behind enemy lines, needed a moonlit night to see where to land. Perhaps most important of all, was good weather. A storm would ground the airplanes, and high waves would swamp landing craft.

March 4, 1944
The Allies make their first major daylight bombing raid on Berlin

June 6, 1944
Over 130,000 American, British, and Canadian troops land in Normandy on D-Day, beginning the liberation of France

Jan. 1944

June 1944

January 1944
American forces attack Monte Cassino and land at Anzio in an attempt to break through German lines and capture Rome

Analyzing TIME LINES

1. **Identifying** On what date did Allied forces land at Normandy to begin liberating France, and what is the date known as?

2. **Determining Cause and Effect** What effect did the successful Allied invasion of Sicily have on politics in Italy?

Given all these requirements, there were only a few days each month to begin the invasion. The first opportunity was from June 5 to 7, 1944. Eisenhower's planning staff referred to the day any operation began by the letter *D*. The invasion date, therefore, came to be known as **D-Day.** Heavy cloud cover, strong winds, and high waves made landing on June 5 impossible. The weather was forecast to improve **briefly** a day later. The Channel would still be rough, but the landing ships and aircraft could operate. After looking at forecasts one last time, shortly after midnight on June 6, 1944, Eisenhower gave the final order: "OK, we'll go."

The Longest Day

Nearly 7,000 ships carrying more than 100,000 soldiers headed for Normandy's coast. At the same time, 23,000 paratroopers were dropped inland, east and west of the beaches. Allied fighter-bombers raced up and down the coast, hitting bridges, bunkers, and radar sites. At dawn, Allied warships began a tremendous barrage. Thousands of shells rained down on the beaches, code-named "Utah," "Omaha," "Gold," "Sword," and "Juno."

The American landing at Utah Beach went well. The German defenses were weak, and in less than three hours the troops had captured the beach and moved inland, suffering fewer than 200 casualties. On the eastern flank, the British and Canadian landings also went well. By the end of the day, British and Canadian forces were several miles inland. Omaha Beach, however, was a different story. Under **intense** German fire, the American assault almost disintegrated. Lieutenant John Bentz Carroll was in the first wave that went ashore:

PRIMARY SOURCE

"Two hundred yards out, we took a direct hit. . . . Somehow or other, the ramp door opened up . . . and the men in front were being struck by machine-gun fire. Everyone started to jump off into the water. . . . The tide was moving us so rapidly. . . . We would grab out on some of those underwater obstructions and mines built on telephone poles and girders, and hang on. We'd take cover, then make a dash through the surf to the next one, fifty feet beyond."

—from *D-Day: Piercing the Atlantic Wall*

General **Omar Bradley,** commander of the American forces landing at Omaha and Utah, began making plans to evacuate. Slowly, however, the American troops began to knock out the German defenses. More landing craft arrived, ramming their way through the obstacles to get to the beach. Nearly 2,500 Americans were either killed or wounded on Omaha, but by early afternoon, Bradley received this message: "Troops formerly pinned down on beaches . . . [are] advancing up heights behind beaches." By the end of the day, nearly 35,000 American troops had landed at Omaha, and another 23,000 had landed at Utah. More than 75,000 British and Canadian troops were on shore as well. The invasion—the largest amphibious operation in history—had succeeded.

Reading Check **Summarizing** What conditions had to be met before Eisenhower could order D-Day to begin?

PRIMARY SOURCE

The United States began island-hopping across the Pacific with the Battle of Tarawa in November 1943. Reporter Robert Sherrod witnessed the savage hand-to-hand fighting:

"A Marine jumped over the seawall and began throwing blocks of fused TNT into a coconut-log pillbox. . . . Two more Marines scaled the seawall, one of them carrying a twin-cylindered tank strapped to their shoulders, the other holding the nozzle of the flame thrower. As another charge of TNT boomed inside the pillbox, causing smoke and dust to billow out, a khaki-clad figure ran out the side entrance. The flame thrower, waiting for him, caught him in its withering stream of intense fire. As soon as it touched him, the [Japanese soldier] flared up like a piece of celluloid. He was dead instantly . . . charred almost to nothingness."

—from *Tarawa: The Story of a Battle*

Driving Japan Back

MAIN Idea American troops slowly regained islands in the Pacific that the Japanese had captured.

HISTORY AND YOU Have you ever had to do a project over? Read to learn about American forces that took back Pacific islands from the Japanese.

While the buildup for invading France was taking place in Britain, American military leaders were also developing a strategy to defeat Japan. The American plan called for a two-pronged attack. The Pacific Fleet, commanded by Admiral Nimitz, would advance through the central Pacific by "hopping" from one island to the next, closer and closer to Japan. Meanwhile, General MacArthur's troops would advance through the Solomon Islands, capture the north coast of New Guinea, and then launch an invasion to retake the Philippines.

Island-Hopping in the Pacific

By the fall of 1943, the navy was ready to launch its island-hopping campaign, but the geography of the central Pacific posed a problem. Many of the islands were coral reef atolls. The water over the coral reef was not always deep enough to allow landing craft to get to the shore. If the landing craft ran aground on the reef, the troops would have to wade to the beach. As some 5,000 United States Marines learned at Tarawa Atoll, wading ashore could cause very high casualties. Tarawa, part of the Gilbert Islands, was the navy's first objective. The Japanese base there had to be captured in order to put air bases in the nearby Marshall Islands.

NATIONAL GEOGRAPHIC **Island-Hopping in the Pacific, 1942–1945**

◀ Marines are shown firing from behind sand bags during the battle of Tarawa. One Marine has just thrown a hand grenade.

SOVIET UNION
Sakhalin
Attu May 11–27, 1943
Kiska
Aleutian Is.
MONGOLIA MANCHURIA
Kuril Is.
Sea of Japan
Beijing
Hiroshima Aug. 6, 1945
Tokyo
Japan surrenders on battleship *Missouri* Sept. 2, 1945
CHINA Yellow R.
Chongqing Nanjing
Shanghai
Nagasaki Aug. 9, 1945
Okinawa Apr. 1– June 22, 1945
Iwo Jima Feb. 19–March 26, 1945
Midway June 4–7, 1942
PACIFIC OCEAN
INDIA
Lashio
BURMA
Hong Kong U.K.
Philippine Sea
Luzon
Manila March 4, 1945 PHILIPPINES
Leyte Gulf Oct. 23–26, 1944
Wake Island U.K.
Saipan June 15–July 9, 1944
Marshall Islands Feb. 1944
Hawaiian Islands
Pearl Harbor
SIAM (THAILAND)
Bangkok
South China Sea
FRENCH INDOCHINA Mindanao
Guam Guam July 21– U.S. Aug. 10, 1944
Palau Is.
Nimitz, Nov. 1943
0   1,000 kilometers
0   1,000 miles
Miller projection
Singapore U.K.
Borneo
MacArthur
Halsey
Tarawa Nov. 20–23, 1943
Nauru Gilbert U.K. Is.
EQUATOR
Sumatra
Batavia
Java
NEW GUINEA
Halsey
Solomon Is.
Guadalcanal Aug. 7, 1942– Feb. 9, 1943
Ellice Is.
INDIAN OCEAN
Darwin
Coral Sea May 4–8, 1942
New Hebrides
Coral Sea
AUSTRALIA

Legend:
- Japanese Empire and conquests
- Farthest extent of Japan's conquests, July 1942
- ◀ Allied forces
- ✳ Major battle
- ◎ Atomic bombing

Analyzing GEOGRAPHY

1. **Place** When Nimitz left Pearl Harbor, what was his destination?
2. **Place** Who controlled Guam in 1942?

People IN HISTORY

The Navajo Code Talkers

When American marines stormed an enemy beach, they used radios to communicate. Using radios, however, meant that the Japanese could intercept and translate the messages. In the midst of the battle, however, there was no time to use a code-machine. Acting upon the suggestion of Philip Johnston, an engineer who had lived on a Navajo reservation as a child, the marines recruited Navajos to serve as "code talkers."

The Navajo language had no written alphabet and was known only to the Navajo and a few missionaries and anthropologists. The Navajo recruits developed code words, using their own language, that stood for military terms. For example, the Navajo word *jay-sho,* or "buzzard," was code for *bomber; lotso,* or "whale," meant *battleship;* and *na-ma-si,* or "potatoes," stood for *grenades.*

Code talkers proved invaluable in combat. They could relay a message in minutes that would have taken a code-machine operator hours to encipher and transmit. At the battle of Iwo Jima, code talkers transmitted more than 800 messages during the first 48 hours as the marines struggled to get ashore under intense bombardment. More than 400 Navajo served in the marine corps as code talkers. Sworn to secrecy, their mission was not revealed until 1971. In 2001 Congress awarded the code talkers the Congressional Gold Medal for their unique contribution during the war.

What advantage did the code talkers provide over traditional forms of communication?

▲ *These Navajo code talkers assigned to a Pacific-based marine regiment relay orders using a field radio.*

When the landing craft hit the reef, at least 20 ships ran aground. The marines had to plunge into shoulder-high water and wade several hundred yards to the beach. Raked by Japanese fire, only one marine in three made it ashore. Once the marines reached the beach, the battle was still far from over.

Although many troops died wading ashore, one vehicle had been able to cross the reef and deliver its troops onto the beaches. The vehicle was a boat with tank tracks, nicknamed the "Alligator." This amphibious tractor, or **amphtrac,** had been invented in the late 1930s to rescue people in Florida swamps. It had never been used in combat, and the navy decided to buy only 200 of them in 1941. If more had been available at Tarawa, American casualties probably would have been much lower.

More than 1,000 marines died on Tarawa. Photos of bodies lying crumpled next to burning landing craft shocked Americans back home. Many people began to wonder how many lives would be lost in defeating Japan.

The next assault—Kwajalein Atoll in the Marshall Islands—went much more smoothly. This time all of the troops went ashore in amphtracs. Although the Japanese resisted fiercely, the marines captured Kwajalein and nearby Eniwetok with far fewer casualties.

After the Marshall Islands, the navy targeted the Mariana Islands. American military planners wanted to use the Marianas as a base for a new heavy bomber, the B-29 Superfortress. The B-29 could fly farther than any other plane in the world. From airfields in the Marianas, B-29s could bomb Japan. Admiral Nimitz decided to invade three of the Mariana Islands: Saipan, Tinian, and Guam. Despite strong Japanese resistance, American troops captured all three by August 1944. A few months later, B-29s began bombing Japan.

MacArthur Returns

As the forces under Admiral Nimitz hopped across the central Pacific, General Douglas MacArthur's troops began their own campaign in the southwest Pacific. The campaign began by invading **Guadalcanal** in the Solomon Islands, east of New Guinea, in August 1942. It continued until early 1944, when MacArthur's troops finally captured enough islands to surround the main Japanese base in the region. In response, the Japanese withdrew their ships and aircraft from the base, although they left 100,000 troops behind to hold the island.

Worried that the navy's advance across the central Pacific was leaving him behind, MacArthur ordered his forces to leap nearly 600 miles (966 km) to capture the Japanese base at Hollandia on the north coast of New Guinea. Shortly after securing New Guinea, MacArthur's troops seized the island of Morotai—the last stop before the Philippines.

To take back the Philippines, the United States assembled an enormous invasion force. In October 1944, more than 700 ships carrying more than 160,000 troops sailed for Leyte Gulf in the Philippines. On October 20, the troops began to land on Leyte, an island on the eastern side of the Philippines. A few hours after the invasion began, MacArthur headed to the beach. Upon reaching the shore, he strode to a radio and spoke into the microphone: "People of the Philippines, I have returned. By the grace of Almighty God, our forces stand again on Philippine soil."

To stop the American invasion, the Japanese sent four aircraft carriers toward the Philippines from the north and secretly dispatched another fleet to the west. Believing the Japanese carriers were leading the main attack, most of the American carriers protecting the invasion left Leyte Gulf and headed north to stop them. Seizing their chance, the Japanese warships to the west raced through the Philippine Islands into Leyte Gulf and ambushed the remaining American ships.

The Battle of Leyte Gulf was the largest naval battle in history. It was also the first time that the Japanese used **kamikaze** attacks. *Kamikaze* means "divine wind" in Japanese. It refers to the great storm that destroyed the Mongol fleet during its invasion of Japan in the thirteenth century. Kamikaze pilots would deliberately crash their planes into American ships, killing themselves but also inflicting severe damage. Luckily for the Americans, just as their situation was becoming desperate, the Japanese commander, believing more American ships were on the way, ordered a retreat.

Although the Japanese fleet had retreated, the campaign to recapture the Philippines from the Japanese was long and grueling. More than 80,000 Japanese were killed; fewer than 1,000 surrendered. MacArthur's troops did not capture Manila until March 1945. The battle left the city in ruins and more than 100,000 Filipino civilians dead. The remaining Japanese retreated into the rugged terrain north of Manila; they were still fighting in August 1945 when word came that Japan had surrendered.

Reading Check **Describing** What strategy did the United States Navy use to advance across the Pacific?

Section 4 REVIEW

Vocabulary

1. **Explain** the significance of: Casablanca Conference, D-Day, Omar Bradley, amphtrac, Guadalcanal, kamikaze.

Main Ideas

2. **Determining Cause and Effect** What event prompted Italy to surrender?

3. **Describing** Why was D-Day's success so vital to an Allied victory?

4. **Summarizing** What was the military goal in the Pacific?

Critical Thinking

5. **Big Ideas** How did the geography of the Pacific affect American strategy?

6. **Organizing** Use a graphic organizer like the one below to explain the importance of each leader listed in the text.

Leader	Significance
Dwight Eisenhower	
George Patton	
George Marshall	
Omar Bradley	
Douglas MacArthur	

7. **Analyzing Visuals** Look at the photo on page 511 of the D-Day landing. What do you observe about the manner of the landing?

Writing About History

8. **Persuasive Writing** Imagine that you are living in Florida and see the potential for the amphtrac in the war. Write a letter to a member of Congress detailing reasons why it would be a good purchase for the marines.

History ONLINE

Study Central™ To review this section, go to glencoe.com and click on Study Central.

GEOGRAPHY & HISTORY

The Battle for Omaha Beach

The selection of a site for the largest amphibious landing in history was one of the biggest decisions of World War II. Allied planners considered coastlines from Denmark to Portugal in search of a sheltered location with firm flat beaches within range of friendly fighter planes in England. There also had to be enough roads and paths to move jeeps and trucks off the beaches and to accommodate the hundreds of thousands of American, Canadian, and British troops set to stream ashore following the invasion. An airfield and a seaport that the Allies could use were also needed. Most important was a reasonable expectation of achieving the element of surprise.

How Did Geography Shape the Battle?

Surrounded at both ends by cliffs that rose wall-like from the sea, Omaha Beach was only four miles long. The entire beach was overlooked by a 150-foot high bluff and there were only five ravines leading from the beach to the top of the bluff.

The Germans made full use of the geographic advantage the 150-foot bluff gave them. They dug trenches and built concrete bunkers for machine guns at the top of the cliffs and positioned them to guard the ravines leading to the beach.

American
British
Canadian
BRITAIN
Dover
Straits of Dover
Portsmouth
Southampton
Shoreham
Calais
Portland
GOLD
JUNO
Dartmouth
OMAHA
SWORD
UTAH
Dieppe
English Channel
Le Havre
Cherbourg
Seine River
St.-Lo Caen
NORMANDY
FRANCE
0   100 kilometers
0   100 miles
Lambert Azimuthal Equal-Area projection

Once ashore they had to cross 300 yards of open beach to the base of the bluff.

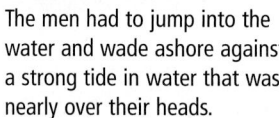

The men had to jump into the water and wade ashore against a strong tide in water that was nearly over their heads.

Analyzing GEOGRAPHY

1. **Location** Why did the Allies choose Normandy as the invasion site?
2. **Human-Environment Interaction** How did geography make the invasion of Omaha Beach difficult?

American troops were carried to Omaha Beach in landing craft. Many of the landing craft came under such intense fire that they opened their front ramp doors early.

The War Ends

Guide to Reading

Big Ideas

Individual Action After fierce military campaigns, President Harry S. Truman decided to use atomic weapons against Japan.

Content Vocabulary
- hedgerow (p. 518)
- napalm (p. 521)
- charter (p. 525)

Academic Vocabulary
- despite (p. 520)
- nuclear (p. 523)

People and Events to Identify
- Battle of the Bulge (p. 518)
- V-E Day (p. 519)
- Harry S. Truman (p. 520)
- Iwo Jima (p. 520)
- Manhattan Project (p. 523)
- V-J Day (p. 524)
- United Nations (p. 524)
- Nuremberg Trials (p. 525)

Reading Strategy

Create an outline of the section, using the major headings as the main points. Follow the structure shown below.

The War Ends
I. The Third Reich Collapses
   A.
   B.
II.
   A.
   B.

Fierce fighting in both Europe and the Pacific during 1945 led to the defeat of the Axis powers. The Allies began war crimes trials and set up a peacekeeping organization to prevent another global war.

The Third Reich Collapses

MAIN Idea The war in Europe ended in spring 1945 after major battles, as the Allies moved west toward Germany.

HISTORY AND YOU Have you ever been in a competition in which you persevered, despite fatigue, to win? Read to learn how the Allies fought in Europe to defeat Germany.

Although D-Day had been a success, it was only the beginning. Surrounding many fields in Normandy were **hedgerows**—dirt walls, several feet thick, covered in shrubbery. The hedgerows had been built to fence in cattle and crops, but they also enabled the Germans to fiercely defend their positions. The battle of the hedgerows ended on July 25, 1944, when 2,500 American bombers blew a hole in the German lines, enabling American tanks to race through the gap.

As the Allies broke out of Normandy, the French Resistance—French civilians who had secretly organized to resist the German occupation of their country—staged a rebellion in Paris. When the Allied forces liberated Paris on August 25, they found the streets filled with French citizens celebrating their victory.

The Battle of the Bulge

As the Allies advanced toward the German border, Hitler decided to stage one last desperate offensive. His goal was to cut off Allied supplies coming through the port of Antwerp, Belgium. The attack began just before dawn on December 16, 1944. Six inches (15 cm) of snow covered the ground, and the weather was bitterly cold. Moving rapidly, the Germans caught the American defenders by surprise. As the German troops raced west, their lines bulged outward, and the attack became known as the **Battle of the Bulge.**

Shortly after the Germans surrounded the Americans, Eisenhower ordered General Patton to rescue them. Three days later, faster than anyone expected in the midst of a snowstorm, Patton's troops slammed into the German lines. As the weather cleared, Allied aircraft began hitting German fuel depots.

On Christmas Eve, out of fuel and weakened by heavy losses, the German troops driving toward Antwerp were forced to halt. Two days later, Patton's troops broke through to the German line. Although

The War Ends in Europe, 1945

The Axis Before the War, 1939

The Axis at its Peak, 1942

The Axis at German Surrender, 1945

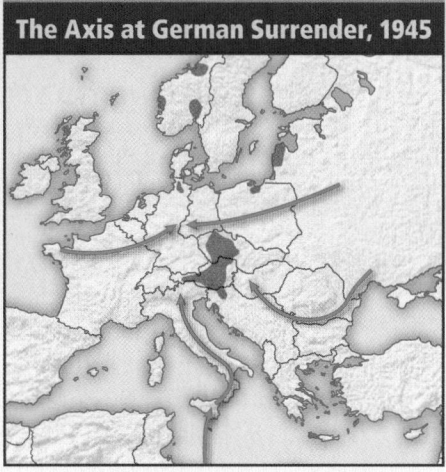

■ Axis-controlled territory
← Allied advances, 1944–45

0   400 kilometers

0   400 miles

Lambert Azimuthal Equal-Area projection

How Many People Died in World War II?

Country	Military Deaths	Civilian Deaths
USSR	11,000,000	6,700,000
Germany	3,250,000	2,350,000
Japan	1,740,000	393,000
China	1,400,000	8,000,000
Poland	110,000	5,300,000
United States	405,000	2,000
Great Britain	306,000	61,000
Italy	227,000	60,000
France	122,000	470,000

Analyzing VISUALS

1. **Comparing** Which nation had the greatest number of civilian casualties?
2. **Analyzing** Why did the United States have so few civilian deaths?

fighting continued for three weeks, the United States had won the Battle of the Bulge. On January 8, the Germans began to withdraw. They had suffered more than 100,000 casualties and lost many tanks and aircraft. They had very few resources left to prevent the Allies from entering Germany.

The War Ends in Europe

While American and British forces fought to liberate France, the Soviets began a massive attack on German troops in Russia. By the time the Battle of the Bulge ended, the Soviets had driven Hitler's forces out of Russia and back across Poland. By February 1945, Soviet troops were only 35 miles (56 km) from Berlin.

As the Soviets crossed Germany's eastern border, American forces attacked Germany's western border. By the end of February 1945, American troops had fought their way to the Rhine River, Germany's last major line of defense in the west. On March 7, American tanks crossed the Rhine.

As German defenses crumbled, American troops raced east to within 70 miles (113 km) of Berlin. On April 16, Soviet troops finally smashed through the German defenses and reached the outskirts of Berlin five days later.

Deep in his Berlin bunker, Adolf Hitler knew the end was near. On April 30, 1945, he committed suicide. Before killing himself, Hitler chose Grand Admiral Karl Doenitz as his successor. Doenitz tried to surrender to the Americans and British while continuing to fight the Soviets, but Eisenhower insisted on unconditional surrender. On May 7, 1945, Germany accepted the terms. The next day— May 8, 1945—was proclaimed **V-E Day,** for "Victory in Europe."

✔ **Reading Check** **Explaining** Why was the Battle of the Bulge such a disastrous defeat for Germany?

Japan Is Defeated

MAIN Idea The United States decided to end the war with Japan by using napalm and atomic bombs.

HISTORY AND YOU When was the last time you had to make a difficult decision, with no really good choice? Read to learn about the decision President Truman made in 1945.

Unfortunately, President Roosevelt did not live to see the defeat of Germany. On April 12, 1945, while vacationing in Warm Springs, Georgia, he died of a stroke. His vice president, **Harry S. Truman,** became president during this difficult time.

The next day, Truman told reporters: "Boys, if you ever pray, pray for me now. . . . When they told me yesterday what had happened, I felt like the moon, the stars, and all the planets had fallen on me."**Despite** his feelings, Truman began at once to make decisions about the war. Although Germany surrendered a few weeks later, the war with Japan continued, and Truman was forced to make some of the most difficult decisions of the war during his first six months in office.

The Battle of Iwo Jima

On November 24, 1944, bombs fell on Tokyo. Above the city flew 80 B-29 Superfortress bombers that had traveled more than 1,500 miles (2,414 km) from new American bases in the Mariana Islands.

At first the B-29s did little damage because they kept missing their targets. By the time the B-29s reached Japan, they did not have enough fuel left to fix their navigational errors or to adjust for high winds. The pilots needed an island closer to Japan so the B-29s could refuel. American military planners decided to invade **Iwo Jima.**

Iwo Jima was perfectly located, roughly halfway between the Marianas and Japan, but its geography was formidable. At its southern tip was a dormant volcano. The terrain was rugged, with rocky cliffs, jagged ravines, and

Winning the War
Against Japan, 1944–1945

April 1, 1945
American troops land on Okinawa

March 9, 1945
Firebombing destroys most of Tokyo

Feb. 1945 ⟩ **April 1945** ⟩ **June 1945** ⟩

October 23–24, 1944
Victory in the Battle of Leyte Gulf enables MacArthur to return to the Philippines

February 19, 1945
U.S. Marines land on Iwo Jima; over 6,800 marines are killed before the island is captured

dozens of caves. Volcanic ash covered the ground. Even worse, the Japanese had built a vast network of concrete bunkers connected by miles of tunnels.

On February 19, 1945, some 60,000 Marines landed on Iwo Jima. As the troops leapt from the amphtracs, they sank up to their ankles in the soft ash. Meanwhile, Japanese artillery began to pound the invaders.

The marines crawled inland, using flamethrowers and explosives to attack the Japanese bunkers. More than 6,800 marines were killed capturing the island. Admiral Nimitz later wrote that, on Iwo Jima, "uncommon valor was a common virtue."

Firebombing Japan

While American engineers prepared airfields on Iwo Jima, General Curtis LeMay, commander of the B-29s based in the Marianas, decided to change strategy. To help the B-29s hit their targets, he ordered them to drop bombs filled with **napalm**—a kind of jellied gasoline. The bombs were designed not only to explode but also to start fires. Even if the B-29s missed their targets, the fires they started would spread to the intended targets.

The use of firebombs was very controversial because the fires would also kill civilians; however, LeMay could think of no other way to destroy Japan's war production quickly. Loaded with firebombs, B-29s attacked Tokyo on March 9, 1945. As strong winds fanned the flames, the firestorm grew so intense that it sucked the oxygen out of the air, asphyxiating thousands. As one survivor later recalled:

PRIMARY SOURCE

"The fires were incredible . . . with flames leaping hundreds of feet into the air. . . . With every passing moment the air became more foul. . . the noise was a continuing crashing roar. . . . Fire-winds filled with burning particles rushed up and down the streets. I watched people . . . running for their lives. . . . The flames raced after them like living things, striking them down. . . . Wherever I turned my eyes, I saw people . . . seeking air to breathe."

—quoted in *New History of World War II*

August 9, 1945
A second atomic bomb is dropped on Japan, destroying the city of Nagasaki

September 2, 1945
The Japanese delegation boards the battleship USS *Missouri* in Tokyo Bay for the official surrender ceremony

August 1945

August 6, 1945
An atomic bomb destroys the Japanese city of Hiroshima

Analyzing TIME LINES

1. **Listing** When was Tokyo destroyed?
2. **Sequencing** How many days lapsed between the dropping of the first and second atomic bombs?

The Tokyo firebombing killed more than 80,000 people and destroyed more than 250,000 buildings. By the end of June 1945, Japan's six most important industrial cities had been firebombed, destroying almost half of their total urban area. By the end of the war, the B-29s had firebombed 67 Japanese cities.

The Invasion of Okinawa

Despite the massive damage the firebombing caused, there were few signs in the spring of 1945 that Japan was ready to quit. Many American officials believed the Japanese would not surrender until Japan had been invaded. To prepare for the invasion, the United States needed a base near Japan to stockpile supplies and build up troops. Iwo Jima was small and still too far away. Military planners chose Okinawa—only 350 miles (563 km) from Japan.

American troops landed on Okinawa on April 1, 1945. Instead of defending the beaches, the Japanese troops took up positions in the island's rugged mountains. To dig the Japanese out of their caves and bunkers, the Americans had to fight their way up steep slopes against constant machine gun and artillery fire. More than 12,000 American soldiers, sailors, and marines died during the fighting, but by June 22, 1945, Okinawa had finally been captured.

The Terms for Surrender

Shortly after the United States captured Okinawa, the Japanese emperor urged his government to find a way to end the war. The biggest problem was the American demand for unconditional surrender. Many Japanese leaders were willing to surrender, but on one condition: the emperor had to stay in power.

American officials knew that the fate of the emperor was the most important issue for the Japanese. Most Americans, however, blamed the emperor for the war and wanted him removed from power. President Truman was reluctant to go against public opinion. Furthermore, he knew the United States was almost ready to test a new weapon that might force Japan to surrender without any conditions. The new weapon was the atomic bomb.

The Manhattan Project

In 1939 Leo Szilard, one of the world's top physicists, learned that German scientists had split the uranium atom. Szilard had been the first scientist to suggest that splitting the atom might release enormous energy. Worried that the Nazis were working on an atomic bomb, Szilard convinced the world's best-known physicist, Albert Einstein, to sign a letter Szilard had drafted and send it to President Roosevelt. In the letter, Einstein warned that by using uranium, "extremely powerful bombs of a new type may . . . be constructed."

Roosevelt responded by setting up a scientific committee to study the issue. The committee remained skeptical until 1941, when they met with British scientists who were already working on an atomic bomb. The British research so impressed the Americans that they

Debates
IN HISTORY

Should America Drop the Atomic Bomb on Japan?

More than 60 years later, people continue to debate what some historians have called the most important event of the twentieth century—President Truman's order to drop atomic bombs on Japan. Did his momentous decision shorten the war and save American lives, as Truman contended, or was it a barbaric and unnecessary show of superior military technology designed to keep the Soviet Union out of Japan?

convinced Roosevelt to begin a program to build an atomic bomb.

The secret American program to build an atomic bomb was code-named the **Manhattan Project** and was headed by General Leslie R. Groves. The first breakthrough came in 1942, when Szilard and Enrico Fermi, another physicist, built the world's first **nuclear** reactor at the University of Chicago. Groves then organized a team of engineers and scientists to build an atomic bomb at a secret laboratory in Los Alamos, New Mexico. J. Robert Oppenheimer led the team. On July 16, 1945, they detonated the world's first atomic bomb in New Mexico.

Hiroshima and Nagasaki

Even before the bomb was tested, American officials began debating how to use it. Admiral William Leahy, chairman of the Joint Chiefs of Staff, opposed using the bomb because it killed civilians indiscriminately. He believed an economic blockade and conventional bombing would convince Japan to surrender. Secretary of War Henry Stimson wanted to warn the Japanese about the bomb while at the same time telling them that they could keep the emperor if they surrendered. Secretary of State James Byrnes, however, wanted to drop the bomb without any warning to shock Japan into surrendering.

President Truman later wrote that he "regarded the bomb as a military weapon and never had any doubts that it should be used." His advisers had warned him to expect massive casualties if the United States invaded Japan. Truman believed it was his duty as president to use every weapon available to save American lives.

YES

Harry S. Truman
President of the United States

PRIMARY SOURCE

"The world will note that the first atomic bomb was dropped on Hiroshima, a military base. . . . If Japan does not surrender, bombs will have to be dropped on her war industries and, unfortunately, thousands of civilian lives will be lost. . . .

Having found the bomb we have used it. We have used it against those who attacked us without warning at Pearl Harbor, against those who have starved and beaten and executed American prisoners of war, against those who have abandoned all pretense of obeying international laws of warfare. We have used it in order to shorten the agony of war, in order to save the lives of thousands and thousands of young Americans."

—from *Public Papers of the Presidents*

NO

William Leahy
Chairman of the Joint Chiefs of Staff

PRIMARY SOURCE

"It is my opinion that the use of this barbarous weapon at Hiroshima and Nagasaki was of no material assistance in our war against Japan. The Japanese were already defeated and ready to surrender because of the effective sea blockade and the successful bombing with conventional weapons. . . .

The lethal possibilities of atomic warfare in the future are frightening. My own feeling was that in being the first to use it, we had adopted an ethical standard common to the barbarians of the Dark Ages. I was not taught to make war in that fashion, and wars cannot be won by destroying women and children."

—from *I Was There*

DBQ Document-Based Questions

1. **Explaining** What reasons does Truman offer to justify the use of the atomic bomb?

2. **Summarizing** Why does Leahy say he was against using the bomb?

3. **Evaluating** Whom do you think makes the more persuasive argument? Explain your answer.

The Allies threatened Japan with "prompt and utter destruction" if the nation did not surrender, but the Japanese did not reply. Truman then ordered the military to drop the bomb. On August 6, 1945, a B-29 bomber named *Enola Gay* dropped an atomic bomb, code-named "Little Boy," on Hiroshima, an important industrial city.

The bomb destroyed about 63 percent of the city. Between 80,000 and 120,000 people died instantly, and thousands more died later from burns and radiation sickness. Three days later, on August 9, the Soviet Union declared war on Japan. Later that day, the United States dropped another atomic bomb, code-named "Fat Man," on the city of Nagasaki, killing between 35,000 and 74,000 people.

Faced with such massive destruction and the shock of the Soviets joining the war, the Japanese emperor ordered his government to surrender. On August 15, 1945—**V-J Day**—Japan surrendered. The long war was over.

✔ **Reading Check** **Analyzing** What arguments did Truman consider when deciding whether to use the atomic bomb?

Building a New World

MAIN Idea The victorious Allies tried to create an organization to prevent future wars.

HISTORY AND YOU What are some of your most noble goals? Read to learn about the goals of the Allied forces after the war.

Well before the war ended, President Roosevelt had begun thinking about what the world would be like after the war. The president had wanted to ensure that war would never again engulf the world.

Creating the United Nations

President Roosevelt believed that a new international political organization could prevent another world war. In 1944, at the Dumbarton Oaks estate in Washington, D.C., delegates from 39 countries met to discuss the new organization, which was to be called the **United Nations** (UN). The delegates at the conference agreed that the UN would have a General Assembly, in which every member

PRIMARY SOURCE
Plans for a Better World

▲ The Nuremberg trials

DBQ **Document-Based Questions**

1. **Identifying** Which right relates to free elections?
2. **Speculating** Why do you think that the right to an education might be so far down on the list?
3. **Evaluating** Which five of the human rights included in the Declaration do you feel are the most important today? Why?

The Universal Declaration of Human Rights
Issued by the United Nations, December 10, 1948

1. All human beings are born free and equal in dignity and rights.
3. Everyone has the right to life, liberty, and security of person.
4. No one shall be held in slavery or servitude . . .
5. No one shall be subjected to torture or to cruel, inhuman or degrading treatment or punishment.
7. All are equal before the law and are entitled without any discrimination to equal protection of the law.
11. Everyone charged with a penal offense has the right to be presumed innocent until proved guilty . . .
13. Everyone has the right to freedom of movement . . .
16. Men and women . . . are entitled to equal rights as to marriage, during marriage and at its dissolution . . .
17. Everyone has the right to own property . . .
18. Everyone has the right to freedom of thought, conscience and religion . . .
19. Everyone has the right to freedom of opinion and expression . . .
20. Everyone has the right to freedom of peaceful assembly and association.
21. The will of the people . . . shall be expressed in periodic and genuine elections which shall be by universal and equal suffrage . . .
23. Everyone has the right to work . . .
25. Everyone has the right to a standard of living adequate for the health and well-being of himself and of his family, including food, clothing, housing and medical care and necessary social services, and the right to security in the event of unemployment, sickness, disability, widowhood, old age or other lack of livelihood . . .
26. Everyone has the right to education . . .

nation in the world would have one vote. The UN would also have a Security Council with 11 members. Five countries would be permanent members of the Security Council: Britain, France, China, the Soviet Union, and the United States—the five big powers that had led the fight against the Axis. These five permanent members would each have veto power.

On April 25, 1945, representatives from 50 countries came to San Francisco to officially organize the United Nations and design its **charter,** or constitution. The General Assembly was given the power to vote on resolutions, to choose the non-permanent members of the Security Council, and to vote on the UN's budget. The Security Council was responsible for international peace and security. It could investigate any international problem and propose settlements. It could also take action to preserve the peace, including asking its members to use military force to uphold a UN resolution.

Soon after its founding, the UN created a Commission on Human Rights and chose Eleanor Roosevelt to serve as its first chair. The Commission drafted the Universal Declaration of Human Rights, and the UN issued it in 1948. The document strongly reflects the ideas and principles that Eleanor Roosevelt espoused during her life. It lists 30 rights that are said to be universally applicable to all human beings in all societies.

Putting the Enemy on Trial

Although the Allies had declared their intention to punish German and Japanese leaders for war crimes, they did not work out the details until the summer of 1945. In August, the United States, Britain, France, and the Soviet Union created the International Military Tribunal (IMT). The Tribunal held trials in Nuremberg, Germany, where Hitler had staged Nazi Party rallies.

Twenty-two leaders of Nazi Germany were prosecuted at the **Nuremberg Trials.** Three were acquitted and seven were given prison sentences. The remaining 12 were sentenced to death. Trials of lower-ranking officials and military officers continued until April 1949. Those trials led to the execution of 24 more German leaders. Another 107 were given prison sentences.

Similar trials were held in Tokyo. The IMT for the Far East charged 25 Japanese leaders with war crimes. Significantly, the Allies did not indict the Japanese emperor. They feared that any attempt to put him on trial would lead to an uprising by the Japanese people. Eighteen Japanese defendants were sentenced to prison. The rest were sentenced to death by hanging.

The war crimes trials punished many of the people responsible for World War II and the Holocaust, but they were also part of the American plan for building a better world. As Robert Jackson, chief counsel for the United States at Nuremberg, observed in his opening statement to the court: "The wrongs we seek to condemn and punish have been so calculated, so malignant and so devastating, that civilization cannot tolerate their being ignored because it cannot survive their being repeated."

✔ **Reading Check**   **Describing** How is the United Nations organized?

Section 5 REVIEW

Vocabulary

1. **Explain** the significance of: hedgerow, Battle of the Bulge, V-E Day, Harry S. Truman, Iwo Jima, napalm, Manhattan Project, V-J Day, United Nations, charter, Nuremberg Trials.

Main Ideas

2. **Explaining** What was the significance of the Battle of the Bulge?

3. **Identifying** What was the advantage of using napalm bombs?

4. **Synthesizing** How was the United Nations designed to prevent global wars?

Critical Thinking

5. **Big Ideas** If you had been a member of President Truman's cabinet, what advice would you have given him about dropping the atomic bomb?

6. **Organizing** Using a graphic organizer like the one below, indicate the steps to victory in Europe and over Japan. Add boxes as needed.

7. **Analyzing Visuals** Look at the photo of the Japanese delegation on page 521. What do you observe about the scene?

Writing About History

8. **Descriptive Writing** Imagine that you are in a large American city when news of victory over Japan comes. Describe the celebrations and the mood of the people.

History ONLINE

Study Central™ To review this section, go to glencoe.com and click on Study Central.

The Pacific

1941
- Japan attacks Pearl Harbor, Dec. 7

1942
- The United States defeats Japan in the Battles of the Coral Sea and Midway

1943
- The United States begins its island-hopping campaign

1944
- The United States retakes the Philippines

1945
- The United States drops the atomic bomb; Japan surrenders on August 15

Europe and North Africa

1941
- Germany invades the Soviet Union

1942
- The Allies turn the tide in the Battle of the Atlantic

1943
- The Allies invade Italy; German forces in North Africa and Stalingrad surrender to Allies

1944
- The Allies invade Normandy on June 6

1945
- Germany surrenders unconditionally on May 7

The Home Front

1941
- President Roosevelt forbids race discrimination in defense industries

1942
- Congress establishes WAAC; War Department relocates Japanese Americans to internment camps

1943
- Race riots occur in Detroit and Los Angeles; Roosevelt establishes OWM

1944
- Supreme Court hears case of *Korematsu* v. *United States*

1945
- Nearly 40 nations sign the United Nations charter

▼ *A convoy of Allied M-3 tanks moves forward.*

▼ *Fire erupts on the* USS Bunker Hill *after a kamikaze attack, May 1945.*

Reviewing Vocabulary

Directions: Choose the word or words that best complete the sentence.

1. One complaint of African Americans at the beginning of World War II was that they were
   - **A** integrated.
   - **B** employed.
   - **C** empowered.
   - **D** disenfranchised.

2. Winston Churchill wanted to attack the _____, or edges, of the German Empire.
   - **A** eastern front
   - **B** periphery
   - **C** left flank
   - **D** western front

3. To aid in the war effort, American citizens accepted the _____ of some items.
   - **A** rationing
   - **B** disappearance
   - **C** abundance
   - **D** commandeering

4. Japanese suicide pilots were known as _____ pilots.
   - **A** Shinto
   - **B** Samurai
   - **C** kamikaze
   - **D** amphtrac

5. Germans fiercely resisted the Allied invasion of France by hiding behind thick, shrubbery-covered dirt walls called _____ that surrounded the fields of Normandy.
   - **A** napalm
   - **B** hedgerows
   - **C** amphtracs
   - **D** guadalcanals

Reviewing Main Ideas

Directions: Choose the best answers to the following questions.

Section 1 *(pp. 486–493)*

6. The Liberty ship was superior to many warships because it was
   - **A** welded instead of riveted.
   - **B** riveted instead of welded.
   - **C** painted in camouflage colors.
   - **D** painted red, white, and blue.

7. African Americans pushed for a _____ victory in the war effort.
   - **A** Tuskegee
   - **B** Triple C
   - **C** Double V
   - **D** Carver

Section 2 *(pp. 494–499)*

8. The Japanese were determined to destroy the American fleet in the Pacific after
   - **A** they were successful at Pearl Harbor.
   - **B** the Americans surrendered at Bataan.
   - **C** the crew of the *Enola Gay* dropped an atomic bomb on Hiroshima.
   - **D** James Doolittle dropped bombs on Tokyo.

9. To prevent huge shipping losses in the Atlantic, Americans used
   - **A** antisubmarine devices.
   - **B** a convoy system.
   - **C** an air force escort.
   - **D** minesweepers.

TEST-TAKING

Look at each question to find clues to support your answer. Try not to get confused by the wording of the question. Then look for an answer that best fits the question.

Need Extra Help?									
If You Missed Questions . . .	1	2	3	4	5	6	7	8	9
Go to Page . . .	491	497	506	515	518	489	492	495–496	499

Section 3 *(pp. 500–507)*

10. During the war, Americans _____ to collect materials that could be used for the war effort.

A planted victory gardens

B held scrap drives

C conserved energy

D sold war bonds

Section 4 *(pp. 508–515)*

11. Where did the Allies begin their invasion of Italy?

A Sicily

B Casablanca

C Tehran

D Normandy

12. Planning for D-Day was complicated by concerns for the

A German army.

B amphtracs.

C weather.

D air forces.

Section 5 *(pp. 518–525)*

13. What was the code name for the plan to build the atomic bomb?

A Manhattan Project

B Doolittle Raid

C Operation Overlord

D V-J Day

14. Which UN body has five permanent members with veto power?

A General Assembly

B Commision on Human Rights

C Security Council

D International Military Tribunal

Critical Thinking

Directions: Choose the best answers to the following questions.

15. The invasion of Normandy was important because it

A brought the Soviet Union into the war.

B forced the Germans to fight a two-front war.

C marked the first successful invasion by sea.

D protected the Pacific fleet.

Base your answer to question 16 on the map below and your knowledge of Chapter 14.

Relocation Camps, 1942–1946

16. Most of the relocation camps were located in what region of the United States?

A the West

B the Southeast

C the Deep South

D the Midwest

17. What was the purpose of the Japanese American Citizens League?

A to fight the Japanese invasion of California

B to fight Roosevelt's order to declare the western United States a military zone

C to help Japanese Americans recover lost property from the relocation

D to encourage Japanese Americans to join the U.S. armed forces

Need Extra Help?								
If You Missed Questions . . .	10	11	12	13	14	15	16	17
Go to Page . . .	507	509–510	511–512	522–523	525	510	R15	504

 GO ON

18. Women were able to serve in noncombat positions in the military and in factories at home because

  A there were not enough men to fill the positions.

  B no one else wanted the jobs.

  C people realized it was unfair to keep them out.

  D women organized, as they did to win the vote.

Analyze the cartoon and answer the question that follows. Base your answer on the cartoon and on your knowledge of Chapter 14.

19. According to the cartoon, why were Americans encouraged to turn out their lights?

  A The British could use the lights to create a blockade.

  B The lights prevented American ships from seeing the British ships.

  C The lights provided a silhouette for ships, making them targets for German submarines.

  D The lights used too much electricity, creating city-wide blackouts.

Document-Based Questions

Directions: Analyze the document and answer the short-answer questions that follow the document.

Many historians believe that the civil rights movement of the 1950s and 1960s had its roots in the "Double V" campaign and the march on Washington. Alexander Allen, a member of the Urban League during the war, believed that World War II was a turning point for African Americans.

> "Up to that point the doors to industrial and economic opportunity were largely closed. Under the pressure of war, the pressures of government policy, the pressures of world opinion, the pressures of blacks themselves and their allies, all this began to change. . . .The war forced the federal government to take a stronger position with reference to discrimination, and things began to change as a result. There was a tremendous attitudinal change that grew out of the war. There had been a new experience for blacks, and many weren't willing to go back to the way it was before."
> —quoted in *Wartime America*

20. How did the war change the status of African Americans in American society?

21. Why do you think the war forced the government to take a stronger position on discrimination in the workplace?

Extended Response

22. World War II was a complex historical event involving nations, people, and decisions from around the world. Write an essay that traces the progress of the war, making sure to include major events and leaders. In the essay, make note of the war's turning points and the use of the atomic bomb. Discuss major decisions of Franklin D. Roosevelt, Winston Churchill, Joseph Stalin, and Charles de Gaulle. To assist you in organizing this essay, construct a time line that includes the battles of Midway, Iwo Jima, Okinawa, the Normandy Invasion, and the Battle of the Bulge.

STOP

History ONLINE

For additional test practice, use Self-Check Quizzes— Chapter 14 at glencoe.com.

Need Extra Help?					
If You Missed Questions . . .	18	19	20	21	22
Go to Page . . .	501	R18	529	R19	484–485

Chapter 15

The Cold War Begins

1945–1960

The world's first nuclear artillery shell is test fired on May 25, 1953. Such tests were common during the early cold war.

1948
- Berlin airlift begins

1950
- McCarthy charges that Communists staff the U.S. State Department
- Korean War begins

1953
- Armistice agreement is reached in Korea

Eisenhower 1953–1961

1945
- Franklin Roosevelt dies

Truman 1945–1953

1947
- Truman Doctrine is declared

U.S. PRESIDENTS

U.S. EVENTS

WORLD EVENTS

1945

1950

March 1945
- Yalta Conference is held to plan postwar world

July 1945
- Potsdam Conference partitions Germany

1948
- State of Israel is created

1949
- Communists take power in China

MAKING CONNECTIONS
How Did the Atomic Bomb Change the World?

The destructiveness of the atomic bomb raised the stakes in military conflicts. Growing tensions between the United States and the Soviet Union after World War II led to a constant threat of nuclear war.

- *How did the atomic bomb change relations between nations?*
- *Do you think the invention of the atomic bomb made the world safer?*

FOLDABLES

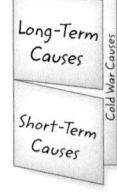

Analyzing Causes Make a Two-Tab Book Foldable that lists the long-term and short-term causes of the Cold War. List the information as you read and review the chapter.

Long-Term Causes

Short-Term Causes

Cold War Causes

1960
- U-2 incident occurs

1955

1960

1956
- Hungarians rebel against the Communist government

1957
- Soviet Union launches Sputnik

History ONLINE Visit glencoe.com and enter *QuickPass*™ code TAVMT5147c15 for Chapter 15 resources.

The Origins of the Cold War

Guide to Reading

Big Ideas
Government and Society Although World War II was nearly over, personal and political differences among Allied leaders and the peoples they represented led to new global challenges.

Content Vocabulary
- satellite nations (p. 537)
- Iron Curtain (p. 537)

Academic Vocabulary
- liberate (p. 532)
- equipment (p. 534)

People and Events to Identify
- Yalta (p. 532)
- Cold War (p. 534)
- Potsdam (p. 536)

Reading Strategy
Categorizing Complete a graphic organizer similar to the one below by filling in the names of the conferences held among the "Big Three" Allies and the outcomes of each.

Conferences	Outcomes

After the war ended, tensions continued to rise over the amount of freedom the Soviets were going to allow the nations they controlled. Leaders of Britain, the United States, and the Soviet Union held conferences but could not resolve this issue.

The Yalta Conference

MAIN Idea Roosevelt, Churchill, and Stalin met at Yalta to discuss Poland, Germany, and the rights of liberated Europe.

HISTORY AND YOU Do you remember Wilson's idealistic Fourteen Points and how they were changed during negotiations after World War I? Read on to learn how negotiations during and after World War II led to results different from what Roosevelt and Truman wanted.

In February 1945, with the war in Europe almost over, Roosevelt, Churchill, and Stalin met at **Yalta**—a Soviet resort on the Black Sea—to plan the postwar world. Although the conference seemed to go well, several agreements reached at Yalta later played an important role in causing the Cold War.

Poland

The first issue discussed at Yalta was what to do about Poland. Shortly after the Germans invaded Poland, the Polish government fled to Britain. In 1944, however, Soviet troops drove back the Germans and entered Poland. As they **liberated** Poland from German control, the Soviets encouraged Polish Communists to set up a new government. This meant there were now two governments claiming the right to govern Poland: one Communist and one non-Communist.

President Roosevelt and Prime Minister Churchill both argued that the Poles should be free to choose their own government. "This is what we went to war against Germany for," Churchill explained, "that Poland should be free and sovereign."

Stalin quickly responded to Churchill's comments. According to Stalin, because Poland was on the Soviet Union's western border, the need for its government to be friendly was a matter of "life and death" from the Soviet point of view. Every time invaders had entered Russia from the west, they had come through Poland. Eventually, the three leaders compromised. Roosevelt and Churchill agreed to recognize the Polish government set up by the Soviets. Stalin agreed that the government would include members of the prewar Polish government and that free elections would be held as soon as possible.

The Yalta Conference, 1945

▲ *Churchill, Roosevelt, and Stalin at Yalta*

The Declaration of Liberated Europe

At Yalta, the Allies issued the Declaration of Liberated Europe. The Soviet Union's failure to uphold the Declaration contributed to the coming of the Cold War. The Declaration contained the following commitments:

• The peoples of Europe will be allowed to create democratic institutions of their own choice, but must destroy all remaining aspects of Nazism and fascism in their societies.

• The United States, Great Britain, and the Soviet Union will help the peoples of Europe to do the following:

  1. Establish peace in their country

  2. Provide aid to people in distress

  3. Form temporary governments that represent all democratic elements of the society and hold free elections to choose a government that responds to the will of the people

• The United States, Great Britain, and the Soviet Union will continue to support the principles expressed in the Atlantic Charter.

NATIONAL GEOGRAPHIC — The Division of Germany, 1945

```
0     100 kilometers
0     100 miles
Albers Equal-Area projection
```

North Sea
Baltic Sea
POLAND
U.K.
NETH.
Elbe R.
Berlin
BELG.

Allied Occupation Zones, 1945–1949
- American
- British
- French
- Soviet
- — Present-day Germany

CZECH.
FRANCE
Rhine R.
Danube R.
SWITZ.
AUSTRIA

```
0     6 kilometers
0     6 miles
```
West Berlin
East Berlin

Analyzing VISUALS

1. **Specifying** In the Declaration of Liberated Europe, what three things did the Big Three promise to help the peoples of Europe do?

2. **Locating** In what zone in the divided Germany was Berlin located?

The Declaration of Liberated Europe

After reaching a compromise on Poland, Roosevelt, Churchill, and Stalin agreed to issue the Declaration of Liberated Europe. The declaration asserted "the right of all people to choose the form of government under which they will live."

The Allies promised that the people of Europe would be allowed "to create democratic institutions of their own choice." They also promised to create temporary governments that represented "all democratic elements" and pledged "the earliest possible establishment through free elections of governments responsive to the will of the people."

Dividing Germany

After discussing Poland and agreeing to a set of principles for liberating Europe, the conference focused on Germany. Roosevelt, Churchill, and Stalin agreed to divide Germany into four zones. Great Britain, the United States, the Soviet Union, and France would each control one zone. The same four countries would also divide the German capital city of Berlin into four zones, even though it was in the Soviet zone.

Although pleased with the decision to divide Germany, Stalin also demanded that Germany pay heavy reparations for the war damage it had caused. Roosevelt agreed, but he insisted reparations be based on Germany's ability to pay. He also suggested, and Stalin agreed, that Germany pay reparations with trade goods and products instead of cash. The Allies would also be allowed to remove industrial machinery, railroad cars, and other **equipment** from Germany as reparations. This decision did not resolve the issue. Over the next few years, arguments about German reparations greatly increased tensions between the United States and the Soviet Union.

Tensions Begin to Rise

The Yalta decisions shaped the expectations of the United States. Two weeks after Yalta, the Soviets pressured the king of Romania into appointing a Communist government. The United States accused the Soviets of violating the Declaration of Liberated Europe.

Soon afterward, the Soviets refused to allow more than three non-Communist Poles to serve in the 18-member Polish government. There was also no indication that they intended to hold free elections in Poland as promised. On April 1, President Roosevelt informed the Soviets that their actions in Poland were not acceptable.

Yalta marked a turning point in Soviet-American relations. President Roosevelt had hoped that an Allied victory and the creation of the United Nations would lead to a more peaceful world. Instead, as the war came to an end, the United States and the Soviet Union became increasingly hostile toward each other. This led to an era of confrontation and competition between the two nations that lasted from about 1946 to 1990. This era became known as the **Cold War.**

Soviet Security Concerns

The tensions between the United States and the Soviet Union led to the Cold War because the two sides had different goals. As the war ended, Soviet leaders became concerned about security. They wanted to keep Germany weak and make sure that the countries between Germany and the Soviet Union were under Soviet control.

Although security concerns influenced their thinking, Soviet leaders were also communists. They believed that communism was a superior economic system that would eventually replace capitalism, and that the Soviet Union should encourage communism in other nations. Soviet leaders also accepted Lenin's theory that capitalist countries would eventually try to destroy communism. This made them suspicious of capitalist nations.

American Economic Issues

While Soviet leaders focused on securing their borders, American leaders focused on economic problems. Many American officials believed that the Depression had caused World War II. Without it, Hitler would never have come to power, and Japan would not have wanted to expand its empire.

Debates
IN HISTORY

Did the Soviet Union Cause the Cold War?

Many people have debated who was responsible for the Cold War. Most Americans, including diplomat George Kennan who had served in Russia, believed that it was Soviet ideology and insecurity that brought on the Cold War. On the other side, communist leaders, such as Stalin's adviser Andrei Zhdanov, believed that capitalism and imperialism caused the Cold War.

American advisers also thought that the Depression became so severe because nations reduced trade. They believed that when nations stop trading, they are forced into war to get resources. By 1945, Roosevelt and his advisers were convinced that economic growth was the key to peace. They wanted to promote economic growth by increasing world trade.

Similar reasoning convinced American leaders to promote democracy and free enterprise. They believed that democratic governments with protections for people's rights made countries more stable and peaceful. They also thought that the free enterprise system, with private property rights and limited government intervention in the economy, was the best route to prosperity.

 Reading Check **Identifying** What did the Allies decide at Yalta?

Truman Takes Control

MAIN Idea Although President Truman took a firm stand against Soviet aggression, Europe remained divided after the war.

HISTORY AND YOU Have you ever had to say no to someone or insist they do something? Read to learn about President Truman's actions at Potsdam.

Eleven days after confronting the Soviets on Poland, President Roosevelt died and Harry S. Truman became president. Truman was strongly anti-Communist. He also believed that World War II had begun because Britain had tried to appease Hitler. He did not intend to make the same mistake with Stalin. "We must stand up to the Russians," he told Secretary of State Edward Stettinius the day after taking office.

YES

George F. Kennan
American Diplomat

PRIMARY SOURCE

"[The] USSR still [believes] in antagonistic 'capitalist encirclement' with which in the long run there can be no permanent peaceful coexistence. . . . At bottom of [the] Kremlin's neurotic view of world affairs is traditional and instinctive Russian sense of insecurity. . . . And they have learned to seek security only in patient but deadly struggle for total destruction of rival power, never in compacts and compromises with it.

. . . In summary, we have here a political force committed fanatically to the belief that . . . it is desirable and necessary that the internal harmony of our society be disrupted, our traditional way of life be destroyed, the international authority of our state be broken, if Soviet power is to be secure."

—Moscow Embassy Telegram #511, 1946

NO

Andrei Zhdanov
Advisor to Stalin

PRIMARY SOURCE

"The more the war recedes into the past, the more distinct becomes . . . the division of the political forces operating on the international arena into two major camps. . . . The principal driving force of the imperialist camp is the U.S.A. . . . The cardinal purpose of the imperialist camp is to strengthen imperialism, to hatch a new imperialist war, to combat socialism and democracy, and to support reactionary and antidemocratic profascist regimes. . . .

. . . As embodiment of a new and superior social system, the Soviet Union reflects in its foreign policy the aspirations of progressive mankind, which desires lasting peace and has nothing to gain from a new war hatched by capitalism."

—from *For a Lasting Peace for a People's Democracy*, no. 1, November 1947

DBQ Document-Based Questions

1. **Paraphrasing** What belief of the Soviets does Kennan say will prevent "permanent peaceful coexistence" with the United States?

2. **Identifying Central Issues** What does Zhdanov say are the goals of the "imperialist camp" led by the United States?

Communist countries

Non-communist countries

—— Iron Curtain

0 — 400 kilometers
0 — 400 miles

Lambert Azimuthal
Equal-Area projection

ICELAND · Reykjavik

NORWAY · Oslo

SWEDEN · Stockholm

FINLAND · Helsinki

Moscow

North Sea

UNITED KINGDOM · Dublin
IRELAND
London

DENMARK · Copenhagen
NETH.
The Hague

Baltic Sea

SOVIET UNION

POLAND · Warsaw
Berlin
EAST GERMANY
Bonn
Brussels
BELG.
WEST GERMANY
Prague
CZECHOSLOVAKIA
Paris
LUX.
FRANCE
Bern
SWITZ.
AUSTRIA · Vienna
HUNGARY · Budapest
ROMANIA · Bucharest
Belgrade
YUGOSLAVIA
BULGARIA · Sofia
ITALY
Rome
Madrid
SPAIN
Corsica
Sardinia
Tiranë
ALBANIA

PRIMARY SOURCE

"A shadow has fallen upon the scenes so lately light by the Allied victory.... From Stettin in the Baltic to Trieste in the Adriatic, an iron curtain has descended across the continent. Behind that line lie all the capitals of the ancient states of Central and Eastern Europe. Warsaw, Berlin, Prague, Vienna, Budapest, Belgrade, Bucharest and Sofia, all these famous cities and the populations around them lie in what I must call the Soviet sphere, and all are subject in one form or another, not only to Soviet influence, but to a very high and, in some cases, increasing measure of control from Moscow....

The Communist parties, which were very small in all these Eastern States of Europe, have been raised to pre-eminence and power far beyond their numbers and are seeking everywhere to obtain totalitarian control....

In front of the iron curtain which lies across Europe are other causes for anxiety... in a great number of countries, far from the Russian frontiers and throughout the world, Communist fifth columns are established and work in ... absolute obedience to the directions they receive from the Communist center.... I do not believe that Soviet Russia desires war. What they desire is the fruits of war and the indefinite expansion of their power and doctrines."

—Winston Churchill, address to Westminster College, Fulton, Missouri, March 5, 1946

DBQ Document-Based Questions

1. **Finding the Main Idea** What was the "iron curtain," and why do you think Churchill described it in that way?

2. **Identifying Central Issues** What "other causes for anxiety" did Churchill say the Soviets were creating?

Ten days later, Truman did exactly that during a meeting with Soviet Foreign Minister Molotov. Truman immediately brought up the issue of Poland and demanded that Stalin hold free elections as he had promised at Yalta. Molotov took the unexpectedly strong message back to Stalin. The meeting marked an important shift in Soviet-American relations and set the stage for further confrontations.

The Potsdam Conference

In July 1945 with the war against Japan still raging, Truman finally met Stalin at **Potsdam,** near Berlin. Both men had come to Potsdam primarily to work out a deal on Germany.

Truman was now convinced that industry was critical to Germany's survival. Unless that nation's economy was allowed to revive, the rest of Europe would never recover, and the German people might turn to communism out of desperation.

Stalin and his advisers were equally convinced that they needed reparations from Germany. The war had devastated the Soviet economy. Soviet troops had begun stripping their zone in Germany of its machinery and industrial equipment for use back home, but Stalin wanted Germany to pay much more.

At the conference, Truman took a firm stand against heavy reparations. He insisted that Germany's industry had to be allowed to recover. Truman suggested that the Soviets take reparations from their zone, while the Allies allowed industry to revive in the other zones. Stalin opposed this idea since the Soviet zone was mostly agricultural. It could not provide all the reparations the Soviets wanted.

To get the Soviets to accept the agreement, Truman offered Stalin a small amount of German industrial equipment from the other zones, but required the Soviets to pay for part of it with food shipments from their zone. He also offered to accept the new German-Polish border the Soviets had established.

Stalin did not like Truman's proposal. At Potsdam, Truman learned that the atomic bomb had been successfully tested, and he hinted to Stalin that the United States had developed a new, powerful weapon. Stalin suspected that Truman was trying to bully him into a deal and that the Americans were trying to limit reparations to keep the Soviets weak.

Despite his suspicions, Stalin had to accept the terms. American and British troops controlled Germany's industrial heartland, and there was no way for the Soviets to get any reparations except by cooperating. Nevertheless, the Potsdam conference marked yet another increase in tensions between the Soviets and the Americans.

The Iron Curtain Descends

Although Truman had won the argument over reparations, he had less success on other issues at Potsdam. The Soviets refused to make any stronger commitments to uphold the Declaration of Liberated Europe. The presence of the Soviet army in Eastern Europe ensured that pro-Soviet Communist governments would eventually be established in Poland, Romania, Bulgaria, Hungary, and Czechoslovakia. "This war is not as in the past," Stalin commented. "Whoever occupies a territory also imposes his own social system. . . . It cannot be otherwise."

The Communist countries of Eastern Europe came to be called **satellite nations** because they were controlled by the Soviets, as satellites are tied by gravity to the planets they orbit. These nations had to remain Communist and friendly to the Soviet Union. They also had to follow policies that the Soviets approved.

After watching the Communist takeover in Eastern Europe, Winston Churchill coined a phrase to describe what had happened. In a 1946 speech delivered in Fulton, Missouri, he referred to an "iron curtain" falling across Eastern Europe. The press picked up the term and, for the next 43 years, when someone referred to the Iron Curtain, they meant the Communist nations of Eastern Europe and the Soviet Union. With the **Iron Curtain** separating the Communist nations of Eastern Europe from the West, the World War II era had come to an end. The Cold War was about to begin.

Reading Check Explaining How did the Potsdam Conference hurt Soviet-American relations?

Section 1 REVIEW

Vocabulary

1. **Explain** the significance of: Yalta, Cold War, Potsdam, satellite nations, Iron Curtain.

Main Ideas

2. **Identifying** At Yalta, what agreement did the "Big Three" come to about Germany's future after World War II?

3. **Summarizing** What concerns made the Soviets suspicious of the Western Allies?

4. **Explaining** How did the Potsdam Conference help bring about the Cold War?

Critical Thinking

5. **Big Ideas** How did different economic systems cause tensions between the United States and the Soviet Union?

6. **Organizing** Use a graphic organizer similar to the one below to list events that led to the Cold War.

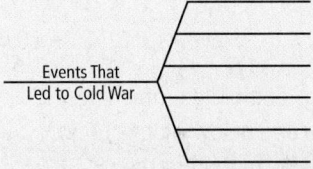

Events That
Led to Cold War

7. **Analyzing Visuals** Study the map on page 536. Why did the Soviet Union want to have control over the countries on its western border?

Writing About History

8. **Expository Writing** Suppose that you are an adviser to Truman. Write a report explaining your interpretation of Churchill's "iron curtain" speech.

History ONLINE

Study Central™ To review this section, go to glencoe.com and click on Study Central.

The Early Cold War Years

President Truman worked to contain communism by supporting Greece, Iran, and West Germany. When Communist North Korea invaded South Korea, Truman and the UN sent troops to aid South Korea.

Guide to Reading

Big Ideas

Trade, War, and Migration As the Cold War began, the United States struggled to oppose Communist aggression in Europe and Asia through political, economic, and military measures.

Content Vocabulary

- containment *(p. 538)*
- limited war *(p. 545)*

Academic Vocabulary

- insecurity *(p. 538)*
- initially *(p. 541)*

People and Events to Identify

- George Kennan *(p. 538)*
- Long Telegram *(p. 538)*
- Marshall Plan *(p. 540)*
- NATO *(p. 541)*
- SEATO *(p. 545)*

Reading Strategy

Sequencing Complete a time line similar to the one below by recording the major events related to the Korean War.

Containing Communism

MAIN Idea The Truman Doctrine offered aid to any nation resisting communism; the Marshall Plan aided European countries in rebuilding.

HISTORY AND YOU Is there a conflict in the world today where you think the United States should intervene? Read on to learn how President Truman adopted policies designed to stop the spread of communism.

Despite growing tensions with the Soviet Union, many American officials continued to believe cooperation with the Soviets was possible. In late 1945 the foreign ministers of the former wartime Allies met first in London, then in Moscow, to discuss the future of Europe and Asia. Although both British and American officials pushed for free elections in Eastern Europe, the Soviets refused to budge. "Our relations with the Russians," the British foreign minister gloomily concluded, "are drifting into the same condition as that in which we had found ourselves with Hitler."

The Long Telegram

Increasingly exasperated by the Soviets' refusal to cooperate, officials at the State Department asked the American Embassy in Moscow to explain Soviet behavior. On February 22, 1946, diplomat **George Kennan** responded with what became known as the **Long Telegram,** a 5,540-word message explaining his views of the Soviets.

According to Kennan, the Soviets' view of the world came from a traditional "Russian sense of **insecurity**" and fear of the West, intensified by the communist ideas of Lenin and Stalin. Because communists believed that they were in a long-term historical struggle against capitalism, Kennan argued, it was impossible to reach any permanent settlement with them.

Kennan therefore proposed what became the basic American policy throughout the Cold War: "a long-term, patient but firm and vigilant **containment** of Russian expansive tendencies." Kennan explained that, in his opinion, the Soviet system had several major economic and political weaknesses. If the United States could keep the Soviets from expanding their power, it would be only a matter of time before the Soviet system would fall apart. Communism could be beaten without going to war. The Long Telegram circulated widely in

The Truman Doctrine

▲ President Truman signs the Foreign Aid Assistance Act, providing aid to Greece and Turkey; the use of aid to support nations resisting Communist pressure became known as the Truman Doctrine.

"The peoples of a number of countries of the world have recently had totalitarian regimes forced upon them against their will. The Government of the United States has made frequent protests against coercion and intimidation, in violation of the Yalta agreement in Poland, Romania, and Bulgaria. At the present moment in world history nearly every nation must choose between alternative ways of life. The choice is too often not a free one. . . . I believe that it must be the policy of the United States to support free peoples who are resisting attempted subjugation by armed minorities or by outside pressures. I believe that we must assist free peoples to work out their own destinies in their own way."

—Truman's address to Congress, March 12, 1947

DBQ Document-Based Questions

1. **Finding the Main Idea** What was the stated goal of the Truman Doctrine?

2. **Drawing Conclusions** Which nation received the most aid through the Marshall Plan? Why do you think this might be?

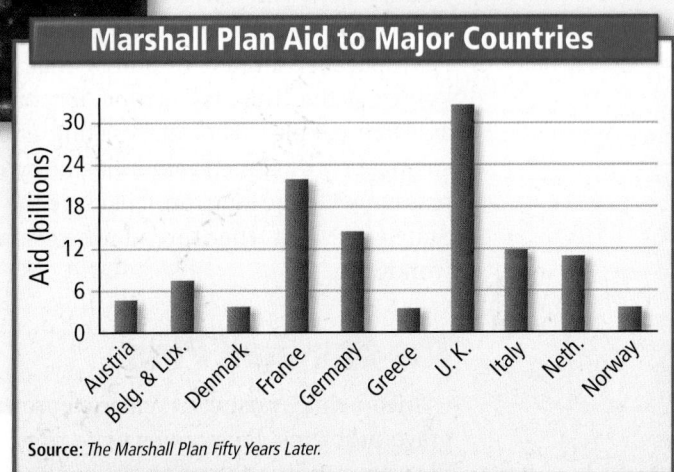

Marshall Plan Aid to Major Countries

Source: *The Marshall Plan Fifty Years Later.*

Truman's administration. The administration based its policy of containment—keeping communism within its present territory through the use of diplomatic, economic, and military actions—on this document.

Crisis in Iran

While Truman's administration discussed Kennan's ideas, a series of crises erupted during the spring and summer of 1946. These crises seemed to prove that Kennan was right about the Soviets. The first crisis began in Iran in March 1946.

During World War II, the United States had put troops in southern Iran while Soviet troops occupied northern Iran to secure a supply line from the Persian Gulf. After the war, instead of withdrawing as promised, the Soviet troops remained in northern Iran. Stalin then began demanding access to Iran's oil supplies. To increase the pressure, Soviet troops helped local Communists in northern Iran establish a separate government.

To American officials, these actions signaled a Soviet push into the Middle East. The secretary of state sent Stalin a strong message demanding that Soviet forces withdraw. At the same time, the battleship USS *Missouri* sailed into the eastern Mediterranean. The pressure seemed to work. Soviet forces withdrew, having been promised a joint Soviet-Iranian oil company, although the Iranian parliament later rejected the plan.

The Truman Doctrine

Frustrated in Iran, Stalin turned northwest to Turkey. There, the straits of the Dardanelles were a vital route from Soviet Black Sea ports to the Mediterranean. For centuries, Russia had wanted to control this strategic route. In August 1946, Stalin demanded joint control of the Dardanelles with Turkey.

For more of the text of Truman's Address to Congress, see page R54 in **Documents in American History.**

Presidential adviser Dean Acheson saw this move as part of a Soviet plan to control the Middle East. He advised Truman to make a show of force. The president ordered the new aircraft carrier *Franklin D. Roosevelt* to join the *Missouri* in protecting Turkey and the eastern Mediterranean.

Meanwhile, Britain tried to help Greece. In August 1946 Greek Communists launched a guerrilla war against the Greek government. British troops helped fight the guerrillas, but in February 1947 Britain informed the United States that it could no longer afford to help Greece due to Britain's weakened postwar economy.

On March 12, 1947, Truman went before Congress to ask for $400 million to fight Communist aggression in Greece and Turkey. His speech outlined a policy that became known as the Truman Doctrine. Its goal was to aid "free peoples who are resisting attempted subjugation by armed minorities or by outside pressures." In the long run, it pledged the United States to fight the spread of communism worldwide.

The Marshall Plan

Meanwhile, postwar Western Europe faced grave problems. Economies were ruined, people were nearing starvation, and political chaos was at hand. In June 1947 Secretary of State George C. Marshall proposed the European Recovery Program, or **Marshall Plan,** which would give European nations American aid to rebuild their economies. Truman saw the Marshall Plan and the Truman Doctrine as "two halves of the same walnut," both essential for containment. Marshall offered help to all nations planning a recovery program:

PRIMARY SOURCE

"Our policy is directed not against any country or doctrine but against hunger, poverty, desperation and chaos. Its purpose should be the revival of a working economy in the world so as to permit the emergence of political and social conditions in which free institutions can exist."

—quoted in *Marshall: Hero for Our Times*

Although the Marshall Plan was offered to the Soviet Union and its satellite nations in Eastern Europe, those nations rejected the offer. Instead, the Soviets developed their own economic program. This action further separated Europe into competing regions. The Marshall Plan pumped billions of dollars worth of supplies, machinery, and food into Western Europe. Western Europe's recovery weakened the appeal of communism and opened new markets for trade.

In his 1949 Inaugural Address, President Truman also proposed assistance for underdeveloped countries outside the war zone. The Point Four Program aimed to make "scientific advances and industrial progress available for the improvement and growth of underdeveloped areas" regardless of region. The Department of State administered Point Four assistances from 1950 until its merger with other foreign aid programs in 1953.

The Berlin Airlift

President Truman and his advisers believed that Western Europe's prosperity depended on Germany's recovery. The Soviets, however, still wanted Germany to pay reparations to the Soviet Union. This dispute brought these nations to the brink of war.

By early 1948, U.S. officials had concluded that the Soviets were trying to undermine Germany's economy. In response, the United States, Great Britain, and France announced that they were merging their zones in Germany and allowing the Germans to have their own government. They also agreed to merge their zones in Berlin and to make West Berlin part of the new German republic.

The new nation was officially called the Federal Republic of Germany, but it became known as West Germany. The Soviet zone eventually became the German Democratic Republic, also known as East Germany. West Germany was not allowed to have a military, but in most respects, it was independent.

The decision to create West Germany convinced the Soviets that they would never get the reparations they wanted. In late June 1948, Soviet troops cut all road and rail traffic to West Berlin hoping to force the United States to either reconsider its decision or abandon West Berlin. President Truman sent bombers with atomic weapons to bases in Britain and the American commander in Germany warned: "If we mean to hold Europe against communism, then we must not budge." The challenge was to keep West Berlin alive without provoking war with the Soviets. Instead of ordering troops to fight their way to Berlin, and thereby triggering war with the Soviet Union, Truman ordered the air force to fly supplies into Berlin instead.

The Berlin airlift began in June 1948 and continued through the spring of 1949, bringing in more than 2 million tons of supplies to the city. Stalin finally lifted the blockade on May 12, 1949. The airlift symbolized American determination to contain communism and not give in to Soviet demands.

NATO

The Berlin blockade convinced many Americans that the Soviets were bent on conquest. The public began to support a military alliance with Western Europe. By April 1949, an agreement had been reached to create the North Atlantic Treaty Organization (NATO)—a mutual defense alliance.

NATO initially included 12 countries: the United States, Canada, Britain, France, Italy, Belgium, Denmark, Portugal, the Netherlands, Norway, Luxembourg, and Iceland. NATO members agreed to come to the aid of any member who was attacked. For the first time in its history, the United States had committed itself to maintaining peace in Europe. Six years later, NATO allowed West Germany to rearm and join its organization. This decision alarmed Soviet leaders. They responded by organizing a military alliance in Eastern Europe known as the Warsaw Pact.

History ONLINE
Student Web Activity Visit glencoe.com and complete the activity on the Berlin Airlift.

✓ Reading Check **Evaluating** What triggered the beginning of the Berlin airlift?

PRIMARY SOURCE
The Berlin Airlift, 1948–1949

After the Soviet Union blockaded West Berlin, the United States delivered 4,000 tons of food, medicine, coal and other supplies that were needed every day to keep the city functioning. A cargo plane had to land with supplies every three and a half minutes. To keep the airlift running, crews stayed onboard and food was brought to them while the planes were unloaded and refueled. Meanwhile, 20,000 volunteers in Berlin built a third airport, enabling the flow of supplies to increase to 13,000 tons a day.

NATIONAL GEOGRAPHIC **NATO Is Born, 1949**

Founding members
Joined 1952
Joined 1955
Warsaw Pact

70°N
ARCTIC CIRCLE
30°W
ICELAND
60°N
20°W
ATLANTIC OCEAN
North Sea
NORWAY
DENMARK
UNITED KINGDOM
NETH.
50°N
BELG.
LUX.
E. GER.
W. GER.
POLAND
SOVIET UNION
CZECH.
FRANCE
HUNGARY
ROMANIA
ITALY
PORTUGAL
40°N
BULGARIA
ALB.
30°E
GREECE
TURKEY
Mediterranean Sea
20°E
10°W
0°
10°E
0 — 600 kilometers
0 — 600 miles
Lambert Azimuthal Equal-Area projection

Analyzing VISUALS

1. **Interpreting** Which nations are the founding members of NATO?

2. **Identifying** Which NATO nations shared a border with one or more Warsaw Pact nations?

The Korean War

MAIN Idea Attempts to keep South Korea free from communism led the United States to military intervention.

HISTORY AND YOU What happens to someone who disobeys a coach, employer, or teacher? Read on to learn what happened to General MacArthur when he criticized the president.

The Cold War eventually spread beyond Europe. Conflicts also emerged in Asia, where events in China and Korea brought about a new attitude toward Japan and sent American troops back into battle in Asia less than five years after World War II had ended.

The Chinese Revolution

In China, Communist forces led by Mao Zedong had been struggling against the Nationalist government led by Chiang Kai-shek since the late 1920s. During World War II, the two sides suspended their war to resist Japanese occupation. With the end of World War II, however, civil war broke out again. Although Mao made great gains, neither side could win nor agree to a compromise.

To prevent a Communist revolution in Asia, the United States sent the Nationalist government $2 billion in aid beginning in the mid-1940s, but the Nationalists squandered this advantage through poor military planning and corruption. By 1949, the Communists had captured the Chinese capital of Beijing, while support for the Nationalists declined.

In August 1949 the U.S. State Department discontinued aid to the Chinese Nationalists. The defeated Nationalists then fled to the small island of Taiwan (Formosa). The victorious Communists established the People's Republic of China in October 1949.

China's fall to communism shocked Americans. To make matters worse, in September 1949 the Soviet Union announced that it had successfully tested its first atomic weapon. Then, early in 1950, the People's Republic of China and the Soviet Union signed a treaty of friendship and alliance. Many Western leaders feared that China and the Soviet Union would support Communist revolutions in other nations.

The United States kept formal diplomatic relations with only the Nationalist Chinese in

The Korean War, 1950–1953

▲ **June–September 1950**

North Korean troops invade South Korea, driving South Korean and UN forces south into a small perimeter around Pusan.

	North Korean-controlled territory
	South Korean-controlled territory
	North Korean advance
	UN counteroffensive
	Front line
	Chinese counteroffensive
	Armistice line

Taiwan. It used its veto power in the UN Security Council to keep representatives of the new Communist People's Republic of China out of the UN, allowing the Nationalists to retain their seat.

New Policies in Japan

The Chinese revolution brought about a significant change in American policy toward Japan. At the end of World War II, General Douglas MacArthur had taken charge of occupied Japan. His mission was to introduce democracy and keep Japan from threatening war again. Once the United States lost China as its chief ally in Asia, it adopted policies to encourage the rapid recovery of Japan's industrial economy. Just as

▲ September–November 1950

Led by General MacArthur, UN troops land behind North Korean lines at the port of Inchon. North Korean forces fall back rapidly, and the UN forces head north into North Korea.

▲ November 1950–January 1951

As UN forces near the Chinese border, Chinese troops cross into North Korea driving the UN back. MacArthur wants to attack Chinese territory. He publicly argues with Truman and is fired.

▲ January 1951–July 1953

Led by U.S. General Matthew Ridgway, the UN forces push the Chinese and North Korean forces out of South Korea. The war bogs down into a stalemate along the 38th parallel.

◄ *Soldiers of the U.S. 2nd Infantry Division man a machine gun near the Chongchun River in Korea, December 15, 1950.*

Analyzing GEOGRAPHY

1. **Human-Environment Interaction** What occurred at the port of Inchon in 1950?

2. **Location** What geographical feature forms the border between China and North Korea?

---

the United States viewed West Germany as the key to defending all of Europe against communism, it saw Japan as the key to defending Asia.

The Korean War Begins

At the end of World War II, American and Soviet forces entered Korea to disarm the Japanese troops stationed there. The Allies divided Korea at the 38th parallel of latitude. Soviet troops controlled the north, while American troops controlled the south.

As the Cold War began, talks to reunify Korea broke down. A Communist Korean government was organized in the north, while an American-backed government controlled the south. Both governments claimed authority over Korea, and border clashes were common. The Soviet Union provided military aid to the North Koreans, who quickly built up an army. On June 25, 1950, North Korean troops invaded the south, rapidly driving back the poorly equipped South Korean forces.

Truman saw the Communist invasion of South Korea as a test of the containment policy and ordered United States naval and air power into action. He then called on the United Nations to act. Truman succeeded because the Soviet delegate was boycotting the UN Security Council over its China policy and was not present to veto the American proposal. With the pledge of UN troops, Truman ordered General MacArthur to send American troops from Japan to Korea.

▲ President Truman, Secretary of State Dean Acheson, and "The Pentagon" are held over the flame of public opinion for firing General MacArthur. "John Q." refers to "John Q. Public," or the American people.

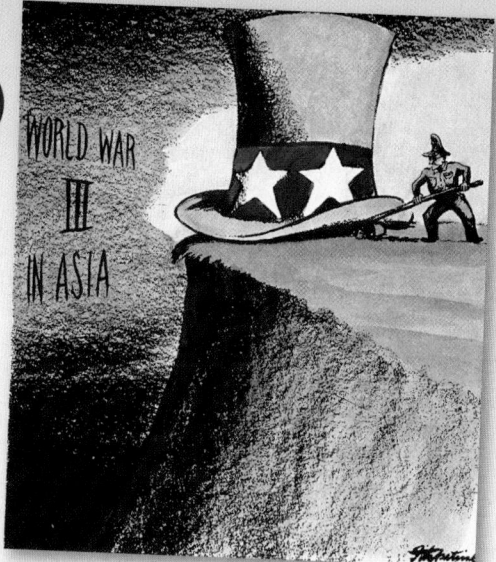

▲ Entitled "Not a General's Job," this cartoon suggests that MacArthur had overstepped his authority in Korea.

Analyzing VISUALS

1. **Identifying Points of View** Which of the cartoons supports President Truman's decision to fire General MacArthur? Explain.

2. **Making Inferences** What does the cartoon on the right imply MacArthur was trying to do in Asia?

The American and South Korean troops were driven back into a small pocket of territory near the port of Pusan. Inside the "Pusan perimeter," as it came to be called, the troops stubbornly resisted the North Korean onslaught, buying time for MacArthur to organize reinforcements.

On September 15, 1950, MacArthur ordered a daring invasion behind enemy lines at the port of Inchon. The Inchon landing took the North Koreans by surprise. Within weeks they were in full retreat back across the 38th parallel. Truman then gave the order to pursue the North Koreans beyond the 38th parallel. MacArthur pushed the North Koreans north to the Yalu River, the border with China.

China Enters the War The Communist People's Republic of China saw the advancing UN troops as a threat and warned the forces to halt their advance. When those warnings were ignored, Chinese forces crossed the Yalu River in November. Hundreds of thousands of Chinese troops flooded across the border, driving the UN forces back across the 38th parallel.

As his troops fell back, an angry MacArthur demanded approval to expand the war against China. He asked for a blockade of Chinese ports, the use of Chiang Kai-shek's Nationalist forces, and the bombing of Chinese cities with atomic weapons.

Truman Fires MacArthur President Truman refused MacArthur's demands because he did not want to expand the war into China or to use the atomic bomb. MacArthur persisted. He publicly criticized the president, arguing that it was a mistake to keep the war limited. "There is no substitute for victory," MacArthur insisted, by which he meant that if the United States was going to go to war, it should use all of its power to win. Keeping a war limited was, in his view, a form of appeasement, and appeasement he argued, "begets new and bloodier war."

Determined to maintain control of policy and to show that the president commanded the military, an exasperated Truman fired MacArthur for insubordination in April 1951. Later, in private conversation, Truman explained:

"I was sorry to have to reach a parting of the way with the big man in Asia, but he asked for it and I had to give it to him."

MacArthur, who remained popular despite being fired, returned home to parades and a hero's welcome. Many Americans criticized the president. Congress and other military leaders, however, supported Truman's decision and his Korean strategy. American policy in Asia remained committed to **limited war**—a war fought to achieve a limited objective, such as containing communism. Truman later explained why he favored limited war in Korea:

PRIMARY SOURCE

"The Kremlin [Soviet Union] is trying, and has been trying for a long time, to drive a wedge between us and the other nations. It wants to see us isolated. It wants to see us distrusted. It wants to see us feared and hated by our allies. Our allies agree with us in the course we are following. They do not believe we should take the initiative to widen the conflict in the Far East. If the United States were to widen the conflict, we might well have to go it alone."

—from "Address to the Civil Defense Conference," May 7, 1951

As Truman also noted, America's allies in Europe were much closer to the Soviet Union. If war broke out, Europe would suffer the most damage and might well be attacked with atomic bombs. This concern—that all-out war in Korea might lead to nuclear war—was the main reason why Truman favored limited war. This concern shaped American foreign policy throughout the Cold War.

Changes in Policy

By mid-1951, the UN forces had pushed the Chinese and North Korean forces back across the 38th parallel. The war then settled down into a series of relatively small battles over hills and other local objectives. In November 1951, peace negotiations began, but an armistice would not be signed until July 1953. More than 33,600 American soldiers died in action in the Korean War, and more than 2,800 died from accidents or disease.

The Korean War marked an important turning point in the Cold War. Until 1950, the United States had preferred to use political pressure and economic aid to contain communism. After the Korean War began, the United States embarked on a major military buildup.

The Korean War also helped expand the Cold War to Asia. Before 1950, the United States had focused on Europe as the most important area in which to contain communism. After the Korean War began, the United States became more militarily involved in Asia. In 1954 the United States signed defense agreements with Japan, South Korea, Taiwan, the Philippines, and Australia, forming the Southeast Asia Treaty Organization (**SEATO**). American aid also began flowing to French forces fighting Communists in Vietnam.

Reading Check **Analyzing** How did President Truman view the Communist invasion of South Korea?

Section 2 REVIEW

Vocabulary

1. **Explain** the significance of: George Kennan, Long Telegram, containment, Marshall Plan, NATO, limited war, SEATO.

Main Ideas

2. **Explaining** How did the Truman Doctrine and the Marshall Plan address the spread of communism?

3. **Describing** What originally led to the formation of two Koreas?

Critical Thinking

4. **Big Ideas** How did the Long Telegram influence U.S. foreign policy?

5. **Categorizing** Use a graphic organizer similar to the one below to list early conflicts between the Soviet Union and the United States.

Conflicts Between the USSR and the U.S.

6. **Analyzing Visuals** Study the maps of the Korean War on pages 542–543. When did the United Nations control the most territory in Korea? When did both sides finally agree on an armistice line?

Writing About History

7. **Persuasive Writing** Write a letter to the editor of a newspaper explaining why you agree or disagree with President Truman's firing of General MacArthur.

History ONLINE

Study Central™ To review this section, go to glencoe.com and click on Study Central.

Section Audio   **Spotlight Video**

The Cold War and American Society

Guide to Reading

Big Ideas
Struggles for Rights In the early part of the Cold War, the fear of communism led to a hunt for spies and to intolerance and suspicion of people with radical ideas in the United States.

Content Vocabulary
• subversion *(p. 546)*
• loyalty review program *(p. 546)*
• perjury *(p. 548)*
• censure *(p. 550)*
• fallout *(p. 553)*

Academic Vocabulary
• manipulate *(p. 547)*
• convince *(p. 548)*

People and Events to Identify
• Red Scare *(p. 546)*
• Alger Hiss *(p. 548)*
• McCarran Act *(p. 550)*
• McCarthyism *(p. 550)*

Reading Strategy
Summarizing As you read, summarize the section content by using the major headings to create an outline similar to the one below.

The Cold War and American Society
I. A New Red Scare
  A. The Loyalty Review Program
  B.
  C.

Fearing subversive activity, the government tried to root out Communists in government, Hollywood, and labor unions, while Americans learned to live with the threat of nuclear attack.

A New Red Scare

MAIN Idea Public accusations and trials followed in the wake of fears of communism and spies.

HISTORY AND YOU Do you remember reading about the fears of communism during the early twentieth century? Read on to learn of a second major scare in the 1950s.

During the 1950s, thousands of ordinary people—from teachers to autoworkers to high government officials—shared a disturbing experience. Rumors and accusations of Communists in the United States and of Communist infiltration of the government tapped into fears that Communists were trying to take over the world.

The **Red Scare** began in September 1945, when a clerk named Igor Gouzenko walked out of the Soviet Embassy in Ottawa, Canada, and defected. Gouzenko carried documents revealing a massive effort by the Soviet Union to infiltrate organizations and government agencies in Canada and the United States, with the specific goal of obtaining information about the atomic bomb.

The Gouzenko case stunned Americans. It implied that spies had infiltrated the American government. Soon, however, the search for spies escalated into a general fear of Communist **subversion.** Subversion is the effort to weaken a society secretly and overthrow its government.

The Loyalty Review Program

In early 1947, just nine days after his powerful speech announcing the Truman Doctrine, the president established a **loyalty review program** to screen all federal employees. Rather than calm public suspicion, Truman's action seemed to confirm fears that Communists had infiltrated the government and helped to increase the fear of communism sweeping the nation.

Between 1947 and 1951, more than 6 million federal employees were screened for their loyalty—a term difficult to define. A person might become a suspect for reading certain books, belonging to various groups, traveling overseas, or even seeing certain foreign films. About 14,000 employees were subject to scrutiny by the Federal Bureau of Investigation (FBI). Some 2,000 employees quit their jobs

▲ **Loyalty and Dissent, Oppenheimer, 1953**

Although he had led the effort to develop the atomic bomb, Dr. Robert Oppenheimer's left-wing views and opposition to the hydrogen bomb led to the suspension of his security clearance and controversial public hearings.

▲ *Hiss v. Chambers*, **1948**

In 1948, Whittaker Chambers, a *TIME* magazine editor and former Communist Party member, testified that U.S. diplomat Alger Hiss was a Communist. Hiss denied being a spy or a member of the Communist Party. Evidence provided by Chambers led to Hiss being convicted of perjury.

Analyzing VISUALS

1. **Summarizing** What were the Rosenbergs accused of and what was the result?

2. **Explaining** Why was Robert Oppenheimer's security clearance suspended?

▶ **The Rosenbergs Are Convicted, 1950**

In 1950 the hunt for spies who had given U.S. nuclear secrets to the Soviets led to the arrest of Julius and Ethel Rosenberg. Accused of running a Soviet spy network, the Rosenbergs became the first civilians executed for espionage in 1953. Their case was controversial and led to public protests.

during the check, many under pressure. Another 212 were fired for "questionable loyalty," although no actual evidence against them was uncovered.

House Un-American Activities Committee (HUAC)

Although the FBI helped screen federal employees, FBI Director J. Edgar Hoover was not satisfied. In 1947 Hoover went before the House Un-American Activities Committee (HUAC). Formed in 1938 to investigate both Communist and Fascist activities in the United States, HUAC was a minor committee until Hoover expanded its importance.

Hoover urged HUAC to hold public hearings on Communist subversion. The committee, Hoover said, could reveal "the diabolic machinations of sinister figures engaged in un-American activities." Hoover's aim was to expose not just Communists but also "Communist sympathizers" and "fellow travelers." Under Hoover's leadership, the FBI sent agents to infiltrate groups suspected of subversion and wiretapped thousands of telephones.

Hollywood on Trial One of HUAC's first hearings in 1947 focused on the film industry as a powerful cultural force that Communists might **manipulate** to spread their ideas and influence. HUAC's interviews routinely began, "Are you now, or have you ever been, a member of the Communist Party?" Future American president Ronald Reagan was head of the Screen Actors Guild at the time and, when called before HUAC, he testified that there were Communists in Hollywood.

During the hearings, ten screenwriters, known as the "Hollywood Ten," used their Fifth Amendment right to protect themselves from self-incrimination and refused to testify. The incident led producers to blacklist, or agree not to hire, anyone who was believed to be a Communist or who refused to cooperate with the committee. In 1950 a pamphlet called *Red Channels* was published, listing 151 blacklisted actors, directors, broadcasters, and screenwriters. The blacklist created an atmosphere of distrust and fear.

Alger Hiss In 1948 Whittaker Chambers, a *TIME* magazine editor and former Communist Party member, testified to HUAC that several government officials were also former Communists or spies.

The most prominent official named by Chambers was **Alger Hiss,** a diplomat who had served in Roosevelt's administration, attended the Yalta conference, and taken part in organizing the United Nations. After Hiss sued him for libel, Chambers testified before a grand jury that, in 1937 and 1938, Hiss had given him secret documents from the State Department. Hiss denied being either a spy or a member of the Communist Party, and he also denied ever having known Chambers.

The committee was ready to drop the investigation until Representative Richard Nixon of California **convinced** his colleagues to continue the hearings to determine whether Hiss or Chambers had lied. Chambers produced copies of secret documents, along with microfilm that he had hidden in a hollow pumpkin on his farm. These "pumpkin papers," Chambers claimed, proved Hiss was lying. A jury agreed and convicted Hiss of **perjury,** or lying under oath.

The Rosenbergs Another sensational spy case centered on accusations that American Communists had sold the secrets of the atomic bomb to the Soviets. Many people did not believe that the Soviet Union could have produced an atomic bomb in 1949 without help. This belief intensified the hunt for spies.

In 1950 the hunt led to a British scientist who admitted sending information to the Soviet Union. After hearing his testimony, the FBI arrested Julius and Ethel Rosenberg, a New York couple who were members of the Communist Party. The government charged them with heading a Soviet spy ring.

The Rosenbergs denied the charges but were condemned to death for espionage. Many people believed that they were not leaders or spies but victims caught up in the wave of anti-Communist frenzy. Appeals, public expressions of support, and pleas for clemency failed, however, and the couple was executed in June 1953.

Project Venona The American public hotly debated the guilt or innocence of individuals, like the Rosenbergs, who were accused of being spies. There was, however, solid evidence of Soviet espionage, although very few Americans knew it at the time. In 1946 American and British cryptographers, working for a project code-named "Venona," cracked the Soviet spy code of the time, enabling them to read approximately 3,000 messages between Moscow and the United States collected during the Cold War.

The messages collected using Project Venona confirmed extensive Soviet spying and an ongoing effort to steal nuclear secrets. The government did not reveal Project Venona's existence until 1995. The Venona documents provided strong evidence that the Rosenbergs were indeed guilty.

The Red Scare Spreads

Following the federal government's example, many state and local governments, universities, businesses, unions, churches, and private organizations began their own efforts to find Communists. The University of California required its 11,000 faculty members to take loyalty oaths and fired 157 who refused to do so. Many Catholic groups became strongly anti-Communist and urged their members to identify Communists within the Church.

The Taft-Hartley Act of 1947 required union leaders to take oaths that they were not Communists, but many union leaders did not object. Instead, they launched their own efforts to purge Communists from their organizations. The president of the CIO called Communist sympathizers "skulking cowards" and "apostles of hate." The CIO eventually expelled 11 unions that refused to remove Communist leaders from their organization.

Reading Check **Explaining** What was the purpose of the loyalty review boards and HUAC?

McCarthyism

MAIN Idea Senator Joseph R. McCarthy used the fear of communism to increase his own power and destroy the reputations of many people.

HISTORY AND YOU Have you ever known anyone who spread untrue stories about others? Read on to find out about the false accusations that Senator McCarthy spread in the early 1950s.

In 1949 the Red Scare intensified even further. In that year, the Soviet Union successfully tested an atomic bomb, and China fell to communism. To many Americans, these events seemed to prove that the United States was losing the Cold War. Deeply concerned, they wanted to know why their government was failing. As a result, many continued to believe that Communists had infiltrated the government and remained undetected.

In February 1950, soon after Alger Hiss's perjury conviction, a little-known Wisconsin senator gave a political speech to a Republican women's group in West Virginia. Halfway through his speech, Senator Joseph R. McCarthy made a surprising statement:

PRIMARY SOURCE

"While I cannot take the time to name all the men in the State Department who have been named as members of the Communist Party and members of a spy ring, I have here in my hand a list of 205 that were known to the Secretary of State as being members of the Communist Party and who nevertheless are still working and shaping the policy of the State Department."

—quoted in *The Fifties*

The Associated Press picked up the statement and sent it to newspapers nationwide. While at an airport, reporters asked McCarthy to see his list of Communists. McCarthy replied that he would be happy to show it to them, but unfortunately, it was in his bag on the plane. In fact, the list never appeared. McCarthy, however, continued to make charges and draw attention.

McCarthy's use of sensationalist charges was not new. When he ran for the Senate in 1946, he accused his opponent, Robert M. La Follette, Jr., of being "communistically inclined." McCarthy did not provide any evidence to support his accusation, but it helped him win the election.

POLITICAL CARTOONS PRIMARY SOURCE
McCarthyism

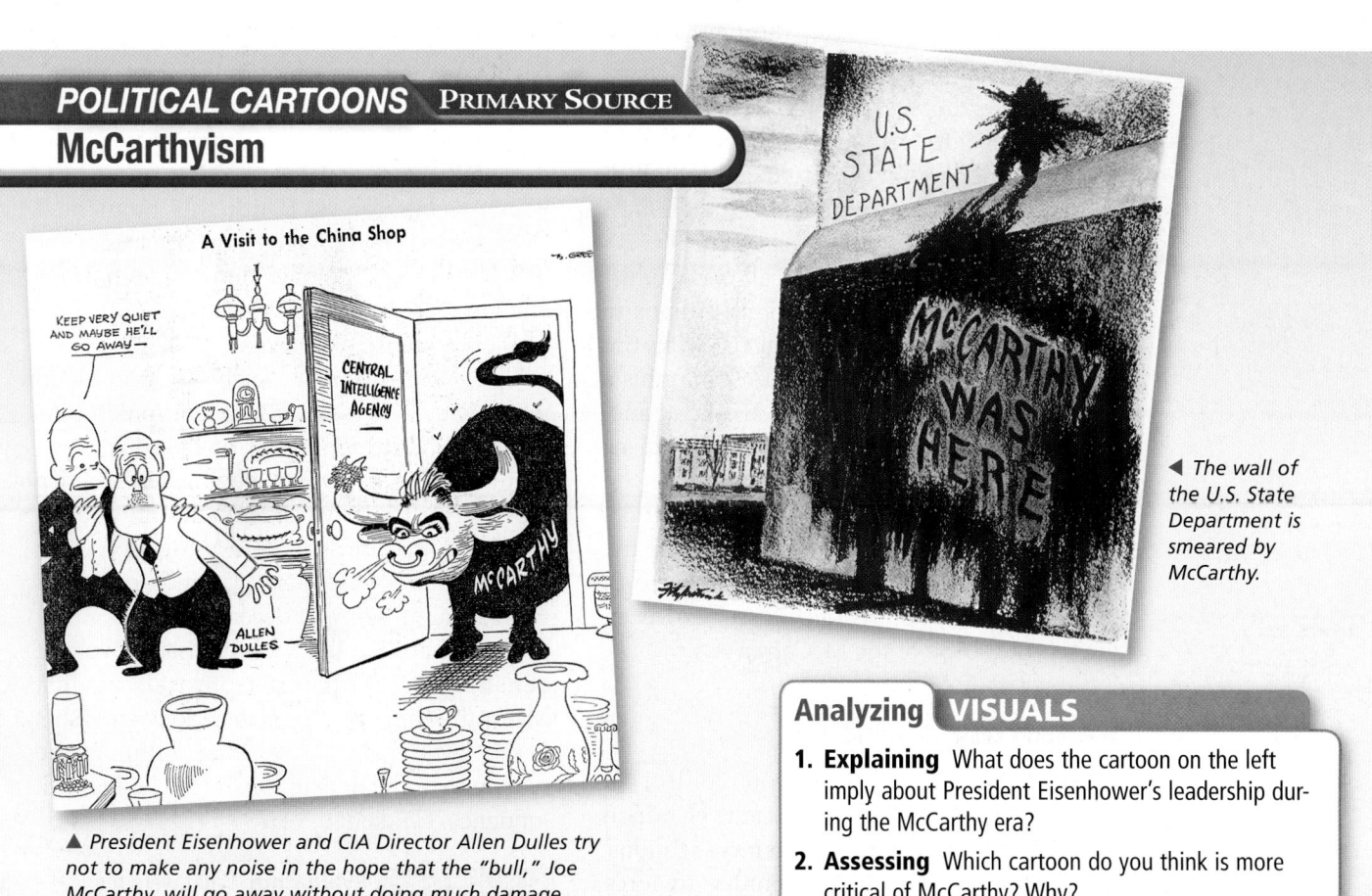

A Visit to the China Shop

KEEP VERY QUIET AND MAYBE HE'LL GO AWAY—

CENTRAL INTELLIGENCE AGENCY

ALLEN DULLES

MCCARTHY

▲ President Eisenhower and CIA Director Allen Dulles try not to make any noise in the hope that the "bull," Joe McCarthy, will go away without doing much damage.

U.S. STATE DEPARTMENT

MCCARTHY WAS HERE

◄ The wall of the U.S. State Department is smeared by McCarthy.

Analyzing VISUALS

1. **Explaining** What does the cartoon on the left imply about President Eisenhower's leadership during the McCarthy era?

2. **Assessing** Which cartoon do you think is more critical of McCarthy? Why?

After becoming a senator, McCarthy continued to proclaim that Communists were a danger both at home and abroad. To some audiences, he distributed a booklet called "The Party of Betrayal," which accused Democratic Party leaders of corruption and of protecting Communists. Secretary of State Dean Acheson was a frequent target. According to McCarthy, Acheson was incompetent and a tool of Stalin. He also wildly accused George C. Marshall, the former army chief of staff and secretary of state, of disloyalty as a member of "a conspiracy so immense as to dwarf any previous such ventures in the history of man."

McCarthy was not alone in making such charges. In the prevailing mood of anxiety about communism, many Americans were ready to believe them.

The McCarran Act

In 1950, with the Korean War underway and McCarthy and others arousing fears of Communist spies, Congress passed the Internal Security Act, usually called the **McCarran Act.** Declaring that "world Communism has as its sole purpose the establishment of a totalitarian dictatorship in America," Senator Pat McCarran of Nevada offered a way to fight "treachery, infiltration, sabotage, and terrorism." The act made it illegal to "combine, conspire, or agree with any other person to perform any act which would substantially contribute to . . . the establishment of a totalitarian government."

The McCarran Act required all Communist Party and "Communist-front" organizations to publish their records and register with the United States attorney general. Communists could not have passports to travel abroad and, in cases of a national emergency, Communists and Communist sympathizers could be arrested and detained. Unwilling to punish people for their opinions, Truman vetoed the bill, but Congress easily overrode his veto in 1950. Later Supreme Court cases, however, limited the scope of the McCarran Act.

McCarthy's Tactics

After the Republicans won control of Congress in 1952, McCarthy became chairman of the Senate subcommittee on investigations. Using the power of his committee to force government officials to testify about alleged Communist influences, McCarthy turned the investigation into a witch hunt—a search for disloyalty based on flimsy evidence and irrational fears. His tactic of damaging reputations with vague and unfounded charges became known as **McCarthyism.**

McCarthy's sensational accusations drew the attention of the press, which put him in the headlines and quoted him widely. When he questioned witnesses, McCarthy would badger them and then refuse to accept their answers. His tactics left a cloud of suspicion that McCarthy and others interpreted as guilt. Furthermore, people were afraid to challenge him for fear of becoming targets themselves.

McCarthy's Downfall

In 1954 McCarthy began to look for Soviet spies in the United States Army. During weeks of televised Army-McCarthy hearings, millions of Americans watched McCarthy question and bully officers, harassing them about trivial details and accusing them of misconduct. His popular support began to fade.

Finally, to strike back at the army's lawyer, Joseph Welch, McCarthy brought up the past of a young lawyer in Welch's firm who had been a member of a Communist-front organization while in law school. Welch, who was fully aware of the young man's past, now exploded at McCarthy for possibly ruining the young man's career: "Until this moment, I think I never really gauged your cruelty or your recklessness. . . . You have done enough. Have you no sense of decency, sir, at long last? Have you left no sense of decency?"

Spectators cheered. Welch had said aloud what many Americans had been thinking. As Senator Stuart Symington of Missouri commented, "The American people have had a look at you for six weeks. You are not fooling anyone." McCarthy had lost the power to arouse fear. Newspaper headlines repeated: "Have you no sense of decency?"

Later that year, the Senate passed a vote of **censure,** or formal disapproval, against McCarthy—one of the most serious criticisms it can level against a member. Although he remained in the Senate, McCarthy had lost all influence. He died in 1957.

✓**Reading Check** **Evaluating** What were the effects of McCarthyism?

ANALYZING SUPREME COURT CASES

Are There Limits on Congressional Power?

★ *Watkins* v. *United States*, 1957

Background to the Case

In 1954 labor organizer John Watkins testified before the House Un-American Activities Committee. He agreed to discuss his own connections with the Communist Party and to identify people he knew who were still members, but he refused to give information about those who were no longer members. Watkins received a misdemeanor conviction for refusing to answer questions "pertinent to the question under inquiry." In 1957 he appealed his case to the Supreme Court.

How the Court Ruled

The Watkins case raised the question: Is it constitutional for a congressional committee to ask any question or investigate any topic, whether or not it is directly related to Congress's law-making function? In a 6-to-1 decision—two members did not participate—the Supreme Court held that the activities of HUAC during its investigations were, indeed, beyond the scope of the stated aims of the committee, as well as the authority of congressional powers.

▲ Senator Joseph McCarthy (above) symbolized the fears of the early 1950s, when communist spies were suspected to have infiltrated all aspects of American society. Together, McCarthy's committee in the Senate and the House Un-American Activities Committee used their power to subpoena people to investigate their loyalty. As a result many reputations were smeared and careers ruined.

PRIMARY SOURCE

The Court's Opinion

"The power of the Congress to conduct investigations is inherent in the legislative process. That power is broad. . . . But, broad as is this power of inquiry, it is not unlimited. There is no general authority to expose the private affairs of individuals without justification in terms of the functions of the Congress. . . . Nor is the Congress a law enforcement or trial agency. These are functions of the executive and judicial departments of government. No inquiry is an end in itself; it must be related to, and in furtherance of, a legitimate task of the Congress. Investigations conducted solely for the personal aggrandizement of the investigators or to "punish" those investigated are indefensible."

—Chief Justice Earl Warren, writing for the majority in
Watkins v. *United States*

PRIMARY SOURCE

Dissenting View

"It may be that at times the House Committee on Un-American Activities has, as the Court says, "conceived of its task in the grand view of its name." And, perhaps, as the Court indicates, the rules of conduct placed upon the Committee by the House admit of individual abuse and unfairness. But that is none of our affair. So long as the object of a legislative inquiry is legitimate and the questions propounded are pertinent thereto, it is not for the courts to interfere with the committee system of inquiry. To hold otherwise would be an infringement on the power given the Congress to inform itself. . . ."

—Justice Tom Campbell Clark, author of the dissenting opinion in
Watkins v. *United States*

DBQ Document-Based Questions

1. **Explaining** On what does Warren say a congressional inquiry must always be based?
2. **Discussing** Why does Clark disagree with the majority opinion?
3. **Making Inferences** What opinion do you think Warren had of HUAC?

Life During the Early Cold War

MAIN Idea Obsessed with fear of a nuclear attack, many Americans took steps to protect themselves.

HISTORY AND YOU Have you ever felt the need to protect yourself from something dangerous or scary? Read to learn more about how Americans tried to deal with their fears during the early 1950s.

The Red Scare and the spread of nuclear weapons had a profound impact on American life in the 1950s. Fear of communism and of nuclear war affected the thinking and choices of many ordinary Americans, as well as their leaders in government. Some Americans responded by preparing to survive a nuclear attack, while others became active in politics in an effort to shape government policy. Writers responded by describing the dangers of atomic war and the threat of communism—sometimes to convince people to take action and sometimes to protest policies they feared might lead to war.

Facing the Bomb

Already upset by the first Soviet atomic test in 1949, Americans were shocked when the Soviets again successfully tested the much more powerful hydrogen bomb, or H-bomb, in 1953. The United States had tested its own H-bomb less than a year earlier.

Americans prepared for a surprise Soviet attack. Schools set aside special areas as bomb shelters. In bomb drills, students learned to

AMERICA CALLING

Take your place in **CIVILIAN DEFENSE**

CONSULT YOUR NEAREST DEFENSE COUNCIL

► In the 1950s school children took part in "duck-and-cover" drills designed to give them a chance at surviving a nuclear blast if they were far enough from the epicenter.

▲ The Civil Defense Agency set up bomb shelters in cities, and made plans to assist survivors after an attack. Today the Civil Defense Agency is known as FEMA—the Federal Emergency Management Agency.

◄ Some Americans invested in personal bomb shelters stocked with food to allow them to survive a bomb blast and the radiation that would follow.

Analyzing VISUALS

1. **Explaining** What was the purpose of the "duck-and-cover" drills and bomb shelters?

2. **Making Inferences** Even if some preparations would not work, why might the government have wanted people to prepare for war?

CANNED FOOD

CANNED WATER

duck under their desks, turn away from the windows, and cover their heads with their hands. These "duck-and-cover" actions were supposed to protect them from a nuclear bomb blast.

Although "duck-and-cover" might have made people feel safe, it would not have protected them from deadly nuclear radiation. According to experts, for every person killed outright by a nuclear blast, four more would die later from **fallout,** the radiation left over after a blast. To protect themselves, some families built backyard fallout shelters and stocked them with canned food.

Popular Culture in the Cold War

Worries about nuclear war and Communist infiltration filled the public's imagination. Cold War themes soon appeared in films, plays, television, the titles of dance tunes, and popular fiction.

In 1953 Arthur Miller's thinly veiled criticism of the Communist witchhunts, *The Crucible,* appeared on Broadway. The play remains popular today as a cautionary tale about how hysteria can lead to false accusations. Matt Cvetic was an FBI undercover informant who secretly infiltrated the Communist Party in Pittsburgh, Pennsylvania. His story captivated magazine readers in the *Saturday Evening Post* in 1950 and came to movie screens the next year as *I Was a Communist for the FBI.* Another suspense film, *Walk East on Beacon* (1951), features the FBI's activities in an espionage case.

In 1953 television took up the theme with a series about an undercover FBI counterspy who was also a Communist Party official. Each week, *I Led Three Lives* kept television viewers on edge. Popular tunes such as "Atomic Boogie" and "Atom Bomb Baby" played on the radio.

In 1954 author Philip Wylie published *Tomorrow!* This novel describes the horrific effects of nuclear war on an unprepared American city. As an adviser on civil defense, Wylie had failed to convince the federal government to play a strong role in building bomb shelters. Frustrated, he wrote his novel to educate the public about the horrors of atomic war.

One of the most famous and enduring works of this period is John Hersey's nonfiction book *Hiroshima.* Originally published as the entire contents of the August 1946 edition of *The New Yorker* magazine, the book provides the firsthand accounts of six survivors of the U.S. dropping of the atomic bomb on Hiroshima, Japan. Not only did it make some Americans question the use of the bomb, *Hiroshima* also underscored the real and personal horrors of a nuclear attack.

At the same time that these fears were haunting Americans, the country was enjoying postwar prosperity and optimism. That spirit, combined with McCarthyism, fears of Communist infiltration, and the threat of atomic attack, made the early 1950s a time of contrasts. As the 1952 election approached, Americans were looking for someone or something that would make them feel secure.

Reading Check **Describing** How did the Cold War affect life in the 1950s?

Vocabulary

1. **Explain** the significance of: Red Scare, subversion, loyalty review program, Alger Hiss, perjury, McCarran Act, McCarthyism, censure, fallout.

Main Ideas

2. **Explaining** What was the result of President Truman's loyalty review program?

3. **Analyzing** Hearings to investigate Communist subversion in what organization led to McCarthy's downfall?

4. **Identifying** What event made Americans fearful of a nuclear attack by the Soviets?

Critical Thinking

5. **Big Ideas** How did the Red Scare and McCarthyism change American society and government?

6. **Organizing** Use a graphic organizer similar to the one below to list the causes and effects of the Red Scare of the 1950s.

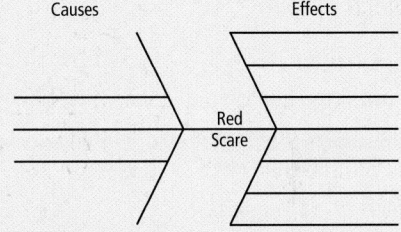

7. **Analyzing Visuals** Study the cartoons on page 549. Which cartoon do you think makes the stronger point? Explain.

Writing About History

8. **Persuasive Writing** Suppose that you are a newspaper editor during the Army-McCarthy hearings. Write an editorial giving reasons why people should support or condemn Senator McCarthy.

History ONLINE

Study Central™ To review this section, go to glencoe.com and click on Study Central.

Eisenhower's Cold War Policies

Guide to Reading

Big Ideas
Science and Technology Nuclear technology enabled Eisenhower to change U.S. military policy, while new missile technology marked the beginning of the space age.

Content Vocabulary
- massive retaliation *(p. 555)*
- brinkmanship *(p. 555)*
- covert *(p. 557)*
- developing nation *(p. 557)*
- military-industrial complex *(p. 559)*

Academic Vocabulary
- imply *(p. 558)*
- response *(p. 559)*

People and Events to Identify
- Central Intelligence Agency *(p. 557)*
- *Sputnik* *(p. 559)*

Reading Strategy
Organizing Complete a concept web similar to the one below by filling in aspects of Eisenhower's Cold War Policies.

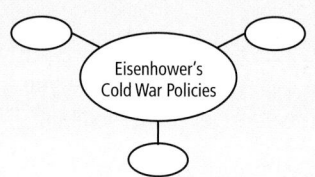

President Eisenhower believed developing new technology to deliver nuclear weapons would help prevent war. He also directed the CIA to use covert operations in the struggle to contain communism.

Massive Retaliation

MAIN Idea Eisenhower fought the Cold War by increasing the U.S. nuclear arsenal and using the threat of nuclear war to end conflicts in Korea, Taiwan, and the Suez.

HISTORY AND YOU Do you know anyone who uses threats to get his or her way? Read further to learn about Eisenhower's use of nuclear threats to achieve foreign policy goals.

By the end of 1952, many Americans were ready for a change in leadership. The Cold War had much to do with that attitude. Many people believed that Truman's foreign policy was not working. The Soviet Union had tested an atomic bomb and consolidated its hold on Eastern Europe. China had fallen to communism, and American troops were fighting in Korea.

Tired of the criticism and uncertain he could win, Truman decided not to run again. The Democrats nominated Adlai Stevenson, governor of Illinois. The Republicans chose Dwight D. Eisenhower, the general who had organized the D-Day invasion. Stevenson had no chance against a national hero who had helped win World War II. Americans wanted someone they could trust to lead the nation in the Cold War. Eisenhower won in a landslide.

"More Bang for the Buck"

The Cold War shaped Eisenhower's thinking from the moment he took office. He was convinced that the key to victory in the Cold War was not simply military might but also a strong economy. The United States had to show the world that free enterprise could produce a better society than communism. At the same time, economic prosperity would prevent Communists from gaining support in the United States and protect society from subversion.

As a professional soldier, Eisenhower knew the costs associated with large-scale conventional war. Preparing for that kind of warfare, he believed, was too expensive. "We cannot defend the nation in a way which will exhaust our economy," the president declared. Instead of maintaining a large and expensive army, the nation "must be prepared to use atomic weapons in all forms." Nuclear weapons, he said, gave "more bang for the buck."

TECHNOLOGY & HISTORY

Cold War Technology President Eisenhower's emphasis on nuclear weapons required new technology to deliver them. Eisenhower wanted to make sure that the United States could wage nuclear war even if the Soviets destroyed American bases in Europe or Asia. This required technology that would allow the U.S. to strike the USSR without needing bases in Europe.

Sixteen missiles were carried in silos located here.

▶ ICBMs

Because bombers could be shot down, Eisenhower also approved the development of intercontinental ballistic missiles (ICBMs) that could reach anywhere in the world in less than 30 minutes. The Atlas missile (right) was the first American ICBM. It was also used to launch the first seven U.S. astronauts. It is still used today to launch satellites.

▲ Long-Range Bombers

In 1955 the U.S. Air Force unveiled the huge B-52 bomber (above), which could fly across continents to drop nuclear bombs. The B-52 is still in use today.

◀ Missile Submarines

Eisenhower also began a program to build submarines capable of launching nuclear missiles from underwater. The Polaris submarine (left) launched in 1960 and carried 16 nuclear missiles.

Analyzing VISUALS

1. **Determining Cause and Effect** How did Eisenhower's nuclear strategy lead to the development of new technologies?
2. **Defining** What is an ICBM and what is its purpose?

The Korean War had convinced Eisenhower that the United States could not contain communism by fighting a series of small wars. Such wars were unpopular and too expensive. Instead, wars had to be prevented from happening in the first place. The best way to do that seemed to be to threaten to use nuclear weapons. This policy came to be called **massive retaliation.**

The new policy enabled Eisenhower to cut military spending from $50 billion to $34 billion. He did this by reducing the size of the army, which was expensive to maintain. At the same time, he increased the U.S. nuclear arsenal from about 1,000 bombs in 1953 to about 18,000 bombs in 1961.

Brinkmanship

President Eisenhower's willingness to threaten nuclear war to maintain peace worried some people. However, Secretary of State John Foster Dulles, the dominant figure in the nation's foreign policy in the 1950s, strongly defended this approach:

PRIMARY SOURCE

"You have to take chances for peace, just as you must take chances in war. Some say that we were brought to the verge of war. Of course we were brought to the verge of war. The ability to get to the verge without getting Into the war Is the necessary art. . . . If you try to run away from it, if you are scared to go to the brink, you are lost. We've had to look it square in the face. . . . We walked to the brink and we looked it in the face. We took strong action."

—quoted in *Rise to Globalism*

Critics called this **brinkmanship**—the willingness to go to the brink of war to force the other side to back down—and argued that it was too dangerous. During several crises, however, President Eisenhower felt compelled to threaten nuclear war.

The Korean War Ends

During his campaign for the presidency, Eisenhower had said, "I shall go to Korea," promising to end the costly and increasingly unpopular war. On December 4, 1952, he kept his promise. Bundled against the freezing Korean winter, the president-elect talked with frontline commanders and their troops.

Eisenhower became convinced that the ongoing battle was costing too many lives and bringing too few victories. He was determined to bring the war to an end. The president then quietly let the Chinese know that the United States might continue the Korean War "under circumstances of our own choosing"—a hint at a nuclear attack.

The threat to go to the brink of nuclear war seemed to work. In July 1953 negotiators signed an armistice. The battle line between the two sides in Korea, which was very near the prewar boundary, became the border between North Korea and South Korea. A "demilitarized zone" (DMZ) separated them. American troops are still based in Korea, helping to defend South Korea's border. There has never been a peace treaty to end the war.

The Taiwan Crisis

Shortly after the Korean War ended, a new crisis erupted in Asia. Although Communists had taken power in mainland China, the Nationalists still controlled Taiwan and several

◄ Turning Point ►

Sputnik Launches a Space Race

As the United States began to develop ICBMs, Americans were stunned to discover that the Soviet Union already had them. On October 4, 1957, the Soviets demonstrated this technology by launching *Sputnik*, the first artificial satellite to orbit Earth.

Worried that the United States was falling behind, Congress created the National Aeronautics and Space Administration (NASA) to coordinate missile research and space exploration. It also passed the National Defense Education Act (NDEA), which provided funds for education in science, math, and foreign languages.

Sputnik marked the beginning of a new era—the use of satellites in space. Both nations in the Cold War began launching satellites to assist in communications and to spy on the other nation. Today, satellites are a vital part of modern communications and travel. They transmit television and cell phone signals, and the satellites of the Global Positioning System (GPS) help ships and airplanes to navigate. Hikers and drivers can also buy GPS receivers to help determine where they are.

ANALYZING HISTORY Do you think missile and satellite technology helped prevent conflict during the Cold War or made the Cold War worse? Create a multimedia presentation on the Space Race and how it has changed American society.

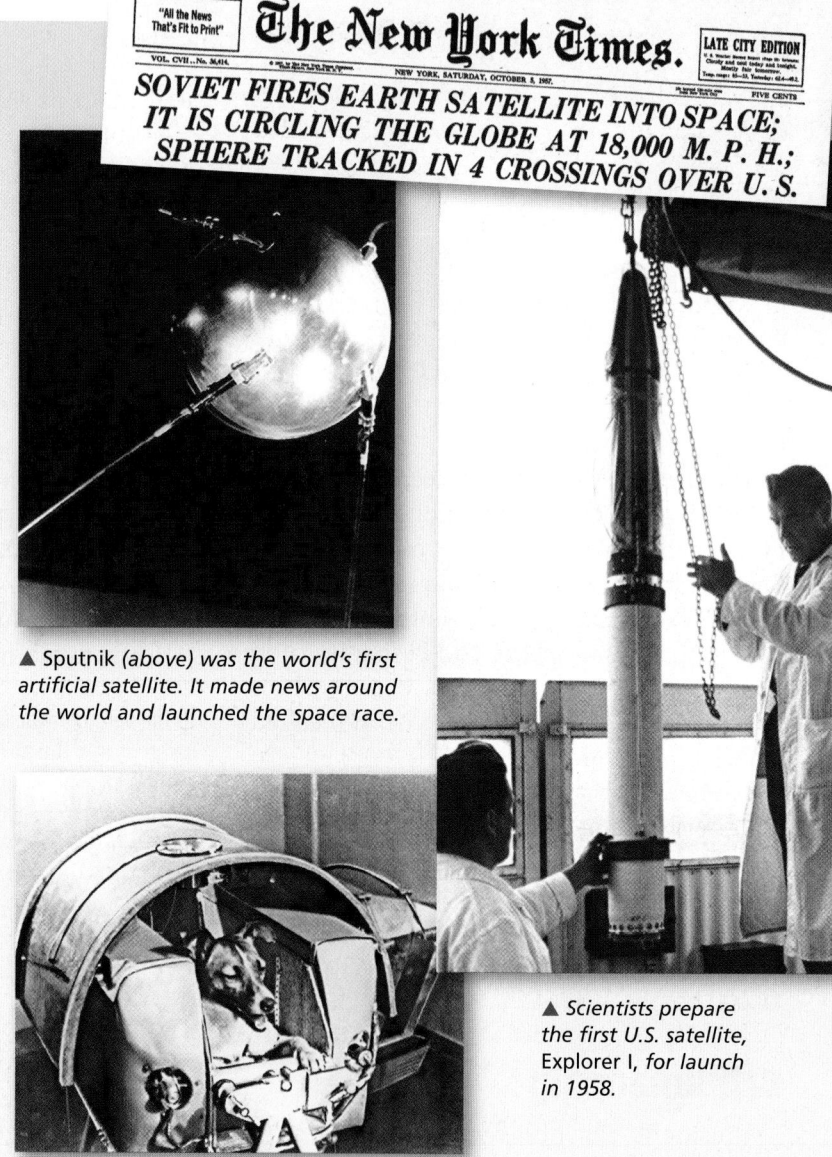

The New York Times.

"All the News That's Fit to Print" LATE CITY EDITION

VOL. CVII..No. 36,414. NEW YORK, SATURDAY, OCTOBER 5, 1957. FIVE CENTS

SOVIET FIRES EARTH SATELLITE INTO SPACE; IT IS CIRCLING THE GLOBE AT 18,000 M. P. H.; SPHERE TRACKED IN 4 CROSSINGS OVER U. S.

▲ *Sputnik (above) was the world's first artificial satellite. It made news around the world and launched the space race.*

▲ *Scientists prepare the first U.S. satellite, Explorer I, for launch in 1958.*

▲ *Sputnik II, launched only a month after Sputnik, carried the first living creature into orbit—an "astro" dog named Laika.*

small islands along China's coast. In the fall of 1954, China threatened to seize two of the islands. Eisenhower saw Taiwan as part of the "anti-Communist barrier" in Asia that needed to be protected at all costs.

When China began shelling the islands and announced that Taiwan would be liberated, Eisenhower asked Congress to authorize the use of force to defend Taiwan. He then warned the Chinese that any attack on Taiwan would be resisted by U.S. naval forces stationed nearby and hinted that they would use nuclear weapons to stop an invasion. Soon afterward, China backed down.

The Suez Crisis

The following year, a serious crisis erupted in the Middle East. Eisenhower's goal in that region was to prevent Arab nations from aligning with the Soviet Union. To build support among Arabs, Secretary of State Dulles offered to help Egypt finance the construction of a dam on the Nile River.

The deal ran into trouble in Congress, however, because Egypt had bought weapons from Communist Czechoslovakia. Dulles was forced to withdraw the offer. A week later, Egyptian troops seized control of the Suez Canal from the Anglo-French company that had controlled it. The Egyptians intended to use the canal's profits to pay for the dam.

The British and French responded quickly to the Suez Crisis. In October 1956, British and French troops invaded Egypt. Eisenhower was furious with Britain and France. The situation became even more dangerous when the Soviet Union threatened rocket attacks on Britain and France and offered to send troops to help Egypt. Eisenhower immediately put U.S. nuclear forces on alert, noting, "If those fellows start something, we may have to hit them— and if necessary, with everything in the bucket."

Under strong pressure from the United States, the British and French called off their invasion. The Soviet Union had won a major diplomatic victory, however, by supporting Egypt. Soon afterward, other Arab nations began accepting Soviet aid as well.

Reading Check **Identifying** What was brinkmanship?

Covert Operations

MAIN Idea Eisenhower directed the Central Intelligence Agency to use covert operations to limit the spread of communism and Soviet influence.

HISTORY AND YOU Do you enjoy reading spy novels? Read on to learn of the development and work of a spy agency in the United States.

President Eisenhower relied on brinkmanship on several occasions, but he knew it could not work in all situations. It could prevent war, but it could not, for example, prevent Communists from staging revolutions within countries. To prevent Communist uprisings in other countries, Eisenhower decided to use **covert,** or hidden, operations conducted by the **Central Intelligence Agency (CIA).**

Many of the CIA's operations took place in **developing nations**—nations with primarily agricultural economies. Many of these countries blamed European imperialism and American capitalism for their problems. Their leaders looked to the Soviet Union as a model of how to industrialize their countries. They often threatened to nationalize, or put under government control, foreign businesses operating in their countries.

One way to stop developing nations from moving into the Communist camp was to provide them with financial aid, as Eisenhower had tried to do in Egypt. In some cases, however, where the threat of communism seemed stronger, the CIA ran covert operations to overthrow anti-American leaders and replace them with pro-American leaders.

Iran and Guatemala

Two examples of covert operations that achieved U.S. objectives took place in Iran and Guatemala. By 1953, Iranian Prime Minister Mohammed Mossadegh had already nationalized the Anglo-Iranian Oil Company. He seemed ready to make an oil deal with the Soviet Union. The pro-American Shah of Iran tried to force Mossadegh out of office, but failed and fled into exile. The CIA quickly sent agents to organize street riots and arrange a coup that ousted Mossadegh and returned the shah to power.

The following year, the CIA intervened in Guatemala. In 1951, with Communist support, Jacobo Arbenz Guzmán was elected president of Guatemala. His land-reform program took over large estates and plantations, including those of the American–owned United Fruit Company. In May 1954, Communist Czechoslovakia delivered arms to Guatemala. The CIA responded by arming the Guatemalan opposition and training them at secret camps in Nicaragua and Honduras. Shortly after these CIA-trained forces invaded Guatemala, Arbenz Guzmán left office.

Trouble in Eastern Europe

Covert operations did not always work as Eisenhower hoped. Stalin died in 1953, and a power struggle began in the Soviet Union. By 1956, Nikita Khrushchev had emerged as the leader of the Soviet Union. That year, Khrushchev delivered a secret speech to Soviet officials. He attacked Stalin's policies and insisted that there were many ways to build a communist society. Although the speech was secret, the CIA obtained a copy of it. With Eisenhower's permission, the CIA arranged for it to be broadcast to Eastern Europe.

Many Eastern Europeans had long been frustrated with Communist rule. Hearing Khrushchev's speech further discredited communism. In June 1956 riots erupted in Eastern Europe. By late October, a full-scale uprising had begun in Hungary. Although Khrushchev was willing to tolerate greater freedom in Eastern Europe, he had never meant to **imply** that the Soviets would tolerate an end to communism in the region. Soon after the uprising began, Soviet tanks rolled into Budapest, the capital of Hungary, and crushed the rebellion.

The Eisenhower Doctrine

The United States was not the only nation using covert means to support its foreign policy. President Gamal Abdel Nasser of Egypt had emerged from the Suez crisis as a hero to the Arab people, and by 1957 he had begun working

PRIMARY SOURCE
The U-2 Incident

In 1960, the Soviet Union shot down an American U-2 spy plane in Soviet air space. The incident led to a dramatic confrontation at the U.S-Soviet summit in Paris in 1960.

◄ Calling President Eisenhower "a thief caught red-handed," Soviet Premier Khrushchev warns the Paris summit that further spy flights will lead to war.

▲ The U-2 (above left) was America's most sophisticated spy plane, able to fly higher than any other plane at the time. The pilot, Francis Gary Powers (above right), was captured but later released.

Analyzing VISUALS

1. **Paraphrasing** What did Nikita Khrushchev say would be the result of further U.S. aerial spying?
2. **Making Inferences** Why was the U-2 used as a spy plane?

with Jordan and Syria to spread pan-Arabism—the idea that all Arab people should be united into one nation. Eisenhower and Dulles worried about Nasser's links to the Soviets and feared that he was laying the groundwork to take control of the Middle East. In late 1957 Eisenhower asked Congress to authorize the use of military force whenever the president thought it necessary to assist Middle East nations resisting Communist aggression. The policy came to be called the Eisenhower Doctrine. It essentially extended the Truman Doctrine and the policy of containment to the Middle East.

In February 1958 Eisenhower's concerns appeared to be confirmed when left-wing rebels, believed to be backed by Nasser and the Soviet Union, seized power in Iraq. Fearing that his government was next, the president of Lebanon asked the United States for help. Eisenhower immediately ordered 5,000 marines to Lebanon to protect its capital, Beirut. At the same time, British forces went into Jordan at the request of King Hussein to protect his government. Once the situation stabilized, the U.S. forces withdrew.

A Spy Plane Is Shot Down

After the Hungarian uprising, Khrushchev reasserted Soviet power and the superiority of communism. Although he had supported "peaceful coexistence" with capitalism, he began accusing the "capitalist countries" of starting a "feverish arms race." In 1957 after the launch of **Sputnik,** Khrushchev boasted, "We will bury capitalism. . . . Your grandchildren will live under communism."

Late the following year, Khrushchev demanded the withdrawal of Allied troops from West Berlin. Secretary of State Dulles rejected Khrushchev's demands. If the Soviets threatened Berlin, Dulles announced, NATO would respond, "if need be by military force." Brinkmanship worked again, and Khrushchev backed down.

At Eisenhower's invitation, Khrushchev visited the United States in late 1959. After the success of that visit, the two leaders agreed to hold a summit in Paris. A summit is a formal face-to-face meeting of leaders from different countries to discuss important issues.

Shortly before the summit was to begin in 1960, the Soviet Union shot down an American U-2 spy plane. At first, Eisenhower claimed that the aircraft was a weather plane that had strayed off course. Then Khrushchev dramatically produced the pilot. Eisenhower refused to apologize, saying the flights had protected American security. In **response,** Khrushchev broke up the summit.

In this climate of heightened tension, President Eisenhower prepared to leave office. In January 1961 he delivered a farewell address to the nation. In the address, he pointed out that a new relationship had developed between the military establishment and the defense industry. He warned Americans to be on guard against the influence of this **military-industrial complex** in a democracy. Although he had avoided war and kept communism contained, Eisenhower was also frustrated: "I confess I lay down my official responsibility in this field with a definite sense of disappointment. . . . I wish I could say that a lasting peace is in sight."

✓ Reading Check **Explaining** In what nations did the United States intervene with covert operations?

Vocabulary

1. **Explain** the significance of: massive retaliation, brinkmanship, covert, Central Intelligence Agency, developing nation, *Sputnik*, military-industrial complex.

Main Ideas

2. **Summarizing** Why did Eisenhower want to depend on nuclear weapons instead of traditional military approaches to war?

3. **Defining** What was the goal of the Eisenhower Doctrine?

Critical Thinking

4. **Big Ideas** How did technology shape Eisenhower's military policy?

5. **Organizing** Use a graphic organizer similar to the one below to list Eisenhower's strategies for containing communism.

6. **Analyzing Visuals** Study the photograph of Khrushchev on page 558. How does this photograph illustrate the U.S. and Soviet relationship at this point in the Cold War?

Writing About History

7. **Persuasive Writing** Suppose that you are a member of Eisenhower's Cabinet. Defend or attack brinkmanship as a foreign policy tactic. Be sure to provide specific reasons for your opinions.

History ONLINE

Study Central™ To review this section, go to glencoe.com and click on Study Central.

Causes of the Cold War

Long-Range Causes

- Both the United States and the Soviet Union believe their economic and political systems are superior.
- Defeat of Germany creates a power vacuum in Europe and leaves U.S. and Soviet forces occupying parts of Europe.
- The U.S. wants to rebuild Europe's economy and support democratic governments to ensure peace and security.
- The USSR wants Germany weak and believes nations on the Soviet border should have Communist governments.

Immediate Causes

- At Yalta, Soviets promise to allow free elections in Eastern Europe but instead gradually impose Communist regimes.
- At Potsdam, Soviets want German reparations, but the U.S. supports rebuilding Germany's economy.
- Soviet troops help Communists in northern Iran, but U.S. pressure forces a withdrawal.
- George Kennan sends the Long Telegram to U.S. officials, explaining that the Soviets need to be contained.
- Soviets send aid to Communist rebels in Greece and demand Turkey share control of the Dardanelles with the USSR; Truman issues the Truman Doctrine and sends aid to Greece and Turkey.

▲ From left to right: British Prime Minister Clement Attlee, U.S. President Harry Truman, and Soviet leader Joseph Stalin at the Potsdam Conference in 1945. The conference contributed to the onset of the Cold War because of disagreements over how to handle postwar Europe.

Effects of the Cold War

Effects in Europe

- U.S. launches the Marshall Plan to rebuild Europe.
- Germany is divided into two separate nations.
- The USSR blockades Berlin; U.S. organizes the Berlin Airlift.
- The U.S. creates NATO; the USSR creates the Warsaw Pact.

Global Effects

- When China falls to communism, the U.S. responds by helping Japan build up its economy and military.
- When Communist North Korea invades South Korea, the U.S. organizes an international force to stop the invasion.

Effects on the United States

- Soviet spies are arrested.
- A new Red Scare leads to laws restricting the Communist Party in the U.S. and to investigations by the House Un-American Activities Committee and Senator Joseph McCarthy.
- Americans practice civil defense; some build bomb shelters.
- President Eisenhower orders the development of new rockets, bombers, and submarines that can carry nuclear weapons.
- Eisenhower uses the CIA to covertly contain communism.

▲ The Soviet Union displays its nuclear capabilities in the form of these short-range missiles during celebrations commemorating the 40th anniversary of the Bolshevik Revolution in 1957. The nuclear arms race was a part of the Cold War for nearly 40 years.

Reviewing Vocabulary

Directions: Choose the word or words that best complete the sentence.

1. After World War II, the Soviet Union wanted to establish a buffer zone of _____ on its European border.

   A developing nations

   B capitalist nations

   C satellite nations

   D demilitarization

2. The policy of _____ became the main approach in U.S. foreign policy toward the Soviet Union during the Cold War.

   A democracy

   B limited war

   C free trade

   D containment

3. Once the Soviet Union tested an atomic bomb, Americans began to fear the effects of _____, assuming they initially survived a nuclear attack.

   A fallout

   B censure

   C subversion

   D duck-and-cover

4. In his farewell address, President Eisenhower warned the American people about the dangers of

   A the Central Intelligence Agency.

   B massive retaliation.

   C the military-industrial complex.

   D brinkmanship.

5. Though a professional soldier, President Eisenhower adopted _____ as the proper way to battle communism.

   A détente

   B implied response

   C inversion

   D massive retaliation

Reviewing Main Ideas

Directions: Choose the best answer for each of the following questions.

Section 1 *(pp. 532–537)*

6. Which of the following was a major outcome of the Yalta Conference?

   A the division of Germany

   B the terms of Germany's surrender

   C the establishment of satellite nations

   D the establishment of NATO

7. At Potsdam, the main conflict was over which of the following?

   A the United Nations

   B the invasion of Japan

   C German reparations

   D nuclear weapons

Section 2 *(pp. 538–545)*

8. George Kennan first suggested which foreign policy?

   A brinkmanship

   B containment

   C massive retaliation

   D the Marshall Plan

9. Which of the following events set off the Korean War?

   A The Japanese invaded South Korea.

   B Soviet-controlled North Korea invaded South Korea.

   C Chinese-controlled North Korea invaded South Korea.

   D The Soviet Union invaded North Korea.

TEST-TAKING TIP

When you first start a test, review it completely so that you can budget your time most efficiently. For example, if there are essay questions at the end, you will want to be sure you leave enough time to write complete answers.

Need Extra Help?									
If You Missed Questions . . .	1	2	3	4	5	6	7	8	9
Go to Page . . .	537	538	552–553	559	555	532–533	536–537	538	543

GO ON

10. What was the underlying goal of the Marshall Plan?

A to contain Soviet expansion in the Middle East and Asia

B to rebuild European economies to prevent the spread of communism

C to monitor the growth of the military-industrial complex in the United States

D to Americanize Western European nations

Section 3 (pp. 546–553)

11. After World War II, the purpose of HUAC was to

A hold public hearings on Communist subversion.

B locate chapters of the Communist Party.

C administer the loyalty review program.

D create the McCarran Act.

12. The McCarran Act required

A every government employee to take a loyalty oath.

B all Communist Party chapters to disband.

C all Communist organizations to register with the government.

D the censure of members of Congress who would not support HUAC.

Section 4 (pp. 554–559)

13. Eisenhower's administration developed an approach to foreign policy based on the threat of nuclear attack, known as

A containment.

B massive retaliation.

C subversion.

D duck-and-cover.

14. The Eisenhower Doctrine extended the Truman Doctrine to which region?

A Asia

B Eastern Europe

C South America

D the Middle East

Critical Thinking

Directions: Choose the best answers to the following questions.

Base your answers to questions 15 and 16 on the map below and on your knowledge of Chapter 15.

Berlin After World War II, 1945

15. Why was Stalin initially able to control access to West Berlin?

A West Berlin was in the Soviet Union.

B West Berlin was ruled by Communists.

C West Berlin was in the Soviet sector of Germany.

D West Berlin had been invaded and occupied by the Red Army.

16. Why did Stalin order a blockade of West Berlin?

A West Berlin was primarily agricultural and would help feed the Soviet army.

B Stalin wanted to unite Berlin and organize free elections for Germany.

C Stalin was afraid of the U.S. nuclear technology and wanted a larger buffer zone.

D Stalin wanted the United States to abandon West Berlin.

Need Extra Help?							
If You Missed Questions . . .	10	11	12	13	14	15	16
Go to Page . . .	540	547	550	554–555	558–559	540–541	540–541

GO ON

17. One historical lesson from the McCarthy era is the realization that

  A loyalty oaths prevent spying.

  B communism is attractive in prosperous times.

  C Communist agents had infiltrated all levels of the U.S. government.

  D public fear of traitors can lead to intolerance and discrimination.

Analyze the cartoon and answer the question that follows. Base your answer on the cartoon and on your knowledge of Chapter 15.

"So Russia Launched a Satellite, but Has It Made Cars With Fins Yet?"

18. In this cartoon, the cartoonist is expressing

  A pride in America's technological know-how.

  B anxiety that America is behind in the space race.

  C a wish for larger, more elaborate cars.

  D the need to share auto technology with Russia.

Document-Based Questions

Directions: Analyze the document and answer the short-answer questions that follow the document.

Margaret Chase Smith, a Republican senator from Maine, was a newcomer and the only woman in the Senate. Smith was upset by McCarthy's behavior and hoped that her colleagues would reprimand him. When they failed to do so, Smith made her "Declaration of Conscience" speech.

> "As a United States Senator, I am not proud of the way in which the Senate has been made a publicity platform for irresponsible sensationalism. I am not proud of the reckless abandon in which unproved charges have been hurled from this side of the aisle. I am not proud of the obviously staged, undignified countercharges that have been attempted in retaliation from the other side of the aisle . . . I am not proud of the way we smear outsiders from the Floor of the Senate and hide behind a cloak of congressional immunity. . . .
>
>   As an American, I am shocked at the way Republicans and Democrats alike are playing directly into the Communist design of 'confuse, divide, and conquer'. . . . I want to see our nation recapture the strength and unity it once had when we fought the enemy instead of ourselves."
>
>   —*from* Declaration of Conscience

19. In the speech, Smith expresses anger with whom? Why?

20. According to Smith, who is really dividing the nation?

Extended Response

21. Many factors contributed to the development of the Cold War, but could it have been avoided? Write a persuasive essay arguing that actions of the United States or the Soviet Union following World War II might have prevented the Cold War, or that it was inevitable.

History ONLINE

For additional test practice, use Self-Check Quizzes—Chapter 15 at glencoe.com.

Need Extra Help?					
If You Missed Questions . . .	17	18	19	20	21
Go to Page . . .	549–550	R18	563	563	532–545

Postwar America

1945–1960

SECTION 1 Truman and Eisenhower
SECTION 2 The Affluent Society
SECTION 3 The Other Side of American Life

Teens enjoy milkshakes while studying in a 1950's-style diner.

U.S. PRESIDENTS
U.S. EVENTS
WORLD EVENTS

1944
• GI Bill is enacted

Truman 1945–1953

1946
• Strikes erupt across country

1947
• Congress passes Taft-Hartley Act over Truman's veto

1951
• The *I Love Lucy* television show airs its first show

1944

1948

1952

1946
• Churchill gives "Iron Curtain" speech

1948
• South Africa introduces apartheid

1952
• Scientists led by Edward Teller develop hydrogen bomb

MAKING CONNECTIONS
What Does It Mean to Be Prosperous?

After World War II, the United States experienced years of steady economic growth. Although not everyone benefited, the economic boom meant most Americans enjoyed more prosperity than earlier generations.

- *How did Americans spend this new wealth?*
- *How does prosperity change the way people live?*

FOLDABLES™

Categorizing Information Make a Folded-Table Foldable on popular culture in the 1950s and present. List the following for both time periods: data on the types of mass media and size of the audiences for them, characteristics of youth culture, and groups represented in the mass media.

Popular Culture	1950s	Present
Mass Media Types		
Youth Culture		
Groups Represented in Media		

Eisenhower
1953–1961

1955
- Salk polio vaccine becomes widely available

1956
- Congress passes Federal Highway Act

1957
- Estimated 40 million television sets in use in the United States

1956

1960

1954
- Gamal Abdel Nasser takes power in Egypt

1956
- Suez Canal crisis

1957
- USSR launches *Sputnik I* and *Sputnik II* satellites

History ONLINE Visit glencoe.com and enter *QuickPass*™ code TAVMT5147c16 for Chapter 16 resources.

Truman and Eisenhower

Guide to Reading

Big Ideas
Economics and Society Following World War II, the federal government supported programs that helped the American economy make the transition from wartime to peacetime production.

Content Vocabulary
- closed shop *(p. 566)*
- right-to-work laws *(p. 567)*
- union shop *(p. 567)*
- dynamic conservatism *(p. 570)*

Academic Vocabulary
- legislator *(p. 566)*
- abandon *(p. 568)*

People and Events to Identify
- GI Bill *(p. 566)*
- "Do-Nothing Congress" *(p. 568)*
- Fair Deal *(p. 569)*
- Federal Highway Act *(p. 571)*

Reading Strategy
Complete a graphic organizer similar to the one below by listing the characteristics of the U.S. postwar economy.

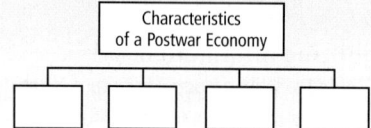

In the postwar era, Congress limited the power of unions and rejected most of President Truman's plan for a "Fair Deal." When Eisenhower became president, he cut back some government programs and launched the interstate highway system.

Return to a Peacetime Economy

MAIN Idea Despite inflation and strikes, the nation was able to shift to a peacetime economy without a recession.

HISTORY AND YOU Do you know you can get help paying for college if you serve in the military? Read to learn about the origins of the "GI Bill" and how it helped World War II veterans get a college education.

After the war many Americans feared the return to a peacetime economy. They worried that, after military production halted and millions of former soldiers glutted the labor market, unemployment and recession might sweep the country. Despite such worries, the economy continued to grow after the war as increased consumer spending helped ward off a recession. After 17 years of an economic depression and wartime shortages, Americans rushed out to buy the consumer goods they had long desired.

The Servicemen's Readjustment Act, popularly called the **GI Bill,** boosted the economy further. The act provided generous funds to veterans to help them establish businesses, buy homes, and attend college. The postwar economy did have problems, particularly in the first couple of years following the end of the war. A greater demand for goods led to higher prices, and this inflation soon triggered labor unrest. As the cost of living rose, workers in the automobile, steel, electrical, and mining industries went on strike for better pay.

Afraid that the nation's energy supply would be drastically reduced because of the striking miners, Truman ordered government seizure of the mines, while pressuring mine owners to grant the union most of its demands. The president also halted a strike that shut down the nation's railroads by threatening to draft the striking workers into the army.

Labor unrest and high prices prompted many Americans to call for a change. The Republicans seized on these sentiments during the 1946 congressional elections, winning control of both houses of Congress for the first time since 1930.

The new conservative Congress quickly set out to curb the power of organized labor. **Legislators** proposed a measure known as the Taft-Hartley Act, which outlawed the **closed shop,** or the practice of forcing business owners to hire only union members. Under this law,

The GI Bill of Rights

One reason the American economy rebounded so quickly after World War II ended was the Servicemen's Readjustment Act of 1944, popularly called the GI Bill of Rights. The act subsidized college tuition and provided zero down-payment, low-interest loans to veterans to help them buy homes and establish businesses.

Veterans flocked to colleges in large numbers after the war. Among them was William Oskay, Jr., (above) who attended Pennsylvania State University in 1946. By 1947, nearly half of all people attending college were veterans. At the University of Iowa (left), 60 percent of students were veterans in 1947. By 1956, when the GI program ended, 7.8 million veterans had used it to attend college. Another 2.4 million veterans used the program to obtain home loans.

Analyzing VISUALS

1. **Calculating** Based on the graph, what was the increase in college enrollments between 1944 and 1950?

2. **Specifying** About how many new homes were constructed in 1950?

College Enrollment

Source: *Historical Statistics of the United States.*

New Home Construction

Source: *Historical Statistics of the United States.*

---

states could pass **right-to-work laws,** which outlawed **union shops** (shops in which new workers were required to join the union). The measure also prohibited featherbedding, the practice of limiting work output in order to create more jobs. Furthermore, the bill forbade unions from using their money to support political campaigns.

When the bill reached Truman, however, he vetoed it, arguing that it was a mistake:

PRIMARY SOURCE

"... [It would] reverse the basic direction of our national labor policy, inject the government into private economic affairs on an unprecedented scale, and conflict with important principles of our democratic society. Its provisions would cause more strikes, not fewer."

—quoted in *The Growth of the American Republic*

The president's concerns did little to sway Congress, which passed the Taft-Hartley Act in 1947 over Truman's veto. Its supporters claimed that the law held irresponsible unions in check, just as the Wagner Act of 1935 had restrained anti-union activities and employers. Labor leaders called the act a "slave labor" law and insisted that it erased many of the gains that unions had made since 1933.

Reading Check **Explaining** Why did Truman veto the Taft-Hartley Act?

History ONLINE
Student Web Activity Visit glencoe.com and complete the activity on the GI Bill.

Truman's Program

MAIN Idea Truman pushed for a "Fair Deal" for Americans, despite the legislative conflicts he had with Congress.

HISTORY AND YOU Do you remember how close the last presidential election was? Read on to learn about Truman's surprise victory in 1948.

The Democratic Party's loss of control in Congress in the 1946 elections did not dampen President Truman's spirits or his plans. Shortly after taking office, Truman had proposed domestic measures seeking to continue the work of Franklin Roosevelt's New Deal. During his tenure in office, Truman worked to push this agenda through Congress.

Truman's Legislative Agenda

Truman's proposals included expansion of Social Security benefits; raising the minimum wage; a program to ensure full employment through aggressive use of federal spending and investment; public housing and slum clearance; and long-range environmental and public works planning. He also proposed a system of national health insurance.

Truman also boldly asked Congress in February 1948 to pass a broad civil rights bill that would protect African Americans' right to vote, abolish poll taxes, and make lynching a federal crime. He issued an executive order barring discrimination in federal employment and ending segregation in the armed forces. Most of Truman's legislative efforts, however, met with little success, as a coalition of Republicans and conservative Southern Democrats defeated many of his proposals.

The Election of 1948

As the 1948 presidential election approached, most observers gave Truman little chance of winning. Some Americans still believed that he lacked the stature for the job, and they viewed his administration as inept.

Divisions within the Democratic Party also seemed to spell disaster for Truman. At the Democratic Convention that summer, two factions **abandoned** the party altogether. Reacting angrily to Truman's support of civil rights, a group of Southern Democrats formed the States' Rights, or Dixiecrat, Party and nominated South Carolina Governor Strom Thurmond for president. At the same time, the party's more liberal members were frustrated by Truman's ineffective domestic policies and critical of his anti-Soviet foreign policy. They formed a new Progressive Party, with Henry A. Wallace as their presidential candidate.

The president's Republican opponent was New York Governor Thomas Dewey, a dignified and popular candidate who seemed unbeatable. After polling 50 political writers, *Newsweek* magazine declared three weeks before the election, "The landslide for Dewey will sweep the country."

Perhaps the only person who gave Truman any chance to win the election was Truman himself. "I know every one of those 50 fellows," he declared about the writers polled in *Newsweek*. "There isn't one of them has enough sense to pound sand in a rat hole." Truman poured his energy into the campaign, traveling more than 20,000 miles by train and making more than 350 speeches. Along the way, he attacked the majority Republican Congress as "do-nothing, good-for-nothing" for refusing to enact his legislative agenda.

Truman's attacks on the "**Do-Nothing Congress**" did not mention that both he and Congress had passed the Truman Doctrine's aid program to Greece and Turkey, as well as the Marshall Plan. Congress had also enacted the National Security Act of 1947, which created the Department of Defense, the National Security Council, and the CIA; established the Joint Chiefs of Staff as a permanent organization; and made the Air Force an independent branch of the military. Congress also passed the Twenty-second Amendment, which limited a president to two terms in office. The 80th Congress did not "do nothing" as Truman charged, but its accomplishments were in areas that did not affect most Americans directly. As a result, Truman's charges began to stick.

With a great deal of support from laborers, African Americans, and farmers, Truman won a narrow but stunning victory over Dewey. Perhaps just as remarkable as the president's victory was the resurgence of the Democratic Party. On election day, Democrats regained control of both houses of Congress.

The Fair Deal

Truman's 1949 State of the Union address repeated the domestic agenda he had put forth previously. "Every segment of our population and every individual," he declared, "has a right to expect from . . . government a fair deal." Whether intentional or not, the president had coined a name—the **Fair Deal**—to set his program apart from the New Deal. In February, he began to send his proposals to Congress.

The 81st Congress did not completely embrace Truman's Fair Deal. Legislators did raise the legal minimum wage to 75¢ an hour. They increased Social Security benefits by 75 percent and extended them to 10 million additional people. Congress also passed the National Housing Act of 1949, which provided for the construction of low-income housing, accompanied by long-term rent subsidies.

Congress refused, however, to pass national health insurance or to provide subsidies for farmers or federal aid for schools. In addition, legislators, led by the same coalition of conservative Republicans and Dixiecrats, opposed Truman's efforts to enact civil rights legislation. His plans for federal aid to education were also not enacted.

✔ **Reading Check** **Summarizing** What did Truman and the Congress accomplish in foreign relations?

PRIMARY SOURCE
The Election of 1948

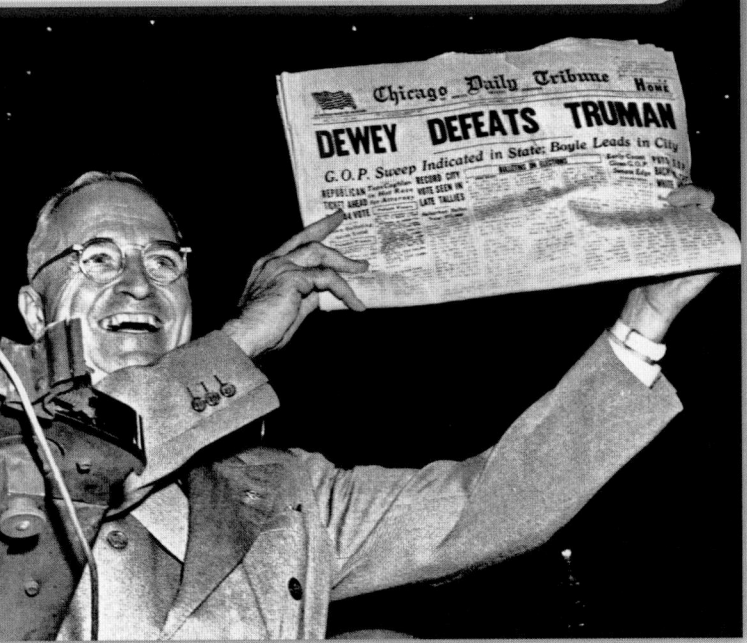

▲ *Harry Truman gleefully displays the erroneous* Chicago Daily Tribune *headline announcing his defeat by Thomas Dewey.*

What Was the Fair Deal?

In 1949 Truman outlined in his State of the Union address an ambitious legislative program that became known as the Fair Deal. Some of its main features were:

- the expansion of Social Security benefits
- an increase in the minimum wage
- a program to ensure full employment
- a program of public housing and slum clearance
- a long-range plan for environmental and public works
- a system of national health insurance
- a broad program of civil rights legislation

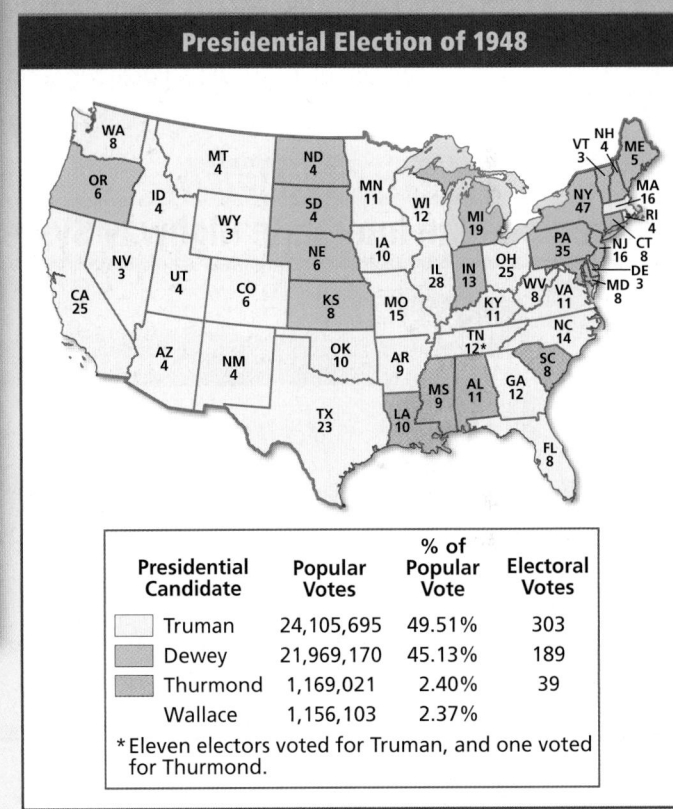

Presidential Election of 1948

Presidential Candidate	Popular Votes	% of Popular Vote	Electoral Votes
Truman	24,105,695	49.51%	303
Dewey	21,969,170	45.13%	189
Thurmond	1,169,021	2.40%	39
Wallace	1,156,103	2.37%	

*Eleven electors voted for Truman, and one voted for Thurmond.

Analyzing VISUALS

1. **Interpreting** In what regions of the nation did Thomas Dewey receive the most votes?

2. **Calculating** What was the difference in percentage of the popular vote received by Truman and Dewey?

The Eisenhower Years

MAIN Idea President Eisenhower cut federal spending, supported business, funded the interstate highway system, and extended some New Deal programs.

HISTORY AND YOU Do you think it is important for a president to have served in the military? Read to learn how Americans chose a war hero as president in the 1950s.

In 1950 the United States went to war in Korea. The war consumed the nation's attention and resources and effectively ended Truman's Fair Deal. By 1952, with the war at a bloody stalemate and his approval rating dropping quickly, Truman declined to run again for the presidency.

With no Democratic incumbent to face, Republicans pinned their hopes for regaining the White House in 1952 on a popular World War II hero: Dwight Eisenhower, former commander of the Allied Forces in Europe. The Democrats nominated Illinois Governor Adlai Stevenson.

The Republicans adopted the slogan: "It's time for a change!" The warm and friendly Eisenhower, known as "Ike," promised to end the war in Korea. "I like Ike" became the Republican rallying cry. Eisenhower won the election in a landslide, carrying the Electoral College, 442 votes to 89. The Republicans also gained an eight-seat majority in the House, while the Senate became evenly divided between Democrats and Republicans.

Eisenhower Takes Office

President Eisenhower had two favorite phrases. "Middle of the road" described his political beliefs and "**dynamic conservatism**" meant balancing economic conservatism with activism in areas that would benefit the country. Eisenhower wasted little time in showing his conservative side. The new president's cabinet appointments included several business

HISTORY AND GEOGRAPHY
Effects of the Interstate Highway System

Interstate Highway System

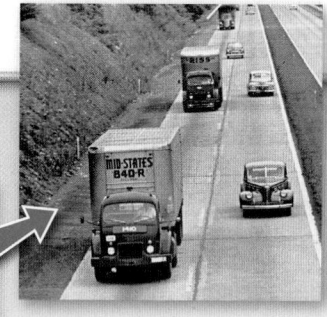

Commercial Trucking *Interstate highways made distribution of goods by transport truck fast and efficient. By the 1990s, trucks moved more than 6 billion tons of goods—mostly by interstate.*

Rise of Suburbs *Interstate highways contributed to the growth of suburbs and urban sprawl. Interstates let people commute long distances from home to work.*

Analyzing GEOGRAPHY

1. **Location** Where were most of the interstate highways built? Why do you think that is?
2. **Movement** In what ways did the interstate highway system change daily life?

Road Culture *Interstate travel encouraged the development of cheap hotel chains, roadside convenience stores, and fast food restaurants located near interstate exits.*

leaders. Under their guidance, Eisenhower ended government price and rent controls, which many conservatives viewed as unnecessary federal regulation of the economy. Eisenhower's administration believed business growth was vital to the nation. His secretary of defense, formerly the president of General Motors, declared to the Senate that "what is good for our country is good for General Motors, and vice versa."

Eisenhower's conservatism showed itself in other ways as well. In an attempt to cut federal spending, the president vetoed a school construction bill and agreed to slash government aid to public housing. Along with these cuts, he supported some modest tax cuts.

Eisenhower also targeted the federal government's continuing aid to businesses, or what he termed "creeping socialism." Shortly after taking office, the president abolished the Reconstruction Finance Corporation (RFC), which since 1932 had lent money to banks, railroads, and other large institutions in financial trouble. Another Depression-era agency, the Tennessee Valley Authority (TVA), also came under Eisenhower's scrutiny. During his presidency, appropriations for the TVA fell from $185 million to $12 million.

In some areas, President Eisenhower took an activist role. For example, he pushed for two large government projects. During the 1950s, as the number of Americans who owned cars increased, so too did the need for greater and more efficient travel routes. In 1956 Congress responded to this growing need by passing the **Federal Highway Act,** the largest public works program in American history. The act appropriated $25 billion for a 10-year effort to construct more than 40,000 miles (64,400 km) of interstate highways. Congress also authorized construction of the Great Lakes–St. Lawrence Seaway to connect the Great Lakes with the Atlantic Ocean through a series of locks on the St. Lawrence River. Three previous presidents had been unable to reach agreements with Canada to build this waterway to aid international shipping. Through Eisenhower's efforts, the two nations finally agreed on a plan to complete the project.

Extending Social Security

Although President Eisenhower cut federal spending and tried to limit the federal government's role in the economy, he agreed to extend the Social Security system to an additional 10 million people. He also extended unemployment compensation to an additional 4 million citizens and agreed to raise the minimum wage and continue to provide some government aid to farmers.

By the time Eisenhower ran for a second term in 1956, the nation had successfully shifted back to a peacetime economy. The battles between liberals and conservatives over whether to continue New Deal policies would continue. In the meantime, however, most Americans focused their energy on enjoying what had become a decade of tremendous prosperity.

Reading Check **Evaluating** What conservative and activist measures did Eisenhower take during his administration?

Section 1 REVIEW

Vocabulary

1. **Explain** the significance of: GI Bill, closed shop, right-to-work laws, union shop, "Do-Nothing Congress," Fair Deal, dynamic conservatism, Federal Highway Act.

Main Ideas

2. **Identifying** What difficulties could have hindered the return to a peacetime economy?

3. **Analyzing** Why did Congress oppose some of Truman's Fair Deal policies?

4. **Describing** How did Eisenhower describe his approach to politics?

Critical Thinking

5. **Big Ideas** How did President Eisenhower aid international shipping during his administration?

6. **Organizing** Use a graphic organizer like the one below to compare the agendas of the Truman and Eisenhower administrations.

Agendas

| Truman | Eisenhower |

7. **Analyzing Visuals** Study the map on page 569. In which part of the country did Strom Thurmond receive the most votes? Why do you think this is?

Writing About History

8. **Persuasive Writing** Assume the role of a member of Congress during Truman's administration. Write a speech convincing Congress to pass or defeat Truman's Fair Deal measures.

History ONLINE

Study Central™ To review this section, go to glencoe.com and click on Study Central.

The Affluent Society

Guide to Reading

Big Ideas
Culture and Beliefs Postwar abundance and new technologies changed American society.

Content Vocabulary
- baby boom *(p. 573)*
- white-collar job *(p. 574)*
- blue-collar worker *(p. 574)*
- multinational corporation *(p. 574)*
- franchise *(p. 574)*
- rock 'n' roll *(p. 577)*
- generation gap *(p. 579)*

Academic Vocabulary
- phenomenon *(p. 572)*
- conform *(p. 574)*

People and Events to Identify
- Levittown *(p. 572)*
- Jonas Salk *(p. 575)*
- Elvis Presley *(p. 577)*
- Jack Kerouac *(p. 579)*

Reading Strategy
Sequencing Use a time line to record major events of science, technology, and popular culture during the 1950s.

For many Americans, the 1950s was a time of affluence, with many new technological breakthroughs. In addition, new forms of entertainment created a generational divide between young people and adults.

American Abundance

MAIN Idea America entered a period of postwar abundance, with expanding suburbs, growing families, and more white-collar jobs.

HISTORY AND YOU Have you ever noticed that every restaurant in a pizza chain looks alike? Read on to learn about the rise of franchises.

The 1950s was a decade of incredible prosperity. Between 1940 and 1955, the average income of American families roughly tripled. Americans in all income brackets—poor, middle-class, and wealthy—experienced this rapid rise in income. In 1958 economist John Kenneth Galbraith published *The Affluent Society,* in which he claimed that the nation's postwar prosperity was a new **phenomenon.** In the past, Galbraith said, all societies had an "economy of scarcity," meaning that a lack of resources and overpopulation had limited economic productivity. Now, the United States had created what Galbraith called an "economy of abundance." New business techniques and improved technology enabled the nation to produce an abundance of goods and services, thereby dramatically raising the standard of living for Americans.

The economic boom of the 1950s provided most Americans with more disposable income than ever before and, as in the 1920s, they began to spend it on new consumer goods, including refrigerators, washing machines, televisions, and air conditioners. Advertising helped fuel the nation's spending spree. Advertising became the fastest-growing industry in the United States, as manufacturers employed new marketing techniques to sell their products. These techniques were carefully planned to whet the consumer's appetite. A second car became a symbol of status, a freezer became a promise of plenty, and mouthwash was portrayed as the key to immediate success.

The Growth of Suburbia

Advertisers targeted consumers who had money to spend. Many of these consumers lived in new mass-produced suburbs that grew up around cities in the 1950s. **Levittown,** New York, was one of the earliest of the mass-produced suburbs. The driving force behind this planned residential community was Bill Levitt, who mass-produced hundreds of simple and similar-looking homes in a potato field 10 miles east of New York City. Between 1947 and 1951, thousands of

A New America: Suburbs and Highways

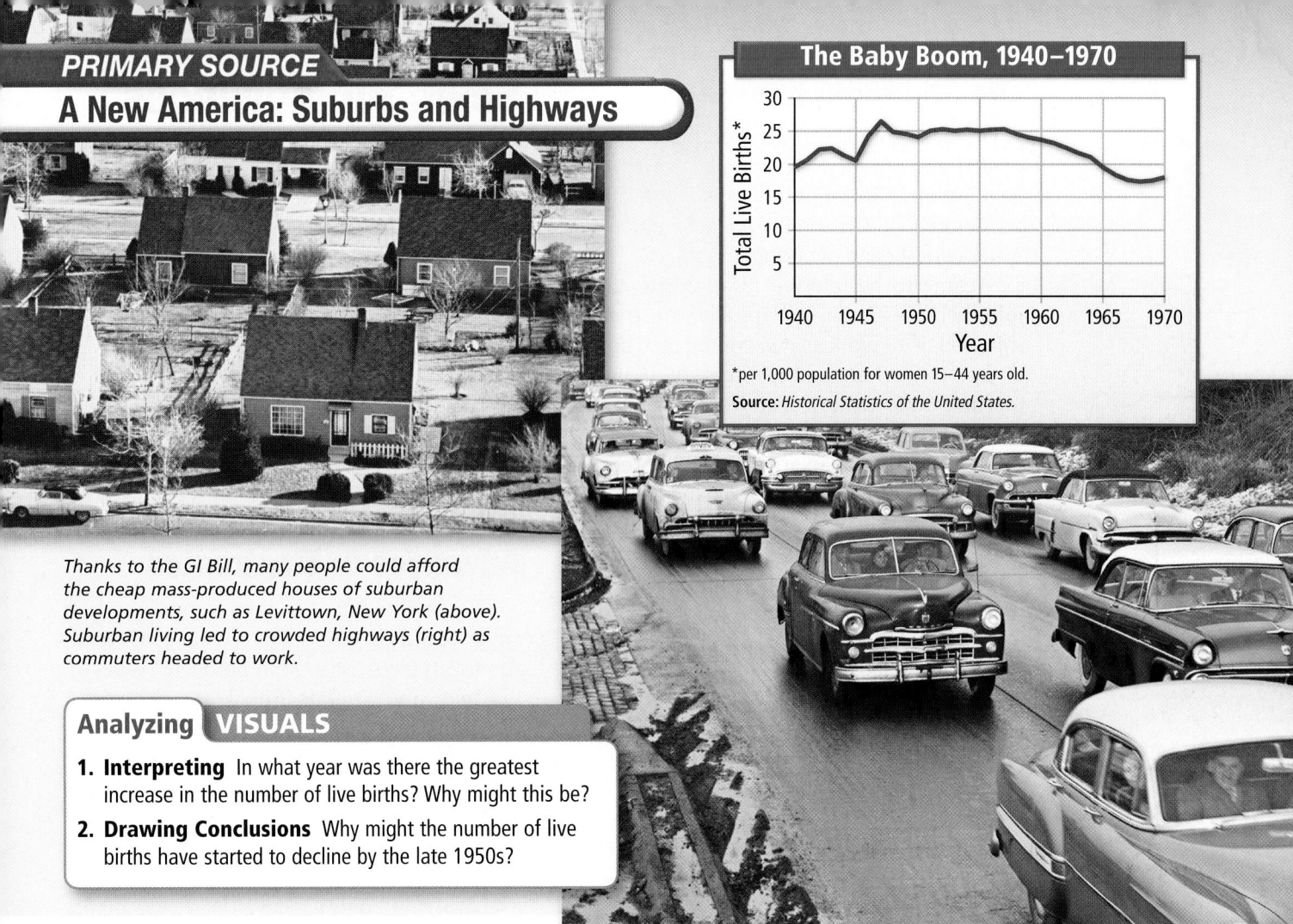

The Baby Boom, 1940–1970

*per 1,000 population for women 15–44 years old.
Source: *Historical Statistics of the United States.*

Thanks to the GI Bill, many people could afford the cheap mass-produced houses of suburban developments, such as Levittown, New York (above). Suburban living led to crowded highways (right) as commuters headed to work.

Analyzing VISUALS

1. **Interpreting** In what year was there the greatest increase in the number of live births? Why might this be?
2. **Drawing Conclusions** Why might the number of live births have started to decline by the late 1950s?

families rushed to buy the inexpensive homes. These new suburbs multiplied throughout the United States. Suburbs became increasingly popular during the 1950s, accounting for about 85 percent of new home construction. The number of suburban dwellers doubled, while the population of cities rose only 10 percent.

Reasons for the rapid growth of suburbia varied. Some people wanted to escape the crime and congestion of city neighborhoods. Others believed the suburbs would provide a better life for themselves and their children. For millions of Americans, the suburbs came to symbolize the American dream.

Affordability was a key reason that home buyers moved to the suburbs. With the GI Bill providing low-interest loans to veterans, buying a new house was more affordable than at any previous time in American history. The government's decision to give income tax deductions for home-mortgage interest payments and property taxes made owning a home even more

attractive. Between 1940 and 1960, the number of Americans who owned their own homes rose from about 41 percent to about 61 percent.

The Baby Boom

The American birthrate exploded after World War II. From 1945 to 1961, a period known as the **baby boom,** more than 65 million children were born in the United States. At the height of the baby boom, a child was born every seven seconds.

Several factors contributed to the baby boom. First, young couples who had delayed marriage during World War II and the Korean War could now marry, buy homes, and begin their families. In addition, the government encouraged the growth of families by offering generous GI benefits for home purchases. Finally, on television and in magazines, popular culture celebrated pregnancy, parenthood, and large families.

The Changing Workplace

Dramatic changes in the workplace accompanied the country's economic growth. The ongoing mechanization of farms and factories accelerated in the 1950s. As a result, more Americans began working in offices. These jobs came to be referred to as **white-collar jobs,** because employees typically wore a white shirt and tie to work, instead of the blue denim of factory workers and laborers. In 1956, for the first time, white-collar workers outnumbered **blue-collar workers.**

Many white-collar employees worked for large corporations. As these businesses competed with each other, some expanded overseas. These **multinational corporations** located themselves closer to important raw materials and benefited from a cheaper labor pool, which made them more competitive.

The 1950s also witnessed the rise of **franchises,** in which a person owns and runs one or several stores of a chain operation. Because many business leaders believed that consumers valued dependability and familiarity, the owners of chain operations often demanded that their franchises present a uniform look and style.

Like franchise owners, many corporate leaders expected their employees to **conform** to company standards. In general, they did not want free-thinking individuals or people who might speak out or criticize the company. Some observers criticized this trend. In his 1950 book *The Lonely Crowd,* sociologist David Riesman argued that this conformity was changing people. Formerly, he claimed, people were "inner-directed," judging themselves on the basis of their own values and the esteem of their families. Now, however, people were becoming "other-directed"—concerned with winning the approval of the corporation or community.

In his 1956 book, *The Organization Man,* William H. Whyte, Jr., attacked the similarity many business organizations cultivated to keep any individual from dominating. "In group doctrine," Whyte wrote, "the strong personality is viewed with overwhelming suspicion," and the person with ideas is considered "a threat."

✔**Reading Check** **Interpreting** Describe two causes and effects of the economic boom of the 1950s.

Scientific Advances

MAIN Idea Computers began a business revolution, and doctors discovered new ways to fight disease.

HISTORY AND YOU Do you own a computer? Read on to learn about the earliest computers.

As the United States experienced many social changes during the postwar era, the nation also witnessed several important scientific advances. In electronics, manufacturing, and medicine, American scientists broke new ground during the 1950s.

Advances in Electronics

The electronics industry made rapid advances after World War II. In 1947 three American physicists—John Bardeen, Walter H. Brattain, and William Shockley—developed the transistor, a tiny electric generator that made it possible to miniaturize radios from large pieces of furniture to small portable items.

The age of computers also dawned in the postwar era. In 1946 scientists working under a U.S. Army contract developed one of the nation's earliest computers—known as ENIAC (Electronic Numerical Integrator and Computer)—to make military calculations. Several years later, a newer model called UNIVAC (Universal Automatic Computer) would process business data and launch the computer revolution. The jet airline age also progressed rapidly with an increased use of plastics and light metals, the development of the jet engine, the swept-back wing design—all of which improved fuel effeciency—and a longer flight range. These developments reduced consumer costs, making airline travel available to the masses.

Medical Miracles

The medical breakthroughs of the 1950s included the development of new, powerful antibiotics and vaccines to fight infection and the introduction of new techniques to fight cancer and heart disease.

Prior to the 1950s, cancer had been thought to be untreatable. The development of radiation treatments and chemotherapy in the 1950s

People IN HISTORY

Dr. Jonas Salk
1914–1995

The man who developed the vaccine for one of the nation's most feared diseases almost did not go into medicine. Jonas Salk enrolled in college as a pre-law student but soon changed his mind. Salk switched his major to premed and went on to become a research scientist.

Every so often, Salk would make rounds in the overcrowded polio wards of a hospital near his lab, where nurses described their feelings of helpless rage. One nurse said, "I can remember how the staff used to kid Dr. Salk—kidding in earnest—telling him to hurry up and do something."

Salk became famous for the polio vaccine he developed in 1952. About becoming a celebrity, Salk observed that it was "a transitory thing and you wait till it blows over. Eventually people will start thinking, 'That poor guy,' and leave me alone. Then I'll be able to get back to my laboratory."

What character traits do you think made Dr. Salk a successful research scientist?

▲ *In the 1940s and 1950s, Americans fought the epidemic of polio cases that struck many children. Here, a device known as an iron lung helps polio patients to breathe.*

---

helped many cancer patients survive. Similarly, treatments for heart disease had eluded scientists for decades, and when someone suffered a heart attack, nothing could be done. In 1950, however, doctors developed cardiopulmonary resuscitation (CPR), a technique that has saved many lives. Doctors also began replacing worn-out heart valves with mechanical valves and implanted the first pacemakers in 1952.

A third disease that had frightened Americans for decades was tuberculosis, a lung disease also known as the white plague. The disease was both highly infectious and contagious, so patients lived in isolation in sanatoriums. In 1956 for the first time, tuberculosis fell from the list of the top ten fatal diseases. New antibiotics and a blood test for the disease finally put an end to fear of tuberculosis.

Polio, too, finally yielded to science. Polio epidemics had been occurring in the United States since 1916. The viral disease had struck Franklin Roosevelt as a young man and forced him to use a wheelchair and wear steel braces on his legs. In the 1940s and 1950s, widespread polio epidemics terrorized the nation. Every summer, polio broke out somewhere in the country. Many died; those who did not were often confined to iron lungs—large metal tanks with pumps that helped patients breathe. Even if they eventually recovered, they were often paralyzed for life.

Each summer, parents searched for ways to safeguard their families from the dreaded disease. Some sent their children to the country to avoid excessive contact with others. Public swimming pools and beaches were closed. Parks and playgrounds across the country stood deserted. Nevertheless, the disease continued to strike. In 1952 a record 58,000 new cases were reported.

Finally, research scientist **Jonas Salk** developed an injectable vaccine to prevent polio. Salk first tested the vaccine on himself, his wife, and his three sons, and then on 2 million schoolchildren. In 1955 the vaccine became available to the general public. American scientist Albert Sabin then developed an oral vaccine for polio. Safer and more convenient than Salk's injection vaccine, the Sabin vaccine became the most common method for preventing the disease. The threat of polio nearly disappeared.

✔ Reading Check **Examining** What medical and technological advances met specific needs in the late 1940s and 1950s?

The New Mass Media

MAIN Idea The rise of television led to changes in the movie and radio industries.

HISTORY AND YOU How many hours of television do you watch weekly? Read to find out about the early days of television broadcasting.

Although regular television broadcasts had begun in the early 1940s, there were few stations, and sets were expensive. There were estimated to be no more than 8,000 sets in use in the entire United States in 1946. By the late 1950s, however, small black-and-white-screened televisions sat in living rooms across the country. Nearly 40 million televisions had been sold by 1957, and more than 80 percent of families had at least one television.

The Rise of Television

Early television programs fell into several main categories, including comedy, action and adventure, and variety entertainment. In 1953 Lucille Ball and her real-life husband, Desi Arnaz, starred in one of the most popular shows ever to air on American television, a situation comedy (sitcom) called *I Love Lucy*. The episode in which Lucy gave birth (which paralleled Lucille Ball's actual pregnancy) had an audience of 44 million viewers. Fewer people tuned in to watch the presidential inauguration the following day.

Comedy proved popular in other formats. Many early comedy shows, such as those starring Bob Hope and Jack Benny, were adapted from radio programs. Variety shows, such as Ed Sullivan's *Toast of the Town,* provided a mix of comedy, music, dance, acrobatics, and juggling. Quiz shows also drew large audiences after the 1955 debut of *The $64,000 Question.* In this show and its many imitators, two contestants tried to answer questions from separate, soundproof booths.

Television viewers also enjoyed action shows. Westerns such as *Hopalong Cassidy, The Lone Ranger,* and *Gunsmoke* grew quickly in popularity. Viewers also enjoyed police shows

PRIMARY SOURCE
Television in the 1950s

▲ *I Love Lucy, a comedy about housewife Lucy, husband Ricky, and friends Fred and Ethel was the most popular show of the 1950s.*

▲ *Howdy Doody was the first network kids' show ever broadcast in color.*

▲ The Adventures of Ozzie and Harriet *was a comedy featuring the life of Ozzie and Harriet Nelson and their sons in a middle-class American suburb. Their portrayal of family life was idealized—father worked, mother stayed at home raising the children, and there was always plenty of food and consumer goods available.*

Analyzing VISUALS

1. **Explaining** How did *The Adventures of Ozzie and Harriet* reflect an idealized American family?

2. **Making Generalizations** To what type of audience were most of these television programs designed to appeal?

such as *Dragnet,* a hugely successful show featuring Detective Joe Friday and his partner hunting down a new criminal each week. By the late 1950s, television news had also become an important vehicle for information, and televised athletic events had made professional and college sports a popular choice for entertainment.

Hollywood Responds

As the popularity of television grew, movies lost viewers. Weekly movie attendance dropped from 82 million in 1946 to 36 million by 1950. By 1960, when some 50 million Americans owned televisions, one-fifth of the nation's movie theaters had closed.

Throughout the 1950s, Hollywood struggled to recapture its audience. When contests, door prizes, and advertising failed to lure people back, Hollywood tried 3-D films that required the audience to wear special glasses. Viewers soon tired of the glasses and the often ridiculous plots of 3-D movies.

Cinemascope—a process that showed movies on large, panoramic screens—finally gave Hollywood something television could not match. Wide-screen, full-color spectacles like *The Robe, The Ten Commandments,* and *Around the World in 80 Days* cost a great deal of money to produce. These blockbusters, however, made up for their cost by attracting huge audiences and netting large profits.

Radio Draws Them In

Television also forced the radio industry to change in order to keep its audience. Television made radio comedies, dramas, and soap operas obsolete. Radio stations responded by broadcasting recorded music, news, weather, sports, and talk shows.

Radio also had one audience that television could not reach—people traveling in their cars. In some ways, the automobile saved the radio industry. People commuting to and from work, running errands, or traveling on long road trips relied on radio for information and entertainment. As a result, radio stations survived and even flourished. The number of radio stations more than doubled between 1948 and 1957.

Reading Check **Identifying** How did the television industry affect the U.S. economy?

New Music and Poetry

MAIN Idea Young people developed their own popular culture based largely on rock 'n' roll music and literature of the beat movement.

HISTORY AND YOU How do the adults you know feel about your favorite music? Read on to learn of the conflicts over musical taste that began during the 1950s.

Many teens in every generation seek to separate themselves from their parents. One way of creating that separation is by embracing different music. In that respect, the 1950s were no different from earlier decades, but the results were different for two reasons.

For the first time, teens had large amounts of disposable income that could be spent on entertainment designed specifically for them. In addition, the new mass media meant that teens across the country could hear the same music broadcast or watch the same television shows. The result was the rise of an independent youth culture separate from adult culture. The new youth culture became an independent market for the entertainment and advertising industries.

Rock 'n' Roll

In 1951 at a record store in downtown Cleveland, Ohio, radio disc jockey Alan Freed noticed white teenagers buying African American rhythm-and-blues records and dancing to the music in the store. Freed convinced his station manager to play the music on the air. Just as the disc jockey had suspected, the listeners went crazy for it. Soon, white artists began making music that stemmed from these African American rhythms and sounds, and a new form of music, **rock 'n' roll,** was born.

With a loud and heavy beat that made it ideal for dancing, along with lyrics about romance, cars, and other themes that appealed to young people, rock 'n' roll became wildly popular with the nation's teens. Before long, teenagers around the country were rushing out to buy recordings from such artists as Buddy Holly, Chuck Berry, and Bill Haley and the Comets. In 1956 teenagers found their first rock 'n' roll hero in **Elvis Presley,** who became known as the "King of Rock 'n' Roll."

For an excerpt from *On the Road*, see page R77 in the **American Literature Library**.

Elvis Presley was born in rural Mississippi and grew up poor in Memphis, Tennessee. While in high school, Presley learned to play guitar and sing by imitating the rhythm-and-blues music he heard on the radio. By 1956, the handsome young Elvis had a record deal with RCA Victor, a movie contract, and had made public appearances on several television shows. At first, the popular television variety show host Ed Sullivan refused to invite Presley to appear, insisting that rock 'n' roll music was not fit for a family-oriented show. When a competing show featuring Presley upset Sullivan's high ratings, however, he relented. He ended up paying Presley $50,000 per performance for three appearances, more than triple the amount he had paid any other performer.

Presley owed his wild popularity as much to his moves as to his music. During his performances he would gyrate his hips and dance in ways that shocked many in the audience. Not surprisingly, parents—many of whom listened to Frank Sinatra and other more mellow, mainstream artists—condemned rock 'n' roll as loud, mindless, and dangerous. The city council of San Antonio, Texas, actually banned rock 'n' roll from the jukeboxes at public swimming pools.

The rock 'n' roll hits that teens bought in record numbers united them in a world their parents did not share. Thus, in the 1950s,

PRIMARY SOURCE
Rock 'n' Roll Sweeps the Nation

African American singers such as Chuck Berry (left), Little Richard (below left), and Fats Domino (below right) became huge stars in the popular music industry of the 1950s.

Bill Haley and His Comets (above) was one of the first popular rock 'n' roll bands. Elvis Presley (left) became rock 'n' roll's first superstar, but many disapproved of his dance moves.

▲ Little Richard

▲ Fats Domino

Analyzing VISUALS

1. **Explaining** Why did adults disapprove of rock 'n' roll?

2. **Describing** How did this disapproval contribute to the generation gap?

rock 'n' roll helped to create what became known as the **generation gap,** or the cultural separation between children and their parents.

The Beat Movement

If rock 'n' roll helped to create a generation gap, a group of mostly white writers and artists who called themselves beats, or beatniks, highlighted a values gap in 1950s America. The term "beat" may have come from the feeling among group members of being "beaten down" by American culture, or from jazz musicians who would say, "I'm beat right down to my socks."

Beat poets, writers, and artists harshly criticized what they considered the sterility and conformity of American life, the meaninglessness of American politics, and the emptiness of popular culture. In 1956, 29-year-old beat poet Allen Ginsberg published a long poem titled "Howl," which blasted modern American life. Another beat member, **Jack Kerouac,** published *On the Road* in 1957. Although Kerouac's book about his freewheeling adventures with a car thief and con artist shocked some readers, the book went on to become a classic in modern American literature. Although the beat movement remained relatively small, it laid the foundations for the more widespread youth cultural rebellion of the 1960s.

African American Entertainers

African American entertainers struggled to find acceptance in a country that often treated them as second-class citizens. With a few notable exceptions, television tended to shut out African Americans. In 1956 NBC gave a popular African American singer named Nat King Cole his own 15-minute musical variety show. In 1958, after 64 episodes, NBC canceled the show after failing to secure a national sponsor for a show hosted by an African American.

African American rock 'n' roll singers faced fewer obstacles. The talented African Americans who recorded hit songs in the 1950s included Chuck Berry, Little Richard, Fats Domino, and Ray Charles. The late 1950s and early 1960s also saw the rise of several female African American groups, including the Crystals, the Shirelles, and the Ronettes. With their catchy, popular sound, these groups were the musical predecessors of the famous late 1960s groups Martha and the Vandellas and the Supremes.

Over time, the music of the early rock 'n' roll artists had a profound influence on popular music throughout the world. Little Richard and Chuck Berry, for example, provided inspiration for the Beatles, whose music swept Britain and the world in the 1960s. Elvis Presley's music transformed generations of rock 'n' roll bands that followed him and other pioneers of rock.

Despite the innovations in music and the economic boom of the 1950s, not all Americans were part of the affluent society. For many of the country's minorities and rural poor, the American dream remained well out of reach.

Reading Check **Summarizing** How did rock 'n' roll help create the generation gap?

Section 2 REVIEW

Vocabulary

1. **Explain** the significance of: Levittown, baby boom, white-collar job, blue-collar worker, multinational corporation, franchise, Jonas Salk, rock 'n' roll, Elvis Presley, generation gap, Jack Kerouac.

Main Ideas

2. **Organizing** Use a graphic organizer like the one below to list the causes and effects of the economic boom of the 1950s.

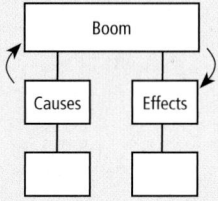

3. **Listing** What major technological breakthroughs occurred in the 1950s?

4. **Explaining** How did television affect other forms of mass media?

5. **Identifying** How did young people of the 1950s express their own culture?

Critical Thinking

6. **Big Ideas** What were the roots of rock 'n' roll, and how did it reach a mass audience?

7. **Analyzing Visuals** Study the photographs on page 576. These programs have been criticized for presenting a one-sided view of American life. Do you agree? Why or why not?

Writing About History

8. **Expository Writing** Assume the role of a media critic in the 1950s, and use the information in this section to write a critique of one television show, movie, music concert, or piece of literature.

History ONLINE

Study Central™ To review this section, go to glencoe.com and click on Study Central.

BETTMANN/CORBIS

Profile

JAMES DEAN *had a brief but spectacular career as a film star. His role in* Rebel Without a Cause *made him an icon for American youth in the mid-50s. In 1955 Dean was killed in a car crash. He was 24.*

"I guess I have as good an insight into this rising generation as any other young man my age. Therefore, when I do play a youth, I try to imitate life. *Rebel Without a Cause* deals with the problems of modern youth. . . . If you want the kids to come and see the picture, you've got to try to reach them on their own grounds. If a picture is psychologically motivated, if there is truth in the relationships in it, then I think that picture will do good."

—*from an interview for* Rebel Without a Cause

VERBATIM

❝It will make a wonderful place for the children to play in, and it will be a good storehouse, too.❞

MRS. RUTH CALHOUN,
mother of three, on her backyard fallout shelter, 1951

❝Riddle: What's college? That's where girls who are above cooking and sewing go to meet a man they can spend their lives cooking and sewing for.❞

ad for Gimbel's department store campus clothes, 1952

❝Radioactive poisoning of the atmosphere and hence annihilation of any life on Earth has been brought within the range of technical possibilities.❞

ALBERT EINSTEIN,
physicist, 1950

❝If the television craze continues with the present level of programs, we are destined to have a nation of morons.❞

DANIEL MARSH,
President of Boston University, 1950

❝Every time the Russians throw an American in jail, the House Un-American Activities Committee throws an American in jail to get even.❞

MORT SAHL,
comedian, 1950s

WINNERS & LOSERS

UNDERWOOD & UNDERWOOD/CORBIS

POODLE CUTS
Short, curly hairstyle gains wide popularity and acceptance

TV GUIDE
New weekly magazine achieves circulation of 6.5 million by 1959

PALMER PAINT COMPANY OF DETROIT
Sells 12 million paint-by-number kits ranging from simple landscapes and portraits to Leonardo da Vinci's The Last Supper

Poodle Cut

THE DUCKTAIL
Banned in several Massachusetts schools in 1957

COLLIER'S
The respected magazine loses circulation, publishes its final edition on January 4, 1957

LEONARDO DA VINCI'S THE LAST SUPPER
Now everyone can paint their own copy to hang in their homes

SUPER STOCK

The Ducktail

1950S WORD PLAY
Translation, Please!
Match the word to its meaning.

Teen-Age Lingo
1. cool
2. hang loose
3. hairy
4. yo-yo

a. a dull person, an outsider
b. worthy of approval
c. formidable
d. don't worry

answers: 1.b; 2.d; 3.c; 4.a

American Scene, 1950–1960
(MILLIONS)

	1950	1960
Children 5–14	24.3	35.5
Girl Scouts & Brownies	1.8	4.0
Bicycle Production	2.0	3.8

BETTMANN/CORBIS

Bomb Shelter

Be Prepared
"Know the Bomb's True Dangers. Know the Steps You Can Take to Escape Them!—You Can Survive."
Government pamphlet, 1950

DIGGING YOUR OWN BOMB SHELTER? Better go shopping. Below is a list of items included with the $3,000 Mark I Kidde Kokoon, designed to accommodate a family of five for a three-to five-day underground stay.

- air blower
- radiation detector
- protective apparel suit
- face respirator
- radiation charts (4)
- hand shovel (for digging out after the blast)
- gasoline driven generator
- gasoline (10 gallons)
- chemical toilet
- toilet chemicals (2 gallons)
- bunks (5)
- mattresses and blankets (5)
- air pump (blowing up mattresses)
- incandescent bulbs (2) 40 watts
- fuses (2) 5 amperes

- clock—non-electric
- first aid kit
- waterless hand cleaner
- sterno stove
- canned water (10 gallons)
- canned food (meat, powdered milk, cereal, sugar, etc.)
- paper products

NUMBERS 1957

3¢ Cost of first-class postage stamp

19¢ Cost of loaf of bread

25¢ Cost of issue of Sports Illustrated

35¢ Cost of movie ticket

50¢ Cost of gallon of milk (delivered)

$2.05 Average hourly wage

$2,845 Cost of new car

POPPERFOTO/ARCHIVE PHOTO

$5,234 Median income for a family of four

$19,500 Median price of a home

CRITICAL THINKING

1. *Predicting* If the number of American children continued to grow, how would that affect bicycle production and Scout membership? How could that growth affect the American economy?

2. *Hypothesizing* How have attitudes towards women changed since the 1952 department store ad for campus clothes? What do you think are some reasons for the change in attitude?

The Other Side of American Life

Guide to Reading

Big Ideas

Economics and Society The postwar prosperity did not extend to all Americans. For some groups, poverty and discrimination continued during the apparent abundance of the 1950s.

Content Vocabulary
- poverty line (p. 582)
- urban renewal (p. 583)
- termination policy (p. 585)
- juvenile delinquency (p. 587)

Academic Vocabulary
- income (p. 582)
- entity (p. 585)

People and Events to Identify
- Lorraine Hansberry (p. 584)
- Bracero Program (p. 584)
- Appalachia (p. 586)

Reading Strategy

Taking Notes As you read about social problems in the United States in the 1950s, use the major headings of this section to create an outline similar to the one below.

> The Other Side of American Life
> I. Poverty Amidst Prosperity
>   A.
>   B.
>   C.
>   D.
>   E.
> II.

During the 1950s, about 20 percent of the American population—particularly people of color and those living in the inner cities and Appalachia—did not share in the general prosperity. Experts also worried about the rise in juvenile delinquency.

Poverty Amidst Prosperity

MAIN Idea Despite the growing affluence of much of the nation, many groups still lived in poverty.

HISTORY AND YOU Are the pockets of poverty in America today the same as they were in the 1950s? Read on to learn about the people and regions most affected by poverty in the 1950s.

The 1950s saw a tremendous expansion of the middle class. At least one in five Americans, or about 30 million people, however, lived below the **poverty line.** This imaginary marker is a figure the government sets to reflect the minimum **income** required to support a family. Such poverty remained invisible to most Americans, who assumed that the country's general prosperity had provided everyone with a comfortable existence.

The writer Michael Harrington, however, made no such assumptions. During the 1950s, Harrington set out to chronicle poverty in the United States. In his book *The Other America,* published in 1962, he alerted those in the mainstream to what he saw in the run-down and hidden communities of the country:

PRIMARY SOURCE

"To be sure, the other America is not impoverished in the same sense as those poor nations where millions cling to hunger as a defense against starvation. . . . That does not change the fact that tens of millions of Americans are, at this very moment, maimed in body and spirit, existing at levels beneath those necessary for human decency. If these people are not starving, they are hungry, and sometimes fat with hunger, for that is what cheap foods do. They are without adequate housing and education and medical care."

—from *The Other America*

The poor included single mothers and the elderly; minorities such as Puerto Ricans and Mexican immigrants; rural Americans—both African American and white—and inner city residents, who remained stuck in crowded slums as wealthier citizens fled to the suburbs. Many Native Americans endured grinding poverty whether they stayed on reservations or migrated to cities.

The Other America

Amid the prosperity of the 1950s, many lived in terrible poverty. While suburbs boomed, the poor, many of whom were minorities, were relegated to inner-city slums. Native Americans suffered extreme poverty and the breakdown of their culture on reservations, while Mexican migrant workers in the Southwest barely made enough to feed, clothe, and shelter themselves and their children.

▲ A poor Navajo family stands outside their home on an Arkansas reservation in 1948.

▲ Children play in the littered streets of a Chicago slum in 1954.

Analyzing VISUALS

1. **Examining** Based on the photos, what aspect of life does it seem the hardest for the poor in America to obtain?

2. **Hypothesizing** What do you think might account for minorities having a lower average income than whites in the United States in the 1940s and 1950s?

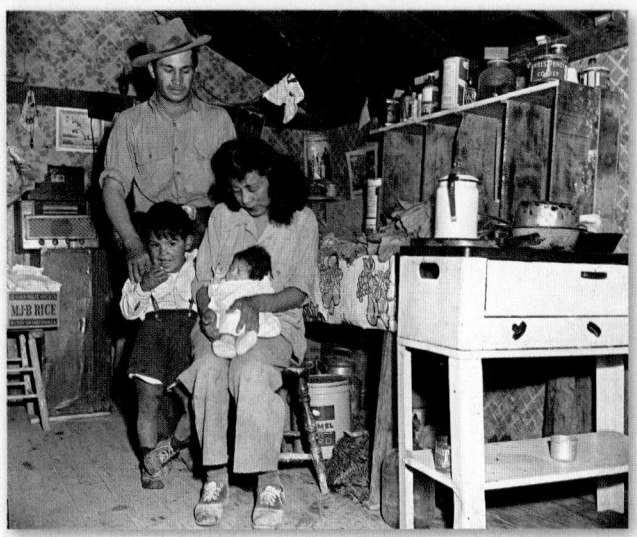

▲ The Cervantes family lived in a one-room shack at a ranch camp near Fresno, California, in 1950.

The Decline of the Inner City

The poverty of the 1950s was most apparent in the nation's urban centers. As middle-class families moved to the suburbs, they left behind the poor and less-educated. Many city centers deteriorated because the taxes that the middle class paid moved out with them. Cities no longer had the tax dollars to provide adequate public transportation, housing, and other services.

When government tried to help inner-city residents, it often made matters worse. During the 1950s, for example, **urban renewal** programs tried to eliminate poverty by tearing down slums and erecting new high-rise buildings for poor residents. These crowded, high-rise projects, however, often created an atmosphere of violence. The government also unwittingly encouraged the residents of public housing to remain poor by evicting them as soon as they began earning a higher income.

In the end, urban renewal programs actually destroyed more housing space than they created. Too often, the wrecking balls destroyed poor people's homes to make way for roadways, parks, universities, tree-lined boulevards, or shopping centers.

African Americans

Many of the citizens left behind in the cities were African American. By 1960, more than 3 million African Americans had migrated from the South to Northern cities in search of greater economic opportunity and to escape violence and racial intimidation. For many of these migrants, however, the economic boom of the war years did not continue in the 1950s.

Long-standing patterns of racial discrimination in schools, housing, hiring, and salaries in the North kept many inner-city African Americans poor. The last hired and the first fired for good jobs, they often remained stuck in the worst-paying occupations. In 1958 African Americans' salaries, on average, were only 51 percent of what whites earned. Poverty and racial discrimination also deprived many African Americans of other benefits, such as decent medical care.

In 1959 the play *A Raisin in the Sun* opened on Broadway. Written by African American author **Lorraine Hansberry,** the play told the story of a working-class African American family struggling against poverty and racism. The title referred to a Langston Hughes poem that wonders what happens to an unrealized dream: "Does it dry up like a raisin in the sun?" The play won the New York Drama Critics Circle Award for the best play of the year. Responding to a correspondent who had seen the play, Lorraine Hansberry wrote: "The ghettos are killing us; not only our dreams . . . but our very bodies. It is not an abstraction to us that the average [African American] has a life expectancy of five to ten years less than the average white."

Hispanics

African Americans were not the only minority group that struggled with poverty. Much of the nation's Hispanic population faced the same problems. During the 1950s and early 1960s, the **Bracero Program** brought nearly 5 million Mexicans to the United States to work on farms and ranches in the Southwest. Braceros were temporary contract workers. Many later returned home, but some 350,000 settled permanently in the United States.

These laborers, who worked on large farms throughout the country, lived with extreme poverty and hardship. They toiled long hours, for little pay, in conditions that were often

PAST & PRESENT

The Inner-City's Ongoing Problems

By the end of the 1950s, many major U.S. cities were in decline. "White flight" and lowered tax revenues, as well as racial discrimination and a lack of sympathy for the less fortunate, combined to create islands of decay and poverty in urban centers.

Although numerous programs were launched in the 1960s to try to improve living conditions and eliminate poverty, the problem has proven more difficult than first anticipated. Fifty years separate the two photos of inner-city slums to the right, yet, tragically, the quality of life has barely changed.

Major Cities With High Poverty Rates, 1960

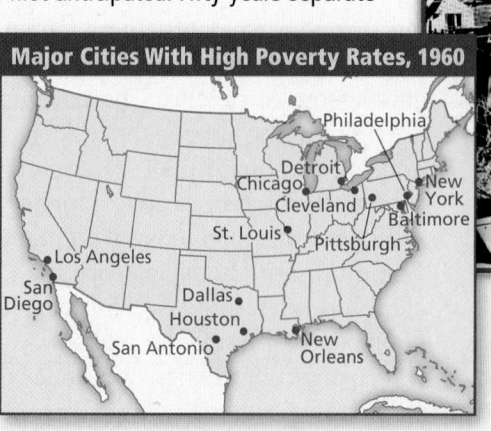

1940

▲ *Even in the 1940s, urban decay was characteristic of many American cities, including Washington, D.C., where people lived in dire poverty within sight of the Capitol.*

unbearable. In *The Other America,* Michael Harrington noted:

PRIMARY SOURCE

"[Migrant laborers] work ten-eleven-twelve hour days in temperatures over one hundred degrees. Sometimes there is no drinking water. . . . Women and children work on ladders and with hazardous machinery. . . . Babies are brought to the field and are placed in 'cradles' of wood boxes."

—from *The Other America*

Away from the fields, many Mexican families lived in small, crudely built shacks, while some did not even have a roof over their heads. "They sleep where they can, some in the open," Harrington noted about one group of migrant workers. "They eat when they can (and sometimes what they can)." The nation paid little attention to the plight of Mexican farm laborers until the 1960s, when the workers began to organize for greater rights.

Native Americans

Native Americans also faced challenges throughout the postwar era. By the middle of the 1900s, Native Americans—who made up less than one percent of the population—were the poorest ethnic group in the nation. Average annual family income for Native American families, for example, was $1,000 less than that of African American families.

After World War II, during which many Native American soldiers had served with distinction, the United States government launched a program to bring Native Americans into mainstream society—whether they wanted to assimilate or not.

Under the plan, which became known as the **termination policy,** the federal government withdrew all official recognition of the Native American groups as legal **entities** and made them subject to the same laws as white citizens. Native American groups were then placed under the responsibility of state governments. At the same time, the government encouraged Native Americans to blend in with the larger society by helping them move off reservations to cities.

Although the idea of integrating Native Americans into mainstream society began with good intentions, some of its supporters had more selfish goals. Speculators and developers sometimes gained rich farmland at the expense of destitute Native American groups.

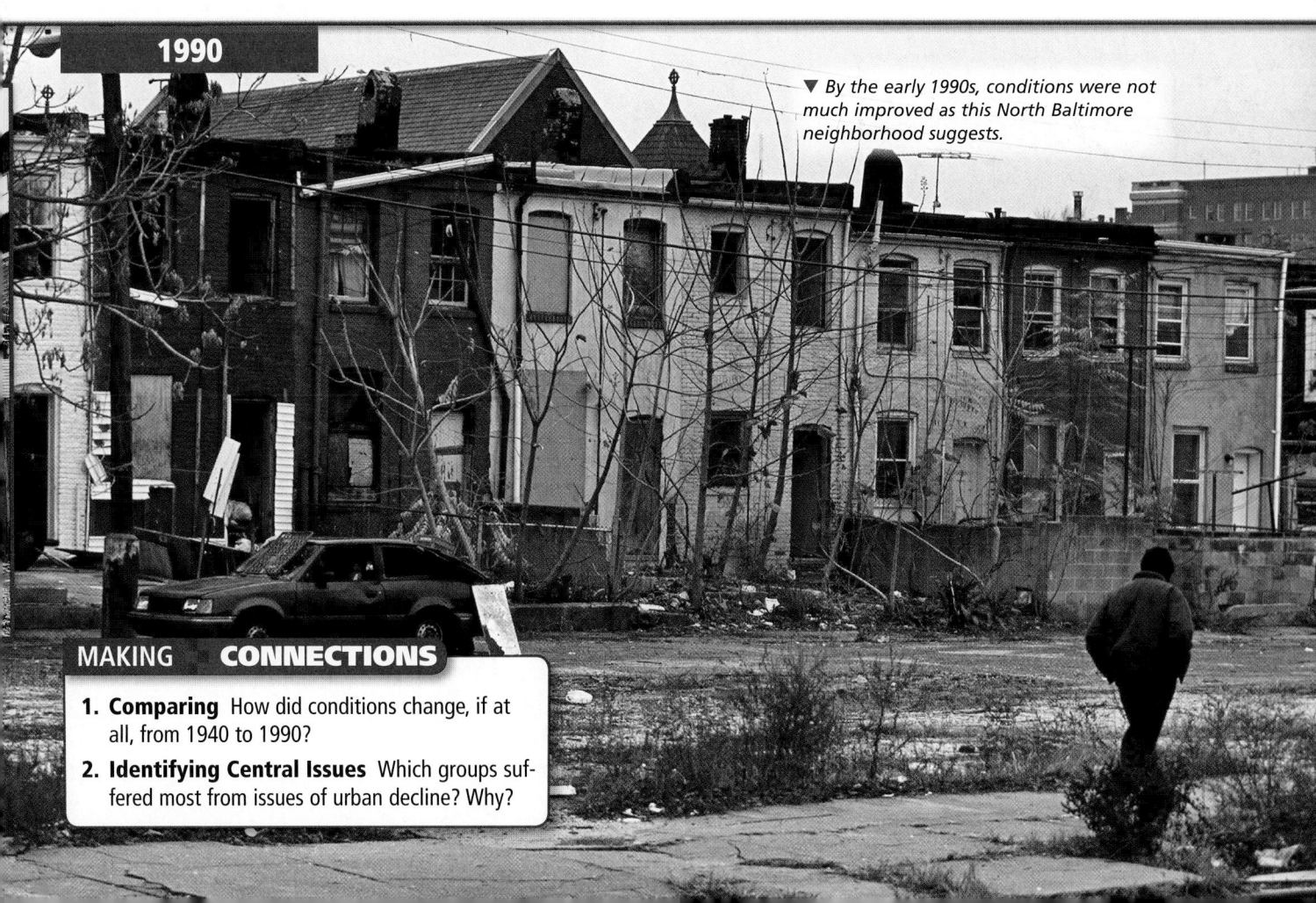

1990

▼ By the early 1990s, conditions were not much improved as this North Baltimore neighborhood suggests.

MAKING CONNECTIONS

1. **Comparing** How did conditions change, if at all, from 1940 to 1990?

2. **Identifying Central Issues** Which groups suffered most from issues of urban decline? Why?

For most Native Americans, termination was a disastrous policy that only deepened their poverty. In the mid-1950s, for example, the Welfare Council of Minneapolis described Native American living conditions in that city as miserable: "One Indian family of five or six, living in two rooms, will take in relatives and friends who come from the reservations seeking jobs until perhaps fifteen people will be crowded into the space."

During the 1950s, Native Americans in Minneapolis could expect to live only 37 years, compared to 46 years for all Minnesota Native Americans and 68 years for other Minneapolis residents. Similar patterns existed elsewhere. Benjamin Reifel, a Sioux, described the despair that the termination policy produced:

PRIMARY SOURCE

"The Indians believed that when the dark clouds of war passed from the skies overhead, their rising tide of expectations, though temporarily stalled, would again reappear. Instead they were threatened by termination. . . . Soaring expectations began to plunge."

—quoted in *The Earth Shall Weep*

Appalachia

Residents of rural **Appalachia** also failed to share in the prosperity of the 1950s. The scenic beauty of the mountainous region, which stretches from New York to Georgia, often hid desperate poverty. Coal mining had long been the backbone of the Appalachian economy. With mechanization of mining in the 1950s, unemployment soared. With no work to be had, some 1.5 million people abandoned Appalachia to seek a better life in the cities. "Whole counties," wrote one reporter, "are precariously held together by a flour-and-dried-milk paste of surplus foods. . . . The men who are no longer needed in the mines and the farmers who cannot compete . . . have themselves become surplus commodities in the mountains."

Appalachia had fewer doctors per thousand people than the rest of the country. Studies revealed high rates of nutritional deficiency and infant mortality. In addition, schooling in the region was considered even worse than in inner-city slums.

Reading Check **Identifying** Which groups were left out of the economic boom of the 1950s?

PRIMARY SOURCE
Poverty in Appalachia

▲ *Eight family members lived in this three-room house lined with newspaper in Appalachia in the 1950s.*

Appalachia

Distressed county, 1960
Other Appalachian county

N.Y.
Pa.
Ohio
Md.
W.Va.
Ky.
Va.
Tenn.
N.C.
S.C.
Miss.
Ga.
Ala.

0   200 kilometers
0   200 miles
Albers Equal-Area projection

Analyzing VISUALS   DBQ

1. **Identifying** Which states had the highest concentration of distressed counties in 1960?

2. **Explaining** What might have accounted for this high number?

Juvenile Delinquency

MAIN Idea Juvenile crime rates rose during the 1950s; a crisis in education occurred when the baby boomers began school.

HISTORY AND YOU Has your school placed a greater emphasis on science and math classes recently? Read to learn about a push in science and math education during the 1950s.

During the 1950s, many middle-class, white Americans found it easy to ignore the poverty and racism that afflicted many of the nation's minorities, since they themselves were removed from it. Some social problems, however, became impossible to ignore.

One problem at this time was a rise in, or at least a rise in the reporting of, **juvenile delinquency**—antisocial or criminal behavior of young people. Between 1948 and 1953, the United States saw a 45 percent rise in juvenile crime rates. A popular 1954 book titled *1,000,000 Delinquents* correctly predicted that in the following year, about 1 million young people would be involved in some kind of criminal activity.

Americans disagreed on what had triggered the rise in delinquency. Experts blamed television, movies, comic books, racism, busy parents, a rising divorce rate, lack of religion, and anxiety over the military draft. Some cultural critics claimed that young people were rebelling against the conformity of their parents. Others blamed a lack of discipline. Doting parents, complained Bishop Fulton J. Sheen, had raised bored children who sought new thrills, such as "alcohol, marijuana, even murder." Still others pointed at social causes, blaming teen violence on poverty. The problem, however, cut across class and racial lines—the majority of car thieves, for example, had grown up in middle-class homes.

Most teens, of course, steered clear of gangs, drugs, and crime. Nonetheless, the public tended to stereotype young people as juvenile delinquents, especially those teens who favored unconventional clothing and long hair, or used street slang.

Concerned about their children, many parents focused on the nation's schools as a possible solution. When baby boomers began entering the school system in the 1950s, enrollments increased by 13 million. School districts struggled to pay for new buildings and hire more teachers.

Americans' education worries only intensified in 1957 after the Soviet Union launched the world's first space satellites, *Sputnik I* and *Sputnik II.* Many Americans felt that the nation had fallen behind its Cold War enemy and blamed what they felt was a lack of technical education in the nation's schools. *Life* magazine proclaimed a "Crisis in Education" and offered a grim warning: "What has long been an ignored national problem, *Sputnik* has made a recognized crisis." In the wake of the *Sputnik* launches, efforts began to improve math and science education. Profound fears about the country's young people, it seemed, dominated the end of a decade that had brought prosperity and progress for many Americans.

Reading Check **Evaluating** What were some suggested explanations of the increase in juvenile crime?

Section 3 REVIEW

Vocabulary

1. **Explain** the significance of: poverty line, urban renewal, Lorraine Hansberry, Bracero Program, termination policy, Appalachia, juvenile delinquency.

Main Ideas

2. **Evaluating** How did the federal government's termination policy affect Native Americans?

3. **Analyzing** What effects did the baby boomers have on schools?

Critical Thinking

4. **Big Ideas** Why did urban renewal fail to improve the lives of the poor in the inner cities?

5. **Organizing** Use a graphic organizer similar to the one below to list groups of Americans left out of the country's postwar economic boom.

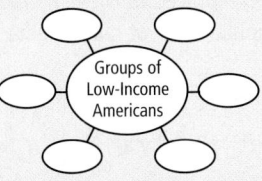

Groups of Low-Income Americans

6. **Analyzing Visuals** Study the photographs on page 583. Why were minority groups hit so hard by poverty, compared to whites, in the 1950s?

Writing About History

7. **Expository Writing** Choose a current social problem that you observe among adolescents. Describe the problem and its causes, and then recommend a solution.

History ONLINE

Study Central™ To review this section, go to glencoe.com and click on Study Central.

Chapter **16** VISUAL SUMMARY

STUDY TO GO You can study anywhere, anytime by downloading quizzes and flashcards to your PDA from glencoe.com.

The Prosperity of the 1950s

Economy and Society

- The GI Bill provided funds and loans to millions of war veterans.
- Consumer spending increased rapidly.
- More Americans owned homes than ever before.

Population Patterns

- The U.S. population experienced a "baby boom."
- Millions of Americans moved out of cities to the suburbs.

Science, Technology, and Medicine

- Improvements in communication, transportation, and electronics allowed Americans to work more efficiently.
- Medical breakthroughs included the polio vaccine, antibiotics, and treatments for tuberculosis, cancer, and heart disease.

Popular Culture

- New forms of music, radio, cinema, and literature emerged.
- Television replaced movies and radio as the nation's new and most popular form of mass media.

▲ *The huge, stylized automobiles of the 1950s, such as this Cadillac convertible, symbolized the good life to many Americans of the time.*

The Problems of the 1950s

Economy and Society

- Workers went on strike for higher wages.
- Congress would not pass Truman's civil rights legislation.
- Eisenhower cut back on New Deal programs.

Population Patterns

- Financially able people moved from crowded cities to new suburbs.
- Poverty increased in the inner city and the poor faced ongoing social problems.
- Crime increased among young people.

Science, Technology, and Medicine

- Poor people in inner cities and rural areas had limited access to modern health care.

Popular Culture

- Not everyone could afford to buy the new consumer goods available, such as televisions.
- African Americans and other minorities were, for the most part, not depicted on television.
- Many television programs promoted stereotypical gender roles.

▲ *While many prospered in the 1950s, many were excluded from achieving the American Dream.*

Reviewing Vocabulary

Directions: Choose the word or words that best complete the sentence.

1. The Taft-Hartley Act outlawed the _____, opening some industries to nonunion workers.

  A closed shop

  B labor unions

  C right-to-work laws

  D open shop

2. During the 1950s, the number of _____ grew, as more Americans worked in offices.

  A computers

  B blue-collar jobs

  C franchises

  D white-collar jobs

3. After World War II, Native Americans suffered from the government policy of _____, which forced them into mainstream society.

  A urban renewal

  B termination

  C migrant work

  D reservation planning

4. _____ tried to eliminate poverty in cities by replacing slums with high-rise buildings for poor residents.

  A Urban renewal

  B Termination policy

  C Franchising

  D Dynamic conservatism

5. The poem "Howl," by Allen Ginsberg, is a work that came out of the _____ movement.

  A rock 'n' roll

  B generation gap

  C beat

  D jazz

Reviewing Main Ideas

Directions: Choose the best answer for each of the following questions.

Section 1 *(pp. 566–571)*

6. Which of the following were two characteristics of the U.S. economy after World War II?

  A high unemployment and scarce goods

  B abundant goods and low unemployment

  C low unemployment and scarce goods

  D abundant goods and high unemployment

7. Which of the following was achieved under Truman's Fair Deal?

  A a large increase in Social Security benefits

  B a broad program of civil rights reforms

  C a decrease in funding for the TVA

  D a federal highway bill

Section 2 *(pp. 572–579)*

8. One major cause of the growth of the suburbs was the

  A rise in blue-collar jobs.

  B Korean War.

  C affordability of homes.

  D television.

9. Jonas Salk developed the first vaccine for which illness?

  A tuberculosis

  B cancer

  C heart disease

  D polio

TEST-TAKING TIP

Before answering, read the entire question and all answer choices. Then choose the answer that makes the most sense.

Need Extra Help?									
If You Missed Questions . . .	1	2	3	4	5	6	7	8	9
Go to Page . . .	566–567	574	585–586	583	579	566–567	569	572–573	574–575

10. How did the post–World War II baby boom affect American society between 1945 and 1960?

   A It decreased the demand for housing.

   B It bankrupted the Social Security system.

   C It increased the need for educational resources.

   D It encouraged people to migrate to the Sun Belt.

11. How did television affect the radio industry?

   A One-fifth of the nation's movie theaters closed.

   B Radio stations started to broadcast soap operas.

   C The number of radio stations increased as the car created a larger audience.

   D Radio stations declined in number as the audience turned to television.

Section 3 *(pp. 582–587)*

12. The imaginary government marker setting the minimum income required to support a family is called the

   A urban renewal.

   B poverty line.

   C income tax.

   D delinquency.

13. The purpose of the Bracero Program was to

   A bring workers into the United States from Mexico.

   B send workers from the United States to Mexico.

   C find housing for new immigrants.

   D deport illegal immigrants.

Critical Thinking

Directions: Choose the best answers to the following questions.

14. The GI Bill boosted the postwar economy by

   A instituting a military draft.

   B providing veterans with generous loans.

   C requiring all veterans to go to college.

   D providing veterans with white-collar jobs.

Base your answers to questions 15 and 16 on the graph below and on your knowledge of Chapter 16.

Suburban Dwellers, 1910–1980

Source: *The First Measured Century.*

15. What trend in the percentage of suburban dwellers does this graph show?

   A Fewer people were moving from the cities to the suburbs each year.

   B More people lived in the suburbs in 1910 than 1950.

   C More people lived in the cities in 1960 than 1950.

   D More people lived in the suburbs in 1980 than 1970.

16. In what year was there approximately twice the percentage of suburban residents as there had been in 1910?

   A 1930

   B 1940

   C 1950

   D 1960

Need Extra Help?							
If You Missed Questions . . .	10	11	12	13	14	15	16
Go to Page . . .	573	577	582	584–585	566–567	R16	R16

17. Many Americans responded to the Soviet launching of *Sputnik* by demanding that schools

A focus more on math and science.

B offer more physical fitness training.

C require students to learn a foreign language.

D require the recitation of the Pledge of Allegiance.

Analyze the cartoon and answer the questions that follow. Base your answers on the cartoon and on your knowledge of Chapter 16.

B. Wiseman

"He never wastes a minute, J.P.—that's his lunch."

18. The main idea of this cartoon is that 1950s white-collar workers were

A lazy and useless.

B unstable and untrustworthy.

C extremely good at what they did.

D overly dedicated to their jobs.

Document-Based Questions

Directions: Analyze the document and answer the short-answer questions that follow the document.

George Gallup, one of the nation's first pollsters, spoke at the University of Iowa in 1953 about the importance of mass media in the United States. Below is an excerpt from his remarks:

> "One of the real threats to America's future place in the world is a citizenry which duly elects to be entertained and not informed. From the time the typical citizen arises and looks at his morning newspaper until he turns off his radio or television set before going to bed, he has unwittingly cast his vote a hundred times for entertainment or for education. Without his knowing it, he has helped to determine the very character of our three most important media of communication—the press, radio, and television."
> —quoted in *Legacy of Freedom, Vol. 2: United States History from Reconstruction to the Present*

19. According to Gallup, what is a threat to the future of the United States in the world?

20. How do American citizens "cast their votes" to determine what is read, seen, and heard in the mass media?

Extended Response

21. Harry Truman was a Democrat, and Dwight Eisenhower was a Republican. However, the two men did not always act along party lines and, in some cases, took similar approaches to governing. In an expository essay, compare and contrast the domestic agendas of these two presidents of the postwar era. Include an introduction and at least three paragraphs with supporting details that explain how Truman's and Eisenhower's ideas and approaches to domestic issues were different and similar.

STOP

History ONLINE

For additional test practice, use Self-Check Quizzes—Chapter 16 at glencoe.com.

Need Extra Help?					
If You Missed Questions . . .	17	18	19	20	21
Go to Page . . .	587	R18	591	591	566–571

A Time of Upheaval
1954–1980

Why It Matters

Americans in the 1960s sought to remake their society. African Americans protested for civil rights and social equality and were soon joined by women's groups, Hispanics, Native Americans, and the disabled, all of whom demanded more equal treatment. At the same time, the federal government launched several new programs, including Medicare, designed to end poverty; and the Supreme Court took a more active role in society, issuing important rulings on civil rights.

Demonstrators block the entrance to the House of Representatives as part of the "May Day" protest against the Vietnam War, 1971

593

Chapter 17

The New Frontier and the Great Society

1961–1968

SECTION 1 The New Frontier

SECTION 2 JFK and the Cold War

SECTION 3 The Great Society

Future President John F. Kennedy waves to a crowd while campaigning, January 1960.

U.S. PRESIDENTS

Kennedy 1961–1963

Nov. 1963
• Kennedy is assassinated; Johnson becomes president

Johnson 1963–1969

U.S. EVENTS

1961
• Bay of Pigs invasion
• Peace Corps is created

1961

Oct. 1962
• Cuban missile crisis

1963

WORLD EVENTS

1961
• Construction of Berlin Wall begins

1964
• South Africa's Nelson Mandela sentenced to life in prison

Chapter Audio

MAKING CONNECTIONS

Can Government Fix Society?

President John F. Kennedy and President Lyndon B. Johnson supported programs intended to end poverty and racism at home and promote democracy abroad. The War on Poverty and the Great Society programs marked the greatest increase in the federal government's role in society since the New Deal. Kennedy's aid programs for developing nations also marked a dramatic shift in American foreign policy towards promoting economic development abroad.

- *How do you think Presidents Kennedy and Johnson changed American society? What programs from the 1960s still exist today?*

FOLDABLES

Categorizing Information Make a Four-Door Book Foldable listing the various programs of Lyndon Johnson's Great Society. Sort the programs into these four categories: War on Poverty, Health and Welfare, Education, and Consumer and Environmental Protection. As you read the chapter, list programs inside your Foldable under the four major categories.

War on Poverty | Health and Welfare
Education | Consumer and Environmental Protection

1965
- Congress establishes Medicare and Medicaid

1966
- Congress passes the Child Nutrition Act

1968
- Lyndon Johnson decides not to run for reelection

1965 — 1967 — 1968

1966
- Indira Gandhi becomes prime minister of India

1968
- Student riots paralyze France

History ONLINE Visit glencoe.com and enter *QuickPass*™ code TAVMT5147c17 for Chapter 17 resources.

Section Audio   Spotlight Video

The New Frontier

Guide to Reading

Big Ideas
Government and Society Under the programs and policies of the Kennedy administration, women, persons with disabilities, and others gained a greater share of civil rights.

Content Vocabulary
• missile gap *(p. 596)*
• reapportionment *(p. 600)*
• due process *(p. 601)*

Academic Vocabulary
• commentator *(p. 596)*
• arbitrary *(p. 601)*

People and Events to Identify
• New Frontier *(p. 597)*
• Earl Warren *(p. 600)*

Reading Strategy
Categorizing As you read about the presidency of John F. Kennedy, complete a graphic organizer similar to the one below by listing the domestic successes and setbacks of his administration.

Successes	Setbacks

In the presidential election campaign of 1960, John F. Kennedy promised to move the nation into "the New Frontier." After narrowly winning the election, Kennedy succeeded in getting only part of his agenda enacted.

The Election of 1960

MAIN Idea In 1960 a youthful John F. Kennedy narrowly defeated Richard M. Nixon in the presidential election.

HISTORY AND YOU Have you ever watched a televised political debate? Did you pay attention to the candidates' looks and mannerisms? Read on to learn how television changed people's perception of candidates.

On September 26, 1960, at 9:30 P.M. Eastern Standard Time, an estimated 75 million people sat indoors, focused on their television sets, watching the first televised presidential debate. The debate marked a new era of television politics.

During the 1960 presidential race, both parties made substantial use of television. The Democrats spent more than $6 million on television and radio spots, while the Republicans spent more than $7.5 million. Not everyone was happy with this new style of campaigning. Television news **commentator** Eric Sevareid complained that the candidates had become "packaged products" and declared, "the Processed Politician has finally arrived."

The candidates in the first televised debate differed in many ways. The Democratic nominee, John F. Kennedy, was a Catholic from a wealthy and influential Massachusetts family. Richard M. Nixon, the Republican nominee and Eisenhower's vice-president, was a Quaker from California; he had grown up in a family that struggled financially. Kennedy seemed outgoing and relaxed, while Nixon struck many as formal and even stiff in manner.

The campaign centered on the economy and the Cold War. Although the candidates presented different styles, they differed little on these two issues. Both promised to boost the economy, and both portrayed themselves as "Cold Warriors," determined to stop the forces of communism. Kennedy expressed concern about a suspected "**missile gap,**" claiming the United States lagged behind the Soviets in weaponry. Nixon warned that the Democrats' fiscal policies would boost inflation, and that only he had the necessary foreign policy experience to guide the nation.

Kennedy's Catholic faith became an issue, as Al Smith's Catholicism had in 1928. The United States had never had a Catholic president, and many Protestants had concerns about Kennedy. Kennedy decided to confront this issue openly in a speech.

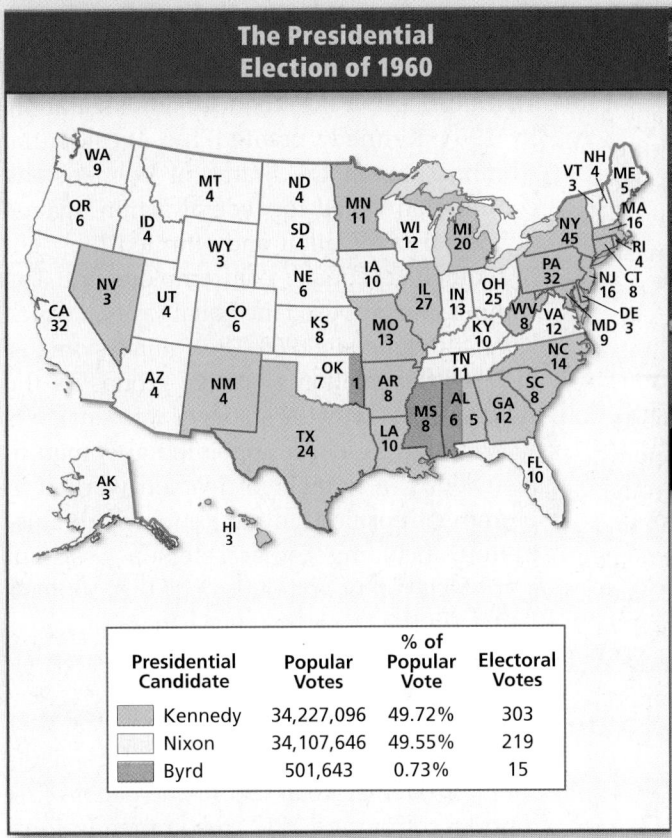

The Presidential Election of 1960

		WA 9									NH	VT 3	ME 5	
OR 6	MT 4	ND 4	MN 11						NY 45		MA 16			
ID 4	WY 3	SD 4	WI 12	MI 20				PA 32		RI 4				
NV 3	UT 4	NE 6	IA 10	IL 27	IN 13	OH 25		NJ 16	CT 8					
CA 32	CO 6	KS 8	MO 13	KY 10	WV 8	VA 12	DE 3	MD 9						
AZ 4	NM 4	OK 7 1	AR 8	TN 11	NC 14									
	TX 24	LA 10	MS 8	AL 6	GA 12	SC 8								
AK 3						FL 10								
HI 3														

Presidential Candidate	Popular Votes	% of Popular Vote	Electoral Votes
Kennedy	34,227,096	49.72%	303
Nixon	34,107,646	49.55%	219
Byrd	501,643	0.73%	15

The Election of 1960

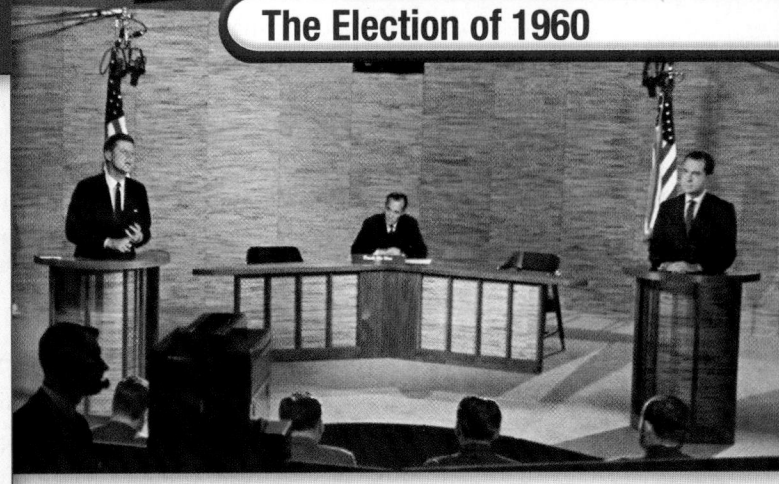

▲ The Kennedy-Nixon debates marked the first televised presidential campaign. Senator Kennedy matched Vice President Nixon's well-known debating skills, grasped facts about the way government worked, and showed he cared about Americans.

Analyzing VISUALS

1. **Assessing** What region of the nation went most solidly Republican?
2. **Identifying** Which states gave one or more electoral votes to Harry Byrd?

"I believe in an America where the separation of the church and state is absolute," he said, "where no Catholic prelate would tell the president, should he be a Catholic, how to act."

The four televised debates influenced the election's outcome, one of the closest in American history. Kennedy won the popular vote by 119,000 out of 68 million votes cast, and the Electoral College by 303 votes to 219.

Despite his narrow victory, John F. Kennedy captured the imagination of the American public as few presidents had before him. During the campaign, many had been taken with Kennedy's youth and optimism, and his Inaugural Address reinforced this impression.

In the speech, the new president declared that "the torch has been passed to a new generation" and called on citizens to take a more active role in making the nation better. "My fellow Americans," he exclaimed, "ask not what your country can do for you—ask what you can do for your country."

✔ Reading Check **Identifying** What were the two main issues of the 1960 presidential election?

Kennedy Takes Office

MAIN Idea Despite an uneasy relationship with Congress, President Kennedy managed to get parts of his domestic agenda passed.

HISTORY AND YOU Do you think there are enough women in top government positions today? Read on to learn how Kennedy's programs were designed to help women.

Upon entering office, President Kennedy set out to implement a legislative agenda that became known as the **New Frontier.** He hoped to increase aid to education, provide health insurance to the elderly, and create a Department of Urban Affairs. He would soon find that transforming lofty ideals into real legislation was no easy task on Capitol Hill.

Although the Democrats had majorities in both houses of Congress, Kennedy was unable to push through many of his programs. Kennedy had trailed Nixon in many Democratic districts and had not helped many Democrats get elected. Those who did win, therefore, did not feel they owed him anything.

Southern Democrats—who were a large part of the Democratic majority in Congress—viewed the New Frontier as too expensive and, together with Republicans, were able to defeat many of Kennedy's proposals. Senator Everett Dirksen, Republican minority leader from Illinois, claimed that Kennedy's efforts to increase the power of the federal government would push the nation down an ominous path.

Successes and Setbacks

Kennedy did achieve some victories, particularly in his efforts to improve the economy. Although the economy had soared through much of the 1950s, it had slowed by the end of the decade. In an effort to increase economic growth and create more jobs, Kennedy advocated deficit spending. The new president convinced Congress to invest more funds in defense and space exploration. Such spending did indeed create more jobs and stimulate economic growth.

In addition, Kennedy asked businesses to hold down prices and labor leaders to hold down pay increases. The labor unions in the steel industry agreed to reduce their demands for higher wages, but several steel companies raised prices sharply. In response, Kennedy threatened to have the Department of Defense buy cheaper foreign steel, and instructed the Justice Department to investigate whether the steel industry was fixing prices. The steel companies backed down and cut their prices, but the victory had strained the president's relations with the business community.

Kennedy also pushed for a cut in tax rates. When opponents argued that a tax cut would help only the wealthy, Kennedy asserted that lower taxes meant businesses would have more money to expand, which would create new jobs and benefit everybody. "A rising tide lifts all boats," Kennedy explained to illustrate how tax cuts would help all Americans.

Congress refused to pass the tax cut because of fears that it would cause inflation. Congress also blocked his plans for health insurance for senior citizens and federal aid to education. However, they did agree to Kennedy's request to raise the minimum wage and his proposal for an Area Redevelopment Act and a Housing Act. These acts helped to create jobs and build low-income housing in poor areas.

Expanding Women's Rights

The issue of women's rights also received attention during the Kennedy administration. In 1961 Kennedy created the Presidential Commission on the Status of Women. The commission called for federal action against gender discrimination and affirmed the right of women to equally paid employment. The commission proposed the Equal Pay Act, which Kennedy signed in 1963. The commission also inspired the creation of similar groups on the state level to study the status of women.

Although he never appointed a woman to his cabinet, a number of women worked in prominent positions in the Kennedy administration, including Esther Peterson, assistant secretary of labor and director of the Women's Bureau of the Department of Labor.

A New View of the Disabled

In 1961 Kennedy convened the President's Panel on Mental Retardation. The panel's first report, containing 112 recommendations, called for funding of research into developmental disabilities and educational and vocational programs for people with developmental disabilities; a greater reliance on residential—as opposed to institutional—treatment centers; and grants to provide prenatal services to women in low-income groups to promote healthy pregnancies.

Responding to the report, Congress enacted the Mental Retardation Facilities and Community Mental Health Centers Construction Act of 1963. This legislation provided grants for construction of research centers; funds to train educational personnel to work with people with developmental disabilities; and grants to states for construction of mental health centers.

In 1962 Eunice Kennedy Shriver, the president's sister, began a day camp at her home for children with developmental disabilities. Camp Shriver, as it was first known, offered people with disabilities a chance to be physically competitive. That effort later grew into the Special Olympics program. The first Special Olympics Games were held in Chicago in 1968.

Reading Check **Evaluating** Why did Kennedy have difficulty getting his agenda enacted?

ANALYZING SUPREME COURT CASES

Does Each Vote Really Count?

★ *Baker* v. *Carr, 1962*
★ *Reynolds* v. *Sims, 1964*

Background of the Cases

Although many more Americans were living in urban areas, most states had not redrawn their political districts to reflect this shift. This gave rural voters more political influence than urban voters. In *Baker* v. *Carr*, the Supreme Court ruled on whether federal courts had jurisdiction in lawsuits seeking to force states to redraw their electoral districts. In *Reynolds* v. *Sims*, the court decided whether uneven electoral districts violated the equal protection clause of the 14th Amendment.

How the Court Ruled

In *Baker* v. *Carr*, the Supreme Court ruled that federal courts can hear lawsuits seeking to force state authorities to redraw electoral districts. In *Reynolds* v. *Sims*, the Court ruled that the inequality of representation in the Alabama legislature did violate the equal protection clause. These rulings forced states to reapportion their political districts according to the principle of "one person, one vote."

▲ The 1962 Supreme Court. Seated left to right, Associate Justices Tom Clark and Hugo Black, Chief Justice Earl Warren, Associate Justices William O. Douglas and John Harlan; standing, left to right, Associate Justices Byron White, William Brennan, Potter Stewart, and Arthur Goldberg. Justices Byron White and Arthur Goldberg were appointed by Kennedy.

PRIMARY SOURCE

The Court's Opinion

"Legislators represent people, not trees or acres. Legislators are elected by voters, not farms or cities or economic interests. As long as ours is a representative form of government . . . the right to elect legislators in a free and unimpaired fashion is a bedrock of our political system. . . .

And, if a State should provide that the votes of citizens in one part of the State should be given two times, or five times, or 10 times the weight of votes of citizens in another part of the State, it could hardly be contended that the right to vote of those residing in the disfavored areas had not been effectively diluted.

—Justice William Brennan, Jr., writing for the court in
Reynolds v. *Sims*

PRIMARY SOURCE

Dissenting Views

"As of 1961, the Constitutions of all but 11 States . . . recognized bases of apportionment other than geographic spread of population. . . . The consequence of today's decision is that . . . state courts, are given blanket authority and the constitutional duty to supervise apportionment. . . . It is difficult to imagine a more intolerable and inappropriate interference by the judiciary with the independent legislatures of the States. . . . [The Court] says only that 'legislators represent people, not trees or acres,' . . . . But it is surely equally obvious . . . that legislators can represent their electors only by speaking for their interests—economic, social, political—many of which do reflect the place where the electors live. . . . These decisions also cut deeply into the fabric of our federalism."

—Justice John Marshall Harlan dissenting in *Reynolds* v. *Sims*

DBQ   Document-Based Questions

1. **Summarizing** What is the main idea of the majority decision in *Reynolds* v. *Sims*?
2. **Explaining** Why does Justice Harlan disagree with the majority in *Reynolds* v. *Sims*?
3. **Making Inferences** How do you think reapportionment according to "one person, one vote" changed state politics?

Warren Court Reforms

MAIN Idea Under Chief Justice Earl Warren, the Supreme Court issued a number of decisions that altered the voting system, expanded due process, and reinterpreted aspects of the First Amendment.

HISTORY AND YOU Do you ever watch cop shows in which police officers read suspects their "Miranda rights"? Read on to learn about the origin of this process.

For further information on the Supreme Court cases referenced on this page, see pages R58–R61 in **Supreme Court Case Summaries.**

In 1953 President Eisenhower nominated **Earl Warren,** governor of California, to be Chief Justice of the United States. Under Warren's leadership, the Supreme Court issued several rulings that dramatically reshaped American politics and society.

"One Man, One Vote"

Some of the Warren Court's more notable decisions concerned **reapportionment,** or the way in which states draw up political districts based on changes in population. By 1960, many more Americans resided in cities and suburbs than in rural areas. Yet many states had failed to change their electoral districts to reflect that population shift.

In Tennessee, for example, a rural county with only 2,340 voters had one representative in the state assembly, while an urban county with 133 times more voters had only seven. Thus, rural voters had far more political influence than urban voters. Some Tennessee voters took the matter to court and their case wound up in the Supreme Court. In *Baker* v. *Carr* (1962), the Court ruled that the federal courts had jurisdiction to hear lawsuits seeking to force states to redraw electoral districts.

The Supreme Court subsequently ruled, in *Reynolds* v. *Sims* (1964), that the current apportionment system in most states was unconstitutional. The Warren Court required states to reapportion electoral districts along the principle of "one man, one vote," so that all citizens' votes would have equal weight. The decision was a momentous one, for it shifted political

What Were the Major Decisions of the Warren Court?

Civil Rights

Brown v. Board of Education (1954)	Declared segregation in public schools unconstitutional
Baker v. Carr (1962)	Established that federal courts can hear lawsuits seeking to force state authorities to redraw electoral districts
Reynolds v. Sims (1964)	Mandated that state legislative districts be approximately equal in population
Heart of Atlanta Motel v. United States (1964)	Upheld the Civil Rights Act of 1964 provision requiring desegregation of public accommodations
Loving v. Virginia (1967)	Forbade state bans on interracial marriage

Due Process

Mapp v. Ohio (1961)	Ruled that unlawfully seized evidence cannot be used in a trial
Gideon v. Wainwright (1963)	Established suspects' right to a court-appointed attorney if suspects were unable to afford one
Escobedo v. Illinois (1964)	Affirmed right of the accused to an attorney during police questioning
Miranda v. Arizona (1966)	Required police to inform suspects of their rights during the arrest process

Freedom of Speech and Religion

Engel v. Vitale (1962)	Banned state-mandated prayer in public schools
Abington School District v. Schempp (1963)	Banned state-mandated Bible reading in public schools
New York Times v. Sullivan (1964)	Restricted circumstances in which celebrities could sue the media

Analyzing VISUALS

1. **Interpreting** How did *Brown* v. *Board of Education* and *Reynolds* v. *Sims* affect the nation?
2. **Summarizing** What three major policy areas did the Warren Court's decisions affect?

power from rural and often conservative areas to urban areas, where more liberal voters resided. The Court's decision also boosted the political power of African Americans and Hispanics, who often lived in cities.

Extending Due Process

In a series of rulings, the Supreme Court began to use the Fourteenth Amendment to apply the Bill of Rights to the states. Originally, the Bill of Rights applied only to the federal government. Many states had their own bills of rights, but some federal rights did not exist at the state level. The Fourteenth Amendment states that "no state shall . . . deprive any person of life, liberty, or property without due process of law." **Due process** means that the law may not treat individuals unfairly, **arbitrarily,** or unreasonably, and that courts must follow proper procedures when trying cases. Due process is meant to ensure that all people are treated the same by the legal system. The Court ruled in several cases that due process meant applying the federal bill of rights to the states.

In 1961 the Supreme Court ruled in *Mapp* v. *Ohio* that state courts could not consider evidence obtained in violation of the federal Constitution. In *Gideon* v. *Wainwright* (1963), the Court ruled that a defendant in a state court had the right to a lawyer, regardless of his or her ability to pay. The following year, in *Escobedo* v. *Illinois,* the justices ruled that suspects must be allowed access to a lawyer and must be informed of their right to remain silent before being questioned by the police. *Miranda* v. *Arizona* (1966) went even further, requiring that authorities immediately inform suspects that they have the right to remain silent; that anything they say can and will be used against them in court; that they have a right to a lawyer; and that, if they cannot afford a lawyer, the court will appoint one for them. Today these warnings are known as the Miranda rights.

Prayer and Privacy

The Supreme Court also handed down decisions that reaffirmed the separation of church and state. The Court applied the First Amendment to the states in *Engel* v. *Vitale* (1962). In this ruling, the Court decided that states could not compose official prayers and require those prayers to be recited in public schools. The following year, in *Abington School District* v. *Schempp*, it ruled against state-mandated Bible readings in public schools. Weighing in on another issue, the Court ruled in *Griswold* v. *Connecticut* (1965) that prohibiting the sale and use of birth-control devices violated citizens' constitutional right to privacy.

As with most rulings of the Warren Court, these decisions delighted some and deeply disturbed others. What most people did agree upon, however, was the Court's pivotal role in shaping national policy. The Warren Court, wrote *New York Times* columnist Anthony Lewis, "has brought about more social change than most Congresses and most Presidents."

✓ Reading Check **Examining** What was the significance of the "One Man, One Vote" ruling?

Section 1 REVIEW

Vocabulary
1. **Explain** the significance of: missile gap, New Frontier, Earl Warren, reapportionment, due process.

Main Ideas
2. **Interpreting** In what ways was the 1960 presidential election a turning point in political campaign history?

3. **Summarizing** What progress was made for women's rights during Kennedy's administration?

4. **Describing** Name three decisions of the Warren Court and explain how each protected civil rights.

Critical Thinking
5. **Big Ideas** What were some successes and failures of Kennedy's New Frontier? How did the new programs change the lives of Americans?

6. **Organizing** Use a graphic organizer similar to the one below to list the economic policies of the Kennedy administration.

Economic Policies	

7. **Analyzing Visuals** Look at the election map on page 597. Which states split their electoral votes?

Writing About History
8. **Expository Writing** In his Inaugural Address, President Kennedy asked his fellow Americans to "ask what you can do for your country." Respond to this statement in an essay.

History ONLINE
Study Central™ To review this section, go to <u>glencoe.com</u> and click on Study Central.

JFK and the Cold War

During the Kennedy Administration, ongoing tensions with the Soviet Union led to crises over Cuba and West Berlin. To contain communism and stay ahead of the Soviet Union in technology, President Kennedy created aid programs for developing nations and expanded the space program.

Guide to Reading

Big Ideas

Economics and Society The Kennedy administration used foreign aid to improve relations with Latin American countries and lessen the appeal of left-wing movements.

Content Vocabulary
- flexible response (p. 602)
- space race (p. 604)

Academic Vocabulary
- conventional (p. 602)
- institute (p. 605)
- remove (p. 607)

People and Events to Identify
- Peace Corps (p. 604)
- Berlin Wall (p. 606)
- Warren Commission (p. 607)

Reading Strategy

Sequencing As you read about the crises of the Cold War, complete a time line similar to the one below to record the major events of the Cold War in the 1950s and early 1960s.

Containing Communism

MAIN Idea President Kennedy developed new programs to combat the spread of communism.

HISTORY AND YOU Would you consider joining the Peace Corps and serving in a foreign country? Read on to learn about Kennedy's diplomatic efforts in Latin America.

When John F. Kennedy entered the White House, he had to devote much of his time to foreign policy. The Cold War with the Soviet Union dominated all other concerns at the time, and Kennedy attempted to stop the spread of communism with a range of programs. These included a **conventional** weaponry program to give the nation's military more flexibility, a program to provide economic aid to Latin America, and the creation of the Peace Corps to help developing nations worldwide.

A More Flexible Response

Kennedy took office at a time of growing global instability. Nationalism was exploding throughout the developing world, and the Soviet Union actively supported "wars of national liberation."

Kennedy felt that Eisenhower had relied too heavily on nuclear weapons, which could be used only in extreme situations. To allow for a "**flexible response**" if nations needed help resisting Communist movements, the president pushed for a buildup of troops and conventional weapons. Kennedy also expanded the Special Forces, an elite army unit created in the 1950s to wage guerrilla warfare in limited conflicts, and allowed the soldiers to wear their distinctive "Green Beret" headgear.

Aid to Other Countries

Kennedy wanted to renew diplomatic focus on Latin America. Conditions in many Latin American societies were not good: Governments were often in the hands of the wealthy few and many

▲ *John F. Kennedy delivers his inaugural speech, January 20, 1961. He spoke of the obligation of his generation to defend liberty. To his right is incoming Vice President Lyndon Johnson.*

PRIMARY SOURCE

"Let the word go forth from this time and place, to friend and foe alike, that the torch has been passed to a new generation of Americans—born in this century, tempered by war, disciplined by a hard and bitter peace, proud of our ancient heritage—and unwilling to witness or permit the slow undoing of those human rights to which this Nation has always been committed. . . . Let every nation know, whether it wishes us well or ill, that we shall pay any price, bear any burden, meet any hardship, support any friend, oppose any foe, in order to assure the survival and the success of liberty. . . .

To those old allies whose cultural and spiritual origins we share, we pledge the loyalty of faithful friends. . . . To those peoples in the huts and villages across the globe struggling to break the bonds of mass misery, we pledge our best efforts to help them help themselves . . . To our sister republics south of our border, we offer a special pledge—to convert our good words into good deeds—in a new alliance for progress—to assist free men and free governments in casting off the chains of poverty. . . .

Now the trumpet summons us again—not as a call to bear arms, though arms we need; not as a call to battle, though embattled we are—but a call to bear the burden of a long twilight struggle, year in and year out, "rejoicing in hope, patient in tribulation"—a struggle against the common enemies of man: tyranny, poverty, disease, and war itself. . . .

And so, my fellow Americans: ask not what your country can do for you—ask what you can do for your country. My fellow citizens of the world: ask not what America will do for you, but what together we can do for the freedom of man."

—Inaugural Address delivered January 20, 1961

DBQ Document-Based Questions

1. **Expressing** What commitment does Kennedy make with respect to human rights?

2. **Classifying** To what three specific groups does Kennedy promise aid, and what aid is promised?

3. **Finding the Main Idea** What does Kennedy indicate are the common enemies of humankind?

---

of their citizens lived in extreme poverty. In some countries, these conditions spurred the growth of left-wing movements aimed at overthrowing their governments.

When the United States became involved in Latin America, it usually did so to help existing governments stay in power and to prevent Communist movements from flourishing. Poor Latin Americans resented this intrusion, just as they resented American corporations, whose presence was seen as a kind of imperialism.

The Alliance for Progress To improve relations between the United States and Latin America, Kennedy proposed an Alliance for Progress, a series of cooperative aid projects with Latin American governments. The alliance was designed to create a "free and prosperous Latin America" that would be more stable and less likely to support Communist-inspired revolutions.

Over a 10-year period, the United States pledged $20 billion to help Latin American countries establish better schools, housing, health care, and fairer land distribution. The results were mixed. In some countries—notably Chile, Colombia, Venezuela, and the Central American republics—the alliance did promote real reform. In others, local rulers used the money to keep themselves in power.

The Peace Corps Another program aimed at helping less-developed nations fight poverty was the **Peace Corps,** an organization that sent Americans to provide humanitarian services in less-developed nations.

After rigorous training, volunteers spent two years in countries that requested assistance. They laid out sewage systems in Bolivia and trained medical technicians in Chad. Others taught English or helped to build roads. Today, the Peace Corps is still active and remains one of Kennedy's most enduring legacies.

The Cold War in Space

In 1961 Yuri Gagarin (YHOO•ree gah•GAHR•ihn), a Soviet astronaut, became the first person to orbit Earth. Again, as in 1957 when they launched *Sputnik,* the first satellite, the Soviets had beaten the United States in the **space race.** President Kennedy worried about the impact of the flight on the Cold War. Soviet successes in space might convince the world that communism was better than capitalism.

Less than six weeks after the Soviet flight, the president went before Congress and declared: "I believe this nation should commit itself to achieving the goal, before this decade is out, of landing a man on the moon."

Kennedy's speech set in motion a massive effort to develop the necessary technology. In 1962 John Glenn became the first American to orbit Earth. Three years later, the United States sent three men into orbit in a capsule called *Apollo. Apollo* was launched using the Saturn V, the most powerful rocket ever built. The Saturn V was able to give both *Apollo* and the lunar module—which astronauts would use to land on the moon—enough velocity to reach the moon.

On July 16, 1969, a Saturn V lifted off in Florida, carrying three American astronauts: Neil Armstrong, Edwin "Buzz" Aldrin, and Michael Collins. On July 20 Armstrong and Aldrin boarded the lunar module, named *Eagle,* and headed down to the moon. Minutes later, Armstrong radioed NASA's flight center in Texas: "Houston . . . the *Eagle* has landed."

Armstrong became the first human being to walk on the moon. As he set foot on the lunar surface, he announced: "That's one small step for a man, one giant leap for mankind." The United States had won the space race and decisively demonstrated its technological superiority over the Soviet Union.

Reading Check **Examining** What global challenges did Kennedy face during his presidency?

TECHNOLOGY & HISTORY

Space Technology Cold War tensions between the United States and the Soviet Union fueled the space race. Both countries vied for superiority in aeronautical technology and dominance in space exploration.

▲ American astronaut John Glenn is loaded into his space capsule, named *Friendship 7,* on February 20, 1962, shortly before being launched into orbit.

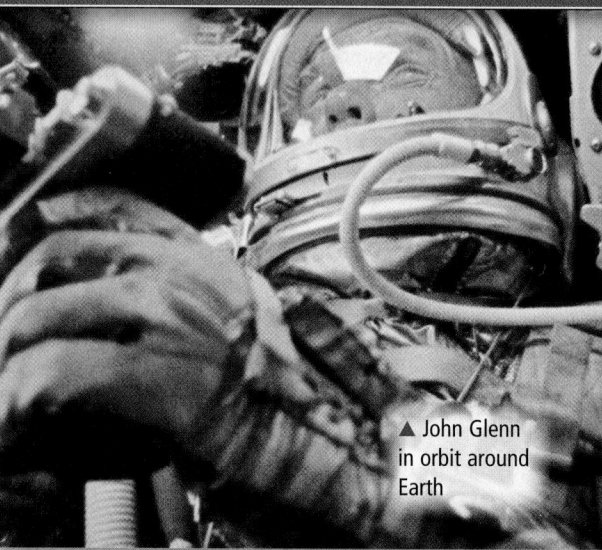

▲ John Glenn in orbit around Earth

◀ NASA recruited seven astronauts for its first manned space program. Each astronaut would ride in a *Mercury* capsule atop an ICBM reconfigured to lift them into space. The first American astronaut to ride into space in the capsule was Alan Shepard. The first American to orbit Earth was John Glenn.

Crises of the Cold War

MAIN Idea President Kennedy faced foreign policy crises in Cuba and Berlin.

HISTORY AND YOU Do you think the embargo against Cuba should be lifted? Read on to learn about the crises President Kennedy faced over Cuba.

President Kennedy's efforts to combat Communist influence in other countries led to some of the most intense crises of the Cold War. At times these crises left Americans and people in many other nations wondering whether the world would survive.

The Bay of Pigs

The first crisis occurred in Cuba, only 90 miles (145 km) from American shores. There, Fidel Castro had overthrown the corrupt Cuban dictator Fulgencio Batista in 1959. Almost immediately, Castro established ties with the Soviet Union, **instituted** drastic land reforms, and seized foreign-owned businesses, many of which were American. Cuba's alliance with the Soviets worried many Americans. The Communists were now too close for comfort, and Soviet premier Nikita Khrushchev was also expressing his intent to strengthen Cuba militarily.

Fearing that the Soviets would use Cuba as a base from which to spread revolution throughout the Western Hemisphere, President Eisenhower had authorized the CIA to secretly train and arm a group of Cuban exiles, known as *La Brigada,* to invade the island. The invasion was intended to set off a popular uprising against Castro.

When Kennedy became president, his advisers approved the plan. In office less than three months and trusting his experts, Kennedy agreed to the operation with some changes. On April 17, 1961, some 1,400 armed Cuban exiles landed at the Bay of Pigs on the south coast of Cuba. The invasion was a disaster. *La Brigada's* boats ran aground on coral reefs; Kennedy canceled their air support to keep the United States' involvement a secret; and the expected popular uprising never happened. Within two days, Castro's forces killed or captured almost all the members of *La Brigada*.

The Bay of Pigs was a dark moment for the Kennedy administration. The action exposed an American plot to overthrow a neighbor's government, and the outcome made the United States look weak and disorganized.

◀ Apollo capsule carried three astronauts.

Lunar Module

▲ Neil Armstrong was the first person to walk on the Moon.

▲ Buzz Aldrin descended to the Moon's surface, July 20, 1969, becoming the second man to walk on the Moon.

▲ To reach the Moon, NASA developed the giant Saturn V rocket, which lifted a three-person capsule, called *Apollo,* and a landing craft, called the Lunar Module, into space. Once *Apollo* and the Lunar Module entered orbit around the Moon, the Lunar Module carried two astronauts from the Apollo capsule down to the Moon's surface.

Analyzing VISUALS

1. **Calculating** What analysis can you make about the size of the space capsules and modules used in space?

2. **Describing** How does the Moon's surface appear in these photos?

3. **Identifying** What was the purpose of the Lunar Module?

The Cuban Missile Crisis, October 1962

NATIONAL GEOGRAPHIC

▲ Fidel Castro in 1963

Soviet missile sites
American quarantine zone

October 27, 1962: a U2 spy plane is shot down over Cuba

UNITED STATES

Gulf of Mexico

Miami

ATLANTIC OCEAN

BAHAMAS

TROPIC OF CANCER

Havana

CUBA

Guantanamo

Site of the Bay of Pigs Invasion: launched Apr. 15, 1961

Caribbean Sea

JAMAICA

HAITI

0   200 kilometers
0   200 miles
Lambert Conformal Equal-Area projection

▼ USS Vesole intercepts a Soviet ship during the U.S. blockade on Cuba.

▲ The presence of missiles in Cuba was confirmed by aerial photographs.

Analyzing GEOGRAPHY

1. **Location** Near what major Cuban city are the missiles placed?
2. **Regions** What is the distance from those missiles to Miami?
3. **Place** Where in Cuba did the Bay of Pigs invasion begin?

Maps In Motion See StudentWorks™ Plus or glencoe.com.

The Berlin Wall Goes Up

Kennedy faced another foreign policy challenge beginning in June 1961, when he met with Soviet Premier Nikita Khrushchev in Vienna, Austria. Khrushchev wanted to stop the flood of Germans pouring out of Communist East Germany into West Berlin. He demanded that the Western powers recognize East Germany and that the United States, Great Britain, and France withdraw from Berlin, a city lying completely within East Germany. Kennedy refused and reaffirmed the West's commitment to West Berlin.

Khrushchev retaliated by building a wall through Berlin, blocking movement between the Soviet sector and the rest of the city. Guards posted along the wall shot at many of those attempting to escape from the East. For nearly 30 years afterward, the **Berlin Wall** stood as a visible symbol of Cold War divisions.

The Cuban Missile Crisis

By far the most terrifying crisis of the Kennedy era occurred the next year. During the summer of 1962, American intelligence agencies learned that Soviet technicians and equipment had arrived in Cuba and that military construction was in progress. On October 22, President Kennedy announced on television that American spy planes had taken aerial photographs showing that the Soviet Union had placed long-range missiles in Cuba. Enemy missiles stationed so close to the United States posed a dangerous threat.

Kennedy ordered a naval blockade to stop the delivery of more missiles, demanded the existing missile sites be dismantled, and warned that if attacked, the United States would respond fully against the Soviet Union. Still, work on the missile sites continued. Nuclear holocaust seemed imminent.

Then, after a flurry of secret negotiations, the Soviet Union offered a deal. It would **remove** the missiles if the United States promised not to invade Cuba and to remove its missiles from Turkey near the Soviet border. The reality was that neither Kennedy nor Khrushchev wanted nuclear war. "Only lunatics . . . who themselves want to perish and before they die destroy the world, could do this," wrote the Soviet leader. On October 28, the leaders reached an agreement. Kennedy publicly agreed not to invade Cuba and privately agreed to remove the Turkish missiles; the Soviets agreed to remove their missiles from Cuba. The world could breathe again.

The Cuban missile crisis forced the United States and the Soviet Union to consider the consequences of nuclear war. In August 1963, the two countries concluded years of negotiation by agreeing to a treaty that banned testing nuclear weapons in the atmosphere.

In the long run, however, the missile crisis had ominous consequences. The humiliating retreat the United States forced on the Soviet leadership undermined the position of Nikita Khrushchev and contributed to his fall from power a year later. The crisis also exposed the Soviets' military inferiority and prompted a dramatic Soviet arms buildup over the next two decades. This buildup contributed to a comparable military increase in the United States in the early 1980s.

Death of a President

Soon after the Senate ratified the test ban treaty, John F. Kennedy's presidency ended shockingly and tragically. On November 22, 1963, Kennedy and his wife traveled to Texas. As the presidential motorcade rode slowly through the crowded streets of Dallas, gunfire rang out. Someone had shot the president twice—once in the throat and once in the head. Horrified government officials sped Kennedy to a nearby hospital, where he was pronounced dead moments later.

Lee Harvey Oswald, the man accused of killing Kennedy, appeared to be a confused and embittered Marxist who had spent time in the Soviet Union. He himself was shot to death while in police custody two days after the assassination. The bizarre situation led some to speculate that the second gunman, local nightclub owner Jack Ruby, killed Oswald to protect others involved in the crime. In 1964 a national commission headed by Chief Justice Warren concluded that Oswald was the lone assassin. The report of the **Warren Commission** left some questions unanswered, and theories about a conspiracy to kill the president have persisted, though none has gained wide acceptance.

In the wake of the assassination, the United States and much of the world went into mourning. Thousands traveled to Washington, D.C., and waited in a line several miles long outside the Capitol to walk silently past the president's flag-draped casket.

Kennedy was president for little more than 1,000 days. Yet he made a profound impression on most Americans. Kennedy's successor, Vice President Lyndon Baines Johnson, set out to promote many of the programs that Kennedy left unfinished.

Reading Check **Summarizing** How was the Cuban missile crisis resolved?

Section 2 REVIEW

Vocabulary

1. **Explain** the significance of: flexible response, Peace Corps, space race, Berlin Wall, Warren Commission.

Main Ideas

2. **Explaining** What were the goals of the Alliance for Progress?

3. **Discussing** How did Kennedy and Khrushchev reach an agreement to end the Cuban missile crisis? What were the details of this agreement?

Critical Thinking

4. **Big Ideas** What was the role of foreign aid in relations between the United States and Latin America?

5. **Organizing** Use a graphic organizer similar to the one below to list the programs that Kennedy used to reduce the threat of nuclear war and to try to stem communism.

6. **Analyzing Visuals** Look at the photograph of John Glenn on page 604. What is the name of his craft, and why do you think the name might have been chosen?

Writing About History

7. **Descriptive Writing** Assume the role of an American citizen during the Cuban missile crisis. Write a journal entry describing the mood of the country during that time.

History ONLINE

Study Central™ To review this section, go to glencoe.com and click on Study Central.

TIME NOTEBOOK

Eyewitness

On May 22, 1964, **PRESIDENT LYNDON JOHNSON** *delivered a speech in Ann Arbor, Michigan, outlining his domestic agenda that would become known as "The Great Society." Speechwriter and policy adviser Richard Goodwin watched the speech on videotape the next morning back in Washington. He recalls his reaction:*

Then, with the cheers, at first muted as if the audience were surprised at their own response, then mounting toward unrestrained, accepting delight, Johnson concluded: "There are those timid souls who say . . . we are condemned to a soulless wealth. I do not agree. We have the power to shape civilization. . . . But we need your will, your labor, your hearts. . . . So let us from this moment begin our work, so that in the future men will look back and say: It was then, after a long and weary way, that man turned the exploits of his genius to the full enrichment of his life."

Watching the film in the White House basement, almost involuntarily I added my applause to the tumultuous acclaim coming from the sound track. . . . I clapped for the President, and for our country.

WHAT IS A PIP, ANYWAY?

Match these rock 'n' roll headliners with their supporting acts.

1. Paul Revere and
2. Martha and
3. Gary Puckett and
4. Gladys Knight and
5. Smokey Robinson and
6. Diana Ross and

a. the Union Gap
b. the Supremes
c. the Miracles
d. the Vandellas
e. the Raiders
f. the Pips

answers: 1. e; 2. d; 3. a; 4. f; 5. c; 6. b

VERBATIM

❝Is there any place we can catch them? What can we do? Are we working 24 hours a day? Can we go around the moon before them?❞

PRESIDENT JOHN F. KENNEDY,
to Lyndon B. Johnson, after hearing that Soviet cosmonaut Yuri Gagarin had orbited the Earth, 1961

❝It was quite a day. I don't know what you can say about a day when you see four beautiful sunsets. . . . This is a little unusual, I think.❞

COLONEL JOHN GLENN,
in orbit, 1962

❝There are tens of millions of Americans who are beyond the welfare state. Taken as a whole there is a culture of poverty . . . bad health, poor housing, low levels of aspiration and high levels of mental distress. Twenty percent of a nation, some 32,000,000.❞

MICHAEL HARRINGTON,
The Culture of Poverty, 1962

❝I have a dream.❞

MARTIN LUTHER KING JR.,
1963

❝I don't see an American dream; . . . I see an American nightmare . . . . Three hundred and ten years we worked in this country without a dime in return.❞

MALCOLM X,
1964

❝The Great Society rests on abundance and liberty for all. It demands an end to poverty and racial injustice.❞

LYNDON B. JOHNSON,
1964

❝In 1962, the starving residents of an isolated Indian village received 1 plow and 1,700 pounds of seeds. They ate the seeds.❞

PEACE CORPS AD,
1965

Space Race

Want to capture some of the glamour and excitement of space exploration? Create a new nickname for your city. You won't be the first.

CITY	NICKNAME
Danbury, CT	Space Age City
Muscle Shoals, AL	Space Age City
Houston, TX	Space City, USA
Galveston, TX	Space Port, USA
Cape Kennedy, FL	Spaceport, USA
Blacksburg, VA	Space Age Community
Huntsville, AL	~~Rocket City, USA~~
	~~Space City, USA~~
	~~Space Capital of the Nation~~
	Space Capital of the World

RALPH MORSE/TIMEPIX

John Glenn, first American to orbit Earth

Milestones

PERFORMED IN ENGLISH, 1962. THE CATHOLIC MASS, following Pope John XXIII's Second Vatican Council. "Vatican II" allows the Latin mass to be translated into local languages around the world.

ENROLLED, 1962. JAMES MEREDITH, at the University of Mississippi, following a Supreme Court ruling that ordered his admission to the previously segregated school. Rioting and a showdown with state officials who wished to bar his enrollment preceded Meredith's entrance to classes.

BROKEN, 1965. 25-DAY FAST BY CÉSAR CHÁVEZ, labor organizer. His protest convinced others to join his nonviolent strike against the grape growers; shoppers boycotted table grapes in sympathy.

STRIPPED, 1967. MUHAMMAD ALI, of his heavyweight champion title, after refusing induction into the army following a rejection of his application for conscientious objector status. The boxer was arrested, given a five-year sentence, and fined $10,000.

PICKETED, 1968. THE MISS AMERICA PAGEANT in Atlantic City, by protesters who believe the contest's emphasis on women's physical beauty is degrading and minimizes the importance of women's intellect.

AP

CRITICAL THINKING

1. Determining Cause and Effect Who did the Voting Rights Act of 1965 help more—whites or African Americans? Explain your answer.

2. Speculating Why do you think President Kennedy was eager to best the Soviets in space?

The Great Society

Guide to Reading

Big Ideas
Individual Action President Lyndon B. Johnson relied on his experience and persuasiveness to get civil rights and antipoverty bills enacted.

Content Vocabulary
- consensus (p. 611)

Academic Vocabulary
- confine (p. 613)
- subsidy (p. 614)

People and Events to Identify
- War on Poverty (p. 611)
- VISTA (p. 612)
- Barry Goldwater (p. 612)
- Great Society (p. 613)
- Medicare (p. 613)
- Medicaid (p. 613)
- Head Start (p. 614)
- Robert Weaver (p. 614)

Reading Strategy
Organizing As you read about Lyndon Johnson's presidency, complete a graphic organizer similar to the one below to list the social and economic programs started during his administration.

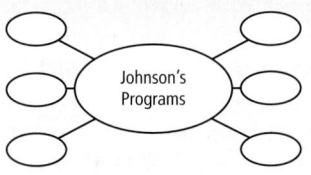
Johnson's Programs

Lyndon B. Johnson had decades of experience in Congress and was skilled in getting legislation enacted. When he became president, he moved quickly to push for passage of a civil rights bill and antipoverty legislation.

Johnson Takes the Reins

MAIN Idea President Johnson's experience in Congress helped him push through a civil rights bill and new laws to fight poverty.

HISTORY AND YOU How do you think someone's early life affects his or her career choices? Read on to learn how Lyndon Johnson's early life prepared him for the presidency.

At 2:38 P.M. on November 22, 1963, just hours after President Kennedy had been pronounced dead, Lyndon B. Johnson stood in the cabin of *Air Force One*, the president's plane, with Kennedy's widow on one side of him and his wife, Claudia, known as "Lady Bird," on the other. Johnson raised his right hand, placed his left hand on a Bible, and took the oath of office.

Within days of the assassination, Johnson appeared before Congress and urged the nation to move forward and build on Kennedy's legacy: "The ideas and ideals which [Kennedy] so nobly represented must and will be translated into effective action," he declared. "John Kennedy's death commands what his life conveyed— that America must move forward."

The United States that President Lyndon B. Johnson inherited from John F. Kennedy appeared to be a booming, bustling place. Away from the nation's affluent suburbs, however, was another country, one inhabited by the poor, the ill-fed, the ill-housed, and the ill-educated. Writer Michael Harrington examined the nation's impoverished areas in his 1962 book, *The Other America*. Harrington claimed that, while the truly poor numbered almost 50 million, they remained largely hidden in city slums, in Appalachia, in the Deep South, and on Native American reservations. Soon after taking office, Lyndon Johnson decided to launch an antipoverty crusade.

Johnson's Leadership Style

Lyndon Baines Johnson was born and raised in the "hill country" of central Texas, near the banks of the Pedernales River. He remained a Texan in his heart, and his style posed a striking contrast with Kennedy's. He was a man of impressive stature who spoke directly, convincingly, and even roughly at times.

The Other America

When President Johnson launched the War on Poverty in 1964, he wanted programs that would help all impoverished Americans, rural and urban.

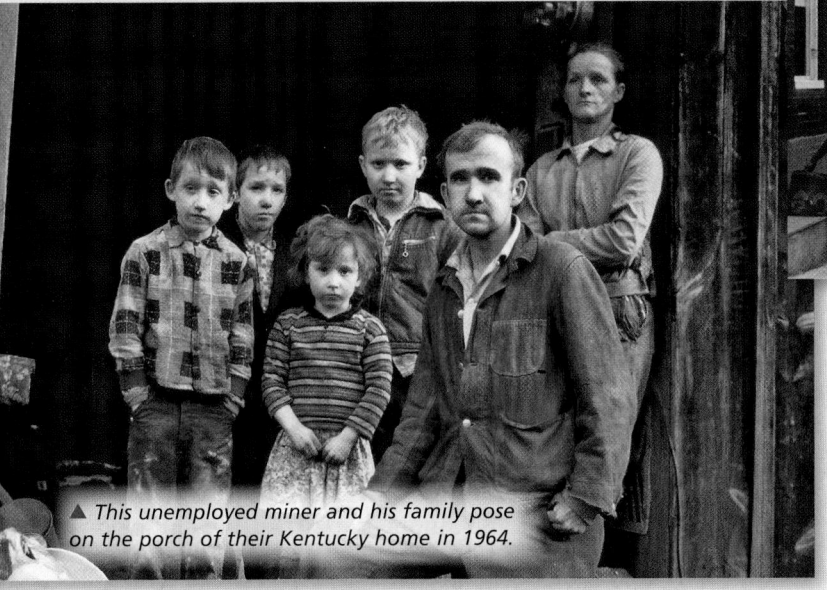

▲ This unemployed miner and his family pose on the porch of their Kentucky home in 1964.

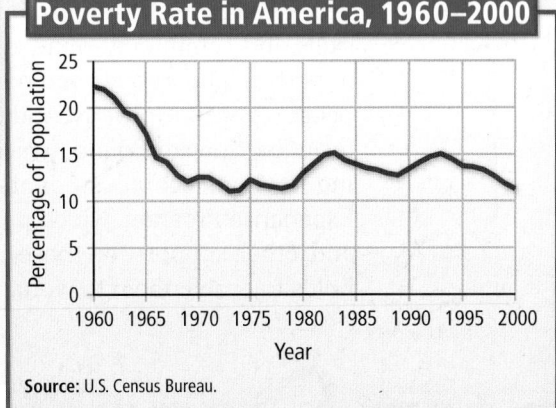

▲ Low-income residents sweep the front stoops of their row houses in Baltimore, Maryland, in the early 1960s.

Analyzing VISUALS   DBQ

1. **Evaluating** Do you find anything hopeful in the photographs shown?
2. **Interpreting** Based on the data in the chart, how successful was Johnson's War on Poverty?

Poverty Rate in America, 1960–2000

Percentage of population (0–25)
Year: 1960 1965 1970 1975 1980 1985 1990 1995 2000

Source: U.S. Census Bureau.

Johnson had honed his style in long years of public service. By the time he became president at age 55, he already had 26 years of congressional experience behind him. He had been a congressional staffer, a member of the House of Representatives, a senator, Senate majority leader, and vice president.

During his career Johnson earned a reputation as a man who got things done. He did favors, twisted arms, bargained, flattered, and threatened. With every technique he could think of, Johnson sought to find **consensus,** or general agreement. His ability to build coalitions had made him one of the most effective and powerful leaders in the Senate's history.

A War on Poverty

Why was this powerful man so concerned about poor people? Although Johnson liked to exaggerate the poor conditions of his child-

hood for dramatic effect, he had in fact known hard times. He had also seen extreme poverty firsthand in a brief career as a teacher in a low-income area. Johnson believed deeply in social action. He felt that a wealthy, powerful government could and should try to improve the lives of its citizens. Kennedy himself had said of Johnson, "He really cares about this nation." Finally, there was Johnson's ambition. He wanted history to portray him as a great president. Attacking poverty was a good place to begin.

Kennedy had plans for an antipoverty program and a civil rights bill before his death. President Johnson knew that any program linked to the slain president would be very popular. In his State of the Union address in 1964, Johnson told his audience: "Unfortunately, many Americans live on the outskirts of hope, some because of their poverty and some because of their color and all too many because of both." He concluded by declaring an "unconditional **War on Poverty** in America."

By the summer of 1964, Johnson had convinced Congress to pass the Economic Opportunity Act. This legislation attacked inadequate public services, illiteracy, and unemployment as three major causes of poverty. The act established 10 new programs within a new government agency, the Office of Economic Opportunity (OEO). Many of the new programs were directed at young Americans living in inner cities.

The Neighborhood Youth Corps provided work-study programs to help underprivileged young men and women earn a high school diploma or college degree. The Job Corps helped unemployed people ages 16–21 acquire job skills. One of the more dramatic programs introduced was **VISTA** (Volunteers in Service to America), which was essentially a domestic Peace Corps. VISTA put young people with skills and community-minded ideals to work in poor neighborhoods and rural areas to help people overcome poverty. Additional programs included Upward Bound, which offered tutoring to high school students, and a Work Experience Program, which provided day care and other support for those in poor households to enable them to work.

The Election of 1964

In April 1964 *Fortune* magazine observed, "Lyndon Johnson has achieved a breadth of public approval few observers would have believed possible when he took office." Johnson had little time to enjoy such praise, for he was soon to run for the office he had first gained through a tragic event.

The Republican candidate in the 1964 election was Senator **Barry Goldwater** of Arizona. Known for his strong conservatism, he set the tone for his campaign when he accepted his party's nomination, declaring, "Extremism in the defense of liberty is no vice! And let me remind you also that moderation in the pursuit of justice is no virtue!"

Few Americans were ready to embrace Goldwater's message, which seemed too aggressive for a nation nervous about nuclear war. On Election Day, Johnson won in a landslide, gaining more than 61 percent of the popular vote and winning all but six states in the Electoral College.

Reading Check **Examining** What inspired the War on Poverty? Why was Johnson able to convince Congress to pass it?

PAST & PRESENT

VISTA Continues the War on Poverty

Volunteers in Service to America (VISTA) began in 1965 as part of President Johnson's War on Poverty. Its focus was to help people help themselves, offering money and programs to low-income communities. Many young people during the idealistic 1960s who weren't able to serve abroad in the Peace Corps program chose instead to work with VISTA. Since the program began, more than 140,000 people have served.

In 1993 VISTA became part of the government agency AmeriCorps. Today, more than 1,200 projects across the nation attempt to make gains in bridging the technology gap, increase housing opportunities, improve health care services, and strengthen community organizations. Volunteers, who must be at least 18, usually work for a year in VISTA-sponsored projects through local, state, or federal agencies or nonprofit, public, or private organizations. In 2006 VISTA had nearly 6,000 volunteers.

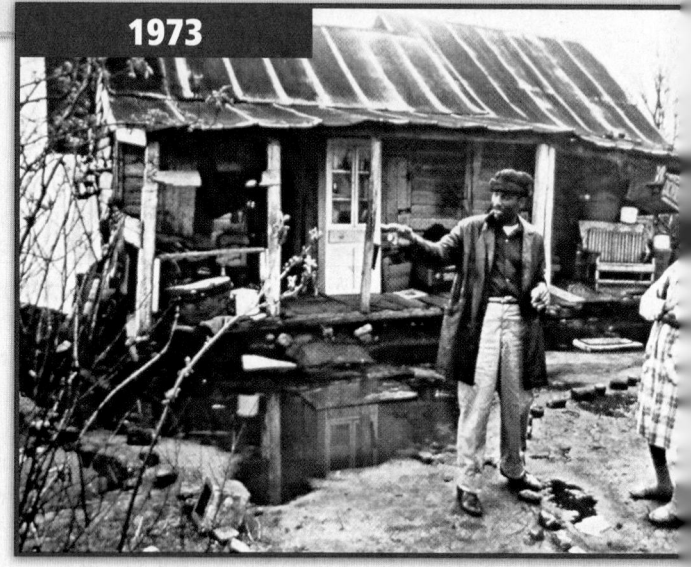

1973

▲ *In 1973, Leroy Sneed was a VISTA member in his hometown of Mitchellville, South Carolina, where he was involved in home-repair and community organizing. Here he talks with a homeowner about rebuilding or repairing her home.*

The Great Society

MAIN Idea Great Society programs provided assistance to disadvantaged Americans.

HISTORY AND YOU What reforms do you think might help reduce poverty today? Read on to learn about the antipoverty programs initiated by President Johnson.

After his election, Johnson began working with Congress to create the "**Great Society**" he had promised during his campaign. In this same period, major goals of the civil rights movement were achieved through the Civil Rights Act of 1964, which barred discrimination of many kinds, and the Voting Rights Act of 1965, which protected voters from discriminatory practices.

Johnson's goals were consistent with the times for several reasons. The civil rights movement had brought the grievances of African Americans to the forefront, reminding many that equality of opportunity had yet to be realized. Economics also supported Johnson's goal. The economy was strong, and many believed it would remain so indefinitely. There was no reason to believe, therefore, that poverty could not be significantly reduced.

Johnson elaborated on the Great Society's goals during a speech at the University of Michigan in May of 1964. It was clear that the president did not intend only to expand relief to the poor or to **confine** government efforts to material things. The president wanted, he said, to build a better society "where leisure is a welcome chance to build and reflect, . . . where the city of man serves not only the needs of the body and the demands of commerce but the desire for beauty and the hunger for community."

This ambitious vision encompassed more than 60 programs that were initiated between 1965 and 1968. Among the most significant programs were **Medicare** and **Medicaid.** Health care reform had been a major issue since the days of Harry Truman. By the 1960s, public support for better health care benefits had solidified. Medicare had especially strong support since it was directed at all senior citizens. In 1965 approximately half of all Americans over the age of 65 had no health insurance.

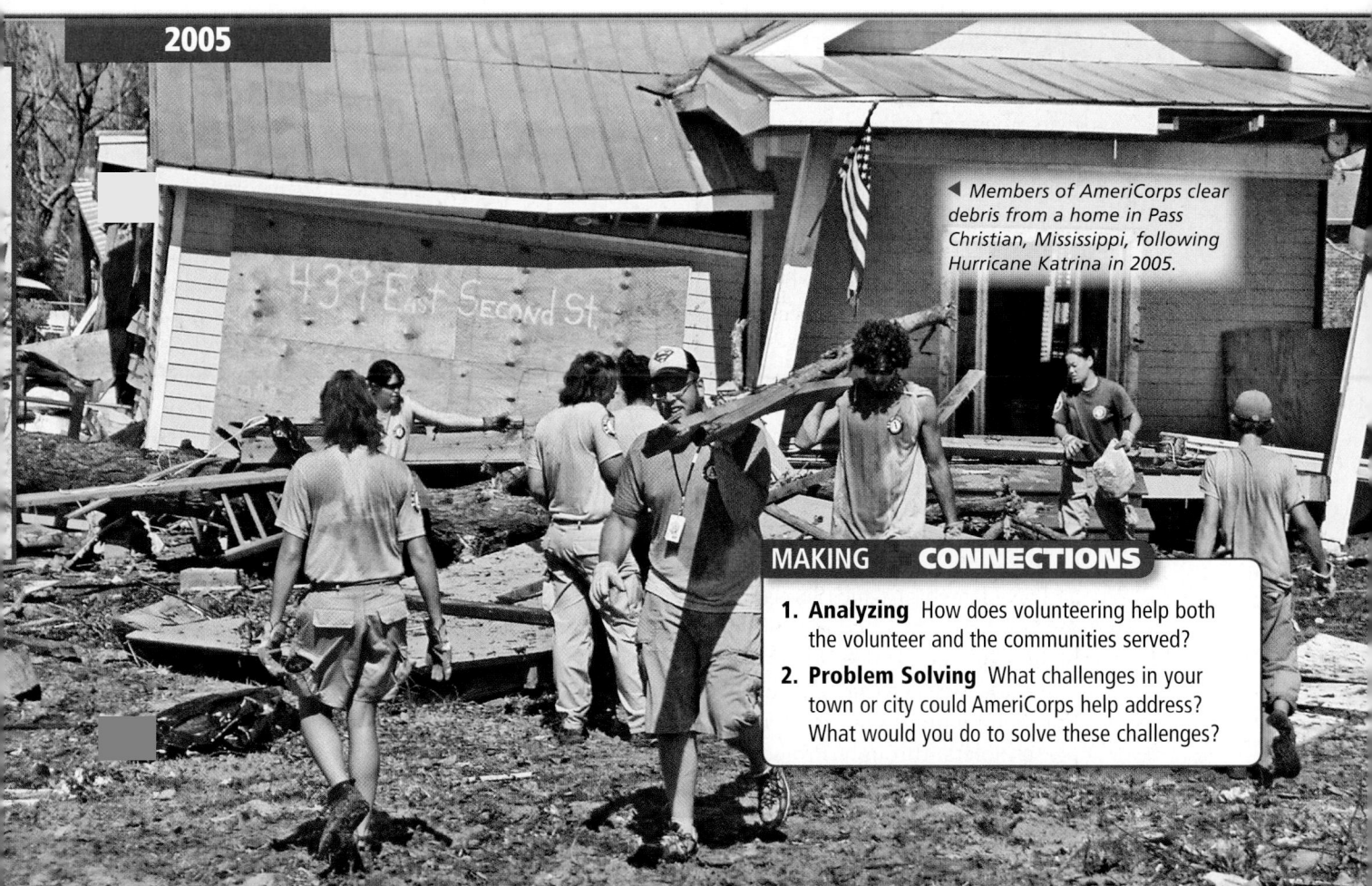

2005

◀ Members of AmeriCorps clear debris from a home in Pass Christian, Mississippi, following Hurricane Katrina in 2005.

MAKING CONNECTIONS

1. **Analyzing** How does volunteering help both the volunteer and the communities served?

2. **Problem Solving** What challenges in your town or city could AmeriCorps help address? What would you do to solve these challenges?

What Was the Great Society?

Health and Welfare

Medicare (1965) established a comprehensive health insurance program for all senior citizens; financed through the Social Security system.

Medicaid (1965) provided health and medical assistance to low-income families; funded through federal and state governments.

Child Nutrition Act (1966) established a school breakfast program and expanded the school lunch and milk programs to improve nutrition.

Education

Elementary and Secondary Education Act (1965) targeted aid to students and funded related activities such as adult education and education counseling.

Higher Education Act (1965) supported college tuition scholarships, student loans, and work-study programs for low- and middle-income students.

Project Head Start (1965) funded a preschool program for disadvantaged children.

The War on Poverty

Office of Economic Opportunity (1964) oversaw many programs to improve life in inner cities, including Job Corps, an education and job training program for at-risk youth.

Housing and Urban Development Act (1965) established new housing subsidy programs and made federal loans and public housing grants easier to obtain.

Demonstration Cities and Metropolitan Development Act (1966) revitalized urban areas through a variety of social and economic programs.

Consumer and Environmental Protection

Water Quality Act and Clean Air Acts (1965) supported development of standards and goals for water and air quality.

Highway Safety Act (1966) improved federal, state, and local coordination and created training standards for emergency medical technicians.

Fair Packaging and Labeling Act (1966) required all consumer products to have true and informative labels.

Analyzing VISUALS

1. **Interpreting** What was the purpose of the Water Quality and Clean Air Acts of 1965?

2. **Evaluating** Which of the Great Society programs do you think had the most effect on American life? Why do you think so?

Johnson convinced Congress to set up Medicare as a health insurance program funded through the Social Security system. Medicare's twin program, Medicaid, financed health care for welfare recipients who were living below the poverty line. Like the New Deal's Social Security program, both programs created what have been called "entitlements," that is, they entitle certain categories of Americans to benefits. Today, the cost of these programs has become a permanent part of the federal budget.

Great Society programs also strongly supported education. For Johnson, who had taught school as a young man, education was a personal passion. Vice President Hubert Humphrey once said that Johnson "was a nut on education.... [He] believed in it, just like some people believe in miracle cures."

The Elementary and Secondary Education Act of 1965 granted millions of dollars to public and private schools for textbooks, library materials, and special education programs. Efforts to improve education also extended to preschoolers through Project **Head Start.**

Administered by the Office of Economic Opportunity, Head Start was directed at disadvantaged children who had "never looked at a picture book or scribbled with a crayon." Another program, Upward Bound, was designed to prepare low-income teenagers for college.

Improvements in health and education were only the beginning of the Great Society programs. Conditions in the cities—poor schools, crime, slum housing, poverty, and pollution—blighted the lives of those who dwelled there. Johnson urged Congress to act on several pieces of legislation addressing urban issues. One created a new cabinet agency, the Department of Housing and Urban Development, in 1965. Its first secretary, **Robert Weaver,** was the first African American to serve in the cabinet. A broad-based program informally called "Model Cities" authorized federal **subsidies** to many cities. The funds, matched by local and state contributions, supported programs to improve transportation, health care, housing, and policing. Since many urban areas lacked sufficient or affordable housing, legislation also authorized about $8 billion to build houses for low- and middle-income people.

One notable Great Society measure changed the composition of the American population: the Immigration Act of 1965. This act eliminated the national origins system established in the 1920s, which had given preference to northern European immigrants. The new measure opened wider the door of the United States to new-comers from all parts of Europe, as well as from Asia and Africa.

The Great Society's Legacy

The Great Society programs touched nearly every aspect of American life and improved thousands, perhaps millions, of lives. In the years since President Johnson left office, however, debate has continued over whether the Great Society was truly a success.

In many ways, the impact of the Great Society was limited. In his rush to accomplish as much as possible, Johnson did not cal-culate exactly how his programs might work. As a result, some of them did not work as well as hoped. Furthermore, the programs grew so quickly they were often unmanageable and difficult to evaluate.

Cities, states, and groups eligible for aid began to expect imme-diate and life-changing benefits. These expectations left many feeling frustrated and angry. Other Americans opposed the mas-sive growth of federal programs and criticized the Great Society for intruding too much into their lives.

A lack of funds also hindered the effectiveness of Great Society programs. When Johnson attempted to fund both his grand domestic agenda and the increasingly costly war in Vietnam, the Great Society eventually suffered. Some Great Society initiatives have survived to the present, however. These include Medicare and Medicaid, two cabinet agencies—the Department of Transportation and the Department of Housing and Urban Development (HUD)—and Project Head Start. Overall, the pro-grams provided some important benefits to poorer communities and gave political and administrative experience to minority groups.

An important legacy of the Great Society was the questions it produced. How can the federal government help disadvantaged citizens? How much government help can a society provide with-out weakening the private sector? How much help can people receive without losing motivation to fight against hardships on their own?

Lyndon Johnson took office determined to change the United States in a way few other presidents had attempted. If he fell short, it was perhaps that the goals he set were so high. In evaluating the administration's efforts, the *New York Times* wrote, "The walls of the ghettos are not going to topple overnight, nor is it possible to wipe out the heritage of generations of social, economic, and educa-tional deprivation by the stroke of a Presidential pen."

Reading Check **Summarizing** What were the Great Society programs, and what was their impact?

Section 3 REVIEW

Vocabulary

1. **Explain** the significance of: consensus, War on Poverty, VISTA, Barry Goldwater, Great Society, Medicare, Medicaid, Head Start, Robert Weaver.

Main Ideas

2. **Analyzing** How did Johnson's War on Poverty strive to ensure greater fairness in American society?

3. **Describing** Which Great Society pro-grams supported education? How did these programs help?

Critical Thinking

4. **Big Ideas** How did President Johnson carry on the ideals of President Kennedy?

5. **Organizing** Use a graphic organizer similar to the one below to list five of the Great Society initiatives that have survived to the present.

Great Society Initiatives

6. **Analyzing Visuals** Look at the graph on page 611. When was poverty at its lowest in the U.S.?

Writing About History

7. **Descriptive Writing** Assume the role of a biographer. Write a chapter in a biogra-phy of Lyndon Johnson in which you com-pare and contrast his leadership style to that of John Kennedy.

History ONLINE

Study Central™ To review this section, go to glencoe.com and click on Study Central.

Domestic Programs of the 1960s

- A growing awareness of poverty, as well as concern for women's rights and the rights of various minority groups, leads to a series of new programs known as the War on Poverty and the Great Society.

- The President's Commission on the Status of Women is established and the Equal Pay Act of 1963 is passed.

- New programs aid the developmentally disabled.

- Office of Economic Opportunity is established to fight poverty, illiteracy, unemployment, and disease.

- Civil Rights Act of 1964 prohibits race discrimination and social segregation, and the Voting Rights Act protects universal suffrage.

- Medicare and Medicaid Acts are passed to provide federal medical aid to senior citizens and poor.

- Elementary and Secondary Education Act is passed to increase aid for public schools.

▲ *VISTA volunteers work to curb delinquency by counseling and helping troubled children and their families.*

▲ *The U.S. Navy ship, the* Vesole, *intercepts the missile-carrying Soviet ship* Potzunov *as it leaves Cuba during the Cuban Missile Crisis.*

Foreign Policy of the 1960s

- Kennedy pledges to end Eisenhower's reliance on nuclear weapons and to use new methods to prevent the spread of communism.

- Kennedy introduces the "flexible response" policy—building up both nuclear missiles and conventional forces.

- The United States pledges aid to struggling Latin American nations.

- Peace Corps sends volunteers to help in poor countries.

- The United States aids Cuban exiles trying to overthrow Castro, but their landing at the Bay of Pigs fails.

- Soviet missiles in Cuba lead to the Cuban missile crisis; the United States blockades Cuba and the Soviets remove the missiles.

- The U.S. and Soviet Union sign the Nuclear Test Ban Treaty.

Supreme Court Cases of the 1960s

- Led by Chief Justice Earl Warren, the Supreme Court makes a series of decisions that dramatically change American society and the federal government's relationship to citizens.

- In *Reynolds* v. *Sims* the Court requires states to adhere to the principle of one person, one vote.

- In four cases, *Mapp* v. *Ohio*, *Gideon* v. *Wainwright*, *Escobedo* v. *Illinois*, and *Miranda* v. *Arizona*, the Court extends due process, giving more protection to those accused of crimes.

- In *Abington School District* v. *Schemp*, the Court rules that states cannot require prayer and Bible readings in public schools.

▲ *Clarence Earl Gideon was denied counsel during a trial in Florida in 1961. His case eventually went to the Supreme Court.*

Reviewing Vocabulary

Directions: Choose the word or words that best completes the sentence.

1. Reapportionment, as ruled on by the Warren Court, is

   A the requirement of separate but equal facilities for schools.

   B the process courts must follow when trying cases to treat individuals fairly.

   C the way in which political districts are drawn based on population changes.

   D the separation of church and state for schools.

2. The policy called _____ helped nations resist Communism by building up conventional troops and weapons.

   A military-industrial complex

   B containment

   C mutual assured destruction

   D flexible response

3. _____ means that the law may not treat individuals unfairly or unreasonably and must treat all individuals equally.

   A Reapportionment

   B Consensus

   C Due process

   D Judicial review

4. Following World War II, the Cold War era featured competition between the United States and the Soviet Union in everything from diplomacy and the military to

   A architecture.

   B the space race.

   C television.

   D population growth.

5. President Johnson was successful at building coalitions and finding a _____ , or general agreement.

   A discord

   B consensus

   C accord

   D variance

Reviewing Main Ideas

Directions: Choose the best answers to the following questions.

Section 1 *(pp. 596–601)*

6. During the presidential election of 1960, Kennedy focused his campaign message on

   A bridging the "missile gap" between the United States and the Soviet Union.

   B continuing the foreign policy of the current administration.

   C how the Democrats' fiscal policies would boost inflation and harm the economy.

   D how Catholicism would influence his decision-making as president.

7. Congress defeated which of the following proposals of Kennedy's New Frontier?

   A raising the minimum wage

   B investing funds in defense and space exploration

   C health care for senior citizens

   D providing funds to build low-income housing

8. The Warren Court decision requiring that a defendant in a state court had the right to a lawyer, regardless of his or her ability to pay, was

   A *Engel* v. *Vitale.*

   B *Griswold* v. *Connecticut.*

   C *Plessy* v. *Ferguson.*

   D *Gideon* v. *Wainwright.*

TEST-TAKING

To answer vocabulary questions 2 and 3, first look at the terms listed as answers. See if you can mentally define each one. Then read the question to select the right answer.

Need Extra Help?								
If You Missed Questions . . .	1	2	3	4	5	6	7	8
Go to Page . . .	600	602	601	604	611	596	598	601

Section 2 (pp. 602–607)

9. Kennedy attempted to reduce the threat of nuclear war and stop the spread of communism by

A withdrawing aid from Latin American countries.

B withdrawing troops from limited military conflicts.

C creating the Peace Corps.

D encouraging growth in the automotive industry to assure that capitalism was superior to communism.

10. How did Soviet Premier Nikita Khrushchev respond when Western powers refused to withdraw from West Berlin?

A He sent long-range missiles to Cuba.

B He had a wall built through Berlin to keep East Germans from escaping to West Berlin.

C He enlisted *La Brigada* to invade Cuba and remove Castro from power.

D He had food and supplies airlifted to Berlin to end a blockade by American forces.

Section 3 (pp. 610–615)

11. Which Johnson program provided work-study opportunities to help young people earn high school diplomas or attend college?

A the Neighborhood Youth Corps

B VISTA

C the Peace Corps

D AmeriCorps

12. Medicare and Medicaid were major accomplishments of

A Franklin Roosevelt's New Deal.

B John F. Kennedy's New Frontier.

C Richard Nixon's New Federalism.

D Lyndon Johnson's Great Society.

13. Which idea was part of Johnson's Great Society?

A eliminating government-funded health care for senior citizens

B providing federal aid for education

C opposing civil rights legislation

D increasing foreign aid to Cuba

Critical Thinking

Directions: Choose the best answers to the following questions.

14. How did the Immigration Reform Act of 1965 change the composition of the American population?

A It set strict limits on the number of immigrants admitted to the United States.

B It did not allow any immigrants to enter the United States from Eastern Europe.

C It continued the national origins system, which gave preference to northern European immigrants.

D It opened the United States to individuals from all over the world, including Asia and Africa.

Base your answer to question 15 on the map below and on your knowledge of Chapter 17.

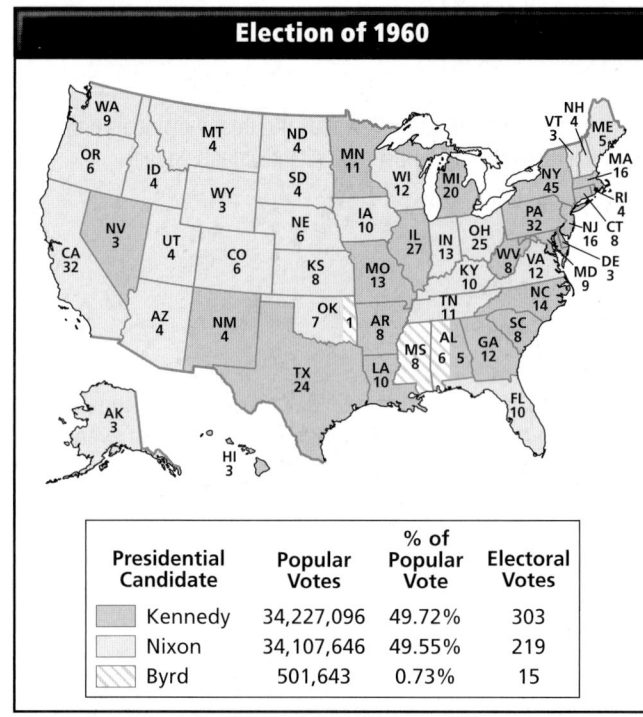

Election of 1960

Presidential Candidate	Popular Votes	% of Popular Vote	Electoral Votes
Kennedy	34,227,096	49.72%	303
Nixon	34,107,646	49.55%	219
Byrd	501,643	0.73%	15

15. Which region of the country gave Kennedy the most electoral votes?

A Pacific Northwest

B Northeast

C Southwest

D Midwest

Need Extra Help?

If You Missed Questions . . .	9	10	11	12	13	14	15
Go to Page . . .	602	606	612	613–614	614	615	R15

GO ON

16. President Lyndon B. Johnson's Great Society is similar to President Franklin D. Roosevelt's New Deal in that both programs

A sought ratification of the Equal Rights Amendment to guarantee equality for women.

B advocated passage of civil rights laws to help African Americans.

C approved efforts by states to reduce taxes for the middle class.

D supported federal funding of programs for the poor.

Analyze the cartoon and answer the question that follows. Base your answer on the cartoon and on your knowledge of Chapter 17.

HERBLOCK'S CARTOON

"Kindly Move Over A Little, Gentlemen"

17. According to the cartoon, what is Johnson trying to do?

A Johnson wants to give more money to the arms race and military establishments.

B Johnson is trying to give health, education, and welfare programs more money.

C Military establishments and arms costs are giving money to social programs.

D Social programs are receiving more money than the military.

Document-Based Questions

Directions: Analyze the document and answer the short-answer questions that follow the document.

Although the standard of living for most Americans rose dramatically throughout the 1960s, some Americans remained mired in poverty. Read the excerpt below in which John Rath discusses his personal experiences with coping with poverty in his sparely furnished room in Chicago:

> *"I come home to an empty room. I don't even have a dog. . . . No, this is not the kind of life I would choose. If a man had a little piece of land or something, a farm, or well . . . anyway, you've got to have something. You sit down in a place like this, you grit your teeth, you follow me? So many of them are doing that, they sit down, they don't know what to do, they go out. I see 'em in the middle of the night, they take a walk. Don't know what to do. Have no home environment, don't have a dog, don't have nothing . . . just a big zero."*
> —quoted in *Division Street: America*

18. What does Rath think might help him to have some purpose in his life?

19. What does he mean when he says: "You sit down in a place like this, you grit your teeth . . . "?

Extended Response

20. Discuss why President Johnson proposed the Great Society and how his initiatives were intended to bring about social change. Then evaluate the extent to which the Great Society succeeded in meeting its goals. Write a well-organized essay that includes an introduction, several paragraphs, and a conclusion. Establish a framework that goes beyond a simple restatement of facts and draws a conclusion about the effectiveness of Johnson's programs.

History ONLINE

For additional test practice, use Self-Check Quizzes—Chapter 17 at glencoe.com.

Need Extra Help?					
If You Missed Questions . . .	16	17	18	19	20
Go to Page . . .	614	R18	619	R19	610–615

The Civil Rights Movement

1954–1968

SECTION 1 The Movement Begins

SECTION 2 Challenging Segregation

SECTION 3 New Civil Rights Issues

Martin Luther King, Jr., and his wife Coretta lead the civil rights march in Selma, Alabama, 1965.

U.S. PRESIDENTS

Eisenhower 1953–1961

Kennedy 1961–1963

1954
- *Brown v. Board of Education* ruling is issued

1955
- Montgomery bus boycott begins in Alabama

1957
- Eisenhower sends troops to Little Rock to ensure integration of a high school

1960
- Greensboro sit-in begins

1963
- The March on Washington, D.C., is held to support the Civil Rights bill

U.S. EVENTS

1953

1957

1961

WORLD EVENTS

1955
- West Germany is admitted to NATO

1957
- Russia launches *Sputnik* into orbit

1960
- France successfully tests nuclear weapons

1962
- Cuban missile crisis erupts

MAKING CONNECTIONS

What Causes Societies to Change?

The civil rights movement gained momentum rapidly after World War II. Decisions by the Supreme Court combined with massive protests by civil rights groups and new federal legislation to finally end racial segregation and disfranchisement in the United States more than 70 years after Southern states had put it in place.

- *Why do you think the civil rights movement made gains in postwar America? What strategies were most effective in winning the battle for civil rights?*

FOLDABLES™

Sequencing Civil Rights Events Create an Accordion Book Foldable to gather information on a time line about various events of the civil rights movement. As you read the chapter, complete the time line by filling in events for roughly 20 years, starting with Roosevelt's Executive Order 8802 of June 1941. The time line should include brief notes on each event.

Johnson
1963–1969

1964
- Civil Rights Act of 1964 passes

1965
- Voting Rights Act passes
- Malcolm X is assassinated

I HAVE A DREAM
Dr. Martin Luther King, Jr.

1968
- Civil Rights Act of 1968 is passed
- Martin Luther King, Jr., is assassinated

1965

1969

1965
- China's Cultural Revolution begins

1967
- Arab-Israeli War brings many Palestinians under Israeli rule

History ONLINE Visit glencoe.com and enter *QuickPass*™ code TAVMT5147c18 for Chapter 18 resources.

Section Audio   **Spotlight Video**

The Movement Begins

Guide to Reading

Big Ideas
Struggles for Rights In the 1950s, African Americans began a movement to win greater legal and social equality.

Content Vocabulary
- "separate but equal" *(p. 622)*
- de facto segregation *(p. 623)*
- sit-in *(p. 624)*

Academic Vocabulary
- facility *(p. 622)*

People and Events to Identify
- Rosa Parks *(p. 622)*
- National Association for the Advancement of Colored People (NAACP) *(p. 622)*
- Thurgood Marshall *(p. 624)*
- Linda Brown *(p. 624)*
- Martin Luther King, Jr. *(p. 626)*
- Southern Christian Leadership Conference (SCLC) *(p. 627)*

Reading Strategy
Organizing Complete a graphic organizer similar to the one below by listing the causes of the civil rights movement.

Civil Rights Movement

After World War II, African Americans and other civil rights supporters challenged segregation in the United States. Their efforts were vigorously opposed by Southern segregationists, but the federal government began to take a firmer stand for civil rights.

The Origins of the Movement

MAIN Idea African Americans won court victories, increased their voting power, and began using "sit-ins" to desegregate public places.

HISTORY AND YOU Are you registered to vote, or do you plan to register when you are 18? Read on to learn how African Americans increased their voting power and worked to desegregate public places.

Prior to the mid 1950s, African Americans struggling for equality had few successes. Jackie Robinson's integration of baseball in 1947 was a dramatic symbol of opportunity, but one baseball player could not transform normal citizens' daily mistreatment. On December 1, 1955, **Rosa Parks** left her job as a seamstress in Montgomery, Alabama, and boarded a bus to go home. In 1955 buses in Montgomery reserved seats in the front for whites and seats in the rear for African Americans. Seats in the middle were open to African Americans, but only if there were few whites on the bus.

Rosa Parks took a seat just behind the white section. Soon, all of the seats on the bus were filled. When the bus driver noticed a white man standing, he told Parks and three other African Americans in her row to get up and let the white man sit down. When Parks did not, the driver then called the Montgomery police.

News of the arrest soon reached E. D. Nixon, a former president of the local chapter of the **National Association for the Advancement of Colored People (NAACP).** Nixon told Parks, "With your permission we can break down segregation on the bus with your case." Parks replied, "If you think it will mean something to Montgomery and do some good, I'll be happy to go along with it."

Rosa Parks did not know that her decision would spark a new era in the civil rights movement. African Americans in Montgomery quickly organized a boycott of the bus system. After decades of segregation and inequality, many African Americans had decided the time had come to demand equal rights.

The struggle would not be easy. The Supreme Court had declared segregation to be constitutional in *Plessy* v. *Ferguson* in 1896. The ruling had established the **"separate but equal"** doctrine. Laws that segregated African Americans were permitted as long as equal **facilities** were provided for them.

People IN HISTORY

Thurgood Marshall
1908–1993

Over his lifetime, Thurgood Marshall made many contributions to the civil rights movement. Perhaps his most famous accomplishment was representing the NAACP in the *Brown* v. *Board of Education* case.

Marshall's speaking style was simple and direct. During the Brown case, Justice Frankfurter asked Marshall for a definition of *equal*. Marshall replied: "*Equal* means getting the same thing, at the same time and in the same place."

Born into a middle-class Baltimore family in 1908, Marshall earned a law degree from Howard University Law School. The school's dean, Charles Hamilton Houston, enlisted Marshall to work for the NAACP. Together, the two laid out the legal strategy for challenging discrimination in many areas of American life. In 1935 Marshall won his first case regarding segregation in state institutions. The decision forced the University of Maryland to integrate. Marshall went on to win 29 of the 32 cases he argued before the Supreme Court, and became known as "Mr. Civil Rights." In 1967 Marshall became the first African American to serve on the Supreme Court, where he continued to be a voice for civil rights. In his view, the Constitution was not perfect, because it had accepted slavery. "The true miracle of the Constitution," he once wrote, "was not the birth of the Constitution, but its life."

How did Thurgood Marshall contribute to the civil rights movement?

The NAACP's Legal Strategy in Action

Even before the famous *Brown* v. *Board of Education* case, Thurgood Marshall had won several cases for the NAACP that chipped away at segregation in the South.

Smith v. *Allwright* (1944): Political parties cannot deny voting rights in party primaries on the basis of race.

Shelley v. *Kraemer* (1948): States cannot enforce private agreements to discriminate on the basis of race in the sale of property.

Sweatt v. *Painter* (1950): Law schools segregated by race are inherently unequal.

After the *Plessy* decision, laws segregating African Americans and whites spread quickly. These laws, nicknamed "Jim Crow" laws, segregated buses, trains, schools, restaurants, pools, parks, and other public facilities. Usually the "Jim Crow" facilities provided for African Americans were of poorer quality than those provided for whites. Areas without laws requiring segregation often had **de facto segregation**—segregation by custom and tradition.

Court Challenges Begin

The civil rights movement had been building for a long time. Since 1909, the NAACP had supported court cases intended to overturn segregation. Over the years, the NAACP achieved some victories. In 1935, for example, the Supreme Court ruled in *Norris* v. *Alabama* that Alabama's exclusion of African Americans from juries violated their right to equal protection under the law. In 1946 the Court ruled in *Morgan* v. *Virginia* that segregation on interstate buses

was unconstitutional. In 1950 it ruled in *Sweatt* v. *Painter* that state law schools had to admit qualified African American applicants, even if parallel black law schools existed.

New Political Power

In addition to a string of court victories, African Americans enjoyed increased political power. Before World War I, most African Americans lived in the South, where they were largely excluded from voting. During the Great Migration, many moved to Northern cities, where they were allowed to vote. Increasingly, Northern politicians sought their votes and listened to their concerns.

During the 1930s, many African Americans benefited from FDR's New Deal programs and began supporting the Democratic Party. This gave the party new strength in the North. This wing of the party was now able to counter Southern Democrats, who often supported segregation.

The Push for Desegregation

During World War II, African American leaders began to use their political power to demand more rights. Their efforts helped end discrimination in wartime factories and increased opportunities for African Americans in the military.

In Chicago in 1942, James Farmer and George Houser founded the Congress of Racial Equality (CORE). CORE began using **sit-ins,** a form of protest first used by union workers in the 1930s. In 1943 CORE attempted to desegregate restaurants that refused to serve African Americans. Using the sit-in strategy, members of CORE went to segregated restaurants. If they were denied service, they sat down and refused to leave. The sit-ins were intended to shame restaurant managers into integrating their restaurants. Using these protests, CORE successfully integrated many restaurants, theaters, and other public facilities in Northern cities including Chicago, Detroit, Denver, and Syracuse.

Brown v. Board of Education

To better understand the court ruling in *Brown v. Board of Education*, read an excerpt from the Court's ruling on page R55 in **Documents in American History.**

After World War II, the NAACP continued to challenge segregation in the courts. From 1939 to 1961, the NAACP's chief counsel and director of its Legal Defense and Education Fund was the brilliant African American attorney **Thurgood Marshall.** After the war, Marshall focused his efforts on ending segregation in public schools.

In 1954 the Supreme Court decided to combine several cases and issue a general ruling on segregation in schools. One of the cases involved a young African American girl named **Linda Brown,** who was denied admission to her neighborhood school in Topeka, Kansas, because of her race. She was told to attend an all-black school across town. With the help of the NAACP, her parents then sued the Topeka school board.

On May 17, 1954, the Supreme Court ruled unanimously in *Brown* v. *Board of Education of Topeka, Kansas,* that segregation in public schools was unconstitutional and violated the equal protection clause of the Fourteenth Amendment. Chief Justice Earl Warren summed up the Court's decision, declaring: "In the field of public education, the doctrine of separate but equal has no place. Separate educational facilities are inherently unequal."

Southern Resistance

The Brown decision marked a dramatic reversal of the precedent established in the *Plessy* v. *Ferguson* case in 1896. *Brown* v. *Board of Education* applied only to public schools, but the ruling threatened the entire system of segregation. Although it convinced many African Americans that the time had come to challenge segregation, it also angered many white Southerners, who became even more determined to defend segregation, regardless of what the Supreme Court ruled.

Although some school districts in border states integrated their schools, anger and opposition was a far more common reaction. In Washington, D.C., Senator Harry F. Byrd of Virginia called on Southerners to adopt "massive resistance" against the ruling. Across the South, hundreds of thousands of white Americans joined citizens' councils to pressure their local governments and school boards into defying the Supreme Court. Many states adopted pupil assignment laws. These laws established elaborate requirements other than race that schools could use to prevent African Americans from attending white schools.

The Supreme Court inadvertently encouraged white resistance when it followed up its decision in *Brown* v. *Board of Education* a year later. The Court ordered school districts to proceed "with all deliberate speed" to end school segregation. The wording was vague enough that many districts were able to keep their schools segregated for many more years.

Massive resistance also appeared in the halls of Congress. In 1956 a group of 101 Southern members of Congress signed the "Southern Manifesto," which denounced the Supreme Court's ruling as "a clear abuse of judicial power" and pledged to use "all lawful means" to reverse the decision. Although the "Southern Manifesto" had no legal standing, the statement encouraged white Southerners to defy the Supreme Court. Not until 1969 did the Supreme Court order all school systems to desegregate "at once" and operate integrated schools "now and hereafter."

Reading Check **Examining** Why was the ruling in *Brown v. Board of Education* so important?

ANALYZING SUPREME COURT CASES

Is Segregation Unconstitutional?

★ *Brown* v. *Board of Education*, 1954

Background to the Cases

One of the most important Supreme Court cases in American history began in 1952, when the Supreme Court agreed to hear the NAACP's case *Brown* v. *Board of Education of Topeka, Kansas,* along with three other cases. They all dealt with the question of whether the principle "separate but equal" established in *Plessy* v. *Ferguson* was constitutional with regard to public schools.

How the Court Ruled

In a unanimous decision in 1954, the Court ruled in favor of Linda Brown and the other plaintiffs. In doing so, it overruled *Plessy* v. *Ferguson* and rejected the idea that equivalent but separate schools for African American and white students were constitutional. The Court held that racial segregation in public schools violates the Fourteenth Amendment's equal protection clause because "Separate educational facilities are inherently unequal." The Court's rejection of "separate but equal" was a major victory for the civil rights movement and led to the overturning of laws requiring segregation in other public places.

▲ *The children involved in the* Brown v. Board of Education *case are shown in this 1953 photograph. They are, from front to back, Vicki Henderson, Donald Henderson, Linda Brown (of the case title), James Emanuel, Nancy Todd, and Katherine Carper. Together, their cases led to the Supreme Court decreeing that public schools could not be segregated on the basis of race.*

<u>PRIMARY SOURCE</u>

The Court's Opinion

"In these days, it is doubtful that any child may reasonably be expected to succeed in life if he is denied the opportunity of an education. Such an opportunity, where the state has undertaken to provide it, is a right which must be made available to all on equal terms. We come then to the question presented: Does segregation of children in public schools solely on the basis of race, even though the physical facilities and other 'tangible' factors may be equal, deprive the children of the minority group of equal educational opportunities? We believe that it does."

—Chief Justice Earl Warren writing for the Court in
Brown v. *Board of Education of Topeka, Kansas*

<u>PRIMARY SOURCE</u>

Dissenting Views

"We regard the decisions of the Supreme Court in the school cases as a clear abuse of judicial power. . . . In the case of *Plessy* v. *Ferguson* in 1896 the Supreme Court expressly declared that under the 14th Amendment no person was denied any of his rights if the States provided separate but equal facilities. . . . This interpretation, restated time and again, became a part of the life of the people of many of the States and confirmed their habits, traditions, and way of life. It is founded on elemental humanity and commonsense, for parents should not be deprived by Government of the right to direct the lives and education of their own children."

—from the "Southern Manifesto"

DBQ Document-Based Questions

1. **Explaining** Why did the Supreme Court find in favor of Linda Brown?
2. **Drawing Conclusions** What is the main argument against the *Brown* decision in the excerpt from the "Southern Manifesto"?
3. **Making Inferences** Do you think that the authors of the "Southern Manifesto" were including African Americans in the last sentence of the excerpt? Why or why not?

The Civil Rights Movement Begins

MAIN Idea The *Brown* v. *Board of Education* ruling ignited protest and encouraged African Americans to challenge other forms of segregation.

HISTORY AND YOU Do you think that one person has the power to change things for the better? Read on to learn how the courage and hard work of individuals helped reform society.

In the midst of the uproar over the *Brown* v. *Board of Education* case, Rosa Parks made her decision to challenge segregation of public transportation. Outraged by Parks's arrest, Jo Ann Robinson, head of a local organization called the Women's Political Council, called on African Americans to boycott Montgomery's buses on the day Rosa Parks appeared in court.

The boycott marked the start of a new era of the civil rights movement among African Americans. Instead of limiting the fight for their rights to court cases, African Americans in large numbers began organizing protests, defying laws that required segregation, and demanding they be treated as equal to whites.

The Montgomery Bus Boycott

The Montgomery bus boycott was a dramatic success. On the afternoon of Rosa Parks's court appearance, several African American leaders formed the Montgomery Improvement Association to run the boycott and to negotiate with city leaders for an end to segregation. They elected a 26-year-old pastor named **Martin Luther King, Jr.,** to lead them.

On the evening of December 5, 1955, a meeting was held at Dexter Avenue Baptist Church, where Dr. King was the pastor. In the deep, resonant tones and powerful phrases that characterized his speaking style, King encouraged the people to continue their protest. "There comes a time, my friends," he said, "when people get tired of being thrown into the abyss of humiliation, where they experience the bleakness of nagging despair." He cautioned, however, that the protest had to be peaceful:

PRIMARY SOURCE

"Now let us say that we are not advocating violence. . . . The only weapon we have in our hands this evening is the weapon of protest. If we were incarcerated behind the iron curtains of a communistic nation—we couldn't do this. If we were trapped in the dungeon of a totalitarian regime—we couldn't do this. But the great glory of American democracy is the right to protest for right!"

—quoted in *Parting the Waters:
America in the King Years*

King had earned a Ph.D. in theology from Boston University. He believed that the only moral way to end segregation and racism was through nonviolent passive resistance. He told his followers, "We must use the weapon of love. We must realize that so many people are taught to hate us that they are not totally responsible for their hate." African Americans, he urged, must say to racists: "We will soon wear you down by our capacity to suffer, and in winning our freedom we will so appeal to your heart and conscience that we will win you in the process."

Turning Point

The Montgomery Bus Boycott

The act of one woman on a bus and the subsequent bus boycott in Montgomery, Alabama, brought civil rights out of the legal arena and turned it into a struggle in which ordinary Americans realized that they could make a difference. Rosa Parks's refusal to give up her seat on the bus to a white man showed that even small acts of defiance could empower people to create change.

The Montgomery bus boycott, which was begun to show support for Parks, became a huge success. It started a chain reaction—the beginning of a mass movement that would dramatically change American society over the next 20 years, and bring to prominence many influential African American leaders, including Martin Luther King, Jr.

ANALYZING HISTORY Drawing Conclusions How did the bus boycott create a mass movement for change?

King drew upon the philosophy and techniques of Indian leader Mohandas Gandhi, who had used nonviolent resistance effectively to challenge British rule in India. Believing in people's ability to transform themselves, King was certain that public opinion would eventually force the government to end segregation.

Stirred by King's powerful words, African Americans in Montgomery continued their boycott for over a year. Instead of riding the bus, they organized car pools or walked to work. Meanwhile, Rosa Parks's legal challenge to bus segregation worked its way through the courts. In November 1956, the Supreme Court affirmed the decision of a special three-judge panel declaring Alabama's laws requiring segregation on buses unconstitutional.

African American Churches

Martin Luther King, Jr., was not the only prominent minister in the bus boycott. Many of the other leaders were African American ministers. The boycott could not have succeeded without the support of the African American churches in the city. As the civil rights movement gained momentum, African American churches continued to play a critical role. They served as forums for many of the protests and planning meetings, and mobilized many of the volunteers for specific civil rights campaigns.

After the Montgomery bus boycott demonstrated that nonviolent protest could be successful, African American ministers led by King established the **Southern Christian Leadership Conference (SCLC)** in 1957. The SCLC set out to eliminate segregation from American society and to encourage African Americans to register to vote. Dr. King served as the SCLC's first president. Under his leadership, the organization challenged segregation at voting booths and in public transportation, housing, and accommodations.

History ONLINE **Student Web Activity** Visit glencoe.com and complete the activity on Rosa Parks.

Reading Check **Summarizing** What role did African American churches play in the civil rights movement?

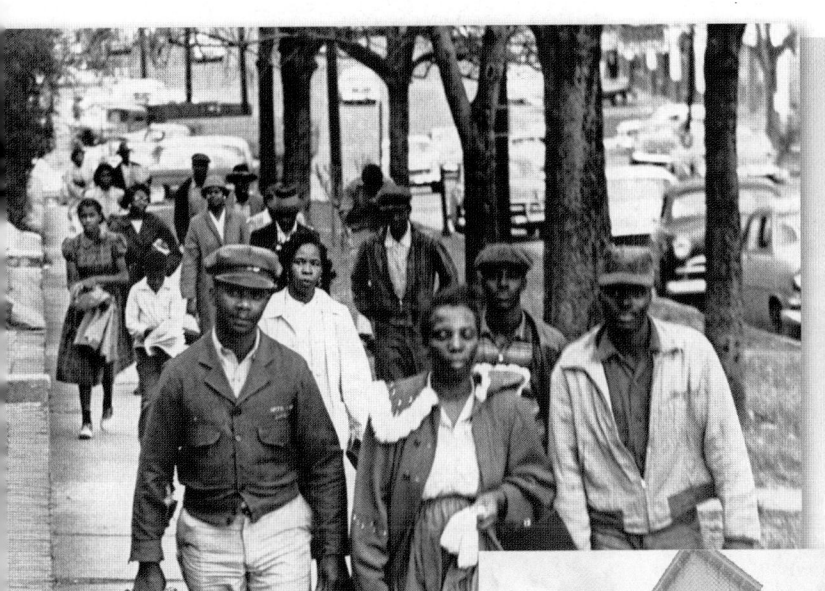

▲ African Americans walk to work during the third month of the Montgomery bus boycott (above). The Dexter Avenue Baptist Church in Montgomery, Alabama (right), was the Reverend Dr. Martin Luther King, Jr.'s, first church as a minister and headquarters for the organizers of the bus boycott.

▲ Rosa Parks rides a newly integrated bus after the successful boycott.

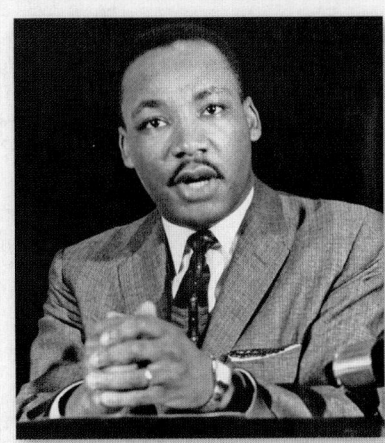

Chapter 18 The Civil Rights Movement **627**

Eisenhower Responds

MAIN Idea President Eisenhower sent the U.S. Army to enforce integration in Arkansas.

HISTORY AND YOU Do you believe that the president should uphold Supreme Court rulings? Read to learn how Eisenhower responded to events in Little Rock, Arkansas.

President Eisenhower sympathized with the civil rights movement and personally disagreed with segregation. Following the precedent set by President Truman, he ordered navy shipyards and veterans' hospitals to desegregate. At the same time, however, Eisenhower disagreed with those who wanted to end segregation through protests and court rulings. He believed segregation and racism would end gradually, as values changed. With the nation in the midst of the Cold War, he worried that challenging white Southerners might divide the nation at a time when the country needed to pull together. Publicly, he refused to endorse the *Brown* v. *Board of Education* decision. Privately, he remarked, "I don't believe you can change the hearts of men with laws or decisions."

Although he believed that the *Brown* v. *Board of Education* decision was wrong, Eisenhower knew he had to uphold the authority of the federal government. As a result, he became the first president since Reconstruction to send troops into the South to protect the rights of African Americans.

Crisis in Little Rock

In September 1957, the school board in Little Rock, Arkansas, won a court order requiring that nine African American students be admitted to Central High, a school with 2,000 white students. The governor of Arkansas, Orval Faubus, was known as a moderate on racial issues, but he was determined to win reelection and began to campaign as a defender of white supremacy. He ordered troops from the Arkansas National Guard to prevent the nine students from entering the school. The next day, as the National Guard troops sur-

PRIMARY SOURCE
Little Rock School Crisis, Arkansas, 1957

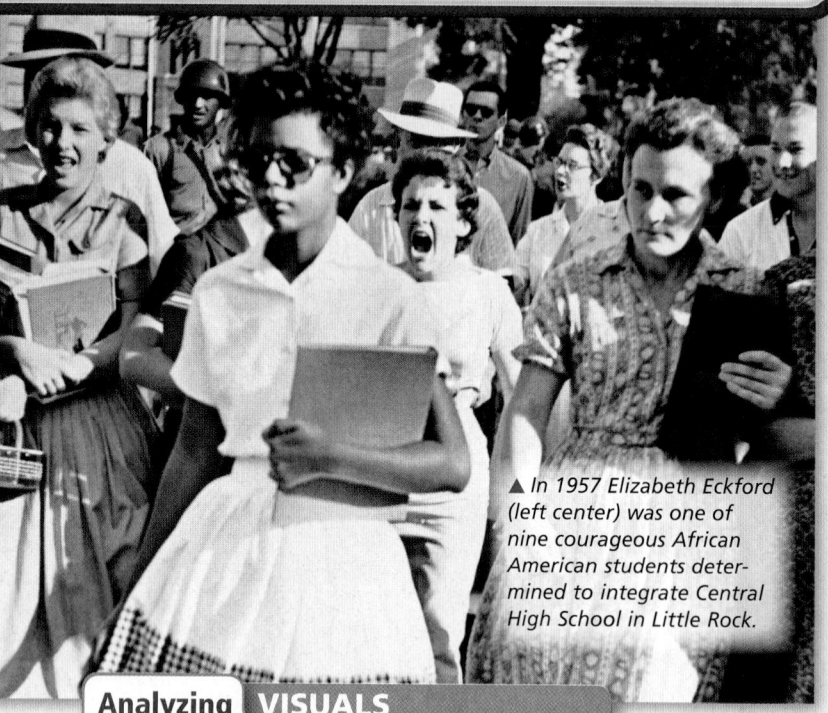

▲ In 1957 Elizabeth Eckford (left center) was one of nine courageous African American students determined to integrate Central High School in Little Rock.

▲ Arkansas governor Orval Faubus sought to block the school's integration. He is shown holding up a paper making his argument that the federal government was abusing its power in forcibly integrating Central High in Little Rock.

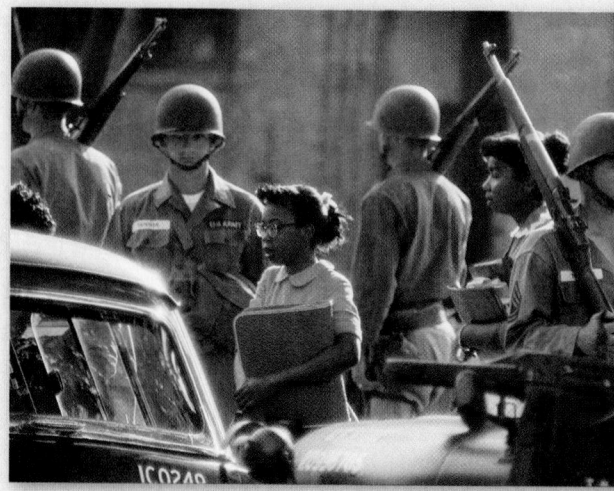

► Federal troops protect African American students at Central High.

Analyzing VISUALS

1. **Explaining** Why do you think the crowd is shouting at Elizabeth Eckford?

2. **Identifying Central Issues** Why did President Eisenhower send troops to Little Rock?

rounded the school, an angry white mob joined the troops to protest and to intimidate the students trying to register.

Faubus had used the armed forces of a state to oppose the federal government—the first such challenge to the Constitution since the Civil War. Eisenhower knew that he could not allow Faubus to defy the federal government. After a conference between Eisenhower and Faubus proved fruitless, the district court ordered the governor to remove the troops. Instead of ending the crisis, however, Faubus simply left the school to the mob. After the African American students entered the building, angry whites beat at least two African American reporters and broke many of the school's windows.

The violence finally convinced President Eisenhower that he had to act. Federal authority had to be upheld. He immediately ordered the Army to send troops to Little Rock. In addition, he federalized the Arkansas National Guard. By nightfall, 1,000 soldiers of the elite 101st Airborne Division had arrived. By 5:00 A.M., the troops had encircled the school, bayonets ready. A few hours later, the nine African American students arrived in an army station wagon and walked into the high school. Federal authority had been upheld, but the troops had to stay in Little Rock for the rest of the school year.

Officials in Little Rock, however, continued to resist integration. Before the start of the following school year, Governor Faubus ordered the three public high schools in Little Rock closed. Steps to integrate the schools in Little Rock resumed only in 1959.

New Civil Rights Legislation

In the same year that the Little Rock crisis began, Congress passed the first civil rights law since Reconstruction. The Civil Rights Act of 1957 was intended to protect the right of African Americans to vote. Eisenhower believed firmly in the right to vote, and he viewed it as his responsibility to protect voting rights. He also knew that if he sent a civil rights bill to Congress, conservative Southern Democrats would try to block the legislation. In 1956 he did send the bill to Congress, hoping not only to split the Democratic Party but also to convince more African Americans to vote Republican.

Several Southern senators did try to stop the Civil Rights Act of 1957, but the Senate majority leader, Democrat Lyndon Johnson, put together a compromise that enabled the act to pass. Although its final form was much weaker than originally intended, the act still brought the power of the federal government into the civil rights debate. It created a civil rights division within the Department of Justice and gave it the authority to seek court injunctions against anyone interfering with the right to vote. It also created the United States Commission on Civil Rights to investigate allegations of denial of voting rights. After the bill passed, the SCLC announced a campaign to register 2 million new African American voters.

✔ **Reading Check** **Explaining** Why did Eisenhower intervene in the Little Rock controversy?

Section 1 REVIEW

Vocabulary

1. **Explain** the significance of: Rosa Parks, NAACP, "separate but equal," de facto segregation, sit-in, Thurgood Marshall, Linda Brown, Martin Luther King, Jr., Southern Christian Leadership Conference.

Main Ideas

2. **Explaining** What was CORE and what were some of its tactics?

3. **Identifying** What event set off the civil rights movement of the 1950s?

4. **Summarizing** Why did Eisenhower send the 101st Airborne Division to Little Rock, Arkansas?

Critical Thinking

5. **Big Ideas** Why did the role of the federal government in civil rights enforcement change?

6. **Organizing** Use a graphic organizer similar to the one below to list the efforts made to end segregation.

Efforts to End Segregation

7. **Analyzing Visuals** Study the photograph of Elizabeth Eckford on page 628. Describe Eckford's demeanor compared to those around her. What might this indicate about her character?

Writing About History

8. **Expository Writing** Assume the role of an African American soldier returning from World War II. Write a letter to the editor of a newspaper describing your expectations of civil rights.

History ONLINE

Study Central™ To review this section, go to glencoe.com and click on Study Central.

Challenging Segregation

I n the early 1960s, the struggle for civil rights intensified. African American citizens and white supporters created organizations that directed protests, targeted specific inequalities, and attracted the attention of the mass media and the government.

The Sit-in Movement

MAIN Idea African American students staged sit-ins and formed the Student Nonviolent Coordinating Committee (SNCC) to organize efforts for desegregation and voter registration throughout the South.

HISTORY AND YOU Would you risk your personal safety to participate in a sit-in? Read on to learn of the response of young people to the sit-in movement of the early 1960s.

In the fall of 1959, four young African Americans—Joseph McNeil, Ezell Blair, Jr., David Richmond, and Franklin McCain—enrolled at North Carolina Agricultural and Technical College, an African American college in Greensboro. The four freshmen spent evenings talking about the civil rights movement. In January 1960, McNeil suggested a sit-in at the whites-only lunch counter in the nearby Woolworth's department store.

"All of us were afraid," Richmond later recalled, "but we went and did it." On February 1, 1960, the four friends entered the Woolworth's. They purchased school supplies and then sat at the lunch counter and ordered coffee. When they were refused service, Blair asked, "I beg your pardon, but you just served us at [the checkout] counter. Why can't we be served at the counter here?" The students stayed at the counter until it closed, and then announced that they would sit at the counter every day until they were given the same service as white customers.

As they left the store, the four were excited. McNeil recalled, "I just felt I had powers within me, a superhuman strength that would come forward." McCain was also energized, saying, "I probably felt better that day than I've ever felt in my life."

News of the daring sit-in at the Woolworth's store spread quickly across Greensboro. The following day, 29 African American students arrived at Woolworth's determined to sit at the counter until served. By the end of the week, over 300 students were taking part.

Starting with just four students, a new mass movement for civil rights had begun. Within two months, sit-ins had spread to 54 cities in nine states. They were staged at segregated stores, restaurants, hotels, and movie theaters. By 1961, sit-ins had been held in more than 100 cities.

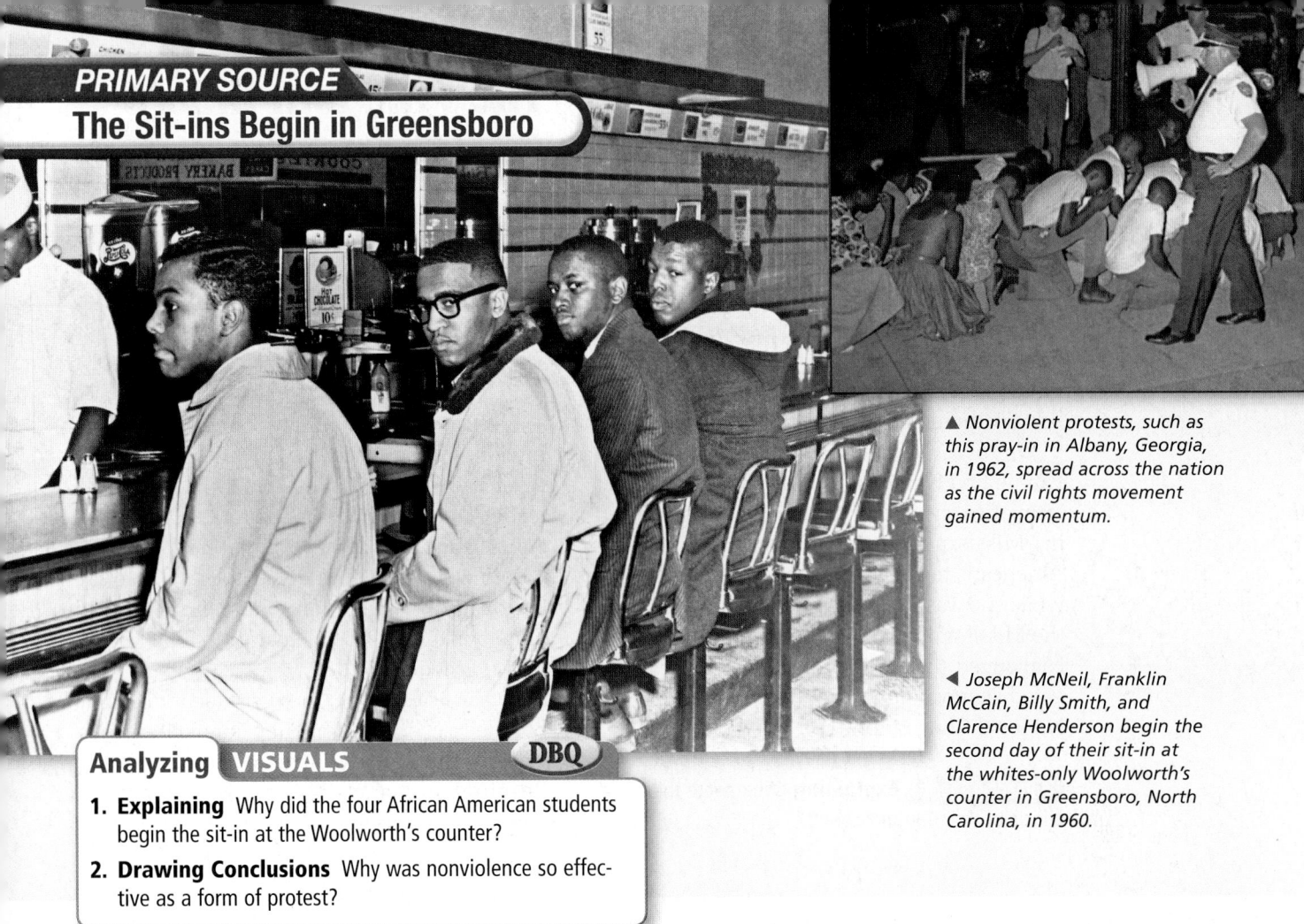

PRIMARY SOURCE
The Sit-ins Begin in Greensboro

▲ Nonviolent protests, such as this pray-in in Albany, Georgia, in 1962, spread across the nation as the civil rights movement gained momentum.

◄ Joseph McNeil, Franklin McCain, Billy Smith, and Clarence Henderson begin the second day of their sit-in at the whites-only Woolworth's counter in Greensboro, North Carolina, in 1960.

Analyzing VISUALS   DBQ

1. **Explaining** Why did the four African American students begin the sit-in at the Woolworth's counter?

2. **Drawing Conclusions** Why was nonviolence so effective as a form of protest?

The sit-in movement brought large numbers of idealistic and energized college students into the civil rights struggle. Many African American students had become discouraged by the slow pace of desegregation. Students like Jesse Jackson, a student leader at North Carolina Agricultural and Technical College, wanted to see things change more quickly. The sit-in offered them a way to take matters into their own hands.

At first, the leaders of the NAACP and the SCLC were nervous about the sit-in campaign. They feared that students did not have the discipline to remain nonviolent if they were provoked enough. For the most part, the students proved them wrong. Those conducting sit-ins were heckled by bystanders, punched, kicked, beaten with clubs, and burned with cigarettes, hot coffee, and acid—but most did not fight back. Their heroic behavior grabbed the nation's attention.

As the sit-ins spread, student leaders in different states realized they needed to coordinate their efforts. The person who brought them together was Ella Baker, a former NAACP official and the executive director of the SCLC. In April 1960 Baker invited student leaders to attend a convention at Shaw University in Raleigh, North Carolina. There she urged students to create their own organization instead of joining the NAACP or the SCLC. Students, she said, had "the right to direct their own affairs and even make their own mistakes."

The students agreed with Baker and established the **Student Nonviolent Coordinating Committee (SNCC).** Among SNCC's early leaders were Marion Barry, who later served as mayor of Washington, D.C., and John Lewis, who later became a member of Congress. African American college students from all across the South made up the majority of SNCC's members, although many whites also joined. Between 1960 and 1965, SNCC played a key role in desegregating public facilities in dozens of Southern communities. SNCC also began sending volunteers into rural areas of the Deep South to **register** African Americans to vote.

The idea for what came to be called the Voter Education Project began with Robert Moses, an SNCC volunteer from New York. Moses pointed out that the civil rights movement tended to focus on urban areas. He urged the SNCC to start helping rural African Americans, who often faced violence if they tried to register to vote. Despite the danger, many SNCC volunteers headed to the Deep South. Moses himself went to Mississippi. Several had their lives threatened; others were beaten, and in 1964, local officials brutally murdered three SNCC workers.

One SNCC organizer, a sharecropper named Fannie Lou Hamer, had been evicted from her farm after registering to vote. She was arrested in Mississippi for urging other African Americans to register. Police severely beat her while she was in jail. She then helped organize the Mississippi Freedom Democratic Party and challenged the legality of Mississippi's segregated Democratic Party at the 1964 Democratic National Convention.

Reading Check **Explaining** What were the effects of the sit-in movement?

The Freedom Riders

MAIN Idea Teams of African Americans and whites rode buses into the South to protest the continued illegal segregation on interstate bus lines.

HISTORY AND YOU Is it acceptable to risk provoking violence in order to advance a cause you support? Read to learn about the violence that erupted against the Freedom Riders and against Martin Luther King, Jr.'s march in Birmingham.

Despite rulings outlawing segregation in interstate bus service, bus travel remained segregated in much of the South. In 1961 CORE leader James Farmer asked teams of African American and white volunteers, many of whom were college students, to travel into the South to draw attention to its refusal to integrate bus terminals. The teams became known as the **Freedom Riders.**

In early May 1961, the first Freedom Riders boarded several southbound interstate buses. When the buses arrived in Anniston, Birmingham, and Montgomery, Alabama, angry white mobs attacked them. The mobs

The Civil Rights Movement, 1954–1965

May 1954
In *Brown* v. *Board of Education,* Supreme Court declares segregated schools unconstitutional

December 1956
Supreme Court declares separate-but-equal doctrine is no longer constitutional

January 1957
Martin Luther King, Jr., and other Southern ministers create SCLC

May 1961
James Farmer organizes the first Freedom Riders to desegregate interstate bus travel

1955 **1957** **1959** **1961**

December 1955
Rosa Parks is arrested and Montgomery Bus Boycott begins

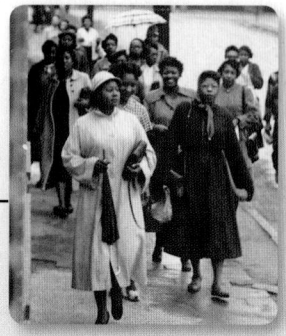

September 1957
Arkansas governor Faubus blocks desegregation of Little Rock High School, forcing Eisenhower to send troops to the school

February 1960
Students in Greensboro, North Carolina, stage a sit-in at a local lunch counter; as sit-ins spread, student leaders form SNCC in April

slit the bus tires and threw rocks at the windows. In Anniston, someone threw a firebomb into one bus, but fortunately no one was killed.

In Birmingham the riders emerged from a bus to face a gang of young men armed with baseball bats, chains, and lead pipes. The gang beat the riders viciously. One witness later reported, "You couldn't see their faces through the blood." The head of the police in Birmingham, Public Safety Commissioner Theophilus Eugene "Bull" Connor, explained that there had been no police at the bus station because it was Mother's Day, and he had given many of his officers the day off. FBI evidence later showed that Connor had contacted the local Ku Klux Klan and told them to beat the Freedom Riders until "it looked like a bulldog got a hold of them."

The violence in Alabama made national news, shocking many Americans. The attack on the Freedom Riders came less than four months after President John F. Kennedy took office. The new president felt compelled to get the violence under control.

Kennedy and Civil Rights

While campaigning for the presidency in 1960, John F. Kennedy promised to actively support the civil rights movement if elected. His brother, Robert F. Kennedy, had used his influence to get Dr. King released from jail after a demonstration in Georgia. African Americans responded by voting overwhelmingly for Kennedy. Their votes helped him narrowly win several key states, including Illinois, which Kennedy carried by only 9,000 votes.

Once in office, however, Kennedy at first seemed as cautious as Eisenhower on civil rights, which disappointed many African Americans. Kennedy knew he needed the support of many Southern senators to get other programs through Congress and that any attempt to push through new civil rights legislation would anger them. Congressional Republicans repeatedly reminded the public of Kennedy's failure to follow through on his campaign promise to push for civil rights for African Americans.

May 1963
Martin Luther King, Jr., leads protests in Birmingham, Alabama; police assault the protestors and King is jailed

March 1965
King leads a march in Selma, Alabama, to build support for a new voting rights law; police brutally attack marchers

August 3, 1965
Congress passes the Voting Rights Act of 1965

1963 ▸ 1965 ▸

September 1962
James Meredith tries to register at University of Mississippi; riots force Kennedy to send troops

August 1963
King delivers his "I Have a Dream" speech during the March on Washington in support of new civil rights act

July 1964
Johnson signs Civil Rights Act of 1964 into law

Analyzing TIME LINES

1. **Identifying** According to the time line, what was the first major event in the civil rights movement?

2. **Analyzing** How many years were there between the *Brown* decision and the passage of the Civil Rights Act of 1964?

3. **Stating** When were the Freedom Riders organized?

Kennedy did, however, name approximately 40 African Americans to high-level positions in the government. He also appointed Thurgood Marshall to a federal judgeship on the Second Circuit Appeals Court in New York—one level below the Supreme Court and the highest judicial position an African American had attained to that point. Kennedy created the Committee on Equal Employment Opportunity (CEEO) to stop the federal bureaucracy from discriminating against African Americans in hiring and promotions.

The Justice Department Takes Action

Although President Kennedy was unwilling to challenge Southern Democrats in Congress, he allowed the Justice Department, run by his brother Robert, to actively support the civil rights movement. Robert Kennedy tried to help African Americans register to vote by having the civil rights division of the Justice Department file lawsuits across the South.

When violence erupted against the Freedom Riders, the Kennedys came to their aid as well, although not at first. At the time the Freedom Riders took action, President Kennedy was preparing for a meeting with Nikita Khrushchev, the leader of the Soviet Union. Kennedy did not want violence in the South to disrupt the meeting by giving the impression that his country was weak and divided.

After the Freedom Riders were attacked in Montgomery, the Kennedys publicly urged them to stop the rides and give everybody a "cooling off" period. James Farmer replied that African Americans "have been cooling off now for 350 years. If we cool off anymore, we'll be in a deep freeze." Instead, he announced that the Freedom Riders planned to head into Mississippi on their next trip.

To stop the violence, President Kennedy made a deal with Senator James Eastland of Mississippi, a strong supporter of segregation. If Eastland would use his influence in Mississippi to prevent violence, Kennedy would not object if the Mississippi police arrested the Freedom Riders. Eastland kept the deal. No violence occurred when the buses arrived in Jackson, Mississippi, but the riders were arrested.

The cost of bailing the Freedom Riders out of jail used up most of CORE's funds, which meant that the rides would have to end unless more money could be found. When Thurgood Marshall learned of the situation, he offered James Farmer the use of the NAACP Legal Defense Fund's huge bail bond account to keep the rides going.

When President Kennedy returned from meeting with Khrushchev and found that the Freedom Riders were still active, he changed his approach. He ordered the Interstate Commerce Commission (ICC) to tighten its regulations against segregated bus terminals. In the meantime, Robert Kennedy ordered the Justice Department to take legal action against Southern cities that maintained segregated bus terminals. The actions of the ICC and the Justice Department finally produced results. By late 1962, segregation in interstate bus travel had come to an end.

James Meredith As the Freedom Riders were trying to desegregate interstate bus lines, efforts continued to integrate Southern schools. On the day John F. Kennedy was inaugurated, an African American air force veteran named **James Meredith** applied for a transfer to the University of Mississippi. Up to that point, the university had avoided complying with the Supreme Court ruling ending segregated education.

In September 1962, Meredith tried to register at the university's admissions office, only to find Ross Barnett, the governor of Mississippi, blocking his path. Meredith had a court order directing the university to register him, but Governor Barnett stated emphatically, "Never! We will never surrender to the evil and illegal forces of tyranny."

Frustrated, President Kennedy dispatched 500 federal marshals to escort Meredith to the campus. Shortly after Meredith and the marshals arrived, an angry white mob attacked the campus, and a full-scale riot erupted. The mob hurled rocks, bottles, bricks, and acid at the marshals. Some people fired shotguns at them. The marshals responded with tear gas, but they were under orders not to fire.

The fighting continued all night. By morning, 160 marshals had been wounded. Reluctantly, Kennedy ordered the army to send several thousand troops to the campus. For the rest of the year, Meredith attended classes at the University of Mississippi under federal guard. He graduated in August.

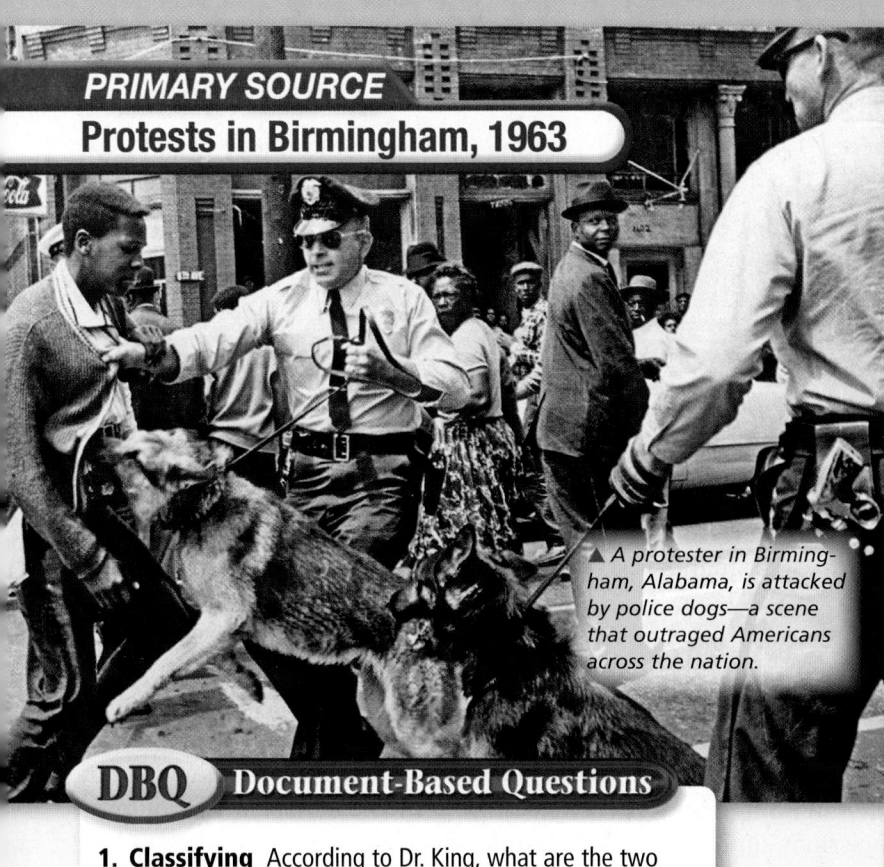

Protests in Birmingham, 1963

A protester in Birmingham, Alabama, is attacked by police dogs—a scene that outraged Americans across the nation.

PRIMARY SOURCE

"Since we so diligently urge people to obey the Supreme Court's decision of 1954 outlawing segregation in the public schools, at first glance it may seem rather paradoxical for us consciously to break laws. One may well ask: "How can you advocate breaking some laws and obeying others?" The answer lies in the fact that there are two types of laws: just and unjust. . . . [and] one has a moral responsibility to disobey unjust laws. I would agree with St. Augustine that 'an unjust law is no law at all.'

. . . . Any law that uplifts human personality is just. Any law that degrades human personality is unjust. All segregation statutes are unjust because segregation distorts the soul and damages the personality. It gives the segregator a false sense of superiority and the segregated a false sense of inferiority. . . . An unjust law is a code that a numerical or power majority group compels a minority group to obey but does not make binding on itself. This is difference made legal. By the same token, a just law is a code that a majority compels a minority to follow and that it is willing to follow itself. This is sameness made legal."

—from Martin Luther King, Jr., "Letter from Birmingham Jail, 1963"

DBQ Document-Based Questions

1. **Classifying** According to Dr. King, what are the two types of laws? What is the difference between them?
2. **Determining Cause and Effect** What does King say are the effects of segregation on the segregator? On the segregated?

Violence in Birmingham

The events in Mississippi frustrated Martin Luther King, Jr., and other civil rights leaders. Although they were pleased that Kennedy had intervened, they were disappointed that the president had not seized the moment to push for a new civil rights law.

Reflecting on the problem, Dr. King came to a difficult decision. It seemed to him that only when violence got out of hand would the federal government intervene. "We've got to have a crisis to bargain with," one of his advisers observed. King agreed. In the spring of 1963, he decided to launch demonstrations in Birmingham, Alabama, knowing they would provoke a violent response. He believed it was the only way to get President Kennedy to actively support civil rights.

The situation in Birmingham was volatile. Public Safety Commissioner Bull Connor, who had arranged for the attack on the Freedom Riders, was now running for mayor. Eight days after the protests began, King was arrested. While in jail, King began writing on scraps of paper that had been smuggled into his cell. The "Letter from Birmingham Jail" that he produced is one of the most eloquent defenses of nonviolent protest ever written.

In his letter, King explained that although the protesters were breaking the law, they were following a higher moral law based on divine justice. Injustice, he insisted, had to be exposed "to the light of human conscience and the air of national opinion before it can be cured."

After King was released, the protests, which had been dwindling, began to grow again. Bull Connor responded with force. He ordered the Birmingham police to use clubs, police dogs, and high-pressure fire hoses on the demonstrators. Millions of Americans watched the graphic violence on the nightly news on television. Outraged by the brutality and worried that the government was losing control, Kennedy ordered his aides to prepare a new civil rights bill.

✔ Reading Check **Evaluating** How did President Kennedy help the civil rights movement?

The Civil Rights Act of 1964

MAIN Idea President Johnson used his political expertise to get the Civil Rights Act of 1964 passed.

HISTORY AND YOU Do you remember the constitutional amendments that granted African Americans civil rights after the Civil War? Read on to learn about new legal steps taken during the 1960s.

Determined to introduce a civil rights bill, Kennedy now waited for a dramatic moment to address the nation on the issue. Alabama's governor, George Wallace, gave the president his chance. At his inauguration as governor, Wallace had stated, "I draw a line in the dust . . . and I say, Segregation now! Segregation tomorrow! Segregation forever!" On June 11, 1963, Wallace stood in front of the University of Alabama's admissions office to block two African Americans from enrolling. He stayed until federal marshals ordered him to move.

The next day a white segregationist murdered Medgar Evers, a civil rights activist in Mississippi. President Kennedy seized the moment to announce his civil rights bill. That evening, he spoke to Americans about a "moral issue . . . as old as the scriptures and as clear as the American Constitution":

PRIMARY SOURCE

"The heart of the question is whether . . . we are going to treat our fellow Americans as we want to be treated. If an American, because his skin is dark, cannot eat lunch in a restaurant open to the public, if he cannot send his children to the best public school available, if he cannot vote for the public officials who represent him . . . then who among us would be content to have the color of his skin changed and stand in his place?

One hundred years of delay have passed since President Lincoln freed the slaves, yet their heirs, their grandsons, are not fully free. . . . And this Nation, for all its hopes and all its boasts, will not be fully free until all its citizens are free. . . . Now the time has come for this Nation to fulfill its promise."

—from Kennedy's White House address, June 11, 1963

The March on Washington

Dr. King realized that Kennedy would have a very difficult time pushing his civil rights bill through Congress. Therefore, he searched for a way to lobby Congress and to build more public support. When A. Philip Randolph suggested a march on Washington, King agreed.

On August 28, 1963, more than 200,000 demonstrators of all races flocked to the nation's capital. The audience heard speeches and sang hymns and songs as they gathered peacefully near the Lincoln Memorial. Dr. King then delivered a powerful speech outlining his dream of freedom and equality for all Americans.

King's speech and the peacefulness and dignity of the March on Washington built momentum for the civil rights bill. Opponents in Congress, however, continued to do what they could to slow the bill down, dragging out their committee investigations and using procedural rules to delay votes.

The Bill Becomes Law

Although the civil rights bill was likely to pass the House of Representatives, where a majority of Republicans and Northern Democrats supported the measure, it faced a much more difficult time in the Senate. There, a small group of determined Southern senators would try to block the bill indefinitely.

In the U.S. Senate, senators are allowed to speak for as long as they like when a bill is being debated. The Senate cannot vote on a bill until all senators have finished speaking. A **filibuster** occurs when a small group of senators take turns speaking and refuse to stop the debate and allow a bill to come to a vote. Today a filibuster can be stopped if at least 60 senators vote for **cloture,** a motion that cuts off debate and forces a vote. In the 1960s, however, 67 senators had to vote for cloture to stop a filibuster. This meant that a minority of senators opposed to civil rights could easily prevent the majority from enacting a new civil rights law.

Worried that the bill would never pass, many African Americans became even more disheartened. Then, President Kennedy was assassinated in Dallas, Texas, on November 22, 1963, and his vice president, Lyndon Johnson, became president. Johnson was from Texas and

Martin Luther King, Jr.'s Address, Washington, 1963

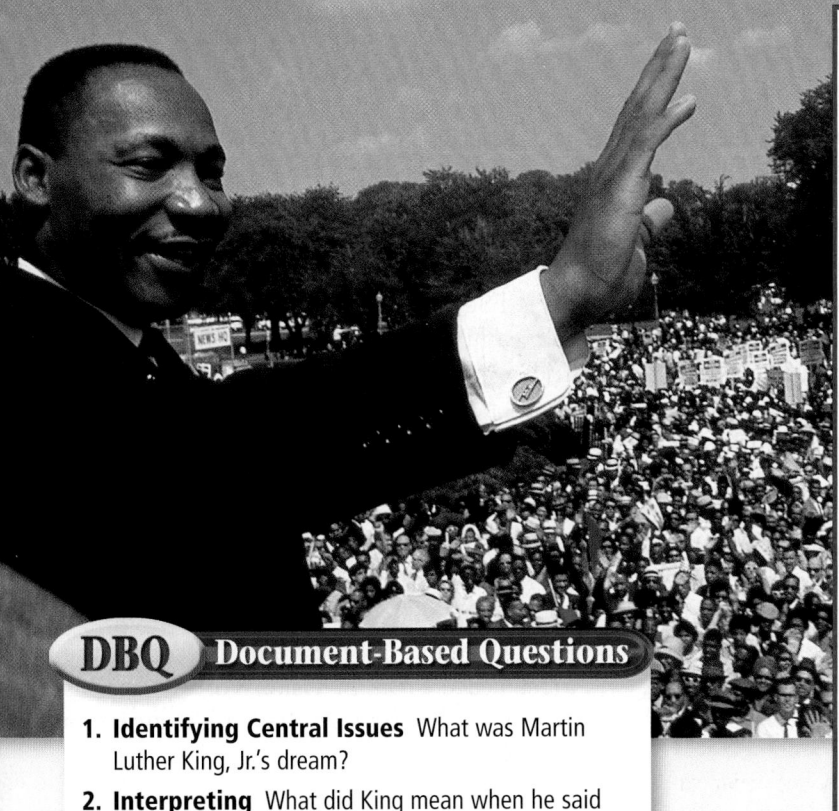

PRIMARY SOURCE

"And so even though we face the difficulties of today and tomorrow, I still have a dream. It is a dream deeply rooted in the American dream.

I have a dream that one day this nation will rise up and live out the true meaning of its creed: 'We hold these truths to be self-evident, that all men are created equal.'

I have a dream that one day on the red hills of Georgia, the sons of former slaves and the sons of former slave owners will be able to sit down together at the table of brotherhood....

I have a dream that my four little children will one day live in a nation where they will not be judged by the color of their skin but by the content of their character.

I have a dream today!

...And when this happens, when we allow freedom to ring, when we let it ring from every village and every hamlet, from every state and every city, we will be able to speed up that day when all of God's children, black men and white men, Jews and Gentiles, Protestants and Catholics, will be able to join hands and sing in the words of the old Negro spiritual:

Free at last! Free at last!

Thank God Almighty, we are free at last!"

—Martin Luther King, Jr.,
"Address in Washington," 1963

DBQ Document-Based Questions

1. **Identifying Central Issues** What was Martin Luther King, Jr.'s dream?

2. **Interpreting** What did King mean when he said that he hoped that one day the nation will "live out the true meaning of its creed"?

had been the leader of the Senate Democrats before becoming vice president. Although he had helped pass the Civil Rights Acts of 1957 and 1960, he had done so by weakening their provisions and by compromising with other Southern senators.

To the surprise of the civil rights movement, Johnson committed himself wholeheartedly to getting Kennedy's program, including the civil rights bill, through Congress. Johnson had served in Congress for many years and was adept at getting legislation enacted. He knew how to build public support, how to put pressure on Congress, and how to use the rules and procedures to get what he wanted.

In February 1964, President Johnson's leadership began to produce results. The civil rights bill passed the House of Representatives by a majority of 290 to 130. The debate then moved to the Senate. In June, after 87 days of filibuster, the Senate finally voted to end debate by a margin of 71 to 29—four votes over the two-thirds needed for cloture. The Senate then eas-

ily passed the bill. On July 2, 1964, President Johnson signed the **Civil Rights Act of 1964** into law.

The Civil Rights Act of 1964 was the most comprehensive civil rights law Congress had ever enacted. It gave the federal government broad power to prevent racial discrimination in a number of areas. The law made segregation illegal in most places of public accommodation, and it gave citizens of all races and nationalities equal access to public facilities. The law gave the U.S. attorney general more power to bring lawsuits to force school desegregation and required private employers to end discrimination in the workplace. It also established the Equal Employment Opportunity Commission (EEOC) as a permanent agency in the federal government. This commission monitors the ban on job discrimination by race, religion, gender, and national origin.

To read more of Martin Luther King, Jr.'s "I Have a Dream" speech, see page R56 in **Documents in American History.**

✓ **Reading Check** **Examining** How did Dr. King lobby Congress to pass a new civil rights act?

The Struggle for Voting Rights

MAIN Idea President Johnson called for a new voting rights law after hostile crowds severely beat civil rights demonstrators.

HISTORY AND YOU Do you remember the tactics Southern states adopted to keep African Americans from voting? Read on to learn about the Voting Rights Act of 1965.

Even after the Civil Rights Act of 1964 was passed, voting rights were far from secure. The act had focused on segregation and job discrimination, and it did little to address voting issues. The Twenty-fourth Amendment, ratified in 1964, helped somewhat by eliminating poll taxes, or fees paid in order to vote, in federal (but not state) elections. African Americans still faced hurdles, however, when they tried to vote. As the SCLC and SNCC stepped up their voter registration efforts in the South, their members were often attacked and beaten, and several were murdered.

Across the South, bombs exploded in African American businesses and churches. Between June and October 1964, arson and bombs destroyed 24 African American churches in Mississippi alone. Convinced that a new law was needed to protect African American voting rights, Dr. King decided to stage another dramatic protest.

The Selma March

In January 1965, the SCLC and Dr. King selected Selma, Alabama, as the focal point for their campaign for voting rights. Although African Americans made up a majority of Selma's population, they comprised only 3 percent of registered voters. To prevent African Americans from registering to vote, Sheriff Jim Clark had deputized and armed dozens of white citizens. His posse terrorized African Americans and frequently attacked demonstrators with clubs and electric cattle prods.

In December 1964, Dr. King received the Nobel Peace Prize in Oslo, Norway, for his work in the civil rights movement. A few weeks

PRIMARY SOURCE
Marching for Freedom, Selma, 1965

Martin Luther King, Jr.

Coretta Scott King, Dr. King's wife

The Civil Rights Act of 1964
- Gave the federal government power to prevent racial discrimination and established the Equal Employment Opportunity Commission (EEOC).
- Made segregation illegal in most places of public accommodation.
- Gave the U.S. attorney general more power to bring lawsuits to force school desegregation.
- Required employers to end workplace discrimination.

The Voting Rights Act of 1965
- Authorized the U.S. attorney general to send federal examiners to register qualified voters.
- Suspended discriminatory devices, such as literacy tests, in counties where less than half of all adults had been allowed to vote.

Analyzing VISUALS

1. **Making Connections** How did the Civil Rights Act of 1964 work to end segregation?

2. **Drawing Conclusions** Why do you think counties where less than half of all adults were allowed to vote were a focus of the Voting Rights Acts of 1965?

later, King announced, "We are not asking, we are demanding the ballot." King's demonstrations in Selma led to the arrest of approximately 2,000 African Americans, including schoolchildren, by Sheriff Clark. Clark's men attacked and beat many of the demonstrators, and Selma quickly became a major story in the national news.

To keep pressure on the president and Congress to act, Dr. King joined with SNCC activists and organized a "march for freedom" from Selma to the state capitol in Montgomery, a distance of about 50 miles (80 km). On Sunday, March 7, 1965, the march began. The SCLC's Hosea Williams and SNCC's John Lewis led 500 protesters toward U.S. Highway 80, the route that marchers had planned to follow to Montgomery.

As the protesters approached the Edmund Pettus Bridge, which led out of Selma, Sheriff Clark ordered them to disperse. While the marchers kneeled in prayer, more than 200 state troopers and deputized citizens rushed the demonstrators. Many were beaten in full view of television cameras. This brutal attack, known later as "Bloody Sunday," left 70 African Americans hospitalized and many more injured.

The nation was stunned as it viewed the shocking footage of law enforcement officers beating peaceful demonstrators. Watching the events from the White House, President Johnson became furious. Eight days later, he appeared before a nationally televised joint session of the legislature to propose a new voting rights law.

The Voting Rights Act of 1965

On August 3, 1965, the House of Representatives passed the voting rights bill by a wide margin. The following day, the Senate also passed the bill. The **Voting Rights Act of 1965** authorized the U.S. attorney general to send federal examiners to register qualified voters, bypassing local officials who often refused to register African Americans. The law also suspended discriminatory devices, such as literacy tests, in counties where less than half of all adults had been registered to vote.

The results were dramatic. By the end of the year, almost 250,000 African Americans had registered as new voters. The number of African American elected officials in the South also increased. In 1965, only about 100 African Americans held elected office; by 1990 more than 5,000 did.

The passage of the Voting Rights Act of 1965 marked a turning point in the civil rights movement. The movement had now achieved its two major legislative goals. Segregation had been outlawed and new federal laws were in place to prevent discrimination and protect voting rights. After 1965, the movement began to shift its focus to the problem of achieving full social and economic equality for African Americans. As part of that effort, the movement turned its attention to the problems of African Americans trapped in poverty and living in ghettos in many of the nation's major cities.

✓ Reading Check **Summarizing** How did the Twenty-fourth Amendment affect African American voting rights?

Section 2 REVIEW

Vocabulary

1. **Explain** the significance of: SNCC, Freedom Riders, James Meredith, filibuster, cloture, Civil Rights Act of 1964, Voting Rights Act of 1965.

Main Ideas

2. **Describing** What was the purpose of the SNCC?

3. **Summarizing** How did the Freedom Riders help the civil rights movement?

4. **Explaining** Why did Dr. King lead the March on Washington in 1963?

5. **Analyzing** What was "Bloody Sunday"? How did President Johnson respond?

Critical Thinking

6. **Big Ideas** How did television help the civil rights movement?

7. **Sequencing** Use a time line similar to the one below to sequence the events in the civil rights movement.

Feb. 1960	Sept. 1962	July 1964

May 1961	Aug. 1963	March 1965

8. **Analyzing Visuals** Study the photographs in this section. What elements of the photographs show the sacrifices African Americans made in the civil rights movement?

Writing About History

9. **Descriptive Writing** Assume the role of a journalist working for a college newspaper in 1960. Write an article for the newspaper describing the sit-in movement, including its participants, goals, and achievements.

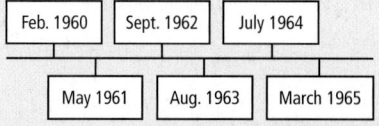

History ONLINE

Study Central™ To review this section, go to <u>glencoe.com</u> and click on Study Central.

ANALYZING PRIMARY SOURCES

The Civil Rights Movement

Although major figures of the civil rights movement such as Martin Luther King, Jr., are widely remembered today, the movement drew its strength from the dedication of grass-roots supporters. In rural and urban areas across the South, ordinary individuals advanced the movement through their participation in marches, boycotts, and voter registration drives. Those who dared to make a stand against discrimination risked being fired from their job, evicted from their home, and becoming the target of physical violence.

Study these primary sources and answer the questions that follow.

PRIMARY SOURCE 1

Public Testimony, 1964

In 1964, the "Mississippi Freedom Democratic Party" challenged the right of Mississippi's established (all white) Democratic Party representatives to seats at the party's national convention on the grounds that African Americans had been systematically denied the right to vote.

"[M]y husband came, and said the plantation owner was raising cain because I had tried to register [to vote] and before he quit talking the plantation owner came, and said, 'Fannie Lou, do you know—did Pap tell you what I said?' And I said, 'Yes sir.' He said, 'I mean that . . . If you don't go down and withdraw . . . well—you might have to go because we are not ready for that.' . . .

And I addressed him and told him and said, 'I didn't try to register for you. I tried to register for myself.'

I had to leave the same night.

On the 10th of September, 1962, 16 bullets was fired into the home of Mr. and Mrs. Robert Tucker for me. That same night two girls were shot in Ruleville, Mississippi. Also Mr. Joe McDonald's house was shot in.

And in June, the 9th, 1963, I had attended a voter registration workshop, was returning back to Mississippi. . . . I stepped off the bus . . . and somebody screamed . . . 'Get that one there,' and when I went to get in the car, when the man told me I was under arrest, he kicked me.

I was carried to the county jail. . . . [The patrolmen] left my cell and it wasn't too long before they came back. He said 'You are from Ruleville all right,' and he used a curse word, he said, 'We are going to beat you until you wish you was dead.'. . .

All of this on account we want to register, to become first-class citizens, and if the freedom Democratic Party is not seated now, I question America, is this America, the land of the free and the home of the brave where we have to sleep with our telephones off the hooks because our lives be threatened daily because we want to live as decent human beings in America?"

—Fannie Lou Hamer testifying before the Credentials Committee of the Democratic National Convention, August 22, 1964

PRIMARY SOURCE 2

Photograph, c. 1964

"Freedom Schools" taught literacy and African American history and encouraged voter registration.

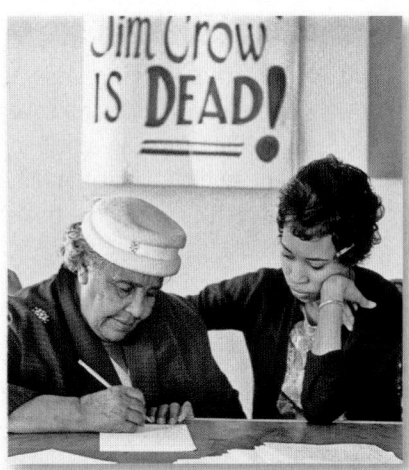

PRIMARY SOURCE 3

Strategy Memo, April 1960

"The choice of the non-violent method, 'the sit-in,' symbolizes both judgment and promise. It is a judgment upon middle-class conventional halfway efforts to deal with radical social evil. It is specifically a judgment upon contemporary civil rights attempts. As one high school student from Chattanooga exclaimed, 'We started because we were tired of waiting for you to act. . . .'"

—James M. Lawson, Jr., "From a Lunch-Counter Stool," April 1960, Student Nonviolent Coordinating Committee Papers

PRIMARY SOURCE 4

Autobiography, 1968

"[At Tougaloo College] I had become very friendly with my social science professor, John Salter, who was in charge of NAACP activities on campus. All during the year, while the NAACP conducted a boycott of the downtown stores in Jackson, I had been one of Salter's most faithful canvassers and church speakers. During the last week of school, he told me that sit-in demonstrations were about to start in Jackson and that he wanted me to be the spokesman for a team that would sit-in at Woolworth's lunch counter. The two other demonstrators would be classmates of mine, Memphis and Pearlena. . . .

Seconds before 11:15 we were occupying three seats at the previously segregated Woolworth's lunch counter. In the beginning the waitresses seemed to ignore us, as if they really didn't know what was going on. Our waitress walked past us a couple of times before she noticed we had started to write our own orders down and realized we wanted service. She asked us what we wanted. We began to read to her from our order slips. She told us that we would be served at the back counter, which was for Negroes.

'We would like to be served here,' I said.

The waitress started to repeat what she had said, then stopped in the middle of the sentence. She turned the lights out behind the counter, and she and the other waitresses almost ran to the back of the store, deserting all their white customers. I guess they thought that violence would start immediately after the whites at the counter realized what was going on.

At noon, students from a nearby white high school started pouring in to Woolworth's. When they first saw us they were sort of surprised. . . . Then the white students started chanting all kinds of anti-Negro slogans. We were called a little bit of everything. . . .

Memphis suggested that we pray. We bowed our heads, and all hell broke loose. A man rushed forward, threw Memphis from his seat, and slapped my face. Then another man who worked in the store threw me against

PRIMARY SOURCE 5

Photograph, 1963

▼ *Lunch counter sit-in May 28, 1963, in Jackson, Mississippi. Seated (from left to right) are John Salter, Joan Trumpauer, and Anne Moody.*

an adjoining counter. . . . The mob started smearing us with ketchup, mustard, sugar, pies, and everything on the counter. . . .

About ninety policemen were standing outside the store; they had been watching the whole thing through the windows, but had not come in to stop the mob or do anything. . . .

After the sit-in, all I could think of was how sick Mississippi whites were. They believed so much in the segregated Southern way of life, they would kill to preserve it. . . . Now I knew it was impossible for me to hate sickness. The whites had a disease, an incurable disease in its final stage. What were our chances against such a disease?"

—Anne Moody, *Coming of Age in Mississippi*

DBQ Document-Based Questions

1. **Identifying** In Source 1, what sorts of repercussions did Fannie Lou Hamer endure for daring to register to vote? How do you think such tactics affected the civil rights movement?

2. **Interpreting** Study the photograph in Source 2. Who seems to be teaching whom? Why do you think the civil rights movement attracted so many young people?

3. **Evaluating** Read the passage in Source 3 and study the photograph in Source 5. Why do you think nonviolent demonstrations were effective for the civil rights movement?

4. **Making Inferences** Read Source 4. Why do you think Anne Moody wanted to try to force integration of the lunch counter? Why would she risk physical harm to do so?

New Civil Rights Issues

Guide to Reading

Big Ideas
Struggles for Rights In the late 1960s, the civil rights movement tried to address the persistent economic inequality of African Americans.

Content Vocabulary
• racism *(p. 642)*
• black power *(p. 644)*

Academic Vocabulary
• enforcement *(p. 646)*

People and Events to Identify
• Kerner Commission *(p. 643)*
• Chicago Movement *(p. 644)*
• Richard J. Daley *(p. 644)*
• Stokely Carmichael *(p. 644)*
• Malcolm X *(p. 645)*
• Black Panthers *(p. 646)*

Reading Strategy
Organizing Complete a graphic organizer like the one below by listing five major violent events in the civil rights movement and their results.

Event	Result

By the mid-1960s, much progress had been made in the arena of civil rights. However, leaders of the movement began to understand that merely winning political rights for African Americans would not completely solve their economic problems. The struggle would continue to try to end economic inequality.

Urban Problems

MAIN Idea African Americans became impatient with the slow pace of change; this frustration sometimes boiled over into riots.

HISTORY AND YOU Have you ever seen news coverage of a riot in the United States or overseas? What triggered the outburst? Read on to learn about the factors that fed into the riots of the 1960s.

Despite the passage of civil rights laws in the 1950s and 1960s, **racism**—prejudice or discrimination toward someone because of his or her race—was still common in American society. Changing the law could not change people's attitudes, nor did it help most African Americans trapped in poverty in the nation's big cities.

In 1965 nearly 70 percent of African Americans lived in large cities. Many had moved from the South to the big cities of the North during the Great Migration of the 1920s and 1940s. There, they often found the same prejudice and discrimination that had plagued them in the South.

Even if African Americans had been allowed to move into white neighborhoods, poverty trapped many of them in inner cities. Many African Americans found themselves channeled into low-paying jobs with little chance of advancement. Those who did better typically found employment as blue-collar workers in factories, but most did not advance beyond that. In 1965 only 15 percent of African Americans held professional, managerial, or clerical jobs, compared to 44 percent of whites. The average income of an African American family was only 55 percent of that of the average white family, and almost half of African Americans lived in poverty. Their unemployment rate was typically twice that of whites.

Poor neighborhoods in the nation's major cities were overcrowded and dirty, leading to higher rates of illness and infant mortality. At the same time, the crime rate increased in the 1960s, particularly in low-income neighborhoods. Juvenile delinquency rates rose, as did the rate of young people dropping out of school. Complicating matters even more was a rise in the number of single-parent households. All poor neighborhoods suffered from these problems, but because

"...SH! AFTER A WHILE THEY'LL GO AWAY!"

Baldy

► Congress is compared to the Roman emperor Nero, who was said to have played music as Rome burned.

◄ Barry Goldwater tries to persuade President Johnson to stop creating programs to end urban poverty.

Analyzing VISUALS   DBQ

1. **Making Inferences** In the cartoon on the left, what does the man suggest about urban problems?

2. **Drawing Conclusions** Based on the cartoon above, what should Congress have done to stop the rioting?

more African Americans lived in poverty, their communities were disproportionately affected.

Many African Americans living in urban poverty knew the civil rights movement had made enormous gains, but when they looked at their own circumstances, nothing seemed to be changing. The movement had raised their hopes, but their everyday problems continued. As a result, their anger and frustration began to rise—until it finally erupted.

The Watts Riot

Just five days after President Johnson signed the Voting Rights Act, a riot erupted in Watts, an African American neighborhood in Los Angeles. Allegations of police brutality had served as the catalyst for this uprising, which lasted for six days and required over 14,000 members of the National Guard and 1,500 law officers to restore order. Rioters burned and looted entire neighborhoods and destroyed about $45 million in property. They killed 34 people and injured about 900 others.

More rioting was yet to come. Riots broke out in dozens of American cities between 1965 and 1968. The worst riot took place in Detroit in 1967. Burning, looting, and skirmishes with police and National Guard members resulted in 43 deaths and over 1,000 wounded.

Eventually the U.S. Army sent in tanks and soldiers armed with machine guns to get control of the situation. Nearly 4,000 fires destroyed 1,300 buildings, and the damage in property loss was estimated at $250 million.

The Kerner Commission

In 1967 President Johnson appointed the National Advisory Commission on Civil Disorders, headed by Governor Otto Kerner of Illinois, to study the causes of the urban riots and to make recommendations to prevent them from happening again. The **Kerner Commission,** as it became known, conducted a detailed study of the problem. The commission blamed racism for most of the problems in the inner city. "Our nation is moving toward two societies, one black, one white—separate and unequal," it concluded.

The commission recommended the creation of 2 million inner-city jobs, the construction of 6 million new units of public housing, and a renewed federal commitment to fight de facto segregation. President Johnson's War on Poverty, which addressed some of the concerns about inner-city jobs and housing, was already underway. Saddled with spending for the Vietnam War, however, Johnson never endorsed the recommendations of the commission.

The Shift to Economic Rights

By the mid-1960s, a number of African American leaders were becoming increasingly critical of Martin Luther King, Jr.'s nonviolent strategy. They felt it had failed to improve the economic position of African Americans. Dr. King came to agree with this criticism, and in 1965 he decided to address economic issues.

Dr. King decided to focus on the problems that African Americans faced in Chicago. King had never conducted a civil rights campaign in the North, but by tackling a large Northern city, he believed he could call greater attention to poverty and other racial problems that lay beneath the urban race riots.

To call attention to the deplorable housing conditions that many African American families faced, Dr. King and his wife Coretta moved into a slum apartment in an African American neighborhood in Chicago. Dr. King and the SCLC hoped to work with local leaders to improve the economic status of African Americans in poor neighborhoods.

The **Chicago Movement,** however, made little headway. When Dr. King led a march through the all-white suburb of Marquette Park to demonstrate the need for open housing, he was met by angry white mobs similar to those in Birmingham and Selma. Mayor **Richard J. Daley** ordered the Chicago police to protect the marchers, and he was determined to prevent violence. He met with Dr. King and proposed a new program to clean up the slums. Associations of realtors and bankers also agreed to promote open housing. In theory, mortgages and rental property would be available to everyone, regardless of race. In practice, little changed.

Reading Check **Describing** How did Dr. King and SCLC leaders hope to address economic concerns?

Black Power

MAIN Idea Impatient with the slower gains of Martin Luther King, Jr.'s movement, many young African Americans called for "black power."

HISTORY AND YOU How did Dr. King work to avoid violence? Read on to find out how some African Americans broke with Dr. King's approach.

Dr. King's failure in Chicago seemed to show that nonviolent protests could do little to solve economic problems. After 1965, many African Americans, especially urban young people, began to turn away from King. Some leaders called for more aggressive forms of protest. Their strategies ranged from armed self-defense to promoting the idea that the government should set aside a number of states where African Americans could live separate from whites. As African Americans became more assertive, some organizations, including CORE and SNCC, voted to expel all whites from leadership positions in their organizations. They believed that African Americans alone should lead their struggle.

Many young African Americans called for **black power,** a term that had many meanings. A few interpreted black power to mean that physical self-defense and even violence were acceptable—a clear rejection of Dr. King's philosophy. To most, including **Stokely Carmichael,** the leader of SNCC in 1966, the term meant that African Americans should control the social, political, and economic direction of their struggle:

PRIMARY SOURCE

"This is the significance of black power as a slogan. For once, black people are going to use the words they want to use—not just the words whites want to hear. . . . The need for psychological equality is the reason why SNCC today believes that blacks must organize in the black community. Only black people can . . . create in the community an aroused and continuing black consciousness. . . ."

—from the *New York Review of Books,* September 1966

Black power stressed pride in the African American cultural group. It emphasized racial distinctiveness rather than assimilation—the process by which minority groups adapt to the dominant culture in a society. African Americans showed pride in their racial heritage by adopting new Afro hairstyles and African-style clothing. Many also took African names. In universities, students demanded that African and African American studies courses be made part of the standard school curriculum. Dr. King and some other leaders criticized black power as a philosophy of hopelessness and despair. The idea was very popular, however, in poor neighborhoods where many African Americans resided.

Malcolm X

By the early 1960s, a young man named **Malcolm X** had become a symbol of the black power movement. Born Malcolm Little in Omaha, Nebraska, he experienced a difficult childhood and adolescence. He drifted into a life of crime and, in 1946, was convicted of burglary and sent to prison for six years.

Prison transformed Malcolm. He began to educate himself and played an active role in the prison debate society. Eventually, he joined the Nation of Islam, commonly known as the Black Muslims, who were led by Elijah Muhammad. Despite their name, the Black

Muslims do not hold the same beliefs as mainstream Muslims. The Nation of Islam preached black nationalism. Like Marcus Garvey in the 1920s, Black Muslims believed that African Americans should separate themselves from whites and form their own self-governing communities.

Shortly after joining the Nation of Islam, Malcolm Little changed his name to Malcolm X. The "X" symbolized the family name of his African ancestors who had been enslaved. He delcared that his true name had been stolen from him by slavery, and he would no longer use the name white society had given him.

The Black Muslims viewed themselves as their own nation and attempted to make themselves as self-sufficient as possible. They ran their own businesses and schools, and published their own newspaper, *Muhammad Speaks.* They encouraged their members to respect each other and to strengthen their families. Black Muslims did not advocate violence, but they did advocate self-defense. Malcolm X's criticisms of white society and the mainstream civil rights movement gained national attention for the Nation of Islam.

PRIMARY SOURCE
Black Power in the 1960s

In the late 1960s, a new group of African American leaders, such as Malcolm X, had lost patience with the slow progress of civil rights and felt that African Americans needed to act more militantly and demand equality, not wait for it to be given.

PRIMARY SOURCE

"Since the black masses here in America are now in open revolt against the American system of segregation, will these same black masses turn toward integration or will they turn toward complete separation? Will these awakened black masses demand integration into the white society that enslaved them or will they demand complete separation from that cruel white society that has enslaved them? Will the exploited and oppressed black masses seek integration with their white exploiters and white oppressors or will these awakened black masses truly revolt and separate themselves completely from this wicked race that has enslaved us?"

—Malcolm X, from his speech "The Black Revolution," 1964

▲ *Medalists Tommie Smith and John Carlos give the black power salute at the 1968 Olympics. Above right, Stokely Carmichael speaks at a protest rally in Mississippi in 1966.*

DBQ Document-Based Questions

1. **Identifying** What are two options Malcolm X thinks African Americans have regarding their relationship with whites?
2. **Drawing Conclusions** Do you think Malcolm X supported integration? Why or why not?

The Civil Rights Movement's Legacy

There have been many changes in the status of African Americans in the United States since the 1960s. Changes have taken place in politics, economics, and education.

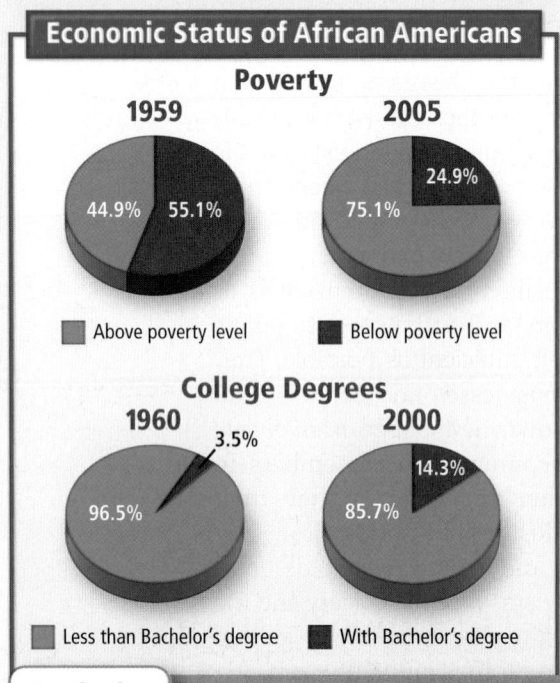

Economic Status of African Americans

Poverty

1959
- 44.9% 55.1%

2005
- 24.9%
- 75.1%

■ Above poverty level   ■ Below poverty level

College Degrees

1960
- 3.5%
- 96.5%

2000
- 14.3%
- 85.7%

■ Less than Bachelor's degree   ■ With Bachelor's degree

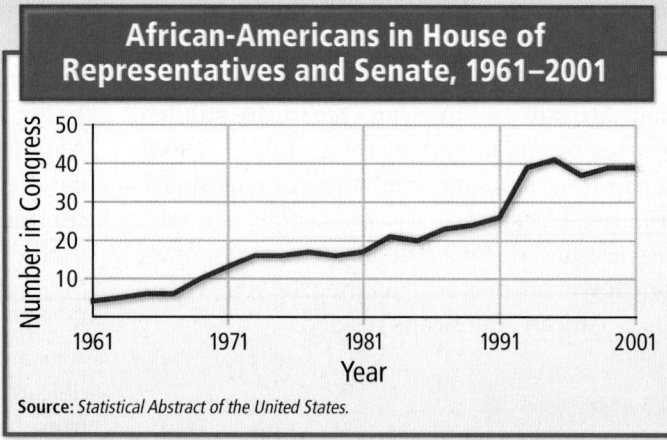

African-Americans in House of Representatives and Senate, 1961–2001

Number in Congress

50, 40, 30, 20, 10

1961   1971   1981   1991   2001

Year

Source: *Statistical Abstract of the United States.*

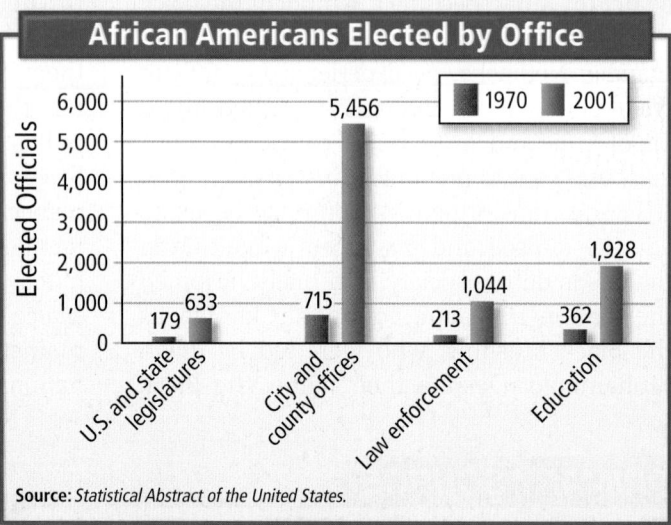

African Americans Elected by Office

Elected Officials

6,000, 5,000, 4,000, 3,000, 2,000, 1,000, 0

■ 1970   ■ 2001

5,456

U.S. and state legislatures: 179, 633
City and county offices: 715
Law enforcement: 213, 1,044
Education: 362, 1,928

Source: *Statistical Abstract of the United States.*

Analyzing VISUALS

1. **Interpreting** In which elected offices did African Americans see the greatest increase in representation?

2. **Drawing Conclusions** Does the data presented suggest that the civil rights movement was a success? Why or why not?

By 1964, Malcolm X had broken with the Black Muslims. Discouraged by scandals involving the Nation of Islam's leader, he went to the Muslim holy city of Makkah (also called Mecca) in Saudi Arabia. After seeing Muslims from many races worshipping together, he concluded that an integrated society was possible after all.

After Malcolm X broke with the Nation of Islam, he continued to criticize the organization. Because of this, organization members shot and killed him in February 1965. Although Malcolm X left the Nation of Islam before his death, his speeches and ideas from those years with the Black Muslims have influenced African Americans to take pride in their own culture and to believe in their ability to make their way in the world.

Malcolm X's ideas influenced a new generation of militant African American leaders who also preached black power, black nationalism, and economic self-sufficiency. In 1966 in Oakland, California, Huey Newton, Bobby Seale, and Eldridge Cleaver organized the **Black Panthers.**

The Black Panthers believed that a revolution was necessary in the United States, and they urged African Americans to arm themselves and prepare to force whites to grant them equal rights. Black Panther leaders called for an end to racial oppression and control of major institutions in the African American community, such as schools, law **enforcement,** housing, and hospitals. Eldridge Cleaver, who served as the minister of culture, articulated many of the organization's aims in his 1967 best-selling book, *Soul on Ice.*

✓ Reading Check **Describing** What disagreements split Dr. Martin Luther King, Jr., and the black power movement?

King Is Assassinated

MAIN Idea After Dr. King was assassinated in Memphis, Tennessee, Congress passed the Civil Rights Act of 1968.

HISTORY AND YOU Do you know someone who remembers Dr. King's assassination? Read about the events surrounding King's death.

By the late 1960s, the civil rights movement had fragmented into dozens of competing organizations with differing philosophies for reaching equality. At the same time, the emergence of black power and the call by some African Americans for violent action angered many white civil rights supporters. This made further legislation to help African Americans economically less likely.

In this atmosphere, Dr. King went to Memphis, Tennessee, to support a strike of African American sanitation workers in March 1968. At the time, the SCLC had been planning a national "Poor People's Campaign" to promote economic advancement for all impoverished Americans. The purpose of this campaign, the most ambitious one that Dr. King would ever lead, was to lobby the federal government to commit billions of dollars to end poverty and unemployment in the United States. People of all races and nationalities were to converge on the nation's capital, as they had in 1963 during the March on Washington, where they would camp out until both Congress and President Johnson agreed to pass the requested legislation to fund the proposal.

On April 4, 1968, as he stood on his hotel balcony in Memphis, Dr. King was assassinated by a sniper. Ironically, the previous night he had told a gathering at a local church, "I've been to the mountaintop. . . . I've looked over and I've seen the Promised Land. I may not get there with you, but I want you to know tonight that we as a people will get to the Promised Land."

Dr. King's death touched off both national mourning and riots in more than 100 cities, including Washington, D.C. The Reverend Ralph Abernathy, who had served as a trusted assistant to Dr. King for many years, led the Poor People's Campaign in King's absence. The demonstration, however, did not achieve any of the major objectives that either King or the SCLC had hoped it would.

In the wake of Dr. King's death, Congress did pass the Civil Rights Act of 1968. The act contained a fair-housing provision outlawing discrimination in housing sales and rentals and gave the Justice Department authority to bring suits against such discrimination.

Dr. King's death marked the end of an era in American history. Although the civil rights movement continued, it lacked the unity of purpose and vision that Dr. King had given it. Under his leadership, and with the help of tens of thousands of dedicated African Americans, many of whom were students, the civil rights movement transformed American society. Although many problems remain to be solved, the achievements of the civil rights movement in the 1950s and 1960s dramatically improved the lives of African Americans, creating opportunities that had not existed before.

Reading Check **Summarizing** What were the goals of the Poor People's Campaign?

Vocabulary

1. **Explain** the significance of: racism, Kerner Commission, Chicago Movement, Richard J. Daley, black power, Stokely Carmichael, Malcolm X, Black Panthers.

Main Ideas

2. **Describing** What were the findings and the recommendations of the Kerner Commission?

3. **Assessing** How did Malcolm X's ideas about the relationship between African Americans and white Americans change by the time of his murder?

4. **Explaining** What was the general effect of Dr. King's assassination?

Critical Thinking

5. **Big Ideas** How was the Civil Rights Act of 1968 designed to improve the economic status of African Americans?

6. **Categorizing** Use a graphic organizer similar to the one below to list the main views of each leader.

Leader	Views
Dr. Martin Luther King, Jr.	
Malcolm X	
Eldridge Cleaver	

7. **Analyzing Visuals** Study the cartoons on page 643. Together, what do they imply about government response and responsibility for the problems of the inner cities?

Writing About History

8. **Expository Writing** Assume the role of a reporter in the late 1960s. Suppose that you have interviewed a follower of Dr. King and a member of the Black Panthers. Write a transcript of each interview.

History ONLINE

Study Central™ To review this section, go to glencoe.com and click on Study Central.

Origins of the Civil Rights Movement

Long-Range Causes

- Widespread racial segregation in the American South
- Lack of voting rights for African Americans in the American South

Immediate Causes

- The arrival of large numbers of African Americans in the North after the Great Migration gives them increased political influence and greater voting power.
- African American contributions during World War II lead many African Americans to believe it is time to take action to demand change.
- NAACP strategy of using lawsuits to weaken segregation scores a major victory in 1954 with the *Brown v. Board of Education* ruling.
- African American churches serve as organizational bases, and pastors rally African Americans and organize protests.

▶ *Linda Brown was the main plaintiff in* Brown v. Board of Education.

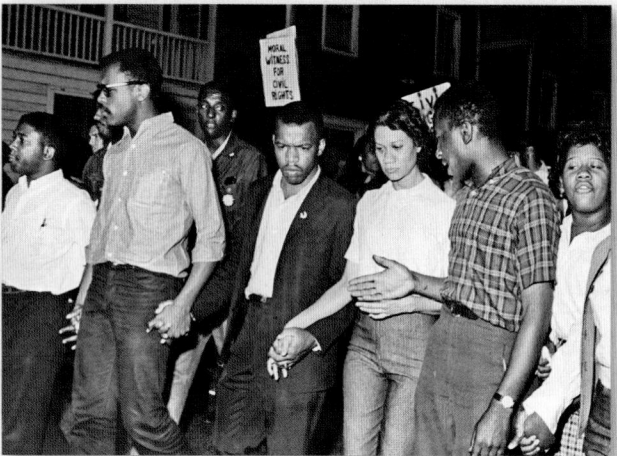

▲ *Civil rights activists march to protest a pro-segregationist speech by Alabama governor George Wallace in 1964.*

Major Events of the Civil Rights Movement

- African American community in Montgomery, Alabama, led by Dr. Martin Luther King, Jr., organizes the Montgomery bus boycott.
- African American students are blocked from entering Little Rock High School. President Eisenhower sends in federal troops and asks Congress to pass the Civil Rights Act of 1957.
- Sit-ins begin in Greensboro, and soon young people are staging sit-ins across the South to integrate public facilities.
- Freedom Riders end segregation on interstate bus travel.
- Martin Luther King, Jr., leads a march in Birmingham, then a March on Washington to support the Civil Rights Act of 1964.
- Martin Luther King, Jr., leads a march in Selma to pressure Congress to pass the Voting Rights Act of 1965.

Major Results of the Civil Rights Movement

- Civil Rights Act of 1957
- Civil Rights Act of 1964
- Voting Rights Act of 1965
- Civil Rights Act of 1968
- End of legal segregation in schools and public facilities
- Restoration of voting rights for African Americans
- Ban on discrimination based on race in the workplace
- Increased federal power to protect civil rights

▲ *A civil rights march in Montgomery, Alabama, in 1965*

Reviewing Vocabulary

Directions: Choose the word or words that best complete the sentence.

1. In *Brown* v. *Board of Education,* the Supreme Court overturned the precedent of _____ established in *Plessy* v. *Ferguson.*

A reading requirements

B de facto segregation

C "separate but equal"

D discrimination

2. During World War II, the Congress of Racial Equality used the _____ to desegregate public restaurants.

A cloture

B sit-in

C filibuster

D March on Washington

3. Some Southern senators used a _____ to try to prevent civil rights legislation from passing.

A filibuster

B cloture

C closed vote

D walk-out

4. Prejudice and discrimination against a person because of his or her race is called

A black power.

B cloture.

C segregation.

D racism.

5. The concept of _____ was supported by militant African American leaders.

A racism

B black power

C nonviolent resistance

D freedom marches

Reviewing Main Ideas

Directions: Choose the best answer to the following questions.

Section 1 *(pp. 622–629)*

6. Which event led to the bus boycott in Montgomery, Alabama?

A a riot in Montgomery

B the CORE sit-in

C the arrest of Rosa Parks

D a church bombing

7. In 1957 the Southern Christian Leadership Conference (SCLC) set out to

A march on Washington and pass a civil rights bill.

B encourage demonstrations and boycotts.

C increase church attendance and promote brotherhood.

D end segregation and encourage voter registration.

8. *Brown* v. *Board of Education* was a significant case because

A it declared it illegal to prevent African Americans from voting.

B it declared it illegal to segregate restaurants.

C it declared it illegal to segregate public schools.

D it declared it illegal to discriminate in the selling of a house.

9. Which of the following statements best describes President Eisenhower's thoughts on civil rights?

A The government should end segregation immediately.

B Integration should only occur in government agencies.

C Segregation and racism would end as generational attitudes changed.

D Only governmental power could change people's beliefs.

TEST-TAKING TIP

Look for clues in the question that help you to eliminate certain answer choices right away. For example, if a question asks for a difference between two political leaders, you know that you can eliminate answer choices that show what they have in common.

Need Extra Help?									
If You Missed Questions . . .	1	2	3	4	5	6	7	8	9
Go to Page . . .	624	624	636–637	642–643	644–645	626	627	624	629

GO ON

Section 2 *(pp. 630–639)*

10. "Bloody Sunday" occurred in reaction to which event?

  A the Selma march

  B the passage of the Civil Rights Act of 1964

  C the March on Washington

  D the assassination of Dr. Martin Luther King, Jr.

11. How did the Civil Rights Act of 1964 help African Americans?

  A The act authorized the U.S. attorney general to send federal employees to register voters.

  B The act suspended literacy tests in counties where less than half of all adults had been allowed to vote.

  C The act outlawed discrimination in housing sales and rentals.

  D The act gave the federal government more power to force school desegregation.

Section 3 *(pp. 642–647)*

12. In response to the race riots in the mid-1960s, the federal government established which of the following?

  A SNCC

  B EEOC

  C Chicago Movement

  D Kerner Commission

13. What did the Nation of Islam, or the Black Muslims, advocate?

  A African Americans should use nonviolent resistance to fight for civil rights.

  B African Americans should separate from whites and form their own self-governing communities.

  C African Americans should use violence to overthrow the government and establish their own nation.

  D African Americans should sue the federal government to establish equality among the nation's citizens.

Critical Thinking

Directions: Choose the best answers to the following questions.

14. Which group worked to fight segregation and other inequalities primarily through the courts?

  A NAACP   **C** SCLC

  B SNCC   **D** CEEO

Base your answers to questions 15 and 16 on the map below and on your knowledge of Chapter 18.

Route of the Freedom Riders, 1961

15. The route of the Freedom Riders focused on which region of the United States?

  A the Midwest

  B the South

  C New England

  D the West

16. The final destination of the Freedom Riders was

  A Montgomery, Alabama.

  B Washington, D.C.

  C Selma, Alabama.

  D Jackson, Mississippi.

Need Extra Help?							
If You Missed Questions . . .	10	11	12	13	14	15	16
Go to Page . . .	638–639	636–637	643–644	645	622–623	R15	R15

17. Huey Newton, Eldridge Cleaver, and Bobby Seale founded which militant African American group?

A the Black Muslims

B the Black Panthers

C SNCC

D the Chicago Movement

Analyze the cartoon and answer the questions that follow. Base your answers on the cartoon and on your knowledge of Chapter 18.

18. In this cartoon, American cities are represented by

A riots.

B water.

C mines.

D ships.

19. Which of the following describes the main idea of this cartoon?

A American cities are being destroyed by racial issues.

B American cities are much like ships.

C American cities need to change direction.

D American cities should avoid racial issues.

Document-Based Questions

Directions: Analyze the document and answer the short-answer questions that follow the document.

On the evening of July 2, 1964, as he prepared to sign the historic Civil Rights Act of 1964, President Lyndon Johnson made a televised address to the American people. Below is an excerpt:

> "I want to take this occasion to talk to you about what . . . [the Civil Rights Act of 1964] means to every American. . . . We believe that all men are created equal. Yet many are denied equal treatment. . . . We believe that all men are entitled to the blessings of liberty. Yet millions are being deprived of those blessings—not because of their own failures, but because of the color of their skin. The reasons are deeply imbedded in history and tradition and the nature of man. We can understand—without rancor or hatred—how this all happened. But it cannot continue. Our Constitution, the foundation of our Republic, forbids it. The principles of our freedom forbid it. Morality forbids it. And the law I will sign tonight forbids it."
>
> —Lyndon Johnson

20. According to Johnson, what are the origins of racism?

21. What does Johnson say forbids the continuation of racism in the United States?

Extended Response

22. Select one of the African American leaders who advocated a more militant approach to the problems of racism in America than did Martin Luther King, Jr. Write an essay comparing and contrasting the ideas of that figure with King's ideas, providing your views on which approach was more effective and why. Your essay should include an introduction and at least three paragraphs with supporting details from the chapter.

STOP

History ONLINE

For additional test practice, use Self-Check Quizzes—Chapter 18 at glencoe.com.

Need Extra Help?						
If You Missed Questions . . .	17	18	19	20	21	22
Go to Page . . .	645–646	R18	R18	651	651	642–647

The Vietnam War
1954–1975

SECTION 1 Going to War in Vietnam

SECTION 2 Vietnam Divides the Nation

SECTION 3 The War Winds Down

American soldiers march up a hill in Vietnam in 1968, as fires behind them send smoke into the air.

U.S. PRESIDENTS

Eisenhower 1953–1961

Kennedy 1961–1963

Johnson 1963–1969

1955
• U.S. military aid and advisers are sent to South Vietnam

1964
• Congress passes Gulf of Tonkin Resolution

1965
• U.S. combat troops arrive in Vietnam

U.S. EVENTS

WORLD EVENTS

1955

1960

1965

1954
• France leaves Indochina; Geneva Accords divide Vietnam in two

1958
• U.S. troops land in Lebanon

1960
• U-2 spy plane is shot down

MAKING CONNECTIONS

Should Citizens Support the Government During Wartime?

During the Cold War, the United States sent troops to Vietnam to stop the spread of communism. Winning in Vietnam proved to be difficult and, as the war dragged on, many Americans began to protest. Eventually, the United States pulled out of Vietnam.

- *Why do you think the United States sent troops to Vietnam?*
- *Why do you think Vietnam divided Americans?*

FOLDABLES

Defining Vietnam Terminology
Make a Vocabulary Book Foldable to aid your review of the Vietnam War. Select terms for a 10-tab Vocabulary Book. Example terms include: *Ho Chi Minh*, *Containment*, and *Gulf of Tonkin Resolution*. Define the terms under the appropriate tab.

1968
- Tet Offensive begins
- Anti-war protest in Chicago

Nixon
1969–1974

1970
- National Guard troops kill student protesters at Kent State

1973
- Last U.S. troops leave Vietnam

1970

1975

1970
- Nixon orders invasion of Cambodia

1975
- Saigon falls to North Vietnamese invasion

History ONLINE Visit glencoe.com and enter *QuickPass*™ code TAVMT5147c19 for Chapter 19 resources.

Chapter 19 The Vietnam War **653**

Going to War in Vietnam

Guide to Reading

Big Ideas
Trade, War, and Migration American involvement in the war in Vietnam was the result of its Cold War strategy.

Content Vocabulary
- domino theory *(p. 655)*
- guerrilla *(p. 655)*
- napalm *(p. 661)*
- Agent Orange *(p. 661)*

Academic Vocabulary
- strategic *(p. 657)*
- traditional *(p. 657)*

People and Events to Identify
- Ho Chi Minh *(p. 654)*
- Dien Bien Phu *(p. 656)*
- Geneva Accords *(p. 656)*
- Ngo Dinh Diem *(p. 656)*
- Vietcong *(p. 657)*
- Gulf of Tonkin Resolution *(p. 658)*
- Ho Chi Minh trail *(p. 661)*

Reading Strategy
Organizing Complete a graphic organizer similar to the one below by providing reasons why the United States aided France in Vietnam.

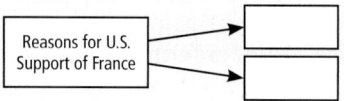

In the late 1940s and early 1950s, most Americans knew little about Indochina, France's colony in Southeast Asia. During the Cold War, however, American officials became concerned the region might fall to communism. Eventually, American troops were sent to fight in Vietnam.

American Involvement in Vietnam

MAIN Idea The Cold War policy of containment led the United States to become increasingly involved in events in Vietnam.

HISTORY AND YOU Have you met anyone who was born in Vietnam? Do you know why he or she left? Read to learn about Vietnam's complicated and tragic history.

In 1940, the Japanese invaded Vietnam. The occupation was only the latest example of foreigners ruling the Vietnamese people. The Chinese Empire had controlled the region for hundreds of years. Then, beginning in the late 1800s and lasting until World War II, France ruled Vietnam as well as neighboring Laos and Cambodia—a region known collectively as French Indochina.

The Growth of Vietnamese Nationalism

The Vietnamese did not want to be ruled by foreigners, and by the early 1900s, nationalism had become a powerful force in the country. The Vietnamese formed several political parties to push for independence or for reform of the French colonial government. One of the leaders of the nationalist movement for almost 30 years was Nguyen Tat Thanh—better known by his assumed name, **Ho Chi Minh.** At the age of 21, Ho Chi Minh traveled to Europe where he lived in London and then Paris. In 1919 he presented a petition for Vietnamese independence at the Versailles Peace Conference, but the peace treaty ignored the issue. Ho Chi Minh later visited the Soviet Union where he became an advocate of communism. In 1930 he returned to Southeast Asia, helped found the Indochinese Communist Party, and worked to overthrow French rule.

Ho Chi Minh's activities made him a wanted man. He fled Indochina and spent several years in exile in the Soviet Union and China. In 1941 he returned to Vietnam. By then, Japan had seized control of the country. Ho Chi Minh organized a nationalist group called the Vietminh. The group united both Communists and non-Communists in the struggle to expel the Japanese forces. Soon afterward, the United States began sending aid to the Vietminh.

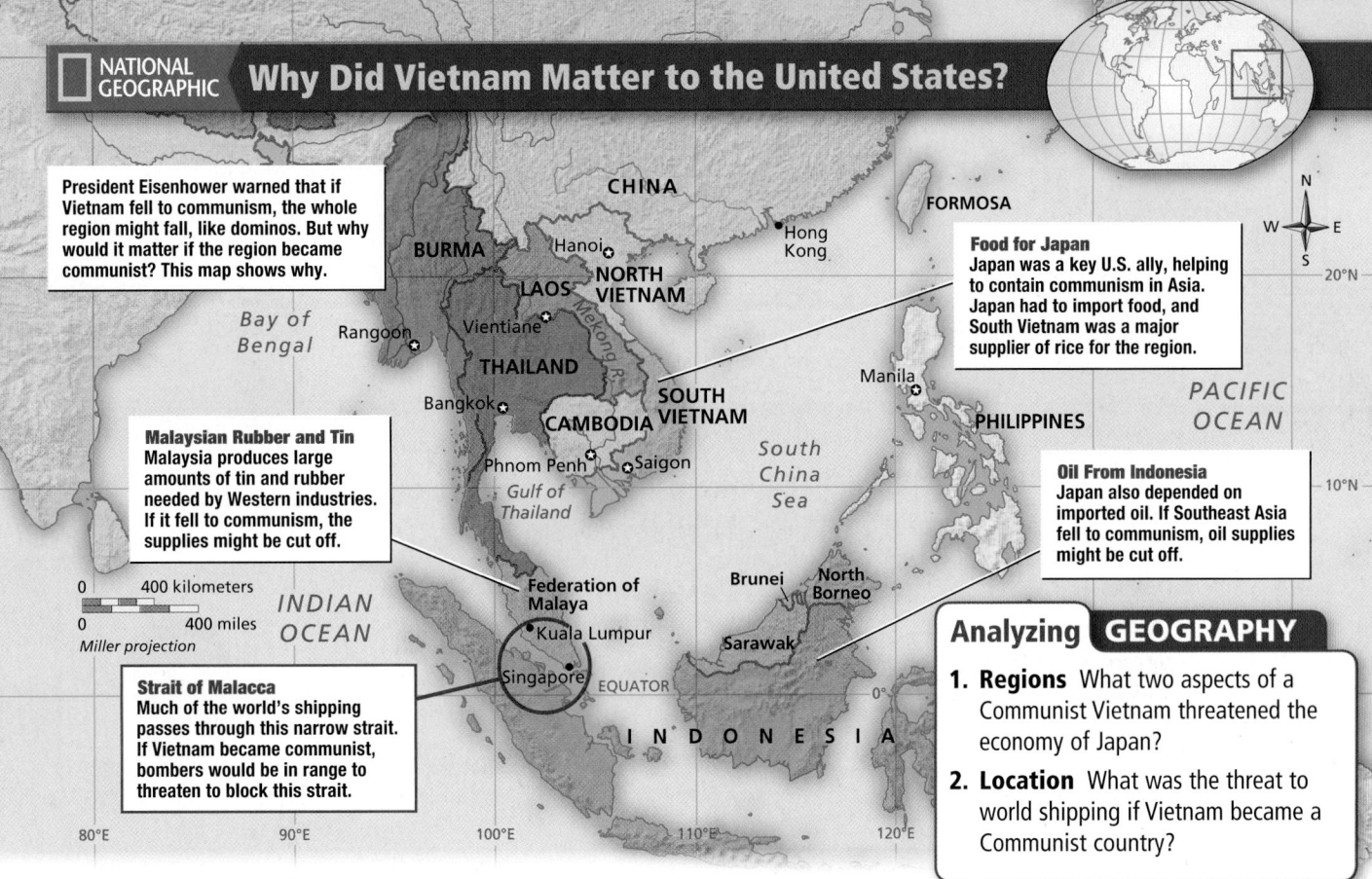

President Eisenhower warned that if Vietnam fell to communism, the whole region might fall, like dominos. But why would it matter if the region became communist? This map shows why.

Food for Japan
Japan was a key U.S. ally, helping to contain communism in Asia. Japan had to import food, and South Vietnam was a major supplier of rice for the region.

Malaysian Rubber and Tin
Malaysia produces large amounts of tin and rubber needed by Western industries. If it fell to communism, the supplies might be cut off.

Oil From Indonesia
Japan also depended on imported oil. If Southeast Asia fell to communism, oil supplies might be cut off.

Strait of Malacca
Much of the world's shipping passes through this narrow strait. If Vietnam became communist, bombers would be in range to threaten to block this strait.

Analyzing GEOGRAPHY

1. **Regions** What two aspects of a Communist Vietnam threatened the economy of Japan?
2. **Location** What was the threat to world shipping if Vietnam became a Communist country?

America Aids the French

When Japan surrendered to the Allies in 1945, it gave up control of Indochina. Ho Chi Minh quickly declared Vietnam to be an independent nation. France, however, had no intention of allowing Vietnam to become independent. Seeking to regain their colonial empire in Southeast Asia, French troops returned to Vietnam in 1946 and drove the Vietminh forces into hiding in the countryside.

The Vietminh fought back against the French-dominated regime and slowly gained control of large areas of the countryside. As the fighting escalated, France appealed to the United States for help. The request put American officials in a difficult position. The United States opposed colonialism. It had pressured the Dutch to give up their empire in Indonesia and supported the British decision to give India independence in 1947. In Vietnam, however, the independence movement had become entangled with the Communist movement. American officials did not want France to control Vietnam, but they also did not want Vietnam to be communist.

Two events convinced President Truman to help France—the fall of China to communism and the outbreak of the Korean War. The latter, in particular, seemed to indicate that the Soviet Union had begun a major push to impose communism on East Asia. Shortly after the Korean War began, Truman authorized military aid to French forces in Vietnam. President Eisenhower continued Truman's policy and defended his decision with what became known as the **domino theory**—the idea that if Vietnam fell to communism, the rest of Southeast Asia would follow:

PRIMARY SOURCE

"You have a row of dominoes set up, you knock over the first one, and what will happen to the last one is the certainty that it will go over very quickly. . . . Asia, after all, has already lost some 450 million of its peoples to Communist dictatorship, and we simply can't afford greater losses."

—President Eisenhower, quoted in *America in Vietnam*

Defeat at Dien Bien Phu

Despite aid from the United States, the French continued to struggle against the Vietminh, who consistently frustrated the French with hit-and-run and ambush tactics. These are the tactics of **guerrillas**, irregular troops who blend into the civilian population and are difficult for regular armies to fight.

CHINA

Dien Bien Phu

BURMA

20°N

Hanoi

LAOS

NORTH VIETNAM

Vientiane

Rangoon

Mekong River

THAILAND

Bangkok

CAMBODIA

SOUTH VIETNAM

South China Sea

Gulf of Thailand

Phnom Penh

Saigon

N
W E
S

0   400 kilometers
0   400 miles
Miller projection

100°E   110°E

▲ Ho Chi Minh, Communist leader of North Vietnam, was determined to reunite Vietnam and began arming Vietcong guerrillas to seize power in South Vietnam.

▲ Mao Zedong, leader of Communist China, supported North Vietnam.

▲ Ngo Dinh Diem, South Vietnam's president, accepted American aid to fight the Vietcong.

Analyzing GEOGRAPHY

1. **Regions** Why do you think Mao supported North Vietnam?
2. **Human-Environment Interaction** What difficulties would North Vietnam face in sending aid to the Vietcong?

The mounting casualties and the inability of the French to defeat the Vietminh made the war very unpopular in France. Finally, in 1954 the struggle reached a turning point when the French commander ordered his forces to occupy the mountain town of **Dien Bien Phu.** Seizing the town would interfere with the Vietminh's supply lines and force them into open battle. Soon afterward, a huge Vietminh force surrounded Dien Bien Phu and began bombarding the town. On May 7, 1954, the French force at Dien Bien Phu fell to the Vietminh. The defeat convinced the French to make peace and withdraw from Indochina.

Geneva Accords

Negotiations to end the conflict were held in Geneva, Switzerland. The **Geneva Accords** divided Vietnam along the 17th parallel, with Ho Chi Minh and the Vietminh in control of North Vietnam and a pro-Western regime in control of the South. In 1956 elections were to be held to reunite the country under a single government. The Geneva Accords also recog-

nized Cambodia's independence. Laos had gained independence in the previous year.

Shortly after the Geneva Accords partitioned Vietnam, the French troops left. The United States became the principal protector of the new government in the South, led by a nationalist leader named **Ngo Dinh Diem** (NOH DIHN deh•EHM). Like Ho Chi Minh, Diem had been educated abroad, but, unlike the North Vietnamese leader, Diem was pro-Western and fiercely anti-Communist. A Catholic, he welcomed the roughly one million North Vietnamese Catholics who migrated south to escape Ho Chi Minh's rule.

The elections mandated by the Geneva Accords never took place. In a special referendum, Diem became president of the new Republic of Vietnam in the South. He then refused to permit the 1956 elections, fearing Ho Chi Minh would win. Eisenhower approved Diem's actions and increased American aid to South Vietnam.

✓ Reading Check **Summarizing** Why did Ho Chi Minh lead a resistance movement against France?

America Becomes Involved in Vietnam

MAIN Idea Political pressures in the United States led the nation to become deeply involved in the civil war in Vietnam.

HISTORY AND YOU Do you have a relative or family friend who fought in the Vietnam War? Read on to find out why the United States got involved in this complicated conflict.

After Ngo Dinh Diem refused to hold national elections and began to crack down on Communist groups in South Vietnam, Ho Chi Minh and the Communists began an armed struggle to reunify the nation. They organized a new guerrilla army of South Vietnamese Communists, which became known as the **Vietcong.** As fighting began between the Vietcong and South Vietnam's forces, President Eisenhower sent hundreds of military advisers to train South Vietnam's army.

Despite American assistance, the Vietcong continued to grow more powerful because many Vietnamese opposed Diem's government. The Vietcong's use of terror was also effective. By 1961, the Vietcong had assassinated thousands of government officials and established control over much of the countryside. In response Diem looked increasingly to the United States for help.

Kennedy Takes Over

On taking office in 1961, President Kennedy continued the nation's policy of support for South Vietnam. Like Presidents Truman and Eisenhower before him, Kennedy saw the Southeast Asian country as vitally important in the battle against communism.

In political terms, Kennedy needed to appear tough on communism, since Republicans often accused Democrats of having lost China to communism during the Truman administration. From 1961 to late 1963, the number of American military personnel in South Vietnam jumped from about 2,000 to around 15,000.

American officials believed that the Vietcong continued to grow because Diem's government was unpopular and corrupt. They urged him to create a more democratic government and to introduce reforms to help Vietnam's peasants. Diem introduced some limited reforms, but they had little effect.

One program Diem introduced, at the urging of American advisers, made the situation worse. The South Vietnamese created special fortified villages known as **strategic** hamlets. These villages were protected by machine guns, bunkers, trenches, and barbed wire. Vietnamese officials then moved villagers to the strategic hamlets. The program proved to be extremely unpopular. Many peasants resented being uprooted from their villages, where they had worked to build farms and where many of their ancestors lay buried.

The Overthrow of Diem

Diem made himself even more unpopular by discriminating against Buddhism, one of the country's most widely practiced religions. In the spring of 1963, Diem, a Catholic, banned the **traditional** religious flags for Buddha's birthday. When Buddhists took to the streets in protest, Diem's police killed 9 people and injured 14 others. In the demonstrations that followed, a Buddhist monk poured gasoline over his robes and set himself on fire, the first of several Buddhists to do so. Images of their self-destruction horrified Americans as they watched the footage on television news reports. These extreme acts of protest were a disturbing sign of the opposition to the Diem regime.

In August 1963 American ambassador Henry Cabot Lodge arrived in Vietnam. He quickly learned that Diem's unpopularity had so alarmed several Vietnamese generals that they were plotting to overthrow him. When Lodge expressed American sympathy for their cause, the generals launched a military coup. They seized power on November 1, 1963, and executed Diem shortly afterward.

Diem's overthrow only made matters worse. Despite his unpopularity with some Vietnamese, Diem had been a respected nationalist and a capable administrator. After his death, South Vietnam's government grew increasingly weak and unstable. The United States became even more deeply involved in order to prop it up. Coincidentally, three weeks after Diem's death, President Kennedy was assassinated. The presidency, as well as the growing problem of Vietnam, now belonged to Kennedy's vice president, Lyndon Johnson.

Johnson and Vietnam

Initially, President Johnson exercised caution and restraint regarding the conflict in Vietnam. "We seek no wider war," he repeatedly promised. At the same time, Johnson was determined to prevent South Vietnam from becoming communist. "The battle against communism," he declared shortly before becoming president, "must be joined ... with strength and determination."

Politics also played a role in Johnson's Vietnam policy. Like Kennedy, Johnson remembered that many Republicans blamed the Truman administration for the fall of China to communism in 1949. Should the Democrats also "lose" Vietnam, Johnson feared, it might cause a "mean and destructive debate that would shatter my Presidency, kill my administration, and damage our democracy."

For the text of the Gulf of Tonkin Resolution see R57 in **Documents in American History.**

The Gulf of Tonkin Resolution On August 2, 1964, President Johnson announced that North Vietnamese torpedo boats had fired on two American destroyers in the Gulf of Tonkin. Two days later, the president reported that another similar attack had taken place. Johnson was campaigning for the presidency and was very sensitive to accusations of being soft on communism. He insisted that North Vietnam's attacks were unprovoked and immediately ordered American aircraft to attack North Vietnamese ships and naval facilities. Johnson did not reveal that the American warships had been helping the South Vietnamese conduct electronic spying and commando raids against North Vietnam.

Johnson then asked Congress for the authority to defend American forces and American allies in Southeast Asia. Congress agreed to Johnson's request with little debate. Most members of Congress agreed with Republican representative Ross Adair of Indiana, who defiantly declared, "The American flag has been fired upon. We will not and cannot tolerate such things."

On August 7, 1964, the Senate and House passed the **Gulf of Tonkin Resolution,** authorizing the president to "take all necessary measures to repel any armed attack against the forces of the United States and to prevent further aggression." With only two dissenting votes, Congress had, in effect, handed its war powers over to the president.

The United States Sends in Troops

Shortly after Congress passed the Gulf of Tonkin Resolution, the Vietcong began to attack bases where American advisers were stationed in South Vietnam. The attacks began in the fall of 1964 and continued to escalate. After a Vietcong attack on a base at Pleiku in February 1965 left eight Americans dead and more than 100 wounded, President Johnson decided to respond. Less than 14 hours after the attack, American aircraft bombed North Vietnam.

After the air strikes, one poll showed that Johnson's approval rating on his handling of Vietnam jumped from 41 percent to 60 percent. Further, nearly 80 percent of Americans agreed that without American assistance, Southeast Asia would fall to the Communists. An equivalent number believed that the United States should send combat troops to Vietnam

Debates IN HISTORY

Should America Fight in Vietnam?

As the war in Vietnam dragged on, Americans became increasingly divided about the nation's role in the conflict. In January 1966, George W. Ball, undersecretary of state to President Johnson, delivered an address to indicate "how we got [into Vietnam] and why we must stay." George Kennan, a former ambassador to the Soviet Union, testified before the Senate Foreign Relations Committee in that same year, arguing that American involvement in Vietnam was "something we would not choose deliberately if the choice were ours to make all over again today."

to prevent that from happening. The president's actions also met with strong approval from his closest advisers, including Secretary of Defense Robert McNamara and National Security Adviser McGeorge Bundy.

Some officials disagreed, chief among them Undersecretary of State George Ball, who initially supported involvement in Vietnam but later turned against it. He warned that if the United States got too involved, it would be difficult to get out. "Once on the tiger's back," he warned, "we cannot be sure of picking the place to dismount."

Most of the advisers who surrounded Johnson, however, firmly believed the nation had a duty to halt communism in Vietnam, both to maintain stability in Southeast Asia and to ensure the United States's continuing power and prestige in the world. In a memo to the president, Bundy argued:

PRIMARY SOURCE

"The stakes in Vietnam are extremely high. The American investment is very large, and American responsibility is a fact of life which is palpable in the atmosphere of Asia, and even elsewhere. The international prestige of the U.S. and a substantial part of our influence are directly at risk in Vietnam."

—quoted in *The Best and the Brightest*

In March 1965, President Johnson expanded American involvement by beginning a sustained bombing campaign against North Vietnam code-named Operation Rolling Thunder. That same month, the president also ordered the first combat troops into Vietnam. American soldiers would now fight alongside South Vietnamese troops against the Vietcong.

Reading Check **Describing** How did politics play a role in President Johnson's Vietnam policy?

YES

George W. Ball
Undersecretary of State

PRIMARY SOURCE

"[T]he conflict in Viet-Nam is a product of the great shifts and changes triggered by the Second World War. . . . [T]he Soviet Union under Stalin exploited the confusion to push out the perimeter of its power and influence in an effort to extend the outer limits of Communist domination by force or the threat of force. . . .

The bloody encounters in [Vietnam] . . . are thus in a real sense battles and skirmishes in a continuing war to prevent one Communist power after another from violating internationally recognized boundary lines fixing the outer limits of Communist dominion. . . .

In the long run our hopes for the people of South Vietnam reflect our hopes for people everywhere. What we seek is a world living in peace and freedom."

—Speech delivered January 30, 1966

NO

George F. Kennan
Former Diplomat

PRIMARY SOURCE

"Vietnam is not a region of major military-industrial importance. . . . Even a situation in which South Vietnam was controlled exclusively by the Vietcong, . . . would not present in my opinion, dangers great enough to justify our direct military intervention.

And to attempt to crush North Vietnamese strength to a point where Hanoi could no longer give any support to Vietcong political activity in the South would. . . have the effect of bringing in Chinese forces at some point. . . .

Our motives are widely misinterpreted; and the spectacle of Americans inflicting grievous injury on the lives of a poor and helpless people. . . produces reactions among millions of people throughout the world profoundly detrimental to the image we would like them to hold of this country."

—Testimony before the Senate Foreign Relations Committee, February 10, 1966

DBQ Document-Based Questions

1. **Summarizing** Why does Ball believe that the United States is justified in fighting in Vietnam?

2. **Explaining** What are the three main points of Kennan's argument?

3. **Contrasting** What is the fundamental difference between the views of Ball and Kennan?

4. **Evaluating** With which position do you agree? Write a paragraph to explain your choice.

A Bloody Stalemate

MAIN Idea The failure of United States forces to defeat the Vietcong and the deaths of thousands of American soldiers led many Americans to question the nation's involvement in Vietnam.

HISTORY AND YOU Have you ever heard people compare a contemporary military conflict to the Vietnam War? Read on to find out why some people fear becoming involved in a similar conflict today.

By the end of 1965, more than 180,000 American combat troops were fighting in Vietnam. In 1966 that number doubled. Since the American military was extremely strong, it marched into Vietnam with great confidence. "America seemed omnipotent then," wrote Philip Caputo, one of the first marines to arrive. "We saw ourselves as the champions of a 'cause that was destined to triumph.'"

Lacking the firepower of the Americans, the Vietcong used ambushes, booby traps, and other guerrilla tactics. Ronald J. Glasser, an American army doctor, described the devastating effects of one booby trap:

PRIMARY SOURCE

"Three quarters of the way through the tangle, a trooper brushed against a two-inch vine, and a grenade slung at chest high went off, shattering the right side of his head and body. . . . Nearby troopers took hold of the unconscious soldier and, half carrying, half dragging him, pulled him the rest of the way through the tangle."

—quoted in *Vietnam, A History*

The Vietcong also frustrated American troops by blending in with the general population and then quickly vanishing. "It was a sheer physical impossibility to keep the enemy from slipping away whenever he wished," explained one American general. Journalist Linda Martin noted, "It's a war where nothing is ever quite certain and nowhere is ever quite safe."

NATIONAL GEOGRAPHIC **The Vietnam War, 1965–1973**

CHINA

Dien Bien Phu
Hanoi
Gulf of Tonkin

LAOS
NORTH VIETNAM

Vientiane

Con Thien 1967

Khe Sanh 1968

Hue 1968

South China Sea

Vinh Huy 1967

Dak To 1967

Cu Nghi 1966

Ia Drang 1965

February 8–March, 1971: Invasion of Laos

THAILAND

May 1–June 29, 1970: Invasion of Cambodia

CAMBODIA

SOUTH VIETNAM

Phnom Penh
Saigon

0   200 kilometers
0   200 miles
Miller projection

20°N

100°E

10°N

110°E

Major U.S. and South Vietnamese troop movement

Major North Vietnamese supply line

Major battle

▲ Although helicopters helped American troops cope with Vietnam's jungles and mountains, napalm bombs (right) were also used to counter the thick foliage.

Analyzing GEOGRAPHY

1. **Places** What countries were invaded during the Vietnam War?

2. **Movement** Why was it difficult to seal South Vietnam's border?

"Search and Destroy"

To counter the Vietcong's tactics, American troops went on "search and destroy" missions. They tried to find enemy troops, bomb their positions, destroy their supply lines, and force them out into the open for combat.

The Vietcong evaded American forces by hiding out in the thick jungle or escaping through tunnels dug in the earth. To take away the Vietcong's ability to hide, American forces literally destroyed the landscape. American planes dropped **napalm**, a jellied gasoline that explodes on contact. They also used **Agent Orange**, a chemical that strips leaves from trees and shrubs, turning farmland and forest into wasteland. For those South Vietnamese still living in the countryside, danger lay on all sides.

United States military leaders underestimated the Vietcong's strength. They also misjudged the enemy's stamina and the support they had among the South Vietnamese. American generals believed that continuously bombing and killing large numbers of Vietcong would destroy the enemy's morale and force them to give up. The guerrillas, however, had no intention of surrendering, and they were willing to accept huge losses to achieve their goals.

The Ho Chi Minh Trail

In the Vietcong's war effort, North Vietnamese support was a major factor. Although the Vietcong forces were made up of many South Vietnamese, North Vietnam provided arms, advisers, and leadership. As Vietcong casualties mounted, North Vietnam began sending North Vietnamese Army units to fight.

North Vietnam sent arms and supplies south by way of a network of jungle paths known as the **Ho Chi Minh trail.** The trail wound through the countries of Cambodia and Laos, bypassing the border between North and South Vietnam. Because the trail passed through countries not directly involved in the war, President Johnson refused to allow a full-scale attack on the trail to shut it down.

North Vietnam itself received military weapons and other support from the Soviet Union and China. One of the main reasons President Johnson refused to order a full-scale invasion of North Vietnam was his fear that such an attack would bring China into the war, as had happened in Korea. By placing limits on the war, however, Johnson made it very difficult to win. Instead of conquering enemy territory, American troops were forced to fight a war of attrition—a strategy of defeating the enemy forces by wearing them down. This strategy led troops to conduct grisly body counts after battles to determine how many enemy soldiers had been killed. The U.S. military began measuring "progress" in the war by the number of enemy dead.

Bombing from American planes killed as many as 220,000 Vietnamese between 1965 and 1967. By the end of 1966, more than 6,700 American soldiers had been killed. The notion of a quick and decisive victory grew increasingly remote. As a result, many citizens back home began to question the nation's involvement in the war.

Reading Check **Describing** What tactics did the United States adopt to fight the Vietcong?

Section 1 REVIEW

Vocabulary

1. **Explain** the significance of: Ho Chi Minh, domino theory, guerrilla, Dien Bien Phu, Geneva Accords, Ngo Dinh Diem, Vietcong, Gulf of Tonkin Resolution, napalm, Agent Orange, Ho Chi Minh trail.

Main Ideas

2. **Explaining** What convinced the French to pull out of Vietnam?

3. **Determining Cause and Effect** What was the result of the overthrow of Diem in Vietnam?

4. **Analyzing** Why did fighting in Vietnam turn into a stalemate by the mid-1960s?

Critical Thinking

5. **Big Ideas** How did American Cold War politics lead to the United States fighting a war in Vietnam?

6. **Sequencing** Use a graphic organizer similar to the one below to sequence events that led to U.S. involvement in Vietnam.

| August 1963 | November 1, 1963 | August 2, 1964 |

| August 7, 1964 | February 1965 | March 1965 |

7. **Analyzing Visuals** Study the map on page 655. Why is China's location significant in relation to the Cold War struggles in Southeast Asia?

Writing About History

8. **Persuasive Writing** Suppose you are a member of Congress in August 1964. Write a statement supporting or opposing the Gulf of Tonkin Resolution.

History ONLINE

Study Central™ To review this section, go to glencoe.com and click on Study Central.

GEOGRAPHY & HISTORY

The Ho Chi Minh Trail

North and South Vietnam were long narrow countries. As a result, the border between them was very narrow and easy to defend. In order to send supplies and troops to the south, the North Vietnamese had to find a way around the border. They achieved this by crossing (illegally) into Laos and Cambodia, two neutral nations to the west, then heading south bypassing South Vietnam's northern border. The mountains and rain forests of the region provided cover for people using the trails and roads that ran south. The Americans referred to the elaborate network of roads, trails, forest paths, bridges, tunnels, and shelters as the Ho Chi Minh Trail.

How Did Geography Influence the Ho Chi Minh Trail?

The Ho Chi Minh Trail followed the topography—or natural physical features—of the region. When viewed from aircraft, the trail often disappeared and blended into the surrounding countryside, making it very difficult to attack. Furthermore, it provided access to multiple points along South Vietnam's long western border, which was much harder for American and South Vietnamese troops to defend. By 1967, an estimated 20,000 Vietnamese soldiers traveled the route each month. The American military tried to disrupt the flow of people and goods, but this proved very difficult to do. By the end of the war, the Ho Chi Minh Trail stretched some 12,000 miles (19,312 km) through the canopied rain forests.

Analyzing GEOGRAPHY

1. **Movement** What diplomatic and international problems were caused by the route of the Ho Chi Minh Trail?

2. **Human-Environment Interaction** What kinds of challenges did the geography of Southeast Asia pose for fighting a war?

▲ In an effort to close the trail and ambush enemy troops using it, American troops set up "firebases" on hilltops overlooking part of the trail. Helicopters helped American troops overcome the region's difficult terrain. They could quickly move men and supplies over the rain forest.

▲ The Vietnamese moved goods along the trail in many ways. Most porters carried goods on their back; others strapped goods to bicycles. Trucks carried supplies and people on wider parts of the trail.

American aircraft tried to destroy troops and vehicles on the trail by dropping bombs, including napalm—a jellied gasoline that would catch fire and burn a wide area.

To deprive the enemy of cover, American aircraft sprayed areas near the trail with defoliants that killed all plant life, leaving a barren area. The most famous chemical used was Agent Orange.

Vietnam Divides the Nation

Guide to Reading

Big Ideas
Group Action Many Americans protested to end their country's involvement in the Vietnam War.

Content Vocabulary
- credibility gap *(p. 664)*
- teach-in *(p. 665)*
- dove *(p. 667)*
- hawk *(p. 667)*

Academic Vocabulary
- media *(p. 664)*
- disproportionate *(p. 665)*

People and Events to Identify
- William Westmoreland *(p. 664)*
- Tet Offensive *(p. 667)*

Reading Strategy
Organizing Complete a graphic organizer similar to the one below to list the reasons for opposition to the Vietnam War.

Reasons for Opposition to Vietnam War

As casualties mounted in Vietnam, many Americans began to protest against the war. Discouraged by domestic conflict over the war, rising violence, and the apparent lack of progress in Vietnam, President Johnson announced he would not seek another term as president.

An Antiwar Movement Emerges

MAIN Idea The Vietnam War produced sharp divisions between Americans who supported the war and those who did not, and the resulting political turmoil led President Johnson to decide not to run again for president.

HISTORY AND YOU Do you know people who did not support the war in Iraq and those who did? Read on to find out how differences over the Vietnam War began to divide the country.

When American troops first entered the Vietnam War in the spring of 1965, many Americans supported the military effort. A Gallup poll published soon afterward showed that 66 percent of Americans approved of the policy in Vietnam. As the war dragged on, however, public support began to drop. Suspicion of the government's truthfulness about the war was a significant reason. Throughout the early years of the war, the American commander in South Vietnam, General **William Westmoreland,** reported that the enemy was on the brink of defeat. In 1967 he confidently declared that the "enemy's hopes are bankrupt" and added, "we have reached an important point where the end begins to come into view."

Contradicting such reports were less optimistic **media** accounts, especially on television. Vietnam was the first "television war," with footage of combat appearing nightly on the evening news. Day after day, millions of people saw images of wounded and dead Americans and began to doubt government reports. In the opinion of many people, a **credibility gap** had developed, meaning it was hard to believe what the Johnson administration said about the war.

Congress, which had given the president a nearly free hand in Vietnam, soon grew uncertain about the war. Beginning in February 1966 the Senate Foreign Relations Committee held "educational" hearings on Vietnam, calling in Secretary of State Dean Rusk and other policy makers to explain the administration's military strategy. The committee also listened to critics, such as American diplomat George Kennan. Although Kennan had helped to create the policy of containment, he argued that Vietnam was not strategically important to the United States.

'CHOPPING BLOCK'

▲ An axe labeled "Vietnam Issue" splits the nation in two.

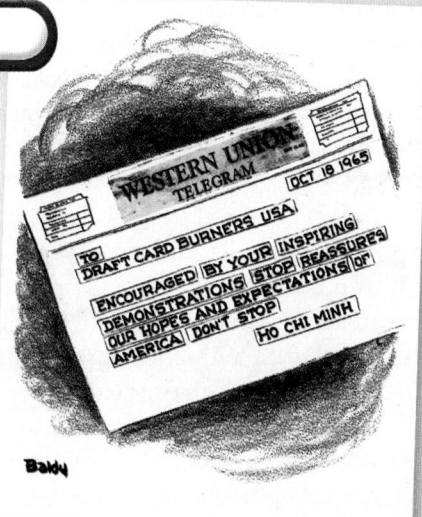

◄ Ho Chi Minh sends a telegram praising antiwar protesters.

Analyzing VISUALS

1. **Finding the Main Idea** What is the main message of the cartoon on the left?

2. **Making Inferences** The cartoon on the right was drawn before the one on the left. Do you think that differences between the two indicate a change in attitude toward antiwar protests? Explain.

Teach-ins Begin

In March 1965, a group of faculty members and students at the University of Michigan joined together in a **teach-in.** They discussed the issues surrounding the war and reaffirmed their reasons for opposing it. In May 1965, 122 colleges held a "National Teach-In" by radio for more than 100,000 antiwar demonstrators.

People who opposed the war did so for different reasons. Some saw the conflict as a civil war in which the United States had no business interfering. Others viewed South Vietnam as a corrupt dictatorship and believed that defending it was immoral and unjust.

Anger at the Draft

Young protesters especially focused on what they saw as an unfair draft system. Until 1969, a college student was often able to defer military service until after graduation. By contrast, young people from working-class families were more likely to be drafted and sent to Vietnam because they were unable to afford college. Draftees in the military were most likely to be assigned to dangerous combat units. In 1969 draftees made up 62 percent of battle deaths.

The majority of soldiers who served in Vietnam, however, were volunteer enlistees. Holding out the military as an avenue to vocational training and upward social mobility, military recruiters encouraged youth in poor and working-class communities to enlist. Thus, a **disproportionate** number of working-class youths, many of them minorities, were among the volunteers who served in Vietnam.

The Vietnam War coincided with the high tide of the civil rights movement, so the treatment of African American soldiers came under scrutiny. Between 1961 and 1966, African Americans constituted about 10 percent of military personnel while African Americans comprised about 13 percent of the total population of the United States. Because African Americans were more likely to be assigned to combat units, however, they accounted for almost 20 percent of combat-related deaths.

This unequal death rate angered African American leaders. In April 1967 Dr. Martin Luther King, Jr. publicly condemned the conflict:

"I speak for the poor of America who are paying the double price of smashed hopes at home and death and corruption in Vietnam. . . . The great initiative in this war is ours. The initiative to stop it must be ours."

—quoted in *A Testament of Hope*

In response, military officials tried to lower the number of African American casualties. At war's end, African Americans made up about 12 percent of America's dead, roughly the same as their national population percentage.

As the war escalated, an increased draft call put many college students at risk. An estimated 500,000 draftees refused to go. Some burned their draft cards, or did not show up for induction, or fled the country. Between 1965 and 1968, officials prosecuted over 3,300 Americans who refused to serve in a war they opposed. In 1969 the government introduced a lottery system in which only those with low lottery numbers were subject to the draft.

Anger against the war was not confined to college campuses. Demonstrators held large and small protests against the war in towns across the country. In April 1965 Students for a Democratic Society (SDS), a left-wing student organization, organized a march on Washington, D.C., that drew over 20,000 people. Two years later, in October 1967, a rally at the Lincoln Memorial drew tens of thousands of protesters as well. When a group of Iowa public school students protested the war by wearing black armbands to school, school district administrators suspended them to maintain "the disciplined atmosphere of the classroom." The Supreme Court decision for the case, *Tinker* v. *Des Moines Independent Community School District* (1969), supported the students' actions, saying that the armbands were a form of symbolic speech, and therefore protected by the First Amendment.

Anger over the draft also fueled discussions about the voting age. Many draftees argued that if they were old enough to fight, they were old enough to vote. In 1971 the Twenty-sixth Amendment to the Constitution was ratified, giving all citizens age 18 and older the right to vote in all state and federal elections.

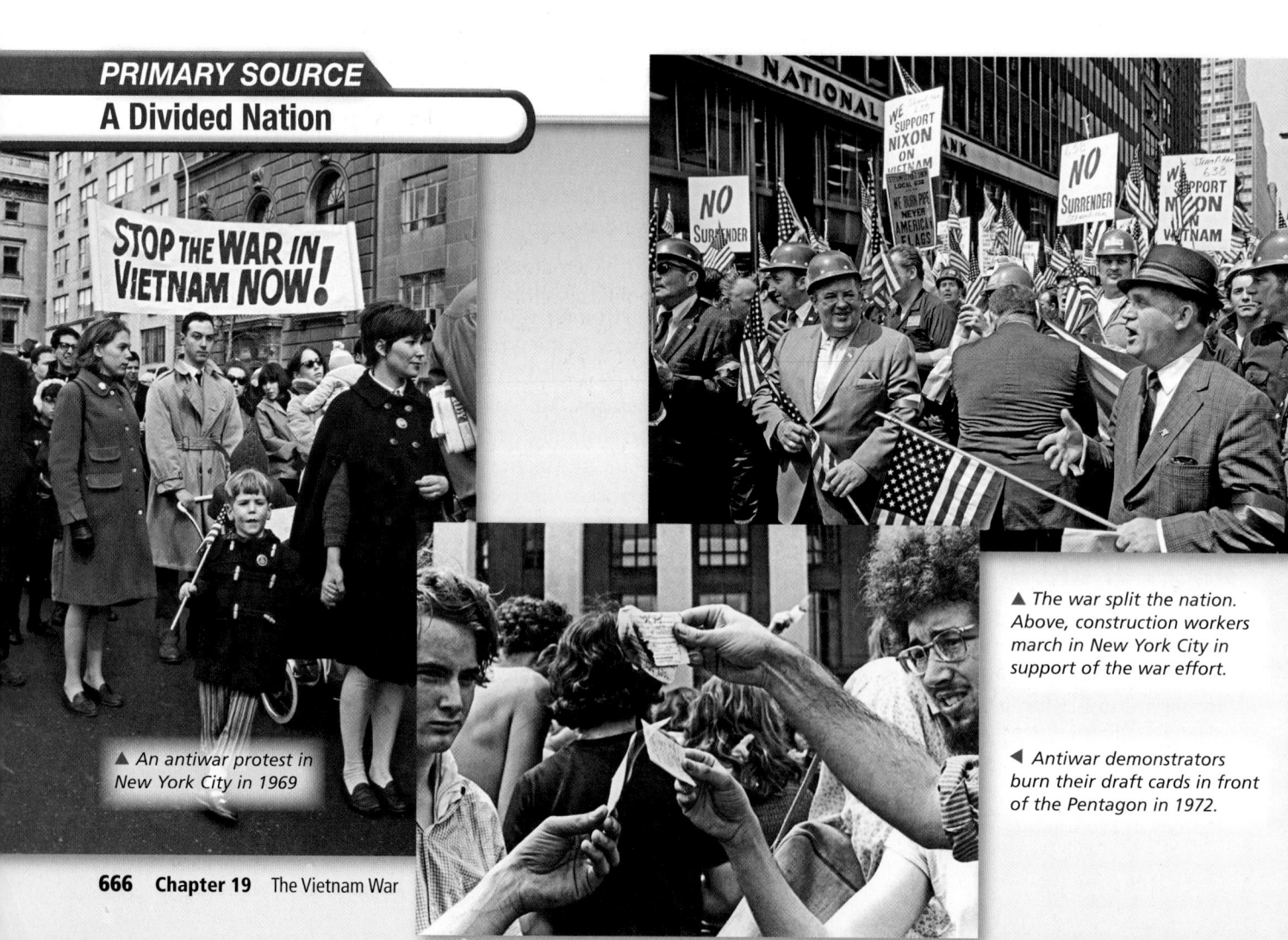

PRIMARY SOURCE

A Divided Nation

▲ An antiwar protest in New York City in 1969

▲ The war split the nation. Above, construction workers march in New York City in support of the war effort.

◄ Antiwar demonstrators burn their draft cards in front of the Pentagon in 1972.

Hawks and Doves

In the face of growing opposition to the war, President Johnson remained determined to continue fighting. He assailed his critics in Congress as "selfish men who want to advance their own interests." He dismissed the college protesters as too naive to appreciate the importance of resisting communism.

The president was not alone in his views. In a poll taken in early 1968, 53 percent of the respondents favored stronger military action in Vietnam, compared to 24 percent who wanted an end to the war. Of those Americans who supported the policy in Vietnam, many openly criticized the protesters for a lack of patriotism.

By 1968 the nation seemed to be divided into two camps. Those who wanted the United States to withdraw from Vietnam were known as **doves.** Those who insisted that the country stay and fight came to be known as **hawks.** As the two groups debated, the war appeared to take a dramatic turn for the worse, and the nation endured a year of shock and crisis.

✔ Reading Check **Explaining** What led to the ratification of the Twenty-sixth Amendment?

Opposition to the Vietnam War

Source: *Statistical Abstract of the United States.*

Analyzing VISUALS

1. **Interpreting** During which two years was opposition to the war lowest? What event occurred around that time?

2. **Synthesizing** In what year did opposition to the war peak? How was this sentiment logically related to the withdrawal of American troops?

1968: The Pivotal Year

MAIN Idea The Tet Offensive increased doubt that the United States could win in Vietnam.

HISTORY AND YOU Have you ever participated in a public-opinion poll? Read how Johnson's plummeting approval rating made him decide not to run for re-election in 1968.

The most turbulent year of the chaotic 1960s was 1968. The year saw a shocking political announcement, two traumatic assassinations, and a political convention held amid strident anti-war demonstrations. First, however, the nation endured a surprise attack in Vietnam.

The Tet Offensive

On January 30, 1968, during Tet, the Vietnamese New Year, the Vietcong and North Vietnamese launched a massive surprise attack. In this **Tet Offensive,** guerrilla fighters attacked most American airbases in South Vietnam and most of the South's major cities. Vietcong even blasted their way into the American embassy in Saigon.

Militarily, Tet was a disaster for the Vietcong. After about a month of fighting, the American and South Vietnamese soldiers repelled the enemy troops, inflicting heavy losses on them. President Johnson triumphantly noted that the enemy's effort had ended in "complete failure." Later, historians confirmed that Tet nearly destroyed the Vietcong.

The North Vietnamese, however, had scored a major political victory. The American people were shocked that an enemy supposedly on the verge of defeat could launch such a large-scale attack. When General Westmoreland requested 209,000 troops in addition to the 500,000 already in Vietnam, he seemed to be admitting the United States could not win.

To make matters worse, the media, which had tried to remain balanced in their war coverage, now openly criticized the effort. "The American people should be getting ready to accept, if they haven't already, the prospect that the whole Vietnam effort may be doomed," declared the *Wall Street Journal.* Television newscaster Walter Cronkite announced that it seemed "more certain than ever that the bloody experience in Vietnam is to end in a stalemate."

The election year 1968 was tumultuous. The country was divided over Vietnam. President Johnson chose not to run again. Protesters fought with police at the Democratic National Convention. Race riots erupted in several American cities and both Martin Luther King, Jr., and Robert Kennedy were killed.

Presidential Election of 1968

Nixon   Humphrey

Presidential Candidate	Popular Votes	% of Popular Vote	Electoral Votes
Nixon	31,710,470	43.60%	301
Humphrey	30,898,055	42.48%	191
Wallace	9,906,473	13.62%	46

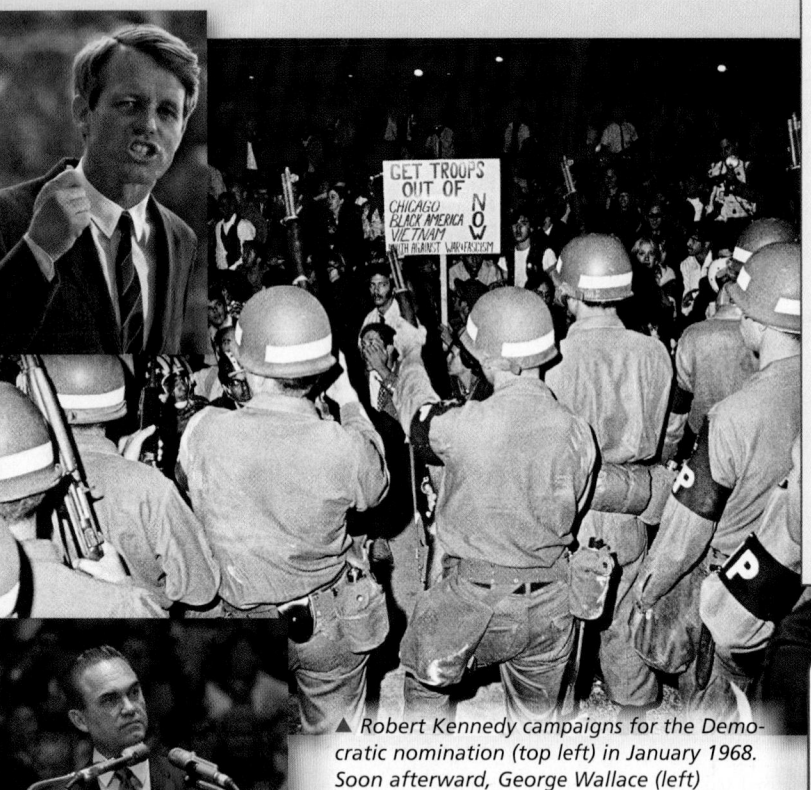

▲ *Robert Kennedy campaigns for the Democratic nomination (top left) in January 1968. Soon afterward, George Wallace (left) entered the race as an independent. Above, police confront protestors at the Democratic National Convention in August 1968.*

Analyzing VISUALS

1. **Regions** In what area of the country did George Wallace receive the most votes?
2. **Regions** Do you think Richard Nixon would have won if Wallace had not been in the race?

Public opinion no longer favored the president. In the weeks following the Tet Offensive, the president's approval rating plummeted to a dismal 35 percent, while support for his handling of the war fell even lower, to 26 percent. The administration's credibility gap now seemed too wide to repair.

Johnson Leaves the Race

With the war growing increasingly unpopular and Johnson's credibility all but gone, some Democrats began looking for an alternative candidate to nominate for president in 1968. In November 1967, even before the Tet disaster, a little-known liberal senator from Minnesota, Eugene McCarthy, became the first dove to declare he would challenge Johnson for the Democratic presidential nomination. In March 1968 McCarthy stunned the nation by winning more than 40 percent of the votes in the New Hampshire primary. Realizing that Johnson was vulnerable, Senator Robert Kennedy, who also opposed the war, quickly entered the race for the Democratic nomination.

With both the country and his own party deeply divided, Johnson addressed the public on television on March 31, 1968. He stunned viewers by announcing, "I have concluded that I should not permit the presidency to become involved in the partisan divisions that are developing in this political year. Accordingly, I shall not seek, and I will not accept, the nomination of my party for another term as your President."

A Season of Violence

Following Johnson's announcement, the nation endured even more shocking events. In April, James Earl Ray was arrested for killing Dr. Martin Luther King, Jr. Just two months later, another assassination rocked the country—that of Robert Kennedy. Kennedy, who appeared to be on his way to winning the Democratic nomination, was gunned down on June 5. The assassin was Sirhan Sirhan, an Arab nationalist angry over the candidate's pro-Israeli remarks a few nights before.

The violence that seemed to plague the country in 1968 culminated with a chaotic and well-publicized clash between antiwar protesters and police at the Democratic National Convention in Chicago. Thousands of protesters surrounded the convention center, demanding that the Democrats adopt an antiwar platform.

Despite the protests, the delegates chose Hubert Humphrey, President Johnson's vice president, as their presidential nominee. Meanwhile, in a park not far from the convention hall, the protesters and police began fighting. As officers tried to disperse demonstrators with tear gas and billy clubs, demonstrators taunted the authorities with the chant, "The whole world is watching!" A subsequent federal investigation of the incident described the event as a "police riot."

Nixon Wins the Presidency

The violence and chaos now associated with the Democratic Party benefited the 1968 Republican presidential candidate, Richard Nixon. Although defeated by John Kennedy in the 1960 election, Nixon had remained active in national politics. A third candidate, Governor George Wallace of Alabama, decided to run in 1968 as an independent. Wallace, an outspoken segregationist, sought to attract Americans who felt threatened by the civil rights movement and urban social unrest.

Public opinion polls gave Nixon a wide lead over Humphrey and Wallace. Nixon's campaign promise to unify the nation and restore law and order appealed to Americans who feared their country was spinning out of control. Nixon also declared that he had a plan for ending the war in Vietnam.

At first Humphrey's support of President Johnson's Vietnam policies hurt his campaign. After Humphrey broke with the president and called for a complete end to the bombing of North Vietnam, he began to move up in the polls. A week before the election, President Johnson helped Humphrey by announcing that the bombing had halted and that a cease-fire would follow.

Johnson's announcement had come too late, however. In the end, Nixon's promises to end the war and restore order at home were enough to sway the American people. On Election Day, Nixon defeated Humphrey by more than 100 electoral votes, although he won the popular vote by a slim margin of 43 percent to 42 percent. Wallace partially accounted for the razor-thin margin by winning 46 electoral votes and more than 13 percent of the popular vote.

Reading Check **Explaining** Why did President Johnson say he would not run for reelection in 1968?

Section 2 REVIEW

Vocabulary

1. **Explain** the significance of: William Westmoreland, credibility gap, teach-in, dove, hawk, Tet Offensive.

Main Ideas

2. **Explaining** Why did some people view the draft as unfair?

3. **Summarizing** What are three important events that made 1968 such a violent year in the United States?

Critical Thinking

4. **Big Ideas** Why did support of the war dwindle by the late 1960s?

5. **Organizing** Use a graphic organizer similar to the one below to list the effects of the Tet Offensive.

```
        ( )        ( )
           \      /
         ( Effects of
           Tet Offensive )
              |
            ( )
```

6. **Analyzing Visuals** Study the cartoon on the right on page 665. What is the message of the telegram beyond its literal meaning?

Writing About History

7. **Expository Writing** Suppose that you are living in 1968. Write a letter to the editor of a local newspaper in which you explain your reasons for either supporting or opposing the Vietnam War.

History ONLINE

Study Central™ To review this section, go to glencoe.com and click on Study Central.

The War Winds Down

Guide to Reading

Big Ideas
Trade, War, and Migration
The Vietnam War changed the way Americans viewed the government and the military, and led them to question how the armed forces were deployed.

Content Vocabulary
- linkage *(p. 670)*
- Vietnamization *(p. 670)*

Academic Vocabulary
- generation *(p. 671)*
- unresolved *(p. 675)*

People and Events to Identify
- Henry Kissinger *(p. 670)*
- Pentagon Papers *(p. 672)*
- War Powers Act *(p. 675)*

Reading Strategy
Organizing Complete a graphic organizer similar to the one below by listing the steps that President Nixon took to end American involvement in Vietnam.

Steps Nixon Took

S hortly after taking office, President Nixon moved to end the nation's involvement in the Vietnam War. The final years of the conflict, however, yielded more bloodshed and turmoil, as well as a growing cynicism in the minds of Americans about the honesty and effectiveness of the United States government.

Nixon Moves to End the War

MAIN Idea While unrest and suspicion of the government grew, the United States finally withdrew its troops from Vietnam.

HISTORY AND YOU Have you ever protested against something you felt was wrong? Read on to find out how college students reacted to what they viewed as a widening of the Vietnam War.

As a first step to fulfilling his campaign promise to end the war, Nixon appointed Harvard professor **Henry Kissinger** as special assistant for national security affairs and gave him wide authority to use diplomacy to end the conflict. Kissinger embarked upon a policy he called **linkage,** which meant improving relations with the Soviet Union and China—suppliers of aid to North Vietnam—so that he could persuade them to cut back on their aid.

Kissinger also rekindled peace talks with the North Vietnamese. In August 1969 Kissinger entered into secret negotiations with North Vietnam's negotiator, Le Duc Tho. In their talks, which dragged on for four years, Kissinger and Le Duc Tho argued over a possible cease-fire, the return of American prisoners of war, and the ultimate fate of South Vietnam.

Meanwhile, Nixon reduced the number of American troops in Vietnam. Known as **Vietnamization,** this process involved the gradual withdrawal of U.S. troops while the South Vietnamese assumed more of the fighting. On June 8, 1969, Nixon announced the withdrawal of 25,000 soldiers, but he was determined to keep a strong American presence in Vietnam to ensure bargaining power during peace negotiations. In support of that goal, the president increased air strikes against North Vietnam and—without informing Congress or the public—began secretly bombing Vietcong sanctuaries in neighboring Cambodia.

Turmoil at Home Continues

Even though the United States had begun scaling back its involvement in Vietnam, the American home front remained divided and volatile, as Nixon's war policies stirred up new waves of protest.

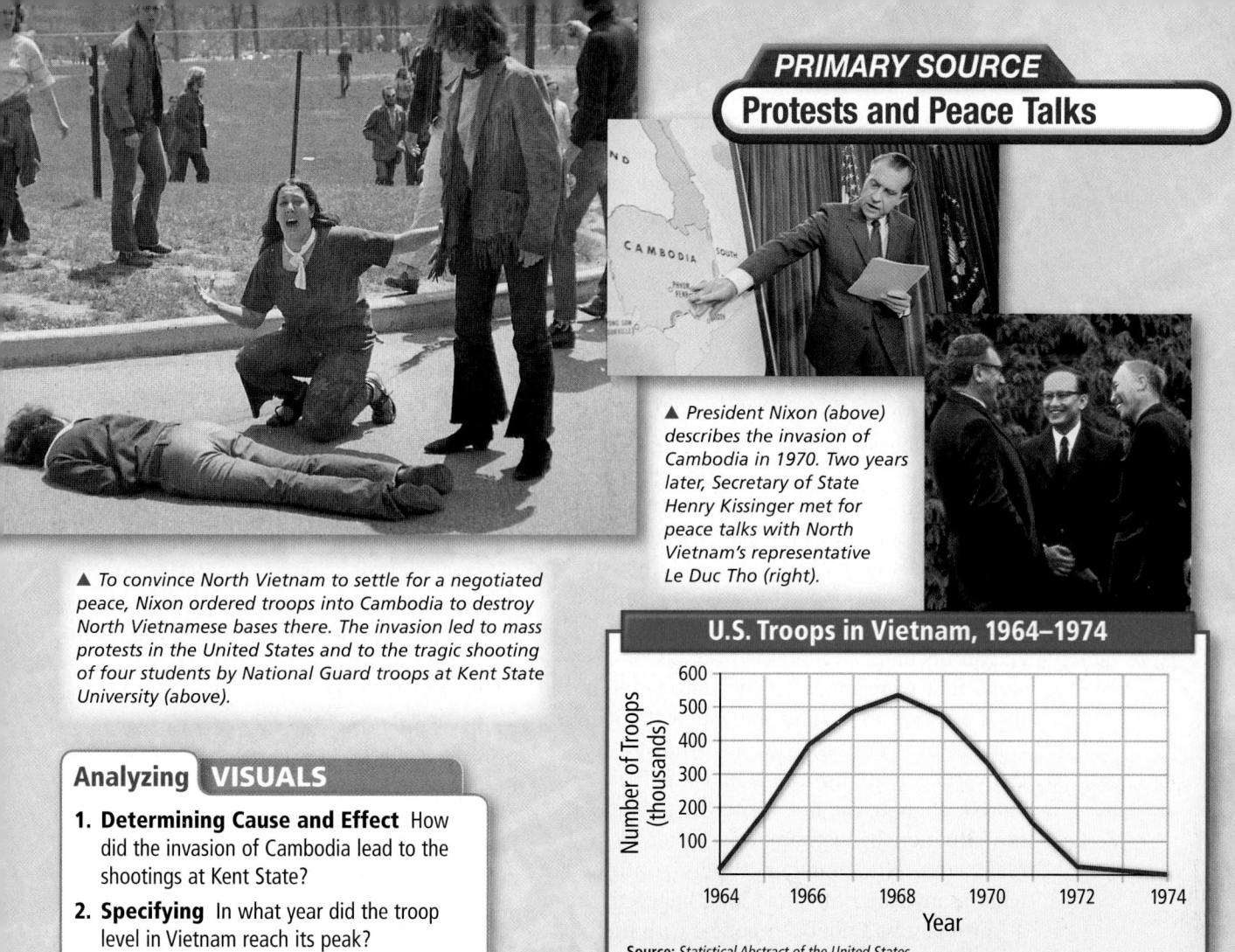

▲ President Nixon (above) describes the invasion of Cambodia in 1970. Two years later, Secretary of State Henry Kissinger met for peace talks with North Vietnam's representative Le Duc Tho (right).

▲ To convince North Vietnam to settle for a negotiated peace, Nixon ordered troops into Cambodia to destroy North Vietnamese bases there. The invasion led to mass protests in the United States and to the tragic shooting of four students by National Guard troops at Kent State University (above).

U.S. Troops in Vietnam, 1964–1974

Source: *Statistical Abstract of the United States.*

Analyzing VISUALS

1. **Determining Cause and Effect** How did the invasion of Cambodia lead to the shootings at Kent State?

2. **Specifying** In what year did the troop level in Vietnam reach its peak?

Massacre at My Lai In late 1969 Americans learned that, in the spring of 1968, an American platoon under the command of Lieutenant William Calley had massacred unarmed South Vietnamese civilians in the hamlet of My Lai. Most of the victims were old men, women, and children. Calley eventually went to prison for his role in the killings.

Most American soldiers acted responsibly and honorably during the war. The actions of a small group, however, convinced many people that the war was brutal and senseless. Jan Barry, a founder of the Vietnam Veterans Against the War, viewed My Lai as a symbol of the dilemma his **generation** faced in the conflict:

PRIMARY SOURCE

"To kill on military orders and be a criminal, or to refuse to kill and be a criminal is the moral agony of America's Vietnam war generation. It is what has forced upward of sixty thousand young Americans, draft resisters and deserters to Canada, and created one hundred thousand military deserters a year...."

—quoted in *Who Spoke Up?*

The Invasion of Cambodia Sparks Protest Americans heard more startling news when Nixon announced in April 1970 that American troops had invaded Cambodia. The troops were ordered to destroy Vietcong military bases there.

Many viewed the Cambodian invasion as a widening of the war, and it set off many protests. At Kent State University on May 4, 1970, Ohio National Guard soldiers, armed with tear gas and rifles, fired on demonstrators without an order to do so. The soldiers killed four students. Ten days later, police killed two African American students during a demonstration at Jackson State College in Mississippi.

In addition to sparking violence on campuses, the invasion of Cambodia cost Nixon significant congressional support. Numerous legislators expressed outrage over the president's failure to notify them of the action. In December 1970 an angry Congress repealed the Gulf of Tonkin Resolution, which had given the president nearly complete power in directing the war in Vietnam.

The Pentagon Papers Support for the war weakened further in 1971 when Daniel Ellsberg, a disillusioned former Defense Department worker, leaked what became known as the **Pentagon Papers** to the *New York Times.* The documents revealed that many government officials during the Johnson administration privately questioned the war while publicly defending it.

The documents contained details of decisions that were made by the presidents and their advisers to expand the war without the consent of Congress. They also showed how the various administrations had tried to convince Congress, the press, and the public that the situation in Vietnam was better than it really was. The Pentagon Papers confirmed what many Americans had long believed: the government had not been honest with them.

The United States Pulls Out

By 1971, polls showed that nearly two-thirds of Americans wanted to end the Vietnam War as quickly as possible. In April 1972 President Nixon dropped his longtime insistence that North Vietnamese troops had to withdraw from South Vietnam before any peace treaty could be signed. In October, less than a month before the presidential election, Kissinger emerged from his secret talks with Le Duc Tho to announce that "peace is at hand."

A month later, Americans went to the polls to decide on a president. Senator George McGovern, the Democratic candidate, was an outspoken critic of the war. He did not appeal to many middle-class Americans, however, who were tired of antiwar protesters. Nixon was reelected in a landslide, winning 60.7 percent of the popular vote.

Just weeks after the presidential election, the peace negotiations broke down. South Vietnam's president, Nguyen Van Thieu, refused to agree to any plan that left North Vietnamese troops in the South. Henry Kissinger tried to win additional concessions from the Communists, but talks broke off on December 16, 1972.

The next day, to force North Vietnam to resume negotiations, the Nixon administration began the most destructive air raids of the entire war. In what became known as the "Christmas bombings," American B-52s dropped thousands of tons of bombs on North Vietnamese targets for 11 straight days, pausing only on Christmas Day.

In the wake of the bombing campaign, the United States and North Vietnam returned to the bargaining table. Thieu finally gave in to American pressure and allowed North Vietnamese troops to remain in the South. On January 27, 1973, the warring sides signed an agreement "ending the war and restoring the peace in Vietnam."

The United States promised to withdraw its troops, and both sides agreed to exchange prisoners of war. The parties did not resolve the issue of South Vietnam's future, however. After almost eight years of war—the longest war in American history—the nation ended its direct involvement in Vietnam.

South Vietnam Falls

Two years after the United States pulled its troops out of Vietnam, the peace agreement collapsed. In March 1975 the North Vietnamese army launched a full-scale invasion of the South. Thieu desperately appealed to Washington, D.C., for help.

President Nixon had assured Thieu during the peace negotiations that the United States "[would] respond with full force should the settlement be violated by North Vietnam." Nixon, however, had resigned under pressure following Watergate, a scandal that broke as the war was winding down. The new president, Gerald Ford, asked for funds to aid the South Vietnamese, but Congress refused.

Without American assistance, the South Vietnamese Army was unable to stop the invasion. On April 30, the North Vietnamese captured Saigon, South Vietnam's capital, and united Vietnam under Communist rule. They then renamed the city Ho Chi Minh City.

Reading Check **Evaluating** What did the Pentagon Papers confirm for many Americans?

★ *New York Times* v. *United States*, 1971

Background to the Case

In 1971 Daniel Ellsberg leaked classified documents, known as the Pentagon Papers, to the *New York Times* and the *Washington Post*. When the newspapers attempted to publish these documents, the Nixon administration argued that publication would threaten national security. The case centered on the First Amendment guarantee of a free press.

How the Court Ruled

In a 6-to-3 per curiam opinion—*per curiam* meaning that the decision was issued by the whole Court and not specific justices—the Court found that the Nixon administration had failed to prove that publication of the Pentagon Papers would imperil the nation in any way. The *New York Times* and the *Washington Post* could publish the Pentagon Papers.

▲ Daniel Ellsberg (above, left) leaked the classified documents known as the Pentagon Papers.

PRIMARY SOURCE

Concurring View

"The Government's power to censor the press [via the First Amendment] was abolished so that the press would remain forever free to censure the Government.... And paramount among the responsibilities of a free press is the duty to prevent any part of the government from deceiving the people and sending them off to distant lands to die of foreign fevers and foreign shot and shell. In my view, far from deserving condemnation for their courageous reporting, the *New York Times*, the *Washington Post*, and other newspapers should be commended for serving the purpose that the Founding Fathers saw so clearly. In revealing the workings of government that led to the Vietnam War, the newspapers did precisely that which the Founders hoped and trusted they would do."

—Justice Hugo Black in *New York Times* v. *United States*

PRIMARY SOURCE

Dissenting View

The First Amendment, after all, is only one part of an entire Constitution. Article II of the great document vests in the Executive Branch primary power over the conduct of foreign affairs and places in that branch the responsibility for the Nation's safety.... What is needed here is a weighing, upon properly developed standards, of the broad right of the press to print and of the very narrow right of the Government to prevent. Such standards are not yet developed. The parties here are in disagreement as to what those standards should be. But even the newspapers concede that there are situations where restraint is in order and is constitutional."

—Justice Harry Blackmun, dissenting in
New York Times v. *United States*

DBQ Document-Based Questions

1. **Explaining** Why did Justice Black agree with the Court's decision? What did he imply about the government's actions?

2. **Contrasting** Why did Justice Blackmun disagree with the Court's decision?

3. **Assessing** Do you think the government can ever justify media censorship, even based on national security concerns? Explain.

The Legacy of Vietnam

MAIN Idea The Vietnam War made a negative impact on the way in which Americans viewed international conflicts, as well as their own government.

History ONLINE **Student Web Activity** Visit glencoe.com and complete the activity on the Vietnam Veterans Memorial.

HISTORY AND YOU Do you think that leaders at the highest levels of the federal government are trustworthy? Read on to find out how the Vietnam War and other events led Americans to lose some trust in their leaders.

"The lessons of the past in Vietnam," President Ford declared in 1975, "have already been learned—learned by Presidents, learned by Congress, learned by the American people—and we should have our focus on the future." Vietnam had a deep and lasting impact on American society.

The War's Human Toll

The United States paid a heavy price for its involvement in Vietnam. The war had cost the nation over $170 billion in direct costs and much more in indirect economic expenses. It had also resulted in the deaths of approximately 58,000 young Americans and the injury of more than 300,000. In Vietnam, around one million North and South Vietnamese soldiers died in the conflict, as did countless civilians.

PRIMARY SOURCE
The Legacy of Vietnam

▲ The Vietnam Veterans Memorial is inscribed with the names of the 58,249 people killed or missing in Vietnam.

The War Powers Act

• Requires the president in all cases to consult with Congress before making any troop commitments

• Requires the president to inform Congress of any commitment of troops abroad within 48 hours

• Requires the president to withdraw troops in 60 to 90 days, unless Congress explicitly approves the troop commitment

▲ Along with returning troops, many freed prisoners of war, or POWs, such as Lt. Colonel Robert Stirm, were joyfully greeted by their families. Sadly, some did not come home and were labeled as MIAs, or "missing in action," and remain so to this day.

Analyzing VISUALS

1. **Explaining** How did the War Powers Act seek to curb the power of the president?

2. **Assessing** Do you think that the legacy of Vietnam has been a lasting one? Why or why not?

Even after they returned home from fighting as in other wars, soldiers found it hard to escape the war's psychological impact. Army Specialist Doug Johnson recalled the problems he faced:

PRIMARY SOURCE

"It took a while for me to recognize that I did suffer some psychological problems in trying to deal with my experience in Vietnam. The first recollection I have of the effect took place shortly after I arrived back in the States. One evening . . . I went to see a movie on post. I don't recall the name of the movie or what it was about, but I remember there was a sad part, and that I started crying uncontrollably. It hadn't dawned on me before this episode that I had. . . succeeded in burying my emotions."

—quoted in *Touched by the Dragon*

One reason why it may have been harder for some Vietnam veterans to readjust to civilian life was that many considered the war a defeat. Many Americans wanted to forget the war. Thus, the sacrifices of many veterans often went unrecognized. There were relatively few welcome-home parades and celebrations after the war.

The war also remained **unresolved** for the American families whose relatives and friends were classified as prisoners of war (POWs) or missing in action (MIA). Despite many official investigations, these families were not convinced that the government had told the truth about POW/MIA policies.

The nation finally began to come to terms with the war almost a decade later. In 1982 the nation dedicated the Vietnam Veterans Memorial in Washington, D.C., a large black granite wall inscribed with the names of those killed and missing in action in the war. "It's a first step to remind America of what we did," veteran Larry Cox of Virginia said at the dedication of the monument.

The War's Impact on the Nation

The war also left its mark on the nation as a whole. In 1973 Congress passed the **War Powers Act** as a way to reestablish some limits on executive power. The act required the president to inform Congress of any commitment of troops abroad within 48 hours, and to withdraw them in 60 to 90 days, unless Congress explicitly approved the troop commitment. No president has recognized this limitation, and the courts have tended to avoid the issue as a strictly political question. Nonetheless, every president since the law's passage has asked Congress to authorize the use of military force before committing ground troops to combat. In general, the war shook the nation's confidence and led some to embrace isolationism, while others began to question the policy of containing communism and instead urged more negotiation with the Soviet Union.

On the domestic front, the Vietnam War increased Americans' cynicism about their government. Many felt the nation's leaders had misled them. Together with Watergate, Vietnam made Americans more wary of their leaders.

Reading Check **Describing** How did the Vietnam War affect Americans' attitudes toward international conflicts?

Section 3 REVIEW

Vocabulary

1. **Explain** the significance of: Henry Kissinger, linkage, Vietnamization, Pentagon Papers, War Powers Act.

Main Ideas

2. **Explaining** Why was the United States unable to help South Vietnam following the full-scale invasion by North Vietnam in 1975?

3. **Describing** How was the aftermath of the Vietnam War different for its veterans than postwar periods had been for veterans of earlier U.S. wars?

Critical Thinking

4. **Big Ideas** Why did Congress pass the War Powers Act? How did it reflect distrust of the executive branch of government?

5. **Organizing** Use a graphic organizer similar to the one below to list the effects of the Vietnam War on the nation.

Effects of Vietnam War

6. **Analyzing Visuals** Study the left photo on page 674. Why do you think it is important for society to have war memorials?

Writing About History

7. **Descriptive Writing** Suppose you are a college student in 1970. Write a journal entry expressing your feelings about the events at Kent State University and Jackson State College.

History ONLINE

Study Central™ To review this section, go to glencoe.com and click on Study Central.

Chapter **19** VISUAL SUMMARY

STUDY TO GO — You can study anywhere, anytime by downloading quizzes and flashcards to your PDA from glencoe.com.

Causes of the Vietnam War

- During World War II, the United States helps the people of Indochina fight the Japanese, who had invaded the region.
- After World War II, France refuses to give independence to the people of Indochina and sends troops to reestablish control.
- Led by Ho Chi Minh, the Vietminh fight the French. Ho Chi Minh wants Vietnam to be independent but also wants to build a Communist society in Vietnam.
- Concerned about the spread of communism, President Eisenhower sends aid to help the French retain control in Vietnam.
- After losing the battle of Dien Bien Phu, France pulls out of Vietnam. The Geneva Accords create North and South Vietnam.
- Ho Chi Minh becomes the leader of North Vietnam and makes it a Communist nation allied with the USSR and China. North Vietnam begins arming guerrillas to fight the South Vietnamese government.
- American leaders become worried that a "domino effect" might cause all of Southeast Asia to fall to communism if South Vietnam falls.
- President Kennedy sharply increases military aid to South Vietnam.
- President Johnson escalates U.S. involvement and gains war powers after the Gulf of Tonkin incident.

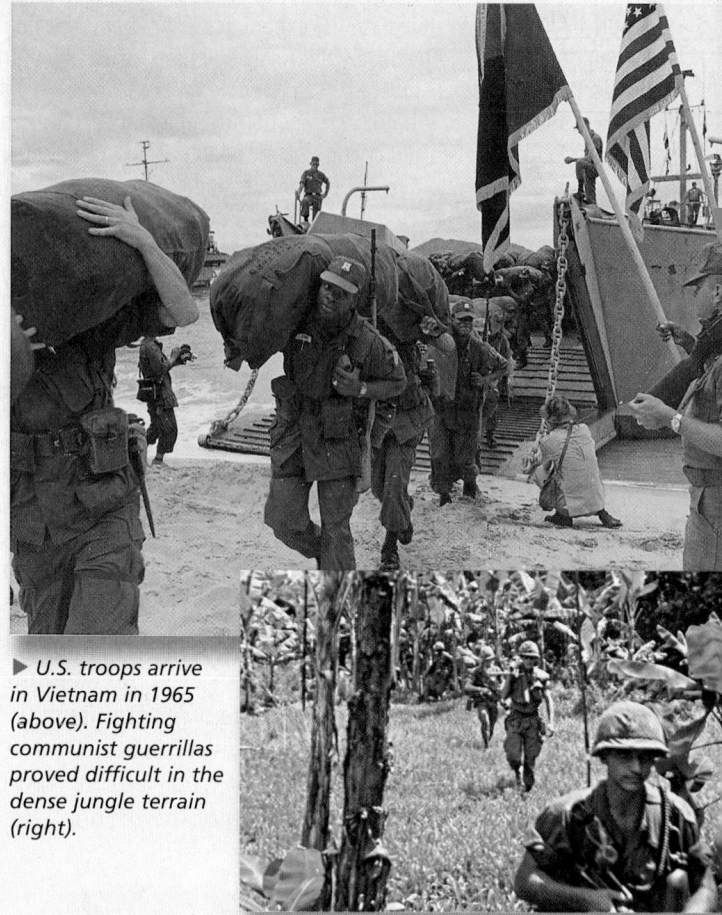

▶ U.S. troops arrive in Vietnam in 1965 (above). Fighting communist guerrillas proved difficult in the dense jungle terrain (right).

▲ The Vietnam Veterans Memorial in Washington, D.C., is a stark reminder of the costs of the Vietnam War.

Effects of the Vietnam War

- Americans applaud President Johnson's response to a Vietcong attack with aggressive air strikes.
- The United States commits over 380,000 ground troops to fighting in Vietnam by the end of 1966.
- American people question the government's honesty about the war, creating the so-called "credibility gap."
- The war casualties and the unfair draft system cause civil unrest.
- The wartime economy hurts domestic spending for programs such as the Great Society.
- President Nixon is elected largely on promises to end the war and unite a divided country.
- Congress passes the War Powers Act to limit the power of the president during wartime.

Reviewing Vocabulary

Directions: Choose the word or words that best complete the sentence.

1. Eisenhower cited the _____ as the reason why the United States had to support South Vietnam.

   A credibility gap

   B self-determination theory

   C domino theory

   D Communist way

2. A person who supported the war effort in Vietnam might be called a

   A hawk.

   B dove.

   C guerrilla.

   D linkage.

3. As the war in Vietnam escalated, a _____ developed as Americans began to find it hard to believe what the Johnson administration said about the conflict.

   A linkage

   B credibility gap

   C domino theory

   D teach-in

4. The Vietcong were Communist _____ located in South Vietnam.

   A elected officials

   B generals

   C diplomats

   D guerrillas

5. President Nixon's plan to withdraw U.S. troops and replace them with South Vietnamese troops was known as

   A linkage.

   B the Tet Offensive.

   C the domino theory.

   D Vietnamization.

Reviewing Main Ideas

Directions: Choose the best answer for each of the following questions.

Section 1 *(pp. 654–661)*

6. Who was the leader of the North Vietnamese?

   A Mao Zedong

   B Ho Chi Minh

   C Dien Bien Phu

   D Ngo Dinh Diem

7. One reason why President Johnson did not order a full-scale attack on North Vietnam was because

   A he did not think that the United States could win.

   B the military lacked the manpower to launch an assault.

   C he did not want to bring China into the war.

   D he did not want to lose the 1968 election.

8. Which of the following temporarily established North and South Vietnam and recognized Cambodia's independence?

   A the Treaty of Paris

   B Gulf of Tonkin Resolution

   C the Truman Doctrine

   D the Geneva Accords

Section 2 *(pp. 664–669)*

9. Many Americans objected to the draft because they believed it

   A forced young men to flee to Canada.

   B unfairly targeted the poor and minorities.

   C did not include women.

   D did not raise the necessary number of troops.

TEST-TAKING TIP

> Do not spend too much time trying to figure out the right answer to a question. Move on, and then come back to that question when you have answered all the questions you do know. If you still do not know the answer, select the one that you think is the most logical.

Need Extra Help?									
If You Missed Questions . . .	1	2	3	4	5	6	7	8	9
Go to Page . . .	665	667	664	657	670	664	658	656	665

10. Which of the following events was significant in turning American public opinion against the war in Vietnam?

A the National Teach-in

B the 1968 Democratic National Convention

C the assassination of President Kennedy

D the Tet Offensive

Section 3 (pp. 670–675)

11. The gradual removal of U.S. troops from Vietnam was known as

A Agent Orange.

B containment.

C linkage.

D Vietnamization.

12. Which of the following was part of the legacy of the Vietnam War?

A Americans' increased cynicism about their government

B Americans' belief that the policy of containment worked

C Americans' confidence that the United States would win the Cold War

D Americans' paranoia about the intentions of the North Vietnamese government

13. The purpose of the War Powers Act was to ensure that the president would

A have greater authority over the military.

B consult Congress before committing troops in extended conflicts.

C have the authority to sign treaties without Senate approval.

D have a freer hand in fighting the spread of communism.

Critical Thinking

Directions: Choose the best answers to the following questions.

14. Why is the Gulf of Tonkin Resolution important?

A It authorized the use of force in Vietnam.

B It ordered U.S. forces to withdraw from Vietnam.

C It divided Vietnam into two countries.

D It required the president to consult Congress before committing troops.

Base your answer to question 15 on the map below and on your knowledge of Chapter 19.

The Vietnam War

15. The Ho Chi Minh trail ran through which two nations?

A Laos and Japan

B Laos and Thailand

C Laos and China

D Laos and Cambodia

Need Extra Help?						
If You Missed Questions . . .	10	11	12	13	14	15
Go to Page . . .	667–668	670	674–675	675	668	R15

GO ON

16. On which idea is the Twenty-sixth Amendment based?

A Women should be allowed to serve in the armed forces.

B The president, not Congress, should decide where and when troops will fight.

C A person who is old enough to fight is old enough to vote.

D A draft is an old-fashioned and unworkable system for selecting soldiers.

Analyze the cartoon and answer the questions that follow. Base your answers on the cartoon and on your knowledge of Chapter 19.

17. This cartoon depicts what aspect of the Vietnam War's effect on the United States?

A disagreements in Congress between hawks and doves

B disagreements among military leaders about war strategy

C disagreements between pro-war and antiwar groups among civilians

D disagreements on Nixon's plan to pull out of Vietnam

18. The cartoonist is expressing the opinion that

A the war was dividing the country.

B President Johnson should ask the country to remain patient during the war.

C Vietnam is a conflict with an easy solution.

D President Johnson is a great leader with a solution to the problems in Vietnam.

Document-Based Questions

Directions: Analyze the document and answer the short-answer questions that follow the document.

In the 1960s many young Americans enlisted or were drafted for military service. Some believed that they had a duty to serve their country. Many had no clear idea of what they were doing or why. In the following excerpt, a young man expresses his thoughts about going to war:

> *"I read a lot of pacifist literature to determine whether or not I was a conscientious objector. I finally concluded that I wasn't....*
>
> *The one clear decision I made in 1968 about me and the war was that if I was going to get out of it, I was going to get out in a legal way. I was not going to defraud the system in order to beat the system. I wasn't going to leave the country, because the odds of coming back looked real slim....*
>
> *With all my terror of going into the Army ... there was something seductive about it, too. I was seduced by World War II and John Wayne movies.... I had been, as we all were, victimized by a romantic, truly uninformed view of war."*
> —quoted in Nam

19. What options did the young man have regarding the war?

20. Do you think World War II movies gave him a realistic view of what fighting in Vietnam would be like?

Extended Response

21. The conflict in Vietnam has been called the first "television war." Americans could watch scenes of death and destruction unfold in front of them from their living rooms. Write an expository essay about how television changed the way Americans view war in general and how it contributed to the unpopularity of the Vietnam War specifically. Your essay should include an introduction and at least three paragraphs that explore this issue.

STOP

History ONLINE

For additional test practice, use Self-Check Quizzes— Chapter 19 at glencoe.com.

Need Extra Help?						
If You Missed Questions . . .	16	17	18	19	20	21
Go to Page . . .	666–667	R18	R18	679	679	664–672

Chapter 20

The Politics of Protest

1960–1980

SECTION 1 Students and the Counterculture

SECTION 2 The Feminist Movement

SECTION 3 Latino Americans Organize

▲ *César Chávez leads a march in Delano, California, in 1966.*

1962
• *Silent Spring* is published

Eisenhower
1953–1961

Kennedy
1961–1963

1963
• *The Feminine Mystique* is published

Johnson
1963–1969

1966
• National Organization for Women and United Farm Workers organized

Nixon
1969–1974

U.S. PRESIDENTS

U.S. EVENTS

WORLD EVENTS

1960

1965

1970

1962
• Cuban missile crisis

1964
• China becomes world's fifth nuclear power

1968
• Soviet Union halts democratic uprising in Czechoslovakia

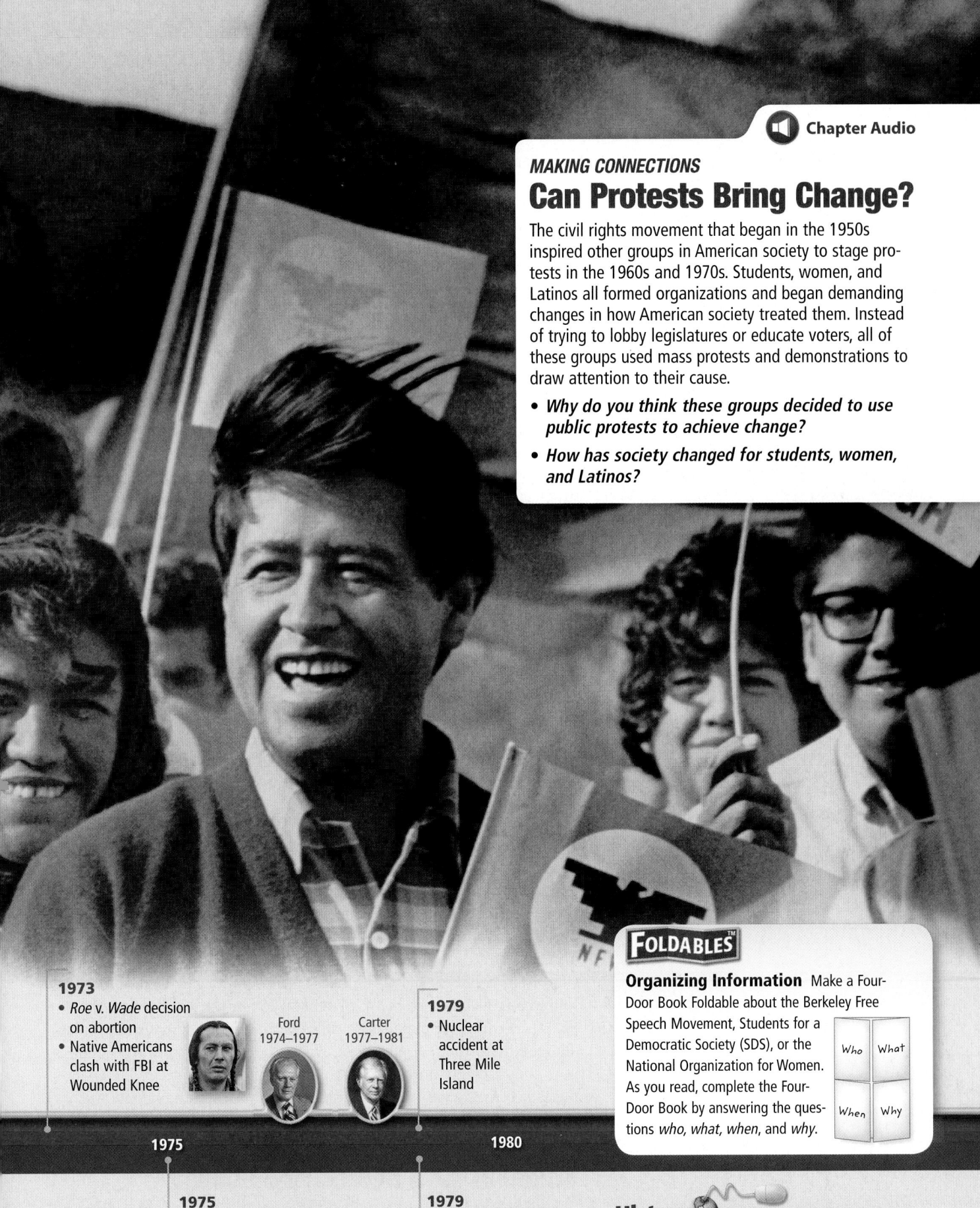

MAKING CONNECTIONS
Can Protests Bring Change?

The civil rights movement that began in the 1950s inspired other groups in American society to stage protests in the 1960s and 1970s. Students, women, and Latinos all formed organizations and began demanding changes in how American society treated them. Instead of trying to lobby legislatures or educate voters, all of these groups used mass protests and demonstrations to draw attention to their cause.

- *Why do you think these groups decided to use public protests to achieve change?*
- *How has society changed for students, women, and Latinos?*

1973
- *Roe* v. *Wade* decision on abortion
- Native Americans clash with FBI at Wounded Knee

Ford
1974–1977

Carter
1977–1981

1979
- Nuclear accident at Three Mile Island

1975

1980

1975
- Last European colonies in Africa gain independence from Portugal

1979
- Ayatollah Khomeini leads revolution against the Shah of Iran

FOLDABLES

Organizing Information Make a Four-Door Book Foldable about the Berkeley Free Speech Movement, Students for a Democratic Society (SDS), or the National Organization for Women. As you read, complete the Four-Door Book by answering the questions *who*, *what*, *when*, and *why*.

Who | What
When | Why

History ONLINE Visit glencoe.com and enter *QuickPass*™ code TAVMT5147c20 for Chapter 20 resources.

Students and the Counterculture

Guide to Reading

Big Ideas
Struggles for Rights During the 1960s, many of the country's young people raised their voices in protest against numerous aspects of American society.

Content Vocabulary
• counterculture *(p. 684)*
• hippies *(p. 684)*
• communes *(p. 685)*

Academic Vocabulary
• rationality *(p. 684)*
• conformity *(p. 685)*

People and Events to Identify
• Port Huron Statement *(p. 683)*
• Tom Hayden *(p. 683)*
• Free Speech Movement *(p. 683)*
• Haight-Ashbury district *(p. 685)*
• Woodstock *(p. 685)*
• Bob Dylan *(p. 685)*

Reading Strategy
Organizing Use the major headings of this section to create an outline similar to the one below.

Students and the Counterculture
I. The Rise of the Youth Movement
  A.
  B.
II.
  A.
  B.

The 1960s was one of the most tumultuous decades in American history. The decade also gave birth to a youth movement that challenged the American political and social system and conventional middle-class values.

The Rise of the Youth Movement

MAIN Idea The youth protest movement of the 1960s included Students for a Democratic Society and the Free Speech Movement.

HISTORY AND YOU Do you know of any groups that work to improve society? Read how the youth of the 1960s protested social injustice.

The roots of the 1960s youth movement stretched back to the 1950s. In the decade after World War II, the country had enjoyed a time of peace and prosperity. Prosperity did not extend to all, however, and some, especially the artists and writers of the beat movement, had openly criticized American society. They believed American society valued conformity over independence and financial gain over spiritual and social advancement.

At the same time, the turmoil of the civil rights movement had raised serious questions about racism in American society, and the nuclear arms race between the United States and the Soviet Union made many of the nation's youth uneasy about the future. For many young people, the events of the 1950s had called into question the wisdom of their parents and their political leaders.

The youth movement originated with the baby boomers, the huge generation born after World War II. By 1970, 58.4 percent of the American population was 34 years old or younger. (By comparison, those 34 or younger in 2000 represented an estimated 48.9 percent.) The early 1960s also saw a rapid increase in enrollment at colleges. The economic boom of the 1950s meant more families could afford to send their children to college. Between 1960 and 1966, enrollment in four-year colleges rose from 3.1 million to almost 5 million. College life gave young people a sense of freedom and independence. It also allowed them to meet and bond with others who shared their feelings about society and fears about the future. It was on college campuses across the nation that youth protest movements began and reached their peak.

Students for a Democratic Society

Some young people were concerned most about the injustices they saw in the country's political and social system. In their view, a small wealthy elite controlled politics, and wealth itself was unfairly

The Student Movement

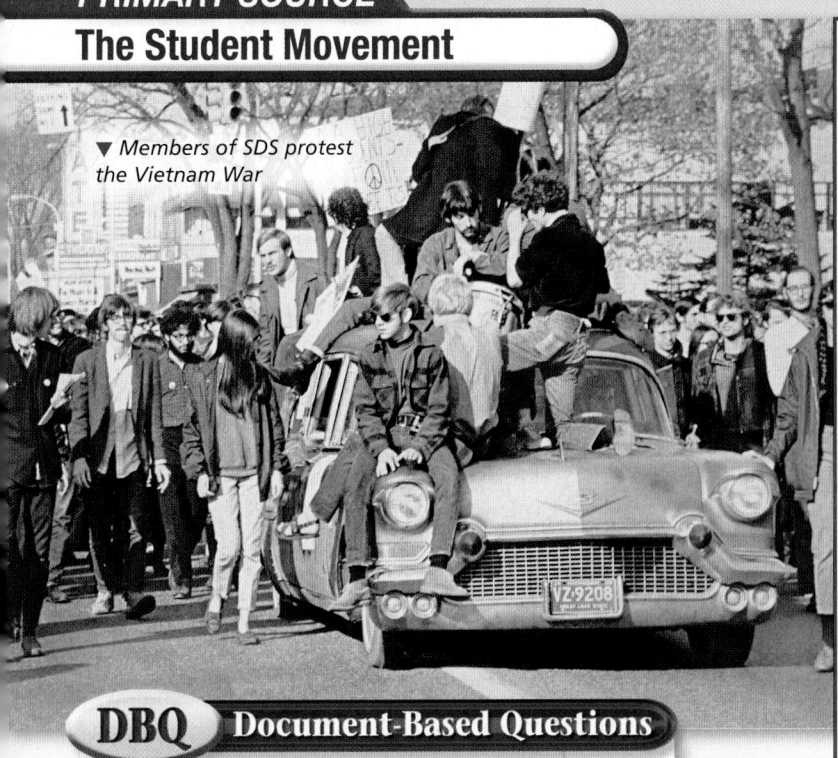

▼ Members of SDS protest the Vietnam War

DBQ Document-Based Questions

1. **Determining Cause and Effect** What two issues led to the activism of the members of SDS?

2. **Summarizing** What were the two goals of the group?

PRIMARY SOURCE

In 1962 Students for a Democratic Society issued the Port Huron Statement explaining SDS and the reasons for their actions:

"We are people of this generation, bred in at least modest comfort, housed now in universities, looking uncomfortably to the world we inherit. . . .

When we were kids the United States was the wealthiest and strongest country in the world . . . Freedom and equality for each individual, government of, by, and for the people—these American values we found good. . . .

As we grew, however, our comfort was penetrated by events too troubling to dismiss. First, the permeating and victimizing fact of human degradation, symbolized by the Southern struggle against racial bigotry, compelled most of us from silence to activism. Second, the enclosing fact of the Cold War, symbolized by the presence of the Bomb, brought awareness that we ourselves, and our friends, and millions of abstract 'others' . . . might die at any time.

. . . Our work is guided by the sense that we may be the last generation in the experiment with living. . . . The search for truly democratic alternatives to the present, and a commitment to social experimentation with them, is a worthy and fulfilling human enterprise, one which moves us and, we hope, others today.

—from the *Port Huron Statement*, 1962

divided. These young people formed what came to be known as the New Left. (The "new" left differed from the "old" left of the 1930s, which had advocated socialism and communism.)

A prominent organization within the New Left was Students for a Democratic Society (SDS), founded in 1959. It defined its views in a 1962 declaration known as the **Port Huron Statement.** Written largely by **Tom Hayden,** editor of the University of Michigan's student newspaper, the declaration called for an end to apathy and urged citizens to stop accepting a country run by big corporations and big government.

SDS chapters focused on protesting the Vietnam War, but they also addressed other issues, including poverty, campus regulations, nuclear power, and racism. In 1968, for example, SDS leaders assisted in an eight-day occupation of several buildings at Columbia University to protest the administration's plan to build a new gym in an area that had served as a neighborhood park near Harlem.

The Free Speech Movement

Another movement that captured the nation's attention in the 1960s was the **Free Speech Movement,** led by Mario Savio and others at the University of California at Berkeley. The movement began when the university decided, in the fall of 1964, to restrict students' rights to distribute literature and to recruit volunteers for political causes on campus. The protesters, however, quickly targeted more general campus matters as well.

Like many college students, those at Berkeley were dissatisfied with practices at their university. Officials divided huge classes into sections taught by graduate students, while many professors claimed they were too busy with research to meet with students. Faceless administrators made rules that were not always easy to obey and imposed punishments for violations. Feeling isolated in this impersonal environment, many Berkeley students rallied to support the Free Speech Movement.

The struggle between Berkeley's students and administrators peaked on December 2, 1964, with a sit-in and powerful speech by Savio. Early the next morning, 600 police officers entered the campus and arrested more than 700 protesters.

The arrests set off an even larger protest movement. Within days, a campus-wide strike had stopped classes and many members of the faculty also voiced their support for the Free Speech Movement. In the face of this growing opposition, the administration gave in to the students' demands.

Soon afterward, the Supreme Court upheld students' rights to freedom of speech and assembly on campuses. In a unanimous vote, the Court upheld the section of the Civil Rights Act assuring these rights in places offering public accommodations, which, by definition, included college campuses. The Berkeley revolt was one of the first major student protests in the 1960s, and it became a model for others. The tactics the Berkeley protesters had used were soon being used in college demonstrations across the country.

Reading Check **Synthesizing** What were three reasons for the growth of the youth movement of the 1960s?

The Counterculture

MAIN Idea Counterculture youths tried to create an alternative to mainstream culture.

HISTORY AND YOU Do you know anyone today who rejects mainstream society? Read on to learn about the ideas of the 1960s counterculture.

While many young Americans in the 1960s sought to reform the system, others rejected it entirely and tried to create a new lifestyle based on flamboyant dress, rock music, drug use, and communal living. They created what became known as the **counterculture** and were commonly called "**hippies.**"

Hippie Culture

Originally, hippies rejected **rationality,** order, and traditional middle-class values. They wanted to build a utopia—a society that was freer, closer to nature, and full of love, empathy, tolerance, and cooperation. Much of this was a reaction to the 1950s stereotype of the white-collar "man in the gray flannel suit" who led a constricted and colorless life.

As the counterculture grew, many newcomers did not understand these ideas. For them, what mattered were the outward signs that

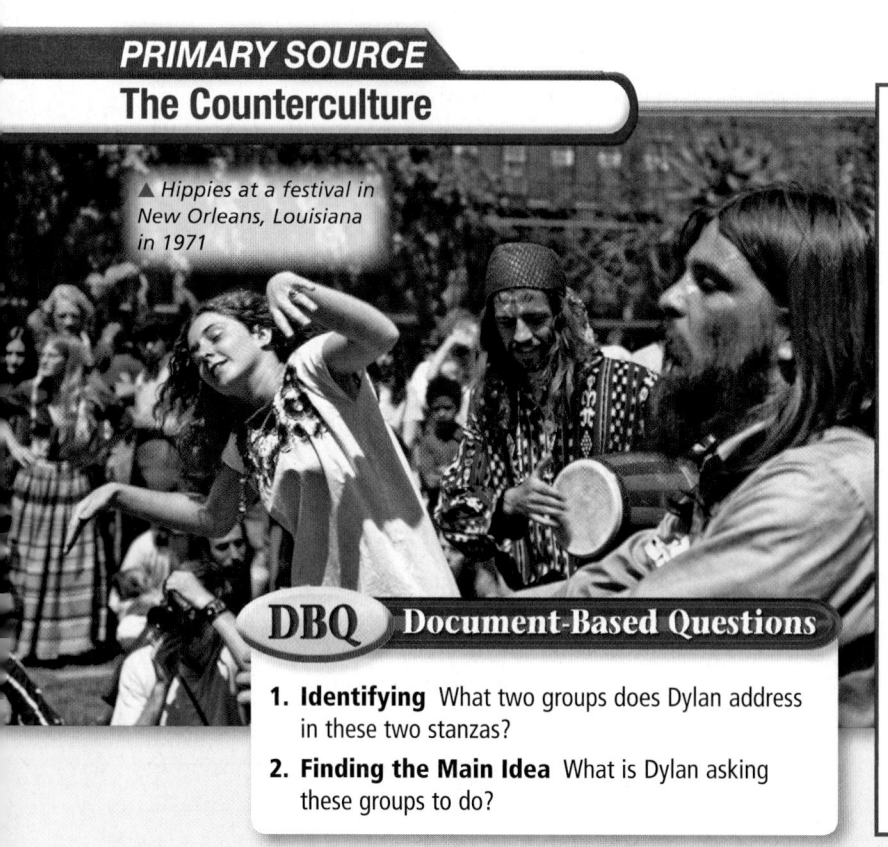

PRIMARY SOURCE
The Counterculture

▲ Hippies at a festival in New Orleans, Louisiana in 1971

Come senators, congressmen
Please heed the call
Don't stand in the doorway
Don't block up the hall
For he that gets hurt
Will be he who has stalled
There's a battle outside
And it is ragin'.
It'll soon shake your windows
And rattle your walls
For the times they are a-changin'.

Come mothers and fathers
Throughout the land
And don't criticize
What you can't understand
Your sons and your daughters
Are beyond your command
Your old road is
Rapidly agin'.
Please get out of the new one
If you can't lend your hand
For the times they are a-changin'.

—from "The Times They Are A-Changin'"

▲ Bob Dylan performs at the Newport Folk Festival in 1965.

DBQ Document-Based Questions

1. **Identifying** What two groups does Dylan address in these two stanzas?

2. **Finding the Main Idea** What is Dylan asking these groups to do?

defined the movement—long hair, Native American headbands, cowboy boots, long dresses, shabby jeans, and the use of drugs.

Many hippies wanted to drop out of society by leaving home and living together in **communes**—group living arrangements in which members shared everything and worked together. Some hippies established rural communes, while others lived together in parks or crowded apartments in large cities. One of the most famous hippie destinations was San Francisco's **Haight-Ashbury district.** By the mid-1960s, thousands of hippies had flocked there.

The Impact of the Counterculture

After a few years, the counterculture movement began to decline. Some urban hippie communities became dangerous places where muggings and other criminal activity took place. The glamour of drug use waned as more and more young people became addicted or died from overdoses. In addition, many people in the movement had gotten older and moved on. Although the counterculture declined without achieving its utopian ideals, it did change some aspects of American culture.

Fashion Protesters and members of the counterculture often expressed themselves with their clothing. By wearing cheap surplus clothes recycled from earlier decades and repaired with patches, they showed that they were rejecting both consumerism and the social class structure. Ethnic clothing was popular for similar reasons. Beads and fringes imitated Native American costumes, while tie-dyed shirts borrowed techniques from India and Africa.

Perhaps the most potent symbol of the era was hair. Long hair, beards, and mustaches on young men symbolized defiance of both 1950s **conformity**—when buzz cuts were popular—and the military, which required all recruits to have short hair. School officials at the time debated the acceptable length of a student's hair. Over time, however, longer hair on men and more individual clothing for both genders became generally accepted. What was once the clothing of defiance became mainstream.

Music Counterculture musicians made use of folk music and the rhythms of rock 'n' roll and wrote heartfelt lyrics that expressed the hopes and fears of their generation. At festivals such as **Woodstock,** held in upstate New York in August 1969, and in Altamont, California, later that year, hundreds of thousands of people gathered to listen to the new music.

Major folk singers included **Bob Dylan,** who became an important voice of the movement, as did singers Joan Baez and Pete Seeger. Rock musicians popular with the counterculture included Jimi Hendrix, Janis Joplin, and The Who. These musicians used electrically amplified instruments that drastically changed the sound of rock, and their innovations continue to influence musicians today.

✔ Reading Check **Evaluating** What lasting impact did the counterculture have on the nation?

Vocabulary

1. **Explain** the significance of: Port Huron Statement, Tom Hayden, Free Speech Movement, counterculture, hippies, communes, Haight-Ashbury district, Woodstock, Bob Dylan.

Main Ideas

2. **Describing** With what issues did SDS concern itself?

3. **Summarizing** What were the core ideals of the members of the counterculture?

Critical Thinking

4. **Big Ideas** How did the U.S. Supreme Court validate the actions of the members of the Free Speech Movement?

5. **Organizing** Use a graphic organizer similar to the one below to list the causes of the youth movement.

Causes

Youth Movement

6. **Analyzing Visuals** Study the image on page 683. Why do you think that older adults were frightened or threatened by the student movement?

Writing About History

7. **Descriptive Writing** Suppose that you are a journalist in the 1960s. Write an article in which you visit a commune and describe the hippie culture of the day.

History ONLINE

Study Central™ To review this section, go to glencoe.com and click on Study Central.

The Feminist Movement

Guide to Reading

Big Ideas
Struggles for Rights Women organized to claim their rights and responsibilities as citizens.

Content Vocabulary
• feminism *(p. 686)*

Academic Vocabulary
• gender *(p. 687)*
• compatible *(p. 691)*

People and Events to Identify
• Equal Pay Act *(p. 687)*
• Betty Friedan *(p. 687)*
• National Organization for Women (NOW) *(p. 688)*
• Gloria Steinem *(p. 688)*
• Equal Rights Amendment (ERA) *(p. 689)*
• Phyllis Schlafly *(p. 690)*
• Title IX *(p. 690)*

Reading Strategy
Categorizing Use a graphic organizer similar to the one below to list the main arguments for and against the Equal Rights Amendment (ERA).

For ERA	Against ERA

By the 1960s, many women had become increasingly dissatisfied with society's perception of women and their place in society. Some women began to join organizations aimed at improving their role in society. The Equal Rights Amendment stirred a national debate.

A Renewed Women's Movement

MAIN Idea Women in the 1960s and 1970s began creating organizations to change society through education and legislative action.

HISTORY AND YOU Have you ever read a book that spurred you to action or got you excited? Read on to learn about a book that helped define and reawaken the women's movement.

African Americans and college students were not the only groups seeking to change American society in the 1960s. By the middle of the decade, a new women's movement had emerged as many women became discontent with their status and treatment in American society. This movement became known as the feminist movement, or the women's liberation movement.

Feminism—the belief that men and women should be equal politically, economically, and socially—had been a weak and often embattled force since the adoption of the Nineteenth Amendment guaranteeing women's voting rights in 1920. Soon after the amendment was ratified, the women's movement split into two camps. For the next 40 years, it had very little political influence.

The onset of World War II provided women with greater opportunity, at least temporarily. With many men enlisted in the army, women became an integral part of the nation's workforce. After the war, however, many women returned to their traditional role of homemaker. Even though 8 million American women had gone to work during the war, the new postwar emphasis on having babies and establishing families discouraged women from seeking employment. Many Americans assumed that a good mother should stay home to raise her children.

Despite the popular emphasis on homemaking, however, the number of women who held jobs outside the home actually increased during the 1950s. Most women who went to work did so in order to help their families maintain their comfortable lifestyles. By 1960, nearly one-third of all married women were part of the paid workforce. Yet many people continued to believe that women, even college-educated women, could better serve society by remaining in the home to influence the next generation of men.

What Caused the Women's Movement?

The women's movement was revitalized in the 1960s, partly because of the efforts of the President's Commission on the Status of Women, and partly because writers, such as Betty Friedan, convinced women the time had come to take action.

▲ President Kennedy meets with Eleanor Roosevelt, Representative Edith Green (center) and Esther Peterson, director of the Women's Bureau at the Department of Labor (right) in early 1962 to discuss the findings of the President's Commission on the Status of Women.

DBQ Document-Based Questions

1. **Making Inferences** What was the "feminine mystique"?
2. **Drawing Conclusions** What do you think "the problem" was?
3. **Hypothesizing** Why might President Kennedy have wanted Eleanor Roosevelt to head the commission studying the status of women?

PRIMARY SOURCE

In 1963 Betty Friedan tried to describe the feelings that would lead to the rebirth of the women's movement:

▲ Betty Friedan, 1972

"The problem lay buried, unspoken, for many years in the minds of American women. . . . Each suburban housewife struggled with it alone. As she made the beds, shopped for groceries, matched slipcover material, ate peanut butter sand-wiches with her children, chauffeured Cub Scouts and Brownies . . . she was afraid to ask even of herself the silent question—'Is this all?'

. . . In the fifteen years after World War II, this mystique of feminine fulfillment became the cherished and self-perpetuating core of contemporary American culture. Millions of women lived their lives in the image of those pretty pictures of the American suburban housewife . . . Words like 'emancipation' and 'career' sounded strange and embarrassing. . . .

But on an April morning in 1959, I heard a mother of four, having coffee with four other mothers in a suburban develop-ment . . . say in a tone of quiet desperation, 'the problem.' And the others knew, without words, that she was not talking about a problem with her husband, or her children, or her home. Suddenly they realized they all shared the same prob-lem, the problem that has no name.

. . . Sometimes a woman would say 'I feel empty somehow . . . incomplete.' Or she would say, 'I feel as if I don't exist.'"
—from *The Feminine Mystique*

Origins of the Movement

By the early 1960s, many women were increasingly resentful of a world where newspaper ads separated jobs by **gender,** banks denied them credit, and, worst of all, they often were paid less for the same work. Women found themselves shut out of higher-paying professions such as law, medicine, and finance. By the mid-1960s, about 47 percent of American women were in the workforce, but three-fourths of them worked in lower paying clerical, sales, or factory jobs, or as cleaning women and hospital attendants.

Workplace Rights One stimulus that invigorated the women's movement was the President's Commission on the Status of Women, established by President Kennedy and headed by Eleanor Roosevelt. The commission's report highlighted the problems faced by women in the workplace and helped create a network of feminist activists who lobbied Congress for women's legislation. In 1963, with the support of organized labor, they won passage of the **Equal Pay Act,** which in most cases outlawed paying men more than women for the same job.

The Feminine Mystique Although many working women were angry about inequality in the workplace, many other women who had stayed home were also discontent. **Betty Friedan** tried to describe the reasons for their discontent in her book *The Feminine Mystique,* published in 1963.

Friedan had traveled around the country interviewing women who had graduated with her from Smith College in 1942. She found that while most of these women reported having everything they could want in life, they still felt unfulfilled.

Friedan's book became a best-seller. Many women began reaching out to one another, pouring out their anger and sadness in what came to be known as consciousness-raising sessions. While they talked informally about their unhappiness, they were also building the base for a nationwide mass movement.

The Civil Rights Act and Women Congress gave the women's movement another boost by including them in the 1964 Civil Rights Act. Title VII of the act outlawed job discrimination not only on the basis of race, color, religion, and national origin, but also on the basis of gender. The law provided a strong legal basis for the changes the women's movement would later demand.

Given the era's attitudes about what kind of work was proper for women, simply having the law on the books was not enough. Even the agency charged with administering the civil rights act—the Equal Employment Opportunity Commission (EEOC)—accepted the idea that jobs could be gender-specific. In 1965 the commission ruled that gender-segregated help-wanted ads were legal.

The Time Is NOW

By June 1966, Betty Friedan returned to an idea that she and other women had been considering—the need for an organization to promote feminist goals. On the back of a napkin she scribbled that it was time "to take the actions needed to bring women into the mainstream of American society, now . . . in fully equal partnership with men." Friedan and others then set out to form the **National Organization for Women** (NOW).

In October 1966, a group of about 300 women and men held the founding conference of NOW. "The time has come," its founders declared, "to confront with concrete action the conditions which now prevent women from enjoying the equality of opportunity and freedom of choice which is their right as individual Americans and as human beings."

The new organization responded to frustrated housewives by demanding greater educational opportunities for women. The group also focused much of its energy on aiding women in the workplace. NOW leaders denounced the exclusion of women from certain professions and from most levels of politics. They lashed out against the practice of paying women less than men for equal work, a practice the Equal Pay Act had not eliminated.

When NOW set out to pass an Equal Rights Amendment to the Constitution, its membership rose to over 200,000. By July 1972, the movement had its own magazine, *Ms.*, which kept readers informed about women's issues. The editor of the magazine was **Gloria Steinem,** an author who became one of the movement's leading figures.

✔ Reading Check **Identifying** What two forces helped bring the women's movement to life again?

Debates IN HISTORY

Should the Equal Rights Amendment Be Ratified?

In the 1970s ratification of the Equal Rights Amendment (ERA) was a hotly debated issue. Organizations such as NOW and other supporters of the amendment fought hard for its ratification. One of these was U.S. Representative Shirley Chisholm, who spoke out in support of the ERA in a speech to Congress in 1970. In 1971 conservative activist Phyllis Schlafly formed the group Stop-ERA to fight the legislation.

Successes and Failures

MAIN Idea The women's movement made gains for women in education and employment but has not achieved complete equality for women.

HISTORY AND YOU Have you ever seen men and women treated differently because of their gender? Read to learn how the women's movement tried to get equal treatment for women in the 1960s and 1970s.

During the late 1960s and early 1970s, the women's movement fought to amend the Constitution and enforce Title VII of the Civil Rights Act, lobbied to repeal laws against abortion, and worked for legislation against gender discrimination in employment, housing, and education. The movement had many successes, but also encountered strong opposition to some of the reforms it wanted.

The Equal Rights Amendment

The women's movement seemed to be off to a strong start when Congress passed the **Equal Rights Amendment** (ERA) in March 1972. The amendment specified that "Equality of rights under the law shall not be denied or abridged by the United States or by any State on account of sex." To become part of the Constitution, the amendment had to be ratified by 38 states. Many states did so—35 by 1979—but by then, significant opposition to the amendment had begun to build up.

Opponents of the ERA argued that it would take away some traditional rights, such as the right to alimony in divorce cases or the right to have single-gender colleges. They also feared it would allow women to be drafted into the military and eliminate laws that provided special protection for women in the workforce.

YES

Shirley Chisholm
Member of the U.S. House of Representatives

PRIMARY SOURCE

"Discrimination against women . . . is so widespread that it seems to many persons normal, natural and right. . . .

It is time we act to assure full equality of opportunity . . . to women.

The argument that this amendment will not solve the problem of sex discrimination is not relevant. . . . Of course laws will not eliminate prejudice from the hearts of human beings. But that is no reason to allow prejudice to continue to be enshrined in our laws. . . . The Constitution they wrote was designed to protect the rights of white, male citizens. As there were no black Founding Fathers, there were no founding mothers—a great pity, on both counts. It is not too late to complete the work they left undone."

—speech before Congress, August 10, 1970

NO

Phyllis Schlafly
Author and Conservative Activist

PRIMARY SOURCE

"This Amendment will absolutely and positively make women subject to the draft. Why any woman would support such a ridiculous and un-American proposal as this is beyond comprehension. . . . Foxholes are bad enough for men, but they certainly are *not* the place for women—and we should reject any proposal which would put them there in the name of 'equal rights.'. . .

Another bad effect of the Equal Rights Amendment is that it will abolish a woman's right to child support and alimony . . .

Under present American laws, the man is *always* required to support his wife and each child he caused to be brought into the world. Why should women abandon these good laws . . . ?"

—from the *Phyllis Schlafly Report*, February 1972

DBQ Document-Based Questions

1. **Summarizing** Why does Chisholm believe that the ERA is necessary?
2. **Explaining** What does Schlafly say was the main flaw in the arguments of the ERA supporters?
3. **Evaluating** With which position do you agree? Write a paragraph to explain your choice.

One outspoken opponent was **Phyllis Schlafly,** who organized the Stop-ERA campaign. By the end of 1979, four states had voted to rescind their approval. Many people had become worried that the amendment would give federal courts too much power to interfere with state laws. Unable to achieve ratification by three-fourths of the states by the deadline set by Congress, the Equal Rights Amendment finally failed in 1982.

Equality in Education

One major achievement of the movement came in the area of education. Kathy Striebel's experience illustrated the discrimination female students often faced in the early 1970s. In 1971 Striebel, a high school junior in St. Paul, Minnesota, wanted to compete for her school's swim team, but the school did not allow girls to join. Kathy's mother, Charlotte, was a member of the local NOW chapter. Through it, she learned that St. Paul had recently banned gender discrimination in education. She filed a grievance with the city's human rights department, and officials required the school to allow Kathy to swim.

For further information on the case of *Roe* v. *Wade*, see page R60 in **Supreme Court Case Summaries.**

Shortly after joining the team, Kathy beat out one of the boys and earned a spot at a meet. As she stood on the block waiting to swim, the opposing coach declared that she was ineligible because the meet was outside St. Paul and thus beyond the jurisdiction of its laws. "They pulled that little girl right off the block," Charlotte Striebel recalled angrily.

Recognizing the problem, leaders of the women's movement lobbied Congress to ban gender discrimination in education. In 1972 Congress responded by passing a law known collectively as the Educational Amendments. One section, **Title IX,** prohibited federally funded schools from discriminating against women in nearly all aspects of its operations, from admissions to athletics.

Right to Privacy and *Roe* v. *Wade*

One aspect of the feminist movement was securing the right to make private decisions, including reproductive decisions. A constitutional right to marital privacy was introduced in 1965 when the Supreme Court outlawed state bans on contraceptives for married couples in *Griswold* v. *Connecticut.* The right to privacy was

---

PRIMARY SOURCE
The Changing Status of Women

Women's roles were changing in society. Although the ERA failed, more women entered the workforce and gender discrimination in schools was banned with the passage of Title IX.

Analyzing VISUALS

1. **Analyzing** By how much did the percentage of working women increase between 1950 and 2000?

2. **Interpreting** What gains, if any, did women make in median income compared to men?

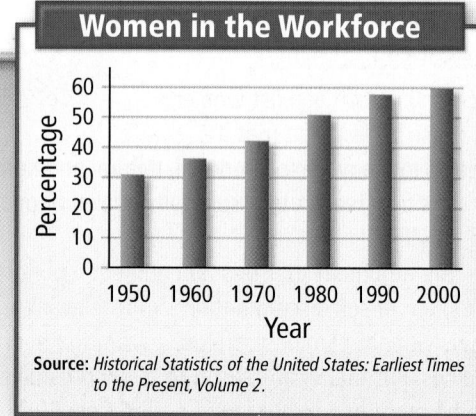

Women in the Workforce

Source: *Historical Statistics of the United States: Earliest Times to the Present, Volume 2.*

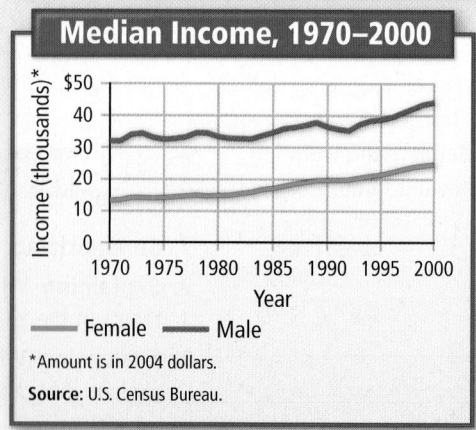

Median Income, 1970–2000

— Female — Male

*Amount is in 2004 dollars.

Source: U.S. Census Bureau.

expanded beyond married couples when activists began challenging laws against abortion. Until 1973, the right to regulate abortion was reserved to the states. This matched the original plan of the Constitution, which reserved all police power—the power to control people and property in the interest of safety, health, welfare, and morals—to the state. Early in the country's history, some abortions were permitted in the early stages of pregnancy, but by the mid-1800s, states had passed laws prohibiting abortion, except to save the life of the mother.

In the late 1960s, some states began adopting more liberal abortion laws. For example, several states allowed abortion if carrying a baby to term might endanger the woman's mental health or if she was a victim of rape or incest. The big change came with the 1973 Supreme Court decision in *Roe* v. *Wade,* which stated that state governments could not regulate abortion during the first three months of pregnancy, a time that was said to be within a woman's constitutional right to privacy. During the second three months of pregnancy, states could regulate abortions on the basis of the health of the mother. States could ban abortion in the final three months except in cases of a medical emergency. Those in favor of abortion rights cheered *Roe* v. *Wade* as a victory, but the issue was far from settled politically. The decision gave rise to the right-to-life movement, whose members consider abortion morally wrong and advocate its total ban.

After the *Roe* v. *Wade* ruling, the two sides began an impassioned battle that continues today. In the 1992 case *Planned Parenthood* v. *Casey,* the Supreme Court modified *Roe* v. *Wade.* The court decided that states could place some restrictions on all abortions, such as requiring doctors to explain the risks and require their patients to give "informed consent," or requiring underage girls to inform their parents before obtaining an abortion. The court struck down laws requiring women to notify their husbands before having an abortion, and abandoned the rule that states could ban abortion only in the final three months. Technology had now made it possible for the fetus to be viable outside the womb much earlier in a pregnancy. States could now restrict abortion based on the viability of the fetus.

The Impact of the Feminist Movement

The women's movement has profoundly changed society. Since the 1970s, many women have pursued college degrees and careers outside of the home, and two-career families are much more common than they were in the 1950s and 1960s. Many employers now offer options to help make work more **compatible** with family life, including flexible hours, on-site child care, and job sharing.

Even with those changes, a significant income gap between men and women still exists. A major reason for the gap is that many working women still hold lower-paying jobs such as bank tellers, administrative assistants, cashiers, schoolteachers, and nurses. It is in professional jobs that women have made the most dramatic gains since the 1970s. By 2000, women made up over 40 percent of the nation's graduates receiving medical or law degrees.

Reading Check **Summarizing** What successes and failures did the women's movement experience during the late 1960s and early 1970s?

Section 2 REVIEW

Vocabulary
1. **Explain** the significance of: feminism, Equal Pay Act, Betty Friedan, National Organization for Women (NOW), Gloria Steinem, Equal Rights Amendment (ERA), Phyllis Schlafly, Title IX.

Main Ideas
2. **Explaining** Why did more women work outside the home in the 1950s?

3. **Explaining** Why were some people against passage of the ERA?

Critical Thinking
4. **Big Ideas** What gains have been made in women's rights since the 1960s?

5. **Organizing** Use a graphic organizer similar to the one below to list the major achievements of the women's movement.

Achievements

6. **Analyzing Visuals** Study the bar graph on page 690. What was the first year in which approximately half of all women were in the workforce?

Writing About History
7. **Persuasive Writing** Assume the role of a supporter or an opponent of the ERA. Write a letter to the editor of your local newspaper to persuade people to support your position.

History ONLINE

Study Central™ To review this section, go to glencoe.com and click on Study Central.

Latino Americans Organize

Guide to Reading

Big Ideas
Struggles for Rights Latinos organized to fight discrimination and to gain access to better education and jobs.

Content Vocabulary
• repatriation (p. 694)
• bilingualism (p. 697)

Academic Vocabulary
• likewise (p. 692)
• adequate (p. 696)

People and Events to Identify
• League of United Latin American Citizens (p. 695)
• American GI Forum (p. 696)
• César Chávez (p. 697)
• Dolores Huerta (p. 697)
• United Farm Workers (p. 697)
• *La Raza Unida* (p. 697)
• Bilingual Education Act (p. 697)

Reading Strategy
Organizing Complete a time line similar to the one below to record major events in the struggle of Latinos for equal civil and political rights.

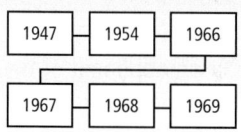

Most Mexican Americans and Mexican immigrants lived in the Southwest, where many faced discrimination in jobs and housing. By the mid-twentieth century, more immigrants arrived from various parts of Latin America. Latinos formed civil rights organizations to challenge discrimination.

Latinos Migrate North

MAIN Idea Mexicans, the largest Spanish-speaking immigrant group, faced discrimination and segregation in the West and Southwest.

HISTORY AND YOU Have you ever heard of immigrants getting their "green cards," which permit them to work in the United States? Read on to learn how the Bracero Program allowed some Mexicans to work on a temporary basis.

Americans of Mexican heritage have lived in what is now the United States since before the founding of the republic. Their numbers steadily increased in the 1800s, in part because the United States acquired territory where Mexicans already lived, and in part because Mexicans began migrating north to live in the United States. In the twentieth century, Mexican immigration rose dramatically.

In 1910 the Mexican Revolution began and the resulting turmoil prompted a wave of emigration from Mexico that lasted more than a decade. During the 1920s, half a million Mexicans immigrated to the United States through official channels, and an unknown number entered the country through other means. Precise population estimates are impossible to determine because many Mexicans frequently moved back and forth across the border.

Not surprisingly, persons of Mexican heritage remained concentrated in the areas that were once the northern provinces of Mexico. In 1930, 90 percent of ethnic Mexicans in the United States lived in Texas, California, Arizona, New Mexico, and Colorado. In Texas, the favorite destinations for Mexican immigrants, cities such as San Antonio and El Paso, had large populations of Mexican Americans and Mexican immigrants. As a result of heavy Mexican immigration, the ethnic Mexican population in Texas grew from 71,062 in 1900 to 683,681 in 1930. Southern California, **likewise,** had a large Spanish-speaking population.

Of course, not all Mexican Americans remained in the West and Southwest. In the 1910s and 1920s, along with Americans of other ethnic backgrounds, many Mexican Americans headed for the cities of the Midwest and Northeast, where they found jobs in factories.

Latinos Arrive in America, 1910–1950

In the twentieth century, Latinos, mainly Mexicans, began to enter the United States in large numbers settling mostly in the West and Southwest. Others, who came from Puerto Rico or Cuba, often settled in the barrios of the large cities in the East.

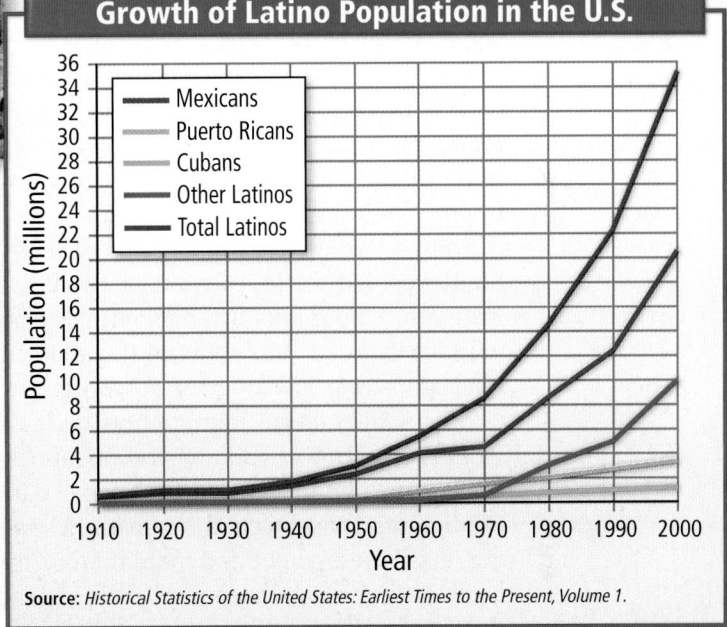

▲ Family of Mexican migrant workers, who came to the United States as part of the Bracero program during World War II

▲ These refugees, guarded by U.S. troops at Fort Bliss, Texas, were some of the more than 500,000 who came to the United States to escape the turmoil of the Mexican Revolution.

Analyzing VISUALS

1. **Interpreting** The U.S. Latino population is made up of which main groups?
2. **Drawing Conclusions** Why have Latino Americans experienced a growing political influence in recent years?

Growth of Latino Population in the U.S.

Legend:
- Mexicans
- Puerto Ricans
- Cubans
- Other Latinos
- Total Latinos

Y-axis: Population (millions), 0 to 36
X-axis: Year, 1910 to 2000

Source: *Historical Statistics of the United States: Earliest Times to the Present, Volume 1.*

Mexicans Face Discrimination

Across the Southwest, most Mexican Americans lived in barrios. Barrios were the product of a combination of the region's history and discrimination against Latinos. Los Angeles, for example, was founded as a Spanish town in 1781. When English-speaking settlers arrived a century later, they built around the older Spanish-speaking district.

Residential segregation, however, also had roots in ethnic discrimination. With heavy Mexican immigration in the early twentieth century, the ethnic Mexican population of Los Angeles grew from 5,000 in 1900 to around 190,000 in 1930. By that time, the Spanish-speaking population was segregated in the eastern part of the city, where most lived in small, dilapidated housing and suffered high rates of infant mortality and disease.

In California and across the Southwest, discrimination in employment meant that most ethnic Mexicans could find work only in low-paying jobs. Many lived in rural areas where they worked as agricultural laborers. Ernesto Galarza was eight years old when his family immigrated to California and settled in Sacramento in 1913. In his autobiography, he recalled the importance of the barrio to new immigrants:

"For the Mexicans the *barrio* was a colony of refugees. We came to know families from Chihuahua, Sonora, Jalisco, and Durango. . . . As poor refugees, their first concern was to find a place to sleep, then to eat and find work. In the *barrio* they were most likely to find all three, for not knowing English, they needed something that was even more urgent than a room, a meal, or a job, and that was information in a language they could understand."

—from *Barrio Boy*

During the Great Depression of the 1930s, approximately one-third of the Mexican population in the United States returned to Mexico. Some left voluntarily, believing it would be easier to get by in Mexico. Many Mexican Americans, however, faced increased hostility and discrimination as unemployment rates soared in the early 1930s.

Then, federal officials launched a series of deportations that not only included immigrants from Mexico but often their American-born children as well. This return to Mexico became known as the **repatriation.**

During World War II, labor shortages in the Southwest led to the creation of the Bracero Program. Under this arrangement, Mexican workers entered into short-term labor contracts, mostly as low-wage farm workers.

Meanwhile, illegal immigration increased. In 1954 Eisenhower's administration launched a program intended to deport illegal Latino immigrants. Police swept through barrios seeking illegal immigrants, and more than 3.7 million Mexicans were deported over the next three years. The raids were criticized in the United States and in Mexico for intimidating people for simply looking "Mexican." In addition, the program often failed to distinguish between individuals legally in the country (some of whom were U.S. citizens) and those who had entered illegally.

Other Latinos Arrive

Although Mexicans remained the largest group of Spanish-speaking newcomers in the 1950s, large numbers of Puerto Ricans arrived as well. American citizens since 1917, Puerto Ricans may move freely within American territory. After World War II, economic troubles in Puerto Rico prompted over a million Puerto Ricans to move to the mainland United States. American factory owners and employment agencies had also begun to recruit in Puerto Rico for workers, and the advent of relatively cheap air travel made immigration easier. The majority of Puerto Ricans settled in New York City. There, they suffered racial discrimination and alarmingly high levels of poverty.

The United States also became home to more than 350,000 Cuban immigrants in the decade after the Cuban Revolution of 1959. Many Cubans fleeing the Communist regime were professionals or business owners who settled in and around Miami, Florida. Most were welcomed in the United States because they were middle class or affluent and viewed as refugees fleeing Communist oppression. In 1960 about 3 million Latinos lived in the United States. By the late 1960s, more than 9 million Latinos lived in the United States.

Reading Check **Summarizing** What were some of the criticisms of Eisenhower's deportation program?

PRIMARY SOURCE
Latinos in the United States

By the late 1960s, approximately 9 million Latinos lived in the United States. Although many were citizens, they still faced segregation, discrimination, and other forms of racial prejudice. However, with their increasing population and through political protest and legal action they began to work to improve conditions.

▲ *Latino dancers in a traditional dance at a fiesta in Taos, New Mexico*

Latinos Organize

MAIN Idea Latino civil rights organizations, such as LULAC and the American GI Forum, fought against discrimination.

HISTORY AND YOU Recall what you learned about the decision in the Supreme Court case *Brown v. Board of Education*. Read on to find out how LULAC filed similar lawsuits challenging discrimination against Mexican Americans.

The Latino community in the West and Southwest included American citizens and immigrant noncitizens. Regardless of their citizenship status, however, people of Mexican heritage were often treated as outsiders by the English-speaking majority. Latinos formed several organizations to work for equal rights and fair treatment.

In 1929 a number of Mexican American organizations came together to create the **League of United Latin American Citizens** (LULAC). The purpose of this organization was to fight discrimination against persons of Latin American ancestry. The organization limited its membership to people of Latin American heritage who were American citizens. LULAC encouraged assimilation into American society and adopted English as its official language.

LULAC achieved many advances for Latinos. One of its early crusades ended segregation of public places in Texas where Mexican Americans (along with African Americans) had been barred from "whites only" sections. The organization also ended the practice of segregating Spanish-speaking children in "Mexican schools."

In *Mendez* v. *Westminster* (1947), a group of Mexican parents won a lawsuit that challenged school segregation in California. Two years later, LULAC filed a similarly successful suit in Texas. During the 1950s, the organization was a frequent and vocal critic of the excesses and abuses of deportation authorities. In 1954 the Supreme Court's ruling in *Hernandez* v. *Texas* extended more rights to Latino citizens. The case ended the exclusion of Mexican Americans from juries in Texas.

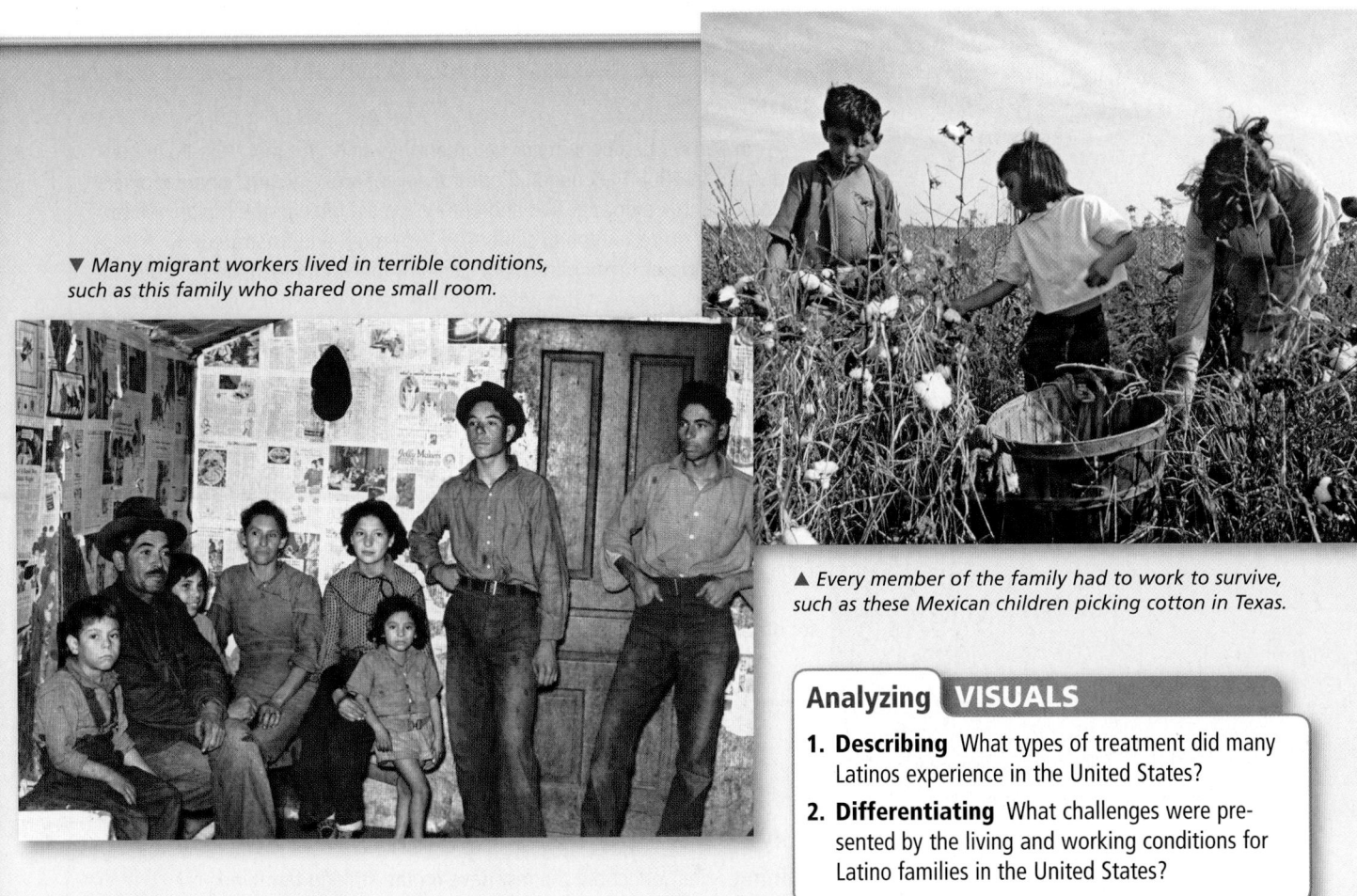

▼ Many migrant workers lived in terrible conditions, such as this family who shared one small room.

▲ Every member of the family had to work to survive, such as these Mexican children picking cotton in Texas.

Analyzing VISUALS

1. **Describing** What types of treatment did many Latinos experience in the United States?

2. **Differentiating** What challenges were presented by the living and working conditions for Latino families in the United States?

History ONLINE
Student Web Activity Visit glencoe.com and complete the activity on protest movements.

Another Latino organization, the **American GI Forum,** was founded to protect the rights of Mexican American veterans. After World War II, Latino veterans were excluded from veterans' organizations and denied medical services by the Veterans Administration.

The GI Forum's first effort to combat racial injustice involved a Mexican American soldier who was killed during World War II. A funeral home refused to hold his funeral because he was Mexican American. The GI Forum drew national attention to the incident and, with the help of Senator Lyndon Johnson, the soldier's remains were buried in Arlington National Cemetery. Initially concerned only with issues directly affecting Latino veterans, the organization later broadened its scope to challenge segregation and other forms of discrimination against all Latinos.

Reading Check **Analyzing** How did American society discriminate against Latinos?

Protests and Progress

MAIN Idea Many Latinos worked as poorly paid agricultural laborers; the United Farm Workers tried to improve their working conditions.

HISTORY AND YOU Do you think the United States should have a national language? Read how school districts set up bilingual education classes to teach immigrant students in their own language while they were still learning English.

As the 1960s began, Latino Americans continued to face prejudice and limited access to **adequate** education, employment, and housing. Encouraged by the achievements of the African American civil rights movement, Latinos launched a series of campaigns to improve their economic situation and end discrimination.

One major campaign was the effort to improve conditions for farmworkers. Most Mexican American farm laborers earned little pay, received few benefits, and had no job

PRIMARY SOURCE
César Chávez Promotes Nonviolence

▲ *Activist César Chávez was instrumental in improving conditions for Latino migrant workers.*

PRIMARY SOURCE

"Farmworkers had been trying to organize a union for more than one hundred years. In 1965 they began a bitter five-year strike against grape growers around Delano, California. Two and one-half years later, in the hungry winter of 1968 with no resolution in sight, they were tired and frustrated.

Among some of them, particularly some of the young men, there began the murmurs of violence. . . . But Cesar rejected that part of our culture 'that tells young men that you're not a man if you don't fight back.' The boycott had followed in the tradition of Cesar's hero, Mahatma Gandhi, whose practice of nonviolence he embraced. And now, like Gandhi, Cesar announced he would undertake a fast . . . .

After twenty-five days, Cesar was carried to a nearby park where the fast ended during a mass with thousands of farmworkers. He had lost thirty-five pounds, but there was no more talk of violence among the farmworkers. . . .

Cesar was too weak to speak, so his statement was read by others in both English and Spanish. 'It is my deepest belief that only by giving our lives do we find life,' they read. 'The truest act of courage . . . is to sacrifice ourselves for others in a totally nonviolent struggle for justice.'"

—Marc Grossman, UFW spokesman, quoted in *Stone Soup for the World*

DBQ Document-Based Questions

1. **Identifying** Whose ideas inspired César Chávez to begin his fast?
2. **Explaining** What effect did the fast have on the striking farmworkers?

security. In the early 1960s, **César Chávez** and **Dolores Huerta** organized two groups that fought for farmworkers. In 1965 the groups went on strike in California to demand union recognition, increased wages, and better benefits.

When employers resisted, Chávez enlisted college students, churches, and civil rights groups to organize a national boycott of table grapes, one of California's main agricultural products. An estimated 17 million citizens stopped buying grapes, and industry profits tumbled. In 1966, under the sponsorship of the American Federation of Labor and Congress of Industrial Organization (AFL-CIO), Chávez and Huerta merged their two organizations into one—the **United Farm Workers** (UFW). The new union kept the boycott going until 1970, when the grape growers finally agreed to raise wages and improve working conditions.

During the 1960s and 1970s, a growing number of Latino youths became involved in civil rights. In 1967 college students in San Antonio, Texas, led by José Angel Gutiérrez, founded the Mexican American Youth Organization (MAYO). MAYO organized walkouts and demonstrations to protest discrimination. In 1968 about 1,000 Mexican American students and teachers in East Los Angeles walked out of their classrooms to protest racism. In Crystal City, Texas, protests organized by MAYO in 1969 led to the creation of bilingual education at the local high school.

MAYO's success and the spread of protests across the West and Southwest convinced Gutiérrez to found a new political party, **La Raza Unida,** or "the United People," in 1969. *La Raza* promoted Latino causes and supported Latino candidates in Texas, California, Colorado, Arizona, and New Mexico. The group mobilized Mexican American voters with calls for job-training programs and greater access to financial institutions. By the early 1970s, it had elected Latinos to local offices in several cities with large Latino populations.

La Raza was part of a larger civil rights movement among Mexican Americans (many of whom began calling themselves Chicanos). This "Brown Power" movement fought against discrimination and celebrated ethnic pride. On September 16, 1969 (Mexican Independence Day), students at the University of California at Berkeley staged a sit-in demanding a Chicano Studies program. Over the next decade, more than 50 universities created programs dedicated to the study of Latinos in the United States.

One issue many Latino leaders promoted in the late 1960s was **bilingualism**—the practice of teaching immigrant students in their own language while they also learned English. Congress supported their arguments, passing the **Bilingual Education Act** in 1968. This act directed school districts to set up classes for immigrants in their own language while they were learning English.

Later, bilingualism became politically controversial. Many Americans worried that bilingualism made it difficult for Latino immigrants to assimilate. Beginning in the 1980s, an English-only movement began, and by the 2000s, legislatures in 25 states had passed laws or amendments making English the official language of their state.

✓**Reading Check** **Explaining** How did Latino Americans increase their economic opportunities in the 1960s?

Section 3 REVIEW

Vocabulary
1. **Explain** the significance of: repatriation, League of United Latin American Citizens, American GI Forum, César Chávez, Dolores Huerta, United Farm Workers, *La Raza Unida*, bilingualism, Bilingual Education Act.

Main Ideas
2. **Identifying** What are the national origins of the three main groups of Latinos in the United States?

3. **Describing** Under what circumstances did the American GI Forum first take action?

4. **Explaining** Why did some Americans worry about the Bilingual Education Act?

Critical Thinking
5. **Big Ideas** How did the judicial system support Latino civil rights in the last century? Cite two relevant court cases and their decisions.

6. **Categorizing** Use a graphic organizer similar to the one below to identify Latino groups and their achievements.

Civil Rights Group	Achievement

7. **Analyzing Visuals** Study the graph on page 693. What was the total U.S. Latino population in 2000? Which group had the largest population?

Writing About History
8. **Expository Writing** Write a magazine article about the conditions that gave rise to the Latino civil rights movement in the postwar period.

History ONLINE

Study Central™ To review this section, go to glencoe.com and click on Study Central.

Causes of the New Protest Movements

- The earlier "beat" movement questioned American values.

- The successes of African Americans' fight for civil rights demonstrated to other groups that change was possible if people demanded change.

- Many in the baby boom generation became frustrated with society as they entered college and began to advocate for social reform.

- The Vietnam War and the draft led many students to join protests.

- Women began to question their position in postwar society. Betty Friedan's book *The Feminine Mystique* influenced many young women.

- The Kennedy administration began to pay attention to women's issues, passing the Equal Pay Act and creating the President's Commission on the Status of Women.

- The Latino American population increased through immigration; Latino newcomers, as well as citizens, faced discrimination.

◀ *SDS leader Mario Savio speaks at a 1966 sit-in.*

▶ *Latinos began to fight for improved labor conditions through the work of the United Farm Workers who held rallies such as this one in 1979.*

Effects of the New Protest Movements

- New student groups, including Students for a Democratic Society (SDS), were formed. Court cases affirmed student rights to free speech on campus.

- New women's groups, such as the National Organization of Women (NOW), emerged. They fought for equal economic rights in the workplace and in society, and they demanded equal opportunities in education.

- A campaign began for the Equal Rights Amendment, but the amendment was not ratified.

- The *Roe* v. *Wade* decision affirmed a constitutional right to abortion, with some limits.

- New Latino organizations emerged, such as the United Farm Workers (UFW) and *La Raza Unida*, fighting for increased economic opportunity and greater representation in political institutions.

- Latinos made substantial gains politically and economically, and many were elected to positions in Congress and state governments.

▲ *Women's rights leaders, such as Bella Abzug (left, in hat) and Betty Friedan (right, in red coat) fought for greater equality for women.*

Reviewing Vocabulary

Directions: Choose the word or words that best complete the sentence.

1. In the 1960s young people known as hippies began the _____ movement.

   A beat

   B counterculture

   C student

   D commune

2. One way that hippies separated themselves from typical society was by living in group arrangements with other hippies known as

   A communes.

   B countercultures.

   C barrios.

   D Woodstocks.

3. A newly energized belief in _____ led to the fight to pass the Equal Rights Amendment.

   A communism

   B environmentalism

   C fascism

   D feminism

4. In the 1930s U.S. officials began to return Mexican immigrants to Mexico in what became known as the

   A counterculture.

   B barrio.

   C repatriation.

   D *La Raza Unida.*

5. Latinos lobbied successfully for the addition of _____ in public education.

   A bilingualism

   B repatriation

   C feminism

   D legalism

Reviewing Main Ideas

Directions: Choose the best answer for each of the following questions.

Section 1 *(pp. 682–685)*

6. SDS was begun by Tom Hayden at which university?

   A Harvard University

   B University of California at Berkeley

   C Kent State University

   D University of Michigan

7. Which of the following was an outgrowth of hippie culture?

   A SDS

   B rock 'n' roll music

   C communes

   D buzz cuts

Section 2 *(pp. 686–691)*

8. The work of the President's Commission on the Status of Women led to

   A the Equal Employment Opportunity Commission.

   B the Equal Rights Amendment.

   C the Equal Pay Act.

   D the National Organization for Women.

9. Title IX of the Educational Amendments prohibited federally funded schools

   A from paying male teachers more than female teachers.

   B from discriminating against minorities.

   C from providing same-gender education.

   D from discriminating on the basis of gender.

TEST-TAKING

Read each question carefully to understand exactly what it is asking. Then review all the answer choices before finally choosing the **best** answer to the question.

Need Extra Help?									
If You Missed Questions . . .	1	2	3	4	5	6	7	8	9
Go to Page . . .	684	685	686–691	694	697	682–683	685	687	690

10. Why did some people oppose the Equal Rights Amendment?

A It said that state governments could not regulate abortion during the first three months of pregnancy.

B It allowed women to go to college and vocational schools for free.

C People feared that it would take away traditional rights such as receiving alimony and exemption from the military draft.

D People feared that more women would choose to stay at home with their families rather than having a career.

Section 3 *(pp. 692–697)*

11. Cuban immigrants arriving after the Cuban Revolution in 1959 were welcomed by Americans because

A there was a shortage of cheap labor.

B they were considered refugees from communism.

C most of them were fluent in English.

D there was a need for more doctors and other professionals.

12. Using a tactic the NAACP had used to advance the rights of African Americans, LULAC fought discrimination against Latinos mainly through

A lobbying efforts.

B demonstrations and other protests.

C the court system.

D periodicals and other mass media.

13. Who was the American GI Forum founded to protect?

A African American veterans

B women veterans

C Mexican American veterans

D Veterans of Pacific Battles

Critical Thinking

Directions: Choose the best answers to the following questions.

14. The Supreme Court upheld the Free Speech protesters' rights to free speech and assembly under which law?

A the Civil Rights Act of 1964

B the Equal Rights Amendment

C the Educational Amendments

D the Twenty-sixth Amendment

Base your answers to questions 15 and 16 on the map below and on your knowledge of Chapter 20.

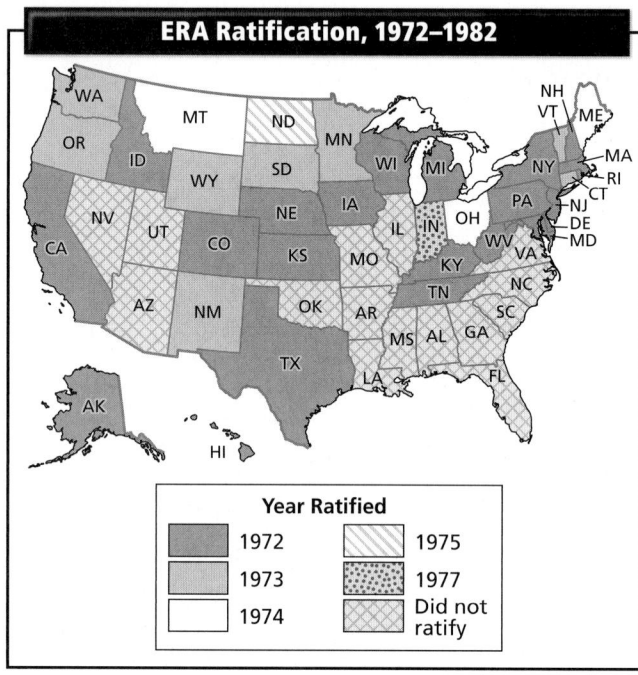

ERA Ratification, 1972–1982

Year Ratified
- 1972
- 1973
- 1974
- 1975
- 1977
- Did not ratify

15. How many states had ratified the ERA by 1977?

A 20 **C** 30

B 25 **D** 35

16. In what region did most states fail to ratify the ERA?

A the South **C** the West

B New England **D** the Midwest

Need Extra Help?							
If You Missed Questions . . .	10	11	12	13	14	15	16
Go to Page . . .	689–690	694–695	695	696	683–684	R15	R15

GO ON

17. The United Farm Workers' boycott against California grape growers was effective because

A the grape growers gave in so quickly to the union's demands.

B no one thought that they could organize so well.

C grapes were a major agricultural product of California.

D the union had the support of the U.S. government.

Base your answers to questions 18 and 19 on the cartoon below and on your knowledge of Chapter 20.

18. What did the cartoonist imply with this cartoon?

A Hippies know a great deal of information.

B Parents do not listen to their children.

C Hippies were wrong to question the older generation when they still accepted money from them.

D The older generation thought hippies were lazy and unintelligent.

19. Based on this cartoon and what you learned in the chapter, which of the following best describes the hippies shown in the cartoon?

A They reject everything about their parents' lifestyle.

B They were most interested in reforming society.

C They only cared about music and communal living.

D They were more interested in the outward signs of a hippie lifestyle.

Document-Based Questions

Directions: Analyze the document and answer the short-answer questions that follow the document.

On December 2, 1964, Mario Savio, the leader of the Free Speech Movement, led a protest at the University of California at Berkeley. Before the protest, Savio made a speech in reaction to comments by Berkeley's president, Clark Kerr. Kerr had said that he would not speak out in favor of students' demands in opposition to the Board of Regents, in the same way that a manager would not speak out against a board of directors. Savio used Kerr's metaphor of the university as a corporation in the following excerpt from his speech:

> "[I]f this is a firm, and if the Board of Regents are the board of directors, and if President Kerr in fact is the manager, then I'll tell you something: the faculty are a bunch of employees, and we're the raw material! But we're a bunch of raw material[s] that don't mean to have any process upon us, don't mean to be made into any product. . . . We're human beings! . . . you've got to put your bodies upon the gears and upon the wheels, upon the levers, upon all the apparatus, and you've got to make it stop. And you've got to indicate to the people who run it, to the people who own it, that unless you're free, the machine will be prevented from working at all!"
>
> —from Mario Savio's speech to Free Speech Movement demonstrators

20. According to Savio, if the university is a company, then what are the students?

21. What is Savio asking his fellow students to do, both literally and figuratively?

Extended Response

22. Write an expository essay explaining why so many protest movements emerged in the United States during the 1960s and 1970s. Your essay should include an introduction and at least three paragraphs that explore this issue, including facts and examples from the chapter.

STOP

History ONLINE

For additional test practice, use Self-Check Quizzes—Chapter 20 at glencoe.com.

Need Extra Help?						
If You Missed Questions . . .	17	18	19	20	21	22
Go to Page . . .	697	R18	701	701	R19	R12

A Changing Society
1968–present

Why It Matters

In the last 40 years, the United States won the Cold War and the Soviet Union collapsed, bringing about dramatic changes in global politics. Americans faced many new challenges, including regional wars, environmental problems, and the rise of international terrorism. At the same time, the rise of modern American conservatism changed America's politics and led to new perspectives on the role of government in modern society.

By the early twenty-first century, American society was becoming increasingly diverse even as technology enabled people to become more interconnected.

Politics and Economics

1968–1980

Secretary of State Henry Kissinger sits with President Richard Nixon in the Oval Office to discuss foreign affairs on September 21, 1973.

U.S. PRESIDENTS

Nixon 1969–1974

Ford 1974–1977

1970
- First Earth Day observed
- Environmental Protection Agency created

1972
- Nixon visits China and the Soviet Union
- Watergate burglars are arrested

1973
- Senate Watergate investigations begin
- AIM and government clash at Wounded Knee, South Dakota

1974
- Nixon resigns

U.S. EVENTS

1970   1972   1974

WORLD EVENTS

1971
- People's Republic of China admitted to UN

1973
- Britain, Ireland, and Denmark join Common Market

1974
- India becomes world's sixth nuclear power

MAKING CONNECTIONS

What Stops Government Abuse of Power?

The Watergate scandal forced Richard Nixon to become the first president to resign from office. The legacy of Watergate, together with the Vietnam War and the economic downturn of the late 1970s, caused many people to distrust the government and worry about the nation's future.

- *How do you think Watergate affected people's attitudes toward government?*
- *Do you think Nixon should have been punished for his role in the scandal?*

FOLDABLES™

Analyzing Cause and Effect After you have read about the Watergate scandal, create a Shutter Fold Foldable to analyze critical information. Write a summary of Watergate events in the large middle section inside the Shutter Foldable. On the left-hand tab, list the causes of the Watergate scandal. On the right-hand tab, list the effects of Watergate on the political system.

1975
- President Ford signs Helsinki Accords

Carter
1977–1981

1979
- Iranian revolutionaries seize U.S. embassy in Tehran

1976

1978

1977
- Human rights manifesto is signed by 241 Czech activists and intellectuals

1979
- Sandinista guerrillas overthrow Nicaraguan dictator Somoza
- Margaret Thatcher becomes prime minister of Great Britain

History ONLINE Visit glencoe.com and enter *QuickPass*™ code TAVMT5147c21 for Chapter 21 resources.

The Nixon Administration

Guide to Reading

Big Ideas

Individual Action One of President Nixon's most dramatic accomplishments was changing the United States's relationship with the People's Republic of China and the Soviet Union.

Content Vocabulary

- revenue sharing *(p. 708)*
- impound *(p. 708)*
- détente *(p. 710)*
- summit *(p. 711)*

Academic Vocabulary

- welfare *(p. 708)*·
- liberal *(p. 708)*

People and Events to Identify

- Southern strategy *(p. 707)*
- New Federalism *(p. 708)*
- Henry Kissinger *(p. 709)*
- Vietnamization *(p. 709)*
- SALT I *(p. 711)*

Reading Strategy

Organizing Complete a graphic organizer similar to the one below by listing Nixon's domestic and foreign policies.

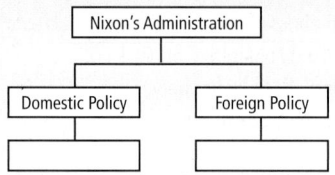

After he won the 1968 presidential election, Richard Nixon sought to restore law and order at home. His greatest accomplishments, however, were in foreign policy, where he worked to ease Cold War tensions with China and the Soviet Union.

Appealing to Middle America

MAIN Idea Nixon won the 1968 election by appealing to a "silent majority" of Americans.

HISTORY AND YOU Do you view your community as politically and socially liberal or conservative? Read on to find out about the strategies Nixon used to convince conservative Southerners to vote for him.

While they did not shout as loudly as the protesters, many Americans supported the government and longed for an end to the violence and turmoil that seemed to be plaguing the nation. The presidential candidate in 1968 who appealed to many of these frustrated citizens was Richard Nixon, a Republican. Nixon aimed many of his campaign messages at these Americans, whom he referred to as "Middle America" and the "silent majority." He promised them "peace with honor" in Vietnam, law and order, a more streamlined government, and a return to more traditional values at home.

Nixon's principal opponent in the 1968 presidential election was Democrat Hubert Humphrey, who had served as vice president under Lyndon Johnson. Nixon also had to wage his campaign against a strong third-party candidate, George Wallace, an experienced Southern politician and avowed supporter of segregation. In a 1964 bid for the Democratic presidential nomination, the former Alabama governor had attracted considerable support.

On Election Day, Wallace captured an impressive 13.5 percent of the popular vote, the best showing of a third-party candidate since 1924. Nixon managed a victory, however, receiving 43.4 percent of the popular vote to Humphrey's 42.7, and 301 electoral votes to Humphrey's 191.

The Southern Strategy

One of the keys to Nixon's victory was his surprisingly strong showing in the South. Even though the South had long been a Democratic stronghold, Nixon had refused to concede the region. To gain Southern support, Nixon had met with powerful South Carolina senator Strom Thurmond and won his backing by promising several things: to appoint only conservatives to the federal

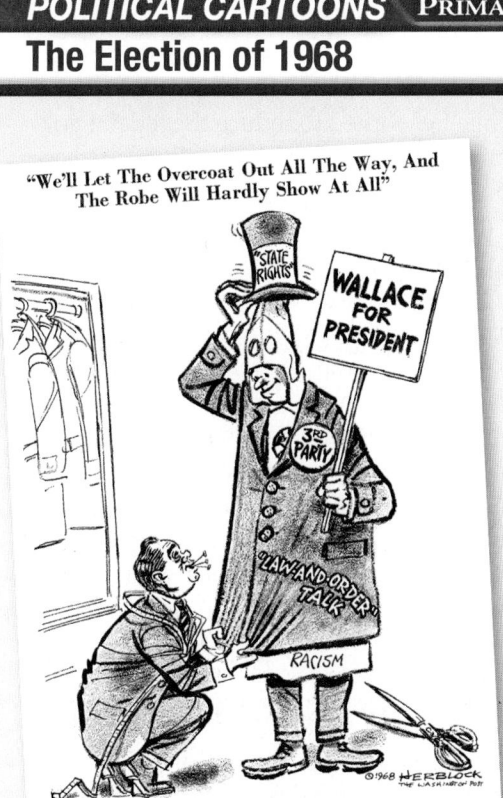

"We'll Let The Overcoat Out All The Way, And The Robe Will Hardly Show At All"

▲ Third-party presidential candidate George Wallace tailors an overcoat to cover the robe worn by one of his supporters.

"...He Doesn't Have Much of a Punch But He's Awful Fast on His Feet!"

▲ Republican Richard Nixon is fast on his feet as he spars with Democrat Hubert Humphrey. The man with the glasses represents John Q. Public, who is speaking to an elephant representing the Republican Party.

Analyzing VISUALS DBQ

1. **Identifying** In the cartoon on the left, what is the cartoonist accusing Wallace of doing?

2. **Identifying Points of View** In the cartoon on the right, do you think the cartoonist approves of Nixon? Why or why not?

courts, to name a Southerner to the Supreme Court, to oppose court-ordered busing, and to choose a vice presidential candidate acceptable to the South. (Nixon ultimately chose Spiro Agnew, governor of the border state of Maryland.)

Nixon's efforts paid off on Election Day. Large numbers of white Southerners deserted the Democratic Party, granting Humphrey only one victory in that region—in Lyndon Johnson's home state of Texas. While Wallace claimed most of the states in the Deep South, Nixon captured Virginia, Tennessee, Kentucky, and North Carolina. Senator Strom Thurmond's support delivered his state of South Carolina for the Republicans as well.

Following his victory, Nixon set out to attract even more Southerners to the Republican Party, an effort that became known as the **Southern strategy.** Toward this end, he kept his agreement with Senator Thurmond and took steps to slow desegregation. During his tenure, Nixon worked to overturn several civil rights policies. He reversed a Johnson administration policy, for example, that had cut off federal funds for racially segregated schools.

A Law-and-Order President

During the campaign, Nixon had also promised to uphold law and order. His administration specifically targeted the nation's antiwar protesters. Attorney General John Mitchell declared that he stood ready to prosecute "hard-line militants" who crossed state lines to stir up riots. Mitchell's deputy, Richard Kleindienst, went even further with the boast, "We're going to enforce the law against draft evaders, against radical students, against deserters, against civil disorders, against organized crime, and against street crime."

President Nixon also went on the attack against the recent Supreme Court rulings that expanded the rights of accused criminals. Nixon openly criticized the Court and its chief justice, Earl Warren. The president promised to fill vacancies on the Supreme Court with judges who would support the rights of law enforcement over the rights of suspected criminals.

When Chief Justice Warren retired shortly after Nixon took office, the president replaced him with Warren Burger, a respected conservative judge. He also placed three other conservative justices on the Court, including one from the South. The Burger Court did not reverse Warren Court rulings on the rights of criminal suspects. It did, however, refuse to expand those rights further. For example, in *Stone* v. *Powell* (1976), it agreed to limits on the rights of defendants to appeal state convictions to the federal judiciary. The Court also continued to uphold capital punishment as constitutional.

The New Federalism

Nixon had campaigned promising to reduce the size of the federal government by dismantling several federal programs and giving more control to state and local governments. Nixon called this the **New Federalism.** He argued that such an approach would make government more effective.

"I reject the patronizing idea that government in Washington, D.C., is inevitably more wise and more efficient than government at the state or local level," Nixon declared. "The idea that a bureaucratic elite in Washington knows what's best for people . . . is really a contention that people cannot govern themselves." Under the New Federalism program, Congress passed a series of **revenue-sharing** bills that granted federal funds to state and local agencies to use.

Although revenue sharing was intended to give state and local agencies more power, over time it gave the federal government new power. As states came to depend on federal funds, the federal government could impose conditions on the states. Unless they met those conditions, their funds would be cut off.

As part of the New Federalism, Nixon sought to close down many of the programs of Johnson's Great Society. He vetoed funding for the Department of Housing and Urban Development, eliminated the Office of Economic Opportunity, and tried unsuccessfully to shut down the Job Corps.

While he worked to reduce the federal government's role, Nixon also sought to increase the power of the executive branch. The president did not have many strong relationships with members of Congress. The fact that the Republicans did not control either house also contributed to struggles with the legislative branch. Nixon often responded by trying to work around Congress. For instance, when Congress appropriated money for programs he opposed, Nixon **impounded,** or refused to release, the funds. By 1973, he had impounded an estimated $15 billion. The Supreme Court eventually declared the practice of impoundment unconstitutional.

The Family Assistance Plan

One federal program Nixon sought to reform was the nation's **welfare** system—Aid to Families with Dependent Children (AFDC). The program had many critics, Republican and Democratic alike. They argued that AFDC was structured so that it was actually better for poor people to apply for benefits than to take a low-paying job. A mother who had such a job, for example, would then have to pay for child care, sometimes leaving her with less income than she had on welfare.

In 1969 Nixon proposed replacing the AFDC with the Family Assistance Plan. The plan called for providing needy families a guaranteed yearly grant of $1,600, which could be supplemented by outside earnings. Many **liberals** applauded the plan as a significant step toward expanding federal responsibility for the poor. Nixon, however, presented the program in a conservative light, arguing it would encourage welfare recipients to become more responsible.

Although the program won approval in the House in 1970, it soon came under harsh attack. Welfare recipients complained that the federal grant was too low, while conservatives, who disapproved of guaranteed income, also criticized the plan. Such opposition led to the program's defeat in the Senate.

Reading Check **Evaluating** How did Nixon's New Federalism differ from Johnson's Great Society?

Nixon's Foreign Policy

MAIN Idea With the support of national security adviser Henry Kissinger, Nixon forged better relationships with China and the Soviet Union.

HISTORY AND YOU How should a president balance his efforts between domestic and foreign affairs? Read on to learn about Nixon's strategies for dealing with communist countries.

Despite Nixon's domestic initiatives, a State Department official later recalled that the president had a "monumental disinterest in domestic policies." Nixon once expressed his hope that a "competent cabinet" of advisers could run the country. This would allow him to focus his energies on foreign affairs.

Nixon and Kissinger

In a move that would greatly influence his foreign policy, Nixon chose as his national security adviser **Henry Kissinger,** a former Harvard professor. Kissinger had served under Presidents Kennedy and Johnson as a foreign policy consultant. Although Secretary of State William Rogers outranked him, Kissinger soon took the lead in helping shape Nixon's foreign policy.

The Nixon Doctrine Nixon and Kissinger shared views on many issues. Both believed abandoning the war in Vietnam would damage the United States's position in the world. Thus, they worked toward a gradual withdrawal while simultaneously training the South Vietnamese to defend themselves.

This policy of **Vietnamization,** as it was called, was then extended globally in what came to be called the Nixon Doctrine. In July 1969, only six months after taking office, Nixon announced that the United States would now expect its allies to take care of their own defense. The United States would uphold all of the alliances it had signed, and would continue to provide military aid and training to allies, but it would no longer "conceive all the plans, design all the programs, execute all the decisions and undertake all the defense of the free nations of the world." America's allies would have to take responsibility for maintaining peace and stability in their own areas of the world.

People IN HISTORY

Henry Kissinger
· 1923–

Born in Germany, Henry Kissinger immigrated to the United States with his family in 1938 to escape Nazi persecution of Jews. During World War II, he served in U.S. military intelligence. After the war, Kissinger attended Harvard University and then joined the faculty there. He held various positions related to government, defense, and international affairs.

After acting as a consultant on national security under Presidents Kennedy and Johnson, Kissinger became President Nixon's national security adviser. In this capacity, he helped to establish the policy of détente with the Soviet Union and China. In 1973 he became secretary of state. Kissinger negotiated the cease-fire with North Vietnam, and along with Le Duc Tho, his co-negotiator, was awarded the Nobel Peace Prize in 1973.

In 1977 Kissinger was awarded the Presidential Medal of Freedom for his services to the nation. Today, he remains an unofficial adviser on international issues to leaders around the world.

How did Henry Kissinger influence foreign policy in the 1970s?

▲ In 1971, Time *magazine celebrated Kissinger as the driving force behind Nixon's trip to China.*

Détente With the Soviet Union and China

▲ President Nixon meets with Soviet premier Brezhnev to discuss limiting the number of nuclear weapons.

The Nuclear Arms Race

Number of nuclear weapons

— United States
— USSR/Russia

Year

Source: *Bulletin of the Atomic Scientists.*

◄ Mao Zedong, leader of China, greets Nixon in Beijing on February 21, 1972.

Analyzing VISUALS

1. **Specifying** In what year did the number of nuclear weapons in the U.S. peak?

2. **Explaining** Why was establishing détente a significant accomplishment?

The New Policy of Détente The Soviet Union was not pleased when Nixon, a man with a history of outspoken anticommunist actions, became president. Nixon was still a staunch anticommunist, but he and Kissinger believed the United States needed to adjust to the growing role of China, Japan, and Western Europe. This emerging "multipolar" world demanded a different approach to American foreign policy.

Both Nixon and Kissinger wanted to continue to contain communism, but they believed that negotiation with Communists offered a better way for the United States to achieve its international goals. Nixon and Kissinger developed a new approach called **détente,** or relaxation of tensions, between the United States and its two major Communist rivals, the Soviet Union and China. In explaining détente to the American people, Nixon said that the United States had to build a better relationship with its main rivals in the interest of world peace:

PRIMARY SOURCE

"We must understand that détente is not a love fest. It is an understanding between nations that have opposite purposes, but which share common interests, including the avoidance of a nuclear war. Such an understanding can work—that is, restrain aggression and deter war—only as long as the potential aggressor is made to recognize that neither aggression nor war will be profitable."

—quoted in *The Limits of Power*

The successes of détente were diminished due to upheavals in smaller nations on the periphery of the Cold War. In Chile, President Salvador Allende was killed during a coup supported by the American CIA. Similarly, the Angolan Civil War, which began in 1975, featured covert aid from the United States. The conflicts in Chile and Angola were examples of proxy wars, conflicts during the Cold War that did not directly involve the United States and the Soviet Union but pursued Cold War aims of the two superpowers.

Nixon Visits China

Détente began with an effort to improve American-Chinese relations. Since 1949, when Communists took power in China, the United States had refused to recognize the Communists as the legitimate rulers. Instead, the American government recognized the exiled regime on the island of Taiwan as the Chinese government. Having long supported this policy, Nixon now set out to reverse it. He began by lifting trade and travel restrictions and withdrawing the Seventh Fleet from defending Taiwan.

After a series of highly secret negotiations between Kissinger and Chinese leaders, Nixon announced that he would visit China in February 1972. During the historic trip, the leaders of both nations agreed to establish "more normal" relations between their countries. In a statement that epitomized the notion of détente, Nixon told his Chinese hosts during a banquet toast, "Let us start a long march together, not in lockstep, but on different roads leading to the same goal, the goal of building a world structure of peace and justice."

In taking this trip, Nixon hoped not only to strengthen ties with the Chinese, but also to encourage the Soviets to more actively pursue diplomacy. Since the 1960s, a rift had developed between the Communist governments of the Soviet Union and China. Troops of the two nations occasionally clashed along their borders. Nixon believed détente with China would encourage Soviet premier Leonid Brezhnev to be more accommodating with the United States.

United States-Soviet Tensions Ease

Nixon's strategy toward the Soviets worked. Shortly after the public learned of American negotiations with China, the Soviets proposed an American-Soviet **summit,** or high-level diplomatic meeting, to be held in May 1972. On May 22, President Nixon flew to Moscow for a weeklong summit, becoming the first American president since World War II to visit the Soviet Union.

During the historic Moscow summit, the two superpowers signed the first Strategic Arms Limitation Treaty, or **SALT I,** a plan to limit nuclear arms the two nations had been working on for years. Nixon and Brezhnev also agreed to increase trade and the exchange of scientific information. Détente profoundly eased tensions between the Soviet Union and the United States.

By the end of Nixon's presidency, one Soviet official admitted that "the United States and the Soviet Union had their best relationship of the whole Cold War period." President Nixon indeed had made his mark on the world stage. As he basked in the glow of his 1972 foreign policy triumphs, however, trouble was brewing on the home front. A scandal was about to engulf his presidency and plunge the nation into one of its greatest constitutional crises.

Reading Check **Summarizing** What were the results of the 1972 American-Soviet summit?

Vocabulary

1. **Explain** the significance of: Southern strategy, New Federalism, revenue sharing, impound, Henry Kissinger, Vietnamization, détente, summit, SALT I.

Main Ideas

2. **Describing** How did President Nixon attempt to increase the power of the presidency?

3. **Explaining** How did Nixon use his visit to China to improve relations with the Soviet Union?

Critical Thinking

4. **Big Ideas** What were the results of Nixon's policy of détente?

5. **Organizing** Use a graphic organizer similar to the one below to describe how President Nixon established détente in the listed countries.

China	
Soviet Union	

6. **Analyzing Visuals** Look at the *Time* cover on page 709. What does the image portray about Nixon's foreign policy?

Writing About History

7. **Expository Writing** Take on the role of a member of President Nixon's staff. Write a press release explaining either Nixon's domestic or foreign policies.

History ONLINE

Study Central™ To review this section, go to glencoe.com and click on Study Central.

The Watergate Scandal

Despite a successful first term, Richard Nixon and his supporters worried about reelection. The tactics they resorted to led the president to become embroiled in a scandal known as Watergate, one of the United States's great constitutional crises.

The Roots of Watergate

MAIN Idea Tactics used by Nixon's supporters to try to ensure his reelection in 1972 led to the Watergate scandal.

HISTORY AND YOU What do you know about Richard Nixon and the Watergate scandal? Read on to learn how the president became involved in this major governmental crisis.

The Watergate scandal is perhaps the most famous scandal in modern American history. It certainly had momentous consequences, as it led to the only time in the nation's history when the president of the United States was forced to resign from office. As reporter Bob Woodward recounts in his book, *All the President's Men*, the scandal began on the morning of June 17, 1972.

Woodward was a young reporter for the *Washington Post* at that time. His editor had ruined his Saturday by asking him to cover a seemingly insignificant but bizarre **incident.** In the early hours of that morning, five men had broken into the Democratic National Committee (DNC) headquarters in the city's Watergate apartment-office complex. Woodward was ordered to attend the arraignment and see if there was a story worth reporting.

As Woodward sat near the back of the courtroom listening to the bail proceedings for the five defendants, the judge asked each man his occupation. One of the men, James McCord, answered that he was retired from government service.

"Where in government?" asked the judge. "CIA," McCord whispered. Woodward sprang to attention. Why was a former agent of the CIA involved in what seemed to be nothing more than a burglary? Over the next two years, Woodward and another reporter, Carl Bernstein, would investigate this question. In so doing, they uncovered a scandal that helped trigger a constitutional crisis and eventually forced President Nixon to resign.

Mounting a Reelection Fight

The Watergate scandal began when the Nixon administration tried to cover up its involvement in the break-in at the Democratic National Committee headquarters, along with other illegal

The Watergate Scandal Erupts

In June 1972, five men were arrested attempting to place wiretaps on phones and stealing information from the Democratic National Headquarters at the Watergate Hotel. The subsequent investigation revealed a cover-up that reached to the White House.

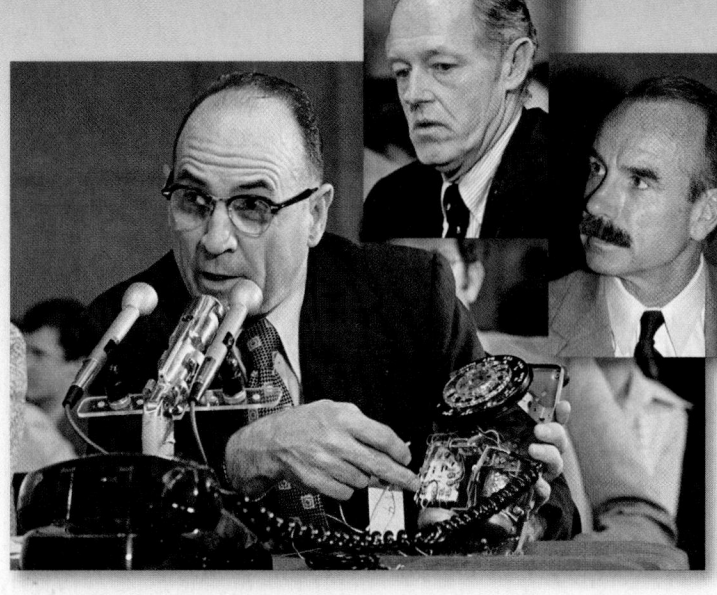

▲ James McCord shows Congress the bugging device he installed. E. Howard Hunt (center) and G. Gordon Liddy (right) also testified.

▲ The Watergate Complex gave its name to the resulting scandal. Security guard Frank Willis (right) reported to police evidence of the break-in.

▶ Counsel to the president John Dean testified that Nixon had been directly involved in the cover-up of the Watergate break-in.

Analyzing VISUALS

1. **Speculating** If you had discovered the break-in, what might make you suspicious about the burglars?

2. **Explaining** Why was John Dean's testimony damaging to the president?

actions. Although the affair began with the Watergate burglary, many scholars believe the roots of the scandal lay in Nixon's character and the atmosphere that he and his advisers created in the White House.

Richard Nixon had fought hard to become president. He had battled back from numerous political defeats, including a loss to John F. Kennedy in the 1960 presidential election. Along the way, Nixon had grown defensive, secretive, and often resentful of his critics.

Furthermore, Nixon had become president when American society was in turmoil. There were race riots, and protests over the Vietnam War continued to consume the country. In Nixon's view, protesters and other "radicals" were trying to bring down his administration. Nixon was so consumed with his opponents that he compiled an "enemies list" filled with

people—from politicians to members of the media—whom he considered a threat to his presidency.

When Nixon began his reelection campaign, his advisers were optimistic. Nixon had just finished triumphant trips to China and the Soviet Union. Former governor George Wallace, who had mounted a strong campaign in 1968, had dropped out of the race after an assassin's bullet paralyzed him, and the Democratic **challenger,** South Dakota Senator George McGovern, was viewed by many as too liberal.

Nixon's reelection was by no means certain, however. The unpopular Vietnam War still raged, and his staffers remembered how close the 1968 election had been. Determined to win at all costs, they began spying on opposition rallies and spreading rumors and false reports about their Democratic opponents.

As part of their efforts to help the president, Nixon's advisers ordered five men to break into the Democratic Party's headquarters at the Watergate complex and steal any sensitive campaign information. They were also to place wiretaps on the office telephones. While the burglars were at work, a security guard making his rounds spotted a piece of tape holding a door lock. The guard ripped off the tape, but when he passed the door later, he noticed that it had been replaced. He quickly called police, who arrived shortly and arrested the men.

The Cover-Up Begins

After the Watergate break-in, the media discovered that one burglar, James McCord, was not only an ex-CIA officer but also a member of the Committee for the Re-election of the President (CRP). Reports soon surfaced that the burglars had been paid from a secret CRP fund controlled by the White House.

At this point, the cover-up began. White House officials destroyed incriminating documents and gave false testimony to investigators. Meanwhile, President Nixon stepped in. The president may not have ordered the break-in, but he did order a cover-up. With Nixon's consent, administration officials asked the CIA to stop the FBI from investigating the source of the money paid to the burglars. The CIA told the FBI that the investigation threatened national security. To combat efforts to block the FBI investigation, the FBI's deputy director, W. Mark Felt, secretly leaked information about Watergate to the Washington Post.

Meanwhile, Nixon's press secretary dismissed the incident as a "third-rate burglary attempt," and the president told the American public, "The White House has had no involvement whatever in this particular incident." The strategy worked. Most Americans believed President Nixon, and despite efforts by the media, in particular the *Washington Post*, to keep the story alive, few people paid much attention during the 1972 presidential campaign. On Election Day, Nixon won reelection by one of the largest margins in history with nearly 61 percent of the popular vote, compared to 37.5 percent for George McGovern.

✓ **Reading Check** **Examining** Why did members of the CRP break into the Democratic National Committee headquarters?

The Cover-Up Unravels

MAIN Idea The president's refusal to cooperate with Congress only focused attention on his possible involvement.

HISTORY AND YOU How far do you think that presidents should be able to go in the name of national security? Read on to learn how Nixon tried to invoke national security concerns to thwart an investigation of his involvement in Watergate.

In early 1973, the Watergate burglars went on trial. Under relentless prodding from federal judge John J. Sirica, McCord agreed to cooperate with the grand jury investigation. He also agreed to testify before the newly created Senate Select Committee on Presidential Campaign Activities. The chairman of the committee was Senator **Sam J. Ervin,** a Democrat from North Carolina.

McCord's testimony opened a floodgate of confessions, and a parade of White House and campaign officials exposed one illegality after another. Foremost among the officials was counsel to the president **John Dean,** a member of the inner circle of the White House who leveled allegations against Nixon himself.

A Summer of Shocking Testimony

In June 1973 John Dean testified before Senator Ervin's committee that former Attorney General John Mitchell had ordered the Watergate break-in and that Nixon had played an active role in attempting to cover up any White House involvement. As a shocked nation absorbed Dean's testimony, the Nixon administration strongly denied the charges.

Because Dean had no evidence to confirm his account, for the next month, the Senate committee attempted to determine who was telling the truth. Then, on July 16, the answer appeared unexpectedly. On that day, White House aide Alexander Butterfield testified that Nixon had ordered a taping system installed in the White House to record all conversations. The president had done so, Butterfield said, to help him write his memoirs after he left office. For members of the committee, however, the tapes would tell them exactly what the president knew and when he knew it, but only if the president could be forced to release them.

ANALYZING SUPREME COURT CASES

Is Executive Privilege Unlimited?

★ *United States* v. *Nixon*, 1974

Background to the Case

In 1974 Special Prosecutor Leon Jaworski issued a subpoena to gain access to tape recordings President Nixon had made of conversations in the Oval Office. Jaworski believed that the tapes would prove the active involvement of the president in the Watergate cover-up. Nixon filed a motion to prevent the subpoena, claiming executive privilege. The case went to district court, but that court withheld judgment pending the decision of the Supreme Court.

How the Court Ruled

In a unanimous 8-to-0 decision (Justice Rehnquist did not take part), the Supreme Court found that executive privilege did not protect Nixon's tape recordings, stating that while the president has a right to protect military secrets and other sensitive material and has a right to some confidentiality, the needs of a criminal trial must take precedence.

▲ The Senate committee overseeing the Watergate investigation, chaired by Senator Sam Ervin (fourth from left at the table), wanted access to Nixon's tape recordings.

PRIMARY SOURCE

The Court's Opinion

"In this case we must weigh the importance of the general privilege of confidentiality of Presidential communications in performance of the President's responsibilities against the inroads of such a privilege on the fair administration of criminal justice. The interest in preserving confidentiality is weighty indeed and entitled to great respect. However, we cannot conclude that advisers will be moved to temper the candor of their remarks by the infrequent occasions of disclosure because of the possibility that such conversations will be called for in the context of a criminal prosecution. On the other hand, the allowance of the privilege to withhold evidence that is demonstrably relevant in a criminal trial would cut deeply into the guarantee of due process of law and gravely impair the basic function of the courts. A President's acknowledged need for confidentiality in the communications of his office is general in nature, whereas the constitutional need for production of relevant evidence in a criminal proceeding is specific and central to the fair adjudication of a particular criminal case in the administration of justice. . . . The President's broad interest in confidentiality of communications will not be vitiated by disclosure of a limited number of conversations preliminarily shown to have some bearing on the pending criminal cases. We conclude that when the ground for asserting privilege as to subpoenaed materials sought for use in a criminal trial is based only on the generalized interest in confidentiality, it cannot prevail over the fundamental demands of due process of law in the fair administration of criminal justice. . . ."

—Chief Justice Warren Burger writing for the Court in
United States v. *Nixon*

DBQ Document-Based Questions

1. **Finding the Main Idea** What is the main point of the decision in *United States* v. *Nixon*?
2. **Summarizing** What does Burger say that executive privilege in this case would violate?
3. **Expressing** Do you agree with the Supreme Court's decision in this case? Explain.

"...DOWN, BOY!..."

Baldy

▲ *The Watergate investigation takes the form of a search dog who has tracked the evidence directly to the president.*

◀ *President Nixon clings to his desk as the Watergate scandal crashes like a tidal wave through the Oval Office.*

©1973 HERBLOCK

Analyzing VISUALS DBQ

1. **Specifying** What does the cartoon on the left use to symbolize the Watergate scandal?
2. **Explaining** What is the meaning of Nixon's appearance and the magnifying glass in the cartoon on the right?

The Case of the Tapes

At first, Nixon refused to hand over the tapes, pleading **executive privilege**—the principle that White House conversations should remain confidential to protect national security. **Special prosecutor** Archibald Cox, the government lawyer appointed by the president to handle the Watergate cases, took Nixon to court in October 1973 to force him to give up the recordings. Nixon ordered Attorney General Elliot Richardson to fire Cox, but Richardson refused and resigned. Nixon then ordered Richardson's deputy to fire Cox, but the deputy resigned as well. Nixon's solicitor general, Robert Bork, finally fired Cox, but the incident, nicknamed the "Saturday Night Massacre" in the press, badly damaged Nixon's reputation with the public.

The fall of 1973 proved to be a disastrous time for Nixon for other reasons, as well. His vice president, Spiro Agnew, was forced to resign in disgrace after investigators learned that he had taken bribes from state contractors while governor of Maryland and that he had continued to accept bribes while serving in Washington. Gerald Ford, the Republican leader of the House of Representatives, became the new vice president.

Nixon Resigns

In an effort to quiet the growing outrage over his actions, President Nixon appointed a new special prosecutor, Texas lawyer Leon Jaworski, who proved no less determined than Cox to obtain the president's tapes. In July the Supreme Court ruled that the president had to turn over the tapes, and Nixon complied.

Several days later, the House Judiciary Committee voted to impeach Nixon, or officially charge him with misconduct. The committee charged Nixon with obstructing justice in the Watergate cover-up; misusing federal agencies to violate the rights of citizens; and defying the authority of Congress by refusing to deliver tapes and other materials as requested. Before the House of Representatives could vote on whether Nixon should be impeached, investigators found indisputable evidence against the president. One of the tapes revealed that on June 23, 1972, just six days after the Watergate burglary, Nixon had ordered the CIA to stop the FBI's investigation. With this news, even the president's strongest supporters conceded that impeachment by the House and conviction in the Senate were inevitable. On August 9, 1974, Nixon resigned his office in disgrace. Gerald Ford took the oath of office and became the nation's 38th president.

The Impact of Watergate

Upon taking office, President Ford urged Americans to put the Watergate scandal behind them. "Our long national nightmare is over," he declared. On September 8, 1974, Ford announced that he would grant a "full, free, and absolute pardon" to Richard Nixon for any crimes he "committed or may have committed or taken part in" while president. "[This] is an American tragedy in which we all have played a part," he told the nation. "It could go on and on and on, or someone must write the end to it."

The Watergate crisis led to new laws intended to limit the power of the executive branch. The **Federal Campaign Act Amendments** limited campaign contributions and established an independent agency to administer stricter election laws. The Ethics in Government Act required financial disclosure by high government officials in all three branches of government. The FBI Domestic Security Investigation Guidelines Act restricted the Bureau's political intelligence-gathering activities. Congress also established a means for appointing an independent counsel to investigate and prosecute wrongdoing by high government officials.

Despite these efforts, Watergate left many Americans with a deep distrust of their public officials. On the other hand, some Americans saw the Watergate affair as proof that in the United States, no person is above the law. As Bob Woodward observed:

PRIMARY SOURCE

"Watergate was probably a good thing for the country; it was a good, sobering lesson. Accountability to the law applies to everyone. The problem with kings and prime ministers and presidents is that they think that they are above it . . . that they have some special rights, and privileges, and status. And a process that says: No. We have our laws and believe them, and they apply to everyone, is a very good thing."

—quoted in *Nixon: An Oral History of His Presidency*

After the ordeal of Watergate, most Americans attempted to put the affair behind them. In the years ahead, however, the nation encountered a host of new troubles, from a stubborn economic recession to a heart-wrenching hostage crisis overseas.

Reading Check **Evaluating** Why did Congress pass new laws after the Watergate scandal?

Section 2 REVIEW

Vocabulary

1. **Explain** the significance of: Sam J. Ervin, John Dean, executive privilege, special prosecutor, Federal Campaign Act Amendments.

Main Ideas

2. **Explaining** How did the Watergate cover-up involve the CIA and the FBI?

3. **Determining Cause and Effect** Why did President Nixon finally resign?

Critical Thinking

4. **Big Ideas** How did the Watergate scandal alter the balance of power between the executive and legislative branches of the federal government?

5. **Organizing** Use a graphic organizer similar to the one below to record the effects of the Watergate scandal.

Effects of Watergate Scandal

6. **Analyzing Visuals** Study the photographs on page 713. How did the Watergate hearings demonstrate the effectiveness of the system of checks and balances?

Writing About History

7. **Descriptive Writing** Take on the role of a television news analyst. Write a script in which you explain the Watergate scandal and analyze the factors that led to it.

History ONLINE

Study Central™ To review this section, go to glencoe.com and click on Study Central.

Ford and Carter

Guide to Reading

Big Ideas
Economics and Society A weakening economy and growing energy crisis marred the terms of Presidents Ford and Carter.

Content Vocabulary
- inflation *(p. 718)*
- embargo *(p. 718)*
- stagflation *(p. 719)*

Academic Vocabulary
- theory *(p. 719)*
- deregulation *(p. 721)*

People and Events to Identify
- OPEC *(p. 718)*
- Helsinki Accords *(p. 720)*
- Department of Energy *(p. 721)*
- Camp David Accords *(p. 723)*

Reading Strategy
Organizing Complete a graphic organizer similar to the one below by listing the causes of economic problems in the 1970s.

By the time Richard Nixon resigned, the boom period Americans had experienced in the previous decades was coming to an end. Through the 1970s, Presidents Gerald R. Ford and Jimmy Carter attempted, with varying levels of success, to lead the United States through both domestic and foreign crises.

The Economic Crisis of the 1970s

MAIN Idea In the 1970s Americans had to face a slowing economy and an end to plentiful, cheap energy.

HISTORY AND YOU Have you ever heard anyone describe their experiences during the energy crisis of the 1970s? Read on to learn how politics and Americans' dependency on oil imports led to a serious crisis.

After World War II, American prosperity seemed normal. This prosperity relied on easy access to global raw materials and a strong manufacturing base at home. In the 1970s, however, prosperity gave way to a decade of hard times.

A Mighty Economic Machine Slows

Economic troubles began in the mid-1960s when President Johnson increased federal deficit spending, to fund both the Vietnam War and the Great Society programs, without raising taxes. This spending spurred **inflation** by pumping large amounts of money into the economy. One measure of inflation, the Consumer Price Index (CPI) calculates the average price of goods and services purchased by households. Comparing CPI on a yearly basis during the 1970s shows that the inflation rate rose more rapidly during this decade.

Another economic blow came when the price of oil began to rise. By 1970, the United States had become dependent on oil imports from the Middle East and Africa. This was not a problem as long as prices remained low, but in 1973, the **Organization of Petroleum Exporting Countries (OPEC)**—a cartel dominated by Arab countries—decided to use oil as a political weapon. In 1973 a war erupted between Israel and its Arab neighbors. OPEC announced an **embargo**, or trade ban, of petroleum to countries that supported Israel. OPEC also raised the price of crude oil by 70 percent, and then by another 130 percent a few months later.

Although the embargo ended within a few months, oil prices continued to rise. The price of a barrel of crude oil rose from $3 in 1973 to $30 in 1980. As oil and gasoline prices rose, Americans had less money for other goods, which contributed to a recession.

The Energy Crisis

OPEC's embargo caused long lines at gas stations and caused inflation to accelerate rapidly. The U.S. government responded by imposing price controls.

▲ The oil embargo and price increases imposed by OPEC, whose members are shown above, severely decreased supply and increased prices in the United States.

Price of Gasoline, 1970–1990

Price (dollars)*

*Price of Leaded Regular Gasoline in Constant 2000 dollars.

Source: Energy Information Administration.

Analyzing VISUALS

1. **Drawing Conclusions** What problems did American consumers face because of the oil embargo?
2. **Specifying** In what year, between 1970 and 1990, did gasoline reach its highest price?

A Stagnant Economy

Another economic problem was the decline of manufacturing. By 1970, many American manufacturing plants were old and less efficient than the plants Japan and Germany had built after World War II. In 1971, for the first time since 1889, the United States imported more than it exported. Unable to compete, many factories closed, and millions of workers lost their jobs. Thus, in the early 1970s, President Nixon faced a new economic problem nicknamed **"stagflation"**—a combination of inflation and a stagnant economy with high unemployment.

Economists who emphasized the demand side of economic **theory,** including supporters of Keynesianism, did not think that inflation and recession could occur at the same time. They believed that demand drives prices and that inflation could only occur in a booming economy when demand for goods was high. As a result, they did not know what fiscal policy the government should pursue. Increased spending might help end the recession, but it would increase inflation. Raising taxes might slow inflation, but it would also keep the economy in recession.

Nixon decided to focus on controlling inflation. The government moved first to cut spending and raise taxes. The president hoped that higher taxes would prompt Americans to spend less, which would ease the demand on goods and drive down prices. Congress and much of the public, however, protested the idea of a tax hike. Nixon then tried to reduce consumer spending by getting the Federal Reserve Board to raise interest rates. When this failed, the president tried to stop inflation by imposing a 90-day freeze on wages and prices and then issuing federal regulations limiting future wage and price increases. This too met with little success.

Reading Check **Explaining** How did President Nixon attempt to stop stagflation?

Ford and Carter Battle the Economic Crisis

MAIN Idea When Gerald Ford failed to solve the nation's problems, Americans turned to political outsider Jimmy Carter to lead the nation.

HISTORY AND YOU Do you think a president should be a Washington insider? Read how being an outsider affected Carter's ability to lead.

When Nixon resigned in 1974, inflation was still high, despite many efforts to reduce prices. Meanwhile, the unemployment rate was over 5 percent. It would now be up to the new president, Gerald Ford, to confront stagflation.

Ford Tries to "Whip" Inflation

By 1975, the American economy was in the worst recession since the Great Depression, with unemployment at nearly 9 percent. Ford responded by launching a plan called WIN—"Whip Inflation Now." He urged Americans to reduce their use of oil and gas, and take steps to conserve energy. The plan had little impact on the economic situation. The president then began cutting government spending and urged the Federal Reserve to raise interest rates to curb inflation. He also sought to balance the budget and keep taxes low. He vetoed more than 50 bills that the Democratic Congress passed during the first two years of his administration. These efforts failed to revive the economy.

Ford's Foreign Policy

In foreign policy, Ford continued Nixon's general strategy. Ford kept Kissinger on as secretary of state and continued to pursue détente with the Soviets and the Chinese. In August 1975, he met with leaders of NATO and the Warsaw Pact to sign the **Helsinki Accords.** Under the accords, the parties recognized the borders of Eastern Europe established at the end of World War II. The Soviets in return promised to uphold certain basic human rights, including the right to move across national borders. The subsequent Soviet failure to uphold these basic rights turned many Americans against détente.

Ford also met with problems in Southeast Asia. In May 1975, soon after Communists seized power in Cambodia, Cambodian forces captured the *Mayaguez,* an American cargo ship traveling near its shores. Calling the seizure an "act of piracy," Ford sent U.S. Marines to retrieve it. Cambodia secretly released the crew shortly before the marines arrived. Unaware the crew was safe, the marines attacked and recaptured the ship, but 41 servicemen died in the battle.

The Election of 1976

The presidential race pitted Gerald Ford against James Earl Carter, Jr., or Jimmy Carter, as he liked to be called. A former governor of Georgia, Carter had no political experience in Washington. Carter took advantage of his outsider status, promising to restore honesty to the federal government. He also promised new programs for energy development, tax reform, welfare reform, and national health care.

Ford characterized Carter as a liberal whose social programs would produce higher rates of inflation and require tax increases. For many voters, however, Carter's image as a moral and upstanding individual, untainted by Washington politics, made him an attractive candidate. In the end, Carter narrowly defeated Ford with 50.1 percent of the popular vote to Ford's 47.9 percent, while capturing 297 electoral votes to Ford's 240.

Carter's Economic Policies

Most of Carter's domestic policies were intended to fix the economy. At first he tried to end the recession and reduce unemployment by increasing government spending and cutting taxes. When inflation surged in 1978, he changed his mind. He delayed the tax cuts and vetoed the spending programs he had himself proposed. He tried to ease inflation by reducing the money supply and raising interest rates. In the end, none of his efforts succeeded.

Carter believed that the nation's most serious problem was its dependence on foreign oil. In one of his first national addresses, he asked Americans to support a "war" against rising energy consumption. "Our decision about energy will test the character of the American people and the ability of the president and Congress to govern this nation," Carter stated.

The Election of 1976

When President Ford failed to solve the nation's economic problems, voters decided to give Washington outsider Jimmy Carter a chance.

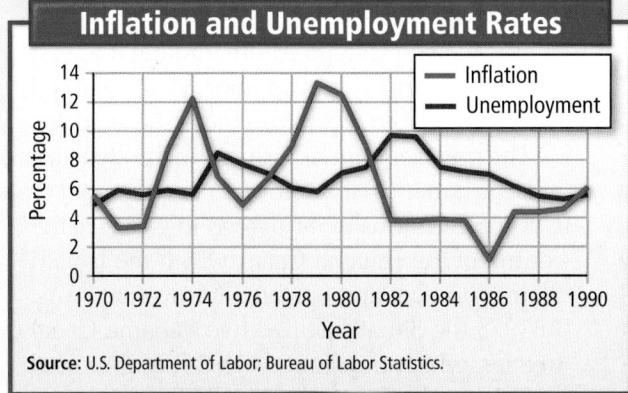

Inflation and Unemployment Rates

Source: U.S. Department of Labor; Bureau of Labor Statistics.

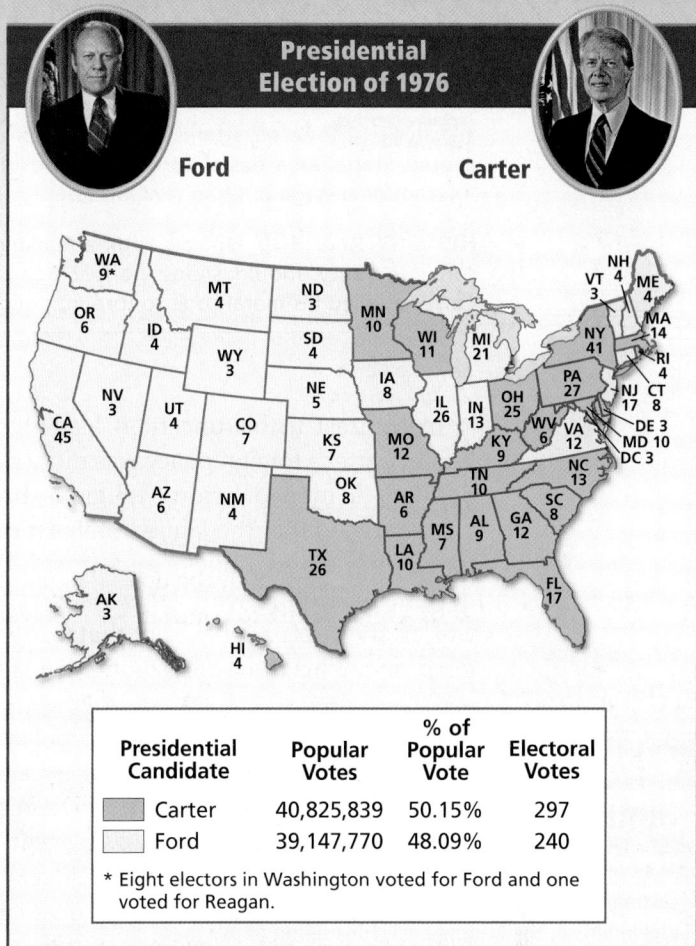

Presidential Election of 1976

Ford   Carter

Presidential Candidate	Popular Votes	% of Popular Vote	Electoral Votes
Carter	40,825,839	50.15%	297
Ford	39,147,770	48.09%	240

* Eight electors in Washington voted for Ford and one voted for Reagan.

Analyzing VISUALS

1. **Analyzing** In what areas of the country did Carter receive the most votes? Why do you think this was so?

2. **Interpreting** What was the trend for both unemployment and inflation after 1976?

Carter proposed a national energy program to conserve oil and to promote the use of coal and renewable energy sources such as solar power. He also convinced Congress to create a **Department of Energy,** and asked Americans to reduce their energy consumption.

Meanwhile, many business leaders and economists urged the president and Congress to deregulate the oil industry. They believed that regulations, first imposed as part of President Nixon's price control plan, made it very difficult for oil companies to make a profit. They claimed they lacked the spare capital needed to invest in new domestic oil wells. This in turn kept the nation dependent on foreign oil.

Carter agreed to support **deregulation** but insisted on a "windfall profits tax" to prevent oil companies from overcharging consumers. Critics argued that the tax conflicted with the basic idea of deregulation, which was to free up capital for use in finding new sources of oil.

In the summer of 1979, instability in the Middle East produced a second major fuel shortage and deepened the nation's economic problems. Under increasing pressure to act, Carter made several proposals in a televised address. In the speech, Carter warned about a "crisis of confidence" that had struck "at the very heart and soul of our national will." The address became known as the "malaise" speech, although Carter had not specifically used that word. Many Americans felt that Carter was blaming the people for his failures.

President Carter's difficulties in solving the nation's economic problems lay partly in his inexperience and inability to work with Congress. Carter, proud of his outsider status, made little effort to reach out to Washington's legislative leaders. As a result, Congress blocked many of his energy proposals. The president also failed to set clear goals for the nation. Instead, he followed a cautious middle course that left people confused. By 1979, public opinion polls showed that Carter's popularity had dropped lower than President Nixon's during Watergate.

Reading Check **Summarizing** To what did President Carter devote much of his domestic agenda?

Carter's Foreign Policy

MAIN Idea Carter attempted to reestablish the United States as a moral force for good on the international stage but had few successes.

HISTORY AND YOU Do you think a leader's personal morality should shape policy? Read how Carter applied his moral code to foreign policy.

In contrast to his uncertain leadership at home, Carter's foreign policy was more clearly defined. A man of strong religious beliefs, Carter argued that the United States must try to be "right and honest and truthful and decent" in dealing with other nations. Yet it was on the international front that Carter suffered one of his most devastating defeats.

Morality in Foreign Policy

President Carter set the tone for his foreign policy in his inaugural speech, when he said, "Our commitment to human rights must be absolute. . . . The powerful must not persecute the weak, and human dignity must be enhanced." Along with his foreign policy team—which included Andrew Young, the first African American ambassador to the United Nations—Carter strove to achieve these goals.

The president put his principles into practice in Latin America. To remove a major symbol of U.S. interventionism, he agreed to give Panama control of the Panama Canal, which the United States had built and operated for over 60 years. In 1978 the Senate ratified two Panama Canal treaties, which transferred control of the canal to Panama on December 31, 1999.

PRIMARY SOURCE
Jimmy Carter and the Middle East

During his administration, Jimmy Carter faced a number of challenges in the Middle East. His foreign policy there met with mixed success.

▲ **The Camp David Accords**

In 1978, Carter helped negotiate a peace treaty between Egypt and Israel. Above, Egyptian President Anwar Sadat, Carter, and Israeli Prime Minister Menachem Begin sign the accords.

▲ **The Soviet Invasion of Afghanistan**

The Soviet invasion of Afghanistan shattered détente. Carter responded by imposing a grain embargo, but it did not force the Soviets to pull back.

▼ **The Iranian Hostage Crisis**

The Ayatollah Khomeini (right) led a revolution in Iran in 1979. Fifty-two Americans were taken hostage. Carter's inability to negotiate their release hurt his reelection campaign.

Analyzing VISUALS

1. **Specifying** What was Carter's major success in foreign policy?

2. **Theorizing** Why was the Middle East a major focus of Carter's foreign policy?

Most dramatically, Carter singled out the Soviet Union as a violator of human rights. He strongly condemned, for example, the Soviet practice of imprisoning those who protested against the government. Relations between the two superpowers suffered a further setback when Soviet troops invaded the Central Asian nation of Afghanistan in December 1979. Carter responded by imposing an embargo on the sale of grain to the Soviet Union and boycotting the 1980 Summer Olympic Games in Moscow. Under the Carter administration, détente eroded further.

Triumph and Failure in the Middle East

It was in the volatile Middle East that President Carter met both his greatest foreign policy triumph and his greatest failure. In 1978 Carter helped broker a historic peace treaty, known as the **Camp David Accords,** between Israel and Egypt—two nations that had been bitter enemies for decades. The treaty was formally signed in 1979. Most other Arab nations in the region opposed the treaty, but it marked a first step to achieving peace in the Middle East.

Just months after the Camp David Accords, Carter had to deal with a crisis in Iran. The United States had long supported Iran's monarch, the Shah, because Iran was a major oil supplier and a buffer against Soviet expansion in the Middle East. The Shah, however, had grown increasingly unpopular in Iran. He was a repressive ruler and had introduced Westernizing reforms to Iranian society. The Islamic clergy fiercely opposed the Shah's reforms. Opposition to the Shah grew, and in January 1979 protesters forced him to flee. An Islamic republic was then declared.

The new regime, led by religious leader Ayatollah Khomeini, distrusted the United States because of its support of the Shah. In November 1979, revolutionaries stormed the American embassy in Tehran and took 52 Americans hostage. The militants threatened to kill the hostages or try them as spies.

The Carter administration tried unsuccessfully to negotiate for the hostages' release. In April 1980, as pressure mounted, Carter approved a daring rescue attempt. To the nation's dismay, the rescue mission failed when several helicopters malfunctioned and one crashed in the desert. Eight servicemen died in the accident. Hamilton Jordan, President Carter's chief of staff, described the atmosphere in the White House the day after the crash. The president "looked exhausted and careworn. . . . The mood at the senior staff meeting was somber and awkward. I sensed that we were all uncomfortable, like when a loved one dies and friends don't know quite what to say."

The crisis continued into the fall of 1980. Every night, news programs reminded viewers how many days the hostages had been held. The president's inability to free them cost him support in the 1980 election. Negotiations continued right up to Carter's last day in office. On January 20, 1981, the day Carter left office, Iran released the Americans, ending their 444 days in captivity.

Reading Check **Summarizing** What was President Carter's main foreign policy theme?

Section 3 REVIEW

Vocabulary

1. **Explain** the significance of: inflation, OPEC, embargo, stagflation, Helsinki Accords, Department of Energy, Camp David Accords.

Main Ideas

2. **Describing** How did the OPEC embargo affect the U.S. economy?

3. **Specifying** What were two ingredients in Carter's failure to achieve success in his domestic policy?

4. **Identifying** What crisis in the Middle East occurred during the Carter administration?

Critical Thinking

5. **Big Ideas** How did Carter attempt to deal with the nation's energy crisis?

6. **Organizing** Complete a graphic organizer by listing the ways in which President Carter applied his human rights ideas to his foreign policy.

Carter's Human Rights Foreign Policy

7. **Analyzing Visuals** Study the photograph of the hostages on page 722. What effect do you think images such as this one had on Americans who were living or traveling in other countries?

Writing About History

8. **Expository Writing** Write an essay identifying what you believe to be Carter's most important foreign policy achievement. Explain your choice.

History ONLINE

Study Central™ To review this section, go to glencoe.com and click on Study Central.

New Approaches to Civil Rights

Guide to Reading

Big Ideas
Struggles for Rights African Americans, Native Americans, and people with disabilities organized to fight discrimination and gain access to better education and jobs.

Content Vocabulary
- busing *(p. 725)*
- affirmative action *(p. 725)*

Academic Vocabulary
- criteria *(p. 726)*
- appropriate *(p. 729)*

People and Events to Identify
- Allan Bakke *(p. 726)*
- Jesse Jackson *(p. 727)*
- Congressional Black Caucus *(p. 727)*
- Shirley Chisholm *(p. 727)*
- American Indian Movement (AIM) *(p. 727)*
- Section 504 *(p. 729)*

Reading Strategy
Sequencing Complete a time line similar to the one below by recording groups in the civil rights movement and their actions.

Throughout the 1960s and 1970s, reforms took place in many areas of society. In this period, minority groups, such as African Americans, Native Americans, and persons with disabilities, began to develop new ways to expand opportunities and assert their civil rights.

African Americans Seek Greater Opportunity

MAIN Idea During the 1960s and 1970s, African Americans built on the civil rights achievements of the 1950s to advance their social, political, and legal status.

HISTORY AND YOU Does your school district have a program of busing? Read on to learn how such programs originated as a way to integrate public schools.

By the end of the 1960s, many African American leaders felt a growing sense of frustration. Although most legal forms of racial discrimination had been dismantled, many African Americans saw little improvement in their daily lives. Increasingly, the problems facing most African Americans lay in their lack of access to good jobs and adequate schooling. As a result, leaders of the civil rights movement began to focus their energies on these problems.

Equal Access to Education

In the 1970s, African Americans began to push harder for improvements in public education and access to good schools. Although the Supreme Court had ordered an end to segregated public schools in the 1954 case *Brown* v. *Board of Education,* many schools remained segregated because children attended schools near where they lived. As a result many schools, especially in the North, remained segregated, not by law, but because whites and African Americans lived in different neighborhoods.

In many cases where de facto segregation existed, the white schools were superior, as Ruth Baston of the NAACP noted in 1965 after visiting Boston schools:

PRIMARY SOURCE

"When we would go to white schools, we'd see these lovely classrooms with a small number of children in each class. The teachers were permanent. We'd see wonderful materials. When we'd go to our schools, we'd see overcrowded classrooms, children sitting out in the corridors. And so then we decided that

Busing to End Segregation

To end segregation in public schools, state courts ordered the busing of children to schools outside of their neighborhoods. Reaction from parents to forced busing was often violent.

DESEGREGATE BOSTON SCHOOLS KEEP THE BUSES ROLLING! STOP THE RACIST AGAINST BLACK
NATIONAL STUDENT COALITION AGAINST RACISM

▲ Supporters of busing took part in the National March on Boston in 1975. The NAACP sponsored the march to mark the anniversary of the Brown v. Board of Education decision, which outlawed segregation in schools.

▲ Anger over busing was particularly virulent in some neighborhoods in Boston, Massachusetts, where police often had to escort school buses along their routes.

Analyzing VISUALS

1. **Explaining** Why were parents in Boston neighborhoods angry over busing?
2. **Making Inferences** Why are protesters holding signs that read "21 years is too long to wait" in the photograph on the right?

---

where there were a large number of white students, that's where the care went. That's where the books went. That's where the money went."

—quoted in *Freedom Bound*

To solve this problem, state courts began ordering local governments to bus children to schools outside their neighborhoods to achieve greater racial balance. The practice led to protests and even riots in several white communities, including Boston. The Supreme Court, however, upheld the constitutionality of **busing** in the 1971 case *Swann* v. *Charlotte-Mecklenburg Board of Education.*

In response, many whites took their children out of public schools or moved to a district where busing had not been imposed. About 20,000 white students left Boston's public system for parochial and private schools. By late 1976, African Americans, Latinos, and other minorities made up the majority of Boston's public school students. This "white flight" also occurred in other cities. When Detroit tried to bus students from one school district to another in 1974, the Court held in *Miliken* v. *Bradley* that busing across district lines was unconstitutional unless districts had been deliberately drawn to create segregation.

Affirmative Action

In addition to supporting busing, civil rights leaders in the 1970s began advocating **affirmative action** as a new way to solve economic and educational discrimination. Enforced through executive orders and federal policies, affirmative action called for companies, schools, and institutions doing business with the federal government to recruit African Americans with the hope that this would lead to improved social and economic status. Officials later expanded affirmative action to include other minority groups and women.

For further information on the case of *Swann* v. *Charlotte-Mecklenburg Board of Education,* see page R61 in the *Supreme Court Case Summaries.*

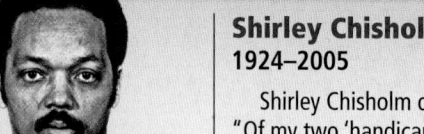

Jesse Jackson
1941–

An ordained Baptist minister, Jesse Jackson first became involved in social causes as an aid to Martin Luther King, Jr. Jackson went on to form Operation PUSH, an organization based in Chicago, which was founded to promote economic opportunities for African Americans. In 1984 he founded the broader National Rainbow Coalition, which advocates for the rights of African Americans, women, and others.

In the 1980s Jackson turned to politics. He ran for the Democratic presidential nomination in 1984 and 1988, placing third and then second to become the most successful African American presidential candidate to that point.

Jackson established the Wall Street Project in 1997 to increase opportunities for minorities in big business. Also in that year, President Clinton selected Jackson as a special envoy to Africa to promote democracy and human rights. In 2000 Jackson received the Presidential Medal of Freedom—the nation's highest civilian honor.

How has Jesse Jackson worked to improve the status of African Americans and promote civil rights for all Americans?

Shirley Chisholm
1924–2005

Shirley Chisholm once remarked, "Of my two 'handicaps,' being female put more obstacles in my path than being black." Her success in challenging both racism and sexism propelled the Brooklyn, New York, native into the national spotlight.

In 1968 Chisholm became the first African American woman to be elected to the United States Congress. There, Chisholm became an ardent defender of several causes, and helped to found the Congressional Black Caucus. She also worked on education and family issues and voted to increase day care programs.

In 1972 Chisholm ran for the Democratic nomination for president. Although she did not win the nomination, she did receive 28 delegates.

After the convention, Chisholm continued her crusade in Congress to help minorities and women for several more terms. She declined to run for re-election in 1982, citing the difficulties of campaigning for liberal issues in an increasingly conservative atmosphere.

On what issues did Shirley Chisholm focus?

Supporters of the policy argued that because so few companies had hired from these groups in the past, they had not necessarily developed the required job skills. If businesses opened their doors wider to minorities, more of them could begin to acquire skills and build better lives.

In one example of affirmative action's impact, Atlanta witnessed a significant increase in minority job opportunities after Maynard Jackson became its first African American mayor in 1973. When Jackson took office, less than one percent of all city contracts went to African Americans, even though they made up about half of Atlanta's population. Jackson used the expansion of the city's airport to redress this imbalance. Through his efforts, small companies and minority firms took on 25 percent of all airport construction work, earning them some $125 million in contracts.

For further information on the case of *University of California Regents v. Bakke,* see page R60 in the *Supreme Court Case Summaries.*

The *Bakke* Case

Affirmative action programs did not go unchallenged, however. Critics viewed them as a form of reverse racial discrimination. They claimed that qualified white male workers and students were kept from jobs, promotions, and places in schools because a certain number of such positions had been set aside for minorities or women.

Affirmative action was addressed by the Supreme Court in 1978. The case began in 1974, after officials at the medical school of the University of California at Davis turned down the admission of a white applicant named **Allan Bakke** for a second time. When Bakke learned that slots had been set aside for minorities, he sued the school. Bakke argued that by admitting minority applicants—some of whom had scored lower than Bakke on their exams—the school had discriminated against him based on his race.

In 1978, in *University of California Regents v. Bakke,* the Supreme Court, in a 5 to 4 ruling, declared that the university had violated Bakke's civil rights. It also ruled, however, that schools had an interest in maintaining a diverse student body. Thus, universities could consider race as one part of their admissions **criteria** as long as they did not use "fixed quotas," such as the slots the UC-Davis Medical School had reserved for minority students.

New Political Leaders

New political leaders emerged in the African American community in the 1970s. **Jesse Jackson,** a former aid to Martin Luther King, Jr., was among this new generation of activists. In 1971 Jackson founded Operation PUSH (People United to Save Humanity), an organization dedicated to registering voters, developing African American businesses, and broadening educational opportunities. In 1984 and 1988, Jackson sought the Democratic presidential nomination. Although both attempts were unsuccessful, he won over millions of voters.

African Americans also became more influential in national politics for the first time since Reconstruction. In 1971 African American members of Congress organized the **Congressional Black Caucus** to more clearly represent their concerns. Another prominent leader of the era was **Shirley Chisholm** of New York. Chisholm was a founding member of the Congressional Black Caucus and the first African American woman to serve in Congress. In 1977 another former assistant to Martin Luther King, Jr., U.S. Representative Andrew Young, was selected by President Carter to become the first African American to serve as U.S. ambassador to the United Nations. He went on to become the mayor of Atlanta. By the early 1980s, African American mayors had been elected in Atlanta, Detroit, Chicago, Los Angeles, New Orleans, Philadelphia, and Washington, D.C.

Another leader who emerged in the 1980s was Louis Farrakhan, a prominent minister of the Nation of Islam. He organized the Million Man March, which attracted an enormous crowd in Washington, D.C., on October 16, 1995. Farrakhan had conceived of the march as a way to promote self-reliance and responsibility among African American men. In addition to Farrakhan, the event featured other prominent speakers, including Jesse Jackson and the poet Maya Angelou.

In 1990, voters in Virginia elected L. Douglas Wilder, who became the first African American to serve as governor of a state. In that same year, David Dinkins took office as the first African American mayor of New York City.

✔ **Reading Check** **Examining** What were the goals of affirmative action policies?

Native Americans Raise Their Voices

MAIN Idea The most impoverished minority group in America, Native Americans, began organizing for civil rights.

HISTORY AND YOU What do you recall about the Black Power Movement in the 1960s? Read on to learn how some Native Americans formed the American Indian Movement.

In 1970 Native Americans were one of the nation's smallest minority groups, constituting less than one percent of the U.S. population, yet they faced enormous problems. The unemployment rate for Native Americans was ten times the national rate. Their average annual family income was $1,000 less than that of African Americans. Unemployment was very high on reservations, where nearly half of all Native Americans lived. Those living in cities often had little education or training. The bleakest statistic of all showed that the life expectancy for Native Americans was almost seven years below the national average.

A Protest Movement Emerges

In 1961 more than 400 members of 67 Native American groups gathered in Chicago to discuss ways to address their problems. They issued a manifesto, known as the Declaration of Indian Purpose, asking for federal programs to create greater economic opportunities on reservations.

Unlike some groups who wanted to be accepted by mainstream society, many Native Americans wanted more independence from it. They took a step toward this goal in 1968 when Congress passed the Indian Civil Rights Act. The legislation guaranteed reservation residents the protections of the Bill of Rights, but it also recognized local reservation law.

Native Americans who viewed the government's efforts as too modest formed more militant groups, which typically employed a more combative style. One such group, the **American Indian Movement (AIM),** staged a symbolic protest in 1969 by occupying the abandoned federal prison on Alcatraz Island in San Francisco Bay for 19 months, claiming ownership "by right of discovery."

The most famous protest by AIM took place at Wounded Knee, South Dakota, where U.S. troops had killed hundreds of Sioux in 1890. In February 1973, AIM members seized the town of Wounded Knee for 70 days. They demanded that the government honor its past treaty obligations to Native Americans and insisted that radical changes be made in the administration of reservations. A brief clash between AIM members and the FBI resulted in two Native Americans dead and several wounded on both sides. Shortly thereafter, the siege came to an end.

Native American Gains

By the mid-1970s, the Native American movement had begun to achieve some of its goals. In 1975 Congress passed the Indian Self-Determination and Educational Assistance Act, which increased funds for Native American education and expanded local control over federal programs. More Native Americans also moved into policy-making positions at the Bureau of Indian Affairs, and the agency pushed for more Native American self-determination.

Native Americans also won several court cases involving land and water rights. The people of the Pueblo of Taos, New Mexico, regained property rights to Blue Lake, a place sacred to their religion. In 1980 a federal court settled a claim of the Passamaquoddy and the Penobscot peoples. The government paid them $81.5 million to relinquish their claim to land in Maine. Other court decisions gave Native American governments the authority to tax businesses on their reservations.

Since Native Americans first began to organize, many reservations have improved their economic conditions by actively developing businesses, such as electric plants, resorts, cattle ranches, and oil and gas wells. More recently, gambling casinos have become a successful enterprise. Because of rulings on sovereignty, Native Americans in some areas are allowed to operate gaming establishments under their own laws even though state laws prevent others from doing so.

✔ **Reading Check** **Analyzing** What conditions led Native Americans to organize in the 1960s?

PRIMARY SOURCE
The Disability Rights Movement

In the 1970s, people with disabilities struggled for greater rights in education, employment, and housing. They met with success in the passage of legislation such as the Rehabilitation Act of 1973.

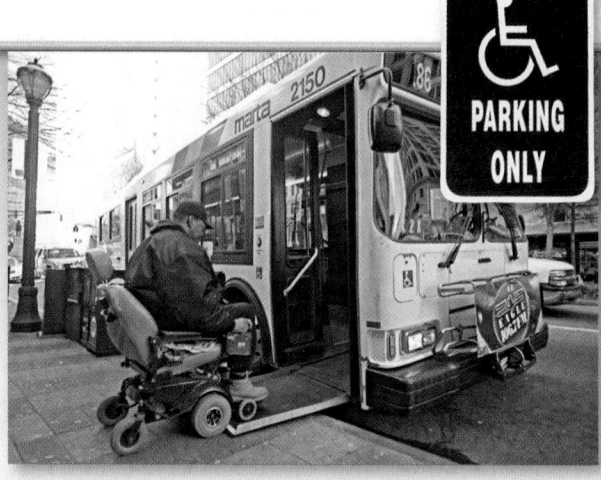

▲ Section 504 of the Rehabilitation Act and, later, the Americans with Disabilities Act specified that disabled people must have equal access to public facilities, such as transportation and parking.

▲ On April 5, 1977, the American Coalition of Citizens with Disabilities organized sit-ins demanding equal rights.

Analyzing VISUALS

1. **Listing** What rights did people with disabilities struggle for in the 1970s?

2. **Specifying** What two accommodations for people with disabilities are shown in the photograph on the right?

The Disability Rights Movement

MAIN Idea During the 1970s, people with disabilities fought for greater rights and access to education and jobs.

HISTORY AND YOU Do you or someone you know have a disability? Read on to learn about how people with disabilities achieved new legislation to help protect their civil rights.

The struggle for disability rights had its early expression in the independent living movement begun at the University of California at Berkeley in the early 1970s. The movement advocated for the right of people of all levels of abilities to choose to live freely in society. This was part of a new attitude that encouraged deinstitutionalization of people with disabilities.

People with disabilities also looked to the federal government to protect their civil rights. Access to public facilities and prohibitions on discrimination in employment led their demands. One victory was passage, in 1968, of the Architectural Barriers Act, which mandated that new buildings constructed with federal funds be accessible to disabled persons. The Rehabilitation Act of 1973 was even more significant. According to **Section 504,** "no otherwise qualified individual with a disability . . . shall . . . be excluded from participation in, be denied the benefits of, or be subjected to discrimination under any program or service or activity receiving Federal financial assistance . . ."

Unfortunately passage of the Rehabilitation Act meant little until procedures for enforcing its provisions were established. As of 1977, the Department of Health, Education, and Welfare (HEW) had issued no such regulations. Frustrated, the American Coalition of Citizens with Disabilities, headed by Frank Bowe, organized protests. On April 5, 1977, some 2,000 persons with disabilities in 10 cities began sit-ins at regional HEW offices. Although most protests lasted only a day or two, protesters in San Francisco maintained their sit-in for over three weeks—leaving only when HEW's director signed the regulations banning discrimination.

Changes also occurred in special education. In 1966 Congress created the Bureau for the Education of the Handicapped, which provided grants to develop programs for educating children with disabilities. In 1975 the Education for All Handicapped Children Act required that all students with disabilities receive a free, **appropriate** education. One trend was to mainstream, or bring into the regular classroom, students with disabilities.

In 1990 Congress enacted the Americans with Disabilities Act. This far-reaching legislation banned discrimination against persons with disabilities in employment, transportation, public education, and telecommunications.

Today, new technologies are important assets to people with disabilities. Innovations such as closed-captioned television broadcasts, devices for telephones, and screen readers allow people with disabilities to access information in new ways.

Reading Check Explaining Why did the American Coalition of Citizens with Disabilities stage sit-ins in 1977?

Section 4 REVIEW

Vocabulary

1. **Explain** the significance of: busing, affirmative action, Allan Bakke, Jesse Jackson, Congressional Black Caucus, Shirley Chisholm, American Indian Movement (AIM), Section 504.

Main Ideas

2. **Specifying** How did some critics characterize affirmative action?

3. **Identifying Central Issues** What was significant about AIM's claim to Alcatraz Island?

4. **Explaining** What was the significance of the independent living movement?

Critical Thinking

5. **Big Ideas** How did the Supreme Court support civil rights during the 1970s?

6. **Organizing** Use a graphic organizer to identify civil rights leaders and their causes.

Civil Rights Leaders	Causes

7. **Analyzing Visuals** Study the images on page 725 of busing in the 1970s. Why do you think reactions to busing were so strong and at times even violent?

Writing About History

8. **Expository Writing** Write a magazine article about conditions that provoked the Native American protest movement of the 1960s and 1970s. Be sure to discuss the movement's goals and activities.

History ONLINE

Study Central™ To review this section, go to glencoe.com and click on Study Central.

Environmentalism

Actions Taken

A mericans became increasingly aware of the damage being done to the environment. Soon environmental issues became national concerns, and individuals, local groups, and the government acted to address the damage and protect natural resources.

The Origins of Environmentalism

MAIN Idea Concerns about the effects of a deadly pesticide, the visible signs of pollution in American cities, and an influential book inspired a movement to protect the environment.

HISTORY AND YOU Do you take action personally or with others to preserve and protect the environment? Read on to learn how one woman inspired the environmental movement.

In 1966 Carol Yannacone of Patchogue, a small community on Long Island, New York, learned that officials were using the powerful pesticide DDT as part of a mosquito control operation at a local lake. Alarmed that the pesticide might poison the lake and local streams, Yannacone and her husband Victor, an attorney, contacted several local scientists who confirmed their suspicions.

The Yannacones then successfully sued to halt the use of the pesticide. In so doing, they had discovered a new strategy for addressing environmental concerns. Shortly after the Yannacones' court victory, the scientists involved in the case established the Environmental Defense Fund and used its contributions for a series of legal actions across the country to halt DDT spraying. Their efforts led to a nationwide ban on the use of the pesticide in 1972.

The effort to ban DDT was only one part of a new environmental movement that took shape in the 1960s and 1970s. The person who helped trigger this new movement was not a political leader or prominent academic, but a soft-spoken marine biologist named **Rachel Carson.** Carson's 1962 book *Silent Spring* assailed the increasing use of pesticides, particularly DDT. She contended that while pesticides curbed insect populations, they also killed birds, fish, and other creatures that might ingest them. Carson warned Americans of a "silent spring," in which there would be no birds left to usher spring in with their songs. *Silent Spring* became a bestseller and one of the most controversial and influential books of the 1960s. The chemical industry was outraged and began an intense campaign to discredit Carson and her arguments.

Many Americans believed Carson's warnings, however, largely because of what they were seeing around them and reading in news reports. Rivers across the nation were no longer safe for

Origins of the Environmentalist Movement

▲ Industrial pollution in cities like Newark, New Jersey (above) led to thick clouds of smog that caused breathing problems for some people. Tired of the dirty air, many Americans began to demand an end to pollution.

▲ Volunteers work to clean up an oil spill off the coast of California in 1969. News of the spill helped mobilize the new environmentalist movement.

◄ In 1969, the Cuyahoga River in Ohio caught fire. The incident gained national attention and contributed to the passage of the Clean Water Act in 1972.

Analyzing VISUALS

1. **Summarizing** What events raised awareness of the need to protect the environment?
2. **Discussing** Why do you think the fire on the Cuyahoga River convinced many people of the need for action?

fishing or swimming. **Smog,** or fog made heavier and darker by smoke and chemical fumes, hung perpetually over many major cities. In the Northwest, timber companies were cutting down acres of forest. In 1969 a major oil spill off Santa Barbara, California, ruined miles of beach and killed scores of birds and aquatic animals. A dike project in Florida's Everglades indirectly killed millions of birds and animals. Pollution and garbage caused nearly all the fish to disappear from Lake Erie. By 1970, many citizens were convinced it was time to do something about protecting the environment.

A Grassroots Effort Begins

Many observers point to April 1970 as the unofficial beginning of the environmentalist movement. That month, the nation held its first Earth Day celebration, a day devoted to addressing environmental concerns. The national response was overwhelming. On 2,000 college campuses, in 10,000 secondary schools, and in hundreds of communities, millions of Americans participated in activities to show their environmental awareness.

After Earth Day, many citizens formed local environmental groups. Long-standing non-profit organizations such as the Audubon Society, the Sierra Club, and the Wilderness Society grew rapidly in membership and political influence. These organizations worked to protect the environment and promote the conservation of natural resources. In 1970 activists started the Natural Resources Defense Council to coordinate a nationwide network of scientists, lawyers, and activists working on environmental issues.

Many communities and businesses responded to these organizations. Many city planners sought to reduce urban sprawl and expand green space. Architects and builders tried to make their structures more energy efficient, and the forestry industry began reforestation programs.

✓ Reading Check **Identifying** What natural resources did environmental groups want to protect?

The Environmental Movement Blossoms

MAIN Idea Pressure from citizens and activist groups led Congress to pass major environmental legislation.

HISTORY AND YOU Can you think of a recent environmental disaster that has been in the news? Read on to learn about two of the worst environmental disasters in American history.

As the environmental movement gained support, the federal government took action. In 1970 President Nixon signed the National Environmental Policy Act, which created the **Environmental Protection Agency (EPA).** The EPA set and enforced pollution standards, promoted research, and directed anti-pollution activities with state and local governments.

The Clean Air Act also became law in 1970 after Congress overrode President Nixon's veto. This act established emissions standards for factories and automobiles. It also ordered all industries to comply with such standards within five years.

In following years, Congress passed two more pieces of significant environmental legislation. The Clean Water Act (1972) restricted the discharge of pollutants into the nation's lakes and rivers, and the Endangered Species Act (1973) established measures for saving threatened animal and plant species. These laws succeeded in reducing smog, and the pollution of many lakes, streams, and rivers declined dramatically.

Love Canal

Despite the flurry of federal environmental legislation, Americans continued to mobilize on the community level throughout the 1970s. One of the most powerful displays of community activism occurred in a housing development near Niagara Falls, New York, known as **Love Canal.**

POLITICAL CARTOONS   PRIMARY SOURCE
A New Focus on the Environment

By the 1970s, the environmental movement was a strong force for change in the nation and around the world. In response, Congress passed a series of laws designed to protect the air, water, and wildlife.

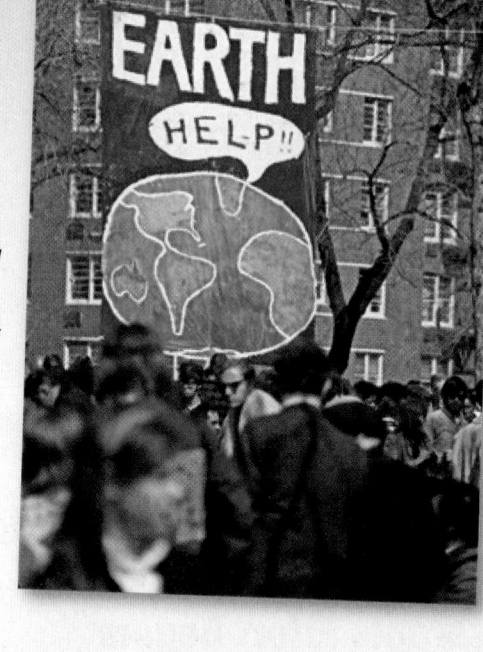

▶ Events, such as the annual Earth Day celebrations, helped environmentalists increase public awareness of environmental problems.

◀ President Ford and others are criticized for supporting industrial interests rather than protecting the environment.

Analyzing VISUALS   DBQ

1. **Identifying** Who does the large figure represent in the cartoon on the left?

2. **Summarizing** What is the main idea being expressed in the Earth Day poster?

During the 1970s, residents of Love Canal began to notice increasingly high incidences of health problems in their community, including nerve damage, blood diseases, cancer, miscarriages, and birth defects. The residents soon learned that their community sat atop a decades-old toxic waste dump. Over time, its hazardous contents had spread through the ground.

Led by a local woman, Lois Gibbs, the residents joined together and demanded that the government take steps to address these health threats. Hindered at first by local and state officials, the residents refused to back down, and by 1978 they had made their struggle known to the entire nation. That year, in the face of mounting public pressure and evidence of the dangers posed by the dump, the state permanently relocated more than 200 families.

In 1980, after hearing protests from the families who still lived near the landfill, President Carter declared Love Canal a federal disaster area and moved over 600 remaining families to new locations. In 1983 Love Canal residents sued the company that had created the dump site and settled the case for $20 million. The site was cleaned up by sealing the waste within an underground bunker and burning homes located above the dumping ground.

Concerns About Nuclear Energy

During the 1970s, a number of citizens also became concerned about the use of nuclear reactors to generate electricity. As nuclear power plants began to dot the nation's landscape, the debate over their use **intensified.** Supporters of nuclear energy hailed it as a cleaner and less expensive **alternative** to **fossil fuels,** such as coal, oil, and natural gas, which are in limited supply. Opponents warned of the risks nuclear energy posed, particularly the devastating consequences of an accidental radiation release into the air.

The debate gained national attention in a shocking fashion in 1979. In the early hours of March 28, one of the reactors at the **Three Mile Island** nuclear facility outside Harrisburg, Pennsylvania, overheated after its cooling system failed. Two days later, as plant officials scrambled to fix the problem, low levels of radiation escaped from the reactor.

Officials evacuated many nearby residents, while others fled on their own. Citizens and community groups expressed outrage at protest rallies. Officials closed down the reactor and sealed the leak. The Nuclear Regulatory Commission, the federal agency that regulates the nuclear power industry, eventually declared the plant safe. President Carter even visited the site in order to allay the public's concerns.

Although no one was hurt, the accident at Three Mile Island had a powerful impact politically. Many people now doubted the safety of nuclear energy. Such doubts have continued. Since Three Mile Island, some 60 nuclear power plants have been shut down or abandoned, and no new facilities have been built since 1973.

Reading Check **Summarizing** What is the environmental movement's main goal?

Section 5 REVIEW

Vocabulary

1. **Explain** the significance of: Rachel Carson, smog, Environmental Protection Agency, Love Canal, fossil fuel, Three Mile Island.

Main Ideas

2. **Summarizing** What were some of the dangers of DDT?

3. **Explaining** Why was Love Canal a dangerous place to live?

Critical Thinking

4. **Big Ideas** What were some groups that lobbied for legislation to protect the environment in the 1960s and 1970s?

5. **Categorizing** Use a graphic organizer similar to the one below to list the environmental laws passed in the 1970s, and explain their purposes.

Environmental Legislation	Purpose

6. **Analyzing Visuals** Study the cartoon on the left-hand side of page 732. What is the meaning of the piece of paper that reads "O.K. Gerald Ford" in the main figure's pocket?

Writing About History

7. **Descriptive Writing** Take on the role of an investigative reporter, and describe the environmental disaster at either Love Canal or Three Mile Island. Explain how community activism brought the issue to the nation's attention.

History ONLINE

Study Central™ To review this section, go to glencoe.com and click on Study Central.

An Era of Challenges

Major Domestic Issues of the 1970s

- A nation is divided and angry over the Vietnam War.
- An energy crisis is triggered by OPEC's raising of oil prices.
- A stagnant economy exists with both inflation and high unemployment.
- Ongoing racial problems occur in major cities.
- Growing awareness of environmental problems including air and water pollution, toxic waste (at Love Canal and other sites), the overuse of pesticides, plus a crisis with the nuclear power plant at Three Mile Island.

Major Foreign Policy Issues of the 1970s

- Cold War tensions continue with the Soviet Union and China.
- The Soviet Union invades Afghanistan.
- War between Israel and its Arab neighbors breaks out in 1973, and ongoing violence occurs in the Middle East.
- A revolution in Iran leads to the taking of American hostages.

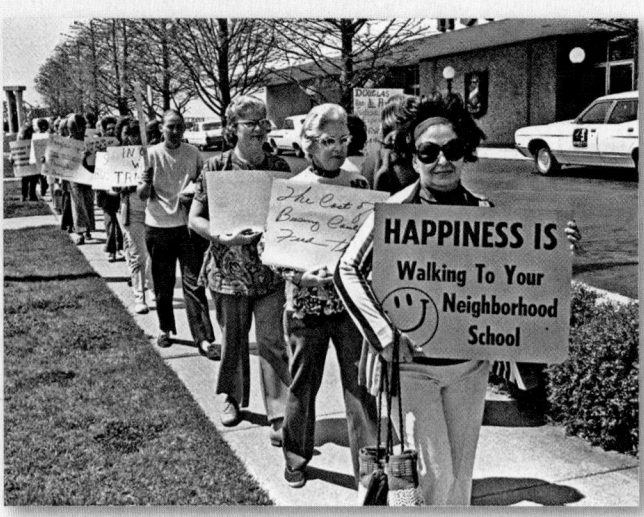

▲ In the 1970s, state courts order the forced desegregation of public schools through busing, despite protests such as the one above in Memphis, Tennessee.

▲ Americans wait in long lines to purchase gasoline during the energy crisis of the 1970s.

◀ The first Earth Day in 1970 is often seen as the start of an organized environmentalist movement, which continues to have a major influence on politics and society today.

New Policies and Activism

Responding to Domestic Issues

- Nixon attempts to win over Southern conservatives, but his administration's determination to win leads to the Watergate cover-up and Nixon's subsequent resignation.
- Ford's WIN campaign fails to overcome inflation.
- Carter urges Americans to conserve energy, creates the Department of Energy, and asks Congress to pass legislation deregulating the oil industry.
- Civil rights leaders propose affirmative action policies to reduce discrimination; the Supreme Court upholds some types of affirmative action in the *Bakke* case.
- Busing begins in northern cities to integrate schools.
- Environmentalist movement begins; Nixon creates the EPA.

Responding to Foreign Policy Issues

- Nixon and Kissinger introduce the policy of détente and begin talks with both the USSR and China.
- Carter mediates negotiations between Israel and Egypt leading to the first Arab-Israeli peace treaty.
- The United States imposes a grain embargo on the USSR for invading Afghanistan and boycotts the Moscow Olympics.
- The hostage crisis with Iran drags on for more than a year; an American rescue attempt fails, and the hostages are not released until Carter leaves office.

Reviewing Vocabulary

Directions: Choose the word or words that best complete the sentence.

1. Richard Nixon used the _____ to attract more Southerners to the Republican Party.

   A détente

   B revenue sharing

   C Southern strategy

   D Dixiecrats

2. In *United States* v. *Nixon*, the Supreme Court found that President Nixon could not invoke _____ to prevent his tapes from being used as evidence in a criminal trial.

   A revenue sharing

   B habeas corpus

   C détente

   D executive privilege

3. During the 1970s, the U.S. economy was threatened by an oil _____ established by OPEC.

   A embargo

   B boycott

   C importation

   D duty

4. _____ was a new way to address the social and economic inequalities that kept African Americans as second-class citizens.

   A Détente

   B The Southern strategy

   C Affirmative action

   D Stagflation

5. In the 1960s and 1970s, environmentalists began to combat issues such as _____ and other types of air pollution.

   A chemical runoff

   B DDT

   C smog

   D toxic waste

Reviewing Main Ideas

Directions: Choose the best answer for each of the following questions.

Section 1 *(pp. 706–711)*

6. Nixon developed a new program to try to make government more efficient known as

   A New Federalism.

   B the Silent Majority.

   C States' Rights.

   D the Great Society.

Section 2 *(pp. 712–717)*

7. Members of the Committee for the Re-election of the President broke into Democratic Party headquarters at the Watergate to

   A leave incriminating evidence of Democratic wrongdoing.

   B install a tape-recording device so that Nixon could write his memoirs.

   C find information to use in the case *United States* v. *Nixon*.

   D steal sensitive information and install wiretaps.

8. In the wake of the Watergate scandal, Congress passed a series of laws to accomplish which of the following goals?

   A to stop tape recordings in the White House

   B to limit the power of the presidency

   C to pardon Richard Nixon for his part in the cover-up

   D to remove police power from the FBI

Section 3 *(pp. 718–723)*

9. In the early 1970s, OPEC began to use oil as a political weapon against countries that

   A would not join their organization.

   B supported Israel's right to exist.

   C refused to pay the new per-barrel oil price.

   D supported Arab countries' disapproval of Israel.

TEST-TAKING

Always manage your time during a test so you can go back and review all your answers.

Need Extra Help?									
If You Missed Questions . . .	1	2	3	4	5	6	7	8	9
Go to Page . . .	706–707	715	718	725	731	708	712–714	717	718

10. To protest the Soviet Union's invasion of Afghanistan, President Carter took which of the following actions?

   A He sent U.S. Army troops to fight with the Afghans.

   B He put NATO forces in Europe on high alert.

   C He approved a buildup of U.S. nuclear weapons.

   D He placed an embargo on grain shipments to the USSR.

Section 4 *(pp. 724–729)*

11. The 1971 case *Swann* v. *Charlotte-Mecklenburg Board of Education* upheld the constitutionality of

   A busing.

   B affirmative action.

   C segregation.

   D revenue sharing.

12. Section 504 of the Rehabilitation Act of 1973 was significant because it

   A set aside money for helping injured veterans in their recovery.

   B mandated physical access to federal buildings.

   C banned discrimination against people with disabilities by any organization receiving federal funds.

   D guaranteed all young people a free and appropriately designed education.

Section 5 *(pp. 730–733)*

13. The unofficial beginning of the environmentalist movement occurred

   A when the Yannacones complained about the use of DDT.

   B on the first Earth Day in 1970.

   C when Congress passed the Clean Air Act.

   D after Love Canal was found to be poisoned.

Critical Thinking

Directions: Choose the best answers to the following questions.

14. What effect did the United States's improved relations with China have on its relations with the Soviet Union?

   A Tensions increased between the two nations.

   B The two nations were able to establish détente.

   C The Warsaw Pact began to break up.

   D The Soviet Union began to boycott American goods.

Base your answer to question 15 on the map below and your knowledge of Chapter 21.

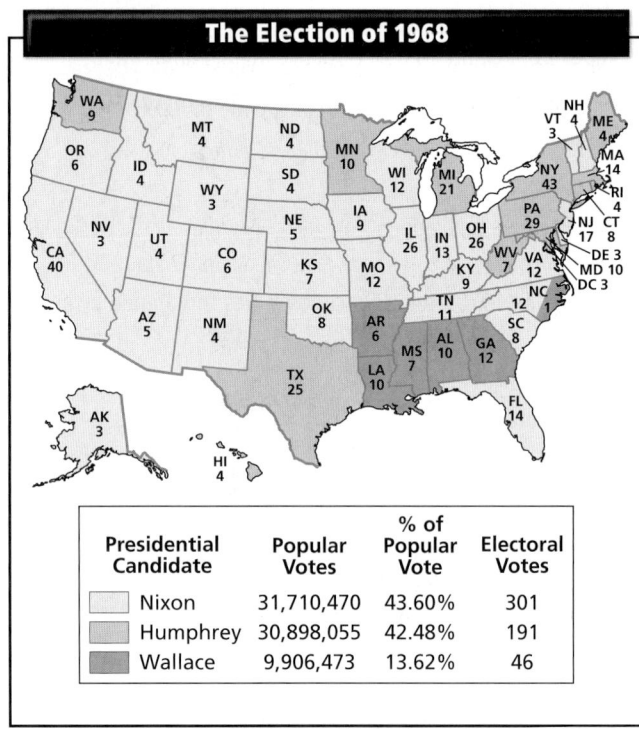

The Election of 1968

Presidential Candidate	Popular Votes	% of Popular Vote	Electoral Votes
Nixon	31,710,470	43.60%	301
Humphrey	30,898,055	42.48%	191
Wallace	9,906,473	13.62%	46

15. In the election of 1968, Nixon received the most support in the

   A North and South.

   B North and Midwest.

   C Midwest and West.

   D South and West.

Need Extra Help?						
If You Missed Questions . . .	10	11	12	13	14	15
Go to Page . . .	723	725	729	730	711	706

16. In 1961, 67 Native American tribes issued the Declaration of Indian Purpose, which

  A demanded federal programs to create greater opportunities on reservations.

  B demanded that the Bill of Rights be recognized on reservations.

  C established the militant group American Indian Movement (AIM).

  D announced their decision to separate completely from the United States.

17. The result of the environmentalist legislation Congress passed in the 1970s was that

  A many corporations went bankrupt.

  B new renewable energy sources were developed.

  C air and water pollution were greatly reduced.

  D Rachel Carson published *Silent Spring*.

Analyze the cartoon and answer the question that follows. Base your answer on the cartoon and on your knowledge of Chapter 21.

Ranan Lurie, 1970.

18. According to this cartoon, who ultimately suffered over the arms buildup between the United States and the Soviet Union?

  A the military-industrial complex

  B the generals of both nations

  C the politicians of both nations

  D the taxpayers of both nations

Document-Based Questions

Directions: Analyze the document and answer the short-answer questions that follow the document.

The following excerpt is from a magazine article that details the growing energy problems in the United States during the 1970s.

> "Evidence of the full dimensions of the energy crisis in this country is becoming more clear every day. . . .
> • As a first step to cut gasoline use, President Nixon was reportedly ready to order closing of service stations nationwide from 9 P.M. Saturday to midnight Sunday. . . .
> • Immediate rationing of gasoline and fuel oil is being urged on the President by top oil-industry executives. . . .
> One major piece of legislation . . . directs the President to take measures necessary to reduce the nation's energy demands by 25 percent within four weeks.
> Speed limits would be cut nationally; lighting and heating of public and commercial buildings would be curtailed; home-owners would be given tax deductions to winterize their homes. . . .
> Other pending measures would impose year-round daylight saving time and would open naval oil reserves for intense exploration."
> —from *U.S. News & World Report*, December 3, 1973

19. What proposals did the U.S. government make to deal with the energy crisis?

20. What lessons do you think the United States might have learned from this crisis?

Extended Response

21. Beginning in the mid 1970s, during what some historians have called a "reverse migration," African Americans moved back to Southern cities. For example, approximately 30,000 African Americans moved to Atlanta, Georgia, during this time. Based on what you have learned about new approaches to civil rights during this period, explain in a persuasive essay what encouraged this change in population movement.

STOP

History ONLINE

For additional test practice, use Self-Check Quizzes—Chapter 21 at glencoe.com.

Need Extra Help?						
If You Missed Questions . . .	16	17	18	19	20	21
Go to Page . . .	727	732	711	737	R19	724–729

Chapter 22

Resurgence of Conservatism

1980–1992

SECTION 1 The New Conservatism

SECTION 2 The Reagan Years

SECTION 3 Life in the 1980s

SECTION 4 The End of the Cold War

President Ronald Reagan, his wife Nancy, Vice-President George H.W. Bush, and his wife Barbara at Reagan's Second Inauguration.

U.S. PRESIDENTS

Carter 1977–1981

Reagan 1981–1989

1979
• Jerry Falwell's "Moral Majority" movement begins

1981
• Launch of *Columbia*, first space shuttle
• American hostages released in Iran

1983
• Reagan announces the Star Wars program
• U.S. Marine barracks bombed in Lebanon

U.S. EVENTS

WORLD EVENTS

1979

1982

1985

1979
• Iranian revolution brings down Shah
• Soviets invade Afghanistan

1980
• War begins between Iran and Iraq

1985
• Mikhail Gorbachev becomes leader of Soviet Union

MAKING CONNECTIONS

Are There Cycles in American Politics?

After several decades where progressive and liberal ideas dominated American politics, conservatism began making a comeback in the 1970s, and in 1980 voters elected the conservative Ronald Reagan president. Reagan's commitment to less government regulation, a stronger military, and uncompromising anticommunism seemed to meet voters' concerns.

- *Why do you think conservative ideas appealed to more Americans in the 1980s?*
- *How do you think conservative ideas have changed society?*

FOLDABLES™

Analyzing Information Create a Folded Chart Foldable to organize information about the government under Ronald Reagan. List domestic and foreign policy for three eras: before the Reagan era, the Reagan administration, and the post-Reagan years.

The Reagan Revolution	Before Reagan	Reagan Era	After Reagan
Domestic Policy			
Foreign Policy			

1986
- Iran-Contra scandal enters the news

1987
- INF Treaty between U.S. and USSR

1988
- More than 35,000 cases of AIDS diagnosed for the year

G. Bush
1989–1993

1991
- Persian Gulf War occurs between Iraq and UN coalition

1988

1991

1989
- Tiananmen Square protest in China
- Communist governments in Eastern Europe collapse

1990
- Germany reunites as one nation

1991
- Soviet Union dissolves

History ONLINE Visit glencoe.com and enter *QuickPass*™ code TAVMT5147c22 for Chapter 22 resources.

The New Conservatism

By the 1980s, new levels of discontent with government and society had left many Americans concerned about the direction of the nation. Some began to call for a return to more conservative approaches and values.

Liberalism and Conservatism

MAIN Idea Conservatives and liberals disagreed on the role of government.

HISTORY AND YOU Do you consider yourself liberal or conservative? Why? Read on to learn more about conservative and liberal ideas of government.

Midge Decter, a New Yorker and a writer for the conservative publication *Commentary*, was appalled at the violence that hit her city on a hot July night in 1977. On the night of July 13, the power failed in New York City. The blackout left millions of people in darkness, and looting and arson rocked the city. City officials and the media blamed the lawlessness on the anger and despair of youth in neglected areas. Decter disagreed:

PRIMARY SOURCE

"[T]hose young men went on their spree of looting because they had been given permission to do so . . . by all the papers and magazines, movies and documentaries—all the outlets for the purveying of enlightened liberal attitude and progressive liberal policy—which had for years and years been proclaiming that race and poverty were sufficient excuses for lawlessness. . . . "

—quoted in *Commentary*, September 1977

Midge Decter's article blaming liberalism for the New York riots illustrates one side of a debate in American politics that continues to the present day. On one side are people who call themselves **liberals;** on the other side are those who identify themselves as **conservatives.** Liberal ideas had dominated American politics in the 1960s, but conservative ideas regained significant support in the 1970s, and in 1980 Ronald Reagan, a strong conservative, was elected president.

Liberalism

In American politics today, people who call themselves liberals believe several basic ideas. In general, liberals believe that the government should regulate the economy to protect people from the

Liberalism vs. Conservatism

▲ Conservatives believe the liberal concern with achieving social equality and alleviating poverty is often taken to excess. They also disapprove of the idea of using the power of government to redistribute wealth from one group to another, preferring that the free market determine the distribution of wealth.

▲ Liberals believe that the conservative concern with keeping taxes low comes at the expense of other social needs and that conservatives who want low taxes are uncaring when it comes to helping the less fortunate.

Analyzing VISUALS

1. **Interpreting** In the cartoon on the left, what is the artist implying about Democratic policies?

2. **Identifying** In the cartoon on the right, what criticisms of tax breaks does the artist illustrate?

power of large corporations and wealthy elites. Liberals also believe that the government, particularly the federal government, should play an active role in helping disadvantaged Americans, partly through social programs and partly by putting more of society's tax burden on wealthier people.

Although liberals favor government intervention in the economy, they are suspicious of any attempt by the government to regulate social behavior. They are strong supporters of free speech and privacy, and are opposed to the government supporting or endorsing religious beliefs. They believe that a diverse society made up of different races, cultures, and ethnic groups will be more creative and energetic.

Liberals often support higher taxes on the wealthy, partly because they believe that those with greater assets should shoulder more of the costs of government and partly because it allows the government to redistribute wealth through government programs and thereby make society more equal.

Conservatism

Unlike liberals, conservatives distrust the power of government. They believe governmental power should be divided into different branches and split between the state and federal levels to limit its ability to intrude into people's lives.

Conservatives believe that when government regulates the economy, it makes the economy less efficient, resulting in less wealth and more poverty. They believe that free enterprise is the best economic system, and argue that if people and businesses are free to make their own economic choices, there will be more wealth and a higher standard of living for everyone.

For this reason, conservatives generally oppose high taxes and government programs that transfer wealth from the rich to those who are less wealthy. They believe that taxes and government programs discourage investment, take away people's incentive to work hard, and reduce the amount of freedom in society.

The more the government regulates the economy, conservatives argue, the more it will have to regulate every aspect of people's behavior. Ultimately, conservatives fear, the government will so restrict people's economic freedom that Americans will no longer be able to improve their standard of living and get ahead in life.

Many conservatives believe that religious faith is vitally important in sustaining society. They believe most social problems result from issues of morality and character—issues, they argue, that are best addressed through commitment to a religious faith and through the private efforts of churches, individuals, and communities to help those in need. Despite this general belief, conservatives do support the use of the governmental police powers to regulate social behavior in some instances.

✓ Reading Check **Contrasting** How do liberal and conservative opinions about government differ?

Conservatism Revives

MAIN Idea Geographical regions tend to support either liberal or conservative ideas.

HISTORY AND YOU Politically, how would you define yourself or the region in which you live? Read on to learn about the growing political power of voters in the Southwest.

During the New Deal era of the 1930s, conservative ideas lost much of their influence in national politics. Following World War II, however, conservatism began to revive.

The Role of the Cold War

Support for conservative ideas began to revive for two major reasons, both related to the Cold War. First, the struggle against communism revived the debate about the role of the government in the economy. Some Americans believed that liberal economic ideas

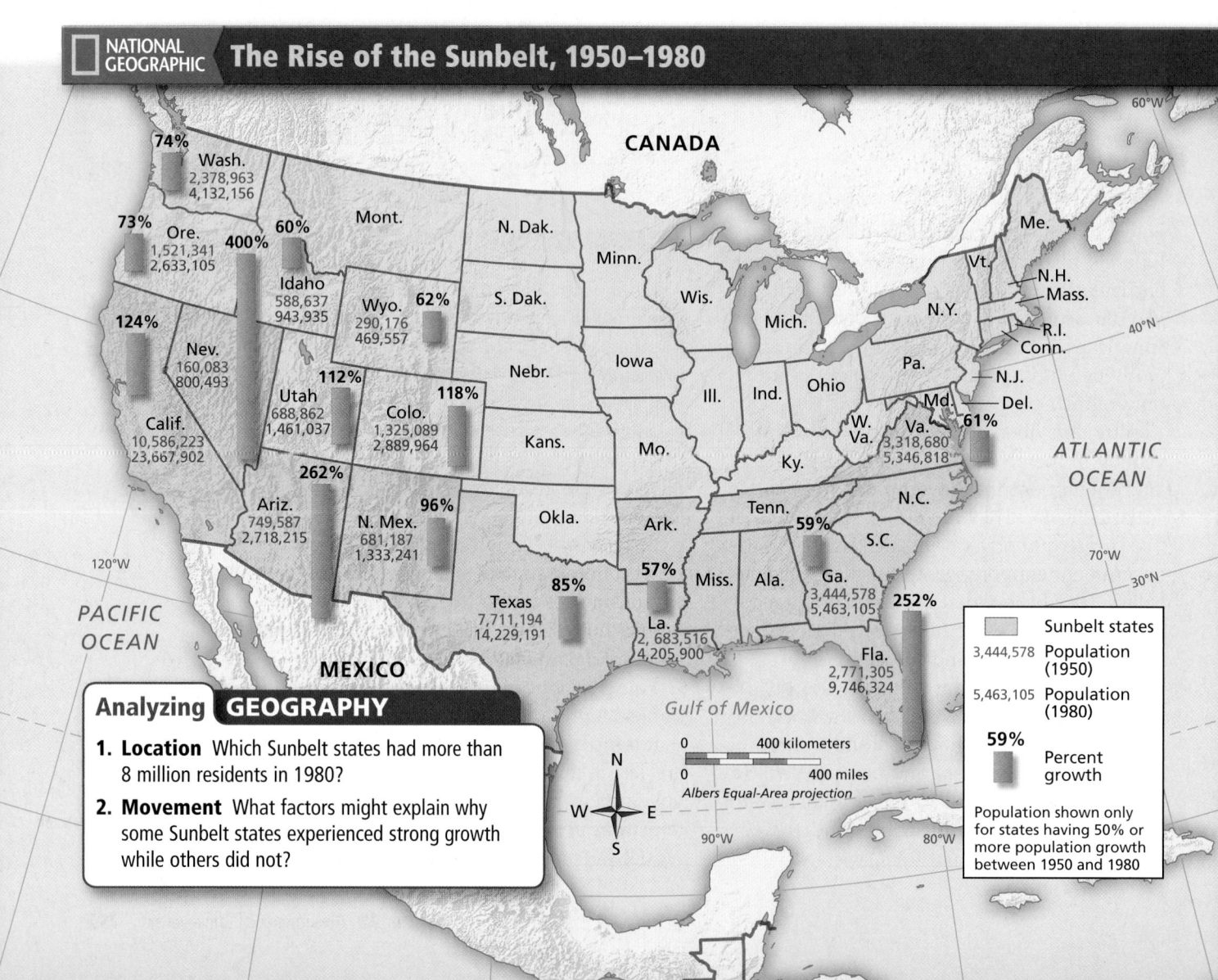

NATIONAL GEOGRAPHIC **The Rise of the Sunbelt, 1950–1980**

Analyzing GEOGRAPHY

1. **Location** Which Sunbelt states had more than 8 million residents in 1980?

2. **Movement** What factors might explain why some Sunbelt states experienced strong growth while others did not?

Legend:
- Sunbelt states
- 3,444,578 Population (1950)
- 5,463,105 Population (1980)
- 59% Percent growth

Population shown only for states having 50% or more population growth between 1950 and 1980 were slowly leading the United States toward communism and set out to stop this trend. They also thought the United States had failed to stop the spread of Soviet power because liberals did not fully understand the need for a strong anticommunist foreign policy.

At the same time, many Americans viewed the Cold War in religious terms. Communism rejects religion and emphasizes the material side of life. To Americans with a deep religious faith, the struggle against communism was a struggle between good and evil. Liberalism, which emphasizes economic welfare, gradually lost the support of many religious Americans, who increasingly turned to conservatism.

Conservatives Organize

In 1955 a young conservative named **William F. Buckley** founded a new magazine called *National Review.* Buckley's magazine helped to revive conservative ideas in the United States. Buckley debated in front of college students and appeared on radio and television shows, spreading conservative ideas to an even wider audience.

Within the Republican Party, conservatives, particularly young conservatives, began to demand a greater role in party decision-making. In 1960 some 90 young conservative leaders met at Buckley's family estate and founded Young Americans for Freedom (YAF), an independent conservative group, to push for their ideas and to support conservative candidates.

By 1964 the new conservative movement had achieved enough influence within the Republican Party to enable the conservative Barry Goldwater to win the nomination for president. To the dismay of the conservatives, however, President Johnson easily defeated Goldwater and won the election in a landslide.

The Rise of the Sunbelt

One of the problems facing conservatives in the 1950s and early 1960s was that their votes were split between the Republicans and the Democrats. Two regions of the country, the South and the West, were more conservative than other areas. Southern conservatives, however, usually voted for the Democrats, while

conservatives in the West voted Republican. This meant that the party that won the heavily populated Northeast would win the election. Since the Northeast strongly supported liberal ideas, both parties were pulled toward liberal policies.

This pattern began to change during World War II, when large numbers of Americans moved south and west to take jobs in the war factories. The movement to the South and West—together known as the **Sunbelt**—continued after the war. As the Sunbelt's economy expanded, Americans living in those regions began to view the federal government differently from people living in the Northeast.

Sunbelt Conservatism

Industry in the Northeast was in decline, leading to the region's nickname—the Rust Belt. This region had higher unemployment than any other, and its cities were congested and polluted. These problems prompted Americans in the Northeast to look to the government for programs and regulations that would help them solve their problems.

In contrast, many Americans in the Sunbelt opposed high taxes and federal regulations that might interfere with their region's growth. Many white Southerners were also angry with the Democrats for supporting civil rights, which they interpreted as an effort by the federal government to impose its policies on the South.

When Barry Goldwater argued in 1964 that the federal government was becoming too strong, many Southerners agreed. For the first time since Reconstruction, they began voting Republican in large numbers. Although Goldwater lost, he showed Republicans that the best way to attract Southern votes was to support conservative policies.

Americans living in the West also responded to conservative criticism of the federal government. Westerners were proud of their frontier heritage and spirit of "rugged individualism." They resented federal environmental regulations that limited ranching, controlled water use, and restricted the development of the region's natural resources. Western anger over such policies inspired the "Sagebrush Rebellion" of the early 1970s—a widespread protest led by conservatives against federal laws that they felt were hindering the region's development.

The Conservative Coalition

The new conservative coalition that emerged in the 1970s was made up of people from the South and West, particularly middle class suburban voters, evangelical Christians, and people concerned about high taxes and resisting the Soviet Union in the Cold War.

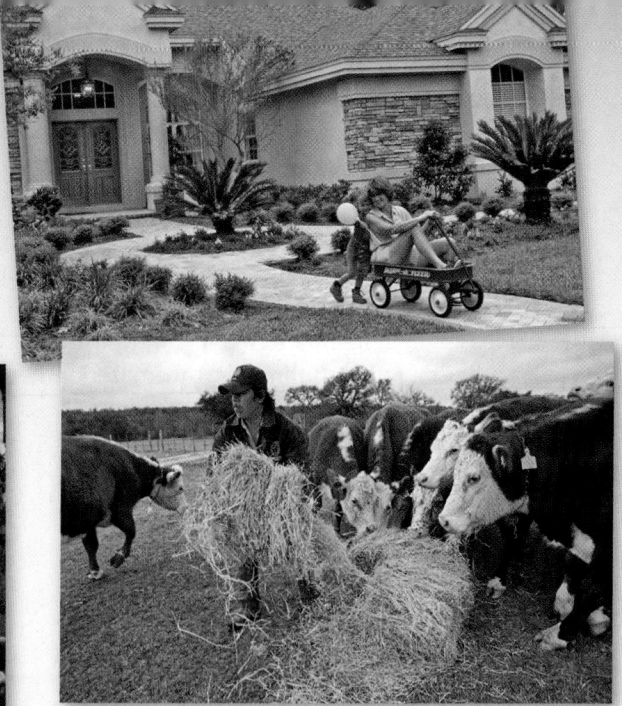

▲ *Voters in the suburbs (top) and rural west (above) increasingly voted conservative in the 1980s.*

▲ *Evangelical Christians including supporters of Jerry Falwell (photo left corner) were a major force behind the conservative resurgence.*

Analyzing VISUALS

1. **Inferring** What do you notice about the ethnicity of most people in the conservative coalition? Why do you think other groups were not as well represented?

2. **Speculating** What groups in the coalition would be most likely to leave it in the future? Why?

By 1980, the population of the Sunbelt had surpassed that of the Northeast. This gave the conservative regions of the country more electoral votes. With Southerners also shifting to the Republican Party, conservatives began to build a coalition that could elect a president.

Suburban Conservatism

As riots erupted and crime soared during the 1960s and 1970s, many Americans moved to suburbs to escape the chaos of the cities. Even there, however, they found the quiet middle-class lifestyle they desired to be in danger. The rapid inflation of the 1970s had caused the buying power of middle-class families to shrink while taxes remained high.

Many Americans resented the taxes they had to pay for New Deal and Great Society programs when they themselves were losing ground economically. In 1978 Howard Jarvis, a conservative activist, launched the first successful tax revolt in California with Proposition 13, a referendum on the state ballot that greatly reduced property taxes.

Soon afterward anti-tax movements appeared in other states, and tax cuts quickly became a national issue. For many Americans, the conservative idea that the government had become too big meant simply that taxes were too high. As conservatives began to call for tax cuts, the middle class flocked to their cause.

The Religious Right

While many Americans turned to conservatism for economic reasons, others were drawn to it because they feared that American society had lost touch with its traditional values. For many Americans of conservative religious faith, the events of the 1960s and 1970s were shocking. The Supreme Court decision in *Roe* v. *Wade,* which established that the right to have an abortion was protected by the Constitution, greatly concerned them. They were also critical of other Supreme Court decisions that limited prayer in public schools and expanded protections for people accused of crimes.

The feminist movement and the push for the Equal Rights Amendment (ERA) also upset some religious Americans because it seemed to represent an assault on the traditional family. Many religious conservatives were shocked by the behavior of some university students in the 1960s, whose contempt for authority seemed to **indicate** a general breakdown in American values and morality. These concerns helped expand the conservative cause into a mass movement.

Although religious conservatives included people of many faiths, the largest group was evangelical Protestants. Evangelicals believe that they are saved from their sins through conversion (which they refer to as being "born again") and a personal commitment to follow Jesus Christ, whose death and resurrection reconciles them to God.

After World War II, a religious revival began in the United States among Protestant evangelicals. Protestant ministers, such as **Billy Graham** and Oral Roberts, built national followings. By the late 1970s, about 70 million Americans described themselves as "born again." Protestant evangelicals owned their own newspapers, magazines, radio stations, and television networks.

Television in particular allowed evangelical ministers to reach a large nationwide audience. These **"televangelists,"** as they were soon called, included Marion "Pat" Robertson, who founded the Christian Broadcasting Network, and **Jerry Falwell,** who used his television show *The Old-Time Gospel Hour* to found a movement that he called the **"Moral Majority."** Using television and mail campaigns, the Moral Majority built up a network of ministers to register new voters who backed conservative candidates and issues. Falwell later claimed to have registered 2 million new voters by 1980.

A New Coalition

By the end of the 1970s, a new conservative coalition of voters had begun to come together. Although the members of this coalition were concerned with many different issues, they were held together by a common belief that American society had somehow lost its way.

The Watergate scandal, high taxes, and special interest politics had undermined many Americans' faith in their government. Rising unemployment, rapid inflation, and the energy crisis had shaken their confidence in the economy. Riots, crime, and drug abuse suggested that society itself was falling apart. The retreat from Vietnam, the hostage crisis in Iran, and the Soviet invasion of Afghanistan seemed to make the nation look weak and helpless internationally. Many Americans were tired of change and upheaval. They wanted **stability** and a return to what they remembered as a better time. For some, the new conservatism and its most prominent spokesperson, Ronald Reagan, offered hope to a nation in distress.

✓ Reading Check **Summarizing** Why did many Americans begin to support the conservative movement?

Section 1 REVIEW

Vocabulary

1. **Explain** the significance of: liberal, conservative, William F. Buckley, Sunbelt, Billy Graham, "televangelist," Jerry Falwell, "Moral Majority."

Main Ideas

2. **Explaining** Why do liberals sometimes support higher taxes on the wealthy?

3. **Determining Cause and Effect** What was the cause of the Sagebrush Rebellion in the 1970s?

Critical Thinking

4. **Big Ideas** What kind of economy do conservatives want?

5. **Organizing** Use a graphic organizer similar to the one below to list conservative beliefs.

Conservative Beliefs

6. **Analyzing Visuals** Study the map of the Sunbelt on page 742. What impact would the migration patterns shown have on representation in the U.S. House of Representatives?

Writing About History

7. **Persuasive Writing** Many conservatives believe that "government that governs least, governs best." Write a paragraph supporting or opposing this statement.

History ONLINE

Study Central™ To review this section, go to glencoe.com and click on Study Central.

The Reagan Years

Guide to Reading

Big Ideas

Trade, War, and Migration During the Cold War, President Reagan reinforced the idea that the United States had to take strong action to resist the spread of Communist influence abroad.

Content Vocabulary

- supply-side economics *(p. 748)*
- budget deficit *(p. 749)*
- "mutual assured destruction" *(p. 753)*

Academic Vocabulary

- confirmation *(p. 750)*
- visible *(p. 751)*

People and Events to Identify

- Reaganomics *(p. 748)*
- Iran-Contra scandal *(p. 752)*
- Mikhail Gorbachev *(p. 753)*

Reading Strategy

Organizing Complete a graphic organizer similar to the one below by filling in the major points of the supply-side theory of economics.

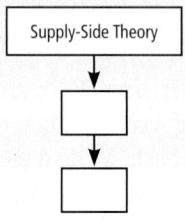

In 1980 Americans elected Ronald Reagan president. Reagan cut taxes, deregulated several industries, and appointed conservative justices. He began a massive military buildup that greatly increased the deficit and sent aid to insurgent groups fighting communism.

The Road to the White House

MAIN Idea President Reagan's experiences in Hollywood and as governor of California led to his successful campaign for the presidency.

HISTORY AND YOU How could a previous career as a movie star help someone get elected to public office? Read on to learn more about the way that President Reagan's background helped to make him an attractive presidential candidate.

In 1926, at age fifteen, Ronald Reagan earned $15 a week working as a lifeguard on the Rock River in Illinois. Being a lifeguard, Reagan later wrote, taught him quite a bit about human nature:

PRIMARY SOURCE

"Lifeguarding provides one of the best vantage points in the world to learn about people. During my career at the park, I saved seventy-seven people. I guarantee you they needed saving—no lifeguard gets wet without good reason. . . . Not many thanked me, much less gave me a reward, and being a little money-hungry, I'd done a little daydreaming about this. They felt insulted. . . . I got to recognize that people hate to be saved. . . ."

—from *Where's the Rest of Me?*

The belief that people do not want to be saved by someone else was one of the ideas that Ronald Reagan took with him to the White House. It reflected his philosophy of self-reliance and independence.

Becoming a Conservative

Reagan grew up in Dixon, Illinois, the son of an Irish American shoe salesman. After graduating from Eureka College in 1932, Reagan worked as a sports broadcaster at an Iowa radio station. In 1937 he took a Hollywood screen test and won a contract from a movie studio. During the next 25 years he made more than 50 movies. As a broadcaster and an actor, Reagan learned how to speak publicly and how to project a strong, attractive image—skills that proved invaluable when he entered politics.

In 1947 Reagan became president of the Screen Actors Guild—the actors' union. Soon afterward, he testified about communism in

The Election of 1980

▼ By 1980, Carter was so unpopular that other Democrats did not want his help in their own campaigns. Reagan soundly defeated Carter in the Election of 1980.

▲ When Ronald Reagan ran for the Republican presidential nomination, he was still best known to most Americans as an actor. Critics said that while he was scripted and polished, he lacked any real substance.

' I PLEDGE TO COME OUT CAMPAIGNING VIGOROUSLY FOR ALL DEMOCRATS I ...'

Analyzing VISUALS

1. **Making Inferences** In the cartoon above, what does the artist infer about Reagan's campaign?

2. **Interpreting** What is the artist in the cartoon to the right saying about Carter's place in the Democratic Party?

Hollywood before the House Un-American Activities Committee. Reagan had been a staunch Democrat and a supporter of the New Deal, but dealing with Communists in the union shifted him toward conservative ideas.

In 1954 Reagan became the host of the television show "General Electric Theater" and agreed to be a motivational speaker for General Electric. As he traveled the country speaking to people, he became increasingly conservative. Over and over again, he said later, he heard average Americans describe how high taxes and government regulations made it impossible for them to get ahead.

By 1964 Reagan had become such a popular national speaker that Barry Goldwater asked him to make a televised speech on behalf of Goldwater's campaign. The speech impressed several wealthy entrepreneurs in California. They convinced Reagan to run for governor of California in 1966 and helped finance his campaign. Reagan won the election and was reelected in 1970. Ten years later he won the Republican presidential nomination.

The Election of 1980

Reagan's campaign appealed to Americans who were frustrated with the economy and worried that the United States had become weak internationally. Reagan promised to cut taxes and increase defense spending. He won the support of social conservatives by calling for a constitutional amendment banning abortion. During one debate with President Carter, Reagan asked voters, "Are you better off than you were four years ago?" On Election Day, the voters answered "No." Reagan won nearly 51 percent of the popular vote and 489 electoral votes, easily defeating Carter in the Electoral College. For the first time since 1954, Republicans also gained control of the Senate.

✔ **Reading Check** **Describing** What event jump-started Ronald Reagan's political career as a conservative leader?

Domestic Policies

MAIN Idea Believing that government was part of the problem, President Reagan cut social service programs, sponsored tax cuts, and deregulated industry.

HISTORY AND YOU Do you think that cutting social programs is a good way to help the economy? Read on to learn more about Reagan's economic policies.

Ronald Reagan believed that the key to restoring the economy and overcoming problems in society was to get Americans to believe in themselves again. He expressed this idea in his Inaugural Address:

PRIMARY SOURCE

"We have every right to dream heroic dreams. . . . You can see heroes every day going in and out of factory gates. Others, a handful in number, produce enough food to feed all of us. . . . You meet heroes across a counter. . . . There are entrepreneurs with faith in themselves and faith in an idea who create new jobs, new wealth and opportunity. . . . Their patriotism is quiet but deep. Their values sustain our national life."

—from Reagan's First Inaugural Address

Reagan also told Americans that they should not expect government to help: "In this present crisis, government is not the solution to our problem. Government is the problem."

Reaganomics

Reagan's first priority was the economy, which was suffering from stagflation—a combination of high unemployment and high inflation. According to most economists, the way to fight unemployment was to increase government spending. Increasing spending, however, made inflation worse. Conservative economists offered two competing ideas for fixing the economy. One group, known as monetarists, argued that inflation was caused by too much money in circulation. They believed the best solution was to raise interest rates. Another group supported **supply-side economics.** They argued that the economy was weak because taxes were too high.

Supply-side economists believed that high taxes took too much money away from investors. If taxes were cut, businesses and investors could use their extra capital to make new investments. Businesses would expand and create new jobs, and the result would be a larger supply of goods for consumers, who would now have more money to spend because of the tax cuts.

Reagan combined monetarism and supply-side economics. He encouraged the Federal Reserve to keep interest rates high, and asked Congress to pass a massive tax cut. Critics called his approach **Reaganomics** or "trickle-down economics." They believed Reagan's policy would help corporations and wealthy Americans, but little wealth would "trickle down" to middle-class or poor Americans.

Reagan made deals with conservative Democrats in the House and moderate Republicans in the Senate. Eventually Congress passed a 25 percent tax cut.

History ONLINE
Student Web Activity Visit glencoe.com and complete the activity on the 1980s.

Debates IN HISTORY

Are Tax Cuts Good for the Economy?

Ronald Reagan believed that government regulation of the economy was harmful and that taxes should be as low as possible to promote private spending and investment. During the 1984 presidential campaign, Reagan ran against Jimmy Carter's vice president, Walter Mondale. In these excerpts from the first debate between the two candidates, Reagan and Mondale discuss their fundamentally different approaches to government. Mondale advocated for tax increases and that is often cited as a main reason why he lost the election.

Cutting Programs Cutting tax rates meant that the government would receive less money, at least until the economy started to grow. This would increase the **budget deficit**—the amount by which expenditures exceed income. To keep the deficit under control, Reagan proposed cuts to social programs. Welfare benefits, including the food-stamp program and the school-lunch program, were cut back. Medicare payments, unemployment compensation, student loans, and housing subsidies were also reduced.

After a struggle, Congress passed most of these cuts. The fight convinced Reagan that he would never get Congress to cut spending enough to balance the budget. He decided that cutting taxes and building up the military were more important than balancing the budget. He accepted a rapidly rising deficit as the price of getting his other programs passed.

Deregulation Reagan believed that excessive government regulation was another cause of the economy's problems. His first act as president was to sign an executive order to end price controls on oil and gasoline. Critics said that ending controls would drive prices up, but in fact they fell. Falling energy prices freed up money for businesses and consumers to spend elsewhere, helping the economy to recover.

Other deregulation soon followed. The Federal Communications Commission stopped trying to regulate the cable television industry. The National Highway Traffic and Safety Administration reduced requirements for air bags and higher fuel efficiency for cars. Carter had already begun deregulating the airline industry, and Reagan encouraged the process, which led to price wars, cheaper fares, and the founding of new airlines.

YES

Ronald Reagan
President

PRIMARY SOURCE

" …[T]he plan that we have had and that we are following is a plan that is based on growth in the economy. . . . Our tax cut, we think, was very instrumental in bringing about this economic recovery.

. . . So, we believe that as we continue to reduce the level of government spending…and, at the same time, as the growth in the economy increases the revenues the government gets, without raising taxes, those two lines will meet. . . . The deficit is the result of excessive government spending. . . . I don't believe that Mr. Mondale has a plan for balancing the budget; he has a plan for raising taxes. . . . And for the 5 years previous to our taking office, taxes doubled in the United States, and the budgets increased $318 billion. So, there is no ratio between taxing and balancing a budget."

—from the first presidential debate, Oct. 7, 1984

NO

Walter Mondale
Presidential candidate

PRIMARY SOURCE

" …[E]ven with historically high levels of economic growth, we will suffer a $263 billion deficit. . . . Real interest rates—the real cost of interest—will remain very, very high, and many economists are predicting that we're moving into a period of very slow growth. . . . I proposed over a hundred billion dollars in cuts in federal spending over 4 years, but I am not going to cut it out of Social Security and Medicare and student assistance and things . . . that people need. . . . The rate of defense spending increase can be slowed. . . . And there are other ways of squeezing this budget without constantly picking on our senior citizens and the most vulnerable in American life."

—from the first presidential debate, Oct. 7, 1984

DBQ Document-Based Questions

1. **Specifying** What does Reagan say his administration has done to improve economic growth?

2. **Explaining** How does Reagan propose to balance the federal budget?

3. **Summarizing** How does Mondale respond to Reagan's plan? What effects does he foresee from that course?

4. **Evaluating** Which approach do you feel will be the most effective? Why? Explain your answer.

People IN HISTORY

Sandra Day O'Connor
1930–

When a Supreme Court vacancy opened up in 1981, President Reagan chose Sandra Day O'Connor, an Arizona appeals court judge. Unlike many Supreme Court justices, O'Connor had broad political experience. Appointed to a state senatorial vacancy in 1969, she successfully ran for the seat and became the state senate's first woman majority leader in 1972. O'Connor won election as a superior court judge in 1974 and was later appointed to the court of appeals.

O'Connor's nomination was opposed by the Moral Majority because she had supported the Equal Rights Amendment (ERA), and had refused to back an anti-abortion amendment, or criticize the decision in *Roe* v. *Wade*. Others, however, praised her legal judgment and conservative approach to the law. As a moderate conservative, she quickly became an important swing vote on the Court, between more liberal and more conservative justices.

Why do you think that O'Connor supported the Equal Rights Amendment?

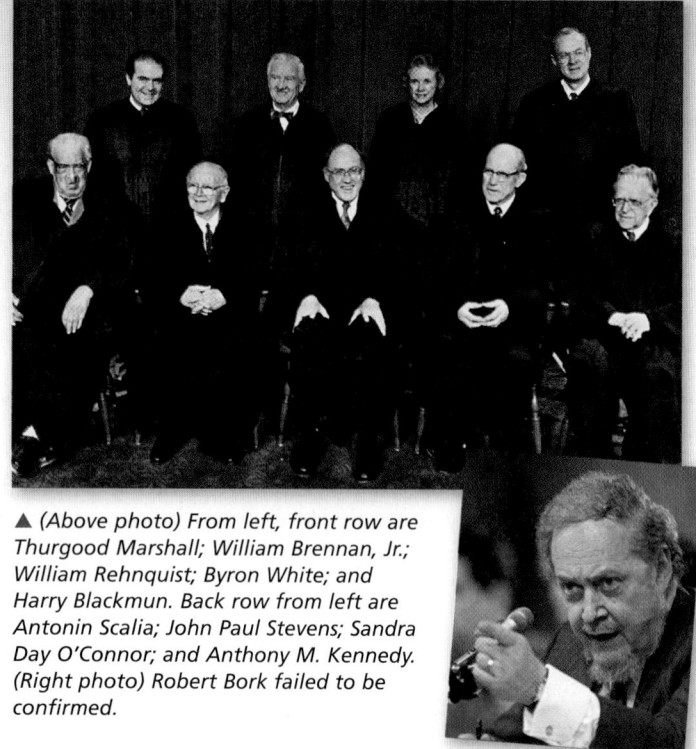

▲ *(Above photo) From left, front row are Thurgood Marshall; William Brennan, Jr.; William Rehnquist; Byron White; and Harry Blackmun. Back row from left are Antonin Scalia; John Paul Stevens; Sandra Day O'Connor; and Anthony M. Kennedy. (Right photo) Robert Bork failed to be confirmed.*

Reagan's secretary of the interior, James Watt, increased the public land that companies could use for oil drilling, mining, and logging. Watt's actions angered environmentalists, as did the EPA's decision to ease regulations on pollution-control equipment and to reduce safety checks on chemicals and pesticides.

In 1983 the economy began to recover. By 1984, the United States had begun the biggest economic expansion in its history up to that time. The median income of families climbed steadily, rising 15 percent by 1989. Five million new businesses and 20 million new jobs were created. By 1988, unemployment had fallen to 5.5 percent, the lowest in 14 years.

Reagan Wins Reelection By 1984, the economic recovery had made Reagan very popular. Democrats nominated Jimmy Carter's vice president, Walter Mondale. He chose as his running mate Representative Geraldine Ferraro, the first woman nominated to run for vice president for a major party. Instead of arguing issues with his opponent, Reagan emphasized the good economy. In an overwhelming landslide, he won about 59 percent of the popular vote and all the electoral votes

except those from Mondale's home state of Minnesota and the District of Columbia.

Shifting the Judicial Balance

Reagan did not apply his conservative ideas only to the economy. He also tried to bring a strict constructionist outlook to the federal judiciary. Reagan wanted judges who followed the original intent of the Constitution. He also changed the Supreme Court by nominating Sandra Day O'Connor, the first woman on the Supreme Court.

In 1986 Chief Justice Warren Burger retired. Reagan chose the most conservative associate justice, William Rehnquist, to succeed him. He then named Antonin Scalia, a conservative, to fill Rehnquist's vacancy. In 1987 his attempt to put Robert Bork on the Court led to a bitter fight in the Senate. Democrats saw Bork as too conservative and blocked his **confirmation.** Reagan then nominated Anthony Kennedy, a moderate, to become the new associate justice.

✔ Reading Check **Explaining** What is supply-side economics?

Reagan Oversees a Military Buildup

MAIN Idea President Reagan began a massive military buildup to weaken the Soviet economy and deter Soviet aggression.

HISTORY AND YOU Do you remember President Eisenhower's warning about the military as he left office? Read to learn how President Reagan sought to use military power to defeat the Soviets.

Reagan also adopted a new foreign policy that rejected both containment and détente. He called the Soviet Union "an evil empire." In his view, the United States should not negotiate with or try to contain evil. It should try to defeat it.

"Peace Through Strength"

In Reagan's opinion, the only option open to the United States in dealing with the Soviet Union was "peace through strength"—a phrase he used during his campaign. The military buildup Reagan launched was the largest peacetime buildup in American history. It cost about $1.5 trillion over five years.

Reagan believed that, if the Soviets tried to match the American buildup, it might put so much pressure on their economy that they would be forced to reform their system or it would collapse. In 1982 Reagan told students at Eureka College that Soviet defense spending would eventually cause the Communist system to fall apart:

PRIMARY SOURCE

"The Soviet empire is faltering because rigid centralized control has destroyed incentives for innovation, efficiency, and individual achievement. . . . But in the midst of social and economic problems, the Soviet dictatorship has forged the largest armed force in the world. It has done so by preempting the human needs of its people and in the end, this course will undermine the foundations of the Soviet system."

—from *A Time for Choosing*

The United States also tried to stop nations from supporting terrorism. After Libya backed a terrorist bombing in Berlin, the United States launched an air attack on Libya on April 14, 1986. The raids killed 37 and injured about 200.

Reagan's military buildup created new jobs in defense industries. Supply-side economists had predicted that, despite the spending, lower taxes combined with cuts in government programs would generate enough growth to increase tax revenues and balance the budget. Tax revenues did rise, but other programs were too popular for Reagan to cut significantly. As a result, the annual budget deficit went from $80 billion to over $200 billion.

The Reagan Doctrine

Reagan also believed that the United States should support guerrilla groups who were fighting to overthrow Communist or pro-Soviet governments. This policy became known as the Reagan Doctrine. This doctrine led to involvement in places as geographically diverse as Africa's Angola, Middle America's Nicaragua and Grenada, and the Middle East's Afghanistan and Lebanon.

Aid to the Afghan Rebels Perhaps the most **visible** example of the Reagan Doctrine was in Afghanistan. In late December 1979 the Soviet Union invaded Afghanistan to support a Soviet-backed government. The Soviets soon found themselves fighting Afghan guerrillas known as the mujahadeen.

President Carter sent about $30 million in military aid to the Afghan guerrillas, but Reagan sent $570 million more. The Soviets were soon trapped in a situation similar to the American experience in Vietnam. As casualties mounted, the war strained the Soviet economy, and in 1988 the Soviets decided to withdraw.

Nicaragua and Grenada Reagan was also concerned about Soviet influence in Nicaragua. Rebels known as the Sandinistas had overthrown a pro-American dictator in Nicaragua in 1979. The Sandinistas set up a socialist government and accepted Cuban and Soviet aid. They then began aiding rebels in nearby El Salvador. The Reagan administration responded by secretly arming an anti-Sandinista guerrilla force known as the contras, from the Spanish word for "counterrevolutionary." When Congress learned of this policy, it banned further aid to the contras.

Reagan's Foreign Policy

President Reagan launched a massive weapons buildup, believing it would weaken the Soviet Union. He also provided aid to Afghan rebels fighting Soviet forces and engaged in a series of meetings with the Soviet leader that produced a nuclear arms treaty (at right).

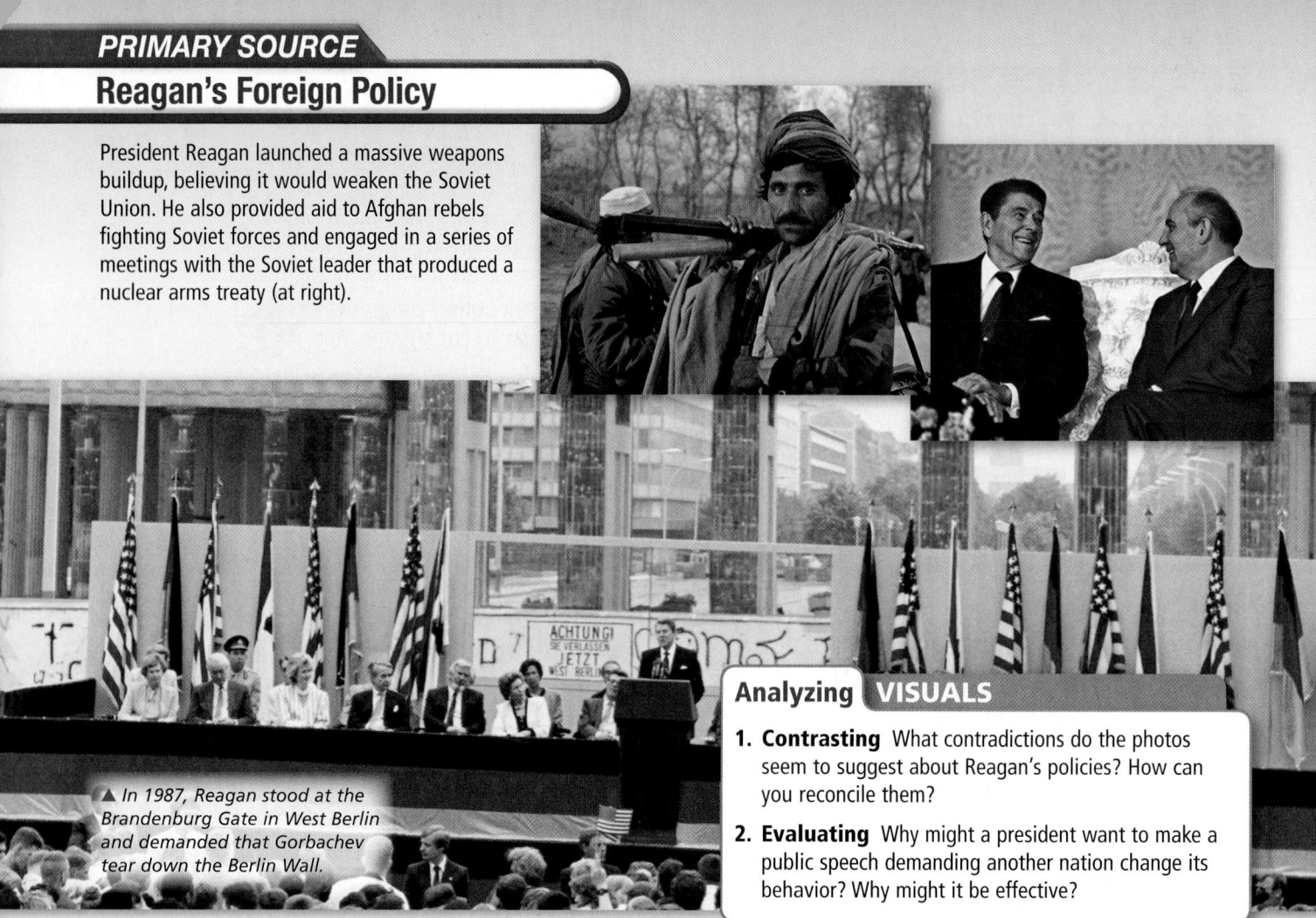

▲ In 1987, Reagan stood at the Brandenburg Gate in West Berlin and demanded that Gorbachev tear down the Berlin Wall.

Analyzing VISUALS

1. **Contrasting** What contradictions do the photos seem to suggest about Reagan's policies? How can you reconcile them?

2. **Evaluating** Why might a president want to make a public speech demanding another nation change its behavior? Why might it be effective?

Aiding the contras was not Reagan's only action in Latin America. In 1983 radical Marxists overthrew the left-wing government on the island of Grenada. In October, Reagan sent in American troops, who quickly defeated the Cuban and Grenadian soldiers. A new anti-Communist government was put in place.

The Iran-Contra Scandal Although Congress had prohibited aid to the Nicaraguan contras, individuals in Reagan's administration continued to illegally support the rebels. They secretly sold weapons to Iran, considered an enemy and sponsor of terrorism, in exchange for the release of American hostages being held in the Middle East. These hostages were taken by the Hezbollah terrorist group because the United States was supporting Israel's involvement in Lebanon's civil war. Profits from these sales were then sent to the contras.

News of the illegal operations broke in November 1986. One of the chief figures in the **Iran-Contra scandal** was Marine colonel Oliver North, an aide to the National Security Council (NSC). He and other senior NSC and CIA officials testified before Congress and admitted to covering up their actions.

President Reagan had approved the sale of arms to Iran, but the congressional investigation concluded that he had had no direct knowledge about the diversion of the money to the contras. The scandal tainted his second term in office.

Arms Control

As part of the military buildup, Reagan decided to place missiles in Western Europe to counter Soviet missiles in Eastern Europe. This decision triggered tens of thousands of protesters to push for a "nuclear freeze"—no more deployment of new nuclear missiles.

Reagan offered to cancel the deployment of the new missiles if the Soviets removed their missiles from Eastern Europe. He also proposed Strategic Arms Reduction Talks (START) to cut the number of missiles on both sides in half. The Soviets refused and walked out of the arms control talks.

"Star Wars" Despite his decision to deploy missiles in Europe, Reagan generally disagreed with the military strategy known as nuclear deterrence, sometimes called **"mutual assured destruction."** This strategy assumed that, as long as the United States and Soviet Union could destroy each other with nuclear weapons, they would be afraid to use them.

Reagan believed that mutual assured destruction was immoral because it depended on the threat to kill massive numbers of people. He also knew that if nuclear war did begin, there would be no way to defend the United States. In March 1983 Reagan proposed the Strategic Defense Initiative (SDI). This plan, nicknamed "Star Wars," called for the development of weapons that could intercept and destroy incoming missiles.

A New Soviet Leader In 1985 **Mikhail Gorbachev** became the leader of the Soviet Union and agreed to resume arms-control talks. Gorbachev believed that the Soviet Union had to reform its economic system or it would soon collapse. It could not afford a new arms race with the United States.

Reagan and Gorbachev met in a series of summits. The first of these was frustrating for both, as they disagreed on many issues. Gorbachev promised to cut back Soviet nuclear forces if Reagan would agree to give up SDI, but Reagan refused.

Reagan then challenged Gorbachev to make reforms. In West Berlin, Reagan stood at the Brandenburg Gate of the Berlin Wall, the symbol of divided Europe, and declared: "General Secretary Gorbachev, if you seek peace, if you seek prosperity for the Soviet Union and Eastern Europe . . . tear down this wall!"

Relations Improve By 1987, Reagan was convinced that Gorbachev did want to reform the Soviet Union and end the arms race. While some politicians distrusted the Soviets, most people welcomed the Cold War thaw and the reduction in the danger of nuclear war. In December 1987 the two leaders signed the Intermediate Range Nuclear Forces (INF) Treaty. It was the first treaty to call for the destruction of nuclear weapons.

No one realized it at the time, but the treaty marked the beginning of the end of the Cold War. With an arms control deal in place, Gorbachev felt confident that Soviet military spending could be reduced. He pushed ahead with economic and political reforms that eventually led to the collapse of communism in Eastern Europe and in the Soviet Union.

With the economy booming, the American military strong, and relations with the Soviet Union rapidly improving, Ronald Reagan's second term came to an end. As he prepared to leave office, Reagan assessed his presidency: "They called it the Reagan revolution. Well, I'll accept that, but for me it always seemed more like the great rediscovery, a rediscovery of our values and our common sense."

Reading Check **Identifying** What was the Reagan Doctrine?

Section 2 REVIEW

Vocabulary

1. **Explain** the significance of: supply-side economics, Reaganomics, budget deficit, Iran-Contra scandal, "mutual assured destruction," Mikhail Gorbachev.

Main Ideas

2. **Specifying** What political office did Ronald Reagan hold before he was elected president?

3. **Explaining** How did Reagan aim to change the Supreme Court?

4. **Summarizing** What was the goal of the U.S. military buildup under President Reagan?

Critical Thinking

5. **Big Ideas** What was President Reagan's approach to foreign policy?

6. **Organizing** Use a graphic organizer similar to the one below to list the ways in which the Reagan Doctrine was implemented.

Reagan Doctrine

7. **Analyzing Visuals** Study the political cartoons on page 747. How do the cartoons portray Reagan and Carter?

Writing About History

8. **Expository Writing** Take on the role of a newspaper editor during the Reagan administration. Write an editorial in which you present your opinion of Reagan's plans for a military buildup.

History ONLINE

Study Central™ To review this section, go to glencoe.com and click on Study Central.

Life in the 1980s

Guide to Reading

Big Ideas
Science and Technology
Achievements in technology during the 1980s symbolized the optimism many associated with the Reagan era.

Content Vocabulary
- yuppie *(p. 754)*
- discount retailing *(p. 755)*

Academic Vocabulary
- via *(p. 756)*
- orientation *(p. 759)*

People and Events to Identify
- Mothers Against Drunk Driving (MADD) *(p. 758)*
- AIDS *(p. 759)*
- Stonewall Riot *(p. 759)*
- American Association of Retired Persons (AARP) *(p. 759)*

Reading Strategy
Organizing Complete a graphic organizer similar to the one below by listing the kinds of social issues that Americans faced in the 1980s.

Social Issues in the 1980s

The 1980s was a period of increased wealth for many, as areas of the economy improved and new technologies came to market. However, cuts in social programs left many Americans in need, leading to a new sense of activism.

A Booming Economy

MAIN Idea Innovation in the retailing and broadcast industries changed American society and generated new businesses and jobs.

HISTORY AND YOU What technological devices are part of your everyday life? Read on to find out about the inventions of the 1980s.

By late 1983, the American economy had revived after the stagflation of the 1970s. Stock prices soared as many companies reported record profits. Stockbrokers, speculators, and real estate developers made multimillion-dollar deals, buying and selling hundreds of companies. Perhaps the most famous real estate developer of the era was Donald Trump, who opened Trump Tower in New York City in 1982. Many of the new moneymakers were young, ambitious, and hardworking. Journalists called them **yuppies,** from "young urban professionals."

The rapid economic growth and emphasis on accumulating wealth in the 1980s was partly caused by the baby boom. By the 1980s, many baby boomers had finished college, entered the job market, and begun building their careers. Young people entering the workforce often placed an emphasis on acquiring goods and getting ahead in their jobs. Because baby boomers were so numerous, their concerns tended to shape the culture.

The strong economic growth of the 1980s mostly benefited middle- and upper-class Americans. As a result, the emphasis on acquiring wealth had another effect on society. From 1967 to 1986, the amount of money earned by the top 5 percent of Americans fluctuated between 15.6 and 17.5 percent of the nation's total income. In the late 1980s, their share of the nation's income began to rise. By the mid-1990s, the top 5 percent of Americans earned well over 21 percent of the nation's income.

A Retail Revolution

In addition to the booming real-estate and stock markets, the economy of the 1980s witnessed a revolution in retail sales. Several entrepreneurs pioneered a new approach to retailing—or selling goods to

The Booming Economy of the 1980s

The American economy grew rapidly in the 1980s for several reasons—lower taxes spurred investment and spending while new methods of retailing lowered prices and new technology led to new businesses and the creation of many new jobs.

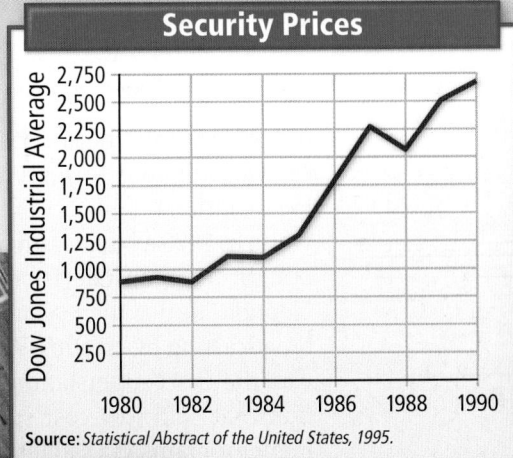

Security Prices

Source: *Statistical Abstract of the United States, 1995.*

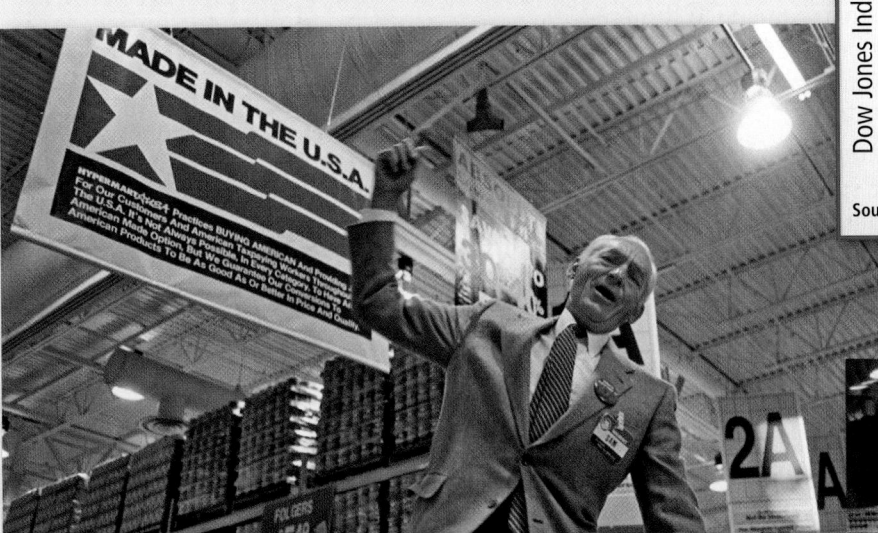

Analyzing VISUALS

1. **Identifying** In what year of the late 1980s did the Dow Jones sharply decline?

2. **Explaining** Examine the photos and then write a brief essay explaining how they demonstrate economic trends of the 1980s.

Discount retail stores (above) and cable television (right) took off in the 1980s, helping to further fuel economic growth.

consumers—that greatly reduced prices for Americans.

This new type of retailing, known as **discount retailing,** had actually begun to emerge in the 1960s—but it did not have a major impact on the economy until the 1980s. Discount retailers sell large quantities of goods at very low prices, trying to sell the goods quickly to turn over their entire inventory in a short period of time. By selling a lot of products at very low prices, they could make more money than traditional retailers who sold fewer products at higher prices. During the 1960s many new discount retail chains were founded, including K Mart, Woolco, Target, and Wal-Mart. Annual sales by discount stores grew from about $2 billion in the mid-1960s to almost $70 billion by 1985.

The most successful discount retailer was Sam Walton, the founder of Wal-Mart. Walton developed a system of distribution centers to rapidly re-supply his stores. He was one of the first retailers to use a computer database to track inventory and sales. By 1985, he was the richest person in the United States.

Others soon copied Walton's approach. By the late 1970s, discount retailers had begun to build huge "superstores" that enabled them to sell large quantities of goods very quickly at low prices. One such entrepreneur was Arthur Blank, who opened Home Depot—a chain of giant home-improvement stores—in 1978. In 1983 Richard Schulze, a former air force officer, used his technical training to found Best Buy, a huge discount retailer of consumer electronics. Dozens of other entrepreneurs started discount stores in other industries. Their innovations created millions of new jobs in the 1980s and helped fuel the era's rapid economic growth.

A Revolution in Media

In the 1980s other entrepreneurs began transforming the news and entertainment industries. Until the late 1970s television viewers were limited to three national networks, local stations, and the public television network. In 1970 a businessman named Ted Turner bought a failing television station in Atlanta, Georgia. Turner then pioneered a new type of broadcasting by creating WTBS in 1975. WTBS was the first "superstation"—a television station that sold low-cost sports and entertainment programs **via** satellite to cable companies throughout the nation.

The Rise of Cable Television Turner's innovation changed broadcasting and helped spread cable television across the country. Dozens of networks soon appeared. Many of the new networks specialized in one type of broadcasting, such as sports (ESPN), movies (HBO), or news. In 1980 Turner himself founded the Cable News Network (CNN)—the first 24-hour, all-news network.

Other new networks focused on specific audiences, such as churchgoers, shoppers, or minorities. In 1980 entrepreneur Robert Johnson created Black Entertainment Television (BET). Johnson—who had been born into a poor, rural family in Mississippi and gone on to earn a master's degree from Princeton University—was convinced that television had tremendous power to promote African American businesses and culture. BET was the first, and is still the largest, African American-owned network on cable television.

In 1981 music and technology merged when Music Television (MTV) went on the air. MTV broadcast performances of songs and images, or music videos. MTV was an instant hit, though the videos it showed were often criticized for violence and sexual content. Many performers began to produce videos along with each of their new albums. Music videos boosted the careers of artists such as Madonna and Michael Jackson.

Rap music was the new sound of the 1980s. This musical style originated in local clubs in New York City's South Bronx. Emphasizing heavy bass and very rhythmic sounds, rap artists did not usually sing but rather spoke over the music and rhythmic beats. Rap's lyrics frequently focused on the African American expe-

PAST & PRESENT

April 1981

New Space Technology

After the series of moon landings of the 1970s, NASA concentrated on the space shuttle. Although it looks like a huge airplane, the shuttle is rocketed into space, then glides back to Earth for another flight. Unlike earlier spacecraft, the shuttle is reusable. Astronauts John Young and Roger Crippen made the first space shuttle flight in April 1981.

Between April 1981 and December 2006, shuttle astronauts completed 114 missions. They have placed many satellites in orbit, including the Hubble Space Telescope, and conducted numerous experiments. Tragedy has struck twice during shuttle missions. In 1986, the space shuttle *Challenger* exploded shortly after liftoff. In 2003, the shuttle *Columbia* came apart while reentering the atmosphere. Seven astronauts died in each of these accidents.

As the shuttle nears the end of its service life, both NASA and several independent companies have begun work on vehicles capable of reaching orbit. Shuttle launches are very expensive and many entrepreneurs are seeking to develop low-cost alternatives to the shuttle that will enable business to move into space and develop new industries there.

▲ On April 12, 1981, the shuttle Columbia *lifted off on the first space shuttle flight.*

rience in the inner city. While rap was initially popular among East Coast African Americans, it grew in popularity, becoming a multimillion-dollar industry that appealed to music lovers across the country.

Technology and Media In the 1980s technology also transformed how people accessed their entertainment. Until the 1980s, most people listened to music on large stereo systems in their homes or relied on radio-station programming when they were driving. In the 1980s, the Sony Walkman made music portable. The Sony Walkman played cassette tapes, but it marked the beginning of a new way for people to access music. In the 1990s, portable compact disc (CD) players replaced the Walkman, and in the early 2000s digital audio players, such as the iPod and MP3 players, advanced the technology even further.

Video technology also began to change. Until the 1980s most people had to watch television shows when they aired. By the end of the 1980s, many people had videocassette recorders (VCRs), enabling them to tape television shows or watch taped films whenever they wished. By the 2000s, VCRs were being replaced by digital video disk (DVD) recorders. The growing use of VCRs changed the movie industry, as people increasingly chose to rent taped movies to watch at home rather than go to the theater.

Even as technology changed the music and television industries, it also brought about a new form of entertainment that competed with music and movies—the video game. Early video games grew out of military computer technology. The first video arcade game was a game called *Pong*, released in 1972. Home video games developed quickly. In the early 1980s sales reached about $3 billion with the sale of games such as *Pac-Man* and *Space Invaders.* Video arcades became the new spot for young people to meet. By the mid-1980s, home video games were able to compete with arcade games in graphics and speed. Video games have continued to grow in popularity to the present day and three major companies—Sony, Nintendo, and Microsoft—have emerged as the major developers of video games and game devices.

Reading Check **Describing** What forms of entertainment gained popularity in the 1980s?

June 2004

In the early 2000s, many private companies were working on building spaceships. SpaceShipOne (below) was the first privately-built ship to carry a person to space. Another company is working on the Goddard (right)—a ship designed to take off and land vertically, without needing wings.

MAKING CONNECTIONS

1. **Analyzing** How has the United States benefited from the space program?

2. **Speculating** What kinds of private businesses might benefit from easy, inexpensive space programs?

New Social Activism

MAIN Idea Social problems affected many people during the 1980s, and new groups formed to try to solve them.

HISTORY AND YOU Does your school have organizations such as Students Against Drunk Driving? Read on to learn more about attempts to limit teen alcohol abuse.

The 1980s was a decade of wealth and prosperity. At the same time, many social problems continued to plague the nation, such as drugs, poverty, homelessness, and disease.

Social Problems

Ongoing problems with drug abuse in the 1980s made many neighborhoods dangerous. Drug users often committed crimes to get money for drugs. Drug use also spread from cities to small towns and rural areas.

Fighting Drugs in Schools In an effort to reduce teen drug use, some schools began searching student bags and lockers for concealed drugs. In 1984 one teen who had been arrested for selling drugs challenged the school's right to search her purse without a warrant. In 1985, the Supreme Court case *New Jersey* v. *T.L.O.* upheld the school's right to search without a warrant if it had probable cause. Although students did have a right to privacy, they did not have the same Fourth Amendment rights as adults. Similarly, the 1995 case of *Vernonia School District* v. *Acton* held that random drug tests do not violate students' Fourth Amendment rights.

Efforts to Stop Drunk Driving Abuse of alcohol was also a serious concern. In 1980 **Mothers Against Drunk Driving (MADD)** was founded to try to stop underage drinking and drunk driving in general. In 1984 Congress cut highway funds to any state that did not raise the legal drinking age to 21. Within four years, all states complied.

The AIDS Epidemic Begins In 1981 researchers identified a disease that caused healthy young people to become sick and die. They named it "acquired immune deficiency syndrome," or **AIDS.** AIDS weakens the

---

The Farm Debt Crisis of the 1980s

Although the high interest rates of the 1980s helped reduce inflation, when they were combined with the low food prices of the era, they created a debt crisis for American farmers who could not make their loan payments and were forced out of business. By the end of the 1980s, the total number of farms in the United States had sharply declined.

Farm Income and Debt

Billions of Dollars*

— Farm Income
— Farm Debt

1975   1980   1985   1990

*In constant 2000 dollars

Source: U.S. Department of Agriculture.

◀ As farmers faced a debt crisis, some began holding demonstrations, such as this one in Washington D.C. in 1984.

Analyzing VISUALS

1. **Hypothesizing** What factors explain why farm debt increased between 1975 and 1980?

2. **Interpreting** What are the farmers at left complaining about?

immune system. HIV, the virus that causes AIDS, is spread through bodily fluids.

In the United States, AIDS was first noticed among homosexual men, but it soon spread among heterosexual men and women. Many people were infected by sexual partners. A few got the disease from blood transfusions. Other victims included drug users who shared needles. Between 1981 and 1988, the Centers for Disease Control and Prevention identified more than 100,000 cases in the United States.

New Activist Groups

AIDS increased the visibility of the country's gay and lesbian community, but some homosexuals had been engaged in efforts to defend their civil rights since the 1960s. On June 27, 1969, New York City police raided a nightclub called the Stonewall Inn. The police had often raided the nightclub because of the sexual **orientation** of its patrons. Frustration among the gay and lesbian onlookers led to a riot. The **Stonewall Riot** marked the beginning of the gay activist movement. Soon after, organizations such as the Gay Liberation Front began efforts to increase tolerance of homosexuality.

Rock 'n' Rollers Become Activists Many musicians and entertainers in the 1980s began using their celebrity to raise awareness about social issues. To help starving people in Ethiopia, Irish rocker Bob Geldof organized musicians in England to present "Band Aid" concerts in 1984. In the next year, the event grew into "Live Aid." People in some 100 countries watched benefit concerts televised from London, Philadelphia, and Sydney, Australia. The organization's theme song, "We Are the World," was a best-seller. In the same year, country singer Willie Nelson organized "Farm Aid" to help American farmers who were going through hard times. Musicians also publicized efforts to end the segregated apartheid social system in South Africa. In the late 1980s, the United States and other nations were attempting to end apartheid in South Africa by imposing economic sanctions against the country.

Senior Citizens Begin to Lobby Another group that became politically active in the 1980s was senior citizens. Decades of improvements in medicine had resulted in more Americans surviving to an older age. In addition, the birthrate had declined, so younger people represented a comparatively smaller proportion of the population. The fact that more Americans were receiving Social Security payments created budget pressures for the government.

Older Americans became very vocal in the political arena, opposing cuts in Social Security or Medicare. Because they tend to vote in large numbers, senior citizens are an influential interest group. Their major lobbying organization is the **American Association of Retired Persons (AARP),** founded in 1958.

✔ Reading Check **Summarizing** On what issues did some entertainers focus in the 1980s?

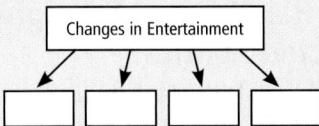

Section 3 REVIEW

Vocabulary

1. **Explain** the significance of: yuppie, discount retailing, Mothers Against Drunk Driving (MADD), AIDS, Stonewall Riot, American Association of Retired Persons (AARP).

Main Ideas

2. **Summarizing** How did retailing change in the 1980s?

3. **Listing** What are three social problems that gained focus in the 1980s?

Critical Thinking

4. **Big Ideas** What new innovations occurred in the consumer electronics industry in the 1980s?

5. **Organizing** Use a graphic organizer similar to the one below to list the changes in entertainment in the 1980s.

```
           Changes in Entertainment
         ┌──────┬──────┬──────┬──────┐
         │      │      │      │      │
         └──────┴──────┴──────┴──────┘
```

6. **Analyzing Visuals** Study the graph of the stock market rise on page 755. How is this graph indicative of what you have read about in this section?

Writing About History

7. **Persuasive Writing** Choose one of the social problems of the 1980s. Write a letter to members of your favorite band asking them to perform a concert to benefit your cause. Your letter should explain why the cause is important.

History ONLINE
Study Central™ To review this section, go to glencoe.com and click on Study Central.

GEOGRAPHY & HISTORY

Urban America on the Move

After World War II, cities grew into vast metropolitan areas—a development referred to as "urban sprawl." Inner cities, often inhabited by lower-income people, lost tax revenue, resulting in deteriorating infrastructure and shortages of affordable housing. As the map shows, many high-growth areas are in Southern Sunbelt states.

In response, some cities sought to improve urban neighborhoods and encourage reinvestment in the city core. These policies have had only limited effect, as suburbs and new "exurbs"—communities located in the country beyond the suburbs, continue to grow.

How Has Urban Geography Affected Politics?

The rapid growth of the suburbs and exurbs plays an important role in American politics. Inner city communities tend to vote for Democrats, while voters in outer suburbs and exurbs tend to vote for Republicans. The reason for this pattern is unclear. In part, it reflects the preference of many minorities who live in the inner city to vote for Democrats. In addition, some political geographers believe that since city-dwellers rely more on government services, they tend to support liberal policies that favor government activism. People in the suburbs and exurbs want more independence and more often distrust government—a conservative perspective. They believe large city governments have done a poor job running schools and controlling crime.

▲ Urban sprawl, traffic congestion, long commutes, and air pollution are part of the price Atlanta paid for rapid growth.

Existing development as of 1993
— Intense
— Moderate
Development since 1993
— Intense
— Moderate

Analyzing GEOGRAPHY

1. **Movement** Which regions experienced the most growth after 1993?

2. **Human-Environment Interaction** How does the urban geography of American cities shape voting patterns and preferences?

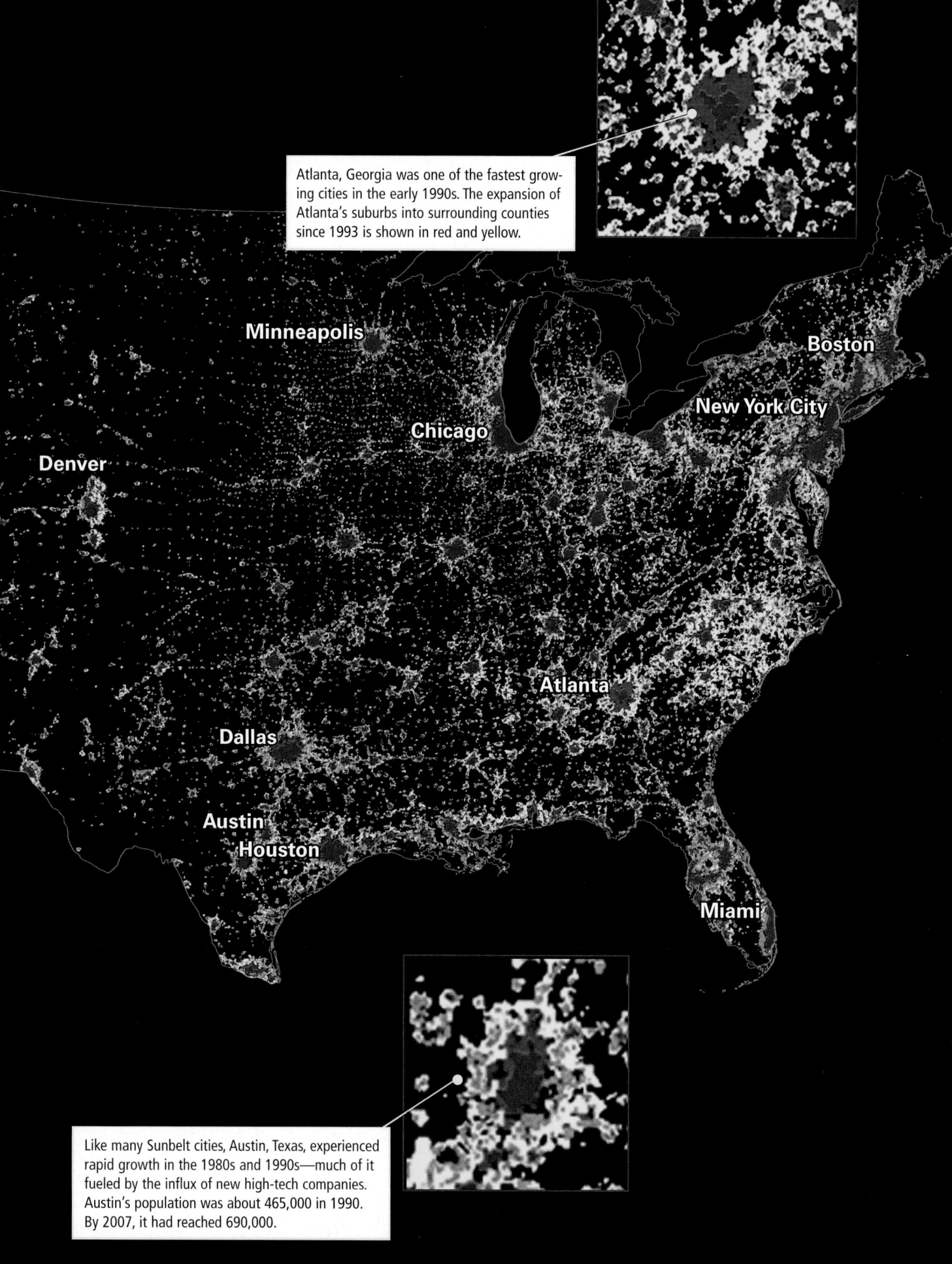

Atlanta, Georgia was one of the fastest growing cities in the early 1990s. The expansion of
Atlanta's suburbs into surrounding counties
since 1993 is shown in red and yellow.

Minneapolis

Boston

New York City

Chicago

Denver

Atlanta

Dallas

Austin

Houston

Miami

Like many Sunbelt cities, Austin, Texas, experienced
rapid growth in the 1980s and 1990s—much of it
fueled by the influx of new high-tech companies.
Austin's population was about 465,000 in 1990.
By 2007, it had reached 690,000.

Section 4

The End of the Cold War

Guide to Reading

Big Ideas
Economics and Society The deficit and an economic slowdown hurt George H.W. Bush's attempt to win reelection in 1992.

Content Vocabulary
- perestroika (p. 763)
- glasnost (p. 763)
- downsizing (p. 766)
- capital gains tax (p. 767)
- grassroots movement (p. 767)

Academic Vocabulary
- initiative (p. 765)
- retain (p. 767)

People and Events to Identify
- Boris Yeltsin (p. 764)
- Tiananmen Square (p. 765)
- Saddam Hussein (p. 765)
- H. Ross Perot (p. 767)

Reading Strategy
Categorizing Complete a graphic organizer similar to the one below by describing U.S. foreign policy in each of the places listed.

Place	Foreign Policy
Soviet Union	
China	
Panama	
Middle East	

I n the late 1980s, the United States faced a series of international crises. The Cold War came to an end in Europe, but events in the Middle East soon led the United States into its first major war since Vietnam.

The Soviet Union Collapses

MAIN Idea The Soviet Union's attempts at reforming its social and economic systems failed, leading to the collapse of the Communist eastern bloc.

HISTORY AND YOU What can you recall about the division of Europe after World War II? Read on to learn about the massive changes that took place in Eastern Europe at the end of the 1980s.

When Ronald Reagan left office, few Americans were thinking about foreign policy. Many generally wanted a continuation of Reagan's domestic policies—low taxes and less government action. When Republicans nominated George H. W. Bush for president in 1988, he reassured Americans he would continue Reagan's policies by making a promise: "Read my lips: No new taxes."

The Democrats hoped to regain the White House in 1988 by promising to help working-class Americans, minorities, and the poor. One candidate for the nomination, civil rights leader Jesse Jackson, tried to create a "rainbow coalition"—a broad group of minorities and the poor—by speaking about homelessness and unemployment. Jackson finished second in the primaries, the first African American to make a serious run for the nomination.

The Democrats nominated Massachusetts governor Michael Dukakis. The Bush campaign portrayed him as too liberal and "soft on crime." The Democrats questioned Bush's leadership abilities, but Bush had Reagan's endorsement and, with the economy still doing well, most Americans felt that Bush was the more able candidate. Bush easily defeated Dukakis in the general election, although Democrats kept control of Congress.

Voters had focused on domestic issues during the election campaign, but soon after taking office President Bush had to focus most of his time and energy on foreign policy as change swept through Eastern Europe and the Cold War came to an abrupt end.

Revolution in Eastern Europe

As president, Bush continued Reagan's policy of cooperation with Soviet leader Mikhail Gorbachev. By the late 1980s, the Soviet economy was suffering from years of inefficient central planning and huge expenditures on the arms race. To save the economy,

NATIONAL GEOGRAPHIC Revolutions in Eastern Europe

◄ The Berlin Wall fell on November 10, 1989.

5. Baltic States became independent, 1991

4. Germany reunited, 1990

3. Berlin Wall torn down, Nov. 1989

1. Democratic elections, 1989

6. Czechoslovakia separated, 1993

2. Non-Communist governments created, 1989

▲ Boris Yeltsin rallies the crowd against the military coup on August 19, 1991.

Analyzing GEOGRAPHY

1. **Regions** Which Eastern European countries abandoned communism first?

2. **Place** Why was the fall of communism in East Germany significant?

Gorbachev instituted **perestroika,** or "restructuring," and allowed some private enterprise and profit making.

The other principle of Gorbachev's plan was **glasnost,** or "openness." It allowed more freedom of religion and speech, enabling people to discuss politics openly. With Gorbachev's support, glasnost spread to Eastern Europe. In 1989 revolutions replaced Communist rulers with democratic governments in Bulgaria, Czechoslovakia, Hungary, Poland, and Romania. The tide of revolution then swept over East Germany, and at midnight on November 9, 1989, guards at the Berlin Wall opened the gates.

Within days, bulldozers leveled the hated symbol of Communist repression. Within a year, East and West Germany had reunited to form one nation—the Federal Republic of Germany.

The Soviet Union Collapses

As Eastern Europe abandoned communism, Gorbachev faced mounting criticism from opponents at home. In August 1991 a group of Communist officials and army officers tried to stage a coup—an overthrow of the government. They arrested Gorbachev and sent troops into Moscow.

In Moscow, Russian president **Boris Yeltsin** defied the coup leaders from his offices in the Russian Parliament. About 50,000 people surrounded the Russian Parliament to protect it from troops. President Bush telephoned Yeltsin to express the support of the United States. Soon afterward, the coup collapsed, and Gorbachev returned to Moscow.

The defeat of the coup brought change swiftly. All 15 Soviet republics declared their independence from the Soviet Union. Yeltsin outlawed the Communist Party in Russia. In late December 1991 Gorbachev announced the end of the Soviet Union. Most of the former Soviet republics then joined in a federation called the Commonwealth of Independent States (CIS). Although CIS member states remained independent, they agreed to form a common economic zone in 1993.

✓ **Reading Check** **Explaining** Why did Mikhail Gorbachev institute the policy of *perestroika*?

A "New World Order"

MAIN Idea Bush used his foreign policy expertise to deal with crises in China, Panama, and the Persian Gulf.

HISTORY AND YOU Do you remember learning about student protests in the 1960s? Read on to learn about a student protest in China.

After the Cold War, the world became increasingly unpredictable. President Bush noted that a "new world order" was emerging. This new world order introduced new military challenges around the globe. For example, U.S. troops led Operation Restore Hope, providing humanitarian assistance and famine relief to refugees in Somalia, which had collapsed when the Cold War motivations were removed. Several other crises requiring military action emerged in China, Panama, and the Middle East.

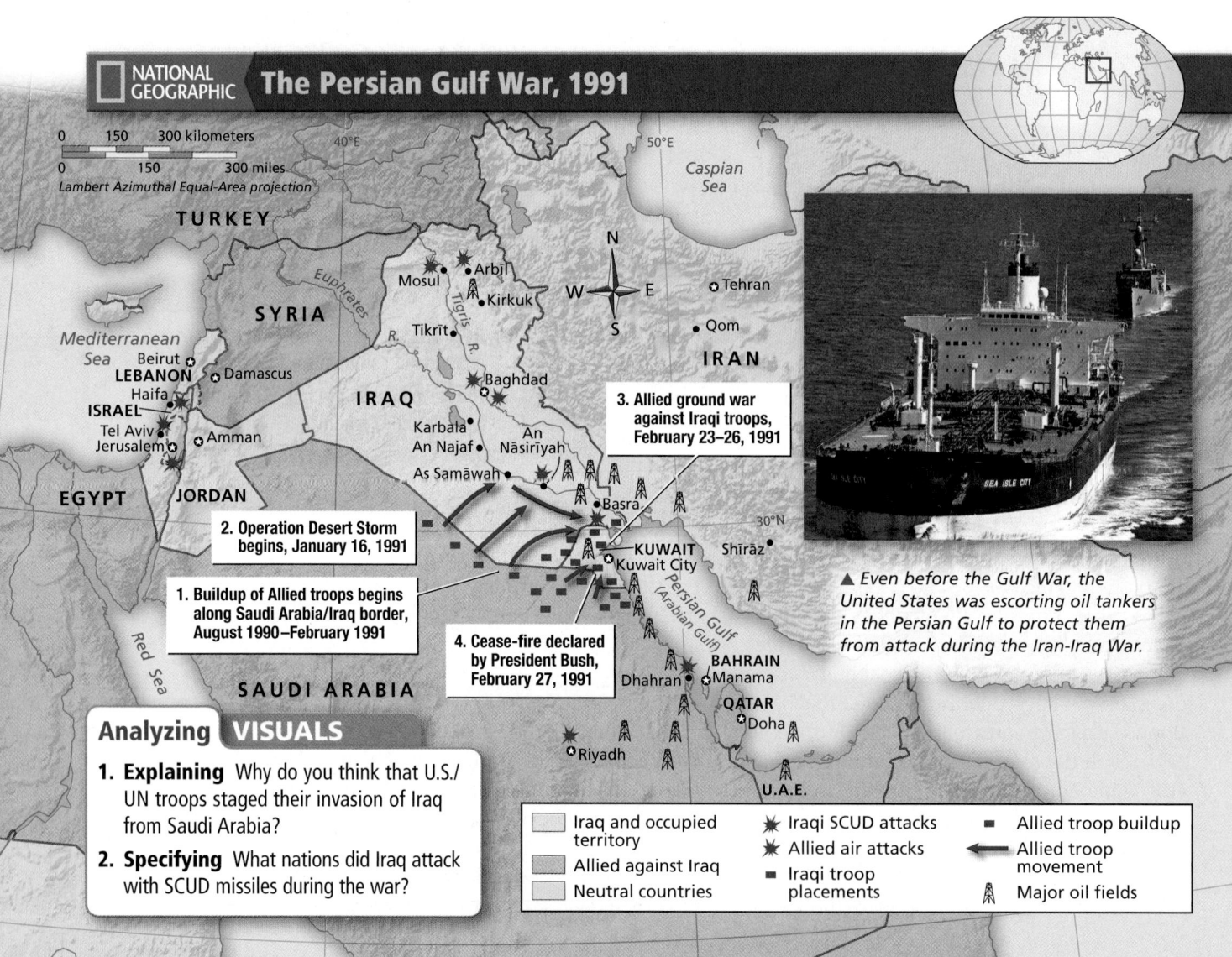

NATIONAL GEOGRAPHIC **The Persian Gulf War, 1991**

0   150   300 kilometers
0   150   300 miles
Lambert Azimuthal Equal-Area projection

3. Allied ground war against Iraqi troops, February 23–26, 1991

2. Operation Desert Storm begins, January 16, 1991

1. Buildup of Allied troops begins along Saudi Arabia/Iraq border, August 1990–February 1991

4. Cease-fire declared by President Bush, February 27, 1991

▲ *Even before the Gulf War, the United States was escorting oil tankers in the Persian Gulf to protect them from attack during the Iran-Iraq War.*

	Iraq and occupied territory	✹ Iraqi SCUD attacks	▬ Allied troop buildup
	Allied against Iraq	✱ Allied air attacks	⬅ Allied troop movement
	Neutral countries	▪ Iraqi troop placements	⚒ Major oil fields

Analyzing VISUALS

1. **Explaining** Why do you think that U.S./UN troops staged their invasion of Iraq from Saudi Arabia?

2. **Specifying** What nations did Iraq attack with SCUD missiles during the war?

Tiananmen Square

Despite the collapse of communism in Eastern Europe and the Soviet Union, China's Communist leaders were determined to stay in power. China's government had relaxed controls on the economy, but it continued to repress political speech and dissent. In May 1989, Chinese students and workers held demonstrations for democracy. The center of the protests was **Tiananmen Square** in Beijing, China's capital. In early June government tanks and soldiers crushed the protests. Many people were killed and hundreds of pro-democracy activists were arrested. Many were later sentenced to death.

Shocked, the United States and several European countries halted arms sales and reduced their diplomatic contacts with China. The World Bank suspended loans. President Bush resisted harsher sanctions, believing that trade and diplomacy would eventually moderate China's behavior.

Panama

While President Bush struggled to deal with global events elsewhere, a crisis developed in Panama. In 1978 the United States had agreed to give Panama control over the Panama Canal by the year 2000. Because of the canal's importance, American officials wanted to make sure Panama's government was both stable and pro-American.

By 1989, Panama's dictator, General Manuel Noriega, had stopped cooperating with the United States. He also aided drug traffickers, cracked down on opponents, and harassed American military personnel defending the canal. In December 1989, Bush ordered American troops to invade Panama. The troops seized Noriega, who was sent to the United States to stand trial on drug charges. The troops then helped the Panamanians hold elections and organize a new government.

The Persian Gulf War

President Bush faced perhaps his most serious crisis in the Middle East. In August 1990 Iraq's dictator, **Saddam Hussein,** sent his army to invade oil-rich Kuwait. American officials feared that the invasion might be only the first step and that Iraq's ultimate goal was to capture Saudi Arabia and its vast oil reserves. American troops rushed to the Middle East and took up positions in Saudi Arabia in response.

President Bush persuaded other UN member countries to join a coalition to stop Iraq. Led by the United States, the United Nations imposed economic sanctions on Iraq and demanded that the Iraqis withdraw. The coalition included troops from the United States, Canada, Europe, and Middle Eastern nations. The UN set a deadline for the Iraqis' withdrawal, after which the coalition would use force to remove them. Congress also voted to authorize the use of force if Iraq did not withdraw.

On October 31, 1990, General Colin Powell, chairman of the Joint Chiefs of Staff, Secretary of Defense Dick Cheney, and other high-ranking officials met with President Bush. It was clear that Iraq would not obey the UN deadline. Powell presented the plan for attacking Iraq. Several advisers gasped at the numbers, which called for over 500,000 American troops. "Mr. President," Powell began, "I wish . . . that I could assure you that air power alone could do it but you can't take that chance. We've gotta take the **initiative** out of the enemy's hands if we're going to go to war." Cheney later recalled that Bush "never hesitated." He looked up from the plans and said simply, "Do it."

On January 16, 1991, the coalition forces launched Operation Desert Storm. Dozens of cruise missiles and thousands of laser-guided bombs fell on Iraq, destroying its air defenses, bridges, artillery, and other military targets. After about six weeks of bombardment, the coalition launched a massive ground attack. Waves of tanks and troop carriers smashed through Iraqi lines and encircled the Iraqi forces defending Kuwait.

The attack killed thousands of Iraqi soldiers, and hundreds of thousands more surrendered. Fewer than 300 coalition troops were killed. Just 100 hours after the ground war began, President Bush declared Kuwait to be liberated. Iraq accepted the coalition's cease-fire terms, and American troops returned home to cheering crowds.

Reading Check **Examining** Why did President Bush take action when Iraqi troops invaded Kuwait?

Domestic Challenges

MAIN Idea To reduce the deficit, President Bush raised taxes, an unpopular decision that helped Bill Clinton win the election.

HISTORY AND YOU How are your school and community designed to provide access for people who use wheelchairs? Read on to find out more about the Americans with Disabilities Act of 1990.

President Bush spent much of his time dealing with foreign policy, but he could not ignore domestic issues. He inherited a growing deficit and a slowing economy. With the Persian Gulf crisis, the economy plunged into a recession and unemployment rose.

The Economy Slows

The recession that began in 1990 was partly caused by the end of the Cold War. As the Soviet threat faded, the United States began reducing its armed forces and canceling orders for military equipment. Thousands of soldiers and defense industry workers were laid off.

Other companies also began **downsizing** —laying off workers and managers to become more efficient. The nation's high level of debt made the recession worse. Americans had borrowed heavily during the 1980s and now faced paying off large debts.

In addition, the huge deficit forced the government to borrow money to pay for its programs. This borrowing kept money from being

HISTORY AND GEOGRAPHY
The Election of 1992

The election of 1992 marked the first time since 1968 that no candidate won at least 50 percent of the popular vote and for much the same reason. A strong third party challenger, Ross Perot (below, center), took votes from both major candidates.

◀ The success of Perot's campaign surprised many Americans.

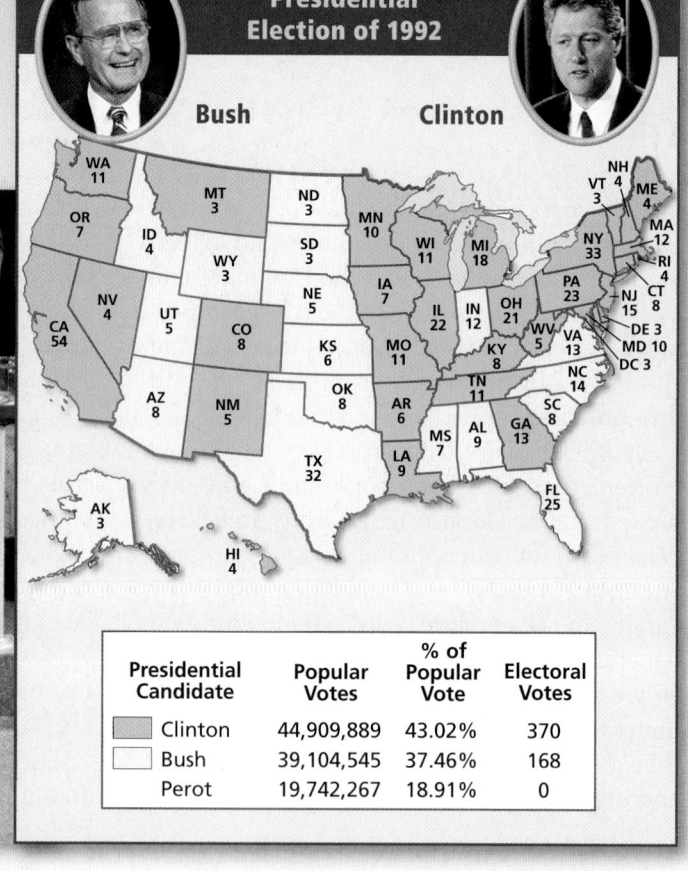

Presidential Election of 1992

Bush   Clinton

Presidential Candidate	Popular Votes	% of Popular Vote	Electoral Votes
Clinton	44,909,889	43.02%	370
Bush	39,104,545	37.46%	168
Perot	19,742,267	18.91%	0

Analyzing VISUALS

1. **Interpreting** What does the cartoon suggest about independent candidates?

2. **Speculating** What factors might explain Clinton's popularity in the Northeast?

available to businesses. The government also had to pay interest on its debt, money that might otherwise have been used to fund programs or boost the economy.

As the economy slowed, hundreds of savings-and-loan institutions collapsed. After President Reagan had allowed them to be deregulated, many had made risky or even dishonest investments. When these investments failed, depositors collected on federal programs to insure deposits. The cost to the public may have reached $500 billion.

Gridlock in Government

Shortly after taking office, Bush tried to improve the economy. He called for a cut in the **capital gains tax**—the tax paid by businesses and investors when they sell stocks or real estate for a profit. Bush believed that the tax cut would encourage businesses to expand. Calling the idea a tax break for the rich, Democrats in Congress defeated it.

Aware that the growing federal deficit was hurting the economy, Bush broke his "no new taxes" campaign pledge. After meeting with congressional leaders, he agreed to a tax increase in exchange for cuts in spending. This decision turned many voters against Bush.

The 1992 Election

Although the recession had weakened his popularity, Bush won the Republican nomination. Bush promised to address voters' economic concerns and he blamed congressional Democrats for the gridlock that seemingly paralyzed the nation's government.

The Democrats nominated Arkansas governor William Jefferson Clinton, despite stories that questioned his character and the fact that he did not serve in Vietnam. Calling himself a "New Democrat" to separate himself from more liberal Democrats, Clinton promised to cut middle-class taxes, reduce government spending, and reform the nation's health care and welfare programs. His campaign repeatedly blamed Bush for the recession.

Some Americans were not happy with either Bush or Clinton. This enabled an independent candidate, billionaire Texas businessman **H. Ross Perot,** to make a strong challenge. Perot stressed the need to end deficit spending. His no-nonsense style appealed to many Americans. A **grassroots movement**—groups of people organizing at the local level—put Perot on the ballot in all 50 states.

Bill Clinton won the election with 43 percent of the popular vote and 370 electoral votes. The Democrats also **retained** control of Congress. Bush won 37 percent of the popular vote, while Perot received 19 percent—the best showing for a third-party candidate since 1912—but no electoral votes.

As the first president born after World War II, the 46-year-old Clinton was the first person from the baby boom generation to enter the White House. It was his task to revive the economy and guide the United States in a rapidly changing world.

Reading Check **Summarizing** Why did President Bush lose popularity as the 1992 election approached?

Section 4 REVIEW

Vocabulary

1. **Explain** the significance of: perestroika, glasnost, Boris Yeltsin, Tiananmen Square, Saddam Hussein, downsizing, capital gains tax, H. Ross Perot, grassroots movement.

Main Ideas

2. **Explaining** How did perestroika and glasnost create conditions that led to the fall of the Soviet Union?

3. **Describing** What actions did the United States take in Panama in 1989?

4. **Determining Cause and Effect** How did the huge deficits from the Reagan years lead to economic problems under George Bush?

Critical Thinking

5. **Big Ideas** How did the economy affect the 1992 election?

6. **Organizing** Use a graphic organizer similar to the one below to list the causes of the recession of the early 1990s.

Budget Problems	Economic Problems	Foreign Developments

7. **Analyzing Visuals** Examine the map on page 764. Which nations have significant oil resources?

Writing About History

8. **Descriptive Writing** Suppose that you are traveling in West Germany in 1989 when the Berlin Wall is being torn down. Write a letter to a friend at home to describe the event and how you think it will affect the United States.

History ONLINE

Study Central™ To review this section, go to glencoe.com and click on Study Central.

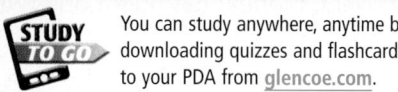

Causes of the New Conservatism

- The Cold War promotes strong foreign policy and an emphasis on minimal government interference in economics.
- Cold War fears of communism encourage many religious Americans to turn to conservative ideas.
- Many Americans are disturbed by the protests, demonstrations, and violence of the 1960s.
- The population growth in the Sunbelt increases support for conservative politicians.
- The rise of an evangelical movement willing to use politics to change society and defend its values helps mobilize conservative voters.
- Frustration with rising taxes and government regulation, especially in the South and West, turns many voters to conservative ideas.
- Both Western conservatives and Southern conservatives come to see the Republican Party as the more conservative party.

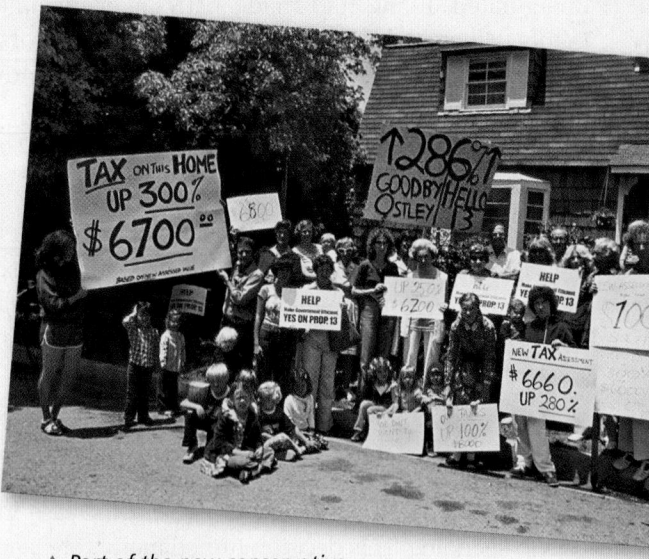

▲ Part of the new conservative movement drew support from Americans who were fed up with high taxes.

▲ The summit between President Reagan and Mikhail Gorbachev created an easing of tensions between the U.S. and Soviet Union.

The Reagan Administration

- Ronald Reagan is elected president in 1980 and 1984.
- Reagan promotes supply-side economics and pushes large tax cuts through Congress.
- Many industries are deregulated, helping spur a boom in the oil, transportation, and communications industries.
- A political debate over cutting government programs rather than expanding them shapes the domestic politics of the era.
- Reagan's administration takes a strong anti-Communist stance in Latin America, the Caribbean, and the Middle East, providing aid to groups that resist communism.
- The nation begins a sustained military buildup to put pressure on the Soviet economy; in addition the United States begins work on anti-missile "Star Wars" technology.
- The failure to cut domestic programs, combined with increased military spending, drives the growing budget deficit to record levels.
- Energy prices fall, the economy grows rapidly, and stock market values soar.
- The farm debt crisis and deregulation of the banks leads to the collapse of many family farms, and many savings and loan institutions.
- Under great economic stress, the Soviet Union introduces perestroika and glasnost; communism falls across Eastern Europe in 1989, and then the Soviet Union collapses in 1991.

Reviewing Vocabulary

Directions: Choose the word or words that best complete the sentence.

1. Political views held by _____ include the belief that the government should regulate the economy to protect people from the power of large corporations.

  A economists

  B liberals

  C conservatives

  D televangelists

2. Reagan based his policies on _____, a philosophy that advocates tax cuts to improve the economy.

  A monetarist economics

  B supply-and-demand economics

  C microeconomics

  D supply-side economics

3. A new business model known as _____ had a major impact on the economy starting in the 1980s.

  A superstations

  B wholesale retailing

  C discount retailing

  D direct mail

4. One part of Mikhail Gorbachev's plan to improve conditions in the Soviet Union was to allow _____, or increased freedom in speech, religion, and political discussion.

  A glasnost

  B perestroika

  C contra

  D rights of assembly

5. To combat the recession of the late 1980s, and searching for greater efficiency, many corporations began laying off employees, a process called

  A downsizing.

  B mass firing.

  C horizontal integration.

  D vertical integration.

Reviewing Main Ideas

Directions: Choose the best answer for each of the following questions.

Section 1 *(pp. 740–745)*

6. One main difference between liberals and conservatives is that, generally,

  A conservatives believe in government regulation of the economy, while liberals do not.

  B liberals believe in government regulation of the economy, while conservatives do not.

  C conservatives believe that all power should be held by the national government, while liberals do not.

  D liberals believe that all power should be held by the states, while conservatives do not.

7. Which of the following two groups had added their support to conservatives by the 1980s?

  A African Americans and urbanites

  B Northerners and Easterners

  C Democrats and women

  D Sunbelters and suburbanites

Section 2 *(pp. 746–753)*

8. Critics of Reagan's economic policy referred to it as "trickle-down economics" because they

  A believed that the plan would work, allowing wealth to "trickle down" to the middle and lower classes.

  B ridiculed the idea that much wealth would "trickle down" to the middle and lower classes.

  C believed that the plan was messy and would cause a great deal of wasteful government spending.

  D agreed that the richest people would share their wealth with the neediest in society.

TEST-TAKING

Read each answer choice and eliminate the ones that simply do not make sense for the given question.

Need Extra Help?

If You Missed Questions . . .	1	2	3	4	5	6	7	8
Go to Page . . .	740–742	748	755	762–763	766	740–742	743	748

9. The Strategic Defense Initiative (SDI) was proposed to strengthen defense by

  A preventing the expansion of Communist countries.

  B re-emphasizing the use of infantry troops in future wars.

  C developing weapons to intercept incoming missiles.

  D severely reducing the number of American troops stationed worldwide.

Section 3 (pp. 754–759)

10. Which technology became available during the 1980s?

  A the digital video recorder

  B the video cassette recorder

  C the personal digital assistant

  D the digital watch

11. A major focus of U.S. social activism in the 1980s was

  A gun control.

  B illiteracy.

  C drug abuse.

  D poverty.

Section 4 (pp. 762–767)

12. The result of the failed Communist coup in Moscow in August 1991 was that

  A Boris Yeltsin became president of the Soviet Union.

  B the Soviet republics declared independence.

  C the Berlin Wall was taken down by bulldozers.

  D the United States sent troops into Saudi Arabia.

13. In response to events in Tiananmen Square in China, the United States and other nations

  A sent weapons and money to the rebels.

  B halted arms sales and reduced their diplomatic contacts with China.

  C made plans for a summit meeting with China to express their concerns.

  D sent in troops to help free the imprisoned protesters.

Critical Thinking

Directions: Choose the best answers to the following questions.

14. The religious right joined the conservative movement because they

  A were concerned about American values and morality.

  B wanted more liberal social welfare programs.

  C felt that the U.S. had been too aggressive with the U.S.S.R.

  D wanted government regulation of local churches.

15. The huge number of baby boomers affected the economy of the 1980s because they

  A were driven to acquire material goods and social success.

  B pushed for increased government spending for the poor.

  C rejected worldly success as members of the Moral Majority.

  D were beginning to draw Social Security benefits.

Base your answer to question 16 on the graph below and your knowledge of Chapter 22.

Military Spending and the Deficit

Legend: Federal Debt; Total Federal Expenses; National Defense

Y-axis: In Hundreds of Billions of Dollars

X-axis: 1980–1992

Sources: Departments of Commerce and Treasury; Office of Management and Budget.

16. How much money was spent on national defense in 1986?

  A approximately 500 billion dollars

  B more than 500 billion dollars

  C approximately 250 billion dollars

  D less than 250 million dollars

Need Extra Help?

If You Missed Questions ...	9	10	11	12	13	14	15	16
Go to Page ...	753	757	758–759	763–764	764–765	744–745	754	R16

GO ON

17. The beginning of the collapse of communism in Eastern Europe is most closely associated with the

A fall of the Berlin Wall.

B admission of Warsaw Pact nations to the North Atlantic Treaty Organization (NATO).

C intervention of the North Atlantic Treaty Organization (NATO) in Yugoslavia.

D formation of the European Union.

Analyze the cartoon and answer the question that follows. Base your answer on the cartoon and on your knowledge of Chapter 22.

'I CAN'T BELIEVE MY EYES!'

18. What is the cartoonist saying about Gorbachev's policies?

A Marx, Lenin, and Stalin would approve of his policies of glasnost and perestroika.

B Marx, Lenin, and Stalin would disapprove of restructuring the Soviet economy and allowing some private enterprise.

C Marx, Lenin, and Stalin would approve of glasnost, or allowing more freedom of religion and speech.

D Marx, Lenin, and Stalin would disapprove of the expansion of communism to Eastern Europe.

Document-Based Questions

Directions: Analyze the document and answer the short-answer questions that follow the document.

President Ronald Reagan addressed the American people at the end of his presidency in 1988. The following is an excerpt from that address:

> The way I see it, there were two great triumphs, two things that I'm proudest of. One is the economic recovery, in which the people of America created—and filled—19 million new jobs. The other is the recovery of our morale. America is respected again. . . .
>
> Common sense told us that when you put a big tax on something, the people will produce less of it. So, we cut the people's tax rates, and the people produced more than ever before. The economy bloomed. . . . Common sense told us that to preserve the peace, we'd have to become strong again after years of weakness and confusion. So, we rebuilt our defenses, and this New Year we toasted the new peacefulness around the globe. . . .
>
> —from *Speaking My Mind*

19. What did Reagan believe were his greatest accomplishments?

20. How did Reagan feel his administration preserved peace?

Extended Response

21. In the late 1980s, the Cold War came to an end with the disintegration of the Warsaw Pact, the fall of the Berlin Wall, and the collapse of the Soviet Union. In an expository essay trace the events that led to the end of this global conflict and explain why you think the conflict ended when it did. In your essay, include an introduction, a conclusion, and at least three paragraphs with details from the chapter.

History ONLINE

For additional test practice, use Self-Check Quizzes—Chapter 22 at glencoe.com.

Need Extra Help?					
If You Missed Questions . . .	17	18	19	20	21
Go to Page . . .	763	R18	771	R19	762–767

A Time of Change

1980–2000

President Bill Clinton looks over the new White House Web site on July 8, 2000

1984
- Apple's Macintosh introduces the mouse and on-screen icons

1981
- IBM introduces their version of the PC or Personal Computer

1986
- Immigration Control and Reform Act passed

1991
- U.S. and other nations liberate Kuwait from Iraqi occupation

G. Bush
1989–1993

U.S. PRESIDENTS

U.S. EVENTS

WORLD EVENTS

| 1980 | 1982 | 1984 | 1986 | 1988 | 1990 | 1992 |

1980
- Lech Walesa organizes trade union Solidarity in Poland

1987
- Soviet Union and United States sign INF Treaty

1989
- The Berlin Wall falls

1990
- The World Wide Web is developed in Switzerland.

MAKING CONNECTIONS
How Has Technology Changed Society?

In the late twentieth century, the development of new technology, including personal computers, mobile phones, and the Internet, revolutionized the way people lived.

- *What other eras in American history experienced rapid technological change?*

- *Has the computer revolution changed society for the better? Why or why not?*

THE WHITE HOUSE

FOLDABLES™

Identifying Technological Changes
Research how computers have changed the way Americans live. Organize the information you learn in a Layered-Look Book Foldable by the following categories: business, communications, and entertainment. Describe how computers are applied in each field and how they have changed the way people live.

The Computer Revolution
Business
Communications
Entertainment

1993
- Mosaic, the first popular Web browser, is released

Clinton
1993–2001

1994
- U.S., Mexico, and Canada found NAFTA

1998
- House of Representatives impeaches President Clinton

1999
- Senate acquits Clinton

G. W. Bush
2001–2009

1994   1996   1998   2000

1993
- Israeli-Palestinian peace accord signed

1995
- Cease-fire signed in Bosnian war

1997
- Britain returns Hong Kong to China

History ONLINE Visit glencoe.com and enter *QuickPass*™ code TAVMT5147c23 for Chapter 23 resources.

The Technological Revolution

Guide to Reading

Big Ideas
Computers, Telecommunications, and the Internet The introduction of the first electronic digital computer in 1946 launched a technological revolution.

Content Vocabulary
- integrated circuit *(p. 774)*
- microprocessor *(p. 774)*
- telecommute *(p. 775)*
- blogs *(p. 777)*

Academic Vocabulary
- device *(p. 774)*
- refinement *(p. 775)*
- communications *(p. 776)*

People and Events to Identify
- ENIAC *(p. 774)*
- Silicon Valley *(p. 774)*
- Steve Jobs *(p. 774)*
- Bill Gates *(p. 775)*

Reading Strategy
Categorizing As you read about the computer age, complete a chart similar to the one below to describe products that revolutionized the computer industry.

	How It Revolutionized Computer Industry
Microprocessors	
Apple II	
Macintosh	
Windows	

The computers we use today bear little resemblance to the first electronic computers that were built in the 1940s. Since the 1980s, computer technology has advanced dramatically, with the creation of home computers and then the expansion of the Internet.

The Computer Changes Society

MAIN Idea A computer revolution changed the workplace and the way people communicate.

HISTORY AND YOU What computer devices do you use regularly? Read on to learn about the earliest electronic computers.

The development of electronic computers began at the end of World War II. The world's first electronic digital computer, called **ENIAC** (Electronic Numerical Integrator and Computer), went into operation in February 1946. ENIAC weighed over 30 tons and was the size of a small house. In early 1959, Robert Noyce designed the first **integrated circuit**—a complete electronic circuit on a single chip of silicon—which made circuits much smaller and very easy to manufacture. Noyce's company was located south of San Francisco. As new companies sprang up nearby to make products using integrated circuits, the region became known as **Silicon Valley.**

In 1968 Noyce and colleague Gordon Moore formed Intel, for "Integrated Electronics," a company that revolutionized the computer industry by combining on a single chip several integrated circuits containing both memory and computing functions. Called **microprocessors,** these new chips made computers much faster and smaller.

Computers for Everyone

Using microprocessor technology, Stephen Wozniak and his 20-year-old friend **Steve Jobs** set out to build a small computer suitable for personal use. In 1976 they founded Apple Computer and completed the Apple I. The following year they introduced the Apple II, the first practical and affordable home computer.

Apple's success sparked intense competition in the computer industry. In 1981 International Business Machines (IBM) introduced its own compact machine, which it called the "Personal Computer" (PC). Apple responded in 1984 with the revolutionary Macintosh, a new model featuring a simplified operating system using on-screen graphic symbols called icons, which users could manipulate with a hand-operated **device** called a mouse.

Computers Beginning in the late 1970s and continuing to the present, changes in computer and telecommunications technology have transformed how people live and work.

▲ Integrated Circuit

The integrated circuit allowed literally millions of tiny circuits to be mass produced and for manufacturers to greatly reduce the size of computer-based products.

◀ Mobile Phone

Microprocessors and digital technology made small mobile phones (cell phones) possible. Improvements in light metals and plastics manufacturing made cell phones and other computerized devices portable. Combined with wireless access to the Internet, the cell phone allows people to stay in communication and to view videos, text messages, and photos no matter where they are.

Personal Computer ▶

The Apple Macintosh introduced in 1984 was the first mass-produced personal computer to use a mouse and on-screen icons to help users interact with the software. The new interface made computers far easier to use and encouraged Americans who were not technically trained to begin using computers. The first mouse (shown above) was invented by Douglas Englebart in 1964.

Analyzing VISUALS

1. **Explaining** What aspects of life do computer-based devices make easier?
2. **Inferring** Why do you think it was important for integrated circuits to be so small?

As Jobs and Wozniak were creating Apple, 19-year-old Harvard dropout **Bill Gates** co-founded Microsoft to design PC software, the instructions used to program computers to perform desired tasks. In 1980 IBM hired Microsoft to develop an operating system for its new PC. Gates paid a Seattle programmer $50,000 for the rights to his software, and with some **refinements,** it became MS-DOS (Microsoft Disk Operating System). In 1985 Microsoft introduced the "Windows" operating system, which enabled PCs to use mouse-activated, on-screen graphic icons.

Compact computers soon transformed the workplace, linking employees within an office or among office branches. They became essential tools in almost all businesses. By the late 1990s, workers used home computers and electronic mail (E-mail) to **"telecommute,"** or do their jobs from home via computer.

New Telecommunications

A parallel revolution in telecommunications coincided with the development of personal computers. In the 1970s, the government started deregulating the telecommunications industry. Then, in 1996 Congress passed the Telecommunications Act, which allowed phone companies to compete with each other and to send television signals. It also allowed cable television companies to offer telephone service. This led to much greater competition, and many new technologies were developed.

One major telecommunications technology that became very popular was the cell phone. Cell phones had been invented in the 1940s, and the first large-scale cellular networks were built in the 1980s, but the phones were large and the service was very expensive. All that began to change in the 1990s.

Wireless digital technology made it possible to miniaturize cell phones, and they quickly became very popular. By the early 2000s, they were in widespread use around the world. Wireless digital technology also made it possible to manufacture small inexpensive satellite dishes that could receive video and radio beamed from orbit into people's homes.

Digital technology rapidly transformed many consumer products. Various companies developed music players, cameras, radios, televisions, and music and video recorders that used digital technology. Because they were digital and relied on computer chips, it became possible to connect them to each other and to computers. Modern cell phones, for example, often have digital cameras built in, and can send and receive E-mail and instant text messages. Computers can play the same videos that can be played on digital television. Further accelerating the interoperability and connections between the technologies was the rise of a global network of interconnected computers that came to be called the Internet.

Reading Check **Describing** How did digital technology change consumer products?

The Rise of the Internet

MAIN Idea A computer resource that linked government agencies developed into the Internet.

HISTORY AND YOU Have you ever used the Internet to do research for a class? Read on to learn about the origins of the Internet.

In 1969 the U.S. Defense Department's Advanced Research Project Agency created a system of networked computers known as ARPANET. The system linked computers at government agencies, defense contractors, and several universities, enabling them to communicate with one another.

In 1986 the National Science Foundation built NSFNet, a network connecting several super computer centers across the country. NSFNet was soon linked to ARPANET, and as the connections to other computer networks across the world grew, the system became known as the Internet. The Internet is not the World Wide Web or E-mail. Those are systems that use the Internet. The Internet is the physical network of computers connected together by phone lines, cable lines, and wireless **communications.**

PRIMARY SOURCE
The Rise of the Internet

As the Internet grew in size and people obtained access to faster computers and faster "broadband" connections, people began to use it for almost everything.

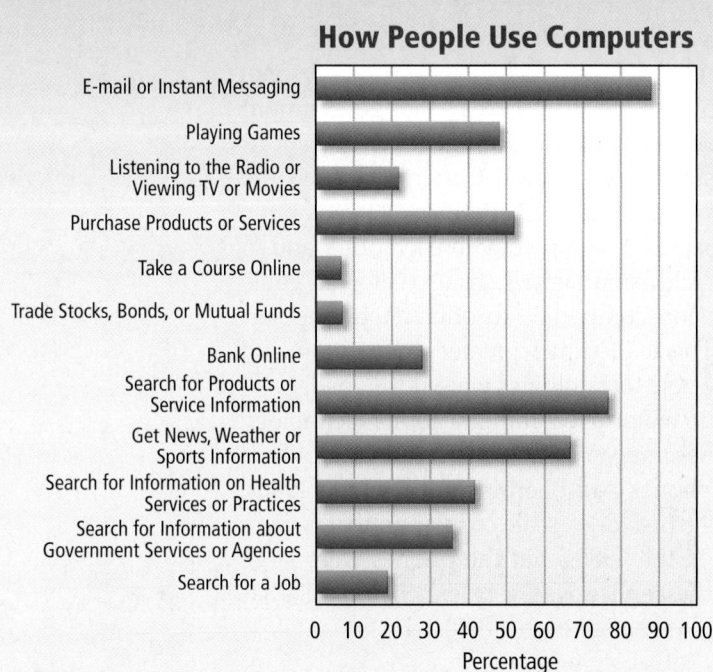

How People Use Computers

- E-mail or Instant Messaging
- Playing Games
- Listening to the Radio or Viewing TV or Movies
- Purchase Products or Services
- Take a Course Online
- Trade Stocks, Bonds, or Mutual Funds
- Bank Online
- Search for Products or Service Information
- Get News, Weather or Sports Information
- Search for Information on Health Services or Practices
- Search for Information about Government Services or Agencies
- Search for a Job

0 10 20 30 40 50 60 70 80 90 100
Percentage

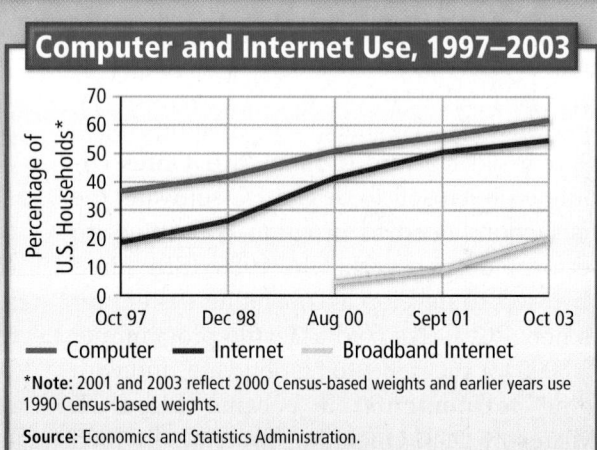

Computer and Internet Use, 1997–2003

Percentage of U.S. Households*

Oct 97 — Dec 98 — Aug 00 — Sept 01 — Oct 03

— Computer — Internet — Broadband Internet

*Note: 2001 and 2003 reflect 2000 Census-based weights and earlier years use 1990 Census-based weights.

Source: Economics and Statistics Administration.

Analyzing VISUALS

1. **Classifying** Which category of activities is the Internet used for the most?

2. **Hypothesizing** Is the growth in the use of the internet slowing or accelerating? Why might this be so?

As personal computers became cheaper and more widely available, more and more people began signing up with Internet Service Providers (ISPs) who could connect their computers to the Internet. By the late 1990s, the Internet had become wildly popular as businesses began experimenting with it to sell goods and services and to improve their productivity and communications. By 2007, more than 1 billion people were regularly using the Internet.

Birth of the World Wide Web

In 1990, researchers at CERN, a physics laboratory in Switzerland, developed a new way to present information on computers linked to the Internet. Known as the World Wide Web, this system used hypertext (what today are referred to as "links" on Web pages) and could be accessed with software known as a Web browser. The system allowed users to post information in the form of Web pages and click on links to jump from Web site to Web site.

Enthusiasm for the World Wide Web spawned a "dot-com" economy. A wide variety of dot-com companies made millions of dollars for stock investors without making any actual profits. Internet-related stocks helped fuel the prosperity of the 1990s, but fell dramatically in 2000 when many unprofitable online companies went out of business. Though the dot-com economy did not last, the computerization of the economy required the American labor force to acquire new skills. This retraining increased productivity as well as the nation's Gross Domestic Product (GDP), the total value of goods and services produced by the domestic economy. The GDP during the mid- to late-1990s rose over twenty percent. This increase was driven by the information technology industry, which includes computer and Internet router manufacturers.

A few companies have, however, become major success stories. Amazon.com, founded by Jeff Bezos, has become a highly successful online bookseller. The companies Google and Yahoo both created search engines that help people locate information on the Web. Many media companies have also found success on the Web in the same way that they did in print and on television —by charging fees for advertising.

The Internet Changes Society

For many people, the World Wide Web has become a way to build a sense of community. People with common interests visit Web sites about those interests to post comments and interact with each other.

Individuals and families share stories and photos about themselves on **blogs**—short for Web logs—Web sites that function as a kind of public diary or notebook. Web sites such as MySpace serve a similar function, while sites such as YouTube enable people to post video clips they want to share with others. Blogs have also led to a renaissance in essay writing and commentary as they enable people to publicly comment on news stories and other events. They have also helped mobilize people for political action. For many, accessing the Web has become a routine and important part of their daily life.

Reading Check **Analyzing** How have the Internet and World Wide Web changed society?

Section 1 REVIEW

Vocabulary

1. **Explain** the significance of: ENIAC, integrated circuit, Silicon Valley, microprocessor, Steve Jobs, Bill Gates, telecommute, blogs.

Main Ideas

2. **Describing** How have personal computers transformed the workplace?

3. **Contrasting** What is the difference between the World Wide Web and the Internet?

Critical Thinking

4. **Big Ideas** How have advances in telecommunications and the rise of the Internet affected the standard of living in the United States?

5. **Organizing** Complete a graphic organizer similar to the one below by listing developments that led to the technological revolution.

Technological Revolution

6. **Analyzing Visuals** Study the photograph of the Apple Computer on page 775. How have computers changed since the 1980s?

Writing About History

7. **Descriptive Writing** Write two paragraphs describing the ways that you and your family use the Internet and how your way of life would be different without it.

History ONLINE

Study Central™ To review this section, go to glencoe.com and click on Study Central.

KIM KOMENICH/GETTY IMAGES

American Notes

In 1985, **RYAN WHITE** *became a symbol of the intolerance that is inflicted on some people suffering from HIV/AIDS.*

Ryan White was 13 years old when he learned that he had contracted HIV through blood products he was taking for hemophilia, a disease he had since birth. At the time, many people thought the AIDS virus could be passed by casual contact—by shaking hands, sneezing, or coughing. Even though AIDS can't be caught that way, people in Ryan's school in Kokomo, Indiana, were afraid to be near him. School officials banned him from classes, and Ryan had to fight in court to win the right to attend school.

In 1987, his family moved to another Indiana town, Cicero, where he was treated more kindly. Ryan died on April 8, 1990. At his funeral, a family friend, Rev. Ray Probasco, said: "It was Ryan who first humanized the disease called AIDS. He allowed us to see the boy who just wanted, more than anything else, to be like other children and to be able to go to school."

VERBATIM

"Just say no."

—NANCY REAGAN,
in 1983, launching her antidrug campaign

"Show me the money!"

—ACTOR CUBA GOODING, JR.'S CHARACTER,
in the 1996 movie Jerry Maguire

"Mr. Gorbachev, tear down this wall!"

—PRESIDENT RONALD REAGAN,
in 1987 addressing the head of the USSR while standing next to the Berlin Wall, which still divided East and West Berlin.

"Can we all get along?"

—RODNEY KING,
pleading in 1992 with the rioters in Los Angeles and other cities, after violence erupted following a jury's acquittal of the police officer who had beaten him.

"We are the world."

—FORTY-FIVE POP STARS,
including Lionel Richie, Ray Charles, and Bruce Springsteen, known as USA for Africa. The group recorded the song "We Are the World" in 1985 to raise money for Africans in need.

"I do not like broccoli. And I haven't liked it since I was a little kid and my mother made me eat it. And I'm President of the United States and I'm not going to eat any more broccoli."

—PRESIDENT GEORGE H. W. BUSH,
1990

FIRSTS IN TECH
Important Dates in the Technology Revolution

1981
Columbia makes the first space shuttle flight

NASA

1982
First use of emoticons in an e-mail:

:-)

and

:-(

1983
Music CDs go on sale in the United States

The first American cell phone system goes into operation

1984
Apple Macintosh computer is released

Steve Jobs presents the first Macintosh computer

AP PHOTO/PAUL SAKUMA

1985
Nintendo Entertainment System comes to America

1991
World Wide Web is created by Tim Berners-Lee of Great Britain

1995
Release of first DVDs (digital video disks)

1997
Dolly the sheep is the first animal made by cloning adult cells

NAJLAH FEANNY/CORBIS

Time Capsule

In 1992, TIME *magazine ran a short story, "Things to Show How We Live Now," as a way to highlight what was important to the public at the time. Here are 15 items from the list. How do they compare with what you think is important?*

REMOTE CONTROL

GARTH BROOKS CD

8-MM CAMCORDER

CASH-MACHINE CARD

INFLATABLE GLOBE

DISPOSABLE CAMERA

DOLPHIN-SAFE TUNA

BAGGY JEANS

PALMTOP COMPUTER

SPF 15 SUNSCREEN

POCKET T-SHIRT

BOTTLED WATER FROM THE ALPS

IN-LINE SKATES

AIR BAG

BEEPER

JAMES KEYSER/GETTY IMAGES

Milestones

LOST, 1986. THE SPACE SHUTTLE *CHALLENGER* exploded 73 seconds after liftoff. Millions watched in horror as the 25th shuttle mission blew up, killing all seven crew members, including high school teacher Christa McAuliffe.

RECONCILED, 1992. U.S. PRESIDENT GEORGE H.W. BUSH AND RUSSIAN PRESIDENT BORIS YELTSIN formally declared an end to the Cold War.

RELEASED, 1981. FIFTY-TWO U.S. HOSTAGES IN IRAN were set free after 444 days in captivity. The crisis played a significant part in Jimmy Carter's failure to win a second presidential term.

AIRED, 1981. FORMER RADIO EXECUTIVES CREATED MTV (MUSIC TELEVISION). They knew that advertisers wanted to reach young people, who loved rock music. So they decided to run music videos on a cable channel.

ERUPTED, 1980. MOUNT ST. HELENS IN WASHINGTON STATE erupted after being dormant for 123 years. A stupendous explosion blew the entire top off the volcano.

NAMED, 1981. SANDRA DAY O'CONNOR became the first female justice on the U.S. Supreme Court after being appointed to the position by President Ronald Reagan.

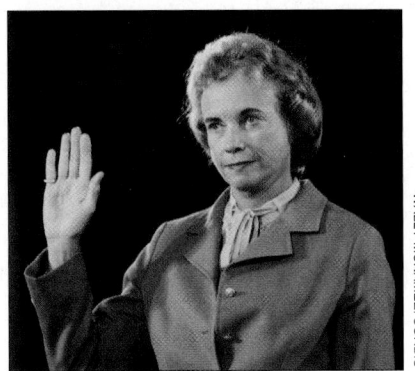

WALLY MCNAMEE/CORBIS

Justice Sandra Day O'Connor

HONORED, 1995. BALTIMORE ORIOLES SHORTSTOP CAL RIPKEN, JR. became a national hero just by going to work every day for 13 years. On September 6, 1995, Ripken showed up at his 2,131st game in a row, breaking the 1939 record set by Lou Gehrig.

NUMBERS

168 Number of people killed in the 1995 bombing of Oklahoma City's Federal Building by two Americans, Terry Nichols and Timothy McVeigh

12 Age of Valerie Ambrose, who won a NASA contest in 1997 by coming up with "Sojourner Truth" as the name for a robot explorer to Mars

11,000,000 Number of gallons of crude oil spilled into Prince William Sound by the tanker *Exxon Valdez* in 1989

NATALIE FOBES/CORBIS

An oil-soaked whale after the Exxon Valdez *spill*

20,000,000 Number of albums Michael Jackson's *Thriller* sold, making it the best-selling record of all time as of 1982

Forever Amount of time former player Pete Rose was banned from baseball after the discovery in 1989 that he was gambling on baseball games

CRITICAL THINKING

1. *Synthesizing* Do you think people's attitudes have changed towards people with HIV/AIDS since 1985? Explain your answer.

2. *Hypothesizing* Why might celebrities be better able than the "average" citizen to focus public attention on serious global issues and problems?

The Clinton Years

Guide to Reading

Big Ideas
Government and Society President Clinton pushed through laws to help families and strengthen gun control, but he also raised taxes and failed to reform health care.

Content Vocabulary
- perjury (p. 785)
- ethnic cleansing (p. 787)

Academic Vocabulary
- modify (p. 781)
- unprecedented (p. 781)
- participant (p. 787)

People and Events to Identify
- AmeriCorps (p. 782)
- Contract with America (p. 783)
- Kenneth Starr (p. 785)
- Dayton Accords (p. 787)

Reading Strategy
Taking Notes As you read about the administration of President Clinton, use the major headings of the section to create an outline similar to the one below.

> **The Clinton Years**
> I. Clinton's Agenda
>   A.
>   B.
>   C.
>   D.
> II.

When William Jefferson Clinton was elected in 1992, he became the first Democrat to win the presidency in 12 years. After achieving only part of his agenda, he faced a new Republican Congress that had very different plans. His second term focused on foreign policy and scandal.

Clinton's Agenda

MAIN Idea President Clinton took office in 1993 with plans for improving health care, cutting the federal deficit, aiding families, and increasing gun control.

HISTORY AND YOU Do you know anyone who has worked for AmeriCorps? Read on to learn about the beginnings of this program.

Only 46 years old when he took office, Bill Clinton was the third-youngest person ever to serve as president and the first of the "baby boom" generation to reach the Oval Office. The new president put forth an ambitious domestic program focusing on five major areas: the economy, the family, education, crime, and health care.

Raising Taxes, Cutting Spending

As he had promised in his election campaign, Clinton focused first on the economy. The problem, in his view, was the federal deficit. Under Reagan and Bush, the deficit had nearly quadrupled, adding billions of dollars annually to the national debt. High deficits forced the government to borrow large sums of money, which helped to drive up interest rates. Clinton believed that the key to economic growth was to lower interest rates. Low interest rates would enable businesses to borrow more money to expand and create more jobs. Low rates would also make it easier for consumers to borrow money for mortgages, car loans, and other items, which in turn would promote economic growth.

One way to bring interest rates down was to reduce the federal deficit. In early 1993, Clinton sent Congress a deficit reduction plan. In trying to cut the deficit, however, Clinton faced a serious problem. About half of all government spending went to entitlement programs, such as Social Security, Medicare, and veterans' benefits. These programs are hard to cut because so many Americans depend on them. Faced with these constraints, Clinton decided to raise taxes, even though he had promised to cut them during his campaign. Clinton proposed raising tax rates for middle- and upper-income Americans and placed new taxes on gasoline, heating oil, and natural

The Debate Over Health Care

During his first term in office, President Clinton launched an ambitious program to reform the nation's health care system. The reforms faced much opposition and never materialized.

▲ President Clinton explains the proposed Health Security card in a speech to Congress in October 1993.

THE ACCIDENT

THE PAIN

THE EMBARRASSMENT

THE REHABILITATION

THE RECOVERY

THE RETURN TO THE SCENE OF THE ACCIDENT AND THE LESSON LEARNED.

I WILL BE SUPER CAUTIOUS FOR THE REST OF MY ADMINISTRATION.

HEALTH CARE REFORM

FOUND OUT YOU WEREN'T INSURED?

▲ The cartoonist shows President Clinton resolving to be very cautious throughout the rest of his administration.

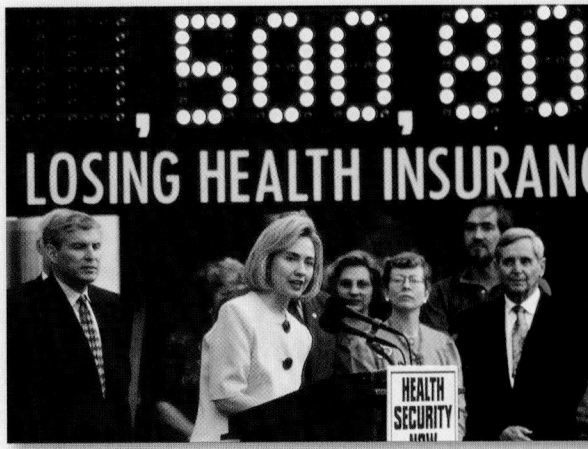

▲ Hillary Clinton speaks about her health care plan in front of a counter showing one person losing health insurance every 1.17 seconds.

Analyzing VISUALS DBQ

1. **Inferring** How does the cartoonist compare Clinton's failed attempt to change health care to an accident?

2. **Analyzing** Why does Clinton resolve to be cautious in the future?

gas. The tax increases were very unpopular, and Republicans in Congress refused to support them. Clinton pressured Democrats, and after many amendments, a **modified** version of Clinton's plan narrowly passed.

Stumbling on Health Care

During his campaign, Clinton had promised to reform the health care system. Some 40 million Americans, or roughly 15 percent of the nation, did not have health insurance. The president created a task force and appointed his wife, Hillary Rodham Clinton, to head it—an **unprecedented** role for a first lady. The

task force developed a plan to guarantee health benefits for all Americans, but it put much of the burden of paying for the benefits on employers. Small-business owners feared they could not afford it. The insurance industry and doctors' organizations also opposed the plan and mounted a nationwide advertising campaign on television and radio to build public opposition to the plan.

Republicans argued that the plan was too complicated, costly, and relied too much on government control. Democrats were divided. Some supported alternative plans, but no plan had enough support to pass. Faced with public opposition, Clinton's plan died without a vote.

Families and Education

Clinton did manage to push several major pieces of legislation through Congress. During his campaign, he had stressed the need to help American families. His first success was the Family Medical Leave Act. This law gave workers up to 12 weeks per year of unpaid family leave for the birth or adoption of a child or for the illness of a family member.

Clinton also persuaded Congress to create the **AmeriCorps** program. This program put students to work improving low-income housing, teaching children to read, and cleaning up the environment. AmeriCorps incorporated the VISTA program that John F. Kennedy had created. AmeriCorps volunteers earn a salary and are awarded a scholarship to continue their education. In September 1994, the first group of AmeriCorps volunteers—some 20,000 in number—began serving in more than 1,000 communities.

Crime and Gun Control

Clinton had also promised to get tough on crime during his campaign, and he strongly endorsed new gun-control laws. Despite strong opposition from many Republicans and the National Rifle Association (NRA), the Democrats in Congress passed a gun-control law known as the Brady Bill. It was named after James Brady, President Reagan's press secretary who had been severely injured by a gunshot during the assassination attempt on the former president. His wife, Sarah Brady, became an advocate of gun control and lobbied Congress to pass the bill. The Brady Handgun Violence Prevention Act imposed a waiting period before people could buy handguns. It also required gun dealers to have police run a background check for a criminal record before selling someone a handgun.

The following year, Clinton introduced another crime bill. The bill provided extra funds for states to build new prisons, and put 100,000 more police officers on the streets. It banned 19 kinds of assault weapons and provided money for crime prevention programs, such as "midnight" basketball leagues that would get young people off the streets.

✓ Reading Check **Explaining** Why did President Clinton's proposed health care plan fail?

Republicans Gain Control of Congress

MAIN Idea Republican victories in Congress led to conflicts between the executive and legislative branches of the federal government.

HISTORY AND YOU Have you ever refused to back down when you felt sure you were in the right? Read on to learn about a showdown between Congress and the president.

Despite his successes, Clinton was very unpopular by late 1994. He had raised taxes, instead of lowering them as he had promised, and he had failed to fix health care. Although the economy was improving, many companies were still downsizing. Several personal issues involving President Clinton further weakened

Debates IN HISTORY

Is a Balanced Budget Amendment a Good Idea?

One of the ideas that congressional Republicans put forth in the "Contract with America" was a balanced budget amendment to the Constitution. A balanced budget amendment would force Congress to pass a federal budget that balanced projected revenues and expenditures. Would such an amendment force Congress to be more responsible in how it spends the taxpayers' money, resulting in a more efficient, limited government? Or, would it dangerously limit Congress's ability to respond to economic and national security emergencies?

public confidence in him. In response, many Americans decided to vote Republican in 1994.

The Contract With America

As the 1994 midterm elections neared, congressional Republicans, led by Newt Gingrich of Georgia, created the **Contract with America.** This program proposed 10 major changes, including lower taxes, welfare reform, tougher anticrime laws, term limits for members of Congress, and a balanced budget amendment. Republicans won a stunning victory—for the first time in 40 years, they had a majority in both houses of Congress.

In their first 100 days in office, House Republicans passed almost the entire Contract with America, but they soon ran into trouble. The Senate defeated several proposals, while the president vetoed others.

The Budget Battle

In 1995 the Republicans clashed with the president over the new federal budget. Clinton vetoed several Republican budget proposals, claiming they cut into social programs too much. Gingrich believed that if Republicans stood firm, the president would back down and approve the budget. Otherwise, the entire federal government would shut down for lack of funds. Clinton, however, refused to budge, and allowed the federal government to close.

By standing firm against Republican budget proposals and allowing the government to shut down, Clinton regained much of the support he had lost in 1994. The Republicans in Congress realized they needed to work with the president to pass legislation. Soon afterward, they reached an agreement with Clinton to balance the budget.

YES

Strom Thurmond
U.S. Senator

PRIMARY SOURCE

"While Congress could achieve a balanced budget by statute, past efforts . . . have failed. It is simply too easy for Congress to change its mind. . . . The constitutional amendment is unyielding in its imposition of discipline on Congress to make the tough decisions necessary to balance the federal budget. Over the past half-century, Congress has demonstrated a total lack of fiscal discipline evidenced by an irrational and irresponsible pattern of spending. This reckless approach has seriously jeopardized the Federal government and threatens the very future of this Nation. As a result, I believe we must look to constitutional protection from a firmly entrenched fiscal policy which threatens the liberties and opportunities of our present and future citizens."

—Statement to the Judiciary Committee, February 16, 1994

NO

Bill Clinton
President

PRIMARY SOURCE

"The balanced budget amendment is, in the first place, bad economics. . . . [T]he Federal deficit depends not just on Congressional decisions, but also on the state of the economy. In particular, the deficit increases automatically whenever the economy weakens. If we try to break this automatic linkage by a Constitutional amendment, we will have to raise taxes and cut expenditures whenever the economy is weak. That not only risks turning minor downturns into serious recessions, but would make recovery from recession far more difficult. Let's be clear: This is not a matter of abstract economic theory. . . . A balanced budget amendment could threaten the livelihoods of millions of Americans. I cannot put them in such peril."

—Letter to Congressional leaders, November 5, 1993

DBQ Document-Based Questions

1. **Finding the Main Idea** Why does Senator Thurmond believe that a constitutional amendment, rather than simply a law, is necessary?

2. **Theorizing** How might Congress's "irresponsible pattern of spending" threaten the nation's future?

3. **Specifying** What specific reasons does President Clinton give to explain his opposition to the balanced budget amendment?

4. **Drawing Conclusions** Which argument do you find more convincing? Why?

In the months before the 1996 election, the president and the Republicans worked together to pass new legislation. In August Congress passed the Health Insurance Portability Act. This act improved health coverage for people who changed jobs and reduced discrimination against people who had pre-existing illnesses.

Later that month, Congress passed the Welfare Reform Act, which limited people to no more than two consecutive years on welfare and required them to work to receive welfare benefits. The law also increased child-care spending and gave tax breaks to companies that hired new employees who had been on welfare.

Clinton Wins Reelection

As the 1996 campaign began, Clinton took credit for the economy. The economic boom of the 1990s was the longest sustained period of growth in American history. Unemployment and inflation fell to their lowest levels in 40 years. The stock market soared, wages rose, crime rates fell, and the number of people on welfare declined. With the economy booming, Clinton's popularity climbed rapidly.

The Republican Party nominated Senator Bob Dole of Kansas, the Republican leader in the Senate, to run against Clinton. Dole chose as his running mate Jack Kemp, a former member of Congress from New York. Dole promised a 15 percent tax cut and attempted to portray Clinton as a tax-and-spend liberal.

H. Ross Perot also ran again as a candidate as he had in the 1992 election. This time he ran as the candidate of the Reform Party, which he had created. Once again Perot made the deficit the main campaign issue.

President Clinton won reelection, winning a little more than 49 percent of the popular vote and 379 electoral votes. Dole received almost 41 percent and 159 electoral votes, and Perot won about 8.4 percent of the popular vote and no electoral votes. Despite Clinton's victory, Republicans retained control of Congress. Two years later, after the 1998 elections, Republicans kept control of Congress, although the Democrats gained 5 seats in the House of Representatives.

Reading Check **Identifying** What two reforms did Clinton and Congress agree to support?

Clinton's Second Term

MAIN Idea Clinton tried to focus the domestic agenda on the needs of children, but personal problems marred his second term.

HISTORY AND YOU Do you remember learning about the impeachment trial of Andrew Johnson? Read on to learn about the second president ever to be impeached.

During Clinton's second term, the economy continued its expansion. As people's incomes rose, so too did the amount of taxes they paid to all levels of government. At the same time, despite their differences, the president and Congress continued to shrink the deficit. In 1997, for the first time in 24 years, the president was able to submit a balanced budget to Congress. Beginning in 1998, the government began to run a surplus—that is, it collected more money than it spent.

Despite these achievements, Clinton's domestic agenda was less aggressive in his second term. Much of his time was spent on foreign policy and in struggling against a personal scandal.

Putting Children First

During his second term, Clinton's domestic agenda shifted toward helping the nation's children. He began by asking Congress to pass a $500 per child tax credit. He also signed the Adoption and Safe Families Act and asked Congress to ban cigarette advertising aimed at children. In August 1997, Clinton signed the Children's Health Insurance Program—a plan to provide health insurance for children whose parents could not afford it.

Clinton also continued his efforts to help American students. "I come from a family where nobody had ever gone to college before," Clinton said. "When I became president, I was determined to do what I could to give every student that chance." To help students, he asked for a tax credit, a large increase in student grants, and an expansion of the Head Start program for disadvantaged preschoolers.

Clinton Is Impeached

The robust economy and his high standing in the polls allowed Clinton to regain the initiative in dealing with Congress. By 1998, how-

Impeaching a President

The Constitution gives Congress the power to remove the president from office "upon impeachment for and conviction of, treason, bribery, or other high crimes and misdemeanors." The House of Representatives has the sole power over impeachment—the formal accusation of wrongdoing in office. If the majority of the House votes to impeach the president, the Senate conducts a trial. A two-thirds vote of those present is needed for conviction. If the president is being impeached, the chief justice of the United States presides.

▲ House Judiciary Committee Chairman, Representative Henry Hyde, stands surrounded by boxes of evidence against President Clinton.

▲ Chief Justice Rehnquist is sworn in for the impeachment trial of President Clinton in the Senate.

Analyzing VISUALS

1. **Hypothesizing** Why do you think the Founders required the House to impeach the president but the Senate to hold the trial?

2. **Theorizing** Why might impeachment only require a majority vote in the House, but conviction requires a two-thirds vote in the Senate?

ever, he had become entangled in a serious scandal that threatened to undermine his presidency.

The scandal began in Clinton's first term, when he was accused of arranging illegal loans for Whitewater Development—an Arkansas real estate company—while he was governor of that state. Attorney General Janet Reno decided that an independent counsel should investigate the president. A special three-judge panel appointed **Kenneth Starr,** a former federal judge, to this position.

In early 1998, a new scandal emerged involving a personal relationship between the president and a White House intern. Some evidence suggested that the president had committed **perjury,** or had lied under oath, about the relationship. The three-judge panel directed Starr to investigate this scandal as well. In September 1998, after examining the evidence, Starr sent his report to the Judiciary Committee of the House of Representatives. Starr argued

that Clinton had obstructed justice, abused his power as president, and committed perjury.

After the 1998 elections, the House began impeachment hearings. Clinton's supporters accused Starr of playing politics. Clinton's accusers argued that the president was accountable if his actions were illegal.

On December 19, 1998, the House of Representatives passed two articles of impeachment, one for perjury and one for obstruction of justice. The vote split almost evenly along party lines, and the case moved to the Senate for trial. On February 12, 1999, the senators cast their votes. The vote was 55 to 45 that Clinton was not guilty of perjury, and 50–50 on the charge of obstruction of justice. Although both votes were well short of the two-thirds needed to remove the president from office, Clinton's reputation had suffered.

✔ **Reading Check** **Examining** What events led to the impeachment of President Clinton?

Clinton Foreign Policy

MAIN Idea During Clinton's second term, the United States worked to end violence in Haiti, southeastern Europe and the Middle East.

HISTORY AND YOU Do you remember when and why NATO was created? Read on to find out how the United States and NATO worked to resolve a crisis in southeastern Europe.

Although Clinton's domestic policies became bogged down in struggles with Congress, he was able to engage in a series of major foreign policy initiatives. On several occasions, President Clinton used force to try to resolve regional conflicts.

The Haitian Intervention

In 1991 military leaders in Haiti overthrew Jean-Bertrand Aristide, the country's first democratically elected president in many decades. Aristide sought refuge in the United States.

Seeking to restore democracy, the Clinton administration convinced the United Nations to impose a trade embargo on Haiti. The embargo created a severe economic crisis in that country. Thousands of Haitian refugees fled to the United States in small boats, and many died at sea. Determined to end the crisis, Clinton ordered an invasion of Haiti. With the troops on the way, former president Jimmy Carter convinced Haiti's rulers to step aside. The American troops then landed to serve as peacekeepers.

Bosnia and Kosovo

The United States also was concerned about mounting tensions in southeastern Europe. During the Cold War, Yugoslavia had been a single federated nation made up of many different ethnic groups under a strong Communist government. In 1991, after the collapse of communism, Yugoslavia split apart.

In Bosnia, one of the former Yugoslav republics, a vicious three-way civil war erupted

PRIMARY SOURCE
Striving for Peace Around the World

With the Cold War over, the Clinton administration focused on bringing stability to the Middle East and southeastern Europe, where religious and ethnic strife had contributed to ongoing violence. In addition, Clinton sent peacekeepers into Haiti to help rebuild the nation's democracy.

▲ Haitians gather outside the fence of the U.S. camp in Haiti to talk to American peacekeepers.

▲ Israeli Prime Minister Yitzhak Rabin and Palestinian leader Yasir Arafat shake hands after signing the 1993 Declaration of Principles.

▼ U.S. troops work with Bosnian Serbs in 1996 to set up boundaries between opposing forces.

Analyzing VISUALS

1. **Predicting** Do you think the United States should intervene in conflicts in the world? What problems can result from such a policy?

2. **Explaining** Why would the United States think intervening in Haiti and Bosnia was important to its own security?

between Orthodox Christian Serbs, Catholic Croatians, and Bosnian Muslims. Despite international pressure, the fighting continued until 1995. The Serbs began what they called **ethnic cleansing**—the brutal expulsion of an ethnic group from a geographic area so that only Serbs lived there. In some cases, Serbian troops slaughtered the Muslims instead of moving them.

The United States convinced its NATO allies that military action was necessary. NATO warplanes attacked the Serbs in Bosnia, forcing them to negotiate. The Clinton administration then arranged peace talks in Dayton, Ohio. The **participants** signed a peace plan known as the **Dayton Accords.** In 1996 some 60,000 NATO troops, including 20,000 Americans, entered Bosnia to enforce the plan.

In 1998 another war erupted, this time in the Serbian province of Kosovo. Kosovo has two major ethnic groups—Serbs and Albanians. Many of the Albanians wanted Kosovo to separate from Serbia. To keep Kosovo in Serbia, Serbian leader Slobodan Milosevic ordered a crackdown. The Albanians then organized their own army to fight back. Worried by Serbian violence against Albanian civilians, President Clinton convinced European leaders that NATO should use force to stop the fighting. In March 1999, NATO began bombing Serbia. In response, Serbia pulled its troops out of Kosovo.

Peacemaking in the Middle East

Although Iraq had been defeated in the Persian Gulf War, Iraqi President Saddam Hussein remained determined to hang onto power. In 1996 Iraqi forces attacked the Kurds, an ethnic group whose homeland lies in northern Iraq. To stop the attacks, the United States fired cruise missiles at Iraqi military targets.

Relations between Israel and the Palestinians were even more volatile. In 1993 Israeli Prime Minister Yitzhak Rabin and Palestine Liberation Organization leader Yasir Arafat reached an agreement. The PLO recognized Israel's right to exist, and Israel recognized the PLO as the representative of the Palestinians. President Clinton then invited Arafat and Rabin to the White House, where they signed the Declaration of Principles—a plan for creating a Palestinian government. Opposition to the peace plan emerged. Radical Palestinians exploded bombs in Israel, killing 256. In 1995 a right-wing Israeli assassinated Prime Minister Rabin.

In 1994, with U.S. help, Jordan and Israel signed a peace treaty. In 1998 Israeli and Palestinian leaders met with President Clinton at the Wye River Plantation in Maryland. The agreement they reached, however, did not address the contested status of Jerusalem or the ultimate dimensions of a projected Israeli withdrawal from the West Bank and Gaza.

In July 2000, President Clinton invited Arafat and Israeli Prime Minister Ehud Barak to Camp David to discuss unresolved issues. Barak agreed to the creation of a Palestinian state in all of Gaza and about 95 percent of the West Bank, but Arafat rejected the deal. In October 2000, a Palestinian uprising began. The region was as far from peace as ever.

✔ **Reading Check** **Identifying** In what three regions of the world did Clinton use force to support his foreign policy?

Section 2 REVIEW

Vocabulary

1. **Explain** the significance of: AmeriCorps, Contract with America, Kenneth Starr, perjury, ethnic cleansing, Dayton Accords.

Main Ideas

2. **Identifying** What were two reasons President Clinton's health care plan failed?

3. **Explaining** Why did the federal government shut down in 1995?

4. **Describing** How could Clinton be impeached but remain in office?

5. **Organizing** Complete a chart similar to the one below by explaining the foreign policy issues facing President Clinton in each of the areas listed.

Region	Issue
Latin America	
Southeastern Europe	
Middle East	

Critical Thinking

6. **Big Ideas** What did President Clinton do to help families during his presidency?

7. **Analyzing Visuals** Study the photograph on page 785 of Clinton's impeachment trial. What elements in the photograph reflect the seriousness of the occasion?

Writing About History

8. **Persuasive Writing** Take on the role of a member of Congress. Write a letter in which you attempt to persuade other lawmakers to vote either for or against the impeachment of President Clinton. Provide reasons for your position.

History ONLINE

Study Central™ To review this section, go to glencoe.com and click on Study Central.

A New Wave of Immigration

Guide to Reading

Big Ideas
Trade, War, and Migration A new immigration law allowed more people to immigrate to the United States.

Content Vocabulary
• migration chains (p. 788)
• refugees (p. 789)
• amnesty (p. 789)

Academic Vocabulary
• illegal (p. 789)
• allocate (p. 790)
• resident (p. 790)

People and Events to Identify
• Immigration Act of 1965 (p. 788)
• Immigration Reform and Control Act of 1986 (p. 789)
• Illegal Immigration Reform and Immigrant Responsibility Act of 1996 (p. 790)

Reading Strategy
Determining Cause and Effect
Use a graphic organizer similar to the one below to list the effects of the Immigration Act of 1965.

In the late twentieth century, the number of immigrants in the United States hit an all time high. Large numbers of non-European immigrants changed the ethnic composition of the United States. Immigration—legal and illegal—emerged as a difficult political issue.

Changes in Immigration Law

MAIN Idea The Immigration Act of 1965 eliminated preferences for certain European immigrants; illegal immigration became a problem.

HISTORY AND YOU Do you remember the controversial elements of the National Origins Act of 1924? Read on to learn how the repeal of the national origins system led to major changes in American society which few people had anticipated.

After the introduction of the national origins quota system in the 1920s, the sources and character of immigration to the United States changed dramatically. For the next few decades, the total number of immigrants arriving annually remained markedly lower. The quota system which gave preference to immigrants from northern and western European countries, although occasionally modified by Congress, remained largely intact until 1965.

In the midst of the flurry of civil rights and antipoverty legislation of the mid-1960s, the **Immigration Act of 1965** received scant attention when it was enacted. The law abolished the national origins quota system. It also gave preference to skilled persons and persons with close relatives who are U.S. citizens—policies which remain in place today. The preference given to the children, spouses, and parents of U.S. citizens meant that **migration chains** were established. As newcomers acquired U.S. citizenship, they too could send for relatives in their home country. Also, for the first time, the legislation introduced limits on immigration from the Western Hemisphere. The act further provided that immigrants could apply for U.S. citizenship after five years of legal residency.

At the time of its passage, few people expected that the new law would radically change the pattern or volume of immigration to the United States. Supporters of the law presented it as an extension of America's growing commitment to equal rights for non-European peoples. As U.S. Representative Philip Burton of California stated, "Just as we sought to eliminate discrimination in our land through the Civil Rights Act, today we seek by phasing out the national origins quota system to eliminate discrimination in immigration to this nation composed of the descendants of immigrants." Supporters of the new law also assumed that the new equal quotas

Estimated Unauthorized Resident Population, 2000

Number of unauthorized immigrants
- 335,000 or more
- 140,000–334,999
- 85,000–139,999
- Fewer than 85,000

Albers Equal-Area projection

Analyzing GEOGRAPHY

1. **Place** According to the map, which states have the largest numbers of unauthorized aliens?

2. **Human-Environment Interaction** What are some geographic factors that could explain why some states attract more immigrants than others?

for non-European nations would generally go unfilled. In fact, immigration from non-European countries soared in subsequent decades.

In addition to those arriving through traditional immigration channels, some newcomers arrived in the United States as **refugees.** Beginning in 1948, refugees from countries ravaged by World War II were admitted, although they were counted as part of their nation's quota. The Cold War led to another class of refugees. According to the McCarran-Walter Act of 1952, anyone who was fleeing a Communist regime could be admitted as a refugee. Refugee policy was further broadened under the Refugee Act of 1980, which defined a refugee as someone leaving his or her country due to a "well founded fear of persecution on account of race, religion, nationality, membership in a particular group, or political opinion."

The growing problem of **illegal** immigration also prompted changes in immigration law. During the Reagan administration, Congress passed the **Immigration Reform and Control Act of 1986.** This law established penalties for employers who knowingly hire unauthorized immigrants and strengthened border controls to prevent illegal entry into the United States. It also established a process to grant **amnesty** (in other words, a pardon) and legal papers to any undocumented alien who could prove that he or she had entered the country before January 1, 1982, and had resided in the United States since then.

Despite these changes, illegal immigration persisted and the number of unauthorized immigrants continued to grow. By 1990, an estimated 3.5 million unauthorized immigrants resided in the United States. By the mid-1990s, Congress was debating new ways to combat illegal immigration.

History ONLINE
Student Skill Activity To learn how to create and modify spreadsheets, visit glencoe.com and complete the skill activity.

The law that resulted from these debates was the **Illegal Immigration Reform and Immigrant Responsibility Act of 1996,** which made several changes to U.S. immigration law. First, it required families sponsoring an immigrant to have an income above the poverty level. Second, it **allocated** more resources to stop illegal immigration, by authorizing an additional 5,000 Border Patrol agents and calling for the construction of a 14-mile fence along the border near San Diego. Third, the law toughened penalties for smuggling people or providing fraudulent documents. Finally, the law made it easier for immigration authorities to deport undocumented aliens.

Another change in immigration law was spurred by the terrorist attacks of September 11, 2001. The USA Patriot Act of 2001 put immigration under the control of the newly created Department of Homeland Security. Furthermore, it tripled the number of Border Patrol agents, Customs Service inspectors, and Immigration and Naturalization Service inspectors along the Canadian border.

Reading Check **Identifying** For what reasons may a foreigner be admitted to the United States as a refugee?

Recent Immigration

MAIN Idea In the late twentieth century, immigrants from Latin America and Asia outnumbered European immigrants.

HISTORY AND YOU Do you remember the reasons that some Americans objected to immigration in the late 1800s? Read on to learn how the debate resurfaced in the 1980s and continues today.

Although immigrants headed for all parts of the United States, certain states experienced a larger influx than others. In 1990, California, Texas, New York, Illinois, and Florida had the highest populations of foreign-born **residents.** High numbers of immigrants also increased the ethnic diversity of these states, as their Latino and Asian populations grew. Among the immigrants who arrived in the 1990s, just over 10 percent came from Europe. More than half of new immigrants came from Latin America, while approximately another 25 percent came from Asia. By 2001, the top five countries of origin for legal immigrants to the United States were Mexico, India, China, the Philippines, and Vietnam.

PRIMARY SOURCE
Securing the Border

After the attacks of September 11, 2001, many Americans became increasingly concerned about border security. Many agreed on the need for increased border patrols. Others proposed building a continuous wall from Texas to California to prevent illegal immigration. Critics of such proposals, however, claimed such actions would not stop people who were determined to enter the country illegally, but rather force them to take more dangerous risks.

▲ On May 27, 2006, a volunteer organization called the Minutemen Civil Defense Corps built a fence along the Mexican border on private property.

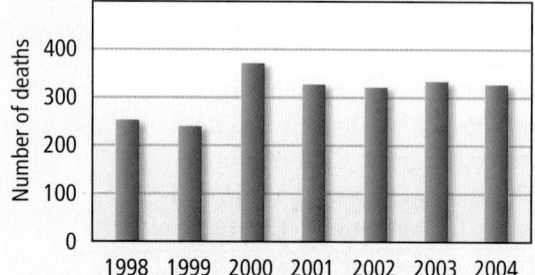

Deaths of Persons Attempting to Cross the Border Illegally

Source: United States Government Accountability Office.

Analyzing VISUALS

1. **Making Connections** Why do you think the organization pictured above decided to call themselves the "minutemen"?

2. **Theorizing** Do you think building a fence along the border would lead to fewer deaths? Why or why not?

Refugees added to the growing immigrant population. In the 25 years following the Cuban Revolution of 1959, more than 800,000 Cubans arrived in the United States. So many of these immigrants settled in the Miami, Florida, area that only the city of Havana, Cuba, is home to more Cubans. In addition, the Vietnam War created refugees. Some 600,000 immigrants from Vietnam, Laos, and Cambodia arrived in the decade after 1974.

In addition to the immigrants entering through legal channels, others arrived without official permission. The largest number of unauthorized immigrants came from Mexico, El Salvador, and Guatemala. The Reagan administration's amnesty program in 1986 had been designed to eliminate the problem of undocumented aliens, but over the next 20 years the number of unauthorized immigrants tripled. American public opinion divided over whether unauthorized immigrants should be able to obtain driver's licenses or send their children to public schools and receive other government services. Some believed that unauthorized immigrants should be deported. Others favored allowing them to apply for temporary work visas so the government could keep track of them, and permitting them to earn permanent residence if they learned English, paid back taxes, and had no criminal record.

In 2006, President George W. Bush made immigration reform a top priority, but members of Congress strongly disagreed over how to solve the problem. A bipartisan majority of the Senate favored legislation that blended tougher enforcement of immigration laws with some form of earned citizenship for the estimated 12 million undocumented aliens living and working in the country. The Senate bill included a provision that undocumented aliens who grew up in the United States and graduated from high school could apply for citizenship. Conservative Republicans who held the majority in the House objected that this would reward illegal behavior. The House rejected any form of amnesty and called for the United States to build a wall along its Mexican border— although the United States had already tripled the size of its border patrol without reducing illegal immigration. As Congress debated a bill that would subject unauthorized aliens to criminal prosecution, Latinos held rallies across the country, carrying signs that read: "We are not criminals."

Advocates of immigration reform promoted alternatives such as expanding quotas through a guest-worker program and establishing a means of legalization for those already in the country. Some undocumented aliens had lived in the United States for years, and had raised families here. Deporting them would mean separating husbands, wives, and children. Some undocumented aliens arrived as children and had lived in the United States most of their lives. Their own children, born in the United States, were native-born citizens even though their parents lacked legal status. Among those who became legal citizens, most wanted other family members to join them, so the reunification of families accounted for three-quarters of all legal immigration.

Reading Check **Explaining** Why did some members of Congress oppose amnesty for undocumented aliens? Why did others support it?

Vocabulary

1. **Explain** the significance of: Immigration Act of 1965, migration chains, refugees, Immigration Reform and Control Act of 1986, amnesty, Illegal Immigration Reform and Immigrant Responsibility Act of 1996.

Main Ideas

2. **Summarizing** What problems arose that caused changes in the immigration laws?

3. **Describing** What alternatives to immigration reform did advocates for reform suggest?

Critical Thinking

4. **Big Ideas** What two acts were instrumental in helping refugees?

5. **Organizing** Use a graphic organizer similar to the one below to list the immigration laws and what they intended.

Immigration Law	Intent
Immigration Act of 1965	
Immigration Reform and Control Act of 1986	
Illegal Immigration Reform and Immigrant Responsibility Act of 1996	

6. **Analyzing Visuals** Study the map on page 789. Research the number of unauthorized immigrants in the United States and create a spreadsheet that lists the states where these immigrants settled and the estimated numbers in 2000 and 2005.

Writing About History

7. **Persuasive Writing** After reading about the problem of illegal immigration, write a letter to your representative in Congress explaining what you feel he or she should do about the problem.

History ONLINE

Study Central™ To review this section, go to glencoe.com and click on Study Central.

ANALYZING PRIMARY SOURCES

The New Immigrants

In the decades since the Immigration Act of 1965 was enacted, the number of immigrants in the United States has risen dramatically. By 2000, immigrants comprised more than 10 percent of the population. The largest groups of these new immigrants came from Latin America and Asia. Immigration has become a topic of political debate. Should the U.S. make it easier to immigrate legally? Should the U.S. decrease the number of persons allowed to immigrate? How should unauthorized immigrants be treated?

Study these primary sources and answer the questions that follow.

PRIMARY SOURCE 1

Oral Interview

"On our third attempt, my wife, children, and I escaped by boat from Vietnam and arrived in Hong Kong, where we remained for three months. Then my brother, who came to America in 1975, sponsored us, and we arrived in America in 1978. . . .

Although in America we live with everything free, to move, to do business, we still have the need to return to Vietnam one day. This is our dream. In Vietnam, before the Communists came, we had a sentimental life, more [mentally] comfortable and cozy, more joyful. . . .

Here in America, we have all the material comforts, very good. But the joy and sentiment are not like we had in Vietnam. There, when we went out from the home, we laughed, we jumped. And we had many relatives and friends to come to see us at home. Here in America, I only know what goes on in my home; my neighbor knows only what goes on in his home. . . . In America, when we go to work, we go in our cars. When we return, we leave our cars and enter our homes [and do not meet neighbors]. We do not need to know what goes on in the houses of our neighbors. That's why we do not have the kind of being at ease that we knew in Vietnam."

—Vietnamese immigrant

PRIMARY SOURCE 3

Oral Interview

"The buzzword is diversity. It's on TV, politics, and this school [university], but then people like me are seen as foreigners and worse, illegals. The logic is if you look Mexican you are an immigrant, don't speak English and are illegal. I get tired of saying that's not me, oh well, except for the Mexican part. I don't look at an Anglo with an Italian name and say, 'Hey, do you speak Italian and when did you come to the United States?'"

—Diana, second-generation Mexican American

PRIMARY SOURCE 2

Photograph, c. 2006

▼ *Tijuana (on the left) lies just south of San Diego; a fence marks the Mexico-U.S. border.*

PRIMARY SOURCE 4

Photograph, 2006

▼ *Jorge Urbina of Nicaragua and his brother Carlos take the oath of citizenship during a naturalization ceremony for 250 immigrants.*

PRIMARY SOURCE 5

Photograph, 2006

▼ *Woman protests illegal immigration.*

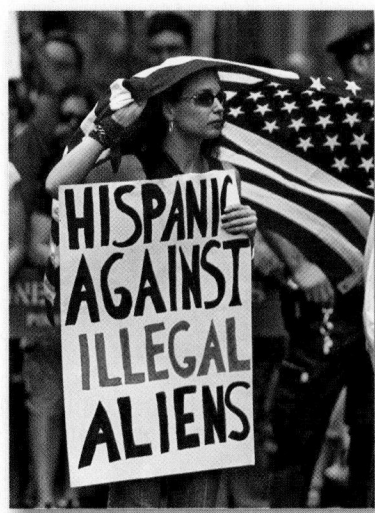

PRIMARY SOURCE 7

Photograph, 2006

▼ *Marchers oppose passage of a bill that would make it a felony to be in the country illegally.*

PRIMARY SOURCE 6

Oral Interview

"Usually we catch young men, who are looking for work to support their families back in Mexico. But more and more we are seeing entire families. They start coming around 7:30 P.M. over the mesa near Cristo Rey Mountain. A steady stream of people all night. We use our night-vision 'infrared' equipment to spot a lot of illegals who would otherwise go unnoticed.

Sometimes border patrolmen ride horseback to patrol these hills. It's an interesting contrast—high-tech infrared machines directing cowboys on horseback. Other times we patrol in small trucks, which provide maneuverability. Before we began using night-vision equipment, aliens had an easier time coming through this area without getting caught. Now we can sit on top of a hill, spot undocumented aliens, then radio for patrol vehicles to come apprehend the groups or individuals after they enter into Texas or New Mexico.

This time of year, in late winter, the aliens try to find work on farms in the Upper Rio Grande Valley. This is the time when farm laborers start pulling weeds and preparing the ground for planting. Between New Year and June, on the northbound highways to Las Cruces, many of the aliens we apprehend are usually agricultural workers or people heading for cities further north, like Denver or Chicago.

Perhaps our greatest concern is the trafficking of drugs tied to the smuggling of illegal aliens. Smuggling of all sorts has become big business in the border regions. Some smugglers have set up networks that may start in Central America or Cuba. We catch illegal immigrants who come from as many as eighty-five countries around the world. Even people from Eastern Europe, who are smuggled in for large fees through South America and Mexico City."

—Michael Teague, U.S. Border Patrol

DBQ Document-Based Questions

1. **Contrasting** How does the speaker in Source 1 contrast his life in America with his life in Vietnam?

2. **Describing** Study the photograph in Source 2. Write a description of the Mexican side of the border and a description of the U.S. side of the border.

3. **Analyzing** Examine Sources 3 and 4. How do they reflect the ethnicities of the new immigrants?

4. **Speculating** Study the photograph in Source 5. What might be some reasons that the woman opposes illegal immigration?

5. **Making Connections** According to the speaker in Source 6, why do so many people risk crossing the border illegally? What other illegal traffic occurs at the border?

An Interdependent World

Guide to Reading

Big Ideas
Economics and Society As the twentieth century drew to a close, world trade and environmentalism became increasingly more important during a period of globalization.

Content Vocabulary
- globalism *(p. 794)*
- euro *(p. 795)*
- global warming *(p. 797)*

Academic Vocabulary
- cited *(p. 796)*
- awareness *(p. 797)*

People and Events to Identify
- North American Free Trade Agreement (NAFTA) *(p. 795)*
- European Union (EU) *(p. 795)*
- Asia Pacific Economic Cooperation (APEC) *(p. 796)*
- World Trade Organization (WTO) *(p. 796)*
- Kyoto Protocol *(p. 797)*

Reading Strategy
Organizing Complete a graphic organizer like the one below to chart the major political and economic problems facing the world at the turn of the century.

Global Concerns

As the world economy became more interconnected in the 1990s, Americans debated whether the elimination of trade barriers was more beneficial or detrimental for the nation. Concerns about environmental damage led to an international conference in Kyoto, Japan.

The New Global Economy

MAIN Idea Regional trade agreements, such as the North American Free Trade Agreement (NAFTA), reflected the growing interdependence of the global economy.

HISTORY AND YOU Do you remember how tariffs were a hotly debated issue in earlier periods of American history? Read on to learn about NAFTA and the fierce political debate it sparked.

In the 1990s Americans began to realize that their relationship with the rest of the world was changing. The economies of individual countries were becoming much more interdependent, and events in one part of the world could dramatically affect the economy of another country thousands of miles away. Computer technology and the Internet played a big role in forging this new global economy. So too did the conviction of many of the world's political and business leaders that free trade and the global exchange of goods contributed to prosperity and economic growth.

At the same time, the Internet and digital satellite technology helped link the world together culturally. For example, people in the United States could read Australian newspapers on the Web, while Chinese students could download American popular music, and an African doctor could consult a British medical database. This idea that the world is becoming increasingly interconnected is sometimes referred to as **globalism,** and the process is called globalization.

Selling American-made goods abroad had long been important to American prosperity. From World War II to the present, Republican and Democratic administrations have worked to lower barriers to international trade. They reasoned that trade helps the American economy: American businesses make money selling goods abroad, and American consumers benefit by having the option to buy goods that are less expensive than those made in the United States. Importing low-cost goods would also keep inflation and interest rates low.

Opponents warned that embracing the global economy would cause manufacturing jobs to move from the United States to nations where wages were low and there were fewer environmental regulations. They suggested that having cheap imports available to buy

The manufacturing of a GM Chevrolet Corvette requires the delivery of components from around the world—an engine from Canada, a transmission from Mexico, electronic switches from Germany, brakes from Australia, and other electronic components from Asia.

would not help those Americans who no longer could find work because their industries had moved overseas. By the 1990s, the debate between supporters of free trade and those who wanted to limit trade had become an important part of American politics.

Regional Blocs

One way to increase international trade was to create regional trade pacts. In 1993 President Clinton convinced Congress to ratify the **North American Free Trade Agreement** (NAFTA). This agreement joined Canada, the United States, and Mexico in a free-trade zone. With NAFTA in operation, exports of American goods to both Canada and Mexico rose dramatically. From 1993 to 2000, it is estimated that combined exports to those two countries rose from $142 to $290 billion, an increase of 104 percent.

Many Americans feared that NAFTA would cause industrial jobs to move to Mexico, where labor costs were lower. Some jobs were indeed lost, as foreign-owned factories, known as *maquiladoras*, opened in Mexico near the American border. At the same time, however, the unemployment rate in the United States began to fall and wages rose. Many American businesses upgraded their technology, and workers shifted to more skilled jobs or to the service industry.

Regional trade blocs also formed in Europe and Asia. In 1993, the **European Union** (EU) was created to promote economic and political cooperation among many European nations. The EU created a common bank and the **euro,** a common currency for member nations. The organization also removed trade barriers between its members and set policies on imports from nations outside the community.

Debating Free Trade

Globalization and the steady reduction of trade barriers between nations has led to many protests and political debates around the globe.

▲ Demonstrators in Seattle protest a meeting of the WTO on November 30, 1999.

Rise of Global Trade and Global GDP

U.S. dollars (billions)

□ GDP ■ Trade

35,000
30,000
25,000
20,000
15,000
10,000
5,000
0

1985 1990 1995 2000 2001

Source: *Australia's Foreign and Trade Policy White Paper.*

Analyzing VISUALS

1. **Identifying Central Issues** How does the graph support those who want free trade? How do the protestors of globalization counter the evidence of the bar graph?

2. **Identifying Points of View** If free trade brings prosperity, what other values might opponents be seeking to protect?

Another trade bloc that came together in the early 1990s was the **Asia Pacific Economic Cooperation** (APEC). It includes most nations that have a coastline on the Pacific Ocean, including the United States, Canada, China, Japan, South Korea, Mexico, and Russia. APEC represented the fastest-growing region in the world and controlled 47 percent of global trade in 2001. APEC began as a forum to promote economic cooperation and lower trade barriers, but major political differences kept its members from acting together.

The World Trade Organization

In 1994 some 120 nations formed the **World Trade Organization** (WTO) to administer international trade agreements and help settle trade disputes. President Clinton convinced Congress to pass legislation enabling the United States to participate in the WTO. Supporters of the WTO **cited** benefits for American consumers, including cheaper imports, new markets, and copyright protection for the American entertainment industry. Opponents noted that the United States would be bound to accept the WTO's rulings in trade disputes even if they hurt the American economy. Despite their concerns, Congress passed the legislation.

Trade With China

China's huge population offered potential as a market for American goods, but many people had reservations about trading with China. These critics cited China's suppression of protests in Tiananmen Square in 1989, its record on human rights, and its threats to invade Taiwan. Despite these concerns, President Clinton argued that expanding trade with China would help bring it into the world community.

After negotiating a new trade agreement, Clinton urged Congress to grant China permanent normal trade relation status. Unions opposed the deal, fearing that inexpensive Chinese goods would flood U.S. markets; conservatives objected to China's military ambitions; and environmentalists worried about pollution from Chinese factories. Over such objections, the bill passed in late 2000.

✓ Reading Check **Analyzing** How did international trade change the world economy?

Global Environmentalism

MAIN Idea As scientists learned that certain chemicals could damage the Earth's ozone layer, they worked to ban their use; concern about global warming became a serious political issue.

HISTORY AND YOU Are there groups in your school or community that work to improve the environment? Read on to learn about efforts to reduce damage to the environment.

The rise of a global economy also increased **awareness** of environmental issues. Environmentalists began thinking of the environment as a global system. Increasingly, they began addressing issues that they believed were of global, not just local, concern.

Concern About Ozone

In the 1980s scientists discovered that chlorofluorocarbons (CFCs) had the ability to break down the ozone layer in the Earth's atmosphere. Ozone is a gas that protects life on Earth from the ultraviolet rays of the sun. At that time, CFCs were widely used in air conditioners and refrigerators. Environmental activists began to push for a ban on CFC production. In the late 1980s, public awareness of the issue increased dramatically when scientists documented a large ozone "hole" over Antarctica. In 1987 the United States and 22 other nations agreed to phase out the production of CFCs and other chemicals that might be weakening the ozone layer.

Global Warming

In the early 1990s, another global environmental issue developed when some scientists found evidence of **global warming**—an increase in average world temperatures over time. Such a rise in temperature could eventually lead to more droughts and other forms of extreme weather. A furious debate began over how to measure the Earth's temperature and what the results meant.

Many experts concluded that carbon dioxide emissions from factories and power plants caused global warming, but others disagreed. The issue became very controversial because the cost of controlling emissions would affect the global economy. Industries would have to pay the cost of further reducing emissions, and those costs would eventually be passed on to consumers. Developing nations trying to industrialize would be hurt the most, but economic growth in wealthier nations would be hurt, too.

Concern about global warming led to an international conference in Kyoto, Japan, in 1997. Thirty-eight nations and the EU signed the Kyoto Protocol promising to reduce emissions, but very few have actually complied with its requirements and reduced their emissions. President Clinton did not submit the Kyoto Protocol to the Senate for ratification because most senators were opposed to it. In 2001 President George W. Bush withdrew the United States from the **Kyoto Protocol,** citing flaws in the treaty.

Reading Check **Describing** Why did environmentalists think CFCs were dangerous?

Section 4 REVIEW

Vocabulary

1. **Explain** the significance of: globalism, North American Free Trade Agreement, European Union, euro, Asia Pacific Economic Cooperation, World Trade Organization, global warming, Kyoto Protocol.

Main Ideas

2. **Explaining** Why was China an important factor in world trade?

3. **Describing** What was the international response to concerns about global warming?

Critical Thinking

4. **Big Ideas** How did NAFTA affect exports of American goods?

5. **Organizing** Complete a graphic organizer by listing and describing the regional trade blocs that formed in the 1990s.

Regional Trade Blocs

6. **Analyzing Visuals** Examine the image on page 796. Why do some people or groups protest globalization?

Writing About History

7. **Expository Writing** Decide which issue of global concern is the most serious. In an essay, explain why you think it is the most serious problem, and provide some possible solutions.

History ONLINE

Study Central™ To review this section, go to glencoe.com and click on Study Central.

A Changing Society

The Technological Revolution

- The invention of the integrated circuit and microprocessors enables small personal computers built by Apple and IBM.
- The telecommunications revolution leads to the development of small portable cell phones, and digital video and audio players.
- The rise of the Internet and World Wide Web provide new ways for people to retrieve information, build communities, and do business.

A New Wave of Immigrants

- New immigration laws in 1965 and 1986 contribute to a rise in Hispanic immigration and an increase in immigrants from Asia, Africa, and the Middle East.
- The American population becomes increasingly culturally diverse.

The Rise of a Global Economy

- Free trade, in combination with the technological revolution, creates a new global marketplace.
- Increasing awareness of the global economy also sparks a new global environmentalist movement.

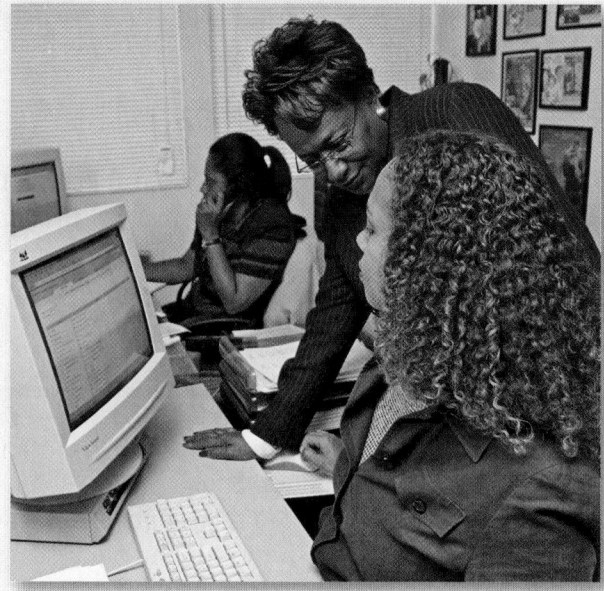

▲ Today, almost all businesses, such as this public relations firm, rely on computers to help employees perform their day-to-day duties.

▲ President Bill Clinton delivers his State of the Union address to a joint session of Congress on January 24, 1995.

The Clinton Years

First-Term Achievements and Failures

- Raised taxes to help cut the deficit
- Proposal for a national health care program fails
- Signed the Family Medical Leave Act into law
- Persuaded Congress to create AmeriCorps
- Signed the Brady Handgun Bill into law
- Worked with Republicans to push the Health Insurance Portability Act and the Welfare Reform Act through Congress

Second-Term Achievements and Failures

- Submits a balanced budget to Congress
- Convinces Congress to pass a new tax credit for children and a children's health insurance program
- Impeached on charges of perjury and obstruction of justice but is acquitted by the Senate

Foreign Policy Achievements

- Dispatched troops to Haiti to restore democracy
- Dispatched troops to Bosnia and bombed Serbia to end the civil war and ethnic cleansing that followed the breakup of Yugoslavia
- Mediated negotiations between Israel and the PLO

Reviewing Vocabulary

Directions: Choose the word or words that best complete the sentence.

1. The company Intel revolutionized computers by combining several integrated circuits on a single chip called a

  A minicomputer.

  B nanocomputer.

  C microprocessor.

  D microcomputer.

2. As the workplace became increasingly reliant on computers, some workers had the option to _____, or work from home via computer.

  A blog

  B allocate

  C telecommute

  D globalize

3. Clinton was impeached because he committed

  A perjury.

  B ethnic cleansing.

  C overtaxation.

  D robbery.

4. The Immigration Reform and Control Act of 1986 granted _____ to immigrants who entered the country before January 1, 1982.

  A leniency

  B citizenship

  C a pardon

  D amnesty

5. The process of the world becoming increasingly interconnected is called

  A globalization.

  B internationalism.

  C Americanism.

  D Nationalism.

Reviewing Main Ideas

Directions: Choose the best answer for each of the following questions.

Section 1 *(pp. 774–777)*

6. The government began to deregulate the telecommunications industry in the

  A 1950s.

  B 1960s.

  C 1970s.

  D 1980s.

7. In 1990, researchers at CERN developed a new way to present information known as

  A the Internet.

  B the computer.

  C the Ethernet.

  D the World Wide Web.

Section 2 *(pp. 780–787)*

8. Democrats passed a law during President Clinton's administration that tightened gun control called

  A the Gun Law.

  B the Anti-Gun Bill.

  C the Brady Bill.

  D the NRA Law.

9. The Contract with America was proposed by

  A Hillary Clinton.

  B President Clinton.

  C Al Gore.

  D Newt Gingrich.

TEST-TAKING

Consider each answer choice individually and cross out choices you have eliminated. You will save time and stop yourself from choosing an answer you have mentally eliminated.

Need Extra Help?

If You Missed Questions . . .	1	2	3	4	5	6	7	8	9
Go to Page . . .	774	775	785	789	794	775	777	782	783

Section 3 *(pp. 788–791)*

10. The Immigration Reform and Control Act of 1986 established

    A admittance of any refugee fleeing a communist regime.

    B legal papers to any undocumented immigrant who could prove he or she entered the country before 1982.

    C the national origins quota system.

    D allocation of more resources to stop illegal immigration.

11. The Illegal Immigration Reform and Immigrant Responsibility Act of 1996

    A relaxed penalties for smuggling people or providing fraudulent documents.

    B established more schools for immigrant children.

    C allocated more resources to stop illegal immigration.

    D called for a wall to be built at the U.S. border.

Section 4 *(pp. 794–797)*

12. Since WWII, Republicans and Democrats have worked to lower barriers to international trade because

    A it helps the American economy.

    B it supports foreign policy.

    C it moves manufacturing jobs overseas.

    D it helps economically depressed countries.

13. Environmentalists were concerned about trade with China because

    A there was concern about the protests in Tiananmen Square.

    B they believed the goods should be manufactured in the United States.

    C there was concern about pollution from Chinese factories.

    D China had made threats to invade Taiwan.

Critical Thinking

Directions: Choose the best answers to the following questions.

14. Which of the following is not an example of digital technology?

    A cell phones that can receive e-mails

    B MP3 players

    C satellite radio

    D newspapers

Base your answers to questions 15 and 16 on the graph below and your knowledge of Chapter 23.

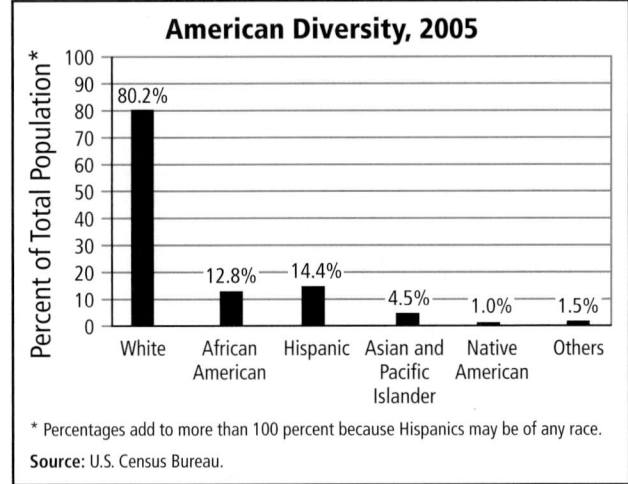

American Diversity, 2005

White: 80.2%
African American: 12.8%
Hispanic: 14.4%
Asian and Pacific Islander: 4.5%
Native American: 1.0%
Others: 1.5%

Percent of Total Population*

* Percentages add to more than 100 percent because Hispanics may be of any race.

Source: U.S. Census Bureau.

15. Which group was the smallest percentage of the population in 2005?

    A African American

    B White

    C Native American

    D Multiracial

16. Why do the percentages add up to more than 100 percent?

    A They did not record data carefully.

    B There can be more than 100 percent.

    C There is no way to determine exact numbers of the population.

    D Hispanics may be of any race.

Need Extra Help?							
If You Missed Questions . . .	10	11	12	13	14	15	16
Go to Page . . .	789	789–790	794–795	796	774–777	R16	R16

GO ON

17. The North American Free Trade Agreement (NAFTA) joined Canada, Mexico and the United States in a free trade zone. Why was this beneficial?

   A Exports to Canada and Mexico increased.

   B Jobs were lost to Mexico.

   C Unemployment in the United States rose.

   D It provided free goods to Canada and Mexico.

Analyze the cartoon and answer the question that follows. Base your answer on the cartoon and on your knowledge of Chapter 23.

18. What is the main idea of this cartoon?

   A Clinton needs to raise taxes to decrease the federal deficit.

   B Clinton should lower taxes to provide relief to taxpapers.

   C Clinton has increased the federal deficit to record levels.

   D The taxpayers are taking advantage of the tax cuts.

19. The presence of increased levels of chlorofluorocarbons (CFCs) concerns scientists because

   A they make the air hard to breathe.

   B they cause global warming.

   C they have the ability to break down ozone.

   D they can enter the water supply.

Document-Based Questions

Directions: Analyze the document and answer the short-answer questions that follow the document.

Global warming became an important topic during the Clinton administration. It was debated across the country, with many different viewpoints.

> *"The world is getting warmer, and by the end of the 21st century could warm by another 6 degrees Celsius (10.8 degrees Fahrenheit). . . . And climate scientists at the heart of the research are now convinced that human action is to blame for some or most of this warming. . . .*
>
> *Everywhere climatologists look—at tree-ring patterns, fossil succession in rock strata, ocean-floor corings…they see evidence of dramatic shifts from cold to hot to cold again. . . . None of these ancient shifts can be blamed on humans. . . . There is still room for argument about the precise role of the sun or other natural cycles in the contribution to global warming. . . .*
>
> —from *World Press Review,* February 2001

20. Why are some scientists not convinced humans are to blame for global warming?

21. What evidence do these scientists cite?

Extended Response

22. After the 1992 election, what did President Clinton's domestic agenda include? Explain in detail the successes and failures of the Clinton administration. Your essay should include an introduction, several paragraphs, and a conclusion. Use relevant facts and details to support your conclusion.

STOP

For additional test practice, use Self-Check Quizzes— Chapter 23 at glencoe.com.

Need Extra Help?						
If You Missed Questions . . .	17	18	19	20	21	22
Go to Page . . .	795	R18	797	797	797	780–782

Chapter 24

A New Century Begins

2001–Present

SECTION 1 America Enters A New Century

SECTION 2 The War on Terrorism Begins

SECTION 3 The Invasion of Iraq

SECTION 4 A Time of Challenges

On September 11, 2006, the Tribute in Light commemorated the fifth anniversary of the attack on the World Trade Center.

November 2000
- A close vote in Florida causes a contested election

G. W. Bush
2001–2009

Sept. 11, 2001
- Terrorists attack World Trade Center and Pentagon

October 2001
- U.S. begins bombing Afghanistan
- Patriot Act enacted

January 2002
- President Bush signs No Child Left Behind Act

March 2003
- U.S. invades Iraq

U.S. PRESIDENTS

U.S. EVENTS

2001

2002

2003

2004

WORLD EVENTS

2001
- Terrorists attack the Indian Parliament

2003
- Israel and PLO sign a cease fire

2004
- Tsunami in Indian Ocean devastates Indonesia and surrounding regions
- Terrorists bomb trains in Spain

MAKING CONNECTIONS

How Does the Passage of Time Affect the Way Events Are Understood?

As the United States entered the twenty-first century, combating terrorism at home and abroad became a national priority. The attacks on the World Trade Center and the Pentagon resulted in wars in Afghanistan and Iraq. The wars as well as new security policies led to great controversy in American politics.

- *What previous events in American history have forced the nation to dramatically change its policies and actions?*

- *How should the United States respond to terrorism to prevent it from happening again?*

FOLDABLES™

Organizing Information Compile facts about the terrorist attacks at the World Trade Center and Pentagon on September 11, 2001. Then, make a Four-Door Book Foldable that explains what, where, when, and why these events occurred.

| Why | What |
| When | Where |

November 2004
- George W. Bush defeats John Kerry in the election

August 2005
- Hurricane Katrina devastates Louisiana and Mississippi; levees fail and New Orleans floods

January 2007
- Nancy Pelosi becomes first female Speaker of the House

2005

2006

2007

2005
- Terrorists bomb London subway system

2006
- Israel invades Lebanon to attack Hezbollah
- Over 1 billion people worldwide use the Internet

History ONLINE Visit glencoe.com and enter *QuickPass*™ code TAVMT5147c24 for Chapter 24 resources.

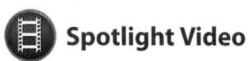
America Enters a New Century

Guide to Reading

Big Ideas
Government and Society A very close presidential election saw a shift in power in the White House, as George W. Bush became the forty-third President of the United States.

Content Vocabulary
- chad *(p. 805)*
- strategic defense *(p. 807)*

Academic Vocabulary
- priority *(p. 807)*
- controversial *(p. 807)*

People and Events to Identify
- Al Gore *(p. 804)*
- George W. Bush *(p. 804)*
- Ralph Nader *(p. 805)*

Reading Strategy
Organizing Complete a graphic organizer similar to the one below by charting the key postelection events culminating in George W. Bush's victory.

I n the election of 2000, Democrat Al Gore faced Republican George W. Bush. After a dispute over the outcome in Florida, Bush became president. Bush then focused on cutting taxes and introducing health care and education reforms.

The Election of 2000

MAIN Idea In one of the closest presidential races in history, involving vote recounts and the Supreme Court, George W. Bush became president.

HISTORY AND YOU Do you think the Electoral College should be modified or eliminated? Read on to learn how the 2000 election ultimately came down to a decision about Florida's disputed electoral votes.

As he prepared to leave office, President Clinton's legacy was uncertain. He had balanced the budget and presided over a period of rapid economic growth. His presidency was marred, however, by the impeachment trial, which had divided the nation and widened the divide between liberals and conservatives. In the election of 2000, that division led to one of the closest elections in American history.

The Candidates Campaign

The Democrats nominated Vice President **Al Gore** for president in 2000. Gore, a former senator from Tennessee, was regarded as a moderate and his Southern roots were expected to help him win votes in the South. For his running mate, Gore chose Senator Joseph Lieberman from Connecticut, the first Jewish American ever to run for vice president on a major party ticket.

The Republican contest for the presidential nomination came down to two men: Governor **George W. Bush** of Texas, son of former president George H.W. Bush, and Senator John McCain of Arizona, a former navy pilot and prisoner of war in North Vietnam. Most Republican leaders endorsed Bush, who was especially popular with conservatives. He easily won the nomination, despite some early McCain victories in the primaries. Bush chose Richard "Dick" Cheney as his vice presidential running mate. Cheney had served as President George H.W. Bush's secretary of defense.

The election campaign revolved around the question of what to do with surplus tax revenues. Both Bush and Gore agreed that Social Security needed reform, but they disagreed on the details. Both promised to cut taxes, although Bush proposed a much larger tax cut than Gore. Both men also promised to improve public education and to support plans to help senior citizens pay for prescription drugs.

Presidential Election of 2000

Gore   Bush

WA 11								NH 4	ME 4
OR 7	MT 3	ND 3	MN 10				VT 3	MA 12	
ID 4		SD 3	WI 11	MI 18		NY 33		RI 4	
NV 4	WY 3	NE 5	IA 7		OH 21	PA 23	NJ 15	CT 8	
CA 54	UT 5	CO 8	KS 6	IL 22	IN 12	WV 5	VA 13	MD 10	DE 3
AZ 8	NM 5	OK 8	MO 11	KY 8	TN 11	NC 14		D.C. 3*	
			AR 6	MS 7	AL 9	GA 13	SC 8		
		TX 32	LA 9						
AK 3						FL 25			
HI 4									

Presidential Candidate	Popular Votes	% of Popular Vote	Electoral Votes
☐ Bush	50,456,002	47.88%	271
☐ Gore	50,999,897	48.40%	266*
Nader	2,882,955	2.74%	0

*One Gore elector from Washington, D.C., abstained from casting an electoral vote.

▲ The recount of the vote in Florida meant vote counters had to examine ballots individually to determine the intention of the voter.

Analyzing VISUALS

1. **Making Generalizations** What characteristics do the states that voted for Bush share? What characteristics do the states that voted for Gore share?

2. **Assessing** Do you think the Florida ballot was easy to understand or confusing? Why?

Frustrated by what he viewed as the fundamental similarities between Bush and Gore, well-known consumer advocate **Ralph Nader** entered the race as the nominee of the Green Party. Nader was known for his strong environmentalist views and his criticism of the power of large corporations. Nader argued that both Bush and Gore depended on campaign funds from large companies and were unwilling to support policies that favored American workers and the environment.

A Close Vote

The 2000 election was one of the closest in American history. No candidate won a majority of the votes cast, but Gore received the most votes, winning 48.4 percent of the popular vote compared to 47.9 percent for Bush. (Nader won about 3 percent of the vote.) To win the presidency, however, candidates must win 270 electoral votes—not lead in the popular vote.

The election came down to the Florida vote—both men needed its 25 electoral votes to win. The results in Florida were so close that state law required a recount of the ballots using vote-counting machines. There were, however, thousands of ballots that had been thrown out because the counting machines could not read the voting cards. Gore then asked for a hand recount of ballots in several strongly Democratic counties. After the machine recount showed Bush still ahead, a battle began over the manual recounts.

Most Florida ballots required voters to punch a hole. The little piece of cardboard punched out of the ballot is called a **chad.** The problem for vote counters was how to count a ballot if the chad was still partially attached. On some, the chad was still in place, and the voter had left only a dimple on the surface. When looking at the ballots, vote counters had to determine what the voter intended—and different counties used different standards.

▲ *The close presidential election of 2000 illustrated clearly how important it is for everyone to exercise the right to vote.*

▲ *The candidates are presented as two turkeys arguing over the results with closed captioning provided to translate what they are saying into what they really mean.*

Analyzing VISUALS **DBQ**

1. **Evaluating** Based on the cartoon on the left, do you think the cartoonist supported Bush or Gore?

2. **Analyzing** Why are the three characters in the cartoon above angry at the man on the right?

Under state law, Florida officials had to certify the results by a certain date. When it became clear that not all of the recounts could be finished in time, Gore went to court to challenge the deadline. The Florida Supreme Court agreed to set a new deadline. At Bush's request, the United States Supreme Court then intervened to decide whether the Florida Supreme Court had acted constitutionally.

While lawyers for Bush and Gore prepared their arguments for the Supreme Court, the hand recounts continued. Despite having more time, not all of the counties where Gore wanted recounts were able to meet the new deadline. On November 26, Florida officials certified Bush the winner by 537 votes.

For more on *Bush v. Gore* read the case summary on page R58 in **Supreme Court Case Summaries.**

Bush v. Gore

Although Bush had been declared the winner in Florida, Gore's lawyers headed back to court arguing that thousands of ballots were still uncounted. The Florida Supreme Court

ordered all Florida counties to begin a hand recount of ballots rejected by the counting machines. As counting began, the United States Supreme Court ordered the recount to stop until it had issued its ruling.

On December 12, in *Bush* v. *Gore,* the United States Supreme Court ruled 7–2 that the hand recounts in Florida violated the equal protection clause of the Constitution. The Court argued that because different vote counters used different standards, the recount did not treat all voters equally.

Both federal law and the Constitution require the electoral votes for president to be cast on a certain day. If Florida missed that deadline, its electoral votes would not count. The Court ruled 5–4 that there was not enough time left to conduct a manual recount that would pass constitutional standards. This ruling left Bush the certified winner in Florida. The next day, Gore conceded the election.

Reading Check **Analyzing** Why did the U.S. Supreme Court stop the manual recounts in Florida?

Bush Becomes President

MAIN Idea George W. Bush supported the enactment of a tax cut, the No Child Left Behind program, and a strategic defense system.

HISTORY AND YOU Have new education policies affected the testing process at your school? Read on to learn more about No Child Left Behind.

On January 20, 2001, George W. Bush became the forty-third president of the United States. In his Inaugural Address, Bush promised to improve the public schools, to cut taxes, to reform Social Security and Medicare, and to build up the nation's defenses.

After taking office, the president's first **priority** was to cut taxes to try to boost the economy. During the election campaign, the stock market dropped sharply, unemployment began to rise, and many new Internet-based companies went out of business. Despite opposition from some Democrats, Congress passed a large $1.35 trillion tax cut to be phased in over 10 years. In the summer of 2001, Americans began receiving tax rebate checks that put about $40 billion back into the economy in an effort to prevent a recession.

Soon after Congress passed the tax cut plan, President Bush proposed two major reforms in education. He wanted public schools to give annual standardized tests, and he wanted to allow parents to use federal funds to pay for private schools if their public schools were doing a poor job. Although Congress refused to give federal funds to private schools, it did vote in favor of annual reading and math tests in public schools for grades 3–8. This law became known as the No Child Left Behind Act.

President Bush also focused on Medicare reform. By the summer of 2002, Congress had introduced a bill adding prescription drug benefits to Medicare. The bill was **controversial.** Some opponents feared it would cost too much, while others argued that it did not go far enough. The program finally became law in November 2003.

Congress also reacted to a rash of corporate scandals—the most famous taking place at a large energy trading company called Enron. Corporate leaders there cost investors and employees billions of dollars before the company went bankrupt. Congress passed a new law—the Public Company Accounting Reform and Investor Protection Act—also known as the Sarbanes-Oxley Act, after the members of Congress who introduced it. The law tightened accounting rules and toughened penalties for dishonest executives.

Shortly after taking office, President Bush also pushed for new military programs designed to meet the needs of the post–Cold War world. One program Bush strongly favored was **strategic defense**—the effort to develop missiles and other devices that could shoot down nuclear missiles. Bush argued that missile defense was needed because many hostile nations were developing long-range missiles.

As the debate about the nation's military programs continued in the summer of 2001, a horrific event changed everything. On September 11, 2001, terrorists crashed passenger jets into the World Trade Center and the Pentagon. A new war had begun.

✔ Reading Check **Explaining** What was President George W. Bush's first priority when he took office?

Section 1 REVIEW

Vocabulary

1. **Explain** the significance of: Al Gore, George W. Bush, Ralph Nader, chad, strategic defense.

Main Ideas

2. **Paraphrasing** What did the U.S. Supreme Court decide in *Bush* v. *Gore?*

3. **Describing** What did the No Child Left Behind Act mandate?

Critical Thinking

4. **Big Ideas** What caused the vote-count controversy in Florida in the 2000 election?

5. **Organizing** Use a graphic organizer similar to the one below by listing President Bush's goals when he took office.

6. **Analyzing Visuals** Study the photos on page 805. Explain how you would change the voting process following the controversy of the 2000 election.

Writing About History

7. **Persuasive Writing** Take on the role of a Supreme Court justice. Write a statement explaining how you voted in *Bush* v. *Gore* and why you took this position.

History ONLINE

Study Central™ To review this section, go to glencoe.com and click on Study Central.

The War on Terrorism Begins

Guide to Reading

Big Ideas
Government and Society Acts of terrorism against the United States prompted George W. Bush to declare "War on Terror."

Content Vocabulary
- terrorism *(p. 810)*
- state-sponsored terrorism *(p. 811)*
- anthrax *(p. 813)*

Academic Vocabulary
- resolve *(p. 809)*
- interpretation *(p. 810)*
- obtain *(p. 812)*

People and Events to Identify
- Osama bin Laden *(p. 809)*
- al-Qaeda *(p. 809)*

Reading Strategy
Organizing Complete a graphic organizer similar to the one below to show causes of terrorism.

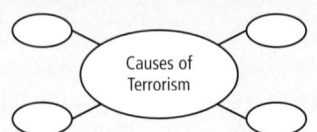

On September 11, 2001, terrorists attacked the United States killing over 3,000 people. The attacks united the nation as Americans worked to help the survivors. President George W. Bush and Congress launched a war on terrorism to prevent such attacks in the future.

September 11, 2001

MAIN Idea The terrorist attacks on the World Trade Center and the Pentagon shocked and alarmed Americans; almost immediately, combating terrorism became the nation's top priority.

HISTORY AND YOU Do you recall learning about the 1919 bombings that triggered government raids and roundups of foreigners? Read on to learn how the United States reacted to the more deadly attacks of 2001.

At 8:45 A.M. Eastern Daylight Time on September 11, 2001, a Boeing 767 passenger jet slammed into the North Tower of the World Trade Center in New York City. As people below gazed in horror, a second plane collided with the South Tower. Soon afterward, a third plane crashed into the Pentagon in Washington, D.C. At 9:50 A.M., the South Tower collapsed in a billowing cloud of dust and debris. The North Tower fell about 40 minutes later. The falling towers killed thousands of people, burying them beneath a vast mound of rubble.

The airplanes did not crash accidentally. Hijackers deliberately crashed them into the buildings. Hijackers also seized a fourth airplane, United Airlines Flight 93, probably hoping to crash it into the White House or the Capitol. Many passengers on Flight 93 had cell phones. After hearing about the World Trade Center, four passengers—Todd Beamer, Thomas Burnett, Jeremy Glick, and Mark Bingham—decided to do something. An operator listening over a cell phone heard Todd Beamer's voice: "Are you ready guys? Let's roll."

Soon afterward, Flight 93 crashed in a field in Pennsylvania. At that moment, Vice President Dick Cheney was in a bunker under the White House. After hearing Flight 93 had crashed, he turned to the others in the room, and said: "I think an act of heroism just took place on that plane."

A National Emergency

The attacks of 9/11, as the day came to be called, killed all 266 passengers and crewmembers on the four hijacked planes. Another 125 people died in the Pentagon. In New York City, nearly 3,000 people died. More Americans were killed in the attacks of September 11,

The Attacks of September 11, 2001

The terrorist attacks of September 11, 2001, altered the lives of millions of Americans and shifted the priorities of the federal government. At home the United States launched a new war against terrorists and their supporters. Globally, the United States took aggressive and preemptive steps to stop terrorism. At home, the balance between civil liberties and national security shifted, with passage of the USA Patriot Act, which gave broad new powers to the federal government.

MAKING CONNECTIONS How are the terrorist attacks and their aftermath still affecting American society and foreign policy?

Above, the South Tower of the World Trade Center bursts into flames after being struck by an airliner while the North Tower burns from an attack a few minutes earlier. At left, one side of the Pentagon was badly damaged. Part of the building later collapsed. At right, after the World Trade Center towers collapsed, the resulting debris coated the city with dust.

2001, than died at Pearl Harbor or on D-Day in World War II.

The attacks shocked Americans, but they responded rapidly to the crisis. Medical workers and firefighters from other cities raced to New York to help. Across the nation, Americans donated blood and collected food, blankets, and other supplies. Within weeks, Americans also donated over $1 billion. From around the world came sympathy. "We are all Americans!" wrote one French journalist.

Everywhere across the nation, Americans put up flags to show their unity and **resolve.** They held candlelight vigils and prayer services as they searched for ways to help. If the terrorists had hoped to divide Americans, they failed. As the Reverend Billy Graham noted at a memorial service, "A tragedy like this could have torn our country apart. But instead it has united us and we have become a family."

The American government also responded quickly to the crisis. All civilian airplanes were grounded. The armed forces were put on high alert. Across the nation, Americans in the National Guard left their civilian jobs and reported for duty. The Air National Guard began patrolling the skies over major cities, and Army National Guard troops were deployed to airports to strengthen security.

On September 14, President Bush declared a national emergency. Congress authorized the use of force to fight whoever had attacked the United States. Intelligence sources and the FBI quickly identified the attacks as the work of a man named **Osama bin Laden** and his organization, **al-Qaeda** (al KY•duh).

ARCTIC OCEAN

NORTH AMERICA

EUROPE

ASIA

PACIFIC OCEAN

ATLANTIC OCEAN

AFRICA

PACIFIC OCEAN

INDIAN OCEAN

AUSTRALIA

1 1993 Bomb at the World Trade Center kills 6

2 1995 Bombs at a U.S.-Saudi facility in Riyadh kill 7

3 1996 Bombing of Khobar Towers barracks in Dhahran, Saudi Arabia, kills 19 Americans

4 1998 Bombings at U.S. embassies in Kenya and Tanzania kill more than 200

5 2000 Attack on the USS *Cole* kills 17 American sailors

6 2001 Hijacked airliners crash into the World Trade Center, the Pentagon, and a field in Pennsylvania killing nearly 3,000

7 2002 Bombing in Bali, Indonesia, kills more than 200

8 2004 Bombing of commuter trains in Madrid, Spain, kills 191

9 2004 Attack on the U.S. Consulate in Jedda, Saudi Arabia, kills 5

10 2005 Bombs on the London subway kill 52

11 2002–present Ongoing attacks against coalition troops and civilians in Afghanistan

12 2003–present Ongoing attacks against coalition troops and civilians in Iraq

Osama bin Laden ▶

Middle East Terrorism and the United States

The attacks on the World Trade Center and the Pentagon were acts of terrorism. **Terrorism** is the use of violence by nongovernmental groups against civilians to achieve a political goal. Terrorist acts are intended to instill fear in people and to force governments into changing their policies.

Although there have been many acts of terrorism in American history, most terrorist attacks on Americans since World War II have been carried out by Middle Eastern groups. The reason Middle Eastern terrorists have targeted Americans can be traced back to events early in the twentieth century.

As oil became important to the American economy in the 1920s, the United States invested heavily in the Middle East oil industry. This industry brought great wealth to the ruling families in some Middle Eastern kingdoms, but most people remained poor. Some

became angry at the United States for supporting the wealthy kingdoms and families.

The rise of the oil industry also led to the spread of Western ideas in the region, and many Muslims feared that their traditional values were being weakened. New movements arose calling for a strict **interpretation** of the Quran—the Muslim holy book—and a return to traditional Muslim religious laws. These Muslim movements wanted to overthrow pro-Western governments in the Middle East and create a pure Islamic society. Muslims who support these movements are referred to as fundamentalist militants. Some militants began using terrorism to achieve their goals.

American support of Israel angered many in the Middle East. In 1947, following the global outrage over the Jewish Holocaust, the UN proposed to divide the British Mandate of Palestine into an Arab state and a Jewish state. The Jews accepted and established Israel in 1948. Arab states responded by attacking Israel. The territory that the UN had proposed as an Arab state came under the control of Israel, Jordan, and Egypt. In the 1950s, Palestinians began staging guerrilla raids and terrorist attacks against Israel. Since the United States gave aid to Israel, it became the target of Muslim hostility. In the 1970s, several Middle East nations realized they could fight Israel and the United States by providing terrorists with money, weapons, and training. This is called **state-sponsored terrorism.** The governments of Libya, Syria, Iraq, and Iran have all sponsored terrorists.

The Rise of Al-Qaeda

In 1979 the Soviet Union invaded Afghanistan. In response, Muslims from across the world headed to Afghanistan to help fight the Soviets. Among them was a wealthy 22-year-old Saudi Arabian named Osama bin Laden. In 1988 he founded an organization called al-Qaeda or "the Base." Al-Qaeda recruited Muslims and channeled money and arms to the Afghan resistance.

Bin Laden believed that superpowers could be beaten. He also believed that Western ideas had contaminated Muslim society and was outraged by Saudi Arabia's decision to allow American troops to be based on Saudi soil after Iraq invaded Kuwait.

At first, bin Laden ran al-Qaeda from camps in Sudan, but in 1996, he moved back to Afghanistan after the Taliban, a militant Muslim fundamentalist group, took power there. Bin Laden dedicated himself to driving Westerners out of the Middle East. In 1998 he called on Muslims to kill Americans. His followers set off bombs at the American embassies in Kenya and Tanzania.

After these bombings, President Clinton ordered cruise missiles fired at terrorist camps in Afghanistan and Sudan, but bin Laden was not deterred. In 1999, al-Qaeda terrorists were arrested while trying to smuggle explosives into the United States in an attempt to bomb Seattle. In October 2000, al-Qaeda terrorists crashed a boat loaded with explosives into the *USS Cole,* an American warship, while it was docked in Yemen. Then, on September 11, 2001, al-Qaeda struck again, hijacking four American passenger planes and executing the most devastating terrorist attack in history.

Reading Check **Explaining** Why was Osama bin Laden able to create a terrorist organization?

A New War Begins

MAIN Idea The war on terrorism involved halting terrorists' access to funding and launching a war in Afghanistan.

HISTORY AND YOU Does your school have plans for coping with an emergency? Read on to learn about the national response to the terrorist attacks.

In an address to Congress on September 20, 2001, President Bush demanded the Taliban regime in Afghanistan turn over bin Laden and his supporters and shut down all terrorist camps. The president then made it clear that although the war on terrorism would start by targeting al-Qaeda, it would not stop there. "It will not end," the president announced, "until every terrorist group of global reach has been found, stopped, and defeated." While Secretary of State Colin Powell began building an international coalition to support the United States, Secretary of Defense Donald Rumsfeld began deploying troops, aircraft, and warships to the Middle East.

The president also announced that the United States would no longer tolerate states that aided terrorists. "From this day forward," the president proclaimed, "any nation that continues to harbor or support terrorism will be regarded by the United States as a hostile regime." The war would not end quickly, but it was a war the nation had to fight:

PRIMARY SOURCE

"Great harm has been done to us. We have suffered great loss. And in our grief and anger we have found our mission and our moment. . . . Our Nation—this generation—will lift a dark threat of violence from our people and our future."

—President George W. Bush, *Address to Joint Session of Congress,* September 20, 2001

In a letter to the *New York Times,* Secretary of Defense Rumsfeld warned Americans that "this will be a war like none other our nation has faced." The enemy, he explained, "is a global network of terrorist organizations and their state sponsors, committed to denying free people the opportunity to live as they choose." Fighting terrorism would not be easy. Military force would be used, but terrorism had to be fought by other means as well.

For a longer excerpt from this speech read, "President Bush's Address to Joint Session of Congress, September 20, 2001" on page R57 of **Documents in American History.**

Responding to 9/11

After the attacks, Americans held vigils and prayer services to remember and honor those who had died. For months after the attacks, Americans closely followed the efforts of firefighters and rescue workers. Despite increased airport security, the attacks left some Americans wary of air travel.

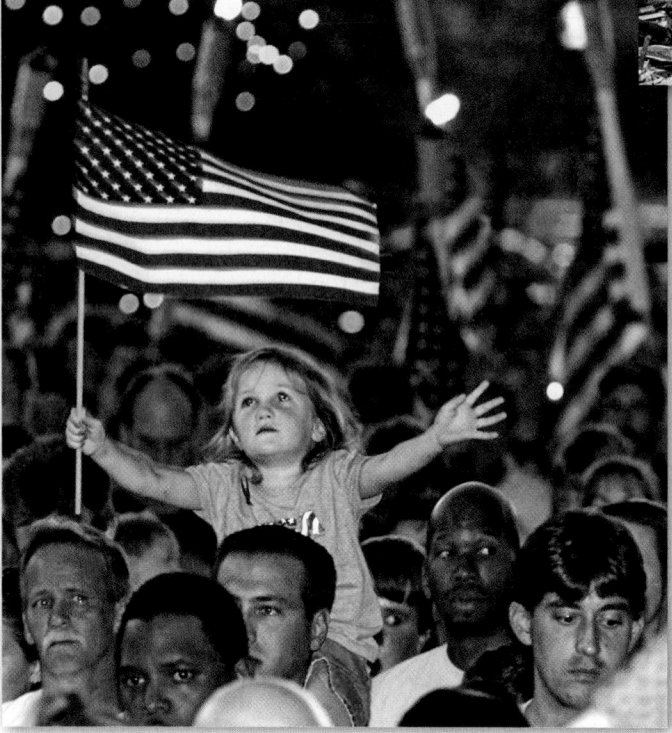

At left, Alana Milawski, waves an American flag during a candlelight vigil in Las Vegas on September 12, 2001. Above, firefighters work in the rubble of the World Trade Center. The attacks led to an increase in airline security (right) resulting in long lines at airports while passengers waited to be screened.

Analyzing VISUALS

1. **Theorizing** Why do you think so many people participated in group vigils and memorials after the attacks?

2. **Evaluating** In what ways were Americans most immediately affected by the attacks of September 11, 2001?

Cutting Terrorist Funding One effective way to fight terrorist groups is to cut off their funding. On September 24, President Bush issued an executive order freezing the financial assets of several individuals and groups suspected of terrorism. As information about terrorist groups increased, more names and organizations were added to the list. President Bush asked other nations to help, and within weeks, some 80 nations had issued orders freezing the assets of the organizations and individuals on the American list.

Homeland Security and the Patriot Act

As part of the effort to protect the American people from further terrorist attacks, President Bush created a new federal agency—the Office of Homeland Security—to coordinate the dozens of federal agencies and departments working to prevent terrorism. He then appointed Pennsylvania governor Tom Ridge to serve as the agency's director.

History ONLINE
Student Web Activity Visit glencoe.com and complete the activity on the war on terrorism.

The president also asked Congress to pass legislation to help law enforcement agencies track down terrorist suspects. Drafting the legislation took time. Congress had to balance Americans' Fourth Amendment protections against unreasonable search and seizure with the need to increase security. President Bush signed the antiterrorist bill—known as the USA Patriot Act—into law in October 2001. In cases involving terrorism, the law permitted secret searches to avoid tipping off suspects and allowed authorities to **obtain** a nationwide search warrant useable in any jurisdiction. The law also made it easier to wiretap suspects and allowed authorities to track Internet communications and seize voice mail.

In the months following the attack, the Office of Homeland Security struggled to coordinate all of the federal agencies fighting terrorism. In June 2002, President Bush asked Congress to combine all of the agencies responsible for the public's safety into a new department called the Department of Homeland Security. The plan called for the largest reorganization of the federal government since 1947, when Congress created the Department of Defense, the National Security Council, and the CIA.

The president's proposal led to an intense debate in Congress, and it did not pass until after the midterm elections in November 2002. The new Department of Homeland Security controls the Coast Guard, the Border Patrol, the Immigration and Naturalization Service, the Customs Service, the Federal Emergency Management Agency, and many other agencies. It also analyzes information collected by the FBI, the CIA, and other intelligence agencies.

Bioterrorism Strikes the United States As the nation struggled to cope with the attacks on the Pentagon and the World Trade Center, another terrorist attack began. On October 5, 2001, a newspaper editor in Florida died from an anthrax infection. **Anthrax** is a type of bacteria. Several nations, including the United States, Russia, and Iraq, have used anthrax to create biological weapons. Antibiotics can cure anthrax, but if left untreated, it can quickly become lethal.

Soon after its appearance in Florida, anthrax was found at the offices of news organizations in New York City. In Washington, D.C., a letter containing anthrax arrived at Senator Tom Daschle's office. It was now clear that terrorists were using the mail to spread anthrax. Traces of anthrax were found at several government buildings. Several postal workers who had handled letters containing anthrax contracted the disease, and two workers died. The FBI began investigating the attack, but no suspects were arrested.

The War in Afghanistan Begins

On October 7, 2001, the United States began bombing al-Qaeda's camps and the Taliban's military forces in Afghanistan. In an address to the nation, President Bush explained that Islam and the Afghan people were not the enemy, and that the United States would send food, medicine, and other supplies to Afghan refugees. The president also explained that the attack on the Taliban was only the beginning. The war on terrorism would continue until victory was achieved:

PRIMARY SOURCE

"Today we focus on Afghanistan, but the battle is broader. Every nation has a choice to make. In this conflict, there is no neutral ground. If any government sponsors the outlaws and killers of innocents, they have become outlaws and murderers, themselves. And they will take that lonely path at their own peril. . . . The battle is now joined on many fronts. We will not waver; we will not tire; we will not falter; and we will not fail. Peace and freedom will prevail. Thank you. May God continue to bless America."

—President George W. Bush, Address to the Nation, October 7, 2001

✔ Reading Check **Outlining** What steps did the president take in response to the terrorist attacks?

Section 2 REVIEW

Vocabulary

1. **Explain** the significance of: Osama bin Laden, al-Qaeda, terrorism, state-sponsored terrorism, anthrax.

Main Ideas

2. **Describing** What factors have contributed to the rise of Middle Eastern terrorist groups?

3. **Listing** What major actions marked the beginning of the United States' war on terrorism?

Critical Thinking

4. **Big Ideas** Why do Islamic fundamentalists in the Middle East disagree with U.S. foreign policy?

5. **Categorizing** Use a graphic organizer similar to the one below to list the responses of individual Americans and the federal government to the attacks on September 11, 2001.

Individuals — Response to 9/11 attacks — Government

6. **Analyzing Visuals** Study the map of terrorist attacks on page 810. How would you describe the scope of al-Qaeda's operation?

Writing About History

7. **Persuasive Writing** The Patriot Act gave law enforcement new ways to fight terrorism. Write a letter to a newspaper explaining why you are either for or against giving up some freedoms in exchange for increased security.

History ONLINE

Study Central™ To review this section, go to glencoe.com and click on Study Central.

The Invasion of Iraq

Guide to Reading

Big Ideas
Trade, War, and Migration In an effort to fight terrorism, the United States launched attacks in both Afghanistan and Iraq.

Content Vocabulary
• weapons of mass destruction (WMD) *(p. 816)*

Academic Vocabulary
• inspector *(p. 817)*
• significantly *(p. 818)*
• eliminate *(p. 819)*

People and Events to Identify
• Northern Alliance *(p. 814)*
• Khalid Shaikh Mohammed *(p. 815)*
• "axis of evil" *(p. 816)*
• Saddam Hussein *(p. 817)*

Reading Strategy
As you read this section on the Invasion of Iraq, complete a graphic organizer similar to the one below to show the different groups in Iraq.

After the attacks of September 11, 2001, the United States invaded Afghanistan, the Central Asian nation that had sheltered many al-Qaeda members. In March 2003, the United States invaded Iraq and toppled the regime of Saddam Hussein.

The War on Terror Continues

MAIN Idea After forcing Taliban leaders in Afghanistan to flee, the United States and its allies sent more troops as peacekeepers and worked to create a stable and democratic government.

HISTORY AND YOU Can you think of a nation or region today where peacekeepers are stationed while a new government is established? Read on to learn about the role of peacekeepers in Afghanistan.

Less than a month after the September 11 attacks, the United States launched a war in Afghanistan with the goal of bringing down the Taliban regime that had sheltered Osama bin Laden and other members of al-Qaeda. Americans also hoped that bin Laden would be captured and brought back for trial in the United States.

While American warplanes bombed the Taliban's forces, the United States began sending military aid to the **Northern Alliance,** a coalition of Afghan groups that had been fighting the Taliban for several years. U.S. Special Forces also entered Afghanistan to advise the Northern Alliance and identify targets for American aircraft. The American bombing campaign quickly shattered the Taliban's defenses. The Northern Alliance then launched a massive attack. In December 2001, the Taliban government collapsed, and surviving Taliban fled to the mountains of Afghanistan.

Rebuilding Afghanistan

After the Taliban fled, the United States and its allies helped local Afghan leaders create a new government. Meanwhile, thousands of American and allied troops arrived to act as peacekeepers. In 2003 NATO took command of peacekeeping in Afghanistan.

Since 2002 Afghanistan has begun to slowly recover from decades of war. The economy has grown rapidly, although the people remain very poor. The United States and its allies have donated some $24 billion to help rebuild the country. In December 2004, Afghanistan held its first nationwide democratic election, and Hamid Karzai was elected president. One year later, the Afghan people elected a National Assembly. Despite these successes, Afghanistan continues to suffer from violence. Taliban insurgents have staged guerrilla

The War in Afghanistan

The United States invaded Afghanistan to overthrow the Taliban regime. Helping to establish a democratic government was the next step.

▲ American soldiers were sent to act as peacekeepers while the new Afghan government tried to establish order in the mountainous country.

▲ The new Afghan constitution granted equal rights to women, including the right to vote.

▶ Hamid Karzai was elected president in 2004.

Analyzing VISUALS

1. **Speculating** What part of their duties do you think these soldiers find most difficult?

2. **Predicting** How may voting rights for women affect the development of the new Afghan government?

attacks and suicide bombings. The Afghan government has little control over the mountainous regions of southern Afghanistan and fighting continues between NATO and Taliban forces in the south.

Bin Laden Goes Into Hiding

According to news reports, American intelligence agencies believe Osama bin Laden crossed into Pakistan to hide in the mountainous region of Waziristan where the local people were friendly to al-Qaeda and the Taliban. Between 2002 and 2006, bin Laden released a number of audiotapes and one videotape urging his followers to continue the fight.

Pakistan has not officially allowed American troops to enter its territory to find bin Laden, although news reports suggest U.S. Special Forces may be operating in the area. Pakistan has itself launched several military operations in Waziristan in search of al-Qaeda and Taliban forces. Although many al-Qaeda operatives have been arrested in Pakistan, Osama bin Laden remains at large.

Tracking Down Al-Qaeda

Since 2001, the United States and its allies have continued their worldwide hunt for al-Qaeda members. Hundreds of people have been captured or killed, including several top leaders of al-Qaeda. In November 2002, the CIA used an unmanned remote-controlled flying drone to fire a missile at a car in Yemen killing everyone in the vehicle. The car had been carrying top al-Qaeda leaders who had planned the attack on the USS *Cole* in 1998.

In 2003, Pakistan and the United States captured **Khalid Shaikh Mohammed**—one of the highest ranking members of al-Qaeda, and the man suspected of planning the September 11 attacks. Between 2002 and 2006, the American government believes that at least 10 major attacks by al-Qaeda, including at least three attacks on the United States and two on Great Britain, have been prevented.

Reading Check Describing What strategy has the United States used to prevent the Taliban from regaining power?

Iraq and Weapons of Mass Destruction

MAIN Idea Concern that Iraq might be producing WMDs that could be given to terrorists led to an ultimatum.

HISTORY AND YOU Do you think the UN is an effective mediator of world affairs? Read on to learn about UN actions before the Iraq War.

The terrorist attacks of September 11, 2001 showed that groups such as al-Qaeda were determined to kill as many Americans as possible. President Bush and his advisers were deeply concerned that terrorist groups might acquire **weapons of mass destruction** (WMD). Weapons of mass destruction can kill large numbers of people all at once. Nuclear, chemical, and biological weapons are all examples of weapons of mass destruction.

During the Cold War, very few nations had weapons of mass destruction, and the United States relied upon a policy of deterrence to prevent their use. The United States announced that if any nation used weapons of mass destruction against the United States, the United States would counterattack with its own weapons of mass destruction. Deterrence worked during the Cold War, but the rise of state-sponsored terrorism created a new problem. If a nation secretly gave weapons of mass destruction to terrorists who then used them against the United States, the American military might not know where the weapons came from, or whom to attack in response.

The "Axis of Evil"

In his State of the Union speech in 2002, President Bush warned that an **"axis of evil"** made up of Iraq, Iran, and North Korea posed a grave threat to the world. Each of these nations had been known to sponsor terrorism, and was suspected of developing weapons of mass destruction. The president warned that "The United States of America will not permit the world's most dangerous regimes to threaten us with the world's most destructive weapons."

Of the three nations in the "axis of evil," the president and his advisers believed Iraq to be the most immediate danger. It had used chem-

THE Global War ON Terror, 2001–2007

Oct. 7, 2001
The United States launches attacks on Taliban positions in Afghanistan

March 20, 2003
American and coalition forces begin the invasion of Iraq

2001 **2002** **2003**

Sept. 11, 2001
Terrorists highjack four planes and attack the World Trade Center and the Pentagon

Nov. 2002
UN Resolution warns Iraq to allow weapons inspectors to return

March 1, 2003
Khalid Shaikh Mohammed, suspected of planning the 9/11 attacks, is captured

Sept. 2003
Eleven countries form the Proliferation Security Initiative to intercept shipments of materials used to make weapons of mass destruction

ical weapons against the Kurds, an ethnic group in northern Iraq, and after the 1991 Gulf War, UN **inspectors** had also found evidence that Iraq had developed biological weapons and had been working on a nuclear bomb.

Between 1991 and 1998, Iraq appeared to be hiding its weapons of mass destruction from UN inspectors. In 1998 the Iraqi government ordered the inspectors to leave the country. In response, President Clinton ordered a massive bombing attack on Iraq to destroy its ability to make such weapons. Despite the attack, intelligence agencies continued to believe Iraq was hiding weapons of mass destruction.

An Ultimatum to Iraq

In 2002 President Bush decided the time had come to deal with Iraq. On September 12, he delivered a speech to the United Nations asking for a new resolution against Iraq. If Iraq's dictator, **Saddam Hussein,** wanted peace he would have to give up Iraq's weapons of mass destruction, readmit the UN weapons inspectors, stop supporting terrorism, and stop oppressing his people. Although he was asking the UN to pass a resolution, the president made it clear that the United States would act with or without UN support.

While the UN Security Council debated a new resolution, President Bush asked Congress to authorize the use of force against Iraq, which it did. With the midterm elections only weeks away, Democrats wanted to focus on the nation's high unemployment rate and the slow economy. Instead, President Bush successfully kept the focus on national security issues. In 2002 Republicans picked up seats in the House of Representatives and regained control of the Senate.

Soon after the American elections, the UN approved a new resolution setting a deadline for Iraq to readmit weapons inspectors. It also required Iraq to declare its weapons of mass destruction, to stop supporting terrorism, and to stop oppressing its people. It threatened "serious consequences" if Iraq did not comply.

✔ **Reading Check** **Analyzing** Why did the United States think stopping the spread of weapons of mass destruction was linked to the war on terror?

Oct. 29, 2004
Osama bin Laden releases a video warning Americans that they will never have security if they continue their attacks

Oct. 2005
American deaths in the war in Iraq surpass 2,000

June 2006
Al-Zarqawi, the leader of al-Qaeda in Iraq, is killed in a U.S. attack

Jan. 2007
President Bush announces he will send 20,000 more troops to Iraq to restore order in Baghdad

2004   2005   2006   2007

Oct., 2004
Iraq Survey Group issues its final report concluding Iraq did not have weapons of mass destruction at the time the war began

Jan. 31, 2005
Iraqis go to the polls in their first free election

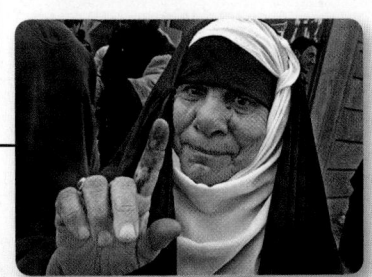

Analyzing TIME LINES

1. **Sequencing** Which happened first—the U.S. attack on Afghanistan or the invasion of Iraq?

2. **Specifying** When did Iraqis hold their first free election?

Confronting Iraq

MAIN Idea Coalition forces defeated the Iraqi military, but then factions in Iraq took up arms against coalition forces and each other.

HISTORY AND YOU In retrospect, do you believe the invasion of Iraq was justified? Read on to learn more about the different stages of the war.

In November 2002, Iraq agreed to readmit UN weapons inspectors. It then submitted a statement admitting it had weapons of mass destruction before the Gulf War, but denying it currently had weapons of mass destruction. Secretary of State Colin Powell declared that Iraq's declaration contained lies and was in "material breach" of the UN resolution.

As the United States and a coalition of some 30 nations prepared for war with Iraq, others at the UN Security Council argued that the inspectors should be given more time to find evidence of Iraq's WMD programs. By March 2003, the inspectors still had found nothing, and the United States began pressing the UN to authorize the use of force against Iraq.

France and Russia, two Security Council members with veto power, refused to back such a resolution. As war became imminent, world opinion divided between those who supported the United States and those who opposed an attack on Iraq. Around the world antiwar protestors staged rallies and marches. Several nations that had supported the United States in its war on terror, and had sent troops to Afghanistan, including France, Germany, and Canada, refused to join the coalition against Iraq. Saudi Arabia and Turkey—both American allies—refused to allow the United States to attack Iraq from their territories. The only nation bordering Iraq that granted permission to use its territory was Kuwait.

The Invasion Begins

On March 20, 2003, the U.S.-led coalition forces attacked Iraq. Over 150,000 American troops, some 45,000 British troops, as well as a few hundred special forces from Australia and Poland took part in the invasion.

Much of the Iraqi army dissolved as soldiers refused to risk their lives for Hussein. A few fierce battles took place, but the Iraqis were unable to slow the coalition advance **significantly.** On May 1, President Bush declared

PRIMARY SOURCE
The Invasion of Iraq

Overthrowing Saddam Hussein to ensure he could not give WMDs to terrorists was the primary objective of the invasion. Ousting his regime, however, proved easier than establishing a new government.

▲ After decades of sham elections, Iraqi voters get to make real choices when they vote during Iraq's 2005 elections.

▲ U.S. and Iraqi soldiers face the difficult challenge of urban warfare in Iraq where the enemy can be very close, hiding behind walls or in buildings.

Analyzing VISUALS

1. **Speculating** What do you suppose these soldiers hope to accomplish in fulfilling their duties?

2. **Predicting** Will regularly-scheduled elections lead to a more stable national government?

that the major combat was over. About 140 Americans and several thousand Iraqis had died. Saddam Hussein was captured in late 2003. After a prolonged trial, an Iraqi court found him guilty of ordering mass executions. He was executed in 2006.

Insurgents and Reconstruction

The quick victory did not end the fighting. Soon after the coalition took control of the country, small groups of Iraqis began staging bombings, sniper attacks, and sporadic battles against coalition forces. Some of the groups carrying out the attacks were former members of Saddam Hussein's military. Others were affiliated with al-Qaeda and other radical Muslim groups who believed the invasion offered a chance to build support in the Muslim world by organizing resistance to the Americans.

Some of the attacks were carried out by militias belonging to the different religious and ethnic groups in Iraq. The majority of Iraq's population is Shia Muslim, but there is a large Sunni Muslim minority as well. The Sunni are themselves divided between Sunni Arabs, who ruled the country under Saddam Hussein's leadership, and Sunni Kurds. The collapse of Hussein's dictatorship renewed old hostilities between these groups, forcing coalition troops to protect them from attacks from each other's militias.

Having gone to war in Iraq to overthrow a tyrant and **eliminate** the possibility of weapons of mass destruction being given to terrorists, the United States found itself trying to suppress an insurgency, prevent a civil war, and establish a new Iraqi government. The United States and its allies spent more than $30 billion to improve Iraq's electrical generating capacity, provide clean water, build schools, and improve health care, but insurgent attacks slowed these efforts. Despite the problems, Iraq's economy began to grow rapidly and a substantial improvement in living standards took place.

Between 2003 and 2006, insurgents killed over 3,000 American soldiers, many more than had died in the initial invasion. Many Americans had expected the war to be over quickly and as the fighting dragged on, support for the war began to decline. The failure to find any weapons of mass destruction also added to the growing controversy as to whether the war was a mistake.

American policy makers now faced a dilemma. If they pulled troops out too soon, Iraq might fall into civil war and provide a safe haven and breeding ground for terrorist groups. At the same time, the longer the United States stayed, the more its presence might stir resentment and support for terrorist groups. The best solution seemed to be to get a functioning and democratic Iraqi government up and running as fast as possible and then train its forces to take over the security of the country. As part of this plan, in January 2005, the Iraqi people went to the polls in huge numbers for the first free elections in their country's history. After much debate, voters then overwhelmingly approved a new constitution in October 2005.

Reading Check **Summarizing** Why did it prove so difficult to end the Iraq War quickly?

Vocabulary

1. **Explain** the significance of: Northern Alliance, Khalid Shaikh Mohammed, weapons of mass destruction, "axis of evil," Saddam Hussein.

Main Ideas

2. **Explaining** Why did the United States send military aid to the Northern Alliance?

3. **Identifying** Why did Bush choose to focus military attention in Iraq?

4. **Summarizing** Why did fighting continue in Iraq after President Bush declared the major combat was over?

Critical Thinking

5. **Big Ideas** Why did the United States declare war on Afghanistan?

6. **Organizing** Use a graphic organizer to list the reasons why President Bush ordered the invasion of Iraq.

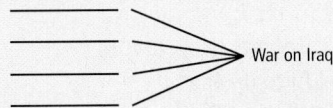

War on Iraq

7. **Analyzing Visuals** Examine the photos on page 818. How does the style of warfare in Iraq differ from the fighting in Afghanistan?

Writing About History

8. **Descriptive Writing** Suppose you are an Iraqi who has recently voted in your first election. Write a journal entry that explains how you feel following your vote.

History ONLINE

Study Central™ To review this section, go to glencoe.com and click on Study Central.

Section 4

A Time of Challenges

After a close campaign, President Bush won a second term in 2004, but scandals and continued difficulties in Iraq helped Democrats win control of Congress in 2006. In 2008, as the economy began experiencing difficulties, voters elected Barack Obama to be president. Obama was the first African American president of the United States.

The Election of 2004

MAIN Idea After a campaign that centered on the war in Iraq and the war on terror, Bush was reelected.

HISTORY AND YOU Have you ever participated in an election at your school? Read on to learn about the election of 2004.

In early 2004, President Bush's approval ratings began to fall. The ongoing war in Iraq and the failure of inspectors to find any weapons of mass destruction weakened his support, as did the scandal at the Iraqi prison of **Abu Ghraib,** where some prisoners were abused by American soldiers. These events gave Democrats the opportunity to mount a serious challenge in the 2004 election.

President Bush and Vice President Cheney were renominated by the Republicans. The Democrats nominated Massachusetts Senator John Kerry for president and North Carolina Senator John Edwards for vice president. Bush promised to cut taxes while continuing the war on terrorism. He opposed abortion and called for a constitutional amendment to ban same-sex marriages. Senator Kerry promised to raise taxes on the wealthy to fund wider health care coverage, and to strengthen Social Security. He also took the opposite stand from Bush on most social issues. Bush's campaign portrayed Kerry as an untrustworthy "flipflopper." Kerry's campaign argued that Bush was too stubborn to change course when events required it.

Although September 11, 2001, had united the nation emotionally, the country remained as divided politically as it had been in 2000. Bush's support was strongest in the South and on the Great Plains, as well as in rural areas and the outer suburbs of major cities. Kerry's base was in the Northeast and on the West Coast, as well as in cities and inner suburbs. Both candidates focused on the upper Midwest where voters were narrowly divided. Nationwide, President Bush won a majority of the popular vote as well as 286 electoral votes. Despite the problems in Iraq, voters felt it safer to stay the course.

✓ Reading Check **Analyzing** Why did President Bush's popularity decline in the year before the 2004 election?

Abu Ghraib and Guantanamo Bay

The revelation that some American troops had mistreated prisoners at the Abu Ghraib prison in Iraq shocked many people. Photographs of prisoners being abused and humiliated diminished the international image of the United States. Similarly, the lack of judicial proceedings and the secrecy surrounding the detainees at Guantanamo Bay prompted international criticism.

▲ Soldiers escort a detainee at Camp X-Ray at the military base at Guantanamo Bay, Cuba.

▲ A U.S. soldier points to prison cells where high risk detainees are held.

Analyzing VISUALS

1. **Interpreting** What might make a detainee "high risk"?
2. **Analyzing** In the photograph above, what elements show the level of security at the detention center?

Security vs. Liberty

MAIN Idea The Supreme Court rejected President Bush's interpretation of the rights and legal status of prisoners at Guantanamo Bay.

HISTORY AND YOU Do you believe all prisoners deserve a right to a trial? Read about the unusual status of prisoners at Guantanamo Bay.

The war on terror heightened the tension between America's national security and its civil liberties. In order to prevent another major terrorist attack, was the government justified in limiting the rights of citizens? Did captured terrorists have any rights at all?

Prisoners at Guantanamo

As American forces captured members of al-Qaeda, a decision had to be made as to what to do with them. In 2004 President Bush decided to hold them at the American military base in **Guantanamo Bay,** Cuba, where they could be interrogated. This decision was very controversial. Some people argued that the prisoners should have the right to a lawyer, formal charges, and eventually a proper trial.

The Bush administration insisted that the prisoners were illegal enemy combatants, not suspects charged with a crime, and as such, they did not have the right to appeal their detentions to an American court. The administration also declared that the **procedures** regarding the treatment of prisoners, as specified in the Geneva Conventions, did not apply to terrorists since they were not part of any nation's armed forces.

The Supreme Court disagreed with the administration. In 2004, in *Rasul* v. *Bush,* the Court ruled that foreign prisoners who claimed they were being unlawfully imprisoned had the right to have their cases heard in court. In response, the Bush administration created military tribunals to hear each detainee's case.

The Supreme Court struck this plan down in 2006 in *Hamdan* v. *Rumsfeld,* ruling that the military tribunals violated the Uniform Code of Military Justice and the Geneva Conventions.

President Bush then asked Congress to establish new tribunals that met the Court's objections. The president agreed that prisoners would have the right to see the evidence against them, and that evidence obtained by torture was inadmissible. The president also agreed to uphold the Geneva Conventions. Congress then passed the Military Commissions Act.

The Military Commissions Act stated that non-citizens captured as enemy combatants had no right to file writs of habeas corpus. If a tribunal determined that they were being lawfully held, they could be held indefinitely without trial. In 2008, in *Boumediene* v. *Bush,* the Supreme Court ruled that the detainees had a right to habeas corpus and declared the section of the Military Commissions Act suspending that right to be unconstitutional.

Domestic Surveillance

As part of the war on terror, the **National Security Agency** (NSA) began wiretapping domestic telephone calls made to overseas locations when they believed one party in the call was a member of al-Qaeda or affiliated with al-Qaeda. When the **monitoring** program became public in 2005, it created a controversy.

Civil rights groups argued that the program violated the Fourth Amendment. They pointed out that Congress had created the Foreign Intelligence Surveillance Court to issue warrants secretly in highly classified security cases. The president argued that the court was too slow and that he had the authority as commander in chief to expand wiretapping to help fight the war on terror. In 2006, a federal judge declared the wiretapping to be unconstitutional, but the following year an appeals court overturned the judge's decision. When Congress began drafting legislation to address the issue, the Bush administration suspended the program and announced that future wiretaps would require a warrant from the Foreign Intelligence Surveillance Court.

Reading Check **Explaining** Why did the Bush administration believe detainees at Guantanamo Bay had no right to take their case to a U.S. court?

Hurricane Katrina was one of the worst natural disasters in the history of the United States. The storm ravaged much of the Gulf Coast region. In New Orleans, the breach of the levees caused even more devastation.

▲ *An aerial photograph shows how the flooding in New Orleans ruined entire neighborhoods.*

A Stormy Second Term

MAIN Idea Bush appointed two new Supreme Court justices; his second term was marred by a hurricane, the ongoing war, and scandals.

HISTORY AND YOU Do you remember Hurricane Katrina? Read on to learn how the handling of the crisis hurt the Bush administration.

Having won a second term with a majority of the popular vote, President Bush concluded the American people had given him a mandate to continue his policies. He began his second term by announcing plans to overhaul the Social Security system and to create a prescription drug program for senior citizens.

Debating Social Security

To fix Social Security, President Bush proposed that workers be allowed to put 4 percent of their income in private accounts rather than in Social Security. This money could then be invested in stocks and bonds. The president

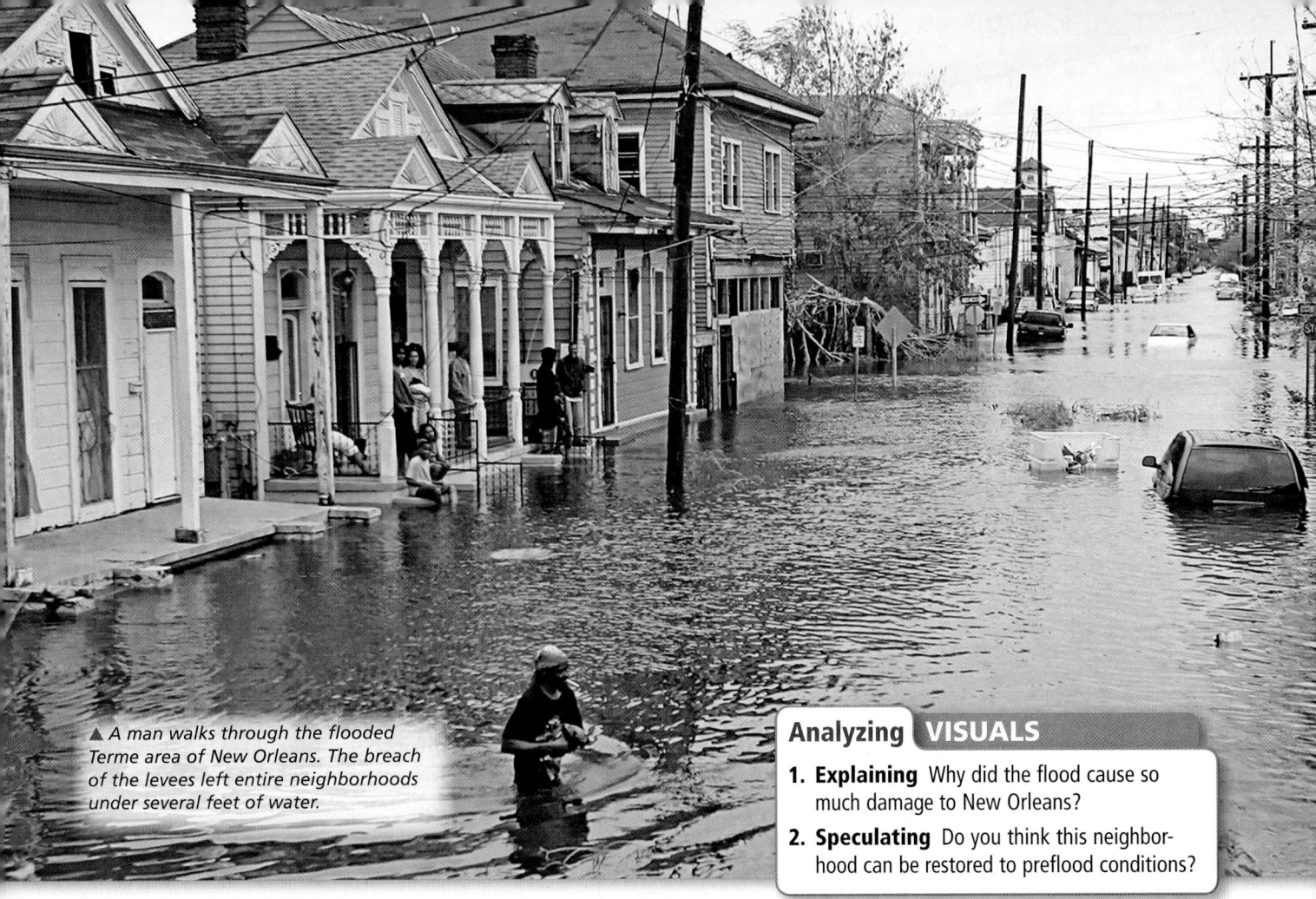

▲ A man walks through the flooded Terme area of New Orleans. The breach of the levees left entire neighborhoods under several feet of water.

Analyzing VISUALS

1. **Explaining** Why did the flood cause so much damage to New Orleans?

2. **Speculating** Do you think this neighborhood can be restored to preflood conditions?

believed that private accounts would grow rapidly and help cover the expected shortfall in Social Security accounts. Democrats argued that the danger to Social Security was overstated and that privatizing any part of Social Security was dangerous. With the American public unenthusiastic, the plan was never brought to a vote in Congress.

Although his plan to reform Social Security failed, President Bush did convince Congress to enact a new prescription drug program for seniors despite the concerns of many of his conservative supporters that the plan would cost too much money. Under the new program, provided by Medicare, people 65 and older can sign up for insurance that helps cover the cost of prescription drugs.

Hurricane Katrina

On August 29, 2005, Hurricane Katrina smashed into the Gulf Coast of the United States, spreading devastation from Florida to Louisiana. The fierce winds, rain, high tides, and storm surges destroyed buildings, roads, and electrical lines, left thousands of people homeless, and cost at least 1,200 lives. After the hurricane had passed, rising waters breached levees protecting the low-lying city of New Orleans. As water flooded the city, those who had stayed behind were forced to flee onto their roofs to await rescue. As the water rose 15 feet in some neighborhoods, many people drowned. Thousands more took shelter in the convention center and at the Superdome, a covered football stadium. There they waited for days without much food, clean water, or information from authorities.

Television news showed the condition of the survivors and asked why the government was not responding more quickly. The mayor of New Orleans was faulted for not issuing a mandatory evacuation until the storm was less than a day away, and for having failed to provide transportation for those who could not leave on their own. The governor of Louisiana argued with federal officials over who was in charge of the state's National Guard units. The Federal Emergency Management Agency (FEMA) seemed unprepared in its response.

Only the Coast Guard seemed able to act, as its helicopters and boats began rescuing stranded citizens. Eventually troops and transportation arrived and moved the evacuees to other cities.

As New Orleans remained flooded, President Bush flew over the devastated areas a few days later. Photographs of the president viewing the scene from high above made him appear detached. With polls showing a sharp drop in confidence in his administration, President Bush fired the head of FEMA and then traveled to New Orleans to pledge federal funds for rebuilding the city.

New Supreme Court Judges

In 2005, President Bush filled two vacancies on the Supreme Court. In the spring of 2005, Justice Sandra Day O'Connor announced her retirement. Although appointed by President Reagan, Justice O'Connor had been a pivotal swing vote on the Court, sometimes siding with conservatives, sometimes with liberals. As her replacement, Bush nominated federal judge **John G. Roberts, Jr.,** a conservative who was well regarded in the Senate. Before the Senate could act, however, Chief Justice William Rehnquist died. Bush then named Roberts to replace him. Roberts easily won Senate confirmation as chief justice.

Again attempting to fill Justice O'Connor's vacancy, President Bush nominated his White House counselor Harriet Miers. Many conservative Republicans were unhappy with Miers because of her lack of experience as a judge. As Republican opposition mounted, President Bush withdrew Miers' name and nominated federal judge **Samuel Alito, Jr.,** a well-known conservative justice. The Senate voted 58 to 42 to confirm Alito.

The 2006 Midterm Elections

The first two years of President Bush's second term had not gone well. He had failed to reform Social Security, and the public was angry with his administration's response to Hurricane Katrina. His prescription drug plan and decision to nominate Harriet Miers to the Supreme Court had angered many conservatives. Many people were also angry at his plan to create a guest-worker program and a path to citizenship for immigrants who had entered the country illegally.

At the same time, Americans had grown frustrated with Congress. The Republican majority seemed awash in scandals. Two Republicans had resigned from Congress after being convicted of corruption, and House Majority Leader Tom DeLay had resigned after being indicted for violating campaign finance laws. Congress also seemed unable to control spending, partly because Republicans and Democrats had been adding an increasing number of **"earmarks"** to spending bills. An earmark requires federal money be spent on a specific project, such as building a bridge, or funding medical research, usually in the sponsor's own state or district.

Problems in Iraq Although government scandals and overspending angered many Americans, the most important reason voters were frustrated was the situation in Iraq. A year earlier, many Americans had taken heart when large numbers of Iraqis had turned out to vote in democratic elections, but their hope for peace in Iraq soon faded. Although the Sunni Kurds and Iraqi Shia generally supported the new Iraqi constitution, it had much less support among Sunni Arabs. Rather than bring peace, the elections were followed by a rise in sectarian violence. In February 2006, the bombing of the Shia Golden Mosque in Samarra set Sunni and Shia militias against each other.

Further complicating the situation was an insurgent group known as Al-Qaeda in Iraq (AQI) that controlled large areas of western Iraq and was determined to defeat American forces and impose a strict militant version of Islam. In addition, the government of Iran had begun covertly sending weapons to the Iraqi insurgents.

The ongoing suicide bombings, kidnappings, and attacks on American soldiers turned a majority of Americans against the war. Democrats demanded the president set a timetable for withdrawing U.S. troops, a policy that President Bush described as "cut and run."

The Democrats Gain Control of Congress Voters expressed their unhappiness with the president and the Republican Congress in 2006. The Democrats won a majority in both the House and the Senate for the first time since 1992. House Democrats then elected California Representative **Nancy Pelosi** to be the first female Speaker of the House of Representatives.

Condoleezza Rice
1954–

Born in Birmingham, Alabama, the same year as the landmark *Brown* v. *Board of Education* decision, Condoleezza Rice rose to become the first African American female secretary of state.

Before becoming involved in politics, Rice had a distinguished career in academia. She started her college studies at age 15 and went on to earn advanced degrees in economics and international studies. Dr. Rice then became a professor at Stanford University. Due to her expertise in Eastern and Central Europe, Rice served as an adviser on foreign affairs to President Ronald Reagan and President George H.W. Bush. She later returned to her post at Stanford.

When George W. Bush decided to run for president, he asked Rice to be his foreign policy adviser. During his first term, she served as head of the National Security Council and supported the attacks on Afghanistan and the invasion of Iraq. She became secretary of state during Bush's second term.

How did Rice's academic studies prepare her for her future role in politics?

Nancy Pelosi
1940–

Originally from Baltimore, Maryland, Nancy Pelosi's interest in politics began at an early age. Her father was a supporter of Democrat Franklin D. Roosevelt's New Deal and held political office.

Pelosi has spent most of her adult life in the San Francisco area. There, she attracted attention as an effective fund-raiser for the Democratic Party. She became the chair of the California State Democratic Party in 1981 and served for two years.

In 1987 she was elected to Congress in a special election to fill a vacancy caused by the death of her predecessor. The following year she was reelected for a full term and has held that office ever since.

In 2002 Pelosi was elected minority whip and tried to forge greater unity among different factions of her party. In that post, she emerged as one of President Bush's toughest critics. When the Democrats regained control of the House of Representatives after the 2006 elections, she became Speaker, the first woman elected to that post.

Why would Pelosi's position give her a platform from which to criticize the president?

Despite promises to end the war and change how Congress operated, Speaker Pelosi and other Democrats opposed to the war were not able to get enough votes to cut funding for the war, or to force the president to set a deadline for pulling the troops out of Iraq. In addition, spending was not reduced and, after a brief moratorium, earmarks were again permitted.

Troops Surge to Iraq The day after the 2006 midterm elections, Secretary of Defense Donald Rumsfeld resigned. Rumsfeld admitted that the war in Iraq was not going well. "In my view it is time for a major adjustment," he wrote. "Clearly what U.S. forces are currently doing in Iraq is not working well enough or fast enough."

President Bush chose Robert Gates to replace Rumsfeld and put a new commander, General David Petraeus, in charge of operations in Iraq. The president then announced a plan to "surge" some 20,000 more troops to Iraq to restore order in Baghdad, where the violence was concentrated.

With the additional troops provided by the surge, General Petraeus began clearing and holding areas of Baghdad that had been plagued by crime and insurgent attacks. At the same time, his forces began reaching out to Sunni groups in western Iraq that had been opposed to the American presence.

By late 2006, Al-Qaeda in Iraq's campaign to impose a militant version of Islam in western Iraq through murder and intimidation had begun to backfire. The Sunni tribes of Anbar—the large western province of Iraq—began working with the American forces to fight the insurgents. Their organization, known as the Anbar Awakening, helped change the course of the war. Increasingly, Sunni militias stopped fighting the Americans and turned against Al-Qaeda in Iraq. In the meantime, Iraq's government continued to make reforms and became increasingly effective, as did the Iraqi army.

By the fall of 2008, violence in Iraq had been dramatically reduced. Coalition forces had handed over control of 12 of Iraq's 18 provinces to the Iraqi government and coalition casualties were lower than at any time since the war began in 2003. The United States began negotiating a new security pact with the Iraqi government to establish the terms and conditions for a continued American presence in the country.

Reading Check **Explaining** What events in the first two years of Bush's second term contributed to Republicans losing control of Congress?

Presidential Election of 2008

Presidential Candidate	Popular Votes	% of Popular Vote	Electoral Votes
Obama	66,057,075	53%	364
McCain	57,839,810	46%	163
Nader	687,124	1%	0

▲ Barack Obama waves to the crowd in Chicago's Grant Park on election night. He is the nation's first African American president.

Analyzing VISUALS

1. **Comparing** Compare Obama's election map to Clinton's 1992 victory and Carter's 1976 victory. What states did Obama win that neither Carter nor Clinton won?

2. **Analyzing** What is the fewest number of states that would have had to switch their votes to McCain for him to win the election?

The Election of 2008

MAIN Idea A major financial crisis and public disapproval of President Bush enabled Barack Obama to win the 2008 election.

HISTORY AND YOU Do you remember Martin Luther King, Jr.'s, dream? Read on to learn about the first African American to become president.

In 2006, a financial crisis began when millions of Americans began to default on their mortgages. The crisis developed because banks had made too many subprime loans—risky loans that were not as likely to be repaid. In addition to the financial crisis, oil prices began to rise steeply. By the summer of 2008, a gallon of gasoline cost nearly twice what it had in 2006. As the 2008 election approached, the economy had replaced the war in Iraq as the most important issue for most Americans.

The Candidates Are Chosen

The election of 2008 was unusual in that neither party had an incumbent president or vice president running for the nomination.

Four Republicans emerged as frontrunners for their party's nomination: former New York mayor Rudy Giuliani, Governor Mike Huckabee of Arkansas, Senator John McCain of Arizona, and Governor Mitt Romney of Massachusetts. With many conservatives split between Romney and Huckabee, John McCain emerged the winner. Many Republican voters admired McCain's heroism during the Vietnam War and believed his reputation as a reformer would help the party win over voters who were angry at President Bush.

Knowing that many conservative Republicans distrusted him, John McCain selected Sarah Palin, the popular conservative governor of

Alaska, to be his running mate. Palin was the first woman to be nominated by the Republican Party to run for vice president.

Three Democrats emerged as frontrunners for their party's nomination: Former First Lady and New York Senator Hillary Clinton; former Senator John Edwards, who had been John Kerry's running mate; and Senator Barack Obama from Illinois. Obama first gained national attention at the 2004 Democratic National Convention, where he delivered the convention's keynote address. His speech greatly impressed Democrats and made Obama a national figure in American politics.

Hillary Clinton was heavily favored to win the 2008 Democratic nomination, but Obama was able to build a large grassroots network of supporters and used the Internet to raise several hundred million dollars, far more than any previous candidate. Clinton tried to portray Obama as inexperienced, but Democrats decided that Obama was more likely to change the country's direction. After winning the nomination, Obama selected Senator Joe Biden of Delaware to be his running mate, probably because Biden's 35 years in the Senate would help offset charges that Obama was too inexperienced to be president.

With the approval ratings of the president and Congress at all-time lows, McCain and Obama both promised change. McCain stressed his experience and reputation for being a maverick—someone who is willing to go against his party and try new approaches to solving problems. Obama argued that McCain's policies were too similar to those of President Bush. Both candidates presented plans that would cut taxes, address the energy crisis, put people back to work, and reform health care.

Obama led in the polls in the summer of 2008, but McCain took the lead following the Republican convention in early September. Obama regained the lead, however, when President Bush announced that the economy was in serious danger because there was no longer enough credit available. In response, Bush and Congress passed a $700 billion dollar bailout for the nation's financial institutions. The crisis increased voter disapproval of the president and the Republican party.

Obama Wins

On election day, Obama won 53% of the popular vote and 364 electoral votes, the biggest victory for a Democratic candidate since 1964. Barack Obama became the first African American to win the presidency. Soon after the networks projected he would win, Obama spoke to his supporters at Grant Park in Chicago:

PRIMARY SOURCE

"... This is our moment. This is our time—to put our people back to work and open doors of opportunity for our kids; to restore prosperity and promote the cause of peace; to reclaim the American Dream and reaffirm that fundamental truth—that out of many, we are one; that while we breathe, we hope, and where we are met with cynicism, and doubt, and those who tell us that we can't, we will respond with that timeless creed that sums up the spirit of a people: Yes We Can."

—Barack Obama, Address at Grant Park, November 4, 2008

✔ Reading Check **Analyzing** What events enabled Obama to win the presidency? Why was his election important in American history?

Section 4 REVIEW

Vocabulary

1. **Explain** the significance of: Abu Ghraib, Guantanamo Bay, National Security Agency, John G. Roberts, Jr., Samuel Alito, Jr., "earmarks," Nancy Pelosi.

Main Ideas

2. **Identifying** What issues did President Bush support in his reelection campaign? What did Kerry support?

3. **Explaining** What did the Supreme Court declare unlawful with the *Hamdan v. Rumsfeld* ruling?

4. **Describing** How did Bush propose to fix Social Security?

Critical Thinking

5. **Big Ideas** Why did Donald Rumsfeld resign as secretary of defense? Who did Bush choose to replace Rumsfeld?

6. **Organizing** Use a graphic organizer like the one below to list the reasons for Republican losses in the 2006 election.

> Reasons for Republican Losses in 2006
> I. The Election of 2004
> II. Security vs. Liberty
>   A.
>   B.

7. **Analyzing Visuals** Examine the map on page 826. How is Obama's victory different from Bush's victory shown on page 805? Which states switched to the Democrats in 2008?

Writing About History

8. **Persuasive Writing** Write a journal entry describing current events that will be read by students 50 years in the future. Be clear and concise with your description of these events.

History ONLINE
Study Central™ To review this section, go to glencoe.com and click on Study Central.

Causes of the Attacks of 9/11

- The rise of the oil industry in the Middle East makes many elites wealthy but leaves many people poor and resentful.
- The oil trade with Europe and the United States brings Western ideas and culture into the Middle East; many feel their traditional Muslim values are being undermined, and militant Muslim movements form.
- The founding of Israel in 1948 angers many Arabs, especially Palestinians. European and American support for Israel angers many in the Middle East.
- The Soviets invade Afghanistan in 1979; Muslims from across the Middle East, including Osama bin Laden, go to fight the Soviet troops.
- Osama bin Laden forms al-Qaeda to help drive the Soviets out of Afghanistan and all Westerners out of the Middle East.
- Iraq invades Kuwait leading to the deployment of American troops in Saudi Arabia, angering Muslim militants, including Osama bin Laden.
- The Soviet pullout from Afghanistan leads to a militant group, the Taliban, taking power and offering aid and shelter to bin Laden.
- Al-Qaeda, based in Afghanistan, stages a series of attacks on Americans, culminating in the attack on September 11, 2001.

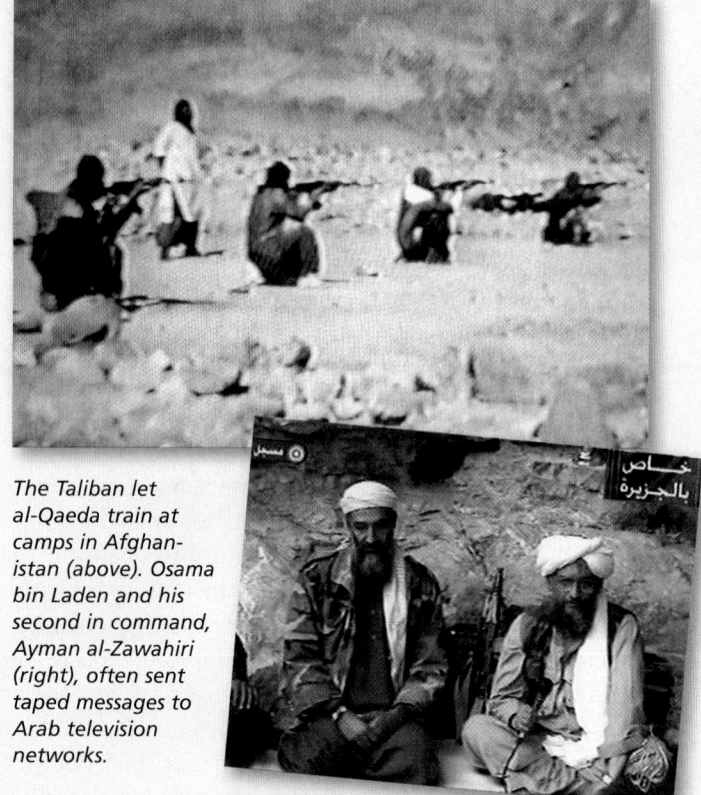

The Taliban let al-Qaeda train at camps in Afghanistan (above). Osama bin Laden and his second in command, Ayman al-Zawahiri (right), often sent taped messages to Arab television networks.

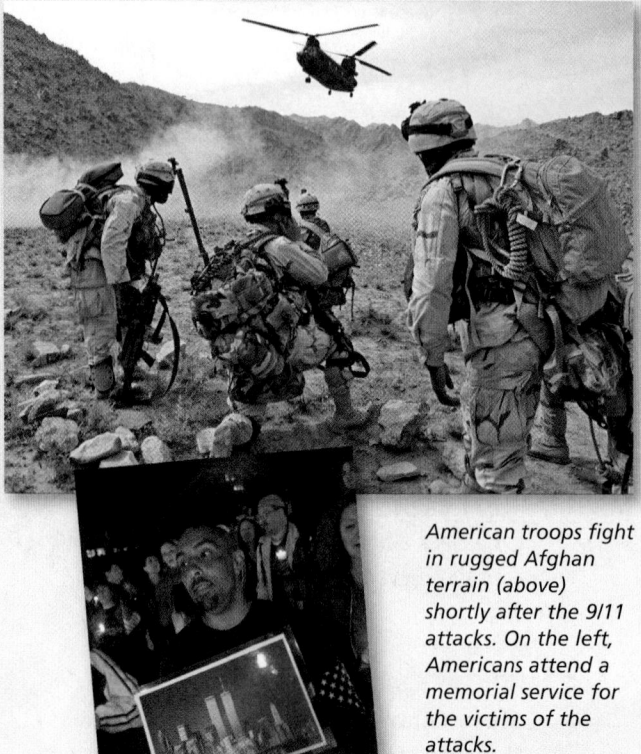

American troops fight in rugged Afghan terrain (above) shortly after the 9/11 attacks. On the left, Americans attend a memorial service for the victims of the attacks.

Effects of the Attacks of 9/11

- Initially, the 9/11 attack unifies Americans and leads to an out-pouring of support to the people of New York.
- President Bush declares a global war on terror to put an end to terrorist groups that threaten Americans.
- The United States launches attacks on the Taliban and helps local forces overthrow their regime. NATO troops then enter Afghanistan to serve as peacekeepers.
- Congress passes the Patriot Act giving the FBI additional powers to help prevent another attack in the United States.
- Congress creates the Department of Homeland Security.
- The Bush administration decides that preventing terrorist groups from getting weapons of mass destruction is a high priority.
- The United States, backed by a coalition of allies, invades Iraq to destroy its weapons of mass destruction.
- The invasion of Iraq is controversial; many traditional allies do not support it, and it divides the American people.
- An insurgency begins in Iraq that keeps American troops fighting for several years.

Review Vocabulary

Directions: Choose the word or words that best complete the sentence.

1. _____ ran for the Green Party in the 2000 presidential election.

   A Al Gore

   B Ralph Nader

   C George W. Bush

   D Dick Cheney

2. Osama bin Laden heads the terrorist group known as

   A Al Jazeera.

   B guerrillas.

   C Hamas.

   D al-Qaeda.

3. The majority of Iraq's population is

   A Shia Muslim.

   B Sunni Muslim.

   C Sunni Arabs.

   D Sunni Kurds.

4. What military base held captured members of al-Qaeda in 2004?

   A Abu Ghraib

   B Guantanamo Bay

   C Pearl Harbor

   D Geneva

5. Projects that spend federal money but usually benefit a single congressional district are known as _____ .

   A gerrymanders

   B earmarks

   C isograms

   D the spoils system

Reviewing Main Ideas

Directions: Choose the best answer for each of the following questions.

Section 1 *(pp. 804–807)*

6. In the 2000 election, Al Gore won

   A the popular vote.

   B a majority of electoral votes.

   C the state of Florida.

   D a pivotal Supreme Court case.

7. After Bush took office, Congress passed which of the following educational reforms?

   A federal funding to parents to pay for private schools if their public school was performing poorly

   B annual standardized testing in reading and math for grades 3–8

   C prohibiting federally funded schools from discriminating against girls and young women

   D transporting children to schools outside their neighborhood to achieve a greater racial balance

Section 2 *(pp. 808–813)*

8. After the bombing of American embassies in Kenya and Tanzania, President Clinton

   A ordered the invasion of Iraq.

   B created the office of Homeland Security.

   C ordered the bombing of terrorist camps in Afghanistan.

   D signed the Patriot Act into law.

TEST-TAKING **TIP**

If a question involves a table, skim the table before reading the question. Then, read the question and interpret the information from the table.

Need Extra Help?								
If You Missed Questions . . .	1	2	3	4	5	6	7	8
Go to Page . . .	805	809	819	821	824	805	807	811

9. In the fall of 2001, bioterrorists attacked news organizations and political figures with

 A smallpox.

 B anthrax.

 C arsenic.

 D radioactive material.

Section 3 (pp. 814–819)

10. President Bush targeted Iraq, one of the three countries in the "axis of evil," before the other two countries because Iraq

 A was the most vulnerable.

 B was responsible for the September 11 attacks.

 C was believed to pose the most imminent danger to the United States.

 D attacked the United States first.

11. Which country was the only nation bordering Iraq to allow the United States to launch offensives from their territory?

 A Saudi Arabia

 B Turkey

 C Iran

 D Kuwait

Section 4 (pp. 820–827)

12. During the 2004 presidential election, George W. Bush's support was strongest in

 A the Northeast.

 B the South and the Great Plains.

 C the Midwest and Great Lakes.

 D all urban areas.

13. Which factor helped Barack Obama win the 2008 election?

 A President Bush's high popularity

 B the U.S. withdrawal from Iraq

 C Hillary Clinton's victory

 D a severe financial crisis

Critical Thinking

Directions: Choose the best answers to the following questions.

14. Which Supreme Court ruling stated that foreign prisoners who claim they were unlawfully imprisoned had the right to have their cases heard in court?

 A *Rasul* v. *Bush*

 B *Bush* v. *Gore*

 C *Hamdan* v. *Rumsfeld*

 D *Gideon* v. *Wainwright*

Base your answer to question 15 on the map below and on your knowledge of Chapter 24.

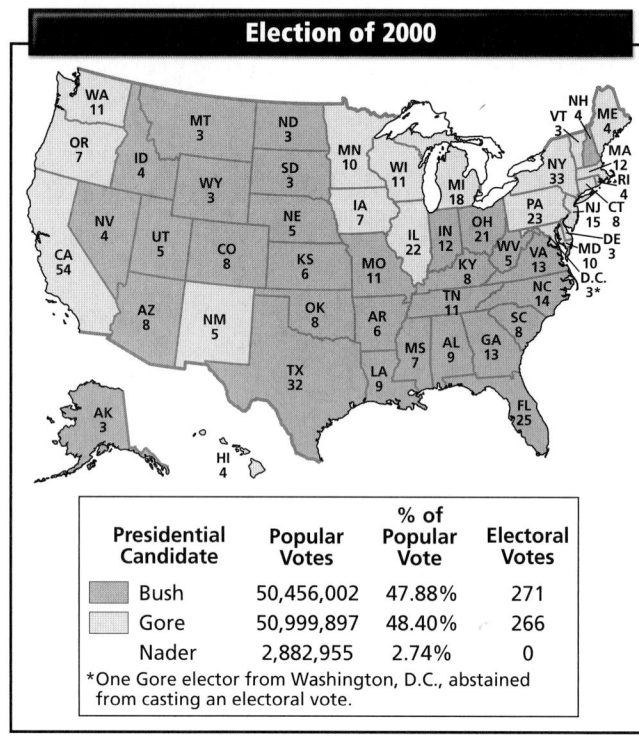

Election of 2000

Presidential Candidate	Popular Votes	% of Popular Vote	Electoral Votes
▮ Bush	50,456,002	47.88%	271
▯ Gore	50,999,897	48.40%	266
Nader	2,882,955	2.74%	0

*One Gore elector from Washington, D.C., abstained from casting an electoral vote.

15. In the election of 2000, George W. Bush won

 A the popular vote.

 B fewer states than Al Gore.

 C a majority of electoral votes.

 D California and New York.

Need Extra Help?

If You Missed Questions . . .	9	10	11	12	13	14	15
Go to Page . . .	813	816	818	821	827	821	805

GO ON

16. Which the following is under the control of the Department of Homeland Security?

A Central Intelligence Agency (CIA)

B Defense Intelligence Agency (DIA)

C Federal Bureau of Investigation (FBI)

D Federal Emergency Management Agency (FEMA)

Analyze the cartoon and answer the question that follows. Base your answer on the cartoon and your knowledge of Chapter 24.

17. According to the cartoon, what is the artist saying about the 2004 presidential election?

A The world is excited about another four years with President Bush.

B The world is disappointed George Bush was reelected.

C The United States made a mistake reelecting Bush.

D Kerry was detached from Middle America therefore he lost the election.

18. Why did the United States think stopping the spread of weapons of mass destruction was linked to the war on terror?

A Saddam Hussein declared an allegiance with al-Qaeda.

B Bin Laden was believed to be hiding in the mountains of Iraq.

C Terrorists might buy or steal weapons of mass destruction and use them against the United States.

D Terrorist groups had already stolen weapons of mass destruction from Iraq.

Document-Based Questions

Directions: Analyze the document and answer the short-answer questions that follow the document.

In October 2001, President Bush signed the highly controversial Patriot Act.

> "If we were to take the position, reflected in provisions in the USA PATRIOT Act, that the government can invade our privacy and gather evidence that can be used against us based on no suspicion whatsoever that we've done anything wrong, but simply because the government wants to gather evidence as part of some generalized, 'anti-terrorism' or 'foreign intelligence' investigation, then we will have rendered that Fourth Amendment principle essentially meaningless."
>
> —Congressman Bob Barr (R-GA),
> "Problems with the USA PATRIOT Act"
>
> "Zero. That's the number of substantiated USA PATRIOT Act civil liberties violations. Extensive congressional oversight found no violations."
>
> —Congressman James Sensenbrenner (R-WI),
> "No rights have been violated"

19. According to Congressman Barr, which constitutional right does the Patriot Act violate and how?

20. What is Congressman Sensenbrenner's response to the accusation that the Patriot Act violates civil rights?

Extended Response

21. The decision to invade Iraq was controversial. Choose to either support a continued U.S. presence in Iraq or immediate troop withdrawal. Write a persuasive essay that includes an introduction and at least three paragraphs that support your position.

History ONLINE

For additional test practice, use Self-Check Quizzes—Chapter 24 at glencoe.com.

Need Extra Help?						
If You Missed Questions . . .	16	17	18	19	20	21
Go to Page . . .	813	R18	816	831	R19	826

Appendix

Contents

Skills Handbook

Skills Handbook
Table of Contents

Critical Thinking Skills

Social Studies Skills

Skills Handbook

Identifying the Main Idea

Why Learn This Skill?

Finding the main idea in a reading passage will help you see the "big picture" by organizing information and determining the most important concepts to remember.

Migrant mother and children in California, 1936

Learning the Skill

Follow these steps to learn how to make a valid generalization. Then answer the questions below.

2. Skim the material to identify its general subject. Look at headings and subheadings.

> In this nation I see tens of millions of its citizens . . . who at this very moment are denied the greater part of what the very lowest standards of today call the necessities of life. I see millions of families trying to live on incomes so meager that the pall of family disaster hangs over them day by day. . . . see one-third of a nation ill-housed, ill-clad, ill-nourished.
>
> It is not in despair that I paint you that picture. I paint it for you in hope—because the Nation, seeing and understanding the injustice in it, proposes to paint it out. We are determined to make every American citizen the subject of his country's interest and concern. . . . The test of our progress is not whether we add more to the abundance of those who have much; it is whether we provide enough for those who have too little.

—Franklin D. Roosevelt, Second Inaugural Address, January 20, 1937

1. Determine the setting of the passage.

3. Notice any details that support a larger idea or issue.

4. Identify the central issue. Ask: What part of the selection conveys the main idea?

As you read the material, ask yourself: What is the purpose of this passage—why was it written?

Practicing the Skill

1. On what occasion was this speech given?

2. When was this speech given?

3. What was the condition of the people mentioned in this passage?

4. What did Roosevelt think should be done about the situation discussed?

Applying the Skill

Bring to class an article about American history from the Internet or another source. Identify the main idea and explain why it is important.

Determining Cause and Effect

Why Learn This Skill?

Determining cause and effect involves considering *why* an event occurred. That helps you analyze how to encourage or prevent the same event in the future. A *cause* is an action or a situation that produces an event. What happens as a result of a cause is an *effect*.

The effect of pesticides on wildlife

Learning the Skill

To identify cause-and-effect relationships, follow these steps:

1. Identify two or more events or developments.

" . . . in 1957, there was a startling wildlife mortality in the wake of a mosquito-control campaign near Duxbury, Mass., followed by a pointless spraying of a DDT/fuel-oil mix over eastern Long Island for eradication of the gypsy moth. Next, an all-out war in the Southern states against the fire ant did such widespread harm to other creatures that its beneficiaries cried for mercy; and after that a great furor arose across the country over the spraying of cranberry plants with aminotri-azole, which led to an Agriculture Department ban against all cranberry marketing just in time for Thanksgiving 1959. . . .

Even before publication [of Rachel Carson's indictment of pesticides, Silent Spring,*] Carson was violently assailed by threats of lawsuits and derision. . . . A huge counterattack was organized and led by . . . the whole chemical industry.* "

—*Time*, March 29, 1999

2. Decide whether one event caused the other. Look for "clue words" such as *because, led to, brought about, so that, after that, produced, as a result of, since, in the wake of, as a result.*

3. Identify the outcomes of events. Remember that some effects have more than one cause, and some causes lead to more than one effect. Also, an effect can become the cause of yet another effect.

Look for logical relationships between events, such as "She overslept, so she missed her bus."

Practicing the Skill

Categorize the items below as *cause, effect, both,* or *neither.*

1. Rachel Carson published *Silent Spring*, criticizing chemical pesticides.

2. Duxbury's wildlife mortality rate rose significantly in 1957.

3. The gypsy moth is a common insect on Long Island.

4. The Agriculture Department banned cranberry marketing.

5. Southern states used pesticides to eradicate the fire ant.

6. The chemical industry threatened Carson with lawsuits.

Applying the Skill

In a newspaper, read an article describing a current event. Determine at least one cause and one effect of that event, and complete a flowchart like the one below.

Cause → Event → Effect

Making Generalizations

Why Learn This Skill?

Generalizations are conclusions that are usually accurate, based on the facts at hand. Generalizations are useful in studying history because they help you see trends. If you say, "Most Mexican immigrants to the United States in the early twentieth century worked in agriculture," that's a generalization. To support it, you could mention that federal funding of irrigation projects in the Southwest in 1902 gave rise to large farms requiring thousands of workers. Not all Mexican immigrants at that time became farmworkers, but many did.

Women workers install fixtures and assemblies to a tail fuselage section of a B-17 bomber at Douglas Aircraft Company's, Long Beach, California, plant.

Learning the Skill

To learn how to make a valid generalization, follow these steps:

1. Identify the subject matter.

2. Collect factual information and examples relevant to the topic.

> The war years had a tremendous impact on women. . . . it was the first time I had a chance to get out of the kitchen and work in industry and make a few bucks. This was something I had never dreamed would happen. In Sapulpa [Oklahoma] all that women had to look forward to was keeping a house and raising families. The war years offered new possibilities. You came out to California, put on your pants and took your lunch pail to a man's job. In Oklahoma a woman's place was in the home, and men went to work and provided. This was the beginning of women's feeling that they could do something more.
>
> —Sybil Lewis, quoted in *The Homefront: America During World War II*

3. Identify similarities among these facts.

Use these similarities to form some general ideas about the subject.

Practicing the Skill

After reading the excerpt above, determine whether each generalization that follows is valid or invalid. Explain your answers.

1. During World War II, women did not want to work outside the home.

2. Women have careers only so that they can afford luxuries.

3. During the war, women had more choices in California than in Oklahoma.

Applying the Skill

Read three editorials in a newspaper and make a generalization about each.

Distinguishing Fact from Opinion

Why Learn This Skill?

To make reasonable judgments about what others say or write, it is important to distinguish facts from opinions. Facts can be proved by evidence such as records, documents, or historical sources. Opinions are based on people's differing values and beliefs.

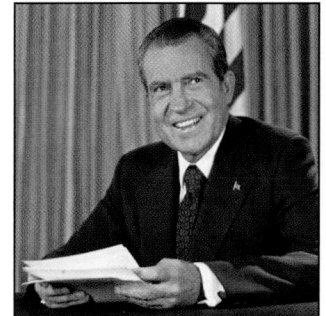

Richard M. Nixon

Learning the Skill

To learn how to separate facts from opinions, follow these steps:

1. Identify the facts. Ask: Which statements can be proved? Where would I find information to verify this statement? If the information is a statistic, it may sound impressive, but you won't know if it's accurate unless you check the source.

> In speaking of the consequences of a precipitate withdrawal [from Vietnam], I mentioned that our allies would lose confidence in America. Far more dangerous, we would lose confidence in ourselves. . . .
>
> In San Francisco a few weeks ago, I saw demonstrators carrying signs reading: "Lose in Vietnam, bring the boys home."
>
> Well, one of the strengths of our free society is that any American has a right to reach that conclusion and to advocate that point of view. But as President of the United States, I would be untrue to my oath of office if I allowed the policy of this Nation to be dictated by the minority who hold that point of view and who try to impose it on the Nation by mounting demonstrations in the street.
>
> . . . If a vocal minority, however fervent its cause, prevails over reason and the will of the majority, this Nation has no future as a free society.
>
> —Richard M. Nixon speech, November 3, 1969

2. Identify opinions by looking for statements of feelings or beliefs. Opinions sometimes contain words like *should, would, could, best, greatest, all, every,* or *always.*

Practicing the Skill

The excerpt above is from a televised speech given by President Richard M. Nixon in 1969, when a Gallup poll showed that 58 percent of Americans believed the Vietnam War was a mistake. Reread the excerpt and answer the questions that follow.

1. Which statements in the passage are factual?

2. Which statements are opinions? Explain.

3. What was the speaker's purpose?

Applying the Skill

Watch a television interview. Then list three facts and three opinions that you hear.

Formulating Questions

Why Learn This Skill?

Asking questions helps you to understand and remember what you read. Learning increases when you ask yourself what is important about the topic and what you would like to know about the people, places, and events.

Jackie Robinson

Learning the Skill

Follow these steps to formulate questions:

1. Think of questions you would like to have answered.

2. Ask *who, what, when, where, why,* and *how* about the main ideas, people, places, and events.

> In 1947 life in America . . . was segregation. . . . But Jackie Robinson, God bless him, was bigger than all of that.
>
> . . . He had to be bigger than the Brooklyn teammates who got up a petition to keep him off the ball club, bigger than the pitchers who threw at him or the base runners who dug their spikes into his shin, bigger than the bench jockeys who hollered for him to . . . shine their shoes, bigger than the so-called fans who . . . wrote him death threats.
>
> . . . Somehow, though, Jackie had the strength to . . . sacrifice his pride for his people's. It was an incredible act of selflessness that brought the races closer together than ever before and shaped the dreams of an entire generation.

—Henry "Hank" Aaron, holder of major-league career home-run record, *Time*, June 14, 1999

3. Reread the section to be sure all your questions have been answered.

Practicing the Skill

The excerpt above is about the first African American major-league baseball player. After reading it, use a chart like the one below and find the answers in the excerpt.

	Question	Answer
Who?		
What?		
Where?		
When?		
Why?		
How?		

Applying the Skill

Select any section of this textbook to read or reread. Make a question chart to help you ask and answer five or more questions about the section as you read.

Analyzing Information

Why Learn This Skill?

The ability to analyze information is important in deciding what you think about a subject. For example, you need to analyze the benefits of social services versus the benefits of small government to decide where you stand on the issue of Social Security.

Gloria Steinem (right) with Adelaide Abankwah, a Ghanian asylum-seeker, in 1999

Learning the Skill

To analyze information, use the following steps:

1. Identify the topic being discussed.

Having spent most of my adult life in social justice movements—from living in post-Gandhian India to working in the civil rights, farm worker and peace movements here, and most of all, in the feminist movement—I've seen constant proof that revolutions are like houses: They can't be built from the top down. Leaders can issue blueprints, which we then adapt to our needs or quietly sabotage. They can prevent us from following our own plan, divide the work force against itself and otherwise slow or stop progress. But what they can't do is create organic and lasting change from the top. Attempts to do so, even in the most authoritarian of systems, eventually end in reversion to old ways, as we see in the countries where Communism and artificial national boundaries were once imposed by Moscow.

—Gloria Steinem, from *The Nation*, July 20–27, 1992

2. Examine how the information is organized. What are the main points?

3. Summarize the information in your own words, and then make a statement of your own based on your understanding of the topic and on what you already know.

Practicing the Skill

After reading the excerpt above, answer the following questions:

1. What topic is being discussed?

2. What are the writer's main points?

3. Summarize the information in this excerpt, and then provide your analysis, based on this information and what you already know about the subject.

Applying the Skill

Select an issue that is currently in the news, such as Social Security, oil prices, global warming, or taxation. Read an article or watch a news segment about the issue. Analyze the information and make a brief statement of your own about the topic. Explain your thinking.

Evaluating Information

Soaring gas prices in the early 2000s frustrated consumers.

Why Learn This Skill?

We live in an information age. Because the amount of information available can be overwhelming, it is sometimes difficult to tell which information is accurate and useful. To do this, you have to evaluate what you read and hear.

Learning the Skill

To figure out how reliable information is, ask yourself the following questions as you read:

> *The single biggest factor in . . . the increase in the inflation rate last year was from one cause: the skyrocketing prices of OPEC oil. We must take whatever actions are necessary to reduce our dependence on foreign oil—and at the same time reduce inflation.*
>
> —former president Jimmy Carter, January 23, 1980

> *Oil prices are so high, becuz big oil companys are tryng to goug us. Greedy oil executives, are driven up prices to get richer.*
>
> —on an individual's Internet "blog"

> *It's certainly clear that high oil prices aren't dulling demand for energy products. According to the Energy Dept.'s Energy Information Administration (EIA), U.S. demand for gasoline in June was 9.5 million barrels per day, a record.*
>
> —*BusinessWeek,* July 7, 2006

1. Is the author or speaker identified? Is he or she an authority on the subject?

2. Is there bias? Does the source unfairly present just one point of view, ignoring any arguments against it?

3. Is the information printed in a credible, reliable publication?

4. Is the information backed up by facts and other sources? Does it seem to be accurate?

5. Is it well written and well edited? Writing filled with errors in spelling, grammar, and punctuation is likely to be careless in other ways, too.

Also notice whether the information is up-to-date.

Practicing the Skill

After reading the statements above, rank them in order of most reliable to least reliable. Explain why you ranked them as you did.

Applying the Skill

Find an advertisement that contains text and bring it to class. In a brief oral presentation, tell the class whether the information in the advertisement is reliable or unreliable, and why.

Making Inferences

Why Learn This Skill?

To *infer* means to evaluate information and arrive at a conclusion. When you make inferences, you "read between the lines," or use clues to figure something out that is not stated directly in the text.

Men read posters at an office of the National Association Opposed to Woman Suffrage.

Learning the Skill

Follow these steps to make inferences:

1. Read carefully for facts and ideas, and list them.

Because the suffrage is not a question of right or of justice, but of policy and expediency. . . .

. . . Because it means simply doubling the vote, and especially the undesirable and corrupt vote of our large cities.

. . . Because the great advance of women in the last century—moral, intellectual and economic—has been made without the vote; which goes to prove that it is not needed for their further advancement along the same lines.

. . . Because our present duties fill up the whole measure of our time and ability, and are such as none but us can perform. Our appreciation of their importance requires us to protest against all efforts to infringe upon our rights by imposing upon us those obligations which can not be . . . performed by us without the sacrifice of the highest interests of our families and our society.

—from Northern California Association Opposed to Woman Suffrage, 1912

2. Summarize the information.

3. Consider what you may already know about the topic.

4. Use your knowledge and insight to develop logical conclusions.

Practicing the Skill

After reading the statement above, answer the following questions:

1. What points do the authors make?

2. Which points does your experience contradict?

3. What inferences might you draw about the women who wrote the document?

Applying the Skill

Read an editorial printed in today's newspaper. What can you infer about the importance of the topic being addressed? Can you tell how the writer feels about the topic? Explain your answer.

Comparing and Contrasting

Why Learn This Skill?

When you make comparisons, you determine similarities among ideas, objects, or events. When you contrast, you are noting differences between ideas, objects, or events. Comparing and contrasting are important skills because they help you choose among several possible alternatives.

Learning the Skill

To compare or contrast items, follow these steps:

1. Select the items to compare or contrast.

2. To compare, determine a common area or areas in which comparisons can be drawn, such as topic, style, or point of view. Look for similarities within these areas.

3. To contrast, look for differences that set the items apart from each other.

Practicing the Skill

After studying the paintings above, answer these questions:

1. How are the paintings similar?

2. How are they different?

3. What do the answers to questions 1 and 2 tell you about the two artists' attitudes toward their subject?

Applying the Skill

Survey 10 of your classmates about an issue in the news, and summarize their responses. Then write a paragraph or two comparing and contrasting their opinions.

Detecting Bias

Why Learn This Skill?

Most people have a point of view, or bias. This bias influences the way they interpret and write about events and issues.

A politician running for reelection, for example, may claim the economy is strong because 20,000 new jobs were created last month. His or her opponent may say the economy is weak because 40,000 people also lost jobs last month. Recognizing bias helps you judge the accuracy of what you hear or read.

Southerners seize abolitionist literature from a local post office in South Carolina in the 1840s.

Learning the Skill

To recognize bias, follow these steps:

1. Consider the author's identity, location, and motivation. Does the writer or a group he or she represents benefit from an outcome supported in the article?

2. Identify statements of fact, if any.

> *The great conservative institution of slavery, so excellent in itself, and so necessary to civil liberty and the dignity of the white race, is one of the grand objects of our struggle. It should never be lost sight of, nor under any pressure should we ever take any step incompatible with the relation of master and slave. . . . Our theory is, that he is better off as a slave; and even if he were not, we could not safely have an emancipated class of them amongst us. Much less can we put arms in his hands. . . . Slavery afterwards would become impossible.*

—Editorial from the Washington, Arkansas, *Telegraph*, January 13, 1865

3. Identify any expressions of opinion or emotion. Look for words with positive or negative overtones for clues about the author's feelings on a topic.

4. Determine the author's point of view.

5. Notice how the author's point of view is reflected in the work.

Practicing the Skill

Read the passage above and then answer the following questions:

1. What is the purpose of this passage?

2. What statements of fact and/or opinion are presented?

3. What evidence of bias do you find?

4. How does the author attempt to convince the audience?

Applying the Skill

Find an editorial in the newspaper that deals with a topic of interest to you. Apply the steps for recognizing bias to the editorial. Write a paragraph summarizing your findings.

Synthesizing Information

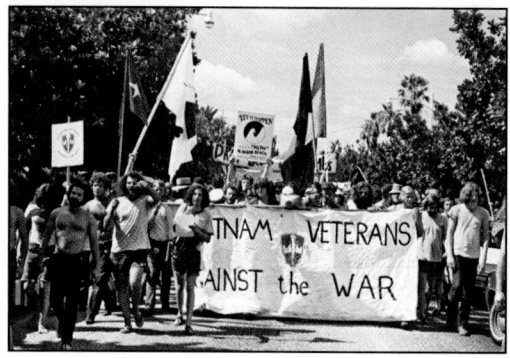

Antiwar rally, Miami Beach, Florida, 1972

Why Learn This Skill?

Synthesizing information involves combining information from two or more sources. Each source may shed new light on other information.

Learning the Skill

Follow these steps to learn how to synthesize information:

1. Analyze each source separately to understand its meaning.

2. Determine what information and whose perspective each source adds to the subject.

Source A *We should declare war on North Vietnam. . . . It's silly talking about how many years we will have to spend in the jungles of Vietnam when we could pave the whole country and put parking stripes on it and still be home for Christmas.*

—future president Ronald Reagan, 1965

Source B *Vietnam presumably taught us that the United States could not serve as the world's policeman; it should also have taught us the dangers of trying to be the world's midwife to democracy when the birth is scheduled to take place under conditions of guerrilla war.*

—Jeane Kirkpatrick, future UN ambassador and foreign policy adviser to Ronald Reagan, 1979

Source C *People say we could have won the [Vietnam] war—we know we could not. People say the anti-war movement harassed and betrayed the soldiers . . . the people who supported the war, the folks who favored intervention, the people who sent us crusading against communism—they betrayed us, their own sons and daughters. Anti-war veterans are the witnesses against them . . . we saw the system was not working, we knew the war had to stop.*

—Ben Chitty, member Vietnam Veterans Against the War, April, 2000

3. Identify points of agreement and disagreement among the sources. Ask: Can Source B or C give me new ways of thinking about Source A?

4. Determine how the sources relate to each other.

Practicing the Skill

After reading the passages above, answer the questions that follow.

1. What is the main subject of each source?

2. Does Source B support or contradict Source A? Does Source C support or contradict source A? Explain.

3. Summarize what you learned from the three sources.

4. Which source do you consider the most reliable? Explain why.

Applying the Skill

Find two sources of information on any period of history that interests you. What are the main ideas in the sources? How does each source add to your understanding of the topic?

Drawing Conclusions

Why Learn This Skill?

A conclusion is a logical understanding that you reach based on details or facts that you read or hear. When you draw conclusions, you use stated information to formulate ideas that are unstated.

Victorian-era house for sale

Learning the Skill

Follow these steps to draw conclusions:

1. Read the text and labels carefully, looking for facts and ideas.

2. Summarize the information. List trends or important facts.

Homeownership in the U.S., 1890–2005

Percentage (y-axis: 0, 10, 20, 30, 40, 50, 60, 70)

Year (x-axis: 1890 1900 1910 1920 1930 1940 1950 1960 1970 1980 1990 1995 2000 2005)

Labels on graph: Earliest Data, Highest Immigration, Roaring '20s, Great Depression, Post World War II Boom, High Inflation, Declining Real Wages

Source: U.S. Bureau of the Census; U.S. Department of Commerce

3. Apply related information that you may already have.

4. Use your knowledge and insight to develop some logical conclusions.

Practicing the Skill

The bar graph above shows the percentage of Americans who owned their own homes during various time periods. Study the graph and answer the following questions:

1. When was the home ownership rate the lowest? Why do you think this was so?

2. During what 20-year period did home ownership rates increase the most? Why do you think this happened?

3. What conclusions can you draw about trends in home ownership?

Applying the Skill

Read one of the People in History profiles in this book. Using the information in the profile, what conclusions can you draw about the life of the person described?

Predicting Consequences

Why Learn This Skill?

Predicting most future events is difficult, but the more information you have, the more accurate your predictions will be. Making good predictions will help you to make better decisions based on their likely outcomes. Using these skills can also help you to understand the outcomes of historical events.

Lois Gibbs

Learning the Skill

To help you make predictions, follow these steps:

1. Gather information about the topic.

> *In the mid-1950s, the Niagara Falls board of education built an elementary school adjacent to a site where Hooker Chemical and Plastics Corporation had dumped more than 22,000 tons of toxic waste. Housing also was built next to the landfill, called Love Canal. Chemicals leached out of the landfill and, by 1976, had shown up in yards and basements.*
>
> *Residents were frequently sick and eventually were found to have extremely high rates of cancer, birth defects, miscarriages, and stillborns. In 1978 Lois Gibbs and other residents began a 3-year battle against Hooker and many levels of government, which claimed the health issues were not related to the chemicals.*
>
> *By 1980, President Jimmy Carter declared Love Canal a federal emergency and more than 1,000 families were relocated and paid for their homes. The tragedy led to "Superfund" legislation that collects taxes from gas and chemical companies, to be used to clean up similar sites.*

2. Use your experience and your knowledge of history and human behavior to predict what consequences could result.

3. Analyze each consequence by asking yourself: How likely is it that this will happen?

Practicing the Skill

1. Do you think the problem described in the passage is likely to reoccur elsewhere?

2. On what do you base your prediction?

3. What are the possible benefits and drawbacks of the "Superfund" legislation described in the passage?

Applying the Skill

Analyze three newspaper articles about an event affecting your community or the nation. Make an educated prediction about what will happen, and explain your reasoning. Then write a letter to the editor, summarizing your prediction. You may want to check back later to see if your prediction came true.

Reading a Special-Purpose Map

Why Learn This Skill?

Special-purpose maps show more than the location of places. They are useful because they show trends or movements of people or things in a concise, visual way.

Learning the Skill

To read a special-purpose map, follow these steps:

1. Read the title to see what topic is illustrated. If the time period being covered is part of the title, notice that.

2. Read the legend and any other text.

3. Notice the movement shown on the map, if any, including the direction of any arrows, where paths lead, or the concentration of several things in certain places.

4. Ask yourself: What have I learned from this map? What can I conclude from this information?

NATIONAL GEOGRAPHIC **Migration in the United States, 1940–1950**

Seattle
Portland
73,000
338,000
NORTHEAST
319,000
385,000
NORTH CENTRAL
Detroit 297,000
Chicago
1,188,000
WEST
New York City
San Francisco
Denver
614,000
1,113,000
449,000
427,000
Washington, D.C.
Los Angeles
San Diego
1,241,000
239,000
Memphis
SOUTH
Fort Worth Dallas
Baton Rouge
Mobile
Houston

Urban Population Increase, 1940–1947
- ☐ 400,000 and over
- ☐ 100,000–199,999
- ☐ 200,000–399,999
- ☐ 50,000–99,999
- ⬅ Population migration between regions

Practicing the Skill

Answer the following questions about the map above:

1. What period in history does the map cover?

2. Was the U.S. population fairly mobile or stationary during this time?

3. Name two cities that gained 400,000 or more residents.

4. From what part of the country did most immigrants to the West come?

Applying the Skill

Study the map in Section 3 of the "Settling the West" chapter. Then answer these questions.

1. Name three states through which Chief Joseph traveled in 1877.

2. What part of the country had the largest number of reservations at this time?

3. What does the map tell you about the compromises Native Americans made to the settlers?

Skills Handbook

Interpreting Graphs

Bar graphs are often used to compare quantities. By presenting similar categories of information visually, often on a grid, they make it easy to see the relationships among the categories.

Why Learn This Skill?

Being able to read bar graphs makes it easy to understand and analyze data quickly.

Learning the Skill

Follow these steps to learn how to understand and use bar graphs. Then answer the questions below.

1. Read the title to see what topic is being illustrated. Notice whether the period of time covered or other information is included within or just below the title.

2. Read the labels to see what categories are being compared, and what measure is being used; for example, dollars, thousands of people, bushels of grain, etc.

3. Notice the numbers that correlate to the ends of the bars.

4. Compare the lengths of the bars and draw a conclusion about the relationships being shown.

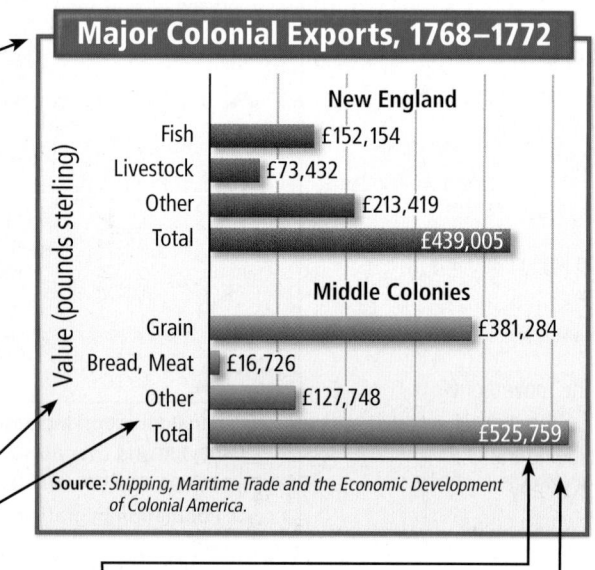

Major Colonial Exports, 1768–1772

Value (pounds sterling)

New England
Fish — £152,154
Livestock — £73,432
Other — £213,419
Total — £439,005

Middle Colonies
Grain — £381,284
Bread, Meat — £16,726
Other — £127,748
Total — £525,759

Source: *Shipping, Maritime Trade and the Economic Development of Colonial America.*

Practicing the Skill

1. What is the topic of this bar graph?

2. In what currency does the graph measure the products?

3. Which type of exports were the least valuable?

4. If you were going into the export business in 1770, which product would you want to export? Why?

Applying the Skill

Ask five students what their favorite food is. Then create a bar graph showing which foods are the most popular.

Sequencing Events

Why Learn This Skill?

Sequencing involves placing facts in the order in which they occurred. Sequencing helps you deal with large quantities of information in an understandable way. In studying history, sequencing can help you understand cause-and-effect relationships among events. This in turn helps analysts to predict outcomes of various events or policies.

John Wilkes Booth escaping Ford's Theatre after shooting President Lincoln

Learning the Skill

To sequence events, follow these steps:

1. Look for dates or clue words: *in 1920, later that year, first, then,* and so on.

2. Arrange facts in the order in which they occurred. Events are not always presented in sequential order. Ask: Would this logically have happened next?

Consider using an organizational tool such as a time line, which makes it easy to see the chronology as well as any cause-and-effect relationships between events.

> *This evening [April 14] at about 9:30 P.M., at Ford's Theatre, the President, while sitting in the private box with Mrs. Lincoln . . . was shot by an assassin, who suddenly entered the box and approached behind the President.*
>
> *The assassin then leaped upon the stage brandishing a large dagger or knife, and made his escape in the rear of the theatre.*
>
> *. . . It is not probable that the President will live through the night.*
>
> *. . . Gen. Grant and wife were advertised to be at the theatre this evening, but he started to Burlington at six o'clock this evening.*
>
> *At a Cabinet meeting, at which Gen. Grant was present, the subject of the state of the country and the prospect of a speedy peace was discussed. The President was very cheerful and hopeful, and spoke very kindly of Gen. Lee and others of the confederacy.*

–War Department statement of April 14, 1865, printed in *New York Times*, April 15

Practicing the Skill

Read the passage above and answer the questions that follow.

1. What dates or clue words in this passage help you determine the sequence of the events?

2. Complete a time line such as the one at right to show the sequence of events described in the selection.

Applying the Skill

Find a newspaper or magazine article about a recent event. Sequence the information presented in the article in a time line or chart.

First Event   Final Event

Interpreting Political Cartoons

Why Learn This Skill?

Political cartoons are drawings that express an opinion about public figures, political issues, or economic or social conditions. They appear in newspapers, magazines, books, and on the Internet. They are intended to convince readers of the artist's or the publication's opinion in an amusing way. Knowing how to interpret a political cartoon is useful because it helps you put issues and candidates in perspective.

Learning the Skill

To interpret a political cartoon, follow these steps:

1. Read the title, caption, conversation balloons, and other text to identify the subject of the cartoon.

2. Identify the characters, people, or symbols shown.

3. Ask yourself: What action is occurring? Who is taking the action?

4. Determine the cartoonist's purpose: is it to persuade, criticize, or just make people think? What idea is the cartoonist trying to get across?

5. Ask yourself whether the publication or the cartoonist has a bias that is being expressed in the cartoon.

Practicing the Skill

Study the cartoon. Then use the cartoon and your knowledge of history to answer the questions that follow.

1. What is the topic of the cartoon?

2. Who are the participants, and what are they doing?

3. What point do you think the cartoonist is trying to make? Is the cartoon relevant to any of today's political issues?

Applying the Skill

Bring a newspaper or magazine to class. With a partner, analyze the message and detect any bias in the cartoons you find.

Analyzing Primary Sources

Why Learn This Skill?

To determine what happened in the past, historians do some detective work. They comb through bits of written and illustrated evidence from the past to reconstruct events. These bits of evidence are called "primary sources." They include letters, diaries, photographs, newspaper articles, ads, and legal documents.

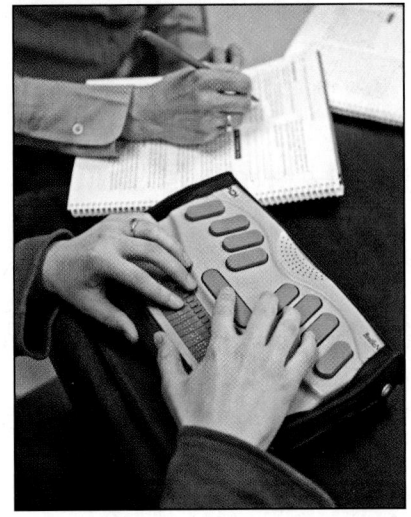

A blind student using a device to take notes in Braille

Learning the Skill

Primary sources yield several important types of information. They often provide details of events or personal perspectives. But remember: any source reflects only one perspective. Before drawing any conclusions, you should examine as many perspectives as possible. To analyze primary sources, follow these steps:

> *No person in the United States shall, on the ground of blindness or severely impaired vision, be denied admission in any course of study by a recipient of Federal financial assistance for any education program or activity; but nothing herein shall be construed to require any such institution to provide any special services to such person because of his blindness or visual impairment.*

—United States Code, Title IX, Education Amendments of 1972

1. Identify the author, the publication, or the document.

2. Determine when and where the document was written or illustrated.

3. Read the document or study the illustration for its content. Try to answer the five "W" questions: Whom is it about? What is it about? When did it happen? Where did it happen? Why did it happen?

Practicing the Skill

The primary source above is a small part of a United States legal document. Read the source and then answer these questions:

1. When was the document written?

2. Who is affected by this document?

3. What is the purpose of this document?

4. Why do you think this document was written?

Applying the Skill

Find a primary source from your past, such as a photo, a report card, an old newspaper clipping, or your first baseball card. Bring the source to class and explain what it shows about that time in your life.

Analyzing Secondary Sources

Painting of Mark Twain by John White

Why Learn This Skill?

This textbook, like many other history books, is a secondary source. It was written by using primary sources to explain the topics covered. The value of a secondary source depends on how well the author has used those primary sources. Learning to analyze secondary sources will help you figure out whether they are presenting topics completely and accurately.

Learning the Skill

Read the passage to the right, which discusses the controversy over the United States's occupation of the Philippines after the Spanish-American War. To analyze secondary sources, ask yourself these questions:

1. Are there references to primary sources in the text? Who are the sources?

2. What insights or biases might these people have?

3. Does the author use the sources effectively to support his or her points?

4. Does the author consider different kinds of sources? Do they represent varying viewpoints?

" *. . . [The anti-imperialists] denounced the extension of American rule by force in the Philippines, not because of what it might do to the Filipinos, but because of what they were convinced it was bound to do to American democratic ideals. They saw in the American seizure and retention of the Islands 'the infamy of the doctrine that a people may be governed without their consent.'. . .*

. . . The expansionists' reply . . . was the twin slogan: duty and destiny. . . . In the words of the archexpansionist Theodore Roosevelt: 'Peace cannot be had until the civilized nations have expanded in some shape over the barbarous nations.'

. . . Mark Twain was one literary figure who was won over . . . 'I left these shores at Vancouver,' he wrote, 'a red-hot imperialist. I wanted the American eagle to go screaming into the Pacific. . . . Why not spread its wings over the Philippines, I asked myself? . . .' But . . . in 1900 he wrote to Joseph Twichell: 'Apparently we are not proposing to set the Filipinos free and give their islands to them. . . . If these things are so, the war out there has no interest for me.' "

—Harold A. Larrabee, in *Historical Viewpoints*

Practicing the Skill

1. What primary sources does the author use?

2. Does the author cite where the quotations he used first appeared?

3. How reliable do you think these sources are?

4. Which source do you agree with?

Applying the Skill

In a newspaper or online, read an in-depth article about a topic that interests you. Then list the primary sources the article uses and analyze how reliable you think they are.

Foldables

FOLDABLES **Dinah Zike's Foldables** are three-dimensional, interactive graphic organizers used to help organize and retain information. Every chapter in your text uses a Foldable to help you identify and learn about the Big Ideas discussed in each section. The following pages provide complete folding instructions for the 14 different Foldables used throughout your Student Edition text.

Table of Contents

Basic Foldable Shapes

Taco Fold   **Hamburger Fold**   **Hot Dog Fold**

Burrito Fold   **Shutter Fold**   **Valley Fold**   **Mountain Fold**

Foldables

Accordion Book

NOTE: *Steps 1 and 2 should be done only if paper is too large to begin with.*

1. Fold the selected paper into *hamburgers*.

2. Cut the paper in half along the fold lines.

3. Fold each section of paper into *hamburgers*, but fold one side one half inch shorter than the other side. This will form a tab that is one half inch long.

4. Fold this tab forward over the shorter side, and then fold it back away from the shorter piece of paper; in other words, fold it the opposite way.

5. To form an *accordion,* glue a straight edge of one section into the *valley* of another section.

NOTE: *Stand the sections on end to form an accordion to help students visualize how to glue them together. (See illustration.)*

Always place the extra tab at the back of the book so you can add more pages later.

Use this book for time lines, student projects that grow, sequencing events or data, and biographies.

Concept-Map Book

1. Fold a sheet of paper along the long or short axis, leaving a two-inch tab uncovered along the top.

2. Fold in half or in thirds.

3. Unfold and cut along the inside fold line(s) to create two or three flaps.

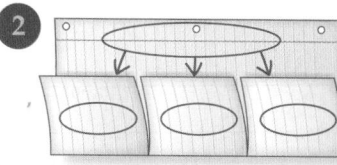

Folded Table or Chart

1. Fold the number of vertical columns needed to make the table or chart.
2. Fold the horizontal rows needed to make the table or chart.
3. Label the rows and columns.

Remember: Tables are organized along vertical and horizontal axes, while charts are organized along one axis, either horizontal or vertical.

Table

Chart

Four-Tab Book

1. Fold a sheet of paper (8½" × 11") in half like a *hot dog.*
2. Fold this long rectangle in half like a *hamburger.*
3. Fold both ends back to touch the *mountain top* or fold it like an *accordion.*
4. On the side with two *valleys* and one *mountain top,* make vertical cuts through one thickness of paper, forming four tabs.

Use this book for data occurring in fours.

Foldables

Four-Door Book

1. Make a *shutter fold* using 11" × 17" or 12" × 18" paper.
2. Fold the *shutter fold* in half like a *hamburger*. Crease well.
3. Open the project and cut along the two inside *valley* folds.
4. These cuts will form four doors on the inside of the project.

Use this fold for data occurring in fours. When folded in half like a *hamburger,* a finished *four-door book* can be glued inside a large (11" × 17") *shutter fold* as part of a larger project.

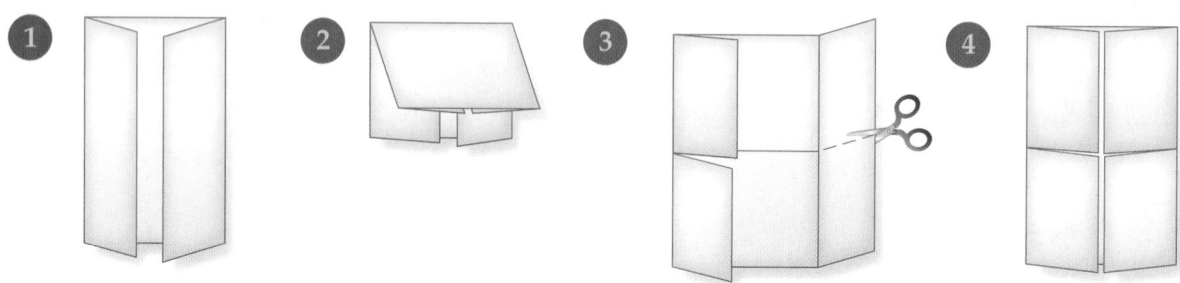

Half-Book

Fold a sheet of paper (8½" × 11") in half.

1. This book can be folded vertically like a *hot dog* or . . .
2. . . . it can be folded horizontally like a *hamburger.*

Use this book for descriptive, expository, persuasive, or narrative writing, as well as for graphs, diagrams, or charts.

Layered-Look Book

1. Stack two sheets of paper (8½" × 11") so that the back sheet is one inch higher than the front sheet.
2. Bring the bottom of both sheets upward and align the edges so that all of the layers or tabs are the same distance apart.
3. When all tabs are an equal distance apart, fold the papers and crease well.
4. Open the papers and glue them together along the *valley*, or inner center fold, or staple them along the *mountain*.

Pocket Book

1. Fold a sheet of paper (8½" × 11") in half like a *hamburger*.
2. Open the folded paper and fold one of the long sides up two inches to form a pocket. Refold along the *hamburger* fold so that the newly formed pockets are on the inside.
3. Glue the outer edges of the two-inch fold with a small amount of glue.
4. **Optional:** Glue a cover around the *pocket book*.

   Variation: Make a multi-paged booklet by gluing several pockets side-by-side. Glue a cover around the multi-paged *pocket book*.

Use 3" × 5" index cards inside the pockets. Store student-made books, such as two-tab books and folded books in the pockets.

Foldables

Sentence Strips

1. Take two sheets of paper (8½" × 11") and fold into *hamburgers*. Cut along the fold lines making four half sheets. *(Use as many half sheets as necessary for additional pages to your book.)*

2. Fold each sheet in half like a *hot dog*.

3. Place the folds side-by-side and staple them together on the left side.

4. One inch from the stapled edge, cut the front page of each folded section up to the *mountain top*. These cuts form flaps that can be raised and lowered.

To make a half-cover, use a sheet of construction paper one inch longer than the book. Glue the back of the last sheet to the construction paper strip leaving one inch, on the left side, to fold over and cover the original staples. Staple this half-cover in place.

Shutter Fold

1. Begin as if you were going to make a *hamburger* but instead of creasing the paper, pinch it to show the midpoint.

2. Fold the outer edges of the paper to meet at the pinch, or mid-point, forming a *shutter fold*.

Use this book for data occurring in twos. Or, make this fold using 11" × 17" paper and smaller books—such as the half-book, journal, and two-tab book—that can be glued inside to create a large project full of student work.

Three-Tab Book

1. Fold a sheet of paper like a *hot dog.*
2. With the paper horizontal, and the fold of the *hot dog* up, fold the right side toward the center, trying to cover one half of the paper.
   NOTE: *If you fold the right edge over first, the final graphic organizer will open and close like a book.*
3. Fold the left side over the right side to make a book with three folds.
4. Open the folded book. Place your hands between the two thicknesses of paper and cut up the two *valleys* on one side only. This will form three tabs.

Use this book for data occurring in threes, and for two-part Venn diagrams.

Variation A:
Draw overlapping circles on the three tabs to make a Venn diagram.

Variation B:
Cut each of the three tabs in half to make a six-tab book.

Trifold Book

1. Fold a sheet of paper (8½" × 11") into thirds.
2. Use this book as is, or cut into shapes. If the trifold is cut, leave plenty of fold on both sides of the designed shape, so the book will open and close in three sections.

Use this book to make charts with three columns or rows, large Venn diagrams, or reports on data occurring in threes.

Foldables

Two-Tab Book

1. Take a *folded book* and cut up the *valley* of the inside fold toward the *mountain top*. This cut forms two large tabs that can be used front and back for writing and illustrations.

2. The book can be expanded by making several of these folds and gluing them side-by-side.

Use this book with data occurring in twos. For example, use it for comparing and contrasting, determining cause and effect, finding similarities and differences, and more.

Vocabulary Book

1. Fold a sheet of notebook paper in half like a *hot dog*.

2. On one side, cut every third line. This results in ten tabs on wide-ruled notebook paper and twelve tabs on college-ruled.

3. Label the tabs.

Presidents of the United States

In this resource you will find portraits of the individuals who served as presidents of the United States, along with their occupations, political party affiliations, and other interesting facts.

**The Republican Party during this period developed into today's Democratic Party. Today's Republican Party originated in 1854.*

1 George Washington

Presidential term: 1789–1797
Lived: 1732–1799
Born in: Virginia
Elected from: Virginia
Occupations: Soldier, Planter
Party: None
Vice President: John Adams

2 John Adams

Presidential term: 1797–1801
Lived: 1735–1826
Born in: Massachusetts
Elected from: Massachusetts
Occupations: Teacher, Lawyer
Party: Federalist
Vice President: Thomas Jefferson

3 Thomas Jefferson

Presidential term: 1801–1809
Lived: 1743–1826
Born in: Virginia
Elected from: Virginia
Occupations: Planter, Lawyer
Party: Republican**
Vice Presidents: Aaron Burr, George Clinton

4 James Madison

Presidential term: 1809–1817
Lived: 1751–1836
Born in: Virginia
Elected from: Virginia
Occupation: Planter
Party: Republican**
Vice Presidents: George Clinton, Elbridge Gerry

5 James Monroe

Presidential term: 1817–1825
Lived: 1758–1831
Born in: Virginia
Elected from: Virginia
Occupation: Lawyer
Party: Republican**
Vice President: Daniel D. Tompkins

6 John Quincy Adams

Presidential term: 1825–1829
Lived: 1767–1848
Born in: Massachusetts
Elected from: Massachusetts
Occupation: Lawyer
Party: Republican**
Vice President: John C. Calhoun

7 Andrew Jackson

Presidential term: 1829–1837
Lived: 1767–1845
Born in: South Carolina
Elected from: Tennessee
Occupations: Lawyer, Soldier
Party: Democratic
Vice Presidents: John C. Calhoun, Martin Van Buren

8 Martin Van Buren

Presidential term: 1837–1841
Lived: 1782–1862
Born in: New York
Elected from: New York
Occupation: Lawyer
Party: Democratic
Vice President: Richard M. Johnson

9 William H. Harrison

Presidential term: 1841
Lived: 1773–1841
Born in: Virginia
Elected from: Ohio
Occupations: Soldier,
    Planter
Party: Whig
Vice President: John Tyler

10 John Tyler

Presidential term: 1841–1845
Lived: 1790–1862
Born in: Virginia
Elected as V.P. from: Virginia
Succeeded Harrison
Occupation: Lawyer
Party: Whig
Vice President: None

11 James K. Polk

Presidential term: 1845–1849
Lived: 1795–1849
Born in: North Carolina
Elected from: Tennessee
Occupation: Lawyer
Party: Democratic
Vice President: George M.
    Dallas

12 Zachary Taylor

Presidential term: 1849–1850
Lived: 1784–1850
Born in: Virginia
Elected from: Louisiana
Occupation: Soldier
Party: Whig
Vice President: Millard
    Fillmore

13 Millard Fillmore

Presidential term: 1850–1853
Lived: 1800–1874
Born in: New York
Elected as V.P. from: New York
Succeeded Taylor
Occupation: Lawyer
Party: Whig
Vice President: None

14 Franklin Pierce

Presidential term: 1853–1857
Lived: 1804–1869
Born in: New Hampshire
Elected from: New Hampshire
Occupation: Lawyer
Party: Democratic
Vice President: William R. King

15 James Buchanan

Presidential term: 1857–1861
Lived: 1791–1868
Born in: Pennsylvania
Elected from: Pennsylvania
Occupation: Lawyer
Party: Democratic
Vice President: John C.
    Breckinridge

16 Abraham Lincoln

Presidential term: 1861–1865
Lived: 1809–1865
Born in: Kentucky
Elected from: Illinois
Occupation: Lawyer
Party: Republican
Vice Presidents: Hannibal
    Hamlin, Andrew Johnson

17 Andrew Johnson

Presidential term: 1865–1869
Lived: 1808–1875
Born in: North Carolina
Elected as V.P. from: Tennessee
Succeeded Lincoln
Occupation: Tailor
Party: Democratic; National Unionist
Vice President: None

U.S. Presidents

18 Ulysses S. Grant

Presidential term: 1869–1877
Lived: 1822–1885
Born in: Ohio
Elected from: Illinois
Occupations: Farmer, Soldier
Party: Republican
Vice Presidents: Schuyler Colfax,
  Henry Wilson

19 Rutherford B. Hayes

Presidential term: 1877–1881
Lived: 1822–1893
Born in: Ohio
Elected from: Ohio
Occupation: Lawyer
Party: Republican
Vice President: William A.
  Wheeler

20 James A. Garfield

Presidential term: 1881
Lived: 1831–1881
Born in: Ohio
Elected from: Ohio
Occupations: Laborer, Professor
Party: Republican
Vice President: Chester A.
  Arthur

21 Chester A. Arthur

Presidential term: 1881–1885
Lived: 1830–1886
Born in: Vermont
Elected as V.P. from: New York
Succeeded Garfield
Occupations: Teacher, Lawyer
Party: Republican
Vice President: None

22 Grover Cleveland

Presidential term: 1885–1889
Lived: 1837–1908
Born in: New Jersey
Elected from: New York
Occupation: Lawyer
Party: Democratic
Vice President: Thomas A.
  Hendricks

23 Benjamin Harrison

Presidential term: 1889–1893
Lived: 1833–1901
Born in: Ohio
Elected from: Indiana
Occupation: Lawyer
Party: Republican
Vice President: Levi P. Morton

24 Grover Cleveland

Presidential term: 1893–1897
Lived: 1837–1908
Born in: New Jersey
Elected from: New York
Occupation: Lawyer
Party: Democratic
Vice President: Adlai E.
  Stevenson

25 William McKinley

Presidential term: 1897–1901
Lived: 1843–1901
Born in: Ohio
Elected from: Ohio
Occupations: Teacher, Lawyer
Party: Republican
Vice Presidents: Garret Hobart,
  Theodore Roosevelt

26 Theodore Roosevelt

Presidential term: 1901–1909
Lived: 1858–1919
Born in: New York
Elected as V.P. from: New York
Succeeded McKinley
Occupations: Historian, Rancher
Party: Republican
Vice President: Charles W.
  Fairbanks

U.S. Presidents

27 William H. Taft

Presidential term: 1909–1913
Lived: 1857–1930
Born in: Ohio
Elected from: Ohio
Occupations: Lawyer
Party: Republican
Vice President: James S. Sherman

28 Woodrow Wilson

Presidential term: 1913–1921
Lived: 1856–1924
Born in: Virginia
Elected from: New Jersey
Occupation: College Professor
Party: Democratic
Vice President: Thomas R. Marshall

29 Warren G. Harding

Presidential term: 1921–1923
Lived: 1865–1923
Born in: Ohio
Elected from: Ohio
Occupations: Newspaper Editor, Publisher
Party: Republican
Vice President: Calvin Coolidge

30 Calvin Coolidge

Presidential term: 1923–1929
Lived: 1872–1933
Born in: Vermont
Elected as V.P. from: Massachusetts, Succeeded Harding
Occupation: Lawyer
Party: Republican
Vice President: Charles G. Dawes

31 Herbert C. Hoover

Presidential term: 1929–1933
Lived: 1874–1964
Born in: Iowa
Elected from: California
Occupation: Engineer
Party: Republican
Vice President: Charles Curtis

32 Franklin D. Roosevelt

Presidential term: 1933–1945
Lived: 1882–1945
Born in: New York
Elected from: New York
Occupation: Lawyer
Party: Democratic
Vice Presidents: John N. Garner, Henry A. Wallace, Harry S. Truman

33 Harry S. Truman

Presidential term: 1945–1953
Lived: 1884–1972
Born in: Missouri
Elected as V.P. from: Missouri Succeeded Roosevelt
Occupations: Clerk, Farmer
Party: Democratic
Vice President: Alben W. Barkley

34 Dwight D. Eisenhower

Presidential term: 1953–1961
Lived: 1890–1969
Born in: Texas
Elected from: New York
Occupation: Soldier
Party: Republican
Vice President: Richard M. Nixon

35 John F. Kennedy

Presidential term: 1961–1963
Lived: 1917–1963
Born in: Massachusetts
Elected from: Massachusetts
Occupations: Author, Reporter
Party: Democratic
Vice President: Lyndon B. Johnson

36 Lyndon B. Johnson

Presidential term: 1963–1969
Lived: 1908–1973
Born in: Texas
Elected as V.P. from: Texas
Succeeded Kennedy
Occupation: Teacher
Party: Democratic
Vice President: Hubert H.
Humphrey

37 Richard M. Nixon

Presidential term: 1969–1974
Lived: 1913–1994
Born in: California
Elected from: New York
Occupation: Lawyer
Party: Republican
Vice Presidents: Spiro T. Agnew,
Gerald R. Ford

38 Gerald R. Ford

Presidential term: 1974–1977
Lived: 1913–2006
Born in: Nebraska
Appointed as V.P. upon Agnew's
resignation; succeeded Nixon
Occupation: Lawyer
Party: Republican
Vice President: Nelson A.
Rockefeller

39 James E. Carter, Jr.

Presidential term: 1977–1981
Lived: 1924–
Born in: Georgia
Elected from: Georgia
Occupations: Business, Farmer
Party: Democratic
Vice President: Walter F.
Mondale

40 Ronald W. Reagan

Presidential term: 1981–1989
Lived: 1911–2004
Born in: Illinois
Elected from: California
Occupations: Actor, Lecturer
Party: Republican
Vice President: George H.W.
Bush

41 George H.W. Bush

Presidential term: 1989–1993
Lived: 1924–
Born in: Massachusetts
Elected from: Texas
Occupation: Business
Party: Republican
Vice President: J. Danforth
Quayle

42 William J. Clinton

Presidential term: 1993–2001
Lived: 1946–
Born in: Arkansas
Elected from: Arkansas
Occupation: Lawyer
Party: Democratic
Vice President: Albert Gore, Jr.

43 George W. Bush

Presidential term: 2001–2009
Lived: 1946–
Born in: Connecticut
Elected from: Texas
Occupation: Business
Party: Republican
Vice President: Richard B.
Cheney

44 Barack Obama

Presidential term: 2009–
Lived: 1961–
Born in: Hawaii
Elected from: Illinois
Occupation: Lawyer
Party: Democratic
Vice President: Joseph R.
Biden, Jr.

U.S. Presidents

United States Facts

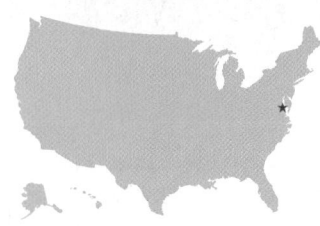

Washington, D.C.
Population: 572,059
Land area: 61 sq. mi.

The states are listed in the order they were admitted to the Union.

Population figures are based on U.S. Bureau of the Census for 2000. House of Representatives figures are from the Clerk of the House of Representatives. States are not drawn to scale.

U.S. Territories

Puerto Rico
Population: 3,808,610
Land area: 3,425 sq. mi.

Guam
Population: 155,000 (est.)
Land area: 209 sq. mi.

U.S. Virgin Islands
Population: 121,000 (est.)
Land area: 134 sq. mi.

American Samoa
Population: 65,000 (est.)
Land area: 77 sq. mi.

1 Delaware
Year Admitted: 1787
Population: 783,600
Land area: 1,955 sq. mi.
Representatives: 1
★ Dover

2 Pennsylvania
Year Admitted: 1787
Population: 12,281,054
Land area: 44,820 sq. mi.
Representatives: 19
Harrisburg ★

3 New Jersey
Year Admitted: 1787
Population: 8,414,350
Land area: 7,419 sq. mi.
Representatives: 13
Trenton ★

4 Georgia
Year Admitted: 1788
Population: 8,186,453
Land area: 57,919 sq. mi.
Representatives: 13
★ Atlanta

5 Connecticut
Year Admitted: 1788
Population: 3,405,565
Land area: 4,845 sq. mi.
Representatives: 5
★ Hartford

6 Massachusetts
Year Admitted: 1788
Population: 6,349,097
Land area: 7,838 sq. mi.
Representatives: 10
Boston ★

7 Maryland
Year Admitted: 1788
Population: 5,296,486
Land area: 9,775 sq. mi.
Representatives: 8
Annapolis ★

8 South Carolina
Year Admitted: 1788
Population: 4,012,012
Land area: 30,111 sq. mi.
Representatives: 6
Columbia ★

9 New Hampshire
Year Admitted: 1788
Population: 1,235,786
Land area: 8,969 sq. mi.
Representatives: 2
Concord ★

10 Virginia
Year Admitted: 1788
Population: 7,078,515
Land area: 39,598 sq. mi.
Representatives: 11
Richmond ★

11 New York
Year Admitted: 1788
Population: 18,976,457
Land area: 47,224 sq. mi.
Representatives: 29
★ Albany

12 North Carolina
Year Admitted: 1789
Population: 8,049,313
Land area: 48,718 sq. mi.
Representatives: 13
Raleigh ★

13 Rhode Island
Year Admitted: 1790
Population: 1,048,319
Land area: 1,045 sq. mi.
Representatives: 2
★ Providence

14 Vermont
Year Admitted: 1791
Population: 608,827
Land area: 9,249 sq. mi.
Representatives: 1
★ Montpelier

15 Kentucky
Year Admitted: 1792
Population: 4,041,769
Land area: 39,732 sq. mi.
Representatives: 6
Frankfort ★

16 Tennessee
Year Admitted: 1796
Population: 5,689,283
Land area: 41,220 sq. mi.
Representatives: 9
★ Nashville

17 Ohio
Year Admitted: 1803
Population: 11,353,140
Land area: 40,953 sq. mi.
Representatives: 18
★ Columbus

18 Louisiana
Year Admitted: 1812
Population: 4,468,976
Land area: 43,566 sq. mi.
Representatives: 7
★ Baton Rouge

19 Indiana
Year Admitted: 1816
Population: 6,080,485
Land area: 35,870 sq. mi.
Representatives: 9
Indianapolis ★

20 Mississippi
Year Admitted: 1817
Population: 2,844,658
Land area: 46,914 sq. mi.
Representatives: 4
★ Jackson

21 Illinois
Year Admitted: 1818
Population: 12,419,293
Land area: 55,593 sq. mi.
Representatives: 19

★ Springfield

22 Alabama
Year Admitted: 1819
Population: 4,447,100
Land area: 50,750 sq. mi.
Representatives: 7

Montgomery ★

23 Maine
Year Admitted: 1820
Population: 1,274,923
Land area: 30,865 sq. mi.
Representatives: 2

★ Augusta

24 Missouri
Year Admitted: 1821
Population: 5,595,211
Land area: 68,898 sq. mi.
Representatives: 9

Jefferson City ★

25 Arkansas
Year Admitted: 1836
Population: 2,673,400
Land area: 52,075 sq. mi.
Representatives: 4

Little Rock ★

26 Michigan
Year Admitted: 1837
Population: 9,938,444
Land area: 56,809 sq. mi.
Representatives: 15

Lansing ★

27 Florida
Year Admitted: 1845
Population: 15,982,378
Land area: 53,997 sq. mi.
Representatives: 25

★ Tallahassee

28 Texas
Year Admitted: 1845
Population: 20,851,820
Land area: 261,914 sq. mi.
Representatives: 32

Austin ★

29 Iowa
Year Admitted: 1846
Population: 2,926,324
Land area: 55,875 sq. mi.
Representatives: 5

★ Des Moines

30 Wisconsin
Year Admitted: 1848
Population: 5,363,675
Land area: 54,314 sq. mi.
Representatives: 8

Madison ★

31 California
Year Admitted: 1850
Population: 33,871,648
Land area: 155,973 sq. mi.
Representatives: 53

Sacramento ★

32 Minnesota
Year Admitted: 1858
Population: 4,919,479
Land area: 79,617 sq. mi.
Representatives: 8

Saint Paul ★

33 Oregon
Year Admitted: 1859
Population: 3,421,399
Land area: 96,003 sq. mi.
Representatives: 5

★ Salem

34 Kansas
Year Admitted: 1861
Population: 2,688,418
Land area: 81,823 sq. mi.
Representatives: 4

Topeka ★

35 West Virginia
Year Admitted: 1863
Population: 1,808,344
Land area: 24,087 sq. mi.
Representatives: 3

★ Charleston

36 Nevada
Year Admitted: 1864
Population: 1,998,257
Land area: 109,806 sq. mi.
Representatives: 3

★ Carson City

37 Nebraska
Year Admitted: 1867
Population: 1,711,263
Land area: 76,878 sq. mi.
Representatives: 3

Lincoln ★

38 Colorado
Year Admitted: 1876
Population: 4,301,261
Land area: 103,730 sq. mi.
Representatives: 7

Denver ★

39 North Dakota
Year Admitted: 1889
Population: 642,200
Land area: 68,994 sq. mi.
Representatives: 1

Bismarck ★

40 South Dakota
Year Admitted: 1889
Population: 754,844
Land area: 75,898 sq. mi.
Representatives: 1

Pierre ★

41 Montana
Year Admitted: 1889
Population: 902,195
Land area: 145,556 sq. mi.
Representatives: 1

★ Helena

42 Washington
Year Admitted: 1889
Population: 5,894,121
Land area: 66,582 sq. mi.
Representatives: 9

★ Olympia

43 Idaho
Year Admitted: 1890
Population: 1,293,953
Land area: 82,751 sq. mi.
Representatives: 2

★ Boise

44 Wyoming
Year Admitted: 1890
Population: 493,782
Land area: 97,105 sq. mi.
Representatives: 1

Cheyenne ★

45 Utah
Year Admitted: 1896
Population: 2,233,169
Land area: 82,168 sq. mi.
Representatives: 3

★ Salt Lake City

46 Oklahoma
Year Admitted: 1907
Population: 3,450,654
Land area: 68,679 sq. mi.
Representatives: 5

Oklahoma City ★

47 New Mexico
Year Admitted: 1912
Population: 1,819,046
Land area: 121,365 sq. mi.
Representatives: 3

★ Santa Fe

48 Arizona
Year Admitted: 1912
Population: 5,130,632
Land area: 113,642 sq. mi.
Representatives: 8

Phoenix ★

49 Alaska
Year Admitted: 1959
Population: 626,932
Land area: 570,374 sq. mi.
Representatives: 1

Juneau ★

50 Hawaii
Year Admitted: 1959
Population: 1,211,537
Land area: 6,432 sq. mi.
Representatives: 2

Honolulu ★

U.S. Facts

Documents of American History

(right) Lincoln's drafts of the Gettysburg Address

Magna Carta

Why They Matter

Documents are often public statements by a president or an official body, such as a legislature, on an important issue. They have become documents because they define a particular issue so well that Americans continue to refer to them. Many documents here address fundamental American beliefs, such as the rights of the individual and the proper limits of government. Other documents, such as the Monroe Doctrine or the Truman Doctrine, address the nation's position and responsibilities in the world.

Documents matter because they are guides to American government and values. Sometimes people study them to learn how Americans came to believe in certain principles. Other times people read documents simply because these writings express certain principles passionately.

Signing the Mayflower Compact

Founding Documents of the American Republic

The first seven documents in this collection represent some of the founding documents of American democracy. Each contributed an essential building block for American political principles. Ultimately these principles were embodied in the Declaration of Independence, the Bill of Rights, and the Constitution.

DOCUMENT	WHY IT MATTERS
The Magna Carta In signing this charter in 1215, King John of England granted his subjects certain permanent liberties or rights, such as the right to a fair trial by a jury of their peers.	Over the centuries, English people believed that the Magna Carta gave them certain rights. They took this idea with them when they settled the American colonies. Some provisions of the Bill of Rights reflect ancient Magna Carta liberties.
The Mayflower Compact In 1620 the Pilgrims signed a compact while still aboard the *Mayflower*. This document laid out a plan for self-government the Pilgrims would use once they landed in America.	This document is the first plan for self-government put into effect in the English colonies. It reflected the idea that government should be based on a consensus of the entire community.
The Fundamental Orders of Connecticut Connecticut settlers agreed they would be governed according to a certain set of laws and through certain institutions. All citizens, not only those of a certain religion, could vote.	This document, the first written constitution drawn up in America, strengthened the colonists' beliefs about governing themselves.
The English Bill of Rights In 1689, after the Glorious Revolution, Parliament forced the king to accept this Bill of Rights guaranteeing basic civil rights.	This document clearly established that English subjects had certain rights and that the king could be removed from power for violating those rights.
Second Treatise of Government English philosopher John Locke wrote this document during the 1680s. One of his basic arguments was that government should be based on a contract between a ruler and those who are ruled. Rebellion is justified if a ruler violates the contract.	During the American Revolution, the colonists drew from Locke's theories of government and especially his ideas about the right to rebel.
The Virginia Statute for Religious Freedom This 1786 statute declared that the state of Virginia should not support Anglicanism or any other religious denomination.	The religious clauses of the Bill of Rights protecting the free exercise of religion and prohibiting an official religion were based on this statute.
The Federalist No. 10 In 1787 James Madison wrote this paper, one of a series arguing for stronger central government as reflected in the new Constitution.	The framework for American government today— a representative government with a strong federal government—was laid out in the Federalist Papers.

 *Use the **American History Primary Source Document Library CD-ROM** to find additional primary sources about American heritage.*

The Magna Carta

The Magna Carta, signed by King John of England in 1215, marked a decisive step forward in the development of English constitutional government. Later it served as a model for the colonists, who carried the Magna Carta's guarantees of political rights to America.

John, by the grace of God, king of England, lord of Ireland, duke of Normandy and Aquitaine, and count of Anjou: to the archbishops, bishops, abbots, earls, barons, justiciaries, foresters, sheriffs, reeves, ministers, and all bailiffs and others his faithful subjects, greeting. . . .

1. We have, in the first place, granted to God, and by this our present charter, confirmed for us and our heirs forever that the English church shall be free. . . .

9. Neither we nor our bailiffs shall seize any land or rent for any debt so long as the debtor's chattels are sufficient to discharge the same. . . .

12. No scutage [tax] or aid shall be imposed in our kingdom unless by the common counsel thereof. . . .

14. For obtaining the common counsel of the kingdom concerning the assessment of aids. . . or of scutage, we will cause to be summoned, severally by our letters, the archbishops, bishops, abbots, earls, and great barons; we will also cause to be summoned generally, by our sheriffs and bailiffs, all those who hold lands directly of us, to meet on a fixed day . . . and at a fixed place. . . .

20. A free man shall be amerced [punished] for a small fault only according to the measure thereof, and for a great crime according to its magnitude. . . . None of these amercements shall be imposed except by the oath of honest men of the neighborhood.

21. Earls and barons shall be amerced only by their peers, and only in proportion to the measure of the offense. . . .

38. In the future no bailiff shall upon his own unsupported accusation put any man to trial without producing credible witnesses to the truth of the accusation.

39. No free man shall be taken, imprisoned, disseised [seized], outlawed, banished, or in any way destroyed, nor will we proceed against or prosecute him, except by the lawful judgment of his peers and by the law of the land.

40. To no one will we sell, to none will we deny or delay, right or justice. . . .

42. In the future it shall be lawful . . . for anyone to leave and return to our kingdom safely and securely by land and water, saving his fealty to us. Excepted are those who have been imprisoned or outlawed according to the law of the land. . . .

61. Whereas we, for the honor of God and the amendment of our realm, and in order the better to allay the discord arisen between us and our barons, have granted all these things aforesaid. . . .

63. Wherefore we will, and firmly charge . . . that all men in our kingdom shall have and hold all the aforesaid liberties, rights, and concessions . . . fully, and wholly to them and their heirs . . . in all things and places forever. . . . It is moreover sworn, as well on our part as on the part of the barons, that all these matters aforesaid will be kept in good faith and without deceit. Witness the above named and many others. Given by our hand in the meadow which is called Runnymede. . . .

The Mayflower Compact

On November 21, 1620, 41 colonists drafted the Mayflower Compact while still aboard the **Mayflower.** *It was the first self-government plan ever put into effect in the English colonies. The compact was drawn up under these circumstances, as described by Governor William Bradford:*

"This day, before we came to harbor, observing some not well affected to unity and concord, but gave some appearance of faction, it was thought good there should be an association and agreement that we should combine together in one body, and to submit to such government and governors as we should by common consent agree to make and choose, and set our hands to this that follows word for word."

In the Name of God, Amen. We, whose names are underwritten, the Loyal Subjects of our dread Sovereign Lord King James, by the Grace of God, of Great Britain, France, and Ireland, King, Defender of the Faith, etc.

Having undertaken for the Glory of God, and Advancement of the Christian Faith, and the honor of our King and Country, a Voyage to plant the first Colony in the northern Parts of Virginia, Do by these Presents, solemnly and mutually, in the Presence of God and one another, covenant and combine ourselves together into a civil Body Politick, for our better Ordering and Preservation, and Furtherance of the Ends aforesaid; And by Virtue hereof do enact, constitute, and frame, such just and equal Laws, Ordinances, Acts, Constitutions, and Offices, from time to time, as shall be thought most meet and convenient for the general Good of the Colony; unto which we promise all due Submission and Obedience. In Witness whereof we have hereunder subscribed our names at Cape Cod the eleventh of November, in the Reign of our Sovereign Lord King James of England, France, and Ireland, the eighteenth and of Scotland, the fifty-fourth. Anno Domini, 1620.

Signing of the Mayflower Compact

The Fundamental Orders of Connecticut

In January 1639, settlers in Connecticut, led by Thomas Hooker, drew up the Fundamental Orders of Connecticut—America's first written constitution. It is essentially a body of laws and a compact among the settlers.

Forasmuch as it has pleased the Almighty God by the wise disposition of His Divine Providence so to order and dispose of things that we, the inhabitants and residents of Windsor, Hartford, and Wethersfield are now cohabiting and dwelling in and upon the river of Conectecotte and the lands thereunto adjoining; and well knowing where a people are gathered together the Word of God requires that, to maintain the peace and union of such a people, there should be an orderly and decent government established according to God, . . . do therefore associate and conjoin ourselves to be as one public state or commonwealth. . . . As also in our civil affairs to be guided and governed according to such laws, rules, orders, and decrees as shall be made, ordered, and decreed, as follows:

1. It is ordered . . . that there shall be yearly two general assemblies or courts; . . . The first shall be called the Court of Election, wherein shall be yearly chosen . . . so many magistrates and other public officers as shall be found requisite. Whereof one to be chosen governor . . . and no other magistrate to be chosen for more than one year; provided always there be six chosen besides the governor . . . by all that are admitted freemen and have taken the oath of fidelity, and do cohabit within this jurisdiction. . . .

4. It is ordered . . . that no person be chosen governor above once in two years, and that the governor be always a member of some approved congregation, and formerly of the magistracy within this jurisdiction; and all the magistrates freemen of this Commonwealth. . . .

5. It is ordered . . . that to the aforesaid Court of Election the several towns shall send their deputies.

. . . Also, the other General Court . . . shall be for making of laws, and any other public occasion which concerns the good of the Commonwealth. . . .

7. It is ordered . . . that . . . the constable or constables of each town shall forthwith give notice distinctly to the inhabitants of the same . . . that . . . they meet and assemble themselves together to elect and choose certain deputies to be at the General Court then following to [manage] the affairs of the Commonwealth; . . .

10. It is ordered . . . that every General Court . . . shall consist of the governor, or someone chosen to moderate the Court, and four other magistrates, at least, with the major part of the deputies of the several towns legally chosen. . . . In which said General Courts shall consist the supreme power of the Commonwealth, and they only shall have power to make laws or repeal them, to grant levies, to admit of freemen, dispose of lands undisposed of to several towns or person, and also shall have power to call either Court or magistrate or any other person whatsoever into question for any misdemeanor. . . .

Connecticut settlers on their way to Hartford

Documents

The English Bill of Rights

In 1689 William of Orange (pictured at right) and his wife Mary became joint rulers of England after accepting a list of conditions that later became known as the English Bill of Rights. This document assured the English people of certain basic civil rights and limited the power of the English monarchy.

An act declaring the rights and liberties of the subject and settling the succession of the crown. Whereas the lords spiritual and temporal and commons assembled at Westminster lawfully, fully and freely representing all the estates of the people of this realm did upon the thirteenth day of February in the year of our Seal of William and Mary Lord one thousand six hundred eighty-eight [-nine] present unto their majesties . . . William and Mary prince and princess of Orange . . . a certain declaration in writing made by the said lords and commons in the words following viz [namely]:

Whereas the late king James the second, by the assistance of divers evil counsellors, judges, and ministers employed by him did endeavor to subvert and extirpate the Protestant religion and the laws and liberties of this kingdom.

By assuming and exercising a power of dispensing with and suspending of laws and the execution of laws without consent of parliament. . . .

By levying money for and to the use of the crown by pretence of prerogative for other time and in other manner than the same was granted by parliament.

By raising and keeping a standing army within this kingdom in time of peace without consent of parliament and quartering soldiers contrary to law. . . .

By violating the freedom of election of members to serve in parliament. . . .

And excessive bail hath been required of persons committed in criminal cases to elude the benefit of the laws made for the liberty of the subjects.

And excessive fines have been imposed.

And illegal and cruel punishments inflicted. . . .

And thereupon the said lords spiritual and temporal and commons . . . do . . . declare that the pretended power of suspending of laws or the execution of laws by regal authority without consent of parliament is illegal. . . .

That levying money for or to the use of the crown . . . without grant of parliament for longer time or in other manner than the same is or shall be granted is illegal.

That it is the right of the subjects to petition the king and all commitments and prosecutions for such petitioning are illegal.

That the raising or keeping a standing army within the kingdom in time of peace unless it be with consent of parliament is against law. . . .

That election of members of parliament ought to be free. . . .

That excessive bail ought not to be required nor excessive fines imposed nor cruel and unusual punishments inflicted. . . .

The said lords . . . do resolve that William and Mary, prince and princess of Orange, be declared king and queen of England, France, and Ireland. . . .

Second Treatise of Government

English philosopher John Locke (above) wrote "Two Treatises of Government" in the early 1680s. Published in 1690, the "Second Treatise of Government" argues that government should be based on an agreement between the people and their ruler, and that if the ruler violates the agreement, a rebellion by the people may be justified.

Of the State of Nature

To understand Political Power right, and to derive it from its Original, we must consider what State all Men are naturally in, and that is, a State of perfect Freedom to order their Actions, and dispose of their Possessions, and Persons as they think fit, within the bounds of the Law of Nature, without asking leave, or depending upon the Will of any other Man. . . .

Of the Beginning of Political Societies

Men being, as has been said, by Nature, all free, equal and independent, no one can be put out of this Estate, and subjected to the Political Power of another, without his own Consent. The only way whereby any one divests himself of his Natural Liberty, and puts on the bonds of Civil Society is by agreeing with other Men to joyn and unite into a Community, for their comfortable, safe, and peaceable living one amongst another, in a secure Enjoyment of their properties, and a greater Security against any that are not of it. This any number of Men may do, because it injures not the Freedom of the rest; they are left as they were in the Liberty of the State of Nature. . . .

Whosoever therefore out of a state of Nature unite into a Community, must be understood to give up all the power, necessary to the ends for which they unite into Society, to the majority of the Community. . . .

Of the Dissolution of Government

Governments are dissolved from within . . . when the Legislative is altered. . . . First, that when such a single Person or Prince sets up his own Arbitrary Will in place of the Laws, which are the Will of the Society, declared by the Legislative, then the Legislative is changed. . . . Secondly, when the Prince hinders the legislative from . . . acting freely, pursuant to those ends, for which it was Constituted, the Legislative is altered. . . . Thirdly, When by the Arbitrary Power of the Prince, the Electors, or ways of Election are altered, without the Consent, and contrary to the common Interest of the People, there also the Legislative is altered. . . .

In these and the like Cases, when the Government is dissolved, the People are at liberty to provide for themselves, by erecting a new Legislative, differing from the other, by the change of Persons, or Form, or both as they shall find it most for their safety and good. For the Society can never, by the fault of another, lose the Native and Original Right it has to preserve itself. . . .

The Virginia Statute for Religious Freedom

This statute, excerpted below, was the basis for the religion clauses in the Bill of Rights. Thomas Jefferson drafted the statute, and James Madison guided it through the Virginia legislature in 1786. The issue it addresses arose when the new state considered whether citizens should continue to support the Anglican Church, as they had in colonial times, or whether they should support any or all other denominations.

Whereas Almighty God hath created the mind free; that all attempts to influence it by temporal punishments . . . tend only to beget habits of hypocrisy and meanness, and are a departure from the plan of the Holy author of our religion; . . . that the impious presumption of legislators and rulers, civil as well as ecclesiastical, who being themselves but fallible and uninspired men, have assumed dominion over the faith of others, setting up their own opinions and modes of thinking as the only true and infallible, and as such endeavouring to impose them on others, hath established and maintained false religions over the greatest part of the world, and through all time; . . . that to compel a man to furnish contributions of money for the propagation of opinions which he disbelieves, is sinful and tyrannical; . . . that our civil rights have no dependence on our religious opinions, any more than our opinions in physics or geometry; that therefore the proscribing any citizen as unworthy the public confidence by laying upon him an incapacity of being called to offices of trust . . . unless he profess or renounce this or that religious opinion, is depriving him injuriously of those privileges and advantages to which in common with his fellow-citizens he has a natural right; that it tends only to corrupt the principles of that religion it is meant to encourage, by bribing with a monopoly of worldly honours and emoluments, those who will externally profess and conform to it . . . :

Be it enacted by the General Assembly, That no man shall be compelled to frequent or support any religious worship, place, or ministry whatsoever, nor shall be enforced, restrained, molested, or burthened in his body or goods, nor shall otherwise suffer on account of his religious opinions or belief; but that all men shall be free to profess, and by argument to maintain, their opinion in matters of religion, and that the same shall in no wise diminish enlarge, or affect their civil capacities. . . .

Thomas Jefferson

The Federalist No. 10

James Madison (pictured at right) wrote several articles for a New York newspaper supporting ratification of the Constitution. In the excerpt below, he argues for the idea of a federal republic as a guard against factions, or overzealous parties, in governing the nation.

The latent causes of faction are thus sown in the nature of man; and we see them everywhere. . . . A zeal for different opinions concerning religion, concerning government, and many other points; . . . an attachment to different leaders ambitiously contending for preeminence and power . . . have, in turn, divided mankind into parties . . . disposed to vex and oppress each other than to cooperate for their common good. . . . But the most common and durable source of factions has been the various and unequal distribution of property. Those who hold and those who are without property have ever formed distinct interests in society. Those who are creditors, and those who are debtors, fall under a like discrimination. A landed interest, a manufacturing interest, a mercantile interest, a moneyed interest, with many lesser interests, grow up of necessity in civilized nations, and divide them into different classes, actuated by different sentiments and views. The regulation of these various and interfering interests forms the principal task of modern legislation and involves the spirit of party and faction in the necessary and ordinary operations of government. . . .

The inference to which we are brought is that the causes of faction cannot be removed and relief is only to be sought in the means of controlling its effects. . . .

By what means is this object attainable? Evidently by one of two only. Either the existence of the same passion or interest in a majority at the same time must be prevented, or the majority, having such coexistent passion or interest, must be rendered, by their number and local situation, unable to concert and carry into effect schemes of oppression. . . .

From this . . . it may be concluded that a pure democracy, by which I mean a society consisting of a small number of citizens, who assemble and administer the government in person, can admit of no cure for the mischiefs of faction. A common passion or interest will, in almost every case, be felt by a majority of the whole; a communication and concert results from the form of government itself; and there is nothing to check the inducements to sacrifice the weaker party or an obnoxious individual. Hence it is that such democracies have ever been spectacles of turbulence and contention. . . .

A republic, by which I mean a government in which the scheme of representation takes place, opens a different prospect and promises the cure for which we are seeking. . . .

The two great points of difference between a democracy and a republic are: first, the delegation of the government in the latter to a small number of citizens elected by the rest; secondly, the greater number of citizens and great sphere of country over which the latter may be extended.

The Federalist No. 51

The author of this Federalist paper is not known. It may have been either James Madison or Alexander Hamilton. The author argues that the Constitution's federal system and separation of powers will protect the rights of the people.

In order to lay a due foundation for that separate and distinct exercise of the different powers of government, which to a certain extent is admitted on all hands to be essential to the preservation of liberty, it is evident that . . . the great security against a gradual concentration of the several powers in the same department, consists in giving to those who administer each department the necessary constitutional means and personal motives to resist encroachments of the others. . . .

Ambition must be made to counteract ambition. . . . A dependence on the people is, no doubt, the primary control on the government; but experience has taught mankind the necessity of auxiliary precautions. . . . The constant aim is to divide and arrange the several offices in such a manner as that each may be a check on the other. . . . In the compound republic of America, the power surrendered by the people is first divided between two distinct governments, and then the portion allotted to each subdivided among distinct and separate departments. . . .

In a free government the security for civil rights must be the same as that for religious rights. It consists in the one case in the multiplicity of interests, and in the other in the multiplicity of sects. . . . In the extended republic of the United States, and among the great variety of interests, parties, and sects which it embraces, a coalition of a majority of the whole society could seldom take place on any other principles than those of justice and the general good. . . . It is no less certain than it is important . . . that the larger the society, provided it lie within a practical sphere, the more duly capable it will be of self-government.

The Federalist No. 59

In this Federalist paper, Alexander Hamilton explains why Congress, and not the states, should have the final say in how federal elections are conducted.

The natural order of the subject leads us to consider . . . that provision of the Constitution which authorizes the national legislature to regulate, in the last resort, the election of its own members. . . . Its propriety rests upon the evidence of this plain proposition, that every government ought to contain in itself the means of its own preservation. . . . Nothing can be more evident, than that an exclusive power of regulating elections for the national government, in the hands of the state legislatures, would leave the existence of the union entirely at their mercy. They could at any moment annihilate it, by neglecting to provide for the choice of persons to administer its affairs. . . .

It is certainly true that the state legislatures, by forbearing the appointment of senators, may destroy the national government. But it will not follow that, because they have a power to do this in one instance, they ought to have it in every other. . . . It is an evil; but it is an evil which could not have been avoided without excluding the states . . . from a place in the organization of the national government. If this had been done, it would doubtless have been interpreted into an entire dereliction of the federal principle; and would certainly have deprived the state governments of that absolute safeguard which they will enjoy under this provision. . . .

Washington's Farewell Address

Washington never orally delivered his Farewell Address. Instead, he arranged to have it printed in a Philadelphia newspaper on September 19, 1796. Designed in part to remove him from consideration for a third presidential term, the address also warned about dangers the new nation was facing, especially the dangers of political parties and sectionalism.

Washington preparing to leave office

Friends and Fellow Citizens:

The period for a new election of a citizen to administer the executive government of the United States being not far distant . . . I should now apprise you of the resolution I have formed to decline being considered. . . .

The unity of government which constitutes you one people is . . . a main pillar in the edifice of your real independence; the support of your tranquility at home, your peace abroad; of your safety; of your prosperity in every shape; of that very liberty which you so highly prize. But as it is easy to foresee that, from different causes and from different quarters, much pains will be taken, many artifices employed to weaken in your minds the conviction of this truth. . . .

The name of American, which belongs to you, in your national capacity, must always exalt the just pride of patriotism more than any appellation derived from local discriminations. . . .

In contemplating the causes which may disturb our Union, it occurs as matter of serious concern that any ground should have been furnished for characterizing parties by geographical discriminations: Northern and Southern; Atlantic and Western; whence designing men may endeavor to excite a belief that there is a real difference of local interests and views. . . .

Let me now take a more comprehensive view and warn you in the most solemn manner against the baneful effects of the spirit of party generally. . . . The alternate domination of one faction over another, sharpened by the spirit of revenge natural to party dissension . . . is itself a frightful despotism. . . .

Of all the dispositions and habits which lead to political prosperity, religion and morality are indispensable supports. . . . A volume could not trace all their connections with private and public felicity. Let it simply be asked where is the security for property, for reputation, for life, if the sense of religious obligation desert the oaths, which are the instruments of investigation in courts of justice? And let us with caution indulge the supposition, that morality can be maintained without religion. Whatever may be conceded to the influence of refined education on minds of peculiar structure—reason and experience both forbid us to expect that national morality can prevail in exclusion of religious principle.

The great rule of conduct for us, in regard to foreign nations, is in extending our commercial relations to have with them as little political connection as possible. . . .

In offering you, my countrymen, these counsels of an old and affectionate friend, I dare not hope that they will make the strong and lasting impression I could wish. . . . But if I may even flatter myself that they may be productive of some partial benefit. . . .

The Kentucky Resolution

The Alien and Sedition Acts of 1798 made it easier for the government to suppress criticism and to arrest political enemies. This Federalist legislation inspired fierce opposition among Republicans, who looked to the state governments to reverse the acts. Two states, Kentucky and Virginia, passed resolutions stating their right to, in effect, disregard federal legislation. The resolutions laid the groundwork for the states' rights often cited during the Civil War. Thomas Jefferson wrote the Kentucky Resolution, excerpted below, which was adopted in 1799.

RESOLVED, . . . that if those who administer the general government be permitted to transgress the limits fixed by that compact, by a total disregard to the special delegations of power therein contained, annihilation of the state governments, and the erection upon their ruins, of a general consolidated government, will be the inevitable consequence; that the principle and construction contended for by sundry of the state legislatures, that the general government is the exclusive judge of the extent of the powers delegated to it, stop nothing short of despotism; . . . that the several states who formed that instrument, being sovereign and independent, have the unquestionable right to judge of its infraction; and that a nullification, by those sovereignties, of all unauthorized acts done under colour of that instrument, is the rightful remedy; . . .

"The Star-Spangled Banner"

Francis Scott Key

During the British bombardment of Fort McHenry during the War of 1812, a young Baltimore lawyer named Francis Scott Key was inspired to write the words to "The Star-Spangled Banner." Although it became popular immediately, it was not until 1931 that Congress officially declared "The Star-Spangled Banner" as the national anthem of the United States.

O! say can you see, by the dawn's early light,

What so proudly we hail'd at the twilight's last gleaming,

Whose broad stripes and bright stars through the perilous fight,

O'er the ramparts we watch'd, were so gallantly streaming?

And the Rockets' red glare, the Bombs bursting in air,

Gave proof through the night that our Flag was still there;

O! say, does that star-spangled Banner yet wave,

O'er the Land of the free, and the home of the brave?

Fort McHenry flag

The Monroe Doctrine

When Spain's power in South America began to weaken, other European nations seemed ready to step in. The United States was developing trade and diplomatic relations with South America, and it wanted to curb European influence there. The following is a statement President Monroe made on the subject in his annual message to Congress on December 2, 1823.

The occasion has been judged proper for asserting, as a principle in which the rights and interests of the United States are involved, that the American continents, by the free and independent condition which they have assumed and maintain, are henceforth not to be considered as subjects for future colonization by any European powers. . . .

. . . We owe it, therefore, to candor and to the amicable relations existing between the United States and those [European] powers to declare that we should consider any attempt on their part to extend their system to any portion of this hemisphere as dangerous to our peace and safety. With the existing colonies or dependencies of any European power we have not interfered and shall not interfere. But with the Governments who have declared their independence and maintain it, and whose independence we have, on great consideration and on just principles, acknowledged, we could not view any interposition for the purpose of oppressing them, or controlling in any other manner their destiny, by any European power in any other light than as the manifestation of an unfriendly disposition toward the United States. . . .

Our policy in regard to Europe, which was adopted at an early stage of the wars which have so long agitated that quarter of the globe, nevertheless remains the same, which is, not to interfere in the internal concerns of any of its powers; to consider the government de facto as the legitimate government for us; to cultivate friendly relations with it, and to preserve those relations by a frank, firm, and manly policy, meeting in all instances the just claims of every power, submitting to injuries from none.

The Seneca Falls Declaration

One of the first documents to call for equal rights for women was the Declaration of Sentiments and Resolutions, issued in 1848 at the Seneca Falls Convention in Seneca Falls, New York. Led by Lucretia Mott and Elizabeth Cady Stanton, the delegates at the convention used the language of the Bill of Rights to call for women's rights.

We hold these truths to be self-evident: that all men and women are created equal; that they are endowed by their Creator with certain inalienable rights; that among these are life, liberty, and the pursuit of happiness; that to secure these rights governments are instituted, deriving their just powers from the consent of the governed. Whenever any form of government becomes destructive of these ends, it is the right of those who suffer from it to refuse allegiance to it, and to insist upon the institution of a new government. . . .

The history of mankind is a history of repeated injuries and usurpations on the part of man toward woman, having in direct object the establishment of an absolute tyranny over her.

Now, in view of this entire disfranchisement . . . we insist that they have immediate admission to all the rights and privileges which belong to them as citizens of the United States. . . .

Lucretia Mott

The Emancipation Proclamation

On January 1, 1863, President Abraham Lincoln issued the Emancipation Proclamation, which freed all enslaved persons in states under Confederate control. The Proclamation was a significant step toward the passage of the Thirteenth Amendment (1865), which ended slavery in the United States.

Whereas, on the 22nd day of September, in the year of our Lord 1862, a proclamation was issued by the President of the United States, containing, among other things, the following, to wit:

That on the 1st day of January, in the year of our Lord 1863, all persons held as slaves within any state or designated part of a state, the people whereof shall then be in rebellion against the United States, shall be then, thenceforward, and forever free; and the executive government of the United States, including the military and naval authority thereof, will recognize and maintain the freedom of such persons and will do no act or acts to repress such persons, or any of them, in any efforts they may make for their actual freedom.

That the executive will, on the 1st day January aforesaid, by proclamation, designate the states and parts of states, if any, in which the people thereof, respectively, shall then be in rebellion against the United States; and the fact that any state or the people thereof shall on that day be in good faith represented in the Congress of the United States by members chosen thereto at elections wherein a majority of the qualified voters of such states shall have participated shall, in the absence of strong countervailing testimony, be deemed conclusive evidence that such state and the people thereof are not then in rebellion against the United States.

Now, therefore, I, Abraham Lincoln, President of the United States, by virtue of the power in me vested as commander in chief of the Army and Navy of the United States, in time of actual armed rebellion against the authority and government of the United States, and as a fit and necessary war measure for suppressing said rebellion, do, on this 1st day of January, in the year of our Lord 1863, and in accordance with my purpose so to do, publicly proclaimed for the full period of 100 days from the day first above mentioned, order, and designate as the states and parts of states wherein the people thereof, respectively, are this day in rebellion against the United States. . . .

And, by virtue of the power and for the purpose aforesaid, I do order and declare that all persons held as slaves within said designated states and parts of states are, and henceforward shall be, free; and that the executive government of the United States, including the military and naval authorities thereof, will recognize and maintain the freedom of said persons. . . .

And upon this act, sincerely believed to be an act of justice, warranted by the Constitution upon military necessity, I invoke the considerate judgment of mankind and the gracious favor of Almighty God. . . .

Abraham Lincoln

The Gettysburg Address

President Abraham Lincoln delivered the Gettysburg Address on November 19, 1863, during the dedication of the Gettysburg National Cemetery. The dedication was in honor of the more than 7,000 Union and Confederate soldiers who died in the Battle of Gettysburg earlier that year. Lincoln's brief speech is often recognized as one of the finest speeches in the English language. It is also one of the most moving speeches in the nation's history.

There are five known manuscript copies of the address, two of which are in the Library of Congress. Scholars debate about which, if any, of the existing manuscripts comes closest to Lincoln's actual words that day.

Four score and seven years ago our fathers brought forth on this continent a new nation, conceived in liberty and dedicated to the proposition that all men are created equal.

Now we are engaged in a great civil war, testing whether that nation or any nation so conceived and so dedicated can long endure. We are met on a great battlefield of that war. We have come to dedicate a portion of that field as a final resting-place for those who here gave their lives that that nation might live. It is altogether fitting and proper that we should do this.

But in a larger sense, we cannot dedicate, we cannot consecrate, we cannot hallow this ground. The brave men, living and dead, who struggled here have consecrated it far above our poor power to add or detract. The world will little note nor long remember what we say here, but it can never forget what they did here. It is for us the living, rather, to be dedicated here to the unfinished work which they who fought here have thus far so nobly advanced. It is rather for us to be here dedicated to the great task remaining before us—that from these honored dead we take increased devotion to that cause for which they gave the last full measure of devotion—that we here highly resolve that these dead shall not have died in vain, that this nation under God shall have a new birth of freedom, and that government of the people, by the people, for the people, shall not perish from the earth.

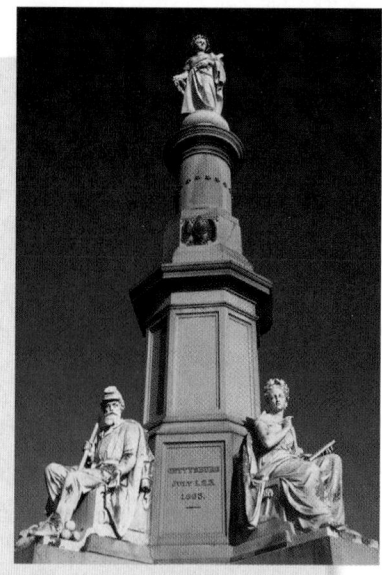

National monument at Gettysburg

The Pledge of Allegiance

Students in a New York City school reciting the Pledge of Allegiance

In 1892 the nation celebrated the 400th anniversary of Columbus's landing in America. In connection with this celebration, Francis Bellamy, a magazine editor, wrote and published the Pledge of Allegiance. The words "under God" were added by Congress in 1954 at the urging of President Dwight D. Eisenhower.

I pledge allegiance to the Flag of the United States of America and to the Republic for which it stands, one Nation under God, indivisible, with liberty and justice for all.

President Harrison on Hawaiian Annexation

An early expression of American imperialism came in the annexation of Hawaii. With the support of the American government, a small number of American troops overthrew the Hawaiian monarchy in January 1893. The excerpt below is from President Benjamin Harrison's written message to Congress. He sent the message along with the treaty for annexation to Congress on February 15, 1893.

I do not deem it necessary to discuss at any length the conditions which have resulted in this decisive action. It has been the policy of the administration not only to respect but to encourage the continuance of an independent government in the Hawaiian Islands so long as it afforded suitable guarantees for the protection of life and property and maintained a stability and strength that gave adequate security against the domination of any other power. . . .

The overthrow of the monarchy was not in any way promoted by this government, but had its origin in what seems to have been a reactionary and revolutionary policy on the part of Queen Liliuokalani, which put in serious peril not only the large and preponderating interests of the United States . . . but all foreign interests. . . . It is quite evident that the monarchy had become effete and the queen's government is weak and inadequate as to be the prey of designing and unscrupulous persons. The restoration of Queen Liliuokalani . . . is undesirable . . . and unless actively supported by the United States would be accompanied by serious disaster and the disorganization of all business interests. The influence and interest of the United States in the islands must be increased and not diminished.

Only two courses are now open—one the establishment of a protectorate by the United States, and the other annexation, full and complete. I think the latter course, which has been adopted in the treaty, will be highly promotive of the best interest of the Hawaiian people and is the only one that will adequately secure the interests of the United States. These interests are not wholly selfish. It is essential that none of the other great powers shall secure these islands. Such a possession would not consist with our safety and with the peace of the world. This view of the situation is so apparent and conclusive that no protest has been heard from any government against proceedings looking to annexation.

The American's Creed

In the patriotic fervor of World War I, national leaders sponsored a contest in which writers submitted ideas for a national creed that would be a brief summary of American beliefs. Of the 3,000 entries, the judges selected that of William Tyler Page as the winner. In a 1918 ceremony in the House of Representatives, the Speaker of the House accepted the creed for the United States.

I believe in the United States of America as a Government of the people, by the people, for the people, whose just powers are derived from the consent of the governed; a democracy in a republic; a sovereign Nation of many sovereign States; a perfect union, one and inseparable; established upon those principles of freedom, equality, justice, and humanity for which American patriots sacrificed their lives and fortunes.

I therefore believe it is my duty to my Country to love it; to support its Constitution; to obey its laws; to respect its flag, and to defend it against all enemies.

The Fourteen Points

On January 8, 1918, President Woodrow Wilson went before Congress to offer a statement of war aims called the Fourteen Points. They reflected Wilson's belief that if the international community accepted certain basic principles of conduct and set up institutions to carry them out, there would be peace in the world.

We entered this war because violations of right had occurred. . . . What we demand in this war, therefore, is . . . that the world be made fit and safe to live in. . . .

The only possible programme, as we see it, is this:

I. Open covenants of peace, openly arrived at, after which there shall be no private international understandings of any kind but diplomacy shall proceed always frankly and in the public view.

II. Absolute freedom of navigation upon the seas, outside territorial waters, alike in peace and in war. . . .

III. The removal, so far as possible, of all economic barriers and the establishment of an equality of trade conditions among all the nations. . . .

IV. Adequate guarantees given and taken that national armaments will be reduced to the lowest point consistent with domestic safety.

V. A free, open-minded, and absolutely impartial adjustment of all colonial claims, based upon a strict observance of the principle that in determining all such questions of sovereignty the interests of the populations concerned must have equal weight with the equitable claims of the government whose title is to be determined.

VI. The evacuation of all Russian territory and . . . opportunity for the independent determination of her own political development and national polity. . . .

VII. Belgium . . . must be evacuated and restored. . . .

VIII. All French territory should be freed and the invaded portions restored, and the wrong done to France by Prussia in 1871 in the matter of Alsace-Lorraine should be righted. . . .

IX. A readjustment of the frontiers of Italy should be effected along clearly recognizable lines of nationality.

X. The peoples of Austria-Hungary . . . should be accorded the freest opportunity of autonomous development.

XI. Roumania, Serbia, and Montenegro should be evacuated; occupied territories restored . . . the relations of the several Balkan states to one another determined by friendly counsel along historically established lines of allegiance and nationality. . . .

XII. The Turkish portions of the present Ottoman Empire should be assured a secure sovereignty. . . .

XIII. An independent Polish state should be erected which should include the territories inhabited by indisputably Polish populations. . . .

XIV. A general association of nations must be formed under specific covenants for the purpose of affording mutual guarantees of political independence and territorial integrity. . . .

Discussion of the Fourteen Points at the Versailles peace conference

The Four Freedoms

President Franklin D. Roosevelt delivered this address on January 6, 1941, in his annual message to Congress. In it, Roosevelt called for a world founded on "four essential human freedoms": freedom of speech and expression, freedom of worship, freedom from want, and freedom from fear.

Just as our national policy in internal affairs has been based upon a decent respect for the rights and dignity of all our fellow men within our gates, so our national policy in foreign affairs has been based on a decent respect for the rights and dignity of all nations, large and small. And the justice of morality must and will win in the end.

Our national policy is this:

First, by an impressive expression of the public will and without regard to partisanship, we are committed to all-inclusive national defense.

Second, by an impressive expression of the public will and without regard to partisanship, we are committed to full support of all those resolute peoples, everywhere, who are resisting aggression and are thereby keeping war away from our Hemisphere. . . .

Third . . . we are committed to the proposition that principles of morality and considerations for our own security will never permit us to acquiesce in a peace dictated by aggressors. . . .

Let us say to the democracies, "We Americans are vitally concerned in your defense of freedom. We are putting forth our energies, our resources, and our organizing powers to give you the strength to regain and maintain a free world. We shall send you, in ever increasing numbers, ships, planes, tanks, guns. This is our purpose and our pledge." In fulfillment of this purpose we will not be intimidated by the threats of dictators that they will regard as a breach of international law and as an act of war our aid to the democracies which dare to resist their aggression. . . .

Caricature of President Roosevelt

In the future days, which we seek to make secure, we look forward to a world founded upon four essential human freedoms.

The first is freedom of speech and expression everywhere in the world.

The second is freedom of every person to worship God in his own way everywhere in the world.

The third is freedom from want, which, translated into world terms, means economic understandings which will secure to every nation a healthy peacetime life for its inhabitants everywhere in the world.

The fourth is freedom from fear—which, translated into world terms, means a worldwide reduction of armaments to such a point and in such a thorough fashion that no nation will be in a position to commit an act of physical aggression against any neighbor—anywhere in the world. . . .

The Truman Doctrine

President Harry S. Truman addressed a joint session of Congress on March 12, 1947, to request aid to fight Communist influence in Greece and Turkey. His message that communism had to be contained represents the central idea of American foreign policy during the Cold War.

The United States has received from the Greek Government an urgent appeal for financial and economic assistance. . . .

When forces of liberation entered Greece they found that the retreating Germans had destroyed virtually all the railways, roads, port facilities, communications, and merchant marine. More than a thousand villages had been burned. Eighty-five percent of the children were tubercular. Livestock, poultry, and draft animals had almost disappeared. Inflation had wiped out practically all savings. As a result of these tragic conditions, a militant minority, exploiting human want and misery, was able to create political chaos which, until now, has made economic recovery impossible.

Greece is today without funds to finance the importation of those goods which are essential to bare subsistence. Under these circumstances the people of Greece cannot make progress in solving their problems of reconstruction. Greece is in desperate need of financial and economic assistance to enable it to resume purchases of food, clothing, fuel and seeds. These are indispensable for the subsistence of its people and are obtainable only from abroad. Greece must have help to import the goods necessary to restore internal order and security, so essential for economic and political recovery. . . .

Meanwhile, the Greek Government is unable to cope with the situation. The Greek army is small and poorly equipped. It needs supplies and equipment if it is to restore the authority of the government throughout Greek territory. Greece must have assistance if it is to become a self-supporting and self-respecting democracy.

The United States must supply that assistance. We have already extended to Greece certain types of relief and economic aid but these are inadequate. There is no other country to which democratic Greece can turn. . . .

No government is perfect. One of the chief virtues of a democracy, however, is that its defects are always visible and under democratic processes can be pointed out and corrected.

The Government of Greece is not perfect. Nevertheless it represents eighty-five percent of the members of the Greek Parliament who were chosen in an election last year. . . .

Greece's neighbor, Turkey, also deserves our attention. The future of Turkey as an independent and economically sound state is clearly no less important to the freedom-loving peoples of the world than the future of Greece. The circumstances in which Turkey finds itself today are considerably different from those of Greece. Turkey has been spared the disasters that have beset Greece. And during the war, the United States and Great Britain furnished Turkey with material aid. Nevertheless, Turkey now needs our support.

. . . To ensure the peaceful development of nations, free from coercion, the United States has taken a leading part in establishing the United Nations. The United Nations is designed to make possible lasting freedom and independence for all its members. We shall not realize our objectives, however, unless we are willing to help free peoples to maintain their free institutions . . . against aggressive movements that seek to impose upon them totalitarian regimes. . . .

This is an investment in world freedom and world peace. . . . The seeds of totalitarian regimes are nurtured by misery and want. They spread and grow in the evil soil of poverty and strife. They reach their full growth when the hope of a people for a better life has died. We must keep that hope alive. . . . If we falter in our leadership, we may endanger the peace of the world—and we shall surely endanger the welfare of our own nation.

Brown v. Board of Education

On May 17, 1954, the Supreme Court ruled in **Brown** *v.* **Board of Education of Topeka, Kansas,** *that racial segregation in public schools was unconstitutional. This decision provided the legal basis for court challenges to segregation in every aspect of American life.*

These cases come to us from the States of Kansas, South Carolina, Virginia, and Delaware. They are premised on different facts and different local conditions, but a common legal question justifies their consideration together in this consolidated opinion.

In each of the cases, minors of the Negro race, through their legal representatives, seek the aid of the courts in obtaining admission to the public schools of their community on a nonsegregated basis. In each instance, they had been denied admission to schools attended by white children under laws requiring or permitting segregation according to race. This segregation was alleged to deprive the plaintiffs of the equal protection of the laws under the Fourteenth Amendment.

The plaintiffs contend that segregated public schools are not "equal" and cannot be made "equal," and that hence they are deprived of the equal protection of the laws. Because of the obvious importance of the question presented, the Court took jurisdiction. . . .

. . . Our decision . . . cannot turn on merely a comparison of these tangible factors in the Negro and white schools involved in each of the cases. We must look instead to the effect of segregation itself on public education.

In approaching this problem, we cannot turn the clock back to 1868 when the Amendment was adopted, or even to 1896 when *Plessy* v. *Ferguson* was written. We must consider public education in the light of its full development and its present place in American life throughout the nation. Only in this way can it be determined if segregation in public schools deprives these plaintiffs of the equal protection of the laws.

Today, education is perhaps the most important function of state and local governments. Compulsory school attendance laws and the great expenditures for education both demonstrate our recognition of the importance of education to our democratic society. . . . In these days, it is doubtful that any child may reasonably be expected to succeed in life if he is denied the opportunity of an education. Such an opportunity, where the state has undertaken to provide it, is a right which must be made available to all on equal terms.

We come then to the question presented: Does segregation of children in public schools solely on the basis of race, even though the physical facilities and other "tangible" factors may be equal, deprive the children of the minority group of equal educational opportunities? We believe that it does.

Linda Brown

. . . We conclude that, in the field of public education, the doctrine of "separate but equal" has no place. Separate educational facilities are inherently unequal. Therefore, we hold that the plaintiff and others similarly situated for whom the actions have been brought are, by reason of the segregation complained of, deprived of the equal protection of the laws guaranteed by the Fourteenth Amendment. . . .

"I Have a Dream"

On August 28, 1963, while Congress was debating broad civil rights legislation, Martin Luther King, Jr., led more than 200,000 people in a march on Washington, D.C. On the steps of the Lincoln Memorial, King gave a stirring speech in which he eloquently spoke of his dreams for African Americans and for the United States.

Martin Luther King, Jr., speaking at the march

Five score years ago, a great American, in whose symbolic shadow we stand, signed the Emancipation Proclamation. This momentous decree came as a great beacon light of hope to millions of Negro slaves who had been seared in the flames of withering injustice. It came as a joyous daybreak to end the long night of captivity.

But one hundred years later, we must face the tragic fact that the Negro is still not free. One hundred years later, the life of the Negro is still sadly crippled by the manacles of segregation and the chains of discrimination. . . .

There are those who are asking the devotees of civil rights, "When will you be satisfied?"

We can never be satisfied as long as the Negro is the victim of the unspeakable horrors of police brutality.

We can never be satisfied as long as our bodies, heavy with the fatigue of travel, cannot gain lodging in the motels of the highways and the hotels of the cities.

We cannot be satisfied as long as the Negro's basic mobility is from a smaller ghetto to a larger one. . . .

We cannot be satisfied as long as a Negro in Mississippi cannot vote and a Negro in New York believes he has nothing for which to vote.

No, no, we are not satisfied, and we will not be satisfied until "justice rolls down like waters and righteousness like a mighty stream." . . .

I say to you today, my friends, so even though we face the difficulties of today and tomorrow, I still have a dream. It is a dream deeply rooted in the American dream.

I have a dream that one day this nation will rise up and live out the true meaning of its creed: "We hold these truths to be self-evident; that all men are created equal."

I have a dream that one day on the red hills of Georgia the sons of former slaves and the sons of former slaveowners will be able to sit down together at the table of brotherhood.

I have a dream that one day even the state of Mississippi, a state sweltering with the heat of injustice and oppression, will be transformed into an oasis of freedom and justice.

I have a dream that my four little children will one day live in a nation where they will not be judged by the color of their skin but by the content of their character. . . .

And when this happens, when we allow freedom to ring, when we let it ring from every village and every hamlet, from every state and every city, we will be able to speed up that day when all of God's children, black men and white men, Jews and Gentiles, Protestants and Catholics, will be able to join hands and sing in the words of the old Negro spiritual, "Free at last! Free at last! Thank God Almighty, we are free at last!"

Gulf of Tonkin Resolution

On August 7, 1964, Congress passed the Gulf of Tonkin Resolution, which stood as the legal basis for the Vietnam War.

Resolved by the Senate and House of Representatives of the United States of America in Congress assembled,

That the Congress approves and supports the determination of the President, as Commander in Chief, to take all necessary measures to repel any armed attack against the forces of the United States and to prevent further aggression.

Section 2. The United States regards as vital to its national interest and to world peace the maintenance of international peace and security in southeast Asia. Consonant with the Constitution of the United States and the Charter of the United Nations and in accordance with its obligations under the Southeast Asia Collective Defense Treaty, the United States is, therefore, prepared, as the President determines, to take all necessary steps, including the use of armed force, to assist any member or protocol state of the Southeast Asia Collective Defense Treaty requesting assistance in defense of its freedom.

President Bush's Address to Joint Session of Congress, September 20, 2001

On September 11, 2001, terrorists crashed airplanes into the World Trade Center in New York City and the Pentagon in Washington, D.C. Thousands of people were killed. In his address, President George W. Bush announced a new kind of war against terrorism.

. . . On September the eleventh, enemies of freedom committed an act of war against our country. . . . Americans have known surprise attacks—but never before on thousands of civilians. All of this was brought upon us in a single day—and night fell on a different world, a world where freedom itself is under attack. . . .

The evidence we have gathered all points to a collection of loosely affiliated terrorist organizations known as al-Qaeda. . . . Our war on terror begins with al-Qaeda, but it does not end there. It will not end until every terrorist group of global reach has been found, stopped, and defeated.

Americans are asking: Why do they hate us? They hate what we see right here in this chamber—a democratically elected government.

Their leaders are self-appointed. They hate our freedoms. . . . By sacrificing human life to serve their radical visions—by abandoning every value except the will to power—they follow in the path of fascism, and Nazism, and totalitarianism. And they will follow that path all the way, to where it ends: in history's unmarked grave of discarded lies.

. . . We will direct every resource at our command—every means of diplomacy, every tool of intelligence, every instrument of law enforcement, every financial influence, and every necessary weapon of war—to the disruption and defeat of the global terror network. . . .

I know there are struggles ahead, and dangers to face. But this country will define our times, not be defined by them. . . . Great harm has been done to us. We have suffered great loss. And in our grief and anger we have found our mission and our moment. . . . Our Nation—this generation—will lift a dark threat of violence from our people and our future. We will rally the world to this cause, by our efforts and by our courage. We will not tire, we will not falter, and we will not fail.

Supreme Court Case Summaries

The following case summaries explain the significance of major Supreme Court cases mentioned in the text.

Abington School District v. Schempp

(1963) struck down a Pennsylvania statute requiring public schools in the state to begin each school day with Bible readings and a recitation of the Lord's Prayer. The Court held that the Constitution's establishment clause leaves religious beliefs and religious practices to each individual's choice and expressly commands that government not intrude into this decision-making process.

Abrams v. United States

(1919) upheld a conviction under the Sedition Act and Espionage Act of 1917. The Court ruled that freedom of speech could be limited if there was a threat to the country.

Baker v. Carr

(1962) established that federal courts can hear suits seeking to force state authorities to redraw electoral districts. In this case, the plaintiff wanted the population of each district to be roughly equal to the population in all other districts. The plaintiff claimed that the votes of voters in the least populous districts counted as much as the votes of voters in the most populous districts.

Brown v. Board of Education

(1954) overruled *Plessy* v. *Ferguson* (1896) and abandoned the separate-but-equal doctrine in the context of public schools. In deciding this case, the Supreme Court rejected the idea that equivalent but separate schools for African Americans and white students would be constitutional. The Court stated that the Fourteenth Amendment's command that all persons be accorded the equal protection of the law (U.S. Const. amend. XIV, sec. 1) is not satisfied by ensuring that African American and white schools "have been equalized, or are being equalized, with respect to buildings, curricula, qualifications, and salaries, and other tangible factors."

The Court then held that racial segregation in public schools violates the equal protection clause because it is inherently unequal. In other words, the separation of schools by race marks the separate race as inferior. The ruling in this case has been extended beyond public education to virtually all public accommodations and activities.

Bush v. Gore

(2000) found that a manual recount of disputed presidential ballots in Florida lacked a uniform standard of judging a voter's intent, thus violating the equal protection clause of the Constitution. The Court also ruled that there was not enough time to conduct a new manual recount that would meet constitutional standards. The case arose when Republican candidate George W. Bush asked the Court to stop a hand recount. This decision ensured that Bush would receive Florida's electoral votes and win the election.

Chisholm v. Georgia

(1793) stripped the immunity of the states to lawsuits in federal court. The Supreme Court held that a citizen of one state could sue another state in federal court without that state consenting to the suit. The Court's decision created a furor and led to the adoption of the Eleventh Amendment, which protects states from federal court suits by citizens of other states.

Dred Scott v. Sandford

(1857) was decided before the Fourteenth Amendment. The Fourteenth Amendment provides that anyone born or naturalized in the United States is a citizen of the nation and of his or her state. In this case, the Supreme Court held that a slave was property, not a citizen, and thus had no rights under the Constitution. The decision was a prime factor leading to the Civil War.

Engel v. Vitale

(1962) held that the establishment clause (U.S. Const. amend. I, cl. 1) was violated by a public school district's practice of starting each school day with a prayer which began, "Almighty God, we acknowledge our dependence upon Thee." The Supreme Court ruled that religion is a personal matter and that government should not align itself with a particular religion in order to prevent religious persecution.

Escobedo v. Illinois (1964) held that Danny Escobedo's right to counsel, as provided by the Sixth Amendment, had been violated. Throughout police questioning, Escobedo asked repeatedly, but unsuccessfully, to see his attorney. The Supreme Court reversed Escobedo's murder conviction, holding that an attorney could have assisted Escobedo in invoking his Fifth Amendment right against self-incrimination. This case served as a forerunner to *Miranda* v. *Arizona*.

Gibbons v. Ogden (1824) made it clear that the authority of Congress to regulate interstate commerce (U.S. Const. art. I, sec. 8, cl. 3) includes the authority to regulate intrastate commercial activity that relates to interstate commerce. Before this case, it was thought that the Constitution would allow a state to close its borders to interstate commercial activity. This ruling says that a state can only regulate internal commercial activity, but Congress can regulate commercial activity that has both intrastate and interstate dimensions.

Gideon v. Wainwright (1963) ruled that poor defendants in criminal cases have the right to a state-paid attorney under the Sixth Amendment. The ruling in this case has been refined to apply only when the defendant, if convicted, can be sentenced to more than six months in jail.

Griswold v. Connecticut (1965) overturned the conviction of two Planned Parenthood employees charged with violating an 1879 state law banning the use of contraceptives. In deciding this case, the Court went beyond the actual words of the Constitution to protect a right—the right to privacy—which is not listed in the Constitution. The case also served as a forerunner to the *Roe* v. *Wade* decision that legalized abortion on the same basis.

Heart of Atlanta Motel, Inc. v. United States (1964) upheld the Civil Rights Act of 1964, which prohibits racial discrimination by those who provide goods, services, and facilities to the public. The Georgia motel in the case drew its business from other states but refused to rent rooms to African Americans. The Supreme Court explained that Congress had the authority to prohibit such discrimination under both the equal protection clause (U.S. Const. amend. XIV, sec. 1) and the commerce clause (art. I, sec. 8, cl. 3). With respect to the commerce clause, the Court explained that Congress had ample evidence to conclude that racial discrimination by hotels and motels impedes interstate commerce.

Korematsu v. United States (1944) allowed the federal government's authority to exclude Japanese Americans, many of whom were citizens, from designated military areas that included almost the entire West Coast. The government defended the orders as a necessary response to Japan's attack on Pearl Harbor. Yet, in upholding the orders, the Court established that government actions that discriminate on the basis of race would be subject to strict scrutiny.

Loving v. Virginia (1967) ruled that state laws that outlaw interracial marriages are unconstitutional under the Fourteenth Amendment. The Court explained that such laws violated the equal protection clause and deprived "citizens of liberty without due process of law." The Court went on to say, "Marriage is one of the basic civil rights of man, fundamental to our very existence and survival."

Mapp v. Ohio (1961) established that evidence seized in violation of the Fourth Amendment could not be used by the prosecution as evidence of a defendant's guilt at the federal, state, or local level.

Marbury v. Madison (1803) established one of the most important principles of American constitutional law. The Supreme Court held that the Court itself has the final say on what the Constitution means. It is also the Supreme Court that has the final say whether or not an act of government—legislative or executive at the federal, state, or local level—violates the Constitution.

Martin v. Hunter's Lessee (1816) affirmed that the Supreme Court has the authority to review state court decisions and is the nation's final court of appeal. The Supreme Court ruled that section 25 of the Judiciary Act of 1789 was constitutional. This section granted the Supreme Court appellate jurisdiction over state courts in certain situations, such as a state court denying the authority of federal law.

McCulloch v. Maryland (1819) established the basis for the expansive authority of Congress. The Supreme Court held that the necessary and proper clause (U.S. Const. art. I, sec. 8, cl. 18) allows Congress to do more than the Constitution specifically authorizes it to do. This case holds that Congress can enact almost any law that will help it achieve the ends established by Article I, Section 8 of the Constitution. For example, Congress has the power to regulate interstate commerce; the necessary and proper clause permits Congress to do so in ways not specified in the Constitution.

Miranda v. Arizona (1966) held that a person in
police custody may not be held unless reminded of his
or her rights. These rights include: 1) the right to remain
silent, 2) the right to an attorney (at government expense if
the person is unable to pay), and 3) that anything the person says after acknowledging that he or she understands
these rights can be used as evidence of guilt at a trial.

The Supreme Court explained that a person alone in
police custody may not understand, even if told, that
he or she can remain silent and thus might be misled
into answering questions. The presence of an attorney is
essential.

Morgan v. Virginia (1946) challenged racial segregation in the South. Irene Morgan was convicted for
refusing to give up her seat on an interstate bus bound
from Virginia to Maryland. The Court ruled that the
Virginia law posed an undue burden on interstate commerce and struck down the statute. However, segregation on southern buses continued on an informal basis.

National Labor Relations Board v. Jones and Laughlin Steel Corp. (1937) upheld
President Franklin Roosevelt's New Deal legislation, the
National Labor Relations Act, which allowed workers
to organize unions in businesses operating or affecting
interstate commerce. Employers were prohibited from
discriminating against their employees because of union
membership. Prior to this case, the Supreme Court had
ruled much New Deal legislation unconstitutional. This
ruling came less than a week after Roosevelt's proposed
court-packing plan. The president intended on "packing" the Supreme Court with additional justices in order
to obtain a pro-New Deal majority on the Court.

New York Times Co. v. Sullivan
(1964) extended the protections afforded to the press
by the free press clause (U.S. Const. amend. I). In this
case, the Supreme Court held that a public official or
public figure suing a publisher for libel (i.e., defamation) must prove that the publisher published a story
that he or she knew was false or published the story in
"reckless disregard of its truth or falsity," which means
that the publisher did not take professionally adequate
steps to determine the story's truth or falsity.

Norris v. Alabama (1935) overturned the conviction of Clarence Norris, an African American sentenced to death for a crime in Alabama. The Supreme
Court held that the grand jury and trial jury had systematically eliminated African American jurors. Thus,
the Court reversed the conviction because it violated the
equal protection clause of the Fourteenth Amendment.

Northern Securities Company v. United States (1904) dealt with
the application of congressional antitrust legislation.
The party involved held three-fourths of the stock in two parallel railroad lines. By a narrow 5–4
decision, the Court upheld the application of the Sherman Antitrust Act. The Court ruled that
the holding company clearly intended to eliminate competition between the two railroads, violating the constitutional right of Congress to regulate interstate commerce.

Plessy v. Ferguson (1896) upheld the separate-but-equal doctrine used by Southern states to perpetuate
segregation after the Civil War officially ended law-mandated segregation. The decision upheld a Louisiana
law requiring passenger trains to have "equal but separated accommodations for the white and colored races."
The Court held that the Fourteenth Amendment's equal
protection clause required only equal public facilities for
the two races, not equal access. This case was overruled
by Brown v. Board of Education (1954).

Regents of the University of California v. Bakke (1978) was the first Supreme Court decision
to suggest that an affirmative action program could be
justified on the basis of diversity. The Court explained
that racial quotas were not permissible under the
equal protection clause of the Fourteenth Amendment.
However, the justices ruled that the diversity rationale
was a legitimate interest that would allow a state medical school to consider an applicant's race in evaluating
his or her application for admission. (Recent Supreme
Court cases suggest that the diversity rationale is no
longer enough to defend an affirmative action program.)

Reynolds v. Sims (1964) extended the one-person, one-vote doctrine announced in Wesberry v.
Sanders to state legislative elections. The Court held
that the inequality of representation in the Alabama
legislature violated the equal protection clause of the
Fourteenth Amendment.

Roe v. Wade (1973) held that women have the
right under various provisions of the Constitution—
most notably, the due process clause of the Fourteenth
Amendment—to decide whether or not to terminate a
pregnancy. The Court's ruling in this case was the most
significant in a long line of decisions over a period of 50
years that recognized a constitutional right of privacy, even
though the word privacy is not found in the Constitution.

Schechter Poultry Corporation v. United States (1935)

overturned the conviction of the employers, who were charged with violating the wage and hour limitations of a law adopted under the authority of the National Industrial Recovery Act. The Court held that because the defendants did not sell poultry in interstate commerce, they were not subject to federal regulations on wages and hours.

Schenck v. United States (1919)

upheld convictions under the Federal Espionage Act. The defendants were charged under the act with distributing leaflets aimed at inciting draft resistance during World War I; their defense was that antidraft speech was protected under the First Amendment.

The Supreme Court unanimously rejected the defense, explaining that whether or not speech is protected depends on the context in which it occurs. Because the defendants' antidraft rhetoric created a "clear and present danger" to the success of the war effort, it was not protected.

Stone v. Powell (1976)

reversed a Court of Appeals decision that evidence was seized illegally and should therefore be excluded. The Court ruled that the defendant was provided a fair and legal opportunity to claim a Fourth Amendment violation before a trial jury. The trial jury found that the search was constitutional and the evidence should not be excluded. The Court stated, "Where the state has provided an opportunity for full and fair litigation of a Fourth Amendment claim, a state prisoner may not be granted federal habeas corpus relief."

Swann v. Charlotte-Mecklenburg Board of Education (1971)

established a new plan to ensure that public schools were not segregated. Many school systems were slow to desegregate after *Brown* v. *Board of Education* and used various tactics to appear to be resolving the problem. This case ordered that busing students, reorganizing school boundaries, and racial ratios all be used as methods to obtain desegregated public school systems.

Sweatt v. Painter (1950)

held that it was unconstitutional for African Americans to be denied admission to the University of Texas Law School based on race. An inferior law school established for African Americans did not give the state justification to deny admission to the main school. This act was a violation of the Fourteenth Amendment.

Wabash v. Illinois (1886)

held that states have no authority to regulate railroad rates for interstate commerce. The Supreme Court held that the commerce clause (U.S. Const. art. I, sec. 8, cl. 3) allowed states to enforce "indirect" but not "direct" burdens on interstate commerce. State railroad rates were ruled "direct" burdens and therefore could not be enforced by states. The decision created a precedent by establishing rate regulation of interstate commerce as an exclusive federal power.

Wickard v. Filburn (1942)

indicated how far the Supreme Court had come in complying with President Franklin Roosevelt's economic philosophies. The Court upheld specific parts of the Second Agricultural Adjustment Act. In its ruling, the Supreme Court held that marketing quotas could be applied to wheat that never left the farm. Using the commerce clause (U.S. Const. art. I, sec. 8, cl. 3) as the basis for its decision, the Court ruled that wheat that never left the farm still had an effect on interstate commerce. Farmers growing their own grain depressed the overall demand and market price of wheat. The decision further extended the power of the commerce clause.

Worcester v. Georgia (1832)

overturned the conviction of Samuel A. Worcester, a missionary among the Cherokee. Worcester was imprisoned under a Georgia law forbidding whites to reside in Cherokee country without taking an oath of allegiance to the state and obtaining a permit. The Supreme Court voided the state law, ruling that the Cherokee were an independent nation based on a federal treaty and free from the jurisdiction of the state. Georgia ignored the decision, and President Jackson refused to enforce it, instead supporting the removal of the Cherokee to the Indian Territory.

American Literature Library

TABLE OF CONTENTS

What Is Literature?

Literature is art created with words. Some people use the term "literature" to include anything written—from newspaper articles and how-to books to pamphlets in a doctor's office. On the other hand, some insist that only creative writing can be literature. Still others suggest that some essays, or written opinions, and even speeches are of such high quality that they may be considered literature.

Just as there are many forms of the visual arts, there are many forms and styles of literature. Reading the literature of a certain period of history helps to bring the people and issues of the time to life.

A Good Story

Have you ever created a story to entertain a younger person? That's fiction: a story invented by the author. Writing that describes or explains real events or activities is referred to as "nonfiction."

The most popular type of fiction is the novel, a long story that usually has many people, or characters, and a complex plot, or action. Novels are written in prose, or everyday language, rather than poetry.

Some novels are inspired by actual events the author witnessed or people he or she has known. But a fiction writer is not attempting to report events or describe people accurately.

By telling a good story, the author tries to lead the reader to discover universal truths. Other types of fiction include short stories and novellas, or short novels.

Time and Timelessness

Some writers set their stories in the present; some write historical novels; others write science fiction tales set in the future. All writers hope their work expresses truths that will be valid long after their lifetimes.

Throughout history, writers have addressed major themes such as good and evil, freedom, religion, power, corruption, love, death, and the relationship of humans to the natural world. Works of literature from a specific period of history often reflect their time in several ways:

- the language used
- the form of the work
- the general attitudes of the characters and the issues they face
- the morality expressed by the outcome

Approaching Poetry

Poetry is writing that is intended first and foremost to evoke emotion, not just convey information or tell a story. The first job of poetry is to create feeling—not to stimulate thought. For this reason it often has a rhythm like music, and it is often easier to understand if read aloud.

Eighteenth- and nineteenth-century poets—and some modern ones—wrote in one of many traditional forms. Each form requires a certain rhyme frequency and pattern of accented syllables, or meter. It also requires a specific number of lines of certain lengths.

Modern poetry does not always follow these conventions; words do not always rhyme, and sometimes the rhythm is to be found in how the words are arranged on the page, not how they sound. Despite these modern touches, the poet's goal remains constant—to evoke specific emotions that illuminate some aspect of life.

The Eras of Literature in American History

Writers reflect world events and issues in their work. Some write directly about those events and issues. Others express values or beliefs that were changed by historical events.

The Early National Period During the early years of the United States, authors often wrote about the challenges of settling a new land. They also focused on religion, morality, and the new form of government. Native Americans already had a rich tradition of oral literature.

After the War of 1812, writers such as James Fennimore Cooper and Washington Irving created a uniquely American style of writing with tales of adventures in the New World. Ralph Waldo Emerson and Henry David Thoreau wrote of the spiritual power of nature.

The Civil War Era During the Civil War and in every decade since, the tragedies of that conflict and the nature of race relations in American society have inspired some of America's best writers, from Mark Twain and Harriet Beecher Stowe in the nineteenth century to William Faulkner and Richard Wright in the twentieth century, and contemporary writers such as August Wilson and Toni Morrison.

Naturalism and Realism As industrialization attracted immigrants from around the globe, writers created art out of the attainment—and the failure—of their dreams. In *The Rise of Silas Lapham*, William Dean Howells told the rags-to-riches story of a Northern industrialist. Early in the twentieth century, "realist" writers, such as Theodore Dreiser, aided the work of Progressive reformers by exposing the underside of industry and the lives of laborers. Other major writers of the era included Mark Twain, Henry James, Stephen Crane, and Edith Wharton.

Modernism in the 1920s and 1930s World War I and its aftermath challenged traditional values, family life, and individual identity. Perhaps the best-known writer of this era is Ernest Hemingway, who along with other "lost generation" writers such as John dos Passos, Gertrude Stein, and F. Scott Fitzgerald described their sense of disillusionment with modern life.

The era also witnessed the appearance of several major African American writers and poets, including Langston Hughes and Claude McKay, in what became known as the Harlem Renaissance.

The tragedy of the Great Depression and the struggles of average Americans to survive provided inspiration for many writers. John Steinbeck's novel *The Grapes of Wrath* about Dust Bowl refugees is perhaps best known.

The second world war spawned a flood of war novels as writers reexamined human beings' relationship to evil, religion, and the meaning of life in the wake of the Jewish Holocaust, and what such an event said about human nature and its capacity for evil.

The 1950s and 1960s In the 1950s, beat writers, such as Jack Kerouac and Tom Robbins, shunned the conformity and materialism of affluent postwar America in favor of spontaneity and experimentation. But history had more shocks in store for American society including the social upheaval of the 1960s, the Vietnam War, and the transformation of a society from one based on reading to a mass-media consumer culture.

Postmodern Writers of Today The events of the late twentieth century led to "postmodern" writing. Postmodern writers are skeptical about any single version of reality in the Information Age. Their writing is full of irony and doubt about modern culture.

Creating a Nation

When white settlers arrived in America, the Native Americans living there already had a highly developed civilization dating back thousands of years. They also had their own form of literature—not written, but handed down from generation to generation orally. A theme common to many Native American stories is their relationship to nature. Many are also parables—stories that use symbols or animals to teach lessons. "Bald Eagle Sends Mud-turtle to the End of the World," written down by Jeremiah Curtin, is an example of a parable.

The second selection here is a portion of a famous speech given by Chief Red Jacket (Native American name Sagoyoweha). Red Jacket was an influential leader of the Seneca nation and the Iroquois confederation of tribes from the 1770s until the 1820s. He fought on the side of the British during the American Revolution, but in the War of 1812, he influenced his people to support the United States.

An ardent advocate of the Native American mode of life, he opposed the introduction of white customs, laws, schools, and especially conversion of Seneca to Christianity. In 1820 or 1821 he successfully petitioned Governor Clinton for the removal of missionaries and white teachers from Buffalo Creek reservation near Buffalo, New York. This speech was given at an 1805 meeting to discuss establishment of missions among six Iroquois nations. In it, Red Jacket argues forcefully for the religious freedom that many white settlers had left Europe to enjoy.

forefathers: ancestors

"Bald Eagle Sends Mud-turtle to the End of the World"

Once upon a time, a bald-headed old man lived on the top of a mountain, and his wife and three children lived near a lake about half way to the summit of the same mountain.

Each day the old man went down to fish in the lake. On his way home he stopped and gave some of the fish to his wife, and thus they lived well and happily. After they had passed many years in this manner, the old man became curious to know how large the world is.

Being chief of his people he called a council, and said, "I want to know how large the world is. I wish some man would volunteer to find out."

One young man said, "I will go and find out."

"Very well," said the chief, "How long will you be gone?"

"I can't tell, for I don't know how far I shall have to travel."

"Go," said the chief, "and when you return you will tell us about your journey."

The young man started and after traveling two moons he came to a country where everything was white—the forests, the water, the grass. It hurt his feet to walk on the white ground, so he hurried back. When he reached home he notified the chief. The chief said, "I don't believe that he has been to the end of the world, but I will call a council and we will hear what he has to say."

When the people were assembled, the young man said: "I did not go very far, but I went as far as I was able." And he told all he knew of the White Country.

The chief said, "We must send another man." . . . Many men were sent, one after another, and each returned with a story a little different from that told by others, but still no one satisfied the chief. At last a man said, "I will start and I will go to the end of the world before I come back."

The chief looked at the man and saw that he was very homely, but very strong, and he said, "I think you will do as you promise. You may go." The chief called a council of the whole nation and each man agreed to make a journey by himself . . . The chief and his men went and were gone forty moons. When they came home a council was held and each told what he had seen. When the man came who had promised to go to the end of the world, he said, "I have been to the end of

Chief Red Jacket's Speech

Chief Red Jacket

the world, I have seen all kinds of people, all kinds of game, all kinds of forests and rivers. I have seen things which no one else has ever seen."

The chief was satisfied. He said, "I am chief of all the people, you will be next to me. You'll be second chief." This was the pay the man got for his journey. He took his position as second chief.

The old chief was Bald Eagle. The first man sent out was Deer. His feet were tender, he could not endure the ice and snow of the White Country. The homely man who went to the end of the world was Mud-turtle.

"BROTHER: Our seats were once large and yours were small. You have now become a great people, and we have scarcely a place left to spread our blankets. You have got our country, but you are not satisfied; you want to force your religion upon us. . . . You say that you are right and we are lost. How do we know this to be true? We understand that your religion is written in a book. If it was intended for us as well as you, why has not the Great Spirit given to us, and not only to us, but why did he not give to our **forefathers,** the knowledge of that book, with the means of understanding it rightly? We only know what you tell us about it. How shall we know when to believe, being so often deceived by the white people.

BROTHER: You say there is but one way to worship and serve the Great Spirit. If there is but one religion, why do you white people differ so much about it? Why not all agreed, as you can all read the book?

BROTHER: We do not understand these things. We are told that your religion was given to your forefathers, and has been handed down from father to son. We also have a religion, which was given to our forefathers, and has been handed down to us their children. We worship in that way. It teaches us to be thankful for all the favors we receive, to love each other, and to be united. We never quarrel about religion.

BROTHER: The Great Spirit has made us all, but He has made a great difference between his white and red children. He has given us different complexions and different customs. To you he has given the arts. To these He has not opened our eyes. . . . Since He has made so great a difference between us in other things, why may we not conclude that he has given us a different religion according to our understanding? The Great Spirit does right. He knows what is best for his children; we are satisfied. . . . We do not wish to destroy your religion, or take it from you. We only want to enjoy our own."

The Young Republic

Sixty years after declaring independence, American culture was still heavily influenced by Europe. In 1836 Ralph Waldo Emerson's groundbreaking essay, "Nature", established a new way for Americans to look at the world. For the first time in history, there was a road-map showing how to escape from traditional cultures and build a new, American identity. A large part of that identity was the belief in indi-viduality, expressed in another Emerson essay, "Self-Reliance," a portion of which follows.

Born in Boston in 1803, Emerson was descended from a long line of New England clergymen. He began his career as a Unitarian minister, but left the church because of doubts about orthodox doctrine. Still, he spent the rest of his life as a teacher of ethics, through his lectures and his writing.

Emerson wrote against the rising tide of American materialism and conformity in his time—themes that are as relevant today as they were a century ago. As he worded it, "Things are in the saddle/And ride mankind."

Emerson is considered the father of a philo-sophical, religious, and literary movement called transcendentalism. Along with Walt Whitman, Henry David Thoreau, Margaret Fuller, and other writers of the day, Emerson believed that the divine spirit was present in every man and in all of nature. In nature, man could intuitively discover all universal laws at work. If God is good and just, then so is man. Evil exists only when man has an imperfect awareness of his essential goodness. This belief led some transcendentalists to social activism.

intuitively: understanding immediately with-out the need of logic or rational thought

particulars: areas of life

asinine: marked by a failure to use intelli-gence or good judgment

loath: unwilling

hobgoblin: a mischievous goblin, or ugly sprite

gazetted: announced in a periodical

"Self-Reliance"
Ralph Waldo Emerson

What I must do is all that concerns me, not what the people think. This rule, equally arduous in actual and in intellectual life, may serve for the whole distinc-tion between greatness and meanness. It is the harder, because you will always find those who think they know what is your duty better than you know it. It is easy in the world to live after the world's opinion; it is easy in solitude to live after our own; but the great man is he who in the midst of the crowd keeps with perfect sweetness the independence of solitude.

The objection to conforming to usages that have become dead to you is that it scatters your force. It loses your time and blurs the impression of your character. If you maintain a dead church, contribute to a dead Bible-society, vote with a great party either for the govern-ment or against it, spread your table like base housekeepers,—under all these screens I have difficulty to detect the precise man you are. And, of course, so much force is withdrawn from your proper life. But do your work, and I shall know you. Do your work, and you shall reinforce yourself. . . .

Well, most men have bound their eyes with one or another handkerchief, and attached themselves to some one of these communities of opinion. This conformity makes them not false in a few **particulars,** authors of a few lies, but false in all particulars. Their every truth is not quite true. . . . Meantime nature is not slow to equip us in the prison-uniform of the party to which we adhere. We come to wear one cut of face and figure, and acquire by degrees the gentlest **asinine** expression . . . the forced smile which we put on in company where we do not feel at ease in answer to conversation which does not interest us. The muscles, not spontaneously moved, but moved by a low usurping wilfulness, grow tight about the outline of the face with the most disagreeable sensation.

For nonconformity the world whips you with its dis-pleasure. And therefore a man must know how to esti-mate a sour face. The by-standers look askance on him in the public street or in the friend's parlour. . . . but the sour faces of the multitude, like their sweet faces, have no deep cause, but are put on and off as the wind blows and a newspaper directs.

Ralph Waldo Emerson

... The other terror that scares us from self-trust is our consistency; a reverence for our past act or word, because the eyes of others have no other data for computing our orbit than our past acts, and we are **loath** to disappoint them. But why ... drag about this corpse of your memory ... ? Suppose you should contradict yourself; what then? It seems to be a rule of wisdom never to rely on your memory alone, scarcely even in acts of pure memory, but to bring the past for judgment into the thousand-eyed present, and live ever in a new day.

... A foolish consistency is the **hobgoblin** of little minds, adored by little statesmen and philosophers and divines. With consistency a great soul has simply nothing to do. He may as well concern himself with his shadow on the wall. Speak what you think now in hard words, and to-morrow speak what to-morrow thinks in hard words again, though it contradict every thing you said to-day.—'Ah, so you shall be sure to be misunderstood.'—Is it so bad, then, to be misunderstood? Pythagoras was misunderstood, and Socrates, and Jesus, and Luther, and Copernicus,

and Galileo, and Newton, and every pure and wise spirit that ever took flesh. To be great is to be misunderstood.

... I hope in these days we have heard the last of conformity and consistency. Let the words be **gazetted** and ridiculous henceforward. ... Man is timid and apologetic; he is no longer upright; he dares not say 'I think,' 'I am,' but quotes some saint or sage. He is ashamed before the blade of grass or the blowing rose. These roses under my window make no reference to former roses or to better ones; they are for what they are; they exist with God to-day. There is no time to them. There is simply the rose; it is perfect in every moment of its existence. ... But man postpones or remembers; he does not live in the present, but with reverted eye laments the past, or, heedless of the riches that surround him, stands on tiptoe to foresee the future. He cannot be happy and strong until he too lives with nature in the present, above time.

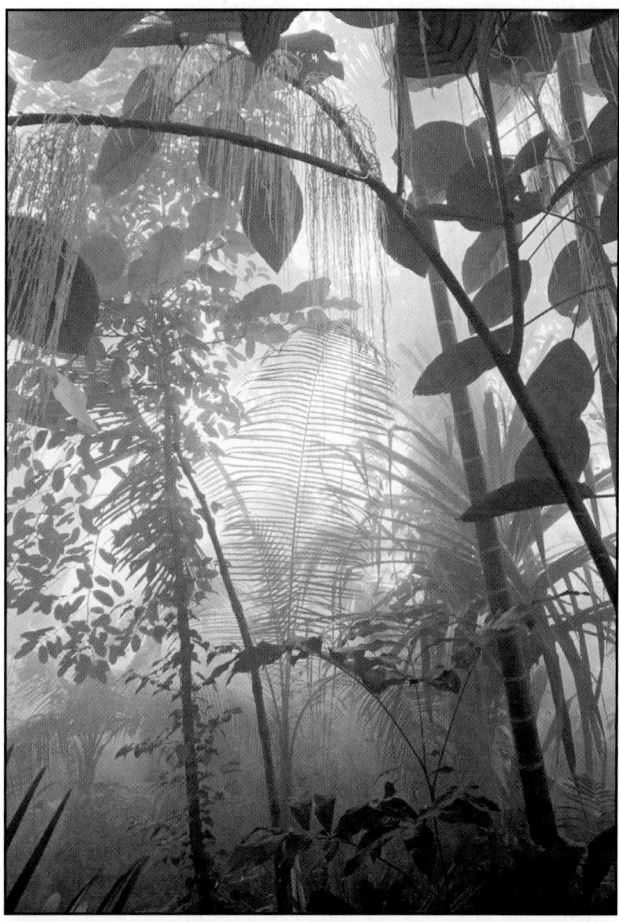

The Crisis of the Union

Harriet Beecher Stowe witnessed the harsh realities of slavery while living in Cincinnati, Ohio, just across the Ohio River from the slave state of Kentucky. Because of these experiences, she became an active abolitionist.

Before the Civil War, many Northerners believed slavery was a constitutionally guaranteed right, and that opposition to it endangered the Union. Even those who agreed with Stowe considered it dangerous to oppose slavery openly and assisted slaveholders in recovering fugitives.

Stowe believed they were able to do this because they did not understand what they were defending. While in church one day in 1851, after she had moved to Brunswick, Maine, she was overcome with a vision of a slave being beaten to death. Sobbing, she ran home and began writing Uncle Tom's Cabin.

The book depicts the life of a long-suffering enslaved person, and the slaveholders and fellow enslaved people in his life. Its 1852 publication attracted threat letters to Stowe, forced closings of bookstores that sold it, and initiated proslavery novels by Southern writers. When Abraham Lincoln met Stowe, he reportedly said, "So this is the little lady who made this big [Civil] war."

In the first year after publication, Uncle Tom's Cabin *sold more than 300,000 copies in the United States. It became the best-selling novel of the nineteenth century, inspired songs and was presented as a play that is still performed today.*

wormwood: A European plant whose leaves yield a bitter oil used to make a liqueur.

dray horse: a horse that hauls heavy loads

Uncle Tom's Cabin
Harriet Beecher Stowe

In this excerpt the enslaved George is visiting his wife, Eliza. They were sold to different slaveholders, but have been allowed to visit each other when not working. George had been hired out to a factory, where he was treated well and had invented a work-saving machine. But when the slaveholder saw George's pride in his accomplishment, he moved George back to the plantation and gave him mindless physical work in order to restore his humility.

Harriet Beecher Stowe

From Chapter 3

You are the handsomest woman I ever saw, and the best one I ever wish to see; but, oh, I wish I'd never seen you, nor you me!"

"O, George, how can you!"

"Yes, Eliza, it's all misery, misery, misery! My life is bitter as **wormwood;** the very life is burning out of me. I'm a poor, miserable, forlorn drudge; I shall only drag you down with me, that's all. What's the use of our trying to do anything, trying to know anything, trying to be anything? What's the use of living? I wish I was dead!"

"O, now, dear George, that is really wicked! I know how you feel about losing your place in the factory, and you have a hard master; but pray be patient, and perhaps something—"

"Patient!" said he, interrupting her; "haven't I been patient? Did I say a word when he came and took me away, for no earthly reason, from the place where everybody was kind to me? I'd paid him truly every cent of my earnings,—and they all say I worked well."

"Well, it *is* dreadful," said Eliza; "but, after all, he is your master, you know."

"My master! and who made him my master? That's what I think of—what right has he to me? I'm a man as much as he is. I'm a better man than he is. I know more about business than he does; I am a better manager than he is; I can read better than he can; I can write a better hand,—and I've learned it all myself, and no thanks to him,—I've learned it in spite of him;

and now what right has he to make a **dray-horse** of me?—to take me from things I can do, and do better than he can, and put me to work that any horse can do? He tries to do it; he says he'll bring me down and humble me, and he puts me to just the hardest, meanest and dirtiest work, on purpose!"

"O, George! George! you frighten me! Why, I never heard you talk so; I'm afraid you'll do something dreadful. I don't wonder at your feelings, at all; but oh, do be careful—do, do—for my sake—for Harry's! . . . O, George, we must have faith. Mistress says that when all things go wrong to us, we must believe that God is doing the very best."

"That's easy to say for people that are sitting on their sofas and riding in their carriages; but let 'em be where I am, I guess it would come some harder. I wish I could be good; but my heart burns, and can't be reconciled, anyhow. You couldn't in my place,—you can't now, if I tell you all I've got to say. You don't know the whole yet."

"What can be coming now?"

"Well, lately Mas'r has been saying that he was a fool to let me marry off the place; that . . . I shall take a wife and settle down on his place . . . or he would sell me down river."

"Why—but you were married to *me* by the minister, as much as if you'd been a white man!" said Eliza, simply.

"Don't you know a slave can't be married? There is no law in this country for that; I can't hold you for my wife, if he chooses to part us. That's why I wish I'd never seen you,—why I wish I'd never been born; it would have been better for us both,—it would have been better for this poor child if he had never been born. All this may happen to him yet!"

"O, but [my] master is so kind!"

"Yes, but who knows?—he may die—and then [our son] may be sold to nobody knows who. What pleasure is it that he is handsome, and smart, and bright? I tell you, Eliza, that a sword will pierce through your soul for every good and pleasant thing your child is or has; it will make him worth too much for you to keep."

The words smote heavily on Eliza's heart; the vision of the trader came before her eyes, and, as if some one had struck her a deadly blow, she turned pale and gasped for breath.

. . . "So, Eliza, my girl," said the husband, mournfully, "bear up, now; and good-by, for I'm going."

"Going, George! Going where?"

"To Canada," said he, straightening himself up; "and when I'm there, I'll buy you; that's all the hope that's left us. You have a kind master, that won't refuse to sell you. I'll buy you and the boy;—God helping me, I will!"

"O, dreadful! if you should be taken?"

"I won't be taken, Eliza; I'll *die* first! I'll be free, or I'll die!"

Eliza flees across the icy Ohio River

The Birth of Modern America

Carl Sandburg was the son of Swedish immigrants who settled in Galesburg, near Chicago. His father worked on the Chicago, Burlington and Quincy railroad at a time when advances in transportation, communications, and manufacturing technology were changing American commerce and life. By the end of the 1800s, the city had become an industrial hub for the lumber, grain, meatpacking, and mail-order businesses.

Sandburg's poem, "Chicago," captures the bustling activity of the city where many African Americans immigrated from the segregated South. It also exposes the evolving urban morality against which many Americans recoiled.

From the time he was a young boy, Sandburg had a variety of jobs—delivering mail, harvesting ice, laying bricks, thrashing wheat, and shining shoes. In 1897 he traveled as a hobo, seeing firsthand the sharp contrast between rich and poor. During his long career, he won two Pulitzer Prizes, one for poetry and another for a five-volume biography of Abraham Lincoln.

*Following "Chicago" is a portion of an address by Samuel Clemens to the citizens of another city—his adopted home, San Francisco. It was written in 1866, as he prepared to revisit the town of his youth, Hannibal, Missouri. In this address, Clemens predicts the changes that he sees beginning to occur as San Francisco evolved from a "straggling town" to a modern **mecca** for multicultural immigration.*

mecca: a center of activity sought as a goal by people with a common interest

heedlessly: without thinking

hither: here

"Chicago"
Carl Sandburg

Hog Butcher for the World,
   Tool Maker, Stacker of Wheat,
   Player with Railroads and the Nation's Freight Handler;
   Stormy, husky, brawling,
   City of the Big Shoulders:

They tell me you are wicked and I believe them, for I
   have seen your painted women under the gas lamps
   luring the farm boys.
And they tell me you are crooked and I answer: Yes, it
   is true I have seen the gunman kill and go free to
   kill again.
And they tell me you are brutal and my reply is: On the
   faces of women and children I have seen the marks
   of wanton hunger.
And having answered so I turn once more to those who
   sneer at this my city, and I give them back the sneer
   and say to them:
Come and show me another city with lifted head singing
   so proud to be alive and coarse and strong and cunning.
Flinging magnetic curses amid the toil of piling job on
   job, here is a tall bold slugger set vivid against the
   little soft cities;
Fierce as a dog with tongue lapping for action, cunning
   as a savage pitted against the wilderness,
      Bareheaded,
      Shoveling,
      Wrecking,
      Planning,
      Building, breaking, rebuilding,
Under the smoke, dust all over his mouth, laughing with
   white teeth,
Under the terrible burden of destiny laughing as a young
   man laughs,
Laughing even as an ignorant fighter laughs who has
   never lost a battle,
Bragging and laughing that under his wrist is the pulse.
   and under his ribs the heart of the people,
      Laughing!
Laughing the stormy, husky, brawling laughter of
   Youth, half-naked, sweating, proud to be Hog
   Butcher, Tool Maker, Stacker of Wheat, Player with
   Railroads and Freight Handler to the Nation.

Chicago grain elevator, 1900

"Farewell"
Samuel Clemens

"I am now about to bid farewell to San Francisco for a season, and to go back to that common home we all tenderly remember in our waking hours and fondly revisit in dreams of the night—a home which is familiar to my recollection, but will be an unknown land to my unaccustomed eyes. I shall share the fate of many another longing exile who wanders back to his early home to find gray hairs where he expected youth, graves where he looked for firesides, grief where he had pictured joy—everywhere change . . . where he had **heedlessly** dreamed that desolating Time had stood still! . . . And while I linger here upon the threshold of this, my new home . . . I accept the warning that mighty changes will have come over this home also when my returning feet shall walk these streets again.

I read the signs of the times, and I, that am no prophet, behold the things that are in store for you. Over slumbering California is stealing the dawn of a radiant future! The great China Mail Line is established, the Pacific Railroad is creeping across the continent, the commerce of the world is about to be revolutionized. California is Crown Princess of the new dispensation! She stands in the centre of the grand highway of the nations; she stands midway between the Old World and the New, and both shall pay her tribute. From the far East and from Europe, multitudes of stout hearts and willing hands are preparing to flock **hither;** to throng her hamlets and villages; to till her fruitful soil; to unveil the riches of her countless mines; to build up an empire on these distant shores that shall shame the bravest dreams of her visionaries. . . . Half the world stands ready to lay its contributions at her feet! Has any other State so brilliant a future? Has any other city a future like San Francisco?

"This straggling town shall be a vast metropolis; this sparsely populated land shall become a crowded hive of busy men; your waste places shall blossom like the rose, and your deserted hills and valleys shall yield bread and wine for unnumbered thousands; railroads shall be spread hither and thither and carry the invigorating blood of commerce to regions that are languishing now; mills and workshops, yea, and factories shall spring up everywhere, and mines that have neither name nor place to-day shall dazzle the world with their affluence. The time is drawing on apace when the clouds shall pass away from your firmament, and a splendid prosperity shall descend like a glory upon the whole land!

"I am bidding the old city and my old friends a kind, but not a sad farewell, for I know that when I see this home again, the changes that will have been wrought upon it . . . will be brighter, happier and prouder a hundred fold than it is this day."

San Francisco, 1890

Imperialism and Progressivism

Theodore Dreiser and other writers, such as Frank Norris and Upton Sinclair, were Progressive Era "muckrakers." They exposed the scandals and corruption of urban American life at the turn of the twentieth century in a literary **genre** *(ZHAHN•ruh) known as American Realism. In this style, writers present everyday life as it actually is, rather than in a* **romanticized** *style, as many earlier writers had done. Norris and Sinclair were also considered naturalist writers, since they believed that humans had to overcome their environment, their ego, and their "brute instincts."*

Dreiser was born "on the wrong side of the tracks," and learned early that middle-class Americans looked on his impoverished family as outsiders. Because of that, his writing shows a compassionate understanding of life's outcasts and failures, and sympathy for those who desperately crave wealth, love, and power. His famous novel, An American Tragedy, *follows the descent of an ordinary young man who commits a ruthless murder, and the social and political pressures that assail him.*

The life of Madeleine, an impoverished young woman, is the theme of this selection, from the short story "Sanctuary." In it we glimpse some of the urban conditions that inspired the work of many progressive reformers of the day.

genre: a category of artistic composition characterized by form, style, or content

romanticized: presented in a fanciful, imaginative way rather than based on fact

"Sanctuary"
Theodore Dreiser

Theodore Dreiser

Primarily, there were the conditions under which [Madeleine] was brought to fifteen years of age: the crowded, scummy tenements; the narrow green-painted halls with their dim gas jets, making the entrance look more like that of a morgue than a dwelling place; the dirty halls and rooms with their green or blue or brown walls painted to save the cost of paper; the bare wooden floors, long since saturated with every type of grease and filth from oleomargarine and suet leaked from cheap fats or meats, to beer and whiskey and tobacco juice. . . .

And then the streets outside—any of the streets by which she had ever been surrounded—block upon block of other red, bare, commonplace tenements crowded to the doors with human life, the space before them sped over by noisy, gassy trucks and vehicles of all kinds. . . .

In this atmosphere were always longshoremen, wagon drivers, sweepers of floors, washers of dishes, waiters, janitors, workers in laundries, factories—mostly in indifferent or decadent or despairing conditions. And all of these people existed, in so far as she ever knew, upon that mysterious, evanescent and fluctuating something known as the weekly wage.

Always about her there had been drunkenness, fighting, complaining, sickness or death; the police coming in, and arresting one and another; the gas man, the rent man, the furniture man, hammering at doors for their due. . . .

It is not surprising that Madeleine came to her twelfth and thirteenth years without any real understanding of the great world about her and without any definite knowledge or skill. Her drunken mother was now more or less dependent upon her, her father having died of pneumonia and her brother and sister having disappeared to do for themselves. . . .

The child actually went hungry at times. . . . a neighbor perceiving her wretched state and suggesting that some extra helpers were wanted in a department store at Christmastime, she applied there, but so wretched were her clothes by now that she was not even considered. . . . she was able to get a place as a servant in a family.

Those who know anything of the life of a domestic know how thoroughly unsatisfactory it is—the leanness, the lack of hope. . . . she had only the kitchen for her chief chamber or a cubbyhole under the roof. . . .

And then, as was natural, love in the guise of youth, a rather sophisticated gallant somewhat above the world in which she was moving, appeared and paid his all but worthless court to her. . . .

A single trip to Wonderland, a single visit to one of its halls where music sounded to the splash of the waves and where he did his best to teach her to dance, a single meal in one of its gaudy, noisy restaurants . . . were given to hope, a new and seemingly realizable dream of happiness implanted in her young mind. The world was happier than she had thought, or could be made so; not all people fought and screamed at each other. There were such things as tenderness, soft words, sweet words.

But the way of so sophisticated a youth with a maid was brief and direct.

. . . Often in this hour she thought of the swift, icy waters of the river, glistening under a winter moon, and then again of the peace and quiet of the House of the Good Shepherd, its shielding remoteness from life, the only true home or sanctuary she had ever known. And so, brooding and repressing occasional sobs, she made her way toward it . . . thinking of the pathetically debasing love-life that was now over— the dream of love that never, never could be again, for her.

* * *

The stark red walls of the institution stood as before, only dim and gray and cold. . . . She had come a long way, drooping, brooding, half-freezing and crying. More than once on the way the hopelessness of her life and her dreams had given her pause, causing her to turn again with renewed determination toward the river—only the vivid and reassuring picture she had retained of this same grim and homely place, its

restricted peace and quiet, the sympathy of Sister St. Agnes and Mother St. Bertha, had carried her on . . . the face of Mother St. Bertha, wrinkled and aweary, appeared at the square opening.

"What is it, my child?" she asked. . . .

"It is Madeleine. I was here four years ago. I was in the girls' ward. I worked in the sewing room."

She was so beaten by life . . . that even now and here she expected little more than an indifference which would send her away again. . . .

"Of course, my child," said the Mother, moving to the door and opening it. "You may come in. But what has happened, child?. . ."

"Mother," pleaded Madeleine wearily, "must I answer now? I am so unhappy! Can't I just have my old dress and my bed for tonight—that little bed under the lamp?"

"Why, yes, dear. . . . Now, my child," she said, "you may undress and bathe. . . . "

In a kind of dumbness of despair she … entered the warm, clean bath which had been provided. She stifled a sob as she did so, and others as she bathed. . . .

. . . Then she was led along other silent passages, once dreary enough but now healing in their sense of peace and rest, and so into the great room set with row upon row of simple white iron beds, covered with their snowy linen . . . beneath which so many like herself were sleeping.

. . . "Oh, Mother," she sobbed as the Sister bent over her, "don't ever make me go out in the world again, will you? You won't will you? I'm so tired! I'm so tired!"

"No, dear, no," soothed the Sister . . . "You need never go out in the world again unless you wish."

Family outside New York City tenement, 1890

Boom and Bust

Writers sometimes create works of fiction inspired by or based on actual events in the news. The story of Nicola Sacco and Bartolomeo Vanzetti, Italian immigrants convicted of murder in 1921, was the inspiration for this selection by John Dos Passos, written in 1936. Large demonstrations were held in support of Sacco and Vanzetti, who claimed they were convicted for being immigrants and anarchists—not for committing a crime. They were executed in 1927, inspiring this passage, as well as the novel, Boston, *by Upton Sinclair.*

Dos Passos used his wartime experience as an ambulance driver in France as the background for several antiwar novels. In his **trilogy,** U.S.A, *he used an experimental form—fragments of songs, news headlines, monologues, and fragments from the lives of unrelated characters—to depict American* **hypocrisy** *and materialism between the two world wars. Dos Passos often combines separate words into one to shade its meaning and for the flow of a line. His* **impressionistic** *writing influenced several generations of American and European novelists.*

The lines in italics in the following passage from U.S.A. *are from actual letters written by Sacco and Vanzetti.*

trilogy: a work of fiction or nonfiction written in three separately published parts, or books

hypocrisy: acting in a way that contradicts what you say you believe in

impressionistic: using vivid details to create a sensory impression rather than objective reality

wardheeler: a worker for a political boss in a ward or local area

U.S.A., "Sacco and Vanzetti Must Die"
John Dos Passos

*S*hall be the human race.

Much I thought of you when I was lying in the death house— the singing, the kind tender voices of the children from the playground where there was all the life and the joy of liberty—just one step from the wall that contains the buried agony of three buried

John Dos Passos

souls. It would remind me so often of you and of your sister and I wish I could see you every moment, but I feel better that you will not come to the death house so that you could not see the horrible picture of three living in agony waiting to be electrocuted.

The Camera Eye

they have clubbed us off the streets   they are stronger   they are rich   they hire and fire the politicians the newspapereditors the old judges the small men with reputations the collegepresidents the **wardheelers** (listen businessmen collegepresidents judges   America will not forget her betrayers) they hire the men with guns   the uniforms the policecars the patrolwagons

all right you have won   you will kill the brave men our friends tonight

there is nothing left to do   we are beaten   we the beaten crowd together in these old dingy schoolrooms on Salem Street shuffle up and down the gritty creaking stairs sit hunched with bowed heads on benches and hear the old words of the haters of oppression   made new in sweat and agony tonight

our work is over   the scribbled phrases   the nights typing releases the smell of the printshop the sharp reek of newsprinted leaflets   the rush for Western Union stringing words into wires the search for stinging words to make you feel who are your oppressors America

America our nation has been beaten by strangers who have turned our language inside out who have taken the clean words our fathers spoke and made them slimy and foul

their hired men sit on the judge's bench they sit back with their feet on the tables under the dome of the State House they are ignorant of our beliefs they have the dollars the guns the armed forces the powerplants

they have built the electricchair and hired the executioner to throw the switch

all right we are two nations

America our nation has been beaten by strangers who have bought the laws and fenced off the meadows and cut down the woods for pulp and turned our pleasant cities into slums and sweated the wealth out of our people and when they want to they hire the executioner to throw the switch

but do they know that the old words of the immigrants are being renewed in blood and agony tonight do they know that the old American speech of the haters of oppression is new tonight in the mouth of an old woman from Pittsburgh of a husky boilermaker from Frisco who hopped freights clear from the Coast to come here in the mouth of a Back Bay social-worker in the mouth of an Italian printer of a hobo from Arkansas   the language of the beaten nation is not forgotten in our ears tonight

the men in the deathhouse made the old words new before they died

If it had not been for these things, I might have lived out my life talking at streetcorners to scorning men. I might have died unknown, unmarked, a failure. This is our career and our triumph. Never in our full life can we hope to do such work for tolerance, for justice, for man's understanding of man as now we do by an accident.

now their work is over   the immigrants haters of oppression lie quiet in black suits in the little undertaking parlor in the North End   the city is quiet   the men of the conquering nation are not to be seen on the streets

they have won why are they scared to be seen on the streets? on the streets you see only the downcast faces of the beaten   the streets belong to the beaten nation   all the way to the cemetery where the bodies of the immigrants are to be burned   we line the curbs in the drizzling rain we crowd the wet sidewalks elbow to elbow silent pale looking with scared eyes at the coffins

we stand defeated America

Nicola Sacco and Bartolomeo Vanzetti being arrested

Global Struggles

Many Jews who survived concentration camps during World War II found it too painful to speak or write about their experiences until many years later. Elie Wiesel (vee•ZEHL) waited for 10 years to write the story of his experiences at Auschwitz, where his family was killed. The first passage is from his 1960 novel, Night. Wiesel was a teenager when the Nazis invaded his town of Sighet in Transylvania in 1944. He became a U.S. citizen in 1963, and won the Nobel Peace Prize in 1986.

World War II had shown the world an unprecedented scale of conflict. The science, technology, and industrialism—which were supposed to advance humanity—had been used instead for mass killing and devastation. It was not surprising that many postwar writers sought alternatives to traditional ways of thinking and writing.

*The Beat Generation—a term coined by Jack Kerouac—was the first modern **subculture**, or "alternative" culture. It was a group of writers during the late 1950s and early 1960s. Rejecting the intellectual, or mental, focus of traditional writing, the Beats sought spontaneity, emotion, and engagement in real, often gritty experience. Their writing has influenced artists, writers, rock musicians, and popular culture ever since.*

In 1947, Kerouac and a friend took a road trip around the country, which inspired his most famous novel, On the Road. Published in 1957, it expresses both the quest for experience and the pessimism of the Beats as they struggled to find meaning in the shadow of the atomic bomb.

subculture: a group that displays behavior different from that of society

Night
Elie Wiesel

And then, one day all foreign Jews were expelled. . . .

Crammed into cattle cars by the Hungarian police, they cried silently. Standing on the station platform, we too were crying. The train disappeared over the horizon; all that was left was thick, dirty smoke.

Behind me, someone said, sighing, "What do you expect? That's war. . . ."

The deportees were quickly forgotten. A few days after they left, it was rumored that they were in Galicia, working, and even that they were content with their fate.

Days went by. Then weeks and months. Life was normal again. A calm, reassuring wind blew through our homes. The shopkeepers were doing good business, the students lived among their books, and the children played in the streets.

One day, as I was about to enter the synagogue, I saw Moishe the Beadle sitting on a bench near the entrance.

He told me what had happened to him and his companions. The train with the deportees had crossed the Hungarian border and, once in Polish territory, had been taken over by the Gestapo. The train had stopped. The Jews were ordered to get off and onto waiting trucks. The trucks headed toward a forest. There everybody was ordered to get out. They were forced to dig huge trenches. When they had finished their work, the men from the Gestapo began theirs. Without passion or haste, they shot their prisoners, who were forced to approach the trench one by one and offer their necks. Infants were tossed into the air and used as targets for the machine guns. This took place in the Galician forest, near Kolomay. How had he, Moishe the Beadle, been able to escape? By a miracle. He was wounded in the leg and left for dead.

Elie Wiesel

On the Road
Jack Kerouac

Later in the afternoon we went out and played baseball with the kids in the sooty field by the Long Island railyard. We also played basketball so frantically the younger boys said, "Take it easy, you don't have to kill yourself." They bounced smoothly all around us and beat us with ease. Dean and I were sweating. At one point Dean fell flat on his face on the concrete court. We huffed and puffed to get the ball away from the boys; they turned and flipped it away. Others darted in and smoothly shot over our heads. We jumped at the basket like maniacs, and the younger boys just reached up and grabbed the ball from our sweating hands and dribbled away. We were like hotrock blackbelly tenorman *Mad* of American back-alley go-music trying to play basketball against Stan Getz and Cool Charlie. They thought we were crazy. Dean and I went back home playing catch from each sidewalk of the street. We tried extra-special catches, diving over bushes and barely missing posts. When a car came by I ran alongside and flipped the ball to Dean just barely behind the vanishing bumper. He darted and caught it and rolled in the grass, and flipped it back for me to catch on the other side of a parked bread truck. I just made it with my meat hand and threw it back so Dean had to whirl and back up and fall on his back across the hedges. Back in the house Dean took his wallet, harrumphed, and handed my aunt the fifteen dollars he owed her from the time we got a speeding ticket in Washington. She was completely surprised and pleased. We had a big supper. "Well, Dean," said my aunt, "I hope you'll be able to take care of your new baby that's coming and stay married this time."

"Yes, yass, yes."

"You can't go all over the country having babies like that. Those poor little things'll grow up helpless. You've got to offer them a chance to live." He looked at his feet and nodded. In the raw red dusk we said good-by, on a bridge over a superhighway.

"I hope you'll be in New York when I get back," I told him.

"All I hope, Dean, is someday we'll be able to live on the same street with our families and get to be a couple of oldtimers together."

"That's right, man—you know that I pray for it completely mindful of the troubles we both had and the troubles coming, as your aunt knows and reminds me. I didn't want the new baby, Inez insisted, and we had a fight. Did you know Marylou got married to a used-car dealer in Frisco and she's having a baby?"

"Yes. We're all getting in there now." Ripples in the upside-down lake of the void, is what I should have said. The bottom of the world is gold and the world is upside down. He took out a snapshot of Camille in Frisco with the new baby girl. The shadow of a man crossed the child on the sunny pavement, two long trouser legs in the sadness. "Who's that?"

"That's only Ed Dunkel. He came back to Galatea, they're gone to Denver now. They spent a day taking pictures."

Ed Dunkel, his compassion unnoticed like the compassion of saints. Dean took out other pictures. I realized these were all the snapshots which our children would look at someday with wonder, thinking their parents had lived smooth, well-ordered, stabilized-within-the-photo lives and got up in the morning to walk proudly on the sidewalks of life, never dreaming the raggedy madness and riot of our actual lives, our actual night, the hell of it, the senseless nightmare road. All of it inside endless and beginningless emptiness. Pitiful forms of ignorance. "Good-by, good-by." Dean walked off in the long red dusk. Locomotives smoked and reeled above him. His shadow followed him, it aped his walk and thoughts and very being. He turned and waved coyly, bashfully. He gave me the boomer's highball, he jumped up and down, he yelled something I didn't catch. He ran around in a circle. All the time he came closer to the concrete corner of the railroad overpass. He made one last signal. I waved back. Suddenly he bent to his life and walked quickly out of sight. I gaped into the bleakness of my own days. I had an awful long way to go too.

A Time of Upheaval

After two world wars many writers began to describe a sense of separateness from nature and a growing sense of personal alienation. The upheaval of societies and cultures brought about by the wars led to a feeling that morality was relative. In other words, what may be immoral in one situation could be considered moral in another situation. These themes, later called modernism by literary critics, showed up in many works of the time.

The early work of poet Adrienne Rich, who was born in 1929 and wrote in careful, more traditional forms, seemed not to be part of this evolving modernist tradition. By the 1960s, her work increasingly confronted themes such as women's role in society, racism, and the Vietnam War, and was written in free verse. In 1973, amid the feminist and civil rights movements, she wrote Diving Into the Wreck, Poems 1971–1972, *which won the National Book Award the next year. The title poem uses the* **metaphor** *of a deep-sea diver to express the goal of looking deeply within to find the truth about ourselves.*

Leroy V. Quintana is a New Mexico native of Mexican ancestry. His poetry draws on his experiences as a Chicano outsider in American society, subject to ethnic and socioeconomic discrimination. His poem here, "Natural History," reflects both his sensitivity to nature and the horrors of the Vietnam War, in which he served during 1967 and 1968.

metaphor: a figure of speech in which one word or image is used to mean something else

sundry: miscellaneous

crenellated: notched

"Diving into the Wreck"
Adrienne Rich

First having read the book of myths,
and loaded the camera,
and checked the edge of the knife-blade,
I put on
the body-armor of black rubber
the absurd flippers
the grave and awkward mask.
I am having to do this
not like Cousteau with his
assiduous team
aboard the sun-flooded schooner
but here alone.

There is a ladder.
The ladder is always there
hanging innocently
close to the side of the schooner.
We know what it is for,
we who have used it.
Otherwise
it is a piece of maritime floss
some **sundry** equipment.

I go down.
Rung after rung and still
the oxygen immerses me
the blue light
the clear atoms
of our human air.
I go down.
My flippers cripple me,
I crawl like an insect down the ladder
and there is no one
to tell me when the ocean
will begin.

First the air is blue and then
it is bluer and then green and then
black I am blacking out and yet
my mask is powerful
it pumps my blood with power
the sea is another story
the sea is not a question of power

I have to learn alone
to turn my body without force
in the deep element.

And now: it is easy to forget
what I came for
among so many who have always
lived here
swaying their **crenellated** fans
between the reefs
and besides
you breathe differently down here.

I came to explore the wreck.
The words are purposes.
The words are maps.
I came to see the damage that was done
and the treasures that prevail.
I stroke the beam of my lamp
slowly along the flank
of something more permanent
than fish or weed

the thing I came for:
the wreck and not the story of the wreck
the thing itself and not the myth

the drowned face always staring
toward the sun
the evidence of damage
worn by salt and away into this threadbare
    beauty
the ribs of the disaster
curving their assertion
among the tentative haunters.

This is the place.
And I am here, the mermaid whose dark hair
streams black, the merman in his armored
    body.
We circle silently
about the wreck
we dive into the hold.
I am she: I am he

whose drowned face sleeps with open eyes
whose breasts still bear the stress
whose silver, copper, vermeil cargo lies
obscurely inside barrels
half-wedged and left to rot
we are the half-destroyed instruments
that once held to a course
the water-eaten log
the fouled compass

We are, I am, you are
by cowardice or courage
the one who find our way
back to this scene
carrying a knife, a camera
a book of myths
in which
our names do not appear.

"Natural History"
Leroy Quintana

To cross a river meant leeches.
A company of NVAs crashing toward you
would be a troop of baboons.
A green snake named Mr. Two Step,
for the number you'd last after bitten.
It was said the NVAs carried flashlights.
One night frightening scores of them
turned out to be a swarm of fireflies.
The whir of birds' wings
turned out to be artillery rounds.
Threw stones at a cobra once,
the sun going down.
Fire at it
and the VC would know our position.
A VC moving slowly in the elephant grass
happened to be a water buffalo.
One night they overran the compound.
Loaded down with grenades, AK-47s
from North Vietnam, mines strapped to their
    chests:
these were only the mosquitos.
The VC only a little more than a whisper's
    reach away,
we called in the Cobras. They came in hissing,
cannons twice as fast as the old gunships.
It was also said the VC kept chickens leashed
    to strings.
So easily frightened they were perfect warning.
One night, shivering uncontrollably with fear,
knowing I would have to kill whatever was
    out there,
walking slowly, scratching.

A Changing Society

Dr. Maya Angelou is a poet, historian, author, actress, playwright, civil-rights activist, producer, and director. Born in St. Louis, Missouri, she has lived in many places. She was a newspaper editor in Egypt and Ghana, and has taught at the University of Ghana and, since 1981, at Wake Forest University in Winston-Salem, North Carolina.

*In the 1960s Dr. Martin Luther King, Jr., asked her to be the Northern coordinator for the Southern Christian Leadership Conference. Angelou gained fame in the United States when her **autobiographical** novel,* I Know Why the Caged Bird Sings, *received critical and popular success when it was published in 1969.*

*Like many modern writers, she focuses a harsh spotlight on characters' frailties, failures, and **dilemmas** in today's complex world. Unlike some, however, she also challenges our strengths and human potential. Former president Bill Clinton commissioned her to read her poem "On the Pulse of the Morning" at his 1993 inauguration. Although Angelou wrote her poem in the last decade of the twentieth century, it shows a focus on personal responsibility and peaceful coexistence that have been her lifelong quests and are her hopes for this millennium.*

autobiographical: written about the person's own life

dilemma: problems caused by a person's situation or world conditions

"On the Pulse of the Morning"

Maya Angelou

Maya Angelou

. . . .
You, created only a little lower than
The angels, have crouched too long in
The bruising darkness
Have lain too long
Facedown in ignorance,
Your mouths spilling words
Armed for slaughter.
. . . .
Come, clad in peace,
And I will sing the songs
The Creator gave to me when I and the
Tree and the Rock were one.
Before cynicism was a bloody sear across your brow
And when you yet knew you still knew nothing.
The River sang and sings on.
. . . .
Here, on the pulse of this new day,
You may have the grace to look up and out
And into your sister's eyes,
And into your brother's face,
Your country,
And say simply
With hope—
Good morning.

"Human Family"

Maya Angelou

I note the obvious differences
in the human family.
Some of us are serious,
some thrive on comedy.

Some declare their lives are lived
as true profundity,
and others claim they really live
the real reality.
. . . .

We love and lose in China,
we weep on England's moors,
and laugh and moan in Guinea,
and thrive on Spanish shores.

We seek success in Finland,
Are born and die in Maine.
In minor ways we differ,
In major we're the same.

I note the obvious differences
between each sort and type,
but we are more alike, my friends,
than we are unalike.

We are more alike, my friends,
than we are unalike.
. . . .

"Equality"

Maya Angelou

You declare you see me dimly
through a glass which will not shine
though I stand before you boldly,
trim in rank and marking time.

You do own to hear me faintly
as a whisper out of range,
while my drums beat out the message
and the rhythms never change.

Equality, and I will be free.
Equality, and I will be free.
. . . .

We have lived a painful history,
we know the shameful past,
but I keep on marching forward,
and you keep on coming last.

Equality, and I will be free.
Equality, and I will be free.

Flag Etiquette

> For Americans, the flag has always had a special meaning. It is a symbol of our nation's freedom and democracy.

Rules and Customs

Over the years, Americans have developed rules and customs concerning the use and display of the flag. One of the most important things every American should remember is to treat the flag with respect.

- The flag should be raised and lowered by hand and displayed only from sunrise to sunset. On special occasions, the flag may be displayed at night, but it should be illuminated.

- The flag may be displayed on all days, weather permitting, particularly on national and state holidays and on historic and special occasions.

- No flag may be flown above the American flag or to the right of it at the same height.

- The flag should never touch the ground or floor beneath it.

- The flag may be flown at half-staff by order of the president, usually to mourn the death of a public official.

- The flag may be flown upside down only to signal distress.

- When the flag becomes old and tattered, it should be destroyed by burning. According to an approved custom, the Union (stars on blue field) is first cut from the flag; then the two pieces, which no longer form a flag, are burned.

Continental Colors
1775-1777

First Stars and Stripes
1777-1795

Betsy Ross Flag
c. 1790

15-Star Flag
1795-1818

20-Star Flag
1818

Great Star Flag
1818

35-Star Flag
1863-1865

38-Star Flag
1877-1890

48-Star Flag
1912-1959

50-Star Flag
1960

Glossary/Glosario

- Content vocabulary terms in this glossary are words that relate to history content. They are **highlighted** yellow in your text.
- Words below that have an asterisk (*) are academic vocabulary terms. They help you understand your school subjects and are **boldfaced** in your text.

abandon • apparent

English	Español

A

*abandon to withdraw protection, support, or help (p. 568)

*abandonar retirar la protección, el apoyo o la ayuda (p. 568)

*academic associated with higher learning at a scholarly institution (p. 308)

*académico relacionado con los estudios superiores en una institución especializada (p. 308)

*access freedom or ability to obtain or make use of (p. 277)

*acceso libertad o capacidad de obtener o hacer uso de (p. 277)

*adapt to change in order to meet the demands of a certain environment or circumstance (p. 162)

*adaptar cambiar para cumplir con las exigencias de cierto entorno o circunstancia (p. 162)

*adequate sufficient for a specific requirement, completed to its minimum requirements (pp. 339, 696)

*adecuado suficiente para un requisito específico, que se completa con los requisitos mínimos (pp. 339, 696)

*advocate to propose a certain position or viewpoint (p. 299)

*abogar proponer cierta posición o punto de vista (p. 299)

affirmative action an active effort to improve employment or educational opportunities for minorities (p. 725)

acción afirmativa un esfuerzo activo para mejorar las oportunidades educacionales y de empleo para las minorías (p. 725)

Agent Orange a chemical defoliant used to clear Vietnamese jungles during the Vietnam War (p. 661)

Agente naranja defoliante químico utilizado para limpiar las junglas vietnamitas durante la Guerra de Vietnam (p. 661)

*allocate to set apart for something specific (p. 790)

*asignar diferenciar para algo específico (p. 790)

allotment a plot of land assigned to an individual or family for cultivation (p. 175)

parcela un terreno asignado a un individuo o familia para su cultivación (p. 175)

*alternative existing or functioning outside the established cultural, social, or economic system (p. 733)

*alternativo que existe o funciona fuera del sistema cultural, social o económico establecido (p. 733)

Americanization causing someone to acquire American traits and characteristics (p. 239)

americanización causar que una persona adquiera características y rasgos americanos (p. 239)

amnesty the act of granting a pardon to a large group of people (pp. 140, 789)

amnistía el acto de otorgar perdón a un número grande de personas (pp. 140, 789)

amphtrac an amphibious tractor used to move troops from ships to shore (p. 514)

amphtrac un tractor anfibio utilizado para mover tropas desde barcos a la orilla del mar (p. 514)

anarchist person who believes that there should be no government (p. 376)

anarquista una persona que cree que no debe haber ningún gobierno (p. 376)

annuity money paid by contract on regular intervals (p. 170)

anualidad dinero pagado por contrato en intervalos regulares (p. 170)

anthrax a bacteria used to create biological weapons (p. 813)

ántrax bacteria utilizada para crear armas biológicas (p. 813)

*apparent appearing to be fact as far as can be understood (p. 423)

*aparente que parece ser cierto dentro de lo que puede comprenderse (p. 423)

Glossary/Glosario

English	**Español**
appeasement accepting demands in order to avoid conflict (p. 461)	**apaciguamiento** demandas aceptadas a fin de evitar conflictos (p. 461)
***appropriate** (adjective) especially suitable or compatible (p. 729)	***apropiado** (adjetivo) especialmente adecuado o compatible (p. 729)
***approximately** an estimation of a figure close to the actual figure (p. 175)	***aproximadamente** cálculo de un número cercano al número real (p. 175)
***arbitrary** existing or coming about seemingly at random or as an unfair or unreasonable act of will (p. 601)	***arbitrario** que existe u ocurre aparentemente al azar o como un acto de voluntad injusto o irrazonable (p. 601)
arbitration settling a dispute by agreeing to accept the decision of an impartial outsider (p. 204)	**arbitraje** arreglar una disputa acordando aceptar la decisión de una persona imparcial (p. 204)
armistice a temporary agreement to end fighting (p. 341)	**armisticio** acuerdo temporal de paz para terminar con una lucha (p. 341)
assembly line a production system with machines and workers arranged so that each person performs an assigned task again and again as the item passes before him or her (p. 368)	**línea de montaje** sistema de producción con máquinas y trabajadores arreglados para que cada persona haga su trabajo designado una y otra vez mientras el artículo pasa frente a ellos (p. 368)
assimilate to absorb a group into the culture of a larger population (p. 175)	**asimilar** incorporar a un grupo dentro de la cultura de una población más grande (p. 175)
***assume** to take for granted or as true (p. 468)	***suponer** dar algo por sentado o considerarlo verdadero (p. 468)
attrition the act of wearing down by constant harassment or attack (p. 129)	**atrición** acto de desalentar por constantes ataques o acoso (p. 129)
***authorities** those who have control over determining and enforcing what is right or wrong (p. 352)	***autoridades** aquéllas que poseen control sobre la determinación y el cumplimiento de lo que es correcto o incorrecto (p. 352)
autonomy the quality or state of being self-governing (p. 270)	**autonomía** la cualidad o el estado de autogobernarse (p. 270)
***awareness** the state of having or showing realization, perception, or knowledge (p. 797)	***conciencia** estado de poseer o mostrar comprensión, percepción o conocimiento (p. 797)

B

baby boom a marked rise in birthrate, such as occurred in the United States following World War II (p. 573)	**auge de nacimientos** aumento marcado en la taza de natalidad, tal como ocurrió en Estados Unidos después de la Segunda Guerra Mundial (p. 573)
bailiff minor officer of the courts (p. 406)	**alguacil** oficial en rango menor de las Cortes (p. 406)
bank holiday closing of banks during the Great Depression to avoid bank runs (p. 424)	**feriado bancario** cierre de bancos durante la Gran Depresión para evitar las corridas bancarias (p. 424)
bank run persistent and heavy demands from a bank's depositors, creditors, or customers (p. 403)	**corrida bancaria** demandas constantes y numerosas por parte de los depositantes, acreedores o clientes de un banco (p. 403)
beats short for "beatniks"; a group of mostly white writers and artists who, in 1950s America, harshly criticized what they considered the sterility and conformity of American life, the meaninglessness of American politics, and the emptiness of popular culture (p. 579)	**beats** nombre corto para "beatniks", un grupo de escritores y artistas en su mayoría blancos quienes en la década de 1950 en Estados Unidos criticaban duramente lo que ellos consideraban la esterilidad y conformismo de la vida estadounidense, el sin sentido de la política estadounidense y el vacío de la cultura popular (p. 579)

*benefit to be useful or profitable (p. 435)

benevolent society an association focusing on spreading the word of God and combating social problems (p. 100)

bilingualism the practice of teaching immigrant students in their own language (p. 697)

Bill of Rights a summary of fundamental rights and privileges guaranteed to a people against violation by the state (p. 78)

binding arbitration process whereby a neutral party hears arguments from two opposing sides and makes a decision that both must accept (p. 438)

black codes laws passed in the South just after the Civil War aimed at controlling freedmen and enabling plantation owners to exploit African American workers (p. 143)

black power the mobilization of the political and economic power of African Americans, especially to compel respect for their rights and to improve their condition (p. 644)

blacklist a list of persons who are disapproved of or who are to be punished or boycotted (p. 201)

blitzkrieg name given to sudden violent offensive attacks the Germans used during World War II; "lightning war" (p. 462)

blockade runner ship that runs through a blockade, usually to smuggle goods through a protected area (p. 130)

blogs online journal where an individual, group, or corporation presents a record of activities, thoughts, or beliefs (p. 777)

blue-collar workers workers in the manual labor field, particularly those requiring protective clothing (p. 574)

blues style of music evolving from African American spirituals and noted for its melancholy sound (p. 390)

bohemian a person (as an artist or writer) leading an unconventional lifestyle (p. 382)

bonanza farm a large, highly profitable wheat farm (p. 169)

*bond a note issued by the government which promises to pay off a loan with interest (p. 242)

*briefly for a short time (p. 512)

brinkmanship the willingness to go to the brink of war to force an opponent to back down (p. 555)

broker state role of the government to work out conflicts among competing interest groups (p. 445)

*beneficiar ser útil o rentable (p. 435)

sociedad de beneficencia una asociación enfocada en llevar la palabra de Dios y combatir problemas sociales (p. 100)

bilingualismo la práctica de enseñar a estudiantes inmigrantes en su propio lenguaje (p. 697)

declaración de derechos resumen de los derechos y privilegios fundamentales que el estado garantiza al pueblo que no se violarán (p. 78)

arbitraje obligatorio proceso por el cual un partido neutral escucha argumentos de dos partidos opositores y toma una decisión que ambos deben aceptar (p. 438)

códigos negros leyes aprobadas en el Sur al terminar la Guerra Civil para controlar a los libertos y permitir a los dueños de plantaciones la explotación de los trabajadores afroamericanos (p. 143)

poder negro movilización del poder económico y político de afroamericanos especialmente para imponer respeto por sus derechos y para mejorar su condiciones (p. 644)

lista negra lista de personas rechazadas o a las que se castigará o boicoteará (p. 201)

guerra relámpago nombre dado a los ataques repentinos ofensivos violentos que los alemanes usaron durante la Segunda Guerra Mundial (p. 462)

forzador de bloqueo un barco que navega a través de un bloqueo, usualmente para pasar contrabando a través de un área protegida (p. 130)

blogs publicación en línea donde un individuo, grupo o empresa presenta un registro de actividades, ideas o creencias (p. 777)

collar azul trabajadors trabajadors de mano de obra, particularmente aquellos que requieren ropa protectora (p. 574)

blues estilo de música que evolucionó de la música espiritual de los afroamericanos, distinguida por su sonido melancólico (p. 390)

bohemio una persona (como artista o escritor) que lleva un estilo de vida poco convencional (p. 382)

granja en bonanza extensa granja de trigo que produce muchas ganancias (p. 169)

*bono una obligación emitida por el gobierno que promete pagar un préstamo con interés (p. 242)

*brevemente por poco tiempo (p. 512)

política arriesgada la buena voluntad para ir al borde de guerra para forzar a un oponente a que se retracte (p. 555)

estado intermediario el papel del gobierno para resolver conflictos entre grupos con intereses competitivos (p. 445)

Glossary/Glosario

Glossary/Glosario

English	**Español**
budget deficit the amount by which expenses exceed income (p. 749)	**déficit del presupuesto** la cantidad por la cual los gastos exceden los ingresos (p. 749)
bull market a long period of rising stock prices (p. 401)	**bolsa al alza** largo período durante el cual los precios de acciones en la bolsa se incrementan (p. 401)
busing a policy of transporting children to schools outside their neighborhoods to achieve greater racial balance (p. 725)	**traslado** obligatorio la política de transportar estudiantes a escuelas fuera de sus vecindarios para alcanzar un balance racial (p. 725)

C

English	**Español**
cabinet a group of advisers to the president (p. 78)	**gabinete** grupo de consejeros al presidente (p. 78)
capital gains tax a federal tax paid by businesses and investors when they sell stocks or real estate (p. 767)	**impuestos a las ganancias del capital** impuesto federal pagado por inversionistas y negocios cuando ellos venden acciones y bienes raíces (p. 767)
carpetbagger name given to many Northerners who moved to the South after the Civil War and supported the Republicans (p. 145)	**carpetbagger** nombre dado a muchos norteños que se mudaron al Sur después de la Guerra Civil y apoyaron a los republicanos (p. 145)
censure to express a formal disapproval of an action (p. 550)	**censura** expresar la desaprobación formal sobre una acción (p. 550)
chad a small piece of cardboard produced by punching a data card (p. 805)	**agujereado** pedazo pequeño de cartón producido taladrando una tarjeta de computadora (p. 805)
*****challenger** one who enters a competition (p. 713)	*****contendiente** el que ingresa a una competencia (p. 713)
charter a constitution (p. 525)	**carta de privilegio** una constitución (p. 525)
checks and balances the system in which each branch of government has the ability to limit the power of the other branches to prevent any from becoming too powerful (p. 38)	**control y balances** sistema en el cual cada ramo de gobierno tiene la habilidad para limitar el poder a los otros ramos para que ninguno vuelva a ser demasiado poderoso (p. 38)
*****cite** to point out as an example in an argument or debate (p. 796)	*****citar** señalar como ejemplo en un argumento o debate (p. 796)
*****civil** of or relating to citizens (p. 109)	*****civil** de los ciudadanos o relativo a ellos (p. 109)
closed shop an agreement in which a company agrees to hire only union members (pp. 206, 566)	**taller cerrado** acuerdo en el que una compañía contrata solamente a miembros del sindicato (pp. 206, 566)
cloture a motion which ends debate and calls for an immediate vote, possible in the U.S. Senate by a vote of 60 senators (p. 636)	**clausura** una moción que termina con el debate y requiere un voto inmediato, posible en el Senado de EE.UU. por un voto de 60 senadores (p. 636)
*****code** a signal or symbol used to represent something that is to be kept secret (p. 496)	*****código** señal o símbolo utilizado para representar algo que se mantendrá en secreto (p. 496)
*****collapse** a sudden loss of force, value, or effect (p. 400)	*****colapso** pérdida repentina de fuerza, valor o efecto (p. 400)
*****colleague** a person who works in the same, or similar, profession (p. 408)	*****colega** persona que trabaja en la misma profesión o en una similar (p. 408)
collective a farm, especially in communist countries, formed from many small holdings collected into a single unit for joint operation under governmental supervision (p. 455)	**granja colectiva** una granja, especialmente en los países comunistas, formada por muchas tierras pequeñas reunidas en una sola unidad para operar conjuntamente bajo la supervisión del gobierno (p. 455)

*commentator one who explains, discusses, or reports in an expository manner, especially news on radio or television (p. 596)

*comisión er the officer in charge of a department or bureau of the public service (p. 145)

committee of correspondence committee organized in each colony to communicate with and unify the colonies (p. 25)

commune a group living arrangement in which members share everything and work together (p. 685)

*communications the various media and processes by which information is exchanged between individuals (p. 776)

*community people with common characteristics living in the same area (p. 413)

*compatible capable of existing in harmony (p. 691)

*concentrate to bring or direct one's powers, efforts, or attention toward a common objective (p. 462)

concentration camp a camp where persons are detained or confined (p. 470)

*conference a meeting of two or more persons for discussing matters of common concern (p. 267)

*confine to enclose or restrain (p. 613)

*confirmation the process of supporting a statement by evidence (p. 750)

*conform to change in a way that fits a standard or authority (p. 574)

*conformity agreement in form, manner, or character (p. 685)

consensus general agreement (p. 611)

conservative a person who believes government power, particularly in the economy, should be limited in order to maximize individual freedom (p. 740)

*constitute to be composed of, made up of, or formed from (p. 207)

*constitutional being in accordance with or regulated by a constitution (p. 78)

*consumer a person who buys what is produced by an economy (p. 196)

containment the policy or process of preventing the expansion of a hostile power (p. 538)

contra Spanish for counterrevolutionary, an anti-Sandinista guerrilla force in Nicaragua (p. 762)

contraband goods whose importation, exportation, or possession is illegal (p. 326)

*controversy a prolonged public dispute (p. 95)

*conventional nonnuclear (p. 602)

*comentarista aquél que explica, discute o informa de manera expositiva, especialmente noticias por radio o televisión (p. 596)

*comisionado funcionario a cargo de un departamento o agencia de servicios públicos (p. 145)

comité de correspondencia comité organizado en cada colonia para comunicar entre las colonias y unificarlas (p. 25)

comuna un arreglo de vivienda en el cual los miembros de un grupo trabajan juntos y comparten todo (p. 685)

*comunicaciones los diferentes medios y procesos mediante los cuales se intercambia información entre individuos (p. 776)

*comunidad personas con características comunes que viven en la misma área (p. 413)

*compatible capaz de existir en armonía (p. 691)

*concentrar orientar los poderes, esfuerzos o atención hacia un objetivo común (p. 462)

campo de concentración un campamento donde personas están detenidas o encerradas (p. 470)

*conferencia reunión entre dos o más personas para discutir asuntos de interés mutuo (p. 267)

*confinar encerrar o contener (p. 613)

*confirmación proceso de sustentar una afirmación con evidencia (p. 750)

*adecuarse cambiar para ajustarse a un estándar o autoridad (p. 574)

*conformidad acuerdo en forma, modo o carácter (p. 685)

consenso acuerdo general (p. 611)

conservador una persona que cree que el poder del gobierno, particularmente en la economía, debe estar limitado para llevar al máximo la libertad individual (p. 740)

*constituir estar compuesto de, hecho de o formado por (p. 207)

*constitucional de acuerdo con una constitución o reglamentado por ella (p. 78)

*consumidor persona que compra lo que produce una economía (p. 196)

contención la política o proceso de prevenir la expansión de un poder hostil (p. 538)

contra contrarevolucionario, la fuerza guerilla anti-Sandinista en Nicaragua (p. 762)

contrabando artículos de los que la importación, exportación o posesión es ilegal (p. 326)

*controversia discusión pública prolongada (p. 95)

*convencional no nuclear (p. 602)

Glossary/Glosario

Glossary/Glosario

English	Español
*convince to bring to belief, consent, or a course of action (p. 548)	***convencer** hacer creer, conseguir el consentimiento o lograr un curso de acción (p. 548)
convoy a group that travels with something, such as a ship, to protect it (p. 339)	**convoy** un grupo que viaja junto con algo, tal como un barco, para protegerlo (p. 339)
convoy system a system in which merchant ships travel with naval vessels for protection (p. 499)	**sistema de convoy** un sistema en el cual barcos mercantes viajan con buques navales para protección (p. 499)
cooperative a store where farmers bought products from each other; an enterprise owned and operated by those who use its services (p. 243)	**cooperativa** tienda donde los granjeros compraban productos el uno del otro; empresa poseída y operada por los que usan sus servicios (p. 243)
cooperative individualism President Hoover's policy of encouraging manufacturers and distributors to form their own organizations and volunteer information to the federal government in an effort to stimulate the economy (p. 365)	**individualismo cooperativo** política del Presidente Hoover para alentar a los manufactureros y distribuidores a formar sus propias organizaciones y pasar información voluntariamente al gobierno federal en un esfuerzo para estimular la economía (p. 365)
*coordinate to harmonize or bring into common action, movement, or condition (p. 503)	***coordinar** armonizar o realizar acciones o movimientos comunes o bien obtener condiciones comunes (p. 503)
corporation an organization that is authorized by law to carry on an activity but treated as though it were a single person (p. 194)	**sociedad anónima** organización autorizada por ley a montar una actividad, tratada como si fuera una sola persona (p. 194)
cost of living the cost of purchasing goods and services essential for survival (p. 348)	**costo de vida** el costo de comprar artículos y servicios esenciales para la supervivencia (p. 348)
cost-plus a government contract to pay a manufacturer the cost to produce an item plus a guaranteed percentage (p. 488)	**costo más** beneficio contrato del gobierno para pagar el costo de fabricación para producir un artículo más un porcentaje garantizado (p. 488)
counterculture a culture with values and beliefs different than the mainstream (p. 684)	**contracultura** una cultura con valores y creencias diferentes de los de la cultura principal (p. 684)
court-packing the act of changing the political balance of power in a nation's judiciary system whereby a national leader, such as the American president, appoints judges who will rule in favor of his or her policies (p. 442)	**recomposición de la corte** acto de modificar el equilibrio político de poder en el sistema judicial de una nación mediante el cual un líder nacional, como el presidente estadounidense, nombra jueces que decidirán a favor de las políticas de éste (p. 442)
covert not openly shown or engaged in (p. 557)	**secreto** no hecho o mostrado abiertamente (p. 557)
creationism the belief that God created the world and everything in it, usually in the way described in Genesis (p. 380)	**creacionismo** la creencia que Dios creó al mundo y todo lo que hay en él, usualmente como se describe en Génesis (p. 380)
credibility gap lack of trust or believability (p. 664)	**barrera de credibilidad** falta de confianza (p. 664)
*credit an amount or sum of money placed at a person's disposal by a bank on condition that it will be repaid with interest (p. 372)	***crédito** monto o suma de dinero que un banco pone a disposición de una persona con la condición de que se devolverá con intereses (p. 372)
*criteria standards on which a judgment or action may be based (p. 726)	***criterios** normas sobre las que puede basarse una opinión o acción (p. 726)
*crucial something considered important or essential (p. 133)	***crucial** algo que se considera importante o fundamental (p. 133)
*currency paper money used as a medium of exchange (p. 243)	***moneda** dinero en papel que se utiliza como medio de cambio (p. 243)

customs duty a tax on imports and exports (p. 23)

derecho de aduana impuesto sobre importaciones y exportaciones (p. 23)

D

de facto segregation segregation by custom and tradition (p. 623)

segregación de facto segregación por costumbre y tradición (p. 623)

deficit spending government practice of spending borrowed money rather than raising taxes, usually an attempt to boost the economy (p. 434)

gastos déficits práctica del gobierno de gastar dinero prestado en vez de aumentar impuestos, usualmente una tentativa para levantar la economía (p. 434)

deflation a decline in the volume of available money or credit that results in lower prices, and, therefore, increases the buying power of money (p. 200)

deflación un decremento de la cantidad de dinero o crédito disponible el cual resulta en precios reducidos y por lo tanto aumenta el poder adquisitivo de la moneda (p. 200)

*****deny** to declare untrue (p. 380)

*****negar** declarar que algo no es cierto (p. 380)

deport to expel individuals from the country (p. 352)

deportar expulsar del país a individuos (p. 352)

*****deregulation** the act or process of removing restrictions or regulations (p. 721)

*****desregulación** acción o proceso de eliminar restricciones o reglamentaciones (p. 721)

*****despite** in spite of (p. 520)

*****a pesar de** pese a que (p. 520)

détente a policy which attempts to relax or ease tensions between nations (p. 710)

détente una política que intenta relajar o borrar la tensión entre naciones (p. 710)

developing nation a nation whose economy is primarily agricultural (p. 557)

nación en desarrollo nación en donde la economía es principalmente agrícola (p. 557)

*****device** a piece of equipment or a mechanism designed to serve a special purpose or perform a special function (p. 774)

*****dispositivo** pieza de un equipo o mecanismo diseñado para servir un propósito especial o para realizar una función específica (p. 774)

direct primary a vote held by all members of a political party to decide their candidate for public office (p. 294)

elección primaria voto tomado por todos los miembros de un partido político para elegir a su candidato para un puesto público (p. 294)

discount retailing selling large quantities of goods at very low prices and trying to sell the goods quickly to turn over their entire inventory in a short period of time (p. 755)

ventas minoristas de descuento vender grandes cantidades de productos a precios muy bajos e intentar realizar ventas rápidas de productos para la rotación del inventario en un corto período de tiempo (p. 755)

*****discrimination** different treatment or preference on a basis other than individual merit (p. 250)

*****discriminación** un trato o preferencia diferente en base a toda cosa diferente del mérito individual (p. 250)

disenfranchise to deprive of the right to vote (p. 491)

privación civil privar el derecho al voto (p. 491)

*****disposable** referring to the money remaining to an individual after deduction of taxes (p. 370)

*****disponible** hace referencia al dinero que le queda a un individuo después de la deducción de impuestos (p. 370)

*****disproportionate** lacking regularity or symmetry in size, degree, or intensity (p. 665)

*****desproporcionado** que carece de regularidad o simetría en tamaño, grado o intensidad (p. 665)

*****distribution** the act or process of being given out or disbursed to clients, customers, or members of a group (p. 194)

*****distribución** acción o proceso de repartir o desembolsar entre clientes, consumidores o miembros de un grupo (p. 194)

*****diverse** being different from one another (p. 382)

*****diferente** ser distinto de otros (p. 382)

dollar diplomacy a policy of joining the business interests of a country with its diplomatic interests abroad (p. 281)

diplomacia del dólar política de juntar los intereses comerciales de un país con sus intereses diplomáticos en el extranjero (p. 281)

English	Español
domino theory the belief that if one nation in Asia fell to the Communists, neighboring countries would follow (p. 655)	**teoría dominó** la creencia que si una nación en Asia se derrumbara ante los comunistas, sus países vecinos hubieran caído en seguida (p. 655)
dove a person in favor of the United States withdrawing from the Vietnam War (p. 667)	**paloma** persona a favor de que Estados Unidos se retirara de la guerra en Vietnam (p. 667)
downsizing reducing a company in size by laying off workers and managers to become more efficient (p. 766)	**reducción de personal** reducción del tamaño de una compañía despidiendo gerentes y trabajadores para llegar a ser una empresa más eficiente (pág. 766)
*****draft** to select a person at random for mandatory military service (p. 332)	*****conscripción** selección de una persona al azar para el servicio militar obligatorio (p. 332)
dry farming a way of farming dry land in which seeds are planted deep in the ground where there is some moisture (p. 168)	**cultivo seco** manera de cultivar tierra seca plantando las semillas en la profundidad de la tierra donde hay algo de humedad (p. 168)
due process a judicial requirement that laws may not treat individuals unfairly, arbitrarily, or unreasonably, and that courts must follow proper procedures and rules when trying cases (p. 601)	**proceso justo** requerimiento judicial de que las leyes no deben tratar individuos injusta, arbitraria, o irracionalmente y que las cortes deben de seguir procesos y reglamentos justos al jurar casos (p. 601)
dynamic conservatism policy of balancing economic conservatism with some activism (p. 570)	**conservatismo dinámico** política de alcanzar un balance entre el conservatismo económico y algún activismo (p. 570)

E

English	Español
"earmark" specifications added by both Republicans and Democrats for the expenditure of federal money for particular projects, such as building a bridge or funding medical research, usually in their own states and districts (p. 824)	**destino de fondos** especificaciones que tanto Republicanos como Demócratas añadieron para el gasto del dinero federal en proyectos particulares, por ejemplo, la construcción de un puente o la financiación de investigaciones médicas, generalmente, en sus propios estados y distritos (p. 824)
economies of scale the reduction in the cost of a good brought about especially by increased production at a given facility (p. 194)	**economía a gran escala** reducción del costo de un producto a causa de la producción aumentada en una fábrica de producción (p. 194)
*****eliminate** to remove or get rid of (p. 819)	*****eliminar** quitar o deshacerse de algo (p. 819)
emancipation the act or process of freeing enslaved persons (p. 102)	**emancipación** el proceso de liberar a personas esclavizadas (p. 102)
embargo a government ban on trade with other countries (p. 718)	**embargo** prohibición gubernamental contra el comercio con otros países (p. 718)
*****emphasis** a special importance given to an object or idea (p. 322)	*****énfasis** importancia especial que se le da a un objeto o idea (p. 322)
*****enforce** to urge or carry out using force (p. 646)	*****hacer cumplir** instar o llevar a cabo por medio de la fuerza (p. 646)
*****ensure** to guarantee or make certain (p. 172)	*****asegurar** garantizar o hacer certero (p. 172)
*****entity** something having independent, separate, or self-contained existence (p. 585)	*****entidad** algo que tiene una existencia independiente, separada y autónoma (p. 585)
entrepreneur one who organizes, manages, and assumes the risks of a business or enterprise (p. 187)	**empresario** persona que organiza, dirige y asume el riesgo de un negocio o empresa (p. 187)

enumerated powers powers listed in the Constitution as belonging to the federal government (p. 79)

poderes enumerados poderes nombrados en la Constitución que pertenecen solamente al gobierno federal (p. 79)

*environmental having to do with the environment; the complex system of plants, animals, water, and soil (p. 304)

*medioambiental relacionado con el medioambiente; el complejo sistema de plantas, animales, agua y suelo (p. 304)

*equipment the articles or physical resources prepared or furnished for a specific task (p. 534)

*equipos artículos o recursos físicos preparados o proporcionados para una tarea específica (p. 534)

*erode to wear away at something until it fades (p. 326)

*erosionar desgastar algo hasta que desaparece (p. 326)

espionage spying, especially to gain government secrets (p. 330)

espionaje espiar, especialmente para obtener secretos gubernamentales (p. 330)

*ethnic relating to large groups of people classed according to common racial, national, tribal, religious, linguistic, or cultural origin or background (p. 216)

*étnico relativo a grandes grupos de personas clasificadas de acuerdo con características comunes de origen racial, de nacionalidad, tribal, religioso, lingüístico o cultural (p. 216)

ethnic cleansing the expulsion, imprisonment, or killing of ethnic minorities by a dominant majority group (p. 787)

purificación étnica expulsión, encarcelamiento o asesinato de minorías étnicas por un grupo mayoritario dominante (p. 787)

euro the basic currency shared by the countries of the European Union since 1999 (p. 795)

eurodólar moneda básica compartida por los países de la Unión Europea desde 1999 (p. 795)

*evolution the scientific theory that humans and other forms of life have evolved over time (pp. 231, 380)

*evolución teoría científica que los humanos y otras formas de vida se han evolucionado tras el tiempo (pp. 231, 380)

executive privilege principle stating that communications of the executive branch should remain confidential to protect national security (p. 716)

privilegio ejecutivo el principio de que las comunicaciones del ramo ejecutivo deben de permanecer confidenciales para proteger la seguridad nacional (p. 716)

*expansion the act or process of increasing or enlarging the extent, number, volume, or scope (p. 263)

*expansión acción o proceso de aumentar o ampliar la extensión, número, volumen o alcance (p. 263)

*exposure the condition of being unprotected, especially from severe weather (p. 99)

*exposición la condición de estar desprotegido, especialmente del mal tiempo (p. 99)

extermination camp a camp where men, women, and children were sent to be executed (p. 470)

campo de exterminación campo donde los hombres, las mujeres, y los niños eran enviados para ser ejecutados (p. 470)

*extract to remove by force (p. 160)

*extraer quitar algo por la fuerza (p. 160)

*facility something that is built, installed, or established to serve a particular purpose (p. 622)

*instalación algo que se construye, instala o establece para servir un propósito especial (p. 622)

fallout radioactive particles dispersed by a nuclear explosion (p. 553)

caída radioactiva partículas radioactivas dispersadas por una explosión nuclear (p. 553)

fascism a political system headed by a dictator that calls for extreme nationalism and racism and no tolerance of opposition (p. 454)

fascismo un sistema político encabezado por un dictador que pide por nacionalismo y racismo extremo y poca tolerancia de la oposición (p. 454)

federalism political system in which power is divided between the national and state governments (p. 37)

federalismo sistema político en el cual el poder está dividido entre los estados y el gobierno federal (p. 37)

feminism the belief that men and women should be equal politically, economically, and socially (p. 686)

feminismo la creencia que los hombres y las mujeres deben ser iguales política, económica y socialmente (p. 686)

filibuster an attempt to kill a bill by having a group of senators take turns speaking continuously so that a vote cannot take place (p. 636)

filibustero un atentado para acabar con un proyecto de ley hablando continuamente a turnos un grupo de senadores para que no pueda haber un voto (p. 636)

*finance to provide money for a project (p. 436)

*financiar proporcionar dinero para un proyecto (p. 436)

English	Español
fireside chats radio broadcasts made by FDR to the American people to explain his initiatives (p. 425)	**pláticas hogareñas** emisiones de radio transmitidas por FDR al pueblo americano para explicar sus iniciativas (p. 425)
flexible response the buildup of conventional troops and weapons to allow a nation to fight a limited war without using nuclear weapons (p. 602)	**respuesta flexible** formación de tropas y armas convencionales para permitir que un país entre en una guerra limitada sin usar armas nucleares (p. 602)
foreclose to take possession of a property from a mortgagor because of defaults on payments (p. 415)	**ejecutar** una hipoteca tomar posesión de una propiedad por falta de pagos hipotecarios (p. 415)
fossil fuel a fuel formed in the earth from decayed plant or animal remains (p. 733)	**combustible fósil** un combustible formado en la tierra de los restos descompuestos de plantas o animales (p. 733)
*__framework__ a set of guidelines to be followed (p. 35)	*__marco__ conjunto de pautas por seguir (p. 35)
franchise the right or license to market a company's goods or services in an area, such as a store of a chain operation (p. 574)	**franquicia** derecho o licencia para comercializar los productos o servicios de una empresa en un área, como una tienda de operación en cadena (p. 574)
*__fundamental__ being of central importance (p. 430)	*__fundamental__ de central importancia (p. 430)

G

English	Español
*__gender__ term applied to the characteristics of a male or female (p. 687)	*__género__ término aplicado a las características de un ser masculino o femenino (p. 687)
general strike a strike involving all the workers in a particular geographic location (p. 349)	**huelga general** una huelga por todos los trabajadores de un lugar geográfico (p. 349)
*__generation__ a classification of people who share the same experience throughout their lives (p. 671)	*__generación__ clasificación de personas que comparten las mismas experiencias a lo largo de sus vidas (p. 671)
generation gap a cultural separation between parents and their children (p. 579)	**barrera generacional** una separación cultural entre padres e hijos (p. 579)
glasnost a Soviet policy permitting open discussion of political and social issues and freer dissemination of news and information (p. 763)	**glasnost** política soviética que permitía discusión abierta de temas políticos y sociales y diseminación más libre de noticias e información (p. 763)
globalism the idea that the world is becoming increasingly interconnected (p. 794)	**globalismo** idea de que el mundo se encuentra cada vez más interconectado (p. 794)
global warming an increase in average world temperatures over time (p. 797)	**calentamiento global** aumento en la temperatura promedio mundial tras un período (p. 797)
gold standard a monetary standard in which one ounce of gold equaled a set number of dollars (p. 424)	**patrón oro norma** monetaria en la cual una onza de oro igualaba a un número fijo de dólares (p. 424)
graduated income tax tax based on the net income of an individual or business and which taxes different income levels at different rates (p. 245)	**impuesto graduado** de utilidades impuesto basado en los ingresos netos de un individuo o empresa en el cual la taza del impuesto se diferencia de acuerdo a diferentes niveles de salario (p. 245)
graft the acquisition of money in dishonest ways, as in bribing a politician (p. 227)	**soborno** adquisición de dinero de manera deshonesta tal como el sobornar a un político (p. 227)
grandfather clause a clause that allowed individuals who did not pass the literacy test to vote if their fathers or grandfathers had voted before Reconstruction began; an exception to a law based on preexisting circumstances (p. 250)	**cláusula de abuelo** cláusula que permitió votar a los que no aprobaron el examen de leer si sus padres o sus abuelos habían votado antes de que empezara la Reconstrucción; excepción a una ley basada en circunstancias preexistentes (p. 250)

grassroots movement a group of people organizing at the local or community level, away from political or cultural centers (p. 767)

movimiento local grupo de personas que se organiza a nivel local y popular lejos de centros políticos o culturales (p. 767)

greenback a piece of U.S. paper money first issued by the North during the Civil War (p. 242)

billete dorso verde billete de papel moneda de EE.UU. expedido por primera vez por el Norte durante la Guerra Civil (p. 242)

gross national product the total value of goods and services produced by a country during a year (p. 182)

producto nacional bruto valor total de bienes y servicios producidos por un país durante un año (p. 182)

*guarantee a statement of assurance (p. 137)

*garantía declaración de seguridad (p. 137)

guerrilla member of an armed band that carries out surprise attacks and sabotage rather than open warfare (pp. 283, 655)

guerrilla banda armada que usa ataques sorpresas o sabotaje en vez de la guerra organizada (pp. 283, 655)

(H)

habeas corpus a legal order for an inquiry to determine whether a person has been lawfully imprisoned (p. 128)

hábeas corpus orden legal para una encuesta para determinar si una persona ha sido encarcelada legalmente (p. 128)

hacienda a huge ranch (p. 164)

hacienda un rancho extenso (p. 164)

hawk someone who believed the United States should continue its military efforts in Vietnam (p. 667)

halcón persona que creía que Estados Unidos debía continuar sus esfuerzos militares en Vietnam (p. 667)

hedgerow row of shrubs or trees surrounding a field, often on a dirt wall (p. 518)

seto fila de arbustos o árboles cercando un campo a menudo sobre un muro de tierra (p. 518)

hemispheric defense zone national policy during World War II that declared the Western Hemisphere to be neutral and that the United States would patrol this region against German submarines (p. 476)

zona de defensa hemisférica política nacional durante la Segunda Guerra Mundial que declaró que el Hemisferio Oeste fue neutral y que Estados Unidos patrullaría esta región en contra de submarinos alemanes (p. 476)

hippies refers to young Americans, especially during the 1960s, who reject the conventions of established society (p. 684)

hippies se refiere a los jóvenes estadounidenses, especialmente durante la década de 1960, que rechazaban las convenciones de la sociedad establecida (p. 684)

hobo a homeless and usually penniless wanderer (p. 406)

vagabundo persona errante sin hogar y usualmente sin dinero (p. 406)

holding company a company whose primary business is owning a controlling share of stock in other companies (p. 198)

compañía de valores compañía de la cual el negocio principal es poseer el control de acciones en otras compañías (p. 198)

homestead method of acquiring a piece of U.S. public land by living on and cultivating it (p. 167)

posesionar método de adquirir una extensión de tierra pública de EEUU viviendo en ella y cultivándola (p. 167)

horizontal integration combining of many firms engaged in the same type of business into one corporation (p. 197)

integración horizontal asociación do firmas competitivas en una sociedad anónima (p. 197)

hydraulic mining method of mining by which water is sprayed at a very high pressure against a hill or mountain, washing away large quantities of dirt, gravel, and rock, and exposing the minerals beneath the surface (p. 161)

minería hidráulica método de minería mediante el que se pulveriza agua a alta presión contra una colina o montaña, lo que elimina grandes cantidades de suciedad, grava y rocas y expone los minerales que se encuentran debajo de la superficie (p. 161)

(I)

*ideology a system of thought that is held by an individual, group, or culture (p. 424)

*ideología sistema de ideas que posee un individuo, grupo o cultura (p. 424)

*illegal not according to or authorized by law (p. 789)

*ilegal que no está de acuerdo con la ley o ésta no lo autoriza (p. 789)

*immigrant one who enters and becomes established in a country other than that of his or her original nationality (p. 214)

*inmigrante aquél que ingresa y se establece en un país que no es su país de origen (p. 214)

Glossary/Glosario

English	Español
impact to make a lasting impression upon an individual or group (p. 392)	*impactar* dejar una impresión duradera en un individuo o grupo (p. 392)
imperialism the actions used by one nation to exercise political or economic control over a smaller or weaker nation (p. 262)	**imperialismo** acciones usadas por una nación para ejercer el control político o económico sobre naciones más pequeñas o débiles (p. 262)
implement to put into action (p. 129)	*implementar* poner en acción (p. 129)
implied powers powers not specifically listed in the Constitution but claimed by the federal government (p. 79)	**poderes implícitos** poderes no nombrados específicamente en la Constitución pero reclamados por el gobierno federal (p. 79)
imply to express indirectly (p. 558)	*insinuar* expresar indirectamente (p. 558)
impound to take possession of (p. 708)	**confiscar** tomar posesión de (p. 708)
incentive something that motivates a person into action (p. 222)	*incentivo* algo que motiva a que una persona realice una acción (p. 222)
incident occurrence of a happening or situation that is a separate unit of experience (p. 712)	*incidente* acontecimiento de un suceso o situación que es una unidad separada de experiencia (p. 712)
income a gain or recurrent benefit usually measured in money derived from capital or labor (p. 582)	*ingresos* ganancia o beneficio recurrente que generalmente se mide en dinero proveniente de capital o trabajo (p. 582)
income tax a tax based on the net income of a person or business (p. 310)	**impuesto de utilidades** impuesto basado en el ingreso neto de una persona o empresa (p. 310)
indentured servant an individual who contracts to work for a colonist for a specified number of years in exchange for transportation to the colonies, food, clothing, and shelter (p. 12)	**sirviente contratado** individuo contratado para trabajar para un colono durante cierto número de años a cambio de transportación a las colonias, alimento, ropa y refugio (p. 12)
indicate to point out, point to, or demonstrate the necessity of (p. 745)	*indicar* señalar, describir o demostrar la necesidad de algo (p. 745)
individualism the thought that no matter what a person's background is, he or she can still become successful (p. 230)	**individualismo** el pensamiento de que sin importar el origen de una persona, ésta puede ser exitosa (p. 230)
industrial union an organization of common laborers and craft workers in a particular industry (p. 201)	**sindicato industrial** organización de trabajadores comunes y obreros calificados en una industria (p. 201)
inflation the loss of value of money (pp. 242, 718)	**inflación** pérdida del valor del dinero (pp. 242, 718)
initial of or relating to the beginning (p. 541)	*inicial* relacionado con el comienzo (p. 541)
initiative the right of citizens to place a measure or issue before the voters or the legislature for approval (p. 295)	**iniciativa** derecho de los ciudadanos de poner una propuesta o tema ante los votantes o la legislatura para su aprobación (p. 295)
injunction a court order whereby one is required to do or to refrain from doing a specified act (p. 205)	**medida cautelar** orden judicial que exige o prohíbe la realización de una acción específica (p. 205)
innovation a new idea or method (p. 168)	*innovación* nueva idea o método (p. 168)
insecurity the state of not being confident or sure (p. 538)	*inseguridad* estado de desconfianza o indecisión (p. 538)
inspector a person appointed to examine foreign facilities, usually in search of weapons (p. 817)	*inspector* persona designada para examinar instalaciones extranjeras, por lo general, en búsqueda de armas (p. 817)

installment buying an item on credit with a monthly plan to pay off the value of the good (p. 405)

pago a plazos compra de un artículo a crédito con un plan de pago mensual para pagar el valor del artículo (p. 405)

*institute to initiate or establish something (p. 605)

*instituir iniciar o establecer algo (p. 605)

insubordination disobedience (p. 307)

insubordinación desobediencia (p. 307)

*integrate to combine two previously separate things (p. 191)

*integrar combinar dos cosas previamente separadas (p. 191)

integrated circuit a complete electronic circuit on a silicon chip that is small and easy to produce (p. 774)

circuito integrado un circuito electrónico completo en un chip de silicona pequeño y fácil de producir (p. 774)

*intense existing in an extreme degree (p. 512)

*intenso que existe en un grado extremo (p. 512)

*intensify to become more frequent and powerful (p. 733)

*intensificar volverse más frecuente y poderoso (p. 733)

internationalism a national policy of actively trading with foreign countries to foster peace and prosperity (p. 459)

internacionalismo política nacional de intercambio comercial activo con países extranjeros para promover la paz y la prosperidad (p. 459)

*interpret to explain the meaning of complex material (p. 38)

*interpretar explicar el significado de materiales complejos (p. 38)

*interpretation the act or process of explaining or telling the meaning of (p. 810)

*interpretación acción o proceso de explicar o decir el significado de algo (p. 810)

*intervene to get involved in the affairs of another (p. 270)

*intervenir involucrarse en los asuntos de otros (p. 270)

*invest to put money into a company in order to gain a future financial reward (p. 401)

*invertir colocar dinero en una empresa con el fin de obtener una recompensa financiera en el futuro (p. 401)

*investigation a systematic examination or official inquiry (p. 363)

*investigación examen sistemático o indagación oficial (p. 363)

*investor one who puts money into a company in order to gain a future financial reward (p. 192)

*inversor aquél que coloca dinero en una empresa con el fin de obtener una recompensa financiera en el futuro (p. 192)

Iron Curtain the political and military barrier that isolated Soviet-controlled countries of Eastern Europe after World War II (p. 537)

cortina de hierro barrera política y militar que aisló a los países de Europa Oriental controlados por los soviéticos después de la Segunda Guerra Mundial (p. 537)

isolationism a national policy of avoiding involvement in world affairs (p. 366)

aislacionismo política nacional de evitar el involucramiento en asuntos mundiales (p. 366)

jazz American style of music that developed from ragtime and blues and which uses syncopated rhythms and melodies (p. 389)

jazz estilo de música americana que se desarrolló de ragtime y blues y que usa melodías y ritmos sincopados (p. 389)

Jim Crow laws statutes or laws created to enforce segregation (p. 250)

Leyes de Jim Crow leyes creadas para reforzar la segregación (p. 250)

jingoism extreme nationalism marked by aggressive foreign policy (p. 271)

patriotismo extremo nacionalismo marcado por la agresiva política extranjera (p. 271)

joint-stock company form of business organization in which many investors pool funds to raise large amounts of money for large projects (p. 8)

compañía por acciones forma de organización de negocios en la cual muchos inversionistas compran acciones para juntar grandes cantidades de dinero para grandes proyectos (p. 8)

judicial review power of the Supreme Court to determine whether laws of Congress are constitutional and to strike down those that are not (p. 83)

revisión judicial derecho de la Suprema Corte para determinar si las leyes del Congreso son constitucionales y para derribar aquellas que no lo son (p. 83)

*justify to prove or to show to be just, right, or reasonable (p. 504)

*justificar probar o demostrar que algo es justo, correcto y razonable (p. 504)

juvenile delinquency antisocial or criminal behavior of young people (p. 587)

delincuencia juvenil comportamiento antisocial o criminal de los jóvenes (p. 587)

Glossary/Glosario

English	Español

K

kamikaze during World War II, a Japanese suicide pilot whose mission was to crash into his target (p. 515)

kamikase durante la Segunda Guerra Mundial un piloto suicida japonés de quien la misión fue chocar en su objetivo (p. 515)

L

labor union an organization of workers formed for the purpose of advancing its members' interests (p. 92)

sindicato organización de trabajadores formada con el propósito de promover los intereses de sus miembros (p. 92)

laissez-faire policy that government should interfere as little as possible in the nation's economy (p. 186)

laissez-faire política que el gobierno debe interferir tan poco como sea posible en la economía del país (p. 186)

land grant a grant of land by the federal government especially for roads, railroads, or agricultural colleges (p. 192)

concesión de tierras una concesión de terrenos por el gobierno federal especialmente para carreteras, vías de ferrocarril y colegios agrícolas (p. 192)

*__legislation__ a proposed law to be voted on by a governing body (p. 295)

*__legislación__ ley propuesta para que un órgano directivo la vote (p. 295)

*__legislator__ one who makes laws as a member of a political, legislative body (p. 566)

*__legislador__ aquél que elabora leyes como miembro de un órgano político legislativo (p. 566)

*__liberal__ a person who generally believes the government should take an active role in the economy and in social programs but should not dictate social behavior (pp. 708, 740)

*__liberal__ persona que generalmente cree que el gobierno debe desempeñar un papel active en la economía y programas sociales pero que el gobierno no debe dictar el comportamiento social (pp. 708, 740)

*__liberate__ to set free (p. 532)

*__liberar__ dejar en libertad (p. 532)

*__likewise__ in a like manner, similarly (p. 692)

*__asimismo__ de la misma manera, igualmente (p. 692)

limited war a war fought with limited commitment of resources to achieve a limited objective, such as containing communism (p. 545)

guerra limitada guerra peleada con compromisos limitados de recursos para alcanzar un objetivo limitado, tal como la contención del comunismo (p. 545)

linkage policy of improving relations with the Soviet Union and China in hopes of persuading them to cut back their aid to North Vietnam (p. 670)

enlace política de mejorar relaciones con la Unión Soviética y China con la esperanza de persuadirlas a que redujeran su ayuda a Vietnam del Norte (p. 670)

lockout a company tool to fight union demands by refusing to allow employees to enter its facilities to work (p. 202)

cierre patronal práctica de una empresa para rechazar las demandas sindicales negándose a permitir a los empleados a entrar al área de trabajo (p. 202)

long drive driving cattle long distances to a railroad depot for fast transport and great profit (p. 163)

manejo largo conducción de ganado por largas distancias a estaciones de ferrocarril para la transportación rápida y grandes ganancias (p. 163)

loyalty review program a policy established by President Truman that authorized the screening of all federal employees to determine their loyalty to the American government (p. 546)

programa de verificación de la lealtad política que estableció el presidente Truman y que autorizaba la investigación de todos los empleados federales para determinar la lealtad de éstos al gobierno estadounidense (p. 546)

lynching an execution performed without lawful approval (p. 252)

linchamiento ejecución hecha sin aprobación legal (p. 252)

M

mandate authorization to act given to a representative (p. 137)

mandato autorización dado a un representante (p. 137)

*manipulate to operate or arrange manually to achieve a desired effect (p. 547)

margin buying a stock by paying only a fraction of the stock price and borrowing the rest (p. 401)

margin call demand by a broker that investors pay back loans made for stocks purchased on margin (p. 401)

martial law the law administered by military forces that is invoked by a government in an emergency (p. 126)

mass media a medium of communication (as in television and radio) intended to reach a wide audience (p. 385)

mass production the production of large quantities of goods using machinery and often an assembly line (p. 368)

massive retaliation a policy of threatening a massive response, including the use of nuclear weapons, against a Communist state trying to seize a peaceful state by force (p. 555)

*media a means of expression or communication, especially in reference to the agencies of mass communication—newspapers, radio, television, and the Internet (p. 664)

*mediate an attempt to resolve conflict between hostile people or groups (p. 445)

microprocessor a computer processor containing both memory and computing functions on a single chip (p. 774)

*migrate to move from one location to another (p. 330)

migration chain the process by which immigrants who have acquired U.S. citizenship can send for relatives in their home country to join them (p. 788)

militarism a policy of aggressive military preparedness (p. 321)

military-industrial complex an informal relationship that some people believe exists between the military and the defense industry to promote greater military spending and influence government policy (p. 559)

minutemen companies of civilian soldiers who boasted they were ready to fight on a minute's notice (p. 26)

missile gap belief that the Soviet Union had more nuclear weapons than the United States (p. 596)

Model T automobile built by the Ford Motor Company from 1908 until 1927 (p. 368)

*modify to make changes or alter (p. 781)

*monitor to observe, oversee, or regulate (p. 822)

monopoly total control of a type of industry by one person or one company (p. 197)

*manipular operar o disponer manualmente para alcanzar un efecto deseado (p. 547)

margen comprar acciones pagando solamente una fracción del precio y pidiendo prestado el resto (p. 401)

llamada de reserva demanda de un accionista a que los inversionistas paguen los préstamos hechos para la compra de acciones al margen (p. 401)

derecho marcial derecho administrado por fuerzas militares que es invocado por un gobierno en una emergencia (p. 126)

medios informativos medios de comunicación (como televisión y radio) con la intención de llegar a la audiencia extensa (p. 385)

fabricación en serie producción de grandes cantidades de productos usando máquinas y a menudo una línea de montaje (p. 368)

represalia masiva una política que amenaza una respuesta masiva, incluyendo el uso de armas nucleares, contra un estado comunista que trata de captar un país pacífico por la fuerza (p. 555)

*medios de comunicación medios de expresión o comunicación, especialmente en referencia a las agencias de comunicación masiva periódicos, radio, televisión e Internet (p. 664)

*mediar intento de resolver un conflicto entre personas o grupos hostiles (p. 445)

microprocesador procesador de computadora que contiene memoria y funciones de computación en un solo chip (p. 774)

*migrar mudarse de un lugar a otro (p. 330)

cadena migratoria proceso mediante el cual los inmigrantes que obtuvieron la ciudadanía estadounidense pueden llamar a sus familiares en sus países de origen para que se les unan (p. 788)

militarismo política de preparación militar agresiva (p. 321)

compejo militar industrial relación informal que algunas personas creen que existe entre lo militar y la industria de defensa para promover mayores gastos militares y para influenciar la política gubernamental (p. 559)

minutemen compañías de soldados civiles que se jactaban de que podrían estar listos para tomar armas en sólo un minuto (p. 26)

diferencia de proyectiles creencia que la Unión Soviética tenía más armas nucleares que Estados Unidos (p. 596)

Modelo T automóvil construido por la Ford Motor Company desde 1908 hasta 1927 (p. 368)

*modificar realizar cambios o alterar (p. 781)

*controlar vigilar, supervisar o regular (p. 822)

monopolio control total de una industria por una persona o una compañía (p. 197)

Glossary/Glosario

English	Español
muckraker a journalist who uncovers abuses and corruption in a society (p. 293)	**muckraker** periodista que revela abusos y corrupción en una sociedad (p. 293)
multinational corporation large corporations with overseas investments (p. 574)	**corporación multinacional** grandes corporaciones de inversión extranjera (p. 574)
"mutual assured destruction" the strategy assuming that, as long as two countries can destroy each other with nuclear weapons, they will be afraid to use them (p. 753)	**destrucción mutua asegurada** estrategia que supone que mientras dos países puedan destruirse mutuamente con armas nucleares, tendrán miedo de utilizarlas (p. 753)

N

English	Español
napalm a jellied gasoline used for bombs (pp. 521, 661)	**napalm** gasolina gelatinosa utilizada para bombas incendiarias (pp. 521, 661)
national self-determination the free choice by the people of a nation of their own future political status (p. 342)	**autodeterminación nacional** es la libre elección que hacen los habitantes de un país sobre su propia situación política futura (p. 342)
nationalism loyalty and devotion to a nation (p. 322)	**nacionalismo** lealtad y devoción a una nación (p. 322)
nativism hostility toward immigrants (p. 376)	**nativismo** sentimientos de hostilidad hacia imigrantes (p. 376)
*****network** an interconnected system (p. 336)	*****red** sistema interconectado (p. 336)
nomad a person who continually moves from place to place, usually in search of food (p. 170)	**nómada** persona que se mueve de un lugar a otro, generalmente en busca de alimentos o pastos (p. 170)
*****nuclear** used in or produced by a nuclear reaction (p. 523)	*****nuclear** que se utiliza en una reacción nuclear o que ésta lo produce (p. 523)

O

English	Español
*****obtain** to gain possession of (p. 812)	*****obtener** lograr posesión de algo (p. 812)
*****ongoing** being actually in process, continuing (p. 393)	*****continuo** que está en proceso, en curso (p. 393)
Open Door policy a policy that allowed each foreign nation in China to trade freely in the other nations' spheres of influence (p. 277)	**política de Puertas Abiertas** política que permitió a cada nación extranjera en China intercambiar libremente en las esferas de influencia de otras naciones (p. 277)
open range vast areas of grassland owned by the federal government (p. 162)	**terreno abierto** gran extensión de pastos propiedad del gobierno federal (p. 162)
open shop a workplace where workers are not required to join a union (p. 374)	**taller abierto** lugar de trabajo donde los trabajadores no son requeridos de ser miembros del sindicato (p. 374)
*****orientation** position relative to a standard (p. 759)	*****orientación** posición relativa a un estándar (p. 759)

P

English	Español
*****participant** one who takes part or shares in something (p. 787)	*****participante** que forma parte de algo o que comparte algo (p. 787)
party boss the person in control of a political machine (p. 227)	**jefe de partido** persona que lleva el control de la maquinaria política (p. 227)
perestroika a policy of economic and government restructuring instituted by Mikhail Gorbachev in the Soviet Union in the 1980s (p. 763)	**perestroika** política de reestructuración económica y gubernamental instituida por Mikhail Gorbachev en la Unión Soviética en los años 1980 (p. 763)

periphery the outer boundary of something (p. 497)

perjury lying when one has sworn under oath to tell the truth (pp. 548, 785)

*phenomenon an exceptional, unusual, or abnormal person, thing, or occurrence (p. 572)

philanthropy providing money to support humanitarian or social goals (p. 232)

Pilgrim a Separatist who journeyed to the American colonies in the 1600s for religious freedom (p. 8)

pocket veto indirectly vetoing a bill by letting a session of Congress expire without signing the bill (p. 142)

polio abbreviated form of poliomyelitis, an acute infectious disease affecting the skeletal muscles, often resulting in permanent disability and deformity (p. 422)

political machine an organization linked to a political party that often controlled local government (p. 227)

poll tax a tax of a fixed amount per person that had to be paid before the person could vote (p. 250)

pool a group sharing in some activity; for example, among railroad owners who made secret agreements and set rates among themselves (p. 196)

popular sovereignty government subject to the will of the people (p. 168); before the Civil War, the idea that people living in a territory had the right to decide by voting if slavery would be allowed there (pp. 37, 107)

populism political movement founded in the 1890s representing mainly farmers, favoring free coinage of silver and government control of railroads and other large industries (p. 242)

poverty line a level of personal or family income below which one is classified as poor by the federal government (p. 582)

*practice to do something repeatedly so it becomes the standard (p. 187)

*prior happening before an event (p. 162)

*procedure a particular way of conducting or engaging in an activity (p. 821)

*prohibit to make illegal by an authority (p. 466)

prohibition laws banning the manufacture, transportation, and sale of alcoholic beverages (p. 299)

propaganda the spreading of ideas about an institution or individual for the purpose of influencing opinion (p. 324)

periferia frontera externa de algo (p. 497)

perjurio mentir cuando uno ha jurado decir la verdad (pp. 548, 785)

*fenómeno persona, cosa o acontecimiento excepcional, inusual o anormal (p. 572)

filantropía proporcionar dinero para apoyar metas humanitarias o sociales (p. 232)

peregrino Separatista que viajó a las colonias americanas durante los años 1600 para libertad religiosa (p. 8)

veto indirecto vetar indirectamente un proyecto de ley permitiendo que una sesión del Congreso expire sin firmar el proyecto (p. 142)

polio abreviatura de poliomielitis, una enfermedad infecciosa aguda que afecta los músculos esqueléticos y a menudo provoca discapacidad y deformidad permanente (p. 422)

maquinaria política organización aliada con un partido político que a menudo controlaba el gobierno local (p. 227)

impuesto de capitación impuesto de cantidad fija por cada persona, el cual tenía que ser pagado antes de que una persona pudiera votar (p. 250)

consorcio grupo compartiendo una actividad; por ejemplo, dueños de ferrocarril que tomaban acuerdos secretos y fijaban tipos entre ellos mismos (p. 196)

soberanía popular teoría política de que el gobierno está sujeto a la voluntad del pueblo (p. 168); antes de la Guerra Civil, la idea de que la gente que vivía en un territorio tenía el derecho de decidir votando si ahí sería permitida la esclavitud (pp. 37, 107)

populismo movimiento político fundado en los años 1890 representando principalmente a los granjeros que favoreció libre acuñación de plata y el control gubernamental de ferrocarriles y otras industrias grandes (p. 242)

línea de pobreza nivel de ingreso individual o familiar bajo del cual uno es clasificado por el gobierno federal como pobre (p. 582)

*práctica es la realización de algo repetidamente hasta que se convierte en hábito (p. 187)

*previo que sucede antes de un acontecimiento (p. 162)

*procedimiento método particular de llevar a cabo una actividad o participar en ella (p. 821)

*prohibir cuando una autoridad dictamina que algo es ilegal (p. 466)

prohibición leyes que prohibían la manufactura, transportación y venta de bebidas alcohólicas (p. 299)

propaganda diseminación de ideas sobre una institución o individuo con el propósito de influenciar la opinión (p. 324)

Glossary/Glosario

Glossary/Glosario

English	Español
proprietary colony a colony owned by an individual (p. 11)	**colonia propietaria** colonia propiedad de un individuo (p. 11)
***prospective** to be likely to, or have intentions to, perform an act (p. 166)	***potencial** que hay probabilidades o se tienen intenciones de realizar una acción (p. 166)
protective tariff tax on imports designed to protect American manufacturers (p. 87)	**arancel protectora** impuesto en importaciones diseñado para proteger a los manufactureros americanos (p. 87)
protectorate a country that is technically independent but is actually under the control of another country (p. 262)	**protectorado** país que es técnicamente independiente pero que en realidad queda bajo el control de otro país (p. 262)
public works projects such as highways, parks, and libraries built with public funds for public use (p. 412)	**obras públicas** proyectos como carreteras, parques y bibliotecas construidos con fondos públicos para uso público (p. 412)
***publish** to make a document available to the general public (p. 233)	***publicar** hacer que un documento esté disponible para el público en general (p. 233)
***purchase** to gain by paying money or its equivalent (p. 474)	***comprar** adquirir algo pagando dinero o su equivalente (p. 474)

R

English	Español
racism prejudice or discrimination against someone because of his or her race (p. 642)	**racismo** prejuicio o discriminación en contra de alguien por su raza (p. 642)
***rationality** the quality or state of being agreeable to reason (p. 684)	***racionalidad** la cualidad o el estado de estar dispuesto a razonar (p. 684)
reapportionment the method states use to draw up political districts based on changes in population (p. 600)	**nueva repartición** método usado por los estados para formar distritos políticos basados en los cambios de población (p. 600)
recall the right that enables voters to remove unsatisfactory elected officials from office (p. 295)	**elección de revocación** derecho que permite a los votantes quitar del cargo a los oficiales elegidos que son inadecuados (p. 295)
***recovery** an economic upturn, as after a depression (p. 442)	***recuperación** repunte económico, como sucede después de una depresión (p. 442)
referendum the practice of letting voters accept or reject measures proposed by the legislature (p. 295)	**referéndum** práctica de permitir a los votantes aceptar o rechazar medidas propuestas por la legislatura (p. 295)
***refinement** the act or process of improving or perfecting (p. 775)	***refinamiento** acción o proceso de mejorar o perfeccionar (p. 775)
refugee someone leaving his or her country due to a "well-founded fear of persecution on account of race, religion, nationality, membership in a particular group, or political opinion." (p. 789)	**refugiado** persona que abandona su país debido a un "miedo fundado de persecución a causa de su raza, religión, nacionalidad, pertenencia a un grupo en particular u opinión política" (p. 789)
***regime** a form of government (p. 460)	***régimen** una forma de gobierno (p. 460)
***register** to file personal information in order to become eligible for an official event (p. 631)	***inscribirse** presentar información personal con el fin de ser elegible para un evento oficial (p. 631)
***regulate** to govern or direct according to rule (p. 302)	***regular** gobernar o dirigir según las normas (p. 302)
relief aid for the needy, welfare (p. 414)	**asistencia pública** ayuda para los necesitados; beneficencia (p. 414)
***relocate** to move to a new place (p. 170)	***trasladar** llevar a un nuevo lugar (p. 170)
***remove** to change the location or position (p. 607)	***quitar** cambiar la ubicación o posición (p. 607)

Glossary/Glosario

reparations payment by the losing country in a war to the winner for the damages caused by the war (p. 344)

indemnización pago hecho por el país perdedor de una guerra al país ganador por los daños causados por la guerra (p. 344)

repatriation being restored or returned to the country of origin, allegiance, or citizenship (p. 694)

repatriación acción de devolver o regresar a una persona a su país de origen, lealtad o ciudadanía (p. 694)

*resident one who lives in a place for some length of time (p. 790)

*residente que vive en un lugar durante algún tiempo (p. 790)

*resolution a formal expression of opinion, will, or intent voted by an official body or assembly (p. 106)

*resolución expresión formal de una opinión, deseo o intención votada por una asamblea u organismo oficial (p. 106)

*resolve to come to an agreement (pp. 342, 809)

*resolver llegar a un acuerdo (pp. 342, 809)

*resource material used in the production process, such as money, people, land, wood, or steel (p. 182)

*recurso material utilizado en el proceso de producción, como dinero, personas, tierra, madera o acero (p. 182)

*response something said or done as a reaction (p. 559)

*respuesta algo que se dice o hace en reacción a algo (p. 559)

*restraint the act of limiting, restricting, or keeping under control (p. 202)

*restricción acción de limitar, impedir o mantener bajo control (p. 202)

*retain to keep in possession (p. 767)

*retener conservar la posesión (p. 767)

*revelation an act of revealing to view or making known (p. 364)

*revelación acción de divulgar para hacer ver o conocer (p. 364)

revenue sharing federal tax money that is distributed among the states (p. 708)

participación en los ingresos dinero de los impuestos federales que se distribuye entre los estados (p. 708)

revenue tariff tax on imports for the purpose of raising money (p. 87)

arancel de ingresos impuesto en las importaciones con el propósito de recaudar dinero (p. 87)

*revise to make changes to an original document (pp. 39, 474)

*revisar realizar cambios a un documento original (pp. 39, 474)

right-to-work law a law making it illegal to require employees to join a union (p. 567)

derecho a trabajar ley que hace ilegal la demanda que los trabajadores se unan a un sindicato (p. 567)

rock 'n' roll popular music usually played on electronically amplified instruments and characterized by a persistent heavily accented beat, much repetition of simple phrases, and often country, folk, and blues elements (p. 577)

rock 'n' roll música popular que generalmente se toca con instrumentos amplificados electrónicamente y se caracteriza por un ritmo persistente y pesadamente acentuado, muchas repeticiones de frases simples y a menudo elementos del Country, Folk y Blues (p. 577)

safety net something that provides security against misfortune; specifically, government relief programs intended to protect against economic disaster (p. 445)

red de seguridad algo que proporciona seguridad en contra de desgracias, específicamente, programas de beneficencia gubernamentales para proteger en contra del desastre económico (p. 445)

satellite nations nations politically and economically dominated or controlled by another more powerful country (p. 537)

países satélite naciones política y económicamente dominadas o controladas por otro país más poderoso (p. 537)

scalawag name given to Southerners who supported Republican Reconstruction of the South (p. 145)

scalawag nombre dado a los sureños que apoyaron la Reconstrucción republicana del Sur (p. 145)

secede to leave or withdraw (p. 97)

separarse abandonar o retirar (p. 97)

secession withdrawal from the Union (p. 108)

secesión retiro de la Unión (p. 108)

segregation the separation or isolation of a race, class, or group (p. 250)

segregación separación o aislamiento de una raza, clase o grupo (p. 250)

Glossary/Glosario

Glossary/Glosario

English | Español

separate-but-equal doctrine established by the 1896 Supreme Court case *Plessy* v. *Ferguson* that permitted laws segregating African Americans as long as equal facilities were provided (p. 622)

separados pero iguales doctrina establecida por la Suprema Corte en el caso *Plessy* contra *Ferguson* en 1896 que las leyes que segregaron a los afroamericanos fueron permitidas si facilidades iguales fueron proporcionadas (p. 622)

separation of powers government principle in which power is divided among different branches (p. 38)

separación de poderes principio de gobierno en el cual el poder está dividido entre diferentes ramos (p. 38)

*series a number of events that come one after another (p. 412)

*serie acontecimientos que suceden uno después de otro (p. 412)

settlement house institution located in a poor neighborhood that provided numerous community services such as medical care, child care, libraries, and classes in English (p. 239)

casa de beneficencia institución establecida en una vecindad pobre que proveía numerosos servicios comunitarios tal como cuidado médico, cuidado de niños, bibliotecas, e instrucción en inglés (p. 239)

sharecropper farmer who works land for an owner who provides equipment and seed and receives a share of the crop (p. 149)

aparcero agricultor que labra la tierra para un dueño que proporciona equipo y semillas y recibe una porción de la cosecha (p. 149)

siege a military blockade of a city or fortified place to force it to surrender (p. 134)

sitio bloqueo militar de una ciudad o un recinto fortificado para forzarlo a rendirse (p. 134)

*significantly to affect something enough to be of some importance (p. 818)

*considerablemente afectar algo lo suficiente como para que sea de importancia (p. 818)

sit-down strike method of boycotting work by sitting down at work and refusing to leave the establishment (p. 438)

huelga de brazos caídos método de boicotear el trabajo por medio de sentarse en el lugar de trabajo y de rehusar a abandonar el establecimiento (p. 438)

sit-in a form of protest involving occupying seats or sitting down on the floor of an establishment (p. 624)

plantón forma de protesta ocupando las sillas o sentándose en el piso de un establecimiento (p. 624)

skyscraper a very tall building (p. 222)

rascacielos edificio de gran altura (p. 222)

slave code a set of laws that formally regulated slavery and defined the relationship between enslaved Africans and free people (p. 18)

código de esclavos leyes aprobadas que regularon formalmente la esclavitud y definieron la relación entre los africanos esclavizados y la gente libre (p. 18)

smog fog made heavier and darker by smoke and chemical fumes (p. 731)

smog niebla hecha más pesada y oscura por el humo y vapores químicos (p. 731)

soap opera a serial drama on television or radio using melodramatic situations (p. 409)

novela drama en serie de radio o televisión utilizando situaciones melodramáticas (p. 409)

Social Darwinism based on Charles Darwin's theories of evolution and natural selection, states that humans have developed through competition and natural selection with only the strongest surviving (pp. 231, 300)

Darwinismo social se basa en las teorías de evolución y de selección natural de Charles Darwin y expresa que los humanos han evolucionado a través de la competencia y de la selección natural, donde sólo sobrevive el más fuerte (pp. 231, 300)

sodbuster a name given to Great Plains farmers (p. 168)

rompeterrón nombre dado a los granjeros de las Grandes Planicies (p. 168)

*source the point at which something is provided (p. 378)

*fuente punto en el que se proporciona algo (p. 378)

space race refers to the Cold War competition over dominance of space exploration capability (p. 604)

carrera espacial se refiere a la competencia durante la Guerra Fría sobre el dominio de la exploración espacial (p. 604)

speakeasy a place where alcoholic beverages are sold illegally (p. 381)

speakeasy lugar donde son vendidas clandestinamente bebidas alcohólicas (p. 381)

special prosecutor a lawyer from outside the government appointed by an attorney general or Congress to investigate a government official for misconduct while in office (p. 716)

speculation act of buying stocks at great risk with the anticipation that the price will rise (p. 401)

sphere of influence section of a country where one foreign nation enjoys special rights and powers (p. 276)

spoils system practice of handing out government jobs to supporters; replacing government employees with the winning candidate's supporters (p. 97)

*stability a state of peace, free from social unrest (p. 745)

stagflation persistent inflation combined with stagnant consumer demand and relatively high unemployment (p. 719)

state-sponsored terrorism violent acts against civilians that are secretly supported by a government in order to attack other nations without going to war (p. 811)

steerage cramped quarters on a ship's lower decks for passengers paying the lowest fares (p. 215)

stock money or capital invested or available for investment or trading (p. 194)

stock market a system for buying and selling stocks in corporations (p. 400)

*strategic necessary to or important in the initiation, conduct, or completion of a military plan (p. 657)

strategic defense a plan to develop missiles and other devices that can shoot down nuclear missiles before they hit the United States (p. 807)

strategic materials materials needed for fighting a war (p. 478)

*strategy a plan or method for achieving a goal (p. 244)

*subsidy money granted by the government to achieve a specific goal that is beneficial to society (p. 614)

subversion a systematic attempt to overthrow a government by using persons working secretly from within (p. 546)

*sufficient enough, adequate (p. 127)

suffrage the right to vote (p. 296)

*sum a specified amount of money (p. 403)

summit a meeting of heads of government (p. 711)

Sunbelt a new industrial region in southern California and the Deep South developing during World War II (p. 502)

fiscal especial un abogado externo al gobierno nombrado por un procurador general o congreso para investigar a un funcionario del gobierno por mala conducta durante sus funciones (p. 716)

especulación acciones compradas con alto riesgo con la anticipación que los precios subirán (p. 401)

esfera de influencia sección de un país donde una nación extranjera tiene derechos y poderes especiales (p. 276)

sistema de despojos práctica de dar puestos gubernamentales a los partidarios; reemplazando a los empleados del gobierno con los partidarios del candidato victorioso (p. 97)

*estabilidad estado de paz, libre de inquietud social (p. 745)

stagflación inflación persistente combinado con la demanda estancada y una taza de desempleo alta (p. 719)

terrorismo patrocinado por el estado actos violentos en contra de civiles que son secretamente apoyados por un gobierno con el motivo de atacar a otras naciones sin entrar en la guerra (p. 811)

tercera clase cuarteles apretados de las cubiertas bajas de un barco para los pasajeros que pagan los pasajes más bajos (p. 215)

reserva dinero o capital invertido o disponible para inversiones u operaciones comerciales (p. 194)

bolsa de valores sistema para comprar y vender acciones de corporaciones (p. 400)

*estratégico necesario o importante para iniciar, realizar o completar un plan militar (p. 657)

defensa estratégica plan para desarrollar proyectiles y otras armas que pueden derribar proyectiles nucleares antes de que estos golpeen en Estados Unidos (p. 807)

materiales estratégicos materiales necesarios para una guerra (p. 478)

*estrategia plan o método para alcanzar una meta (p. 244)

*subsidio dinero que otorga el gobierno para alcanzar una meta específica que beneficia a la sociedad (p. 614)

subversión intento sistemático para derrocar un gobierno utilizando personas que trabajan secretamente desde adentro (p. 546)

*suficiente bastante, adecuado (p. 127)

sufragio derecho al voto (p. 296)

*suma cantidad específica de dinero (p. 403)

cumbre junta de jefes de gobiernos (p. 711)

Región Solada nueva región industrial en el sur de California y el Bajo Sur que se desarrolló durante la Segunda Guerra Mundial (p. 502)

Glossary/Glosario

Glossary/Glosario

English	**Español**
supply-side economics economic theory that lower taxes will boost the economy as businesses and individuals invest their money, thereby creating higher tax revenue (pp. 365, 748)	**economía de oferta teoría** económica de que los impuestos bajos levantarían la economía invirtiendo su dinero los negocios y los individuos, así creando un alto ingreso del impuesto (pp. 365, 748)
***suspend** to temporarily stop an operation (p. 406)	***suspender** detener temporalmente una operación (p. 406)
***symbolize** to represent, express, or identify by a symbol (p. 390)	***simbolizar** representar, expresar o identificar por medio de un símbolo (p. 390)

T

English	**Español**
***target** something or someone fired on or marked for attack (p. 498)	***objetivo** algo o alguien a quien se dispara o a quien se marca para atacar (p. 498)
teach-in an extended meeting or class held to discuss a social or political issue (p. 665)	**plantón educacional** junta o clase extendida para discutir un asunto político o social (p. 665)
***technique** a method of achieving a desired task (p. 409)	***técnica** método para lograr una tarea determinada (p. 409)
telecommute to work at home by means of an electronic linkup with a central office (p. 775)	**viajar electrónicamente** trabajar en casa por medio de conexión electrónica con una oficina central (p. 775)
televangelist an evangelist who conducts regularly televised religious programs (p. 745)	**televangelista** evangelista que transmite regularmente programas evangélicos por televisión (p. 745)
temperance moderation in or abstinence from alcohol (p. 100)	**templanza** moderación o abstinencia del uso del alcohol (p. 100)
tenement multifamily apartments, usually dark, crowded, and barely meeting minimum living standards (p. 225)	**casa de vecindad** apartamentos para varias familias, normalmente obscuros, apretados que apenas cumplen con los estándares mínimos de viviendas (p. 225)
termination policy a government policy to bring Native Americans into mainstream society by withdrawing recognition of Native American groups as legal entities (p. 585)	**política de terminación** política gubernamental para traer a los Nativos Americanos dentro de la sociedad principal retirando el reconocimiento de los grupos Nativos Americanos como entidades legales (p. 585)
terrorism the use of violence by nongovernmental groups against civilians to achieve a political goal by instilling fear and frightening governments into changing policies (p. 810)	**terrorismo** el uso de violencia por grupos no del gobierno en contra de civiles para alcanzar una meta política impartiendo miedo y amenazando gobiernos para que cambien su política (p. 810)
***theory** a hypothesis meant for argument or investigation (p. 719)	***teoría** hipótesis pensada para un argumento o investigación (p. 719)
time zone a geographical region in which the same standard time is kept (p. 191)	**huso horario** región geográfica en la cual la misma norma horaria es mantenida (p. 191)
trade union an organization of workers with the same trade or skill (p. 201)	**gremio** organización de trabajadores con el mismo oficio o destreza (p. 201)
***traditional** relating to cultural continuity in social attitudes, customs, and institutions (p. 657)	***tradicional** relativo a la continuidad cultural en las actitudes sociales, costumbres e instituciones (p. 657)
***transport** to convey from one place to another (p. 465)	***transportar** llevar de un lugar a otro (p. 465)
***transportation** method of travel from one place to another (p. 86)	***transporte** método para viajar de un lugar a otro (p. 86)

triangular trade a three-way trade route that exchanged goods between the American colonies and two other trading partners (p. 16)

comercio triangular una ruta comercial de tres ramas para intercambiar productos entre las colonias americanas y otros dos asociados comerciales (p. 16)

*trigger to cause an action that causes a greater reaction (p. 227)

*desencadenar provocar una acción que desencadena una reacción mayor (p. 227)

trust a combination of firms or corporations formed by a legal agreement, especially to reduce competition (p. 198)

cártel combinación de empresas o sociedades anónimas formada por acuerdo legal, especialmente para reducir la competición (p. 198)

*unconstitutional not in accordance with or authorized by the constitution of a state or society (p. 312)

*inconstitucional que no está de acuerdo con la constitución de un estado o sociedad o no posee la autorización de ésta (p. 312)

unfair trade practices trading practices which derive a gain at the expense of the competition (p. 311)

prácticas comerciales injustas prácticas comerciales que ganan el beneficio perjudicando a la competencia (p. 311)

*unify to bring a group together with a similar goal or thought pattern (p. 385)

*unificar juntar a un grupo con un objetivo o patrones de pensamiento similares (p. 385)

union shop a business that requires employees to join a union (p. 567)

taller sindicalizado comercio que requiere que los trabajadores se unan al sindicato (p. 567)

*unresolved not cleared up, understandable, or dealt with successfully (p. 675)

*no resuelto no esclarecido, no comprensible o tratado con éxito (p. 675)

urban renewal government programs that attempt to eliminate poverty and revitalize urban areas (p. 583)

renovación urbana programas gubernamentales que intentan eliminar la pobreza y revitalizar las áreas urbanas (p. 583)

*vehicle a means of carrying or transporting something (p. 489)

*vehículo medio para llevar o transportar algo (p. 489)

vertical integration the combining of companies that supply equipment and services needed for a particular industry (p. 197)

integración vertical asociación de compañías que abastecen equipo y servicios necesarios a una industria particular (p. 197)

veto power of the chief executive to reject laws passed by the legislature (p. 38)

veto poder del jefe del ejecutivo de rechazar leyes aprobadas por la legislatura (p. 38)

*via to have come by or through (p. 756)

*vía haber llegado mediante o a través de (p. 756)

victory garden gardens planted by American citizens during war to raise vegetables for home use, leaving more for the troops (pp. 328, 507)

huerto de victoria huertos plantados por ciudadanos americanos durante la guerra para cultivar vegetales para usar en casa así dejando más para las tropas (pp. 328, 507)

victory suit a men's suit with no vest, no cuffs, a short jacket, and narrow lapels, worn during World War II in order to save fabric for the war effort (p. 504)

victory suit traje de hombre sin chaleco ni puños, con una chaqueta corta y solapas angostas que se vestía durante la Segunda Guerra Mundial para ahorrar tela para la guerra (p. 504)

Vietnamization the process of making South Vietnam assume more of the war effort by slowly withdrawing American troops from Vietnam (p. 670)

vietnamización el proceso de hacer que el Vietnam del Sur asumiera más de los esfuerzos de la guerra sacando poco a poco a las tropas americanas de Vietnam (p. 670)

vigilance committee group of ordinary citizens formed by local law enforcement officers and tasked with finding criminals and bringing them to justice (p. 159)

comité de vigilancia grupo de ciudadanos comunes formado por funcionarios locales encargados del cumplimiento de la ley, que deben encontrar criminales y ponerlos a disposición de la justicia (p. 159)

Glossary/Glosario

Glossary/Glosario

English	**Español**
*violation the disregard or breaking of the law (p. 460)	*violación ignorar o quebrantar la ley (p. 460)
*virtually almost entirely, nearly (p. 471)	*prácticamente casi por completo, por poco (p. 471)
*visible what can be seen (p. 751)	*visible lo que puede verse (p. 751)

W

English	**Español**
war on poverty antipoverty program under President Lyndon Johnson (p. 611)	guerra contra la pobreza programa anti-pobreza bajo el Presidente Lyndon Johnson (p. 611)
weapons of mass destruction (WMD) weapons, including nuclear, chemical, and biological, that can kill large numbers of people all at once (p. 816)	armas de destrucción masiva (ADM) armas, incluidas las nucleares, químicas y biológicas, que pueden matar una gran cantidad de personas a la vez (p. 816)
*welfare aid in the form of money or necessities for those in need, especially disadvantaged social groups (p. 708)	*asistencia social ayuda en forma de dinero o necesidades para los necesitados; grupos sociales que se encuentran especialmente en desventaja (p. 708)
welfare capitalism system in which companies enable employees to buy stock, participate in profit sharing, and receive benefits such as medical care common in the 1920s (p. 374)	capitalismo de beneficencia sistema en el cual las compañías permiten a los trabajadores comprar acciones, compartir las ganancias, y recibir beneficios tal como atención médica, común en los años 1920 (p. 374)
white-collar jobs jobs in fields not requiring work clothes or protective clothing, such as sales (p. 574)	collar blanco trabajos trabajos que no requieren ropa de protección o de trabajo, asi como los vendedores (p. 574)
*widespread having influence on or affecting a large group; widely diffused or prevalent (p. 349)	*generalizar influir sobre algo/alguien o afectar a un grupo numeroso (p. 349)

Y

English	**Español**
yellow journalism type of sensational, biased, and often false reporting for the sake of attracting readers (p. 269)	periodismo amarillista tipo de reportaje sensacional, tendencioso, y a menudo falso con el propósito de atraer a los lectores (p. 269)
yuppie a young college-educated adult who is employed in a well-paying profession and who lives and works in or near a large city (p. 754)	yuppie adulto joven educado en la universidad empleado en una profesión de buen salario y que vive y trabaja en o cerca de una ciudad grande (p. 754)

Z

English	**Español**
zoot suit men's clothing of extreme cut typically consisting of a thigh-length jacket with wide padded shoulders and peg pants with narrow cuffs (p. 504)	zoot suit vestimenta de hombre de corte extremo que consiste típicamente de una chaqueta a la altura de los muslos con hombreras anchas y pantalón pirata con bocamanga angosta (p. 504)

Index

Italicized page numbers refer to illustrations. The following abbreviations are used in the index:
m = map; c = chart; p = photograph or picture; g = graph; crt = cartoon; ptg = painting; q = quote

Index

Index

Index

Index

Index

Johnson, Claudia "Lady Bird," 610

Johnson, Doug, q675

Johnson, Hugh, 429

Johnson, James Weldon, 350

Johnson, Lyndon B., p608; Civil Rights Act (1957), 629; civil rights movement and, 636–37, 639; economy and, 718; election of 1968, q668; Kerner Commission and, 643–44; presidency of, 607, 608, 610–15; Vietnam and, 658–59, q658

Johnson, Robert, 756

joint-stock companies, 8

Joliet, Louis, 8

Jones, Bobby, 385

Jones, Mary Harris "Mother," 207, 306

Joplin, Scott, 233

Joseph, Chief, 174, q174

journalism, 269, 293

judicial branch, 37, 38, 39, 78, 82, 750. See also Supreme Court, U.S.

judicial nationalism, 88

judicial review, Supreme Court and, 82–83

judicial system, American colonies and, 25

Judiciary Act (1789), 78

Jungle, The (Sinclair), 302, q302

Justice Department, civil rights movement and, 634

juvenile delinquency, 504, 587

Kaiser, Henry, 489

kamikaze attacks, 515

Kansas, 248–49

Kansas-Nebraska Act, 111

Karzai, Hamid, 814, p815

Kasserine Pass, Battle of, 498

Kearney, Denis, 219

Keating-Owen Child Labor Act (1916), 312

Kelley, Oliver H., 243

Kellogg, Frank, 367

Kellogg-Briand Pact, 367

Kelly Act (1925), 372

Kemp, Jack, 784

Kennan, George F., p535, q535, 538, 658, p659, q659, 664

Kennecott Copper Mine, 161

Kennedy, Anthony, 750

Kennedy, Jacqueline, 610

Kennedy, John F., p594–95, p597, p603, q603, p608, q636; civil rights movement and, 633–34, 635; Cold War and, 602–7; election of 1960, 596–97; Vietnam and, 657; women's rights and, 687

Kennedy, Robert F., 633, 634, 668, p668

Kent State University, p671

Kentucky, 126, 131

Kerner, Otto, 643

Kerner Commission, 643–44

Kerouac, Jack, 579

Kerry, John, 820

Key, Francis Scott, 83

Keynes, John Maynard, 442

Khrushchev, Nikita, 558, p558, 559, 605, 607, 634

King, Coretta Scott, p638

King, Henry, q248–49

King, Martin Luther, Jr., q608, p620–21, q626, p627, p637; Birmingham protests and, 635, q635; death of, 647; economic rights and, 644; March on Selma, p638; March on Washington, 636; Montgomery bus boycott, 626–27; Robert Kennedy and, 633; Vietnam War and, q666

King, Rodney, q778

King Philip's War, 11

Kings Mountain, Battle of, 29

Kissinger, Henry, 670, p671, 672, 709, p709, 710, 711, 720

Kitty Hawk, USS, 278, p279

Kleindienst, Richard, 707

Knights of Labor, 204

Know-Nothing Party, 91, 111

Knox, Frank, 486

Korea, 276

Korean War, 542–45, m542–43, crt544, 555, 556, 570, 655

Korematsu, Fred, 504

Korematsu v. United States (1944), 504, 505, q505

Kosovo, 787

Kristallnacht, 467–68, p467, q467

Ku Klux Klan, 147, 377, p377, 633

Kurds, the, 787, 817, 827

Kuwait, 765

Kyoto Protocol, 797

labor laws, 298–99

laborors, common, 200

labor unions, 92, 200–207, 208, 298, 301; in the 1920s, 374; in the 1950s, 566–67; Clayton Antitrust Act (1914), 311; communism and, 548; immigration and, 218; Kennedy and, 598; membership, g202; the New Deal and, 429, 437–39, g438; populism and, 245; post-World War I, 346–47; United Farm Workers, 697; World War I and, 329; World War II and, 506

Lafayette, Marquis de, 339, 340

La Follette, Robert M., 294, q295

La Follette, Robert M., Jr., 549

laissez-faire economics, 186–87, 231

Lakota Sioux people, 171–72, 173–74

Lamont, Thomas W., 325

land grants, to railroads, m191, 192

Landon, Alfred, 441

land ownership, 13, 88, 164–65

Lange, Dorothea, 409

Langley, Samuel, 370–71

languages: bilingualism, 697; Native American, 6

Lanham Act (1940), 503

Lansing, Robert, 324, p325, q325

Laos, 656, 661

La Raza Unida (the United People), 697

La Salle, René-Robert Cavalier de, 8

Las Gorras Blancas, 165

Last Spike Ceremony, p189, 190

Latimer, Lewis, 184

Latin America: Cold War and, 602–3; debts, national and, 280; Jimmy Carter and, 723; Monroe Doctrine, 88; Panama Canal and, 280; U.S. diplomacy and, 267, 281–82, m281; U.S. investment in, g281

Latino Americans. See Hispanic Americans

law enforcement, 782. See also crime

Lawrence strike, c205, 207

Lawson, James M., Jr., q640

League of Nations, 343, 345, 366

League of United Latin American Citizens (LULAC), 695

Leahy, William, p523, q523

leaseholds, 276–77

Lecompton constitution, 113

Le Duc Tho, 670, p671, 672

Lee, Richard Henry, 41

Lee, Robert E., 113, 126, 132, 133, 134–35, 136, p136, 137, 138–139

Legal Tender Act, 127

legislative branch, 37, 38–39. See also Congress, U.S.

LeMay, Curtis, 521

Lend-Lease Act, 476, 478

Lenin, Vladimir, 339, 455

Letter from Birmingham Jail (King), 635, q635

letters of marque, 29

Levitt, Bill, 572

Levittown, New York, 572–73, p573

Lewis, Anthony, q601

Lewis, John, 631, 639

Lewis, John L., 438

Lewis, Sinclair, 384

Lewis and Clark expedition, p82

Lexington and Concord, Battles of, 26

Leyte Gulf, Battle of, 515

liberalism, 740–41, crt741

Liberator, The (newspaper), 102–3

Liberty Bonds, 329, c329

Liberty Party, 106, 108

Liberty ships, p488, 489, q489

Liddy, G. Gordon, p713

Lieberman, Joseph, 804

lightbulb, p184

Liliuokalani, Queen of Hawaii, 266, p266

limited war, 545

Lincoln, Abraham, p132, p135, p141; assassination of, 137;

Index

Index

Index

Index

Index

Index

Acknowledgments and Photo Credits

TEXT AND ART

317 From *The Century* by Peter Jennings, copyright © 1998 by ABC Television Network Group, a division of Capitol Cities, Inc. Used by permission of Doubleday, a division of Random House, Inc. 383 Reprinted with the permission of Scribner, an imprint of Simon & Schuster Adult Publishing Group, from *The Great Gatsby* by F. Scott Fitzgerald. Copyright 1925 by Charles Scribner's Sons. Copyright renewed 1953 by Frances Scott Fitzgerald Lanahan. 383 Excerpt from Part I of "The Hollow Men" in *Collected Poems 1909-1962* by T.S. Eliot, copyright 1936 by Harcourt, Inc., and renewed 1964 by T.S. Eliot, reprinted by permission of the publisher. 389 Excerpt from *Dust Tracks on a Road* by Zora Neale Hurston. Copyright 1942 by Zora Neale Hurston, renewed © 1970 by John C. Hurston. Reprinted by permission of HarperCollins Publishers. 389 "If we must die" by Claude McKay, courtesy of the Literary Representative for the Works of Claude McKay, Schomburg Center for Research in Black Culture, The New York Public Library, Astor, Lennox and Tilden Foundations. 389 "I, Too" from *The Collected Poems of Langston Hughes* by Langston Hughes, edited by Arnold Rampersad with David Roessel, Associate Editor, copyright © 1994 by The Estate of Langston Hughes. Used by permission of Alfred A. Knopf, a division of Random House, Inc. 402 From *1929: the Year of the Great Crash* by William K. Klingman. Copyright © 1989 by William K. Klingman. Reprinted by permission of HarperCollins Publishers. 409 Excerpt from *Dust to Eat: Drought and Depression in the 1930s* by Michael L. Cooper. Copyright © 2004 by Michael L. Cooper. Reprinted by permission of Clarion Books, an imprint of Houghton Mifflin Company. All rights reserved. 432 "Gardiner C. Means" and "Raymond Moley" from *Hard Times* by Studs Terkel. Copyright © 1970, 1986 by Studs Terkel. Reprinted by permission of Donadio & Olson, Inc. 449 Excerpt from *The Autobiography of Eleanor Roosevelt* by Eleanor Roosevelt. Copyright 1937, 1949, © 1958, 1961 by Anna Eleanor Roosevelt. Copyright © 1958 by Curtis Publishing Company. Reprinted by permission of HarperCollins Publishers. 467 from "Kristallnacht" by Frederic Morton. *The New York Times*, November 10, 1978. Copyright © 1978 The New York Times Company. Reprinted by permission. 473 "Luther D. Fletcher" from *World War II: From the Battle Front to the Home Front, Arkansans Tell Their Stories*, copyright © 1995 by Kay B. Hall. Reprinted by permission of the University of Arkansas Press. 619 "John Rath, 61" from *Division Street* by Studs Terkel. Copyright © 1967 by Studs Terkel. Reprinted by permission of Donadio & Olson, Inc. 635 637 Reprinted by arrangement with The Heirs to the Estate of Martin Luther King Jr., c/o Writers house as agent for the proprietor New York, NY. Copyright 1963 Martin Luther King, Jr.; copyright renewed 1991 Coretta Scott King. 641 From *Coming of Age in Mississippi* by Anne Moody, copyright © 1968 by Anne Moody. Used by permission of Doubleday, a division of Random House, Inc. 645 Copyright © 1971 by Merlin House, Inc./Seaver Books. Reprinted from *The End of White World Supremacy* by Malcolm X, edited by Imam Benjamin Karim. Published by Seaver Books, New York, New York. 684 from "The Times They Are A-Changin'" by Bob Dylan. Copyright © 1963; renewed 1991 Special Rider Music. All rights reserved. International copyright secured. Reprinted by permission. 687 From The Feminine Mystique by Betty Friedan. Copyright © 1983, 1974, 1973, 1963 by Betty Friedan. Used by permission of W.W. Norton & Company, Inc. 793 "The Tortilla Curtain", from *New Americans: An Oral History* by Al Santoli, copyright © 1988 by Al Santoli. Used by permission of Viking Penguin, a division of Penguin Group (USA) Inc. 801 from "A Grim Picture" by Tim Radford. *The Guardian*, November, 15, 2000. Copyright Guardian News & Media Ltd, 2000. Reprinted by permission. R7 From "Why I'm Not Running for President" by Gloria Steinem, from the July 20, 1992 issue of *The Nation*. Reprinted by permission. For subscription information call 1-800-333-8536. Portions of each week's Nation magazine can be accessed at http://www.thenation.com. R74 "The Camera Eye (50)" from *The Big Money*, copyright 1933, 1934, 1935, 1936 and © renewed 1963, 1964 by John Dos Passos. Reprinted by permission of Lucy Dos Passos Coggin. R77 "Part Four – 1" from *On the Road* by Jack Kerouac, copyright © 1955, 1957 by Jack Kerouac; renewed © 1983 by Stella Kerouac, renewed © 1985 by Stella Kerouac and Jan Kerouac. Used by permission of Viking Penguin, a division of Penguin Group (USA) Inc. R80 From *On the Pulse of Morning* by Maya Angelou, copyright © 1993 by Maya Angelou. Used by permission of Random House, Inc.

Glencoe would like to acknowledge the artists and agencies that participated in illustrating this program: American Artists Reps Inc.; Deborah Wolfe Ltd/illustrationOnLine.com; GeoNova LLC.

PHOTO CREDITS

Abbreviation Key: BC: Bettmann/CORBIS; GI: Getty Images; LOC: Library of Congress

Cover (tl)BC, (tc)Bob Adelman/Magnum Photos, (tr)David Turnley/CORBIS, (cl)Catherine Karnow/CORBIS, (c cr) GI, (b)Fine Art Photographic Library, London/Art Resource, NY; vi (t)Boltin Picture Library/Bridgeman Art Library, (b)Painting by Don Troiani, www.historicalartprints.com; vii (t)Lowell Georgia/CORBIS, (c)William Henry Jackson/Cardoza Fine Art Gallery, (b)CORBIS; viii (t)Nagasaki Museum of History and Culture, (c)The Granger Collection, New York, (b)CORBIS; ix (t)Howard A. Thain/Collection of the New York Historical Society/Bridgeman Art Library, (c)Roger-Viollet/Topham/The Image Works, (b)BC; x (t)Mary Evans Picture Library, (c)BC, (b)SuperStock; xi (t)Wally McNamee/CORBIS, (c) Bob Adelman/Magnum Photos, (b)Larry Burrows/Time Life Pictures/GI; xii (t)Eli Reed/Magnum Photos, (c)The White House/Handout/GI, (b)Brooks Kraft/CORBIS; xxiii GI; xxiv (b)Pierce Rafferty/Petrified Collection/GI, (bkgd)Owaki/Kulla/CORBIS; xxv (t)Dynamic Graphics Group/Creatas/Alamy Images, (b)Eric Foltz/iStockphoto; A20 (t)ThinkStock/SuperStock, (cl)Janet Foster/Masterfile, (cr)Mark Tomalty/Masterfile, (bl)Jurgen Freund/Nature Picture Library, (br)age fotostock/SuperStock; GH2 BananaStock/PictureQuest; GH16-1 Boltin Picture Library/Bridgeman Art Library; 2 Galleria degli Uffizi, Florence/Bridgeman Art Library; 2-3 SuperStock; 3 Michael Nicholson/CORBIS; 5 (tl)George Catlin/GI, (tr bl) The Granger Collection, New York, (br)Photograph courtesy of the Schwarz Gallery, Philadelphia; 7 (inset) The Granger Collection, New York, (bkgd)The City of Plainfield, NJ; 9 (tl)Sheffield Galleries and Museums Trust, UK/Bridgeman Art Library, (tr)Adam Woolfitt/Robert Harding World Imagery/CORBIS, (b)National Maritime Museum, London; 10 (l)Kean Collection/GI, (r)Schlesinger Library, Radcliffe Institute, Harvard University/Bridgeman Art Library; 14 (t)CORBIS, (c)PunchStock, (bl)C Squared Studios/GI, (br)Iconotec/Alamy Images; 15 (l to r, t to b) GI, (2 13)LOC, LC-USZ62-242, (3)Ingram Publishing/Alamy Images, (4)Brand X Pictures/PunchStock, (5)Artville/GI, (6)Alan and Sandy Carey/GI, (7)Dynamic Graphics Group/IT Stock Free/Alamy Images, (8)PunchStock, (9)PhotoAlto/GI, (10)CORBIS, (11)GI, (12) C Squared Studios/GI, (14)Creativ Studio Heinemann/GI, (15)Alamy Images, (16)Image Source Pink/GI; 18 The Granger Collection, New York; 19 (l)Ariadne Van Zandbergen/GI, (r)Bridgeman Art Library; 20 GI; 23 (l)LOC, LC-USZC4-5315, (r)LOC; 24 25 BC; 27 (l)National Portrait Gallery/SuperStock, (r)The Granger Collection, New York; 28 35 The Granger Collection, New York; 42 (t)Erich Lessing/Art Resource, NY, (c)SuperStock, (b)The Granger Collection, New York; 45 American Antiquarian Society; 47 Comstock/PunchStock; 51 53 Brooks Kraft/CORBIS; 57 John Aikins/CORBIS; 76-77 akg-images; 81 BC; 82 The Granger Collection, New York; 87 The Landis Valley Museum; 89 The Granger Collection, New York; 90 (l)BC, (r)Underwood & Underwood/CORBIS; 91 (l)Eric Long/National Museum of American History, Smithsonian Institution, (c)The Granger Collection, New York, (r)courtesy of the National Museum of American History, Washington, D.C.; 96 The Granger Collection, New York; 97 (inset)Gary I. Rothstein/Reuters/CORBIS, (bkgd)Monika Graff/The Image Works; 98 SuperStock; 101 Art Archive/Culver Pictures/Napoleon Sarony; 102 (tl)BC, (tc tr) The Granger Collection, New York, (b)Collection of J. Paul Getty Museum; 105 Bridgeman Art Library; 106 LOC; 108 (l)California State Library, Sacramento, (r)LOC; 108-109 The Granger Collection, New York; 109 (t)Bridgeman Art Library, (b)The Granger Collection, New York; 110 (l)Syracuse Newspapers/Dick Blume/The Image Works, (r)BC; 112 Currier and Ives/LOC; 114 The New York Public Library; 115 (t)BC, (b)Missouri Historical Society, St. Louis; 116 (t)American Textile History Museum, Lowell, MA, (cl cr) BC, (b)Picture History; 119 The New York Historical Society; 120 (l)Museum of the Confederacy, (r)LOC, (LC-DIG-cwpb-06233); 120-121 Minnesota Historical Society/CORBIS; 123 Museum of American Political Life/Photo by Steve Laschever; 124 (tl)BC, (tr b) The Granger Collection, New York; 125 (tl)Henry Horner Lincoln Collection, (tr)Art Archive/Culver Pictures, (b)Bridgeman Art Library; 127 (l)Medford Historical Society Collection/CORBIS; (r)BC; 128 (tl)Collection of David & Kevin Kyle, (tc)Military & Historical Image Bank/Don Troiani, (tr)Medford Historical Society Collection/CORBIS, (b)War Department/National Archives/Time Life Pictures/GI; 131 LOC; 132 (tl)LOC, (tr b)BC; 134 BC; 135 CORBIS; 136 (l)BC, (r)The Granger Collection, New York; 141 (t)CORBIS, (cl)Art

Archive/National Archives Washington, DC, (cr b) LOC; **143** (tl)Flip Schulke/CORBIS, (tc)Flip Schulke/Black Star, (tr)AP Images, (bl br)BC; **146** The Granger Collection, New York; **148** CORBIS; **150** (tl)The Granger Collection, New York, (tr)Bridgeman Art Library, (cl)CORBIS, (cr)Kunstler Enterprises, Ltd, (bl)LOC, LC-USZC4-1519, (br)Picture History; **153** LOC, **154-155** William Henry Jackson/Cardoza Fine Art Gallery; **156** The Granger Collection, New York; **156-157** Lowell Georgia/CORBIS; **160** LOC, LC-USZ62-9889; **161** (t)Calvin Larsen/Photo Researchers, (b)Scott T. Smith/CORBIS; **162-163** BC; **164** (l)Art Archive/Bill Manns, (r)GI; **167** Minnesota Historical Society/CORBIS; **168** (l)State Historical Society of Wisconsin, (r)akg-images; **173** (l)GI, (r)CORBIS; **174** (l)CORBIS, (r)The Granger Collection, New York; **176** (t b) The Granger Collection, New York, (c)CORBIS; **180** National Railway Museum/Science & Society Museum; **180-181** LOC, LC-USZ62-77541; **184** (t)Mary Evans Picture Library, (bl)The Granger Collection, New York, (bcl)Time Life Pictures/GI, (bcr)BC, (br)Schenectady Museum; Hall of Electrical History Foundation/CORBIS; **185** (tl)BC, (tr)Mary Evans Picture Library, (b)George Eastman House; **186** (l)LOC, LC-USZ62-99122, (r)LOC, LC-USZ62-99407; **189** (tl)Union Pacific Museum, (tr) Private Collection, Peter Newark American Pictures/Bridgeman Art Library, (bl)GI, (bc)Union Pacific Museum, (br)BC; **192** GI; **195** BC; **198** (l)SuperStock, (r)CORBIS; **201** (l tr)CORBIS, (br)Hulton Archive/GI; **206** CORBIS; **208** (l)Union Pacific Museum, (c)CORBIS, (b)Hulton Archive/GI; **211** Stock Montage/Hulton Archive/GI; **212-213** CORBIS; **213** (t)Shore Line Trolley Museum Library, Sprague Collection, (b)London Stereoscopic Company/GI; **216** (l)Michael Maslan Historic Photographs/CORBIS, (tr)Art Archive/ Culver Pictures, (br)The Granger Collection, New York; **218** The Granger Collection, New York; **220** (t)Picture Research Consultants, (b)Brown Brothers Sterling, PA; **221** OSU Cartoon Research Library; **223** (tl)CORBIS, (tr)Museum of the City of New York/CORBIS, (b)LOC, LC-USZ-54088; **224** Hulton-Deutsch Collection/CORBIS; **225** (tl)CORBIS, (tr)BC, (b)The Granger Collection, New York; **226** The Granger Collection, New York; **231** (l)LOC, LC-USZ62-15566, (r)Frank & Marie Wood/The Picture Bank; **232** Geofferey Clements/CORBIS; **233** Museum of Art, Rhode Island School of Design; Jesse Metcalf and Walter H. Kimball Funds; **235** (l)The Granger Collection, New York, (r)GI; **237** (l)CORBIS, (r)Duke University; **238** (l)The Granger Collection, New York, (r)AP Images; **243** The Everett Collection; **244** The Granger Collection, New York; **246** (tl tr)CORBIS, (b)GI; **249** The Granger Collection, New York; **251** Snark/Art Resource, NY; **252** Brown Brothers; **254** (t)Brown Brothers, (c)Picture Research Consultants, (b)Lewis W. Hine/George Eastman House/GI; **257** Picture Research Consultants; **258-259** Franklin D Roosevelt Library; **260-261** CORBIS; **263** (t)CORBIS, (b)The Mariners' Museum/CORBIS; **265** (l)Nagasaki Museum of History and Culture, (r)James G. Evans/Chicago History Museum (1932.21); **266** (l)Hawaii State Archives, (r)The Granger Collection, New York; **269** (l)LOC, LC-USZ62-99767; (tr)The Granger Collection, New York, (br)Kurz & Allison/The Granger Collection, New York; **270** BC; **271** (l)Hulton Archive/GI, (r)LOC; **273** (l)LOC, LC-USZ62-62631), (r)GI; **274** (l)LOC, LC-USZC4-5392, (r)LOC, LC-USZ62-91465); **277**The Granger Collection, New York; **278** BC; **279** Koichi Kamoshida/GI; **282** The Granger Collection, New York; **285** Morton Beebe/CORBIS; **286** (t)BC, (c b)Time Life Pictures/GI; **289** CORBIS; **290** (t)Museum of the City of New York Print Archives, (b)Key Color/Index Stock Imagery; **290-291** Jessie Beals/Schlesinger Library, Radcliffe Institute, Harvard University/Bridgeman Art Library; **293** (t)BC, (b)Hulton-Deutsch Collection/CORBIS; **294-295** LOC, LC-USZ62-56437; **296** (t)LOC, LC-USZ62-46713, (bl)LOC, LC-USZ62-106109, (br)LOC, LC-ISZ62-28195; **297** BC; **298** (l)Keystone/GI, (r)UNITE HERE Archives, Kheel Center, Cornell University; **301** LOC, LC-USZC4-434; **303** The Granger Collection, New York; **305** (l)BC, (r)The Granger Collection, New York; **306** CORBIS; **309** (t)CORBIS, (b)The Granger Collection, New York; **312** (t)Underwood & Underwood/CORBIS, (b)BC; **314** (t)BC, (c)LOC, Prints & Photographs Division (LC-USZ62-83858), (b)CORBIS; **317** LOC, LC-USZC4-6425; **318** (t)The Mariners' Museum/CORBIS, (b)BC; **318-319** 319 BC; **322** (l)CORBIS, (c r)BC; **323** BC; **325** (l)LOC, LC-DIG-ggbain-05650, (r)CORBIS; **326** (tl b)BC, (tr)CORBIS; **329** (l)Swim Ink 2, LLC/CORBIS, (r)K.J. Historical/CORBIS, (bkgd)BC; **331** BC; **332** (l)LOC, LC-USZ62-116442, (r)LOC, LC-USZC4-2426; **334** (t)LOC, LC-USZC4-1539, (b)LOC, LC-USZ62-91465); **335** LOC, LC-USZC4-9861; **338** (l)Australian War Memorial Negative Number, E00921, (r)Hulton-Deutsch Collection/CORBIS; **339 341** BC; **344** (l)By Permission of the Marcus Family, (r)LOC/© 1919, The Washington Post. Reprinted with permission; **349** Underwood & Underwood/CORBIS; **350** Brown Brothers; **351** Neville Elder/CORBIS; **352** (l cr)White House Historical Association, (cl)Underwood & Underwood/CORBIS, (r)CORBIS; **354** (t)BC, (c b)CORBIS; **357** Chicago Tribune; **358-359** Howard A. Thain/Collection of the New York Historical Society/Bridgeman Art Library; **360** CORBIS; **360-361** Roger-Viollet/Topham/The Image Works; **361** National Air and Space Museum/Smithsonian Institution;

363 364 The Granger Collection, New York; **369** (tl)Hirz/GI, (tr bl)FPG/Hulton Archive/GI, (cl)Hulton Archive/GI, (cr)Topham/The Image Works, (br)The Granger Collection, New York; **370** (l)Hulton Archive/GI, (cl)The Image Works, (cr)SSPL/The Image Works, (r)Ohio Historical Society; **371** (tl)Mary Evans Picture Library, (tr)LOC, LC-USZ62-119950, (c)Huntington Library/SuperStock, (b)Minnesota Historical Society; **372** The Granger Collection, New York, **373** (l)Frank & Marie-Therese Wood/The Picture Bank, (r)The Granger Collection, New York; **374** Hulton Archive/GI, **377** (l)BC, (r)LOC, LC-USZ62-52584, **378** Underwood & Underwood/CORBIS; **379** (l)Mary Evans Picture Library, (r)Columbus Dispatch/Ohio Historical Society; **380** (l)LOC/GI, (r)CORBIS, **383** Francis G. Mayer/CORBIS; **384** (tl)Culver Pictures/SuperStock, (tc)National Archives, (tr)Art Archive/Culver Pictures, (b)The Kobal Collection; **389** The Granger Collection, New York; **390** (l)Art Archive/Culver Pictures, (tr br)Frank Driggs Collection/GI; **391** (l)Frank Driggs Collection/GI, (c)Sasha/GI, (r)Underwood & Underwood/CORBIS; **394** (t)Mary Evans Picture Library, (c)Frank Driggs Collection/GI, (b)General Photographic Agency/GI; **397** LOC/© 1925, The Washington Post. Reprinted with Permission; **398-399 399** BC; **401** (l)The Granger Collection, New York, (r)Underwood & Underwood/LOC; **402** Hulton-Deutsch Collection/CORBIS; **403** (l)BC, (r)American Stock/GI; **407** (l)Chicago Historical Society, (r)Hulton Archive/GI; **408** (l)BC, (r)Margaret Bourke-White/Time Life Pictures/GI; **411** Russell Lee/CORBIS; **413** (l)The Granger Collection, New York, (r)GI; **414** (l)BC, (tr)AP Images, (b)Picture History; **416** (t)Mary Evans Picture Library, (c)BC, (b)Scherl/SVBilderdienst/The Image Works; **419** John T. McCutcheon/The Granger Collection, New York; **420** (t)CORBIS, (b)akg-images; **420-421 421** BC; **423** Underwood & Underwood/CORBIS; **425** BC; **426** (tl)Picture History, (tr)LOC, LC-USF34-032948-D, (b)MPI/GI; **427** (tl b)BC, (tr)Underwood & Underwood/CORBIS; **429** (inset)CORBIS, (bkgd)Tom Brakefield/GI; **430** The Granger Collection, New York; **432** The Granger Collection, New York; **433** (l)LOC, LC-DIG-ppmsca-12896, (r)The Granger Collection, New York; **435** (l c)BC, (r)The Granger Collection, New York; **437** (l)The Granger Collection, New York, (r)CORBIS; **438 441** BC; **443** The Granger Collection, New York; **444** (tl)BC, (tr)courtesy FDIC, (b)courtesy FHA; **446** (t)Underwood & Underwood/CORBIS, (c)U.S. Forest Service,(b)BC; **449 450-451** The Granger Collection, New York; **452** Keystone/GI; **452-453** Mary Evans Picture Library; **453** (t)USHMM, (b)LOC, LC-USZ62-89348; **457** (t)The Granger Collection, New York, (b)BC; **458** BC; **461** CORBIS; **463** (l c) BC, (r)The Granger Collection, New York; **464** (tl)Art Archive, (tr b)BC; **467** (l r)Mary Evans Picture Library, (bkgd)Roger Foley; **468** (l)Yivo Institute for Jewish Research, (r)Yad Vashem Photo Archives, courtesy of USHMM Photo Archives; **468-469** Roger Foley; **469** (l)AFP/ GI, (r)National Archives: Suitland, courtesy of the United States Holocaust Memorial Museum; **470** USHMM; **472** National Archives; **473** (l)USHMM, (r)David Olere/The Beate Klarsfeld Foundation; **475** (l)The Granger Collection, New York, (r)LOC, LC-USZ62-52601; **476** SuperStock; **478** (t)CORBIS, (bl br)GI; **480** The Granger Collection, New York; **483** Chicago Historical Society; **484 484-485** BC; **485** CORBIS; **487** BC; **488** Time & Life Pictures/GI; **490** BC; **491** (l)US Army Photo, (r)BC; **492** (l)Peter Stackpole/Time Life Pictures/GI, (r)CORBIS; **495** CORBIS; **497** Art Archive/National Archives Washington, DC; **498** (t)CORBIS, (b)Art Archive; **501** (l)LOC, LC-DIG-fsac-1a34953, (c)GI, (r)CORBIS; **502-503** John Vachon/Anthony Potter Collection/GI; **505** GI; **506** (l)United Artists/The Kobal Collection, (c)Walt Disney Pictures/The Kobal Collection, (r)CORBIS; **510** (t) BC, (bl)CORBIS, (br)GI; **511** (t)Art Archive, (b)Ullstein Bild/The Granger Collection, New York; **512-513 514** CORBIS; **520** Digital Stock/CORBIS; **521** (tl b)CORBIS, (tr)Naval Historical Foundation; **523** (l)Art Archive/Culver Pictures, (r)GI; **524** CORBIS; **526** (l)LOC, LC-DIG-fsac-1a35223, (r)LOC, LC-DIG-fsac-1a35297; **529** Dr. Seuss Collection/Mandeville Special Collections Library/University of California, San Diego; **530** (t)BC, (b)Picture Research Consultants; **530-531** BC, **531** Smithsonian Institution; **533** The Granger Collection, New York; **535** (l)BC, (r)Hulton-Deutsch Collection/CORBIS; **539** GI; **541** Time Life Pictures/GI; **543** BC; **544** The Granger Collection, New York; **547** CORBIS; **549** (l)Weber and Beyer/CORBIS, (r)The Granger Collection, New York; **551** BC; **552** (t)LOC, LC-USZC4-4431, (c b)BC; **555** (l c)CORBIS, (r)U.S. Air Force Photo; **556** (t)The Granger Collection, New York, (cl)NSSDC/NASA, (cr)Donald Uhbrock/Time Life Pictures/GI, (b)BC; **558** (tl)NASA, (tr)Time Life Pictures/GI, (b)CORBIS; **560** (t)Picture Research Consultants, (b)BC; **563** Ross Lewis Milwaukee Public Library; **564** (t)FPG/GI, (b)CORBIS; **564-565** SuperStock; **565** Natural Museum of American History/Smithsonian Institution; **567** (l)GI, (r)CORBIS; **569** CORBIS; **570** (tl)Masterfile, (tr)Time Life Pictures/GI, (bl)J R Eyerman/Time Life Pictures/GI, (br)Marvin Koner/CORBIS; **573** (l)Time Life Pictures/GI, (r)CORBIS; **575** BC; **576** (l)BC, (c)National Museum of American History/Smithsonian Institution, (r)The Kobal Collection; **578** (tl)Brown Brothers, (tr)Michael Ochs Archives/CORBIS, (bl)BC, (bc)Photofest, (br)Michael

Ochs Archives/CORBIS; **583** (tl tr)Time Life Pictures/GI, (b)AP Images; **584** BC; **585** Thomas Hoepker/Magnum Photos; **586** National Archives; **588** (t)SuperStock, (b)Time Life Pictures/GI; **591** B. Wiseman/from Hey, Can't You Forget Business? by Charles Preston, ©1953, E.P. Dutton & Co., Inc.; **592-593** Wally McNamee/CORBIS; **594** (tl)Art Resource, NY, (tc)GI, (tr b)AP Images; **594-595** Time Life Pictures/GI; **597 599** BC; **603** George Silk/Time Life Pictures/GI; **604** (l)GI, (c)CORBIS SYGMA, (r)CORBIS; **605** (l)CORBIS SYGMA, (cl)BC, (cr r)CORBIS; **606** (tl)Rene Burri/Magnum Photos, (tr)AP Images, (b)Carl Mydans/Time Life Pictures/GI; **611** (l)John Dominis/Time Life Pictures/GI,(r)CORBIS; **612** Americorps VISTA Archives; **613** Corporation photo by Peter Shifter, Office of Public Affairs/AmeriCorps; **616** (t)AmeriCorps Archive, (c)Carl Mydans/ Time Life Pictures/GI, (b)Flip Schulke/Black Star; **619** LOC; **620** (l)Carl Iwaski/Time Life Pictures/GI, (r)Art Resource, NY; **620-621** Bob Adelman/Magnum Photos; **621** Collection of Janice L. and David J. Frent; **623** Time Life Pictures/GI; **625** Carl Iwaski/ Time Life Pictures/GI; **627** (tl tr br)Don Craven/Time Life Pictures/GI, (bl)Flip Schulke/CORBIS; **628** (tl tr)CORBIS, (b)BC; **631** (l)CORBIS, (r)AP Images; **632** (t br)BC, (bl)Don Craven/Time Life Pictures/GI; **633** (tl)Charles Moore 1963/Black Star, (tr)Steve Schapiro, (b)BC; **635** Bill Hudson/AP Images; **637** Francis Miller/Time Life Pictures/GI; **638** Flip Schulke/ CORBIS; **640** Eve Arnold/Magnum Photos; **641** The Everett Collection; **643** (l)Atlanta Constitution, 1964, Clifford H. "Baldy" Baldowski Editorial Cartoons. Courtesy of the Richard B. Russell Library for Political Research and Studies, The University of Georgia Libraries, (r)A 1967 Herblock Cartoon, copyright by The Herb Block Foundation; **645** (l) Robert Parent/Time Life Pictures/GI, (c)AP Images, (r)Flip Schulke/CORBIS; **648** (t)Carl Iwaski/ Time Life Pictures/GI, (c)Francis Miller/Time Life Pictures/GI, (b)Flip Schulke/CORBIS; **651** Jon Kennedy/Arkansas Democrat-Gazette; **652** (t)Art Resource, NY, (b)Naval Historical Foundation; **652-653** Larry Burrows/Time Life Pictures/GI; **656** (tl)BC, (tr)AFP/GI, (b)AP Images; **659** (l)Popperfoto/ Alamy Images, (r)CORBIS; **660** (t)MPI/GI, (b)Larry Burrows/Time Life Pictures/GI; **663** (l)BC, (r)AP Images; **665** (l)LOC/Tom Francis Darcy, Newsday/Reprinted with permission from LA Times Reprints, (r)Atlanta Constitution, Oct 18 1965, Clifford H. "Baldy" Baldowski Editorial Cartoons. Courtesy of the Richard B. Russell Library for Political Research and Studies, The University of Georgia Libraries; **666** (l b)Bernard Gotfryd/GI, (c)Hulton Archive/GI, (r)Paul Fusco/Magnum Photos; **668** (tl)CORBIS, (tr cr)BC, (cl)Bob Gomel/Time Life Pictures/GI; **671** (l)John Filo, (c)David Kennerly/ BC, (r)Dirck Halstead/Time Life Pictures/GI; **673** (tl)BC, (tr)Time Life Pictures/GI, (b)The Granger Collection, New York; **674** (l)Alex Wong/GI, (r)Sal Veder/AP Images; **676** (t)AP Images, (c)Art Archive/Dept Defence Washington, (b)Wally McNamee/CORBIS; **679** The Granger Collection, New York; **680** (l)Art Resource, NY, (r)Charles Gatewood/The Image Works; **680-681** Take Stock; **681** AP Images; **683** BC; **684** (l)Vince Streano/CORBIS, (r)Andrew DeLory/Hulton Archive/GI; **687** (l)BC, (r)Charles Gatewood/The Image Works; **689** AP Images; **690** BC; **693** CORBIS; **694** LOC; **695** (l)CORBIS, (r)Jim Sugar/CORBIS; **696** Arthur Schatz/Time Life Pictures/ GI; **698** (t c)BC, (b)Steve Northup/Time Life Pictures/GI; **701** Jack Knox Estate/OSU Cartoon Research Library; **702-703** Michael Goldman/ Masterfile; **704** (l)Hulton Archive/GI, (r)BC; **704-705** AP Images; **705** Tom Ebenhoh/Black Star; **707** (l)A 1968 Herblock Cartoon, copyright by The Herb Block Foundation, (r)Atlanta Constitution, 1968 Oct 17, Clifford H. "Baldy" Baldowski Editorial Cartoons. Courtesy of the Richard B. Russell Library for Political Research and Studies, The University of Georgia Libraries; **709** (l)BC, (tr)Time Life Pictures/GI; **710** (l)Dirck Halstead/Liasion/GI, (r)AFP/GI; **713** (tl cr b) BC, (tr)Robert Maass/CORBIS, (cl)Adam Woolfitt/CORBIS, (c)Dennis Brack/Black Star; **715** Mark Godfrey/The Images Works; **716** (l)A 1973 Herblock Cartoon, copyright by The Herb Block Foundation, (r)Atlanta Constitution, 1973, Clikfford H. "Baldy" Baldowski Editorial Cartoons. Courtesy of the Richard B. Russell Library for Political Research and Studies, The University of Georgia Libraries; **719** (l)Jason Laure/Woodfin Camp/Time Life Pictures/GI, (c r)BC; **721** (l)Brown Brothers, (r)Karl Schumacher/Time Life Pictures/GI; **722** (t)M. Lipschitz/AP Images, (cl)David Rubinger/ CORBIS, (cr)Sergio Gaudenti/Kipa/CORBIS, (b)MPI/GI; **725** (l)AP Images,(r)Scherl/SV-Bilderndienst/The Image Works; **726** (l)PA/Topham/ The Images Works, (r)Charles Gatewood/The Image Works; **728** (l)Wally McNamee/CORBIS, (c)Ed Kashi/CORBIS, (r)Brand X/SuperStock; **731** (l c)BC, (r)Charles E. Rotkin/CORBIS; **732** (l)A 1975 Herblock Cartoon, copyright by The Herb Block Foundation, (r)Hulton Archive/GI; **734** (t)Charles Gatewood/The Image Works, (c)BC, (b)Julian Wasser/Time Life Pictures/ GI; **737** Ranan R. Lurie, Cartoonews International Syndicate, New York City; **738** (t) AP Images, (b)Peter Turnley/CORBIS; **738-739** Eli Reed/ Magnum Photos; **739** Lana Harris/AP Images; **741** (l)Gary McCoy/Cagle Cartoons, (r)Chris Slane/Cagle Cartoons; **744** (t)Index Stock Imagery, (bl)Cynthia Johnson/Time Life Pictures/GI, (bc)Annie Griffiths Belt, (br)Joe Raedle/Newsmakers GI; **747** (t)Atlanta Constitution, 1976 Apr. 6, Clifford H. "Baldy" Baldowski Editorial Cartoons. Courtesy of the Richard B.

Russell Library for Political Research and Studies, The University of Georgia Libraries, (b)Atlanta Constitution, 1981 Oct 18, Clifford H. "Baldy" Baldowski Editorial Cartoons. Courtesy of the Richard B. Russell Library for Political Research and Studies, The University of Georgia Libraries; **749** (l)Wally McNamee/CORBIS, (r)Roger Ressmeyer/CORBIS; **750** (tl)Wally McNamee/ CORBIS, (tr)Bob Daughtery/AP Images, (b)BC; **752** (tl)Robert Nickelsberg/ Time Life Pictures/GI, (tr)Dirck Halstead/Time Life Pictures/GI, (b)CORBIS; **755** (l)Eli Reichman/Time Life Pictures/GI, (r)Bob Krist/ CORBIS; **756** NASA/AP Images; **757** (inset)Blue Origin, (bkgd)HANDOUT/ epa/CORBIS; **758** BC; **760** AP Images; **763** (l)Stephan Ferry/Liasion/GI, (r)Diane-Lu Hovasse/AFP/GI; **764** Thomas Hartwell/Time Life Pictures/ GI; **766** (tl)Owen Franken/CORBIS, (tr)Markowitz Jeffrey/CORBIS SYGMA; (c)Wally McNamee/CORBIS, (b)Mike Lane/Cagle Cartoons; **768** (t)Tony Korody/Time Life Pictures/GI, (c)BC, (b)Alain Nogues/CORBIS SYGMA; **771** LOC, LC-DIG-ppmsc-07930, **772** (tl)Roger Ressmeyer/CORBIS, (tr)Spec. Robert Elliott/CORBIS, (b)David Brauchli/Reuters/CORBIS; **772-773** The White House/Handout/GI; **773** Official White House Photo by Eric Draper; **775** (tl)Ed Young/CORBIS, (tr)Douglas Engelbart/Bootstrap Alliance, (bl)TWPhoto/CORBIS, (br)Roger Ressmeyer/CORBIS; **781** (l)TOLES © 1997 The Washington Post. Reprinted with permission of UNIVERSAL PRESS SYNDICATE. All rights reserved, (tr)Wally McNamee/CORBIS, (br)Markowitz Jeffrey/CORBIS SYGMA; **783** (l)Terry Ashe/Time Life Pictures/GI, (r)SuperStock; **785** (l)Wally McNamee/CORBIS, (r)Joe Marquette/AP Images; **786** (l)Peter Turnley/CORBIS, (tr)Les Stone/CORBIS SYGMA, (br)Leif Skoogfors/CORBIS; **790** David Kadlubowski/CORBIS; **792** (l) Fred Greaves/Reuters/CORBIS, (r)Carlos Barria/Reuters/CORBIS; **793** (t)Stanley Rogouski, (b)Michael Newman/PhotoEdit; **795** (t)GI, (b)Transtock/Alamy Images; **796** Hamilton Karie/CORBIS SYGMA; **798** (t)Michael Newman/ PhotoEdit, (b)Ron Edmonds/AP Images; **801** TOLES © 1998 The Washington Post. Reprinted with permission of UNIVERSAL PRESS SYNDICATE. All rights reserved; **802** (l)Alan Diaz/AP Images, (c)Evan Vucci/AP Images, (r)Dimas Ardian/GI; **802-803** Michael Macor/San Francisco Chronicle/ CORBIS; **802** Official White House Photo by Eric Draper; **805** (t)Colin Braley/ Reuters/CORBIS, (bl bc)Ron Sachs/CNP/CORBIS, (br)Najlah Feanny/ CORBIS; **806** Daryl Cagle/Cagle Cartoons; **809** (t)Reuters/Sean Adair/ CORBIS, (bl)Ron Sachs/CNP/CORBIS, (br)Stan Honda/AFP/GI; **810** AP Images; **812** (t)Matthew McDermott/CORBIS, (bl)Reuters/CORBIS, (br)Steve Liss/CORBIS; **815** (t)Alexandra Boulat/VII/AP Images, (bl)Scott Peterson/ GI, (br)David Guttenfelder/AP Images; **816** (t)Ali Haider/AP Images, (b)Reuters/Jeff Christensen/CORBIS; **817** (tl)Al Jazeera via APTN/AP Images, (tr)Lynsey Addario/CORBIS, (b)Wathiq Khuzaie/GI; **818** (l)Lauren Frayer/ AP Images, (r)Khalid al-Mousily/Reuters/CORBIS; **821** (l)Khampha Bouaphanh/Knight Ridder/Tribune/Pool/Reuters/CORBIS, (r)Brooks Kraft/CORBIS; **822** Smiley N. Pool/Dallas Morning News/CORBIS; **823** Rick Wilking/Reuters/CORBIS; **824** (l)Wathiq Khuzaie/GI, (r)Nancy Kaserman/ZUMA/CORBIS; **826** (tl)Bruno Vincent/GI, (tr)Evan Agostini/GI, (b) Chris McGrath/GI; **828** (t)AFP/GI, (cl)Kamal Kishore/AP Images, (cr)Al Jazeera/AP Images, (b)Evan Agostini/ImageDirect/C; **831** Olie Johannson/ Political Cartoons; **R2** LOC, LC-USF34-T01-009095-C; **R3** Art Shay/Time Life Pictures/GI; **R4** LOC, LC-DIG-fsac-1a35337; **R5** Wally McNamee/ CORBIS; **R6** Photo File/MLB Photos/GI; **R7** Stan Honda/AFP/GI; **R8** GI; **R9** CORBIS; **R10** (l)Comstock/CORBIS, (r)Art Archive/ Reina Sofia Museum, Madrid; **R11** CORBIS; **R12 R13** BC; **R14** Harry Scull Jr./GI; **R17** The Granger Collection, New York; **R18** Clifford K. Berryman/National Archives; **R19** Scott, Lituchy/Star Ledger/CORBIS; **R20** Smithsonian Intstitution/CORBIS; **R32 R33** White House Historical Association; **R33** (bl)Official White House Photo by Eric Draper, (br)Brooks Kraft/CORBIS; **R36** (tl)National Archives, (tr)Illinois State Historical Library, (b)Private Collection; **R39** Private Collection; **R40** The Wadsworth Atheneum; **R41 R42** Bridgeman Art Library; **R43 R44** National Portrait Gallery, Smithsonian Institution/Art Resource, NY; **R46** Chicago Historical Society; **R47** (l)Maryland Historical Society, Baltimore, Maryland, (r)National Museum of American History/Armed Forces History Collections/ Smithsonian Institution; **R48** Picture Research Consultants; **R49** LOC; **R50** (t)Andre Jenny/Focus Group/PictureQuest, (b)BC; **R52** National Portrait Gallery, Smithsonian Institution, Washington, D.C./Art Resource, NY; **R53** Courtesy Franklin D. Roosevelt Library; **R55** Carl Iwaski/Time Life Pictures/GI; **R56** Francis Miller/Time Life Pictures/GI; **R58 R60** GI; **R61** Picture Research Consultants; **R65** Stock Montage/GI; **R67** (t)Stock Montage/GI, (b)Frans Lanting/CORBIS; **R68** BC; **R69** Collection of the New York Historical Society/Bridgeman Art Library; **R71** (t)Erling Larson/GI, (b)Henry Guttmann/GI; **R72** Keystone/GI; **R73** General Photographic Agency/GI; **R74** Ray Fisher/Time Life Pictures/GI; **R75** Hulton Archive/ GI; **R76** Stephen Jaffe/AFP/GI; **R80** Mitchell Gerber/CORBIS; **Timeline Presidential Paintings** White House Historical Association.

Photo Credits